Software Engineering

A PRACTITIONER'S APPROACH

FIFTH EDITION

软件工程

实践者之路

第 5 版

Roger S. Pressman, Ph.D.

清华大学出版社
McGraw-Hill Companies, Inc.

(京)新登字 158 号

北京市版权局著作权合同登记号: 01-2000-3919

书 名: Software Engineering A Practitioner's Approach, 5th ed.
软件工程 实践者之路
作 者: Roger S. Pressman
出版者: 清华大学出版社(北京清华大学学研大厦,邮编 100084)
http://www.tup.tsinghua.edu.cn
印刷者: 北京牛山世兴印刷厂
发行者: 新华书店总店北京发行所
开 本: 787×960 1/16 印张: 56
版 次: 2001 年 1 月第 1 版 2002 年 10 月第 3 次印刷
书 号: ISBN 7-302-04139-3/TP·2442
印 数: 6501～9000
定 价: 79.00 元

You get much more than a textbook when you use

SOFTWARE ENGINEERING
A PRACTITIONER'S APPROACH, 5/e

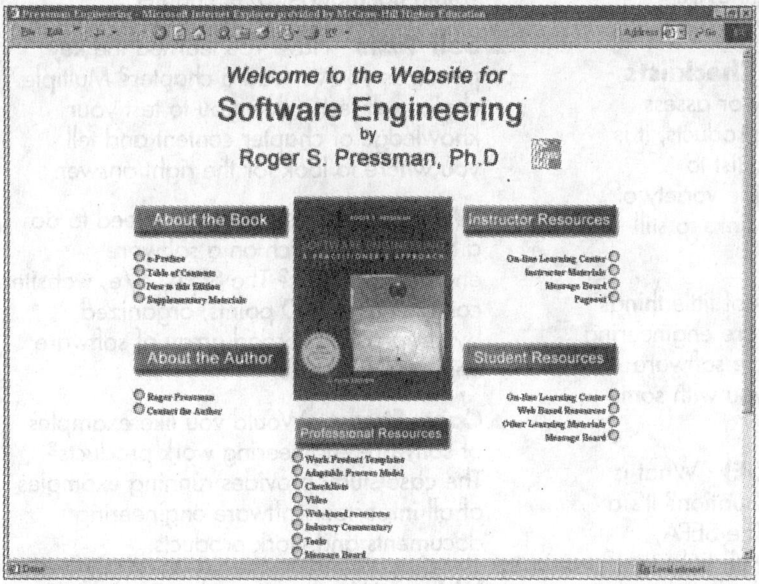

SEPA, 5/e, is accompanied by a comprehensive software engineering website, designed to provide valuable resources for students, instructors, and software professionals. Among the many resources you will be able to use as a reader of SEPA, 5/e, are:

Instructor Resources

- ▲ **Instructor's Guide** - A complete Instructor's Guide for SEPA, 5/e, is available for download. The Guide includes chapter by chapter discussion of the book, suggestions for various course structures and term projects, teaching guidelines, and selected solutions to problems.
- ▲ **Powerpoint Slides** - A full set of MS powerpoint slides may be downloaded to supplement your lecture presentations.
- ▲ **Test Bank** - A collection of suggested test questions (with answers) is provided.
- ▲ **Tiny Tools** - A collection of simple software engineering tools that serve to implement approaches and techniques presented in SEPA, 5/e, is provided.
- ▲ **Page Out** - A tool that enables you to develop your own course specific website.
- ▲ **Message Board** - The message board allows communication among instructors who are using SEPA, 5/e, for teaching purposes.

The SEPA, 5/e, website is an important source of software engineering information, a gateway to additional information on the Web, and an important part of the learning experience.

Visit the SEPA, 5/e, website at http://www.mhhe.com/engcs/compsci/pressman

Professional Resources

- **Documents/Work Product Templates** - If you need examples of the format and content of software engineering work products, they're provided for download.
- **Software Engineering Checklists** - When you conduct a review or assess software engineering work products, it is a good idea to have a checklist to guide your evaluation. A wide variety of checklists are provided and links to still more are also included.
- **Tiny Tools** - There are lots of little things that lead to success in software engineering work. This collection of simple software engineering tools will help you with some of them.
- **Professional Tools (CASE)** - What is the best CASE tool for our situation? It's a commonly asked question. The SEPA, 5/e, website provides you with links to hundreds of CASE tools and more than a few tools comparisons.
- **Software Engineering Resources** - If you need to do some research or take an on-line tutorial, the SEPA, 5/e, website contains over 500 pointers to a broad array of software engineering topics.
- **Adaptable Process Model** - The adaptable process model is a comprehensive process template that can be tuned to your organization's needs.
- **An Industry Quality Video Curriculum** - An industry quality video curriculum, already used at hundreds of major companies worldwide, is available to augment SEPA, 5/e. Information about this product is available at the website.
- **Industry Commentary** - A collection of short essays, extracted from a number of industry sources, is provided to help spur thoughtful debate.

Student Resources

- **Study Guide** - Need a quick review during exam time? The study guide can help by summarizing key points presented within each SEPA, 5/e, chapter.
- **Self-Tests** - Have you learned the key points as you've read a chapter? Multiple choice self-tests allow you to test your knowledge of chapter content and tell you where to look for the right answer.
- **Web-based Resources** - Need to do a bit more research on a software engineering topic? The SEPA, 5/e, website contains over 500 points, organized by chapter, to a broad array of software engineering topics.
- **Case Study** - Would you like examples of software engineering work products? The case study provides running examples of all important software engineering documents and work products.
- **Video** - Want to hear what Dr. Pressman has to say on a software engineering topic? Take a look!
- **Supplementary Content** - Need even more information? The site contains a collection of supplementary materials that expand on topics presented within the book.
- **Message Board** - Want to talk with other readers? The message board allows Q&A among students and others and provides a useful mechanism for informal communication.

出 版 者 的 话

今天，我们的大学生、研究生和教学、科研工作者，面临的是一个国际化的信息时代。他们将需要随时查阅大量的外文资料；会有更多的机会参加国际性学术交流活动；接待外国学者；走上国际会议的讲坛。作为科技工作者，他们不仅应有与国外同行进行口头和书面交流的能力，更为重要的是，他们必须具备极强的查阅外文资料获取信息的能力。有鉴于此，在原国家教委所颁布的“大学英语教学大纲”中有一条规定：专业阅读应作为必修课程开设。同时，在大纲中还规定了这门课程的学时和教学要求。有些高校除开设“专业阅读”课之外，还在某些专业课拟进行英语授课。但教、学双方都苦于没有一定数量的合适的英文原版教材作为教学参考书。为满足这方面的需要，我们陆续精选了一批国外计算机科学方面最新版本的著名教材，进行影印出版。我社获得国外著名出版公司和原著作者的授权将国际先进水平的教材引入我国高等学校，为师生们提供了教学用书，相信会对高校教材改革产生积极的影响。

我们欢迎高校师生将使用影印版教材的效果、意见反馈给我们，更欢迎国内专家、教授积极向我社推荐国外优秀计算机教育教材，以利我们将《大学计算机教育丛书(影印版)》做得更好，更适合高校师生的需要。

清华大学出版社

《大学计算机教育丛书(影印版)》项目组

1999.6

ABOUT THE AUTHOR

Roger S. Pressman is an internationally recognized authority in software process improvement and software engineering technologies. For over three decades, he has worked as a software engineer, a manager, a professor, an author, and a consultant, focusing on software engineering issues.

As an industry practitioner and manager, Dr. Pressman worked on the development of CAD/CAM systems for advanced engineering and manufacturing applications. He has also held positions with responsibility for scientific and systems programming.

After receiving a Ph.D. in engineering from the University of Connecticut, Dr. Pressman moved to academia where he became Bullard Associate Professor of Computer Engineering at the University of Bridgeport and director of the university's Computer-Aided Design and Manufacturing Center.

Dr. Pressman is currently president of R.S. Pressman & Associates, Inc., a consulting firm specializing in software engineering methods and training. He serves as principle consultant, helping companies establish effective software engineering practices. He also designed and developed the company's software engineering training and process improvement products—*Essential Software Engineering,* a complete video curriculum that is among the industry's most comprehensive treatments of the subject, and *Process Advisor,* a self-directed system for software engineering process improvement. Both products are used by hundreds of companies worldwide.

Dr. Pressman has written many technical papers, is a regular contributor to industry periodicals, and is author of six books. In addition to *Software Engineering: A Practitioner's Approach,* he has written *A Manager's Guide to Software Engineering* (McGraw-Hill), an award-winning book that uses a unique Q&A format to present management guidelines for instituting and understanding software engineering technology; *Making Software Engineering Happen* (Prentice-Hall), the first book to address the critical management problems associated with software process improvement; and *Software Shock* (Dorset House), a treatment that focuses on software and its impact on business and society. Dr. Pressman is on the Editorial Boards of *IEEE Software* and the *Cutter IT Journal,* and for many years, was editor of the "Manager" column in *IEEE Software.*

Dr. Pressman is a well-known speaker, keynoting a number of major industry conferences. He has presented tutorials at the International Conference on Software Engineering and at many other industry meetings. He is a member of the ACM, IEEE, and Tau Beta Pi, Phi Kappa Phi, Eta Kappa Nu, and Pi Tau Sigma.

CONTENTS AT A GLANCE

TABLE OF CONTENTS

PART TWO—MANAGING SOFTWARE PROJECTS 53

CHAPTER 3 PROJECT MANAGEMENT CONCEPTS 55

CHAPTER 4 SOFTWARE PROCESS AND PROJECT METRICS 79

CHAPTER 11 ANALYSIS CONCEPTS AND PRINCIPLES 271

CHAPTER 12 ANALYSIS MODELING 299

CHAPTER 13 DESIGN CONCEPTS AND PRINCIPLES 335

CHAPTER 14 ARCHITECTURAL DESIGN 365

CHAPTER 19 TECHNICAL METRICS FOR SOFTWARE 507

PART FOUR—OBJECT-ORIENTED SOFTWARE ENGINEERING 539

CHAPTER 20 OBJECT-ORIENTED CONCEPTS AND PRINCIPLES 541

CHAPTER 21 OBJECT-ORIENTED ANALYSIS 571

CHAPTER 22 OBJECT-ORIENTED DESIGN 603

CHAPTER 23 OBJECT-ORIENTED TESTING 631

CHAPTER 24 TECHNICAL METRICS FOR OBJECT-ORIENTED SYSTEMS 653

CHAPTER 32 THE ROAD AHEAD 845

PREFACE

When a computer software succeeds—when it meets the needs of the people who use it, when it performs flawlessly over a long period of time, when it is easy to modify and even easier to use—it can and does change things for the better. But when software fails—when its users are dissatisfied, when it is error prone, when it is difficult to change and even harder to use—bad things can and do happen. We all want to build software that makes things better, avoiding the bad things that lurk in the shadow of failed efforts. To succeed, we need discipline when software is designed and built. We need an engineering approach.

In the 20 years since the first edition of this book was written, software engineering has evolved from an obscure idea practiced by a relatively small number of zealots to a legitimate engineering discipline. Today, it is recognized as a subject worthy of serious research, conscientious study, and tumultuous debate. Throughout the industry, *software engineer* has replaced *programmer* as the job title of preference. Software process models, software engineering methods, and software tools have been adopted successfully across a broad spectrum of industry applications.

Although managers and practitioners alike recognize the need for a more disciplined approach to software, they continue to debate the manner in which discipline is to be applied. Many individuals and companies still develop software haphazardly, even as they build systems to service the most advanced technologies of the day. Many professionals and students are unaware of modern methods. And as a result, the quality of the software that we produce suffers and bad things happen. In addition, debate and controversy about the true nature of the software engineering approach continue. The status of software engineering is a study in contrasts. Attitudes have changed, progress has been made, but much remains to be done before the discipline reaches full maturity.

The fifth edition of *Software Engineering: A Practitioner's Approach* is intended to serve as a guide to a maturing engineering discipline. The fifth edition, like the four editions that preceded it, is intended for both students and practitioners, retaining its appeal as a guide to the industry professional and a comprehensive introduction to the student at the upper level undergraduate or first year graduate level. The format and style of the fifth edition have undergone significant change, making the presentation more reader-friendly and the content more easily accessible.

The fifth edition is considerably more than a simple update. The book has been revised to accommodate the dramatic growth in the field and to emphasize new and important software engineering practices. In addition, a comprehensive Web site has been developed to complement the content of the book. The Web site, which I call

SepaWeb, can be found at **http://www.mhhe.com/pressman.** Designed to be used in conjunction with the fifth edition of *Software Engineering: A Practitioner's Approach,* SepaWeb provides a broad array of software engineering resources that will benefit instructors, students, and industry professionals.

Like all Web sites, SepaWeb will evolve over time, but the following major content areas will always be present: (1) a broad array of *instructor resources* including a comprehensive on-line *Instructor's Guide* and supplementary teaching materials (e.g., slide presentations to supplement lectures, video-based instructional aids); (2) a wide variety of *student resources* including an extensive on-line learning center (encompassing study guides, Web-based resources, and self-tests), an evolving collection of "tiny tools," a case study, and additional supplementary content; and (3) a detailed collection of *professional resources* including outlines (and samples of) software engineering documents and other work products, a useful set of software engineering checklists, a catalog of software engineering (CASE) tools, a comprehensive collection of Web-based resources, and an "adaptable process model" that provides a detailed task breakdown of the software engineering process. In addition, SepaWeb will contain other goodies that are currently in development.

The 32 chapters of the fifth edition have been organized into five parts. This has been done to compartmentalize topics and assist instructors who may not have the time to complete the entire book in one term. Part One, The Product and the Process, presents an introduction to the software engineering milieu. It is intended to introduce the subject matter, and more important, to present concepts that will be necessary for later chapters. Part Two, Managing Software Projects, presents topics that are relevant to those who plan, manage, and control a software development project. Part Three, Conventional Methods for Software Engineering, presents the classical analysis, design, and testing methods that some view as the "conventional" school of software engineering. Part Four, Object-Oriented Software Engineering, presents object-oriented methods across the entire software engineering process, including analysis, design, and testing. Part Five, Advanced Software Engineering Topics, presents dedicated chapters that address formal methods, cleanroom software engineering, component-based software engineering, client/server software engineering, Web engineering, reengineering, and CASE.

The five-part organization of the fifth edition enables an instructor to "cluster" topics based on available time and student need. An entire one-term course can be built around one or more of the five parts. For example, a "design course" might emphasize only Part Three or Part Four; a "methods course" might present selected chapters in Parts Three, Four, and Five. A "management course" would stress Parts One and Two. By organizing the fifth edition in this way, I attempted to provide an instructor with a number of teaching options. SepaWeb can and should be used to supplement the content that is chosen from the book.

An *Instructor's Guide* for *Software Engineering: A Practitioner's Approach* is available from SepaWeb. The *Instructor's Guide* presents suggestions for conducting various types of software engineering courses, recommendations for a variety of software projects to be conducted in conjunction with a course, solutions to selected problems, and a number of teaching aids.

A comprehensive video curriculum, *Essential Software Engineering,* is available to complement this book. The video curriculum has been designed for industry training and has been modularized to enable individual software engineering topics to be presented on an as-needed, when-needed basis. Further information on the video can be obtained by mailing the request card at the back of this book.[1]

My work on the five editions of *Software Engineering: A Practitioner's Approach* has been the longest continuing technical project of my life. Even when the writing stops, information extracted from the technical literature continues to be assimilated and organized. For this reason, my thanks to the many authors of books, papers, and articles as well as a new generation of contributors to electronic media (newsgroups, e-newsletters, and the World Wide Web) who have provided me with additional insight, ideas, and commentary over the past 20 years. Many have been referenced within the pages of each chapter. All deserve credit for their contribution to this rapidly evolving field. I also wish to thank the reviewers of the fifth edition: Donald H. Kraft, Louisiana State University; Panos E. Livadas, University of Florida; Joseph Lambert, Pennsylvania State University; Kenneth L. Modesitt, University of Michigan—Dearborn; and, James Purtilo, University of Maryland. Their comments and criticism have been invaluable. Special thanks and acknowledgement also go to Bruce Maxim of the University of Michigan—Dearborn, who assisted me in developing the Web site that accompanies this book. Bruce is responsible for much of its design and pedagogical content.

The content of the fifth edition of *Software Engineering: A Practitioner's Approach* has been shaped by industry professionals, university professors, and students who have used earlier editions of the book and have taken the time to communicate their suggestions, criticisms, and ideas. My thanks to each of you. In addition, my personal thanks go to our many industry clients worldwide, who certainly teach me as much or more than I can teach them.

As the editions of this book have evolved, my sons, Mathew and Michael, have grown from boys to men. Their maturity, character, and success in the real world have been an inspiration to me. Nothing has filled me with more pride. And finally, to Barbara, my love and thanks for encouraging still another edition of "the book."

Roger S. Pressman

---

1 If the request card is missing, please visit the R. S. Pressman & Associates, Inc. Web site at http://www.rspa.com/ese or e-mail a request for information to info@rspa.com.

USING THIS BOOK

The fifth edition of *Software Engineering: A Practitioner's Approach* (SEPA) has been redesigned to enhance your reading experience and to provide integrated links to the SEPA Web site, http://www.mhhe.com/pressman/. SepaWeb contains a wealth of useful supplementary information for readers of the book and a broad array of resources (e.g., an *Instructor's Guide,* classroom slides, and video supplements) for instructors who have adopted SEPA for classroom use.

A comprehensive video curriculum, *Essential Software Engineering,* is available to complement this book. The video curriculum has been designed for industry training and has been modularized to enable individual software engineering topics to be presented on an as-needed, when-needed basis. Further information on the video can be obtained by mailing the request card at the back of this book.[1]

Throughout the book, you will encounter marginal icons that should be interpreted in the following manner:

KEY POINT
Used to emphasize an important point in the body of the text.

The **keypoint** icon will help you to find important points quickly.

WebRef
For pointers that will take you directly to Web resources

The **WebRef** icon provides direct pointers to important software engineering related Web sites.

ADVICE
Practical advice from the real world of software engineering.

The **advice** icon provides pragmatic guidance that can help you make the right decision or avoid common problems while building software.

SEPA WEB
A selected topic

The **SepaWeb** pointer indicates that further information about the noted topic is available at the SEPA Web site.

Where can I find the answer?

The **question mark** icon asks common questions that are answered in the body of the text.

SEPA WEB CHECKLIST

The **SepaWeb.checklists** icon points you to detailed checklists that will help you to assess the software engineering work you're doing and the work products you produce.

XRef
Provides an important cross reference within the book.

The **xref** icon will point you to another part of the book where information relevant to the current discussion can be found.

Quote:
"Important words"

The **quote** icon presents interesting quotes that have relevance to the topic at hand.

SEPA WEB DOCUMENT

The **SepaWeb.documents** icon points you to detailed document outlines, descriptions and examples contained within the SEPA Web site.

---

1 If the card is missing, please visit the R.S. Pressman & Associates, Inc. Web site at http://www.rspa.com/ese, or e-mail to info@rspa.com.

PART

One

THE PRODUCT AND THE PROCESS

In this part of *Software Engineering: A Practitioner's Approach,* you'll learn about the product that is to be engineered and the process that provides a framework for the engineering technology. The following questions are addressed in the chapters that follow:

- What is computer software . . . really?
- Why do we struggle to build high-quality computer-based systems?
- How can we categorize application domains for computer software?
- What myths about software still exist?
- What is a "software process"?
- Is there a generic way to assess the quality of a process?
- What process models can be applied to software development?
- How do linear and iterative process models differ?
- What are their strengths and weaknesses?
- What advanced process models have been proposed for software engineering work?

Once these questions are answered, you'll be better prepared to understand the management and technical aspects of the engineering discipline to which the remainder of this book is dedicated.

CHAPTER

1 THE PRODUCT

KEY CONCEPTS

The warnings began more than a decade before the event, but no one paid much attention. With less than two years to the deadline, the media picked up the story. Then government officials voiced their concern, business and industry leaders committed vast sums of money, and finally, dire warnings of pending catastrophe penetrated the public's consciousness. Software, in the guise of the now-infamous Y2K bug, would fail and, as a result, stop the world as we then knew it.

As we watched and wondered during the waning months of 1999, I couldn't help thinking of an unintentionally prophetic paragraph contained on the first page of the fourth edition of this book. It stated:

> Computer software has become a driving force. It is the engine that drives business decision making. It serves as the basis for modern scientific investigation and engineering problem solving. It is a key factor that differentiates modern products and services. It is embedded in systems of all kinds: transportation, medical, telecommunications, military, industrial processes, entertainment, office products, . . . the list is almost endless. Software is virtually inescapable in a modern world. And as we move into the twenty-first century, it will become the driver for new advances in everything from elementary education to genetic engineering.

QUICK LOOK

What is it? Computer software is the product that software engineers design and build. It encompasses programs that execute within a computer of any size and architecture, documents that encompass hard-copy and virtual forms, and data that combine numbers and text but also includes representations of pictorial, video, and audio information.

Who does it? Software engineers build it, and virtually everyone in the industrialized world uses it either directly or indirectly.

Why is it important? Because it affects nearly every aspect of our lives and has become pervasive in our commerce, our culture, and our everyday activities.

What are the steps? You build computer software like you build any successful product, by applying a process that leads to a high-quality result that meets the needs of the people who will use the product. You apply a software engineering approach.

What is the work product? From the point of view of a software engineer, the work product is the programs, documents, and data that are computer software. But from the user's viewpoint, the work product is the resultant information that somehow makes the user's world better.

How do I ensure that I've done it right? Read the remainder of this book, select those ideas applicable to the software that you build, and apply them to your work.

In the five years since the fourth edition of this book was written, the role of software as the "driving force" has become even more obvious. A software-driven Internet has spawned its own $500 billion economy. In the euphoria created by the promise of a new economic paradigm, Wall Street investors gave tiny "dot-com" companies billion dollar valuations before these start-ups produced a dollar in sales. New software-driven industries have arisen and old ones that have not adapted to the new driving force are now threatened with extinction. The United States government has litigated against the software's industry's largest company, just as it did in earlier eras when it moved to stop monopolistic practices in the oil and steel industries.

Quote:
"Ideas and technological discoveries are the driving engines of economic growth."
The Wall Street Journal

Software's impact on our society and culture continues to be profound. As its importance grows, the software community continually attempts to develop technologies that will make it easier, faster, and less expensive to build high-quality computer programs. Some of these technologies are targeted at a specific application domain (e.g., Web-site design and implementation); others focus on a technology domain (e.g., object-oriented systems); and still others are broad-based (e.g., operating systems such as LINUX). However, we have yet to develop a software technology that does it all, and the likelihood of one arising in the future is small. And yet, people bet their jobs, their comfort, their safety, their entertainment, their decisions, and their very lives on computer software. It better be right.

This book presents a framework that can be used by those who build computer software—people who must get it right. The technology encompasses a process, a set of methods, and an array of tools that we call *software engineering.*

1.1 THE EVOLVING ROLE OF SOFTWARE

Today, software takes on a dual role. It is a product and, at the same time, the vehicle for delivering a product. As a product, it delivers the computing potential embodied by computer hardware or, more broadly, a network of computers that are accessible by local hardware. Whether it resides within a cellular phone or operates inside a mainframe computer, software is an information transformer—producing, managing, acquiring, modifying, displaying, or transmitting information that can be as simple as a single bit or as complex as a multimedia presentation. As the vehicle used to deliver the product, software acts as the basis for the control of the computer (operating systems), the communication of information (networks), and the creation and control of other programs (software tools and environments).

KEY POINT
Software is both a product and a vehicle for delivering a product.

Software delivers the most important product of our time—information. Software transforms personal data (e.g., an individual's financial transactions) so that the data can be more useful in a local context; it manages business information to enhance competitiveness; it provides a gateway to worldwide information networks (e.g., Internet) and provides the means for acquiring information in all of its forms.

The role of computer software has undergone significant change over a time span of little more than 50 years. Dramatic improvements in hardware performance, profound changes in computing architectures, vast increases in memory and storage capacity, and a wide variety of exotic input and output options have all precipitated more sophisticated and complex computer-based systems. Sophistication and complexity can produce dazzling results when a system succeeds, but they can also pose huge problems for those who must build complex systems.

> **Quote:**
> "For I dipped into the future, far as the human eye could see, Saw the vision of the world, and all the wonder that would be."
> **Tennyson**

Popular books published during the 1970s and 1980s provide useful historical insight into the changing perception of computers and software and their impact on our culture. Osborne [OSB79] characterized a "new industrial revolution." Toffler [TOF80] called the advent of microelectronics part of "the third wave of change" in human history, and Naisbitt [NAI82] predicted a transformation from an industrial society to an "information society." Feigenbaum and McCorduck [FEI83] suggested that information and knowledge (controlled by computers) would be the focal point for power in the twenty-first century, and Stoll [STO89] argued that the "electronic community" created by networks and software was the key to knowledge interchange throughout the world.

> **Quote:**
> "Computers make it easy to do a lot of things, but most of the things that they make it easier to do don't need to be done."
> **Andy Rooney**

As the 1990s began, Toffler [TOF90] described a "power shift" in which old power structures (governmental, educational, industrial, economic, and military) disintegrate as computers and software lead to a "democratization of knowledge." Yourdon [YOU92] worried that U.S. companies might loose their competitive edge in software-related businesses and predicted "the decline and fall of the American programmer." Hammer and Champy [HAM93] argued that information technologies were to play a pivotal role in the "reengineering of the corporation." During the mid-1990s, the pervasiveness of computers and software spawned a rash of books by "neo-Luddites" (e.g., *Resisting the Virtual Life,* edited by James Brook and Iain Boal and *The Future Does Not Compute* by Stephen Talbot). These authors demonized the computer, emphasizing legitimate concerns but ignoring the profound benefits that have already been realized. [LEV95]

During the later 1990s, Yourdon [YOU96] re-evaluated the prospects for the software professional and suggested the "the rise and resurrection" of the American programmer. As the Internet grew in importance, his change of heart proved to be correct. As the twentieth century closed, the focus shifted once more, this time to the impact of the Y2K "time bomb" (e.g., [YOU98b], [DEJ98], [KAR99]). Although the predictions of the Y2K doomsayers were incorrect, their popular writings drove home the pervasiveness of software in our lives. Today, "ubiquitous computing" [NOR98] has spawned a generation of information appliances that have broadband connectivity to the Web to provide "a blanket of connectedness over our homes, offices and motorways" [LEV99]. Software's role continues to expand.

The lone programmer of an earlier era has been replaced by a team of software specialists, each focusing on one part of the technology required to deliver a complex application. And yet, the same questions asked of the lone programmer are being asked when modern computer-based systems are built:

- Why does it take so long to get software finished?
- Why are development costs so high?
- Why can't we find all the errors before we give the software to customers?
- Why do we continue to have difficulty in measuring progress as software is being developed?

These, and many other questions,[1] are a manifestation of the concern about software and the manner in which it is developed—a concern that has lead to the adoption of software engineering practice.

1.2 SOFTWARE

In 1970, less than 1 percent of the public could have intelligently described what "computer software" meant. Today, most professionals and many members of the public at large feel that they understand software. But do they?

? How should we define *software*?

A textbook description of software might take the following form: *Software is (1) instructions (computer programs) that when executed provide desired function and performance, (2) data structures that enable the programs to adequately manipulate information, and (3) documents that describe the operation and use of the programs.* There is no question that other, more complete definitions could be offered. But we need more than a formal definition.

1.2.1 Software Characteristics

To gain an understanding of software (and ultimately an understanding of software engineering), it is important to examine the characteristics of software that make it different from other things that human beings build. When hardware is built, the human creative process (analysis, design, construction, testing) is ultimately translated into a physical form. If we build a new computer, our initial sketches, formal design drawings, and breadboarded prototype evolve into a physical product (chips, circuit boards, power supplies, etc.).

Software is a logical rather than a physical system element. Therefore, software has characteristics that are considerably different than those of hardware:

KEY POINT
Software is engineered, not manufactured.

1. Software is developed or engineered, it is not manufactured in the classical sense.

Although some similarities exist between software development and hardware manufacture, the two activities are fundamentally different. In both activities, high qual-

---

1 In an excellent book of essays on the software business, Tom DeMarco [DEM95] argues the counterpoint. He states: "Instead of asking 'why does software cost so much?' we need to begin asking 'What have we done to make it possible for today's software to cost so little?' The answer to that question will help us continue the extraordinary level of achievement that has always distinguished the software industry."

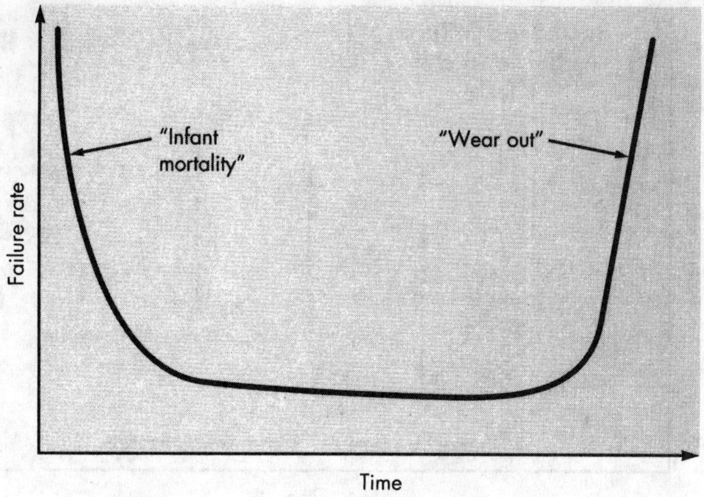

FIGURE 1.1
Failure curve for hardware

ity is achieved through good design, but the manufacturing phase for hardware can introduce quality problems that are nonexistent (or easily corrected) for software. Both activities are dependent on people, but the relationship between people applied and work accomplished is entirely different (see Chapter 7). Both activities require the construction of a "product" but the approaches are different.

Software costs are concentrated in engineering. This means that software projects cannot be managed as if they were manufacturing projects.

KEY POINT
Software doesn't wear out, but it does deteriorate.

2. Software doesn't "wear out."

Figure 1.1 depicts failure rate as a function of time for hardware. The relationship, often called the "bathtub curve," indicates that hardware exhibits relatively high failure rates early in its life (these failures are often attributable to design or manufacturing defects); defects are corrected and the failure rate drops to a steady-state level (ideally, quite low) for some period of time. As time passes, however, the failure rate rises again as hardware components suffer from the cumulative affects of dust, vibration, abuse, temperature extremes, and many other environmental maladies. Stated simply, the hardware begins to wear out.

Software is not susceptible to the environmental maladies that cause hardware to wear out. In theory, therefore, the failure rate curve for software should take the form of the "idealized curve" shown in Figure 1.2. Undiscovered defects will cause high failure rates early in the life of a program. However, these are corrected (ideally, without introducing other errors) and the curve flattens as shown.The idealized curve is a gross oversimplification of actual failure models (see Chapter 8 for more information) for software. However, the implication is clear—software doesn't wear out. But it does deteriorate!

This seeming contradiction can best be explained by considering the "actual curve" shown in Figure 1.2. During its life, software will undergo change (maintenance). As

FIGURE 1.2
Idealized and actual failure curves for software

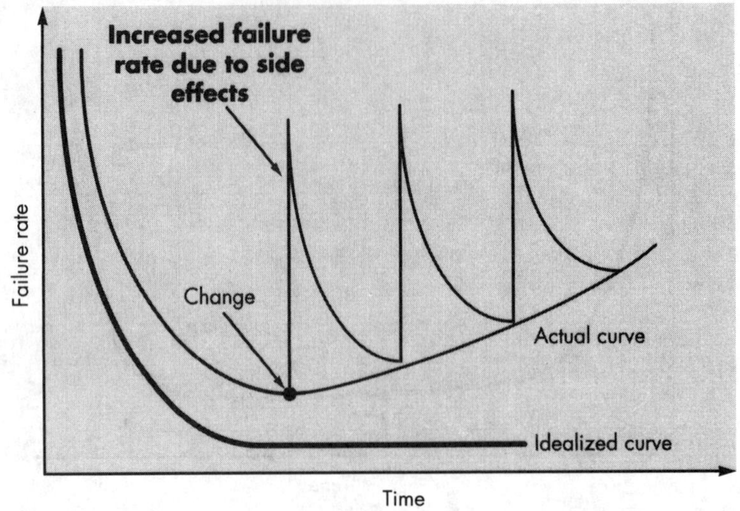

KEY POINT
Software engineering methods strive to reduce the magnitude of the spikes and the slope of the actual curve in Figure 1.2.

changes are made, it is likely that some new defects will be introduced, causing the failure rate curve to spike as shown in Figure 1.2. Before the curve can return to the original steady-state failure rate, another change is requested, causing the curve to spike again. Slowly, the minimum failure rate level begins to rise—the software is deteriorating due to change.

Another aspect of wear illustrates the difference between hardware and software. When a hardware component wears out, it is replaced by a spare part. There are no software spare parts. Every software failure indicates an error in design or in the process through which design was translated into machine executable code. Therefore, software maintenance involves considerably more complexity than hardware maintenance.

KEY POINT
Most software continues to be custom built.

3. Although the industry is moving toward component-based assembly, most software continues to be custom built.

Consider the manner in which the control hardware for a computer-based product is designed and built. The design engineer draws a simple schematic of the digital circuitry, does some fundamental analysis to assure that proper function will be achieved, and then goes to the shelf where catalogs of digital components exist. Each integrated circuit (called an *IC* or a *chip*) has a part number, a defined and validated function, a well-defined interface, and a standard set of integration guidelines. After each component is selected, it can be ordered off the shelf.

As an engineering discipline evolves, a collection of standard design components is created. Standard screws and off-the-shelf integrated circuits are only two of thousands of standard components that are used by mechanical and electrical engineers as they design new systems. The reusable components have been created so that the engineer can concentrate on the truly innovative elements of a design, that is, the parts of the design that represent something new. In the hardware world, component reuse is a natural part of the engineering process. In the software world, it is something that has only begun to be achieved on a broad scale.

A software component should be designed and implemented so that it can be reused in many different programs. In the 1960s, we built scientific subroutine libraries that were reusable in a broad array of engineering and scientific applications. These subroutine libraries reused well-defined algorithms in an effective manner but had a limited domain of application. Today, we have extended our view of reuse to encompass not only algorithms but also data structure. Modern reusable components encapsulate both data and the processing applied to the data, enabling the software engineer to create new applications from reusable parts. For example, today's graphical user interfaces are built using reusable components that enable the creation of graphics windows, pull-down menus, and a wide variety of interaction mechanisms. The data structure and processing detail required to build the interface are contained with a library of reusable components for interface construction.

XRef
Software reuse is discussed in Chapter 13. Component-based software engineering is presented in Chapter 27.

1.2.2 Software Applications

Software may be applied in any situation for which a prespecified set of procedural steps (i.e., an algorithm) has been defined (notable exceptions to this rule are expert system software and neural network software). Information content and determinacy are important factors in determining the nature of a software application. Content refers to the meaning and form of incoming and outgoing information. For example, many business applications use highly structured input data (a database) and produce formatted "reports." Software that controls an automated machine (e.g., a numerical control) accepts discrete data items with limited structure and produces individual machine commands in rapid succession.

Information determinacy refers to the predictability of the order and timing of information. An engineering analysis program accepts data that have a predefined order, executes the analysis algorithm(s) without interruption, and produces resultant data in report or graphical format. Such applications are determinate. A multiuser operating system, on the other hand, accepts inputs that have varied content and arbitrary timing, executes algorithms that can be interrupted by external conditions, and produces output that varies as a function of environment and time. Applications with these characteristics are indeterminate.

It is somewhat difficult to develop meaningful generic categories for software applications. As software complexity grows, neat compartmentalization disappears. The following software areas indicate the breadth of potential applications:

System software. System software is a collection of programs written to service other programs. Some system software (e.g., compilers, editors, and file management utilities) process complex, but determinate, information structures. Other systems applications (e.g., operating system components, drivers, telecommunications processors) process largely indeterminate data. In either case, the system software area is characterized by heavy interaction with computer hardware; heavy usage by multiple users; concurrent operation that requires scheduling, resource sharing, and sophisticated process management; complex data structures; and multiple external interfaces.

Real-time software. Software that monitors/analyzes/controls real-world events as they occur is called *real time.* Elements of real-time software include a data gathering component that collects and formats information from an external environment, an analysis component that transforms information as required by the application, a control/output component that responds to the external environment, and a monitoring component that coordinates all other components so that real-time response (typically ranging from 1 millisecond to 1 second) can be maintained.

WebRef

One of the most comprehensive libraries of shareware/freeware can be found at **www.shareware.com**

Business software. Business information processing is the largest single software application area. Discrete "systems" (e.g., payroll, accounts receivable/payable, inventory) have evolved into management information system (MIS) software that accesses one or more large databases containing business information. Applications in this area restructure existing data in a way that facilitates business operations or management decision making. In addition to conventional data processing application, business software applications also encompass interactive computing (e.g., point-of-sale transaction processing).

Engineering and scientific software. Engineering and scientific software have been characterized by "number crunching" algorithms. Applications range from astronomy to volcanology, from automotive stress analysis to space shuttle orbital dynamics, and from molecular biology to automated manufacturing. However, modern applications within the engineering/scientific area are moving away from conventional numerical algorithms. Computer-aided design, system simulation, and other interactive applications have begun to take on real-time and even system software characteristics.

Embedded software. Intelligent products have become commonplace in nearly every consumer and industrial market. Embedded software resides in read-only memory and is used to control products and systems for the consumer and industrial markets. Embedded software can perform very limited and esoteric functions (e.g., keypad control for a microwave oven) or provide significant function and control capability (e.g., digital functions in an automobile such as fuel control, dashboard displays, and braking systems).

Personal computer software. The personal computer software market has burgeoned over the past two decades. Word processing, spreadsheets, computer graphics, multimedia, entertainment, database management, personal and business financial applications, external network, and database access are only a few of hundreds of applications.

Web-based software. The Web pages retrieved by a browser are software that incorporates executable instructions (e.g., CGI, HTML, Perl, or Java), and data (e.g., hypertext and a variety of visual and audio formats). In essence, the network becomes a massive computer providing an almost unlimited software resource that can be accessed by anyone with a modem.

Artificial intelligence software. Artificial intelligence (AI) software makes use of nonnumerical algorithms to solve complex problems that are not amenable to computation or straightforward analysis. Expert systems, also called knowledge-based systems, pattern recognition (image and voice), artificial neural networks, theorem proving, and game playing are representative of applications within this category.

1.3 SOFTWARE: A CRISIS ON THE HORIZON?

Quote:

"The most likely way for the world to be destroyed, most experts agree, is by accident. That's where we come in; we're computer professionals. We cause accidents."

Nathaniel Borenstein

Many industry observers (including this author) have characterized the problems associated with software development as a "crisis." More than a few books (e.g., [GLA97], [FLO97], [YOU98a]) have recounted the impact of some of the more spectacular software failures that have occurred over the past decade. Yet, the great successes achieved by the software industry have led many to question whether the term *software crisis* is still appropriate. Robert Glass, the author of a number of books on software failures, is representative of those who have had a change of heart. He states [GLA98]: "I look at my failure stories and see exception reporting, spectacular failures in the midst of many successes, a cup that is [now] nearly full."

It is true that software people succeed more often than they fail. It also true that the software crisis predicted 30 years ago never seemed to materialize. What we really have may be something rather different.

The word *crisis* is defined in *Webster's Dictionary* as "a turning point in the course of anything; decisive or crucial time, stage or event." Yet, in terms of overall software quality and the speed with which computer-based systems and products are developed, there has been no "turning point," no "decisive time," only slow, evolutionary change, punctuated by explosive technological changes in disciplines associated with software.

The word *crisis* has another definition: "the turning point in the course of a disease, when it becomes clear whether the patient will live or die." This definition may give us a clue about the real nature of the problems that have plagued software development.

What we really have might be better characterized as a chronic affliction.[2] The word *affliction* is defined as "anything causing pain or distress." But the definition of the adjective *chronic* is the key to our argument: "lasting a long time or recurring often; continuing indefinitely." It is far more accurate to describe the problems we have endured in the software business as a chronic affliction than a crisis.

Regardless of what we call it, the set of problems that are encountered in the development of computer software is not limited to software that "doesn't function

2 This terminology was suggested by Professor Daniel Tiechrow of the University of Michigan in a talk presented in Geneva, Switzerland, April 1989.

properly." Rather, the affliction encompasses problems associated with how we develop software, how we support a growing volume of existing software, and how we can expect to keep pace with a growing demand for more software.

We live with this affliction to this day—in fact, the industry prospers in spite of it. And yet, things would be much better if we could find and broadly apply a cure.

1.4 SOFTWARE MYTHS

Quote:

"In the absence of meaningful standards, a new industry like software comes to depend instead on folklore."

Tom DeMarco

Many causes of a software affliction can be traced to a mythology that arose during the early history of software development. Unlike ancient myths that often provide human lessons well worth heeding, software myths propagated misinformation and confusion. Software myths had a number of attributes that made them insidious; for instance, they appeared to be reasonable statements of fact (sometimes containing elements of truth), they had an intuitive feel, and they were often promulgated by experienced practitioners who "knew the score."

Today, most knowledgeable professionals recognize myths for what they are—misleading attitudes that have caused serious problems for managers and technical people alike. However, old attitudes and habits are difficult to modify, and remnants of software myths are still believed.

Management myths. Managers with software responsibility, like managers in most disciplines, are often under pressure to maintain budgets, keep schedules from slipping, and improve quality. Like a drowning person who grasps at a straw, a software manager often grasps at belief in a software myth, if that belief will lessen the pressure (even temporarily).

Myth: We already have a book that's full of standards and procedures for building software, won't that provide my people with everything they need to know?

Reality: The book of standards may very well exist, but is it used? Are software practitioners aware of its existence? Does it reflect modern software engineering practice? Is it complete? Is it streamlined to improve time to delivery while still maintaining a focus on quality? In many cases, the answer to all of these questions is "no."

Myth: My people have state-of-the-art software development tools, after all, we buy them the newest computers.

Reality: It takes much more than the latest model mainframe, workstation, or PC to do high-quality software development. Computer-aided software engineering (CASE) tools are more important than hardware for achieving good quality and productivity, yet the majority of software developers still do not use them effectively.

Myth: If we get behind schedule, we can add more programmers and catch up (sometimes called the *Mongolian horde concept*).

Reality: Software development is not a mechanistic process like manufacturing. In the words of Brooks [BRO75]: "adding people to a late software project makes it

WebRef

The Software Project Managers Network at **www.spmn.com** can help you dispel these and other myths.

later." At first, this statement may seem counterintuitive. However, as new people are added, people who were working must spend time educating the newcomers, thereby reducing the amount of time spent on productive development effort. People can be added but only in a planned and well-coordinated manner.

Myth: If I decide to outsource[3] the software project to a third party, I can just relax and let that firm build it.

Reality: If an organization does not understand how to manage and control software projects internally, it will invariably struggle when it outsources software projects.

Customer myths. A customer who requests computer software may be a person at the next desk, a technical group down the hall, the marketing/sales department, or an outside company that has requested software under contract. In many cases, the customer believes myths about software because software managers and practitioners do little to correct misinformation. Myths lead to false expectations (by the customer) and ultimately, dissatisfaction with the developer.

ADVICE

Work very hard to understand what you have to do before you start. You may not be able to develop every detail, but the more you know, the less risk you take.

Myth: A general statement of objectives is sufficient to begin writing programs—we can fill in the details later.

Reality: A poor up-front definition is the major cause of failed software efforts. A formal and detailed description of the information domain, function, behavior, performance, interfaces, design constraints, and validation criteria is essential. These characteristics can be determined only after thorough communication between customer and developer.

Myth: Project requirements continually change, but change can be easily accommodated because software is flexible.

Reality: It is true that software requirements change, but the impact of change varies with the time at which it is introduced. Figure 1.3 illustrates the impact of change. If serious attention is given to up-front definition, early requests for change can be accommodated easily. The customer can review requirements and recommend modifications with relatively little impact on cost. When changes are requested during software design, the cost impact grows rapidly. Resources have been committed and a design framework has been established. Change can cause upheaval that requires additional resources and major design modification, that is, additional cost. Changes in function, performance, interface, or other characteristics during implementation (code and test) have a severe impact on cost. Change, when requested after software is in production, can be over an order of magnitude more expensive than the same change requested earlier.

XRef

The management and control of change is considered in detail in Chapter 9.

3 The term "outsourcing" refers to the widespread practice of contracting software development work to a third party—usually a consulting firm that specializes in building custom software for its clients.

FIGURE 1.3
The impact of change

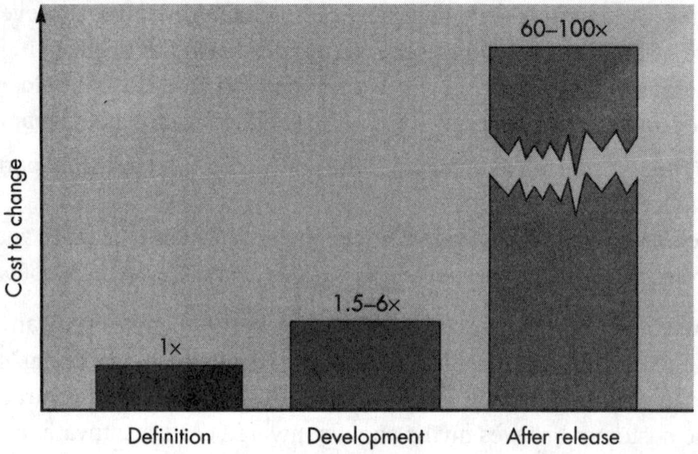

Practitioner's myths. Myths that are still believed by software practitioners have been fostered by 50 years of programming culture. During the early days of software, programming was viewed as an art form. Old ways and attitudes die hard.

Myth: Once we write the program and get it to work, our job is done.
Reality: Someone once said that "the sooner you begin 'writing code', the longer it'll take you to get done." Industry data ([LIE80], [JON91], [PUT97]) indicate that between 60 and 80 percent of all effort expended on software will be expended after it is delivered to the customer for the first time.

ADVICE
Whenever you think, we don't have time for software engineering discipline, ask yourself: "Will we have time to do it over again?"

Myth: Until I get the program "running" I have no way of assessing its quality.
Reality: One of the most effective software quality assurance mechanisms can be applied from the inception of a project—the *formal technical review.* Software reviews (described in Chapter 8) are a "quality filter" that have been found to be more effective than testing for finding certain classes of software defects.

Myth: The only deliverable work product for a successful project is the working program.
Reality: A working program is only one part of a *software configuration* that includes many elements. Documentation provides a foundation for successful engineering and, more important, guidance for software support.

Myth: Software engineering will make us create voluminous and unnecessary documentation and will invariably slow us down.
Reality: Software engineering is not about creating documents. It is about creating quality. Better quality leads to reduced rework. And reduced rework results in faster delivery times.

Many software professionals recognize the fallacy of the myths just described. Regrettably, habitual attitudes and methods foster poor management and technical practices, even when reality dictates a better approach. Recognition of software realities is the first step toward formulation of practical solutions for software engineering.

1.5 SUMMARY

Software has become the key element in the evolution of computer-based systems and products. Over the past 50 years, software has evolved from a specialized problem solving and information analysis tool to an industry in itself. But early "programming" culture and history have created a set of problems that persist today. Software has become the limiting factor in the continuing evolution of computer-based systems. Software is composed of programs, data, and documents. Each of these items comprises a configuration that is created as part of the software engineering process. The intent of software engineering is to provide a framework for building software with higher quality.

REFERENCES

[BRO75] Brooks, F., *The Mythical Man-Month,* Addison-Wesley, 1975.

[DEJ98] De Jager, P. et al., *Countdown Y2K: Business Survival Planning for the Year 2000,* Wiley, 1998.

[DEM95] DeMarco, T., *Why Does Software Cost So Much?* Dorset House, 1995, p. 9.

[FEI83] Feigenbaum, E.A. and P. McCorduck, *The Fifth Generation,* Addison-Wesley, 1983.

[FLO97] Flowers, S., *Software Failure, Management Failure—Amazing Stories and Cautionary Tales,* Wiley, 1997.

[GLA97] Glass, R.L., *Software Runaways,* Prentice-Hall, 1997.

[GLA98] Glass, R.L., "Is There Really a Software Crisis?" *IEEE Software,* vol. 15, no. 1, January 1998, pp. 104–105.

[HAM93] Hammer, M., and J. Champy, *Reengineering the Corporation,* HarperCollins Publishers, 1993.

[JON91] Jones, C., *Applied Software Measurement,* McGraw-Hill, 1991.

[KAR99] Karlson, E. and J. Kolber, *A Basic Introduction to Y2K: How the Year 2000 Computer Crisis Affects YOU,* Next Era Publications, 1999.

[LEV95] Levy, S., "The Luddites Are Back," *Newsweek,* July 12, 1995, p. 55.

[LEV99] Levy, S., "The New Digital Galaxy," *Newsweek,* May 31, 1999, p. 57.

[LIE80] Lientz, B. and E. Swanson, *Software Maintenance Management,* Addison-Wesley, 1980.

[NAI82] Naisbitt, J., *Megatrends,* Warner Books, 1982.

[NOR98] Norman, D., *The Invisible Computer,* MIT Press, 1998.

[OSB79] Osborne, A., *Running Wild—The Next Industrial Revolution,* Osborne/McGraw-Hill, 1979.

[PUT97] Putnam, L. and W. Myers, *Industrial Strength Software,* IEEE Computer Society Press, 1997.

[STO89] Stoll, C., *The Cuckoo's Egg,* Doubleday, 1989.

[TOF80] Toffler, A., *The Third Wave,* Morrow, 1980.

[TOF90] Toffler, A., *Powershift,* Bantam Publishers, 1990.

[YOU92] Yourdon, E., *The Decline and Fall of the American Programmer,* Yourdon Press, 1992.

[YOU96] Yourdon, E., *The Rise and Resurrection of the American Programmer,* Yourdon Press, 1996.

[YOU98a] Yourdon, E., *Death March Projects,* Prentice-Hall, 1998.

[YOU98b] Yourdon, E. and J. Yourdon, *Time Bomb 2000,* Prentice-Hall, 1998.

PROBLEMS AND POINTS TO PONDER

1.1. Software is the differentiating characteristic in many computer-based products and systems. Provide examples of two or three products and at least one system in which software, not hardware, is the differentiating element.

1.2. In the 1950s and 1960s, computer programming was an art form learned in an apprenticelike environment. How have the early days affected software development practices today?

1.3. Many authors have discussed the impact of the "information era." Provide a number of examples (both positive and negative) that indicate the impact of software on our society. Review one of the pre-1990 references in Section 1.1 and indicate where the author's predictions were right and where they were wrong.

1.4. Choose a specific application and indicate: (a) the software application category (Section 1.2.2) into which it fits; (b) the data content associated with the application; and (c) the information determinacy of the application.

1.5. As software becomes more pervasive, risks to the public (due to faulty programs) become an increasingly significant concern. Develop a realistic doomsday scenario (other than Y2K) where the failure of a computer program could do great harm (either economic or human).

1.6. Peruse the Internet newsgroup comp.risks and prepare a summary of risks to the public that have recently been discussed. An alternate source is *Software Engineering Notes* published by the ACM.

1.7. Write a paper summarizing recent advances in one of the leading edge software application areas. Potential choices include: advanced Web-based applications, virtual reality, artificial neural networks, advanced human interfaces, intelligent agents.

1.8. The "myths" noted in Section 1.4 are slowly fading as the years pass, but others are taking their place. Attempt to add one or two "new" myths to each category.

FURTHER READINGS AND INFORMATION SOURCES

Literally thousands of books are written about computer software. The vast majority discuss programming languages or software applications, but a few discuss software itself. Pressman and Herron (*Software Shock,* Dorset House, 1991) presented an early discussion (directed at the layperson) of software and the way professionals build it.

Negroponte's (*Being Digital,* Alfred A. Knopf, 1995) best-selling book provides a view of computing and its overall impact in the twenty-first century. Books by Norman [NOR98] and Bergman (*Information Appliances and Beyond,* Academic Press/Morgan Kaufmann, 2000) suggest that the widespread impact of the PC will decline as information appliances and pervasive computing connect everyone in the industrialized world and almost every "appliance" that they own to a new Internet infrastructure.

Minasi (*The Software Conspiracy: Why Software Companies Put out Faulty Products, How They Can Hurt You, and What You Can Do,* McGraw-Hill, 2000) argues that the "modern scourge" of software bugs can be eliminated and suggests ways to accomplish this. DeMarco (*Why Does Software Cost So Much?* Dorset House, 1995) has produced a collection of amusing and insightful essays on software and the process through which it is developed.

A wide variety of information sources on software-related topics and management is available on the Internet. An up-to-date list of World Wide Web references that are relevant to software can be found at the SEPA Web site:

http://www.mhhe.com/engcs/compsci/pressman/resources/product.mhtml

CHAPTER

2 THE PROCESS

KEY CONCEPTS

In a fascinating book that provides an economist's view of software and software engineering, Howard Baetjer, Jr. [BAE98], comments on the software process:

> Because software, like all capital, is embodied knowledge, and because that knowledge is initially dispersed, tacit, latent, and incomplete in large measure, software development is a social learning process. The process is a dialogue in which the knowledge that must become the software is brought together and embodied in the software. The process provides interaction between users and designers, between users and evolving tools, and between designers and evolving tools [technology]. It is an iterative process in which the evolving tool itself serves as the medium for communication, with each new round of the dialogue eliciting more useful knowledge from the people involved.

Indeed, building computer software is an iterative learning process, and the outcome, something that Baetjer would call "software capital," is an embodiment of knowledge collected, distilled, and organized as the process is conducted.

QUICK LOOK

What is it? When you build a product or system, it's important to go through a series of predictable steps—a road map that helps you create a timely, high-quality result. The road map that you follow is called a '*software process*.'

Who does it? Software engineers and their managers adapt the process to their needs and then follow it. In addition, the people who have requested the software play a role in the software process.

Why is it important? Because it provides stability, control, and organization to an activity that can, if left uncontrolled, become quite chaotic.

What are the steps? At a detailed level, the process that you adopt depends on the software you're building. One process might be appropriate for creating software for an aircraft avionics system, while an entirely different process would be indicated for the creation of a Web site.

What is the work product? From the point of view of a software engineer, the work products are the programs, documents, and data produced as a consequence of the software engineering activities defined by the process.

How do I ensure that I've done it right? A number of software process assessment mechanisms enable organizations to determine the "maturity" of a software process. However, the quality, timeliness, and long-term viability of the product you build are the best indicators of the efficacy of the process that you use.

But what exactly is a software process from a technical point of view? Within the context of this book, we define a *software process* as a framework for the tasks that are required to build high-quality software. Is *process* synonymous with software engineering? The answer is "yes" and "no." A software process defines the approach that is taken as software is engineered. But software engineering also encompasses technologies that populate the process—technical methods and automated tools.

More important, software engineering is performed by creative, knowledgeable people who should work within a defined and mature software process that is appropriate for the products they build and the demands of their marketplace. The intent of this chapter is to provide a survey of the current state of the software process and pointers to more detailed discussion of management and technical topics presented later in this book.

2.1 SOFTWARE ENGINEERING: A LAYERED TECHNOLOGY

> **Quote:**
> "More than a discipline or a body of knowledge, engineering is a verb, an action word, a way of approaching a problem."
> **Scott Whitmire**

Although hundreds of authors have developed personal definitions of *software engineering,* a definition proposed by Fritz Bauer [NAU69] at the seminal conference on the subject still serves as a basis for discussion:

> [Software engineering is] the establishment and use of sound engineering principles in order to obtain economically software that is reliable and works efficiently on real machines.

Almost every reader will be tempted to add to this definition. It says little about the technical aspects of software quality; it does not directly address the need for customer satisfaction or timely product delivery; it omits mention of the importance of measurement and metrics; it does not state the importance of a mature process. And yet, Bauer's definition provides us with a baseline. What "sound engineering principles" can be applied to computer software development? How do we "economically" build software so that it is "reliable"? What is required to create computer programs that work "efficiently" on not one but many different "real machines"? These are the questions that continue to challenge software engineers.

The IEEE [IEE93] has developed a more comprehensive definition when it states:

> **?** How do we define ***software engineering?***

> Software Engineering: (1) The application of a systematic, disçiplined, quantifiable approach to the development, operation, and maintenance of software; that is, the application of engineering to software. (2) The study of approaches as in (1).

2.1.1 Process, Methods, and Tools

Software engineering is a layered technology. Referring to Figure 2.1, any engineering approach (including software engineering) must rest on an organizational commitment to quality. Total quality management and similar philosophies foster a continuous process improvement culture, and this culture ultimately leads to the

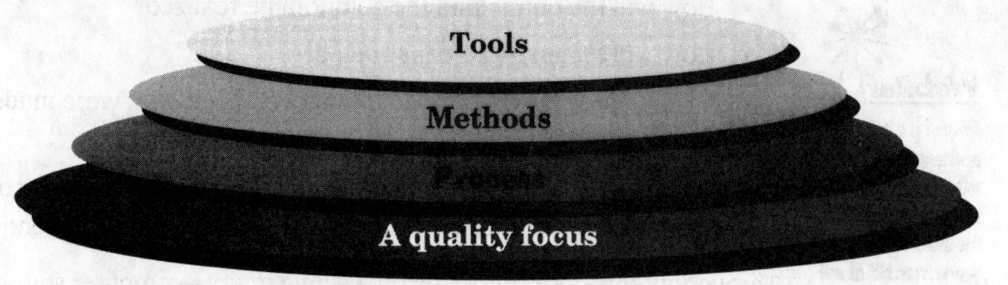

FIGURE 2.1 Software engineering layers

development of increasingly more mature approaches to software engineering. The bedrock that supports software engineering is a quality focus.

The foundation for software engineering is the *process* layer. Software engineering process is the glue that holds the technology layers together and enables rational and timely development of computer software. Process defines a framework for a set of *key process areas* (KPAs) [PAU93] that must be established for effective delivery of software engineering technology. The key process areas form the basis for management control of software projects and establish the context in which technical methods are applied, work products (models, documents, data, reports, forms, etc.) are produced, milestones are established, quality is ensured, and change is properly managed.

KEY POINT Software engineering encompasses a process, management and technical methods, and tools.

Software engineering *methods* provide the technical how-to's for building software. Methods encompass a broad array of tasks that include requirements analysis, design, program construction, testing, and support. Software engineering methods rely on a set of basic principles that govern each area of the technology and include modeling activities and other descriptive techniques.

Software engineering *tools* provide automated or semi-automated support for the process and the methods. When tools are integrated so that information created by one tool can be used by another, a system for the support of software development, called *computer-aided software engineering,* is established. CASE combines software, hardware, and a software engineering database (a repository containing important information about analysis, design, program construction, and testing) to create a software engineering environment analogous to CAD/CAE (computer-aided design/engineering) for hardware.

2.1.2 A Generic View of Software Engineering

Engineering is the analysis, design, construction, verification, and management of technical (or social) entities. Regardless of the entity to be engineered, the following questions must be asked and answered:

- What is the problem to be solved?
- What characteristics of the entity are used to solve the problem?

WebRef
Crosstalk is a journal that provides pragmatic software engineering advice and comment. On-line issues are available at **www.stsc.hill.af.mil**

- How will the entity (and the solution) be realized?
- How will the entity be constructed?
- What approach will be used to uncover errors that were made in the design and construction of the entity?
- How will the entity be supported over the long term, when corrections, adaptations, and enhancements are requested by users of the entity.

Throughout this book, we focus on a single entity—computer software. To engineer software adequately, a software engineering process must be defined. In this section, the generic characteristics of the software process are considered. Later in this chapter, specific process models are addressed.

KEY POINT
Software is engineered by applying three distinct phases that focus on definition, development, and support.

The work associated with software engineering can be categorized into three generic phases, regardless of application area, project size, or complexity. Each phase addresses one or more of the questions noted previously.

The *definition phase* focuses on *what.* That is, during definition, the software engineer attempts to identify what information is to be processed, what function and performance are desired, what system behavior can be expected, what interfaces are to be established, what design constraints exist, and what validation criteria are required to define a successful system. The key requirements of the system and the software are identified. Although the methods applied during the definition phase will vary depending on the software engineering paradigm (or combination of paradigms) that is applied, three major tasks will occur in some form: system or information engineering (Chapter 10), software project planning (Chapters 3, 5, 6, and 7), and requirements analysis (Chapters 11, 12, and 21).

Quote:
"Einstein argued that there must be a simplified explanation of nature, because God is not capricious or arbitrary. No such faith comforts the software engineer. Much of the complexity that he must master is arbitrary complexity."
Fred Brooks

The *development phase* focuses on *how*. That is, during development a software engineer attempts to define how data are to be structured, how function is to be implemented within a software architecture, how procedural details are to be implemented, how interfaces are to be characterized, how the design will be translated into a programming language (or nonprocedural language), and how testing will be performed. The methods applied during the development phase will vary, but three specific technical tasks should always occur: software design (Chapters 13–16, and 22), code generation, and software testing (Chapters 17, 18, and 23).

The *support phase* focuses on *change* associated with error correction, adaptations required as the software's environment evolves, and changes due to enhancements brought about by changing customer requirements. The support phase reapplies the steps of the definition and development phases but does so in the context of existing software. Four types of change are encountered during the support phase:

Correction. Even with the best quality assurance activities, it is likely that the customer will uncover defects in the software. *Corrective maintenance* changes the software to correct defects.

Adaptation. Over time, the original environment (e.g., CPU, operating system, business rules, external product characteristics) for which the software was developed is likely to change. *Adaptive maintenance* results in modification to the software to accommodate changes to its external environment.

Enhancement. As software is used, the customer/user will recognize additional functions that will provide benefit. *Perfective maintenance* extends the software beyond its original functional requirements.

ADVICE

When you use the term maintenance, recognize that it's much more than simply fixing bugs.

Prevention. Computer software deteriorates due to change, and because of this, *preventive maintenance,* often called *software reengineering,* must be conducted to enable the software to serve the needs of its end users. In essence, preventive maintenance makes changes to computer programs so that they can be more easily corrected, adapted, and enhanced.

In addition to these support activities, the users of software require continuing support. In-house technical assistants, telephone-help desks, and application-specific Web sites are often implemented as part of the support phase.

Today, a growing population of legacy programs[1] is forcing many companies to pursue software reengineering strategies (Chapter 30). In a global sense, software reengineering is often considered as part of business process reengineering.

The phases and related steps described in our generic view of software engineering are complemented by a number of *umbrella activities.* Typical activities in this category include:

- Software project tracking and control
- Formal technical reviews
- Software quality assurance
- Software configuration management
- Document preparation and production
- Reusability management
- Measurement
- Risk management

SEPA WEB

Umbrella activities

Umbrella activities are applied throughout the software process and are discussed in Parts Two and Five of this book.

2.2 THE SOFTWARE PROCESS

A software process can be characterized as shown in Figure 2.2. A *common process framework* is established by defining a small number of framework activities that are applicable to all software projects, regardless of their size or complexity. A number of *task sets*—each a collection of software engineering work tasks, project milestones,

1 The term *legacy programs* is a euphemism for older, often poorly designed and documented software that is business critical and must be supported over many years.

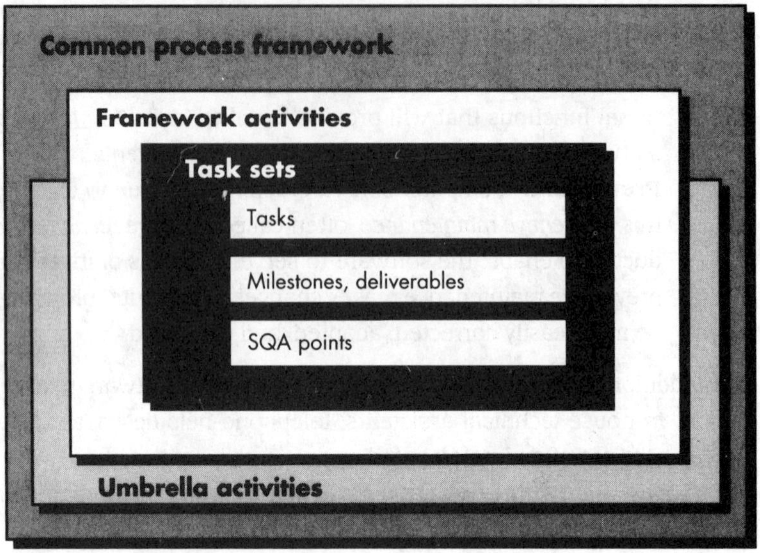

FIGURE 2.2 The software process

work products, and quality assurance points—enable the framework activities to be adapted to the characteristics of the software project and the requirements of the project team. Finally, umbrella activities—such as software quality assurance, software configuration management, and measurement[2]—overlay the process model. Umbrella activities are independent of any one framework activity and occur throughout the process.

ADVICE *Select a common process framework that is tuned to the product, the people, and the project.*

In recent years, there has been a significant emphasis on "process maturity." The Software Engineering Institute (SEI) has developed a comprehensive model predicated on a set of software engineering capabilities that should be present as organizations reach different levels of process maturity. To determine an organization's current state of process maturity, the SEI uses an assessment that results in a five point grading scheme. The grading scheme determines compliance with a *capability maturity model* (CMM) [PAU93] that defines key activities required at different levels of process maturity. The SEI approach provides a measure of the global effectiveness of a company's software engineering practices and establishes five process maturity levels that are defined in the following manner:

Level 1: Initial. The software process is characterized as ad hoc and occasionally even chaotic. Few processes are defined, and success depends on individual effort.

Level 2: Repeatable. Basic project management processes are established to track cost, schedule, and functionality. The necessary process discipline is in place to repeat earlier successes on projects with similar applications.

---

2 These topics are discussed in detail in later chapters.

WebRef
The SEI offers a wide array of process-related information at **www.sei.cmu.edu**

Level 3: Defined. The software process for both management and engineering activities is documented, standardized, and integrated into an organizationwide software process. All projects use a documented and approved version of the organization's process for developing and supporting software. This level includes all characteristics defined for level 2.

Level 4: Managed. Detailed measures of the software process and product quality are collected. Both the software process and products are quantitatively understood and controlled using detailed measures. This level includes all characteristics defined for level 3.

Level 5: Optimizing. Continuous process improvement is enabled by quantitative feedback from the process and from testing innovative ideas and technologies. This level includes all characteristics defined for level 4.

The five levels defined by the SEI were derived as a consequence of evaluating responses to the SEI assessment questionnaire that is based on the CMM. The results of the questionnaire are distilled to a single numerical grade that provides an indication of an organization's process maturity.

ADVICE
Every organization should strive to achieve the intent of the SEI CMM. However, implementing every aspect of the model may be overkill in your situation.

The SEI has associated key process areas (KPAs) with each of the maturity levels. The KPAs describe those software engineering functions (e.g., software project planning, requirements management) that must be present to satisfy good practice at a particular level. Each KPA is described by identifying the following characteristics:

- *Goals*—the overall objectives that the KPA must achieve.
- *Commitments*—requirements (imposed on the organization) that must be met to achieve the goals or provide proof of intent to comply with the goals.
- *Abilities*—those things that must be in place (organizationally and technically) to enable the organization to meet the commitments.
- *Activities*—the specific tasks required to achieve the KPA function.
- *Methods for monitoring implementation*—the manner in which the activities are monitored as they are put into place.
- *Methods for verifying implementation*—the manner in which proper practice for the KPA can be verified.

Eighteen KPAs (each described using these characteristics) are defined across the maturity model and mapped into different levels of process maturity. The following KPAs should be achieved at each process maturity level:[3]

Process maturity level 2

- Software configuration management
- Software quality assurance

3 Note that the KPAs are additive. For example, process maturity level 4 contains all level 3 KPAs plus those noted for level 2.

- Software subcontract management
- Software project tracking and oversight
- Software project planning
- Requirements management

Process maturity level 3

WebRef
A tabular version of the complete SEI-CMM, including all goals, commitments, abilities, and activities, is available at **sepo.nosc.mil/CMMmatrices.html**

- Peer reviews
- Intergroup coordination
- Software product engineering
- Integrated software management
- Training program
- Organization process definition
- Organization process focus

Process maturity level 4

- Software quality management
- Quantitative process management

Process maturity level 5

- Process change management
- Technology change management
- Defect prevention

Each of the KPAs is defined by a set of *key practices* that contribute to satisfying its goals. The key practices are policies, procedures, and activities that must occur before a key process area has been fully instituted. The SEI defines *key indicators* as "those key practices or components of key practices that offer the greatest insight into whether the goals of a key process area have been achieved." Assessment questions are designed to probe for the existence (or lack thereof) of a key indicator.

2.3 SOFTWARE PROCESS MODELS

Quote:
"Too often, software work follows the first law of bicycling: No matter where you're going, it's uphill and against the wind."
author unknown

To solve actual problems in an industry setting, a software engineer or a team of engineers must incorporate a development strategy that encompasses the process, methods, and tools layers described in Section 2.1.1 and the generic phases discussed in Section 2.1.2. This strategy is often referred to as a *process model* or a *software engineering paradigm*. A process model for software engineering is chosen based on the nature of the project and application, the methods and tools to be used, and the controls and deliverables that are required. In an intriguing paper on the nature of the software process, L. B. S. Raccoon [RAC95] uses fractals as the basis for a discussion of the true nature of the software process.

FIGURE 2.3

(a) The phases of a problem solving loop [RAC95]

(b) The phases within phases of the problem solving loop [RAC95]

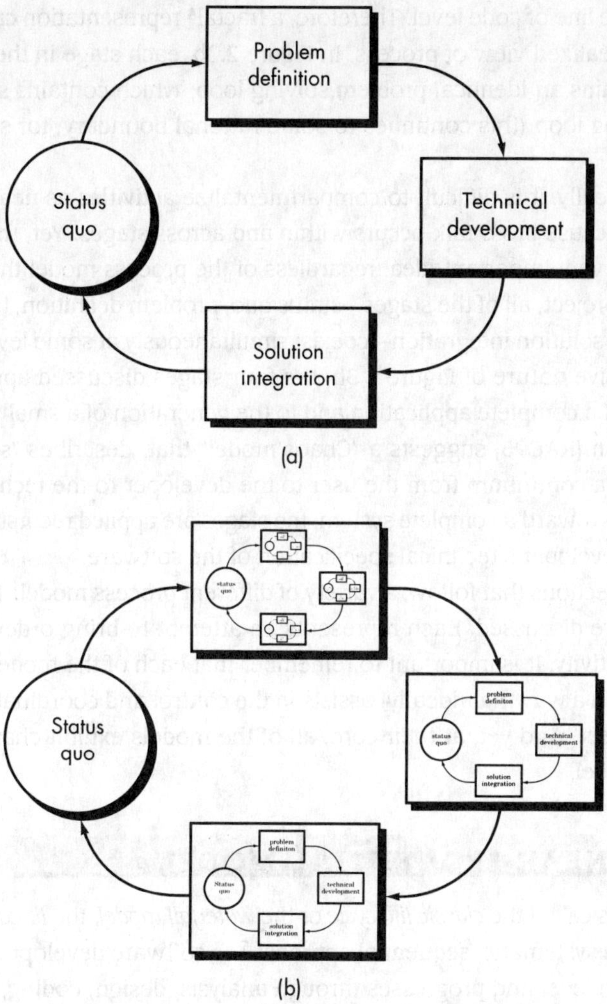

All software development can be characterized as a problem solving loop (Figure 2.3a) in which four distinct stages are encountered: status quo, problem definition, technical development, and solution integration. Status quo "represents the current state of affairs" [RAC95]; problem definition identifies the specific problem to be solved; technical development solves the problem through the application of some technology, and solution integration delivers the results (e.g., documents, programs, data, new business function, new product) to those who requested the solution in the first place. The generic software engineering phases and steps defined in Section 2.1.2 easily map into these stages.

This problem solving loop applies to software engineering work at many different levels of resolution. It can be used at the macro level when the entire application is considered, at a mid-level when program components are being engineered, and even at the line of code level. Therefore, a fractal[4] representation can be used to provide an idealized view of process. In Figure 2.3b, each stage in the problem solving loop contains an identical problem solving loop, which contains still another problem solving loop (this continues to some rational boundary; for software, a line of code).

Realistically, it is difficult to compartmentalize activities as neatly as Figure 2.3b implies because cross talk occurs within and across stages. Yet, this simplified view leads to a very important idea: regardless of the process model that is chosen for a software project, all of the stages—status quo, problem definition, technical development, and solution integration—coexist simultaneously at some level of detail. Given the recursive nature of Figure 2.3b, the four stages discussed apply equally to the analysis of a complete application and to the generation of a small segment of code.

KEY POINT

All stages of a software process—status quo, problem definition, technical development, and solution integration—coexist simultaneously at some level of detail.

Raccoon [RAC95] suggests a "Chaos model" that describes "software development [as] a continuum from the user to the developer to the technology." As work progresses toward a complete system, the stages are applied recursively to user needs and the developer's technical specification of the software.

In the sections that follow, a variety of different process models for software engineering are discussed. Each represents an attempt to bring order to an inherently chaotic activity. It is important to remember that each of the models has been characterized in a way that (ideally) assists in the control and coordination of a real software project. And yet, at their core, all of the models exhibit characteristics of the Chaos model.

2.4 THE LINEAR SEQUENTIAL MODEL

Sometimes called the *classic life cycle* or the *waterfall model,* the *linear sequential model* suggests a systematic, sequential approach[5] to software development that begins at the system level and progresses through analysis, design, coding, testing, and support. Figure 2.4 illustrates the linear sequential model for software engineering. Modeled after a conventional engineering cycle, the linear sequential model encompasses the following activities:

System/information engineering and modeling. Because software is always part of a larger system (or business), work begins by establishing requirements for all system elements and then allocating some subset of these requirements to software. This system view is essential when software must interact with other elements such as hardware, people, and databases. System engineering and analysis encompass requirements gathering at the system level with a small amount of top level

4 Fractals were originally proposed for geometric representations. A pattern is defined and then applied recursively at successively smaller scales; patterns fall inside patterns.

5 Although the original waterfall model proposed by Winston Royce [ROY70] made provision for "feedback loops," the vast majority of organizations that apply this process model treat it as if it were strictly linear.

FIGURE 2.4
The linear sequential model

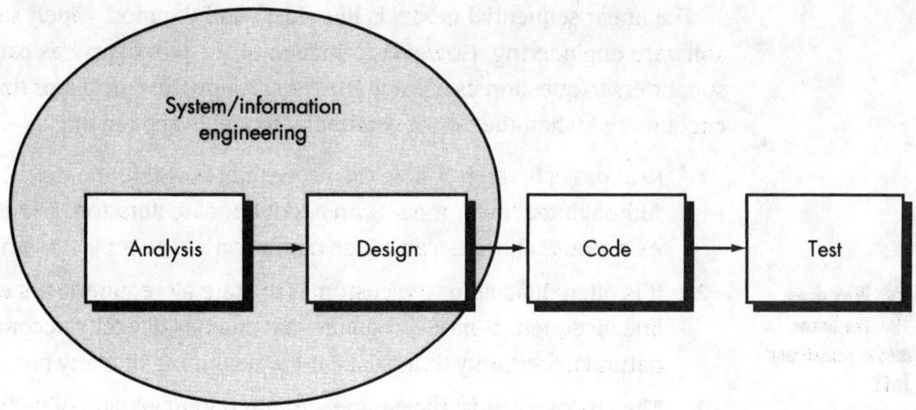

design and analysis. Information engineering encompasses requirements gathering at the strategic business level and at the business area level.

Software requirements analysis. The requirements gathering process is intensified and focused specifically on software. To understand the nature of the program(s) to be built, the software engineer ("analyst") must understand the information domain (described in Chapter 11) for the software, as well as required function, behavior, performance, and interface. Requirements for both the system and the software are documented and reviewed with the customer.

Design. Software design is actually a multistep process that focuses on four distinct attributes of a program: data structure, software architecture, interface representations, and procedural (algorithmic) detail. The design process translates requirements into a representation of the software that can be assessed for quality before coding begins. Like requirements, the design is documented and becomes part of the software configuration.

ADVICE

Although the linear model is often derided as "old fashioned," it remains a reasonable approach when requirements are well understood.

Code generation. The design must be translated into a machine-readable form. The code generation step performs this task. If design is performed in a detailed manner, code generation can be accomplished mechanistically.

Testing. Once code has been generated, program testing begins. The testing process focuses on the logical internals of the software, ensuring that all statements have been tested, and on the functional externals; that is, conducting tests to uncover errors and ensure that defined input will produce actual results that agree with required results.

Support. Software will undoubtedly undergo change after it is delivered to the customer (a possible exception is embedded software). Change will occur because errors have been encountered, because the software must be adapted to accommodate changes in its external environment (e.g., a change required because of a new operating system or peripheral device), or because the customer requires functional or performance enhancements. Software support/maintenance reapplies each of the preceding phases to an existing program rather than a new one.

The linear sequential model is the oldest and the most widely used paradigm for software engineering. However, criticism of the paradigm has caused even active supporters to question its efficacy [HAN95]. Among the problems that are sometimes encountered when the linear sequential model is applied are:

? Why does the linear model sometimes fail?

1. Real projects rarely follow the sequential flow that the model proposes. Although the linear model can accommodate iteration, it does so indirectly. As a result, changes can cause confusion as the project team proceeds.
2. It is often difficult for the customer to state all requirements explicitly. The linear sequential model requires this and has difficulty accommodating the natural uncertainty that exists at the beginning of many projects.
3. The customer must have patience. A working version of the program(s) will not be available until late in the project time-span. A major blunder, if undetected until the working program is reviewed, can be disastrous.

In an interesting analysis of actual projects Bradac [BRA94], found that the linear nature of the classic life cycle leads to "blocking states" in which some project team members must wait for other members of the team to complete dependent tasks. In fact, the time spent waiting can exceed the time spent on productive work! The blocking state tends to be more prevalent at the beginning and end of a linear sequential process.

Each of these problems is real. However, the classic life cycle paradigm has a definite and important place in software engineering work. It provides a template into which methods for analysis, design, coding, testing, and support can be placed. The classic life cycle remains a widely used procedural model for software engineering. While it does have weaknesses, it is significantly better than a haphazard approach to software development.

2.5 THE PROTOTYPING MODEL

Often, a customer defines a set of general objectives for software but does not identify detailed input, processing, or output requirements. In other cases, the developer may be unsure of the efficiency of an algorithm, the adaptability of an operating system, or the form that human/machine interaction should take. In these, and many other situations, a *prototyping paradigm* may offer the best approach.

The prototyping paradigm (Figure 2.5) begins with requirements gathering. Developer and customer meet and define the overall objectives for the software, identify whatever requirements are known, and outline areas where further definition is mandatory. A "quick design" then occurs. The quick design focuses on a representation of those aspects of the software that will be visible to the customer/user (e.g., input approaches and output formats). The quick design leads to the construction of

FIGURE 2.5
The prototyping paradigm

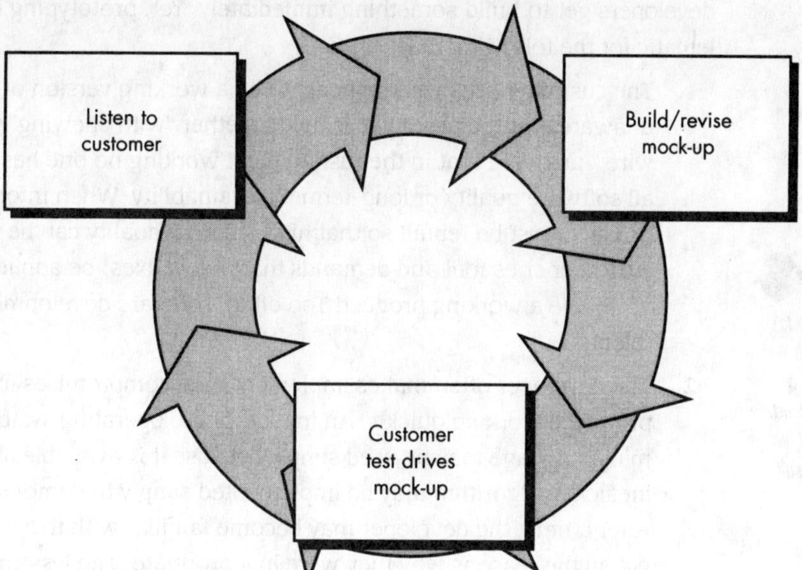

a prototype. The prototype is evaluated by the customer/user and used to refine requirements for the software to be developed. Iteration occurs as the prototype is tuned to satisfy the needs of the customer, while at the same time enabling the developer to better understand what needs to be done.

ADVICE

When your customer has a legitimate need but is clueless about the details, develop a prototype as a first step.

Ideally, the prototype serves as a mechanism for identifying software requirements. If a working prototype is built, the developer attempts to use existing program fragments or applies tools (e.g., report generators, window managers) that enable working programs to be generated quickly.

But what do we do with the prototype when it has served the purpose just described? Brooks [BRO75] provides an answer:

> In most projects, the first system built is barely usable. It may be too slow, too big, awkward in use or all three. There is no alternative but to start again, smarting but smarter, and build a redesigned version in which these problems are solved . . . When a new system concept or new technology is used, one has to build a system to throw away, for even the best planning is not so omniscient as to get it right the first time. The management question, therefore, is not whether to build a pilot system and throw it away. You will do that. The only question is whether to plan in advance to build a throwaway, or to promise to deliver the throwaway to customers . . .

The prototype can serve as "the first system." The one that Brooks recommends we throw away. But this may be an idealized view. It is true that both customers and developers like the prototyping paradigm. Users get a feel for the actual system and developers get to build something immediately. Yet, prototyping can also be problematic for the following reasons:

1. The customer sees what appears to be a working version of the software, unaware that the prototype is held together "with chewing gum and baling wire," unaware that in the rush to get it working no one has considered overall software quality or long-term maintainability. When informed that the product must be rebuilt so that high levels of quality can be maintained, the customer cries foul and demands that "a few fixes" be applied to make the prototype a working product. Too often, software development management relents.

ADVICE

Resist pressure to extend a rough prototype into a production product. Quality almost always suffers as a result.

2. The developer often makes implementation compromises in order to get a prototype working quickly. An inappropriate operating system or programming language may be used simply because it is available and known; an inefficient algorithm may be implemented simply to demonstrate capability. After a time, the developer may become familiar with these choices and forget all the reasons why they were inappropriate. The less-than-ideal choice has now become an integral part of the system.

Although problems can occur, prototyping can be an effective paradigm for software engineering. The key is to define the rules of the game at the beginning; that is, the customer and developer must both agree that the prototype is built to serve as a mechanism for defining requirements. It is then discarded (at least in part) and the actual software is engineered with an eye toward quality and maintainability.

2.6 THE RAD MODEL

Rapid application development (RAD) is an incremental software development process model that emphasizes an extremely short development cycle. The RAD model is a "high-speed" adaptation of the linear sequential model in which rapid development is achieved by using component-based construction. If requirements are well understood and project scope is constrained, the RAD process enables a development team to create a "fully functional system" within very short time periods (e.g., 60 to 90 days) [MAR91]. Used primarily for information systems applications, the RAD approach encompasses the following phases [KER94]:

Business modeling. The information flow among business functions is modeled in a way that answers the following questions: What information drives the business process? What information is generated? Who generates it? Where does the information go? Who processes it? Business modeling is described in more detail in Chapter 10.

Data modeling. The information flow defined as part of the business modeling phase is refined into a set of data objects that are needed to support the business. The char-

FIGURE 2.6
The RAD model

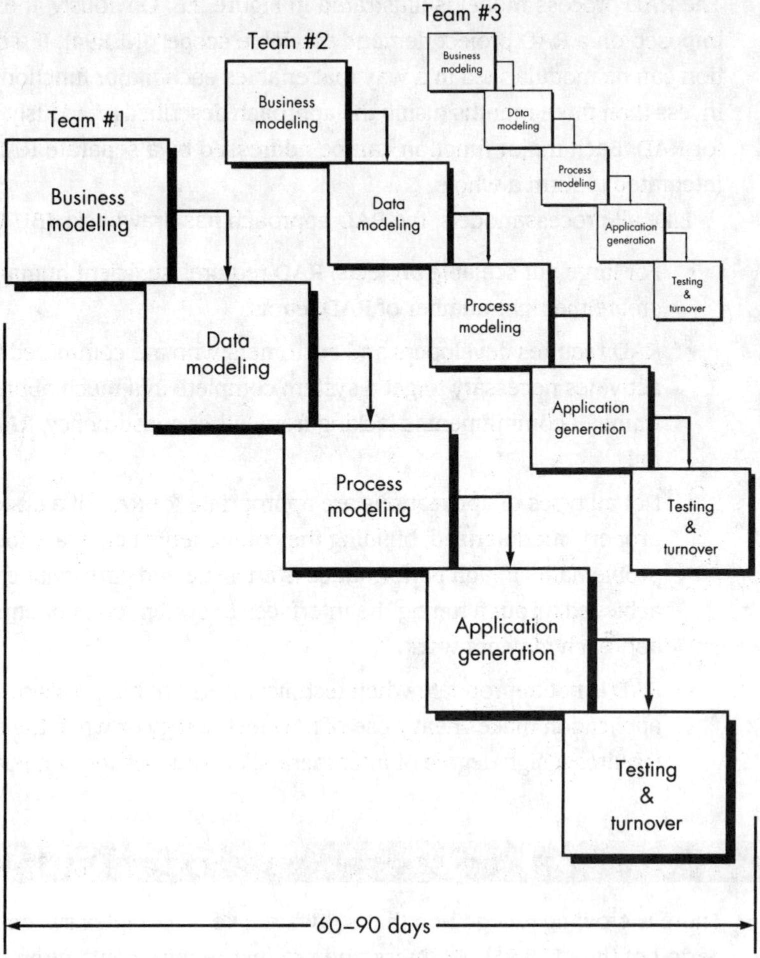

acteristics (called *attributes*) of each object are identified and the relationships between these objects defined. Data modeling is considered in Chapter 12.

Process modeling. The data objects defined in the data modeling phase are transformed to achieve the information flow necessary to implement a business function. Processing descriptions are created for adding, modifying, deleting, or retrieving a data object.

Application generation. RAD assumes the use of fourth generation techniques (Section 2.10). Rather than creating software using conventional third generation programming languages the RAD process works to reuse existing program components (when possible) or create reusable components (when necessary). In all cases, automated tools are used to facilitate construction of the software.

Testing and turnover. Since the RAD process emphasizes reuse, many of the program components have already been tested. This reduces overall testing time. However, new components must be tested and all interfaces must be fully exercised.

The RAD process model is illustrated in Figure 2.6. Obviously, the time constraints imposed on a RAD project demand "scalable scope" [KER94]. If a business application can be modularized in a way that enables each major function to be completed in less than three months (using the approach described previously), it is a candidate for RAD. Each major function can be addressed by a separate RAD team and then integrated to form a whole.

Like all process models, the RAD approach has drawbacks [BUT94]:

XRef
RAD makes heavy use of reusable components. For further information on component-based development, see Chapter 27.

- For large but scalable projects, RAD requires sufficient human resources to create the right number of RAD teams.
- RAD requires developers and customers who are committed to the rapid-fire activities necessary to get a system complete in a much abbreviated time frame. If commitment is lacking from either constituency, RAD projects will fail.
- Not all types of applications are appropriate for RAD. If a system cannot be properly modularized, building the components necessary for RAD will be problematic. If high performance is an issue and performance is to be achieved through tuning the interfaces to system components, the RAD approach may not work.
- RAD is not appropriate when technical risks are high. This occurs when a new application makes heavy use of new technology or when the new software requires a high degree of interoperability with existing computer programs.

2.7 EVOLUTIONARY SOFTWARE PROCESS MODELS

There is growing recognition that software, like all complex systems, evolves over a period of time [GIL88]. Business and product requirements often change as development proceeds, making a straight path to an end product unrealistic; tight market deadlines make completion of a comprehensive software product impossible, but a limited version must be introduced to meet competitive or business pressure; a set of core product or system requirements is well understood, but the details of product or system extensions have yet to be defined. In these and similar situations, software engineers need a process model that has been explicitly designed to accommodate a product that evolves over time.

The linear sequential model (Section 2.4) is designed for straight-line development. In essence, this waterfall approach assumes that a complete system will be delivered after the linear sequence is completed. The prototyping model (Section 2.5) is designed to assist the customer (or developer) in understanding requirements. In general, it is not designed to deliver a production system. The evolutionary nature of software is not considered in either of these classic software engineering paradigms.

Evolutionary models are iterative. They are characterized in a manner that enables software engineers to develop increasingly more complete versions of the software.

2.7.1 The Incremental Model

The *incremental model* combines elements of the linear sequential model (applied repetitively) with the iterative philosophy of prototyping. Referring to Figure 2.7, the incremental model applies linear sequences in a staggered fashion as calendar time progresses. Each linear sequence produces a deliverable "increment" of the software [MDE93]. For example, word-processing software developed using the incremental paradigm might deliver basic file management, editing, and document production functions in the first increment; more sophisticated editing and document production capabilities in the second increment; spelling and grammar checking in the third increment; and advanced page layout capability in the fourth increment. It should be noted that the process flow for any increment can incorporate the prototyping paradigm.

KEY POINT

The incremental model delivers software in small but usable pieces, called "increments." In general, each increment builds on those that have already been delivered.

When an incremental model is used, the first increment is often a *core product.* That is, basic requirements are addressed, but many supplementary features (some known, others unknown) remain undelivered. The core product is used by the customer (or undergoes detailed review). As a result of use and/or evaluation, a plan is developed for the next increment. The plan addresses the modification of the core product to better meet the needs of the customer and the delivery of additional features and functionality. This process is repeated following the delivery of each increment, until the complete product is produced.

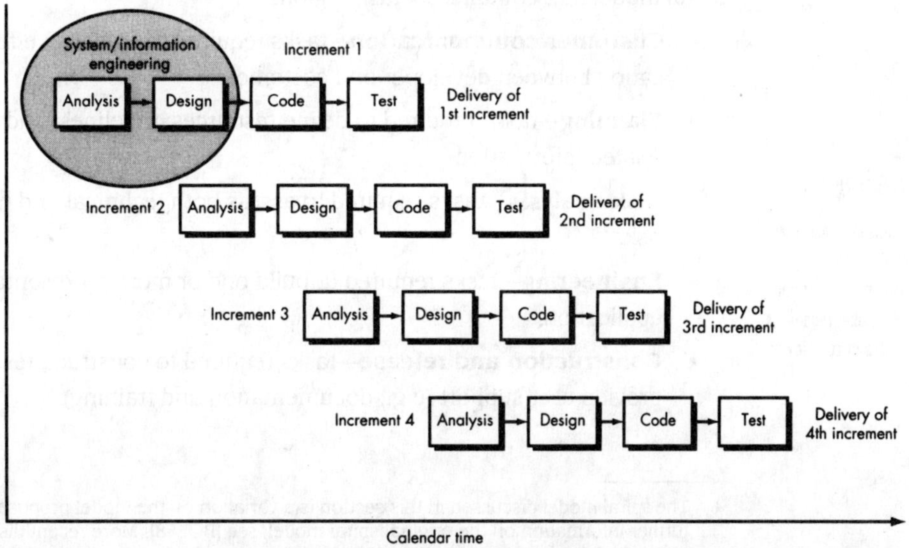

FIGURE 2.7
The incremental model

ADVICE

When you encounter a difficult deadline that cannot be changed, the incremental model is a good paradigm to consider.

The incremental process model, like prototyping (Section 2.5) and other evolutionary approaches, is iterative in nature. But unlike prototyping, the incremental model focuses on the delivery of an operational product with each increment. Early increments are stripped down versions of the final product, but they do provide capability that serves the user and also provide a platform for evaluation by the user.

Incremental development is particularly useful when staffing is unavailable for a complete implementation by the business deadline that has been established for the project. Early increments can be implemented with fewer people. If the core product is well received, then additional staff (if required) can be added to implement the next increment. In addition, increments can be planned to manage technical risks. For example, a major system might require the availability of new hardware that is under development and whose delivery date is uncertain. It might be possible to plan early increments in a way that avoids the use of this hardware, thereby enabling partial functionality to be delivered to end-users without inordinate delay.

2.7.2 The Spiral Model

The *spiral model,* originally proposed by Boehm [BOE88], is an evolutionary software process model that couples the iterative nature of prototyping with the controlled and systematic aspects of the linear sequential model. It provides the potential for rapid development of incremental versions of the software. Using the spiral model, software is developed in a series of incremental releases. During early iterations, the incremental release might be a paper model or prototype. During later iterations, increasingly more complete versions of the engineered system are produced.

A spiral model is divided into a number of framework activities, also called *task regions.*[6] Typically, there are between three and six task regions. Figure 2.8 depicts a spiral model that contains six task regions:

KEY POINT

Framework activities apply to every software project you undertake, regardless of size or complexity.

- **Customer communication**—tasks required to establish effective communication between developer and customer.
- **Planning**—tasks required to define resources, timelines, and other project-related information.
- **Risk analysis**—tasks required to assess both technical and management risks.
- **Engineering**—tasks required to build one or more representations of the application.
- **Construction and release**—tasks required to construct, test, install, and provide user support (e.g., documentation and training).

---

6 The spiral model discussed in this section is a variation on the model proposed by Boehm. For further information on the original spiral model, see [BOE88]. More recent discussion of Boehm's spiral model can be found in [BOE98].

FIGURE 2.8
A typical spiral model

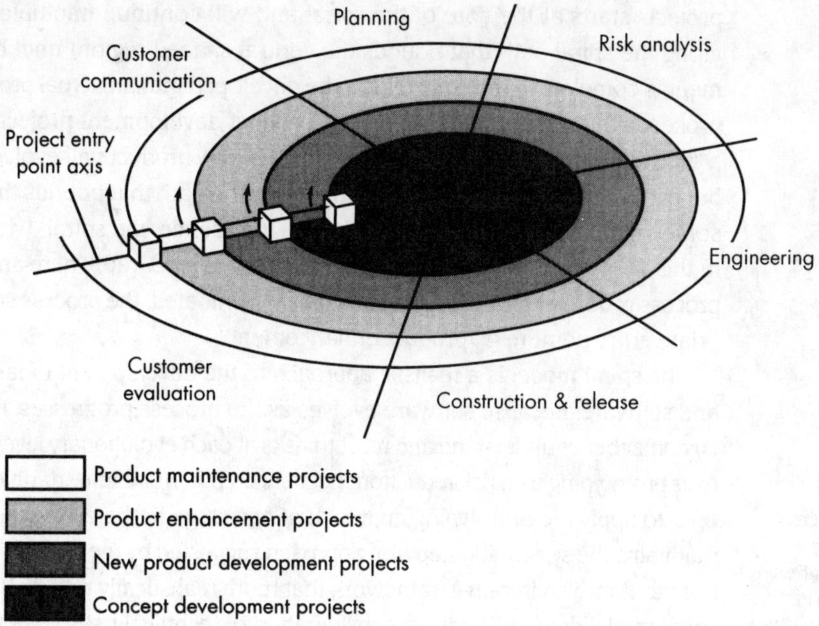

- **Customer evaluation**—tasks required to obtain customer feedback based on evaluation of the software representations created during the engineering stage and implemented during the installation stage.

What is a "task set"?

Each of the regions is populated by a set of work tasks, called a *task set,* that are adapted to the characteristics of the project to be undertaken. For small projects, the number of work tasks and their formality is low. For larger, more critical projects, each task region contains more work tasks that are defined to achieve a higher level of formality. In all cases, the umbrella activities (e.g., software configuration management and software quality assurance) noted in Section 2.2 are applied.

As this evolutionary process begins, the software engineering team moves around the spiral in a clockwise direction, beginning at the center. The first circuit around the spiral might result in the development of a product specification; subsequent passes around the spiral might be used to develop a prototype and then progressively more sophisticated versions of the software. Each pass through the planning region results in adjustments to the project plan. Cost and schedule are adjusted based on feedback derived from customer evaluation. In addition, the project manager adjusts the planned number of iterations required to complete the software.

Adaptable process model

Unlike classical process models that end when software is delivered, the spiral model can be adapted to apply throughout the life of the computer software. An alternative view of the spiral model can be considered by examining the *project entry point axis,* also shown in Figure 2.8. Each cube placed along the axis can be used to represent the starting point for different types of projects. A "concept development project" starts at the core of the spiral and will continue (multiple iterations occur along the spiral path that bounds the central shaded region) until concept development is complete. If the concept is to be developed into an actual product, the process proceeds through the next cube (new product development project entry point) and a "new development project" is initiated. The new product will evolve through a number of iterations around the spiral, following the path that bounds the region that has somewhat lighter shading than the core. In essence, the spiral, when characterized in this way, remains operative until the software is retired. There are times when the process is dormant, but whenever a change is initiated, the process starts at the appropriate entry point (e.g., product enhancement).

The spiral model is a realistic approach to the development of large-scale systems and software. Because software evolves as the process progresses, the developer and customer better understand and react to risks at each evolutionary level. The spiral model uses prototyping as a risk reduction mechanism but, more important, enables the developer to apply the prototyping approach at any stage in the evolution of the product. It maintains the systematic stepwise approach suggested by the classic life cycle but incorporates it into an iterative framework that more realistically reflects the real world. The spiral model demands a direct consideration of technical risks at all stages of the project and, if properly applied, should reduce risks before they become problematic.

XRef
Evolutionary models, such as the spiral model, are particularly well-suited to the development of object-oriented systems. See Part Four for details.

But like other paradigms, the spiral model is not a panacea. It may be difficult to convince customers (particularly in contract situations) that the evolutionary approach is controllable. It demands considerable risk assessment expertise and relies on this expertise for success. If a major risk is not uncovered and managed, problems will undoubtedly occur. Finally, the model has not been used as widely as the linear sequential or prototyping paradigms. It will take a number of years before efficacy of this important paradigm can be determined with absolute certainty.

2.7.3 The WINWIN Spiral Model

The spiral model discussed in Section 2.7.2 suggests a framework activity that addresses customer communication. The objective of this activity is to elicit project requirements from the customer. In an ideal context, the developer simply asks the customer what is required and the customer provides sufficient detail to proceed. Unfortunately, this rarely happens. In reality, the customer and the developer enter into a process of negotiation, where the customer may be asked to balance functionality, performance, and other product or system characteristics against cost and time to market.

KEY POINT
Eliciting software requirements demands negotiation. Successful negotiation occurs when both sides "win".

The best negotiations strive for a "win-win" result.[7] That is, the customer wins by getting the system or product that satisfies the majority of the customer's needs and the developer wins by working to realistic and achievable budgets and deadlines.

---

7 Dozens of books have been written on negotiating skills (e.g., [FIS91], [DON96], [FAR97]). It is one of the more important things that a young (or old) engineer or manager can learn. Read one.

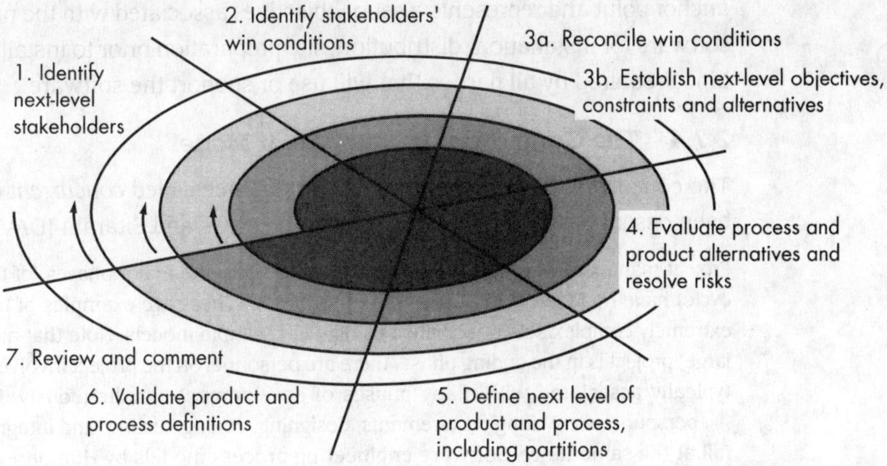

FIGURE 2.9
The WINWIN spiral model [BOE98].

Boehm's WINWIN spiral model [BOE98] defines a set of negotiation activities at the beginning of each pass around the spiral. Rather than a single customer communication activity, the following activities are defined:

SEPA WEB
Negotiating skills

1. Identification of the system or subsystem's key "stakeholders."[8]
2. Determination of the stakeholders' "win conditions."
3. Negotiation of the stakeholders' win conditions to reconcile them into a set of win-win conditions for all concerned (including the software project team).

Successful completion of these initial steps achieves a win-win result, which becomes the key criterion for proceeding to software and system definition. The WINWIN spiral model is illustrated in Figure 2.9.

In addition to the emphasis placed on early negotiation, the WINWIN spiral model introduces three process milestones, called *anchor points* [BOE96], that help establish the completion of one cycle around the spiral and provide decision milestones before the software project proceeds.

In essence, the anchor points represent three different views of progress as the project traverses the spiral. The first anchor point, *life cycle objectives* (LCO), defines a set of objectives for each major software engineering activity. For example, as part of LCO, a set of objectives establishes the definition of top-level system/product requirements. The second anchor point, *life cycle architecture* (LCA), establishes objectives that must be met as the system and software architecture is defined. For example, as part of LCA, the software project team must demonstrate that it has evaluated the applicability of off-the-shelf and reusable software components and considered their impact on architectural decisions. *Initial operational capability* (IOC) is the third

8 A stakeholder is anyone in the organization that has a direct business interest in the system or product to be built and will be rewarded for a successful outcome or criticized if the effort fails.

anchor point and represents a set of objectives associated with the preparation of the software for installation/distribution, site preparation prior to installation, and assistance required by all parties that will use or support the software.

2.7.4 The Concurrent Development Model

The concurrent development model, sometimes called *concurrent engineering,* has been described in the following manner by Davis and Sitaram [DAV94]:

> Project managers who track project status in terms of the major phases [of the classic life cycle] have no idea of the status of their projects. These are examples of trying to track extremely complex sets of activities using overly simple models. Note that although . . . [a large] project is in the coding phase, there are personnel on the project involved in activities typically associated with many phases of development simultaneously. For example, . . . personnel are writing requirements, designing, coding, testing, and integration testing [all at the same time]. Software engineering process models by Humphrey and Kellner [[HUM89], [KEL89]] have shown the concurrency that exists for activities occurring during any one phase. Kellner's more recent work [KEL91] uses statecharts [a notation that represents the states of a process] to represent the concurrent relationship existent among activities associated with a specific event (e.g., a requirements change during late development), but fails to capture the richness of concurrency that exists across all software development and management activities in the project. . . . Most software development process models are driven by time; the later it is, the later in the development process you are. [A concurrent process model] is driven by user needs, management decisions, and review results.

The concurrent process model can be represented schematically as a series of major technical activities, tasks, and their associated states. For example, the engineering activity defined for the spiral model (Section 2.7.2) is accomplished by invoking the following tasks: prototyping and/or analysis modeling, requirements specification, and design.[9]

Figure 2.10 provides a schematic representation of one activity with the concurrent process model. The activity—analysis—may be in any one of the states[10] noted at any given time. Similarly, other activities (e.g., design or customer communication) can be represented in an analogous manner. All activities exist concurrently but reside in different states. For example, early in a project the *customer communication* activity (not shown in the figure) has completed its first iteration and exists in the **awaiting changes** state. The *analysis* activity (which existed in the **none** state while initial customer communication was completed) now makes a transition into the **under development** state. If, however, the customer indicates that changes in requirements must be made, the *analysis* activity moves from the **under development** state into the **awaiting changes** state.

The concurrent process model defines a series of events that will trigger transitions from state to state for each of the software engineering activities. For example,

---

9 It should be noted that analysis and design are complex tasks that require substantial discussion. Parts Three and Four of this book consider these topics in detail.

10 A state is some externally observable mode of behavior.

FIGURE 2.10
One element of the concurrent process model

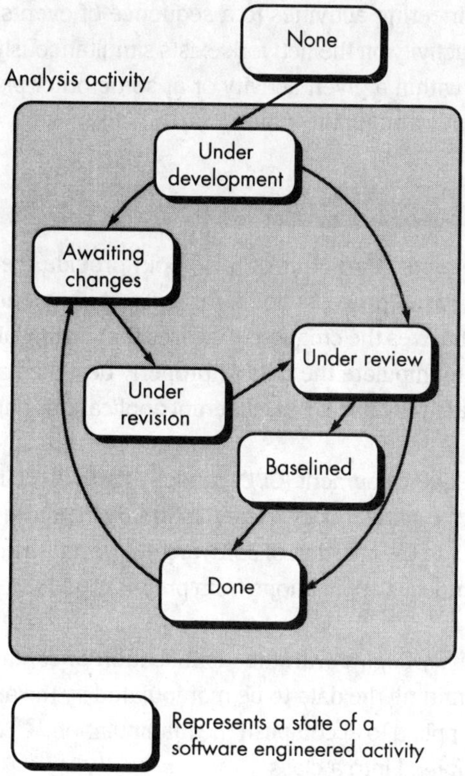

during early stages of design, an inconsistency in the analysis model is uncovered. This generates the event *analysis model correction* which will trigger the *analysis* activity from the **done** state into the **awaiting changes** state.

The concurrent process model is often used as the paradigm for the development of client/server[11] applications (Chapter 28). A client/server system is composed of a set of functional components. When applied to client/server, the concurrent process model defines activities in two dimensions [SHE94]: a system dimension and a component dimension. System level issues are addressed using three activities: design, assembly, and use. The component dimension is addressed with two activities: design and realization. Concurrency is achieved in two ways: (1) system and component activities occur simultaneously and can be modeled using the state-oriented approach described previously; (2) a typical client/server application is implemented with many components, each of which can be designed and realized concurrently.

In reality, the concurrent process model is applicable to all types of software development and provides an accurate picture of the current state of a project. Rather than

---

11 In a client/server applications, software functionality is divided between clients (normally PCs) and a server (a more powerful computer) that typically maintains a centralized database.

confining software engineering activities to a sequence of events, it defines a network of activities. Each activity on the network exists simultaneously with other activities. Events generated within a given activity or at some other place in the activity network trigger transitions among the states of an activity.

2.8 COMPONENT-BASED DEVELOPMENT

Object-oriented technologies (Part Four of this book) provide the technical framework for a component-based process model for software engineering. The object-oriented paradigm emphasizes the creation of classes that encapsulate both data and the algorithms used to manipulate the data. If properly designed and implemented, object-oriented classes are reusable across different applications and computer-based system architectures.

XRef

The underlying technology for CBD is discussed in Part Four of this book. A more detailed discussion of the CBD process is presented in Chapter 27.

The component-based development (CBD) model (Figure 2.11) incorporates many of the characteristics of the spiral model. It is evolutionary in nature [NIE92], demanding an iterative approach to the creation of software. However, the component-based development model composes applications from prepackaged software components (called *classes*).

The engineering activity begins with the identification of candidate classes. This is accomplished by examining the data to be manipulated by the application and the algorithms that will be applied to accomplish the manipulation.[12] Corresponding data and algorithms are packaged into a class.

FIGURE 2.11
Component-based development

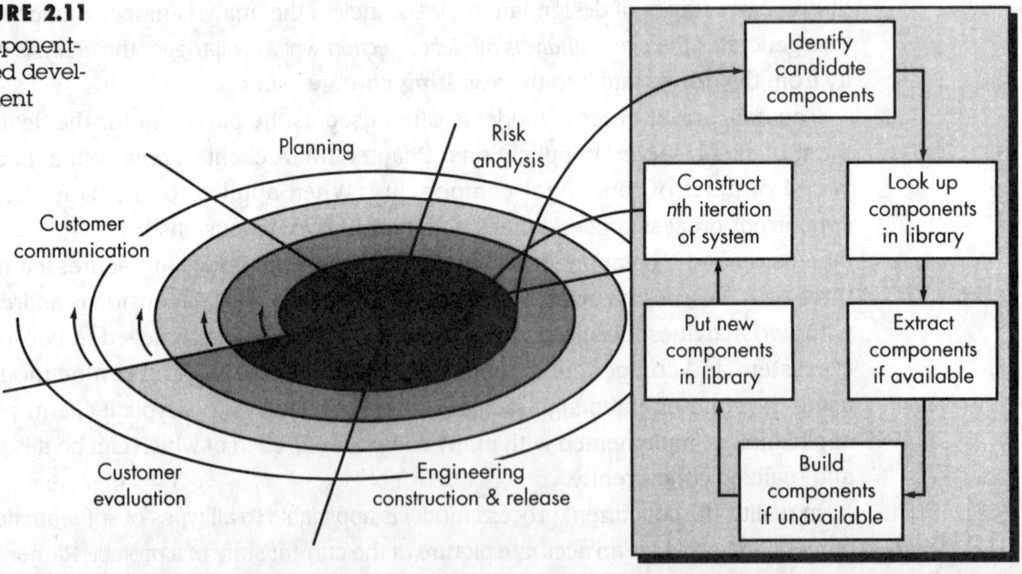

12 This is a simplified description of class definition. For a more detailed discussion, see Chapter 20.

Classes created in past software engineering projects are stored in a class library or repository (Chapter 31). Once candidate classes are identified, the class library is searched to determine if these classes already exist. If they do, they are extracted from the library and reused. If a candidate class does not reside in the library, it is engineered using object-oriented methods (Chapters 21–23). The first iteration of the application to be built is then composed, using classes extracted from the library and any new classes built to meet the unique needs of the application. Process flow then returns to the spiral and will ultimately re-enter the component assembly iteration during subsequent passes through the engineering activity.

The component-based development model leads to software reuse, and reusability provides software engineers with a number of measurable benefits. Based on studies of reusability, QSM Associates, Inc., reports component assembly leads to a 70 percent reduction in development cycle time; an 84 percent reduction in project cost, and a productivity index of 26.2, compared to an industry norm of 16.9. [YOU94] Although these results are a function of the robustness of the component library, there is little question that the component-based development model provides significant advantages for software engineers.

XRef
UML is discussed in some detail in Chapters 21 and 22.

The *unified software development process* [JAC99] is representative of a number of component-based development models that have been proposed in the industry. Using the *Unified Modeling Language* (UML), the unified process defines the components that will be used to build the system and the interfaces that will connect the components. Using a combination of iterative and incremental development, the unified process defines the function of the system by applying a scenario-based approach (from the user point of view). It then couples function with an architectural framework that identifies the form the the software will take.

2.9 THE FORMAL METHODS MODEL

XRef
Formal methods are discussed in Chapters 25 and 26.

The formal methods model encompasses a set of activities that leads to formal mathematical specification of computer software. Formal methods enable a software engineer to specify, develop, and verify a computer-based system by applying a rigorous, mathematical notation. A variation on this approach, called *cleanroom software engineering* [MIL87, DYE92], is currently applied by some software development organizations.

When formal methods (Chapters 25 and 26) are used during development, they provide a mechanism for eliminating many of the problems that are difficult to overcome using other software engineering paradigms. Ambiguity, incompleteness, and inconsistency can be discovered and corrected more easily, not through ad hoc review but through the application of mathematical analysis. When formal methods are used during design, they serve as a basis for program verification and therefore enable the software engineer to discover and correct errors that might go undetected.

Although it is not destined to become a mainstream approach, the formal methods model offers the promise of defect-free software. Yet, the following concerns about its applicability in a business environment have been voiced:

1. The development of formal models is currently quite time consuming and expensive.
2. Because few software developers have the necessary background to apply formal methods, extensive training is required.
3. It is difficult to use the models as a communication mechanism for technically unsophisticated customers.

These concerns notwithstanding, it is likely that the formal methods approach will gain adherents among software developers who must build safety-critical software (e.g., developers of aircraft avionics and medical devices) and among developers that would suffer severe economic hardship should software errors occur.

2.10 FOURTH GENERATION TECHNIQUES

The term *fourth generation techniques* (4GT) encompasses a broad array of software tools that have one thing in common: each enables the software engineer to specify some characteristic of software at a high level. The tool then automatically generates source code based on the developer's specification. There is little debate that the higher the level at which software can be specified to a machine, the faster a program can be built. The 4GT paradigm for software engineering focuses on the ability to specify software using specialized language forms or a graphic notation that describes the problem to be solved in terms that the customer can understand.

Currently, a software development environment that supports the 4GT paradigm includes some or all of the following tools: nonprocedural languages for database query, report generation, data manipulation, screen interaction and definition, code generation; high-level graphics capability; spreadsheet capability, and automated generation of HTML and similar languages used for Web-site creation using advanced software tools. Initially, many of the tools noted previously were available only for very specific application domains, but today 4GT environments have been extended to address most software application categories.

Like other paradigms, 4GT begins with a requirements gathering step. Ideally, the customer would describe requirements and these would be directly translated into an operational prototype. But this is unworkable. The customer may be unsure of what is required, may be ambiguous in specifying facts that are known, and may be unable or unwilling to specify information in a manner that a 4GT tool can consume.

For this reason, the customer/developer dialog described for other process models remains an essential part of the 4GT approach.

For small applications, it may be possible to move directly from the requirements gathering step to implementation using a nonprocedural fourth generation language (4GL) or a model composed of a network of graphical icons. However, for larger efforts, it is necessary to develop a design strategy for the system, even if a 4GL is to be used. The use of 4GT without design (for large projects) will cause the same difficulties (poor quality, poor maintainability, poor customer acceptance) that have been encountered when developing software using conventional approaches.

ADVICE

Even though you use a 4GT, you still have to emphasize solid software engineering by doing analysis, design, and testing.

Implementation using a 4GL enables the software developer to represent desired results in a manner that leads to automatic generation of code to create those results. Obviously, a data structure with relevant information must exist and be readily accessible by the 4GL.

To transform a 4GT implementation into a product, the developer must conduct thorough testing, develop meaningful documentation, and perform all other solution integration activities that are required in other software engineering paradigms. In addition, the 4GT developed software must be built in a manner that enables maintenance to be performed expeditiously.

Like all software engineering paradigms, the 4GT model has advantages and disadvantages. Proponents claim dramatic reduction in software development time and greatly improved productivity for people who build software. Opponents claim that current 4GT tools are not all that much easier to use than programming languages, that the resultant source code produced by such tools is "inefficient," and that the maintainability of large software systems developed using 4GT is open to question.

There is some merit in the claims of both sides and it is possible to summarize the current state of 4GT approaches:

1. The use of 4GT is a viable approach for many different application areas. Coupled with computer-aided software engineering tools and code generators, 4GT offers a credible solution to many software problems.
2. Data collected from companies that use 4GT indicate that the time required to produce software is greatly reduced for small and intermediate applications and that the amount of design and analysis for small applications is also reduced.
3. However, the use of 4GT for large software development efforts demands as much or more analysis, design, and testing (software engineering activities) to achieve substantial time savings that result from the elimination of coding.

To summarize, fourth generation techniques have already become an important part of software engineering. When coupled with component-based development approaches (Section 2.8), the 4GT paradigm may become the dominant approach to software development.

2.11 PROCESS TECHNOLOGY

The process models discussed in the preceding sections must be adapted for use by a software project team. To accomplish this, process technology tools have been developed to help software organizations analyze their current process, organize work tasks, control and monitor progress, and manage technical quality [BAN95].

Process technology tools allow a software organization to build an automated model of the common process framework, task sets, and umbrella activities discussed in Section 2.3. The model, normally represented as a network, can then be analyzed to determine typical work flow and examine alternative process structures that might lead to reduced development time or cost.

Once an acceptable process has been created, other process technology tools can be used to allocate, monitor, and even control all software engineering tasks defined as part of the process model. Each member of a software project team can use such tools to develop a checklist of work tasks to be performed, work products to be produced, and quality assurance activities to be conducted. The process technology tool can also be used to coordinate the use of other computer-aided software engineering tools (Chapter 31) that are appropriate for a particular work task.

2.12 PRODUCT AND PROCESS

If the process is weak, the end product will undoubtedly suffer, but an obsessive overreliance on process is also dangerous. In a brief essay, Margaret Davis [DAV95] comments on the duality of product and process:

> **Quote:** "[If it is developed thoughtlessly and applied mindlessly, process can become] the death of common sense."
> **Philip K. Howard**

About every ten years, give or take five, the software community redefines "the problem" by shifting its focus from product issues to process issues. Thus, we have embraced structured programming languages (product) followed by structured analysis methods (process) followed by data encapsulation (product) followed by the current emphasis on the Software Engineering Institute's Software Development Capability Maturity Model (process).

While the natural tendency of a pendulum is to come to rest at a point midway between two extremes, the software community's focus constantly shifts because new force is applied when the last swing fails. These swings are harmful in and of themselves because they confuse the average software practitioner by radically changing what it means to perform the job let alone perform it well. The swings also do not solve "the problem" for they are doomed to fail as long as product and process are treated as forming a dichotomy instead of a duality.

There is precedence in the scientific community to advance notions of duality when contradictions in observations cannot be fully explained by one competing theory or another. The dual nature of light, which seems to be simultaneously particle and wave, has been accepted since the 1920's when Louis de Broglie proposed it. I believe that the observations we can make on the artifacts of software and its development demonstrate a fundamental duality between product and process. You can never derive or understand the full artifact, its context, use, meaning, and worth if you view it as only a process or only a product . . .

All of human activity may be a process, but each of us derives a sense of self worth from those activities that result in a representation or instance that can be used or appreciated either by more than one person, used over and over, or used in some other context not considered. That is, we derive feelings of satisfaction from reuse of our products by ourselves or others.

Thus, while the rapid assimilation of reuse goals into software development potentially increases the satisfaction software practitioners derive from their work, it also increases the urgency for acceptance of the duality of product and process. Thinking of a reusable artifact as only product or only process either obscures the context and ways to use it or obscures the fact that each use results in product that will, in turn, be used as input to some other software development activity. Taking one view over the other dramatically reduces the opportunities for reuse and, hence, loses the opportunity for increasing job satisfaction.

Quote:
"Any activity becomes creative when the doer cares about doing it right, or doing it better."
John Updike

People derive as much (or more) satisfaction from the creative process as they do from the end product. An artist enjoys the brush strokes as much the framed result. A writer enjoys the search for the proper metaphor as much as the finished book. A creative software professional should also derive as much satisfaction from the process as the end-product.

The work of software people will change in the years ahead. The duality of product and process is one important element in keeping creative people engaged as the transition from programming to software engineering is finalized.

2.13 SUMMARY

Software engineering is a discipline that integrates process, methods, and tools for the development of computer software. A number of different process models for software engineering have been proposed, each exhibiting strengths and weaknesses, but all having a series of generic phases in common. The principles, concepts, and methods that enable us to perform the process that we call *software engineering* are considered throughout the remainder of this book.

REFERENCES

[BAE98] Baetjer, Jr., H., *Software as Capital,* IEEE Computer Society Press, 1998, p. 85.

[BAN95] Bandinelli, S. et al., "Modeling and Improving an Industrial Software Process," *IEEE Trans. Software Engineering,* vol. SE-21, no. 5, May 1995, pp. 440–454.

[BOE88] Boehm, B., "A Spiral Model for Software Development and Enhancement," *Computer,* vol. 21, no. 5, May 1988, pp. 61–72.

[BOE96] Boehm, B., "Anchoring the Software Process," *IEEE Software,* vol. 13, no. 4, July 1996, pp. 73–82.

[BOE98] Boehm, B., "Using the WINWIN Spiral Model: A Case Study," *Computer,* vol. 31, no. 7, July 1998, pp. 33–44.

[BRA94] Bradac, M., D. Perry, and L. Votta, "Prototyping a Process Monitoring Experiment," *IEEE Trans. Software Engineering,* vol. SE-20, no. 10, October 1994, pp. 774–784.

[BRO75] Brooks, F., *The Mythical Man-Month,* Addison-Wesley, 1975.

[BUT94] Butler, J., "Rapid Application Development in Action," *Managing System Development,* Applied Computer Research, vol. 14, no. 5, May 1994, pp. 6–8.

[DAV94] Davis, A. and P. Sitaram, "A Concurrent Process Model for Software Development," *Software Engineering Notes,* ACM Press, vol. 19, no. 2, April 1994, pp. 38–51.

[DAV95] Davis, M.J., "Process and Product: Dichotomy or Duality," *Software Engineering Notes,* ACM Press, vol. 20, no. 2, April 1995, pp. 17–18.

[DON96] Donaldson, M.C. and M. Donaldson, *Negotiating for Dummies,* IDG Books Worldwide, 1996.

[DYE92] Dyer, M., *The Cleanroom Approach to Quality Software Development,* Wiley, 1992.

[FAR97] Farber, D.C., *Common Sense Negotiation: The Art of Winning Gracefully,* Bay Press, 1997.

[FIS91] Fisher, R., W. Ury, and B. Patton, *Getting to Yes: Negotiating Agreement Without Giving In,* 2nd edition, Penguin USA, 1991.

[GIL88] Gilb, T., *Principles of Software Engineering Management,* Addison-Wesley, 1988.

[HAN95] Hanna, M., "Farewell to Waterfalls," *Software Magazine,* May 1995, pp. 38–46.

[HUM89] Humphrey, W. and M. Kellner, "Software Process Modeling: Principles of Entity Process Models," *Proc. 11th Intl. Conference on Software Engineering,* IEEE Computer Society Press, pp. 331–342.

[IEE93] *IEEE Standards Collection: Software Engineering,* IEEE Standard 610.12—1990, IEEE, 1993.

[JAC99] Jacobson, I, Booch, G., and J. Rumbaugh, *The Unified Software Development Process,* Addison-Wesley, 1999.

[KEL89] Kellner, M., *Software Process Modeling: Value and Experience,* SEI Technical Review—1989, SEI, 1989.

[KEL91] Kellner, M., "Software Process Modeling Support for Management Planning and Control," *Proc. 1st Intl. Conf. on the Software Process,* IEEE Computer Society Press, 1991, pp. 8–28.

[KER94] Kerr, J. and R. Hunter, *Inside RAD,* McGraw-Hill, 1994.

[MAR91] Martin, J., *Rapid Application Development,* Prentice-Hall, 1991.

[MDE93] McDermid, J. and P. Rook, "Software Development Process Models," in *Software Engineer's Reference Book,* CRC Press, 1993, pp. 15/26–15/28.

[MIL87] Mills, H.D., M. Dyer, and R. Linger, "Cleanroom Software Engineering," *IEEE Software,* September 1987, pp. 19–25.

[NAU69] Naur, P. and B. Randall (eds.), *Software Engineering: A Report on a Conference Sponsored by the NATO Science Committee,* NATO, 1969.

[NIE92] Nierstrasz, O., S. Gibbs, and D. Tsichritzis, "Component-Oriented Software Development," *CACM,* vol. 35, no. 9, September 1992, pp. 160–165.

[PAU93] Paulk, M. et al., "Capability Maturity Model for Software," Software Engineering Institute, Carnegie Mellon University, Pittsburgh, PA, 1993.

[RAC95] Raccoon, L.B.S., "The Chaos Model and the Chaos Life Cycle," *ACM Software Engineering Notes,* vol. 20., no. 1, January, 1995, pp. 55–66.

[ROY70] Royce, W.W., "Managing the Development of Large Software Systems: Concepts and Techniques," *Proc. WESCON,* August 1970.

[SHE94] Sheleg, W., "Concurrent Engineering: A New Paradign for C/S Development," *Application Development Trends,* vol. 1, no. 6, June 1994, pp. 28–33.

[YOU94] Yourdon, E., "Software Reuse," *Application Development Strategies,* vol. 6, no. 12, December 1994, pp. 1–16.

PROBLEMS AND POINTS TO PONDER

2.1. Figure 2.1 places the three software engineering layers on top of a layer entitled *a quality focus.* This implies an organization quality program such as Total Quality Management. Do a bit of research and develop an outline of the key tenets of a Total Quality Management program.

2.2. Is there ever a case when the generic phases of the software engineering process don't apply? If so, describe it.

2.3. The SEI's capability maturity model is an evolving document. Do some research and determine if any new KPAs have been added since the publication of this book.

2.4. The Chaos model suggests that a problem solving loop can be applied at any degree of resolution. Discuss the way in which you would apply the loop to (1) understand requirements for a word-processing product; (2) develop an advanced spelling/grammar checking component for the word processor; (3) generate code for a program module that determines the subject, predicate, and object in an English language sentence.

2.5. Which of the software engineering paradigms presented in this chapter do you think would be most effective? Why?

2.6. Provide five examples of software development projects that would be amenable to prototyping. Name two or three applications that would be more difficult to prototype.

2.7. The RAD model is often tied to CASE tools. Research the literature and provide a summary of a typical CASE tool that supports RAD.

2.8. Propose a specific software project that would be amenable to the incremental model. Present a scenario for applying the model to the software.

2.9. As you move outward along the process flow path of the spiral model, what can you say about the software that is being developed or maintained?

2.10. Many people believe that the only way in which order of magnitude improvements in software quality and productivity will be achieved is through component-based development. Find three or four recent papers on the subject and summarize them for the class.

2.11. Describe the concurrent development model in your own words.

2.12. Provide three examples of fourth generation techniques.

2.13. Which is more important—the product or the process?

FURTHER READINGS AND INFORMATION SOURCES

The current state of the art in software engineering can best be determined from monthly publications such as *IEEE Software, Computer,* and the *IEEE Transactions on Software Engineering.* Industry periodicals such as *Application Development Trends, Cutter IT Journal* and *Software Development* often contain articles on software engineering topics. The discipline is 'summarized' every year in the *Proceedings of the International Conference on Software Engineering,* sponsored by the IEEE and ACM and is discussed in depth in journals such as *ACM Transactions on Software Engineering and Methodology, ACM Software Engineering Notes,* and *Annals of Software Engineering.*

Many software engineering books have been published in recent years. Some present an overview of the entire process while others delve into a few important topics to the exclusion of others. Three anthologies that cover a wide range of software engineering topics are

Keyes, J., (ed.), *Software Engineering Productivity Handbook,* McGraw-Hill, 1993.

McDermid, J., (ed.), *Software Engineer's Reference Book,* CRC Press, 1993.

Marchiniak, J.J. (ed.), *Encyclopedia of Software Engineering,* Wiley, 1994.

Gautier (*Distributed Engineering of Software,* Prentice-Hall, 1996) provides suggestions and guidelines for organizations that must develop software across geographically dispersed locations.

On the lighter side, a book by Robert Glass (*Software Conflict,* Yourdon Press, 1991) presents amusing and controversial essays on software and the software engineering process. Pressman and Herron (*Software Shock,* Dorset House, 1991) consider software and its impact on individuals, businesses, and government.

The Software Engineering Institute (SEI is located at Carnegie-Mellon University) has been chartered with the responsibility of sponsoring a software engineering monograph series. Practitioners from industry, government, and academia are contributing important new work. Additional software engineering research is conducted by the Software Productivity Consortium.

A wide variety of software engineering standards and procedures have been published over the past decade. The *IEEE Software Engineering Standards* contains standards that cover almost every important aspect of the technology. ISO 9000-3 guidelines provide guidance for software organizations that require registration to the ISO 9001 quality standard. Other software engineering standards can be obtained from the Department of Defense, the FAA, and other government and nonprofit agencies. Fairclough (*Software Engineering Guides,* Prentice-Hall, 1996) provides a detailed reference to software engineering standards produced by the European Space Agency (ESA).

A wide variety of information sources on software engineering and the software process is available on the Internet. An up-to-date list of World Wide Web references that are relevant to the software process can be found at the SEPA Web site: **http://www.mhhe.com/engcs/compsci/pressman/resources/process.mhtml**

PART

Two

MANAGING SOFTWARE PROJECTS

In this part of *Software Engineering: A Practitioner's Approach,* we consider the management techniques required to plan, organize, monitor, and control software projects. In the chapters that follow, you'll get answers to the following questions:

- How must the people, process, and problem be managed during a software project?
- What are software metrics and how can they be used to manage a software project and the software process?
- How does a software team generate reliable estimates of effort, cost, and project duration?
- What techniques can be used to formally assess the risks that can have an impact on project success?
- How does a software project manager select the set of software engineering work tasks?
- How is a project schedule created?
- How is quality defined so that it can be controlled?
- What is software quality assurance?
- Why are formal technical reviews so important?
- How is change managed during the development of computer software and after delivery to the customer?

Once these questions are answered, you'll be better prepared to manage software projects in a way that will lead to timely delivery of a high-quality product.

CHAPTER

3 PROJECT MANAGEMENT CONCEPTS

KEY CONCEPTS

- critical practices . . 74
- common process framework 70
- coordination 65
- problem decomposition . . . 67
- process decomposition . . . 70
- scope 67
- software team . . 60
- team leader 59
- team structure . . . 60
- team toxicity 63
- W^5HH principle . . 73

In the preface to his book on software project management, Meiler Page-Jones [PAG85] makes a statement that can be echoed by many software engineering consultants:

> I've visited dozens of commercial shops, both good and bad, and I've observed scores of data processing managers, again, both good and bad. Too often, I've watched in horror as these managers futilely struggled through nightmarish projects, squirmed under impossible deadlines, or delivered systems that outraged their users and went on to devour huge chunks of maintenance time.

What Page-Jones describes are symptoms that result from an array of management and technical problems. However, if a post mortem were to be conducted for every project, it is very likely that a consistent theme would be encountered: project management was weak.

In this chapter and the six that follow, we consider the key concepts that lead to effective software project management. This chapter considers basic software project management concepts and principles. Chapter 4 presents process and project metrics, the basis for effective management decision making. The techniques that are used to estimate cost and resource requirements and establish an effective project plan are discussed in Chapter 5. The man-

QUICK LOOK

What is it? Although many of us (in our darker moments) take Dilbert's view of "management," it remains a very necessary activity when computer-based systems and products are built. Project management involves the planning, monitoring, and control of the people, process, and events that occur as software evolves from a preliminary concept to an operational implementation.

Who does it? Everyone "manages" to some extent, but the scope of management activities varies with the person doing it. A software engineer manages her day-to-day activities, planning, monitoring, and controlling technical tasks. Project managers plan, monitor, and control the work of a team of software engineers. Senior managers coordinate the interface between the business and the software professionals.

Why is it important? Building computer software is a complex undertaking, particularly if it involves many people working over a relatively long time. That's why software projects need to be managed.

What are the steps? Understand the four P's—people, product, process, and project. People must be organized to perform software work effectively. Communication with the customer must occur so that product scope and requirements are understood. A process must be selected that is appropriate for the people and the product. The project must be planned by estimating effort and calendar time to accomplish work tasks: defining work products, establishing quality checkpoints, and

QUICK LOOK

establishing mechanisms to monitor and control work defined by the plan.

What is the work product? A project plan is produced as management activities commence. The plan defines the process and tasks to be conducted, the people who will do the work, and the mechanisms for assessing risks, controlling change, and evaluating quality.

How do I ensure that I've done it right? You're never completely sure that the project plan is right until you've delivered a high-quality product on time and within budget. However, a project manager does it right when he encourages software people to work together as an effective team, focusing their attention on customer needs and product quality.

agement activities that lead to effective risk monitoring, mitigation, and management are presented in Chapter 6. Chapter 7 discusses the activities that are required to define project tasks and establish a workable project schedule. Finally, Chapters 8 and 9 consider techniques for ensuring quality as a project is conducted and controlling changes throughout the life of an application.

3.1 THE MANAGEMENT SPECTRUM

Effective software project management focuses on the four P's: people, product, process, and project. The order is not arbitrary. The manager who forgets that software engineering work is an intensely human endeavor will never have success in project management. A manager who fails to encourage comprehensive customer communication early in the evolution of a project risks building an elegant solution for the wrong problem. The manager who pays little attention to the process runs the risk of inserting competent technical methods and tools into a vacuum. The manager who embarks without a solid project plan jeopardizes the success of the product.

3.1.1 The People

Quote:
"There exists enormous variability in the ability of different people to perform programming tasks."
Bill Curtis

The cultivation of motivated, highly skilled software people has been discussed since the 1960s (e.g., [COU80], [WIT94], [DEM98]). In fact, the "people factor" is so important that the Software Engineering Institute has developed a *people management capability maturity model* (PM-CMM), "to enhance the readiness of software organizations to undertake increasingly complex applications by helping to attract, grow, motivate, deploy, and retain the talent needed to improve their software development capability" [CUR94].

The people management maturity model defines the following key practice areas for software people: recruiting, selection, performance management, training, compensation, career development, organization and work design, and team/culture development. Organizations that achieve high levels of maturity in the people management area have a higher likelihood of implementing effective software engineering practices.

The PM-CMM is a companion to the software capability maturity model (Chapter 2) that guides organizations in the creation of a mature software process. Issues associated with people management and structure for software projects are considered later in this chapter.

3.1.2 The Product

XRef

A taxonomy of application areas that spawn software "products" is discussed in Chapter 1.

Before a project can be planned, product[1] objectives and scope should be established, alternative solutions should be considered, and technical and management constraints should be identified. Without this information, it is impossible to define reasonable (and accurate) estimates of the cost, an effective assessment of risk, a realistic breakdown of project tasks, or a manageable project schedule that provides a meaningful indication of progress.

The software developer and customer must meet to define product objectives and scope. In many cases, this activity begins as part of the system engineering or business process engineering (Chapter 10) and continues as the first step in software requirements analysis (Chapter 11). Objectives identify the overall goals for the product (from the customer's point of view) without considering how these goals will be achieved. Scope identifies the primary data, functions and behaviors that characterize the product, and more important, attempts to *bound* these characteristics in a quantitative manner.

Once the product objectives and scope are understood, alternative solutions are considered. Although very little detail is discussed, the alternatives enable managers and practitioners to select a "best" approach, given the constraints imposed by delivery deadlines, budgetary restrictions, personnel availability, technical interfaces, and myriad other factors.

3.1.3 The Process

KEY POINT

Framework activities are populated with tasks, milestones, work products, and quality assurance points.

A software process (Chapter 2) provides the framework from which a comprehensive plan for software development can be established. A small number of framework activities are applicable to all software projects, regardless of their size or complexity. A number of different task sets—tasks, milestones, work products, and quality assurance points—enable the framework activities to be adapted to the characteristics of the software project and the requirements of the project team. Finally, umbrella activities—such as software quality assurance, software configuration management, and measurement—overlay the process model. Umbrella activities are independent of any one framework activity and occur throughout the process.

3.1.4 The Project

We conduct planned and controlled software projects for one primary reason—it is the only known way to manage complexity. And yet, we still struggle. In 1998, industry data indicated that 26 percent of software projects failed outright and 46 percent experienced cost and schedule overruns [REE99]. Although the success rate for

---

1 In this context, the term *product* is used to encompass any software that is to be built at the request of others. It includes not only software products but also computer-based systems, embedded software, and problem-solving software (e.g., programs for engineering/scientific problem solving).

software projects has improved somewhat, our project failure rate remains higher than it should be.[2]

In order to avoid project failure, a software project manager and the software engineers who build the product must avoid a set of common warning signs, understand the critical success factors that lead to good project management, and develop a commonsense approach for planning, monitoring and controlling the project. Each of these issues is discussed in Section 3.5 and in the chapters that follow.

3.2 PEOPLE

In a study published by the IEEE [CUR88], the engineering vice presidents of three major technology companies were asked the most important contributor to a successful software project. They answered in the following way:

> **Quote:** "Companies that sensibly manage their investment in people will prosper in the long run."
> **Tom DeMarco & Tim Lister**

VP 1: I guess if you had to pick one thing out that is most important in our environment, I'd say it's not the tools that we use, it's the people.

VP 2: The most important ingredient that was successful on this project was having smart people . . . very little else matters in my opinion. . . . The most important thing you do for a project is selecting the staff . . . The success of the software development organization is very, very much associated with the ability to recruit good people.

VP 3: The only rule I have in management is to ensure I have good people—real good people—and that I grow good people—and that I provide an environment in which good people can produce.

Indeed, this is a compelling testimonial on the importance of people in the software engineering process. And yet, all of us, from senior engineering vice presidents to the lowliest practitioner, often take people for granted. Managers argue (as the preceding group had) that people are primary, but their actions sometimes belie their words. In this section we examine the players who participate in the software process and the manner in which they are organized to perform effective software engineering.

3.2.1 The Players

The software process (and every software project) is populated by players who can be categorized into one of five constituencies:

1. **Senior managers** who define the business issues that often have significant influence on the project.

---

2 Given these statistics, it's reasonable to ask how the impact of computers continues to grow exponentially and the software industry continues to post double digit sales growth. Part of the answer, I think, is that a substantial number of these "failed" projects are ill-conceived in the first place. Customers lose interest quickly (because what they requested wasn't really as important as they first thought), and the projects are cancelled.

2. **Project (technical) managers** who must plan, motivate, organize, and control the practitioners who do software work.

3. **Practitioners** who deliver the technical skills that are necessary to engineer a product or application.

4. **Customers** who specify the requirements for the software to be engineered and other *stakeholders* who have a peripheral interest in the outcome.

5. **End-users** who interact with the software once it is released for production use.

Every software project is populated by people who fall within this taxonomy. To be effective, the project team must be organized in a way that maximizes each person's skills and abilities. And that's the job of the team leader.

3.2.2 Team Leaders

Project management is a people-intensive activity, and for this reason, competent practitioners often make poor team leaders. They simply don't have the right mix of people skills. And yet, as Edgemon states: "Unfortunately and all too frequently it seems, individuals just fall into a project manager role and become accidental project managers." [EDG95]

? What do we look for when we select someone to lead a software project?

In an excellent book of technical leadership, Jerry Weinberg [WEI86] suggests a MOI model of leadership:

Motivation. The ability to encourage (by "push or pull") technical people to produce to their best ability.

Organization. The ability to mold existing processes (or invent new ones) that will enable the initial concept to be translated into a final product.

Ideas or innovation. The ability to encourage people to create and feel creative even when they must work within bounds established for a particular software product or application.

Quote:

"In simplest terms, a leader is one who knows where he wants to go, and gets up, and goes."

John Erskine

Weinberg suggests that successful project leaders apply a problem solving management style. That is, a software project manager should concentrate on understanding the problem to be solved, managing the flow of ideas, and at the same time, letting everyone on the team know (by words and, far more important, by actions) that quality counts and that it will not be compromised.

Another view [EDG95] of the characteristics that define an effective project manager emphasizes four key traits:

Problem solving. An effective software project manager can diagnose the technical and organizational issues that are most relevant, systematically structure a solution or properly motivate other practitioners to develop the solution, apply lessons learned from past projects to new situations, and remain flexible enough to change direction if initial attempts at problem solution are fruitless.

Managerial identity. A good project manager must take charge of the project. She must have the confidence to assume control when necessary and the assurance to allow good technical people to follow their instincts.

ADVICE

A software wizard may not have the temperament or desire to be a team leader. Don't force the wizard to become one.

Achievement. To optimize the productivity of a project team, a manager must reward initiative and accomplishment and demonstrate through his own actions that controlled risk taking will not be punished.

Influence and team building. An effective project manager must be able to "read" people; she must be able to understand verbal and nonverbal signals and react to the needs of the people sending these signals. The manager must remain under control in high-stress situations.

3.2.3 The Software Team

Quote:

"Not every group is a team, and not every team is effective."
Glenn Parker

There are almost as many human organizational structures for software development as there are organizations that develop software. For better or worse, organizational structure cannot be easily modified. Concern with the practical and political consequences of organizational change are not within the software project manager's scope of responsibility. However, the organization of the people directly involved in a new software project is within the project manager's purview.

The following options are available for applying human resources to a project that will require n people working for k years:

1. n individuals are assigned to m different functional tasks, relatively little combined work occurs; coordination is the responsibility of a software manager who may have six other projects to be concerned with.
2. n individuals are assigned to m different functional tasks ($m < n$) so that informal "teams" are established; an ad hoc team leader may be appointed; coordination among teams is the responsibility of a software manager.
3. n individuals are organized into t teams; each team is assigned one or more functional tasks; each team has a specific structure that is defined for all teams working on a project; coordination is controlled by both the team and a software project manager.

How should a software team be organized?

Although it is possible to voice arguments for and against each of these approaches, a growing body of evidence indicates that a formal team organization (option 3) is most productive.

The "best" team structure depends on the management style of your organization, the number of people who will populate the team and their skill levels, and the overall problem difficulty. Mantei [MAN81] suggests three generic team organizations:

Democratic decentralized (DD). This software engineering team has no permanent leader. Rather, "task coordinators are appointed for short durations and then replaced by others who may coordinate different tasks." Decisions on problems and approach are made by group consensus. Communication among team members is horizontal.

Controlled decentralized (CD). This software engineering team has a defined leader who coordinates specific tasks and secondary leaders that have responsibility for subtasks. Problem solving remains a group activity, but implementation of solutions is partitioned among subgroups by the team leader. Communication among subgroups and individuals is horizontal. Vertical communication along the control hierarchy also occurs.

Controlled Centralized (CC). Top-level problem solving and internal team coordination are managed by a team leader. Communication between the leader and team members is vertical.

Mantei [MAN81] describes seven project factors that should be considered when planning the structure of software engineering teams:

What factors should we consider when structuring a software team?

- The difficulty of the problem to be solved.
- The size of the resultant program(s) in lines of code or function points (Chapter 4).
- The time that the team will stay together (team lifetime).
- The degree to which the problem can be modularized.
- The required quality and reliability of the system to be built.
- The rigidity of the delivery date.
- The degree of sociability (communication) required for the project.

Because a centralized structure completes tasks faster, it is the most adept at handling simple problems. Decentralized teams generate more and better solutions than individuals. Therefore such teams have a greater probability of success when working on difficult problems. Since the CD team is centralized for problem solving, either a CD or CC team structure can be successfully applied to simple problems. A DD structure is best for difficult problems.

Because the performance of a team is inversely proportional to the amount of communication that must be conducted, very large projects are best addressed by teams with a CC or CD structures when subgrouping can be easily accommodated.

ADVICE

It's often better to have a few small, well-focused teams than a single large team.

The length of time that the team will "live together" affects team morale. It has been found that DD team structures result in high morale and job satisfaction and are therefore good for teams that will be together for a long time.

The DD team structure is best applied to problems with relatively low modularity, because of the higher volume of communication needed. When high modularity is possible (and people can do their own thing), the CC or CD structure will work well.

CC and CD teams have been found to produce fewer defects than DD teams, but these data have much to do with the specific quality assurance activities that are applied by the team. Decentralized teams generally require more time to complete a project than a centralized structure and at the same time are best when high sociability is required.

Constantine [CON93] suggests four "organizational paradigms" for software engineering teams:

Quote:

"Working with people is difficult, but not impossible."

Peter Drucker

1. A *closed paradigm* structures a team along a traditional hierarchy of authority (similar to a CC team). Such teams can work well when producing software that is quite similar to past efforts, but they will be less likely to be innovative when working within the closed paradigm.
2. The *random paradigm* structures a team loosely and depends on individual initiative of the team members. When innovation or technological breakthrough is required, teams following the random paradigm will excel. But such teams may struggle when "orderly performance" is required.
3. The *open paradigm* attempts to structure a team in a manner that achieves some of the controls associated with the closed paradigm but also much of the innovation that occurs when using the random paradigm. Work is performed collaboratively, with heavy communication and consensus-based decision making the trademarks of open paradigm teams. Open paradigm team structures are well suited to the solution of complex problems but may not perform as efficiently as other teams.
4. The *synchronous paradigm* relies on the natural compartmentalization of a problem and organizes team members to work on pieces of the problem with little active communication among themselves.

As an historical footnote, the earliest software team organization was a controlled centralized (CD) structure originally called the *chief programmer team.* This structure was first proposed by Harlan Mills and described by Baker [BAK72]. The nucleus of the team was composed of a *senior engineer* (the chief programmer), who plans, coordinates and reviews all technical activities of the team; *technical staff* (normally two to five people), who conduct analysis and development activities; and a *backup engineer,* who supports the senior engineer in his or her activities and can replace the senior engineer with minimum loss in project continuity.

XRef

The role of the librarian exists regardless of team structure. See Chapter 9 for details.

The chief programmer may be served by one or more specialists (e.g., telecommunications expert, database designer), support staff (e.g., technical writers, clerical personnel), and a *software librarian.* The librarian serves many teams and performs the following functions: maintains and controls all elements of the software configuration (i.e., documentation, source listings, data, storage media); helps collect and format software productivity data; catalogs and indexes reusable software components; and assists the teams in research, evaluation, and document preparation. The importance of a librarian cannot be overemphasized. The librarian acts as a controller, coordinator, and potentially, an evaluator of the software configuration.

A variation on the democratic decentralized team has been proposed by Constantine [CON93], who advocates teams with creative independence whose approach to work might best be termed *innovative anarchy.* Although the free-spirited approach to software work has appeal, channeling creative energy into a high-performance team must be a central goal of a software engineering organization. To achieve a high-performance team:

Quote:
"No matter what the problem is, it's always a people problem."
Jerry Weinberg

- Team members must have trust in one another.
- The distribution of skills must be appropriate to the problem.
- Mavericks may have to be excluded from the team, if team cohesiveness is to be maintained.

Regardless of team organization, the objective for every project manager is to help create a team that exhibits cohesiveness. In their book, *Peopleware,* DeMarco and Lister [DEM98] discuss this issue:

> We tend to use the word *team* fairly loosely in the business world, calling any group of people assigned to work together a "team." But many of these groups just don't seem like teams. They don't have a common definition of success or any identifiable team spirit. What is missing is a phenomenon that we call *jell.*
>
> A jelled team is a group of people so strongly knit that the whole is greater than the sum of the parts . . .
>
> Once a team begins to jell, the probability of success goes way up. The team can become unstoppable, a juggernaut for success . . . They don't need to be managed in the traditional way, and they certainly don't need to be motivated. They've got momentum.

DeMarco and Lister contend that members of jelled teams are significantly more productive and more motivated than average. They share a common goal, a common culture, and in many cases, a "sense of eliteness" that makes them unique.

ADVICE
Jelled teams are the ideal, but they're not easy to achieve. At a minimum, be certain to avoid a "toxic environment."

But not all teams jell. In fact, many teams suffer from what Jackman calls "team toxicity" [JAC98]. She defines five factors that "foster a potentially toxic team environment":

1. A frenzied work atmosphere in which team members waste energy and lose focus on the objectives of the work to be performed.
2. High frustration caused by personal, business, or technological factors that causes friction among team members.
3. "Fragmented or poorly coordinated procedures" or a poorly defined or improperly chosen process model that becomes a roadblock to accomplishment.

4. Unclear definition of roles resulting in a lack of accountability and resultant finger-pointing.
5. "Continuous and repeated exposure to failure" that leads to a loss of confidence and a lowering of morale.

Jackman suggests a number of antitoxins that address these all-too-common problems.

? How do we avoid "toxins" that often infect a software team?

To avoid a frenzied work environment, the project manager should be certain that the team has access to all information required to do the job and that major goals and objectives, once defined, should not be modified unless absolutely necessary. In addition, bad news should not be kept secret but rather, delivered to the team as early as possible (while there is still time to react in a rational and controlled manner).

Although frustration has many causes, software people often feel it when they lack the authority to control their situation. A software team can avoid frustration if it is given as much responsibility for decision making as possible. The more control over process and technical decisions given to the team, the less frustration the team members will feel.

An inappropriately chosen software process (e.g., unnecessary or burdensome work tasks or poorly chosen work products) can be avoided in two ways: (1) being certain that the characteristics of the software to be built conform to the rigor of the process that is chosen and (2) allowing the team to select the process (with full recognition that, once chosen, the team has the responsibility to deliver a high-quality product).

Quote:
"Do or do not; there is no try."
Yoda (Star Wars)

The software project manager, working together with the team, should clearly refine roles and responsibilities before the project begins. The team itself should establish its own mechanisms for accountability (formal technical reviews[3] are an excellent way to accomplish this) and define a series of corrective approaches when a member of the team fails to perform.

Every software team experiences small failures. The key to avoiding an atmosphere of failure is to establish team-based techniques for feedback and problem solving. In addition, failure by any member of the team must be viewed as a failure by the team itself. This leads to a team-oriented approach to corrective action, rather than the finger-pointing and mistrust that grows rapidly on toxic teams.

In addition to the five toxins described by Jackman, a software team often struggles with the differing human traits of its members. Some team members are extroverts, others are introverted. Some people gather information intuitively, distilling broad concepts from disparate facts. Others process information linearly, collecting and organizing minute details from the data provided. Some team members are comfortable making decisions only when a logical, orderly argument is presented. Others are intuitive, willing to make a decision based on "feel." Some practitioners want

3 Formal technical reviews are discussed in detail in Chapter 8.

a detailed schedule populated by organized tasks that enable them to achieve closure for some element of a project. Others prefer a more spontaneous environment in which open issues are okay. Some work hard to get things done long before a milestone date, thereby avoiding stress as the date approaches, while others are energized by the rush to make a last minute deadline. A detailed discussion of the psychology of these traits and the ways in which a skilled team leader can help people with opposing traits to work together is beyond the scope of this book.[4] However, it is important to note that recognition of human differences is the first step toward creating teams that jell.

3.2.4 Coordination and Communication Issues

There are many reasons that software projects get into trouble. The *scale* of many development efforts is large, leading to complexity, confusion, and significant difficulties in coordinating team members. *Uncertainty* is common, resulting in a continuing stream of changes that ratchets the project team. *Interoperability* has become a key characteristic of many systems. New software must communicate with existing software and conform to predefined constraints imposed by the system or product.

These characteristics of modern software—scale, uncertainty, and interoperability—are facts of life. To deal with them effectively, a software engineering team must establish effective methods for coordinating the people who do the work. To accomplish this, mechanisms for formal and informal communication among team members and between multiple teams must be established. Formal communication is accomplished through "writing, structured meetings, and other relatively non-interactive and impersonal communication channels" [KRA95]. Informal communication is more personal. Members of a software team share ideas on an ad hoc basis, ask for help as problems arise, and interact with one another on a daily basis.

Kraul and Streeter [KRA95] examine a collection of project coordination techniques that are categorized in the following manner:

Formal, impersonal approaches include software engineering documents and deliverables (including source code), technical memos, project milestones, schedules, and project control tools (Chapter 7), change requests and related documentation (Chapter 9), error tracking reports, and repository data (see Chapter 31).

? How do we coordinate the actions of team members?

Formal, interpersonal procedures focus on quality assurance activities (Chapter 8) applied to software engineering work products. These include status review meetings and design and code inspections.

Informal, interpersonal procedures include group meetings for information dissemination and problem solving and "collocation of requirements and development staff."

---

4 An excellent introduction to these issues as they relate to software project teams can be found in [FER98].

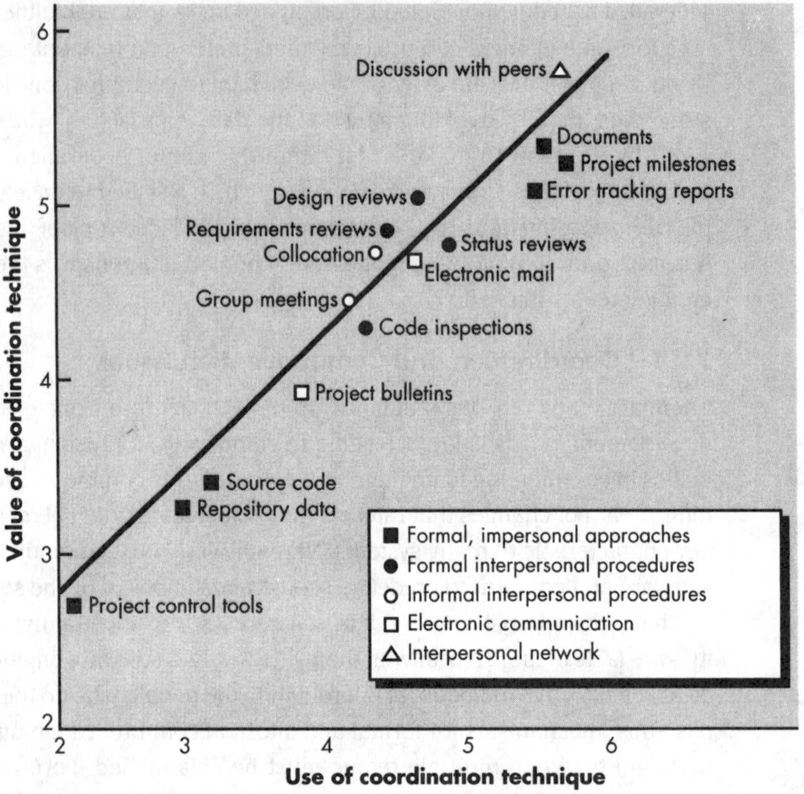

FIGURE 3.1 Value and Use of Coordination and Communication Techniques

Electronic communication encompasses electronic mail, electronic bulletin boards, and by extension, video-based conferencing systems.

Interpersonal networking includes informal discussions with team members and those outside the project who may have experience or insight that can assist team members.

To assess the efficacy of these techniques for project coordination, Kraul and Streeter studied 65 software projects involving hundreds of technical staff. Figure 3.1 (adapted from [KRA95]) expresses the value and use of the coordination techniques just noted. Referring to figure, the perceived value (rated on a seven point scale) of various coordination and communication techniques is plotted against their frequency of use on a project. Techniques that fall above the regression line were "judged to be relatively valuable, given the amount that they were used" [KRA95]. Techniques that fell below the line were perceived to have less value. It is interesting to note that interpersonal networking was rated the technique with highest coordination and communication value. It is also important to note that early software quality assurance mechanisms (requirements and design reviews) were perceived to have more value than later evaluations of source code (code inspections).

3.3 THE PRODUCT

A software project manager is confronted with a dilemma at the very beginning of a software engineering project. Quantitative estimates and an organized plan are required, but solid information is unavailable. A detailed analysis of software requirements would provide necessary information for estimates, but analysis often takes weeks or months to complete. Worse, requirements may be fluid, changing regularly as the project proceeds. Yet, a plan is needed "now!"

Therefore, we must examine the product and the problem it is intended to solve at the very beginning of the project. At a minimum, the scope of the product must be established and bounded.

3.3.1 Software Scope

The first software project management activity is the determination of *software scope.* Scope is defined by answering the following questions:

ADVICE

If you can't bound a characteristic of the software you intend to build, list the characteristic as a major project risk.

Context. How does the software to be built fit into a larger system, product, or business context and what constraints are imposed as a result of the context?

Information objectives. What customer-visible data objects (Chapter 11) are produced as output from the software? What data objects are required for input?

Function and performance. What function does the software perform to transform input data into output? Are any special performance characteristics to be addressed?

Software project scope must be unambiguous and understandable at the management and technical levels. A statement of software scope must be bounded. That is, quantitative data (e.g., number of simultaneous users, size of mailing list, maximum allowable response time) are stated explicitly; constraints and/or limitations (e.g., product cost restricts memory size) are noted, and mitigating factors (e.g., desired algorithms are well understood and available in C++) are described.

3.3.2 Problem Decomposition

KEY POINT

In order to develop a reasonable project plan, you have to functionally decompose the problem to be solved.

Problem decomposition, sometimes called *partitioning* or *problem elaboration,* is an activity that sits at the core of software requirements analysis (Chapter 11). During the scoping activity no attempt is made to fully decompose the problem. Rather, decomposition is applied in two major areas: (1) the functionality that must be delivered and (2) the process that will be used to deliver it.

Human beings tend to apply a divide and conquer strategy when they are confronted with a complex problems. Stated simply, a complex problem is partitioned into smaller problems that are more manageable. This is the strategy that applies as project planning begins. Software functions, described in the statement of scope, are evaluated and refined to provide more detail prior to the beginning of estimation

(Chapter 5). Because both cost and schedule estimates are functionally oriented, some degree of decomposition is often useful.

XRef
A useful technique for problem decomposition, called a *grammatical parse,* is presented in Chapter 12.

As an example, consider a project that will build a new word-processing product. Among the unique features of the product are continuous voice as well as keyboard input, extremely sophisticated "automatic copy edit" features, page layout capability, automatic indexing and table of contents, and others. The project manager must first establish a statement of scope that bounds these features (as well as other more mundane functions such as editing, file management, document production, and the like). For example, will continuous voice input require that the product be "trained" by the user? Specifically, what capabilities will the copy edit feature provide? Just how sophisticated will the page layout capability be?

As the statement of scope evolves, a first level of partitioning naturally occurs. The project team learns that the marketing department has talked with potential customers and found that the following functions should be part of automatic copy editing: (1) spell checking, (2) sentence grammar checking, (3) reference checking for large documents (e.g., Is a reference to a bibliography entry found in the list of entries in the bibliography?), and (4) section and chapter reference validation for large documents. Each of these features represents a subfunction to be implemented in software. Each can be further refined if the decomposition will make planning easier.

3.4 THE PROCESS

The generic phases that characterize the software process—definition, development, and support—are applicable to all software. The problem is to select the process model that is appropriate for the software to be engineered by a project team. In Chapter 2, a wide array of software engineering paradigms were discussed:

ADVICE
Once the process model is chosen, populate it with the minimum set of work tasks and work products that will result in a high-quality product—avoid process overkill!

- the linear sequential model
- the prototyping model
- the RAD model
- the incremental model
- the spiral model
- the WINWIN spiral model
- the component-based development model
- the concurrent development model
- the formal methods model
- the fourth generation techniques model

The project manager must decide which process model is most appropriate for (1) the customers who have requested the product and the people who will do the work,

(2) the characteristics of the product itself, and (3) the project environment in which the software team works. When a process model has been selected, the team then defines a preliminary project plan based on the set of common process framework activities. Once the preliminary plan is established, process decomposition begins. That is, a complete plan, reflecting the work tasks required to populate the framework activities must be created. We explore these activities briefly in the sections that follow and present a more detailed view in Chapter 7.

3.4.1 Melding the Product and the Process

Project planning begins with the melding of the product and the process. Each function to be engineered by the software team must pass through the set of framework activities that have been defined for a software organization. Assume that the organization has adopted the following set of framework activities (Chapter 2):

ADVICE

Remember: framework activities are applied on every project—no exceptions.

- *Customer communication*—tasks required to establish effective requirements elicitation between developer and customer.
- *Planning*—tasks required to define resources, timelines, and other project-related information.
- *Risk analysis*—tasks required to assess both technical and management risks.
- *Engineering*—tasks required to build one or more representations of the application.
- *Construction and release*—tasks required to construct, test, install, and provide user support (e.g., documentation and training).
- *Customer evaluation*—tasks required to obtain customer feedback based on evaluation of the software representations created during the engineering activity and implemented during the construction activity.

KEY POINT

Product and process decomposition occur simultaneously as the project plan evolves.

The team members who work on a product function will apply each of the framework activities to it. In essence, a matrix similar to the one shown in Figure 3.2 is created. Each major product function (the figure notes functions for the word-processing software discussed earlier) is listed in the left-hand column. Framework activities are listed in the top row. Software engineering work tasks (for each framework activity) would be entered in the following row.[5] The job of the project manager (and other team members) is to estimate resource requirements for each matrix cell, start and end dates for the tasks associated with each cell, and work products to be produced as a consequence of each task. These activities are considered in Chapters 5 and 7.

5 It should be noted that work tasks must be adapted to the specific needs of a project. Framework activities always remain the same, but work tasks will be selected based on a number of adaptation criteria. This topic is discussed further in Chapter 7 and at the SEPA Web site.

FIGURE 3.2
Melding the Problem and the Process

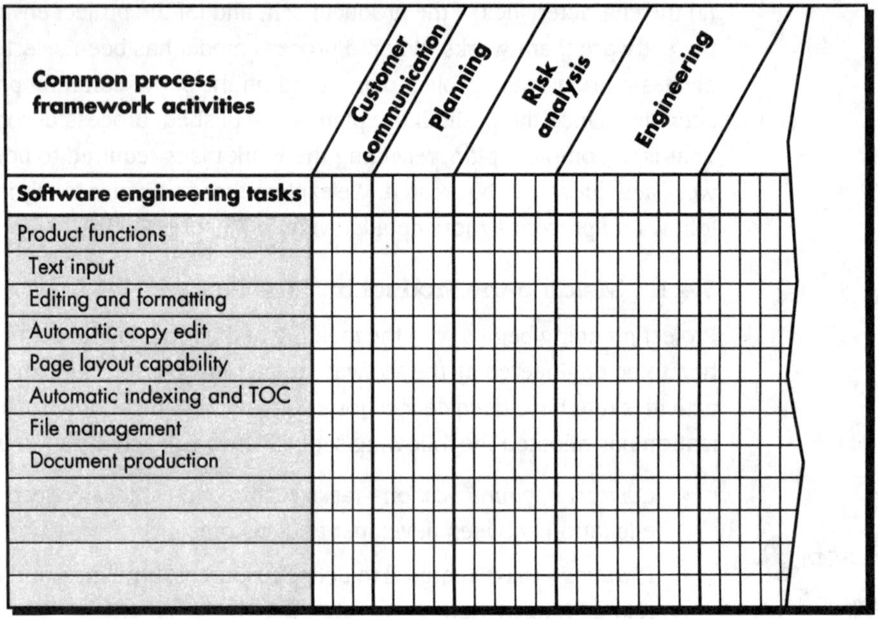

3.4.2 Process Decomposition

A software team should have a significant degree of flexibility in choosing the software engineering paradigm that is best for the project and the software engineering tasks that populate the process model once it is chosen. A relatively small project that is similar to past efforts might be best accomplished using the linear sequential approach. If very tight time constraints are imposed and the problem can be heavily compartmentalized, the RAD model is probably the right option. If the deadline is so tight that full functionality cannot reasonably be delivered, an incremental strategy might be best. Similarly, projects with other characteristics (e.g., uncertain requirements, breakthrough technology, difficult customers, significant reuse potential) will lead to the selection of other process models.[6]

ADVICE

Always apply the CPF, regardless of project size, criticality, or type. Work tasks may vary, but the CPF does not.

Once the process model has been chosen, the common process framework (CPF) is adapted to it. In every case, the CPF discussed earlier in this chapter—customer communication, planning, risk analysis, engineering, construction and release, customer evaluation—can be fitted to the paradigm. It will work for linear models, for iterative and incremental models, for evolutionary models, and even for concurrent or component assembly models. The CPF is invariant and serves as the basis for all software work performed by a software organization.

But actual work tasks do vary. Process decomposition commences when the project manager asks, "How do we accomplish this CPF activity?" For example, a small,

---

6 Recall that project characteristics also have a strong bearing on the structure of the team that is to do the work. See Section 3.2.3.

relatively simple project might require the following work tasks for the *customer communication* activity:

1. Develop list of clarification issues.
2. Meet with customer to address clarification issues.
3. Jointly develop a statement of scope.
4. Review the statement of scope with all concerned.
5. Modify the statement of scope as required.

These events might occur over a period of less than 48 hours. They represent a process decomposition that is appropriate for the small, relatively simple project.

Now, we consider a more complex project, which has a broader scope and more significant business impact. Such a project might require the following work tasks for the customer communication activity:

SEPA WEB: Adaptable process model

1. Review the customer request.
2. Plan and schedule a formal, facilitated meeting with the customer.
3. Conduct research to specify the proposed solution and existing approaches.
4. Prepare a "working document" and an agenda for the formal meeting.
5. Conduct the meeting.
6. Jointly develop mini-specs that reflect data, function, and behavioral features of the software.
7. Review each mini-spec for correctness, consistency, and lack of ambiguity.
8. Assemble the mini-specs into a scoping document.
9. Review the scoping document with all concerned.
10. Modify the scoping document as required.

Both projects perform the framework activity that we call "customer communication," but the first project team performed half as many software engineering work tasks as the second.

3.5 THE PROJECT

Quote:
"At least 7 of 10 signs of IS project failures are determined before a design is developed or a line of code is written . . ."
John Reel

In order to manage a successful software project, we must understand what can go wrong (so that problems can be avoided) and how to do it right. In an excellent paper on software projects, John Reel [REE99] defines ten signs that indicate that an information systems project is in jeopardy:

1. Software people don't understand their customer's needs.
2. The product scope is poorly defined.
3. Changes are managed poorly.

4. The chosen technology changes.
5. Business needs change [or are ill-defined].
6. Deadlines are unrealistic.
7. Users are resistant.
8. Sponsorship is lost [or was never properly obtained].
9. The project team lacks people with appropriate skills.
10. Managers [and practitioners] avoid best practices and lessons learned.

Jaded industry professionals often refer to the 90–90 rule when discussing particularly difficult software projects: The first 90 percent of a system absorbs 90 percent of the allotted effort and time. The last 10 percent takes the other 90 percent of the allotted effort and time [ZAH94]. The seeds that lead to the 90–90 rule are contained in the signs noted in the preceeding list.

But enough negativity! How does a manager act to avoid the problems just noted? Reel [REE99] suggests a five-part commonsense approach to software projects:

1. **Start on the right foot.** This is accomplished by working hard (very hard) to understand the problem that is to be solved and then setting realistic objects and expectations for everyone who will be involved in the project. It is reinforced by building the right team (Section 3.2.3) and giving the team the autonomy, authority, and technology needed to do the job.

WebRef
A broad array of resources that can help both neophyte and experienced project managers can be found at **www.pmi.org**, **www.4pm.com**, and **www.projectmanagement.com**

2. **Maintain momentum.** Many projects get off to a good start and then slowly disintegrate. To maintain momentum, the project manager must provide incentives to keep turnover of personnel to an absolute minimum, the team should emphasize quality in every task it performs, and senior management should do everything possible to stay out of the team's way.[7]
3. **Track progress.** For a software project, progress is tracked as work products (e.g., specifications, source code, sets of test cases) are produced and approved (using formal technical reviews) as part of a quality assurance activity. In addition, software process and project measures (Chapter 4) can be collected and used to assess progress against averages developed for the software development organization.
4. **Make smart decisions.** In essence, the decisions of the project manager and the software team should be to "keep it simple." Whenever possible, decide to use commercial off-the-shelf software or existing software components, decide to avoid custom interfaces when standard approaches are

7 The implication of this statement is that bureacracy is reduced to a minimum, extraneous meetings are eliminated, and dogmatic adherence to process and project rules is eliminated. The team should be allowed to do its thing.

available, decide to identify and then avoid obvious risks, and decide to allocate more time than you think is needed to complex or risky tasks (you'll need every minute).

5. **Conduct a postmortem analysis.** Establish a consistent mechanism for extracting lessons learned for each project. Evaluate the planned and actual schedules, collect and analyze software project metrics, get feedback from team members and customers, and record findings in written form.

3.6 THE W^5HH PRINCIPLE

In an excellent paper on software process and projects, Barry Boehm [BOE96] states: "you need an organizing principle that scales down to provide simple [project] plans for simple projects." Boehm suggests an approach that addresses project objectives, milestones and schedules, responsibilities, management and technical approaches, and required resources. He calls it the WWWWWHH principle, after a series of questions that lead to a definition of key project characteristics and the resultant project plan:

? What questions need to be answered in order to develop a project plan?

Why is the system being developed? The answer to this question enables all parties to assess the validity of business reasons for the software work. Stated in another way, does the business purpose justify the expenditure of people, time, and money?

What will be done, by when? The answers to these questions help the team to establish a project schedule by identifying key project tasks and the milestones that are required by the customer.

Who is responsible for a function? Earlier in this chapter, we noted that the role and responsibility of each member of the software team must be defined. The answer to this question helps accomplish this.

Where are they organizationally located? Not all roles and responsibilities reside within the software team itself. The customer, users, and other stakeholders also have responsibilities.

How will the job be done technically and managerially? Once product scope is established, a management and technical strategy for the project must be defined.

How much of each resource is needed? The answer to this question is derived by developing estimates (Chapter 5) based on answers to earlier questions.

Software Project Plan

Boehm's W^5HH principle is applicable regardless of the size or complexity of a software project. The questions noted provide an excellent planning outline for the project manager and the software team.

3.7 CRITICAL PRACTICES

The Airlie Council[8] has developed a list of "critical software practices for performance-based management." These practices are "consistently used by, and considered critical by, highly successful software projects and organizations whose 'bottom line' performance is consistently much better than industry averages" [AIR99]. In an effort to enable a software organization to determine whether a specific project has implemented critical practices, the Airlie Council has developed a set of "QuickLook" questions [AIR99] for a project:[9]

Airlie Project Quicklook

Formal risk management. What are the top ten risks for this project? For each of the risks, what is the chance that the risk will become a problem and what is the impact if it does?

Empirical cost and schedule estimation. What is the current estimated size of the application software (excluding system software) that will be delivered into operation? How was it derived?

Metric-based project management. Do you have in place a metrics program to give an early indication of evolving problems? If so, what is the current requirements volatility?

Earned value tracking. Do you report monthly earned value metrics? If so, are these metrics computed from an activity network of tasks for the entire effort to the next delivery?

Defect tracking against quality targets. Do you track and periodically report the number of defects found by each inspection (formal technical review) and execution test from program inception and the number of defects currently closed and open?

People-aware program management. What is the average staff turnover for the past three months for each of the suppliers/developers involved in the development of software for this system?

If a software project team cannot answer these questions or answers them inadequately, a thorough review of project practices is indicated. Each of the critical practices just noted is addressed in detail throughout Part Two of this book.

3.8 SUMMARY

Software project management is an umbrella activity within software engineering. It begins before any technical activity is initiated and continues throughout the definition, development, and support of computer software.

8 The Airlie Council is a team of software engineering experts chartered by the U.S. Department of Defense to help develop guidelines for best practices in software project management and software engineering.

9 Only those critical practices associated with "project integrity" are noted here. Other best practices will be discussed in later chapters.

Four P's have a substantial influence on software project management—people, product, process, and project. People must be organized into effective teams, motivated to do high-quality software work, and coordinated to achieve effective communication. The product requirements must be communicated from customer to developer, partitioned (decomposed) into their constituent parts, and positioned for work by the software team. The process must be adapted to the people and the problem. A common process framework is selected, an appropriate software engineering paradigm is applied, and a set of work tasks is chosen to get the job done. Finally, the project must be organized in a manner that enables the software team to succeed.

The pivotal element in all software projects is people. Software engineers can be organized in a number of different team structures that range from traditional control hierarchies to "open paradigm" teams. A variety of coordination and communication techniques can be applied to support the work of the team. In general, formal reviews and informal person-to-person communication have the most value for practitioners.

The project management activity encompasses measurement and metrics, estimation, risk analysis, schedules, tracking, and control. Each of these topics is considered in the chapters that follow.

REFERENCES

[AIR99] Airlie Council, "Performance Based Management: The Program Manager's Guide Based on the 16-Point Plan and Related Metrics," Draft Report, March 8, 1999.

[BAK72] Baker, F.T., "Chief Programmer Team Management of Production Programming," *IBM Systems Journal,* vol. 11, no. 1, 1972, pp. 56–73.

[BOE96] Boehm, B., "Anchoring the Software Process," *IEEE Software,* vol. 13, no. 4, July 1996, pp. 73–82.

[CON93] Constantine, L., "Work Organization: Paradigms for Project Management and Organization, *CACM,* vol. 36, no. 10, October 1993, pp. 34–43.

[COU80] Cougar, J. and R. Zawacki, *Managing and Motivating Computer Personnel,* Wiley, 1980.

[CUR88] Curtis, B. et al., "A Field Study of the Software Design Process for Large Systems," *IEEE Trans. Software Engineering,* vol. SE-31, no. 11, November 1988, pp. 1268–1287.

[CUR94] Curtis, B., et al., *People Management Capability Maturity Model,* Software Engineering Institute, 1994.

[DEM98] DeMarco, T. and T. Lister, *Peopleware,* 2nd ed., Dorset House, 1998.

[EDG95] Edgemon, J., "Right Stuff: How to Recognize It When Selecting a Project Manager," *Application Development Trends,* vol. 2, no. 5, May 1995, pp. 37–42.

[FER98] Ferdinandi, P.L., "Facilitating Communication," *IEEE Software,* September 1998, pp. 92–96.

[JAC98] Jackman, M., "Homeopathic Remedies for Team Toxicity," *IEEE Software,* July 1998, pp. 43–45.

[KRA95] Kraul, R. and L. Streeter, "Coordination in Software Development," *CACM,* vol. 38, no. 3, March 1995, pp. 69–81.

[MAN81] Mantei, M., "The Effect of Programming Team Structures on Programming Tasks," *CACM,* vol. 24, no. 3, March 1981, pp. 106–113.

[PAG85] Page-Jones, M., *Practical Project Management,* Dorset House, 1985, p. vii.

[REE99] Reel, J.S., "Critical Success Factors in Software Projects, *IEEE Software,* May, 1999, pp. 18–23.

[WEI86] Weinberg, G., *On Becoming a Technical Leader,* Dorset House, 1986.

[WIT94] Whitaker, K., *Managing Software Maniacs,* Wiley, 1994.

[ZAH94] Zahniser, R., "Timeboxing for Top Team Performance," *Software Development,* March 1994, pp. 35–38.

PROBLEMS AND POINTS TO PONDER

3.1. Based on information contained in this chapter and your own experience, develop "ten commandments" for empowering software engineers. That is, make a list of ten guidelines that will lead to software people who work to their full potential.

3.2. The Software Engineering Institute's people management capability maturity model (PM-CMM) takes an organized look at "key practice areas" that cultivate good software people. Your instructor will assign you one KPA for analysis and summary.

3.3. Describe three real-life situations in which the customer and the end-user are the same. Describe three situations in which they are different.

3.4. The decisions made by senior management can have a significant impact on the effectiveness of a software engineering team. Provide five examples to illustrate that this is true.

3.5. Review a copy of Weinberg's book [WEI86] and write a two- or three-page summary of the issues that should be considered in applying the MOI model.

3.6. You have been appointed a project manager within an information systems organization. Your job is to build an application that is quite similar to others your team has built, although this one is larger and more complex. Requirements have been thoroughly documented by the customer. What team structure would you choose and why? What software process model(s) would you choose and why?

3.7. You have been appointed a project manager for a small software products company. Your job is to build a breakthrough product that combines virtual reality hardware with state-of-the-art software. Because competition for the home entertainment market is intense, there is significant pressure to get the job done. What team structure would you choose and why? What software process model(s) would you choose and why?

3.8. You have been appointed a project manager for a major software products company. Your job is to manage the development of the next generation version of its widely used word-processing software. Because competition is intense, tight deadlines have been established and announced. What team structure would you choose and why? What software process model(s) would you choose and why?

3.9. You have been appointed a software project manager for a company that services the genetic engineering world. Your job is to manage the development of a new software product that will accelerate the pace of gene typing. The work is R&D oriented, but the goal to to produce a product within the next year. What team structure would you choose and why? What software process model(s) would you choose and why?

3.10. Referring to Figure 3.1, based on the results of the referenced study, documents are perceived to have more use than value. Why do you think this occurred and what can be done to move the documents data point above the regression line in the graph? That is, what can be done to improve the perceived value of documents?

3.11. You have been asked to develop a small application that analyzes each course offered by a university and reports the average grade obtained in the course (for a given term). Write a statement of scope that bounds this problem.

3.12. Do a first level functional decomposition of the page layout function discussed briefly in Section 3.3.2.

FURTHER READINGS AND INFORMATION SOURCES

An excellent four volume series written by Weinberg (*Quality Software Management,* Dorset House, 1992, 1993, 1994, 1996) introduces basic systems thinking and management concepts, explains how to use measurements effectively, and addresses "congruent action," the ability to establish "fit" between the manager's needs, the needs of technical staff, and the needs of the business. It will provide both new and experienced managers with useful information. Brooks (*The Mythical Man-Month,* Anniversary Edition, Addison-Wesley, 1995) has updated his classic book to provide new insight into software project and management issues. Purba and Shah (*How to Manage a Successful Software Project,* Wiley, 1995) present a number of case studies that indicate why some projects succeed and others fail. Bennatan (*Software Project Management in a Client/Server Environment,* Wiley, 1995) discusses special management issues associated with the development of client/server systems.

It can be argued that the most important aspect of software project management is people management. The definitive book on this subject has been written by

DeMarco and Lister [DEM98], but the following books on this subject have been published in recent years and are worth examining:

Beaudouin-Lafon, M., *Computer Supported Cooperative Work,* Wiley-Liss, 1999.

Carmel, E., *Global Software Teams: Collaborating Across Borders and Time Zones,* Prentice Hall, 1999.

Humphrey, W.S., *Managing Technical People: Innovation, Teamwork, and the Software Process,* Addison-Wesley, 1997.

Humphrey, W.S., *Introduction to the Team Software Process,* Addison-Wesley, 1999.

Jones, P.H., *Handbook of Team Design: A Practitioner's Guide to Team Systems Development,* McGraw-Hill, 1997.

Karolak, D.S., *Global Software Development: Managing Virtual Teams and Environments,* IEEE Computer Society, 1998.

Mayer, M., *The Virtual Edge: Embracing Technology for Distributed Project Team Success,* Project Management Institute Publications, 1999.

Another excellent book by Weinberg [WEI86] is must reading for every project manager and every team leader. It will give you insight and guidance in ways to do your job more effectively. House (*The Human Side of Project Management,* Addison-Wesley, 1988) and Crosby *(Running Things: The Art of Making Things Happen,* McGraw-Hill, 1989) provide practical advice for managers who must deal with human as well as technical problems.

Even though they do not relate specifically to the software world and sometimes suffer from over-simplification and broad generalization, best-selling "management" books by Drucker (*Management Challenges for the 21st Century,* Harper Business, 1999), Buckingham and Coffman (*First, Break All the Rules: What the World's Greatest Managers Do Differently,* Simon and Schuster, 1999) and Christensen (*The Innovator's Dilemma,* Harvard Business School Press, 1997) emphasize "new rules" defined by a rapidly changing economy, Older titles such as *The One-Minute Manager* and *In Search of Excellence* continue to provide valuable insights that can help you to manage people issues more effectively.

A wide variety of information sources on software project issues are available on the Internet. An up-to-date list of World Wide Web references that are relevant to the software projects can be found at the SEPA Web site:

http://www.mhhe.com/engcs/compsci/pressman/resources/project-mgmt.mhtml

CHAPTER

4 SOFTWARE PROCESS AND PROJECT METRICS

KEY CONCEPTS

Measurement is fundamental to any engineering discipline, and software engineering is no exception. Measurement enables us to gain insight by providing a mechanism for objective evaluation. Lord Kelvin once said:

> When you can measure what you are speaking about and express it in numbers, you know something about it; but when you cannot measure, when you cannot express it in numbers, your knowledge is of a meager and unsatisfactory kind: it may be the beginning of knowledge, but you have scarcely, in your thoughts, advanced to the stage of a science.

The software engineering community has finally begun to take Lord Kelvin's words to heart. But not without frustration and more than a little controversy!

Software metrics refers to a broad range of measurements for computer software. Measurement can be applied to the software process with the intent of improving it on a continuous basis. Measurement can be used throughout a software project to assist in estimation, quality control, productivity assessment, and project control. Finally, measurement can be used by software engineers to help assess the quality of technical work products and to assist in tactical decision making as a project proceeds.

QUICK LOOK

What is it? Software process and product metrics are quantitative measures that enable software people to gain insight into the efficacy of the software process and the projects that are conducted using the process as a framework. Basic quality and productivity data are collected. These data are then analyzed, compared against past averages, and assessed to determine whether quality and productivity improvements have occurred. Metrics are also used to pinpoint problem areas so that remedies can be developed and the software process can be improved.

Who does it? Software metrics are analyzed and assessed by software managers. Measures are often collected by software engineers.

Why is it important? If you don't measure, judgement can be based only on subjective evaluation. With measurement, trends (either good or bad) can be spotted, better estimates can be made, and true improvement can be accomplished over time.

What are the steps? Begin by defining a limited set of process, project, and product measures that are easy to collect. These measures are often normalized using either size- or function-oriented metrics. The result is analyzed and compared to past averages for similar projects performed within the organization. Trends are assessed and conclusions are generated.

▶

QUICK LOOK

What is the work product? A set of software metrics that provide insight into the process and understanding of the project.

How do I ensure that I've done it right? By applying a consistent, yet simple measurement scheme that is never to be used to assess, reward, or punish individual performance.

XRef

Technical metrics for software engineering are presented in Chapters 19 and 24.

Within the context of software project management, we are concerned primarily with productivity and quality metrics—measures of software development "output" as a function of effort and time applied and measures of the "fitness for use" of the work products that are produced. For planning and estimating purposes, our interest is historical. What was software development productivity on past projects? What was the quality of the software that was produced? How can past productivity and quality data be extrapolated to the present? How can it help us plan and estimate more accurately?

In their guidebook on software measurement, Park, Goethert, and Florac [PAR96] discuss the reasons that we measure:

> There are four reasons for measuring software processes, products, and resources: to characterize, to evaluate, to predict, or to improve.
>
> We characterize to gain understanding of processes, products, resources, and environments, and to establish baselines for comparisons with future assessments.
>
> We evaluate to determine status with respect to plans. Measures are the sensors that let us know when our projects and processes are drifting off track, so that we can bring them back under control. We also evaluate to assess achievement of quality goals and to assess the impacts of technology and process improvements on products and processes.
>
> We predict so that we can plan. Measuring for prediction involves gaining understandings of relationships among processes and products and building models of these relationships, so that the values we observe for some attributes can be used to predict others. We do this because we want to establish achievable goals for cost, schedule, and quality—so that appropriate resources can be applied. Predictive measures are also the basis for extrapolating trends, so estimates for cost, time, and quality can be updated based on current evidence. Projections and estimates based on historical data also help us analyze risks and make design/cost trade-offs.
>
> We measure to improve when we gather quantitative information to help us identify roadblocks, root causes, inefficiencies, and other opportunities for improving product quality and process performance.

Quote:

"Software metrics let you know when to laugh and when to cry."
Tom Gilb

4.1 MEASURES, METRICS, AND INDICATORS

Although the terms *measure, measurement,* and *metrics* are often used interchangeably, it is important to note the subtle differences between them. Because *measure* can be used either as a noun or a verb, definitions of the term can become confusing. Within the software engineering context, a measure provides a quantitative indication of the extent, amount, dimension, capacity, or size of some attribute of a product or process. Measurement is the act of determining a measure. The *IEEE Standard Glossary of Software Engineering Terms* [IEE93] defines *metric* as "a quantitative measure of the degree to which a system, component, or process possesses a given attribute."

Quote:
"Not everything that can be counted counts, and not everything that counts can be counted."
Albert Einstein

When a single data point has been collected (e.g., the number of errors uncovered in the review of a single module), a measure has been established. Measurement occurs as the result of the collection of one or more data points (e.g., a number of module reviews are investigated to collect measures of the number of errors for each). A software metric relates the individual measures in some way (e.g., the average number of errors found per review or the average number of errors found per person-hour expended on reviews.[1]

A software engineer collects measures and develops metrics so that indicators will be obtained. An *indicator* is a metric or combination of metrics that provide insight into the software process, a software project, or the product itself [RAG95]. An indicator provides insight that enables the project manager or software engineers to adjust the process, the project, or the process to make things better.

For example, four software teams are working on a large software project. Each team must conduct design reviews but is allowed to select the type of review that it will use. Upon examination of the metric, errors found per person-hour expended, the project manager notices that the two teams using more formal review methods exhibit an errors found per person-hour expended that is 40 percent higher than the other teams. Assuming all other parameters equal, this provides the project manager with an indicator that formal review methods may provide a higher return on time investment than another, less formal review approach. She may decide to suggest that all teams use the more formal approach. The metric provides the manager with insight. And insight leads to informed decision making.

4.2 METRICS IN THE PROCESS AND PROJECT DOMAINS

Measurement is commonplace in the engineering world. We measure power consumption, weight, physical dimensions, temperature, voltage, signal-to-noise ratio . . . the list is almost endless. Unfortunately, measurement is far less common in the software engineering world. We have trouble agreeing on what to measure and trouble evaluating measures that are collected.

---

1 This assumes that another measure, person-hours expended, is collected for each review.

WebRef
A comprehensive software metrics guidebook can be downloaded from **www.ivv.nasa.gov/SWG/resources/NASA-GB-001-94.pdf**

Metrics should be collected so that process and product indicators can be ascertained. *Process indicators* enable a software engineering organization to gain insight into the efficacy of an existing process (i.e., the paradigm, software engineering tasks, work products, and milestones). They enable managers and practitioners to assess what works and what doesn't. Process metrics are collected across all projects and over long periods of time. Their intent is to provide indicators that lead to long-term software process improvement.

Project indicators enable a software project manager to (1) assess the status of an ongoing project, (2) track potential risks, (3) uncover problem areas before they go "critical," (4) adjust work flow or tasks, and (5) evaluate the project team's ability to control quality of software work products.

In some cases, the same software metrics can be used to determine project and then process indicators. In fact, measures that are collected by a project team and converted into metrics for use during a project can also be transmitted to those with responsibility for software process improvement. For this reason, many of the same metrics are used in both the process and project domain.

4.2.1 Process Metrics and Software Process Improvement

The only rational way to improve any process is to measure specific attributes of the process, develop a set of meaningful metrics based on these attributes, and then use the metrics to provide indicators that will lead to a strategy for improvement. But before we discuss software metrics and their impact on software process improvement, it is important to note that process is only one of a number of "controllable factors in improving software quality and organizational performance [PAU94]."

KEY POINT
The skill and motivation of the people doing the work are the most important factors that influence software quality.

Referring to Figure 4.1, process sits at the center of a triangle connecting three factors that have a profound influence on software quality and organizational performance. The skill and motivation of people has been shown [BOE81] to be the single most influential factor in quality and performance. The complexity of the product can have a substantial impact on quality and team performance. The technology (i.e., the software engineering methods) that populate the process also has an impact. In addition, the process triangle exists within a circle of environmental conditions that include the development environment (e.g., CASE tools), business conditions (e.g., deadlines, business rules), and customer characteristics (e.g., ease of communication).

? How do I measure the effectiveness of a software process?

We measure the efficacy of a software process indirectly. That is, we derive a set of metrics based on the outcomes that can be derived from the process. Outcomes include measures of errors uncovered before release of the software, defects delivered to and reported by end-users, work products delivered (productivity), human effort expended, calendar time expended, schedule conformance, and other measures. We also derive process metrics by measuring the characteristics of specific software engineering tasks. For example, we might measure the effort and time spent

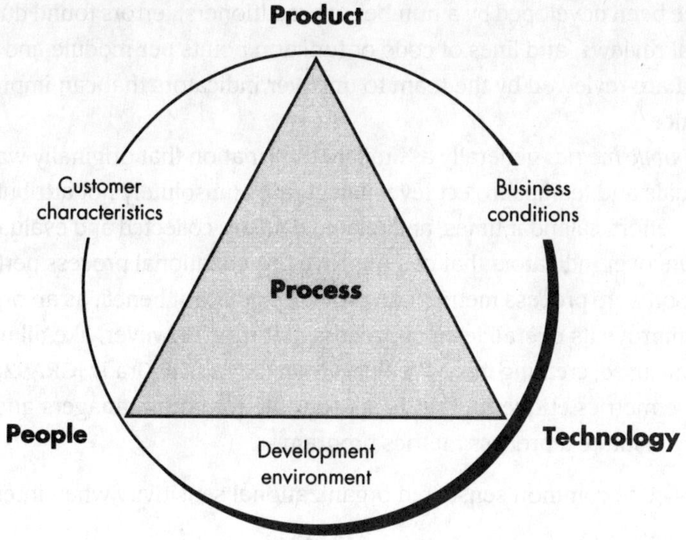

FIGURE 4.1 Determinants for software quality and organizational effectiveness (adapted from [PAU94])

performing the umbrella activities and the generic software engineering activities described in Chapter 2.

Grady [GRA92] argues that there are "private and public" uses for different types of process data. Because it is natural that individual software engineers might be sensitive to the use of metrics collected on an individual basis, these data should be private to the individual and serve as an indicator for the individual only. Examples of *private metrics* include defect rates (by individual), defect rates (by module), and errors found during development.

The "private process data" philosophy conforms well with the *personal software process* approach proposed by Humphrey [HUM95]. Humphrey describes the approach in the following manner:

> The personal software process (PSP) is a structured set of process descriptions, measurements, and methods that can help engineers to improve their personal performance. It provides the forms, scripts, and standards that help them estimate and plan their work. It shows them how to define processes and how to measure their quality and productivity. A fundamental PSP principle is that everyone is different and that a method that is effective for one engineer may not be suitable for another. The PSP thus helps engineers to measure and track their own work so they can find the methods that are best for them.

Humphrey recognizes that software process improvement can and should begin at the individual level. Private process data can serve as an important driver as the individual software engineer works to improve.

Some process metrics are private to the software project team but public to all team members. Examples include defects reported for major software functions (that have been developed by a number of practitioners), errors found during formal technical reviews, and lines of code or function points per module and function.[2] These data are reviewed by the team to uncover indicators that can improve team performance.

KEY POINT
Public metrics enable an organization to make strategic changes that improve the software process and tactical changes during a software project.

Public metrics generally assimilate information that originally was private to individuals and teams. Project level defect rates (absolutely not attributed to an individual), effort, calendar times, and related data are collected and evaluated in an attempt to uncover indicators that can improve organizational process performance.

Software process metrics can provide significant benefit as an organization works to improve its overall level of process maturity. However, like all metrics, these can be misused, creating more problems than they solve. Grady [GRA92] suggests a "software metrics etiquette" that is appropriate for both managers and practitioners as they institute a process metrics program:

? What guidelines should be applied when we collect software metrics?

- Use common sense and organizational sensitivity when interpreting metrics data.
- Provide regular feedback to the individuals and teams who collect measures and metrics.
- Don't use metrics to appraise individuals.
- Work with practitioners and teams to set clear goals and metrics that will be used to achieve them.
- Never use metrics to threaten individuals or teams.
- Metrics data that indicate a problem area should not be considered "negative." These data are merely an indicator for process improvement.
- Don't obsess on a single metric to the exclusion of other important metrics.

WebRef
SSPI and other quality related information is available through the American Society for Quality at **www.asq.org**

As an organization becomes more comfortable with the collection and use of process metrics, the derivation of simple indicators gives way to a more rigorous approach called *statistical software process improvement* (SSPI). In essence, SSPI uses software failure analysis to collect information about all errors and defects[3] encountered as an application, system, or product is developed and used. Failure analysis works in the following manner:

1. All errors and defects are categorized by origin (e.g., flaw in specification, flaw in logic, nonconformance to standards).
2. The cost to correct each error and defect is recorded.

---

2 See Sections 4.3.1 and 4.3.2 for detailed discussions of LOC and function point metrics.

3 As we discuss in Chapter 8, an *error* is some flaw in a software engineering work product or deliverable that is uncovered by software engineers before the software is delivered to the end-user. A *defect* is a flaw that is uncovered after delivery to the end-user.

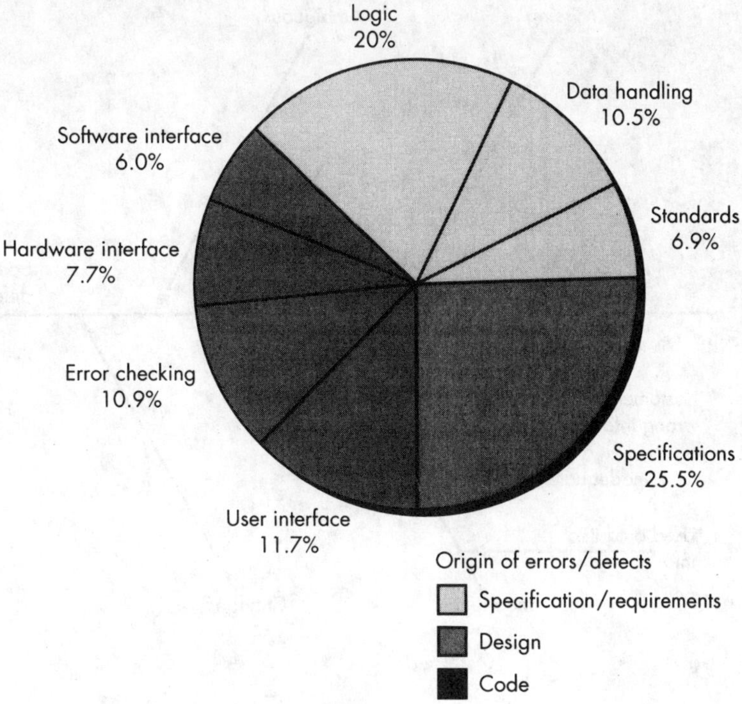

FIGURE 4.2 Causes of defects and their origin for four software projects [GRA94]

ADVICE *You can't improve your approach to software engineering unless you understand where you're strong and where you're weak. Use SSPI techniques to gain that understanding.*

3. The number of errors and defects in each category is counted and ranked in descending order.
4. The overall cost of errors and defects in each category is computed.
5. Resultant data are analyzed to uncover the categories that result in highest cost to the organization.
6. Plans are developed to modify the process with the intent of eliminating (or reducing the frequency of) the class of errors and defects that is most costly.

Following steps 1 and 2, a simple defect distribution can be developed (Figure 4.2) [GRA94]. For the pie-chart noted in the figure, eight causes of defects and their origin (indicated by shading) are shown. Grady suggests the development of a *fishbone diagram* [GRA92] to help in diagnosing the data represented in the frequency diagram. Referring to Figure 4.3, the spine of the diagram (the central line) represents the quality factor under consideration (in this case specification defects that account for 25 percent of the total). Each of the ribs (diagonal lines) connecting to the spine indicate potential causes for the quality problem (e.g., missing requirements, ambiguous specification, incorrect requirements, changed requirements). The spine and ribs notation is then added to each of the major ribs of the diagram to expand upon the cause noted. Expansion is shown only for the *incorrect* cause in Figure 4.3.

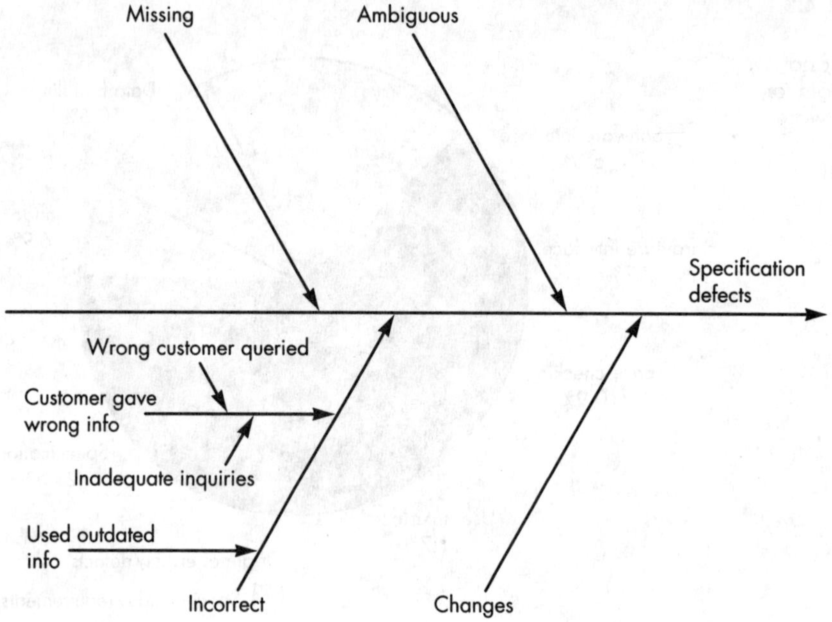

FIGURE 4.3 A fishbone diagram (adapted from [GRA92])

The collection of process metrics is the driver for the creation of the fishbone diagram. A completed fishbone diagram can be analyzed to derive indicators that will enable a software organization to modify its process to reduce the frequency of errors and defects.

4.2.2 Project Metrics

Software process metrics are used for strategic purposes. Software project measures are tactical. That is, project metrics and the indicators derived from them are used by a project manager and a software team to adapt project work flow and technical activities.

XRef
Project estimation techniques are discussed in Chapter 5.

The first application of project metrics on most software projects occurs during estimation. Metrics collected from past projects are used as a basis from which effort and time estimates are made for current software work. As a project proceeds, measures of effort and calendar time expended are compared to original estimates (and the project schedule). The project manager uses these data to monitor and control progress.

As technical work commences, other project metrics begin to have significance. Production rates represented in terms of pages of documentation, review hours, function points, and delivered source lines are measured. In addition, errors uncovered during each software engineering task are tracked. As the software evolves from specification into design, technical metrics (Chapters 19 and 24) are collected to assess

How should we use metrics during the project itself?

design quality and to provide indicators that will influence the approach taken to code generation and testing.

The intent of project metrics is twofold. First, these metrics are used to minimize the development schedule by making the adjustments necessary to avoid delays and mitigate potential problems and risks. Second, project metrics are used to assess product quality on an ongoing basis and, when necessary, modify the technical approach to improve quality.

As quality improves, defects are minimized, and as the defect count goes down, the amount of rework required during the project is also reduced. This leads to a reduction in overall project cost.

Another model of software project metrics [HET93] suggests that every project should measure:

- *Inputs*—measures of the resources (e.g., people, environment) required to do the work.
- *Outputs*—measures of the deliverables or work products created during the software engineering process.
- *Results*—measures that indicate the effectiveness of the deliverables.

In actuality, this model can be applied to both process and project. In the project context, the model can be applied recursively as each framework activity occurs. Therefore the output from one activity becomes input to the next. Results metrics can be used to provide an indication of the usefulness of work products as they flow from one framework activity (or task) to the next.

4.3 SOFTWARE MEASUREMENT

Measurements in the physical world can be categorized in two ways: direct measures (e.g., the length of a bolt) and indirect measures (e.g., the "quality" of bolts produced, measured by counting rejects). Software metrics can be categorized similarly.

What is the difference between direct and indirect measures?

Direct measures of the software engineering process include cost and effort applied. Direct measures of the product include lines of code (LOC) produced, execution speed, memory size, and defects reported over some set period of time. *Indirect measures* of the product include functionality, quality, complexity, efficiency, reliability, maintainability, and many other "-abilities" that are discussed in Chapter 19.

The cost and effort required to build software, the number of lines of code produced, and other direct measures are relatively easy to collect, as long as specific conventions for measurement are established in advance. However, the quality and functionality of software or its efficiency or maintainability are more difficult to assess and can be measured only indirectly.

We have already partitioned the software metrics domain into process, project, and product metrics. We have also noted that product metrics that are private to an individual are often combined to develop project metrics that are public to a software team. Project metrics are then consolidated to create process metrics that are public to the software organization as a whole. But how does an organization combine metrics that come from different individuals or projects?

ADVICE *Because many factors influence software work, don't use metrics to compare individuals or teams.*

To illustrate, we consider a simple example. Individuals on two different project teams record and categorize all errors that they find during the software process. Individual measures are then combined to develop team measures. Team A found 342 errors during the software process prior to release. Team B found 184 errors. All other things being equal, which team is more effective in uncovering errors throughout the process? Because we do not know the size or complexity of the projects, we cannot answer this question. However, if the measures are normalized, it is possible to create software metrics that enable comparison to broader organizational averages.

4.3.1 Size-Oriented Metrics

? What data should we collect to derive size-oriented metrics?

Size-oriented software metrics are derived by normalizing quality and/or productivity measures by considering the *size* of the software that has been produced. If a software organization maintains simple records, a table of size-oriented measures, such as the one shown in Figure 4.4, can be created. The table lists each software development project that has been completed over the past few years and corresponding measures for that project. Referring to the table entry (Figure 4.4) for project alpha: 12,100 lines of code were developed with 24 person-months of effort at a cost of $168,000. It should be noted that the effort and cost recorded in the table represent all software engineering activities (analysis, design, code, and test), not just coding. Further information for project alpha indicates that 365 pages of documentation were developed, 134 errors were recorded before the software was released, and 29 defects

Project	LOC	Effort	$(000)	Pp. doc.	Errors	Defects	People
alpha	12,100	24	168	365	134	29	3
beta	27,200	62	440	1224	321	86	5
gamma	20,200	43	314	1050	256	64	6
⋮	⋮	⋮	⋮	⋮	⋮		

FIGURE 4.4
Size-oriented metrics

were encountered after release to the customer within the first year of operation. Three people worked on the development of software for project alpha.

Metrics collection template

In order to develop metrics that can be assimilated with similar metrics from other projects, we choose lines of code as our normalization value. From the rudimentary data contained in the table, a set of simple size-oriented metrics can be developed for each project:

- Errors per KLOC (thousand lines of code).
- Defects[4] per KLOC.
- $ per LOC.
- Page of documentation per KLOC.

In addition, other interesting metrics can be computed:

- Errors per person-month.
- LOC per person-month.
- $ per page of documentation.

KEY POINT

Size-oriented metrics are widely used, but debate about their validity and applicability continues.

Size-oriented metrics are not universally accepted as the best way to measure the process of software development [JON86]. Most of the controversy swirls around the use of lines of code as a key measure. Proponents of the LOC measure claim that LOC is an "artifact" of all software development projects that can be easily counted, that many existing software estimation models use LOC or KLOC as a key input, and that a large body of literature and data predicated on LOC already exists. On the other hand, opponents argue that LOC measures are programming language dependent, that they penalize well-designed but shorter programs, that they cannot easily accommodate nonprocedural languages, and that their use in estimation requires a level of detail that may be difficult to achieve (i.e., the planner must estimate the LOC to be produced long before analysis and design have been completed).

4.3.2 Function-Oriented Metrics

WebRef

Comprehensive information on function points can be obtained at **www.ifpug.org**

Function-oriented software metrics use a measure of the functionality delivered by the application as a normalization value. Since 'functionality' cannot be measured directly, it must be derived indirectly using other direct measures. Function-oriented metrics were first proposed by Albrecht [ALB79], who suggested a measure called the *function point.* Function points are derived using an empirical relationship based on countable (direct) measures of software's information domain and assessments of software complexity.

Function points are computed [IFP94] by completing the table shown in Figure 4.5. Five information domain characteristics are determined and counts are provided in

4 A defect occurs when quality assurance activities (e.g., formal technical reviews) fail to uncover an error in a work product produced during the software process.

FIGURE 4.5
Computing function points

Measurement parameter	Count		Weighting factor Simple	Average	Complex		
Number of user inputs		×	3	4	6	=	
Number of user outputs		×	4	5	7	=	
Number of user inquiries		×	3	4	6	=	
Number of files		×	7	10	15	=	
Number of external interfaces		×	5	7	10	=	
Count total						→	

the appropriate table location. Information domain values are defined in the following manner:[5]

KEY POINT
Function points are derived from direct measures of the information domain.

Number of user inputs. Each user input that provides distinct application-oriented data to the software is counted. Inputs should be distinguished from inquiries, which are counted separately.

Number of user outputs. Each user output that provides application-oriented information to the user is counted. In this context output refers to reports, screens, error messages, etc. Individual data items within a report are not counted separately.

Number of user inquiries. An inquiry is defined as an on-line input that results in the generation of some immediate software response in the form of an on-line output. Each distinct inquiry is counted.

Number of files. Each logical master file (i.e., a logical grouping of data that may be one part of a large database or a separate file) is counted.

Number of external interfaces. All machine readable interfaces (e.g., data files on storage media) that are used to transmit information to another system are counted.

Once these data have been collected, a complexity value is associated with each count. Organizations that use function point methods develop criteria for determining whether a particular entry is simple, average, or complex. Nonetheless, the determination of complexity is somewhat subjective.

To compute function points (FP), the following relationship is used:

$$FP = \text{count total} \times [0.65 + 0.01 \times \Sigma(F_i)] \quad (4\text{-}1)$$

where count total is the sum of all FP entries obtained from Figure 4.5.

5 In actuality, the definition of information domain values and the manner in which they are counted are a bit more complex. The interested reader should see [IFP94] for details.

The F_i (i = 1 to 14) are "complexity adjustment values" based on responses to the following questions [ART85]:

1. Does the system require reliable backup and recovery?
2. Are data communications required?
3. Are there distributed processing functions?
4. Is performance critical?
5. Will the system run in an existing, heavily utilized operational environment?
6. Does the system require on-line data entry?
7. Does the on-line data entry require the input transaction to be built over multiple screens or operations?
8. Are the master files updated on-line?
9. Are the inputs, outputs, files, or inquiries complex?
10. Is the internal processing complex?
11. Is the code designed to be reusable?
12. Are conversion and installation included in the design?
13. Is the system designed for multiple installations in different organizations?
14. Is the application designed to facilitate change and ease of use by the user?

Each of these questions is answered using a scale that ranges from 0 (not important or applicable) to 5 (absolutely essential). The constant values in Equation (4-1) and the weighting factors that are applied to information domain counts are determined empirically.

Once function points have been calculated, they are used in a manner analogous to LOC as a way to normalize measures for software productivity, quality, and other attributes:

- Errors per FP.
- Defects per FP.
- $ per FP.
- Pages of documentation per FP.
- FP per person-month.

4.3.3 Extended Function Point Metrics

KEY POINT Extending function points are used for engineering, real-time, and control-oriented applications.

The function point measure was originally designed to be applied to business information systems applications. To accommodate these applications, the data dimension (the information domain values discussed previously) was emphasized to the exclusion of the functional and behavioral (control) dimensions. For this reason, the function point measure was inadequate for many engineering and embedded systems (which emphasize function and control). A number of extensions to the basic function point measure have been proposed to remedy this situation.

A function point extension called *feature points* [JON91], is a superset of the function point measure that can be applied to systems and engineering software applications.

The feature point measure accommodates applications in which algorithmic complexity is high. Real-time, process control and embedded software applications tend to have high algorithmic complexity and are therefore amenable to the feature point.

To compute the feature point, information domain values are again counted and weighted as described in Section 4.3.2. In addition, the feature point metric counts a new software characteristic—*algorithms*. An *algorithm* is defined as "a bounded computational problem that is included within a specific computer program" [JON91]. Inverting a matrix, decoding a bit string, or handling an interrupt are all examples of algorithms.

WebRef

A useful FAQ on function points (and extended function points) can be obtained at **http://ourworld.compuserve.com/homepages/softcomp/**

Another function point extension for real-time systems and engineered products has been developed by Boeing. The Boeing approach integrates the data dimension of software with the functional and control dimensions to provide a function-oriented measure amenable to applications that emphasize function and control capabilities. Called the *3D function point* [WHI95], characteristics of all three software dimensions are "counted, quantified, and transformed" into a measure that provides an indication of the functionality delivered by the software.[6]

The *data dimension* is evaluated in much the same way as described in Section 4.3.2. Counts of retained data (the internal program data structure; e.g., files) and external data (inputs, outputs, inquiries, and external references) are used along with measures of complexity to derive a data dimension count. The *functional dimension* is measured by considering "the number of internal operations required to transform input to output data" [WHI95]. For the purposes of 3D function point computation, a "transformation" is viewed as a series of processing steps that are constrained by a set of semantic statements. The *control dimension* is measured by counting the number of transitions between states.[7]

A state represents some externally observable mode of behavior, and a transition occurs as a result of some event that causes the software or system to change its mode of behavior (i.e., to change state). For example, a wireless phone contains software that supports auto dial functions. To enter the *auto-dial* state from a *resting state,* the user presses an **Auto** key on the keypad. This event causes an LCD display to prompt for a code that will indicate the party to be called. Upon entry of the code and hitting the **Dial** key (another event), the wireless phone software makes a transition to the *dialing* state. When computing 3D function points, transitions are not assigned a complexity value.

To compute 3D function points, the following relationship is used:

$$\text{index} = I + O + Q + F + E + T + R \qquad (4\text{-}2)$$

---

6 It should be noted that other extensions to function points for application in real-time software work (e.g., [ALA97]) have also been proposed. However, none of these appears to be widely used in the industry.

7 A detailed discussion of the behavioral dimension, including states and state transitions, is presented in Chapter 12.

FIGURE 4.6
Determining the complexity of a transformation for 3D function points [WHI95].

Processing steps \ Semantic statements	1–5	6–10	11+
1–10	Low	Low	Average
11–20	Low	Average	High
21+	Average	High	High

where *I, O, Q, F, E, T*, and *R* represent complexity weighted values for the elements discussed already: inputs, outputs, inquiries, internal data structures, external files, transformation, and transitions, respectively. Each complexity weighted value is computed using the following relationship:

$$\text{complexity weighted value} = N_{il}W_{il} + N_{ia}W_{ia} + N_{ih}W_{ih} \qquad (4\text{-}3)$$

where N_{il}, N_{ia}, and N_{ih} represent the number of occurrences of element *i* (e.g., outputs) for each level of complexity (low, medium, high); and W_{il}, W_{ia}, and W_{ih} are the corresponding weights. The overall complexity of a transformation for 3D function points is shown in Figure 4.6.

It should be noted that function points, feature points, and 3D function points represent the same thing—"functionality" or "utility" delivered by software. In fact, each of these measures results in the same value if only the data dimension of an application is considered. For more complex real-time systems, the feature point count is often between 20 and 35 percent higher than the count determined using function points alone.

The function point (and its extensions), like the LOC measure, is controversial. Proponents claim that FP is programming language independent, making it ideal for applications using conventional and nonprocedural languages; that it is based on data that are more likely to be known early in the evolution of a project, making FP more attractive as an estimation approach. Opponents claim that the method requires some "sleight of hand" in that computation is based on subjective rather than objective data; that counts of the information domain (and other dimensions) can be difficult to collect after the fact; and that FP has no direct physical meaning—it's just a number.

4.4 RECONCILING DIFFERENT METRICS APPROACHES

The relationship between lines of code and function points depends upon the programming language that is used to implement the software and the quality of the design. A number of studies have attempted to relate FP and LOC measures. To quote Albrecht and Gaffney [ALB83]:

> The thesis of this work is that the amount of function to be provided by the application (program) can be estimated from the itemization of the major components[8] of data to be used or provided by it. Furthermore, this estimate of function should be correlated to both the amount of LOC to be developed and the development effort needed.

The following table [JON98] provides rough estimates of the average number of lines of code required to build one function point in various programming languages:

If I know the number of LOC, is it possible to estimate the number of function points?

Programming Language	LOC/FP (average)
Assembly language	320
C	128
COBOL	106
FORTRAN	106
Pascal	90
C++	64
Ada95	53
Visual Basic	32
Smalltalk	22
Powerbuilder (code generator)	16
SQL	12

ADVICE *Use backfiring data judiciously. It is far better to compute FP using the methods discussed earlier.*

A review of these data indicates that one LOC of C++ provides approximately 1.6 times the "functionality" (on average) as one LOC of FORTRAN. Furthermore, one LOC of a Visual Basic provides more than three times the functionality of a LOC for a conventional programming language. More detailed data on the relationship between FP and LOC are presented in [JON98] and can be used to "backfire" (i.e., to compute the number of function points when the number of delivered LOC are known) existing programs to determine the FP measure for each.

LOC and FP measures are often used to derive productivity metrics. This invariably leads to a debate about the use of such data. Should the LOC/person-month (or FP/person-month) of one group be compared to similar data from another? Should managers appraise the performance of individuals by using these metrics? The answers

8 It is important to note that "the itemization of major components" can be interpreted in a variety of ways. Some software engineers who work in an object-oriented development environment (Part Four) use the number of classes or objects as the dominant size metric. A maintenance organization might view project size in terms of the number of engineering change orders (Chapter 9). An information systems organization might view the number of business processes affected by an application.

to these questions is an emphatic "No!" The reason for this response is that many factors influence productivity, making for "apples and oranges" comparisons that can be easily misinterpreted.

Function points and LOC based metrics have been found to be relatively accurate predictors of software development effort and cost. However, in order to use LOC and FP for estimation (Chapter 5), a historical baseline of information must be established.

4.5 METRICS FOR SOFTWARE QUALITY

The overriding goal of software engineering is to produce a high-quality system, application, or product. To achieve this goal, software engineers must apply effective methods coupled with modern tools within the context of a mature software process. In addition, a good software engineer (and good software engineering managers) must measure if high quality is to be realized.

WebRef

An excellent source of information on software quality and related topics (including metrics) can be found at **www.qualityworld.com**

The quality of a system, application, or product is only as good as the requirements that describe the problem, the design that models the solution, the code that leads to an executable program, and the tests that exercise the software to uncover errors. A good software engineer uses measurement to assess the quality of the analysis and design models, the source code, and the test cases that have been created as the software is engineered. To accomplish this real-time quality assessment, the engineer must use technical measures (Chapters 19 and 24) to evaluate quality in objective, rather than subjective ways.

XRef

A detailed discussion of software quality assurance activities is presented in Chapter 8.

The project manager must also evaluate quality as the project progresses. Private metrics collected by individual software engineers are assimilated to provide project-level results. Although many quality measures can be collected, the primary thrust at the project level is to measure errors and defects. Metrics derived from these measures provide an indication of the effectiveness of individual and group software quality assurance and control activities.

Metrics such as work product (e.g., requirements or design) errors per function point, errors uncovered per review hour, and errors uncovered per testing hour provide insight into the efficacy of each of the activities implied by the metric. Error data can also be used to compute the *defect removal efficiency* (DRE) for each process framework activity. DRE is discussed in Section 4.5.3.

4.5.1 An Overview of Factors That Affect Quality

Over 25 years ago, McCall and Cavano [MCC78] defined a set of quality factors that were a first step toward the development of metrics for software quality. These factors assess software from three distinct points of view: (1) product operation (using it), (2) product revision (changing it), and (3) product transition (modifying it to work in a different environment; i.e., "porting" it). In their work, the authors describe the relationship between these quality factors (what they call a *framework*) and other aspects of the software engineering process:

> First, the framework provides a mechanism for the project manager to identify what qualities are important. These qualities are attributes of the software in addition to its functional correctness and performance which have life cycle implications. Such factors as maintainability and portability have been shown in recent years to have significant life cycle cost impact . . .
>
> Secondly, the framework provides a means for quantitatively assessing how well the development is progressing relative to the quality goals established . . .
>
> Thirdly, the framework provides for more interaction of QA personnel throughout the development effort . . .
>
> Lastly, . . . quality assurance personal can use indications of poor quality to help identify [better] standards to be enforced in the future.

KEY POINT

Surprisingly, the factors that defined software quality in the 1970s are the same factors that continue to define software quality in the first decade of this century.

A detailed discussion of McCall and Cavano's framework, as well as other quality factors, is presented in Chapter 19. It is interesting to note that nearly every aspect of computing has undergone radical change as the years have passed since McCall and Cavano did their seminal work in 1978. But the attributes that provide an indication of software quality remain the same.

What does this mean? If a software organization adopts a set of quality factors as a "checklist" for assessing software quality, it is likely that software built today will still exhibit quality well into the first few decades of this century. Even as computing architectures undergo radical change (as they surely will), software that exhibits high quality in operation, transition, and revision will continue to serve its users well.

4.5.2 Measuring Quality

Although there are many measures of software quality, correctness, maintainability, integrity, and usability provide useful indicators for the project team. Gilb [GIL88] suggests definitions and measures for each.

Correctness. A program must operate correctly or it provides little value to its users. Correctness is the degree to which the software performs its required function. The most common measure for correctness is defects per KLOC, where a defect is defined as a verified lack of conformance to requirements. When considering the overall quality of a software product, defects are those problems reported by a user of the program after the program has been released for general use. For quality assessment purposes, defects are counted over a standard period of time, typically one year.

Maintainability. Software maintenance accounts for more effort than any other software engineering activity. Maintainability is the ease with which a program can be corrected if an error is encountered, adapted if its environment changes, or enhanced if the customer desires a change in requirements. There is no way to measure maintainability directly; therefore, we must use indirect measures. A simple time-oriented metric is *mean-time-to-change* (MTTC), the time it takes to analyze the change request, design an appropriate modification, implement the change, test it, and distribute the change to all users. On average, programs that are maintainable will have a lower MTTC (for equivalent types of changes) than programs that are not maintainable.

Hitachi [TAJ81] has used a cost-oriented metric for maintainability called *spoilage*—the cost to correct defects encountered after the software has been released to its end-users. When the ratio of spoilage to overall project cost (for many projects) is plotted as a function of time, a manager can determine whether the overall maintainability of software produced by a software development organization is improving. Actions can then be taken in response to the insight gained from this information.

Integrity. Software integrity has become increasingly important in the age of hackers and firewalls. This attribute measures a system's ability to withstand attacks (both accidental and intentional) to its security. Attacks can be made on all three components of software: programs, data, and documents.

To measure integrity, two additional attributes must be defined: threat and security. *Threat* is the probability (which can be estimated or derived from empirical evidence) that an attack of a specific type will occur within a given time. *Security* is the probability (which can be estimated or derived from empirical evidence) that the attack of a specific type will be repelled. The integrity of a system can then be defined as

$$\text{integrity} = \text{summation}\ [(1 - \text{threat}) \times (1 - \text{security})]$$

where threat and security are summed over each type of attack.

Usability. The catch phrase "user-friendliness" has become ubiquitous in discussions of software products. If a program is not user-friendly, it is often doomed to failure, even if the functions that it performs are valuable. Usability is an attempt to quantify user-friendliness and can be measured in terms of four characteristics: (1) the physical and or intellectual skill required to learn the system, (2) the time required to become moderately efficient in the use of the system, (3) the net increase in productivity (over the approach that the system replaces) measured when the system is used by someone who is moderately efficient, and (4) a subjective assessment (sometimes obtained through a questionnaire) of users attitudes toward the system. Detailed discussion of this topic is contained in Chapter 15.

The four factors just described are only a sampling of those that have been proposed as measures for software quality. Chapter 19 considers this topic in additional detail.

4.5.3 Defect Removal Efficiency

A quality metric that provides benefit at both the project and process level is defect removal efficiency (DRE). In essence, DRE is a measure of the filtering ability of quality assurance and control activities as they are applied throughout all process framework activities.

When considered for a project as a whole, DRE is defined in the following manner:

What is defect removal efficiency?

$$DRE = E/(E + D) \tag{4-4}$$

where E is the number of errors found before delivery of the software to the end-user and D is the number of defects found after delivery.

The ideal value for DRE is 1. That is, no defects are found in the software. Realistically, D will be greater than 0, but the value of DRE can still approach 1. As E increases (for a given value of D), the overall value of DRE begins to approach 1. In fact, as E increases, it is likely that the final value of D will decrease (errors are filtered out before they become defects). If used as a metric that provides an indicator of the filtering ability of quality control and assurance activities, DRE encourages a software project team to institute techniques for finding as many errors as possible before delivery.

DRE can also be used within the project to assess a team's ability to find errors before they are passed to the next framework activity or software engineering task. For example, the requirements analysis task produces an analysis model that can be reviewed to find and correct errors. Those errors that are not found during the review of the analysis model are passed on to the design task (where they may or may not be found). When used in this context, we redefine DRE as

ADVICE

Use DRE as a measure of the efficacy of your early SQA activities. If DRE is low during analysis and design, spend some time improving the way you conduct formal technical reviews.

$$DRE_i = E_i/(E_i + E_{i+1}) \tag{4-5}$$

where E_i is the number of errors found during software engineering activity i and E_{i+1} is the number of errors found during software engineering activity $i+1$ that are traceable to errors that were not discovered in software engineering activity i.

A quality objective for a software team (or an individual software engineer) is to achieve DRE_i that approaches 1. That is, errors should be filtered out before they are passed on to the next activity.

4.6 INTEGRATING METRICS WITHIN THE SOFTWARE PROCESS

The majority of software developers still do not measure, and sadly, most have little desire to begin. As we noted earlier in this chapter, the problem is cultural. Attempting to collect measures where none had been collected in the past often precipitates resistance. "Why do we need to do this?" asks a harried project manager. "I don't see the point," complains an overworked practitioner.

In this section, we consider some arguments for software metrics and present an approach for instituting a metrics collection program within a software engineering organization. But before we begin, some words of wisdom are suggested by Grady and Caswell [GRA87]:

> Some of the things we describe here will sound quite easy. Realistically, though, establishing a successful company-wide software metrics program is hard work. When we say that you must wait at least three years before broad organizational trends are available, you get some idea of the scope of such an effort.

The caveat suggested by the authors is well worth heeding, but the benefits of measurement are so compelling that the hard work is worth it.

4.6.1 Arguments for Software Metrics

Why is it so important to measure the process of software engineering and the product (software) that it produces? The answer is relatively obvious. If we do not measure, there no real way of determining whether we are improving. And if we are not improving, we are lost.

By requesting and evaluating productivity and quality measures, senior management can establish meaningful goals for improvement of the software engineering process. In Chapter 1 we noted that software is a strategic business issue for many companies. If the process through which it is developed can be improved, a direct impact on the bottom line can result. But to establish goals for improvement, the current status of software development must be understood. Hence, measurement is used to establish a process baseline from which improvements can be assessed.

Quote:
"We manage things 'by the numbers' in many aspects of our lives. . . . These numbers give us insight and help steer our actions."
Michael Mah
Larry Putnam

The day-to-day rigors of software project work leave little time for strategic thinking. Software project managers are concerned with more mundane (but equally important) issues: developing meaningful project estimates, producing higher-quality systems, getting product out the door on time. By using measurement to establish a project baseline, each of these issues becomes more manageable. We have already noted that the baseline serves as a basis for estimation. Additionally, the collection of quality metrics enables an organization to "tune" its software process to remove the "vital few" causes of defects that have the greatest impact on software development.[9]

At the project and technical levels (in the trenches), software metrics provide immediate benefit. As the software design is completed, most developers would be anxious to obtain answers to the questions such as

- Which user requirements are most likely to change?
- Which components in this system are most error prone?
- How much testing should be planned for each component?
- How many errors (of specific types) can I expect when testing commences?

---

9 These ideas have been formalized into an approach called *statistical software quality assurance* and are discussed in detail in Chapter 8.

Answers to these questions can be determined if metrics have been collected and used as a technical guide. In later chapters, we examine how this is done.

4.6.2 Establishing a Baseline

By establishing a metrics baseline, benefits can be obtained at the process, project, and product (technical) levels. Yet the information that is collected need not be fundamentally different. The same metrics can serve many masters. The metrics baseline consists of data collected from past software development projects and can be as simple as the table presented in Figure 4.4 or as complex as a comprehensive database containing dozens of project measures and the metrics derived from them.

? What critical information can metrics provide for a developer?

To be an effective aid in process improvement and/or cost and effort estimation, baseline data must have the following attributes: (1) data must be reasonably accurate—"guestimates" about past projects are to be avoided; (2) data should be collected for as many projects as possible; (3) measures must be consistent, for example, a line of code must be interpreted consistently across all projects for which data are collected; (4) applications should be similar to work that is to be estimated—it makes little sense to use a baseline for batch information systems work to estimate a real-time, embedded application.

4.6.3 Metrics Collection, Computation, and Evaluation

KEY POINT Baseline metrics data should be collected from a large, representative sampling of past software projects.

The process for establishing a baseline is illustrated in Figure 4.7. Ideally, data needed to establish a baseline has been collected in an ongoing manner. Sadly, this is rarely the case. Therefore, data collection requires a historical investigation of past projects to reconstruct required data. Once measures have been collected (unquestionably the most difficult step), metrics computation is possible. Depending on the breadth of measures collected, metrics can span a broad range of LOC or FP metrics as well as other quality- and project-oriented metrics. Finally, metrics must be evaluated and applied during estimation, technical work, project control, and process improvement. Metrics evaluation focuses on the underlying reasons for the results obtained and produces a set of indicators that guide the project or process.

4.7 MANAGING VARIATION: STATISTICAL PROCESS CONTROL

Because the software process and the product it produces both are influenced by many parameters (e.g., the skill level of practitioners, the structure of the software team, the knowledge of the customer, the technology that is to be implemented, the tools to be used in the development activity), metrics collected for one project or product will not be the same as similar metrics collected for another project. In fact, there is often significant variability in the metrics we collect as part of the software process.

FIGURE 4.7
Software metrics collection process

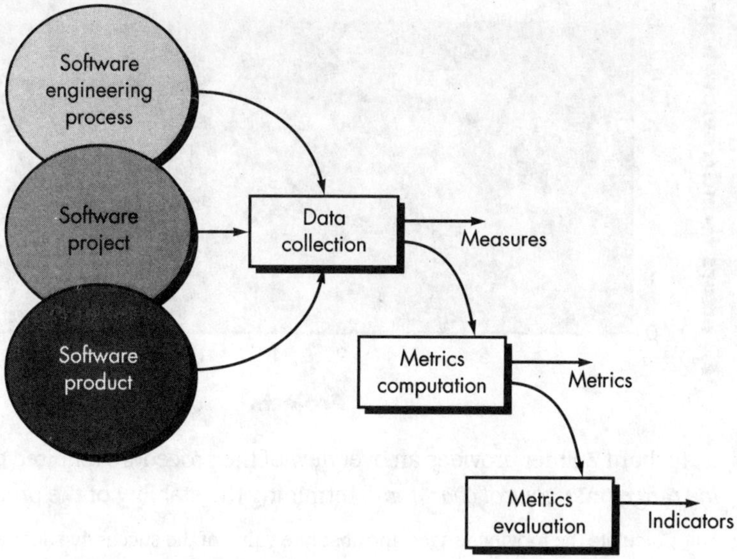

Quote:
"If I had to reduce my message for management to just a few words, I'd say it all had to do with reducing variation."
W. Edwards Deming

Since the same process metrics will vary from project to project, how can we tell if improved (or degraded) metrics values that occur as consequence of improvement activities are having a quantitative impact? How do we know whether we're looking at a statistically valid trend or whether the "trend" is simply a result of statistical noise? When are changes (either positive or negative) to a particular software metric meaningful?

A graphical technique is available for determining whether changes and variation in metrics data are meaningful. Called the *control chart* and developed by Walter Shewart in the 1920s,[10] this technique enables individuals interested in software process improvement to determine whether the dispersion (variability) and "location" (moving average) of process metrics are *stable* (i.e., the process exhibits only natural or controlled changes) or *unstable* (i.e., the process exhibits out-of-control changes and metrics cannot be used to predict performance). Two different types of control charts are used in the assessment of metrics data [ZUL99]: (1) the moving range control chart and (2) the individual control chart.

? How can we be sure that the metrics we collect are statistically valid?

To illustrate the control chart approach, consider a software organization that collects the process metric, errors uncovered per review hour, E_r. Over the past 15 months, the organization has collected E_r for 20 small projects in the same general software development domain. The resultant values for E_r are represented in Figure 4.8. In the figure, E_r varies from a low of 1.2 for project 3 to a high of 5.9 for project 17. In an effort to improve the effectiveness of reviews, the software organization provided training and mentoring to all project team members beginning with project 11.

10 It should be noted that, although the control chart was originally developed for manufacturing processes, it is equally applicable for software processes.

FIGURE 4.8
Metrics data for errors uncovered per review hour

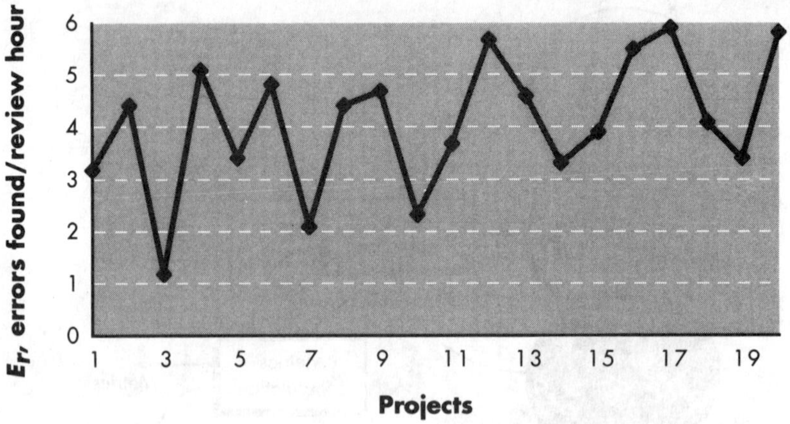

Richard Zultner provides an overview of the procedure required to develop a *moving range* (mR) *control chart* for determining the stability of the process [ZUL99]:

> 1. Calculate the moving ranges: the absolute value of the successive differences between each pair of data points . . . Plot these moving ranges on your chart.
>
> 2. Calculate the mean of the moving ranges . . . plot this ("mR bar") as the center line on your chart.
>
> 3. Multiply the mean by 3.268. Plot this line as the *upper control limit* [UCL]. This line is three standard deviations above the mean.

Quote:
"If we can't tell signals from noise, how will we ever know if changes to the process are improvement—or illusions?"
Richard Zultner

Using the data represented in Figure 4.8 and the steps suggested by Zultner, we develop an mR control chart shown in Figure 4.9. The mR bar (mean) value for the moving range data is 1.71. The upper control limit is 5.58.

To determine whether the process metrics dispersion is stable, a simple question is asked: Are all the moving range values inside the UCL? For the example noted, the answer is "yes." Hence, the metrics dispersion is stable.

The individual control chart is developed in the following manner:[11]

1. Plot individual metrics values as shown in Figure 4.8.
2. Compute the average value, A_m, for the metrics values.
3. Multiply the mean of the mR values (the mR bar) by 2.660 and add A_m computed in step 2. This results in the *upper natural process limit* (UNPL). Plot the UNPL.
4. Multiply the mean of the mR values (the mR bar) by 2.660 and subtract this amount from A_m computed in step 2. This results in the *lower natural process limit* (LNPL). Plot the LNPL. If the LNPL is less than 0.0, it need not be plotted unless the metric being evaluated takes on values that are less than 0.0.
5. Compute a standard deviation as $(\text{UNPL} - A_m)/3$. Plot lines one and two standard deviations above and below A_m. If any of the standard deviation

11 The discussion that follows is a summary of steps suggested by Zultner [ZUL99].

FIGURE 4.9
Moving range control chart

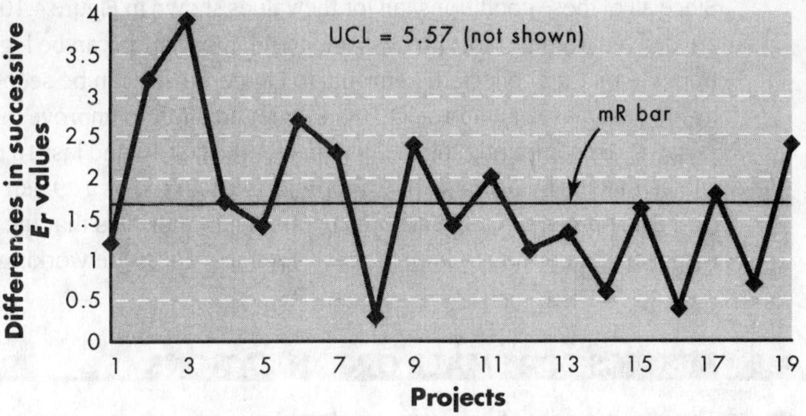

FIGURE 4.10
Individual control chart

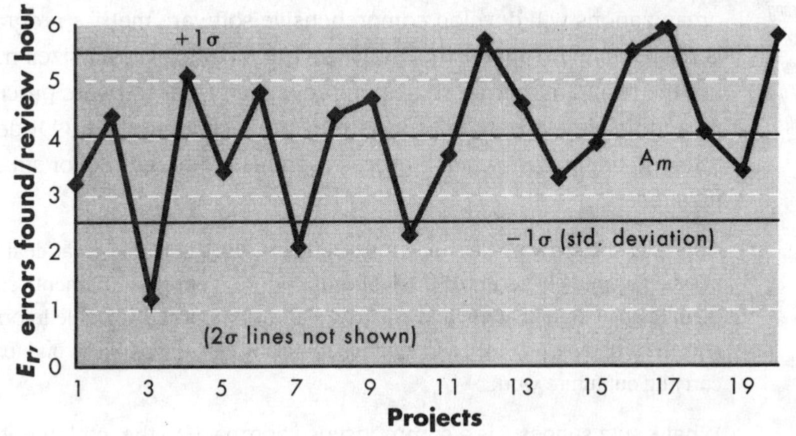

lines is less than 0.0, it need not be plotted unless the metric being evaluated takes on values that are less than 0.0.

WebRef
The *Common Control Chart Cookbook* covers the topic at some length and can be found at **www.sytsma.com/tqmtools/ctlchtprinciples.html**

Applying these steps to the data represented in Figure 4.8, we derive an *individual control chart* as shown in Figure 4.10.

Zultner [ZUL99] reviews four criteria, called *zone rules,* that may be used to evaluate whether the changes represented by the metrics indicate a process that is in control or out of control. If any of the following conditions is true, the metrics data indicate a process that is out of control:

1. A single metrics value lies outside the UNPL.
2. Two out of three successive metrics values lie more than two standard deviations away from A_m.
3. Four out of five successive metrics values lie more than one standard deviation away from A_m.
4. Eight consecutive metrics values lie on one side of A_m.

Since all of these conditions fail for the values shown in Figure 4.10, the metrics data are derived from a stable process and trend information can be legitimately inferred from the metrics collected. Referring to Figure 4.10, it can be seen that the variability of E_r decreases after project 10 (i.e., after an effort to improve the effectiveness of reviews). By computing the mean value for the first 10 and last 10 projects, it can be shown that the mean value of E_r for projects 11–20 shows a 29 percent improvement over E_r for projects 1–10. Since the control chart indicates that the process is stable, it appears that efforts to improve review effectiveness are working.

4.8 METRICS FOR SMALL ORGANIZATIONS

ADVICE

If you're just starting to collect software metrics, remember to keep it simple. If you bury yourself with data, your metrics effort will fail.

The vast majority of software development organizations have fewer than 20 software people. It is unreasonable, and in most cases unrealistic, to expect that such organizations will develop comprehensive software metrics programs. However, it is reasonable to suggest that software organizations of all sizes measure and then use the resultant metrics to help improve their local software process and the quality and timeliness of the products they produce. Kautz [KAU99] describes a typical scenario that occurs when metrics programs are suggested for small software organizations:

> Originally, the software developers greeted our activities with a great deal of skepticism, but they eventually accepted them because we kept our measurements simple, tailored them to each organization, and ensured that they produced valuable information. In the end, the programs provided a foundation for taking care of customers and for planning and carrying out future work.

What Kautz suggests is a commonsense approach to the implementation of any software process related activity: keep it simple, customize to meet local needs, and be sure it adds value. In the paragraphs that follow, we examine how these guidelines relate to metrics for small shops.

How do I derive a set of "simple" software metrics?

"Keep it simple" is a guideline that works reasonably well in many activities. But how do we derive a "simple" set of software metrics that still provides value, and how can we be sure that these simple metrics will meet the needs of a particular software organization? We begin by focusing not on measurement but rather on results. The software group is polled to define a single objective that requires improvement. For example, "reduce the time to evaluate and implement change requests." A small organization might select the following set of easily collected measures:

- Time (hours or days) elapsed from the time a request is made until evaluation is complete, t_{queue}.
- Effort (person-hours) to perform the evaluation, W_{eval}.
- Time (hours or days) elapsed from completion of evaluation to assignment of change order to personnel, t_{eval}.

- Effort (person-hours) required to make the change, W_{change}.
- Time required (hours or days) to make the change, t_{change}.
- Errors uncovered during work to make change, E_{change}.
- Defects uncovered after change is released to the customer base, D_{change}.

Once these measures have been collected for a number of change requests, it is possible to compute the total elapsed time from change request to implementation of the change and the percentage of elapsed time absorbed by initial queuing, evaluation and change assignment, and change implementation. Similarly, the percentage of effort required for evaluation and implementation can be determined. These metrics can be assessed in the context of quality data, E_{change} and D_{change}. The percentages provide insight into where the change request process slows down and may lead to process improvement steps to reduce t_{queue}, W_{eval}, t_{eval}, W_{change}, and/or E_{change}. In addition, the defect removal efficiency can be computed as

$$\text{DRE} = E_{change} / (E_{change} + D_{change})$$

DRE can be compared to elapsed time and total effort to determine the impact of quality assurance activities on the time and effort required to make a change.

For small groups, the cost of collecting measures and computing metrics ranges from 3 to 8 percent of project budget during the learning phase and then drops to less than 1 percent of project budget after software engineers and project managers have become familiar with the metrics program [GRA99]. These costs can show a substantial return on investment if the insights derived from metrics data lead to meaningful process improvement for the software organization.

4.9 ESTABLISHING A SOFTWARE METRICS PROGRAM

The Software Engineering Institute has developed a comprehensive guidebook [PAR96] for establishing a "goal-driven" software metrics program. The guidebook suggests the following steps:

WebRef
A Guidebook for Goal-Driven Software Measurement can be downloaded from **www.sei.cmu.edu**

1. Identify your business goals.
2. Identify what you want to know or learn.
3. Identify your subgoals.
4. Identify the entities and attributes related to your subgoals.
5. Formalize your measurement goals.
6. Identify quantifiable questions and the related indicators that you will use to help you achieve your measurement goals.
7. Identify the data elements that you will collect to construct the indicators that help answer your questions.
8. Define the measures to be used, and make these definitions operational.

9. Identify the actions that you will take to implement the measures.
10. Prepare a plan for implementing the measures.

A detailed discussion of these steps is best left to the SEI's guidebook. However, a brief overview of key points is worthwhile.

KEY POINT
The software metrics you choose are driven by the business or technical goals you wish to accomplish.

Because software supports business functions, differentiates computer-based systems or products, or acts as a product in itself, goals defined for the business can almost always be traced downward to specific goals at the software engineering level. For example, consider a company that makes advanced home security systems which have substantial software content. Working as a team, software engineering and business managers can develop a list of prioritized business goals:

1. Improve our customers' satisfaction with our products.
2. Make our products easier to use.
3. Reduce the time it takes us to get a new product to market.
4. Make support for our products easier.
5. Improve our overall profitability.

The software organization examines each business goal and asks: "What activities do we manage or execute and what do we want to improve within these activities?" To answer these questions the SEI recommends the creation of an "entity-question list" in which all things (entities) within the software process that are managed or influenced by the software organization are noted. Examples of entities include development resources, work products, source code, test cases, change requests, software engineering tasks, and schedules. For each entity listed, software people develop a set of questions that assess quantitative characteristics of the entity (e.g., size, cost, time to develop). The questions derived as a consequence of the creation of an entity-question list lead to the derivation of a set of subgoals that relate directly to the entities created and the activities performed as part of the software process.

Consider the fourth goal: "Make support for our products easier." The following list of questions might be derived for this goal [PAR96]:

- Do customer change requests contain the information we require to adequately evaluate the change and then implement it in a timely manner?
- How large is the change request backlog?
- Is our response time for fixing bugs acceptable based on customer need?
- Is our change control process (Chapter 9) followed?
- Are high-priority changes implemented in a timely manner?

Based on these questions, the software organization can derive the following subgoal: Improve the performance of the change management process. The software process entities and attributes that are relevant to the subgoal are identified and measurement goals associated with them are delineated.

The SEI [PAR96] provides detailed guidance for steps 6 through 10 of its goal-driven measurement approach. In essence, a process of stepwise refinement is applied in which goals are refined into questions that are further refined into entities and attributes that are then refined into metrics.

4.10 SUMMARY

Measurement enables managers and practitioners to improve the software process; assist in the planning, tracking, and control of a software project; and assess the quality of the product (software) that is produced. Measures of specific attributes of the process, project, and product are used to compute software metrics. These metrics can be analyzed to provide indicators that guide management and technical actions.

Process metrics enable an organization to take a strategic view by providing insight into the effectiveness of a software process. Project metrics are tactical. They enable a project manager to adapt project work flow and technical approach in a real-time manner.

Both size- and function-oriented metrics are used throughout the industry. Size-oriented metrics use the line of code as a normalizing factor for other measures such as person-months or defects. The function point is derived from measures of the information domain and a subjective assessment of problem complexity.

Software quality metrics, like productivity metrics, focus on the process, the project, and the product. By developing and analyzing a metrics baseline for quality, an organization can correct those areas of the software process that are the cause of software defects.

Metrics are meaningful only if they have been examined for statistical validity. The control chart is a simple method for accomplishing this and at the same time examining the variation and location of metrics results.

Measurement results in cultural change. Data collection, metrics computation, and metrics analysis are the three steps that must be implemented to begin a metrics program. In general, a goal-driven approach helps an organization focus on the right metrics for its business. By creating a metrics baseline—a database containing process and product measurements—software engineers and their managers can gain better insight into the work that they do and the product that they produce.

REFERENCES

[ALA97] Alain, A., M. Maya, J.M. Desharnais, and S. St. Pierre, "Adapting Function Points to Real-Time Software," *American Programmer,* vol. 10, no. 11, November 1997, pp. 32–43.

[ALB79] Albrecht, A.J., "Measuring Application Development Productivity," *Proc. IBM Application Development Symposium,* Monterey, CA, October 1979, pp. 83–92.

[ALB83] Albrecht, A.J. and J.E. Gaffney, "Software Function, Source Lines of Code and Development Effort Prediction: A Software Science Validation," *IEEE Trans. Software Engineering,* November 1983, pp. 639–648.

[ART85] Arthur, L.J., *Measuring Programmer Productivity and Software Quality,* Wiley-Interscience, 1985.

[BOE81] Boehm, B., *Software Engineering Economics,* Prentice-Hall, 1981.

[GRA87] Grady, R.B. and D.L. Caswell, *Software Metrics: Establishing a Company-wide Program,* Prentice-Hall, 1987.

[GRA92] Grady, R.G., *Practical Software Metrics for Project Management and Process Improvement,* Prentice-Hall, 1992.

[GRA94] Grady, R., "Successfully Applying Software Metrics," *Computer,* vol. 27, no. 9, September 1994, pp. 18–25.

[GRA99] Grable, R., et al., "Metrics for Small Projects: Experiences at SED," *IEEE Software,* March 1999, pp. 21–29.

[GIL88] Gilb, T., *Principles of Software Project Management,* Addison-Wesley, 1988.

[HET93] Hetzel, W., *Making Software Measurement Work,* QED Publishing Group, 1993.

[HUM95} Humphrey, W., *A Discipline for Software Engineering,* Addison-Wesley, 1995.

[IEE93] *IEEE Software Engineering Standards,* Standard 610.12-1990, pp. 47–48.

[IFP94] *Function Point Counting Practices Manual,* Release 4.0, International Function Point Users Group, 1994.

[JON86] Jones, C., *Programming Productivity,* McGraw-Hill, 1986.

[JON91] Jones, C., *Applied Software Measurement,* McGraw-Hill, 1991.

[JON98] Jones, C., *Estimating Software Costs,* McGraw-Hill, 1998.

[KAU99] Kautz, K., "Making Sense of Measurement for Small Organizations," *IEEE Software,* March 1999, pp. 14–20.

[MCC78] McCall, J.A. and J.P. Cavano, "A Framework for the Measurement of Software Quality," ACM Software Quality Assurance Workshop, November 1978.

[PAR96] Park, R.E., W.B. Goethert, and W.A. Florac, *Goal Driven Software Measurement—A Guidebook,* CMU/SEI-96-BH-002, Software Engineering Institute, Carnegie Mellon University, August 1996.

[PAU94] Paulish, D. and A. Carleton, "Case Studies of Software Process Improvement Measurement," *Computer,* vol. 27, no. 9, September 1994, pp. 50–57.

[RAG95] Ragland, B., "Measure, Metric or Indicator: What's the Difference?" *Crosstalk,* vol. 8, no. 3, March 1995, p. 29–30.

[TAJ81] Tajima, D. and T. Matsubara, "The Computer Software Industry in Japan," *Computer,* May 1981, p. 96.

[WHI95] Whitmire, S.A., "An Introduction to 3D Function Points", *Software Development,* April 1995, pp. 43–53.

[ZUL99] Zultner, R.E., "What Do Our Metrics Mean?" *Cutter IT Journal,* vol. 12, no. 4, April 1999, pp. 11–19.

PROBLEMS AND POINTS TO PONDER

4.1. Suggest three measures, three metrics, and corresponding indicators that might be used to assess an automobile.

4.2. Suggest three measures, three metrics, and corresponding indicators that might be used to assess the service department of an automobile dealership.

4.3. Describe the difference between process and project metrics in your own words.

4.4. Why should some software metrics be kept "private"? Provide examples of three metrics that should be private. Provide examples of three metrics that should be public.

4.5. Obtain a copy of Humphrey (*Introduction to the Personal Software Process,* Addison-Wesley, 1997) and write a one- or two-page summary that outlines the PSP approach.

4.6. Grady suggests an etiquette for software metrics. Can you add three more rules to those noted in Section 4.2.1?

4.7. Attempt to complete the fishbone diagram shown in Figure 4.3. That is, following the approach used for "incorrect" specifications, provide analogous information for "missing, ambiguous, and changed" specifications.

4.8. What is an indirect measure and why are such measures common in software metrics work?

4.9. Team A found 342 errors during the software engineering process prior to release. Team B found 184 errors. What additional measures would have to be made for projects A and B to determine which of the teams eliminated errors more efficiently? What metrics would you propose to help in making the determination? What historical data might be useful?

4.10. Present an argument against lines of code as a measure for software productivity. Will your case hold up when dozens or hundreds of projects are considered?

4.11. Compute the function point value for a project with the following information domain characteristics:

Number of user inputs: 32
Number of user outputs: 60
Number of user inquiries: 24
Number of files: 8
Number of external interfaces: 2

Assume that all complexity adjustment values are average.

4.12. Compute the 3D function point value for an embedded system with the following characteristics:

Internal data structures: 6
External data structure: 3

Number of user inputs: 12
Number of user outputs: 60
Number of user inquiries: 9
Number of external interfaces: 3
Transformations: 36
Transitions: 24

Assume that the complexity of these counts is evenly divided between low, average, and high.

4.13. The software used to control a photocopier requires 32,000 of C and 4,200 lines of Smalltalk. Estimate the number of function points for the software inside the photocopier.

4.14. McCall and Cavano (Section 4.5.1) define a "framework" for software quality. Using information contained in this and other books, expand each of the three major "points of view" into a set of quality factors and metrics.

4.15. Develop your own metrics (do not use those presented in this chapter) for correctness, maintainability, integrity, and usability. Be sure that they can be translated into quantitative values.

4.16. Is it possible for spoilage to increase while at the same time defects/KLOC decrease? Explain.

4.17. Does the LOC measure make any sense when fourth generation techniques are used? Explain.

4.18. A software organization has DRE data for 15 projects over the past two years. The values collected are 0.81, 0.71, 0.87, 0.54, 0.63, 0.71, 0.90, 0.82, 0.61, 0.84, 0.73, 0.88, 0.74, 0.86, 0.83. Create mR and individual control charts to determine whether these data can be used to assess trends.

FURTHER READINGS AND INFORMATION SOURCES

Software process improvement (SPI) has received a significant amount of attention over the past decade. Since measurement and software metrics are key to successfully improving the software process, many books on SPI also discuss metrics. Worthwhile additions to the literature include:

Burr, A. and M. Owen, *Statistical Methods for Software Quality,* International Thomson Publishing, 1996.

El Emam, K. and N. Madhavji (eds.), *Elements of Software Process Assessment and Improvement,* IEEE Computer Society, 1999.

Florac, W.A. and A.D. Carleton, *Measuring the Software Process: Statistical Process Control for Software Process Improvement,* Addison-Wesley, 1999.

Garmus, D. and D. Herron, *Measuring the Software Process: A Practical Guide to Functional Measurements,* Prentice-Hall, 1996.

Humphrey, W., *Introduction to the Team Software Process,* Addison-Wesley Longman, 2000.

Kan, S.H., *Metrics and Models in Software Quality Engineering,* Addison-Wesley, 1995.

Humphrey [HUM95], Yeh (*Software Process Control,* McGraw-Hill, 1993), Hetzel [HET93], and Grady [GRA92] discuss how software metrics can be used to provide the indicators necessary to improve the software process. Putnam and Myers (*Executive Briefing: Controlling Software Development,* IEEE Computer Society, 1996) and Pulford and his colleagues (*A Quantitative Approach to Software Management,* Addison-Wesley, 1996) discuss process metrics and their use from a management point of view.

Weinberg (*Quality Software Management,* Volume 2: *First Order Measurement,* Dorset House, 1993) presents a useful model for observing software projects, ascertaining the meaning of the observation, and determining its significance for tactical and strategic decisions. Garmus and Herron (*Measuring the Software Process,* Prentice-Hall, 1996) discuss process metrics with an emphasis on function point analysis. The Software Productivity Consortium (*The Software Measurement Guidebook,* Thomson Computer Press, 1995) provides useful suggestions for instituting an effective metrics approach. Oman and Pfleeger (*Applying Software Metrics,* IEEE Computer Society Press, 1997) have edited an excellent anthology of important papers on software metrics. Park, et al. [PAR96] have developed a detailed guidebook that provides step-by-step suggestions for instituting a software metrics program for software process improvement.

The newsletter *IT Metrics* (edited by Howard Rubin and published by Cutter Information Services) presents useful commentary on the state of software metrics in the industry. The magazines *Cutter IT Journal* and *Software Development* have regular articles and entire features dedicated to software metrics.

A wide variety of information sources on software process and project metrics are available on the Internet. An up-to-date list of World Wide Web references that are relevant to the software process and project metrics can be found at the SEPA Web site:

http://www.mhhe.com/engcs/compsci/pressman/resources/process-metrics.mhtml

CHAPTER

5 SOFTWARE PROJECT PLANNING

KEY CONCEPTS

Software project management begins with a set of activities that are collectively called *project planning.* Before the project can begin, the manager and the software team must estimate the work to be done, the resources that will be required, and the time that will elapse from start to finish. Whenever estimates are made, we look into the future and accept some degree of uncertainty as a matter of course. To quote Frederick Brooks [BRO75]:

> . . . our techniques of estimating are poorly developed. More seriously, they reflect an unvoiced assumption that is quite untrue, i.e., that all will go well. . . . because we are uncertain of our estimates, software managers often lack the courteous stubbornness to make people wait for a good product.

Although estimating is as much art as it is science, this important activity need not be conducted in a haphazard manner. Useful techniques for time and effort estimation do exist. Process and project metrics can provide historical perspective and powerful input for the generation of quantitative estimates. Past experience (of all people involved) can aid immeasurably as estimates are developed and reviewed. Because estimation lays a foundation for all other project planning activities and project planning provides the road map for successful software engineering, we would be ill-advised to embark without it.

QUICK LOOK

What is it? Software project planning actually encompasses all of the activities we discuss in Chapters 5 through 9. However, in the context of this chapter, planning involves estimation—your attempt to determine how much money, how much effort, how many resources, and how much time it will take to build a specific software-based system or product.

Who does it? Software managers—using information solicited from customers and software engineers and software metrics data collected from past projects.

Why is it important? Would you build a house without knowing how much you were about to spend? Of course not, and since most computer-based systems and products cost considerably more to build than a large house, it would seem reasonable to develop an estimate before you start creating the software.

What are the steps? Estimation begins with a description of the scope of the product. Until the scope is "bounded" it's not possible to develop a meaningful estimate. The problem is then decomposed into a set of smaller problems and each of these is estimated using historical data and experience as guides. It is advisable to generate your estimates using at least two different methods (as a cross check). Problem complexity and risk are considered before a final estimate is made.

What is the work product? A simple table delineating the tasks to be performed, the functions to be

QUICK LOOK

implemented, and the cost, effort, and time involved for each is generated. A list of required project resources is also produced.

How do I ensure that I've done it right? That's hard, because you won't really know until the project has been completed. However, if you have experience and follow a systematic approach, generate estimates using solid historical data, create estimation data points using at least two different methods, and factor in complexity and risk, you can feel confident that you've given it your best shot.

5.1 OBSERVATIONS ON ESTIMATING

A leading executive was once asked what single characteristic was most important when selecting a project manager. His response: "a person with the ability to know what will go wrong before it actually does . . ." We might add: "and the courage to estimate when the future is cloudy."

Estimation of resources, cost, and schedule for a software engineering effort requires experience, access to good historical information, and the courage to commit to quantitative predictions when qualitative information is all that exists. Estimation carries inherent risk[1] and this risk leads to uncertainty.

Quote:

"Good estimating approaches and solid historical data offer the best hope that reality will win over impossible demands."

Capers Jones

Project complexity has a strong effect on the uncertainty inherent in planning. Complexity, however, is a relative measure that is affected by familiarity with past effort. The first-time developer of a sophisticated e-commerce application might consider it to be exceedingly complex. However, a software team developing its tenth e-commerce Web site would consider such work run of the mill. A number of quantitative software complexity measures have been proposed [ZUS97]. Such measures are applied at the design or code level and are therefore difficult to use during software planning (before a design and code exist). However, other, more subjective assessments of complexity (e.g., the function point complexity adjustment factors described in Chapter 4) can be established early in the planning process.

Project size is another important factor that can affect the accuracy and efficacy of estimates. As size increases, the interdependency among various elements of the software grows rapidly.[2] Problem decomposition, an important approach to estimating, becomes more difficult because decomposed elements may still be formidable. To paraphrase Murphy's law: "What can go wrong will go wrong"—and if there are more things that can fail, more things will fail.

KEY POINT

Project complexity, project size, and the degree of structural uncertainty all affect the reliability of estimates.

The *degree of structural uncertainty* also has an effect on estimation risk. In this context, structure refers to the degree to which requirements have been solidified, the ease with which functions can be compartmentalized, and the hierarchical nature of the information that must be processed.

---

1 Systematic techniques for risk analysis are presented in Chapter 6.

2 Size often increases due to the "scope creep" that occurs when the customer changes requirements. Increases in project size can have a geometric impact on project cost and schedule (M. Mah, personal communication).

Quote:

"It is the mark of an instructed mind to rest satisfied with the degree of precision which the nature of a subject admits, and not to seek exactness when only an approximation of the truth is possible."

Aristotle

The availability of historical information has a strong influence on estimation risk. By looking back, we can emulate things that worked and improve areas where problems arose. When comprehensive software metrics (Chapter 4) are available for past projects, estimates can be made with greater assurance, schedules can be established to avoid past difficulties, and overall risk is reduced.

Risk is measured by the degree of uncertainty in the quantitative estimates established for resources, cost, and schedule. If project scope is poorly understood or project requirements are subject to change, uncertainty and risk become dangerously high. The software planner should demand completeness of function, performance, and interface definitions (contained in a *System Specification*). The planner, and more important, the customer should recognize that variability in software requirements means instability in cost and schedule.

However, a project manager should not become obsessive about estimation. Modern software engineering approaches (e.g., evolutionary process models) take an iterative view of development. In such approaches, it is possible[3] to revisit the estimate (as more information is known) and revise it when the customer makes changes to requirements.

5.2 PROJECT PLANNING OBJECTIVES

ADVICE

The more you know, the better you estimate. Therefore, update your estimates as the project progresses.

The objective of software project planning is to provide a framework that enables the manager to make reasonable estimates of resources, cost, and schedule. These estimates are made within a limited time frame at the beginning of a software project and should be updated regularly as the project progresses. In addition, estimates should attempt to define best case and worst case scenarios so that project outcomes can be bounded.

The planning objective is achieved through a process of information discovery that leads to reasonable estimates. In the following sections, each of the activities associated with software project planning is discussed.

5.3 SOFTWARE SCOPE

The first activity in software project planning is the determination of software scope. Function and performance allocated to software during system engineering (Chapter 10) should be assessed to establish a project scope that is unambiguous and understandable at the management and technical levels. A statement of software scope must be *bounded.*

Software scope describes the data and control to be processed, function, performance, constraints, interfaces, and reliability. Functions described in the statement

3 This is not meant to imply that it is always politically acceptable to modify initial estimates. A mature software organization and its managers recognize that change is not free. And yet, many customers demand (incorrectly) that an estimate once made must be maintained regardless of changing circumstances.

of scope are evaluated and in some cases refined to provide more detail prior to the beginning of estimation. Because both cost and schedule estimates are functionally oriented, some degree of decomposition is often useful. Performance considerations encompass processing and response time requirements. Constraints identify limits placed on the software by external hardware, available memory, or other existing systems.

5.3.1 Obtaining Information Necessary for Scope

Things are always somewhat hazy at the beginning of a software project. A need has been defined and basic goals and objectives have been enunciated, but the information necessary to define scope (a prerequisite for estimation) has not yet been delineated.

The most commonly used technique to bridge the communication gap between the customer and developer and to get the communication process started is to conduct a preliminary meeting or interview. The first meeting between the software engineer (the analyst) and the customer can be likened to the awkwardness of a first date between two adolescents. Neither person knows what to say or ask; both are worried that what they do say will be misinterpreted; both are thinking about where it might lead (both likely have radically different expectations here); both want to get the thing over with; but at the same time, both want it to be a success.

? How should we initiate communication between the developer and the customer?

Yet, communication must be initiated. Gause and Weinberg [GAU89] suggest that the analyst start by asking *context-free questions;* that is, a set of questions that will lead to a basic understanding of the problem, the people who want a solution, the nature of the solution desired, and the effectiveness of the first encounter itself.

The first set of context-free questions focuses on the customer, the overall goals and benefits. For example, the analyst might ask:

- Who is behind the request for this work?
- Who will use the solution?
- What will be the economic benefit of a successful solution?
- Is there another source for the solution?

The next set of questions enables the analyst to gain a better understanding of the problem and the customer to voice any perceptions about a solution:

- How would you (the customer) characterize "good" output that would be generated by a successful solution?
- What problem(s) will this solution address?
- Can you show me (or describe) the environment in which the solution will be used?
- Will any special performance issues or constraints affect the way the solution is approached?

The final set of questions focuses on the effectiveness of the meeting. Gause and Weinberg call these "meta-questions" and propose the following (abbreviated) list:

- Are you the right person to answer these questions? Are answers "official"?
- Are my questions relevant to the problem that you have?
- Am I asking too many questions?
- Can anyone else provide additional information?
- Should I be asking you anything else?

These questions (and others) will help to "break the ice" and initiate the communication that is essential to establish the scope of the project. But a question and answer meeting format is not an approach that has been overwhelmingly successful. In fact, the Q&A session should be used for the first encounter only and then be replaced by a meeting format that combines elements of problem solving, negotiation, and specification.

XRef
Requirements elicitation techniques are discussed in Chapter 11.

Customers and software engineers often have an unconscious "us and them" mindset. Rather than working as a team to identify and refine requirements, each constituency defines its own "territory" and communicates through a series of memos, formal position papers, documents, and question and answer sessions. History has shown that this approach works poorly. Misunderstandings abound, important information is omitted, and a successful working relationship is never established.

With these problems in mind, a number of independent investigators have developed a team-oriented approach to requirements gathering that can be applied to help establish the scope of a project. Called *facilitated application specification techniques* (FAST), this approach encourages the creation of a joint team of customers and developers who work together to identify the problem, propose elements of the solution, negotiate different approaches, and specify a preliminary set of requirements.

5.3.2 Feasibility

Quote:
"It's 106 miles to Chicago, we got a full tank of gas, half a pack of cigarettes, it's dark and we're wearing sunglasses. Hit it."
The Blues Brothers

Once scope has been identified (with the concurrence of the customer), it is reasonable to ask: "Can we build software to meet this scope? Is the project feasible?" All too often, software engineers rush past these questions (or are pushed past them by impatient managers or customers), only to become mired in a project that is doomed from the onset. Putnam and Myers [PUT97a] address this issue when they write:

> . . . not everything imaginable is feasible, not even in software, evanescent as it may appear to outsiders. On the contrary, software feasibility has four solid dimensions: *Technology*—Is a project technically feasible? Is it within the state of the art? Can defects be reduced to a level matching the application's needs? *Finance*—Is it financially feasible? Can development be completed at a cost the software organization, its client, or the market can afford? *Time*—Will the project's time-to-market beat the competition? *Resources*—Does the organization have the resources needed to succeed?

> For some projects in established areas the answers are easy. You have done projects like this one before. After a few hours or sometimes a few weeks of investigation, you are sure you can do it again.
>
> Projects on the margins of your experience are not so easy. A team may have to spend several months discovering what the central, difficult-to-implement requirements of a new application actually are. Do some of these requirements pose risks that would make the project infeasible? Can these risks be overcome? The feasibility team ought to carry initial architecture and design of the high-risk requirements to the point at which it can answer these questions. In some cases, when the team gets negative answers, a reduction in requirements may be negotiated.
>
> Meantime, the cartoon people [senior managers] are drumming their fingers nervously on their large desks. Often, they wave their fat cigars in a lordly manner and yell impatiently through the smoke screen, "Enough. Do it!"
>
> Many of the projects that appear in the newspapers a few years later as whopping failures got started this way.

ADVICE

Technical feasibility is important, but business need is even more important. It does no good to build a high tech system or product that no one really wants.

Putnam and Myers correctly suggest that scoping is not enough. Once scope is understood, the software team and others must work to determine if it can be done within the dimensions just noted. This is a crucial, although often overlooked, part of the estimation process.

5.3.3 A Scoping Example

Communication with the customer leads to a definition of the data and control that are processed, the functions that must be implemented, the performance and constraints that bound the system, and related information. As an example, consider software for a conveyor line sorting system (CLSS). The statement of scope for CLSS follows:

> The conveyor line sorting system (CLSS) sorts boxes moving along a conveyor line. Each box is identified by a bar code that contains a part number and is sorted into one of six bins at the end of the line. The boxes pass by a sorting station that contains a bar code reader and a PC. The sorting station PC is connected to a shunting mechanism that sorts the boxes into the bins. Boxes pass in random order and are evenly spaced. The line is moving at five feet per minute. CLSS is depicted schematically in Figure 5.1.
>
> CLSS software receives input information from a bar code reader at time intervals that conform to the conveyor line speed. Bar code data will be decoded into box identification format. The software will do a look-up in a part number database containing a maximum of 1000 entries to determine proper bin location for the box currently at the reader (sorting station). The proper bin location is passed to a sorting shunt that will position boxes in the appropriate bin. A record of the bin destination for each box will be maintained for later recovery and reporting. CLSS software will also receive input from a pulse tachometer that will be used to synchronize the control signal to the shunting mechanism. Based on the number of pulses generated between the sorting station and the shunt, the software will produce a control signal to the shunt to properly position the box.

FIGURE 5.1
A conveyor line sorting system

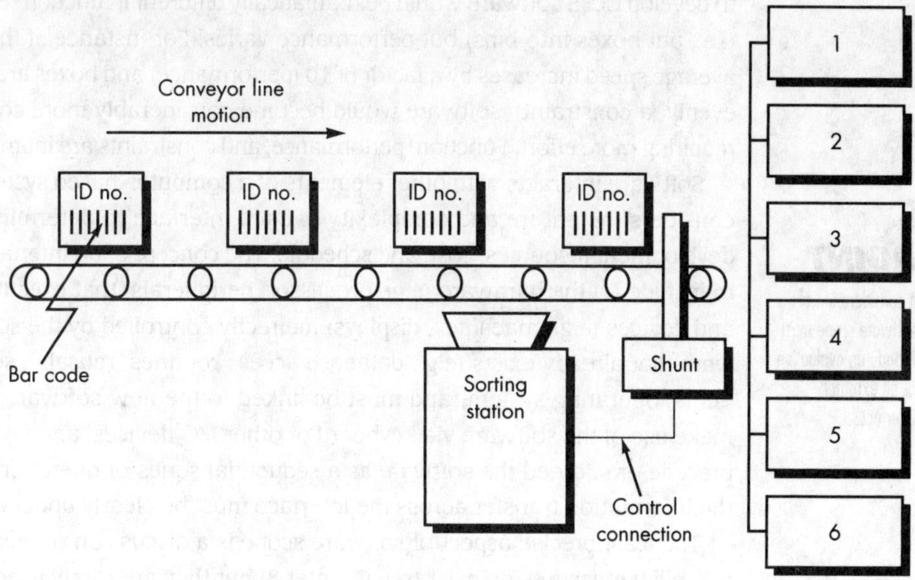

The project planner examines the statement of scope and extracts all important software functions. This process, called *decomposition,* was discussed in Chapter 3 and results in the following functions:[4]

- Read bar code input.
- Read pulse tachometer.
- Decode part code data.
- Do database look-up.
- Determine bin location.
- Produce control signal for shunt.
- Maintain record of box destinations.

ADVICE
Adjust estimates to reflect difficult performance requirements and design constraints, even if scope is otherwise simple.

In this case, performance is dictated by conveyor line speed. Processing for each box must be completed before the next box arrives at the bar code reader. The CLSS software is constrained by the hardware it must access (the bar code reader, the shunt, the PC), the available memory, and the overall conveyor line configuration (evenly spaced boxes).

Function, performance, and constraints must be evaluated together. The same function can precipitate an order of magnitude difference in development effort when considered in the context of different performance bounds. The effort and cost required

4 In reality, the functional decomposition is performed during system engineering (Chapter 10). The planner uses information derived from the *System Specification* to define software functions.

to develop CLSS software would be dramatically different if function remains the same (i.e., put boxes into bins) but performance varies. For instance, if the conveyor line average speed increases by a factor of 10 (performance) and boxes are no long spaced evenly (a constraint), software would become considerably more complex—thereby requiring more effort. Function, performance, and constraints are intimately connected.

KEY POINT

A consideration of software scope must include an evaluation of all external interfaces.

Software interacts with other elements of a computer-based system. The planner considers the nature and complexity of each interface to determine any effect on development resources, cost, and schedule. The concept of an interface is interpreted to include (1) the hardware (e.g., processor, peripherals) that executes the software and devices (e.g., machines, displays) indirectly controlled by the software, (2) software that already exists (e.g., database access routines, reusable software components, operating system) and must be linked to the new software, (3) people that make use of the software via keyboard or other I/O devices, and (4) procedures that precede or succeed the software as a sequential series of operations. In each case, the information transfer across the interface must be clearly understood.

The least precise aspect of software scope is a discussion of reliability. Software reliability measures do exist (see Chapter 8) but they are rarely used at this stage of a project. Classic hardware reliability characteristics like *mean-time-between-failures* (MTBF) can be difficult to translate to the software domain. However, the general nature of the software may dictate special considerations to ensure "reliability." For example, software for an air traffic control system or the space shuttle (both human-rated systems) must not fail or human life may be lost. An inventory control system or word-processor software should not fail, but the impact of failure is considerably less dramatic. Although it may not be possible to quantify software reliability as precisely as we would like in the statement of scope, we can use the nature of the project to aid in formulating estimates of effort and cost to assure reliability.

? What is the primary source of information for determining scope?

If a *System Specification* (see Chapter 10) has been properly developed, nearly all information required for a description of software scope is available and documented before software project planning begins. In cases where a specification has not been developed, the planner must take on the role of system analyst to determine attributes and bounds that will influence estimation tasks.

5.4 RESOURCES

The second software planning task is estimation of the resources required to accomplish the software development effort. Figure 5.2 illustrates development resources as a pyramid. The *development environment*—hardware and software tools—sits at the foundation of the resources pyramid and provides the infrastructure to support the development effort. At a higher level, we encounter reusable *software components*—software building blocks that can dramatically reduce development costs and accelerate delivery. At the top of the pyramid is the primary resource—*people*. Each resource is specified with four characteristics: description of the resource, a state-

FIGURE 5.2
Project resources

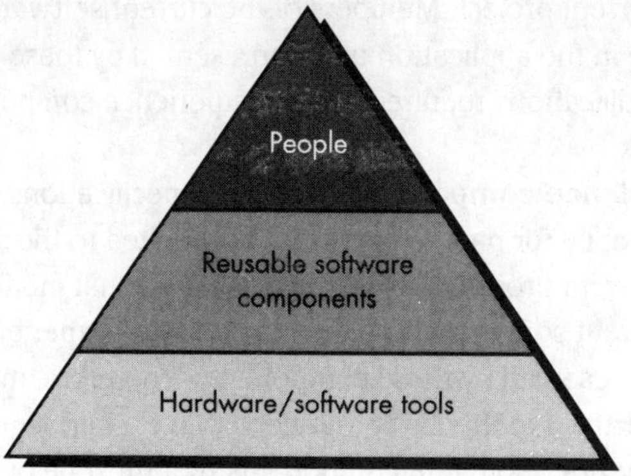

ment of availability, time when the resource will be required; duration of time that resource will be applied. The last two characteristics can be viewed as a time window. Availability of the resource for a specified window must be established at the earliest practical time.

5.4.1 Human Resources

XRef
The roles software people play and the team organizations that they populate are discussed in Chapter 3.

The planner begins by evaluating scope and selecting the skills required to complete development. Both organizational position (e.g., manager, senior software engineer) and specialty (e.g., telecommunications, database, client/server) are specified. For relatively small projects (one person-year or less), a single individual may perform all software engineering tasks, consulting with specialists as required.

The number of people required for a software project can be determined only after an estimate of development effort (e.g., person-months) is made. Techniques for estimating effort are discussed later in this chapter.

5.4.2 Reusable Software Resources

KEY POINT
To be reused effectively, software components must be cataloged, standardized, and validated.

Component-based software engineering (CBSE)[5] emphasizes reusability—that is, the creation and reuse of software building blocks [HOO91]. Such building blocks, often called *components*, must be cataloged for easy reference, standardized for easy application, and validated for easy integration.

Bennatan [BEN92] suggests four software resource categories that should be considered as planning proceeds:

Off-the-shelf components. Existing software that can be acquired from a third party or that has been developed internally for a past project. COTS (commercial off-the-shelf) components are purchased from a third party, are ready for use on the current project, and have been fully validated.

Full-experience components. Existing specifications, designs, code, or test data developed for past projects that are similar to the software to be

5 Component-based software engineering is considered in detail in Chapter 27.

built for the current project. Members of the current software team have had full experience in the application area represented by these components. Therefore, modifications required for full-experience components will be relatively low-risk.

Partial-experience components. Existing specifications, designs, code, or test data developed for past projects that are related to the software to be built for the current project but will require substantial modification. Members of the current software team have only limited experience in the application area represented by these components. Therefore, modifications required for partial-experience components have a fair degree of risk.

New components. Software components that must be built by the software team specifically for the needs of the current project.

The following guidelines should be considered by the software planner when reusable components are specified as a resource:

? What issues should we consider when we plan to reuse existing software components?

1. If off-the-shelf components meet project requirements, acquire them. The cost for acquisition and integration of off-the-shelf components will almost always be less than the cost to develop equivalent software.[6] In addition, risk is relatively low.
2. If full-experience components are available, the risks associated with modification and integration are generally acceptable. The project plan should reflect the use of these components.
3. If partial-experience components are available, their use for the current project must be analyzed. If extensive modification is required before the components can be properly integrated with other elements of the software, proceed carefully—risk is high. The cost to modify partial-experience components can sometimes be greater than the cost to develop new components.

Ironically, reusable software components are often neglected during planning, only to become a paramount concern during the development phase of the software process. It is better to specify software resource requirements early. In this way technical evaluation of the alternatives can be conducted and timely acquisition can occur.

5.4.3 Environmental Resources

The environment that supports the software project, often called the *software engineering environment* (SEE), incorporates hardware and software. Hardware provides a platform that supports the tools (software) required to produce the work products that are an outcome of good software engineering practice.[7] Because most software

6 When existing software components are used during a project, the overall cost reduction can be dramatic. In fact, industry data indicate that cost, time to market, and the number of defects delivered to the field all are reduced.

7 Other hardware—the target environment—is the computer on which the software will execute when it has been released to the end-user.

organizations have multiple constituencies that require access to the SEE, a project planner must prescribe the time window required for hardware and software and verify that these resources will be available.

When a computer-based system (incorporating specialized hardware and software) is to be engineered, the software team may require access to hardware elements being developed by other engineering teams. For example, software for a numerical control (NC) used on a class of machine tools may require a specific machine tool (e.g., an NC lathe) as part of the validation test step; a software project for advanced page-layout may need a digital-typesetting system at some point during development. Each hardware element must be specified by the software project planner.

5.5 SOFTWARE PROJECT ESTIMATION

> **Quote:**
> "In an age of outsourcing and increased competition, the ability to estimate more accurately . . . has emerged as a critical survival factor for many IT groups."
> **Rob Thomsett**

In the early days of computing, software costs constituted a small percentage of the overall computer-based system cost. An order of magnitude error in estimates of software cost had relatively little impact. Today, software is the most expensive element of virtually all computer-based systems. For complex, custom systems, a large cost estimation error can make the difference between profit and loss. Cost overrun can be disastrous for the developer.

Software cost and effort estimation will never be an exact science. Too many variables—human, technical, environmental, political—can affect the ultimate cost of software and effort applied to develop it. However, software project estimation can be transformed from a black art to a series of systematic steps that provide estimates with acceptable risk.

To achieve reliable cost and effort estimates, a number of options arise:

1. Delay estimation until late in the project (obviously, we can achieve 100% accurate estimates after the project is complete!).
2. Base estimates on similar projects that have already been completed.
3. Use relatively simple decomposition techniques to generate project cost and effort estimates.
4. Use one or more empirical models for software cost and effort estimation.

Unfortunately, the first option, however attractive, is not practical. Cost estimates must be provided "up front." However, we should recognize that the longer we wait, the more we know, and the more we know, the less likely we are to make serious errors in our estimates.

The second option can work reasonably well, if the current project is quite similar to past efforts and other project influences (e.g., the customer, business conditions, the SEE, deadlines) are equivalent. Unfortunately, past experience has not always been a good indicator of future results.

The remaining options are viable approaches to software project estimation. Ideally, the techniques noted for each option should be applied in tandem; each used as a cross-check for the other. *Decomposition techniques* take a "divide and conquer" approach to software project estimation. By decomposing a project into major functions and related software engineering activities, cost and effort estimation can be performed in a stepwise fashion. *Empirical estimation models* can be used to complement decomposition techniques and offer a potentially valuable estimation approach in their own right. A model is based on experience (historical data) and takes the form

$$d = f(v_i)$$

where d is one of a number of estimated values (e.g., effort, cost, project duration) and v_i are selected independent parameters (e.g., estimated LOC or FP).

Automated estimation tools implement one or more decomposition techniques or empirical models. When combined with a graphical user interface, automated tools provide an attractive option for estimating. In such systems, the characteristics of the development organization (e.g., experience, environment) and the software to be developed are described. Cost and effort estimates are derived from these data.

SEPA WEB: Estimation tools

Each of the viable software cost estimation options is only as good as the historical data used to seed the estimate. If no historical data exist, costing rests on a very shaky foundation. In Chapter 4, we examined the characteristics of some of the software metrics that provide the basis for historical estimation data.

5.6 DECOMPOSITION TECHNIQUES

Software project estimation is a form of problem solving, and in most cases, the problem to be solved (i.e., developing a cost and effort estimate for a software project) is too complex to be considered in one piece. For this reason, we decompose the problem, recharacterizing it as a set of smaller (and hopefully, more manageable) problems.

In Chapter 3, the decomposition approach was discussed from two different points of view: decomposition of the problem and decomposition of the process. Estimation uses one or both forms of partitioning. But before an estimate can be made, the project planner must understand the scope of the software to be built and generate an estimate of its "size."

5.6.1 Software Sizing

KEY POINT

The "size" of software to be built can be estimated using a direct measure, LOC, or an indirect measure, FP.

The accuracy of a software project estimate is predicated on a number of things: (1) the degree to which the planner has properly estimated the size of the product to be built; (2) the ability to translate the size estimate into human effort, calendar time, and dollars (a function of the availability of reliable software metrics from past projects); (3) the degree to which the project plan reflects the abilities of the software team; and (4) the stability of product requirements and the environment that supports the software engineering effort.

In this section, we consider the *software sizing* problem. Because a project estimate is only as good as the estimate of the size of the work to be accomplished, sizing represents the project planner's first major challenge. In the context of project planning, size refers to a quantifiable outcome of the software project. If a direct approach is taken, size can be measured in LOC. If an indirect approach is chosen, size is represented as FP.

Putnam and Myers [PUT92] suggest four different approaches to the sizing problem:

? How do we size the software that we're planning to build?

"Fuzzy logic" sizing. This approach uses the approximate reasoning techniques that are the cornerstone of fuzzy logic. To apply this approach, the planner must identify the type of application, establish its magnitude on a qualitative scale, and then refine the magnitude within the original range. Although personal experience can be used, the planner should also have access to a historical database of projects[8] so that estimates can be compared to actual experience.

Function point sizing. The planner develops estimates of the information domain characteristics discussed in Chapter 4.

Standard component sizing. Software is composed of a number of different "standard components" that are generic to a particular application area. For example, the standard components for an information system are subsystems, modules, screens, reports, interactive programs, batch programs, files, LOC, and object-level instructions. The project planner estimates the number of occurrences of each standard component and then uses historical project data to determine the delivered size per standard component. To illustrate, consider an information systems application. The planner estimates that 18 reports will be generated. Historical data indicates that 967 lines of COBOL [PUT92] are required per report. This enables the planner to estimate that 17,000 LOC will be required for the reports component. Similar estimates and computation are made for other standard components, and a combined size value (adjusted statistically) results.

Change sizing. This approach is used when a project encompasses the use of existing software that must be modified in some way as part of a project. The planner estimates the number and type (e.g., reuse, adding code, changing code, deleting code) of modifications that must be accomplished. Using an "effort ratio" [PUT92] for each type of change, the size of the change may be estimated.

Putnam and Myers suggest that the results of each of these sizing approaches be combined statistically to create a *three-point* or *expected value* estimate. This is accomplished by developing optimistic (low), most likely, and pessimistic (high) values for size and combining them using Equations (5-1) described in the next section.

---

8 See Section 5.9 for a discussion of estimating tools that make use of a historical database and the other sizing techniques discussed in this section..

5.6.2 Problem-Based Estimation

In Chapter 4, lines of code and function points were described as measures from which productivity metrics can be computed. LOC and FP data are used in two ways during software project estimation: (1) as an estimation variable to "size" each element of the software and (2) as baseline metrics collected from past projects and used in conjunction with estimation variables to develop cost and effort projections.

? What do LOC- and FP-oriented estimation have in common?

LOC and FP estimation are distinct estimation techniques. Yet both have a number of characteristics in common. The project planner begins with a bounded statement of software scope and from this statement attempts to decompose software into problem functions that can each be estimated individually. LOC or FP (the estimation variable) is then estimated for each function. Alternatively, the planner may choose another component for sizing such as classes or objects, changes, or business processes affected.

ADVICE

When collecting productivity metrics for projects, be sure to establish a taxonomy of project types. This will enable you to compute domain-specific averages, making estimation more accurate.

Baseline productivity metrics (e.g., LOC/pm or FP/pm[9]) are then applied to the appropriate estimation variable, and cost or effort for the function is derived. Function estimates are combined to produce an overall estimate for the entire project.

It is important to note, however, that there is often substantial scatter in productivity metrics for an organization, making the use of a single baseline productivity metric suspect. In general, LOC/pm or FP/pm averages should be computed by project domain. That is, projects should be grouped by team size, application area, complexity, and other relevant parameters. Local domain averages should then be computed. When a new project is estimated, it should first be allocated to a domain, and then the appropriate domain average for productivity should be used in generating the estimate.

The LOC and FP estimation techniques differ in the level of detail required for decomposition and the target of the partitioning. When LOC is used as the estimation variable, decomposition[10] is absolutely essential and is often taken to considerable levels of detail. The following decomposition approach has been adapted from Phillips [PHI98]:[11]

KEY POINT

For LOC estimates, decomposition focuses on software functions.

```
define product scope;
identify functions by decomposing scope;
do while functions remain
        select a function_j
        assign all functions to subfunctions list;
```

9 The acronym *pm* stands for person-month.

10 In general, problem functions are decomposed. However, a list of standard components (Section 5.6.1) may be used instead.

11 The informal process design language noted here is intended to illustrate the general approach for sizing. It does not consider every logical contingency.

```
do while subfunctions remain
    select subfunction_k
    if subfunction_k resembles subfunction_d described in a historical data base
    then    note historical cost, effort, size (LOC or FP) data for subfunction_d;
            adjust historical cost, effort, size data based on any differences;
            use adjusted cost, effort, size data to derive partial estimate, E_p;
            project estimate = sum of {E_p};
    else    if cost, effort, size (LOC or FP) for subfunction_k can be estimated
            then derive partial estimate, E_p;
            project estimate = sum of {E_p};
            else subdivide subfunction_k into smaller subfunctions;
            add these to subfunctions list;
            endif
    endif
    enddo
enddo
```

This decomposition approach assumes that all functions can be decomposed into subfunctions that will resemble entries in a historical data base. If this is not the case, then another sizing approach must be applied. The greater the degree of partitioning, the more likely reasonably accurate estimates of LOC can be developed.

KEY POINT
For FP estimates, decomposition focuses on information domain characteristics.

For FP estimates, decomposition works differently. Rather than focusing on function, each of the information domain characteristics—inputs, outputs, data files, inquiries, and external interfaces—as well as the 14 complexity adjustment values discussed in Chapter 4 are estimated. The resultant estimates can then be used to derive a FP value that can be tied to past data and used to generate an estimate.

Regardless of the estimation variable that is used, the project planner begins by estimating a range of values for each function or information domain value. Using historical data or (when all else fails) intuition, the planner estimates an optimistic, most likely, and pessimistic size value for each function or count for each information domain value. An implicit indication of the degree of uncertainty is provided when a range of values is specified.

? How do I compute the expected value for software size?

A three-point or expected value can then be computed. The *expected value* for the estimation variable (size), *S*, can be computed as a weighted average of the optimistic (s_{opt}), most likely (s_m), and pessimistic (s_{pess}) estimates. For example,

$$S = (s_{opt} + 4s_m + s_{pess})/6 \tag{5-1}$$

gives heaviest credence to the "most likely" estimate and follows a beta probability distribution. We assume that there is a very small probability the actual size result will fall outside the optimistic or pessimistic values.

Once the expected value for the estimation variable has been determined, historical LOC or FP productivity data are applied. Are the estimates correct? The only reasonable answer to this question is: "We can't be sure." Any estimation technique, no matter how sophisticated, must be cross-checked with another approach. Even then, common sense and experience must prevail.

5.6.3 An Example of LOC-Based Estimation

As an example of LOC and FP problem-based estimation techniques, let us consider a software package to be developed for a computer-aided design application for mechanical components. A review of the *System Specification* indicates that the software is to execute on an engineering workstation and must interface with various computer graphics peripherals including a mouse, digitizer, high resolution color display and laser printer.

Using the *System Specification* as a guide, a preliminary statement of software scope can be developed:

> The CAD software will accept two- and three-dimensional geometric data from an engineer. The engineer will interact and control the CAD system through a user interface that will exhibit characteristics of good human/machine interface design. All geometric data and other supporting information will be maintained in a CAD database. Design analysis modules will be developed to produce the required output, which will be displayed on a variety of graphics devices. The software will be designed to control and interact with peripheral devices that include a mouse, digitizer, laser printer, and plotter.

This statement of scope is preliminary—it is *not* bounded. Every sentence would have to be expanded to provide concrete detail and quantitative bounding. For example, before estimation can begin the planner must determine what "characteristics of good human/machine interface design" means or what the size and sophistication of the "CAD database" are to be.

ADVICE

Many modern applications reside on a network or are part of a client/server architecture. Therefore, be sure that your estimates include the effort required for the development of "infrastructure" software.

For our purposes, we assume that further refinement has occurred and that the following major software functions are identified:

- User interface and control facilities (UICF)
- Two-dimensional geometric analysis (2DGA)
- Three-dimensional geometric analysis (3DGA)
- Database management (DBM)
- Computer graphics display facilities (CGDF)
- Peripheral control function (PCF)
- Design analysis modules (DAM)

Following the decomposition technique for LOC, an estimation table, shown in Figure 5.3, is developed. A range of LOC estimates is developed for each function. For example, the range of LOC estimates for the 3D geometric analysis function is optimistic—4600 LOC, most likely—6900 LOC, and pessimistic—8600 LOC.

FIGURE 5.3
Estimation table for the LOC method

Function	Estimated LOC
User interface and control facilities (UICF)	2,300
Two-dimensional geometric analysis (2DGA)	5,300
Three-dimensional geometric analysis (3DGA)	6,800
Database management (DBM)	3,350
Computer graphics display facilities (CGDF)	4,950
Peripheral control function (PCF)	2,100
Design analysis modules (DAM)	8,400
Estimated lines of code	*33,200*

ADVICE

Do not succumb to the temptation to use this result as your estimate. You should derive another estimate using a different method.

Applying Equation (5-1), the expected value for the 3D geometric analysis function is 6800 LOC. Other estimates are derived in a similar fashion. By summing vertically in the estimated LOC column, an estimate of 33,200 lines of code is established for the CAD system.

A review of historical data indicates that the organizational average productivity for systems of this type is 620 LOC/pm. Based on a burdened labor rate of $8000 per month, the cost per line of code is approximately $13. Based on the LOC estimate and the historical productivity data, the total estimated project cost is $431,000 and the estimated effort is 54 person-months.[12]

5.6.4 An Example of FP-Based Estimation

WebRef
Information on FP cost estimating tools can be obtained at **www.spr.com**

Decomposition for FP-based estimation focuses on information domain values rather than software functions. Referring to the function point calculation table presented in Figure 5.4, the project planner estimates inputs, outputs, inquiries, files, and external interfaces for the CAD software. For the purposes of this estimate, the complexity weighting factor is assumed to be average. Figure 5.4 presents the results of this estimate.

FIGURE 5.4
Estimating information domain values

Information domain value	Opt.	Likely	Pess.	Est. count	Weight	FP count
Number of inputs	20	24	30	24	4	97
Number of outputs	12	15	22	16	5	78
Number of inquiries	16	22	28	22	5	88
Number of files	4	4	5	4	10	42
Number of external interfaces	2	2	3	2	7	15
Count total						*320*

12 Estimates are rounded-off to the nearest $1,000 and person-month. Arithmetic precision to the nearest dollar or tenth of a month is unrealistic.

Each of the complexity weighting factors is estimated and the complexity adjustment factor is computed as described in Chapter 4:

Factor	Value
Backup and recovery	4
Data communications	2
Distributed processing	0
Performance critical	4
Existing operating environment	3
On-line data entry	4
Input transaction over multiple screens	5
Master files updated on-line	3
Information domain values complex	5
Internal processing complex	5
Code designed for reuse	4
Conversion/installation in design	3
Multiple installations	5
Application designed for change	5
Complexity adjustment factor	1.17

Finally, the estimated number of FP is derived:

$$FP_{\text{estimated}} = \text{count-total} \times [0.65 + 0.01 \times \Sigma\ (F_i)]$$
$$FP_{\text{estimated}} = 375$$

The organizational average productivity for systems of this type is 6.5 FP/pm. Based on a burdened labor rate of $8000 per month, the cost per FP is approximately $1230. Based on the LOC estimate and the historical productivity data, the total estimated project cost is $461,000 and the estimated effort is 58 person-months.

5.6.4 Process-Based Estimation

The most common technique for estimating a project is to base the estimate on the process that will be used. That is, the process is decomposed into a relatively small set of tasks and the effort required to accomplish each task is estimated.

XRef
A common process framework (CPF) is discussed in Chapter 2.

Like the problem-based techniques, process-based estimation begins with a delineation of software functions obtained from the project scope. A series of software process activities must be performed for each function. Functions and related software process activities may be represented as part of a table similar to the one presented in Figure 3.2.

Once problem functions and process activities are melded, the planner estimates the effort (e.g., person-months) that will be required to accomplish each software process activity for each software function. These data constitute the central matrix of the table in Figure 3.2. Average labor rates (i.e., cost/unit effort) are then applied to the effort estimated for each process activity. It is very likely the labor rate will vary for each task. Senior staff heavily involved in early activities are generally more expensive than junior staff involved in later design tasks, code generation, and early testing.

FIGURE 5.5
Process-based estimation table

Activity →	CC	Planning	Risk analysis	Engineering		Construction release		CE	Totals
Task →				Analysis	Design	Code	Test		
Function ↓									
UICF				0.50	2.50	0.40	5.00	n/a	8.40
2DGA				0.75	4.00	0.60	2.00	n/a	7.35
3DGA				0.50	4.00	1.00	3.00	n/a	8.50
CGDF				0.50	3.00	1.00	1.50	n/a	6.00
DBM				0.50	3.00	0.75	1.50	n/a	5.75
PCF				0.25	2.00	0.50	1.50	n/a	4.25
DAM				0.50	2.00	0.50	2.00	n/a	5.00
Totals	0.25	0.25	0.25	3.50	20.50	4.50	16.50		46.00
% effort	1%	1%	1%	8%	45%	10%	36%		

CC = customer communication CE = customer evaluation

ADVICE

If time permits, use greater granularity when specifying tasks in Figure 5.5, such as breaking analysis into its major tasks and estimating each separately.

Costs and effort for each function and software process activity are computed as the last step. If process-based estimation is performed independently of LOC or FP estimation, we now have two or three estimates for cost and effort that may be compared and reconciled. If both sets of estimates show reasonable agreement, there is good reason to believe that the estimates are reliable. If, on the other hand, the results of these decomposition techniques show little agreement, further investigation and analysis must be conducted.

5.6.5 An Example of Process-Based Estimation

To illustrate the use of process-based estimation, we again consider the CAD software introduced in Section 5.6.3. The system configuration and all software functions remain unchanged and are indicated by project scope.

Referring to the completed process-based table shown in Figure 5.5, estimates of effort (in person-months) for each software engineering activity are provided for each CAD software function (abbreviated for brevity). The engineering and construction release activities are subdivided into the major software engineering tasks shown. Gross estimates of effort are provided for customer communication, planning, and risk analysis. These are noted in the total row at the bottom of the table. Horizontal and vertical totals provide an indication of estimated effort required for analysis, design, code, and test. It should be noted that 53 percent of all effort is expended on front-end engineering tasks (requirements analysis and design), indicating the relative importance of this work.

Based on an average burdened labor rate of \$8,000 per month, the total estimated project cost is \$368,000 and the estimated effort is 46 person-months. If desired, labor rates could be associated with each software process activity or software engineering task and computed separately.

ADVICE

Do not expect that all estimates will agree within a percent or two. If the estimates are within a 20 percent band, they can be reconciled into a single value.

Total estimated effort for the CAD software range from a low of 46 person-months (derived using a process-based estimation approach) to a high of 58 person-months (derived using an FP estimation approach). The average estimate (using all three approaches) is 53 person-months. The maximum variation from the average estimate is approximately 13 percent.

What happens when agreement between estimates is poor? The answer to this question requires a re-evaluation of information used to make the estimates. Widely divergent estimates can often be traced to one of two causes:

1. The scope of the project is not adequately understood or has been misinterpreted by the planner.
2. Productivity data used for problem-based estimation techniques is inappropriate for the application, obsolete (in that it no longer accurately reflects the software engineering organization), or has been misapplied.

The planner must determine the cause of divergence and then reconcile the estimates.

5.7 EMPIRICAL ESTIMATION MODELS

KEY POINT

An estimation model reflects the population of projects from which it has been derived. Therefore, the model is domain sensitive.

An *estimation model* for computer software uses empirically derived formulas to predict effort as a function of LOC or FP. Values for LOC or FP are estimated using the approach described in Sections 5.6.2 and 5.6.3. But instead of using the tables described in those sections, the resultant values for LOC or FP are plugged into the estimation model.

The empirical data that support most estimation models are derived from a limited sample of projects. For this reason, no estimation model is appropriate for all classes of software and in all development environments. Therefore, the results obtained from such models must be used judiciously.[13]

5.7.1 The Structure of Estimation Models

A typical estimation model is derived using regression analysis on data collected from past software projects. The overall structure of such models takes the form [MAT94]

$$E = A + B \times (ev)^C \qquad (5\text{-}2)$$

where *A*, *B*, and *C* are empirically derived constants, *E* is effort in person-months, and *ev* is the estimation variable (either LOC or FP). In addition to the relationship noted in Equation (5-2), the majority of estimation models have some form of project adjust-

13 In general, an estimation model should be calibrated for local conditions. The model should be run using the results of completed projects. Data predicted by the model should be compared to actual results and the efficacy of the model (for local conditions) should be assessed. If agreement is not good, model coefficients and exponents must be recomputed using local data.

ment component that enables E to be adjusted by other project characteristics (e.g., problem complexity, staff experience, development environment). Among the many LOC-oriented estimation models proposed in the literature are

$E = 5.2 \times (\text{KLOC})^{0.91}$	Walston-Felix model
$E = 5.5 + 0.73 \times (\text{KLOC})^{1.16}$	Bailey-Basili model
$E = 3.2 \times (\text{KLOC})^{1.05}$	Boehm simple model
$E = 5.288 \times (\text{KLOC})^{1.047}$	Doty model for KLOC > 9

ADVICE

None of these models should be used without careful calibration to your environment.

FP-oriented models have also been proposed. These include

$E = -13.39 + 0.0545\ \text{FP}$	Albrecht and Gaffney model
$E = 60.62 \times 7.728 \times 10^{-8}\ \text{FP}^3$	Kemerer model
$E = 585.7 + 15.12\ \text{FP}$	Matson, Barnett, and Mellichamp model

A quick examination of these models indicates that each will yield a different result[14] for the same values of LOC or FP. The implication is clear. Estimation models must be calibrated for local needs!

5.7.2 The COCOMO Model

In his classic book on "software engineering economics," Barry Boehm [BOE81] introduced a hierarchy of software estimation models bearing the name COCOMO, for *COnstructive COst MOdel*. The original COCOMO model became one of the most widely used and discussed software cost estimation models in the industry. It has evolved into a more comprehensive estimation model, called *COCOMO II* [BOE96, BOE00]. Like its predecessor, COCOMO II is actually a hierarchy of estimation models that address the following areas:

Application composition model. Used during the early stages of software engineering, when prototyping of user interfaces, consideration of software and system interaction, assessment of performance, and evaluation of technology maturity are paramount.

Early design stage model. Used once requirements have been stabilized and basic software architecture has been established.

Post-architecture-stage model. Used during the construction of the software.

WebRef

Detailed information on COCOMO II, including downloadable software, can be obtained at **sunset.usc.edu/COCOMOII/cocomo.html**

Like all estimation models for software, the COCOMO II models require sizing information. Three different sizing options are available as part of the model hierarchy: object points, function points, and lines of source code.

The COCOMO II application composition model uses object points and is illustrated in the following paragraphs. It should be noted that other, more

14 Part of the reason is that these models are often derived from relatively small populations of projects in only a few application domains.

TABLE 5.1
Complexity weighting for object types [BOE96]

Object type	Complexity weight		
	Simple	Medium	Difficult
Screen	1	2	3
Report	2	5	8
3GL component			10

sophisticated estimation models (using FP and KLOC) are also available as part of COCOMO II.

What is an "object point"?

Like function points (Chapter 4), the *object point* is an indirect software measure that is computed using counts of the number of (1) screens (at the user interface), (2) reports, and (3) components likely to be required to build the application. Each object instance (e.g., a screen or report) is classified into one of three complexity levels (i.e., simple, medium, or difficult) using criteria suggested by Boehm [BOE96]. In essence, complexity is a function of the number and source of the client and server data tables that are required to generate the screen or report and the number of views or sections presented as part of the screen or report.

Once complexity is determined, the number of screens, reports, and components are weighted according to Table 5.1. The object point count is then determined by multiplying the original number of object instances by the weighting factor in Table 5.1 and summing to obtain a total object point count. When component-based development or general software reuse is to be applied, the percent of reuse (%reuse) is estimated and the object point count is adjusted:

NOP = (object points) x [(100 − %reuse)/100]

where NOP is defined as new object points.

To derive an estimate of effort based on the computed NOP value, a "productivity rate" must be derived. Table 5.2 presents the productivity rate

PROD = NOP/person-month

TABLE 5.2
Productivity rates for object points [BOE96]

Developer's experience/capability	Very low	Low	Nominal	High	Very high
Environment maturity/capability	Very low	Low	Nominal	High	Very high
PROD	4	7	13	25	50

for different levels of developer experience and development environment maturity. Once the productivity rate has been determined, an estimate of project effort can be derived as

estimated effort = NOP/PROD

In more advanced COCOMO II models,[15] a variety of scale factors, cost drivers, and adjustment procedures are required. A complete discussion of these is beyond the scope of this book. The interested reader should see [BOE00] or visit the COCOMO II Web site.

5.7.3 The Software Equation

The software equation [PUT92] is a dynamic multivariable model that assumes a specific distribution of effort over the life of a software development project. The model has been derived from productivity data collected for over 4000 contemporary software projects. Based on these data, an estimation model of the form

$$E = [\text{LOC} \times B^{0.333}/P]^3 \times (1/t^4) \qquad (5\text{-}3)$$

where E = effort in person-months or person-years
t = project duration in months or years
B = "special skills factor"[16]
P = "productivity parameter" that reflects:

- Overall process maturity and management practices
- The extent to which good software engineering practices are used
- The level of programming languages used
- The state of the software environment
- The skills and experience of the software team
- The complexity of the application

WebRef
Information on software cost estimation tools that have evolved from the software equation can be obtained at
www.qsm.com

Typical values might be P = 2,000 for development of real-time embedded software; P = 10,000 for telecommunication and systems software; P = 28,000 for business systems applications.[17] The productivity parameter can be derived for local conditions using historical data collected from past development efforts.

It is important to note that the software equation has two independent parameters: (1) an estimate of size (in LOC) and (2) an indication of project duration in calendar months or years.

---

15 As noted earlier, these models use FP and KLOC counts for the size variable.

16 B increases slowly as "the need for integration, testing, quality assurance, documentation, and management skills grow [PUT92]." For small programs (KLOC = 5 to 15), B = 0.16. For programs greater than 70 KLOC, B = 0.39.

17 It is important to note that the productivity parameter can be empirically derived from local project data.

To simplify the estimation process and use a more common form for their estimation model, Putnam and Myers [PUT92] suggest a set of equations derived from the software equation. Minimum development time is defined as

$$t_{min} = 8.14\ (LOC/P)^{0.43} \text{ in months for } t_{min} > 6 \text{ months} \quad (5\text{-}4a)$$
$$E = 180\ Bt^3 \text{ in person-months for } E \geq 20 \text{ person-months} \quad (5\text{-}4b)$$

Note that t in Equation (5-4b) is represented in years.

Using Equations (5-4) with $P = 12{,}000$ (the recommended value for scientific software) for the CAD software discussed earlier in this chapter,

$$t_{min} = 8.14\ (33200/12000)^{0.43}$$
$$t_{min} = 12.6 \text{ calendar months}$$
$$E = 180 \times 0.28 \times (1.05)^3$$
$$E = 58 \text{ person-months}$$

The results of the software equation correspond favorably with the estimates developed in Section 5.6. Like the COCOMO model noted in the preceding section, the software equation has evolved over the past decade. Further discussion of an extended version of this estimation approach can be found in [PUT97b].

5.8 THE MAKE/BUY DECISION

In many software application areas, it is often more cost effective to acquire than develop computer software. Software engineering managers are faced with a *make/buy decision* that can be further complicated by a number of acquisition options: (1) software may be purchased (or licensed) off-the-shelf, (2) "full-experience" or "partial-experience" software components (see Section 5.4.2) may be acquired and then modified and integrated to meet specific needs, or (3) software may be custom built by an outside contractor to meet the purchaser's specifications.

ADVICE

There are times when off-the-shelf software provides a "perfect" solution except for a few special features that you can't live without. In many cases, it's worth living without the special features!

The steps involved in the acquisition of software are defined by the criticality of the software to be purchased and the end cost. In some cases (e.g., low-cost PC software), it is less expensive to purchase and experiment than to conduct a lengthy evaluation of potential software packages. For more expensive software products, the following guidelines can be applied:

1. Develop specifications for function and performance of the desired software. Define measurable characteristics whenever possible.

2. Estimate the internal cost to develop and the delivery date.

3a. Select three or four candidate applications that best meet your specifications.

3b. Select reusable software components that will assist in constructing the required application.

4. Develop a comparison matrix that presents a head-to-head comparison of key functions. Alternatively, conduct benchmark tests to compare candidate software.
5. Evaluate each software package or component based on past product quality, vendor support, product direction, reputation, and the like.
6. Contact other users of the software and ask for opinions.

In the final analysis, the make/buy decision is made based on the following conditions: (1) Will the delivery date of the software product be sooner than that for internally developed software? (2) Will the cost of acquisition plus the cost of customization be less than the cost of developing the software internally? (3) Will the cost of outside support (e.g., a maintenance contract) be less than the cost of internal support? These conditions apply for each of the acquisition options.

5.8.1 Creating a Decision Tree

? Is there a systematic way to sort through the options associated with the make/buy decision?

The steps just described can be augmented using statistical techniques such as *decision tree analysis* [BOE89]. For example, Figure 5.6 depicts a decision tree for a software-based system, *X*. In this case, the software engineering organization can (1) build system *X* from scratch, (2) reuse existing "partial-experience" components to construct the system, (3) buy an available software product and modify it to meet local needs, or (4) contract the software development to an outside vendor.

FIGURE 5.6
A decision tree to support the make/buy decision

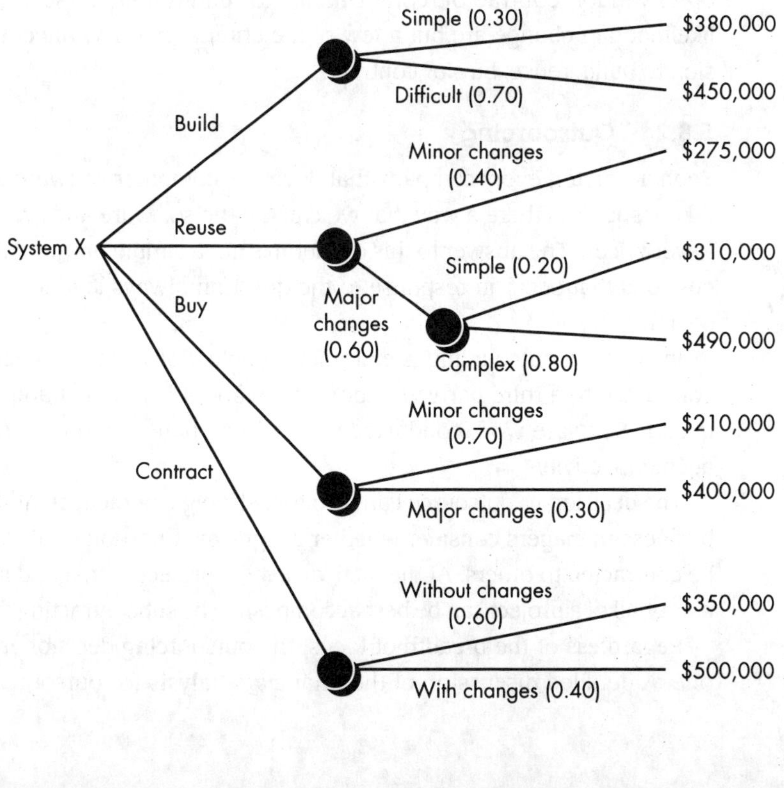

If the system is to be built from scratch, there is a 70 percent probability that the job will be difficult. Using the estimation techniques discussed earlier in this chapter, the project planner projects that a difficult development effort will cost $450,000. A "simple" development effort is estimated to cost $380,000. The expected value for cost, computed along any branch of the decision tree, is

$$\text{expected cost} = \Sigma\ (\text{path probability})_i \times (\text{estimated path cost})_i$$

where i is the decision tree path. For the build path,

$$\text{expected cost}_{\text{build}} = 0.30\ (\$380\text{K}) + 0.70\ (\$450\text{K}) = \$429\text{K}$$

WebRef

An excellent tutorial on decision tree analysis can be found at **www.demon.co.uk/mindtool/dectree.html**

Following other paths of the decision tree, the projected costs for reuse, purchase and contract, under a variety of circumstances, are also shown. The expected costs for these paths are

$$\text{expected cost}_{\text{reuse}} = 0.40\ (\$275\text{K}) + 0.60\ [0.20(\$310\text{K}) + 0.80(\$490\text{K})] = \$382\text{K}$$
$$\text{expected cost}_{\text{buy}} = 0.70(\$210\text{K}) + 0.30(\$400\text{K})] = \$267\text{K}$$
$$\text{expected cost}_{\text{contract}} = 0.60(\$350\text{K}) + 0.40(\$500\text{K})] = \$410\text{K}$$

Based on the probability and projected costs that have been noted in Figure 5.6, the lowest expected cost is the "buy" option.

It is important to note, however, that many criteria—not just cost— must be considered during the decision-making process. Availability, experience of the developer/vendor/contractor, conformance to requirements, local "politics," and the likelihood of change are but a few of the criteria that may affect the ultimate decision to build, reuse, buy, or contract.

5.8.2 Outsourcing

Quote:

"As a rule, outsourcing requires even more skillful management than in-house development."

Steve McConnell

Sooner or later, every company that develops computer software asks a fundamental question: "Is there a way that we can get the software and systems we need at a lower price?" The answer to this question is not a simple one, and the emotional discussions that occur in response to the question always lead to a single word: outsourcing.

In concept, outsourcing is extremely simple. Software engineering activities are contracted to a third party who does the work at lower cost and, hopefully, higher quality. Software work conducted within a company is reduced to a contract management activity.

The decision to outsource can be either strategic or tactical. At the strategic level, business managers consider whether a significant portion of all software work can be contracted to others. At the tactical level, a project manager determines whether part or all of a project can be best accomplished by subcontracting the software work.

Regardless of the breadth of focus, the outsourcing decision is often a financial one. A detailed discussion of the financial analysis for outsourcing is beyond the scope of this book and is best left to others (e.g., [MIN95]). However, a brief review of the pros and cons of the decision is worthwhile.

WebRef
Useful information (papers, pointers) on outsourcing can be found at **www.outsourcing.com**

On the positive side, cost savings can usually be achieved by reducing the number of software people and the facilities (e.g., computers, infrastructure) that support them. On the negative side, a company loses some control over the software that it needs. Since software is a technology that differentiates its systems, services, and products, a company runs the risk of putting the fate of its competitiveness into the hands of a third party.

The trend toward outsourcing will undoubtedly continue. The only way to blunt the trend is to recognize that software work is extremely competitive at all levels. The only way to survive is to become as competitive as the outsourcing vendors themselves.

5.9 AUTOMATED ESTIMATION TOOLS

The decomposition techniques and empirical estimation models described in the preceding sections are available as part of a wide variety of software tools. These automated estimation tools allow the planner to estimate cost and effort and to perform "what-if" analyses for important project variables such as delivery date or staffing. Although many automated estimation tools exist, all exhibit the same general characteristics and all perform the following six generic functions [JON96]:

SEPA WEB
Estimation tools

1. **Sizing of project deliverables.** The "size" of one or more software work products is estimated. Work products include the external representation of software (e.g., screen, reports), the software itself (e.g., KLOC), functionality delivered (e.g., function points), descriptive information (e.g. documents).
2. **Selecting project activities.** The appropriate process framework (Chapter 2) is selected and the software engineering task set is specified.
3. **Predicting staffing levels.** The number of people who will be available to do the work is specified. Because the relationship between people available and work (predicted effort) is highly nonlinear, this is an important input.
4. **Predicting software effort.** Estimation tools use one or more models (e.g., Section 5.7) that relate the size of the project deliverables to the effort required to produce them.
5. **Predicting software cost.** Given the results of step 4, costs can be computed by allocating labor rates to the project activities noted in step 2.
6. **Predicting software schedules.** When effort, staffing level, and project activities are known, a draft schedule can be produced by allocating labor across software engineering activities based on recommended models for effort distribution (Chapter 7).

When different estimation tools are applied to the same project data, a relatively large variation in estimated results is encountered. More important, predicted values sometimes are significantly different than actual values. This reinforces the notion that the output of estimation tools should be used as one "data point" from which estimates are derived—not as the only source for an estimate.

5.10 SUMMARY

The software project planner must estimate three things before a project begins: how long it will take, how much effort will be required, and how many people will be involved. In addition, the planner must predict the resources (hardware and software) that will be required and the risk involved.

The statement of scope helps the planner to develop estimates using one or more techniques that fall into two broad categories: decomposition and empirical modeling. Decomposition techniques require a delineation of major software functions, followed by estimates of either (1) the number of LOC, (2) selected values within the information domain, (3) the number of person-months required to implement each function, or (4) the number of person-months required for each software engineering activity. Empirical techniques use empirically derived expressions for effort and time to predict these project quantities. Automated tools can be used to implement a specific empirical model.

Accurate project estimates generally use at least two of the three techniques just noted. By comparing and reconciling estimates derived using different techniques, the planner is more likely to derive an accurate estimate. Software project estimation can never be an exact science, but a combination of good historical data and systematic techniques can improve estimation accuracy.

REFERENCES

[BEN92] Bennatan, E.M., *Software Project Management: A Practitioner's Approach,* McGraw-Hill, 1992.

[BOE81] Boehm, B., *Software Engineering Economics,* Prentice-Hall, 1981.

[BOE89] Boehm, B., *Risk Management,* IEEE Computer Society Press, 1989.

[BOE96] Boehm, B., "Anchoring the Software Process," *IEEE Software,* vol. 13, no. 4, July 1996, pp. 73–82.

[BOE00] Boehm, B., et al., *Software Cost Estimation in COCOMO II,* Prentice-Hall, 2000.

[BRO75] Brooks, F., *The Mythical Man-Month,* Addison-Wesley, 1975.

[GAU89] Gause, D.C. and G.M. Weinberg, *Exploring Requirements: Quality Before Design,* Dorset House, 1989.

[HOO91] Hooper, J. and R.O. Chester, *Software Reuse: Guidelines and Methods,* Plenum Press, 1991.

[JON96] Jones, C., "How Software Estimation Tools Work," *American Programmer,* vol. 9, no. 7, July 1996, pp. 19–27.

[MAT94] Matson, J., B. Barrett, and J. Mellichamp, "Software Development Cost Estimation Using Function Points," *IEEE Trans. Software Engineering,* vol. SE-20, no. 4, April 1994, pp. 275–287.

[MIN95] Minoli, D., *Analyzing Outsourcing,* McGraw-Hill, 1995.

[PHI98] Phillips, D., *The Software Project Manager's Handbook,* IEEE Computer Society Press, 1998.

[PUT92] Putnam, L. and W. Myers, *Measures for Excellence,* Yourdon Press, 1992.

[PUT97a] Putnam, L. and W. Myers, "How Solved Is the Cost Estimation Problem?" *IEEE Software,* November 1997, pp. 105–107.

[PUT97b] Putnam, L. and W. Myers, *Industrial Strength Software: Effective Management Using Measurement,* IEEE Computer Society Press, 1997.

[ZUS97] Zuse, H., *A Framework for Software Measurement,* deGruyter, 1997.

PROBLEMS AND POINTS TO PONDER

5.1. Assume that you are the project manager for a company that builds software for consumer products. You have been contracted to build the software for a home security system. Write a statement of scope that describes the software. Be sure your statement of scope is bounded. If you're unfamiliar with home security systems, do a bit of research before you begin writing. *Alternate:* Replace the home security system with another problem that is of interest to you.

5.2. Software project complexity is discussed briefly in Section 5.1. Develop a list of software characteristics (e.g., concurrent operation, graphical output) that affect the complexity of a project. Prioritize the list.

5.3. Performance is an important consideration during planning. Discuss how performance can be interpreted differently depending upon the software application area.

5.4. Do a functional decomposition of the home security system software you described in problem 5.1. Estimate the size of each function in LOC. Assuming that your organization produces 450 LOC/pm with a burdened labor rate of $7000 per person-month, estimate the effort and cost required to build the software using the LOC-based estimation technique described in Section 5.6.3.

5.5. Using the 3D function point measure described in Chapter 4, compute the number of FP for the home security system software and derive effort and cost estimates using the FP-based estimation technique described in Section 5.6.4.

5.6. Use the COCOMO II model to estimate the effort required to build software for a simple ATM that produces 12 screens, 10 reports, and will require approximately

80 software components. Assume average complexity and average developer/environment maturity. Use the application composition model with object points.

5.7. Use the software equation to estimate the home security system software. Assume that Equations (5-4) are applicable and that $P = 8000$.

5.8. Compare the effort estimates derived in problems 5.4, 5.5, and 5.7. Develop a single estimate for the project using a three-point estimate. What is the standard deviation and how does it affect your degree of certainty about the estimate?

5.9. Using the results obtained in problem 5.8, determine whether it's reasonable to expect that the software can be built within the next six months and how many people would have to be used to get the job done.

5.10. Develop a spreadsheet model that implements one or more of the estimation techniques described in this chapter. Alternatively, acquire one or more on-line models for estimation from Web-based sources.

5.11. *For a project team,* develop a software tool that implements each of the estimation techniques developed in this chapter.

5.12. It seems odd that cost and schedule estimates are developed during software project planning—before detailed software requirements analysis or design has been conducted. Why do you think this is done? Are there circumstances when it should not be done?

5.13. Recompute the expected values noted for the decision tree in Figure 5.6 assuming that every branch has a 50–50 probability. Would this change your final decision?

FURTHER READINGS AND INFORMATION SOURCES

Most software project management books contain discussions of project estimation. Jones (*Estimating Software Costs,* McGraw-Hill, 1998) has written the most comprehensive treatment of the subject published to date. His book contains models and data that are applicable to software estimating in every application domain. Roetzheim and Beasley (*Software Project Cost and Schedule Estimating: Best Practices,* Prentice-Hall, 1997) present many useful models and suggest step-by-step guidelines for generating the best possible estimates.

Phillips [PHI98], Bennatan (*On Time, Within Budget: Software Project Management Practices and Techniques,* Wiley, 1995), Whitten (*Managing Software Development Projects: Formula for Success,* Wiley, 1995), Wellman (*Software Costing,* Prentice-Hall, 1992), and Londeix (*Cost Estimation for Software Development,* Addison-Wesley, 1987) contain useful information on software project planning and estimation.

Putnam and Myer's detailed treatment of software cost estimating ([PUT92] and [PUT97b]) and Boehm's books on software engineering economics ([BOE81] and

COCOMO II [BOE00]) describe empirical estimation models. These books provide detailed analysis of data derived from hundreds of software projects. An excellent book by DeMarco (*Controlling Software Projects,* Yourdon Press, 1982) provides valuable insight into the management, measurement, and estimation of software projects. Sneed (*Software Engineering Management,* Wiley, 1989) and Macro (*Software Engineering: Concepts and Management,* Prentice-Hall, 1990) consider software project estimation in considerable detail.

Lines-of-code cost estimation is the most commonly used approach in the industry. However, the impact of the object-oriented paradigm (see Part Four) may invalidate some estimation models. Lorenz and Kidd (*Object-Oriented Software Metrics,* Prentice-Hall, 1994) and Cockburn (*Surviving Object-Oriented Projects,* Addison-Wesley, 1998) consider estimation for object-oriented systems.

A wide variety of information sources on software planning and estimation is available on the Internet. An up-to-date list of World Wide Web references that are relevant to software estimation can be found at the SEPA Web site:
http://www.mhhe.com/engcs/compsci/pressman/resources/project-plan.mhtml

CHAPTER

6 RISK ANALYSIS AND MANAGEMENT

KEY CONCEPTS

In his book on risk analysis and management, Robert Charette [CHA89] presents a conceptual definition of risk:

> First, risk concerns future happenings. Today and yesterday are beyond active concern, as we are already reaping what was previously sowed by our past actions. The question is, can we, therefore, by changing our actions today, create an opportunity for a different and hopefully better situation for ourselves tomorrow. This means, second, that risk involves change, such as in changes of mind, opinion, actions, or places . . . [Third,] risk involves choice, and the uncertainty that choice itself entails. Thus paradoxically, risk, like death and taxes, is one of the few certainties of life.

When risk is considered in the context of software engineering, Charette's three conceptual underpinnings are always in evidence. The future is our concern—what risks might cause the software project to go awry? Change is our concern—how will changes in customer requirements, development technologies, target computers, and all other entities connected to the project affect timeliness and overall success? Last, we must grapple with choices—what methods and tools should we use, how many people should be involved, how much emphasis on quality is "enough"?

QUICK LOOK

What is it? Risk analysis and management are a series of steps that help a software team to understand and manage uncertainty. Many problems can plague a software project. A risk is a potential problem—it might happen, it might not. But, regardless of the outcome, it's a really good idea to identify it, assess its probability of occurrence, estimate its impact, and establish a contingency plan should the problem actually occur.

Who does it? Everyone involved in the software process—managers, software engineers, and customers—participate in risk analysis and management.

Why is it important? Think about the Boy Scout motto: "Be prepared." Software is a difficult undertaking. Lots of things can go wrong, and frankly, many often do. It's for this reason that being prepared—understanding the risks and taking proactive measures to avoid or manage them—is a key element of good software project management.

What are the steps? Recognizing what can go wrong is the first step, called "risk identification." Next, each risk is analyzed to determine the likelihood that it will occur and the damage that it will do if it does occur. Once this information is established, risks are ranked, by probability and impact. Finally, a plan is developed to manage those risks with high probability and high impact.

What is the work product? A risk mitigation, monitoring, and management (RMMM) plan or

QUICK LOOK

a set of risk information sheets is produced.

How do I ensure that I've done it right? The risks that are analyzed and managed should be derived from thorough study of the people, the product, the process, and the project. The RMMM should be revisited as the project proceeds to ensure that risks are kept up to date. Contingency plans for risk management should be realistic.

Peter Drucker [DRU75] once said, "While it is futile to try to eliminate risk, and questionable to try to minimize it, it is essential that the risks taken be the right risks." Before we can identify the "right risks" to be taken during a software project, it is important to identify all risks that are obvious to both managers and practitioners.

6.1 REACTIVE VS. PROACTIVE RISK STRATEGIES

Reactive risk strategies have been laughingly called the "Indiana Jones school of risk management" [THO92]. In the movies that carried his name, Indiana Jones, when faced with overwhelming difficulty, would invariably say, "Don't worry, I'll think of something!" Never worrying about problems until they happened, Indy would react in some heroic way.

Quote:

"If you don't actively attack the risks, they will actively attack you."

Tom Gilb

Sadly, the average software project manager is not Indiana Jones and the members of the software project team are not his trusty sidekicks. Yet, the majority of software teams rely solely on reactive risk strategies. At best, a reactive strategy monitors the project for likely risks. Resources are set aside to deal with them, should they become actual problems. More commonly, the software team does nothing about risks until something goes wrong. Then, the team flies into action in an attempt to correct the problem rapidly. This is often called a *fire fighting mode.* When this fails, "crisis management" [CHA92] takes over and the project is in real jeopardy.

A considerably more intelligent strategy for risk management is to be proactive. A proactive strategy begins long before technical work is initiated. Potential risks are identified, their probability and impact are assessed, and they are ranked by importance. Then, the software team establishes a plan for managing risk. The primary objective is to avoid risk, but because not all risks can be avoided, the team works to develop a contingency plan that will enable it to respond in a controlled and effective manner. Throughout the remainder of this chapter, we discuss a proactive strategy for risk management.

6.2 SOFTWARE RISKS

Although there has been considerable debate about the proper definition for software risk, there is general agreement that risk always involves two characteristics [HIG95]:

- *Uncertainty*—the risk may or may not happen; that is, there are no 100% probable risks.[1]
- *Loss*—if the risk becomes a reality, unwanted consequences or losses will occur.

When risks are analyzed, it is important to quantify the level of uncertainty and the degree of loss associated with each risk. To accomplish this, different categories of risks are considered.

What types of risks are we likely to encounter as the software is built?

Project risks threaten the project plan. That is, if project risks become real, it is likely that project schedule will slip and that costs will increase. Project risks identify potential budgetary, schedule, personnel (staffing and organization), resource, customer, and requirements problems and their impact on a software project. In Chapter 5, project complexity, size, and the degree of structural uncertainty were also defined as project (and estimation) risk factors.

Technical risks threaten the quality and timeliness of the software to be produced. If a technical risk becomes a reality, implementation may become difficult or impossible. Technical risks identify potential design, implementation, interface, verification, and maintenance problems. In addition, specification ambiguity, technical uncertainty, technical obsolescence, and "leading-edge" technology are also risk factors. Technical risks occur because the problem is harder to solve than we thought it would be.

Business risks threaten the viability of the software to be built. Business risks often jeopardize the project or the product. Candidates for the top five business risks are (1) building a excellent product or system that no one really wants (market risk), (2) building a product that no longer fits into the overall business strategy for the company (strategic risk), (3) building a product that the sales force doesn't understand how to sell, (4) losing the support of senior management due to a change in focus or a change in people (management risk), and (5) losing budgetary or personnel commitment (budget risks). It is extremely important to note that simple categorization won't always work. Some risks are simply unpredictable in advance.

Quote:

"[Today,] no one has the luxury of getting to know a task so well that it holds no surprises, and surprises mean risk."
Stephen Grey

Another general categorization of risks has been proposed by Charette [CHA89]. *Known risks* are those that can be uncovered after careful evaluation of the project plan, the business and technical environment in which the project is being developed, and other reliable information sources (e.g., unrealistic delivery date, lack of documented requirements or software scope, poor development environment). *Predictable risks* are extrapolated from past project experience (e.g., staff turnover, poor communication with the customer, dilution of staff effort as ongoing maintenance requests are serviced). *Unpredictable risks* are the joker in the deck. They can and do occur, but they are extremely difficult to identify in advance.

---

1 A risk that is 100 percent probable is a constraint on the software project.

6.3 RISK IDENTIFICATION

Risk identification is a systematic attempt to specify threats to the project plan (estimates, schedule, resource loading, etc.). By identifying known and predictable risks, the project manager takes a first step toward avoiding them when possible and controlling them when necessary.

ADVICE

Although generic risks are important to consider, usually the product-specific risks cause the most headaches. Be certain to spend the time to identify as many product-specific risks as possible.

There are two distinct types of risks for each of the categories that have been presented in Section 6.2: generic risks and product-specific risks. *Generic risks* are a potential threat to every software project. *Product-specific risks* can be identified only by those with a clear understanding of the technology, the people, and the environment that is specific to the project at hand. To identify product-specific risks, the project plan and the software statement of scope are examined and an answer to the following question is developed: "What special characteristics of this product may threaten our project plan?"

One method for identifying risks is to create a *risk item checklist.* The checklist can be used for risk identification and focuses on some subset of known and predictable risks in the following generic subcategories:

- *Product size*—risks associated with the overall size of the software to be built or modified.
- *Business impact*—risks associated with constraints imposed by management or the marketplace.
- *Customer characteristics*—risks associated with the sophistication of the customer and the developer's ability to communicate with the customer in a timely manner.
- *Process definition*—risks associated with the degree to which the software process has been defined and is followed by the development organization.
- *Development environment*—risks associated with the availability and quality of the tools to be used to build the product.
- *Technology to be built*—risks associated with the complexity of the system to be built and the "newness" of the technology that is packaged by the system.
- *Staff size and experience*—risks associated with the overall technical and project experience of the software engineers who will do the work.

SEPA WEB

Risk item checklist

The risk item checklist can be organized in different ways. Questions relevant to each of the topics can be answered for each software project. The answers to these questions allow the planner to estimate the impact of risk. A different risk item checklist format simply lists characteristics that are relevant to each generic subcategory. Finally, a set of "risk components and drivers" [AFC88] are listed along with their probability of occurrence. Drivers for performance, support, cost, and schedule are discussed in answer to later questions.

Quote:
"Risk management is project management for adults."
Tim Lister

A number of comprehensive checklists for software project risk have been proposed in the literature (e.g., [SEI93], [KAR96]). These provide useful insight into generic risks for software projects and should be used whenever risk analysis and management is instituted. However, a relatively short list of questions [KEI98] can be used to provide a preliminary indication of whether a project is "at risk."

6.3.1 Assessing Overall Project Risk

The following questions have derived from risk data obtained by surveying experienced software project managers in different part of the world [KEI98]. The questions are ordered by their relative importance to the success of a project.

? Is the software project we're working on at serious risk?

1. Have top software and customer managers formally committed to support the project?
2. Are end-users enthusiastically committed to the project and the system/product to be built?
3. Are requirements fully understood by the software engineering team and their customers?
4. Have customers been involved fully in the definition of requirements?
5. Do end-users have realistic expectations?
6. Is project scope stable?
7. Does the software engineering team have the right mix of skills?
8. Are project requirements stable?
9. Does the project team have experience with the technology to be implemented?
10. Is the number of people on the project team adequate to do the job?
11. Do all customer/user constituencies agree on the importance of the project and on the requirements for the system/product to be built?

WebRef
Risk Radar is a risk management database that helps project managers identify, rank, and communicate project risks. It can be found at **www.spmn.com/rsktrkr.html**

If any one of these questions is answered negatively, mitigation, monitoring, and management steps should be instituted without fail. The degree to which the project is at risk is directly proportional to the number of negative responses to these questions.

6.3.2 Risk Components and Drivers

The U.S. Air Force [AFC88] has written a pamphlet that contains excellent guidelines for software risk identification and abatement. The Air Force approach requires that the project manager identify the risk drivers that affect software risk components—

performance, cost, support, and schedule. In the context of this discussion, the risk components are defined in the following manner:

- *Performance risk*—the degree of uncertainty that the product will meet its requirements and be fit for its intended use.
- *Cost risk*—the degree of uncertainty that the project budget will be maintained.
- *Support risk*—the degree of uncertainty that the resultant software will be easy to correct, adapt, and enhance.
- *Schedule risk*—the degree of uncertainty that the project schedule will be maintained and that the product will be delivered on time.

The impact of each risk driver on the risk component is divided into one of four impact categories—negligible, marginal, critical, or catastrophic. Referring to Figure 6.1 [BOE89],

<table>
<tr><th colspan="2">Components / Category</th><th>Performance</th><th>Support</th><th>Cost</th><th>Schedule</th></tr>
<tr><td rowspan="2">Catastrophic</td><td>1</td><td colspan="2">Failure to meet the requirement would result in mission failure</td><td colspan="2">Failure results in increased costs and schedule delays with expected values in excess of $500K</td></tr>
<tr><td>2</td><td>Significant degradation to nonachievement of technical performance</td><td>Nonresponsive or unsupportable software</td><td>Significant financial shortages, budget overrun likely</td><td>Unachievable IOC</td></tr>
<tr><td rowspan="2">Critical</td><td>1</td><td colspan="2">Failure to meet the requirement would degrade system performance to a point where mission success is questionable</td><td colspan="2">Failure results in operational delays and/or increased costs with expected value of $100K to $500K</td></tr>
<tr><td>2</td><td>Some reduction in technical performance</td><td>Minor delays in software modifications</td><td>Some shortage of financial resources, possible overruns</td><td>Possible slippage in IOC</td></tr>
<tr><td rowspan="2">Marginal</td><td>1</td><td colspan="2">Failure to meet the requirement would result in degradation of secondary mission</td><td colspan="2">Costs, impacts, and/or recoverable schedule slips with expected value of $1K to $100K</td></tr>
<tr><td>2</td><td>Minimal to small reduction in technical performance</td><td>Responsive software support</td><td>Sufficient financial resources</td><td>Realistic, achievable schedule</td></tr>
<tr><td rowspan="2">Negligible</td><td>1</td><td colspan="2">Failure to meet the requirement would create inconvenience or nonoperational impact</td><td colspan="2">Error results in minor cost and/or schedule impact with expected value of less than $1K</td></tr>
<tr><td>2</td><td>No reduction in technical performance</td><td>Easily supportable software</td><td>Possible budget underrun</td><td>Early achievable IOC</td></tr>
</table>

Note: (1) The potential consequence of undetected software errors or faults.
(2) The potential consequence if the desired outcome is not achieved.

FIGURE 6.1 Impact assessment [BOE89]

a characterization of the potential consequences of errors (rows labeled 1) or a failure to achieve a desired outcome (rows labeled 2) are described. The impact category is chosen based on the characterization that best fits the description in the table.

6.4 RISK PROJECTION

Risk projection, also called *risk estimation,* attempts to rate each risk in two ways—the likelihood or probability that the risk is real and the consequences of the problems associated with the risk, should it occur. The project planner, along with other managers and technical staff, performs four risk projection activities: (1) establish a scale that reflects the perceived likelihood of a risk, (2) delineate the consequences of the risk, (3) estimate the impact of the risk on the project and the product, and (4) note the overall accuracy of the risk projection so that there will be no misunderstandings.

6.4.1 Developing a Risk Table

A risk table provides a project manager with a simple technique for risk projection.[2] A sample risk table is illustrated in Figure 6.2.

Risks	Category	Probability	Impact	RMMM
Size estimate may be significantly low	PS	60%	2	
Larger number of users than planned	PS	30%	3	
Less reuse than planned	PS	70%	2	
End-users resist system	BU	40%	3	
Delivery deadline will be tightened	BU	50%	2	
Funding will be lost	CU	40%	1	
Customer will change requirements	PS	80%	2	
Technology will not meet expectations	TE	30%	1	
Lack of training on tools	DE	80%	3	
Staff inexperienced	ST	30%	2	
Staff turnover will be high	ST	60%	2	
•				
•				
•				

Impact values:
1—catastrophic
2—critical
3—marginal
4—negligible

FIGURE 6.2 Sample risk table prior to sorting

2 The risk table should be implemented as a spreadsheet model. This enables easy manipulation and sorting of the entries.

FIGURE 6.3
Risk and management concern

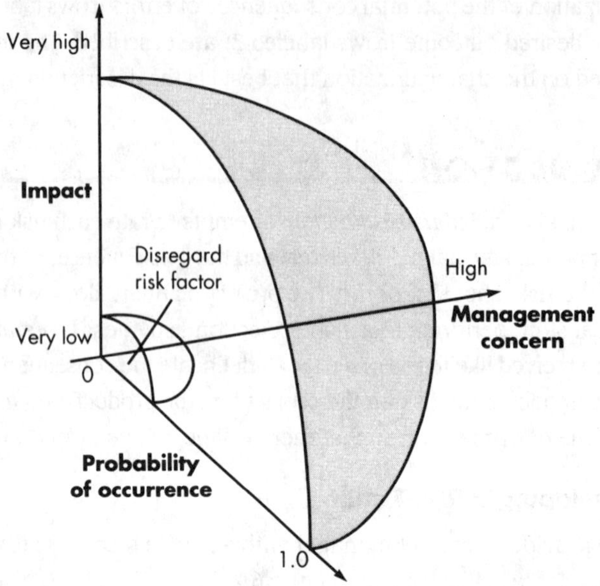

ADVICE

Think hard about the software you're about to build and ask yourself, "What can go wrong?" Create your own list and ask other members of the software team to do the same.

A project team begins by listing all risks (no matter how remote) in the first column of the table. This can be accomplished with the help of the risk item checklists referenced in Section 6.3. Each risk is categorized in the second column (e.g., PS implies a project size risk, BU implies a business risk). The probability of occurrence of each risk is entered in the next column of the table. The probability value for each risk can be estimated by team members individually. Individual team members are polled in round-robin fashion until their assessment of risk probability begins to converge.

Next, the impact of each risk is assessed. Each risk component is assessed using the characterization presented in Figure 6.1, and an impact category is determined. The categories for each of the four risk components—performance, support, cost, and schedule—are averaged[3] to determine an overall impact value.

KEY POINT

The risk table is sorted by probability and impact to rank risks.

Once the first four columns of the risk table have been completed, the table is sorted by probability and by impact. High-probability, high-impact risks percolate to the top of the table, and low-probability risks drop to the bottom. This accomplishes first-order risk prioritization.

The project manager studies the resultant sorted table and defines a cutoff line. The *cutoff line* (drawn horizontally at some point in the table) implies that only risks that lie above the line will be given further attention. Risks that fall below the line are re-evaluated to accomplish second-order prioritization. Referring to Figure 6.3, risk impact and probability have a distinct influence on management concern. A risk fac-

3 A weighted average can be used if one risk component has more significance for the project.

tor that has a high impact but a very low probability of occurrence should not absorb a significant amount of management time. However, high-impact risks with moderate to high probability and low-impact risks with high probability should be carried forward into the risk analysis steps that follow.

Quote: "Failure to prepare is preparing to fail." **Ben Franklin**

All risks that lie above the cutoff line must be managed. The column labeled RMMM contains a pointer into a *Risk Mitigation, Monitoring and Management Plan* or alternatively, a collection of risk information sheets developed for all risks that lie above the cutoff. The RMMM plan and risk information sheets are discussed in Sections 6.5 and 6.6.

Risk probability can be determined by making individual estimates and then developing a single consensus value. Although that approach is workable, more sophisticated techniques for determining risk probability have been developed [AFC88]. Risk drivers can be assessed on a qualitative probability scale that has the following values: impossible, improbable, probable, and frequent. Mathematical probability can then be associated with each qualitative value (e.g., a probability of 0.7 to 1.0 implies a highly probable risk).

6.4.2 Assessing Risk Impact

Three factors affect the consequences that are likely if a risk does occur: its nature, its scope, and its timing. The *nature* of the risk indicates the problems that are likely if it occurs. For example, a poorly defined external interface to customer hardware (a technical risk) will preclude early design and testing and will likely lead to system integration problems late in a project. The *scope* of a risk combines the severity (just how serious is it?) with its overall distribution (how much of the project will be affected or how many customers are harmed?). Finally, the *timing* of a risk considers when and for how long the impact will be felt. In most cases, a project manager might want the "bad news" to occur as soon as possible, but in some cases, the longer the delay, the better.

Returning once more to the risk analysis approach proposed by the U.S. Air Force [AFC88], the following steps are recommended to determine the overall consequences of a risk:

? How do we assess the consequences of a risk?

1. Determine the average probability of occurrence value for each risk component.
2. Using Figure 6.1, determine the impact for each component based on the criteria shown.
3. Complete the risk table and analyze the results as described in the preceding sections.

The overall *risk exposure,* RE, is determined using the following relationship [HAL98]:

$$RE = P \times C$$

where *P* is the probability of occurrence for a risk, and *C* is the the cost to the project should the risk occur.

For example, assume that the software team defines a project risk in the following manner:

Risk identification. Only 70 percent of the software components scheduled for reuse will, in fact, be integrated into the application. The remaining functionality will have to be custom developed.

Risk probability. 80% (likely).

Risk impact. 60 reusable software components were planned. If only 70 percent can be used, 18 components would have to be developed from scratch (in addition to other custom software that has been scheduled for development). Since the average component is 100 LOC and local data indicate that the software engineering cost for each LOC is $14.00, the overall cost (impact) to develop the components would be 18 x 100 x 14 = $25,200.

Risk exposure. *RE* = 0.80 x 25,200 ~ $20,200.

ADVICE

Compare RE for all risks to the cost estimate for the project. If RE is greater than 50 percent of project cost, the viability of the project must be evaluated.

Risk exposure can be computed for each risk in the risk table, once an estimate of the cost of the risk is made. The total risk exposure for all risks (above the cutoff in the risk table) can provide a means for adjusting the final cost estimate for a project. It can also be used to predict the probable increase in staff resources required at various points during the project schedule.

The risk projection and analysis techniques described in Sections 6.4.1 and 6.4.2 are applied iteratively as the software project proceeds. The project team should revisit the risk table at regular intervals, re-evaluating each risk to determine when new circumstances cause its probability and impact to change. As a consequence of this activity, it may be necessary to add new risks to the table, remove some risks that are no longer relevant, and change the relative positions of still others.

6.4.3 Risk Assessment

At this point in the risk management process, we have established a set of triplets of the form [CHA89]:

$$[r_i, l_i, x_i]$$

where r_i is risk, l_i is the likelihood (probability) of the risk, and x_i is the impact of the risk. During risk assessment, we further examine the accuracy of the estimates that were made during risk projection, attempt to rank the risks that have been uncovered, and begin thinking about ways to control and/or avert risks that are likely to occur.

For assessment to be useful, a *risk referent level* [CHA89] must be defined. For most software projects, the risk components discussed earlier—performance, cost, support, and schedule—also represent risk referent levels. That is, there is a level for per-

FIGURE 6.4
Risk referent level

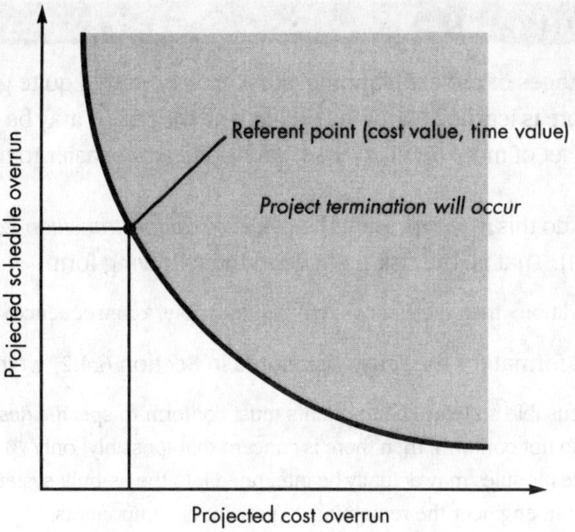

KEY POINT The risk referent level establishes your tolerance for pain. Once risk exposure exceeds the referent level, the project may be terminated.

formance degradation, cost overrun, support difficulty, or schedule slippage (or any combination of the four) that will cause the project to be terminated. If a combination of risks create problems that cause one or more of these referent levels to be exceeded, work will stop. In the context of software risk analysis, a risk referent level has a single point, called the *referent point* or *break point,* at which the decision to proceed with the project or terminate it (problems are just too great) are equally weighted. Figure 6.4 represents this situation graphically.

In reality, the referent level can rarely be represented as a smooth line on a graph. In most cases it is a region in which there are areas of uncertainty; that is, attempting to predict a management decision based on the combination of referent values is often impossible. Therefore, during risk assessment, we perform the following steps:

1. Define the risk referent levels for the project.
2. Attempt to develop a relationship between each (r_i, l_i, x_i) and each of the referent levels.
3. Predict the set of referent points that define a region of termination, bounded by a curve or areas of uncertainty.
4. Try to predict how compound combinations of risks will affect a referent level.

A detailed discussion of risk referent level is best left to books that are dedicated to risk analysis (e.g., [CHA89], [ROW88]).

6.5 RISK REFINEMENT

During early stages of project planning, a risk may be stated quite generally. As time passes and more is learned about the project and the risk, it may be possible to refine the risk into a set of more detailed risks, each somewhat easier to mitigate, monitor, and manage.

What is a good way to describe a risk?

One way to do this is to represent the risk in *condition-transition-consequence* (CTC) format [GLU94]. That is, the risk is stated in the following form:

Given that <condition> then there is concern that (possibly) <consequence>.

Using the CTC format for the reuse risk noted in Section 6.4.2, we can write:

Given that all reusable software components must conform to specific design standards and that some do not conform, then there is concern that (possibly) only 70 percent of the planned reusable modules may actually be integrated into the as-built system, resulting in the need to custom engineer the remaining 30 percent of components.

This general condition can be refined in the following manner:

Subcondition 1. Certain reusable components were developed by a third party with no knowledge of internal design standards.

Subcondition 2. The design standard for component interfaces has not been solidified and may not conform to certain existing reusable components.

Subcondition 3. Certain reusable components have been implemented in a language that is not supported on the target environment.

The consequences associated with these refined subconditions remains the same (i.e., 30 percent of software components must be customer engineered), but the refinement helps to isolate the underlying risks and might lead to easier analysis and response.

6.6 RISK MITIGATION, MONITORING, AND MANAGEMENT

All of the risk analysis activities presented to this point have a single goal—to assist the project team in developing a strategy for dealing with risk. An effective strategy must consider three issues:

Quote:

"If I take so many precautions, it is because I leave nothing to chance."
Napolean

- risk avoidance
- risk monitoring
- risk management and contingency planning

If a software team adopts a proactive approach to risk, avoidance is always the best strategy. This is achieved by developing a plan for *risk mitigation*. For example, assume that high staff turnover is noted as a project risk, r_1. Based on past history and management intuition, the likelihood, l_1, of high turnover is estimated to be 0.70 (70 percent, rather high) and the impact, x_1, is projected at level 2. That is, high turnover will have a critical impact on project cost and schedule.

To mitigate this risk, project management must develop a strategy for reducing turnover. Among the possible steps to be taken are

WebRef
An excellent FAQ on risk management can be obtained at **www.sei.cmu.edu/organization/programs/sepm/risk/risk.faq.html**

- Meet with current staff to determine causes for turnover (e.g., poor working conditions, low pay, competitive job market).
- Mitigate those causes that are under our control before the project starts.
- Once the project commences, assume turnover will occur and develop techniques to ensure continuity when people leave.
- Organize project teams so that information about each development activity is widely dispersed.
- Define documentation standards and establish mechanisms to be sure that documents are developed in a timely manner.
- Conduct peer reviews of all work (so that more than one person is "up to speed").
- Assign a backup staff member for every critical technologist.

As the project proceeds, risk monitoring activities commence. The project manager monitors factors that may provide an indication of whether the risk is becoming more or less likely. In the case of high staff turnover, the following factors can be monitored:

Quote:
"We are ready for an unforseen event that may or may not occur."
Dan Quayle

- General attitude of team members based on project pressures.
- The degree to which the team has jelled.
- Interpersonal relationships among team members.
- Potential problems with compensation and benefits.
- The availability of jobs within the company and outside it.

In addition to monitoring these factors, the project manager should monitor the effectiveness of risk mitigation steps. For example, a risk mitigation step noted here called for the definition of documentation standards and mechanisms to be sure that documents are developed in a timely manner. This is one mechanism for ensuring continuity, should a critical individual leave the project. The project manager should monitor documents carefully to ensure that each can stand on its own and that each imparts information that would be necessary if a newcomer were forced to join the software team somewhere in the middle of the project.

Risk management and contingency planning assumes that mitigation efforts have failed and that the risk has become a reality. Continuing the example, the project is well underway and a number of people announce that they will be leaving. If the mitigation strategy has been followed, backup is available, information is documented, and knowledge has been dispersed across the team. In addition, the project manager may temporarily refocus resources (and readjust the project schedule) to those functions that are fully staffed, enabling newcomers who must be added to the team to "get up to speed." Those individuals who are leaving are asked to stop all work and spend their last weeks in "knowledge transfer mode." This might include video-based knowledge capture, the development of "commentary documents," and/or meeting with other team members who will remain on the project.

ADVICE

If RE for a specific risk is less than the cost of risk mitigation, don't try to mitigate the risk but continue to monitor it.

It is important to note that RMMM steps incur additional project cost. For example, spending the time to "backup" every critical technologist costs money. Part of risk management, therefore, is to evaluate when the benefits accrued by the RMMM steps are outweighed by the costs associated with implementing them. In essence, the project planner performs a classic cost/benefit analysis. If risk aversion steps for high turnover will increase both project cost and duration by an estimated 15 percent, but the predominant cost factor is "backup," management may decide not to implement this step. On the other hand, if the risk aversion steps are projected to increase costs by 5 percent and duration by only 3 percent management will likely put all into place.

For a large project, 30 or 40 risks may identified. If between three and seven risk management steps are identified for each, risk management may become a project in itself! For this reason, we adapt the Pareto 80–20 rule to software risk. Experience indicates that 80 percent of the overall project risk (i.e., 80 percent of the potential for project failure) can be accounted for by only 20 percent of the identified risks. The work performed during earlier risk analysis steps will help the planner to determine which of the risks reside in that 20 percent (e.g., risks that lead to the highest risk exposure). For this reason, some of the risks identified, assessed, and projected may not make it into the RMMM plan—they don't fall into the critical 20 percent (the risks with highest project priority).

6.7 SAFETY RISKS AND HAZARDS

Risk is not limited to the software project itself. Risks can occur after the software has been successfully developed and delivered to the customer. These risks are typically associated with the consequences of software failure in the field.

In the early days of computing, there was reluctance to use computers (and software) to control safety critical processes such as nuclear reactors, aircraft flight control, weapons systems, and large-scale industrial processes. Although the probability of failure of a well-engineered system was small, an undetected fault in a computer-based control or monitoring system could result in enormous economic damage or, worse, significant human injury or loss of life. But the cost and functional benefits of computer-based control and monitoring far outweigh the risk. Today, computer hardware and software are used regularly to control safety critical systems.

WebRef

A voluminous database containing all entries from the ACM's Forum on Risks to the Public can be found at **catless.ncl.ac.uk/Risks/search.html**

When software is used as part of a control system, complexity can increase by an order of magnitude or more. Subtle design faults induced by human error—something that can be uncovered and eliminated in hardware-based conventional control—become much more difficult to uncover when software is used.

Software safety and *hazard analysis* [LEV95] are software quality assurance activities (Chapter 8) that focus on the identification and assessment of potential hazards that may affect software negatively and cause an entire system to fail. If hazards can be identified early in the software engineering process, software design features can be specified that will either eliminate or control potential hazards.

6.8 THE RMMM PLAN

A risk management strategy can be included in the software project plan or the risk management steps can be organized into a separate *Risk Mitigation, Monitoring and Management Plan*. The RMMM plan documents all work performed as part of risk analysis and is used by the project manager as part of the overall project plan.

SEPA WEB DOCUMENT RMMM Plan

Some software teams do not develop a formal RMMM document. Rather, each risk is documented individually using a *risk information sheet* (RIS) [WIL97]. In most cases, the RIS is maintained using a database system, so that creation and information entry, priority ordering, searches, and other analysis may be accomplished easily. The format of the RIS is illustrated in Figure 6.5.

Once RMMM has been documented and the project has begun, risk mitigation and monitoring steps commence. As we have already discussed, risk mitigation is a problem avoidance activity. Risk monitoring is a project tracking activity with three primary objectives: (1) to assess whether predicted risks do, in fact, occur; (2) to ensure that risk aversion steps defined for the risk are being properly applied; and (3) to collect information that can be used for future risk analysis. In many cases, the problems that occur during a project can be traced to more than one risk. Another job of risk monitoring is to attempt to allocate *origin* (what risk(s) caused which problems throughout the project).

6.9 SUMMARY

Whenever a lot is riding on a software project, common sense dictates risk analysis. And yet, most software project managers do it informally and superficially, if they do it at all. The time spent identifying, analyzing, and managing risk pays itself back in many ways: less upheaval during the project, a greater ability to track and control a project, and the confidence that comes with planning for problems before they occur.

FIGURE 6.5
Risk information sheet [WIL97]

Risk information sheet			
Risk ID: P02-4-32	Date: 5/9/02	Prob: 80%	Impact: high

Description:
Only 70 percent of the software components scheduled for reuse will, in fact, be integrated into the application. The remaining functionality will have to be custom developed.

Refinement/context:
Subcondition 1: Certain reusable components were developed by a third party with no knowledge of internal design standards.
Subcondition 2: The design standard for component interfaces has not been solidified and may not conform to certain existing reusable components.
Subcondition 3: Certain reusable components have been implemented in a language that is not supported on the target environment.

Mitigation/monitoring:
1. Contact third party to determine conformance with design standards.
2. Press for interface standards completion; consider component structure when deciding on interface protocol.
3. Check to determine number of components in subcondition 3 category; check to determine if language support can be acquired.

Management/contingency plan/trigger:
RE computed to be $20,200. Allocate this amount within project contingency cost. Develop revised schedule assuming that 18 additional components will have to be custom built; allocate staff accordingly.
Trigger: Mitigation steps unproductive as of 7/1/02

Current status:
5/12/02: Mitigation steps initiated.

Originator: D. Gagne	Assigned: B. Laster

Risk analysis can absorb a significant amount of project planning effort. Identification, projection, assessment, management, and monitoring all take time. But the effort is worth it. To quote Sun Tzu, a Chinese general who lived 2500 years ago, "If you know the enemy and know yourself, you need not fear the result of a hundred battles." For the software project manager, the enemy is risk.

REFERENCES

[AFC88] *Software Risk Abatement,* AFCS/AFLC Pamphlet 800-45, U.S. Air Force, September 30, 1988.

[BOE89] Boehm, B.W., *Software Risk Management,* IEEE Computer Society Press, 1989.

[CHA89] Charette, R.N., *Software Engineering Risk Analysis and Management,* McGraw-Hill/Intertext, 1989.

[CHA92] Charette, R.N., "Building Bridges over Intelligent Rivers," *American Programmer,* vol. 5, no. 7, September, 1992, pp. 2–9.

[DRU75] Drucker, P., *Management,* W. H. Heinemann, 1975.

[GIL88] Gilb, T., *Principles of Software Engineering Management,* Addison-Wesley, 1988.

[GLU94] Gluch, D.P., "A Construct for Describing Software Development Risks," CMU/SEI-94-TR-14, Software Engineering Institute, 1994.

[HAL98] Hall, E.M., *Managing Risk: Methods for Software Systems Development,* Addison-Wesley, 1998.

[HIG95] Higuera, R.P., "Team Risk Management," *CrossTalk,* U.S. Dept. of Defense, January 1995, p. 2–4.

[KAR96] Karolak, D.W., *Software Engineering Risk Management,* IEEE Computer Society Press, 1996.

[KEI98] Keil, M., et al., "A Framework for Identifying Software Project Risks," *CACM,* vol. 41, no. 11, November 1998, pp. 76–83.

[LEV95] Leveson, N.G., *Safeware: System Safety and Computers,* Addison-Wesley, 1995.

[ROW88] Rowe, W.D., *An Anatomy of Risk,* Robert E. Krieger Publishing Co., 1988.

[SEI93] "Taxonomy-Based Risk Identification," Software Engineering Institute, CMU/SEI-93-TR-6, 1993.

[THO92] Thomsett, R., "The Indiana Jones School of Risk Management," *American Programmer,* vol. 5, no. 7, September 1992, pp. 10–18.

[WIL97] Williams, R.C, J.A. Walker, and A.J. Dorofee, "Putting Risk Management into Practice," *IEEE Software,* May 1997, pp. 75–81.

PROBLEMS AND POINTS TO PONDER

6.1. Provide five examples from other fields that illustrate the problems associated with a reactive risk strategy.

6.2. Describe the difference between "known risks" and "predictable risks."

6.3. Add three additional questions or topics to each of the risk item checklists presented at the SEPA Web site.

6.4. You've been asked to build software to support a low-cost video editing system. The system accepts videotape as input, stores the video on disk, and then allows the user to do a wide range of edits to the digitized video. The result can then be output to tape. Do a small amount of research on systems of this type and then make a list of technology risks that you would face as you begin a project of this type.

6.5. You're the project manager for a major software company. You've been asked to lead a team that's developing "next generation" word-processing software (see Section 3.4.2 for a brief description). Create a risk table for the project.

6.6. Describe the difference between risk components and risk drivers.

6.7. Develop a risk mitigation strategy and specific risk mitigation activities for three of the risks noted in Figure 6.2.

6.8. Develop a risk monitoring strategy and specific risk monitoring activities for three of the risks noted in Figure 6.2. Be sure to identify the factors that you'll be monitoring to determine whether the risk is becoming more or less likely.

6.9. Develop a risk management strategy and specific risk management activities for three of the risks noted in Figure 6.2.

6.10. Attempt to refine three of the risks noted in Figure 6.2 and then create risk information sheets for each.

6.11. Represent three of the risks noted in Figure 6.2 using a CTC format.

6.12. Recompute the risk exposure discussed in Section 6.4.2 when cost/LOC is $16 and the probability is 60 percent.

6.13. Can you think of a situation in which a high-probability, high-impact risk would not be considered as part of your RMMM plan?

6.14. Referring the the risk referent shown on Figure 6.4, would the curve always have the symmetric arc shown or would there be situations in which the curve would be more distorted. If so, suggest a scenario in which this might happen.

6.15. Do some research on software safety issues and write a brief paper on the subject. Do a Web search to get current information.

6.16. Describe five software application areas in which software safety and hazard analysis would be a major concern.

FURTHER READINGS AND INFORMATION SOURCES

The software risk management literature has expanded significantly in recent years. Hall [HAL98] presents one of the more thorough treatments of the subject. Karolak [KAR96] has written a guidebook that introduces an easy-to-use risk analysis model with worthwhile checklists and questionnaires. A useful snapshot of risk assessment has been written by Grey (*Practical Risk Assessment for Project Management,* Wiley, 1995). His abbreviated treatment provides a good introduction to the subject. Additional books worth examining include

Chapman, C.B. and S. Ward, *Project Risk Management: Processes, Techniques and Insights,* Wiley, 1997.

Schuyler, J.R., *Decision Analysis in Projects,* Project Management Institute Publications, 1997.

Wideman, R.M. (editor), *Project & Program Risk Management: A Guide to Managing Project Risks and Opportunities,* Project Management Institute Publications, 1998.

Capers Jones (*Assessment and Control of Software Risks,* Prentice-Hall, 1994) presents a detailed discussion of software risks that includes data collected from hundreds of software projects. Jones defines 60 risk factors that can affect the outcome of software projects. Boehm [BOE89] suggests excellent questionnaire and checklist formats that can prove invaluable in identifying risk. Charette [CHA89] presents a detailed treatment of the mechanics of risk analysis, calling on probability theory and statistical techniques to analyze risks. In a companion volume, Charette (*Application Strategies for Risk Analysis,* McGraw-Hill, 1990) discusses risk in the context of both system and software engineering and suggests pragmatic strategies for risk management. Gilb (*Principles of Software Engineering Management,* Addison-Wesley, 1988) presents a set of "principles" (which are often amusing and sometimes profound) that can serve as a worthwhile guide for risk management.

The March 1995 issue of *American Programmer,* the May 1997 issue of *IEEE Software,* and the June 1998 issue of the *Cutter IT Journal* all are dedicated to risk management.

The Software Engineering Institute has published many detailed reports and guidebooks on risk analysis and management. The Air Force Systems Command pamphlet AFSCP 800-45 [AFC88] describes risk identification and reduction techniques. Every issue of the *ACM Software Engineering Notes* has a section entitled "Risks to the Public" (editor, P.G. Neumann). If you want the latest and best software horror stories, this is the place to go.

A wide variety of information sources on risk analysis and management is available on the Internet. An up-to-date list of World Wide Web references that are relevant to risk can be found at the SEPA Web site:

http://www.mhhe.com/engcs/compsci/pressman/resources/risk.mhtml

CHAPTER

7 PROJECT SCHEDULING AND TRACKING

KEY CONCEPTS

In the late 1960s, a bright-eyed young engineer was chosen to "write" a computer program for an automated manufacturing application. The reason for his selection was simple. He was the only person in his technical group who had attended a computer programming seminar. He knew the ins and outs of assembly language and FORTRAN but nothing about software engineering and even less about project scheduling and tracking.

His boss gave him the appropriate manuals and a verbal description of what had to be done. He was informed that the project must be completed in two months.

He read the manuals, considered his approach, and began writing code. After two weeks, the boss called him into his office and asked how things were going.

"Really great," said the young engineer with youthful enthusiasm, "This was much simpler than I thought. I'm probably close to 75 percent finished."

The boss smiled. "That's really terrific," he said, encouraging the young engineer to keep up the good work. They planned to meet again in a week's time.

A week later the boss called the engineer into his office and asked, "Where are we?"

QUICK LOOK

What is it? You've selected an appropriate process model, you've identified the software engineering tasks that have to be performed, you estimated the amount of work and the number of people, you know the deadline, you've even considered the risks. Now it's time to connect the dots. That is, you have to create a network of software engineering tasks that will enable you to get the job done on time. Once the network is created, you have to assign responsibility for each task, make sure it gets done, and adapt the network as risks become reality. In a nutshell, that's software project scheduling and tracking.

Who does it? At the project level, software proj-ect managers using information solicited from software engineers. At an individual level, software engineers themselves.

Why is it important? In order to build a complex system, many software engineering tasks occur in parallel, and the result of work performed during one task may have a profound effect on work to be conducted in another task. These interdependencies are very difficult to understand without a schedule. It's also virtually impossible to assess progress on a moderate or large software project without a detailed schedule.

What are the steps? The software engineering tasks dictated by the software process model are refined for the functionality to be built. Effort and duration are allocated to each task and a task network (also called an "activity network") is

QUICK LOOK

created in a manner that enables the software team to meet the delivery deadline established.

What is the work product? The project schedule and related information are produced.

How do I ensure that I've done it right? Proper scheduling requires that (1) all tasks appear in the network, (2) effort and timing are intelligently allocated to each task, (3) interdependencies between tasks are properly indicated, (4) resources are allocated for the work to be done, and (5) closely spaced milestones are provided so that progress can be tracked.

"Everything's going well," said the youngster, "but I've run into a few small snags. I'll get them ironed out and be back on track soon."

"How does the deadline look?" the boss asked.

"No problem," said the engineer. "I'm close to 90 percent complete."

If you've been working in the software world for more than a few years, you can finish the story. It'll come as no surprise that the young engineer[1] stayed 90 percent complete for the entire project duration and finished (with the help of others) only one month late.

This story has been repeated tens of thousands of times by software developers during the past three decades. The big question is why?

7.1 BASIC CONCEPTS

Although there are many reasons why software is delivered late, most can be traced to one or more of the following root causes:

- An unrealistic deadline established by someone outside the software development group and forced on managers and practitioner's within the group.
- Changing customer requirements that are not reflected in schedule changes.
- An honest underestimate of the amount of effort and/or the number of resources that will be required to do the job.
- Predictable and/or unpredictable risks that were not considered when the project commenced.
- Technical difficulties that could not have been foreseen in advance.
- Human difficulties that could not have been foreseen in advance.
- Miscommunication among project staff that results in delays.
- A failure by project management to recognize that the project is falling behind schedule and a lack of action to correct the problem.

Quote:

"Excessive or irrational schedules are probably the single most destructive influence in all of software."

Capers Jones

Aggressive (read "unrealistic") deadlines are a fact of life in the software business. Sometimes such deadlines are demanded for reasons that are legitimate, from the

1 If you're wondering whether this story is autobiographical, it is!

point of view of the person who sets the deadline. But common sense says that legitimacy must also be perceived by the people doing the work.

7.1.1 Comments on "Lateness"

Napoleon once said: "Any commander in chief who undertakes to carry out a plan which he considers defective is at fault; he must put forth his reasons, insist on the plan being changed, and finally tender his resignation rather than be the instrument of his army's downfall." These are strong words that many software project managers should ponder.

Quote: "I love deadlines. I like the whooshing sound they make as they fly by." **Douglas Adams**

The estimation and risk analysis activities discussed in Chapters 5 and 6, and the scheduling techniques described in this chapter are often implemented under the constraint of a defined deadline. If best estimates indicate that the deadline is unrealistic, a competent project manager should "protect his or her team from undue [schedule] pressure . . . [and] reflect the pressure back to its originators" [PAG85].

To illustrate, assume that a software development group has been asked to build a real-time controller for a medical diagnostic instrument that is to be introduced to the market in nine months. After careful estimation and risk analysis, the software project manager comes to the conclusion that the software, as requested, will require 14 calendar months to create with available staff. How does the project manager proceed?

It is unrealistic to march into the customer's office (in this case the likely customer is marketing/sales) and demand that the delivery date be changed. External market pressures have dictated the date, and the product must be released. It is equally foolhardy to refuse to undertake the work (from a career standpoint). So, what to do?

The following steps are recommended in this situation:

? What should we do when management demands that we make a deadline that is impossible?

1. Perform a detailed estimate using historical data from past projects. Determine the estimated effort and duration for the project.
2. Using an incremental process model (Chapter 2), develop a software engineering strategy that will deliver critical functionality by the imposed deadline, but delay other functionality until later. Document the plan.
3. Meet with the customer and (using the detailed estimate), explain why the imposed deadline is unrealistic. Be certain to note that all estimates are based on performance on past projects. Also be certain to indicate the percent improvement that would be required to achieve the deadline as it currently exists.[2] The following comment is appropriate:

   "I think we may have a problem with the delivery date for the XYZ controller software. I've given each of you an abbreviated breakdown of production

---

2 If the percent of improvement is 10 to 25 percent, it may actually be possible to get the job done. But, more likely, the percent of improvement in team performance must be greater than 50 percent. This is an unrealistic expectation.

rates for past projects and an estimate that we've done a number of different ways. You'll note that I've assumed a 20 percent improvement in past production rates, but we still get a delivery date that's 14 calendar months rather than 9 months away."

4. Offer the incremental development strategy as an alternative:

"We have a few options, and I'd like you to make a decision based on them. First, we can increase the budget and bring on additional resources so that we'll have a shot at getting this job done in nine months. But understand that this will increase risk of poor quality due to the tight timeline.[3] Second, we can remove a number of the software functions and capabilities that you're requesting. This will make the preliminary version of the product somewhat less functional, but we can announce all functionality and then deliver over the 14 month period. Third, we can dispense with reality and wish the project complete in nine months. We'll wind up with nothing that can be delivered to a customer. The third option, I hope you'll agree, is unacceptable. Past history and our best estimates say that it is unrealistic and a recipe for disaster."

XRef

Incremental process models are described in Chapter 2.

There will be some grumbling, but if solid estimates based on good historical data are presented, it's likely that negotiated versions of option 1 or 2 will be chosen. The unrealistic deadline evaporates.

7.1.2 Basic Principles

Fred Brooks, the well-known author of *The Mythical Man-Month* [BRO95], was once asked how software projects fall behind schedule. His response was as simple as it was profound: "One day at a time."

The reality of a technical project (whether it involves building a hydroelectric plant or developing an operating system) is that hundreds of small tasks must occur to accomplish a larger goal. Some of these tasks lie outside the mainstream and may be completed without worry about impact on project completion date. Other tasks lie on the "critical" path.[4] If these "critical" tasks fall behind schedule, the completion date of the entire project is put into jeopardy.

ADVICE

The tasks required to achieve the project manager's objective should not be performed manually. There are many excellent project scheduling tools. Use them.

The project manager's objective is to define all project tasks, build a network that depicts their interdependencies, identify the tasks that are critical within the network, and then track their progress to ensure that delay is recognized "one day at a time." To accomplish this, the manager must have a schedule that has been defined at a degree of resolution that enables the manager to monitor progress and control the project.

Software project scheduling is an activity that distributes estimated effort across the planned project duration by allocating the effort to specific software engineering tasks.

---

3 You might also add that adding more people does not reduce calendar time proportionally.

4 The critical path will be discussed in greater detail later in this chapter.

It is important to note, however, that the schedule evolves over time. During early stages of project planning, a *macroscopic schedule* is developed. This type of schedule identifies all major software engineering activities and the product functions to which they are applied. As the project gets under way, each entry on the macroscopic schedule is refined into a *detailed schedule.* Here, specific software tasks (required to accomplish an activity) are identified and scheduled.

Quote:
"Overly optimistic scheduling doesn't result in shorter actual schedules, it results in longer ones."
Steve McConnell

Scheduling for software engineering projects can be viewed from two rather different perspectives. In the first, an end-date for release of a computer-based system has already (and irrevocably) been established. The software organization is constrained to distribute effort within the prescribed time frame. The second view of software scheduling assumes that rough chronological bounds have been discussed but that the end-date is set by the software engineering organization. Effort is distributed to make best use of resources and an end-date is defined after careful analysis of the software. Unfortunately, the first situation is encountered far more frequently than the second.

Like all other areas of software engineering, a number of basic principles guide software project scheduling:

KEY POINT
When you develop a schedule, compartmentalize the work, represent task interdependencies, allocate effort and time to each task, define responsibilities for the work to be done, and define outcomes and milestones.

Compartmentalization. The project must be compartmentalized into a number of manageable activities and tasks. To accomplish compartmentalization, both the product and the process are decomposed (Chapter 3).

Interdependency. The interdependency of each compartmentalized activity or task must be determined. Some tasks must occur in sequence while others can occur in parallel. Some activities cannot commence until the work product produced by another is available. Other activities can occur independently.

Time allocation. Each task to be scheduled must be allocated some number of work units (e.g., person-days of effort). In addition, each task must be assigned a start date and a completion date that are a function of the interdependencies and whether work will be conducted on a full-time or part-time basis.

Effort validation. Every project has a defined number of staff members. As time allocation occurs, the project manager must ensure that no more than the allocated number of people have been scheduled at any given time. For example, consider a project that has three assigned staff members (e.g., 3 person-days are available per day of assigned effort[5]). On a given day, seven concurrent tasks must be accomplished. Each task requires 0.50 person days of effort. More effort has been allocated than there are people to do the work.

Defined responsibilities. Every task that is scheduled should be assigned to a specific team member.

5 In reality, less than three person-days are available because of unrelated meetings, sickness, vacation, and a variety of other reasons. For our purposes, however, we assume 100 percent availability.

Defined outcomes. Every task that is scheduled should have a defined outcome. For software projects, the outcome is normally a work product (e.g., the design of a module) or a part of a work product. Work products are often combined in deliverables.

Defined milestones. Every task or group of tasks should be associated with a project milestone. A milestone is accomplished when one or more work products has been reviewed for quality (Chapter 8) and has been approved.

Each of these principles is applied as the project schedule evolves.

7.2 THE RELATIONSHIP BETWEEN PEOPLE AND EFFORT

In a small software development project a single person can analyze requirements, perform design, generate code, and conduct tests. As the size of a project increases, more people must become involved. (We can rarely afford the luxury of approaching a ten person-year effort with one person working for ten years!)

ADVICE

If you must add people to a late project, be certain that you've assigned them work that is highly compartmentalized.

There is a common myth (discussed in Chapter 1) that is still believed by many managers who are responsible for software development effort: "If we fall behind schedule, we can always add more programmers and catch up later in the project." Unfortunately, adding people late in a project often has a disruptive effect on the project, causing schedules to slip even further. The people who are added must learn the system, and the people who teach them are the same people who were doing the work. While teaching, no work is done, and the project falls further behind.

In addition to the time it takes to learn the system, more people increase the number of communication paths and the complexity of communication throughout a project. Although communication is absolutely essential to successful software development, every new communication path requires additional effort and therefore additional time.

7.2.1 An Example

Consider four software engineers, each capable of producing 5000 LOC/year when working on an individual project. When these four engineers are placed on a team project, six potential communication paths are possible. Each communication path requires time that could otherwise be spent developing software. We shall assume that team productivity (when measured in LOC) will be reduced by 250 LOC/year for each communication path, due to the overhead associated with communication. Therefore, team productivity is 20,000 − (250 x 6) = 18,500 LOC/year—7.5 percent less than what we might expect.[6]

---

6 It is possible to pose a counterargument: Communication, if it is effective, can enhance the quality of the work being performed, thereby reducing the amount of rework and increasing the individual productivity of team members. The jury is still out!

KEY POINT
The relationship between the number of people working on a software project and overall productivity is not linear.

The one-year project on which the team is working falls behind schedule, and with two months remaining, two additional people are added to the team. The number of communication paths escalates to 14. The productivity input of the new staff is the equivalent of 840 x 2 = 1680 LOC for the two months remaining before delivery. Team productivity now is 20,000 + 1680 − (250 x 14) = 18,180 LOC/year.

Although the example is a gross oversimplification of real-world circumstances, it does illustrate another key point: The relationship between the number of people working on a software project and overall productivity is not linear.

Based on the people/work relationship, are teams counterproductive? The answer is an emphatic "no," if communication improves software quality. In fact, formal technical reviews (see Chapter 8) conducted by software teams can lead to better analysis and design, and more important, can reduce the number of errors that go undetected until testing (thereby reducing testing effort). Hence, productivity and quality, when measured by time to project completion and customer satisfaction, can actually improve.

7.2.2. An Empirical Relationship

Recalling the software equation [PUT92] that was introduced in Chapter 5, we can demonstrate the highly nonlinear relationship between chronological time to complete a project and human effort applied to the project. The number of delivered lines of code (source statements), L, is related to effort and development time by the equation:

$$L = P \times E^{1/3} t^{4/3}$$

where E is development effort in person-months, P is a productivity parameter that reflects a variety of factors that lead to high-quality software engineering work (typical values for P range between 2,000 and 12,000), and t is the project duration in calendar months.

Rearranging this software equation, we can arrive at an expression for development effort E:

ADVICE
As the deadline becomes tighter and tighter, you reach a point at which the work cannot be completed on schedule, regardless of the number of people doing the work. Face reality and define a new delivery date.

$$E = L^3 / (P^3 t^4) \qquad (7\text{-}1)$$

where E is the effort expended (in person-years) over the entire life cycle for software development and maintenance and t is the development time in years. The equation for development effort can be related to development cost by the inclusion of a burdened labor rate factor ($/person-year).

This leads to some interesting results. Consider a complex, real-time software project estimated at 33,000 LOC, 12 person-years of effort. If eight people are assigned to the project team, the project can be completed in approximately 1.3 years. If, however, we extend the end-date to 1.75 years, the highly nonlinear nature of the model described in Equation (7-1) yields:

$$E = L^3 / (P^3 t^4) \sim 3.8 \text{ person-years.}$$

This implies that, by extending the end-date six months, we can reduce the number of people from eight to four! The validity of such results is open to debate, but the implication is clear: Benefit can be gained by using fewer people over a somewhat longer time span to accomplish the same objective.

7.2.3 Effort Distribution

? How much effort should be expended on each of the major software engineering tasks?

Each of the software project estimation techniques discussed in Chapter 5 leads to estimates of work units (e.g., person-months) required to complete software development. A recommended distribution of effort across the definition and development phases is often referred to as the *40–20–40 rule.*[7] Forty percent of all effort is allocated to front-end analysis and design. A similar percentage is applied to back-end testing. You can correctly infer that coding (20 percent of effort) is de-emphasized.

This effort distribution should be used as a guideline only. The characteristics of each project must dictate the distribution of effort. Work expended on project planning rarely accounts for more than 2–3 percent of effort, unless the plan commits an organization to large expenditures with high risk. Requirements analysis may comprise 10–25 percent of project effort. Effort expended on analysis or prototyping should increase in direct proportion with project size and complexity. A range of 20 to 25 percent of effort is normally applied to software design. Time expended for design review and subsequent iteration must also be considered.

Because of the effort applied to software design, code should follow with relatively little difficulty. A range of 15–20 percent of overall effort can be achieved. Testing and subsequent debugging can account for 30–40 percent of software development effort. The criticality of the software often dictates the amount of testing that is required. If software is human rated (i.e., software failure can result in loss of life), even higher percentages are typical.

7.3 DEFINING A TASK SET FOR THE SOFTWARE PROJECT

A number of different process models were described in Chapter 2. These models offer different paradigms for software development. Regardless of whether a software team chooses a linear sequential paradigm, an iterative paradigm, an evolutionary paradigm, a concurrent paradigm or some permutation, the process model is populated by a set of tasks that enable a software team to define, develop, and ultimately support computer software.

No single set of tasks is appropriate for all projects. The set of tasks that would be appropriate for a large, complex system would likely be perceived as overkill for a small, relatively simple software product. Therefore, an effective software process

7 Today, more than 40 percent of all project effort is often recommended for analysis and design tasks for large software development projects. Hence, the name *40–20–40* no longer applies in a strict sense.

should define a collection of task sets, each designed to meet the needs of different types of projects.

KEY POINT
A "task set" is a collection of software engineering tasks, milestones, and deliverables.

A *task set* is a collection of software engineering work tasks, milestones, and deliverables that must be accomplished to complete a particular project. The task set to be chosen must provide enough discipline to achieve high software quality. But, at the same time, it must not burden the project team with unnecessary work.

Task sets are designed to accommodate different types of projects and different degrees of rigor. Although it is difficult to develop a comprehensive taxonomy of software project types, most software organizations encounter the following projects:

1. *Concept development projects* that are initiated to explore some new business concept or application of some new technology.
2. *New application development projects* that are undertaken as a consequence of a specific customer request.
3. *Application enhancement projects* that occur when existing software undergoes major modifications to function, performance, or interfaces that are observable by the end-user.
4. *Application maintenance projects* that correct, adapt, or extend existing software in ways that may not be immediately obvious to the end-user.
5. *Reengineering projects* that are undertaken with the intent of rebuilding an existing (legacy) system in whole or in part.

Even within a single project type, many factors influence the task set to be chosen. When taken in combination, these factors provide an indication of the degree of rigor with which the software process should be applied.

7.3.1 Degree of Rigor

KEY POINT
The task set will grow in size and complexity as the degree of rigor grows.

Even for a project of a particular type, the *degree of rigor* with which the software process is applied may vary significantly. The degree of rigor is a function of many project characteristics. As an example, small, non-business-critical projects can generally be addressed with somewhat less rigor than large, complex business-critical applications. It should be noted, however, that all projects must be conducted in a manner that results in timely, high-quality deliverables. Four different degrees of rigor can be defined:

Casual. All process framework activities (Chapter 2) are applied, but only a minimum task set is required. In general, umbrella tasks will be minimized and documentation requirements will be reduced. All basic principles of software engineering are still applicable.

Structured. The process framework will be applied for this project. Framework activities and related tasks appropriate to the project type will be applied and umbrella activities necessary to ensure high quality will be applied. SQA, SCM, documentation, and measurement tasks will be conducted in a streamlined manner.

Strict. The full process will be applied for this project with a degree of discipline that will ensure high quality. All umbrella activities will be applied and robust work products will be produced.

ADVICE

If everything is an emergency, there's something wrong with your software process or with the people who manage the business or both.

Quick reaction. The process framework will be applied for this project, but because of an emergency situation[8] only those tasks essential to maintaining good quality will be applied. "Back-filling" (i.e., developing a complete set of documentation, conducting additional reviews) will be accomplished after the application/product is delivered to the customer.

The project manager must develop a systematic approach for selecting the degree of rigor that is appropriate for a particular project. To accomplish this, project adaptation criteria are defined and a task set selector value is computed.

7.3.2 Defining Adaptation Criteria

Adaptation criteria are used to determine the recommended degree of rigor with which the software process should be applied on a project. Eleven adaptation criteria [PRE99] are defined for software projects:

- Size of the project
- Number of potential users
- Mission criticality
- Application longevity
- Stability of requirements
- Ease of customer/developer communication
- Maturity of applicable technology
- Performance constraints
- Embedded and nonembedded characteristics
- Project staff
- Reengineering factors

SEPA WEB

Adaptable Process Model

Each of the adaptation criteria is assigned a grade that ranges between 1 and 5, where 1 represents a project in which a small subset of process tasks are required and overall methodological and documentation requirements are minimal, and 5 represents a project in which a complete set of process tasks should be applied and overall methodological and documentation requirements are substantial.

---

8 Emergency situations should be rare (they should not occur on more than 10 percent of all work conducted within the software engineering context). An emergency is not the same as a project with tight time constraints.

TABLE 7.1 COMPUTING THE TASK SET SELECTOR

Adaptation Criteria	Grade	Weight	Entry Point Multiplier					Product
			Conc.	NDev.	Enhan.	Maint.	Reeng.	
Size of project	___	1.20	0	1	1	1	1	___
Number of users	___	1.10	0	1	1	1	1	___
Business criticality	___	1.10	0	1	1	1	1	___
Longevity	___	0.90	0	1	1	0	0	___
Stability of requirements	___	1.20	0	1	1	1	1	___
Ease of communication	___	0.90	1	1	1	1	1	___
Maturity of technology	___	0.90	1	1	0	0	1	___
Performance constraints	___	0.80	0	1	1	0	1	___
Embedded/nonembedded	___	1.20	1	1	1	0	1	___
Project staffing	___	1.00	1	1	1	1	1	___
Interoperability	___	1.10	0	1	1	1	1	___
Reengineering factors	___	1.20	0	0	0	0	1	___
Task set selector (TSS)								___

7.3.3 Computing a Task Set Selector Value

To select the appropriate task set for a project, the following steps should be conducted:

? How do we choose the appropriate task set for our project?

1. Review each of the adaptation criteria in Section 7.3.2 and assign the appropriate grades (1 to 5) based on the characteristics of the project. These grades should be entered into Table 7.1.
2. Review the weighting factors assigned to each of the criteria. The value of a weighting factor ranges from 0.8 to 1.2 and provides an indication of the relative importance of a particular adaptation criterion to the types of software developed within the local environment. If modifications are required to better reflect local circumstances, they should be made.
3. Multiply the grade entered in Table 7.1 by the *weighting factor* and by the *entry point multiplier* for the type of project to be undertaken. The entry point multiplier takes on a value of 0 or 1 and indicates the relevance of the adaptation criterion to the project type. The result of the product

   grade x weighting factor x entry point multiplier

   is placed in the Product column of Table 7.1 for each adaptation criteria individually.
4. Compute the average of all entries in the Product column and place the result in the space marked *task set selector* (TSS). This value will be used to help select the task set that is most appropriate for the project.

TABLE 7.2 COMPUTING THE TASK SET SELECTOR—AN EXAMPLE

Adaptation Criteria	Grade	Weight	Entry Point Multiplier					Product
			Conc.	NDev.	Enhan.	Maint.	Reeng.	
Size of project	2	1.2		1				2.4
Number of users	3	1.1		1				3.3
Business criticality	4	1.1		1				4.4
Longevity	3	0.9		1				2.7
Stability of requirements	2	1.2		1				2.4
Ease of communication	2	0.9		1				1.8
Maturity of technology	2	0.9		1				1.8
Performance constraints	3	0.8		1				2.4
Embedded/nonembedded	3	1.2		1				3.6
Project staffing	2	1.0		1				2.0
Interoperability	4	1.1		1				4.4
Reengineering factors	0	1.2		0				0.0
Task set selector (TSS)								**2.8**

7.3.4 Interpreting the TSS Value and Selecting the Task Set

Once the task set selector is computed, the following guidelines can be used to select the appropriate task set for a project:

Task set selector value	Degree of rigor
TSS < 1.2	casual
1.0 < TSS < 3.0	structured
TSS > 2.4	strict

ADVICE

If the task set selector value is in an overlap area, it usually is OK to choose the less formal degree of rigor, unless project risk is high.

The overlap in TSS values from one recommended task set to another is purposeful and is intended to illustrate that sharp boundaries are impossible to define when making task set selections. In the final analysis, the task set selector value, past experience, and common sense must all be factored into the choice of the task set for a project.

Table 7.2 illustrates how TSS might be computed for a hypothetical project. The project manager selects the grades shown in the Grade column. The project type is *new application development.* Therefore, entry point multipliers are selected from the NDev column. The entry in the Product column is computed using

Grade x Weight x NewDev entry point multiplier

The value of TSS (computed as the average of all entries in the product column) is 2.8. Using the criteria discussed previously, the manager has the option of using either the structured or the strict task set. The final decision is made once all project factors have been considered.

7.4 SELECTING SOFTWARE ENGINEERING TASKS

In order to develop a project schedule, a task set must be distributed on the project time line. As we noted in Section 7.3, the task set will vary depending upon the project type and the degree of rigor. Each of the project types described in Section 7.3 may be approached using a process model that is linear sequential, iterative (e.g., the prototyping or incremental models), or evolutionary (e.g., the spiral model). In some cases, one project type flows smoothly into the next. For example, concept development projects that succeed often evolve into new application development projects. As a new application development project ends, an application enhancement project sometimes begins. This progression is both natural and predictable and will occur regardless of the process model that is adopted by an organization. Therefore, the major software engineering tasks described in the sections that follow are applicable to all process model flows. As an example, we consider the software engineering tasks for a concept development project.

An adaptable process model (APM) includes a variety of task sets and is available for your use.

Concept development projects are initiated when the potential for some new technology must be explored. There is no certainty that the technology will be applicable, but a customer (e.g., marketing) believes that potential benefit exists. Concept development projects are approached by applying the following major tasks:

Concept scoping determines the overall scope of the project.

Preliminary concept planning establishes the organization's ability to undertake the work implied by the project scope.

Technology risk assessment evaluates the risk associated with the technology to be implemented as part of project scope.

Proof of concept demonstrates the viability of a new technology in the software context.

Concept implementation implements the concept representation in a manner that can be reviewed by a customer and is used for "marketing" purposes when a concept must be sold to other customers or management.

Customer reaction to the concept solicits feedback on a new technology concept and targets specific customer applications.

A quick scan of these tasks should yield few surprises. In fact, the software engineering flow for concept development projects (and for all other types of projects as well) is little more than common sense.

The software team must understand what must be done (scoping); then the team (or manager) must determine whether anyone is available to do it (planning), consider the risks associated with the work (risk assessment), prove the technology in some way (proof of concept), and implement it in a prototypical manner so that the customer can evaluate it (concept implementation and customer evaluation). Finally, if the concept is viable, a production version (translation) must be produced.

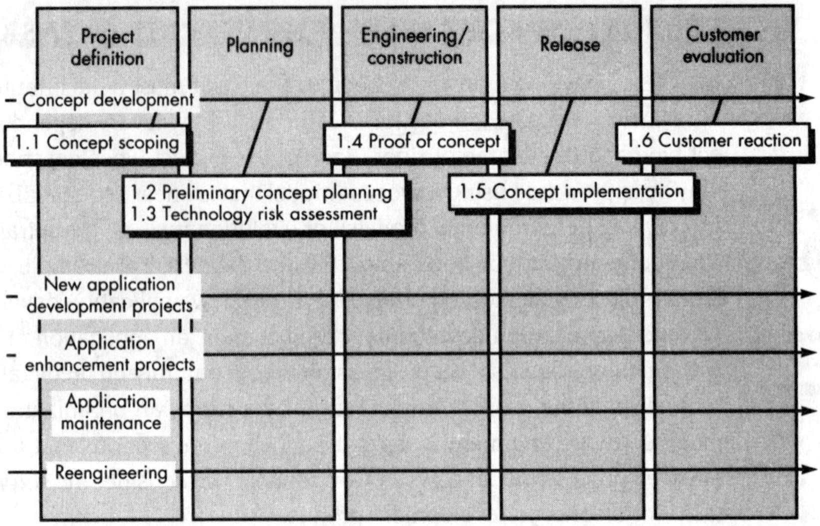

FIGURE 7.1 Concept development tasks in a linear sequential model

It is important to note that concept development framework activities are iterative in nature. That is, an actual concept development project might approach these activities in a number of planned increments, each designed to produce a deliverable that can be evaluated by the customer.

If a linear process model flow is chosen, each of these increments is defined in a repeating sequence as illustrated in Figure 7.1. During each sequence, umbrella activities (described in Chapter 2) are applied; quality is monitored; and at the end of each sequence, a deliverable is produced. With each iteration, the deliverable should converge toward the defined end product for the concept development stage. If an evolutionary model is chosen, the layout of tasks 1.1 through 1.6 would appear as shown in Figure 7.2. Major software engineering tasks for other project types can be defined and applied in a similar manner.

7.5 REFINEMENT OF MAJOR TASKS

The major tasks described in Section 7.4 may be used to define a macroscopic schedule for a project. However, the macroscopic schedule must be refined to create a detailed project schedule. Refinement begins by taking each major task and decomposing it into a set of subtasks (with related work products and milestones).

As an example of task decomposition, consider *concept scoping* for a development project, discussed in Section 7.4. Task refinement can be accomplished using an outline format, but in this book, a process design language approach is used to illustrate the flow of the concept scoping activity:

FIGURE 7.2
Concept development tasks using an evolutionary model

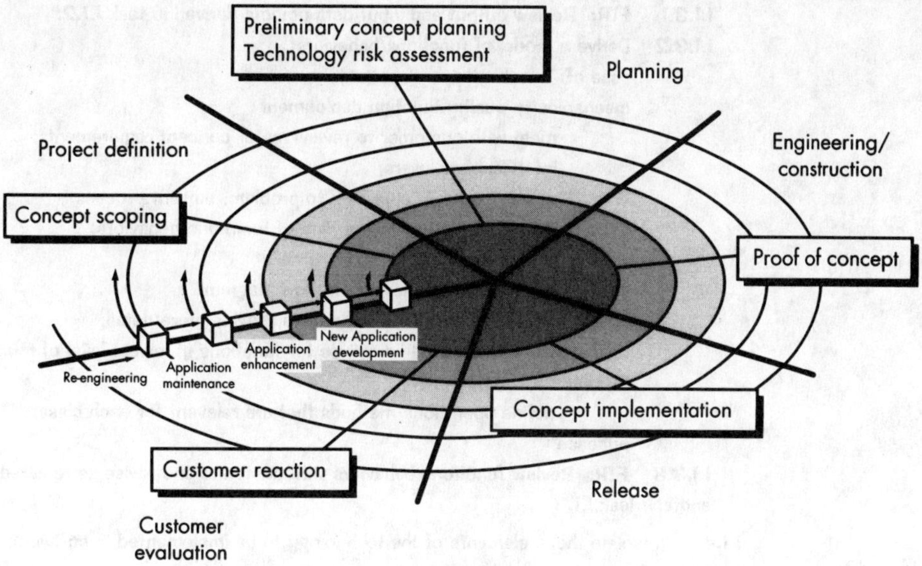

Task definition: Task I.1 Concept Scoping

I.1.1 Identify need, benefits and potential customers;

I.1.2 Define desired output/control and input events that drive the application;

Begin Task I.1.2

I.1.2.1 FTR: Review written description of need[9]

I.1.2.2 Derive a list of customer visible outputs/inputs

case of: mechanics

mechanics = quality function deployment

meet with customer to isolate major concept requirements;

interview end-users;

observe current approach to problem, current process;

review past requests and complaints;

mechanics = structured analysis

make list of major data objects;

define relationships between objects;

define object attributes;

mechanics = object view

make list of problem classes;

develop class hierarchy and class connections;

define attributes for classes;

endcase

I.1.2.3 FTR: Review outputs/inputs with customer and revise as required;

endtask Task I.1.2

I.1.3 Define the functionality/behavior for each major function;

Begin Task I.1.3

The adaptable process model (APM) contains a complete process design language description for all software engineering tasks.

9 FTR indicates that a formal technical review (Chapter 8) is to be conducted.

```
    I.1.3.1   FTR: Review output and input data objects derived in task I.1.2;
    I.1.3.2   Derive a model of functions/behaviors;
              case of: mechanics
              mechanics = quality function deployment
                  meet with customer to review major concept requirements;
                  interview end-users;
                  observe current approach to problem, current process;
                  develop a hierarchical outline of functions/behaviors;
              mechanics = structured analysis
                  derive a context level data flow diagram;
                  refine the data flow diagram to provide more detail;
                  write processing narratives for functions at lowest level of refinement;
              mechanics = object view
                  define operations/methods that are relevant for each class;
              endcase
    I.1.3.3   FTR: Review functions/behaviors with customer and revise as required;
    endtask Task I.1.3
  I.1.4     Isolate those elements of the technology to be implemented in software;
  I.1.5     Research availability of existing software;
  I.1.6     Define technical feasibility;
  I.1.7     Make quick estimate of size;
  I.1.8     Create a Scope Definition;
endTask definition:  Task I.1
```

The tasks and subtasks noted in the process design language refinement form the basis for a detailed schedule for the concept scoping activity.

7.6 DEFINING A TASK NETWORK

KEY POINT
The task network is a useful mechanism for depicting intertask dependencies and determining the critical path.

Individual tasks and subtasks have interdependencies based on their sequence. In addition, when more than one person is involved in a software engineering project, it is likely that development activities and tasks will be performed in parallel. When this occurs, concurrent tasks must be coordinated so that they will be complete when later tasks require their work product(s).

A *task network,* also called an *activity network,* is a graphic representation of the task flow for a project. It is sometimes used as the mechanism through which task sequence and dependencies are input to an automated project scheduling tool. In its simplest form (used when creating a macroscopic schedule), the task network depicts major software engineering tasks. Figure 7.3 shows a schematic task network for a concept development project.

The concurrent nature of software engineering activities leads to a number of important scheduling requirements. Because parallel tasks occur asynchronously, the planner must determine intertask dependencies to ensure continuous progress toward completion. In addition, the project manager should be aware of those tasks that lie on the critical path. That is, tasks that must be completed on schedule if the project

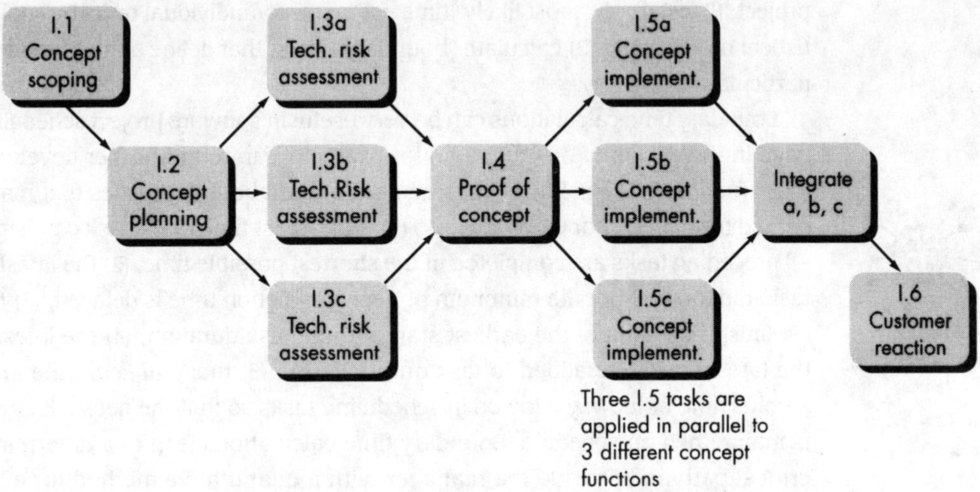

FIGURE 7.3 A task network for concept development

as a whole is to be completed on schedule. These issues are discussed in more detail later in this chapter.

It is important to note that the task network shown in Figure 7.3 is macroscopic. In a detailed task network (a precursor to a detailed schedule), each activity shown in Figure 7.3 would be expanded. For example, Task I.1 would be expanded to show all tasks detailed in the refinement of Tasks I.1 shown in Section 7.5.

7.7 SCHEDULING

ADVICE

For all but the simplest projects, scheduling should be done with the aid of a project scheduling tool.

Scheduling of a software project does not differ greatly from scheduling of any multitask engineering effort. Therefore, generalized project scheduling tools and techniques can be applied with little modification to software projects.

Program evaluation and review technique (PERT) and *critical path method* (CPM) [MOD83] are two project scheduling methods that can be applied to software development. Both techniques are driven by information already developed in earlier project planning activities:

- Estimates of effort
- A decomposition of the product function
- The selection of the appropriate process model and task set
- Decomposition of tasks

Interdependencies among tasks may be defined using a task network. Tasks, sometimes called the project *work breakdown structure* (WBS), are defined for the product as a whole or for individual functions.

Both PERT and CPM provide quantitative tools that allow the software planner to (1) determine the *critical path*—the chain of tasks that determines the duration of the project; (2) establish "most likely" time estimates for individual tasks by applying statistical models; and (3) calculate "boundary times" that define a time "window" for a particular task.

Boundary time calculations can be very useful in software project scheduling. Slippage in the design of one function, for example, can retard further development of other functions. Riggs [RIG81] describes important boundary times that may be discerned from a PERT or CPM network: (1) the earliest time that a task can begin when all preceding tasks are completed in the shortest possible time, (2) the latest time for task initiation before the minimum project completion time is delayed, (3) the earliest finish—the sum of the earliest start and the task duration, (4) the latest finish—the latest start time added to task duration, and (5) the *total float*—the amount of surplus time or leeway allowed in scheduling tasks so that the network critical path is maintained on schedule. Boundary time calculations lead to a determination of critical path and provide the manager with a quantitative method for evaluating progress as tasks are completed.

SEPA WEB: CASE tools project/scheduling and planning

Both PERT and CPM have been implemented in a wide variety of automated tools that are available for the personal computer [THE93]. Such tools are easy to use and make the scheduling methods described previously available to every software project manager.

7.7.1 Timeline Charts

When creating a software project schedule, the planner begins with a set of tasks (the work breakdown structure). If automated tools are used, the work breakdown is input as a task network or task outline. Effort, duration, and start date are then input for each task. In addition, tasks may be assigned to specific individuals.

KEY POINT A timeline chart enables you to determine what tasks will be conducted at a given point in time.

As a consequence of this input, a *timeline chart,* also called a *Gantt chart,* is generated. A timeline chart can be developed for the entire project. Alternatively, separate charts can be developed for each project function or for each individual working on the project.

Figure 7.4 illustrates the format of a timeline chart. It depicts a part of a software project schedule that emphasizes the concept scoping task (Section 7.5) for a new word-processing (WP) software product. All project tasks (for concept scoping) are listed in the left-hand column. The horizontal bars indicate the duration of each task. When multiple bars occur at the same time on the calendar, task concurrency is implied. The diamonds indicate milestones.

Once the information necessary for the generation of a timeline chart has been input, the majority of software project scheduling tools produce *project tables*—a tabular listing of all project tasks, their planned and actual start- and end-dates, and a variety of related information (Figure 7.5). Used in conjunction with the timeline chart, project tables enable the project manager to track progress.

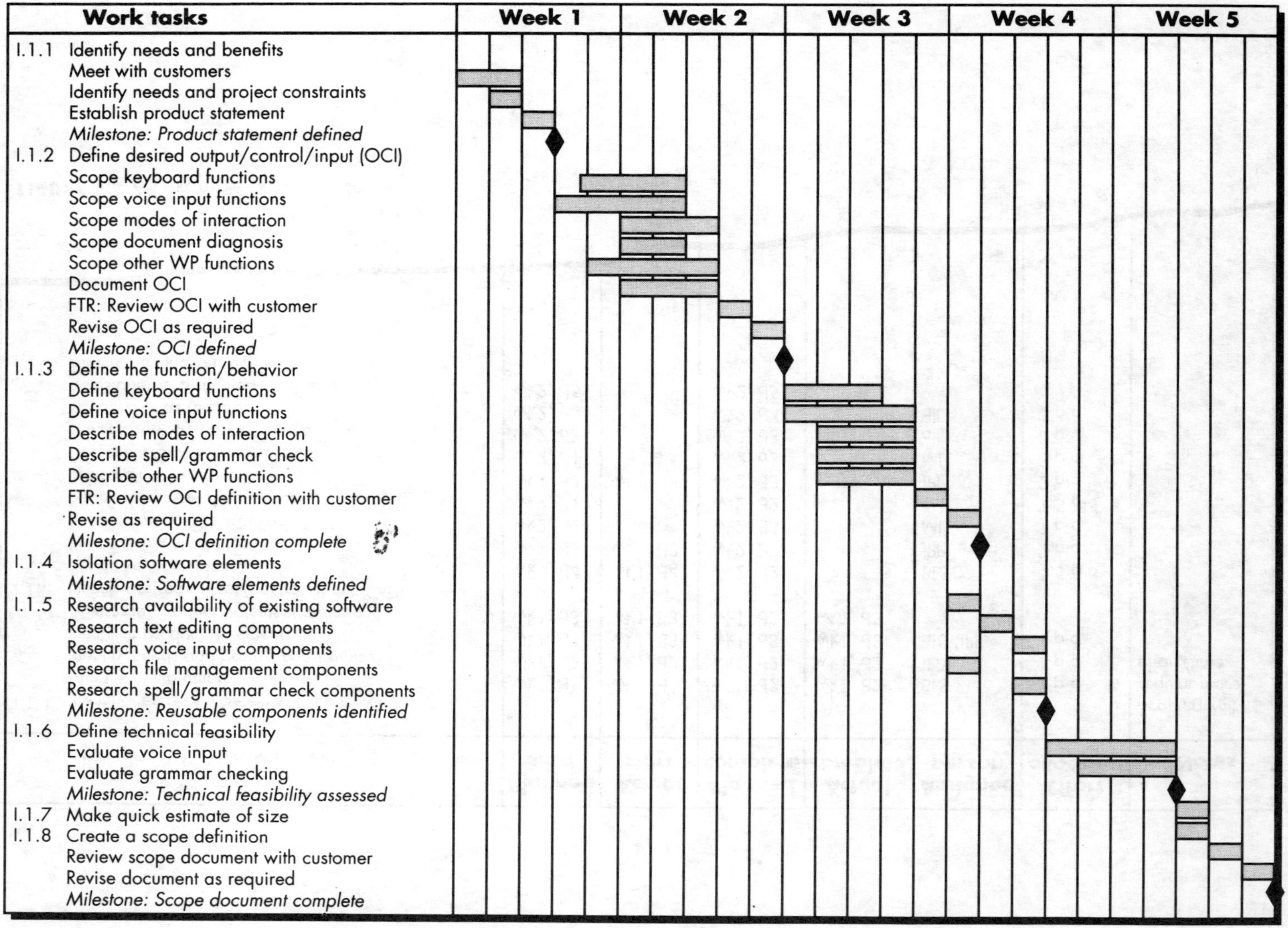

FIGURE 7.4 An example timeline chart

Work tasks	Planned start	Actual start	Planned complete	Actual complete	Assigned person	Effort allocated	Notes
1.1.1 Identify needs and benefits							Scoping will require more effort/time
Meet with customers	wk1, d1	wk1, d1	wk1, d2	wk1, d2	BLS	2 p-d	
Identify needs and project constraints	wk1, d2	wk1, d2	wk1, d2	wk1, d2	JPP	1 p-d	
Establish product statement	wk1, d3	wk1, d3	wk1, d3	wk1, d3	BLS/JPP	1 p-d	
Milestone: Product statement defined	wk1, d3	wk1, d3	wk1, d3	wk1, d3			
1.1.2 Define desired output/control/input (OCI)							
Scope keyboard functions	wk1, d4	wk1, d4	wk2, d2		BLS	1.5 p-d	
Scope voice input functions	wk1, d3	wk1, d3	wk2, d2		JPP	2 p-d	
Scope modes of interaction	wk2, d1		wk2, d3		MLL	1 p-d	
Scope document diagnostics	wk2, d1		wk2, d2		BLS	1.5 p-d	
Scope other WP functions	wk1, d4	wk1, d4	wk2, d3		JPP	2 p-d	
Document OCI	wk2, d1		wk2, d3		MLL	3 p-d	
FTR: Review OCI with customer	wk2, d3		wk2, d3		all	3 p-d	
Revise OCI as required	wk2, d4		wk2, d4		all	3 p-d	
Milestone: OCI defined	wk2, d5		wk2, d5				
1.1.3 Define the function/behavior							

FIGURE 7.5 An example project table

7.7.2 Tracking the Schedule

The project schedule provides a road map for a software project manager. If it has been properly developed, the project schedule defines the tasks and milestones that must be tracked and controlled as the project proceeds. Tracking can be accomplished in a number of different ways:

Quote:

"The basic rule of software status reporting can be summarized in a single phrase: 'No surprises!'."

Capers Jones

- Conducting periodic project status meetings in which each team member reports progress and problems.
- Evaluating the results of all reviews conducted throughout the software engineering process.
- Determining whether formal project milestones (the diamonds shown in Figure 7.4) have been accomplished by the scheduled date.
- Comparing actual start-date to planned start-date for each project task listed in the resource table (Figure 7.5).
- Meeting informally with practitioners to obtain their subjective assessment of progress to date and problems on the horizon.
- Using earned value analysis (Section 7.8) to assess progress quantitatively.

In reality, all of these tracking techniques are used by experienced project managers.

Control is employed by a software project manager to administer project resources, cope with problems, and direct project staff. If things are going well (i.e., the project is on schedule and within budget, reviews indicate that real progress is being made and milestones are being reached), control is light. But when problems occur, the project manager must exercise control to reconcile them as quickly as possible. After a problem has been diagnosed,[10] additional resources may be focused on the problem area: staff may be redeployed or the project schedule can be redefined.

ADVICE

The best indicator of progress is the completion and successful review of a defined software work product.

When faced with severe deadline pressure, experienced project managers sometimes use a project scheduling and control technique called *time-boxing* [ZAH95]. The time-boxing strategy recognizes that the complete product may not be deliverable by the predefined deadline. Therefore, an incremental software paradigm (Chapter 2) is chosen and a schedule is derived for each incremental delivery.

The tasks associated with each increment are then time-boxed. This means that the schedule for each task is adjusted by working backward from the delivery date for the increment. A "box" is put around each task. When a task hits the boundary of its time box (plus or minus 10 percent), work stops and the next task begins.

The initial reaction to the time-boxing approach is often negative: "If the work isn't finished, how can we proceed?" The answer lies in the way work is accomplished. By the time the time-box boundary is encountered, it is likely that 90 percent of the

---

10 It is important to note that schedule slippage is a symptom of some underlying problem. The rôle of the project manager is to diagnose the underlying problem and act to correct it.

task has been completed.[11] The remaining 10 percent, although important, can (1) be delayed until the next increment or (2) be completed later if required. Rather than becoming "stuck" on a task, the project proceeds toward the delivery date.

7.8 EARNED VALUE ANALYSIS

KEY POINT

Earned value provides a quantitative indication of progress.

In Section 7.7.2, we discussed a number of qualitative approaches to project tracking. Each provides the project manager with an indication of progress, but an assessment of the information provided is somewhat subjective. It is reasonable to ask whether there is a quantitative technique for assessing progress as the software team progresses through the work tasks allocated to the project schedule. In fact, a technique for performing quantitative analysis of progress does exist. It is called *earned value analysis* (EVA).

Humphrey [HUM95] discusses earned value in the following manner:

> The earned value system provides a common value scale for every [software project] task, regardless of the type of work being performed. The total hours to do the whole project are estimated, and every task is given an earned value based on its estimated percentage of the total.

Stated even more simply, earned value is a measure of progress. It enables us to assess the "percent of completeness" of a project using quantitative analysis rather than rely on a gut feeling. In fact, Fleming and Koppleman [FLE98] argue that earned value analysis "provides accurate and reliable readings of performance from as early as 15 percent into the project."

To determine the earned value, the following steps are performed:

? How do I compute earned value to assess progress?

1. The *budgeted cost of work scheduled* (BCWS) is determined for each work task represented in the schedule. During the estimation activity (Chapter 5), the work (in person-hours or person-days) of each software engineering task is planned. Hence, $BCWS_i$ is the effort planned for work task *i*. To determine progress at a given point along the project schedule, the value of BCWS is the sum of the $BCWS_i$ values for all work tasks that should have been completed by that point in time on the project schedule.

2. The BCWS values for all work tasks are summed to derive the budget at completion, BAC. Hence,

$$BAC = \Sigma\ (BCWS_k) \text{ for all tasks } k$$

3. Next, the value for *budgeted cost of work performed* (BCWP) is computed. The value for BCWP is the sum of the BCWS values for all work tasks that have actually been completed by a point in time on the project schedule.

---

11 A cynic might recall the saying: "The first 90 percent of a system takes 90 percent of the time. The last 10 percent of the system takes 90 percent of the time."

Wilkens [WIL99] notes that "the distinction between the BCWS and the BCWP is that the former represents the budget of the activities that were planned to be completed and the latter represents the budget of the activities that actually were completed." Given values for BCWS, BAC, and BCWP, important progress indicators can be computed:

Schedule performance index, SPI = BCWP/BCWS

Schedule variance, SV = BCWP – BCWS

SPI is an indication of the efficiency with which the project is utilizing scheduled resources. An SPI value close to 1.0 indicates efficient execution of the project schedule. SV is simply an absolute indication of variance from the planned schedule.

WebRef
A wide array of earned value analysis resources (comprehensive bibliography, papers, hotlinks) can be found at **www.acq.osd.mil/pm/**

Percent scheduled for completion = BCWS/BAC

provides an indication of the percentage of work that should have been completed by time *t*.

Percent complete = BCWP/BAC

provides a quantitative indication of the percent of completeness of the project at a given point in time, *t*.

It is also possible to compute the *actual cost of work performed,* ACWP. The value for ACWP is the sum of the effort actually expended on work tasks that have been completed by a point in time on the project schedule. It is then possible to compute

Cost performance index, CPI = BCWP/ACWP

Cost variance, CV = BCWP – ACWP

A CPI value close to 1.0 provides a strong indication that the project is within its defined budget. CV is an absolute indication of cost savings (against planned costs) or shortfall at a particular stage of a project.

Like over-the-horizon radar, earned value analysis illuminates scheduling difficulties before they might otherwise be apparent. This enables the software project manager to take corrective action before a project crisis develops.

7.9 ERROR TRACKING

KEY POINT
Error tracking allows you to compare current work with past efforts and provides a quantitative indication of the quality of the work being conducted.

Throughout the software process, a project team creates work products (e.g., requirements specifications or prototype, design documents, source code). But the team also creates (and hopefully corrects) errors associated with each work product. If error-related measures and resultant metrics are collected over many software projects, a project manager can use these data as a baseline for comparison against error data collected in real time. Error tracking can be used as one means for assessing the status of a current project.

In Chapter 4, the concept of defect removal efficiency was discussed. To review briefly, the software team performs formal technical reviews (and, later, testing) to find and correct errors, *E,* in work products produced during software engineering tasks. Any errors that are not uncovered (but found in later tasks) are considered to be defects, *D*. Defect removal efficiency (Chapter 4) has been defined as

$$\text{DRE} = E/(E + D)$$

DRE is a process metric that provides a strong indication of the effectiveness of quality assurance activities, but DRE and the error and defect counts associated with it can also be used to assist a project manager in determining the progress that is being made as a software project moves through its scheduled work tasks.

Let us assume that a software organization has collected error and defect data over the past 24 months and has developed averages for the following metrics:

- Errors per requirements specification page, E_{req}
- Errors per component—design level, E_{design}
- Errors per component—code level, E_{code}
- DRE—requirements analysis
- DRE—architectural design
- DRE—component level design
- DRE—coding

As the project progresses through each software engineering step, the software team records and reports the number of errors found during requirements, design, and code reviews. The project manager calculates current values for E_{req}, E_{design}, and E_{code}. These are then compared to averages for past projects. If current results vary by more than 20% from the average, there may be cause for concern and there is certainly cause for investigation.

For example, if $E_{req} = 2.1$ for project X, yet the organizational average is 3.6, one of two scenarios is possible: (1) the software team has done an outstanding job of developing the requirements specification or (2) the team has been lax in its review approach. If the second scenario appears likely, the project manager should take immediate steps to build additional design time[12] into the schedule to accommodate the requirements defects that have likely been propagated into the design activity.

ADVICE

The more quantitative your approach to project tracking and control, the more likely you'll be able to foresee potential problems and respond to them proactively. Use earned value and tracking metrics.

These error tracking metrics can also be used to better target review and/or testing resources. For example, if a system is composed of 120 components, but 32 of these component exhibit E_{design} values that have substantial variance from the average, the project manager might elect to dedicate code review resources to the 32 components and allow others to pass into testing with no code review. Although all components should undergo code review in an ideal setting, a selective approach (reviewing only those modules that have suspect quality based on the E_{design} value) might be an effective means for recouping lost time and/or saving costs for a project that has gone over budget.

12 In reality, the extra time will be spent reworking requirements defects, but the work will occur when the design is underway.

7.10 THE PROJECT PLAN

Each step in the software engineering process should produce a deliverable that can be reviewed and that can act as a foundation for the steps that follow. The *Software Project Plan* is produced at the culmination of the planning tasks. It provides baseline cost and scheduling information that will be used throughout the software process.

Software Project Plan

The *Software Project Plan* is a relatively brief document that is addressed to a diverse audience. It must (1) communicate scope and resources to software management, technical staff, and the customer; (2) define risks and suggest risk aversion techniques; (3) define cost and schedule for management review; (4) provide an overall approach to software development for all people associated with the project; and (5) outline how quality will be ensured and change will be managed.

A presentation of cost and schedule will vary with the audience addressed. If the plan is used only as an internal document, the results of each estimation technique can be presented. When the plan is disseminated outside the organization, a reconciled cost breakdown (combining the results of all estimation techniques) is provided. Similarly, the degree of detail contained within the schedule section may vary with the audience and formality of the plan.

It is important to note that the *Software Project Plan* is *not* a static document. That is, the project team revisits the plan repeatedly—updating risks, estimates, schedules and related information—as the project proceeds and more is learned.

7.11 SUMMARY

Scheduling is the culmination of a planning activity that is a primary component of software project management. When combined with estimation methods and risk analysis, scheduling establishes a road map for the project manager.

Scheduling begins with process decomposition. The characteristics of the project are used to adapt an appropriate task set for the work to be done. A task network depicts each engineering task, its dependency on other tasks, and its projected duration. The task network is used to compute the critical path, a timeline chart and a variety of project information. Using the schedule as a guide, the project manager can track and control each step in the software process.

REFERENCES

[BRO95] Brooks, M., *The Mythical Man-Month,* Anniversary Edition, Addison-Wesley, 1995.

[FLE98] Fleming, Q.W. and J.M. Koppelman, "Earned Value Project Management," *Crosstalk,* vol. 11, no. 7, July 1998, p. 19.

[HUM95] Humphrey, W., *A Discipline for Software Engineering,* Addison-Wesley, 1995.

[PAG85] Page-Jones, M., *Practical Project Management,* Dorset House, 1985, pp. 90–91.

[PRE99] Pressman, R.S., *Adaptable Process Model,* R.S. Pressman & Associates, 1999.

[PUT92] Putnam, L. and W. Myers, *Measures for Excellence,* Yourdon Press, 1992.

[RIG81] Riggs, J., *Production Systems Planning, Analysis and Control,* 3rd ed., Wiley, 1981.

[THE93] The', L., "Project Management Software That's IS Friendly," *Datamation,* October 1, 1993, pp. 55–58.

[WIL99] Wilkens, T.T., "Earned Value, Clear and Simple," Primavera Systems, April 1, 1999, p. 2.

[ZAH95] Zahniser, R., "Time-Boxing for Top Team Performance," *Software Development,* March 1995, pp. 34–38.

PROBLEMS AND POINTS TO PONDER

7.1. "Unreasonable" deadlines are a fact of life in the software business. How should you proceed if you're faced with one?

7.2. What is the difference between a macroscopic schedule and a detailed schedule. Is it possible to manage a project if only a macroscopic schedule is developed? Why?

7.3. Is there ever a case where a software project milestone is not tied to a review? If so, provide one or more examples.

7.4. In Section 7.2.1, we present an example of the "communication overhead" that can occur when multiple people work on a software project. Develop a counterexample that illustrates how engineers who are well-versed in good software engineering practices and use formal technical reviews can increase the production rate of a team (when compared to the sum of individual production rates). Hint: You can assume that reviews reduce rework and that rework can account for 20–40 percent of a person's time.

7.5. Although adding people to a late software project can make it later, there are circumstances in which this is not true. Describe them.

7.6. The relationship between people and time is highly nonlinear. Using Putnam's software equation (described in Section 7.2.2), develop a table that relates number of people to project duration for a software project requiring 50,000 LOC and 15 person-years of effort (the productivity parameter is 5000 and B = 0.37). Assume that the software must be delivered in 24 months plus or minus 12 months.

7.7. Assume that you have been contracted by a university to develop an on-line course registration system (OLCRS). First, act as the customer (if you're a student, that should be easy!) and specify the characteristics of a good system. (Alternatively, your instructor will provide you with a set of preliminary requirements for the system.) Using the estimation methods discussed in Chapter 5, develop an effort and duration estimate for OLCRS. Suggest how you would:

a. Define parallel work activities during the OLCRS project.
b. Distribute effort throughout the project.
c. Establish milestones for the project.

7.8. Using Section 7.3 as a guide compute the TSS for OLCRS. Be sure to show all of your work. Select a project type and an appropriate task set for the project.

7.9. Define a task network for OLCRS, or alternatively, for another software project that interests you. Be sure to show tasks and milestones and to attach effort and duration estimates to each task. If possible, use an automated scheduling tool to perform this work.

7.10. If an automated scheduling tool is available, determine the critical path for the network defined in problem 7.7.

7.11. Using a scheduling tool (if available) or paper and pencil (if necessary), develop a timeline chart for the OLCRS project.

7.12. Refine the task called "technology risk assessment" in Section 7.4 in much the same way as concept scoping was refined in Section 7.5.

7.13. Assume you are a software project manager and that you've been asked to compute earned value statistics for a small software project. The project has 56 planned work tasks that are estimated to require 582 person-days to complete. At the time that you've been asked to do the earned value analysis, 12 tasks have been completed. However the project schedule indicates that 15 tasks should have been completed. The following scheduling data (in person-days) are available:

Task	Planned effort	Actual effort
1	12.0	12.5
2	15.0	11.0
3	13.0	17.0
4	8.0	9.5
5	9.5	9.0
6	18.0	19.0
7	10.0	10.0
8	4.0	4.5
9	12.0	10.0
10	6.0	6.5
11	5.0	4.0
12	14.0	14.5
13	16.0	—
14	6.0	—
15	8.0	—

Compute the SPI, schedule variance, percent scheduled for completion, percent complete, CPI, and cost variance for the project.

7.14. Is it possible to use DRE as a metric for error tracking throughout a software project? Discuss the pros and cons of using DRE for this purpose.

FURTHER READINGS AND INFORMATION SOURCES

McConnell (*Rapid Development,* Microsoft Press, 1996) presents an excellent discussion of the issues that lead to overly optimistic software project scheduling and what you can do about it. O'Connell (*How to Run Successful Projects II: The Silver Bullet,* Prentice-Hall, 1997) presents a step-by-step approach to project management that will help you to develop a realistic schedule for your projects.

Project scheduling issues are covered in most books on software project management. McConnell (*Software Project Survival Guide,* Microsoft Press, 1998), Hoffman and Beaumont (*Application Development: Managing a Project's Life Cycle,* Midrange Computing, 1997), Wysoki and his colleagues (*Effective Project Management,* Wiley, 1995), and Whitten (*Managing Software Development Projects,* 2nd ed., Wiley, 1995) consider the topic in detail. Boddie (*Crunch Mode,* Prentice-Hall, 1987) has written a book for all managers who "have 90 days to do a six month project."

Worthwhile information on project scheduling can also be obtained in general purpose project management books. Among the many offerings available are

Kerzner, H., *Project Management: A Systems Approach to Planning, Scheduling, and Controlling,* Wiley, 1998.

Lewis, J.P., *Mastering Project Management: Applying Advanced Concepts of Systems Thinking, Control and Evaluation,* McGraw-Hill, 1998.

Fleming and Koppelman (*Earned Value Project Management,* Project Management Institute Publications, 1996) discuss the use of earned value techniques for project tracking and control in considerable detail.

A wide variety of information sources on project scheduling and management is available on the Internet. An up-to-date list of World Wide Web references that are relevant to scheduling can be found at the SEPA Web site:
http://www.mhhe.com/engcs/compsci/pressman/resources/project-sched.mhtml

CHAPTER

8 SOFTWARE QUALITY ASSURANCE

KEY CONCEPTS

The software engineering approach described in this book works toward a single goal: to produce high-quality software. Yet many readers will be challenged by the question: "What is software quality?"

Philip Crosby [CRO79], in his landmark book on quality, provides a wry answer to this question:

> The problem of quality management is not what people don't know about it. The problem is what they think they do know . . .
>
> In this regard, quality has much in common with sex. Everybody is for it. (Under certain conditions, of course.) Everyone feels they understand it. (Even though they wouldn't want to explain it.) Everyone thinks execution is only a matter of following natural inclinations. (After all, we do get along somehow.) And, of course, most people feel that problems in these areas are caused by other people. (If only they would take the time to do things right.)

Some software developers continue to believe that software quality is something you begin to worry about after code has been generated. Nothing could be further from the truth! *Software quality assurance* (SQA) is an umbrella activity (Chapter 2) that is applied throughout the software process.

QUICK LOOK

What is it? It's not enough to talk the talk by saying that software quality is important, you have to (1) explicitly define what is meant when you say "software quality," (2) create a set of activities that will help ensure that every software engineering work product exhibits high quality, (3) perform quality assurance activities on every software project, (4) use metrics to develop strategies for improving your software process and, as a consequence, the quality of the end product.

Who does it? Everyone involved in the software engineering process is responsible for quality.

Why is it important? You can do it right, or you can do it over again. If a software team stresses quality in all software engineering activities, it reduces the amount of rework that it must do. That results in lower costs, and more importantly, improved time-to-market.

What are the steps? Before software quality assurance activities can be initiated, it is important to define 'software quality' at a number of different levels of abstraction. Once you understand what quality is, a software team must identify a set of SQA activities that will filter errors out of work products before they are passed on.

What is the work product? A Software Quality Assurance Plan is created to define a software team's SQA strategy. During analysis, design, and code generation, the primary SQA work product is the formal technical review summary report. During

QUICK LOOK

testing, test plans and procedures are produced. Other work products associated with process improvement may also be generated.

How do I ensure that I've done it right? Find errors before they become defects! That is, work to improve your defect removal efficiency (Chapters 4 and 7), thereby reducing the amount of rework that your software team has to perform.

SQA encompasses (1) a quality management approach, (2) effective software engineering technology (methods and tools), (3) formal technical reviews that are applied throughout the software process, (4) a multitiered testing strategy, (5) control of software documentation and the changes made to it, (6) a procedure to ensure compliance with software development standards (when applicable), and (7) measurement and reporting mechanisms.

In this chapter, we focus on the management issues and the process-specific activities that enable a software organization to ensure that it does "the right things at the right time in the right way."

8.1 QUALITY CONCEPTS[1]

It has been said that no two snowflakes are alike. Certainly when we watch snow falling it is hard to imagine that snowflakes differ at all, let alone that each flake possesses a unique structure. In order to observe differences between snowflakes, we must examine the specimens closely, perhaps using a magnifying glass. In fact, the closer we look, the more differences we are able to observe.

Quote:

"People forget how fast you did a job—but they always remember how well you did it."
Howard Newton.

This phenomenon, *variation between samples,* applies to all products of human as well as natural creation. For example, if two "identical" circuit boards are examined closely enough, we may observe that the copper pathways on the boards differ slightly in geometry, placement, and thickness. In addition, the location and diameter of the holes drilled in the boards varies as well.

All engineered and manufactured parts exhibit variation. The variation between samples may not be obvious without the aid of precise equipment to measure the geometry, electrical characteristics, or other attributes of the parts. However, with sufficiently sensitive instruments, we will likely come to the conclusion that no two samples of any item are exactly alike.

Variation control is the heart of quality control. A manufacturer wants to minimize the variation among the products that are produced, even when doing something relatively simple like duplicating diskettes. Surely, this cannot be a problem—duplicat-

1 This section, written by Michael Stovsky, has been adapted from "Fundamentals of ISO 9000," a workbook developed for *Essential Software Engineering,* a video curriculum developed by R. S. Pressman & Associates, Inc. Reprinted with permission.

ing diskettes is a trivial manufacturing operation, and we can guarantee that exact duplicates of the software are always created.

Or can we? We need to ensure the tracks are placed on the diskettes within a specified tolerance so that the overwhelming majority of disk drives can read the diskettes. In addition, we need to ensure the magnetic flux for distinguishing a zero from a one is sufficient for read/write heads to detect. The disk duplication machines can, and do, wear and go out of tolerance. So even a "simple" process such as disk duplication may encounter problems due to variation between samples.

KEY POINT

Controlling variation is the key to a high-quality product. In the software context, we strive to control the variation in the process we apply, the resources we expend, and the quality attributes of the end product.

But how does this apply to software work? How might a software development organization need to control variation? From one project to another, we want to minimize the difference between the predicted resources needed to complete a project and the actual resources used, including staff, equipment, and calendar time. In general, we would like to make sure our testing program covers a known percentage of the software, from one release to another. Not only do we want to minimize the number of defects that are released to the field, we'd like to ensure that the variance in the number of bugs is also minimized from one release to another. (Our customers will likely be upset if the third release of a product has ten times as many defects as the previous release.) We would like to minimize the differences in speed and accuracy of our hotline support responses to customer problems. The list goes on and on.

8.1.1 Quality

The *American Heritage Dictionary* defines *quality* as "a characteristic or attribute of something." As an attribute of an item, quality refers to measurable characteristics—things we are able to compare to known standards such as length, color, electrical properties, and malleability. However, software, largely an intellectual entity, is more challenging to characterize than physical objects.

Nevertheless, measures of a program's characteristics do exist. These properties include cyclomatic complexity, cohesion, number of function points, lines of code, and many others, discussed in Chapters 19 and 24. When we examine an item based on its measurable characteristics, two kinds of quality may be encountered: quality of design and quality of conformance.

Quote:

"It takes less time to do a thing right than explain why you did it wrong."
Henry Wadsworth Longfellow

Quality of design refers to the characteristics that designers specify for an item. The grade of materials, tolerances, and performance specifications all contribute to the quality of design. As higher-grade materials are used, tighter tolerances and greater levels of performance are specified, the design quality of a product increases, if the product is manufactured according to specifications.

Quality of conformance is the degree to which the design specifications are followed during manufacturing. Again, the greater the degree of conformance, the higher is the level of quality of conformance.

In software development, quality of design encompasses requirements, specifications, and the design of the system. Quality of conformance is an issue focused primarily on implementation. If the implementation follows the design and the resulting system meets its requirements and performance goals, conformance quality is high.

But are quality of design and quality of conformance the only issues that software engineers must consider? Robert Glass [GLA98] argues that a more "intuitive" relationship is in order:

User satisfaction = compliant product + good quality + delivery within budget and schedule

At the bottom line, Glass contends that quality is important, but if the user isn't satisfied, nothing else really matters. DeMarco [DEM99] reinforces this view when he states: "A product's quality is a function of how much it changes the world for the better." This view of quality contends that if a software product provides substantial benefit to its end-users, they may be willing to tolerate occasional reliability or performance problems.

8.1.2 Quality Control

What is software quality control?

Variation control may be equated to quality control. But how do we achieve quality control? *Quality control* involves the series of inspections, reviews, and tests used throughout the software process to ensure each work product meets the requirements placed upon it. Quality control includes a feedback loop to the process that created the work product. The combination of measurement and feedback allows us to tune the process when the work products created fail to meet their specifications. This approach views quality control as part of the manufacturing process.

Quality control activities may be fully automated, entirely manual, or a combination of automated tools and human interaction. A key concept of quality control is that all work products have defined, measurable specifications to which we may compare the output of each process. The feedback loop is essential to minimize the defects produced.

8.1.3 Quality Assurance

WebRef
A wide variety of software quality resources can be found at **www.qualitytree.com/links/links.htm**

Quality assurance consists of the auditing and reporting functions of management. The goal of quality assurance is to provide management with the data necessary to be informed about product quality, thereby gaining insight and confidence that product quality is meeting its goals. Of course, if the data provided through quality assurance identify problems, it is management's responsibility to address the problems and apply the necessary resources to resolve quality issues.

8.1.4 Cost of Quality

The *cost of quality* includes all costs incurred in the pursuit of quality or in performing quality-related activities. Cost of quality studies are conducted to provide a baseline for the current cost of quality, identify opportunities for reducing the cost of quality, and provide a normalized basis of comparison. The basis of normalization is almost always dollars. Once we have normalized quality costs on a dollar basis, we have the necessary data to evaluate where the opportunities lie to improve our processes. Furthermore, we can evaluate the effect of changes in dollar-based terms.

What are the components of the cost of quality?

Quality costs may be divided into costs associated with prevention, appraisal, and failure. *Prevention costs* include

- quality planning
- formal technical reviews
- test equipment
- training

Appraisal costs include activities to gain insight into product condition the "first time through" each process. Examples of appraisal costs include

- in-process and interprocess inspection
- equipment calibration and maintenance
- testing

ADVICE

Don't be afraid to incur significant prevention costs. Rest assured that your investment will provide an excellent return.

Failure costs are those that would disappear if no defects appeared before shipping a product to customers. Failure costs may be subdivided into internal failure costs and external failure costs. *Internal failure costs* are incurred when we detect a defect in our product prior to shipment. Internal failure costs include

- rework
- repair
- failure mode analysis

External failure costs are associated with defects found after the product has been shipped to the customer. Examples of external failure costs are

- complaint resolution
- product return and replacement
- help line support
- warranty work

As expected, the relative costs to find and repair a defect increase dramatically as we go from prevention to detection to internal failure to external failure costs. Figure 8.1, based on data collected by Boehm [BOE81] and others, illustrates this phenomenon.

Anecdotal data reported by Kaplan, Clark, and Tang [KAP95] reinforces earlier cost statistics and is based on work at IBM's Rochester development facility:

FIGURE 8.1
Relative cost of correcting an error

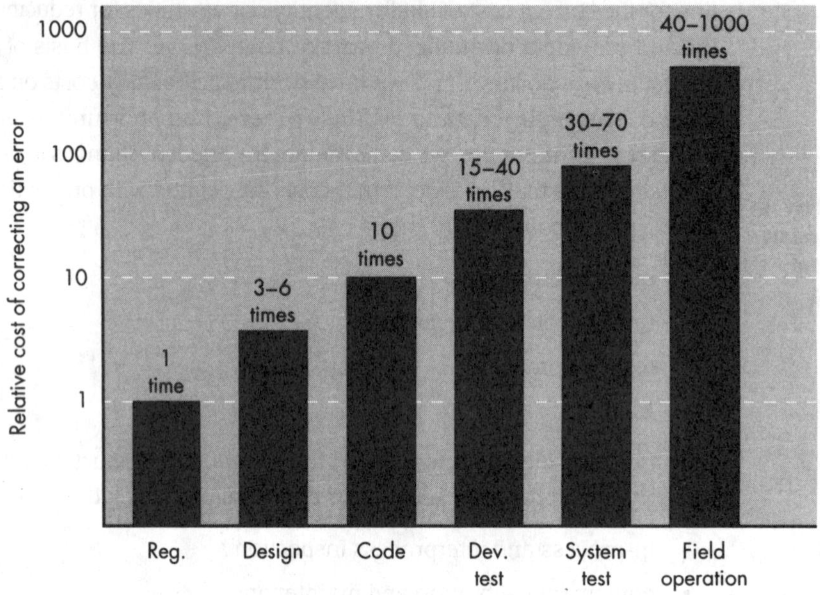

ADVICE

Testing is necessary, but it's also a very expensive way to find errors. Spend time finding errors early in the process and you may be able to significantly reduce testing and debugging costs.

A total of 7053 hours was spent inspecting 200,000 lines of code with the result that 3112 potential defects were prevented. Assuming a programmer cost of $40.00 per hour, the total cost of preventing 3112 defects was $282,120, or roughly $91.00 per defect.

Compare these numbers to the cost of defect removal once the product has been shipped to the customer. Suppose that there had been no inspections, but that programmers had been extra careful and only one defect per 1000 lines of code [significantly better than industry average] escaped into the shipped product. That would mean that 200 defects would still have to be fixed in the field. At an estimated cost of $25,000 per field fix, the cost would be $5 million, or approximately 18 times more expensive than the total cost of the defect prevention effort.

It is true that IBM produces software that is used by hundreds of thousands of customers and that their costs for field fixes may be higher than those for software organizations that build custom systems. This in no way negates the results just noted. Even if the average software organization has field fix costs that are 25 percent of IBM's (most have no idea what their costs are!), the cost savings associated with quality control and assurance activities are compelling.

8.2 THE QUALITY MOVEMENT

Today, senior managers at companies throughout the industrialized world recognize that high product quality translates to cost savings and an improved bottom line. However, this was not always the case. The quality movement began in the 1940s with the seminal work of W. Edwards Deming [DEM86] and had its first true test in Japan. Using Deming's ideas as a cornerstone, the Japanese developed a systematic

KEY POINT

TQM can be applied to computer software. The TQM approach stresses continuous process improvement.

approach to the elimination of the root causes of product defects. Throughout the 1970s and 1980s, their work migrated to the western world and was given names such as "total quality management" (TQM).[2] Although terminology differs across different companies and authors, a basic four step progression is normally encountered and forms the foundation of any good TQM program.

The first step, called *kaizen,* refers to a system of continuous process improvement. The goal of *kaizen* is to develop a process (in this case, the software process) that is visible, repeatable, and measurable.

The second step, invoked only after *kaizen* has been achieved, is called *atarimae hinshitsu.* This step examines intangibles that affect the process and works to optimize their impact on the process. For example, the software process may be affected by high staff turnover, which itself is caused by constant reorganization within a company. Maybe a stable organizational structure could do much to improve the quality of software. *Atarimae hinshitsu* would lead management to suggest changes in the way reorganization occurs.

WebRef

A wide variety of resources for continuous process improvement and TQM can be found at **deming.eng.clemson.edu/**

While the first two steps focus on the process, the next step, called *kansei* (translated as "the five senses"), concentrates on the user of the product (in this case, software). In essence, by examining the way the user applies the product *kansei* leads to improvement in the product itself and, potentially, to the process that created it.

Finally, a step called *miryokuteki hinshitsu* broadens management concern beyond the immediate product. This is a business-oriented step that looks for opportunity in related areas identified by observing the use of the product in the marketplace. In the software world, *miryokuteki hinshitsu* might be viewed as an attempt to uncover new and profitable products or applications that are an outgrowth from an existing computer-based system.

For most companies *kaizen* should be of immediate concern. Until a mature software process (Chapter 2) has been achieved, there is little point in moving to the next steps.

8.3 SOFTWARE QUALITY ASSURANCE

Even the most jaded software developers will agree that high-quality software is an important goal. But how do we define quality? A wag once said, "Every program does something right, it just may not be the thing that we want it to do."

Many definitions of software quality have been proposed in the literature. For our purposes, *software quality* is defined as

? How do we define software quality?

> Conformance to explicitly stated functional and performance requirements, explicitly documented development standards, and implicit characteristics that are expected of all professionally developed software.

---

2 See [ART92] for a comprehensive discussion of TQM and its use in a software context and [KAP95] for a discussion of the use of the Baldrige Award criteria in the software world.

There is little question that this definition could be modified or extended. In fact, a definitive definition of software quality could be debated endlessly. For the purposes of this book, the definition serves to emphasize three important points:

1. Software requirements are the foundation from which quality is measured. Lack of conformance to requirements is lack of quality.
2. Specified standards define a set of development criteria that guide the manner in which software is engineered. If the criteria are not followed, lack of quality will almost surely result.
3. A set of implicit requirements often goes unmentioned (e.g., the desire for ease of use and good maintainability). If software conforms to its explicit requirements but fails to meet implicit requirements, software quality is suspect.

8.3.1 Background Issues

Quote:

"We made too many wrong mistakes."

Yogi Berra

Quality assurance is an essential activity for any business that produces products to be used by others. Prior to the twentieth century, quality assurance was the sole responsibility of the craftsperson who built a product. The first formal quality assurance and control function was introduced at Bell Labs in 1916 and spread rapidly throughout the manufacturing world. During the 1940s, more formal approaches to quality control were suggested. These relied on measurement and continuous process improvement as key elements of quality management.

Today, every company has mechanisms to ensure quality in its products. In fact, explicit statements of a company's concern for quality have become a marketing ploy during the past few decades.

WebRef

An in-depth tutorial and wide-ranging resources for quality management can be found at **www.management.gov.**

The history of quality assurance in software development parallels the history of quality in hardware manufacturing. During the early days of computing (1950s and 1960s), quality was the sole responsibility of the programmer. Standards for quality assurance for software were introduced in military contract software development during the 1970s and have spread rapidly into software development in the commercial world [IEE94]. Extending the definition presented earlier, software quality assurance is a "planned and systematic pattern of actions" [SCH98] that are required to ensure high quality in software. The scope of quality assurance responsibility might best be characterized by paraphrasing a once-popular automobile commercial: "Quality Is Job #1." The implication for software is that many different constituencies have software quality assurance responsibility—software engineers, project managers, customers, salespeople, and the individuals who serve within an SQA group.

The SQA group serves as the customer's in-house representative. That is, the people who perform SQA must look at the software from the customer's point of view. Does the software adequately meet the quality factors noted in Chapter 19? Has software development been conducted according to pre-established standards? Have technical disciplines properly performed their roles as part of the SQA activity? The SQA group attempts to answer these and other questions to ensure that software quality is maintained.

8.3.2 SQA Activities

Software quality assurance is composed of a variety of tasks associated with two different constituencies—the software engineers who do technical work and an SQA group that has responsibility for quality assurance planning, oversight, record keeping, analysis, and reporting.

Software engineers address quality (and perform quality assurance and quality control activities) by applying solid technical methods and measures, conducting formal technical reviews, and performing well-planned software testing. Only reviews are discussed in this chapter. Technology topics are discussed in Parts Three through Five of this book.

The charter of the SQA group is to assist the software team in achieving a high-quality end product. The Software Engineering Institute [PAU93] recommends a set of SQA activities that address quality assurance planning, oversight, record keeping, analysis, and reporting. These activities are performed (or facilitated) by an independent SQA group that:

? What is the role of an SQA group?

Prepares an SQA plan for a project. The plan is developed during project planning and is reviewed by all interested parties. Quality assurance activities performed by the software engineering team and the SQA group are governed by the plan. The plan identifies

- evaluations to be performed
- audits and reviews to be performed
- standards that are applicable to the project
- procedures for error reporting and tracking
- documents to be produced by the SQA group
- amount of feedback provided to the software project team

Participates in the development of the project's software process description. The software team selects a process for the work to be performed. The SQA group reviews the process description for compliance with organizational policy, internal software standards, externally imposed standards (e.g., ISO-9001), and other parts of the software project plan.

Reviews software engineering activities to verify compliance with the defined software process. The SQA group identifies, documents, and tracks deviations from the process and verifies that corrections have been made.

Audits designated software work products to verify compliance with those defined as part of the software process. The SQA group reviews selected work products; identifies, documents, and tracks deviations; verifies that corrections have been made; and periodically reports the results of its work to the project manager.

Ensures that deviations in software work and work products are documented and handled according to a documented procedure. Deviations may be encountered in the project plan, process description, applicable standards, or technical work products.

Records any noncompliance and reports to senior management. Noncompliance items are tracked until they are resolved.

In addition to these activities, the SQA group coordinates the control and management of change (Chapter 9) and helps to collect and analyze software metrics.

8.4 SOFTWARE REVIEWS

ADVICE

Like water filters, FTRs tend to retard the "flow" of software engineering activities. Too few and the flow is "dirty." Too many and the flow slows to a trickle. Use metrics to determine which reviews work and which may not be effective. Take the ineffective ones out of the flow.

Software reviews are a "filter" for the software engineering process. That is, reviews are applied at various points during software development and serve to uncover errors and defects that can then be removed. Software reviews "purify" the software engineering activities that we have called *analysis, design,* and *coding*. Freedman and Weinberg [FRE90] discuss the need for reviews this way:

> Technical work needs reviewing for the same reason that pencils need erasers: *To err is human.* The second reason we need technical reviews is that although people are good at catching some of their own errors, large classes of errors escape the originator more easily than they escape anyone else. The review process is, therefore, the answer to the prayer of Robert Burns:
>
> *O wad some power the giftie give us*
> *to see ourselves as other see us*
>
> A review—any review—is a way of using the diversity of a group of people to:
>
> 1. Point out needed improvements in the product of a single person or team;
> 2. Confirm those parts of a product in which improvement is either not desired or not needed;
> 3. Achieve technical work of more uniform, or at least more predictable, quality than can be achieved without reviews, in order to make technical work more manageable.

Many different types of reviews can be conducted as part of software engineering. Each has its place. An informal meeting around the coffee machine is a form of review, if technical problems are discussed. A formal presentation of software design to an audience of customers, management, and technical staff is also a form of review. In this book, however, we focus on the *formal technical review,* sometimes called a *walkthrough* or an *inspection.* A formal technical review is the most effective filter from a quality assurance standpoint. Conducted by software engineers (and others) for software engineers, the FTR is an effective means for improving software quality.

8.4.1 Cost Impact of Software Defects

The *IEEE Standard Dictionary of Electrical and Electronics Terms* (IEEE Standard 100-1992) defines a *defect* as "a product anomaly." The definition for *fault* in the hardware context can be found in IEEE Standard 610.12-1990:

> (a) A defect in a hardware device or component; for example, a short circuit or broken wire. (b) An incorrect step, process, or data definition in a computer program. Note: This definition is used primarily by the fault tolerance discipline. In common usage, the terms "error" and "bug" are used to express this meaning. See also: data-sensitive fault; program-sensitive fault; equivalent faults; fault masking; intermittent fault.

Within the context of the software process, the terms *defect* and *fault* are synonymous. Both imply a quality problem that is discovered *after* the software has been released to end-users (or to another activity in the software process). In earlier chapters, we used the term *error* to depict a quality problem that is discovered by software engineers (or others) before the software is released to the end-user (or to another activity in the software process).

The primary objective of formal technical reviews is to find errors during the process so that they do not become defects after release of the software. The obvious benefit of formal technical reviews is the early discovery of errors so that they do not propagate to the next step in the software process.

KEY POINT

The primary objective of an FTR is to find errors before they are passed on to another software engineering activity or released to the customer.

A number of industry studies (by TRW, Nippon Electric, Mitre Corp., among others) indicate that design activities introduce between 50 and 65 percent of all errors (and ultimately, all defects) during the software process. However, formal review techniques have been shown to be up to 75 percent effective [JON86] in uncovering design flaws. By detecting and removing a large percentage of these errors, the review process substantially reduces the cost of subsequent steps in the development and support phases.

To illustrate the cost impact of early error detection, we consider a series of relative costs that are based on actual cost data collected for large software projects [IBM81].[3] Assume that an error uncovered during design will cost 1.0 monetary unit to correct. Relative to this cost, the same error uncovered just before testing commences will cost 6.5 units; during testing, 15 units; and after release, between 60 and 100 units.

3 Although these data are more than 20 years old, they remain applicable in a modern context.

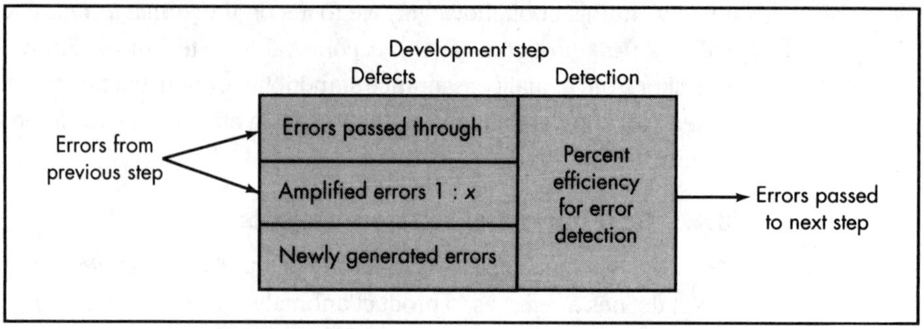

FIGURE 8.2 Defect amplification model

8.4.2 Defect Amplification and Removal

A defect amplification model [IBM81] can be used to illustrate the generation and detection of errors during the preliminary design, detail design, and coding steps of the software engineering process. The model is illustrated schematically in Figure 8.2. A box represents a software development step. During the step, errors may be inadvertently generated. Review may fail to uncover newly generated errors and errors from previous steps, resulting in some number of errors that are passed through. In some cases, errors passed through from previous steps are amplified (amplification factor, *x*) by current work. The box subdivisions represent each of these characteristics and the percent of efficiency for detecting errors, a function of the thoroughness of the review.

Quote: "Some maladies, as doctors say, at their beginning are easy to cure but difficult to recognize . . . but in the course of time when they have not at first been recognized and treated, become easy to recognize but difficult to cure." **Niccolo Machiavelli**

Figure 8.3 illustrates a hypothetical example of defect amplification for a software development process in which no reviews are conducted. Referring to the figure, each test step is assumed to uncover and correct 50 percent of all incoming errors without introducing any new errors (an optimistic assumption). Ten preliminary design defects are amplified to 94 errors before testing commences. Twelve latent errors are released to the field. Figure 8.4 considers the same conditions except that design and code reviews are conducted as part of each development step. In this case, ten initial preliminary design errors are amplified to 24 errors before testing commences. Only three latent errors exist. Recalling the relative costs associated with the discovery and correction of errors, overall cost (with and without review for our hypothetical example) can be established. The number of errors uncovered during each of the steps noted in Figures 8.3 and 8.4 is multiplied by the cost to remove an error (1.5 cost units for design, 6.5 cost units before test, 15 cost units during test, and 67 cost units after release). Using these data, the total cost for development and maintenance when reviews are conducted is 783 cost units. When no reviews are conducted, total cost is 2177 units—nearly three times more costly.

To conduct reviews, a software engineer must expend time and effort and the development organization must spend money. However, the results of the preceding example leave little doubt that we can pay now or pay much more later. Formal tech-

FIGURE 8.3
Defect amplification, no reviews

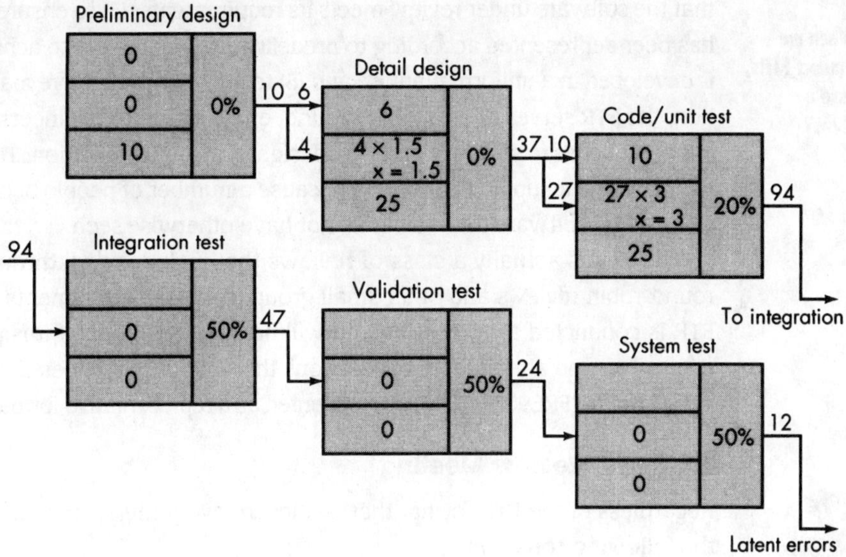

FIGURE 8.4
Defect amplification, reviews conducted

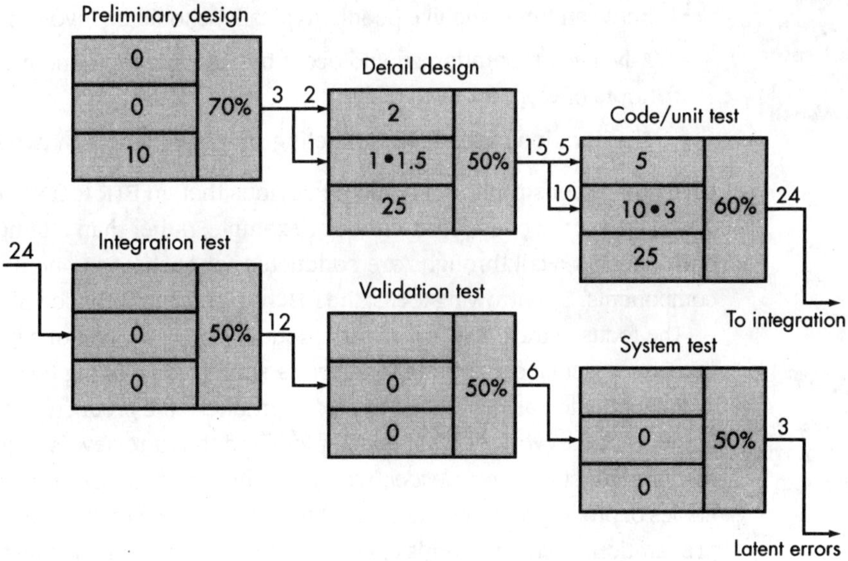

nical reviews (for design and other technical activities) provide a demonstrable cost benefit. They should be conducted.

8.5 FORMAL TECHNICAL REVIEWS

A formal technical review is a software quality assurance activity performed by software engineers (and others). The objectives of the FTR are (1) to uncover errors in function, logic, or implementation for any representation of the software; (2) to verify

When we conduct FTRs, what are our objectives?

that the software under review meets its requirements; (3) to ensure that the software has been represented according to predefined standards; (4) to achieve software that is developed in a uniform manner; and (5) to make projects more manageable. In addition, the FTR serves as a training ground, enabling junior engineers to observe different approaches to software analysis, design, and implementation. The FTR also serves to promote backup and continuity because a number of people become familiar with parts of the software that they may not have otherwise seen.

The FTR is actually a class of reviews that includes walkthroughs, inspections, round-robin reviews and other small group technical assessments of software. Each FTR is conducted as a meeting and will be successful only if it is properly planned, controlled, and attended. In the sections that follow, guidelines similar to those for a walkthrough [FRE90], [GIL93] are presented as a representative formal technical review.

8.5.1 The Review Meeting

Quote: "A meeting is too often an event where minutes are taken and hours are wasted." **author unknown**

Regardless of the FTR format that is chosen, every review meeting should abide by the following constraints:

- Between three and five people (typically) should be involved in the review.
- Advance preparation should occur but should require no more than two hours of work for each person.
- The duration of the review meeting should be less than two hours.

Given these constraints, it should be obvious that an FTR focuses on a specific (and small) part of the overall software. For example, rather than attempting to review an entire design, walkthroughs are conducted for each component or small group of components. By narrowing focus, the FTR has a higher likelihood of uncovering errors.

KEY POINT The FTR focuses on a relatively small portion of a work product.

The focus of the FTR is on a work product (e.g., a portion of a requirements specification, a detailed component design, a source code listing for a component). The individual who has developed the work product—the *producer*—informs the project leader that the work product is complete and that a review is required. The project leader contacts a *review leader,* who evaluates the product for readiness, generates copies of product materials, and distributes them to two or three reviewers for advance preparation. Each reviewer is expected to spend between one and two hours reviewing the product, making notes, and otherwise becoming familiar with the work. Concurrently, the review leader also reviews the product and establishes an agenda for the review meeting, which is typically scheduled for the next day.

WebRef The NASA SATC *Formal Inspection Guidebook* can be downloaded from **satc.gsfc.nasa.gov/fi/fipage.html**

The review meeting is attended by the review leader, all reviewers, and the producer. One of the reviewers takes on the role of the *recorder;* that is, the individual who records (in writing) all important issues raised during the review. The FTR begins with an introduction of the agenda and a brief introduction by the producer. The producer then proceeds to "walk through" the work product, explaining the material, while reviewers raise issues based on their advance preparation. When valid problems or errors are discovered, the recorder notes each.

At the end of the review, all attendees of the FTR must decide whether to (1) accept the product without further modification, (2) reject the product due to severe errors (once corrected, another review must be performed), or (3) accept the product provisionally (minor errors have been encountered and must be corrected, but no additional review will be required). The decision made, all FTR attendees complete a sign-off, indicating their participation in the review and their concurrence with the review team's findings.

8.5.2 Review Reporting and Record Keeping

During the FTR, a reviewer (the recorder) actively records all issues that have been raised. These are summarized at the end of the review meeting and a review issues list is produced. In addition, a formal technical review summary report is completed. A *review summary report* answers three questions:

1. What was reviewed?
2. Who reviewed it?
3. What were the findings and conclusions?

Technical Review Summary Report and Issues List

The review summary report is a single page form (with possible attachments). It becomes part of the project historical record and may be distributed to the project leader and other interested parties.

The *review issues list* serves two purposes: (1) to identify problem areas within the product and (2) to serve as an action item checklist that guides the producer as corrections are made. An issues list is normally attached to the summary report.

It is important to establish a follow-up procedure to ensure that items on the issues list have been properly corrected. Unless this is done, it is possible that issues raised can "fall between the cracks." One approach is to assign the responsibility for follow-up to the review leader.

8.5.3 Review Guidelines

Guidelines for the conduct of formal technical reviews must be established in advance, distributed to all reviewers, agreed upon, and then followed. A review that is uncontrolled can often be worse that no review at all. The following represents a minimum set of guidelines for formal technical reviews:

ADVICE

Don't point out errors harshly. One way to be gentle is to ask a question that enables the producer to discover his or her own error.

1. *Review the product, not the producer.* An FTR involves people and egos. Conducted properly, the FTR should leave all participants with a warm feeling of accomplishment. Conducted improperly, the FTR can take on the aura of an inquisition. Errors should be pointed out gently; the tone of the meeting should be loose and constructive; the intent should not be to embarrass or belittle. The review leader should conduct the review meeting to ensure that the proper tone and attitude are maintained and should immediately halt a review that has gotten out of control.

2. *Set an agenda and maintain it.* One of the key maladies of meetings of all types is *drift.* An FTR must be kept on track and on schedule. The review leader is chartered with the responsibility for maintaining the meeting schedule and should not be afraid to nudge people when drift sets in.

3. *Limit debate and rebuttal.* When an issue is raised by a reviewer, there may not be universal agreement on its impact. Rather than spending time debating the question, the issue should be recorded for further discussion off-line.

Quote:
"It is one of the most beautiful compensations of life, that no man can sincerely try to help another without helping himself."
Ralph Waldo Emerson

4. *Enunciate problem areas, but don't attempt to solve every problem noted.* A review is not a problem-solving session. The solution of a problem can often be accomplished by the producer alone or with the help of only one other individual. Problem solving should be postponed until after the review meeting.

5. *Take written notes.* It is sometimes a good idea for the recorder to make notes on a wall board, so that wording and priorities can be assessed by other reviewers as information is recorded.

6. *Limit the number of participants and insist upon advance preparation.* Two heads are better than one, but 14 are not necessarily better than 4. Keep the number of people involved to the necessary minimum. However, all review team members must prepare in advance. Written comments should be solicited by the review leader (providing an indication that the reviewer has reviewed the material).

FTR Checklists

7. *Develop a checklist for each product that is likely to be reviewed.* A checklist helps the review leader to structure the FTR meeting and helps each reviewer to focus on important issues. Checklists should be developed for analysis, design, code, and even test documents.

8. *Allocate resources and schedule time for FTRs.* For reviews to be effective, they should be scheduled as a task during the software engineering process. In addition, time should be scheduled for the inevitable modifications that will occur as the result of an FTR.

9. *Conduct meaningful training for all reviewers.* To be effective all review participants should receive some formal training. The training should stress both process-related issues and the human psychological side of reviews. Freedman and Weinberg [FRE90] estimate a one-month learning curve for every 20 people who are to participate effectively in reviews.

10. *Review your early reviews.* Debriefing can be beneficial in uncovering problems with the review process itself. The very first product to be reviewed should be the review guidelines themselves.

Because many variables (e.g., number of participants, type of work products, timing and length, specific review approach) have an impact on a successful review, a software organization should experiment to determine what approach works best in a local context. Porter and his colleagues [POR95] provide excellent guidance for this type of experimentation.

8.6 FORMAL APPROACHES TO SQA

In the preceding sections, we have argued that software quality is everyone's job; that it can be achieved through competent analysis, design, coding, and testing, as well as through the application of formal technical reviews, a multitiered testing strategy, better control of software work products and the changes made to them, and the application of accepted software engineering standards. In addition, quality can be defined in terms of a broad array of quality factors and measured (indirectly) using a variety of indices and metrics.

XRef
Techniques for formal specification of software are considered in Chapter 25. Correctness proofs are considered in Chapter 26.

Over the past two decades, a small, but vocal, segment of the software engineering community has argued that a more formal approach to software quality assurance is required. It can be argued that a computer program is a mathematical object [SOM96]. A rigorous syntax and semantics can be defined for every programming language, and work is underway to develop a similarly rigorous approach to the specification of software requirements. If the requirements model (specification) and the programming language can be represented in a rigorous manner, it should be possible to apply mathematic proof of correctness to demonstrate that a program conforms exactly to its specifications.

Attempts to prove programs correct are not new. Dijkstra [DIJ76] and Linger, Mills, and Witt [LIN79], among others, advocated proofs of program correctness and tied these to the use of structured programming concepts (Chapter 16).

8.7 STATISTICAL SOFTWARE QUALITY ASSURANCE

Statistical quality assurance reflects a growing trend throughout industry to become more quantitative about quality. For software, statistical quality assurance implies the following steps:

? What steps are required to perform statistical SQA?

1. Information about software defects is collected and categorized.
2. An attempt is made to trace each defect to its underlying cause (e.g., nonconformance to specifications, design error, violation of standards, poor communication with the customer).
3. Using the Pareto principle (80 percent of the defects can be traced to 20 percent of all possible causes), isolate the 20 percent (the "vital few").
4. Once the vital few causes have been identified, move to correct the problems that have caused the defects.

Quote:

"20 percent of the code has 80 percent of the defects. Find them, fix them!"

Lowell Arthur

This relatively simple concept represents an important step towards the creation of an adaptive software engineering process in which changes are made to improve those elements of the process that introduce error.

To illustrate this, assume that a software engineering organization collects information on defects for a period of one year. Some of the defects are uncovered as software is being developed. Others are encountered after the software has been released to its end-users. Although hundreds of different errors are uncovered, all can be tracked to one (or more) of the following causes:

WebRef

The Chinese Association for Software Quality presents one of the most comprehensive quality Web sites at **www.casq.org**

- incomplete or erroneous specifications (IES)
- misinterpretation of customer communication (MCC)
- intentional deviation from specifications (IDS)
- violation of programming standards (VPS)
- error in data representation (EDR)
- inconsistent component interface (ICI)
- error in design logic (EDL)
- incomplete or erroneous testing (IET)
- inaccurate or incomplete documentation (IID)
- error in programming language translation of design (PLT)
- ambiguous or inconsistent human/computer interface (HCI)
- miscellaneous (MIS)

To apply statistical SQA, Table 8.1 is built. The table indicates that IES, MCC, and EDR are the *vital few* causes that account for 53 percent of all errors. It should be noted, however, that IES, EDR, PLT, and EDL would be selected as the vital few causes if only serious errors are considered. Once the vital few causes are determined, the software engineering organization can begin corrective action. For example, to correct MCC, the software developer might implement facilitated application specification techniques (Chapter 11) to improve the quality of customer communication and specifications. To improve EDR, the developer might acquire CASE tools for data modeling and perform more stringent data design reviews.

It is important to note that corrective action focuses primarily on the vital few. As the vital few causes are corrected, new candidates pop to the top of the stack.

Statistical quality assurance techniques for software have been shown to provide substantial quality improvement [ART97]. In some cases, software organizations have achieved a 50 percent reduction per year in defects after applying these techniques.

In conjunction with the collection of defect information, software developers can calculate an *error index* (EI) for each major step in the software process [IEE94]. After analysis, design, coding, testing, and release, the following data are gathered:

E_i = the total number of errors uncovered during the ith step in the software engineering process

TABLE 8.1 DATA COLLECTION FOR STATISTICAL SQA

	Total		Serious		Moderate		Minor	
Error	**No.**	**%**	**No.**	**%**	**No.**	**%**	**No.**	**%**
IES	205	22%	34	27%	68	18%	103	24%
MCC	156	17%	12	9%	68	18%	76	17%
IDS	48	5%	1	1%	24	6%	23	5%
VPS	25	3%	0	0%	15	4%	10	2%
EDR	130	14%	26	20%	68	18%	36	8%
ICI	58	6%	9	7%	18	5%	31	7%
EDL	45	5%	14	11%	12	3%	19	4%
IET	95	10%	12	9%	35	9%	48	11%
IID	36	4%	2	2%	20	5%	14	3%
PLT	60	6%	15	12%	19	5%	26	6%
HCI	28	3%	3	2%	17	4%	8	2%
MIS	56	6%	0	0%	15	4%	41	9%
Totals	942	100%	128	100%	379	100%	435	100%

S_i = the number of serious errors
M_i = the number of moderate errors
T_i = the number of minor errors
PS = size of the product (LOC, design statements, pages of documentation) at the ith step
w_s, w_m, w_t = weighting factors for serious, moderate, and trivial errors, where recommended values are $w_s = 10$, $w_m = 3$, $w_t = 1$. The weighting factors for each phase should become larger as development progresses. This rewards an organization that finds errors early.

At each step in the software process, a *phase index*, PI_i, is computed:

$$PI_i = w_s (S_i/E_i) + w_m (M_i/E_i) + w_t (T_i/E_i)$$

The *error index* is computed by calculating the cumulative effect on each PI_i, weighting errors encountered later in the software engineering process more heavily than those encountered earlier:

$$EI = \Sigma(i \times PI_i)/PS$$
$$= (PI_1 + 2PI_2 + 3PI_3 + \ldots iPI_i)/PS$$

The error index can be used in conjunction with information collected in Table 8.1 to develop an overall indication of improvement in software quality.

The application of the statistical SQA and the Pareto principle can be summarized in a single sentence: *Spend your time focusing on things that really matter, but first be sure that you understand what really matters!*

A comprehensive discussion of statistical SQA is beyond the scope of this book. Interested readers should see [SCH98], [KAP95], or [KAN95].

8.8 SOFTWARE RELIABILITY

There is no doubt that the reliability of a computer program is an important element of its overall quality. If a program repeatedly and frequently fails to perform, it matters little whether other software quality factors are acceptable.

WebRef
The Reliability Analysis Center provides much useful information on reliability, maintainability, supportability, and quality at **rac.iitri.org**

Software reliability, unlike many other quality factors, can be measured directed and estimated using historical and developmental data. *Software reliability* is defined in statistical terms as "the probability of failure-free operation of a computer program in a specified environment for a specified time" [MUS87]. To illustrate, program X is estimated to have a reliability of 0.96 over eight elapsed processing hours. In other words, if program X were to be executed 100 times and require eight hours of elapsed processing time (execution time), it is likely to operate correctly (without failure) 96 times out of 100.

Whenever software reliability is discussed, a pivotal question arises: What is meant by the term *failure?* In the context of any discussion of software quality and reliability, failure is nonconformance to software requirements. Yet, even within this definition, there are gradations. Failures can be only annoying or catastrophic. One failure can be corrected within seconds while another requires weeks or even months to correct. Complicating the issue even further, the correction of one failure may in fact result in the introduction of other errors that ultimately result in other failures.

8.8.1 Measures of Reliability and Availability

KEY POINT
Software reliability problems can almost always be traced to errors in design or implementation.

Early work in software reliability attempted to extrapolate the mathematics of hardware reliability theory (e.g., [ALV64]) to the prediction of software reliability. Most hardware-related reliability models are predicated on failure due to wear rather than failure due to design defects. In hardware, failures due to physical wear (e.g., the effects of temperature, corrosion, shock) are more likely than a design-related failure. Unfortunately, the opposite is true for software. In fact, all software failures can be traced to design or implementation problems; wear (see Chapter 1) does not enter into the picture.

There has been debate over the relationship between key concepts in hardware reliability and their applicability to software (e.g., [LIT89], [ROO90]). Although an irrefutable link has yet be be established, it is worthwhile to consider a few simple concepts that apply to both system elements.

If we consider a computer-based system, a simple measure of reliability is *mean-time-between-failure* (MTBF), where

$$\text{MTBF} = \text{MTTF} + \text{MTTR}$$

The acronyms MTTF and MTTR are mean-time-to-failure and mean-time-to-repair, respectively.

Why is MTBF a more useful metric than defects/KLOC?

Many researchers argue that MTBF is a far more useful measure than defects/KLOC or defects/FP. Stated simply, an end-user is concerned with failures, not with the total error count. Because each error contained within a program does not have the same failure rate, the total error count provides little indication of the reliability of a system. For example, consider a program that has been in operation for 14 months. Many errors in this program may remain undetected for decades before they are discovered. The MTBF of such obscure errors might be 50 or even 100 years. Other errors, as yet undiscovered, might have a failure rate of 18 or 24 months. Even if every one of the first category of errors (those with long MTBF) is removed, the impact on software reliability is negligible.

In addition to a reliability measure, we must develop a measure of availability. *Software availability* is the probability that a program is operating according to requirements at a given point in time and is defined as

$$\text{Availability} = [\text{MTTF}/(\text{MTTF} + \text{MTTR})] \times 100\%$$

The MTBF reliability measure is equally sensitive to MTTF and MTTR. The availability measure is somewhat more sensitive to MTTR, an indirect measure of the maintainability of software.

8.8.2 Software Safety

Leveson [LEV86] discusses the impact of software in safety critical systems when she writes:

> Before software was used in safety critical systems, they were often controlled by conventional (nonprogrammable) mechanical and electronic devices. System safety techniques are designed to cope with random failures in these [nonprogrammable] systems. Human design errors are not considered since it is assumed that all faults caused by human errors can be avoided completely or removed prior to delivery and operation.

Quote:

"I cannot imagine any condition which would cause this ship to founder. Modern shipbuilding has gone beyond that."

E.I. Smith, captain of the Titanic

When software is used as part of the control system, complexity can increase by an order of magnitude or more. Subtle design faults induced by human error—something that can be uncovered and eliminated in hardware-based conventional control—become much more difficult to uncover when software is used.

Software safety is a software quality assurance activity that focuses on the identification and assessment of potential hazards that may affect software negatively and cause an entire system to fail. If hazards can be identified early in the software engineering process, software design features can be specified that will either eliminate or control potential hazards.

A modeling and analysis process is conducted as part of software safety. Initially, hazards are identified and categorized by criticality and risk. For example, some of the hazards associated with a computer-based cruise control for an automobile might be

- causes uncontrolled acceleration that cannot be stopped
- does not respond to depression of brake pedal (by turning off)

- does not engage when switch is activated
- slowly loses or gains speed

WebRef
Worthwhile papers on software safety (and a detailed glossary) can be found at **www.rstcorp.com/hotlist/topics-safety.html**

Once these system-level hazards are identified, analysis techniques are used to assign severity and probability of occurrence.[4] To be effective, software must be analyzed in the context of the entire system. For example, a subtle user input error (people are system components) may be magnified by a software fault to produce control data that improperly positions a mechanical device. If a set of external environmental conditions are met (and only if they are met), the improper position of the mechanical device will cause a disastrous failure. Analysis techniques such as *fault tree analysis* [VES81], *real-time logic* [JAN86], or *petri net models* [LEV87] can be used to predict the chain of events that can cause hazards and the probability that each of the events will occur to create the chain.

Once hazards are identified and analyzed, safety-related requirements can be specified for the software. That is, the specification can contain a list of undesirable events and the desired system responses to these events. The role of software in managing undesirable events is then indicated.

? What is the difference between software reliability and software safety?

Although software reliability and software safety are closely related to one another, it is important to understand the subtle difference between them. Software reliability uses statistical analysis to determine the likelihood that a software failure will occur. However, the occurrence of a failure does not necessarily result in a hazard or mishap. Software safety examines the ways in which failures result in conditions that can lead to a mishap. That is, failures are not considered in a vacuum, but are evaluated in the context of an entire computer-based system.

A comprehensive discussion of software safety is beyond the scope of this book. Those readers with further interest should refer to Leveson's [LEV95] book on the subject.

8.9 MISTAKE-PROOFING FOR SOFTWARE

If William Shakespeare had commented on the modern software engineer's condition, he might have written: "To err is human, to find the error quickly and correct it is divine." In the 1960s, a Japanese industrial engineer, Shigeo Shingo [SHI86], working at Toyota, developed a quality assurance technique that led to the prevention and/or early correction of errors in the manufacturing process. Called *poka-yoke* (mistake-proofing), Shingo's concept makes use of *poka-yoke* devices—mechanisms that lead to (1) the prevention of a potential quality problem before it occurs or (2) the rapid detection of quality problems if they are introduced. We encounter *poka-yoke* devices in our everyday lives (even if we are unaware of the concept). For exam-

4 This approach is analogous to the risk analysis approach described for software project management in Chapter 6. The primary difference is the emphasis on technology issues as opposed to project-related topics.

ple, the ignition switch for an automobile will not work if an automatic transmission is in gear (a *prevention device*); an auto's warning beep will sound if the seat belts are not buckled (a *detection device*).

An effective *poka-yoke* device exhibits a set of common characteristics:

WebRef
A comprehensive collection of *poka-yoke* resources can be obtained at **www.campbell.berry.edu/faculty/jgrout/pokayoke.shtml**

- **It is simple and cheap.** If a device is too complicated or expensive, it will not be cost effective.
- **It is part of the process.** That is, the *poka-yoke* device is integrated into an engineering activity.
- **It is located near the process task where the mistakes occur.** Thus, it provides rapid feedback and error correction.

Although *poka-yoke* was originally developed for use in "zero quality control" [SHI86] for manufactured hardware, it can be adapted for use in software engineering. To illustrate, we consider the following problem [ROB97]:

A software products company sells application software to an international market. The pull-down menus and associated mnemonics provided with each application must reflect the local language. For example, the English language menu item for "Close" has the mnemonic "C" associated with it. When the application is sold in a French-speaking country, the same menu item is "Fermer" with the mnemonic "F." To implement the appropriate menu entry for each locale, a "localizer" (a person conversant in the local language and terminology) translates the menus accordingly. The problem is to ensure that (1) each menu entry (there can be hundreds) conforms to appropriate standards and that there are no conflicts, regardless of the language that is used.

The use of *poka-yoke* for testing various application menus implemented in different languages as just described is discussed in a paper by Harry Robinson [ROB97]:[5]

We first decided to break the menu testing problem down into parts that we could solve. Our first advance on the problem was to understand that there were two separate aspects to the message catalogs. There was the content aspect: the simple text translations, such as changing "Close" to "Fermer." Since the test team was not fluent in the 11 target languages, we had to leave this aspect to the language experts.

The second aspect of the message catalogs was the structure, the syntax rules that a properly constructed target catalog must obey. Unlike content, it would be possible for the test team to verify the structural aspects of the catalogs.

As an example of what is meant by structure, consider the labels and mnemonics of an application menu. A menu is made up of labels and associated mnemonics. Each menu, regardless of its contents or its locale, must obey the following rules listed in the Motif Style Guide:

- Each mnemonic must be contained in its associated label
- Each mnemonic must be unique within the menu

5 The paragraphs that follow have been excerpted (with minor editing) from [ROB97] with the permission of the author.

- Each mnemonic must be a single character
- Each mnemonic must be in ASCII

These rules are invariant across locales, and can be used to verify that a menu is constructed correctly in the target locale.

There were several possibilities for how to mistake-proof the menu mnemonics:

Prevention device. We could write a program to generate mnemonics automatically, given a list of the labels in each menu. This approach would prevent mistakes, but the problem of choosing a good mnemonic is difficult and the effort required to write the program would not be justified by the benefit gained.

Prevention device. We could write a program that would prevent the localizer from choosing mnemonics that did not meet the criteria. This approach would also prevent mistakes, but the benefit gained would be minimal; incorrect mnemonics are easy enough to detect and correct after they occur.

Detection device. We could provide a program to verify that the chosen menu labels and mnemonics meet the criteria above. Our localizers could run the programs on their translated message catalogs before sending the catalogs to us. This approach would provide very quick feedback on mistakes, and it is likely as a future step.

Detection device. We could write a program to verify the menu labels and mnemonics, and run the program on message catalogs after they are returned to us by the localizers. This approach is the path we are currently taking. It is not as efficient as some of the above methods, and it can require communication back and forth with the localizers, but the detected errors are still easy to correct at this point.

Several small poka-yoke scripts were used as poka-yoke devices to validate the structural aspects of the menus. A small poka-yoke script would read the table, retrieve the mnemonics and labels from the message catalog, and compare the retrieved strings against the established criteria noted above.

The poka-yoke scripts were small (roughly 100 lines), easy to write (some were written in under an hour) and easy to run. We ran our poka-yoke scripts against 16 applications in the default English locale plus 11 foreign locales. Each locale contained 100 menus, for a total of 1200 menus. The poka-yoke devices found 311 mistakes in menus and mnemonics. Few of the problems we uncovered were earth-shattering, but in total they would have amounted to a large annoyance in testing and running our localized applications.

This example depicts a *poka-yoke* device that has been integrated into software engineering testing activity. The *poka-yoke* technique can be applied at the design, code, and testing levels and provides an effective quality assurance filter.

8.10 THE ISO 9000 QUALITY STANDARDS[6]

A *quality assurance system* may be defined as the organizational structure, responsibilities, procedures, processes, and resources for implementing quality management

6 This section, written by Michael Stovsky, has been adapted from "Fundamentals of ISO 9000" and "ISO 9001 Standard," workbooks developed for *Essential Software Engineering,* a video curriculum developed by R. S. Pressman & Associates, Inc. Reprinted with permission.

[ANS87]. Quality assurance systems are created to help organizations ensure their products and services satisfy customer expectations by meeting their specifications. These systems cover a wide variety of activities encompassing a product's entire life cycle including planning, controlling, measuring, testing and reporting, and improving quality levels throughout the development and manufacturing process. ISO 9000 describes quality assurance elements in generic terms that can be applied to any business regardless of the products or services offered.

WebRef
Extensive links to ISO 9000/9001 resources can be found at **www.tantara.ab.ca/iso_list.htm**

The ISO 9000 standards have been adopted by many countries including all members of the European Community, Canada, Mexico, the United States, Australia, New Zealand, and the Pacific Rim. Countries in Latin and South America have also shown interest in the standards.

After adopting the standards, a country typically permits only ISO registered companies to supply goods and services to government agencies and public utilities. Telecommunication equipment and medical devices are examples of product categories that must be supplied by ISO registered companies. In turn, manufacturers of these products often require their suppliers to become registered. Private companies such as automobile and computer manufacturers frequently require their suppliers to be ISO registered as well.

To become registered to one of the quality assurance system models contained in ISO 9000, a company's quality system and operations are scrutinized by third party auditors for compliance to the standard and for effective operation. Upon successful registration, a company is issued a certificate from a registration body represented by the auditors. Semi-annual surveillance audits ensure continued compliance to the standard.

8.10.1 The ISO Approach to Quality Assurance Systems

The ISO 9000 quality assurance models treat an enterprise as a network of interconnected processes. For a quality system to be ISO compliant, these processes must address the areas identified in the standard and must be documented and practiced as described.

KEY POINT
ISO 9000 describes what must be done to be compliant, but it does not describe how it must be done.

ISO 9000 describes the elements of a quality assurance system in general terms. These elements include the organizational structure, procedures, processes, and resources needed to implement quality planning, quality control, quality assurance, and quality improvement. However, ISO 9000 does not describe how an organization should implement these quality system elements. Consequently, the challenge lies in designing and implementing a quality assurance system that meets the standard and fits the company's products, services, and culture.

8.10.2 The ISO 9001 Standard

ISO 9001 is the quality assurance standard that applies to software engineering. The standard contains 20 requirements that must be present for an effective quality assurance system. Because the ISO 9001 standard is applicable to all engineering disciplines, a special set of ISO guidelines (ISO 9000-3) have been developed to help interpret the standard for use in the software process.

ISO 9000 for Software

The requirements delineated by ISO 9001 address topics such as management responsibility, quality system, contract review, design control, document and data control, product identification and traceability, process control, inspection and testing, corrective and preventive action, control of quality records, internal quality audits, training, servicing, and statistical techniques. In order for a software organization to become registered to ISO 9001, it must establish policies and procedures to address each of the requirements just noted (and others) and then be able to demonstrate that these policies and procedures are being followed. For further information on ISO 9001, the interested reader should see [HOY98], [SCH97], or [SCH94].

8.11 THE SQA PLAN

The *SQA Plan* provides a road map for instituting software quality assurance. Developed by the SQA group, the plan serves as a template for SQA activities that are instituted for each software project.

The SQA plan

A standard for SQA plans has been recommended by the IEEE [IEE94]. Initial sections describe the purpose and scope of the document and indicate those software process activities that are covered by quality assurance. All documents noted in the *SQA Plan* are listed and all applicable standards are noted. The management section of the plan describes SQA's place in the organizational structure, SQA tasks and activities and their placement throughout the software process, and the organizational roles and responsibilities relative to product quality.

The documentation section describes (by reference) each of the work products produced as part of the software process. These include

- project documents (e.g., project plan)
- models (e.g., ERDs, class hierarchies)
- technical documents (e.g., specifications, test plans)
- user documents (e.g., help files)

In addition, this section defines the minimum set of work products that are acceptable to achieve high quality.

The standards, practices, and conventions section lists all applicable standards and practices that are applied during the software process (e.g., document standards, coding standards, and review guidelines). In addition, all project, process, and (in some instances) product metrics that are to be collected as part of software engineering work are listed.

The reviews and audits section of the plan identifies the reviews and audits to be conducted by the software engineering team, the SQA group, and the customer. It provides an overview of the approach for each review and audit.

The test section references the *Software Test Plan and Procedure* (Chapter 18). It also defines test record-keeping requirements. Problem reporting and corrective action defines procedures for reporting, tracking, and resolving errors and defects, and identifies the organizational responsibilities for these activities.

The remainder of the *SQA Plan* identifies the tools and methods that support SQA activities and tasks; references software configuration management procedures for controlling change; defines a contract management approach; establishes methods for assembling, safeguarding, and maintaining all records; identifies training required to meet the needs of the plan; and defines methods for identifying, assessing, monitoring, and controlling risk.

8.12 SUMMARY

Software quality assurance is an umbrella activity that is applied at each step in the software process. SQA encompasses procedures for the effective application of methods and tools, formal technical reviews, testing strategies and techniques, *poka-yoke* devices, procedures for change control, procedures for assuring compliance to standards, and measurement and reporting mechanisms.

SQA is complicated by the complex nature of software quality—an attribute of computer programs that is defined as "conformance to explicitly and implicitly specified requirements." But when considered more generally, software quality encompasses many different product and process factors and related metrics.

Software reviews are one of the most important SQA activities. Reviews serve as filters throughout all software engineering activities, removing errors while they are relatively inexpensive to find and correct. The formal technical review is a stylized meeting that has been shown to be extremely effective in uncovering errors.

To properly conduct software quality assurance, data about the software engineering process should be collected, evaluated, and disseminated. Statistical SQA helps to improve the quality of the product and the software process itself. Software reliability models extend measurements, enabling collected defect data to be extrapolated into projected failure rates and reliability predictions.

In summary, we recall the words of Dunn and Ullman [DUN82]: "Software quality assurance is the mapping of the managerial precepts and design disciplines of quality assurance onto the applicable managerial and technological space of software engineering." The ability to ensure quality is the measure of a mature engineering discipline. When the mapping is successfully accomplished, mature software engineering is the result.

REFERENCES

[ALV64] Alvin, W.H. von (ed.), *Reliability Engineering,* Prentice-Hall, 1964.

[ANS87] ANSI/ASQC A3-1987, Quality Systems Terminology, 1987.

[ART92] Arthur, L.J., *Improving Software Quality: An Insider's Guide to TQM,* Wiley, 1992.

[ART97] Arthur, L.J., "Quantum Improvements in Software System Quality, *CACM,* vol. 40, no. 6, June 1997, pp. 47–52.

[BOE81] Boehm, B., *Software Engineering Economics,* Prentice-Hall, 1981.

[CRO79] Crosby, P., *Quality Is Free,* McGraw-Hill, 1979.

[DEM86] Deming, W.E., *Out of the Crisis,* MIT Press, 1986.

[DEM99] DeMarco, T., "Management Can Make Quality (Im)possible," *Cutter IT Summit,* Boston, April 1999.

[DIJ76] Dijkstra, E., *A Discipline of Programming,* Prentice-Hall, 1976.

[DUN82] Dunn, R. and R. Ullman, *Quality Assurance for Computer Software,* McGraw-Hill, 1982.

[FRE90] Freedman, D.P. and G.M. Weinberg, *Handbook of Walkthroughs, Inspections and Technical Reviews,* 3rd ed., Dorset House, 1990.

[GIL93] Gilb, T. and D. Graham, *Software Inspections,* Addison-Wesley, 1993.

[GLA98] Glass, R., "Defining Quality Intuitively," *IEEE Software,* May 1998, pp. 103–104, 107.

[HOY98] Hoyle, D., *ISO 9000 Quality Systems Development Handbook: A Systems Engineering Approach,* Butterworth-Heinemann, 1998.

[IBM81] "Implementing Software Inspections," course notes, IBM Systems Sciences Institute, IBM Corporation, 1981.

IEE94] *Software Engineering Standards,* 1994 ed., IEEE Computer Society, 1994.

[JAN86] Jahanian, F. and A.K. Mok, "Safety Analysis of Timing Properties of Real-Time Systems", *IEEE Trans. Software Engineering,* vol. SE-12, no. 9, September 1986, pp. 890–904.

[JON86] Jones, T.C., *Programming Productivity,* McGraw-Hill, 1986.

[KAN95] Kan, S.H., *Metrics and Models in Software Quality Engineering,* Addison-Wesley, 1995.

[KAP95] Kaplan, C., R. Clark, and V. Tang, *Secrets of Software Quality: 40 Innovations from IBM,* McGraw-Hill, 1995.

[LEV86] Leveson, N.G., "Software Safety: Why, What, and How," *ACM Computing Surveys,* vol. 18, no. 2, June 1986, pp. 125–163.

[LEV87] Leveson, N.G. and J.L. Stolzy, "Safety Analysis Using Petri Nets, *IEEE Trans. Software Engineering,* vol. SE-13, no. 3, March 1987, pp. 386–397.

[LEV95] Leveson, N.G., *Safeware: System Safety And Computers,* Addison-Wesley, 1995.

[LIN79] Linger, R., H. Mills, and B. Witt, *Structured Programming,* Addison-Wesley, 1979.

[LIT89] Littlewood, B., "Forecasting Software Reliability," in *Software Reliability: Modeling and Identification,* (S. Bittanti, ed.), Springer-Verlag, 1989, pp. 141–209.

[MUS87] Musa, J.D., A. Iannino, and K. Okumoto, *Engineering and Managing Software with Reliability Measures,* McGraw-Hill, 1987.

[POR95] Porter, A., H. Siy, C.A. Toman, and L.G. Votta, "An Experiment to Assess the Cost-Benefits of Code Inspections in Large Scale Software Development," Proc. *Third ACM SIGSOFT Symposium on the Foundations of Software Engineering,* Washington, D.C., October 1996, ACM Press, pp. 92–103.

[ROB97] Robinson, H., "Using Poka-Yoke Techniques for Early Error Detection," *Proc. Sixth International Conference on Software Testing Analysis and Review* (STAR'97), 1997, pp. 119–142.

[ROO90] Rook, J., *Software Reliability Handbook,* Elsevier, 1990.

[SCH98] Schulmeyer, G.C. and J.I. McManus (eds.), *Handbook of Software Quality Assurance,* 3rd ed., Prentice-Hall, 1998.

[SCH94] Schmauch, C.H., *ISO 9000 for Software Developers,* ASQC Quality Press, 1994.

[SCH97] Schoonmaker, S.J., *ISO 9001 for Engineers and Designers,* McGraw-Hill, 1997.

[SHI86] Shigeo Shingo, *Zero Quality Control: Source Inspection and the Poka-yoke System,* Productivity Press, 1986.

[SOM96] Somerville, I., *Software Engineering,* 5th ed., Addison-Wesley, 1996.

[VES81] Veseley, W.E., et al., *Fault Tree Handbook,* U.S. Nuclear Regulatory Commission, NUREG-0492, January 1981.

PROBLEMS AND POINTS TO PONDER

8.1. Early in this chapter we noted that "variation control is the heart of quality control." Since every program that is created is different from every other program, what are the variations that we look for and how do we control them?

8.2. Is it possible to assess the quality of software if the customer keeps changing what it is supposed to do?

8.3. Quality and reliability are related concepts but are fundamentally different in a number of ways. Discuss them.

8.4. Can a program be correct and still not be reliable? Explain.

8.5. Can a program be correct and still not exhibit good quality? Explain.

8.6. Why is there often tension between a software engineering group and an independent software quality assurance group? Is this healthy?

8.7. You have been given the responsibility for improving the quality of software across your organization. What is the first thing that you should do? What's next?

8.8. Besides counting errors, are there other countable characteristics of software that imply quality? What are they and can they be measured directly?

8.9. A formal technical review is effective only if everyone has prepared in advance. How do you recognize a review participant who has not prepared? What do you do if you're the review leader?

8.10. Some people argue that an FTR should assess programming style as well as correctness. Is this a good idea? Why?

8.11. Review Table 8.1 and select four vital few causes of serious and moderate errors. Suggest corrective actions using information presented in other chapters.

8.12. An organization uses a five-step software engineering process in which errors are found according to the following percentage distribution:

Step	Percentage of errors found
1	20%
2	15%
3	15%
4	40%
5	10%

Using Table 8.1 information and this percentage distribution, compute the overall defect index for the organization. Assume PS = 100,000.

8.13. Research the literature on software reliability and write a paper that describes one software reliability model. Be sure to provide an example.

8.14. The MTBF concept for software is open to criticism. Can you think of a few reasons why?

8.15. Consider two safety critical systems that are controlled by computer. List at least three hazards for each that can be directly linked to software failures.

8.16. Using Web and print resources, develop a 20 minute tutorial on *poka-yoke* and present it to your class.

8.17. Suggest a few *poka-yoke* devices that might be used to detect and/or prevent errors that are commonly encountered prior to "sending" an e-mail message.

8.18. Acquire a copy of ISO 9001 and ISO 9000-3. Prepare a presentation that discusses three ISO 9001 requirements and how they apply in a software context.

FURTHER READINGS AND INFORMATION SOURCES

Books by Moriguchi (*Software Excellence: A Total Quality Management Guide,* Productivity Press, 1997) and Horch (*Practical Guide to Software Quality Management,* Artech Publishing, 1996) are excellent management-level presentations on the benefits of formal quality assurance programs for computer software. Books by Deming [DEM86] and Crosby [CRO79] do not focus on software, but both books are must reading for senior managers with software development responsibility. Gluckman and Roome (*Everyday Heroes of the Quality Movement,* Dorset House, 1993) humanizes quality issues by telling the story of the players in the quality process. Kan *(Metrics and Models in Software Quality Engineering,* Addison-Wesley, 1995) presents a quantitative view of software quality.

Tingley (*Comparing ISO 9000, Malcolm Baldrige, and the SEI CMM for Software,* Prentice-Hall, 1996) provides useful guidance for organizations that are striving to improve their quality management processes. Oskarsson (*An ISO 9000 Approach to Building Quality Software,* Prentice-Hall, 1995) discusses the ISO standard as it applies to software.

Dozens of books have been written about software quality issues in recent years. The following is a small sampling of useful sources:

Clapp, J.A., et al., *Software Quality Control, Error Analysis and Testing,* Noyes Data Corp., 1995.

Dunn, R.H. and R.S. Ullman, *TQM for Computer Software,* McGraw-Hill, 1994.

Fenton, N., R. Whitty, and Y. Iizuka, *Software Quality Assurance and Measurement: Worldwide Industrial Applications,* Chapman & Hall, 1994.

Ferdinand, A.E., *Systems, Software, and Quality Engineering,* Van Nostrand-Reinhold, 1993.

Ginac, F.P., *Customer Oriented Software Quality Assurance,* Prentice-Hall, 1998.

Ince, D. , *ISO 9001 and Software Quality Assurance,* McGraw-Hill, 1994.

Ince, D., *An Introduction to Software Quality Assurance and Its Implementation,* McGraw-Hill, 1994.

Jarvis, A. and V. Crandall, *Inroads to Software Quality: "How to" Guide and Toolkit,* Prentice-Hall, 1997.

Sanders, J., *Software Quality: A Framework for Success in Software Development,* Addison-Wesley, 1994.

Sumner, F.H., *Software Quality Assurance,* Macmillan, 1993.

Wallmuller, E., *Software Quality Assurance: A Practical Approach,* Prentice-Hall, 1995.

Weinberg, G.M., *Quality Software Management,* four volumes, Dorset House, 1992, 1993, 1994, 1996.

Wilson, R.C., *Software Rx: Secrets of Engineering Quality Software,* Prentice-Hall, 1997.

An anthology edited by Wheeler, Brykczynski, and Meeson (*Software Inspection: Industry Best Practice,* IEEE Computer Society Press, 1996) presents useful information on this important SQA activity. Friedman and Voas (*Software Assessment,* Wiley, 1995) discuss both theoretical underpinnings and practical methods for ensuring the reliability and safety of computer programs.

Musa (*Software Reliability Engineering: More Reliable Software, Faster Development and Testing,* McGraw-Hill, 1998) has written a practical guide to applied software reliability techniques. Anthologies of important papers on software reliability have been edited by Kapur et al. (*Contributions to Hardware and Software Reliability Modelling,* World Scientific Publishing Co., 1999), Gritzalis (*Reliability, Quality and Safety of Software-Intensive Systems,* Kluwer Academic Publishers, 1997), and Lyu (*Handbook of Software Reliability Engineering,* McGraw-Hill, 1996). Storey (*Safety-Critical Computer Systems,* Addison-Wesley, 1996) and Leveson [LEV95] continue to be the most comprehensive discussions of software safety published to date.

In addition to [SHI86], the *poka-yoke* technique for mistake-proofing software is discussed by Shingo (*The Shingo Production Management System: Improving Process Functions,* Productivity Press, 1992) and Shimbun *(Poka-Yoke: Improving Product Quality by Preventing Defects,* Productivity Press, 1989).

A wide variety of information sources on software quality assurance, software reliability, and related subjects is available on the Internet. An up-to-date list of World Wide Web references that are relevant to software quality can be found at the SEPA Web site:

http://www.mhhe.com/engcs/compsci/pressman/resources/sqa.mhtml

CHAPTER

9 SOFTWARE CONFIGURATION MANAGEMENT

Change is inevitable when computer software is built. And change increases the level of confusion among software engineers who are working on a project. Confusion arises when changes are not analyzed before they are made, recorded before they are implemented, reported to those with a need to know, or controlled in a manner that will improve quality and reduce error. Babich [BAB86] discusses this when he states:

> The art of coordinating software development to minimize . . . confusion is called *configuration management.* Configuration management is the art of identifying, organizing, and controlling modifications to the software being built by a programming team. The goal is to maximize productivity by minimizing mistakes.

Software configuration management (SCM) is an umbrella activity that is applied throughout the software process. Because change can occur at any time, SCM activities are developed to (1) identify change, (2) control change, (3) ensure that change is being properly implemented, and (4) report changes to others who may have an interest.

It is important to make a clear distinction between software support and software configuration management. Support is a set of software engineering activities that occur after software has been delivered to the customer and put

QUICK LOOK

What is it? When you build computer software, change happens. And because it happens, you need to control it effectively. Software configuration management (SCM) is a set of activities designed to control change by identifying the work products that are likely to change, establishing relationships among them, defining mechanisms for managing different versions of these work products, controlling the changes imposed, and auditing and reporting on the changes made.

Who does it? Everyone involved in the software engineering process is involved with SCM to some extent, but specialized support positions are sometimes created to manage the SCM process.

Why is it important? If you don't control change, it controls you. And that's never good. It's very easy for a stream of uncontrolled changes to turn a well-run software project into chaos. For that reason, SCM is an essential part of good project management and solid software engineering practice.

What are the steps? Because many work products are produced when software is built, each must be uniquely identified. Once this is accomplished, mechanisms for version and change control can be established. To ensure that quality is maintained as changes are made, the process is audited; and to ensure that those with a need to know are informed about changes, reporting is conducted.

QUICK LOOK

What is the work product? The Software Configuration Management Plan defines the project strategy for SCM. In addition, when formal SCM is invoked, the change control process produces software change requests and reports and engineering change orders.

How do I ensure that I've done it right? When every work product can be accounted for, traced, and controlled; when every change can be tracked and analyzed; when everyone who needs to know about a change has been informed—you've done it right.

into operation. Software configuration management is a set of tracking and control activities that begin when a software engineering project begins and terminate only when the software is taken out of operation.

A primary goal of software engineering is to improve the ease with which changes can be accommodated and reduce the amount of effort expended when changes must be made. In this chapter, we discuss the specific activities that enable us to manage change.

9.1 SOFTWARE CONFIGURATION MANAGEMENT

The output of the software process is information that may be divided into three broad categories: (1) computer programs (both source level and executable forms); (2) documents that describe the computer programs (targeted at both technical practitioners and users), and (3) data (contained within the program or external to it). The items that comprise all information produced as part of the software process are collectively called a *software configuration.*

Quote:

"There is nothing permanent except change."

Heraclitus 500 B.C.

As the software process progresses, the number of *software configuration items* (SCIs) grows rapidly. A *System Specification* spawns a *Software Project Plan* and *Software Requirements Specification* (as well as hardware related documents). These in turn spawn other documents to create a hierarchy of information. If each SCI simply spawned other SCIs, little confusion would result. Unfortunately, another variable enters the process—*change.* Change may occur at any time, for any reason. In fact, the First Law of System Engineering [BER80] states: "No matter where you are in the system life cycle, the system will change, and the desire to change it will persist throughout the life cycle."

What is the origin of these changes? The answer to this question is as varied as the changes themselves. However, there are four fundamental sources of change:

- New business or market conditions dictate changes in product requirements or business rules.
- New customer needs demand modification of data produced by information systems, functionality delivered by products, or services delivered by a computer-based system.

- Reorganization or business growth/downsizing causes changes in project priorities or software engineering team structure.
- Budgetary or scheduling constraints cause a redefinition of the system or product.

Software configuration management is a set of activities that have been developed to manage change throughout the life cycle of computer software. SCM can be viewed as a software quality assurance activity that is applied throughout the software process. In the sections that follow, we examine major SCM tasks and important concepts that help us to manage change.

9.1.1 Baselines

ADVICE *Most software changes are justified. Don't bemoan changes. Rather, be certain that you have mechanisms in place to handle them.*

Change is a fact of life in software development. Customers want to modify requirements. Developers want to modify the technical approach. Managers want to modify the project strategy. Why all this modification? The answer is really quite simple. As time passes, all constituencies know more (about what they need, which approach would be best, how to get it done and still make money). This additional knowledge is the driving force behind most changes and leads to a statement of fact that is difficult for many software engineering practitioners to accept: Most changes are justified!

A *baseline* is a software configuration management concept that helps us to control change without seriously impeding justifiable change. The IEEE (IEEE Std. No. 610.12-1990) defines a baseline as:

> A specification or product that has been formally reviewed and agreed upon, that thereafter serves as the basis for further development, and that can be changed only through formal change control procedures.

One way to describe a baseline is through analogy:

> Consider the doors to the kitchen in a large restaurant. One door is marked OUT and the other is marked IN. The doors have stops that allow them to be opened only in the appropriate direction.
>
> If a waiter picks up an order in the kitchen, places it on a tray and then realizes he has selected the wrong dish, he may change to the correct dish quickly and informally before he leaves the kitchen.
>
> If, however, he leaves the kitchen, gives the customer the dish and then is informed of his error, he must follow a set procedure: (1) look at the check to determine if an error has occurred, (2) apologize profusely, (3) return to the kitchen through the IN door, (4) explain the problem, and so forth.

KEY POINT A software engineering work product becomes a baseline only after it has been reviewed and approved.

A baseline is analogous to the kitchen doors in the restaurant. Before a software configuration item becomes a baseline, change may be made quickly and informally. However, once a baseline is established, we figuratively pass through a swinging one-way door. Changes can be made, but a specific, formal procedure must be applied to evaluate and verify each change.

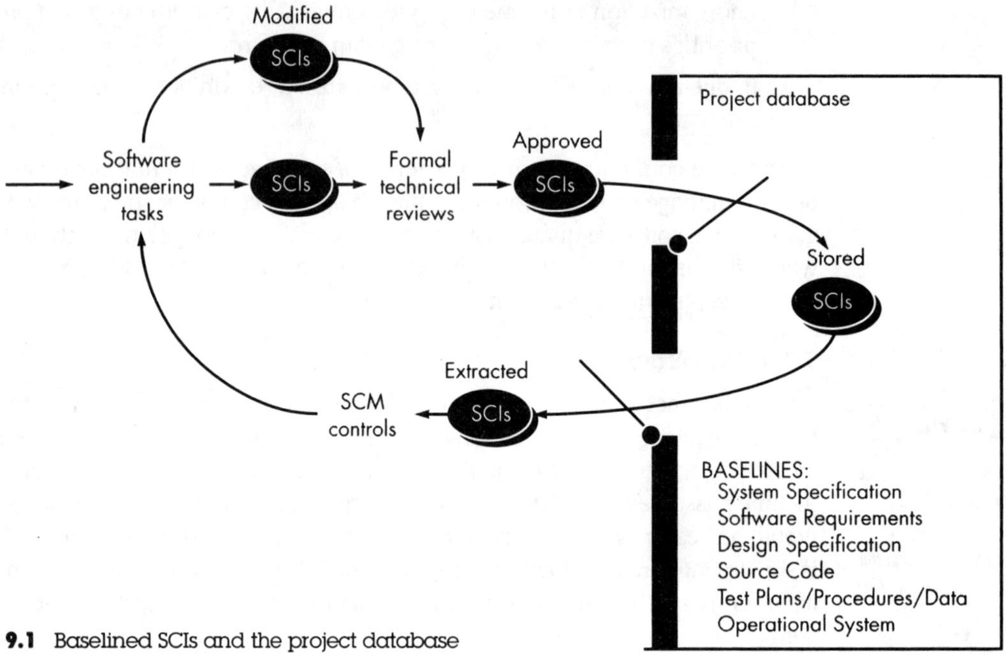

FIGURE 9.1 Baselined SCIs and the project database

In the context of software engineering, a baseline is a milestone in the development of software that is marked by the delivery of one or more software configuration items and the approval of these SCIs that is obtained through a formal technical review (Chapter 8). For example, the elements of a *Design Specification* have been documented and reviewed. Errors are found and corrected. Once all parts of the specification have been reviewed, corrected and then approved, the *Design Specification* becomes a baseline. Further changes to the program architecture (documented in the *Design Specification*) can be made only after each has been evaluated and approved. Although baselines can be defined at any level of detail, the most common software baselines are shown in Figure 9.1.

ADVICE

Be sure that the project database is maintained in a centralized, controlled location.

The progression of events that lead to a baseline is also illustrated in Figure 9.1. Software engineering tasks produce one or more SCIs. After SCIs are reviewed and approved, they are placed in a *project database* (also called a *project library* or *software repository*). When a member of a software engineering team wants to make a modification to a baselined SCI, it is copied from the project database into the engineer's private work space. However, this extracted SCI can be modified only if SCM controls (discussed later in this chapter) are followed. The arrows in Figure 9.1 illustrate the modification path for a baselined SCI.

9.1.2 Software Configuration Items

We have already defined a software configuration item as information that is created as part of the software engineering process. In the extreme, a SCI could be considered to be a single section of a large specification or one test case in a large suite of

FIGURE 9.2
Configuration objects

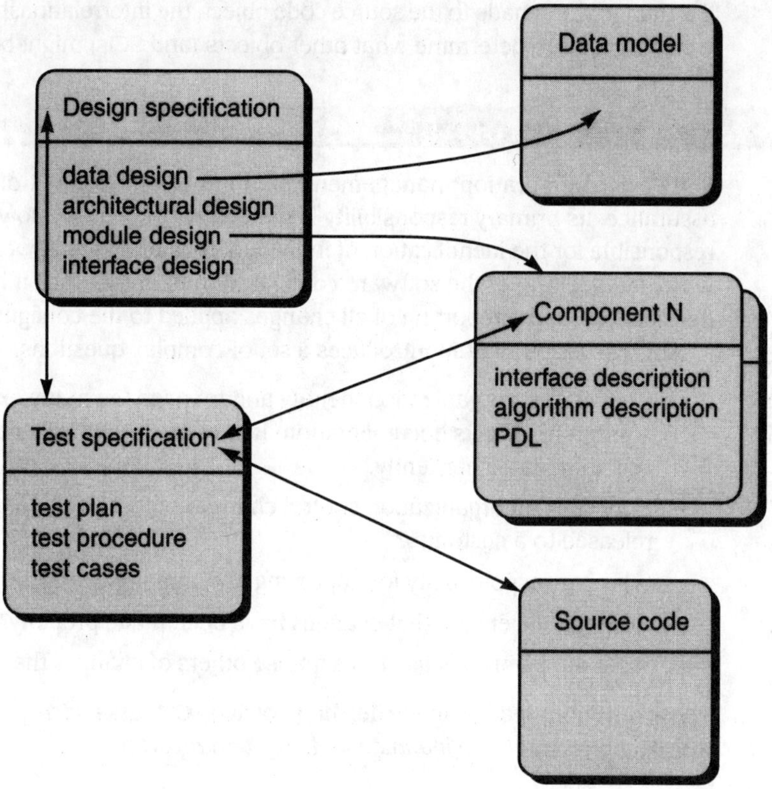

tests. More realistically, an SCI is a document, a entire suite of test cases, or a named program component (e.g., a C++ function or an Ada package).

Software Configuration Items

In addition to the SCIs that are derived from software work products, many software engineering organizations also place software tools under configuration control. That is, specific versions of editors, compilers, and other CASE tools are "frozen" as part of the software configuration. Because these tools were used to produce documentation, source code, and data, they must be available when changes to the software configuration are to be made. Although problems are rare, it is possible that a new version of a tool (e.g., a compiler) might produce different results than the original version. For this reason, tools, like the software that they help to produce, can be baselined as part of a comprehensive configuration management process.

In reality, SCIs are organized to form *configuration objects* that may be cataloged in the project database with a single name. A configuration object has a name, attributes, and is "connected" to other objects by relationships. Referring to Figure 9.2, the configuration objects, **Design Specification, data model, component N, source code** and **Test Specification** are each defined separately. However, each of the objects is related to the others as shown by the arrows. A curved arrow indicates a *compositional relation.* That is, **data model** and **component N** are part of the object **Design Specification.** A double-headed straight arrow indicates an interrelationship

If a change were made to the source code object, the interrelationships enable a software engineer to determine what other objects (and SCIs) might be affected.[1]

9.2 THE SCM PROCESS

Software configuration management is an important element of software quality assurance. Its primary responsibility is the control of change. However, SCM is also responsible for the identification of individual SCIs and various versions of the software, the auditing of the software configuration to ensure that it has been properly developed, and the reporting of all changes applied to the configuration.

Any discussion of SCM introduces a set of complex questions:

WebRef
The *Configuration Management Yellow Pages* contains the most comprehensive listing of SCM resources on the Web at **www.cs.colorado.edu/users/andre/configuration_management.html**

- How does an organization identify and manage the many existing versions of a program (and its documentation) in a manner that will enable change to be accommodated efficiently?
- How does an organization control changes before and after software is released to a customer?
- Who has responsibility for approving and ranking changes?
- How can we ensure that changes have been made properly?
- What mechanism is used to appraise others of changes that are made?

These questions lead us to the definition of five SCM tasks: *identification, version control, change control, configuration auditing,* and *reporting.*

9.3 IDENTIFICATION OF OBJECTS IN THE SOFTWARE CONFIGURATION

To control and manage software configuration items, each must be separately named and then organized using an object-oriented approach. Two types of objects can be identified [CHO89]: *basic objects* and *aggregate objects.*[2] A basic object is a "unit of text" that has been created by a software engineer during analysis, design, code, or test. For example, a basic object might be a section of a requirements specification, a source listing for a component, or a suite of test cases that are used to exercise the code. An aggregate object is a collection of basic objects and other aggregate objects. Referring to Figure 9.2, **Design Specification** is an aggregate object. Conceptually, it can be viewed as a named (identified) list of pointers that specify basic objects such as **data model** and **component N**.

Each object has a set of distinct features that identify it uniquely: a name, a description, a list of resources, and a "realization." The object name is a character string that identifies the object unambiguously. The object description is a list of data items that identify

1 These relationships are defined within the database. The structure of the project database will be discussed in greater detail in Chapter 31.

2 The concept of an aggregate object [GUS89] has been proposed as a mechanism for representing a complete version of a software configuration.

- the SCI type (e.g., document, program, data) represented by the object
- a project identifier
- change and/or version information

KEY POINT

The interrelationships established for configuration objects allow a software engineer to assess the impact of change.

Resources are "entities that are provided, processed, referenced or otherwise required by the object [CHO89]." For example, data types, specific functions, or even variable names may be considered to be object resources. The realization is a pointer to the "unit of text" for a basic object and null for an aggregate object.

Configuration object identification must also consider the relationships that exist between named objects. An object can be identified as **<part-of>** an aggregate object. The relationship **<part-of>** defines a hierarchy of objects. For example, using the simple notation

E-R diagram 1.4 <part-of> data model;
data model <part-of> design specification;

we create a hierarchy of SCIs.

XRef

Data models and data flow diagrams are discussed in Chapter 12.

It is unrealistic to assume that the only relationships among objects in an object hierarchy are along direct paths of the hierarchical tree. In many cases, objects are interrelated across branches of the object hierarchy. For example, a data model is interrelated to data flow diagrams (assuming the use of structured analysis) and also interrelated to a set of test cases for a specific equivalence class. These cross structural relationships can be represented in the following manner:

data model <interrelated> data flow model;
data model <interrelated> test case class m;

In the first case, the interrelationship is between a composite object, while the second relationship is between an aggregate object (**data model**) and a basic object (**test case class m**).

The interrelationships between configuration objects can be represented with a *module interconnection language* (MIL) [NAR87]. A MIL describes the interdependencies among configuration objects and enables any version of a system to be constructed automatically.

The identification scheme for software objects must recognize that objects evolve throughout the software process. Before an object is baselined, it may change many times, and even after a baseline has been established, changes may be quite frequent. It is possible to create an *evolution graph* [GUS89] for any object. The evolution graph describes the change history of an object, as illustrated in Figure 9.3. Configuration object 1.0 undergoes revision and becomes object 1.1. Minor corrections and changes result in versions 1.1.1 and 1.1.2, which is followed by a major update that is object 1.2. The evolution of object 1.0 continues through 1.3 and 1.4, but at the same time, a major modification to the object results in a new evolutionary path, version 2.0. Both versions are currently supported.

Changes may be made to any version, but not necessarily to all versions. How does the developer reference all components, documents, and test cases for version 1.4? How does the marketing department know what customers currently have

FIGURE 9.3
Evolution graph

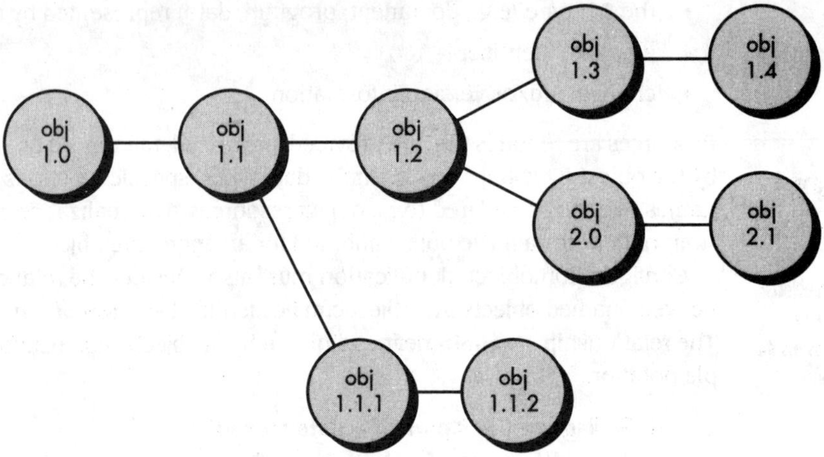

version 2.1? How can we be sure that changes to the version 2.1 source code are properly reflected in the corresponding design documentation? A key element in the answer to all these questions is identification.

CASE Tools—SCM

A variety of automated SCM tools has been developed to aid in identification (and other SCM) tasks. In some cases, a tool is designed to maintain full copies of only the most recent version. To achieve earlier versions (of documents or programs) changes (cataloged by the tool) are "subtracted" from the most recent version [TIC82]. This scheme makes the current configuration immediately available and allows other versions to be derived easily.

9.4 VERSION CONTROL

Version control combines procedures and tools to manage different versions of configuration objects that are created during the software process. Clemm [CLE89] describes version control in the context of SCM:

> Configuration management allows a user to specify alternative configurations of the software system through the selection of appropriate versions. This is supported by associating attributes with each software version, and then allowing a configuration to be specified [and constructed] by describing the set of desired attributes.

ADVICE

The naming scheme you establish for SCIs should incorporate the version number.

These "attributes" mentioned can be as simple as a specific version number that is attached to each object or as complex as a string of Boolean variables (switches) that indicate specific types of functional changes that have been applied to the system [LIE89].

One representation of the different versions of a system is the evolution graph presented in Figure 9.3. Each node on the graph is an aggregate object, that is, a complete version of the software. Each version of the software is a collection of SCIs (source code, documents, data), and each version may be composed of different variants. To illustrate this concept, consider a version of a simple program that is com-

FIGURE 9.4
Object pool representation of components, variants, and versions [REI89]

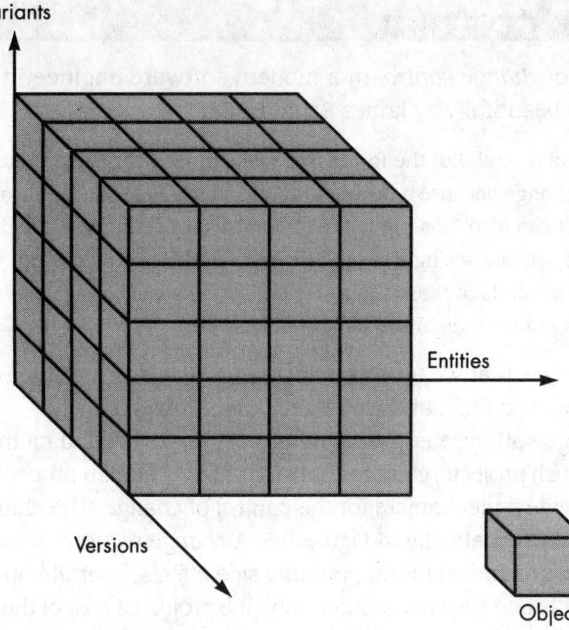

posed of entities 1, 2, 3, 4, and 5.[3] Entity 4 is used only when the software is implemented using color displays. Entity 5 is implemented when monochrome displays are available. Therefore, two variants of the version can be defined: (1) entities 1, 2, 3, and 4; (2) entities 1, 2, 3, and 5.

Quote:
"Any change, even a change for the better, is always accompanied by drawbacks and discomforts."
Arnold Bennett

To construct the appropriate *variant* of a given version of a program, each entity can be assigned an "attribute-tuple"—a list of features that will define whether the entity should be used when a particular variant of a software version is to be constructed. One or more attributes is assigned for each variant. For example, a color attribute could be used to define which entity should be included when color displays are to be supported.

Another way to conceptualize the relationship between entities, variants and versions (revisions) is to represent them as an *object pool* [REI89]. Referring to Figure 9.4, the relationship between configuration objects and entities, variants and versions can be represented in a three-dimensional space. An entity is composed of a collection of objects at the same revision level. A variant is a different collection of objects at the same revision level and therefore coexists in parallel with other variants. A new version is defined when major changes are made to one or more objects.

A number of different automated approaches to version control have been proposed over the past decade. The primary difference in approaches is the sophistication of the attributes that are used to construct specific versions and variants of a system and the mechanics of the process for construction.

3 In this context, the term *entity* refers to all composite objects and basic objects that exist for a baselined SCI. For example, an "input" entity might be constructed with six different software components, each responsible for an input subfunction.

9.5 CHANGE CONTROL

The reality of *change control* in a modern software engineering context has been summed up beautifully by James Bach [BAC98]:

> Change control is vital. But the forces that make it necessary also make it annoying. We worry about change because a tiny perturbation in the code can create a big failure in the product. But it can also fix a big failure or enable wonderful new capabilities. We worry about change because a single rogue developer could sink the project; yet brilliant ideas originate in the minds of those rogues, and a burdensome change control process could effectively discourage them from doing creative work.

Quote:
"The art of progress is to preserve order amid change and to preserve change amid order."
Alfred North Whitehead

Bach recognizes that we face a balancing act. Too much change control and we create problems. Too little, and we create other problems.

For a large software engineering project, uncontrolled change rapidly leads to chaos. For such projects, change control combines human procedures and automated tools to provide a mechanism for the control of change. The change control process is illustrated schematically in Figure 9.5. A *change request*[4] is submitted and evaluated to assess technical merit, potential side effects, overall impact on other configuration objects and system functions, and the projected cost of the change. The results of the evaluation are presented as a *change report,* which is used by a *change control authority* (CCA)—a person or group who makes a final decision on the status and priority of the change. An *engineering change order* (ECO) is generated for each approved change. The ECO describes the change to be made, the constraints that must be respected, and the criteria for review and audit. The object to be changed is "checked out" of the project database, the change is made, and appropriate SQA activities are applied. The object is then "checked in" to the database and appropriate version control mechanisms (Section 9.4) are used to create the next version of the software.

ADVICE
Confusion leads to errors—some of them very serious. Access and synchronization control avoid confusion. Implement them both, even if your approach has to be simplified to accommodate your development culture.

The "check-in" and "check-out" process implements two important elements of change control—access control and synchronization control. *Access control* governs which software engineers have the authority to access and modify a particular configuration object. *Synchronization control* helps to ensure that parallel changes, performed by two different people, don't overwrite one another [HAR89].

Access and synchronization control flow are illustrated schematically in Figure 9.6. Based on an approved change request and ECO, a software engineer *checks out* a configuration object. An access control function ensures that the software engineer has authority to check out the object, and synchronization control *locks* the object in the project database so that no updates can be made to it until the currently checked-out version has been replaced. Note that other copies can be checked-out, but other updates cannot be made. A copy of the baselined object, called the *extracted version,*

---

4 Although many change requests are submitted during the software support phase, we take a broader view in this discussion. A request for change can occur at any time during the software process.

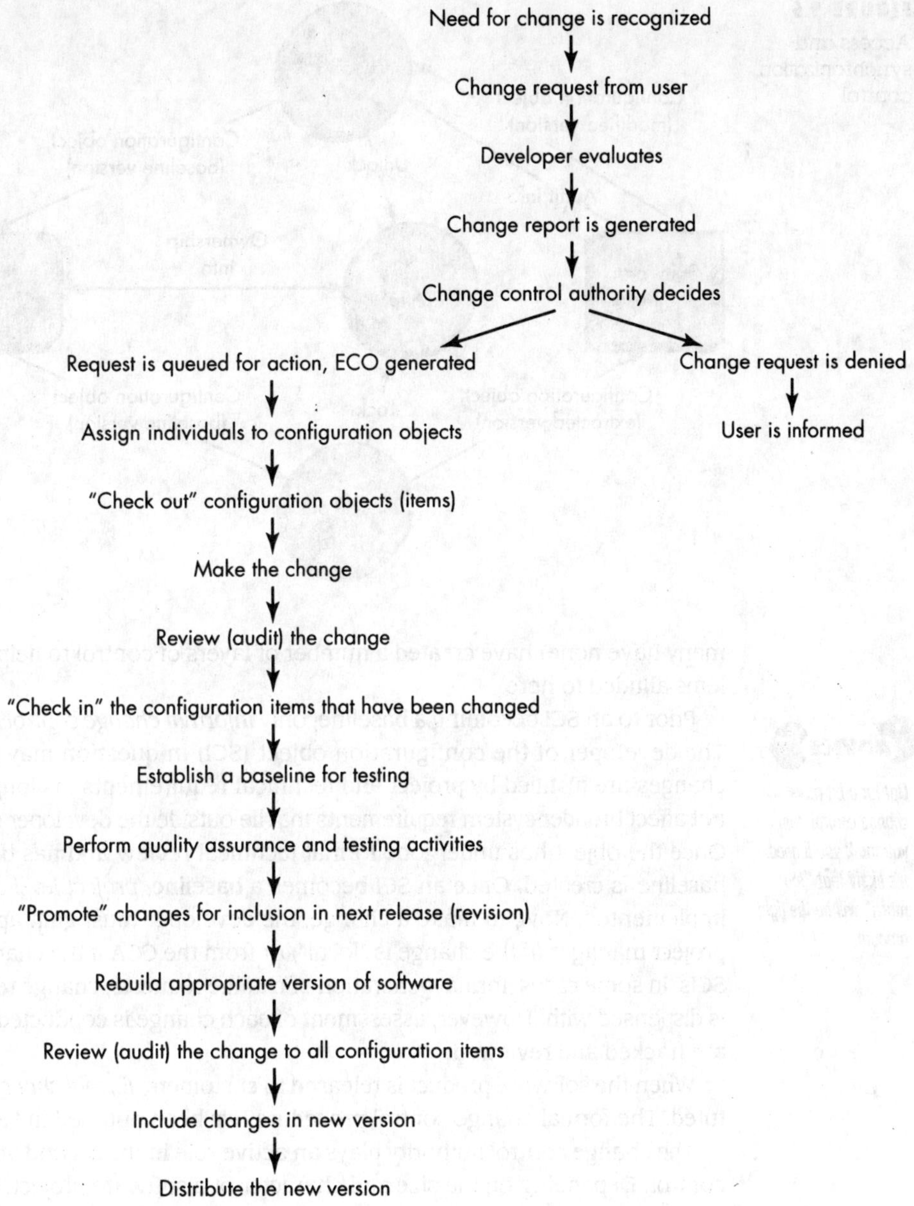

FIGURE 9.5
The change control process

is modified by the software engineer. After appropriate SQA and testing, the modified version of the object is *checked in* and the new baseline object is unlocked.

Some readers may begin to feel uncomfortable with the level of bureaucracy implied by the change control process description. This feeling is not uncommon. Without proper safeguards, change control can retard progress and create unnecessary red tape. Most software developers who have change control mechanisms (unfortunately,

FIGURE 9.6
Access and synchronization control

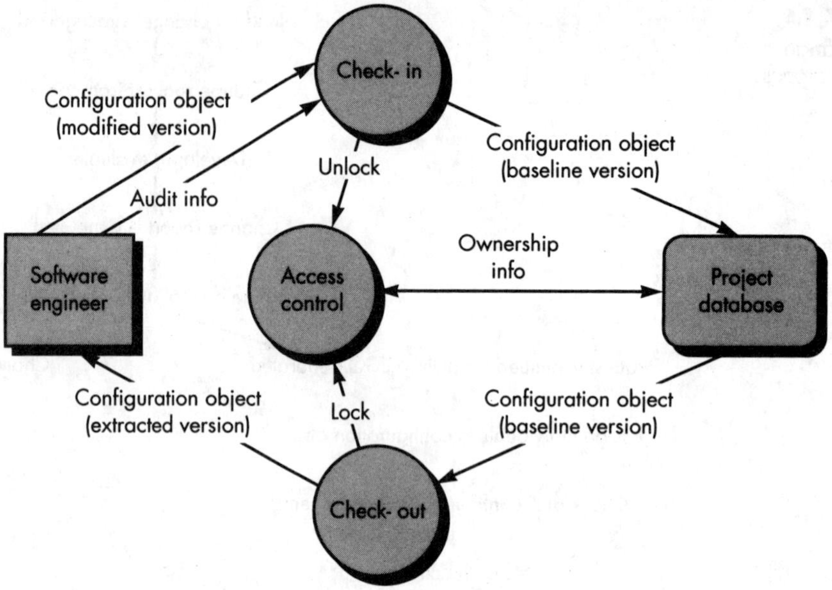

many have none) have created a number of layers of control to help avoid the problems alluded to here.

ADVICE

Opt for a bit more change control than you think you'll need. It's likely that "too much" will be the right amount.

Prior to an SCI becoming a baseline, only *informal change control* need be applied. The developer of the configuration object (SCI) in question may make whatever changes are justified by project and technical requirements (as long as changes do not affect broader system requirements that lie outside the developer's scope of work). Once the object has undergone formal technical review and has been approved, a baseline is created. Once an SCI becomes a baseline, *project level change control* is implemented. Now, to make a change, the developer must gain approval from the project manager (if the change is "local") or from the CCA if the change affects other SCIs. In some cases, formal generation of change requests, change reports, and ECOs is dispensed with. However, assessment of each change is conducted and all changes are tracked and reviewed.

When the software product is released to customers, *formal change control* is instituted. The formal change control procedure has been outlined in Figure 9.5.

Quote:

"Change is inevitable, except from vending machines."
Bumper sticker

The change control authority plays an active role in the second and third layers of control. Depending on the size and character of a software project, the CCA may be composed of one person—the project manager—or a number of people (e.g., representatives from software, hardware, database engineering, support, marketing). The role of the CCA is to take a global view, that is, to assess the impact of change beyond the SCI in question. How will the change affect hardware? How will the change affect performance? How will the change modify customer's perception of the product? How will the change affect product quality and reliability? These and many other questions are addressed by the CCA.

9.6 CONFIGURATION AUDIT

Identification, version control, and change control help the software developer to maintain order in what would otherwise be a chaotic and fluid situation. However, even the most successful control mechanisms track a change only until an ECO is generated. How can we ensure that the change has been properly implemented? The answer is twofold: (1) formal technical reviews and (2) the software configuration audit.

The formal technical review (presented in detail in Chapter 8) focuses on the technical correctness of the configuration object that has been modified. The reviewers assess the SCI to determine consistency with other SCIs, omissions, or potential side effects. A formal technical review should be conducted for all but the most trivial changes.

? What are the primary questions that we ask during a configuration audit?

A *software configuration audit* complements the formal technical review by assessing a configuration object for characteristics that are generally not considered during review. The audit asks and answers the following questions:

1. Has the change specified in the ECO been made? Have any additional modifications been incorporated?
2. Has a formal technical review been conducted to assess technical correctness?
3. Has the software process been followed and have software engineering standards been properly applied?
4. Has the change been "highlighted" in the SCI? Have the change date and change author been specified? Do the attributes of the configuration object reflect the change?
5. Have SCM procedures for noting the change, recording it, and reporting it been followed?
6. Have all related SCIs been properly updated?

In some cases, the audit questions are asked as part of a formal technical review. However, when SCM is a formal activity, the SCM audit is conducted separately by the quality assurance group.

9.7 STATUS REPORTING

Configuration status reporting (sometimes called *status accounting*) is an SCM task that answers the following questions: (1) What happened? (2) Who did it? (3) When did it happen? (4) What else will be affected?

The flow of information for configuration status reporting (CSR) is illustrated in Figure 9.5. Each time an SCI is assigned new or updated identification, a CSR entry is made. Each time a change is approved by the CCA (i.e., an ECO is issued), a CSR entry is made. Each time a configuration audit is conducted, the results are reported as part of the CSR task. Output from CSR may be placed in an on-line database [TAY85], so that software developers or maintainers can access change information by keyword category. In addition, a CSR report is generated on a regular basis and is intended to keep management and practitioners appraised of important changes.

ADVICE

Develop a "need to know list" for every SCI and keep it up-to-date. When a change is made, be sure that everyone on the list is informed.

Configuration status reporting plays a vital role in the success of a large software development project. When many people are involved, it is likely that "the left hand not knowing what the right hand is doing" syndrome will occur. Two developers may attempt to modify the same SCI with different and conflicting intents. A software engineering team may spend months of effort building software to an obsolete hardware specification. The person who would recognize serious side effects for a proposed change is not aware that the change is being made. CSR helps to eliminate these problems by improving communication among all people involved.

9.8 SCM STANDARDS

Over the past two decades a number of software configuration management standards have been proposed. Many early SCM standards, such as MIL-STD-483, DOD-STD-480A and MIL-STD-1521A, focused on software developed for military applications. However, more recent ANSI/IEEE standards, such as ANSI/IEEE Stds. No. 828-1983, No. 1042-1987, and Std. No. 1028-1988 [IEE94], are applicable for nonmilitary software and are recommended for both large and small software engineering organizations.

9.9 SUMMARY

Software configuration management is an umbrella activity that is applied throughout the software process. SCM identifies, controls, audits, and reports modifications that invariably occur while software is being developed and after it has been released to a customer. All information produced as part of software engineering becomes part of a software configuration. The configuration is organized in a manner that enables orderly control of change.

The software configuration is composed of a set of interrelated objects, also called software configuration items, that are produced as a result of some software engineering activity. In addition to documents, programs, and data, the development environment that is used to create software can also be placed under configuration control.

Once a configuration object has been developed and reviewed, it becomes a baseline. Changes to a baselined object result in the creation of a new version of that object. The evolution of a program can be tracked by examining the revision history of all configuration objects. Basic and composite objects form an object pool from which variants and versions are created. Version control is the set of procedures and tools for managing the use of these objects.

Change control is a procedural activity that ensures quality and consistency as changes are made to a configuration object. The change control process begins with a change request, leads to a decision to make or reject the request for change, and culminates with a controlled update of the SCI that is to be changed.

The configuration audit is an SQA activity that helps to ensure that quality is maintained as changes are made. Status reporting provides information about each change to those with a need to know.

REFERENCES

[BAB86] Babich, W.A., *Software Configuration Management,* Addison-Wesley, 1986.

[BAC98] Bach, J., "The Highs and Lows of Change Control," *Computer,* vol. 31, no. 8, August 1998, pp. 113–115.

[BER80] Bersoff, E.H., V.D. Henderson, and S.G. Siegel, *Software Configuration Management,* Prentice-Hall, 1980.

[CHO89] Choi, S.C. and W. Scacchi, "Assuring the Correctness of a Configured Software Description," *Proc. 2nd Intl. Workshop on Software Configuration Management,* ACM, Princeton, NJ, October 1989, pp. 66–75.

[CLE89] Clemm, G.M., "Replacing Version Control with Job Control," *Proc. 2nd Intl. Workshop on Software Configuration Management,* ACM, Princeton, NJ, October 1989, pp. 162–169.

[GUS89] Gustavsson, A., "Maintaining the Evoluation of Software Objects in an Integrated Environment," *Proc. 2nd Intl. Workshop on Software Configuration Management,* ACM, Princeton, NJ, October 1989, pp. 114–117.

[HAR89] Harter, R., "Configuration Management," *HP Professional,* vol. 3, no. 6, June 1989.

[IEE94] *Software Engineering Standards,* 1994 edition, IEEE Computer Society, 1994.

[LIE89] Lie, A. et al., "Change Oriented Versioning in a Software Engineering Database," *Proc. 2nd Intl. Workshop on Software Configuration Management,* ACM, Princeton, NJ, October, 1989, pp. 56–65.

[NAR87] Narayanaswamy, K. and W. Scacchi, "Maintaining Configurations of Evolving Software Systems," *IEEE Trans. Software Engineering,* vol. SE-13, no. 3, March 1987, pp. 324–334.

[REI89] Reichenberger, C., "Orthogonal Version Management," *Proc. 2nd Intl. Workshop on Software Configuration Management,* ACM, Princeton, NJ, October 1989, pp. 137–140.

[TAY85] Taylor, B., "A Database Approach to Configuration Management for Large Projects," *Proc. Conf. Software Maintenance—1985,* IEEE, November 1985, pp. 15–23.

[TIC82] Tichy, W.F., "Design, Implementation and Evaluation of a Revision Control System," *Proc. 6th Intl. Conf. Software Engineering,* IEEE, Tokyo, September 1982, pp. 58–67.

PROBLEMS AND POINTS TO PONDER

9.1. Why is the First Law of System Engineering true? How does it affect our perception of software engineering paradigms.

9.2. Discuss the reasons for baselines in your own words.

9.3. Assume that you're the manager of a small project. What baselines would you define for the project and how would you control them?

9.4. Design a project database system that would enable a software engineer to store, cross reference, trace, update, change, and so forth all important software configuration items. How would the database handle different versions of the same program? Would source code be handled differently than documentation? How will two developers be precluded from making different changes to the same SCI at the same time?

9.5. Do some research on object-oriented databases and write a paper that describes how they can be used in the context of SCM.

9.6. Use an E-R model (Chapter 12) to describe the interrelationships among the SCIs (objects) listed in Section 9.1.2.

9.7. Research an existing SCM tool and describe how it implements control for versions, variants, and configuration objects in general.

9.8. The relations **<part-of>** and **<interrelated>** represent simple relationships between configuration objects. Describe five additional relationships that might be useful in the context of a project database.

9.9. Research an existing SCM tool and describe how it implements the mechanics of version control. Alternatively, read two or three of the papers on SCM and describe the different data structures and referencing mechanisms that are used for version control.

9.10. Using Figure 9.5 as a guide, develop an even more detailed work breakdown for change control. Describe the role of the CCA and suggest formats for the change request, the change report, and the ECO.

9.11. Develop a checklist for use during configuration audits.

9.12. What is the difference between an SCM audit and a formal technical review? Can their function be folded into one review? What are the pros and cons?

FURTHER READINGS AND INFORMATION SOURCES

One of the few books that have been written about SCM in recent years is by Brown, et al. (*AntiPatterns and Patterns in Software Configuration Management,* Wiley, 1999). The authors discuss the things not to do (antipatterns) when implementing an SCM process and then consider their remedies.

Lyon (*Practical CM: Best Configuration Management Practices for the 21st Century,* Raven Publishing, 1999) and Mikkelsen and Pherigo (*Practical Software Configuration Management: The Latenight Developer's Handbook,* Allyn & Bacon, 1997) provide pragmatic tutorials on important SCM practices. Ben-Menachem (*Software Configuration Management Guidebook,* McGraw-Hill, 1994), Vacca (*Implementing a Successful Configuration Change Management Program,* I. S. Management Group, 1993), and Ayer and Patrinnostro (*Software Configuration Management,* McGraw-Hill, 1992) present good overviews for those who need further introduction to the subject. Berlack (*Soft-*

ware Configuration Management, Wiley, 1992) presents a useful survey of SCM concepts, emphasizing the importance of the repository and tools in the management of change. Babich [BAB86] provides an abbreviated, yet effective, treatment of pragmatic issues in software configuration management.

Buckley (*Implementing Configuration Management,* IEEE Computer Society Press, 1993) considers configuration management approaches for all system elements—hardware, software, and firmware—with detailed discussions of major CM activities. Rawlings (*SCM for Network Development Environments,* McGraw-Hill, 1994) is the first SCM book to address the subject with a specific emphasis on software development in a networked environment. Whitgift (*Methods and Tools for Software Configuration Management,* Wiley, 1991) contains reasonable coverage of all important SCM topics, but is distinguished by discussion of repository and CASE environment issues. Arnold and Bohner (*Software Change Impact Analysis,* IEEE Computer Society Press, 1996) have edited an anthology that discusses how to analyze the impact of change within complex software-based systems.

Because SCM identifies and controls software engineering documents, books by Nagle (*Handbook for Preparing Engineering Documents: From Concept to Completion,* IEEE, 1996), Watts (*Engineering Documentation Control Handbook: Configuration Management for Industry,* Noyes Publications, 1993), Ayer and Patrinnostro (*Documenting the Software Process,* McGraw-Hill, 1992) provide a complement to more-focused SCM texts. The March 1999 edition of *Crosstalk* contains a number of useful articles on SCM.

A wide variety of information sources on software configuration management and related subjects is available on the Internet. An up-to-date list of World Wide Web references that are relevant to SCM can be found at the SEPA Web site:
http://www.mhhe.com/engcs/compsci/pressman/resources/scm.mhtml

CHAPTER

10 SYSTEM ENGINEERING

KEY CONCEPTS

Almost 500 years ago, Machiavelli said: "there is nothing more difficult to take in hand, more perilous to conduct or more uncertain in its success, than to take the lead in the introduction of a new order of things." During the past 50 years, computer-based systems have introduced a new order. Although technology has made great strides since Machiavelli spoke, his words continue to ring true.

Software engineering occurs as a consequence of a process called *system engineering*. Instead of concentrating solely on software, system engineering focuses on a variety of elements, analyzing, designing, and organizing those elements into a system that can be a product, a service, or a technology for the transformation of information or control.

The system engineering process is called *business process engineering* when the context of the engineering work focuses on a business enterprise. When a product (in this context, a product includes everything from a wireless telephone to an air traffic control system) is to be built, the process is called *product engineering*.

Both business process engineering and product engineering attempt to bring order to the development of computer-based systems. Although each is applied in a different application domain, both strive to put software into context. That

QUICK LOOK

What is it? Before software can be engineered, the "system" in which it resides must be understood. To accomplish this, the overall objective of the system must be determined; the role of hardware, software, people, database, procedures, and other system elements must be identified; and operational requirements must be elicited, analyzed, specified, modeled, validated, and managed. These activities are the foundation of system engineering.

Who does it? A system engineer works to understand system requirements by working with the customer, future users, and other stakeholders.

Why is it important? There's an old saying: "You can't see the forest for the trees." In this context, the "forest" is the system, and the trees are the technology elements (including software) that are required to realize the system. If you rush to build technology elements before you understand the system, you'll undoubtedly make mistakes that will disappoint your customer. Before you worry about the trees, understand the forest.

What are the steps? Objectives and more detailed operational requirements are identified by eliciting information from the customer; requirements are analyzed to assess their clarity, completeness, and consistency; a specification, often incorporating a system model, is created and then validated by both practitioners and customers. Finally, system requirements are managed to ensure that changes are properly controlled.

QUICK LOOK

What is the work product? An effective representation of the system must be produced as a consequence of system engineering. This can be a prototype, a specification or even a symbolic model, but it must communicate the operational, functional, and behavioral characteristics of the system to be built and provide insight into the system architecture.

How do I ensure that I've done it right? Perform requirements engineering steps, including requirements elicitation, that lead to a solid specification. Then review all system engineering work products for clarity, completeness, and consistency. As important, expect changes to the system requirements and manage them using solid SCM (Chapter 9) methods.

is, both business process engineering and product engineering[1] work to allocate a role for computer software and, at the same time, to establish the links that tie software to other elements of a computer-based system.

In this chapter, we focus on the management issues and the process-specific activities that enable a software organization to ensure that it does the right things at the right time in the right way.

10.1 COMPUTER-BASED SYSTEMS

The word *system* is possibly the most overused and abused term in the technical lexicon. We speak of political systems and educational systems, of avionics systems and manufacturing systems, of banking systems and subway systems. The word tells us little. We use the adjective describing system to understand the context in which the word is used. *Webster's Dictionary* defines *system* in the following way:

> 1. a set or arrangement of things so related as to form a unity or organic whole; 2. a set of facts, principles, rules, etc., classified and arranged in an orderly form so as to show a logical plan linking the various parts; 3. a method or plan of classification or arrangement; 4. an established way of doing something; method; procedure . . .

Five additional definitions are provided in the dictionary, yet no precise synonym is suggested. *System* is a special word.

Borrowing from Webster's definition, we define a *computer-based system* as

> A set or arrangement of elements that are organized to accomplish some predefined goal by processing information.

The goal may be to support some business function or to develop a product that can be sold to generate business revenue. To accomplish the goal, a computer-based system makes use of a variety of system elements:

1 In reality, the term *system engineering* is often used in this context. However, in this book, the term *system engineering* is generic and is used to encompass both business process engineering and product engineering.

Software. Computer programs, data structures, and related documentation that serve to effect the logical method, procedure, or control that is required.

Hardware. Electronic devices that provide computing capability, the interconnectivity devices (e.g., network switches, telecommunications devices) that enable the flow of data, and electromechanical devices (e.g., sensors, motors, pumps) that provide external world function.

ADVICE

Don't be lured into taking a "software-centric" view. Begin by considering all elements of a system before you concentrate on software.

People. Users and operators of hardware and software.

Database. A large, organized collection of information that is accessed via software.

Documentation. Descriptive information (e.g., hardcopy manuals, on-line help files, Web sites) that portrays the use and/or operation of the system.

Procedures. The steps that define the specific use of each system element or the procedural context in which the system resides.

The elements combine in a variety of ways to transform information. For example, a marketing department transforms raw sales data into a profile of the typical purchaser of a product; a robot transforms a command file containing specific instructions into a set of control signals that cause some specific physical action. Creating an information system to assist the marketing department and control software to support the robot both require system engineering.

One complicating characteristic of computer-based systems is that the elements constituting one system may also represent one macro element of a still larger system. The macro element is a computer-based system that is one part of a larger computer-based system. As an example, we consider a "factory automation system" that is essentially a hierarchy of systems. At the lowest level of the hierarchy we have a numerical control machine, robots, and data entry devices. Each is a computer-based system in its own right. The elements of the numerical control machine include electronic and electromechanical hardware (e.g., processor and memory, motors, sensors), software (for communications, machine control, interpolation), people (the machine operator), a database (the stored NC program), documentation, and procedures. A similar decomposition could be applied to the robot and data entry device. Each is a computer-based system.

KEY POINT

Complex systems are actually a hierarchy of macro elements that are themselves systems.

At the next level in the hierarchy, a manufacturing cell is defined. The manufacturing cell is a computer-based system that may have elements of its own (e.g., computers, mechanical fixtures) and also integrates the macro elements that we have called numerical control machine, robot, and data entry device.

To summarize, the manufacturing cell and its macro elements each are composed of system elements with the generic labels: software, hardware, people, database, procedures, and documentation. In some cases, macro elements may share a generic element. For example, the robot and the NC machine both might be managed by a single operator (the people element). In other cases, generic elements are exclusive to one system.

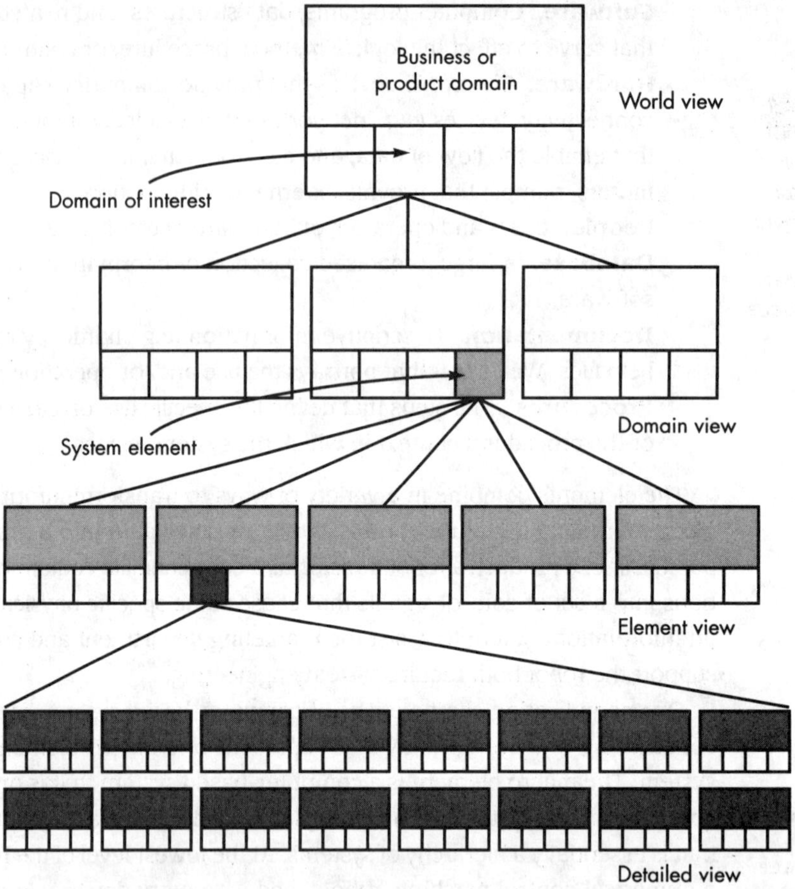

FIGURE 10.1
The system engineering hierarchy

The role of the system engineer is to define the elements for a specific computer-based system in the context of the overall hierarchy of systems (macro elements). In the sections that follow, we examine the tasks that constitute computer system engineering.

10.2 THE SYSTEM ENGINEERING HIERARCHY

Regardless of its domain of focus, system engineering encompasses a collection of top-down and bottom-up methods to navigate the hierarchy illustrated in Figure 10.1. The system engineering process usually begins with a "world view." That is, the entire business or product domain is examined to ensure that the proper business or technology context can be established. The world view is refined to focus more fully on specific domain of interest. Within a specific domain, the need for targeted system elements (e.g., data, software, hardware, people) is analyzed. Finally, the analysis, design, and construction of a targeted system element is initiated. At the top of the hierarchy, a very broad context is established and, at the bottom, detailed technical activities, performed by the relevant engineering discipline (e.g., hardware or software engineering), are conducted.[2]

Stated in a slightly more formal manner, the world view (WV) is composed of a set of domains (D_i), which can each be a system or system of systems in its own right.

$$WV = \{D_1, D_2, D_3, \ldots, D_n\}$$

Each domain is composed of specific elements (E_j) each of which serves some role in accomplishing the objective and goals of the domain or component:

KEY POINT Good system engineering begins with a clear understanding of context—the world view— and then progressively narrows focus until technical detail is understood.

$$D_i = \{E_1, E_2, E_3, \ldots, E_m\}$$

Finally, each element is implemented by specifying the technical components (C_k) that achieve the necessary function for an element:

$$E_j = \{C_1, C_2, C_3, \ldots, C_k\}$$

In the software context, a component could be a computer program, a reusable program component, a module, a class or object, or even a programming language statement.

It is important to note that the system engineer narrows the focus of work as he or she moves downward in the hierarchy just described. However, the world view portrays a clear definition of overall functionality that will enable the engineer to understand the domain, and ultimately the system or product, in the proper context.

10.2.1 System Modeling

System engineering is a modeling process. Whether the focus is on the world view or the detailed view, the engineer creates models that [MOT92]

? What does a system engineering model accomplish?

- Define the processes that serve the needs of the view under consideration.
- Represent the behavior of the processes and the assumptions on which the behavior is based.
- Explicitly define both exogenous and endogenous input[3] to the model.
- Represent all linkages (including output) that will enable the engineer to better understand the view.

To construct a system model, the engineer should consider a number of restraining factors:

2 In some situations, however, system engineers must first consider individual system elements and/or detailed requirements. Using this approach, subsystems are described bottom up by first considering constituent detailed components of the subsystem.

3 *Exogenous* inputs link one constituent of a given view with other constituents at the same level or other levels; *endogenous* input links individual components of a constituent at a particular view.

1. *Assumptions* that reduce the number of possible permutations and variations, thus enabling a model to reflect the problem in a reasonable manner. As an example, consider a three-dimensional rendering product used by the entertainment industry to create realistic animation. One domain of the product enables the representation of 3D human forms. Input to this domain encompasses the ability to specify movement from a live human actor, from video, or by the creation of graphical models. The system engineer makes certain assumptions about the range of allowable human movement (e.g., legs cannot be wrapped around the torso) so that the range of inputs and processing can be limited.

KEY POINT
A system engineer considers the following factors when developing alternative solutions: assumptions, simplifications, limitations, constraints, and customer preferences.

2. *Simplifications* that enable the model to be created in a timely manner. To illustrate, consider an office products company that sells and services a broad range of copiers, faxes, and related equipment. The system engineer is modeling the needs of the service organization and is working to understand the flow of information that spawns a service order. Although a service order can be derived from many origins, the engineer categorizes only two sources: internal demand and external request. This enables a simplified partitioning of input that is required to generate the service order.
3. *Limitations* that help to bound the system. For example, an aircraft avionics system is being modeled for a next generation aircraft. Since the aircraft will be a two-engine design, the monitoring domain for propulsion will be modeled to accommodate a maximum of two engines and associated redundant systems.
4. *Constraints* that will guide the manner in which the model is created and the approach taken when the model is implemented. For example, the technology infrastructure for the three-dimensional rendering system described previously is a single G4-based processor. The computational complexity of problems must be constrained to fit within the processing bounds imposed by the processor.
5. *Preferences* that indicate the preferred architecture for all data, functions, and technology. The preferred solution sometimes comes into conflict with other restraining factors. Yet, customer satisfaction is often predicated on the degree to which the preferred approach is realized.

The resultant system model (at any view) may call for a completely automated solution, a semi-automated solution, or a nonautomated approach. In fact, it is often possible to characterize models of each type that serve as alternative solutions to the problem at hand. In essence, the system engineer simply modifies the relative influence of different system elements (people, hardware, software) to derive models of each type.

10.2.2 System Simulation

In the late 1960s, R. M. Graham [GRA69] made a distressing comment about the way we build computer-based systems: "We build systems like the Wright brothers built airplanes—build the whole thing, push it off a cliff, let it crash, and start over again." In fact, for at least one class of system—the *reactive system*—we continue to do this today.

ADVICE

If simulation capability is unavailable for a reactive system, project risk increases. Consider using an iterative process model that will enable you to deliver a working product in the first iteration and then use other iterations to tune its performance.

Many computer-based systems interact with the real world in a reactive fashion. That is, real-world events are monitored by the hardware and software that form the computer-based system, and based on these events, the system imposes control on the machines, processes, and even people who cause the events to occur. Real-time and embedded systems often fall into the reactive systems category.

Unfortunately, the developers of reactive systems sometimes struggle to make them perform properly. Until recently, it has been difficult to predict the performance, efficiency, and behavior of such systems prior to building them. In a very real sense, the construction of many real-time systems was an adventure in "flying." Surprises (most of them unpleasant) were not discovered until the system was built and "pushed off a cliff." If the system crashed due to incorrect function, inappropriate behavior, or poor performance, we picked up the pieces and started over again.

Many systems in the reactive category control machines and/or processes (e.g., commercial aircraft or petroleum refineries) that must operate with an extremely high degree of reliability. If the system fails, significant economic or human loss could occur. For this reason, the approach described by Graham is both painful and dangerous.

Today, software tools for system modeling and simulation are being used to help to eliminate surprises when reactive, computer-based systems are built. These tools are applied during the system engineering process, while the role of hardware and software, databases and people is being specified. Modeling and simulation tools enable a system engineer to "test drive" a specification of the system. The technical details and specialized modeling techniques that are used to enable a test drive are discussed briefly in Chapter 31.

SEPA WEB

CASE Tools
Modeling & Simulation

10.3 BUSINESS PROCESS ENGINEERING: AN OVERVIEW

The goal of business process engineering (BPE) is to define architectures that will enable a business to use information effectively. Michael Guttman [GUT99] describes the challenge when he states:

> [T]oday's computing environment consists of computing power that's distributed over an enterprise-wide array of heterogeneous processing units, scaled and configured for a wide variety of tasks. Variously known as client-server computing, distributed processing, and enterprise networking (to name just a few overused terms), this new environment promised businesses the greater functionality and flexibility they demanded.

> However, the price for this change is largely borne by the IT [information technology] organizations that must support this polyglot configuration. Today, each IT organization must become, in effect, its own systems integrator and architect. It must design, implement, and support its own unique configuration of heterogeneous computing resources, distributed logically and geographically throughout the enterprise, and connected by an appropriate enterprise-wide networking scheme.
>
> Moreover, this configuration can be expected to change continuously, but unevenly, across the enterprise, due to changes in business requirements and in computing technology. These diverse and incremental changes must be coordinated across a distributed environment consisting of hardware and software supplied by dozens, if not hundreds, of vendors. And, of course, we expect these changes to be seamlessly incorporated without disrupting normal operations and to scale gracefully as those operations expand.

When taking a world view of a company's information technology needs, there is little doubt that system engineering is required. Not only is the specification of the appropriate computing architecture required, but the software architecture that populates the "unique configuration of heterogeneous computing resources" must be developed. Business process engineering is one approach for creating an overall plan for implementing the computing architecture [SPE93].

KEY POINT
Three different architectures are developed during BPE: data architecture, application architecture, and technology infrastructure.

Three different architectures must be analyzed and designed within the context of business objectives and goals:

- data architecture
- applications architecture
- technology infrastructure

XRef
Data objects are discussed in detail in Chapter 12.

The *data architecture* provides a framework for the information needs of a business or business function. The individual building blocks of the architecture are the data objects that are used by the business. A data object contains a set of attributes that define some aspect, quality, characteristic, or descriptor of the data that are being described. For example, an information engineer might define the data object **customer.** To more fully describe **customer,** the following attributes are defined:

Object: Customer
Attributes:
- **name**
- **company name**
- **job classification and purchase authority**
- **business address and contact information**
- **product interest(s)**
- **past purchase(s)**
- **date of last contact**
- **status of contact**

Once a set of data objects is defined, their relationships are identified. A *relationship* indicates how objects are connected to one another. As an example, consider the objects: **customer,** and **product A.** The two objects can be connected by the relationship *purchases;* that is, a customer purchases product A or product A is purchased by a customer. The data objects (there may be hundreds or even thousands for a major business activity) flow between business functions, are organized within a database, and are transformed to provide information that serves the needs of the business.

XRef
A detailed discussion of software architecture is presented in Chapter 14.

The *application architecture* encompasses those elements of a system that transform objects within the data architecture for some business purpose. In the context of this book, we consider the application architecture to be the system of programs (software) that performs this transformation. However, in a broader context, the application architecture might incorporate the role of people (who are information transformers and users) and business procedures that have not been automated.

The *technology infrastructure* provides the foundation for the data and application architectures. The infrastructure encompasses the hardware and software that are used to support the application and data. This includes computers, operating systems, networks, telecommunication links, storage technologies, and the architecture (e.g., client/server) that has been designed to implement these technologies.

ADVICE
As a software engineer, you may never get involved in ISP or BAA. However, if it's clear that these activities haven't been done, inform the stakeholders that the project risk is very high.

To model the system architectures described earlier, a hierarchy of business process engineering activities is defined. Referring to Figure 10.2, the world view is achieved through *information strategy planning* (ISP). ISP views the entire business as an entity and isolates the domains of the business (e.g., engineering, manufacturing, marketing, finance, sales) that are important to the overall enterprise. ISP defines the data objects that are visible at the enterprise level, their relationships, and how they flow between the business domains [MAR90].

The domain view is addressed with a BPE activity called *business area analysis* (BAA). Hares [HAR93] describes BAA in the following manner:

> BAA is concerned with identifying in detail data (in the form of entity [data object] types) and function requirements (in the form of processes) of selected business areas [domains] identified during ISP and ascertaining their interactions (in the form of matrices). It is only concerned with specifying what is required in a business area.

SEPA WEB
Business Process Engineering

As the system engineer begins BAA, the focus narrows to a specific business domain. BAA views the business area as an entity and isolates the business functions and procedures that enable the business area to meet its objectives and goals. BAA, like ISP, defines data objects, their relationships, and how data flow. But at this level, these characteristics are all bounded by the business area being analyzed. The outcome of BAA is to isolate areas of opportunity in which information systems may support the business area.

Once an information system has been isolated for further development, BPE makes a transition into software engineering. By invoking a *business system design* (BSD) step, the basic requirements of a specific information system are modeled and these requirements are translated into data architecture, applications architecture, and technology infrastructure.

FIGURE 10.2
The business process engineering hierarchy

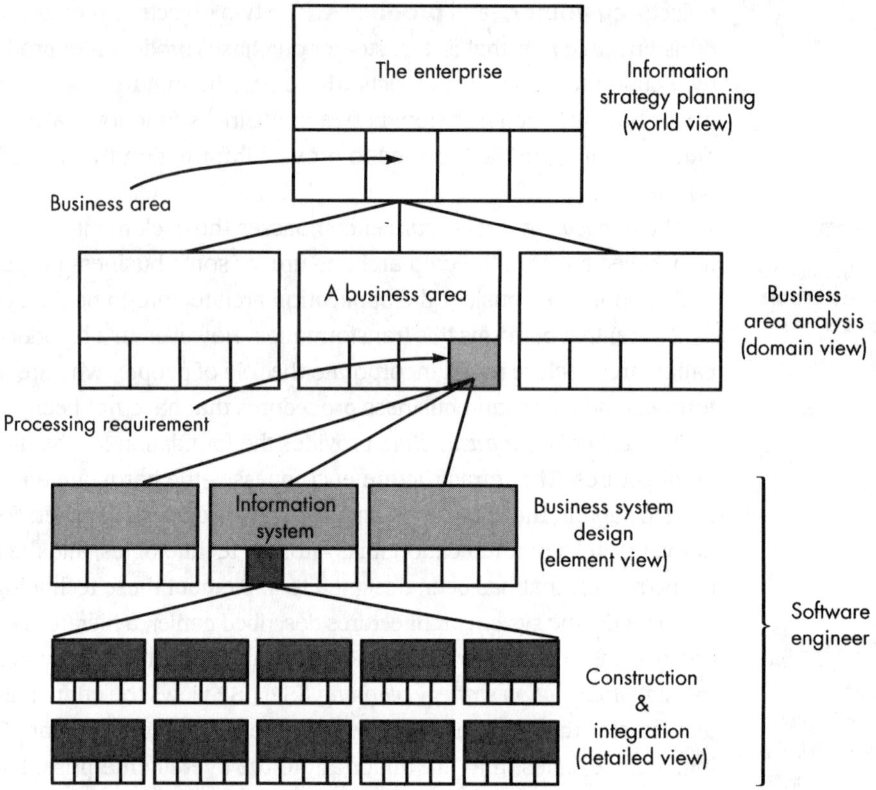

The final BPE step—*construction and integration* focuses on implementation detail. The architecture and infrastructure are implemented by constructing an appropriate database and internal data structures, by building applications using software components, and by selecting appropriate elements of a technology infrastructure to support the design created during BSD. Each of these system components must then be integrated to form a complete information system or application. The integration activity also places the new information system into the business area context, performing all user training and logistics support to achieve a smooth transition.[4]

10.4 PRODUCT ENGINEERING: AN OVERVIEW

The goal of product engineering is to translate the customer's desire for a set of defined capabilities into a working product. To achieve this goal, product engineering—like

4 It should be noted that the terminology (adapted from [MAR90]) used in Figure 10.2 is associated with information engineering, the predecessor of modern BPE. However, the area of focus implied by each activity noted is addressed by all who consider the subject.

FIGURE 10.3
The product engineering hierarchy

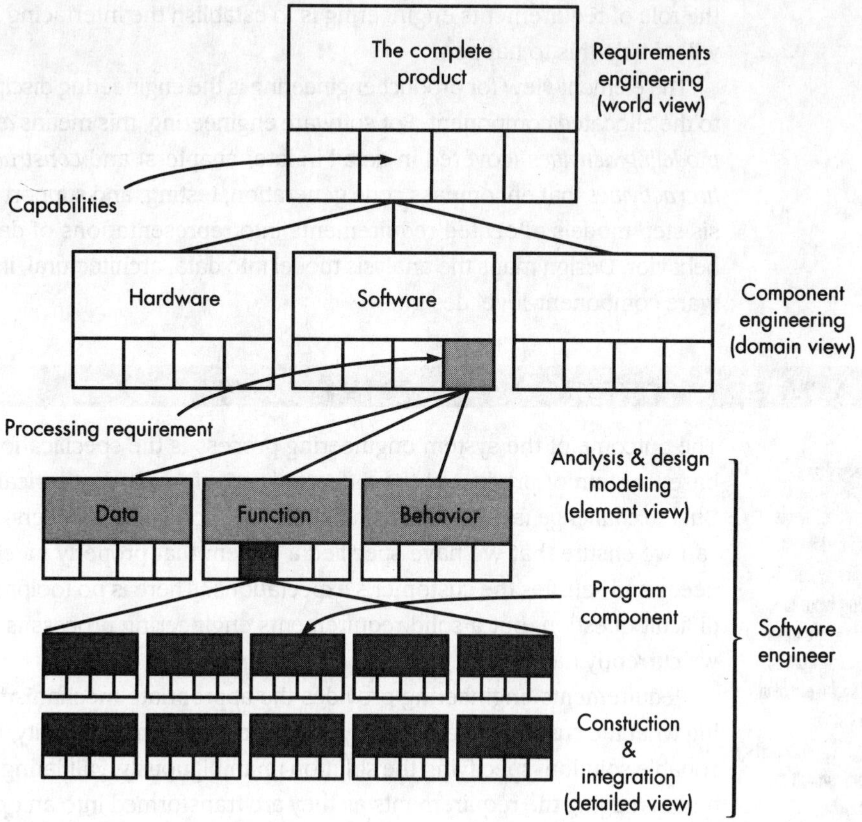

business process engineering—must derive architecture and infrastructure. The architecture encompasses four distinct system components: software, hardware, data (and databases), and people. A support infrastructure is established and includes the technology required to tie the components together and the information (e.g., documents, CD-ROM, video) that is used to support the components.

Referring to Figure 10.3, the world view is achieved through *requirements engineering.* The overall requirements of the product are elicited from the customer. These requirements encompass information and control needs, product function and behavior, overall product performance, design and interfacing constraints, and other special needs. Once these requirements are known, the job of requirements engineering is to allocate function and behavior to each of the four components noted earlier.

Once allocation has occurred, *system component engineering* commences. System component engineering is actually a set of concurrent activities that address each of the system components separately: software engineering, hardware engineering, human engineering, and database engineering. Each of these engineering disciplines takes a domain-specific view, but it is important to note that the engineering disciplines must establish and maintain active communication with one another. Part of the role of requirements engineering is to establish the interfacing mechanisms that will enable this to happen.

The element view for product engineering is the engineering discipline itself applied to the allocated component. For software engineering, this means *analysis and design modeling activities* (covered in detail in later chapters) and *construction and integration activities* that encompass code generation, testing, and support steps. The analysis step models allocated requirements into representations of data, function, and behavior. Design maps the analysis model into data, architectural, interface, and software component-level designs.

10.5 REQUIREMENTS ENGINEERING

Quote:

"The hardest single part of building a software system is deciding what to build. . . . No other part of the work so cripples the resulting system if done wrong. No other part is more difficult to rectify later.

Fred Brooks

The outcome of the system engineering process is the specification of a computer-based system or product at the different levels described generically in Figure 10.1. But the challenge facing system engineers (and software engineers) is profound: How can we ensure that we have specified a system that properly meets the customer's needs and satisfies the customer's expectations? There is no foolproof answer to this difficult question, but a solid requirements engineering process is the best solution we currently have.

Requirements engineering provides the appropriate mechanism for understanding what the customer wants, analyzing need, assessing feasibility, negotiating a reasonable solution, specifying the solution unambiguously, validating the specification, and managing the requirements as they are transformed into an operational system [THA97]. The requirements engineering process can be described in five distinct steps [SOM97]:

- requirements elicitation
- requirements analysis and negotiation
- requirements specification
- system modeling
- requirements validation
- requirements management

WebRef

A detailed report entitled "Issues in Requirements Elicitation" can be downloaded from **www.sei.cmu.edu/publications/documents/92.reports/92.tr.012.html**

10.5.1 Requirements Elicitation

It certainly seems simple enough—ask the customer, the users, and others what the objectives for the system or product are, what is to be accomplished, how the system or product fits into the needs of the business, and finally, how the system or product is to be used on a day-to-day basis. But it isn't simple—it's very hard.

Christel and Kang [CRI92] identify a number of problems that help us understand why requirements elicitation is difficult:

Why is it so difficult to gain a clear understanding of what the customer wants?

- *Problems of scope.* The boundary of the system is ill-defined or the customers/users specify unnecessary technical detail that may confuse, rather than clarify, overall system objectives.
- *Problems of understanding.* The customers/users are not completely sure of what is needed, have a poor understanding of the capabilities and limitations of their computing environment, don't have a full understanding of the problem domain, have trouble communicating needs to the system engineer, omit information that is believed to be "obvious," specify requirements that conflict with the needs of other customers/users, or specify requirements that are ambiguous or untestable.
- *Problems of volatility.* The requirements change over time.

To help overcome these problems, system engineers must approach the requirements gathering activity in an organized manner.

Sommerville and Sawyer [SOM97] suggest a set of detailed guidelines for requirements elicitation, which are summarized in the following steps:

ADVICE Be sure you've assessed overall feasibility before you expend effort and time eliciting detailed requirements.

- Assess the business and technical feasibility for the proposed system.
- Identify the people who will help specify requirements and understand their organizational bias.
- Define the technical environment (e.g., computing architecture, operating system, telecommunications needs) into which the system or product will be placed.
- Identify "domain constraints" (i.e., characteristics of the business environment specific to the application domain) that limit the functionality or performance of the system or product to be built.
- Define one or more requirements elicitation methods (e.g., interviews, focus groups, team meetings).
- Solicit participation from many people so that requirements are defined from different points of view; be sure to identify the rationale for each requirement that is recorded.
- Identify ambiguous requirements as candidates for prototyping.
- Create usage scenarios (see Chapter 11) to help customers/users better identify key requirements.

XRef Requirements elicitation methods are presented in Chapter 11.

The work products produced as a consequence of the requirements elicitation activity will vary depending on the size of the system or product to be built. For most systems, the work products include

- A statement of need and feasibility.
- A bounded statement of scope for the system or product.

- A list of customers, users, and other stakeholders who participated in the requirements elicitation activity.
- A description of the system's technical environment.
- A list of requirements (preferably organized by function) and the domain constraints that apply to each.
- A set of usage scenarios that provide insight into the use of the system or product under different operating conditions.
- Any prototypes developed to better define requirements.

Each of these work products is reviewed by all people who have participated in the requirements elicitation.

10.5.2 Requirements Analysis and Negotiation

Once requirements have been gathered, the work products noted earlier form the basis for *requirements analysis.* Analysis categorizes requirements and organizes them into related subsets; explores each requirement in relationship to others; examines requirements for consistency, omissions, and ambiguity; and ranks requirements based on the needs of customers/users.

What questions must be asked and answered during requirements analysis?

As the requirements analysis activity commences, the following questions are asked and answered:

- Is each requirement consistent with the overall objective for the system/product?
- Have all requirements been specified at the proper level of abstraction? That is, do some requirements provide a level of technical detail that is inappropriate at this stage?
- Is the requirement really necessary or does it represent an add-on feature that may not be essential to the objective of the system?
- Is each requirement bounded and unambiguous?
- Does each requirement have attribution? That is, is a source (generally, a specific individual) noted for each requirement?
- Do any requirements conflict with other requirements?
- Is each requirement achievable in the technical environment that will house the system or product?
- Is each requirement testable, once implemented?

SEPA WEB CHECKLIST
Requirements Analysis

It isn't unusual for customers and users to ask for more than can be achieved, given limited business resources. It also is relatively common for different customers or users to propose conflicting requirements, arguing that their version is "essential for our special needs."

ADVICE

If different customers/users cannot agree on requirements, the risk of failure is very high. Proceed with extreme caution.

The system engineer must reconcile these conflicts through a process of negotiation. Customers, users and stakeholders are asked to rank requirements and then discuss conflicts in priority. Risks associated with each requirement are identified and analyzed (see Chapter 6 for details). Rough guestimates of development effort are made and used to assess the impact of each requirement on project cost and delivery time. Using an iterative approach, requirements are eliminated, combined, and/or modified so that each party achieves some measure of satisfaction.

10.5.3 Requirements Specification

In the context of computer-based systems (and software), the term *specification* means different things to different people. A specification can be a written document, a graphical model, a formal mathematical model, a collection of usage scenarios, a prototype, or any combination of these.

SEPA WEB Negotiation Techniques

Some suggest that a "standard template" [SOM97] should be developed and used for a system specification, arguing that this leads to requirements that are presented in a consistent and therefore more understandable manner. However, it is sometimes necessary to remain flexible when a specification is to be developed. For large systems, a written document, combining natural language descriptions and graphical models may be the best approach. However, usage scenarios may be all that are required for smaller products or systems that reside within well-understood technical environments.

SEPA WEB DOCUMENT System Specification

The *System Specification* is the final work product produced by the system and requirements engineer. It serves as the foundation for hardware engineering, software engineering, database engineering, and human engineering. It describes the function and performance of a computer-based system and the constraints that will govern its development. The specification bounds each allocated system element. The *System Specification* also describes the information (data and control) that is input to and output from the system.

10.5.4 System Modeling

Assume for a moment that you have been asked to specify all requirements for the construction of a gourmet kitchen. You know the dimensions of the room, the location of doors and windows, and the available wall space. You could specify all cabinets and appliances and even indicate where they are to reside in the kitchen. Would this be a useful specification?

The answer is obvious. In order to fully specify what is to be built, you would need a meaningful model of the kitchen, that is, a blueprint or three-dimensional rendering that shows the position of the cabinets and appliances and their relationship to one another. From the model, it would be relatively easy to assess the efficiency of work flow (a requirement for all kitchens), the aesthetic "look" of the room (a personal, but very important requirement).

We build system models for much the same reason that we would develop a blueprint or 3D rendering for the kitchen. It is important to evaluate the system's components in relationship to one another, to determine how requirements fit into this picture, and to assess the "aesthetics" of the system as it has been conceived. Further discussion of system modeling is presented in Section 10.6.

10.5.5 Requirements Validation

The work products produced as a consequence of requirements engineering (a system specification and related information) are assessed for quality during a validation step. *Requirements validation* examines the specification to ensure that all system requirements have been stated unambiguously; that inconsistencies, omissions, and errors have been detected and corrected; and that the work products conform to the standards established for the process, the project, and the product.

ADVICE

A key concern during requirements validation is consistency. Use the system model to ensure that requirements have been consistently stated.

The primary requirements validation mechanism is the formal technical review (Chapter 8). The review team includes system engineers, customers, users, and other stakeholders who examine the system specification[5] looking for errors in content or interpretation, areas where clarification may be required, missing information, inconsistencies (a major problem when large products or systems are engineered), conflicting requirements, or unrealistic (unachievable) requirements.

Although the requirements validation review can be conducted in any manner that results in the discovery of requirements errors, it is useful to examine each requirement against a set of checklist questions. The following questions represent a small subset of those that might be asked:

SEPA WEB CHECKLIST

Requirements

- Are requirements stated clearly? Can they be misinterpreted?
- Is the source (e.g., a person, a regulation, a document) of the requirement identified? Has the final statement of the requirement been examined by or against the original source?
- Is the requirement bounded in quantitative terms?
- What other requirements relate to this requirement? Are they clearly noted via a cross-reference matrix or other mechanism?
- Does the requirement violate any domain constraints?
- Is the requirement testable? If so, can we specify tests (sometimes called *validation criteria*) to exercise the requirement?
- Is the requirement traceable to any system model that has been created?
- Is the requirement traceable to overall system/product objectives?

5 In reality, many FTRs are conducted as the system specification is developed. It is best for the review team to examine small portions of the specification, so that attention can be focused on a specific aspect of the requirements.

- Is the system specification structured in a way that leads to easy understanding, easy reference, and easy translation into more technical work products?
- Has an index for the specification been created?
- Have requirements associated with system performance, behavior, and operational characteristics been clearly stated? What requirements appear to be implicit?

Checklist questions like these help ensure that the validation team has done everything possible to conduct a thorough review of each requirement.

WebRef

An article entitled "Making Requirements Management Work for You" contains pragmatic guidelines: **stsc.hill.af.mil/crosstalk/1999/apr/davis.asp**

10.5.6 Requirements Management

In the preceding chapter, we noted that requirements for computer-based systems change and that the desire to change requirements persists throughout the life of the system. *Requirements management* is a set of activities that help the project team to identify, control, and track requirements and changes to requirements at any time as the project proceeds. Many of these activities are identical to the software configuration management techniques discussed in Chapter 9.

Like SCM, requirements management begins with identification. Each requirement is assigned a unique identifier that might take the form

<requirement type><requirement #>

KEY POINT

Many requirements management activities are borrowed from SCM.

where requirement type takes on values such as F = functional requirement, D = data requirement, B = behavioral requirement, I = interface requirement, and P = output requirement. Hence, a requirement identified as F09 indicates a functional requirement assigned requirement number 9.

Once requirements have been identified, traceability tables are developed. Shown schematically in Figure 10.4, each traceability table relates identified requirements to one or more aspects of the system or its environment. Among many possible traceability tables are the following:

ADVICE

When a system is large and complex, determining the "connections" among requirements can be a daunting task. Use traceability tables to make the job a bit easier.

Features traceability table. Shows how requirements relate to important customer observable system/product features.

Source traceability table. Identifies the source of each requirement.

Dependency traceability table. Indicates how requirements are related to one another.

Subsystem traceability table. Categorizes requirements by the subsystem(s) that they govern.

Interface traceability table. Shows how requirements relate to both internal and external system interfaces.

In many cases, these traceability tables are maintained as part of a requirements database so that they may be quickly searched to understand how a change in one requirement will affect different aspects of the system to be built.

FIGURE 10.4 Generic traceability table

Requirement \ Specific aspect of the system or its environment	A01	A02	A03	A04	A05				Aii
R01			✓		✓				
R02	✓		✓						
R03	✓			✓					✓
R04		✓			✓				
R05	✓	✓		✓					✓
Rnn	✓		✓						

10.6 SYSTEM MODELING

Every computer-based system can be modeled as an information transform using an input-processing-output template. Hatley and Pirbhai [HAT87] have extended this view to include two additional system features—user interface processing and maintenance and self-test processing. Although these additional features are not present for every computer-based system, they are very common, and their specification makes any system model more robust.

XRef
Other system modeling methods take an object-oriented view. The UML approach can be applied at the system level and is discussed in Chapters 21 and 22.

Using a representation of input, processing, output, user interface processing, and self-test processing, a system engineer can create a model of system components that sets a foundation for later steps in each of the engineering disciplines.

To develop the system model, a *system model template* [HAT87] is used. The system engineer allocates system elements to each of five processing regions within the template: (1) user interface, (2) input, (3) system function and control, (4) output, and (5) maintenance and self-test. The format of the architecture template is shown in Figure 10.5.

Like nearly all modeling techniques used in system and software engineering, the system model template enables the analyst to create a hierarchy of detail. A *system context diagram* (SCD) resides at the top level of the hierarchy. The context diagram "establishes the information boundary between the system being implemented and the environment in which the system is to operate" [HAT87]. That is, the SCD defines all external producers of information used by the system, all external consumers of information created by the system, and all entities that communicate through the interface or perform maintenance and self-test.

FIGURE 10.5
System model template [HAT87]

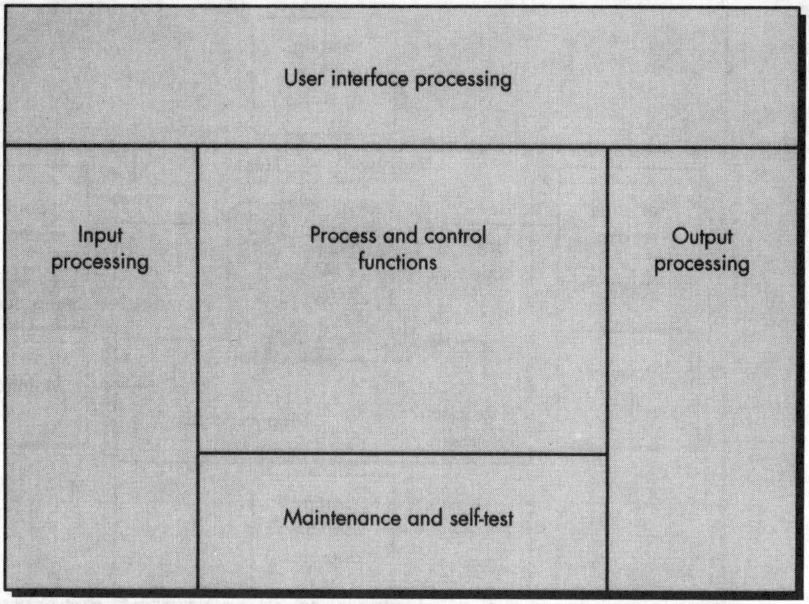

To illustrate the use of the SCD, consider the conveyor line sorting system that was introduced in Chapter 5. The system engineer is presented with the following (somewhat nebulous) statement of objectives for CLSS:

> CLSS must be developed such that boxes moving along a conveyor line will be identified and sorted into one of six bins at the end of the line. The boxes will pass by a sorting station where they will be identified. Based on an identification number printed on the side of the box (an equivalent bar code is provided), the boxes will be shunted into the appropriate bins. Boxes pass in random order and are evenly spaced. The line is moving slowly.

ADVICE

The SCD provides a "big picture" view of the system you must build. Every detail need not be specified at this level. Refine the SCD hierarchically to elaborate the system.

For this example, CLSS is extended and makes use of a personal computer at the sorting station site. The PC executes all CLSS software, interacts with the bar code reader to read part numbers on each box, interacts with the conveyor line monitoring equipment to acquire conveyor line speed, stores all part numbers sorted, interacts with a sorting station operator to produce a variety of reports and diagnostics, sends control signals to the shunting hardware to sort the boxes, and communicates with a central factory automation mainframe. The SCD for CLSS (extended) is shown in Figure 10.6.

Each box shown in Figure 10.6 represents an *external entity*—that is, a producer or consumer of system information. For example, the bar code reader produces information that is input to the CLSS system. The symbol for the entire system (or, at lower levels, major subsystems) is a rectangle with rounded corners. Hence, CLSS is represented in the processing and control region at the center of the SCD. The labeled

FIGURE 10.6
System context diagram for CLSS (extended)

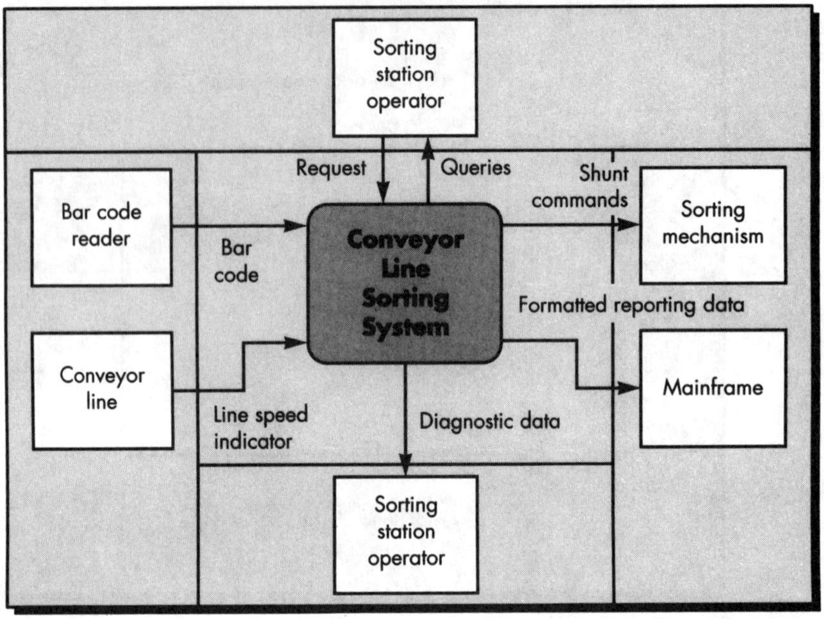

arrows shown in the SCD represent information (data and control) as it moves from the external environment into the CLSS system. The external entity *bar code reader* produces input information that is labeled **bar code**. In essence, the SCD places any system into the context of its external environment.

XRef
The SFD is a precursor to the data flow diagram, discussed in Chapter 12.

The system engineer refines the system context diagram by considering the shaded rectangle in Figure 10.6 in more detail. The major subsystems that enable the conveyor line sorting system to function within the context defined by the SCD are identified. Referring to Figure 10.7, the major subsystems are defined in a *system flow diagram* (SFD) that is derived from the SCD. Information flow across the regions of the SCD is used to guide the system engineer in developing the SFD—a more detailed "schematic" for CLSS. The system flow diagram shows major subsystems and important lines of information (data and control) flow. In addition, the system template partitions the subsystem processing into each of the five regions discussed earlier. At this stage, each of the subsystems can contain one or more system elements (e.g., hardware, software, people) as allocated by the system engineer.

WebRef
A useful white paper on Hatley-Pirbhai method can be found at **www.hasys.com/papers/hp_description.html**

The initial system flow diagram becomes the top node of a hierarchy of SFDs. Each rounded rectangle in the original SFD can be expanded into another architecture template dedicated solely to it. This process is illustrated schematically in Figure 10.8. Each of the SFDs for the system can be used as a starting point for subsequent engineering steps for the subsystem that has been described.

FIGURE 10.7 System flow diagram for CLSS (extended)

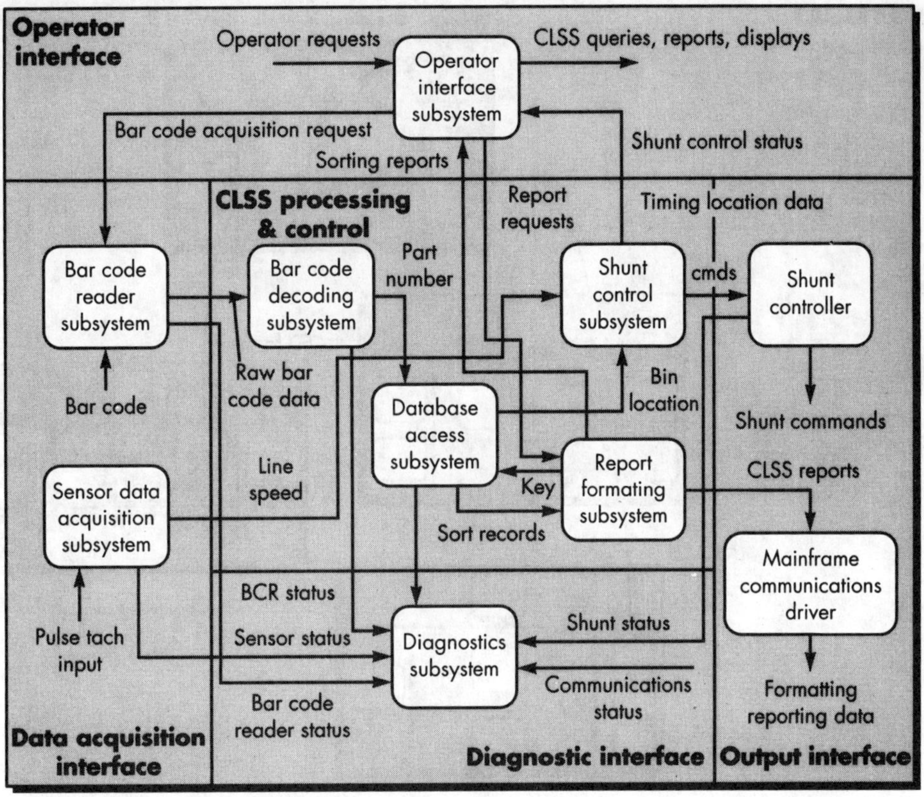

Subsystems and the information that flows between them can be specified (bounded) for subsequent engineering work. A narrative description of each subsystem and a definition of all data that flow between subsystems become important elements of the *System Specification*.

10.7 SUMMARY

A high-technology system encompasses a number of elements: software, hardware, people, database, documentation, and procedures. System engineering helps to translate a customer's needs into a model of a system that makes use of one or more of these elements.

System engineering begins by taking a "world view." A business domain or product is analyzed to establish all basic business requirements. Focus is then narrowed to a "domain view," where each of the system elements is analyzed individually. Each element is allocated to one or more engineering components, which are then addressed by the relevant engineering discipline.

FIGURE 10.8
Building an SFD hierarchy

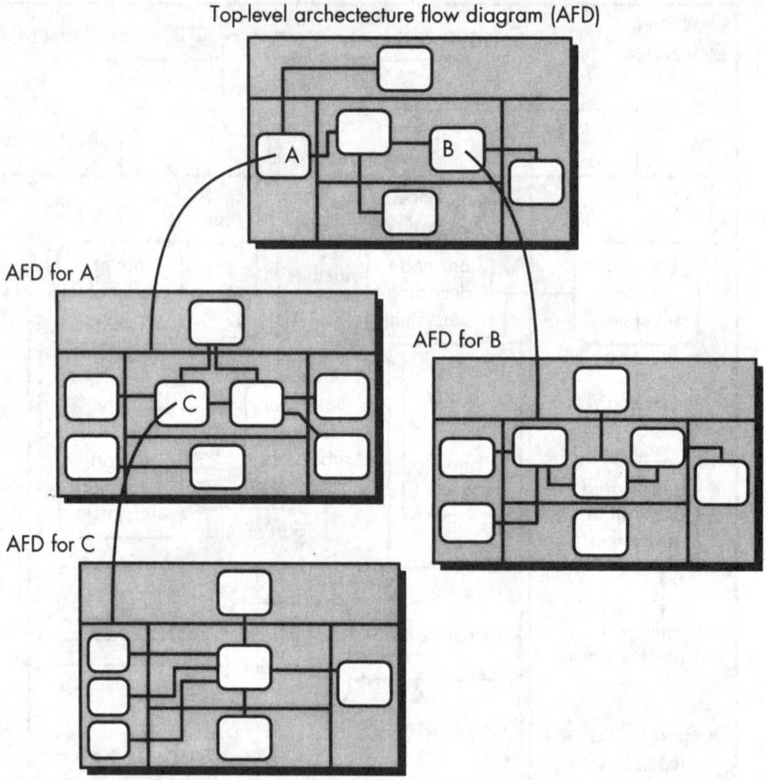

Business process engineering is a system engineering approach that is used to define architectures that enable a business to use information effectively. The intent of business process engineering is to derive comprehensive data architecture, application architecture, and technology infrastructure that will meet the needs of the business strategy and the objectives and goals of each business area. Business process engineering encompasses information strategy planning (ISP), business area analysis (BAA), and application specific analysis that is actually part of software engineering.

Product engineering is a system engineering approach that begins with system analysis. The system engineer identifies the customer's needs, determines economic and technical feasibility, and allocates function and performance to software, hardware, people, and databases—the key engineering components.

System engineering demands intense communication between the customer and the system engineer. This is achieved through a set of activities that are called requirements engineering—elicitation, analysis and negotiation, specification, modeling, validation, and management.

After requirements have been isolated, a system model is produced and representations of each major subsystem can be developed. The system engineering task culminates with the creation of a *System Specification*—a document that forms the foundation for all engineering work that follows.

REFERENCES

[CRI92] Christel, M.G. and K.C. Kang, "Issues in Requirements Elicitation," Software Engineering Institute, CMU/SEI-92-TR-12 7, September 1992.

[GRA69] Graham, R.M., in *Proceedings 1969. NATO Conference on Software Engineering,* 1969.

[GUT99] Guttman, M., "Architectural Requirements for a Changing Business World," *Research Briefs from Cutter Consortium* (an on-line service), June 1, 1999.

[HAR93] Hares, J.S., *Information Engineering for the Advanced Practitioner,* Wiley, 1993, pp. 12–13.

[HAT87] Hatley, D.J. and I.A. Pirbhai, *Strategies for Real-Time System Specification,* Dorset House, 1987.

[MAR90] Martin, J., *Information Engineering: Book II—Planning and Analysis,* Prentice-Hall, 1990.

[MOT92] Motamarri, S., "Systems Modeling and Description," *Software Engineering Notes,* vol. 17, no. 2, April 1992, pp. 57–63.

[SOM97] Somerville, I. and P. Sawyer, *Requirements Engineering,* Wiley, 1997.

[SPE93] Spewak, S., *Enterprise Architecture Planning,* QED Publishing, 1993.

[THA97] Thayer, R.H. and M. Dorfman, *Software Requirements Engineering,* 2nd ed., IEEE Computer Society Press, 1997.

PROBLEMS AND POINTS TO PONDER

10.1. Find as many single-word synonyms for the word *system* as you can. Good luck!

10.2. Build a hierarchical "system of systems" for a system, product, or service with which you are familiar. Your hierarchy should extend down to simple system elements (hardware, software, etc.) along at least one branch of the "tree."

10.3. Select any large system or product with which you are familiar. Define the set of domains that describe the world view of the system or product. Describe the set of elements that make up one or two domains. For one element, identify the technical components that must be engineered.

10.4. Select any large system or product with which you are familiar. State the assumptions, simplifications, limitations, constraints, and preferences that would have to be made to build an effective (and realizable) system model.

10.5. Business process engineering strives to define data and application architecture as well as technology infrastructure. Describe what each of these terms means and provide an example.

10.6. Information strategy planning begins with the definitions of objectives and goals. Provide examples of each from the business domain.

10.7. A system engineer can come from one of three sources: the system developer, the customer, or some outside organization. Discuss the pros and cons that apply to each source. Describe an "ideal" system engineer.

10.8. Your instructor will distribute a high-level description of a computer-based system or product:

a. Develop a set of questions that you should ask as a system engineer.

b. Propose at least two different allocations for the system based on answers to your questions.

c. In class, compare your allocation to those of fellow students.

10.9. Develop a checklist for attributes to be considered when the "feasibility" of a system or product is to be evaluated. Discuss the interplay among attributes and attempt to provide a method for grading each so that a quantitative "feasibility number" may be developed.

10.10. Research the accounting techniques that are used for a detailed cost/benefit analysis of a computer-based system that will require some hardware manufacturing and assembly. Attempt to write a "cookbook" set of guidelines that a technical manager could apply.

10.11. Develop a system context diagram and system flow diagrams for the computer-based system of your choice (or one assigned by your instructor).

10.12. Write a system module narrative that would be contained in system diagram specifications for one or more of the subsystems defined in the SFDs developed for Problem 10.11.

10.13. Research the literature on CASE tools and write a brief paper describing how modeling and simulation tools work. Alternate: Collect literature from two or more CASE vendors that sell modeling and simulation tools and assess the similarities and differences.

10.14. Based on documents provided by your instructor, develop an abbreviated *System Specification* for one of the following computer-based systems:

a. a nonlinear, digital video-editing system

b. a digital scanner for a personal computer

c. an electronic mail system

d. a university registration system

e. an Internet access provider

f. an interactive hotel reservation system

g. a system of local interest

Be sure to create the system models described in Section 10.6.

10.15. Are there characteristics of a system that cannot be established during system engineering activities? Describe the characteristics, if any, and explain why a consideration of them must be delayed until later engineering steps.

10.16. Are there situations in which formal system specification can be abbreviated or eliminated entirely? Explain.

FURTHER READINGS AND INFORMATION SOURCES

Relatively few books have been published on system engineering in recent years. Among those that have appeared are

Blanchard, B.S., *System Engineering Management,* 2nd ed., Wiley, 1997.

Rechtin, E. and M.W. Maier, *The Art of Systems Architecting,* CRC Press, 1996.

Weiss, D., et al., *Software Product-Line Engineering,* Addison-Wesley, 1999.

Books by Armstrong and Sage (*Introduction to Systems Engineering,* Wiley, 1997), Martin (*Systems Engineering Guidebook,* CRC Press, 1996), Wymore (*Model-Based Systems Engineering,* CRC Press, 1993), Lacy (*System Engineering Management,* McGraw-Hill, 1992), Aslaksen and Belcher (*Systems Engineering,* Prentice-Hail, 1992), Athey (*Systematic Systems Approach,* Prentice-Hall, 1982), and Blanchard and Fabrycky (*Systems Engineering and Analysis,* Prentice-Hall, 1981) present the system engineering process (with a distinct engineering emphasis) and provide worthwhile guidance.

In recent years, information engineering texts have been replaced by books that focus on business process engineering. Scheer (*Business Process Engineering: Reference Models for Industrial Enterprises,* Springer-Verlag, 1998) describes business process modeling methods for enterprise-wide information systems. Lozinsky (*Enterprise-wide Software Solutions: Integration Strategies and Practices,* Addison-Wesley, 1998) addresses the use of software packages as a solution that allows a company to migrate from legacy systems to modern business processes. Martin (*Information Engineering,* 3 volumes, Prentice-Hall, 1989, 1990, 1991) presents a comprehensive discussion of information engineering topics. Books by Hares [HAR93], Spewak [SPE93], and Flynn and Fragoso-Diaz (*Information Modeling: An International Perspective,* Prentice-Hall, 1996) also treat the subject in detail.

Davis and Yen (*The Information System Consultant's Handbook: Systems Analysis and Design,* CRC Press, 1998) present encyclopedic coverage of system analysis and design issues in the information systems domain. An excellent IEEE tutorial by Thayer and Dorfman [THA97] discusses the interrelationship between system and software-level requirements analysis issues. A earlier volume by the same authors (*Standards, Guidelines and Examples: System and Software Requirements Engineering,* IEEE Computer Society Press, 1990) presents a comprehensive discussion of standards and guidelines for analysis work.

For those readers actively involved in systems work or interested in a more sophisticated treatment of the topic, Gerald Weinberg's books (*An Introduction to General*

System Thinking, Wiley-Interscience, 1976 and *On the Design of Stable Systems,* Wiley-Interscience, 1979) have become classics and provide an excellent discussion of "general systems thinking" that implicitly leads to a general approach to system analysis and design. More recent books by Weinberg (*General Principles of Systems Design,* Dorset House, 1988 and *Rethinking Systems Analysis and Design,* Dorset House, 1988) continue in the tradition of his earlier work.

A wide variety of information sources on system engineering and related subjects is available on the Internet. An up-to-date list of World Wide Web references that are relevant to system engineering, information engineering, business process engineering, and product engineering can be found at the SEPA Web site:
http://www.mhhe.com/engcs/compsci/pressman/resources/syseng.mhtml

CHAPTER

11 ANALYSIS CONCEPTS AND PRINCIPLES

KEY CONCEPTS

Software requirements engineering is a process of discovery, refinement, modeling, and specification. The system requirements and role allocated to software—initially established by the system engineer—are refined in detail. Models of the required data, information and control flow, and operational behavior are created. Alternative solutions are analyzed and a complete analysis model is created. Donald Reifer [REI94] describes the software requirement engineering process in the following way:

> Requirements engineering is the systematic use of proven principles, techniques, languages, and tools for the cost effective analysis, documentation, and on-going evolution of user needs and the specification of the external behavior of a system to satisfy those user needs. Notice that like all engineering disciplines, requirements engineering is not conducted in a sporadic, random or otherwise haphazard fashion, but instead is the systematic use of proven approaches.

Both the software engineer and customer take an active role in software requirements engineering—a set of activities that is often referred to as *analysis.* The customer attempts to reformulate a sometimes nebulous system-level description of data, function, and behavior into concrete detail. The developer acts as interrogator, consultant, problem solver, and negotiator.

QUICK LOOK

What is it? The overall role of software in a larger system is identified during system engineering (Chapter 10). However, it's necessary to take a harder look at software's role—to understand the specific requirements that must be achieved to build high-quality software. That's the job of software requirements analysis. To perform the job properly, you should follow a set of underlying concepts and principles.

Who does it? Generally, a software engineer performs requirements analysis. However, for complex business applications, a "system analyst"—trained in the business aspects of the application domain—may perform the task.

Why is it important? If you don't analyze, it's highly likely that you'll build a very elegant software solution that solves the wrong problem. The result is: wasted time and money, personal frustration, and unhappy customers.

What are the steps? Data, functional, and behavioral requirements are identified by eliciting information from the customer. Requirements are refined and analyzed to assess their clarity, completeness, and consistency. A specification incorporating a model of the software is created and then validated by both software engineers and customers/users.

What is the work product? An effective representation of the software must be produced as a

QUICK LOOK

consequence of requirements analysis. Like system requirements, software requirements can be represented using a prototype, a specification or even a symbolic model.

How do I ensure that I've done it right? Software requirements analysis work products must be reviewed for clarity, completeness, and consistency.

Quote:

"This sentence contradicts itself—no actually it doesn't."

Douglas Hofstadter

Requirements analysis and specification may appear to be a relatively simple task, but appearances are deceiving. Communication content is very high. Chances for misinterpretation or misinformation abound. Ambiguity is probable. The dilemma that confronts a software engineer may best be understood by repeating the statement of an anonymous (infamous?) customer: "I know you believe you understood what you think I said, but I am not sure you realize that what you heard is not what I meant."

11.1 REQUIREMENTS ANALYSIS

Requirements analysis is a software engineering task that bridges the gap between system level requirements engineering and software design (Figure 11.1). Requirements engineering activities result in the specification of software's operational characteristics (function, data, and behavior), indicate software's interface with other system elements, and establish constraints that software must meet. Requirements analysis allows the software engineer (sometimes called *analyst* in this role) to refine the software allocation and build models of the data, functional, and behavioral domains that will be treated by software. Requirements analysis provides the software designer with a representation of information, function, and behavior that can be translated to data, architectural, interface, and component-level designs. Finally, the requirements specification provides the developer and the customer with the means to assess quality once software is built.

Quote:

"We spend a lot of time—the majority of total project time—not implementing or testing, but trying to decide what to build."

Brian Lawrence

Software requirements analysis may be divided into five areas of effort: (1) problem recognition, (2) evaluation and synthesis, (3) modeling, (4) specification, and (5) review. Initially, the analyst studies the *System Specification* (if one exists) and the *Software Project Plan*. It is important to understand software in a system context and to review the software scope that was used to generate planning estimates. Next, communication for analysis must be established so that problem recognition is ensured. The goal is recognition of the basic problem elements as perceived by the customer/users.

Problem evaluation and solution synthesis is the next major area of effort for analysis. The analyst must define all externally observable data objects, evaluate the flow and content of information, define and elaborate all software functions, understand software behavior in the context of events that affect the system, establish system

FIGURE 11.1
Analysis as a bridge between system engineering and software design

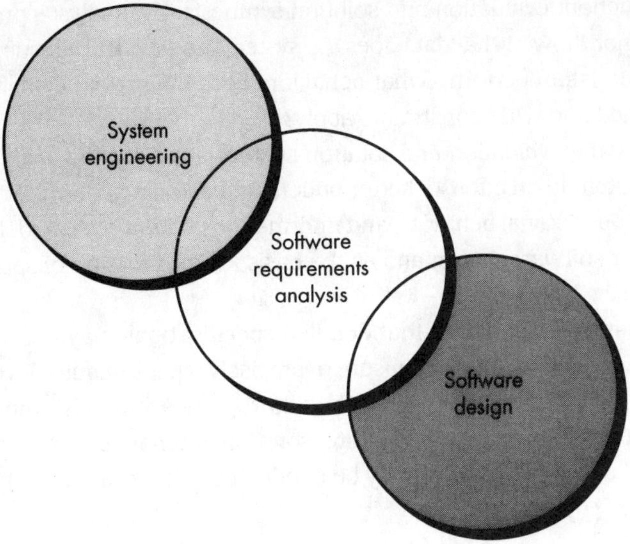

interface characteristics, and uncover additional design constraints. Each of these tasks serves to describe the problem so that an overall approach or solution may be synthesized.

For example, an inventory control system is required for a major supplier of auto parts. The analyst finds that problems with the current manual system include (1) inability to obtain the status of a component rapidly, (2) two- or three-day turnaround to update a card file, (3) multiple reorders to the same vendor because there is no way to associate vendors with components, and so forth. Once problems have been identified, the analyst determines what information is to be produced by the new system and what data will be provided to the system. For instance, the customer desires a daily report that indicates what parts have been taken from inventory and how many similar parts remain. The customer indicates that inventory clerks will log the identification number of each part as it leaves the inventory area.

ADVICE

Expect to do a bit of design during requirements analysis and a bit of requirements analysis during design.

Upon evaluating current problems and desired information (input and output), the analyst begins to synthesize one or more solutions. To begin, the data objects, processing functions, and behavior of the system are defined in detail. Once this information has been established, basic architectures for implementation are considered. A client/server approach would seem to be appropriate, but does the software to support this architecture fall within the scope outlined in the *Software Plan*? A database management system would seem to be required, but is the user/customer's need for associativity justified? The process of evaluation and synthesis continues until both analyst and customer feel confident that software can be adequately specified for subsequent development steps.

What should be my primary focus at this stage?

Throughout evaluation and solution synthesis, the analyst's primary focus is on "what," not "how." What data does the system produce and consume, what functions must the system perform, what behaviors does the system exhibit, what interfaces are defined and what constraints apply?[1]

During the evaluation and solution synthesis activity, the analyst creates models of the system in an effort to better understand data and control flow, functional processing, operational behavior, and information content. The model serves as a foundation for software design and as the basis for the creation of specifications for the software.

In Chapter 2, we noted that detailed specifications may not be possible at this stage. The customer may be unsure of precisely what is required. The developer may be unsure that a specific approach will properly accomplish function and performance. For these, and many other reasons, an alternative approach to requirements analysis, called *prototyping,* may be conducted. We discuss prototyping later in this chapter.

11.2 REQUIREMENTS ELICITATION FOR SOFTWARE

Before requirements can be analyzed, modeled, or specified they must be gathered through an elicitation process. A customer has a problem that may be amenable to a computer-based solution. A developer responds to the customer's request for help. Communication has begun. But, as we have already noted, the road from communication to understanding is often full of potholes.

11.2.1 Initiating the Process

Quote:
"He who asks a question is a fool for five minutes; he who does not ask a question remains a fool forever."
Chinese Proverb

The most commonly used requirements elicitation technique is to conduct a meeting or interview. The first meeting between a software engineer (the analyst) and the customer can be likened to the awkwardness of a first date between two adolescents. Neither person knows what to say or ask; both are worried that what they do say will be misinterpreted; both are thinking about where it might lead (both likely have radically different expectations here); both want to get the thing over with, but at the same time, both want it to be a success.

Yet, communication must be initiated. Gause and Weinberg [GAU89] suggest that the analyst start by asking *context-free questions.* That is, a set of questions that will lead to a basic understanding of the problem, the people who want a solution, the nature of the solution that is desired, and the effectiveness of the first encounter itself. The first set of context-free questions focuses on the customer, the overall goals, and the benefits. For example, the analyst might ask:

1 Davis [DAV93] argues that the terms *what* and *how* are too vague. For an interesting discussion of this issue, the reader should refer to his book.

- Who is behind the request for this work?
- Who will use the solution?
- What will be the economic benefit of a successful solution?
- Is there another source for the solution that you need?

These questions help to identify all stakeholders who will have interest in the software to be built. In addition, the questions identify the measurable benefit of a successful implementation and possible alternatives to custom software development.

The next set of questions enables the analyst to gain a better understanding of the problem and the customer to voice his or her perceptions about a solution:

Quote:

"Plain question and plain answer make the shortest road out of most perplexities."

Mark Twain

- How would you characterize "good" output that would be generated by a successful solution?
- What problem(s) will this solution address?
- Can you show me (or describe) the environment in which the solution will be used?
- Will special performance issues or constraints affect the way the solution is approached?

The final set of questions focuses on the effectiveness of the meeting. Gause and Weinberg [GAU89] call these *meta-questions* and propose the following (abbreviated) list:

ADVICE

If a system or product will serve many users, be absolutely certain that requirements are elicited from a representative cross-section of users. If only one user defines all requirements, acceptance risk is high.

- Are you the right person to answer these questions? Are your answers "official"?
- Are my questions relevant to the problem that you have?
- Am I asking too many questions?
- Can anyone else provide additional information?
- Should I be asking you anything else?

These questions (and others) will help to "break the ice" and initiate the communication that is essential to successful analysis. But a question and answer meeting format is not an approach that has been overwhelmingly successful. In fact, the Q&A session should be used for the first encounter only and then replaced by a meeting format that combines elements of problem solving, negotiation, and specification. An approach to meetings of this type is presented in the next section.

11.2.2 Facilitated Application Specification Techniques

Too often, customers and software engineers have an unconscious "us and them" mind-set. Rather than working as a team to identify and refine requirements, each constituency defines its own "territory" and communicates through a series of memos, formal position papers, documents, and question and answer sessions. History has shown that this approach doesn't work very well. Misunderstandings abound, important information is omitted, and a successful working relationship is never established.

WebRef
One approach to FAST is called "joint application design" (JAD). A detailed discussion of JAD can be found at
www.bee.net/bluebird/jaddoc.htm

It is with these problems in mind that a number of independent investigators have developed a team-oriented approach to requirements gathering that is applied during early stages of analysis and specification. Called *facilitated application specification techniques* (FAST), this approach encourages the creation of a joint team of customers and developers who work together to identify the problem, propose elements of the solution, negotiate different approaches and specify a preliminary set of solution requirements [ZAH90]. FAST has been used predominantly by the information systems community, but the technique offers potential for improved communication in applications of all kinds.

Many different approaches to FAST have been proposed.[2] Each makes use of a slightly different scenario, but all apply some variation on the following basic guidelines:

What makes a FAST meeting different from an ordinary meeting?

- A meeting is conducted at a neutral site and attended by both software engineers and customers.
- Rules for preparation and participation are established.
- An agenda is suggested that is formal enough to cover all important points but informal enough to encourage the free flow of ideas.
- A "facilitator" (can be a customer, a developer, or an outsider) controls the meeting.
- A "definition mechanism" (can be work sheets, flip charts, or wall stickers or an electronic bulletin board, chat room or virtual forum) is used.
- The goal is to identify the problem, propose elements of the solution, negotiate different approaches, and specify a preliminary set of solution requirements in an atmosphere that is conducive to the accomplishment of the goal.

Quote:
"Facts do not cease to exist because they are ignored."
Aldous Huxley

To better understand the flow of events as they occur in a typical FAST meeting, we present a brief scenario that outlines the sequence of events that lead up to the meeting, occur during the meeting, and follow the meeting.

Initial meetings between the developer and customer (Section 11.2.1) occur and basic questions and answers help to establish the scope of the problem and the overall perception of a solution. Out of these initial meetings, the developer and customer write a one- or two-page "product request." A meeting place, time, and date for FAST are selected and a facilitator is chosen. Attendees from both the development and customer/user organizations are invited to attend. The product request is distributed to all attendees before the meeting date.

---

2 Two of the more popular approaches to FAST are joint application development (JAD), developed by IBM and the METHOD, developed by Performance Resources, Inc., Falls Church, VA.

KEY POINT
Before the FAST meeting, make a list of objects, services, constraints, and performance criteria.

While reviewing the request in the days before the meeting, each FAST attendee is asked to make a list of *objects* that are part of the environment that surrounds the system, other objects that are to be produced by the system, and objects that are used by the system to perform its functions. In addition, each attendee is asked to make another list of *services* (processes or functions) that manipulate or interact with the objects. Finally, lists of *constraints* (e.g., cost, size, business rules) and *performance criteria* (e.g., speed, accuracy) are also developed. The attendees are informed that the lists are not expected to be exhaustive but are expected to reflect each person's perception of the system.

As an example,[3] assume that a FAST team working for a consumer products company has been provided with the following product description:

> Our research indicates that the market for home security systems is growing at a rate of 40 percent per year. We would like to enter this market by building a microprocessor-based home security system that would protect against and/or recognize a variety of undesirable "situations" such as illegal entry, fire, flooding, and others. The product, tentatively called *SafeHome,* will use appropriate sensors to detect each situation, can be programmed by the homeowner, and will automatically telephone a monitoring agency when a situation is detected.

In reality, considerably more information would be provided at this stage. But even with additional information, ambiguity would be present, omissions would likely exist, and errors might occur. For now, the preceding "product description" will suffice.

The FAST team is composed of representatives from marketing, software and hardware engineering, and manufacturing. An outside facilitator is to be used.

KEY POINT
Objects are manipulated by services and must "live" within the constraints and performance defined by the FAST team.

Each person on the FAST team develops the lists described previously. Objects described for *SafeHome* might include smoke detectors, window and door sensors, motion detectors, an alarm, an event (a sensor has been activated), a control panel, a display, telephone numbers, a telephone call, and so on. The list of services might include setting the alarm, monitoring the sensors, dialing the phone, programming the control panel, reading the display (note that services act on objects). In a similar fashion, each FAST attendee will develop lists of constraints (e.g., the system must have a manufactured cost of less than $80, must be user-friendly, must interface directly to a standard phone line) and performance criteria (e.g., a sensor event should be recognized within one second, an event priority scheme should be implemented).

As the FAST meeting begins, the first topic of discussion is the need and justification for the new product—everyone should agree that the product is justified. Once agreement has been established, each participant presents his or her lists for discussion. The lists can be pinned to the walls of the room using large sheets of paper, stuck to the walls using adhesive backed sheets, or written on a wall board. Alternatively, the lists may have been posted on an electronic bulletin board or posed in

---

3 This example (with extensions and variations) will be used to illustrate important software engineering methods in many of the chapters that follow. As an exercise, it would be worthwhile to conduct your own FAST meeting and develop a set of lists for it.

a chat room environment for review prior to the meeting. Ideally, each list entry should be capable of being manipulated separately so that lists can be combined, entries can be deleted and additions can be made. At this stage, critique and debate are strictly prohibited.

ADVICE

Avoid the impulse to shoot down a customer's idea as "too costly" or "impractical." The idea here is to negotiate a list that is acceptable to all. To do this, you must keep an open mind.

After individual lists are presented in one topic area, a combined list is created by the group. The combined list eliminates redundant entries, adds any new ideas that come up during the discussion, but does not delete anything. After combined lists for all topic areas have been created, discussion—coordinated by the facilitator—ensues. The combined list is shortened, lengthened, or reworded to properly reflect the product/system to be developed. The objective is to develop a *consensus list* in each topic area (objects, services, constraints, and performance). The lists are then set aside for later action.

Once the consensus lists have been completed, the team is divided into smaller subteams; each works to develop *mini-specifications* for one or more entries on each of the lists.[4] Each mini-specification is an elaboration of the word or phrase contained on a list. For example, the mini-specification for the *SafeHome* object **control panel** might be

- mounted on wall
- size approximately 9 × 5 inches
- contains standard 12-key pad and special keys
- contains LCD display of the form shown in sketch [not presented here]
- all customer interaction occurs through keys
- used to enable and disable the system
- software provides interaction guidance, echoes, and the like
- connected to all sensors

Each subteam then presents each of its mini-specs to all FAST attendees for discussion. Additions, deletions, and further elaboration are made. In some cases, the development of mini-specs will uncover new objects, services, constraints, or performance requirements that will be added to the original lists. During all discussions, the team may raise an issue that cannot be resolved during the meeting. An issues list is maintained so that these ideas will be acted on later.

After the mini-specs are completed, each FAST attendee makes a list of *validation criteria* for the product/system and presents his or her list to the team. A consensus list of validation criteria is then created. Finally, one or more participants (or outsiders) is assigned the task of writing the complete draft specification using all inputs from the FAST meeting.

Quote:

"The beginning is the most important part of the work."

Plato

---

4 An alternative approach results in the creation of use-cases. See Section 11.2.4 for details.

FAST is not a panacea for the problems encountered in early requirements elicitation. But the team approach provides the benefits of many points of view, instantaneous discussion and refinement, and is a concrete step toward the development of a specification.

11.2.3 Quality Function Deployment

KEY POINT

QFD defines requirements in a way that maximizes customer satisfaction.

Quality function deployment (QFD) is a quality management technique that translates the needs of the customer into technical requirements for software. Originally developed in Japan and first used at the Kobe Shipyard of Mitsubishi Heavy Industries, Ltd., in the early 1970s, QFD "concentrates on maximizing customer satisfaction from the software engineering process [ZUL92]." To accomplish this, QFD emphasizes an understanding of what is valuable to the customer and then deploys these values throughout the engineering process. QFD identifies three types of requirements [ZUL92]:

ADVICE

Everyone wants to implement lots of exciting requirements, but be careful. That's how "requirements creep" sets in. On the other hand, often the exciting requirements lead to a breakthrough product!

Normal requirements. The objectives and goals that are stated for a product or system during meetings with the customer. If these requirements are present, the customer is satisfied. Examples of normal requirements might be requested types of graphical displays, specific system functions, and defined levels of performance.

Expected requirements. These requirements are implicit to the product or system and may be so fundamental that the customer does not explicitly state them. Their absence will be a cause for significant dissatisfaction. Examples of expected requirements are: ease of human/machine interaction, overall operational correctness and reliability, and ease of software installation.

Exciting requirements. These features go beyond the customer's expectations and prove to be very satisfying when present. For example, word processing software is requested with standard features. The delivered product contains a number of page layout capabilities that are quite pleasing and unexpected.

WebRef

The QFD Institute is an excellent source for information: **www.qfdi.org**

In actuality, QFD spans the entire engineering process [AKA90]. However, many QFD concepts are applicable to the requirements elicitation activity. We present an overview of only these concepts (adapted for computer software) in the paragraphs that follow.

In meetings with the customer, *function deployment* is used to determine the value of each function that is required for the system. *Information deployment* identifies both the data objects and events that the system must consume and produce. These are tied to the functions. Finally, *task deployment* examines the behavior of the system or product within the context of its environment. *Value analysis* is conducted to determine the relative priority of requirements determined during each of the three deployments.

QFD uses customer interviews and observation, surveys, and examination of historical data (e.g., problem reports) as raw data for the requirements gathering activity. These data are then translated into a table of requirements—called the *customer voice table*—that is reviewed with the customer. A variety of diagrams, matrices, and evaluation methods are then used to extract expected requirements and to attempt to derive exciting requirements [BOS91].

11.2.4 Use-Cases

KEY POINT

A use-case is a scenario that describes how software is to be used in a given situation.

As requirements are gathered as part of informal meetings, FAST, or QFD, the software engineer (analyst) can create a set of scenarios that identify a thread of usage for the system to be constructed. The scenarios, often called *use-cases* [JAC92], provide a description of how the system will be used.

To create a use-case, the analyst must first identify the different types of people (or devices) that use the system or product. These *actors* actually represent roles that people (or devices) play as the system operates. Defined somewhat more formally, an actor is anything that communicates with the system or product and that is external to the system itself.

SEPA WEB DOCUMENT

Use-Cases

It is important to note that an actor and a user are not the same thing. A typical user may play a number of different roles when using a system, whereas an actor represents a class of external entities (often, but not always, people) that play just one role. As an example, consider a machine operator (a user) who interacts with the control computer for a manufacturing cell that contains a number of robots and numerically controlled machines. After careful review of requirements, the software for the control computer requires four different modes (roles) for interaction: programming mode, test mode, monitoring mode, and troubleshooting mode. Therefore, four actors can be defined: programmer, tester, monitor, and troubleshooter. In some cases, the machine operator can play all of these roles. In others, different people may play the role of each actor.

KEY POINT

Use-cases are defined from an actor's point of view. An actor is a role that people (users) or devices play as they interact with the software.

Because requirements elicitation is an evolutionary activity, not all actors are identified during the first iteration. It is possible to identify primary actors [JAC92] during the first iteration and secondary actors as more is learned about the system. Primary actors interact to achieve required system function and derive the intended benefit from the system. They work directly and frequently with the software. Secondary actors support the system so that primary actors can do their work.

Once actors have been identified, use-cases can be developed. The use-case describes the manner in which an actor interacts with the system. Jacobson [JAC92] suggests a number of questions that should be answered by the use-case:

- What main tasks or functions are performed by the actor?
- What system information will the actor acquire, produce, or change?
- Will the actor have to inform the system about changes in the external environment?

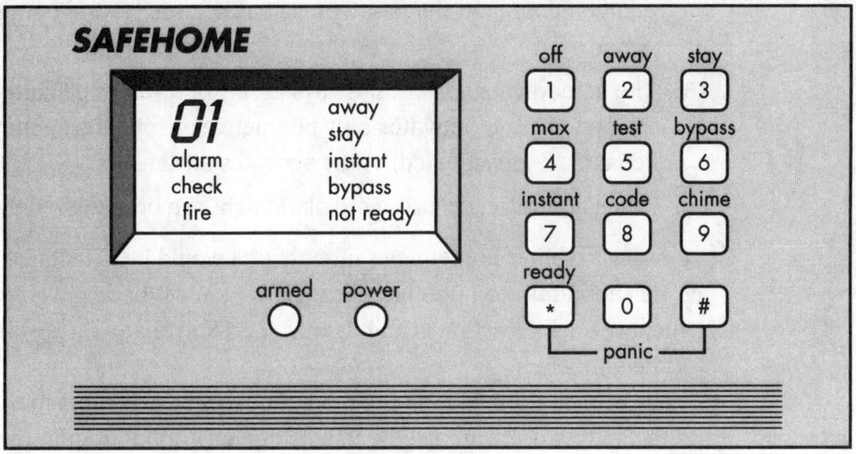

FIGURE 11.2 SafeHome control panel

- What information does the actor desire from the system?
- Does the actor wish to be informed about unexpected changes?

WebRef
A detailed discussion of use-cases, including examples, guidelines, and templates is presented at **members.aol.com/acockburn/papers/OnUseCases.htm**

In general, a use-case is simply a written narrative that describes the role of an actor as interaction with the system occurs.

Recalling basic *SafeHome* requirements (Section 11.2.2), we can define three actors: the homeowner (the user), sensors (devices attached to the system), and the monitoring and response subsystem (the central station that monitors *SafeHome*). For the purposes of this example, we consider only the **homeowner** actor. The homeowner interacts with the product in a number of different ways:

- enters a password to allow all other interactions
- inquires about the status of a security zone
- inquires about the status of a sensor
- presses the panic button in an emergency
- activates/deactivates the security system

A use-case for *system activation* follows:

1. The homeowner observes a prototype of the *SafeHome* control panel (Figure 11.2) to determine if the system is ready for input. If the system is not ready, the homeowner must physically close windows/doors so that the ready indicator is present. [A *not ready* indicator implies that a sensor is open; i.e., that a door or window is open.]
2. The homeowner uses the keypad to key in a four-digit password. The password is compared with the valid password stored in the system. If the password is incorrect, the control panel will beep once and reset itself for

additional input. If the password is correct, the control panel awaits further action.

3. The homeowner selects and keys in *stay* or *away* (see Figure 11.2) to activate the system. *Stay* activates only perimeter sensors (inside motion detecting sensors are deactivated). *Away* activates all sensors.
4. When activation occurs, a red alarm light can be observed by the homeowner.

Use-cases for other homeowner interactions would be developed in a similar manner. It is important to note that each use-case must be reviewed with care. If some element of the interaction is ambiguous, it is likely that a review of the use-case will indicate a problem.

Each use-case provides an unambiguous scenario of interaction between an actor and the software. It can also be used to specify timing requirements or other constraints for the scenario. For example, in the use-case just noted, requirements indicate that activation occurs 30 seconds after the *stay* or *away* key is hit. This information can be appended to the use-case.

Use-cases describe scenarios that will be perceived differently by different actors. Wyder [WYD96] suggests that quality function deployment can be used to develop a weighted priority value for each use-case. To accomplish this, use-cases are evaluated from the point of view of all actors defined for the system. A priority value is assigned to each use-case (e.g., a value from 1 to 10) by each of the actors.[5] An average priority is then computed, indicating the perceived importance of each of the use-cases. When an iterative process model is used for software engineering, the priorities can influence which system functionality is delivered first.

11.3 ANALYSIS PRINCIPLES

Over the past two decades, a large number of analysis modeling methods have been developed. Investigators have identified analysis problems and their causes and have developed a variety of modeling notations and corresponding sets of heuristics to overcome them. Each analysis method has a unique point of view. However, all analysis methods are related by a set of operational principles:

? What are the underlying principles that guide analysis work?

1. The information domain of a problem must be represented and understood.
2. The functions that the software is to perform must be defined.
3. The behavior of the software (as a consequence of external events) must be represented.
4. The models that depict information, function, and behavior must be partitioned in a manner that uncovers detail in a layered (or hierarchical) fashion.

5 Ideally, this evaluation should be performed by individuals from the organization or business function represented by an actor.

5. The analysis process should move from essential information toward implementation detail.

By applying these principles, the analyst approaches a problem systematically. The information domain is examined so that function may be understood more completely. Models are used so that the characteristics of function and behavior can be communicated in a compact fashion. Partitioning is applied to reduce complexity. Essential and implementation views of the software are necessary to accommodate the logical constraints imposed by processing requirements and the physical constraints imposed by other system elements.

In addition to these operational analysis principles, Davis [DAV95a] suggests a set[6] of guiding principles for requirements engineering:

- *Understand the problem before you begin to create the analysis model.* There is a tendency to rush to a solution, even before the problem is understood. This often leads to elegant software that solves the wrong problem!
- *Develop prototypes that enable a user to understand how human/machine interaction will occur.* Since the perception of the quality of software is often based on the perception of the "friendliness" of the interface, prototyping (and the iteration that results) are highly recommended.
- *Record the origin of and the reason for every requirement.* This is the first step in establishing traceability back to the customer.
- *Use multiple views of requirements.* Building data, functional, and behavioral models provide the software engineer with three different views. This reduces the likelihood that something will be missed and increases the likelihood that inconsistency will be recognized.
- *Rank requirements.* Tight deadlines may preclude the implementation of every software requirement. If an incremental process model (Chapter 2) is applied, those requirements to be delivered in the first increment must be identified.
- *Work to eliminate ambiguity.* Because most requirements are described in a natural language, the opportunity for ambiguity abounds. The use of formal technical reviews is one way to uncover and eliminate ambiguity.

Quote:
"A computer will do what you tell it to do, but that may be much different from what you had in mind."
Joseph Weizenbaum

A software engineer who takes these principles to heart is more likely to develop a software specification that will provide an excellent foundation for design.

11.3.1 The Information Domain

All software applications can be collectively called *data processing*. Interestingly, this term contains a key to our understanding of software requirements. Software is built

6 Only a small subset of Davis's requirements engineering principles are noted here. For more information, see [DAV95a].

to process data, to transform data from one form to another; that is, to accept input, manipulate it in some way, and produce output. This fundamental statement of objective is true whether we build batch software for a payroll system or real-time embedded software to control fuel flow to an automobile engine.

KEY POINT

The information domain of a problem encompasses data items or objects that contain numbers, text, images, audio, video, or any combination of these.

It is important to note, however, that software also processes events. An event represents some aspect of system control and is really nothing more than Boolean data—it is either on or off, true or false, there or not there. For example, a pressure sensor detects that pressure exceeds a safe value and sends an alarm signal to monitoring software. The alarm signal is an event that controls the behavior of the system. Therefore, data (numbers, text, images, sounds, video, etc.) and control (events) both reside within the information domain of a problem.

The first operational analysis principle requires an examination of the information domain and the creation of a *data model.* The information domain contains three different views of the data and control as each is processed by a computer program: (1) information content and relationships (the data model), (2) information flow, and (3) information structure. To fully understand the information domain, each of these views should be considered.

ADVICE

To begin your understanding of the information domain, the first question to be asked is: "What information does this system produce as output?"

Information content represents the individual data and control objects that constitute some larger collection of information transformed by the software. For example, the data object, **paycheck,** is a composite of a number of important pieces of data: the payee's name, the net amount to be paid, the gross pay, deductions, and so forth. Therefore, the content of **paycheck** is defined by the attributes that are needed to create it. Similarly, the content of a control object called **system status** might be defined by a string of bits. Each bit represents a separate item of information that indicates whether or not a particular device is on- or off-line.

Data and control objects can be related to other data and control objects. For example, the data object paycheck has one or more relationships with the objects timecard, employee, bank, and others. During the analysis of the information domain, these relationships should be defined.

Information flow represents the manner in which data and control change as each moves through a system. Referring to Figure 11.3, input objects are transformed to intermediate information (data and/or control), which is further transformed to output. Along this transformation path (or paths), additional information may be introduced from an existing data store (e.g., a disk file or memory buffer). The transformations applied to the data are functions or subfunctions that a program must perform. Data and control that move between two transformations (functions) define the interface for each function.

Information structure represents the internal organization of various data and control items. Are data or control items to be organized as an *n*-dimensional table or as a hierarchical tree structure? Within the context of the structure, what information is related to other information? Is all information contained within a single structure or

FIGURE 11.3
Information flow and transformation

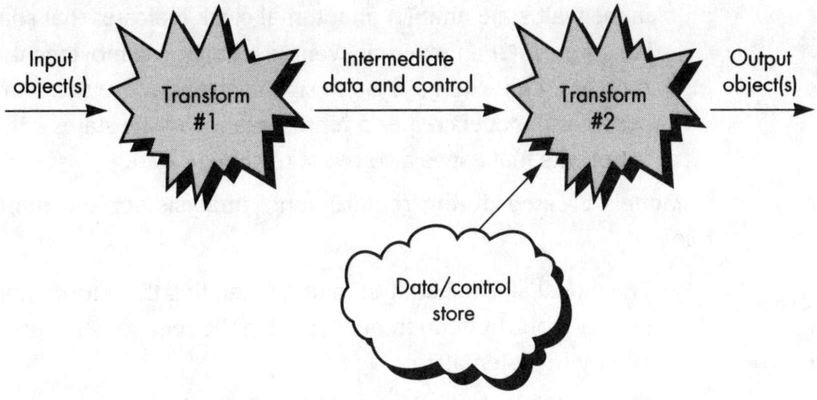

are distinct structures to be used? How does information in one information structure relate to information in another structure? These questions and others are answered by an assessment of information structure. It should be noted that data structure, a related concept discussed later in this book, refers to the design and implementation of information structure within the software.

11.3.2 Modeling

We create functional models to gain a better understanding of the actual entity to be built. When the entity is a physical thing (a building, a plane, a machine), we can build a model that is identical in form and shape but smaller in scale. However, when the entity to be built is software, our model must take a different form. It must be capable of representing the information that software transforms, the functions (and subfunctions) that enable the transformation to occur, and the behavior of the system as the transformation is taking place.

The second and third operational analysis principles require that we build models of function and behavior.

? What types of models do we create during requirements analysis?

Functional models. Software transforms information, and in order to accomplish this, it must perform at least three generic functions: input, processing, and output. When functional models of an application are created, the software engineer focuses on problem specific functions. The functional model begins with a single context level model (i.e., the name of the software to be built). Over a series of iterations, more and more functional detail is provided, until a thorough delineation of all system functionality is represented.

Behavioral models. Most software responds to events from the outside world. This stimulus/response characteristic forms the basis of the behavioral model. A computer program always exists in some state—an externally observable mode of behavior (e.g., waiting, computing, printing, polling) that is changed only when some event occurs. For example, software will remain in the wait state until (1) an internal clock indicates that some time interval has passed, (2) an external event (e.g., a mouse movement) causes an interrupt, or (3) an external system signals the software to act in some manner. A behavioral model creates a representation of the states of the software and the events that cause a software to change state.

Models created during requirements analysis serve a number of important roles:

How do we use the models we create during requirements analysis?

- The model aids the analyst in understanding the information, function, and behavior of a system, thereby making the requirements analysis task easier and more systematic.
- The model becomes the focal point for review and, therefore, the key to a determination of completeness, consistency, and accuracy of the specifications.
- The model becomes the foundation for design, providing the designer with an essential representation of software that can be "mapped" into an implementation context.

The analysis methods that are discussed in Chapters 12 and 21 are actually modeling methods. Although the modeling method that is used is often a matter of personal (or organizational) preference, the modeling activity is fundamental to good analysis work.

11.3.3 Partitioning

KEY POINT
Partitioning is a process that results in the elaboration of data, function, or behavior. It may be performed horizontally or vertically.

Problems are often too large and complex to be understood as a whole. For this reason, we tend to partition (divide) such problems into parts that can be easily understood and establish interfaces between the parts so that overall function can be accomplished. The fourth operational analysis principle suggests that the information, functional, and behavioral domains of software can be partitioned.

In essence, *partitioning* decomposes a problem into its constituent parts. Conceptually, we establish a hierarchical representation of function or information and then partition the uppermost element by (1) exposing increasing detail by moving vertically in the hierarchy or (2) functionally decomposing the problem by moving horizontally in the hierarchy. To illustrate these partitioning approaches, let us reconsider the *SafeHome* security system described in Section 11.2.2. The software allocation for *SafeHome* (derived as a consequence of system engineering and FAST activities) can be stated in the following paragraphs:

SafeHome software enables the homeowner to configure the security system when it is installed, monitors all sensors connected to the security system, and interacts with the homeowner through a keypad and function keys contained in the *SafeHome* control panel shown in Figure 11.2.

FIGURE 11.4
Horizontal partitioning of SafeHome function

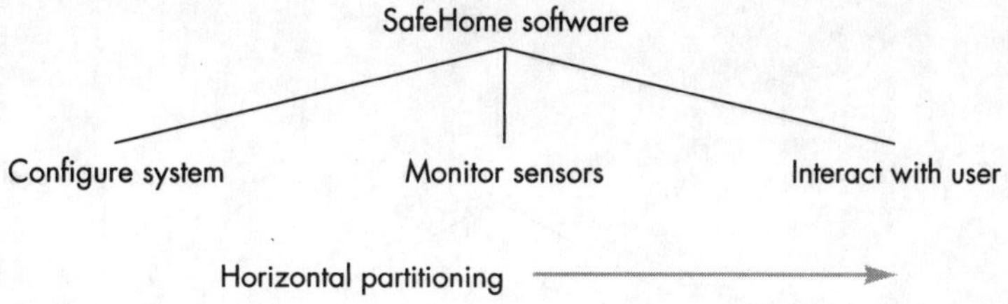

During installation, the *SafeHome* control panel is used to "program" and configure the system. Each sensor is assigned a number and type, a master password is programmed for arming and disarming the system, and telephone number(s) are input for dialing when a sensor event occurs.

When a sensor event is recognized, the software invokes an audible alarm attached to the system. After a delay time that is specified by the homeowner during system configuration activities, the software dials a telephone number of a monitoring service, provides information about the location, reporting the nature of the event that has been detected. The telephone number will be redialed every 20 seconds until telephone connection is obtained.

All interaction with *SafeHome* is managed by a user-interaction subsystem that reads input provided through the keypad and function keys, displays prompting messages on the LCD display, displays system status information on the LCD display. Keyboard interaction takes the following form . . .

The requirements for *SafeHome* software may be analyzed by partitioning the information, functional, and behavioral domains of the product. To illustrate, the functional domain of the problem will be partitioned. Figure 11.4 illustrates a *horizontal decomposition* of *SafeHome* software. The problem is partitioned by representing constituent *SafeHome* software functions, moving horizontally in the functional hierarchy. Three major functions are noted on the first level of the hierarchy.

Quote:
"Furious activity is no substitute for understanding."
H. H. Williams

The subfunctions associated with a major *SafeHome* function may be examined by exposing detail vertically in the hierarchy, as illustrated in Figure 11.5. Moving downward along a single path below the function *monitor sensors,* partitioning occurs vertically to show increasing levels of functional detail.

The partitioning approach that we have applied to *SafeHome* functions can also be applied to the information domain and behavioral domain as well. In fact, partitioning of information flow and system behavior (discussed in Chapter 12) will provide additional insight into software requirements. As the problem is partitioned, interfaces between functions are derived. Data and control items that move across an interface should be restricted to inputs required to perform the stated function and outputs that are required by other functions or system elements.

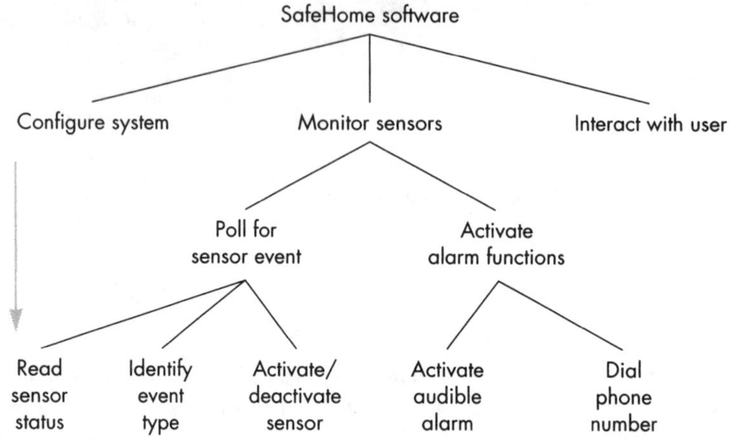

FIGURE 11.5 Vertical partitioning of SafeHome function

11.3.4 Essential and Implementation Views[7]

ADVICE *Avoid the temptation to move directly to the implementation view, assuming that the essence of the problem is obvious. Specifying implementation detail too quickly reduces your options and increases risk.*

An *essential view* of software requirements presents the functions to be accomplished and information to be processed without regard to implementation details. For example, the essential view of the *SafeHome* function *read sensor status* does not concern itself with the physical form of the data or the type of sensor that is used. In fact, it could be argued that read status would be a more appropriate name for this function, since it disregards details about the input mechanism altogether. Similarly, an essential data model of the data item **phone number** (implied by the function *dial phone number*) can be represented at this stage without regard to the underlying data structure (if any) used to implement the data item. By focusing attention on the essence of the problem at early stages of requirements engineering, we leave our options open to specify implementation details during later stages of requirements specification and software design.

The *implementation view* of software requirements presents the real world manifestation of processing functions and information structures. In some cases, a physical representation is developed as the first step in software design. However, most computer-based systems are specified in a manner that dictates accommodation of certain implementation details. A *SafeHome* input device is a perimeter sensor (not a watch dog, a human guard, or a booby trap). The sensor detects illegal entry by sensing a break in an electronic circuit. The general characteristics of the sensor should be noted as part of a software requirements specification. The analyst must recognize the constraints imposed by predefined system elements (the sensor) and consider the implementation view of function and information when such a view is appropriate.

7 Many people use the terms *logical* and *physical* views to connote the same concept.

We have already noted that software requirements engineering should focus on what the software is to accomplish, rather than on how processing will be implemented. However, the implementation view should not necessarily be interpreted as a representation of how. Rather, an implementation model represents the current mode of operation; that is, the existing or proposed allocation for all system elements. The essential model (of function or data) is generic in the sense that realization of function is not explicitly indicated.

11.4 SOFTWARE PROTOTYPING

Quote:
"Developers may build and test against specifications but users accept or reject against current and actual operational realities."
Bernard Boar

Analysis should be conducted regardless of the software engineering paradigm that is applied. However, the form that analysis takes will vary. In some cases it is possible to apply operational analysis principles and derive a model of software from which a design can be developed. In other situations, requirements elicitation (via FAST, QFD, use-cases, or other "brainstorming" techniques [JOR89]) is conducted, analysis principles are applied, and a model of the software to be built, called a *prototype,* is constructed for customer and developer assessment. Finally, some circumstances require the construction of a prototype at the beginning of analysis, since the model is the only means through which requirements can be effectively derived. The model then evolves into production software.

11.4.1 Selecting the Prototyping Approach

The prototyping paradigm can be either close-ended or open-ended. The close-ended approach is often called *throwaway prototyping.* Using this approach, a prototype serves solely as a rough demonstration of requirements. It is then discarded, and the software is engineered using a different paradigm. An open-ended approach, called *evolutionary prototyping,* uses the prototype as the first part of an analysis activity that will be continued into design and construction. The prototype of the software is the first evolution of the finished system.

? What do I look for to determine whether or not prototyping is a viable approach?

Before a close-ended or open-ended approach can be chosen, it is necessary to determine whether the system to be built is amenable to prototyping. A number of prototyping candidacy factors [BOA84] can be defined: application area, application complexity, customer characteristics, and project characteristics.[8]

In general, any application that creates dynamic visual displays, interacts heavily with a user, or demands algorithms or combinatorial processing that must be developed in an evolutionary fashion is a candidate for prototyping. However, these application areas must be weighed against application complexity. If a candidate application (one that has the characteristics noted) will require the development of tens of thousands of lines of code before any demonstrable function can be performed, it is likely

8 A useful discussion of other candidacy factors—"when to prototype"— can be found in [DAV95b].

FIGURE 11.6 Selecting the appropriate prototyping approach

Question	Throwaway prototype	Evolutionary prototype	Additional preliminary work required
Is the application domain understood?	Yes	Yes	No
Can the problem be modeled?	Yes	Yes	No
Is the customer certain of basic system requirements?	Yes/No	Yes/No	No
Are requirements established and stable?	No	Yes	Yes
Are any requirements ambiguous?	Yes	No	Yes
Are there contradictions in the requirements?	Yes	No	Yes

to be too complex for prototyping.[9] If, however, the complexity can be partitioned, it may still be possible to prototype portions of the software.

Because the customer must interact with the prototype in later steps, it is essential that (1) customer resources be committed to the evaluation and refinement of the prototype and (2) the customer is capable of making requirements decisions in a timely fashion. Finally, the nature of the development project will have a strong bearing on the efficacy of prototyping. Is project management willing and able to work with the prototyping method? Are prototyping tools available? Do developers have experience with prototyping methods? Andriole [AND92] suggests six questions (Figure 11.6) and indicates typical sets of answers and the corresponding suggested prototyping approach.

11.4.2 Prototyping Methods and Tools

For software prototyping to be effective, a prototype must be developed rapidly so that the customer may assess results and recommend changes. To conduct rapid prototyping, three generic classes of methods and tools (e.g., [AND92], [TAN89]) are available:

Fourth generation techniques. Fourth generation techniques (4GT) encompass a broad array of database query and reporting languages, program and application generators, and other very high-level nonprocedural languages. Because 4GT enable the software engineer to generate executable code quickly, they are ideal for rapid prototyping.

Reusable software components. Another approach to rapid prototyping is to assemble, rather than build, the prototype by using a set of existing software components. Melding prototyping and program component reuse will

9 In some cases, extremely complex prototypes can be constructed rapidly by using fourth generation techniques or reusable software components.

work only if a library system is developed so that components that do exist can be cataloged and then retrieved. It should be noted that an existing software product can be used as a prototype for a "new, improved" competitive product. In a way, this is a form of reusability for software prototyping.

Formal specification and prototyping environments. Over the past two decades, a number of formal specification languages and tools have been developed as a replacement for natural language specification techniques. Today, developers of these formal languages are in the process of developing interactive environments that (1) enable an analyst to interactively create language-based specifications of a system or software, (2) invoke automated tools that translate the language-based specifications into executable code, and (3) enable the customer to use the prototype executable code to refine formal requirements.

11.5 SPECIFICATION

There is no doubt that the mode of specification has much to do with the quality of solution. Software engineers who have been forced to work with incomplete, inconsistent, or misleading specifications have experienced the frustration and confusion that invariably results. The quality, timeliness, and completeness of the software suffers as a consequence.

11.5.1 Specification Principles

Specification, regardless of the mode through which we accomplish it, may be viewed as a representation process. Requirements are represented in a manner that ultimately leads to successful software implementation. A number of specification principles, adapted from the work of Balzer and Goodman [BAL86], can be proposed:

ADVICE

In most cases, it is unreasonable to expect that the specification will "cross every t and dot every i." It should, however, capture the essense of what the customer requires.

1. Separate functionality from implementation.
2. Develop a model of the desired behavior of a system that encompasses data and the functional responses of a system to various stimuli from the environment.
3. Establish the context in which software operates by specifying the manner in which other system components interact with software.
4. Define the environment in which the system operates and indicate how "a highly intertwined collection of agents react to stimuli in the environment (changes to objects) produced by those agents" [BAL86].
5. Create a cognitive model rather than a design or implementation model. The cognitive model describes a system as perceived by its user community.
6. Recognize that "the specifications must be tolerant of incompleteness and augmentable." A specification is always a model—an abstraction—of some

real (or envisioned) situation that is normally quite complex. Hence, it will be incomplete and will exist at many levels of detail.

7. Establish the content and structure of a specification in a way that will enable it to be amenable to change.

This list of basic specification principles provides a basis for representing software requirements. However, principles must be translated into realization. In the next section we examine a set of guidelines for creating a specification of requirements.

11.5.2 Representation

We have already seen that software requirements may be specified in a variety of ways. However, if requirements are committed to paper or an electronic presentation medium (and they almost always should be!) a simple set of guidelines is well worth following:

What are a few basic guidelines for representing requirements?

Representation format and content should be relevant to the problem. A general outline for the contents of a *Software Requirements Specification* can be developed. However, the representation forms contained within the specification are likely to vary with the application area. For example, a specification for a manufacturing automation system might use different symbology, diagrams and language than the specification for a programming language compiler.

Information contained within the specification should be nested. Representations should reveal layers of information so that a reader can move to the level of detail required. Paragraph and diagram numbering schemes should indicate the level of detail that is being presented. It is sometimes worthwhile to present the same information at different levels of abstraction to aid in understanding.

Diagrams and other notational forms should be restricted in number and consistent in use. Confusing or inconsistent notation, whether graphical or symbolic, degrades understanding and fosters errors.

Representations should be revisable. The content of a specification will change. Ideally, CASE tools should be available to update all representations that are affected by each change.

Investigators have conducted numerous studies (e.g., [HOL95], [CUR85]) on human factors associated with specification. There appears to be little doubt that symbology and arrangement affect understanding. However, software engineers appear to have individual preferences for specific symbolic and diagrammatic forms. Familiarity often lies at the root of a person's preference, but other more tangible factors such as spatial arrangement, easily recognizable patterns, and degree of formality often dictate an individual's choice.

11.5.3 The Software Requirements Specification

The *Software Requirements Specification* is produced at the culmination of the analysis task. The function and performance allocated to software as part of system engineering are refined by establishing a complete information description, a detailed functional description, a representation of system behavior, an indication of performance requirements and design constraints, appropriate validation criteria, and other information pertinent to requirements. The National Bureau of Standards, IEEE (Standard No. 830-1984), and the U.S. Department of Defense have all proposed candidate formats for software requirements specifications (as well as other software engineering documentation).

The *Introduction* of the software requirements specification states the goals and objectives of the software, describing it in the context of the computer-based system. Actually, the Introduction may be nothing more than the software scope of the planning document.

Software Requirements Specification

The *Information Description* provides a detailed description of the problem that the software must solve. Information content, flow, and structure are documented. Hardware, software, and human interfaces are described for external system elements and internal software functions.

A description of each function required to solve the problem is presented in the *Functional Description.* A processing narrative is provided for each function, design constraints are stated and justified, performance characteristics are stated, and one or more diagrams are included to graphically represent the overall structure of the software and interplay among software functions and other system elements. The *Behavioral Description* section of the specification examines the operation of the software as a consequence of external events and internally generated control characteristics.

ADVICE

When you develop validation criteria, answer the following question: "How would I recognize a successful system if it were dropped on my desk tomorrow?"

Validation Criteria is probably the most important and, ironically, the most often neglected section of the *Software Requirements Specification.* How do we recognize a successful implementation? What classes of tests must be conducted to validate function, performance, and constraints? We neglect this section because completing it demands a thorough understanding of software requirements—something that we often do not have at this stage. Yet, specification of validation criteria acts as an implicit review of all other requirements. It is essential that time and attention be given to this section.

Finally, the specification includes a *Bibliography and Appendix.* The bibliography contains references to all documents that relate to the software. These include other software engineering documentation, technical references, vendor literature, and standards. The appendix contains information that supplements the specifications. Tabular data, detailed description of algorithms, charts, graphs, and other material are presented as appendixes.

In many cases the *Software Requirements Specification* may be accompanied by an executable prototype (which in some cases may replace the specification), a paper prototype or a *Preliminary User's Manual.* The *Preliminary User's Manual* presents the software as a black box. That is, heavy emphasis is placed on user input and the resultant output. The manual can serve as a valuable tool for uncovering problems at the human/machine interface.

11.6 SPECIFICATION REVIEW

A review of the *Software Requirements Specification* (and/or prototype) is conducted by both the software developer and the customer. Because the specification forms the foundation of the development phase, extreme care should be taken in conducting the review.

The review is first conducted at a macroscopic level; that is, reviewers attempt to ensure that the specification is complete, consistent, and accurate when the overall information, functional, and behavioral domains are considered. However, to fully explore each of these domains, the review becomes more detailed, examining not only broad descriptions but the way in which requirements are worded. For example, when specifications contain "vague terms" (e.g., *some, sometimes, often, usually, ordinarily, most,* or *mostly*), the reviewer should flag the statements for further clarification.

Software Requirements Specification Review

Once the review is complete, the *Software Requirements Specification* is "signed-off" by both the customer and the developer. The specification becomes a "contract" for software development. Requests for changes in requirements after the specification is finalized will not be eliminated. But the customer should note that each after-the-fact change is an extension of software scope and therefore can increase cost and/or protract the schedule.

Even with the best review procedures in place, a number of common specification problems persist. The specification is difficult to "test" in any meaningful way, and therefore inconsistency or omissions may pass unnoticed. During the review, changes to the specification may be recommended. It can be extremely difficult to assess the global impact of a change; that is, how a change in one function affects requirements for other functions. Modern software engineering environments (Chapter 31) incorporate CASE tools that have been developed to help solve these problems.

11.7 SUMMARY

Requirements analysis is the first technical step in the software process. It is at this point that a general statement of software scope is refined into a concrete specification that becomes the foundation for all software engineering activities that follow.

Analysis must focus on the information, functional, and behavioral domains of a problem. To better understand what is required, models are created, the problem is partitioned, and representations that depict the essence of requirements and, later, implementation detail, are developed.

In many cases, it is not possible to completely specify a problem at an early stage. Prototyping offers an alternative approach that results in an executable model of the software from which requirements can be refined. To properly conduct prototyping special tools and techniques are required.

The *Software Requirements Specification* is developed as a consequence of analysis. Review is essential to ensure that the developer and the customer have the same perception of the system. Unfortunately, even with the best of methods, the problem is that the problem keeps changing.

REFERENCES

[AKA90] Akao, Y., ed., *Quality Function Deployment: Integrating Customer Requirements in Product Design* (translated by G. Mazur), Productivity Press, 1990.

[AND92] Andriole, S., *Rapid Application Prototyping,* QED, 1992.

[BAL86] Balzer, R. and N. Goodman, "Principles of Good Specification and Their Implications for Specification Languages," in *Software Specification Techniques* (Gehani, N. and A. McGetrick, eds.), Addison-Wesley, 1986, pp. 25–39.

[BOA84] Boar, B., *Application Prototyping,* Wiley-Interscience,1984.

[BOS91] Bossert, J.L., *Quality Function Deployment: A Practitioner's Approach,* ASQC Press, 1991.

[CUR85] Curtis, B., *Human Factors in Software Development,* IEEE Computer Society Press, 1985.

[DAV93] Davis, A., *Software Requirements: Objects, Functions and States,* Prentice-Hall, 1993.

[DAV95a] Davis, A., *201 Principles of Software Development,* McGraw-Hill, 1995.

[DAV95b] Davis, A., "Software Prototyping," in *Advances in Computers,* volume 40, Academic Press, 1995.

[GAU89] Gause, D.C. and G.M. Weinberg, *Exploring Requirements: Quality Before Design,* Dorset House, 1989.

[HOL95] Holtzblatt, K. and E. Carmel (eds.), "Requirements Gathering: The Human Factor," special issue of *CACM*, vol. 38, no. 5, May 1995.

[JAC92] Jacobson, I., *Object-Oriented Software Engineering,* Addison-Wesley, 1992.

[JOR89] Jordan, P.W., et al., "Software Storming: Combining Rapid Prototyping and Knowledge Engineering," *IEEE Computer,* vol. 22, no. 5, May 1989, pp. 39–50.

[REI94] Reifer, D.J., "Requirements Engineering," in *Encyclopedia of Software Engineering* (J.J. Marciniak, ed.), Wiley, 1994, pp. 1043–1054.

[TAN89] Tanik, M.M. and R.T. Yeh (eds.), "Rapid Prototyping in Software Development," special issue of *IEEE Computer,* vol. 22, no. 5, May 1989.

[WYD96] Wyder, T., "Capturing Requirements with Use-Cases," *Software Development,* February 1996, pp. 37–40.

[ZAH90] Zahniser, R.A., "Building Software in Groups," *American Programmer,* vol. 3, nos. 7–8, July-August 1990.

[ZUL92] Zultner, R., "Quality Function Deployment for Software: Satisfying Customers," *American Programmer,* February 1992, pp. 28–41.

PROBLEMS AND POINTS TO PONDER

11.1. Software requirements analysis is unquestionably the most communication-intensive step in the software process. Why does the communication path frequently break down?

11.2. There are frequently severe political repercussions when software requirements analysis (and/or system analysis) begins. For example, workers may feel that job security is threatened by a new automated system. What causes such problems? Can the analysis task be conducted so that politics is minimized?

11.3. Discuss your perceptions of the ideal training and background for a systems analyst.

11.4. Throughout this chapter we refer to the "customer." Describe the "customer" for information systems developers, for builders of computer-based products, for systems builders. Be careful here, there may be more to this problem than you first imagine!

11.5. Develop a facilitated application specification techniques "kit." The kit should include a set of guidelines for conducting a FAST meeting and materials that can be used to facilitate the creation of lists and any other items that might help in defining requirements.

11.6. Your instructor will divide the class into groups of four or six students. Half of the group will play the role of the marketing department and half will take on the role of software engineering. Your job is to define requirements for the *SafeHome* security system described in this chapter. Conduct a FAST meeting using the guidelines presented in this chapter.

11.7. Is it fair to say that a *Preliminary User's Manual* is a form of prototype? Explain your answer.

11.8. Analyze the information domain for *SafeHome.* Represent (using any notation that seems appropriate) information flow in the system, information content, and any information structure that is relevant.

11.9. Partition the functional domain for *SafeHome.* First perform horizontal partitioning; then perform vertical partitioning.

11.10. Create essential and implementation representations of the *SafeHome* system.

11.11. Build a paper prototype (or a real prototype) for *SafeHome.* Be sure to depict owner interaction and overall system function.

11.12. Try to identify software components of *SafeHome* that might be "reusable" in other products or systems. Attempt to categorize these components.

11.13. Develop a written specification for *SafeHome* using the outline provided at the SEPA Web site. (Note: Your instructor will suggest which sections to complete at this time.) Be sure to apply the questions that are described for the specification review.

11.14. How did your requirements differ from others who attempted a solution for *SafeHome?* Who built a "Chevy"—who built a "Cadillac"?

FURTHER READINGS AND INFORMATION SOURCES

Books that address requirements engineering provide a good foundation for the study of basic analysis concepts and principles. Thayer and Dorfman (*Software Requirements Engineering,* 2nd ed., IEEE Computer Society Press, 1997) present a worthwhile anthology on the subject. Graham and Graham (*Requirements Engineering and Rapid Development,* Addison-Wesley, 1998) emphasize rapid development and the use of object-oriented methods in their discussion of requirements engineering, while MacCauley (*Requirements Engineering,* Springer-Verlag, 1996) presents a brief academic treatment of the subject.

In years past, the literature emphasized requirements modeling and specification methods, but today, equal emphasis has been given to effective methods for software requirements elicitation. Wood and Silver (*Joint Application Development,* 2nd ed., Wiley, 1995) have written the definitive treatment of joint application development. Cohen and Cohen (*Quality Function Deployment,* Addison-Wesley, 1995), Terninko (*Step-by-Step QFD: Customer-Driven Product Design,* Saint Lucie Press, 1997), Gause and Weinberg [GAU89], and Zahniser [ZAH90] discuss the mechanics of effective meetings, methods for brainstorming, and elicitation approaches that can be used to clarify results and a variety of other useful issues. Use-cases have become an important part of object-oriented requirements analysis, but they can be used regardless of the implementation technology selected. Rosenburg and Scott (*Use-Case Driven Object Modeling with UML: A Practical Approach,* Addison-Wesley, 1999), Schneider et al. (*Applying Use-Cases: A Practical Guide,* Addison-Wesley, 1998), and Texel and Williams (*Use-Cases Combined With Booch/OMT/UML,* Prentice-Hall, 1997) provide detailed guidance and many useful examples.

Information domain analysis is a fundamental principle of requirements analysis. Books by Mattison (*The Object-Oriented Enterprise*, McGraw-Hill, 1994), Tillman (*A Practical Guide to Logical Data Modeling,* McGraw-Hill, 1993), and Modell (*Data Analysis, Data Modeling and Classification,* McGraw-Hill, 1992) cover various aspects of this important subject.

A recent book by Harrison (*Prototyping and Software Development,* Springer-Verlag, 1999) provides a modern perspective on software prototyping. Two books by Connell and Shafer (*Structured Rapid Prototyping,* Prentice-Hall, 1989) and (*Object-Oriented Rapid Prototyping,* Yourdon Press, 1994) show how this important analysis technique can be used in both conventional and object-oriented environments. Other books by Pomberger et al. (*Object Orientation and Prototyping in Software Engineering,* Prentice-Hall, 1996) and Krief et al. (*Prototyping with Objects,* Prentice-Hall, 1996) examine prototyping from the object-oriented perspective. The *IEEE Proceedings of the International Workshop on Rapid System Prototyping* (published yearly) presents current research in the area.

A wide variety of information sources on requirements analysis and related subjects is available on the Internet. An up-to-date list of World Wide Web references that are relevant to analysis concepts and methods can be found at the SEPA Web site:

http://www.mhhe.com/engcs/compsci/pressman/resources/reqm.mhtml

CHAPTER

12 ANALYSIS MODELING

KEY CONCEPTS

At a technical level, software engineering begins with a series of modeling tasks that lead to a complete specification of requirements and a comprehensive design representation for the software to be built. The *analysis model,* actually a set of models, is the first technical representation of a system. Over the years many methods have been proposed for analysis modeling. However, two now dominate. The first, *structured analysis,* is a classical modeling method and is described in this chapter. The other approach, *object-oriented analysis,* is considered in detail in Chapter 21. Other commonly used analysis methods are noted in Section 12.8.

Structured analysis is a model building activity. Applying the operational analysis principles discussed in Chapter 11, we create and partition data, functional, and behavioral models that depict the essence of what must built. Structured analysis is not a single method applied consistently by all who use it. Rather, it is an amalgam that evolved over more than 30 years.

In his seminal book on the subject, Tom DeMarco [DEM79] describes structured analysis in this way:

> Looking back over the recognized problems and failings of the analysis phase, I suggest that we need to make the following additions to our set of analysis phase goals:

QUICK LOOK

What is it? The written word is a wonderful vehicle for communication, but it is not necessarily the best way to represent the requirements for computer software. Analysis modeling uses a combination of text and diagrammatic forms to depict requirements for data, function, and behavior in a way that is relatively easy to understand, and more important, straightforward to review for correctness, completeness, and consistency.

Who does it? A software engineer (sometimes called an analyst) builds the model using requirements elicited from the customer.

Why is it important? To validate software requirements, you need to examine them from a number of different points of view. Analysis modeling represents requirements in three "dimensions" thereby increasing the probability that errors will be found, that inconsistency will surface, and that omissions will be uncovered.

What are the steps? Data, functional, and behavioral requirements are modeled using a number of different diagrammatic formats. Data modeling defines data objects, attributes, and relationships. Functional modeling indicates how data are transformed within a system. Behavioral modeling depicts the impact of events. Once preliminary models are created, they are refined and analyzed to assess their clarity, completeness, and consistency. A specification incorporating the

QUICK LOOK

model is created and then validated by both software engineers and customers/users.

What is the work product? Data object descriptions, entity relationship diagrams, data flow diagrams, state transition diagrams, process specifications, and control specifications are created as part of the analysis modeling activity.

How do I ensure that I've done it right? Analysis modeling work products must be reviewed for correctness, completeness, and consistency.

- The products of analysis must be highly maintainable. This applies particularly to the Target Document [software requirements specifications].
- Problems of size must be dealt with using an effective method of partitioning. The Victorian novel specification is out.
- Graphics have to be used whenever possible.
- We have to differentiate between logical [essential] and physical [implementation] considerations . . .

  At the very least, we need . . .
- Something to help us partition our requirements and document that partitioning before specification . . .
- Some means of keeping track of and evaluating interfaces . . .
- New tools to describe logic and policy, something better than narrative text . . .

There is probably no other software engineering method that has generated as much interest, been tried (and often rejected and then tried again) by as many people, provoked as much criticism, and sparked as much controversy. But the method has prospered and has gained a substantial following in the software engineering community.

12.1 A BRIEF HISTORY

> **Quote:**
> "The problem is not that there are problems. The problem is expecting otherwise and thinking that having problems is a problem."
> **Theodore Rubin**

Like many important contributions to software engineering, structured analysis was not introduced with a single landmark paper or book. Early work in analysis modeling was begun in the late 1960s and early 1970s, but the first appearance of the structured analysis approach was as an adjunct to another important topic—"structured design." Researchers (e.g., [STE74], [YOU78]) needed a graphical notation for representing data and the processes that transformed it. These processes would ultimately be mapped into a design architecture.

The term *structured analysis,* originally coined by Douglas Ross, was popularized by DeMarco [DEM79]. In his book on the subject, DeMarco introduced and named the key graphical symbols and the models that incorporated them. In the years that followed, variations of the structured analysis approach were suggested by Page-Jones [PAG80], Gane and Sarson [GAN82], and many others. In every instance, the method focused on information systems applications and did not provide an adequate notation to address the control and behavioral aspects of real-time engineering problems.

By the mid-1980s, real-time "extensions" were introduced by Ward and Mellor [WAR85] and later by Hatley and Pirbhai [HAT87]. These extensions resulted in a more robust analysis method that could be applied effectively to engineering problems. Attempts to develop one consistent notation have been suggested [BRU88], and modernized treatments have been published to accommodate the use of CASE tools [YOU89].

12.2 THE ELEMENTS OF THE ANALYSIS MODEL

The analysis model must achieve three primary objectives: (1) to describe what the customer requires, (2) to establish a basis for the creation of a software design, and (3) to define a set of requirements that can be validated once the software is built. To accomplish these objectives, the analysis model derived during structured analysis takes the form illustrated in Figure 12.1.

At the core of the model lies the *data dictionary*—a repository that contains descriptions of all data objects consumed or produced by the software. Three different diagrams surround the the core. The *entity relation diagram* (ERD) depicts relationships between data objects. The ERD is the notation that is used to conduct the data

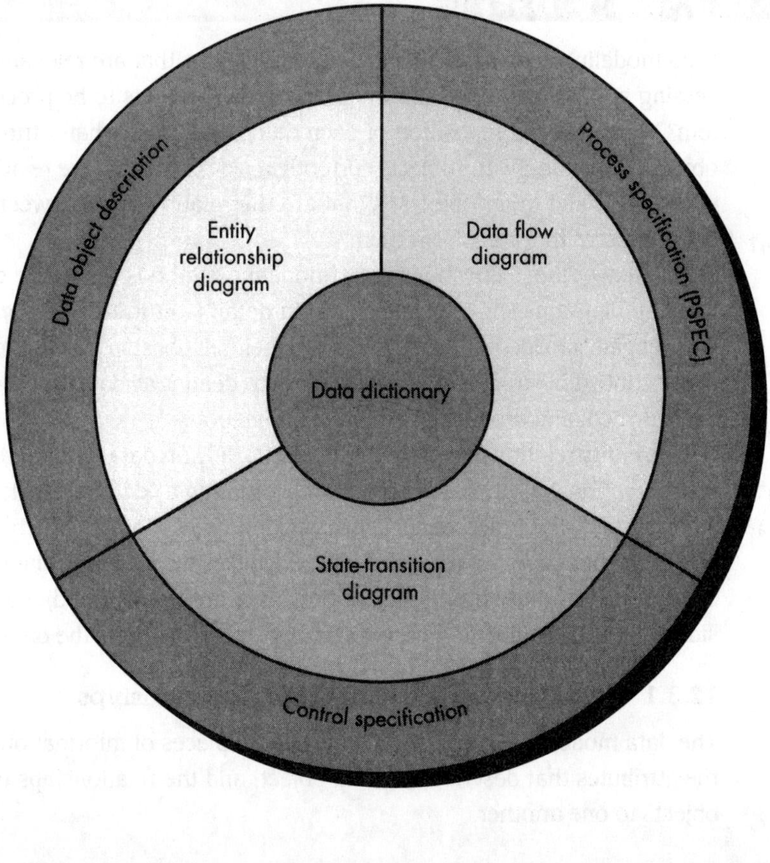

FIGURE 12.1
The structure of the analysis model

modeling activity. The attributes of each data object noted in the ERD can be described using a data object description.

The *data flow diagram* (DFD) serves two purposes: (1) to provide an indication of how data are transformed as they move through the system and (2) to depict the functions (and subfunctions) that transform the data flow. The DFD provides additional information that is used during the analysis of the information domain and serves as a basis for the modeling of function. A description of each function presented in the DFD is contained in a *process specification* (PSPEC).

The *state transition diagram* (STD) indicates how the system behaves as a consequence of external events. To accomplish this, the STD represents the various modes of behavior (called *states*) of the system and the manner in which transitions are made from state to state. The STD serves as the basis for behavioral modeling. Additional information about the control aspects of the software is contained in the *control specification* (CSPEC).

The analysis model encompasses each of the diagrams, specifications, descriptions, and the dictionary noted in Figure 12.1. A more detailed discussion of these elements of the analysis model is presented in the sections that follow.

12.3 DATA MODELING

What questions does data modeling answer?

Data modeling answers a set of specific questions that are relevant to any data processing application. What are the primary data objects to be processed by the system? What is the composition of each data object and what attributes describe the object? Where do the the objects currently reside? What are the relationships between each object and other objects? What are the relationships between the objects and the processes that transform them?

Quote:

"The power of the ER approach is its ability to describe entities in the real world of the business and the relationships between them."

Martin Modell

To answer these questions, data modeling methods make use of the entity relationship diagram. The ERD, described in detail later in this section, enables a software engineer to identify data objects and their relationships using a graphical notation. In the context of structured analysis, the ERD defines all data that are entered, stored, transformed, and produced within an application.

The entity relationship diagram focuses solely on data (and therefore satisfies the first operational analysis principles), representing a "data network" that exists for a given system. The ERD is especially useful for applications in which data and the relationships that govern data are complex. Unlike the data flow diagram (discussed in Section 12.4 and used to represent how data are transformed), data modeling considers data independent of the processing that transforms the data.

12.3.1 Data Objects, Attributes, and Relationships

The data model consists of three interrelated pieces of information: the data object, the attributes that describe the data object, and the relationships that connect data objects to one another.

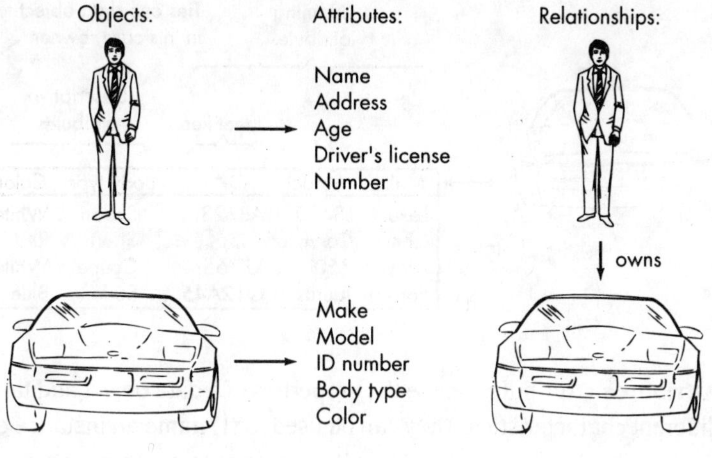

FIGURE 12.2 Data objects, attributes and relationships

Data objects. A *data object* is a representation of almost any composite information that must be understood by software. By *composite information,* we mean something that has a number of different properties or attributes. Therefore, width (a single value) would not be a valid data object, but dimensions (incorporating height, width, and depth) could be defined as an object.

KEY POINT

A data object is a representation of any composite information that is processed by computer software.

A data object can be an external entity (e.g., anything that produces or consumes information), a thing (e.g., a report or a display), an occurrence (e.g., a telephone call) or event (e.g., an alarm), a role (e.g., salesperson), an organizational unit (e.g., accounting department), a place (e.g., a warehouse), or a structure (e.g., a file). For example, a person or a car (Figure 12.2) can be viewed as a data object in the sense that either can be defined in terms of a set of attributes. The data object description incorporates the data object and all of its attributes.

WebRef

Useful information on data modeling can be found at **www.datamodel.org**

Data objects (represented in bold) are related to one another. For example, **person** can *own* **car**, where the relationship *own* connotes a specific "connection" between **person** and **car**. The relationships are always defined by the context of the problem that is being analyzed.

A data object encapsulates data only—there is no reference within a data object to operations that act on the data.[1] Therefore, the data object can be represented as a table as shown in Figure 12.3. The headings in the table reflect attributes of the object. In this case, a car is defined in terms of make, model, ID number, body type, color and owner. The body of the table represents specific instances of the data object. For example, a Chevy Corvette is an instance of the data object **car.**

1 This distinction separates the data object from the *class* or *object* defined as part of the object-oriented paradigm discussed in Part Four of this book.

FIGURE 12.3 Tabular representation of data objects

Make	Model	ID#	Body type	Color	Owner
Lexus	LS400	AB123. . .	Sedan	White	RSP
Chevy	Corvette	X456. . .	Sports	Red	CCD
BMW	750iL	XZ765. . .	Coupe	White	LJL
Ford	Taurus	Q12A45. . .	Sedan	Blue	BLF

KEY POINT

Attributes name a data object, describe its characteristics, and in some cases, make reference to another object.

Attributes. Attributes define the properties of a data object and take on one of three different characteristics. They can be used to (1) name an instance of the data object, (2) describe the instance, or (3) make reference to another instance in another table. In addition, one or more of the attributes must be defined as an *identifier*—that is, the identifier attribute becomes a "key" when we want to find an instance of the data object. In some cases, values for the identifier(s) are unique, although this is not a requirement. Referring to the data object **car**, a reasonable identifier might be the ID number.

The set of attributes that is appropriate for a given data object is determined through an understanding of the problem context. The attributes for **car** might serve well for an application that would be used by a Department of Motor Vehicles, but these attributes would be useless for an automobile company that needs manufacturing control software. In the latter case, the attributes for **car** might also include ID number, body type and color, but many additional attributes (e.g., interior code, drive train type, trim package designator, transmission type) would have to be added to make car a meaningful object in the manufacturing control context.

KEY POINT

Relationships indicate the manner in which data objects are "connected" to one another.

Relationships. Data objects are connected to one another in different ways. Consider two data objects, **book** and **bookstore**. These objects can be represented using the simple notation illustrated in Figure 12.4a. A connection is established between **book** and **bookstore** because the two objects are related. But what are the relationships? To determine the answer, we must understand the role of books and bookstores within the context of the software to be built. We can define a set of object/relationship pairs that define the relevant relationships. For example,

- A bookstore orders books.
- A bookstore displays books.
- A bookstore stocks books.
- A bookstore sells books.
- A bookstore returns books.

FIGURE 12.4
Relationships

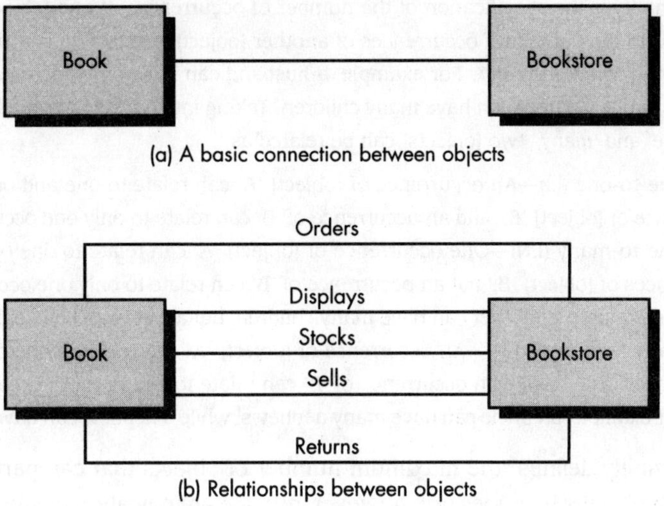

The relationships *orders, displays, stocks, sells,* and *returns* define the relevant connections between **book** and **bookstore**. Figure 12.4b illustrates these object/relationship pairs graphically.

It is important to note that object/relationship pairs are bidirectional. That is, they can be read in either direction. A bookstore orders books or books are ordered by a bookstore.[2]

12.3.2 Cardinality and Modality

The elements of data modeling—data objects, attributes, and relationships— provide the basis for understanding the information domain of a problem. However, additional information related to these basic elements must also be understood.

We have defined a set of objects and represented the object/relationship pairs that bind them. But a simple pair that states: **object X** *relates* to **object Y** does not provide enough information for software engineering purposes. We must understand how many occurrences of **object X** are related to how many occurrences of **object Y.** This leads to a data modeling concept called *cardinality.*

Cardinality. The data model must be capable of representing the number of occurrences objects in a given relationship. Tillmann [TIL93] defines the *cardinality* of an object/relationship pair in the following manner:

2 To avoid ambiguity, the manner in which a relationship is labeled must be considered. For example, if context is not considered for a bidirectional relation, Figure 12.4b could be misinterpreted to mean that books order bookstores. In such cases, rephrasing is necessary.

Cardinality is the specification of the number of occurrences of one [object] that can be related to the number of occurrences of another [object]. Cardinality is usually expressed as simply 'one' or 'many.' For example, a husband can have only one wife (in most cultures), while a parent can have many children. Taking into consideration all combinations of 'one' and 'many,' two [objects] can be related as

- One-to-one (l:l)—An occurrence of [object] 'A' can relate to one and only one occurrence of [object] 'B,' and an occurrence of 'B' can relate to only one occurrence of 'A.'
- One-to-many (l:N)—One occurrence of [object] 'A' can relate to one or many occurrences of [object] 'B,' but an occurrence of 'B' can relate to only one occurrence of 'A.' For example, a mother can have many children, but a child can have only one mother.
- Many-to-many (M:N)—An occurrence of [object] 'A' can relate to one or more occurrences of 'B,' while an occurrence of 'B' can relate to one or more occurrences of 'A.' For example, an uncle can have many nephews, while a nephew can have many uncles.

Cardinality defines "the maximum number of objects that can participate in a relationship" [TIL93]. It does not, however, provide an indication of whether or not a particular data object must participate in the relationship. To specify this information, the data model adds modality to the object/relationship pair.

Modality. The *modality* of a relationship is 0 if there is no explicit need for the relationship to occur or the relationship is optional. The modality is 1 if an occurrence of the relationship is mandatory. To illustrate, consider software that is used by a local telephone company to process requests for field service. A customer indicates that there is a problem. If the problem is diagnosed as relatively simple, a single repair action occurs. However, if the problem is complex, multiple repair actions may be required. Figure 12.5 illustrates the relationship, cardinality, and modality between the data objects **customer** and **repair action.**

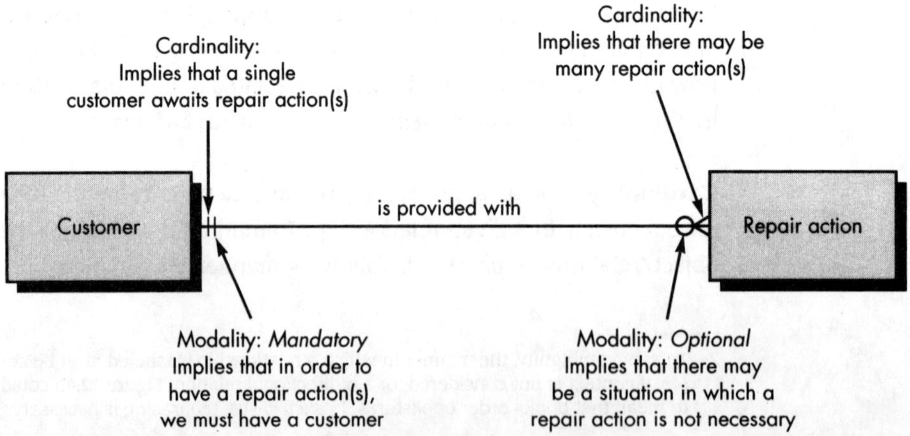

FIGURE 12.5
Cardinality and modality

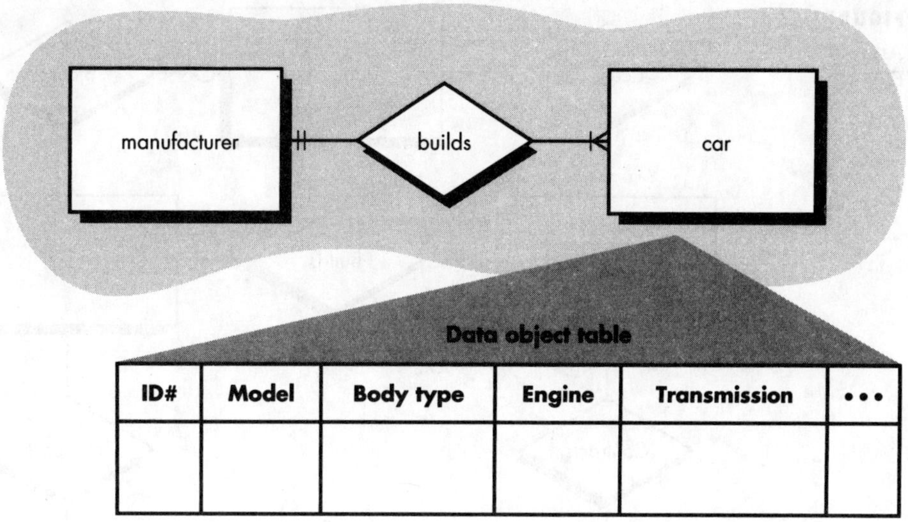

FIGURE 12.6
A simple ERD and data object table (Note: In this ERD the relationship *builds* is indicated by a diamond)

Referring to the figure, a one to many cardinality relationship is established. That is, a single customer can be provided with zero or many repair actions. The symbols on the relationship connection closest to the data object rectangles indicate cardinality. The vertical bar indicates one and the three-pronged fork indicates many. Modality is indicated by the symbols that are further away from the data object rectangles. The second vertical bar on the left indicates that there must be a customer for a repair action to occur. The circle on the right indicates that there may be no repair action required for the type of problem reported by the customer.

KEY POINT
The primary purpose of the ERD is to represent entities (data objects) and their relationships with one another.

12.3.3 Entity/Relationship Diagrams

The object/relationship pair (discussed in Section 12.3.1) is the cornerstone of the data model. These pairs can be represented graphically using the *entity/relationship diagram*. The ERD was originally proposed by Peter Chen [CHE77] for the design of relational database systems and has been extended by others. A set of primary components are identified for the ERD: data objects, attributes, relationships, and various type indicators. The primary purpose of the ERD is to represent data objects and their relationships.

Rudimentary ERD notation has already been introduced in Section 12.3. Data objects are represented by a labeled rectangle. Relationships are indicated with a labeled line connecting objects. In some variations of the ERD, the connecting line contains a diamond that is labeled with the relationship. Connections between data objects and relationships are established using a variety of special symbols that indicate cardinality and modality (Section 12.3.2).

The relationship between the data objects **car** and **manufacturer** would be represented as shown in Figure 12.6. One manufacturer builds one or many cars. Given

FIGURE 12.7
An expanded ERD

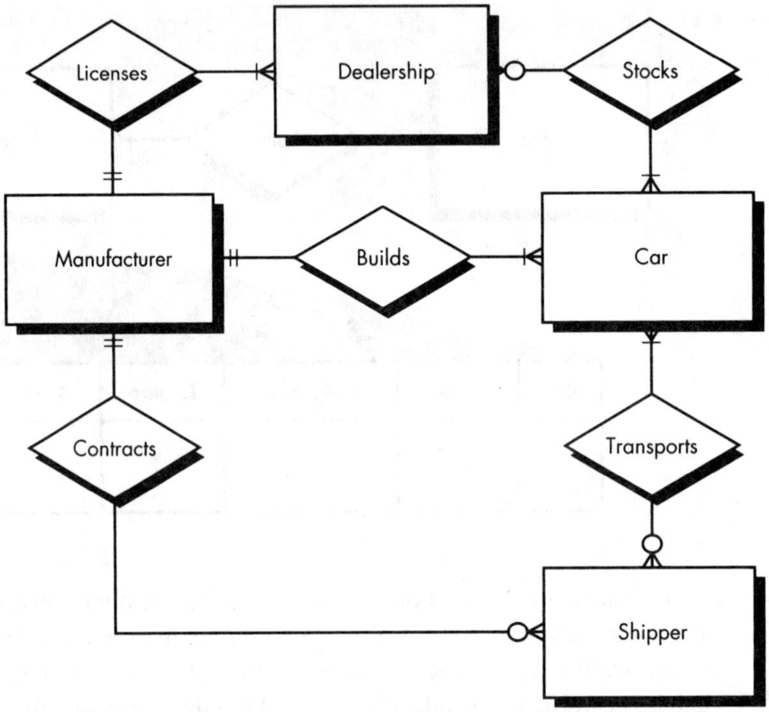

the context implied by the ERD, the specification of the data object **car** (data object table in Figure 12.6) would be radically different from the earlier specification (Figure 12.3). By examining the symbols at the end of the connection line between objects, it can be seen that the modality of both occurrences is mandatory (the vertical lines).

ADVICE

Develop the ERD iteratively by refining both data objects and the relationships that connect them.

Expanding the model, we represent a grossly oversimplified ERD (Figure 12.7) of the distribution element of the automobile business. New data objects, **shipper** and **dealership,** are introduced. In addition, new relationships—*transports, contracts, licenses,* and *stocks*—indicate how the data objects shown in the figure associate with one another. Tables for each of the data objects contained in the ERD would have to be developed according to the rules introduced earlier in this chapter.

In addition to the basic ERD notation introduced in Figures 12.6 and 12.7, the analyst can represent *data object type hierarchies.* In many instances, a data object may actually represent a class or category of information. For example, the data object **car** can be categorized as domestic, European, or Asian. The ERD notation shown in Figure 12.8 represents this categorization in the form of a hierarchy [ROS85].

ERD notation also provides a mechanism that represents the associativity between objects. An *associative data object* is represented as shown in Figure 12.9. In the figure, each of the data objects that model the individual subsystems is associated with the data object **car.**

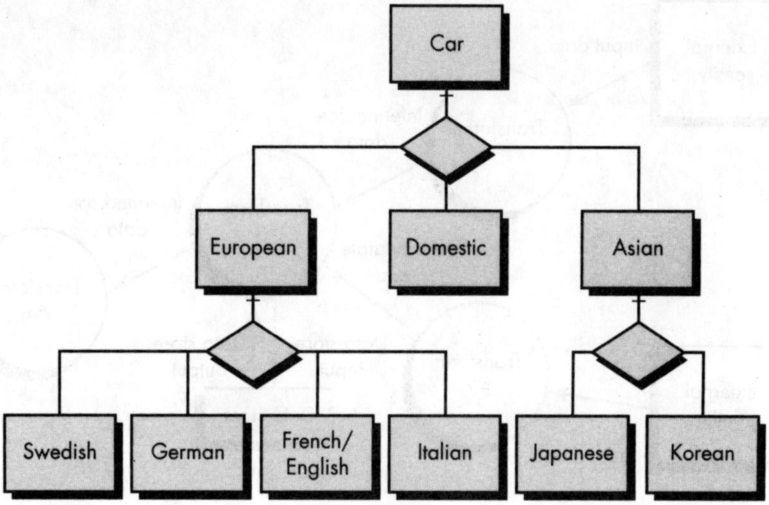

FIGURE 12.8 Data object-type hierarchies

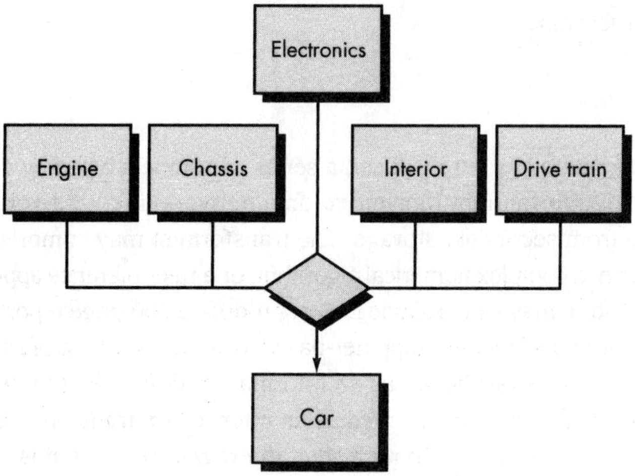

FIGURE 12.9 Associative data objects

Data modeling and the entity relationship diagram provide the analyst with a concise notation for examining data within the context of a software application. In most cases, the data modeling approach is used to create one piece of the analysis model, but it can also be used for database design and to support any other requirements analysis methods.

12.4 FUNCTIONAL MODELING AND INFORMATION FLOW

Information is transformed as it flows through a computer-based system. The system accepts input in a variety of forms; applies hardware, software, and human elements to transform it; and produces output in a variety of forms. Input may be a control

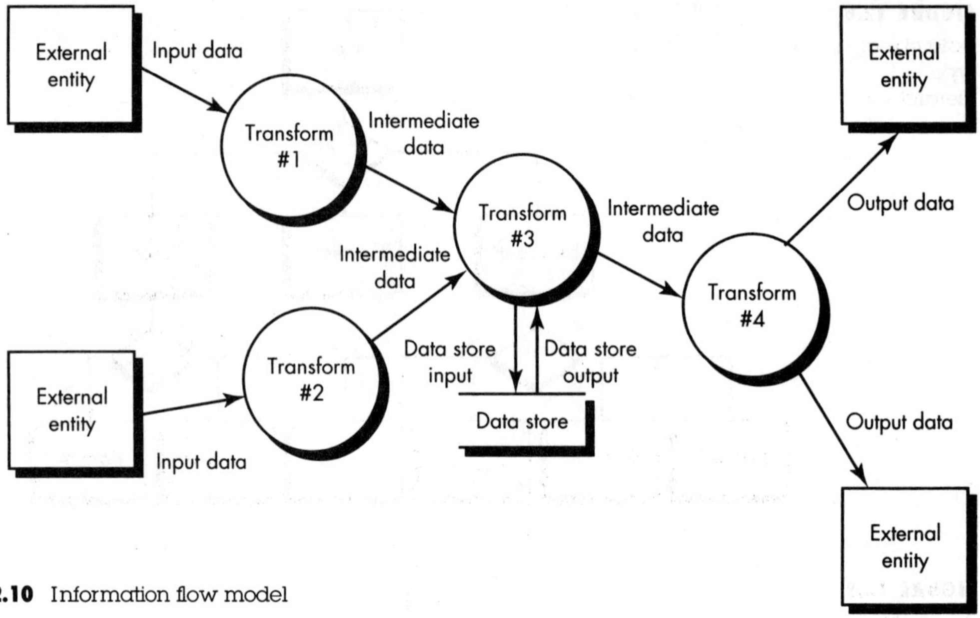

FIGURE 12.10 Information flow model

signal transmitted by a transducer, a series of numbers typed by a human operator, a packet of information transmitted on a network link, or a voluminous data file retrieved from secondary storage. The transform(s) may comprise a single logical comparison, a complex numerical algorithm, or a rule-inference approach of an expert system. Output may light a single LED or produce a 200-page report. In effect, we can create a *flow model* for any computer-based system, regardless of size and complexity.

Structured analysis began as an information flow modeling technique. A computer-based system is represented as an information transform as shown in Figure 12.10. A rectangle is used to represent an *external entity;* that is, a system element (e.g., hardware, a person, another program) or another system that produces information for transformation by the software or receives information produced by the software. A circle (sometimes called a *bubble*) represents a *process* or *transform* that is applied to data (or control) and changes it in some way. An arrow represents one or more *data items* (data objects). All arrows on a data flow diagram should be labeled. The double line represents a data store—stored information that is used by the software. The simplicity of DFD notation is one reason why structured analysis techniques are widely used.

ADVICE

The DFD is not procedural. That is, do not try to represent conditional processing or loops with this diagrammatic form. Simply show the flow of data.

It is important to note that no explicit indication of the sequence of processing or conditional logic is supplied by the diagram. Procedure or sequence may be implicit in the diagram, but explicit logical details are generally delayed until software design. It is important not to confuse a DFD with the flowchart.

12.4.1 Data Flow Diagrams

KEY POINT

The DFD provides a mechanism for information flow modeling and functional modeling.

As information moves through software, it is modified by a series of transformations. A *data flow diagram* is a graphical representation that depicts information flow and the transforms that are applied as data move from input to output. The basic form of a data flow diagram, also known as a *data flow graph* or a *bubble chart,* is illustrated in Figure 12.10.

The data flow diagram may be used to represent a system or software at any level of abstraction. In fact, DFDs may be partitioned into levels that represent increasing information flow and functional detail. Therefore, the DFD provides a mechanism for functional modeling as well as information flow modeling. In so doing, it satisfies the second operational analysis principle (i.e., creating a functional model) discussed in Chapter 11.

ADVICE

Refinement from one DFD level to the next should follow an approximate 1:5 ratio, reducing as the refinement proceeds.

A level 0 DFD, also called a *fundamental system model* or a *context model,* represents the entire software element as a single bubble with input and output data indicated by incoming and outgoing arrows, respectively. Additional processes (bubbles) and information flow paths are represented as the level 0 DFD is partitioned to reveal more detail. For example, a level 1 DFD might contain five or six bubbles with interconnecting arrows. Each of the processes represented at level 1 is a subfunction of the overall system depicted in the context model.

As we noted earlier, each of the bubbles may be refined or layered to depict more detail. Figure 12.11 illustrates this concept. A fundamental model for system *F* indicates the primary input is *A* and ultimate output is *B*. We refine the *F* model into transforms f_1 to f_7. Note that *information flow continuity* must be maintained; that is, input

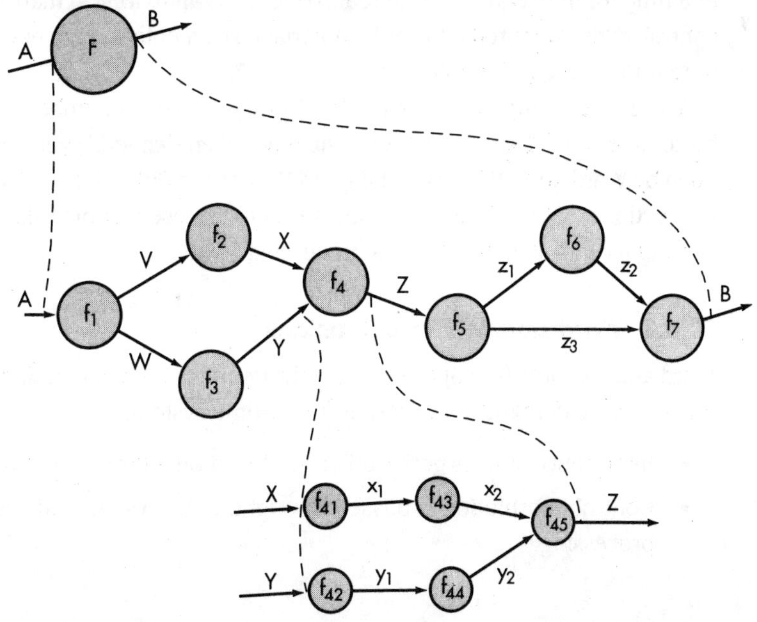

FIGURE 12.11
Information flow refinement

ADVICE

Although information flow continuity must be maintained, recognize that a data item represented at one level may be refined into its constituent parts at the next level.

and output to each refinement must remain the same. This concept, sometimes called *balancing,* is essential for the development of consistent models. Further refinement of f_4 depicts detail in the form of transforms f_{41} to f_{45}. Again, the input (*X*, *Y*) and output (*Z*) remain unchanged.

The basic notation used to develop a DFD is not in itself sufficient to describe requirements for software. For example, an arrow shown in a DFD represents a data object that is input to or output from a process. A data store represents some organized collection of data. But what is the content of the data implied by the arrow or depicted by the store? If the arrow (or the store) represents a collection of objects, what are they? These questions are answered by applying another component of the basic notation for structured analysis—the *data dictionary.* The use of the data dictionary is discussed later in this chapter.

DFD graphical notation must be augmented with descriptive text. A *process specification* (PSPEC) can be used to specify the processing details implied by a bubble within a DFD. The process specification describes the input to a function, the algorithm that is applied to transform the input, and the output that is produced. In addition, the PSPEC indicates restrictions and limitations imposed on the process (function), performance characteristics that are relevant to the process, and design constraints that may influence the way in which the process will be implemented.

12.4.2 Extensions for Real-Time Systems

Many software applications are time dependent and process as much or more control-oriented information as data. A real-time system must interact with the real world in a time frame dictated by the real world. Aircraft avionics, manufacturing process control, consumer products, and industrial instrumentation are but a few of hundreds of real-time software applications.

To accommodate the analysis of real-time software, a number of extensions to the basic notation for structured analysis have been defined. These extensions, developed by Ward and Mellor [WAR85] and Hatley and Pirbhai [HAT87] and illustrated in the sections that follow, enable the analyst to represent control flow and control processing as well as data flow and processing.

12.4.3 Ward and Mellor Extensions

Ward and Mellor [WAR85] extend basic structured analysis notation to accommodate the following demands imposed by a real-time system:

- Information flow is gathered or produced on a time-continuous basis.
- Control information is passed throughout the system and associated control processing.

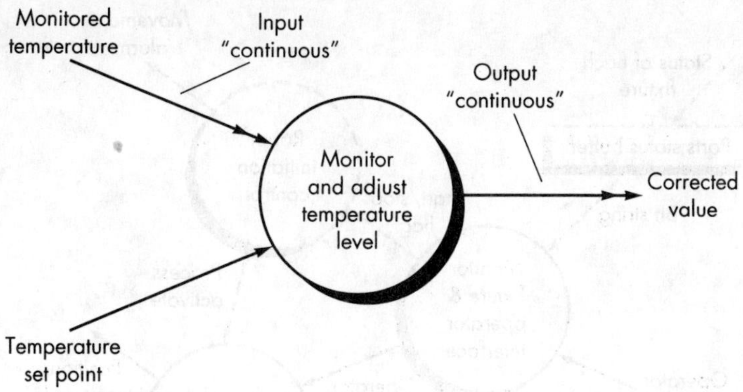

FIGURE 12.12 Time-continuous data flow

- Multiple instances of the same transformation are sometimes encountered in multitasking situations.
- Systems have states and a mechanism causes transition between states.

KEY POINT

To adequately model a real-time system, structured analysis notation must be available for time-continuous data and event processing.

In a significant percentage of real-time applications, the system must monitor time-continuous information generated by some real-world process. For example, a real-time test monitoring system for gas turbine engines might be required to monitor turbine speed, combustor temperature, and a variety of pressure probes on a continuous basis. Conventional data flow notation does not make a distinction between discrete data and time-continuous data. One extension to basic structured analysis notation, shown in Figure 12.12, provides a mechanism for representing *time-continuous data flow.* The double headed arrow is used to represent time-continuous flow while a single headed arrow is used to indicate discrete data flow. In the figure, **monitored temperature** is measured continuously while a single value for **temperature set point** is also provided. The process shown in the figure produces a time-continuous output, **corrected value.**

The distinction between discrete and time-continuous data flow has important implications for both the system engineer and the software designer. During the creation of the system model, a system engineer will be better able to isolate those processes that may be performance critical (it is often likely that the input and output of time-continuous data will be performance sensitive). As the physical or implementation model is created, the designer must establish a mechanism for collection of time-continuous data. Obviously, the digital system collects data in a quasi-continuous fashion using techniques such as high-speed polling. The notation indicates where analog-to-digital hardware will be required and which transforms are likely to demand high-performance software.

In conventional data flow diagrams, control or event flows are not represented explicitly. In fact, the software engineer is cautioned to specifically exclude the

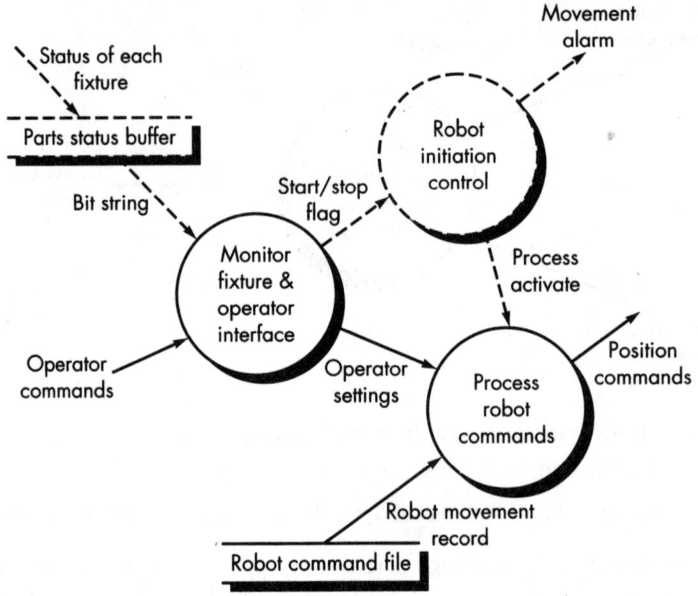

FIGURE 12.13 Data and control flows using Ward and Mellor notation [WAR85]

representation of control flow from the data flow diagram. This exclusion is overly restrictive when real-time applications are considered, and for this reason, a specialized notation for representing event flows and control processing has been developed. Continuing the convention established for data flow diagrams, data flow is represented using a solid arrow. *Control flow,* however, is represented using a dashed or shaded arrow. A process that handles only control flows, called a *control process,* is similarly represented using a dashed bubble.

Quote: "The environment of a real-time system often contains devices that act as the senses of the system." **Paul Ward and Stephen Mellor**

Control flow can be input directly to a conventional process or into a control process. Figure 12.13 illustrates control flow and processing as it would be represented using Ward and Mellor notation. The figure illustrates a top-level view of a data and control flow for a manufacturing cell. As components to be assembled by a robot are placed on fixtures, a status bit is set within a **parts status buffer** (a control store) that indicates the presence or absence of each component. Event information contained within the **parts status buffer** is passed as a bit string to a process, *monitor fixture and operator interface.* The process will read **operator commands** only when the control information, bit string, indicates that all fixtures contain components. An event flag, **start/stop flag,** is sent to *robot initiation control,* a control process that enables further command processing. Other data flows occur as a consequence of the **process activate** event that is sent to *process robot commands.*

In some situations multiple instances of the same control or data transformation process may occur in a real-time system. This can occur in a multitasking environment when tasks are spawned as a result of internal processing or external events. For example, a number of part status buffers may be monitored so that different robots can be signaled at the appropriate time. In addition, each robot may have its own robot control system. The Ward and Mellor notation used to represent *multiple equivalent instances* simply overlays process (or control process) bubbles to indicate multiplicity.

12.4.4 Hatley and Pirbhai Extensions

The Hatley and Pirbhai [HAT87] extensions to basic structured analysis notation focus less on the creation of additional graphical symbols and more on the representation and specification of the control-oriented aspects of the software. The dashed arrow is once again used to represent control or event flow. Unlike Ward and Mellor, Hatley and Pirbhai suggest that dashed and solid notation be represented separately. Therefore, a *control flow diagram* is defined. The CFD contains the same processes as the DFD, but shows control flow, rather than data flow. Instead of representing control processes directly within the flow model, a notational reference (a solid bar) to a *control specification* (CSPEC) is used. In essence, the solid bar can be viewed as a "window" into an "executive" (the CSPEC) that controls the processes (functions) represented in the DFD based on the event that is passed through the window. The CSPEC, described in detail in Section 12.6.4, is used to indicate (1) how the software behaves when an event or control signal is sensed and (2) which processes are invoked as a consequence of the occurrence of the event. A process specification is used to describe the inner workings of a process represented in a flow diagram.

KEY POINT

The CFD shows how events move through a system. The CSPEC indicates how software behaves as a consequence of events and what processes come into play to manage events.

Using the notation described in Figures 12.12 and 12.13, along with additional information contained in PSPECs and CSPECs, Hatley and Pirbhai create a model of a real-time system. Data flow diagrams are used to represent data and the processes that manipulate it. Control flow diagrams show how events flow among processes and illustrate those external events that cause various processes to be activated. The interrelationship between the process and control models is shown schematically in Figure 12.14. The process model is "connected" to the control model through data conditions. The control model is "connected" to the process model through process activation information contained in the CSPEC.

A *data condition* occurs whenever data input to a process result in control output. This situation is illustrated in Figure 12.15, part of a flow model for an automated monitoring and control system for pressure vessels in an oil refinery. The process *check and convert pressure* implements the algorithm described in the PSPEC pseudocode shown. When the **absolute tank pressure** is greater than an allowable maximum, an **above pressure** event is generated. Note that when Hatley and Pirbhai notation is used, the data flow is shown as part of a DFD, while the control flow is noted separately as part of a control flow diagram. As we noted earlier, the vertical solid bar into which the **above pressure** event flows is a pointer to the CSPEC. Therefore, to determine what happens when this event occurs, we must check the CSPEC.

The control specification (CSPEC) contains a number of important modeling tools. A *process activation table* (described in Section 12.6.4) is used to indicate which

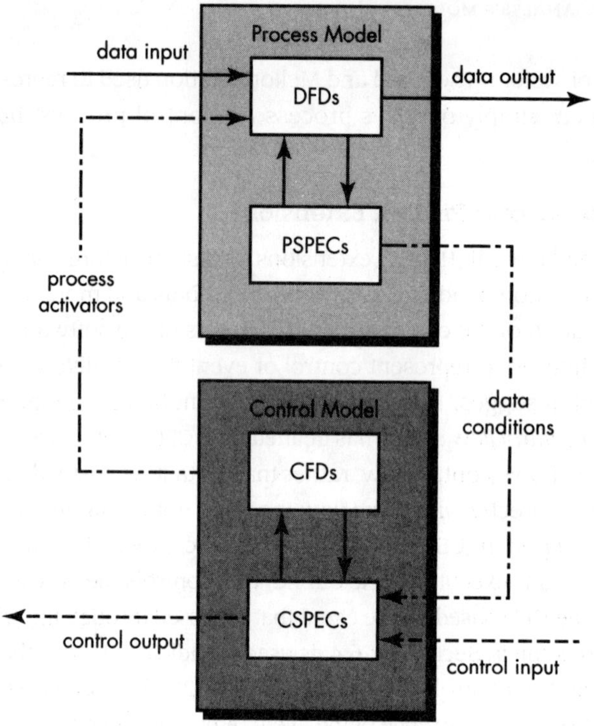

FIGURE 12.14 The relationship between data and control models [HAT87]

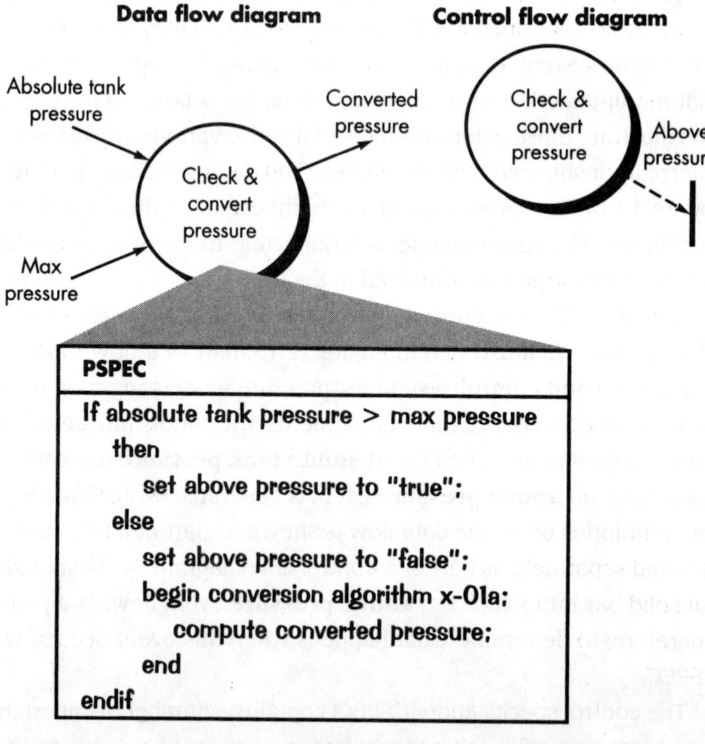

FIGURE 12.15 Data conditions

FIGURE 12.16 Level 1 CFD for photocopier software

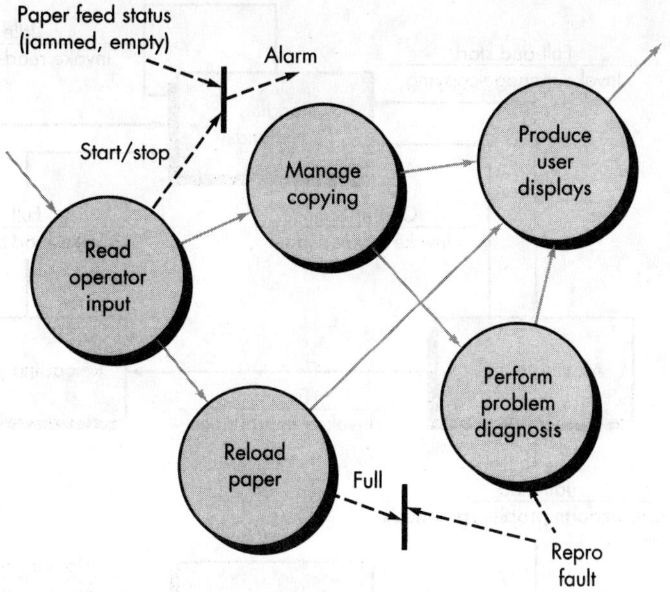

processes are activated by a given event. For example, a process activation table (PAT) for Figure 12.15 might indicate that the **above pressure** event would cause a process *reduce tank pressure* (not shown) to be invoked. In addition to the PAT, the CSPEC may contain a state transition diagram. The STD is a behavioral model that relies on the definition of a set of system states and is described in the following section.

12.5 BEHAVIORAL MODELING

? How do I model the software's reaction to some external event?

Behavioral modeling is an operational principle for all requirements analysis methods. Yet, only extended versions of structured analysis ([WAR85], [HAT87]) provide a notation for this type of modeling. The state transition diagram represents the behavior of a system by depicting its states and the events that cause the system to change state. In addition, the STD indicates what actions (e.g., process activation) are taken as a consequence of a particular event.

A state is any observable mode of behavior. For example, states for a monitoring and control system for pressure vessels described in Section 12.4.4 might be *monitoring state, alarm state, pressure release state,* and so on. Each of these states represents a mode of behavior of the system. A state transition diagram indicates how the system moves from state to state.

To illustrate the use of the Hatley and Pirbhai control and behavioral extensions, consider software embedded within an office photocopying machine. A simplified representation of the control flow for the photocopier software is shown in Figure 12.16. Data flow arrows have been lightly shaded for illustrative purposes, but in reality they are not shown as part of a control flow diagram.

FIGURE 12.17
State transition diagram for photocopier software

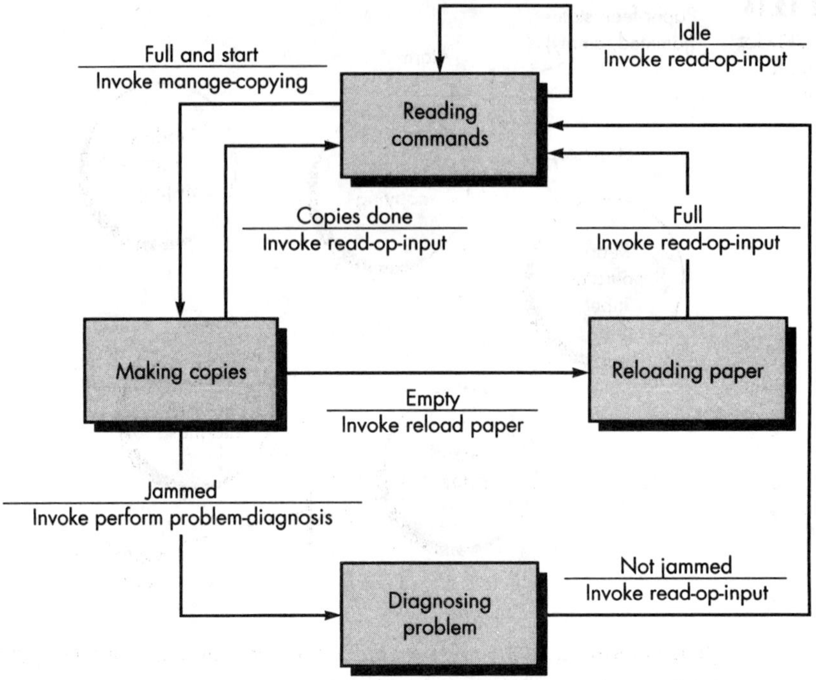

Control flows are shown entering and exiting individual processes and the vertical bar representing the CSPEC "window." For example, the **paper feed status** and **start/stop** events flow into the CSPEC bar. This implies that each of these events will cause some process represented in the CFD to be activated. If we were to examine the CSPEC internals, the **start/stop** event would be shown to activate/deactivate the *manage copying* process. Similarly, the **jammed** event (part of **paper feed status**) would activate *perform problem diagnosis.* It should be noted that all vertical bars within the CFD refer to the same CSPEC. An event flow can be input directly into a process as shown with **repro fault.** However, this flow does not activate the process but rather provides control information for the process algorithm.

Quote:

"The only thing missing is a state of confusion."

A reviewer upon puzzling over an extremely complex STD.

A simplified state transition diagram for the photocopier software is shown in Figure 12.17. The rectangles represent system states and the arrows represent transitions between states. Each arrow is labeled with a ruled expression. The top value indicates the event(s) that cause the transition to occur. The bottom value indicates the action that occurs as a consequence of the event. Therefore, when the paper tray is **full** and the **start** button is pressed, the system moves from the *reading commands* state to the *making copies* state. Note that states do not necessarily correspond to processes on a one-to-one basis. For example, the state *making copies* would encompass both the *manage copying* and *produce user displays* processes shown in Figure 12.16.

12.6 THE MECHANICS OF STRUCTURED ANALYSIS

ADVICE

The analysis model allows a reviewer to examine software requirements from three different points of view. Therefore, be certain to use ERDs, DFDs, and STDs when you build the model.

In the previous section, we discussed basic and extended notation for structured analysis. To be used effectively in software requirements analysis, this notation must be combined with a set of heuristics that enable a software engineer to derive a good analysis model. To illustrate the use of these heuristics, an adapted version of the Hatley and Pirbhai [HAT87] extensions to the basic structured analysis notation will be used throughout the remainder of this chapter.

In the sections that follow, we examine each of the steps that should be applied to develop complete and accurate models using structured analysis. Through this discussion, the notation introduced in Section 12.4 will be used, and other notational forms, alluded to earlier, will be presented in some detail.

12.6.1 Creating an Entity/Relationship Diagram

The entity/relationship diagram enables a software engineer to fully specify the data objects that are input and output from a system, the attributes that define the properties of these objects, and their relationships. Like most elements of the analysis model, the ERD is constructed in an iterative manner. The following approach is taken:

What steps are required to build an ERD?

1. During requirements elicitation, customers are asked to list the "things" that the application or business process addresses. These "things" evolve into a list of input and output data objects as well as external entities that produce or consume information.
2. Taking the objects one at a time, the analyst and customer define whether or not a connection (unnamed at this stage) exists between the data object and other objects.
3. Wherever a connection exists, the analyst and the customer create one or more object/relationship pairs.
4. For each object/relationship pair, cardinality and modality are explored.
5. Steps 2 through 4 are continued iteratively until all object/relationships have been defined. It is common to discover omissions as this process continues. New objects and relationships will invariably be added as the number of iterations grows.
6. The attributes of each entity are defined.
7. An entity relationship diagram is formalized and reviewed.
8. Steps 1 through 7 are repeated until data modeling is complete.

To illustrate the use of these basic guidelines, the *SafeHome* security system example, discussed in Chapter 11, will be used. Referring back to the processing narrative

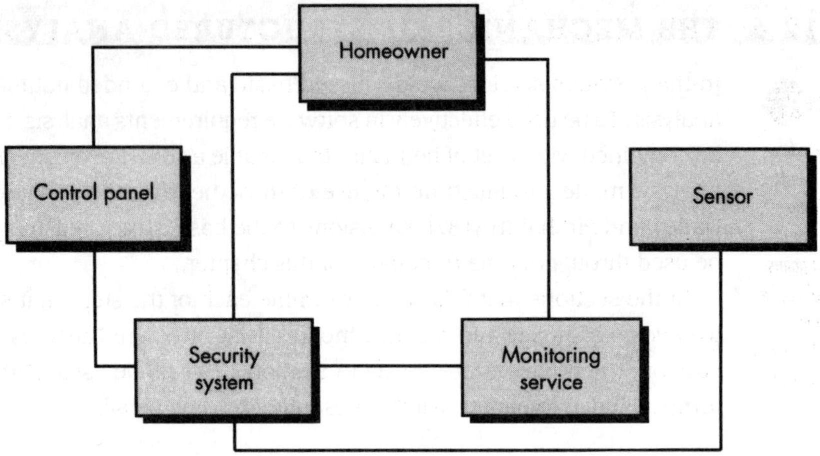

FIGURE 12.18 Establishing connections

for *SafeHome* (Section 11.3.3), the following (partial) list of "things" are relevant to the problem:

- homeowner
- control panel
- sensors
- security system
- monitoring service

Taking these "things" one at a time, connections are explored. To accomplish this, each object is drawn and lines connecting the objects are noted. For example, referring to Figure 12.18, a direct connection exists between **homeowner** and **control panel, security system,** and **monitoring service.** A single connection exists between **sensor** and **security system**, and so forth.

Once all connections have been defined, one or more object/relationship pairs are identified for each connection. For example, the connection between **sensor** and **security system** is determined to have the following object/relationship pairs:

security system *monitors* **sensor**
security system *enables/disables* **sensor**
security system *tests* **sensor**
security system *programs* **sensor**

Each of these object/relationship pairs is analyzed to determine cardinality and modality. For example, considering the object/relationship pair **security system** *monitors* **sensor,** the cardinality between **security system** and **sensor** is one to many. The modality is one occurrence of **security system** (mandatory) and at least one occurrence of **sensor** (mandatory). Using the ERD notation introduced in Section 12.3, the

FIGURE 12.19 Developing relationships and cardinality/ modality

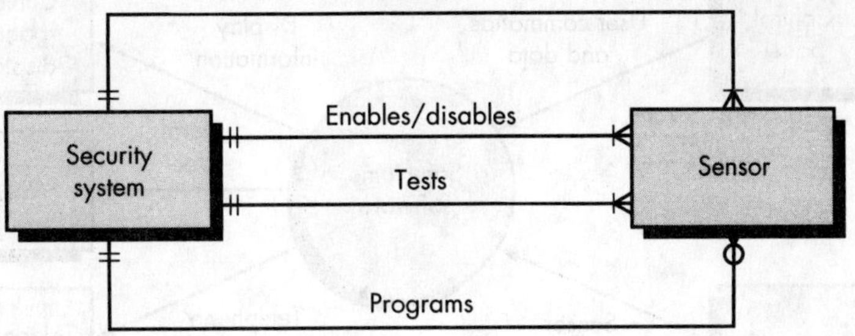

connecting line between **security system** and **sensor** would be modified as shown in Figure 12.19. Similar analysis would be applied to all other data objects.

Each object is studied to determine its attributes. Since we are considering the software that must support *SafeHome,* the attributes should focus on data that must be stored to enable the system to operate. For example, the **sensor** object might have the following attributes: sensor type, internal identification number, zone location, and alarm level.

12.6.2 Creating a Data Flow Model

The data flow diagram enables the software engineer to develop models of the information domain and functional domain at the same time. As the DFD is refined into greater levels of detail, the analyst performs an implicit functional decomposition of the system, thereby accomplishing the fourth operational analysis principle for function. At the same time, the DFD refinement results in a corresponding refinement of data as it moves through the processes that embody the application.

? Are there any useful guidelines for creating DFDs?

A few simple guidelines can aid immeasurably during derivation of a data flow diagram: (1) the level 0 data flow diagram should depict the software/system as a single bubble; (2) primary input and output should be carefully noted; (3) refinement should begin by isolating candidate processes, data objects, and stores to be represented at the next level; (4) all arrows and bubbles should be labeled with meaningful names; (5) information flow continuity must be maintained from level to level, and (6) one bubble at a time should be refined. There is a natural tendency to overcomplicate the data flow diagram. This occurs when the analyst attempts to show too much detail too early or represents procedural aspects of the software in lieu of information flow.

Again considering the *SafeHome* product, a level 0 DFD for the system is shown in Figure 12.20. The primary external entities (boxes) produce information for use by the system and consume information generated by the system. The labeled arrows represent data objects or data object type hierarchies. For example, **user commands and data** encompasses all configuration commands, all activation/deactivation

FIGURE 12.20
Context-level DFD for SafeHome

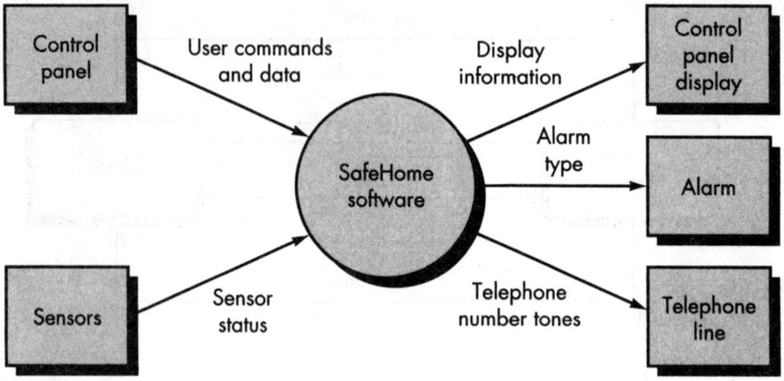

commands, all miscellaneous interactions, and all data that are entered to qualify or expand a command.

The level 0 DFD is now expanded into a level 1 model. But how do we proceed? A simple, yet effective approach is to perform a "grammatical parse" on the processing narrative that describes the context level bubble. That is, we isolate all nouns (and noun phrases) and verbs (and verb phrases) in the *SafeHome* narrative originally presented in Chapter 11. To illustrate, we again reproduce the processing narrative underlining the first occurrence of all nouns and italicizing the first occurrence of all verbs.[3]

ADVICE

The grammatical parse is not foolproof, but it will provide you with an excellent jump start if you're struggling to define data objects and transforms.

SafeHome software *enables* the homeowner to *configure* the security system when it is *installed, monitors* all sensors *connected* to the security system, and *interacts* with the homeowner through a keypad and function keys *contained* in the SafeHome control panel shown in Figure 11.2.

During installation, the SafeHome control panel is *used* to "*program*" and *configure* the system. Each sensor is *assigned* a number and type, a master password is programmed for *arming* and *disarming* the system, and telephone number(s) are *input* for *dialing* when a sensor event occurs.

When a sensor event is *recognized*, the software *invokes* an audible alarm attached to the system. After a delay time that is *specified* by the homeowner during system configuration activities, the software dials a telephone number of a monitoring service, *provides* information about the location, *reporting* the nature of the event that has been detected. The telephone number will be *redialed* every 20 seconds until telephone connection is *obtained.*

All interaction with SafeHome is *managed* by a user-interaction subsystem that *reads* input provided through the keypad and function keys, *displays* prompting messages on the LCD display, displays system status information on the LCD display. Keyboard interaction takes the following form . . .

Referring to the "grammatical parse," a pattern begins to emerge. All verbs are *SafeHome* processes; that is, they may ultimately be represented as bubbles in a sub-

3 It should be noted that nouns and verbs that are synonyms or have no direct bearing on the modeling process are omitted.

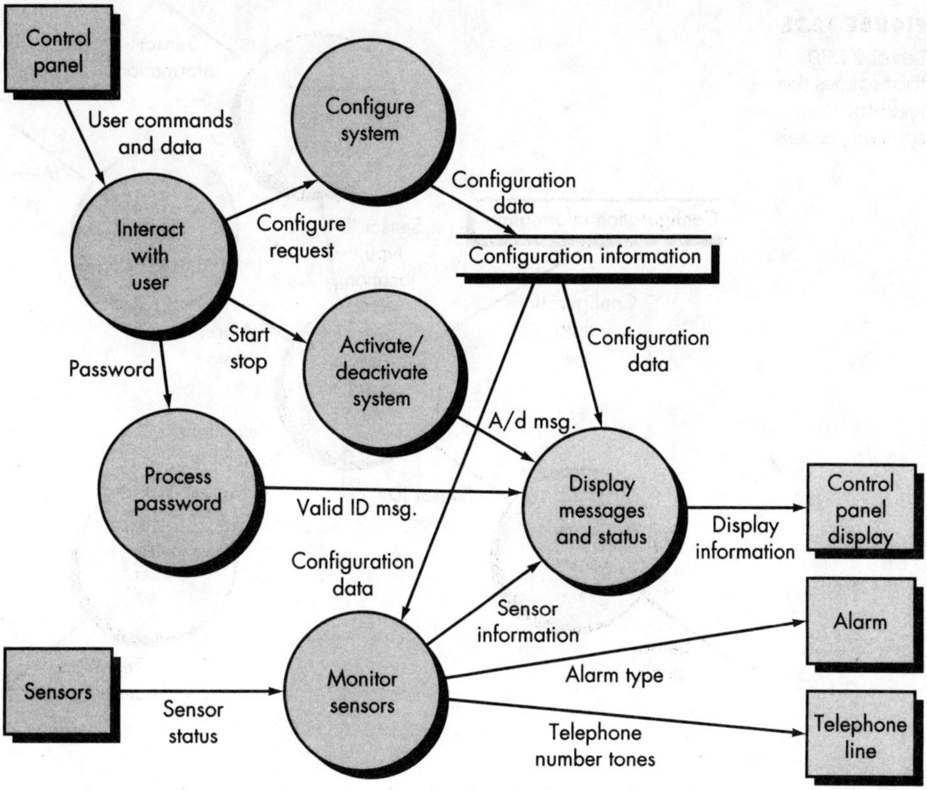

FIGURE 12.21 Level 1 DFD for SafeHome

ADVICE *Be certain that the processing narrative you intend to parse is written at the same level of abstraction throughout.*

sequent DFD. All nouns are either external entities (boxes), data or control objects (arrows), or data stores (double lines). Note further that nouns and verbs can be attached to one another (e.g., **sensor** is assigned number and type). Therefore, by performing a grammatical parse on the processing narrative for a bubble at any DFD level, we can generate much useful information about how to proceed with the refinement to the next level. Using this information, a level 1 DFD is shown in Figure 12.21. The context level process shown in Figure 12.20 has been expanded into six processes derived from an examination of the grammatical parse. Similarly, the information flow between processes at level 1 has been derived from the parse.

It should be noted that information flow continuity is maintained between levels 0 and 1. Elaboration of the content of inputs and output at DFD levels 0 and 1 is postponed until Section 12.7.

The processes represented at DFD level 1 can be further refined into lower levels. For example, the process *monitor sensors* can be refined into a level 2 DFD as shown in Figure 12.22. Note once again that information flow continuity has been maintained between levels.

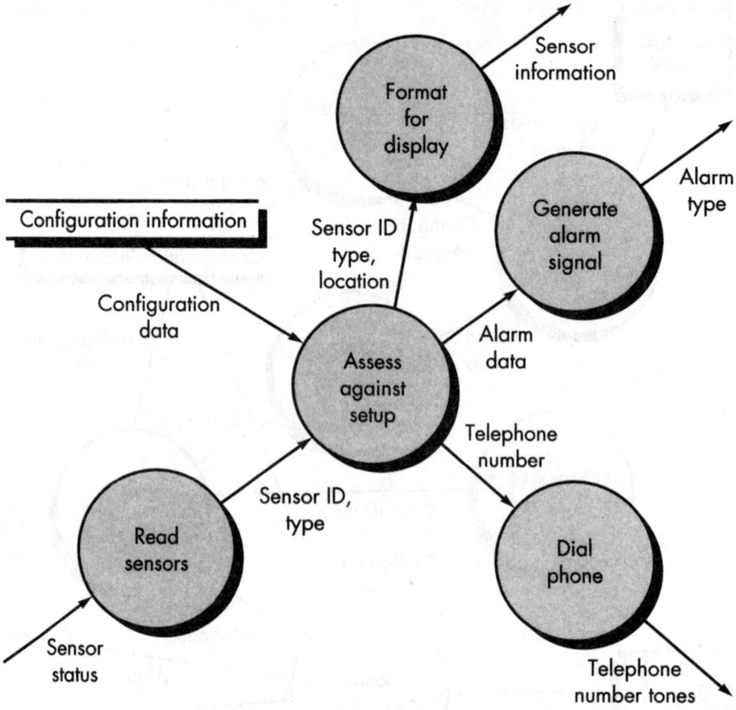

FIGURE 12.22 Level 2 DFD that refines the monitor sensors process

The refinement of DFDs continues until each bubble performs a simple function. That is, until the process represented by the bubble performs a function that would be easily implemented as a program component. In Chapter 13, we discuss a concept, called *cohesion,* that can be used to assess the simplicity of a given function. For now, we strive to refine DFDs until each bubble is "single-minded."

12.6.3 Creating a Control Flow Model

For many types of data processing applications, the data model and the data flow diagram are all that is necessary to obtain meaningful insight into software requirements. As we have already noted, however, a large class of applications are "driven" by events rather than data; produce control information rather than reports or displays, and process information with heavy concern for time and performance. Such applications require the use of control flow modeling in addition to data flow modeling.

The graphical notation required to create a control flow diagram was presented in Section 12.4.4. To review the approach for creating a CFD, a data flow model is "stripped" of all data flow arrows. Events and control items (dashed arrows) are then added to the diagram and a "window" (a vertical bar) into the control specification is shown. But how are events selected?

We have already noted that an event or control item is implemented as a Boolean value (e.g., true or false, on or off, 1 or 0) or a discrete list of conditions (empty, jammed, full). To select potential candidate events, the following guidelines are suggested:

? How do I select potential events for a CFD, STD, and CSPEC?

- List all sensors that are "read" by the software.
- List all interrupt conditions.
- List all "switches" that are actuated by an operator.
- List all data conditions.
- Recalling the noun/verb parse that was applied to the processing narrative, review all "control items" as possible CSPEC inputs/outputs.
- Describe the behavior of a system by identifying its states; identify how each state is reached; and define the transitions between states.
- Focus on possible omissions—a very common error in specifying control; for example, ask: "Is there any other way I can get to this state or exit from it?"

A level 1 CFD for *SafeHome* software is illustrated in Figure 12.23. Among the events and control items noted are **sensor event** (i.e., a sensor has been tripped), **blink flag** (a signal to blink the LCD display), and **start/stop switch** (a signal to turn the system on or off). When the event flows into the CSPEC window from the outside world, it implies that the CSPEC will activate one or more of the processes shown in the CFD. When a control item emanates from a process and flows into the CSPEC window, control and activation of some other process or an outside entity is implied.

12.6.4 The Control Specification

The control specification (CSPEC) represents the behavior of the system (at the level from which it has been referenced) in two different ways. The CSPEC contains a state transition diagram that is a sequential specification of behavior. It can also contain a program activation table—a combinatorial specification of behavior. The underlying attributes of the CSPEC were introduced in Section 12.4.4. It is now time to consider an example of this important modeling notation for structured analysis.

Figure 12.24 depicts a state transition diagram for the level 1 control flow model for *SafeHome.* The labeled transition arrows indicate how the system responds to events as it traverses the four states defined at this level. By studying the STD, a software engineer can determine the behavior of the system and, more important, can ascertain whether there are "holes" in the specified behavior. For example, the STD (Figure 12.24) indicates that the only transition from the *reading user input* state occurs when the **start/stop switch** is encountered and a transition to the *monitoring system status* state occurs. Yet, there appears to be no way, other than the occurrence of **sensor event**, that will allow the system to return to *reading user input.* This is an

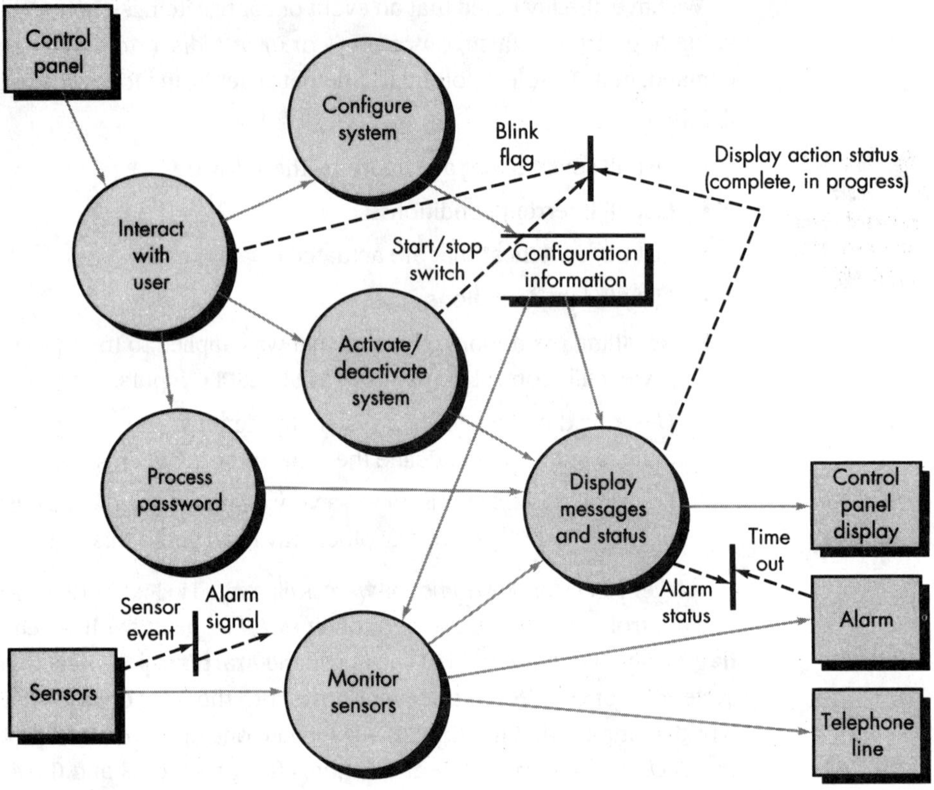

FIGURE 12.23 Level 1 CFD for SafeHome

FIGURE 12.24 State transition diagram for SafeHome

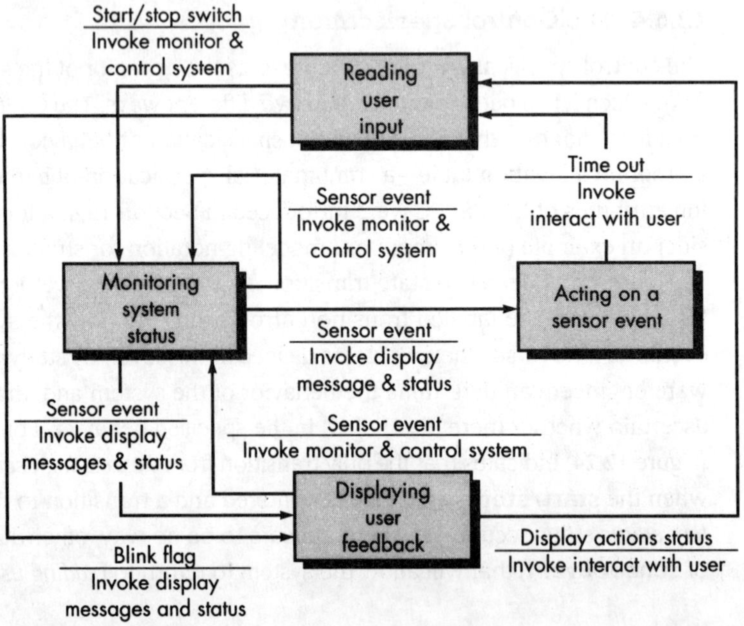

error in specification and would, we hope, be uncovered during review and corrected. Examine the STD to determine whether there are any other anomalies.

A somewhat different mode of behavioral representation is the process activation table. The PAT represents information contained in the STD in the context of processes, not states. That is, the table indicates which processes (bubbles) in the flow model will be invoked when an event occurs. The PAT can be used as a guide for a designer who must build an executive that controls the processes represented at this level. A PAT for the level 1 flow model of *SafeHome* software is shown in Figure 12.25.

The CSPEC describes the behavior of the system, but it gives us no information about the inner working of the processes that are activated as a result of this behavior. The modeling notation that provides this information is discussed in the next section.

12.6.5 The Process Specification

The process specification (PSPEC) is used to describe all flow model processes that appear at the final level of refinement. The content of the process specification can include narrative text, a *program design language* (PDL) description of the process algorithm, mathematical equations, tables, diagrams, or charts. By providing a PSPEC to accompany each bubble in the flow model, the software engineer creates a "mini-spec" that can serve as a first step in the creation of the *Software Requirements Specification* and as a guide for design of the software component that will implement the process.

Input events						
Sensor event	0	0	0	0	1	0
Blink flag	0	0	1	1	0	0
Start/stop switch	0	1	0	0	0	0
Display action status						
Complete	0	0	0	1	0	0
In progress	0	0	1	0	0	0
Time out	0	0	0	0	0	1
Output						
Alarm signal	0	0	0	0	1	0
Process activation						
Monitor and control system	0	1	0	0	1	1
Activate/deactivate system	0	1	0	0	0	0
Display messages and status	1	0	1	1	1	1
Interact with user	1	0	0	1	0	1

FIGURE 12.25 Process activation table for SafeHome

To illustrate the use of the PSPEC, consider the *process password* transform represented in the flow model for *SafeHome* (Figure 12.21). The PSPEC for this function might take the form:

PSPEC: process password

The *process password* transform performs all password validation for the *SafeHome* system. *Process password* receives a four-digit password from the *interact with user* function. The password is first compared to the master password stored within the system. If the master password matches, <valid id message = true> is passed to the *message and status display* function. If the master password does not match, the four digits are compared to a table of secondary passwords (these may be assigned to house guests and/or workers who require entry to the home when the owner is not present). If the password matches an entry within the table, <valid id message = true> is passed to the *message and status display* function. If there is no match, <valid id message = false> is passed to the *message and status display function.*

If additional algorithmic detail is desired at this stage, a program design language representation may also be included as part of the PSPEC. However, many believe that the PDL version should be postponed until component design commences.

12.7 THE DATA DICTIONARY

The analysis model encompasses representations of data objects, function, and control. In each representation data objects and/or control items play a role. Therefore, it is necessary to provide an organized approach for representing the characteristics of each data object and control item. This is accomplished with the data dictionary.

The data dictionary has been proposed as a quasi-formal grammar for describing the content of objects defined during structured analysis. This important modeling notation has been defined in the following manner [YOU89]:

> The *data dictionary* is an organized listing of all data elements that are pertinent to the system, with precise, rigorous definitions so that both user and system analyst will have a common understanding of inputs, outputs, components of stores and [even] intermediate calculations.

? How do I represent the content of the data objects I've identified?

Today, the data dictionary is always implemented as part of a CASE "structured analysis and design tool." Although the format of dictionaries varies from tool to tool, most contain the following information:

- *Name*—the primary name of the data or control item, the data store or an external entity.
- *Alias*—other names used for the first entry.
- *Where-used/how-used*—a listing of the processes that use the data or control item and how it is used (e.g., input to the process, output from the process, as a store, as an external entity.

- *Content description*—a notation for representing content.
- *Supplementary information*—other information about data types, preset values (if known), restrictions or limitations, and so forth.

Once a data object or control item name and its aliases are entered into the data dictionary, consistency in naming can be enforced. That is, if an analysis team member decides to name a newly derived data item **xyz,** but **xyz** is already in the dictionary, the CASE tool supporting the dictionary posts a warning to indicate duplicate names. This improves the consistency of the analysis model and helps to reduce errors.

"Where-used/how-used" information is recorded automatically from the flow models. When a dictionary entry is created, the CASE tool scans DFDs and CFDs to determine which processes use the data or control information and how it is used. Although this may appear unimportant, it is actually one of the most important benefits of the dictionary. During analysis there is an almost continuous stream of changes. For large projects, it is often quite difficult to determine the impact of a change. Many a software engineer has asked, "Where is this data object used? What else will have to change if we modify it? What will the overall impact of the change be?" Because the data dictionary can be treated as a database, the analyst can ask "where used/how used" questions, and get answers to these queries.

CASE Tools
Structured Analysis

The notation used to develop a content description is noted in the following table:

Data Construct	**Notation**	**Meaning**
	=	is composed of
Sequence	+	and
Selection	[|]	either-or
Repetition	{ }^{n}	*n* repetitions of
	( )	optional data
	* ... *	delimits comments

The notation enables a software engineer to represent composite data in one of the three fundamental ways that it can be constructed:

1. As a sequence of data items.
2. As a selection from among a set of data items.
3. As a repeated grouping of data items. Each data item entry that is represented as part of a sequence, selection, or repetition may itself be another composite data item that needs further refinement within the dictionary.

To illustrate the use of the data dictionary, we return to the level 2 DFD for the *monitor system* process for *SafeHome,* shown in Figure 12.22. Referring to the figure, the data item **telephone number** is specified as input. But what exactly is a telephone number? It could be a 7-digit local number, a 4-digit extension, or a 25-digit long distance carrier sequence. The data dictionary provides us with a precise definition of **telephone number** for the DFD in question. In addition it indicates where and how this data item is used and any supplementary information that is relevant to it. The data dictionary entry begins as follows:

name:	telephone number
aliases:	none
where used/how used:	assess against set-up (output)
	dial phone (input)

description:

telephone number = [local number|long distance number]
local number = prefix + access number
long distance number = 1 + area code + local number
area code = [800 | 888 | 561]
prefix = *a three digit number that never starts with 0 or 1*
access number = * any four number string *

The content description is expanded until all composite data items have been represented as elementary items (items that require no further expansion) or until all composite items are represented in terms that would be well-known and unambiguous to all readers. It is also important to note that a specification of elementary data often restricts a system. For example, the definition of area code indicates that only three area codes (two toll-free and one in South Florida) are valid for this system.

The data dictionary defines information items unambiguously. Although we might assume that the telephone number represented by the DFD in Figure 12.22 could accommodate a 25-digit long distance carrier access number, the data dictionary content description tells us that such numbers are not part of the data that may be used.

For large computer-based systems, the data dictionary grows rapidly in size and complexity. In fact, it is extremely difficult to maintain a dictionary manually. For this reason, CASE tools should be used.

12.8 OTHER CLASSICAL ANALYSIS METHODS

Over the years, many other worthwhile software requirements analysis methods have been used throughout the industry. While all follow the operational analysis principles discussed in Chapter 11, each uses a different notation and a unique set of heuristics for deriving the analysis model. An overview of three important analysis methods:

SEPA WEB: DSSD, JSD, and SADT

- *Data Structured Systems Development* (DSSD) [WAR81], [ORR81]
- *Jackson System Development* (JSD) [JAC83]
- *Structured Analysis and Design Technique* (SADT) [ROS77], [ROS85]

is presented within the SEPA Web site for those readers interested in a broader view of analysis modeling.

12.9 SUMMARY

Structured analysis, a widely used method of requirements modeling, relies on data modeling and flow modeling to create the basis for a comprehensive analysis model. Using entity-relationship diagrams, the software engineer creates a representation of all data objects that are important for the system. Data and control flow diagrams are used as a basis for representing the transformation of data and control. At the same time, these models are used to create a functional model of the software and to provide a mechanism for partitioning function. A behavioral model is created using the state transition diagram, and data content is developed with a data dictionary. Process and control specifications provide additional elaboration of detail.

The original notation for structured analysis was developed for conventional data processing applications, but extensions have made the method applicable to real-time systems. Structured analysis is supported by an array of CASE tools that assist in the creation of each element of the model and also help to ensure consistency and correctness.

REFERENCES

[BRU88] Bruyn, W. et al., "ESML: An Extended Systems Modeling Language Based on the Data Flow Diagram," *ACM Software Engineering Notes,* vol. 13, no. 1, January 1988, pp. 58–67.

[CHE77] Chen, P., *The Entity-Relationship Approach to Logical Database Design,* QED Information Systems, 1977.

[DEM79] DeMarco, T., *Structured Analysis and System Specification,* Prentice-Hall, 1979.

[GAN82] Gane, T. and C. Sarson, *Structured Systems Analysis,* McDonnell Douglas, 1982.

[HAT87] Hatley, D.J. and I.A. Pirbhai, *Strategies for Real-Time System Specification,* Dorset House, 1987.

[JAC83] Jackson, M.A., *System Development,* Prentice-Hall, 1983.

[ORR81] Orr, K.T., *Structured Requirements Definition,* Ken Orr & Associates, Inc., 1981.

[PAG80] Page-Jones, M., *The Practical Guide to Structured Systems Design,* Yourdon Press, 1980.

[ROS77] Ross, D. and K. Schoman, "Structured Analysis for Requirements Definition," *IEEE Trans. Software Engineering,* vol. SE-3, no. 1, January 1977, pp. 6–15.

[ROS85] Ross, D. "Applications and Extensions of SADT," *IEEE Computer,* vol. 18, no. 4, April 1984, pp. 25–35.

[STE74] Stevens, W.P., G.J. Myers, and L.L. Constantine, "Structured Design," *IBM Systems Journal,* vol. 13, no. 2, 1974, pp. 115–139.

[TIL93] Tillmann, G., *A Practical Guide to Logical Data Modeling,* McGraw-Hill, 1993.

[WAR81] Warnier, J.D., *Logical Construction of Systems,* Van Nostrand-Reinhold, 1981.

[WAR85] Ward, P.T. and S.J. Mellor, *Structured Development for Real-Time Systems* (three volumes), Yourdon Press, 1985.

[YOU78] Yourdon, E.N. and Constantine, L.L., *Structured Design,* Yourdon Press, 1978.

[YOU89] Yourdon, E.N., *Modern Structured Analysis,* Prentice-Hall, 1990.

PROBLEMS AND POINTS TO PONDER

12.1. Acquire at least three of the references discussed in Section 12.1 and write a brief paper that outlines how the perception of structured analysis has changed over time. As a concluding section, suggest ways that you think the method will change in the future.

12.2. You have been asked to build one of the following systems:

a. A network-based course registration system for your university.
b. A Web-based order-processing system for a computer store.
c. A simple invoicing system for a small business.
d. Software that replaces a Rolodex and is built into a wireless phone.
e. An automated cookbook that is built into an electric range or microwave.

Select the system that is of interest to you and develop an entity/relationship diagram that describes data objects, relationships, and attributes.

12.3. What is the difference between cardinality and modality?

12.4. Draw a context-level model (level 0 DFD) for one of the five systems that are listed in Problem 12.2. Write a context-level processing narrative for the system.

12.5. Using the context-level DFD developed in Problem 12.4, develop level 1 and level 2 data flow diagrams. Use a "grammatical parse" on the context-level processing narrative to get yourself started. Remember to specify all information flow by labeling all arrows between bubbles. Use meaningful names for each transform.

12.6. Develop a CFDs, CSPECs, PSPECs, and a data dictionary for the system you selected in Problem 12.2. Try to make your model as complete as possible.

12.7. Does the information flow continuity concept mean that, if one flow arrow appears as input at level 0, then one flow arrow must appear as input at subsequent levels? Discuss your answer.

12.8. Using the Ward and Mellor extensions, redraw the flow model contained in Figure 12.16. How will you accommodate the CSPEC that is implied in Figure 12.16? Ward and Mellor do not use this notation.

12.9. Using the Hatley and Pirbhai extensions, redraw the flow model contained in Figure 12.13. How will you accommodate the control process (dashed bubble) that is implied in Figure 12.13? Hatley and Pirbhai do not use this notation.

12.10. Describe an event flow in your own words.

12.11. Develop a complete flow model for the photocopier software discussed in Section 12.5. You may use either the Ward and Mellor or Hatley and Pirbhai method. Be certain to develop a detailed state transition diagram for the system.

12.12. Complete the processing narratives for the analysis model for *SafeHome* software shown in Figure 12.21. Describe the interaction mechanics between the user and the system. Will your additional information change the flow models for *SafeHome* presented in this chapter? If so, how?

12.13. The department of public works for a large city has decided to develop a Web-based *pothole tracking and repair system* (PHTRS). A description follows:

> Citizens can log onto a Web site and report the location and severity of potholes. As potholes are reported they are logged within a "public works department repair system" and are assigned an identifying number, stored by street address, size (on a scale of 1 to 10), location (middle, curb, etc.), district (determined from street address), and repair priority (determined from the size of the pothole). Work order data are associated with each pothole and includes pothole location and size, repair crew identifying number, number of people on crew, equipment assigned, hours applied to repair, hole status (work in progress, repaired, temporary repair, not repaired), amount of filler material used and cost of repair (computed from hours applied, number of people, material and equipment used). Finally, a damage file is created to hold information about reported damage due to the pothole and includes citizen's name, address, phone number, type of damage, dollar amount of damage. PHTRS is an on-line system; all queries are to be made interactively.

Using structured analysis notation, develop a complete analysis model for PHTRS.

12.14. Next generation software for a word-processing system is to be developed. Do a few hours of research on the application area and conduct a FAST meeting (Chapter 11) with your fellow students to develop requirements (your instructor will help you coordinate this). Build a requirements model of the system using structured analysis.

12.15. Software for a video game is to be developed. Proceed as in Problem 12.14.

12.16. Contact four or five vendors that sell CASE tools for structured analysis. Review their literature and write a brief paper that summarizes generic features that seem to distinguish one tool from another.

FURTHER READINGS AND INFORMATION SOURCES

Dozens of books have been published on structured analysis. All cover the subject adequately, but only a few do a truly excellent job. DeMarco's book [DEM79] remains a good introduction to the basic notation. Books by Hoffer et al. (*Modern Systems Analysis and Design,* Addison-Wesley, 2nd ed., 1998), Kendall and Kendall (*Systems Analysis and Design,* 2nd ed., Prentice-Hall, 1998), Davis and Yen (*The Information System Consultant's Handbook: Systems Analysis and Design,* CRC Press, 1998), Modell (*A Professional's Guide to Systems Analysis,* 2nd ed., McGraw-Hill, 1996), Robertson and Robertson (*Complete Systems Analysis,* 2 volumes, Dorset House, 1994), and Page-Jones (*The Practical Guide to Structured Systems Design,* 2nd ed., Prentice-Hall, 1988) are worthwhile references. Yourdon's book on the subject [YOU89] remains among the most comprehensive coverage published to date.

For an engineering emphasis [WAR85] and [HAT87] are the books of preference. However, Edwards (*Real-Time Structured Methods: Systems Analysis,* Wiley, 1993) also covers the analysis of real-time systems in considerable detail, presenting a number of useful examples drawn from actual applications.

Many variations on structured analysis have evolved over the last decade. Cutts (*Structured Systems Analysis and Design Methodology,* Van Nostrand-Reinhold, 1990) and Hares (*SSADM for the Advanced Practitioner,* Wiley, 1990) describe SSADM, a variation on structured analysis that is widely used in the United Kingdom and Europe.

Flynn et al. (*Information Modeling: An International Perspective,* Prentice-Hall, 1996), Reingruber and Gregory (*Data Modeling Handbook,* Wiley, 1995) and Tillman [TIL93] present detailed tutorials for creating industry-quality data models. Kim and Salvatore ("Comparing Data Modeling Formalisms," *Communications of the ACM,* June 1995) have written an excellent comparison of data modeling methods. An interesting book by Hay (*Data Modeling Patterns,* Dorset House, 1995) presents typical data model "patterns" that are encountered in many different businesses. A detailed treatment of behavioral modeling can be found in Kowal (*Behavior Models: Specifying User's Expectations,* Prentice-Hall, 1992).

A wide variety of information sources on structured analysis and related subjects is available on the Internet. An up-to-date list of World Wide Web references that are relevant to analysis concepts and methods can be found at the SEPA Web site:
http://www.mhhe.com/engcs/compsci/pressman/resources/reqm-analysis.mhtml

CHAPTER 13 DESIGN CONCEPTS AND PRINCIPLES

KEY CONCEPTS

The designer's goal is to produce a model or representation of an entity that will later be built. The process by which the design model is developed is described by Belady [BEL81]:

> [T]here are two major phases to any design process: diversification and convergence. Diversification is the *acquisition* of a repertoire of alternatives, the raw material of design: components, component solutions, and knowledge, all contained in catalogs, textbooks, and the mind. During convergence, the designer chooses and combines appropriate elements from this repertoire to meet the design objectives, as stated in the requirements document and as agreed to by the customer. The second phase is the gradual *elimination* of all but one particular configuration of components, and thus the creation of the final product.

Diversification and convergence combine intuition and judgment based on experience in building similar entities, a set of principles and/or heuristics that guide the way in which the model evolves, a set of criteria that enables quality to be judged, and a process of iteration that ultimately leads to a final design representation.

Software design, like engineering design approaches in other disciplines, changes continually as new methods, better analysis, and broader understanding

QUICK LOOK

What is it? Design is a meaningful engineering representation of something that is to be built. It can be traced to a customer's requirements and at the same time assessed for quality against a set of predefined criteria for "good" design. In the software engineering context, design focuses on four major areas of concern: data, architecture, interfaces, and components. The concepts and principles discussed in this chapter apply to all four.

Who does it? Software engineers design computer-based systems, but the skills required at each level of design work are different. At the data and architectural level, design focuses on patterns as they apply to the application to be built. At the interface level, human ergonomics often dictate our design approach. At the component level, a "programming approach" leads us to effective data and procedural designs.

Why is it important? You wouldn't attempt to build a house without a blueprint, would you? You'd risk confusion, errors, a floor plan that didn't make sense, windows and doors in the wrong place . . . a mess. Computer software is considerably more complex than a house; hence, we need a blueprint—the design.

What are the steps? Design begins with the requirements model. We work to transform this model into four levels of design detail: the data structure,

QUICK LOOK the system architecture, the interface representation, and the component level detail. During each design activity, we apply basic concepts and principles that lead to high quality.

What is the work product? Ultimately, a Design Specification is produced. The specification is composed of the design models that describe data, architecture, interfaces, and components. Each is a work product of the design process.

How do I ensure that I've done it right? At each stage, software design work products are reviewed for clarity, correctness, completeness, and consistency with the requirements and with one another.

evolve. Software design methodologies lack the depth, flexibility, and quantitative nature that are normally associated with more classical engineering design disciplines. However, methods for software design do exist, criteria for design quality are available, and design notation can be applied. In this chapter, we explore the fundamental concepts and principles that are applicable to all software design. Chapters 14, 15, 16, and 22 examine a variety of software design methods as they are applied to architectural, interface, and component-level design.

13.1 SOFTWARE DESIGN AND SOFTWARE ENGINEERING

Quote:
"The most common miracles of software engineering are the transitions from analysis to design and design to code."
Richard Dué

Software design sits at the technical kernel of software engineering and is applied regardless of the software process model that is used. Beginning once software requirements have been analyzed and specified, software design is the first of three technical activities—design, code generation, and test—that are required to build and verify the software. Each activity transforms information in a manner that ultimately results in validated computer software.

Each of the elements of the analysis model (Chapter 12) provides information that is necessary to create the four design models required for a complete specification of design. The flow of information during software design is illustrated in Figure 13.1. Software requirements, manifested by the data, functional, and behavioral models, feed the design task. Using one of a number of design methods (discussed in later chapters), the design task produces a data design, an architectural design, an interface design, and a component design.

The *data design* transforms the information domain model created during analysis into the data structures that will be required to implement the software. The data objects and relationships defined in the entity relationship diagram and the detailed data content depicted in the data dictionary provide the basis for the data design activity. Part of data design may occur in conjunction with the design of software architecture. More detailed data design occurs as each software component is designed.

The *architectural design* defines the relationship between major structural elements of the software, the "design patterns" that can be used to achieve the requirements

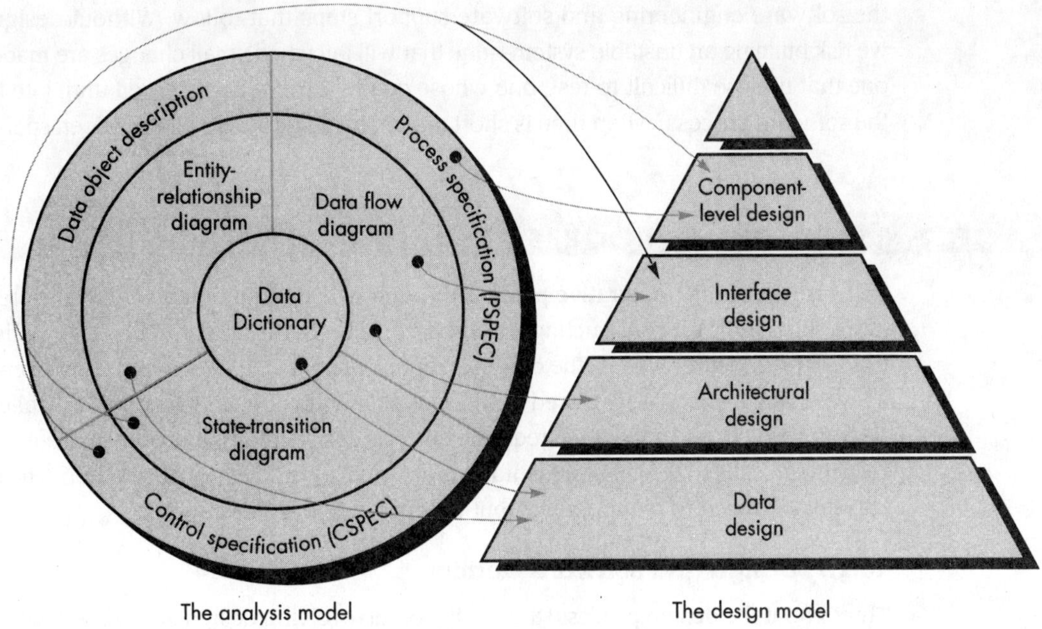

FIGURE 13.1 Translating the analysis model into a software design

that have been defined for the system, and the constraints that affect the way in which architectural design patterns can be applied [SHA96]. The architectural design representation—the framework of a computer-based system—can be derived from the system specification, the analysis model, and the interaction of subsystems defined within the analysis model.

The *interface design* describes how the software communicates within itself, with systems that interoperate with it, and with humans who use it. An interface implies a flow of information (e.g., data and/or control) and a specific type of behavior. Therefore, data and control flow diagrams provide much of the information required for interface design.

The *component-level design* transforms structural elements of the software architecture into a procedural description of software components. Information obtained from the PSPEC, CSPEC, and STD serve as the basis for component design.

During design we make decisions that will ultimately affect the success of software construction and, as important, the ease with which software can be maintained. But why is design so important?

The importance of software design can be stated with a single word—*quality.* Design is the place where quality is fostered in software engineering. Design provides us with representations of software that can be assessed for quality. Design is the only way that we can accurately translate a customer's requirements into a finished software product or system. Software design serves as the foundation for all the software engineering and software support steps that follow. Without design, we risk building an unstable system—one that will fail when small changes are made; one that may be difficult to test; one whose quality cannot be assessed until late in the software process, when time is short and many dollars have already been spent.

13.2 THE DESIGN PROCESS

Software design is an iterative process through which requirements are translated into a "blueprint" for constructing the software. Initially, the blueprint depicts a holistic view of software. That is, the design is represented at a high level of abstraction—a level that can be directly traced to the specific system objective and more detailed data, functional, and behavioral requirements. As design iterations occur, subsequent refinement leads to design representations at much lower levels of abstraction. These can still be traced to requirements, but the connection is more subtle.

13.2.1 Design and Software Quality

Throughout the design process, the quality of the evolving design is assessed with a series of formal technical reviews or design walkthroughs discussed in Chapter 8. McGlaughlin [MCG91] suggests three characteristics that serve as a guide for the evaluation of a good design:

Quote:
"To achieve a good design, people have to think the right way about how to conduct the design activity."
Katharine Whitehead

- The design must implement all of the explicit requirements contained in the analysis model, and it must accommodate all of the implicit requirements desired by the customer.
- The design must be a readable, understandable guide for those who generate code and for those who test and subsequently support the software.
- The design should provide a complete picture of the software, addressing the data, functional, and behavioral domains from an implementation perspective.

Each of these characteristics is actually a goal of the design process. But how is each of these goals achieved?

In order to evaluate the quality of a design representation, we must establish technical criteria for good design. Later in this chapter, we discuss design quality criteria in some detail. For the time being, we present the following guidelines:

? Are there generic guidelines that will lead to a good design?

1. A design should exhibit an architectural structure that (1) has been created using recognizable design patterns, (2) is composed of components that exhibit good design characteristics (these are discussed later in this chapter), and (3) can be implemented in an evolutionary fashion, thereby facilitating implementation and testing.

> **Quote:**
> "There are two ways of constructing a software design: One way is to make it so simple that there are obviously no deficiencies, and the other way is to make it so complicated that there are no obvious deficiencies. The first method is far more difficult."
> **C. A. R. Hoare**

2. A design should be modular; that is, the software should be logically partitioned into elements that perform specific functions and subfunctions.
3. A design should contain distinct representations of data, architecture, interfaces, and components (modules).
4. A design should lead to data structures that are appropriate for the objects to be implemented and are drawn from recognizable data patterns.
5. A design should lead to components that exhibit independent functional characteristics.
6. A design should lead to interfaces that reduce the complexity of connections between modules and with the external environment.
7. A design should be derived using a repeatable method that is driven by information obtained during software requirements analysis.

These criteria are not achieved by chance. The software design process encourages good design through the application of fundamental design principles, systematic methodology, and thorough review.

13.2.2 The Evolution of Software Design

The evolution of software design is a continuing process that has spanned the past four decades. Early design work concentrated on criteria for the development of modular programs [DEN73] and methods for refining software structures in a top-down manner [WIR71]. Procedural aspects of design definition evolved into a philosophy called *structured programming* [DAH72], [MIL72]. Later work proposed methods for the translation of data flow [STE74] or data structure [JAC75], [WAR74] into a design definition. Newer design approaches (e.g., [JAC92], [GAM95]) proposed an object-oriented approach to design derivation. Today, the emphasis in software design has been on software architecture [SHA96], [BAS98] and the design patterns that can be used to implement software architectures [GAM95], [BUS96], [BRO98].

? What characteristics are common to all design methods?

Many design methods, growing out of the work just noted, are being applied throughout the industry. Like the analysis methods presented in Chapter 12, each software design method introduces unique heuristics and notation, as well as a somewhat parochial view of what characterizes design quality. Yet, all of these methods have a number of common characteristics: (1) a mechanism for the translation of analysis model into a design representation, (2) a notation for representing functional components and their interfaces, (3) heuristics for refinement and partitioning, and (4) guidelines for quality assessment.

Regardless of the design method that is used, a software engineer should apply a set of fundamental principles and basic concepts to data, architectural, interface, and component-level design. These principles and concepts are considered in the sections that follow.

13.3 DESIGN PRINCIPLES

Software design is both a process and a model. The design *process* is a sequence of steps that enable the designer to describe all aspects of the software to be built. It is important to note, however, that the design process is not simply a cookbook. Creative skill, past experience, a sense of what makes "good" software, and an overall commitment to quality are critical success factors for a competent design.

The design *model* is the equivalent of an architect's plans for a house. It begins by representing the totality of the thing to be built (e.g., a three-dimensional rendering of the house) and slowly refines the thing to provide guidance for constructing each detail (e.g., the plumbing layout). Similarly, the design model that is created for software provides a variety of different views of the computer software.

Basic design principles enable the software engineer to navigate the design process. Davis [DAV95] suggests a set[1] of principles for software design, which have been adapted and extended in the following list:

- **The design process should not suffer from "tunnel vision."** A good designer should consider alternative approaches, judging each based on the requirements of the problem, the resources available to do the job, and the design concepts presented in Section 13.4.
- **The design should be traceable to the analysis model.** Because a single element of the design model often traces to multiple requirements, it is necessary to have a means for tracking how requirements have been satisfied by the design model.
- **The design should not reinvent the wheel.** Systems are constructed using a set of design patterns, many of which have likely been encountered before. These patterns should always be chosen as an alternative to reinvention. Time is short and resources are limited! Design time should be invested in representing truly new ideas and integrating those patterns that already exist.
- **The design should "minimize the intellectual distance" [DAV95] between the software and the problem as it exists in the real world.** That is, the structure of the software design should (whenever possible) mimic the structure of the problem domain.
- **The design should exhibit uniformity and integration.** A design is uniform if it appears that one person developed the entire thing. Rules of style and format should be defined for a design team before design work begins. A design is integrated if care is taken in defining interfaces between design components.

KEY POINT

Design consistency and uniformity are crucial when large systems are to be built. A set of design rules should be established for the software team before work begins.

---

1 Only a small subset of Davis's design principles are noted here. For more information, see [DAV95].

- **The design should be structured to accommodate change.** The design concepts discussed in the next section enable a design to achieve this principle.
- **The design should be structured to degrade gently, even when aberrant data, events, or operating conditions are encountered.** Well-designed software should never "bomb." It should be designed to accommodate unusual circumstances, and if it must terminate processing, do so in a graceful manner.
- **Design is not coding, coding is not design.** Even when detailed procedural designs are created for program components, the level of abstraction of the design model is higher than source code. The only design decisions made at the coding level address the small implementation details that enable the procedural design to be coded.
- **The design should be assessed for quality as it is being created, not after the fact.** A variety of design concepts (Section 13.4) and design measures (Chapters 19 and 24) are available to assist the designer in assessing quality.

XRef
Guidelines for conducting effective design reviews are presented in Chapter 8.

- **The design should be reviewed to minimize conceptual (semantic) errors.** There is sometimes a tendency to focus on minutiae when the design is reviewed, missing the forest for the trees. A design team should ensure that major conceptual elements of the design (omissions, ambiguity, inconsistency) have been addressed before worrying about the syntax of the design model.

When these design principles are properly applied, the software engineer creates a design that exhibits both external and internal quality factors [MEY88]. *External quality factors* are those properties of the software that can be readily observed by users (e.g., speed, reliability, correctness, usability).[2] *Internal quality factors* are of importance to software engineers. They lead to a high-quality design from the technical perspective. To achieve internal quality factors, the designer must understand basic design concepts.

13.4 DESIGN CONCEPTS

A set of fundamental software design concepts has evolved over the past four decades. Although the degree of interest in each concept has varied over the years, each has stood the test of time. Each provides the software designer with a foundation from which more sophisticated design methods can be applied. Each helps the software engineer to answer the following questions:

- What criteria can be used to partition software into individual components?
- How is function or data structure detail separated from a conceptual representation of the software?
- What uniform criteria define the technical quality of a software design?

2 A more detailed discussion of quality factors is presented in Chapter 19.

M. A. Jackson once said: "The beginning of wisdom for a [software engineer] is to recognize the difference between getting a program to work, and getting it right" [JAC75]. Fundamental software design concepts provide the necessary framework for "getting it right."

13.4.1 Abstraction

Quote:
"Abstraction is one of the fundamental ways that we as humans cope with complexity."
Grady Booch

When we consider a modular solution to any problem, many *levels of abstraction* can be posed. At the highest level of abstraction, a solution is stated in broad terms using the language of the problem environment. At lower levels of abstraction, a more procedural orientation is taken. Problem-oriented terminology is coupled with implementation-oriented terminology in an effort to state a solution. Finally, at the lowest level of abstraction, the solution is stated in a manner that can be directly implemented. Wasserman [WAS83] provides a useful definition:

> [T]he psychological notion of "abstraction" permits one to concentrate on a problem at some level of generalization without regard to irrelevant low level details; use of abstraction also permits one to work with concepts and terms that are familiar in the problem environment without having to transform them to an unfamiliar structure . . .

Each step in the software process is a refinement in the level of abstraction of the software solution. During system engineering, software is allocated as an element of a computer-based system. During software requirements analysis, the software solution is stated in terms "that are familiar in the problem environment." As we move through the design process, the level of abstraction is reduced. Finally, the lowest level of abstraction is reached when source code is generated.

As we move through different levels of abstraction, we work to create procedural and data abstractions. A *procedural abstraction* is a named sequence of instructions that has a specific and limited function. An example of a procedural abstraction would be the word *open* for a door. *Open* implies a long sequence of procedural steps (e.g., walk to the door, reach out and grasp knob, turn knob and pull door, step away from moving door, etc.).

ADVICE
As a designer, work hard to derive both procedural and data abstractions that serve the problem at hand, but that also can be reused in other situations.

A *data abstraction* is a named collection of data that describes a data object (Chapter 12). In the context of the procedural abstraction *open*, we can define a data abstraction called **door**. Like any data object, the data abstraction for **door** would encompass a set of attributes that describe the door (e.g., door type, swing direction, opening mechanism, weight, dimensions). It follows that the procedural abstraction *open* would make use of information contained in the attributes of the data abstraction **door**.

Many modern programming languages provide mechanisms for creating abstract data types. For example, the Ada package is a programming language mechanism that provides support for both data and procedural abstraction. The original abstract data type is used as a template or generic data structure from which other data structures can be instantiated.

Control abstraction is the third form of abstraction used in software design. Like procedural and data abstraction, control abstraction implies a program control mechanism without specifying internal details. An example of a control abstraction is the *synchronization semaphore* [KAI83] used to coordinate activities in an operating system. The concept of the control abstraction is discussed briefly in Chapter 14.

13.4.2 Refinement

Stepwise refinement is a top-down design strategy originally proposed by Niklaus Wirth [WIR71]. A program is developed by successively refining levels of procedural detail. A hierarchy is developed by decomposing a macroscopic statement of function (a procedural abstraction) in a stepwise fashion until programming language statements are reached. An overview of the concept is provided by Wirth [WIR71]:

> In each step (of the refinement), one or several instructions of the given program are decomposed into more detailed instructions. This successive decomposition or refinement of specifications terminates when all instructions are expressed in terms of any underlying computer or programming language . . . As tasks are refined, so the data may have to be refined, decomposed, or structured, and it is natural to refine the program and the data specifications in parallel.
>
> Every refinement step implies some design decisions. It is important that . . . the programmer be aware of the underlying criteria (for design decisions) and of the existence of alternative solutions . . .

ADVICE

There is a tendency to move immediately to full detail, skipping the refinement steps. This leads to errors and omissions and makes the design much more difficult to review. Perform stepwise refinement.

The process of program refinement proposed by Wirth is analogous to the process of refinement and partitioning that is used during requirements analysis. The difference is in the level of implementation detail that is considered, not the approach.

Refinement is actually a process of *elaboration.* We begin with a statement of function (or description of information) that is defined at a high level of abstraction. That is, the statement describes function or information conceptually but provides no information about the internal workings of the function or the internal structure of the information. Refinement causes the designer to elaborate on the original statement, providing more and more detail as each successive refinement (elaboration) occurs.

Abstraction and refinement are complementary concepts. Abstraction enables a designer to specify procedure and data and yet suppress low-level details. Refinement helps the designer to reveal low-level details as design progresses. Both concepts aid the designer in creating a complete design model as the design evolves.

13.4.3 Modularity

The concept of modularity in computer software has been espoused for almost five decades. Software architecture (described in Section 13.4.4) embodies modularity; that is, software is divided into separately named and addressable components, often called *modules,* that are integrated to satisfy problem requirements.

It has been stated that "modularity is the single attribute of software that allows a program to be intellectually manageable" [MYE78]. Monolithic software (i.e., a large program composed of a single module) cannot be easily grasped by a reader. The number of control paths, span of reference, number of variables, and overall complexity would make understanding close to impossible. To illustrate this point, consider the following argument based on observations of human problem solving.

Let $C(x)$ be a function that defines the perceived complexity of a problem x, and $E(x)$ be a function that defines the effort (in time) required to solve a problem x. For two problems, p_1 and p_2, if

$$C(p_1) > C(p_2) \qquad (13\text{-}1a)$$

it follows that

$$E(p_1) > E(p_2) \qquad (13\text{-}1b)$$

As a general case, this result is intuitively obvious. It does take more time to solve a difficult problem.

Quote:

"There's always an easy solution to every human problem—neat, plausible, and wrong."

H. L. Mencken

Another interesting characteristic has been uncovered through experimentation in human problem solving. That is,

$$C(p_1 + p_2) > C(p_1) + C(p_2) \qquad (13\text{-}2)$$

Expression (13-2) implies that the perceived complexity of a problem that combines p_1 and p_2 is greater than the perceived complexity when each problem is considered separately. Considering Expression (13-2) and the condition implied by Expressions (13-1), it follows that

$$E(p_1 + p_2) > E(p_1) + E(p_2) \qquad (13\text{-}3)$$

This leads to a "divide and conquer" conclusion—it's easier to solve a complex problem when you break it into manageable pieces. The result expressed in Expression (13-3) has important implications with regard to modularity and software. It is, in fact, an argument for modularity.

ADVICE

Don't overmodularize. The simplicity of each module will be overshadowed by the complexity of integration.

It is possible to conclude from Expression (13-3) that, if we subdivide software indefinitely, the effort required to develop it will become negligibly small! Unfortunately, other forces come into play, causing this conclusion to be (sadly) invalid. Referring to Figure 13.2, the effort (cost) to develop an individual software module does decrease as the total number of modules increases. Given the same set of requirements, more modules means smaller individual size. However, as the number of modules grows, the effort (cost) associated with integrating the modules also grows. These characteristics lead to a total cost or effort curve shown in the figure. There is a number, M, of modules that would result in minimum development cost, but we do not have the necessary sophistication to predict M with assurance.

FIGURE 13.2
Modularity and software cost

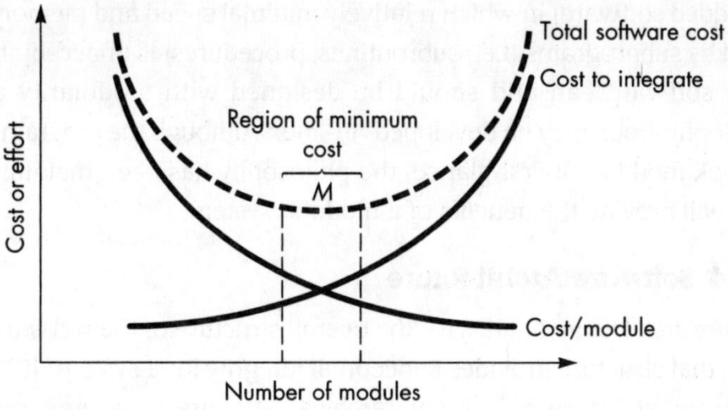

The curves shown in Figure 13.2 do provide useful guidance when modularity is considered. We should modularize, but care should be taken to stay in the vicinity of *M*. Undermodularity or overmodularity should be avoided. But how do we know "the vicinity of M"? How modular should we make software? The answers to these questions require an understanding of other design concepts considered later in this chapter.

XRef
Design methods are discussed in Chapters 14, 15, 16, and 22.

Another important question arises when modularity is considered. How do we define an appropriate module of a given size? The answer lies in the method(s) used to define modules within a system. Meyer [MEY88] defines five criteria that enable us to evaluate a design method with respect to its ability to define an effective modular system:

? How can we evaluate a design method to determine if it will lead to effective modularity?

Modular decomposability. If a design method provides a systematic mechanism for decomposing the problem into subproblems, it will reduce the complexity of the overall problem, thereby achieving an effective modular solution.

Modular composability. If a design method enables existing (reusable) design components to be assembled into a new system, it will yield a modular solution that does not reinvent the wheel.

Modular understandability. If a module can be understood as a standalone unit (without reference to other modules), it will be easier to build and easier to change.

Modular continuity. If small changes to the system requirements result in changes to individual modules, rather than systemwide changes, the impact of change-induced side effects will be minimized.

Modular protection. If an aberrant condition occurs within a module and its effects are constrained within that module, the impact of error-induced side effects will be minimized.

Finally, it is important to note that a system may be designed modularly, even if its implementation must be "monolithic." There are situations (e.g., real-time software, embedded software) in which relatively minimal speed and memory overhead introduced by subprograms (i.e., subroutines, procedures) is unacceptable. In such situations, software can and should be designed with modularity as an overriding philosophy. Code may be developed "in-line." Although the program source code may not look modular at first glance, the philosophy has been maintained and the program will provide the benefits of a modular system.

13.4.4 Software Architecture

WebRef
The STARS *Software Architecture Technology Guide* provides in-depth information and resources at **www-ast.tds-gn.lmco.com/arch/guide.html**

Software architecture alludes to "the overall structure of the software and the ways in which that structure provides conceptual integrity for a system" [SHA95a]. In its simplest form, architecture is the hierarchical structure of program components (modules), the manner in which these components interact and the structure of data that are used by the components. In a broader sense, however, *components* can be generalized to represent major system elements and their interactions.[3]

One goal of software design is to derive an architectural rendering of a system. This rendering serves as a framework from which more detailed design activities are conducted. A set of architectural patterns enable a software engineer to reuse design-level concepts.

Quote:
"A software architecture is the development work product that gives the highest return on investment with respect to quality, schedule and cost."
Len Bass et al.

Shaw and Garlan [SHA95a] describe a set of properties that should be specified as part of an architectural design:

Structural properties. This aspect of the architectural design representation defines the components of a system (e.g., modules, objects, filters) and the manner in which those components are packaged and interact with one another. For example, objects are packaged to encapsulate both data and the processing that manipulates the data and interact via the invocation of methods.

Extra-functional properties. The architectural design description should address how the design architecture achieves requirements for performance, capacity, reliability, security, adaptability, and other system characteristics.

Families of related systems. The architectural design should draw upon repeatable patterns that are commonly encountered in the design of families of similar systems. In essence, the design should have the ability to reuse architectural building blocks.

KEY POINT
Five different types of models are used to represent the architectural design.

Given the specification of these properties, the architectural design can be represented using one or more of a number of different models [GAR95]. *Structural models* represent architecture as an organized collection of program components. *Framework models* increase the level of design abstraction by attempting to identify repeatable architectural design frameworks (patterns) that are encountered in similar types of applications. *Dynamic models* address the behavioral aspects of the program architecture, indicating how the structure or system configuration may change as a function of external events. *Process models* focus on the design of the business

3 For example, the architectural components of a client/server system are represented at a different level of abstraction. See Chapter 28 for details.

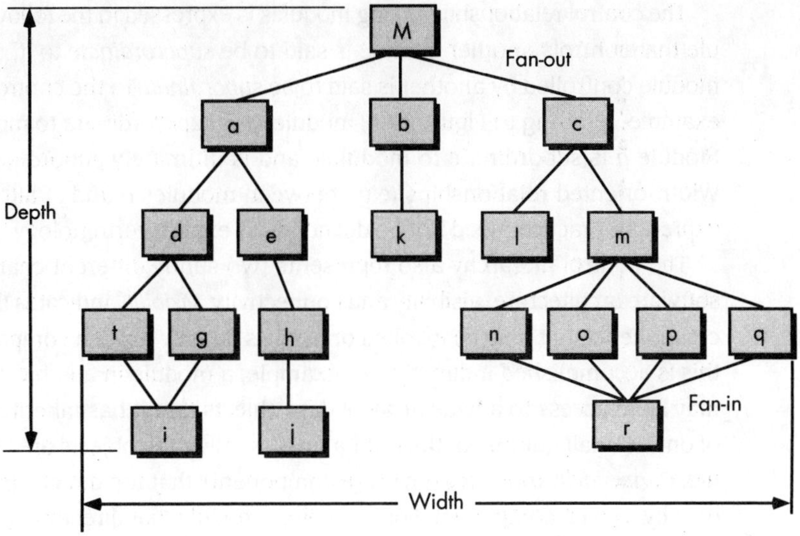

FIGURE 13.3 Structure terminology for a call and return architectural style

or technical process that the system must accommodate. Finally, *functional models* can be used to represent the functional hierarchy of a system.

A number of different *architectural description languages* (ADLs) have been developed to represent these models [SHA95b]. Although many different ADLs have been proposed, the majority provide mechanisms for describing system components and the manner in which they are connected to one another.

13.4.5 Control Hierarchy

XRef
A detailed discussion of architectural styles and patterns is presented in Chapter 14.

Control hierarchy, also called *program structure,* represents the organization of program components (modules) and implies a hierarchy of control. It does not represent procedural aspects of software such as sequence of processes, occurrence or order of decisions, or repetition of operations; nor is it necessarily applicable to all architectural styles.

ADVICE
If you develop object-oriented software, the structural measures noted here do not apply. However, others (considered in Part Four) are applicable.

Different notations are used to represent control hierarchy for those architectural styles that are amenable to this representation. The most common is the treelike diagram (Figure 13.3) that represents hierarchical control for call and return architectures.[4] However, other notations, such as Warnier-Orr [ORR77] and Jackson diagrams [JAC83] may also be used with equal effectiveness. In order to facilitate later discussions of structure, we define a few simple measures and terms. Referring to Figure 13.3, *depth* and *width* provide an indication of the number of levels of control and overall *span of control*, respectively. *Fan-out* is a measure of the number of modules that are directly controlled by another module. *Fan-in* indicates how many modules directly control a given module.

4 A call and return architecture (Chapter 14) is a classic program structure that decomposes function into a control hierarchy where a "main" program invokes a number of program components, which in turn may invoke still other components.

The control relationship among modules is expressed in the following way: A module that controls another module is said to be *superordinate* to it, and conversely, a module controlled by another is said to be *subordinate* to the controller [YOU79]. For example, referring to Figure 13.3, module *M* is superordinate to modules *a, b,* and *c.* Module *h* is subordinate to module *e* and is ultimately subordinate to module *M.* Width-oriented relationships (e.g., between modules *d* and *e*) although possible to express in practice, need not be defined with explicit terminology.

The control hierarchy also represents two subtly different characteristics of the software architecture: visibility and connectivity. *Visibility* indicates the set of program components that may be invoked or used as data by a given component, even when this is accomplished indirectly. For example, a module in an object-oriented system may have access to a wide array of data objects that it has inherited, but makes use of only a small number of these data objects. All of the objects are visible to the module. *Connectivity* indicates the set of components that are directly invoked or used as data by a given component. For example, a module that directly causes another module to begin execution is connected to it.[5]

13.4.6 Structural Partitioning

If the architectural style of a system is hierarchical, the program structure can be partitioned both horizontally and vertically. Referring to Figure 13.4a, *horizontal partitioning* defines separate branches of the modular hierarchy for each major program function. *Control modules,* represented in a darker shade are used to coordinate communication between and execution of the functions. The simplest approach to horizontal partitioning defines three partitions—input, data transformation (often called *processing*) and output. Partitioning the architecture horizontally provides a number of distinct benefits:

? What are the benefits of horizontal partitioning?

- software that is easier to test
- software that is easier to maintain
- propagation of fewer side effects
- software that is easier to extend

Because major functions are decoupled from one another, change tends to be less complex and extensions to the system (a common occurrence) tend to be easier to accomplish without side effects. On the negative side, horizontal partitioning often causes more data to be passed across module interfaces and can complicate the overall control of program flow (if processing requires rapid movement from one function to another).

5 In Chapter 20, we explore the concept of inheritance for object-oriented software. A program component can inherit control logic and/or data from another component without explicit reference in the source code. Components of this sort would be visible but not directly connected. A structure chart (Chapter 14) indicates connectivity.

FIGURE 13.4
Structural partitioning

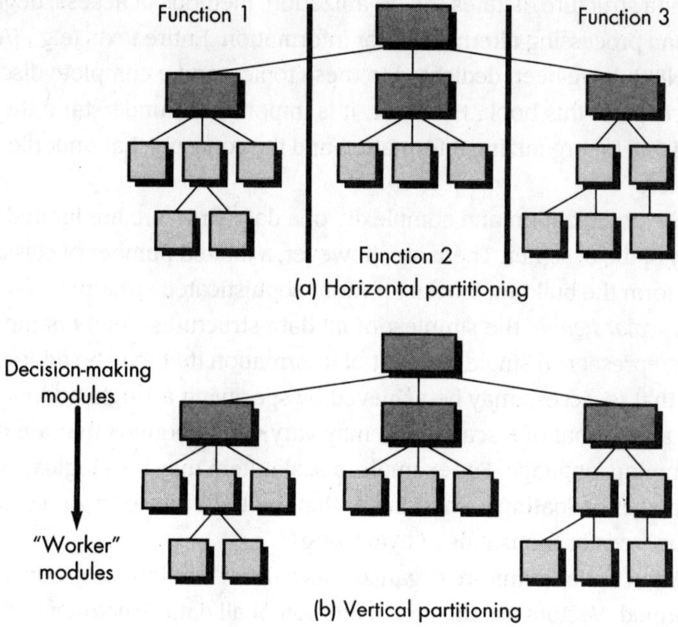

Vertical partitioning (Figure 13.4b), often called *factoring,* suggests that control (decision making) and work should be distributed top-down in the program structure. Top-level modules should perform control functions and do little actual processing work. Modules that reside low in the structure should be the workers, performing all input, computation, and output tasks.

KEY POINT
"Worker" modules tend to change more frequently than control modules. By placing the workers low in the structure, side effects (due to change) are reduced.

The nature of change in program structures justifies the need for vertical partitioning. Referring to Figure 13.4b, it can be seen that a change in a control module (high in the structure) will have a higher probability of propagating side effects to modules that are subordinate to it. A change to a worker module, given its low level in the structure, is less likely to cause the propagation of side effects. In general, changes to computer programs revolve around changes to input, computation or transformation, and output. The overall control structure of the program (i.e., its basic behavior is far less likely to change). For this reason vertically partitioned structures are less likely to be susceptible to side effects when changes are made and will therefore be more maintainable—a key quality factor.

13.4.7 Data Structure

Data structure is a representation of the logical relationship among individual elements of data. Because the structure of information will invariably affect the final procedural design, data structure is as important as program structure to the representation of software architecture.

Data structure dictates the organization, methods of access, degree of associativity, and processing alternatives for information. Entire texts (e.g., [AHO83], [KRU84], [GAN89]) have been dedicated to these topics, and a complete discussion is beyond the scope of this book. However, it is important to understand the classic methods available for organizing information and the concepts that underlie information hierarchies.

The organization and complexity of a data structure are limited only by the ingenuity of the designer. There are, however, a limited number of classic data structures that form the building blocks for more sophisticated structures.

Quote:
"The order and connection of ideas is the same as the order and connection of things."
Baruch Spinoza

A *scalar item* is the simplest of all data structures. As its name implies, a scalar item represents a single element of information that may be addressed by an identifier; that is, access may be achieved by specifying a single address in memory. The size and format of a scalar item may vary within bounds that are dictated by a programming language. For example, a scalar item may be a logical entity one bit long, an integer or floating point number that is 8 to 64 bits long, or a character string that is hundreds or thousands of bytes long.

When scalar items are organized as a list or contiguous group, a *sequential vector* is formed. Vectors are the most common of all data structures and open the door to variable indexing of information.

When the sequential vector is extended to two, three, and ultimately, an arbitrary number of dimensions, an *n-dimensional space* is created. The most common *n*-dimensional space is the two-dimensional matrix. In many programming languages, an *n*-dimensional space is called an *array*.

Items, vectors, and spaces may be organized in a variety of formats. A *linked list* is a data structure that organizes noncontiguous scalar items, vectors, or spaces in a manner (called *nodes*) that enables them to be processed as a list. Each node contains the appropriate data organization (e.g., a vector) and one or more pointers that indicate the address in storage of the next node in the list. Nodes may be added at any point in the list by redefining pointers to accommodate the new list entry.

ADVICE
Spend at least as much time designing data structures as you intend to spend designing the algorithms to manipulate them. If you do, you'll save time in the long run.

Other data structures incorporate or are constructed using the fundamental data structures just described. For example, a *hierarchical data structure* is implemented using multilinked lists that contain scalar items, vectors, and possibly, *n*-dimensional spaces. A hierarchical structure is commonly encountered in applications that require information categorization and associativity.

It is important to note that data structures, like program structure, can be represented at different levels of abstraction. For example, a stack is a conceptual model of a data structure that can be implemented as a vector or a linked list. Depending on the level of design detail, the internal workings of a **stack** may or may not be specified.

FIGURE 13.5
Procedure is layered

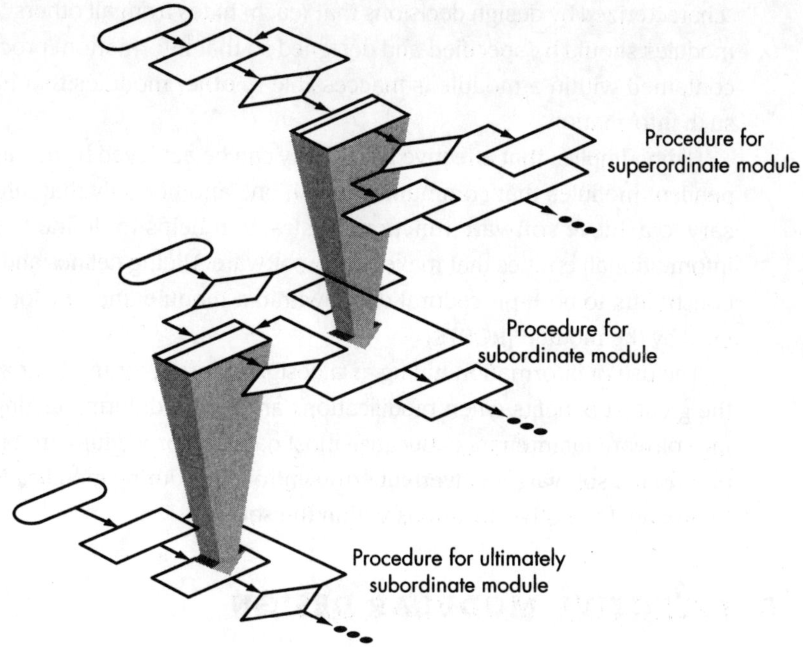

13.4.8 Software Procedure

Program structure defines control hierarchy without regard to the sequence of processing and decisions. Software procedure focuses on the processing details of each module individually. Procedure must provide a precise specification of processing, including sequence of events, exact decision points, repetitive operations, and even data organization and structure.

There is, of course, a relationship between structure and procedure. The processing indicated for each module must include a reference to all modules subordinate to the module being described. That is, a procedural representation of software is layered as illustrated in Figure 13.5.[6]

13.4.9 Information Hiding

The concept of modularity leads every software designer to a fundamental question: "How do we decompose a software solution to obtain the best set of modules?" The principle of *information hiding* [PAR72] suggests that modules be

6 This is not true for all architectural styles. For example, hierarchical layering of procedure is not encountered in object-oriented architectures.

"characterized by design decisions that (each) hides from all others." In other words, modules should be specified and designed so that information (procedure and data) contained within a module is inaccessible to other modules that have no need for such information.

Hiding implies that effective modularity can be achieved by defining a set of independent modules that communicate with one another only that information necessary to achieve software function. Abstraction helps to define the procedural (or informational) entities that make up the software. Hiding defines and enforces access constraints to both procedural detail within a module and any local data structure used by the module [ROS75].

The use of information hiding as a design criterion for modular systems provides the greatest benefits when modifications are required during testing and later, during software maintenance. Because most data and procedure are hidden from other parts of the software, inadvertent errors introduced during modification are less likely to propagate to other locations within the software.

13.5 EFFECTIVE MODULAR DESIGN

All the fundamental design concepts described in the preceding section serve to precipitate modular designs. In fact, modularity has become an accepted approach in all engineering disciplines. A modular design reduces complexity (see Section 13.4.3), facilitates change (a critical aspect of software maintainability), and results in easier implementation by encouraging parallel development of different parts of a system.

13.5.1 Functional Independence

The concept of *functional independence* is a direct outgrowth of modularity and the concepts of abstraction and information hiding. In landmark papers on software design Parnas [PAR72] and Wirth [WIR71] allude to refinement techniques that enhance module independence. Later work by Stevens, Myers, and Constantine [STE74] solidified the concept.

ADVICE

A module is "single minded" if you can describe it with a simple sentence—subject, predicate, object.

Functional independence is achieved by developing modules with "single-minded" function and an "aversion" to excessive interaction with other modules. Stated another way, we want to design software so that each module addresses a specific subfunction of requirements and has a simple interface when viewed from other parts of the program structure. It is fair to ask why independence is important. Software with effective modularity, that is, independent modules, is easier to develop because function may be compartmentalized and interfaces are simplified (consider the ramifications when development is conducted by a team). Independent modules are easier to maintain (and test) because secondary effects caused by design or code modification are limited, error propagation is reduced, and reusable modules are possible. To summarize, functional independence is a key to good design, and design is the key to software quality.

Independence is measured using two qualitative criteria: cohesion and coupling. *Cohesion* is a measure of the relative functional strength of a module. *Coupling* is a measure of the relative interdependence among modules.

13.5.2 Cohesion

Cohesion is a natural extension of the information hiding concept described in Section 13.4.9. A cohesive module performs a single task within a software procedure, requiring little interaction with procedures being performed in other parts of a program. Stated simply, a cohesive module should (ideally) do just one thing.

KEY POINT

Cohesion is a qualitative indication of the degree to which a module focuses on just one thing.

Cohesion may be represented as a "spectrum." We always strive for high cohesion, although the mid-range of the spectrum is often acceptable. The scale for cohesion is nonlinear. That is, low-end cohesiveness is much "worse" than middle range, which is nearly as "good" as high-end cohesion. In practice, a designer need not be concerned with categorizing cohesion in a specific module. Rather, the overall concept should be understood and low levels of cohesion should be avoided when modules are designed.

At the low (undesirable) end of the spectrum, we encounter a module that performs a set of tasks that relate to each other loosely, if at all. Such modules are termed *coincidentally cohesive.* A module that performs tasks that are related logically (e.g., a module that produces all output regardless of type) is *logically cohesive.* When a module contains tasks that are related by the fact that all must be executed with the same span of time, the module exhibits *temporal cohesion.*

As an example of low cohesion, consider a module that performs error processing for an engineering analysis package. The module is called when computed data exceed prespecified bounds. It performs the following tasks: (1) computes supplementary data based on original computed data, (2) produces an error report (with graphical content) on the user's workstation, (3) performs follow-up calculations requested by the user, (4) updates a database, and (5) enables menu selection for subsequent processing. Although the preceding tasks are loosely related, each is an independent functional entity that might best be performed as a separate module. Combining the functions into a single module can serve only to increase the likelihood of error propagation when a modification is made to one of its processing tasks.

ADVICE

If you concentrate on only one thing during component-level design, make it cohesion.

Moderate levels of cohesion are relatively close to one another in the degree of module independence. When processing elements of a module are related and must be executed in a specific order, *procedural cohesion* exists. When all processing elements concentrate on one area of a data structure, *communicational cohesion* is present. High cohesion is characterized by a module that performs one distinct procedural task.

As we have already noted, it is unnecessary to determine the precise level of cohesion. Rather it is important to strive for high cohesion and recognize low cohesion so that software design can be modified to achieve greater functional independence.

FIGURE 13.6 Types of coupling

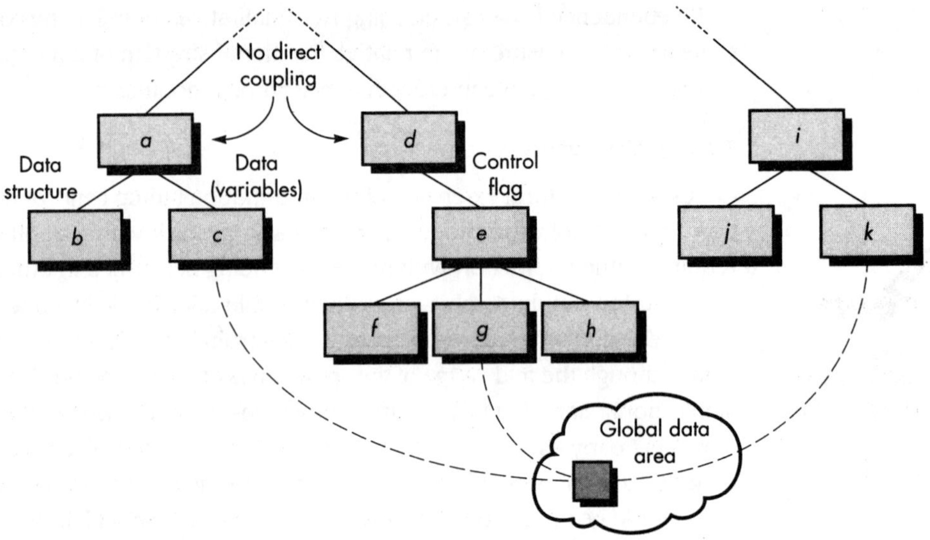

13.5.3 Coupling

Coupling is a measure of interconnection among modules in a software structure. Coupling depends on the interface complexity between modules, the point at which entry or reference is made to a module, and what data pass across the interface.

KEY POINT Coupling is a qualitative indication of the degree to which a module is connected to other modules and to the outside world.

In software design, we strive for lowest possible coupling. Simple connectivity among modules results in software that is easier to understand and less prone to a "ripple effect" [STE74], caused when errors occur at one location and propagate through a system.

Figure 13.6 provides examples of different types of module coupling. Modules *a* and *d* are subordinate to different modules. Each is unrelated and therefore no direct coupling occurs. Module *c* is subordinate to module *a* and is accessed via a conventional argument list, through which data are passed. As long as a simple argument list is present (i.e., simple data are passed; a one-to-one correspondence of items exists), low coupling (called *data coupling*) is exhibited in this portion of structure. A variation of data coupling, called *stamp coupling,* is found when a portion of a data structure (rather than simple arguments) is passed via a module interface. This occurs between modules *b* and *a*.

ADVICE *Highly coupled systems lead to debugging nightmares. Avoid them.*

At moderate levels, coupling is characterized by passage of control between modules. *Control coupling* is very common in most software designs and is shown in Figure 13.6 where a "control flag" (a variable that controls decisions in a subordinate or superordinate module) is passed between modules *d* and *e*.

Relatively high levels of coupling occur when modules are tied to an environment external to software. For example, I/O couples a module to specific devices, formats, and communication protocols. *External coupling* is essential, but should be limited to a small number of modules with a structure. High coupling also occurs when a number of modules reference a global data area. *Common coupling,* as this mode is called, is shown in Figure 13.6. Modules *c, g,* and *k* each access a data item in a global data area (e.g., a disk file or a globally accessible memory area). Module *c* initializes the item. Later module *g* recomputes and updates the item. Let's assume that an error occurs and *g* updates the item incorrectly. Much later in processing module, *k* reads the item, attempts to process it, and fails, causing the software to abort. The apparent cause of abort is module *k*; the actual cause, module *g.* Diagnosing problems in structures with considerable common coupling is time consuming and difficult. However, this does not mean that the use of global data is necessarily "bad." It does mean that a software designer must be aware of potential consequences of common coupling and take special care to guard against them.

The highest degree of coupling, *content coupling,* occurs when one module makes use of data or control information maintained within the boundary of another module. Secondarily, content coupling occurs when branches are made into the middle of a module. This mode of coupling can and should be avoided.

The coupling modes just discussed occur because of design decisions made when structure was developed. Variants of external coupling, however, may be introduced during coding. For example, *compiler coupling* ties source code to specific (and often nonstandard) attributes of a compiler; *operating system* (OS) *coupling* ties design and resultant code to operating system "hooks" that can create havoc when OS changes occur.

13.6 DESIGN HEURISTICS FOR EFFECTIVE MODULARITY

Once program structure has been developed, effective modularity can be achieved by applying the design concepts introduced earlier in this chapter. The program structure can be manipulated according to the following set of heuristics:

> **Quote:**
> "The notion that good [design] techniques restrict creativity is like saying that an artist can paint without learning the details of form or a musician does not need knowledge of music theory."
> **Marvin Zelkowitz et al.**

1. *Evaluate the "first iteration" of the program structure to reduce coupling and improve cohesion.* Once the program structure has been developed, modules may be exploded or imploded with an eye toward improving module independence. An *exploded module* becomes two or more modules in the final program structure. An *imploded module* is the result of combining the processing implied by two or more modules.

   An exploded module often results when common processing exists in two or more modules and can be redefined as a separate cohesive module. When high coupling is expected, modules can sometimes be imploded to reduce passage of control, reference to global data, and interface complexity.

2. *Attempt to minimize structures with high fan-out; strive for fan-in as depth increases.* The structure shown inside the cloud in Figure 13.7 does not make effective use of factoring. All modules are "pancaked" below a single control

FIGURE 13.7
Program structures

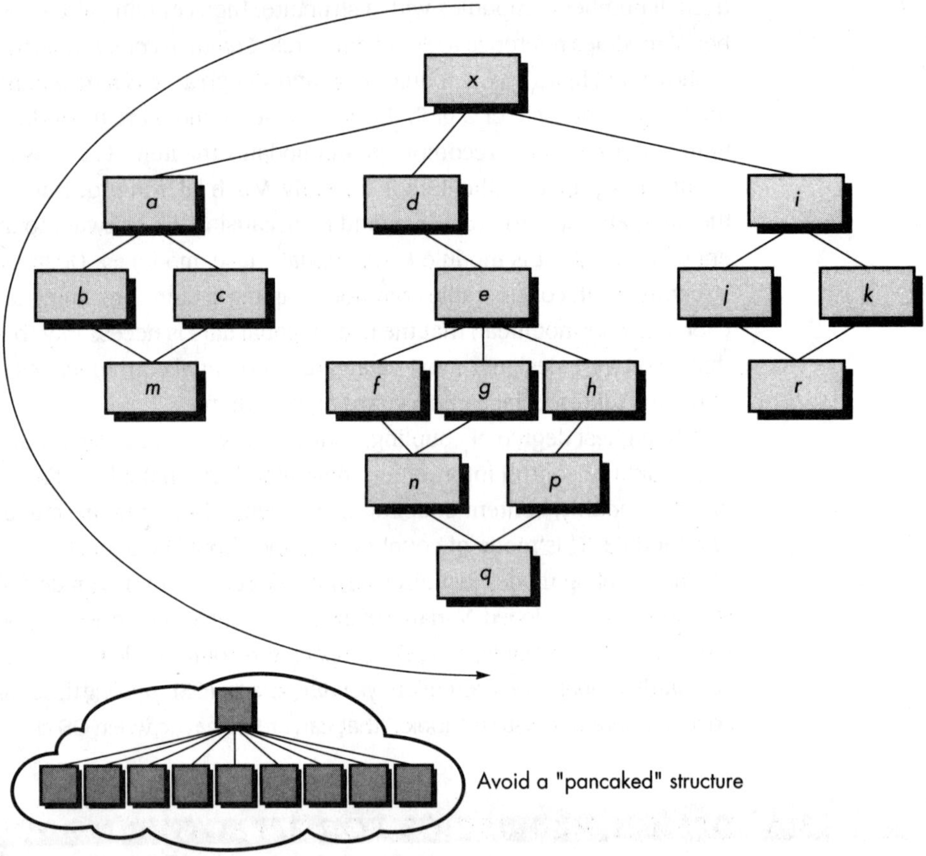

module. In general, a more reasonable distribution of control is shown in the upper structure. The structure takes an oval shape, indicating a number of layers of control and highly utilitarian modules at lower levels.

3. *Keep the scope of effect of a module within the scope of control of that module.* The *scope of effect* of module *e* is defined as all other modules that are affected by a decision made in module *e.* The *scope of control* of module *e* is all modules that are subordinate and ultimately subordinate to module *e.* Referring to Figure 13.7, if module *e* makes a decision that affects module *r,* we have a violation of this heuristic, because module *r* lies outside the scope of control of module *e.*

4. *Evaluate module interfaces to reduce complexity and redundancy and improve consistency.* Module interface complexity is a prime cause of software errors. Interfaces should be designed to pass information simply and should be consistent with the function of a module. Interface inconsistency (i.e., seemingly

unrelated data passed via an argument list or other technique) is an indication of low cohesion. The module in question should be reevaluated.

5. *Define modules whose function is predictable, but avoid modules that are overly restrictive.* A module is predictable when it can be treated as a black box; that is, the same external data will be produced regardless of internal processing details.[7] Modules that have internal "memory" can be unpredictable unless care is taken in their use.

WebRef

A detailed report on software design methods including a discussion of all design concepts and principles found in this chapter can be obtained at **www.dacs.dtic.mil/techs/design/Design.ToC.html**

A module that restricts processing to a single subfunction exhibits high cohesion and is viewed with favor by a designer. However, a module that arbitrarily restricts the size of a local data structure, options within control flow, or modes of external interface will invariably require maintenance to remove such restrictions.

6. *Strive for "controlled entry" modules* by *avoiding "pathological connections."* This design heuristic warns against content coupling. Software is easier to understand and therefore easier to maintain when module interfaces are constrained and controlled. *Pathological connection* refers to branches or references into the middle of a module.

13.7 THE DESIGN MODEL

The design principles and concepts discussed in this chapter establish a foundation for the creation of the design model that encompasses representations of data, architecture, interfaces, and components. Like the analysis model before it, each of these design representations is tied to the others, and all can be traced back to software requirements.

In Figure 13.1, the design model was represented as a pyramid. The symbolism of this shape is important. A pyramid is an extremely stable object with a wide base and a low center of gravity. Like the pyramid, we want to create a software design that is stable. By establishing a broad foundation using data design, a stable mid-region with architectural and interface design, and a sharp point by applying component-level design, we create a design model that is not easily "tipped over" by the winds of change.

It is interesting to note that some programmers continue to design implicitly, conducting component-level design as they code. This is akin to taking the design pyramid and standing it on its point—an extremely unstable design results. The smallest change may cause the pyramid (and the program) to topple.

The methods that lead to the creation of the design model are presented in Chapters 14, 15, 16, and 22 (for object-oriented systems). Each method enables the designer

7 A "black box" module is a procedural abstraction.

to create a stable design that conforms to fundamental concepts that lead to high-quality software.

13.8 DESIGN DOCUMENTATION

The *Design Specification* addresses different aspects of the design model and is completed as the designer refines his representation of the software. First, the overall scope of the design effort is described. Much of the information presented here is derived from the *System Specification* and the analysis model (*Software Requirements Specification*).

Next, the data design is specified. Database structure, any external file structures, internal data structures, and a cross reference that connects data objects to specific files are all defined.

Software Design Specification

The architectural design indicates how the program architecture has been derived from the analysis model. In addition, structure charts are used to represent the module hierarchy (if applicable).

The design of external and internal program interfaces is represented and a detailed design of the human/machine interface is described. In some cases, a detailed prototype of a GUI may be represented.

Components—separately addressable elements of software such as subroutines, functions, or procedures—are initially described with an English-language processing narrative. The processing narrative explains the procedural function of a component (module). Later, a procedural design tool is used to translate the narrative into a structured description.

The *Design Specification* contains a requirements cross reference. The purpose of this cross reference (usually represented as a simple matrix) is (1) to establish that all requirements are satisfied by the software design and (2) to indicate which components are critical to the implementation of specific requirements.

The first stage in the development of test documentation is also contained in the design document. Once program structure and interfaces have been established, we can develop guidelines for testing of individual modules and integration of the entire package. In some cases, a detailed specification of test procedures occurs in parallel with design. In such cases, this section may be deleted from the *Design Specification.*

Design constraints, such as physical memory limitations or the necessity for a specialized external interface, may dictate special requirements for assembling or packaging of software. Special considerations caused by the necessity for program overlay, virtual memory management, high-speed processing, or other factors may cause modification in design derived from information flow or structure. In addition, this section describes the approach that will be used to transfer software to a customer site.

The final section of the *Design Specification* contains supplementary data. Algorithm descriptions, alternative procedures, tabular data, excerpts from other documents, and other relevant information are presented as a special note or as a separate appendix. It may be advisable to develop a *Preliminary Operations/Installation Manual* and include it as an appendix to the design document.

13.8 SUMMARY

Design is the technical kernel of software engineering. During design, progressive refinements of data structure, architecture, interfaces, and procedural detail of software components are developed, reviewed, and documented. Design results in representations of software that can be assessed for quality.

A number of fundamental software design principles and concepts have been proposed over the past four decades. Design principles guide the software engineer as the design process proceeds. Design concepts provide basic criteria for design quality.

Modularity (in both program and data) and the concept of abstraction enable the designer to simplify and reuse software components. Refinement provides a mechanism for representing successive layers of functional detail. Program and data structure contribute to an overall view of software architecture, while procedure provides the detail necessary for algorithm implementation. Information hiding and functional independence provide heuristics for achieving effective modularity.

We conclude our discussion of design fundamentals with the words of Glenford Myers [MYE78]:

> We try to solve the problem by rushing through the design process so that enough time will be left at the end of the project to uncover errors that were made because we rushed through the design process . . .

The moral is this: Don't rush through it! Design is worth the effort.

We have not concluded our discussion of design. In the chapters that follow, design methods are discussed. These methods, combined with the fundamentals in this chapter, form the basis for a complete view of software design.

REFERENCES

[AHO83] Aho, A.V., J. Hopcroft, and J. Ullmann, *Data Structures and Algorithms,* Addison-Wesley, 1983.

[BAS98] Bass, L., P. Clements, and R. Kazman, *Software Architecture in Practice,* Addison-Wesley, 1998.

[BEL81] Belady, L., Foreword to *Software Design: Methods and Techniques* (L.J. Peters, author), Yourdon Press, 1981.

[BRO98] Brown, W.J., et al., *Anti-Patterns,* Wiley, 1998.

[BUS96] Buschmann, F. et al., *Pattern-Oriented Software Architecture,* Wiley, 1996.

[DAH72] Dahl, O., E. Dijkstra, and C. Hoare, *Structured Programming,* Academic Press, 1972.

[DAV95] Davis, A., *201 Principles of Software Development,* McGraw-Hill, 1995.

[DEN73] Dennis, J., "Modularity," in *Advanced Course on Software Engineering* (F.L. Bauer, ed.), Springer-Verlag, New York, 1973, pp. 128–182.

[GAM95] Gamma, E. et al., *Design Patterns,* Addison-Wesley, 1995.

[GAN89] Gonnet, G., *Handbook of Algorithms and Data Structures,* 2nd ed., Addison-Wesley, 1989.

[GAR95] Garlan, D. and M. Shaw, "An Introduction to Software Architecture," *Advances in Software Engineering and Knowledge Engineering,* vol. I (V. Ambriola and G. Tortora, eds.), World Scientific Publishing Company, 1995.

[JAC75] Jackson, M.A., *Principles of Program Design,* Academic Press, 1975.

[JAC83] Jackson, M.A., *System Development,* Prentice-Hall, 1983.

[JAC92] Jacobson, I., *Object-Oriented Software Engineering,* Addison-Wesley, 1992.

[KAI83] Kaiser, S.H., *The Design of Operating Systems for Small Computer Systems,* Wiley-Interscience, 1983, pp. 594 ff.

[KRU84] Kruse, R.L., *Data Structures and Program Design,* Prentice-Hall, 1984.

[MCG91] McGlaughlin, R., "Some Notes on Program Design," *Software Engineering Notes,* vol. 16, no. 4, October 1991, pp. 53–54.

[MEY88] Meyer, B., *Object-Oriented Software Construction,* Prentice-Hall, 1988.

[MIL72] Mills, H.D., "Mathematical Foundations for Structured Programming," Technical Report FSC 71-6012, IBM Corp., Federal Systems Division, Gaithersburg, Maryland, 1972.

[MYE78] Myers, G., *Composite Structured Design,* Van Nostrand,1978.

[ORR77] Orr, K.T., *Structured Systems Development,* Yourdon Press, 1977.

[PAR72] Parnas, D.L., "On Criteria to Be Used in Decomposing Systems into Modules," *CACM,* vol. 14, no. 1, April 1972, pp. 221–227.

[ROS75] Ross, D., J. Goodenough, and C. Irvine, "Software Engineering: Process, Principles and Goals," *IEEE Computer,* vol. 8, no. 5, May 1975.

[SHA95a] Shaw, M. and D. Garlan, "Formulations and Formalisms in Software Architecture," *Volume 1000—Lecture Notes in Computer Science,* Springer-Verlag, 1995.

[SHA95b] Shaw, M. et al., "Abstractions for Software Architecture and Tools to Support Them," *IEEE Trans. Software Engineering,* vol. SE-21, no. 4, April 1995, pp. 314–335.

[SHA96] Shaw, M. and D. Garlan, *Software Architecture,* Prentice-Hall, 1996.

[SOM89] Sommerville, I., *Software Engineering,* 3rd ed., Addison-Wesley, 1989.

[STE74] Stevens, W., G. Myers, and L. Constantine, "Structured Design," *IBM Systems Journal,* vol. 13, no. 2, 1974, pp. 115–139.

[WAR74] Warnier, J., *Logical Construction of Programs,* Van Nostrand-Reinhold, 1974.

[WAS83] Wasserman, A., "Information System Design Methodology," in *Software Design Techniques* (P. Freeman and A. Wasserman, eds.), 4th ed., IEEE Computer Society Press, 1983, p. 43.

[WIR71] Wirth, N., "Program Development by Stepwise Refinement," *CACM,* vol. 14, no. 4, 1971, pp. 221–227.

[YOU79] Yourdon, E., and L. Constantine, *Structured Design,* Prentice-Hall, 1979.

PROBLEMS AND POINTS TO PONDER

13.1. Do you design software when you "write" a program? What makes software design different from coding?

13.2. Develop three additional design principles to add to those noted in Section 13.3.

13.3. Provide examples of three data abstractions and the procedural abstractions that can be used to manipulate them.

13.4. Apply a "stepwise refinement approach" to develop three different levels of procedural abstraction for one or more of the following programs:

a. Develop a check writer that, given a numeric dollar amount, will print the amount in words normally required on a check.

b. Iteratively solve for the roots of a transcendental equation.

c. Develop a simple round-robin scheduling algorithm for an operating system.

13.5. Is there a case when Expression (13-2) may not be true? How might such a case affect the argument for modularity?

13.6. When should a modular design be implemented as monolithic software? How can this be accomplished? Is performance the only justification for implementation of monolithic software?

13.7. Develop at least five levels of abstraction for one of the following software problems:

a. A video game of your choosing.

b. A 3D transformation package for computer graphics applications.

c. A programming language interpreter.

d. A two degree of freedom robot controller.

e. Any problem mutually agreeable to you and your instructor.

As the level of abstraction decreases, your focus may narrow so that at the last level (source code) only a single task need be described.

13.8. Obtain the original Parnas paper [PAR72] and summarize the software example that he uses to illustrate decomposition of a system into modules. How is information hiding used to achieve the decomposition?

13.9. Discuss the relationship between the concept of information hiding as an attribute of effective modularity and the concept of module independence.

13.10. Review some of your recent software development efforts and grade each module (on a scale of 1—low to 7—high). Bring in samples of your best and worst work.

13.11. A number of high-level programming languages support the internal procedure as a modular construct. How does this construct affect coupling? information hiding?

13.12. How are the concepts of coupling and software portability related? Provide examples to support your discussion.

13.13. Discuss how structural partitioning can help to make software more maintainable.

13.14. What is the purpose of developing a program structure that is factored?

13.15. Describe the concept of information hiding in your own words.

13.16. Why is it a good idea to keep the scope of effect of a module within its scope of control?

FURTHER READINGS AND INFORMATION SOURCES

Donald Norman has written two books (*The Design of Everyday Things,* Doubleday, 1990, and *The Psychology of Everyday Things,* HarperCollins, 1988) that have become classics in the design literature and "must" reading for anyone who designs anything that humans use. Adams (*Conceptual Blockbusting,* 3rd ed., Addison-Wesley, 1986) has written a book that is essential reading for designers who want to broaden their way of thinking. Finally, a classic text by Polya (*How to Solve It,* 2nd ed., Princeton University Press, 1988) provides a generic problem-solving process that can help software designers when they are faced with complex problems.

Following in the same tradition, Winograd et al. (*Bringing Design to Software,* Addison-Wesley, 1996) discusses software designs that work, those that don't, and why. A fascinating book edited by Wixon and Ramsey (*Field Methods Casebook for Software Design,* Wiley, 1996) suggests field research methods (much like those used by anthropologists) to understand how end-users do the work they do and then design software that meets their needs. Beyer and Holtzblatt (*Contextual Design: A Customer-Centered Approach to Systems Designs,* Academic Press, 1997) offer another view of software design that integrates the customer/user into every aspect of the software design process.

McConnell (*Code Complete,* Microsoft Press, 1993) presents an excellent discussion of the practical aspects of designing high-quality computer software. Robertson (*Simple Program Design*, 3rd ed., Boyd and Fraser Publishing, 1999) presents an introductory discussion of software design that is useful for those beginning their study of the subject.

An excellent historical survey of important papers on software design is contained in an anthology edited by Freeman and Wasserman (*Software Design Techniques,* 4th ed., IEEE, 1983). This tutorial reprints many of the classic papers that have formed the basis for current trends in software design. Good discussions of software design fundamentals can be found in books by Myers [MYE78], Peters (*Software Design: Methods and Techniques,* Yourdon Press, 1981), Macro (*Software Engineering: Concepts and

Management, Prentice-Hall, 1990), and Sommerville (*Software Engineering,* Addison-Wesley, 5th ed., 1996).

Mathematically rigorous treatments of computer software and design fundamentals may be found in books by Jones (*Software Development: A Rigorous Approach,* Prentice-Hall, 1980), Wulf (*Fundamental Structures of Computer Science,* Addison-Wesley, 1981), and Brassard and Bratley (*Fundamental of Algorithmics,* Prentice-Hall, 1995). Each of these texts helps to supply a necessary theoretical foundation for our understanding of computer software.

Kruse (*Data Structures and Program Design,* Prentice-Hall, 1994) and Tucker et al. (*Fundamentals of Computing II: Abstraction, Data Structures, and Large Software Systems,* McGraw-Hill, 1995) present worthwhile information on data structures. Measures of design quality, presented from both the technical and management perspectives, are considered by Card and Glass (*Measuring Software Design Quality,* Prentice-Hall, 1990).

A wide variety of information sources on software design and related subjects is available on the Internet. An up-to-date list of World Wide Web references that are relevant to design concepts and methods can be found at the SEPA Web site:
http://www.mhhe.com/engcs/compsci/pressman/resources/design-principles.mhtml

CHAPTER

14 ARCHITECTURAL DESIGN

KEY CONCEPTS

Design has been described as a multistep process in which representations of data and program structure, interface characteristics, and procedural detail are synthesized from information requirements. This description is extended by Freeman [FRE80]:

> [D]esign is an activity concerned with making major decisions, often of a structural nature. It shares with programming a concern for abstracting information representation and processing sequences, but the level of detail is quite different at the extremes. Design builds coherent, well planned representations of programs that concentrate on the interrelationships of parts at the higher level and the logical operations involved at the lower levels . . .

As we have noted in the preceding chapter, design is information driven. Software design methods are derived from consideration of each of the three domains of the analysis model. The data, functional, and behavioral domains serve as a guide for the creation of the software design.

Methods required to create "coherent, well planned representations" of the data and architectural layers of the design model are presented in this chapter. The objective is to provide a systematic approach for the derivation of the architectural design—the preliminary blueprint from which software is constructed.

QUICK LOOK

What is it? Architectural design represents the structure of data and program components that are required to build a computer-based system. It considers the architectural style that the system will take, the structure and properties of the components that constitute the system, and the interrelationships that occur among all architectural components of a system.

Who does it? Although a software engineer can design both data and architecture, the job is often allocated to specialists when large, complex systems are to be built. A database or data warehouse designer creates the data architecture for a system. The "system architect" selects an appropriate architectural style for the requirements derived during system engineering and software requirements analysis.

Why is it important? In the *Quick Look* for the last chapter, we asked: "You wouldn't attempt to build a house without a blueprint, would you?" You also wouldn't begin drawing blueprints by sketching the plumbing layout for the house. You'd need to look at the big picture—the house itself—before you worry about details. That's what architectural design does—it provides you with the big picture and ensures that you've got it right.

What are the steps? Architectural design begins with data design and then proceeds to the derivation of one or more representations of the ▶

QUICK LOOK

architectural structure of the system. Alternative architectural styles or patterns are analyzed to derive the structure that is best suited to customer requirements and quality attributes. Once an alternative has been selected, the architecture is elaborated using an architectural design method.

What is the work product? An architecture model encompassing data architecture and program structure is created during architectural design. In addition, component properties and relationships (interactions) are described.

How do I ensure that I've done it right? At each stage, software design work products are reviewed for clarity, correctness, completeness, and consistency with requirements and with one another.

14.1 SOFTWARE ARCHITECTURE

In their landmark book on the subject, Shaw and Garlan [SHA96] discuss software architecture in the following manner:

> Ever since the first program was divided into modules, software systems have had architectures, and programmers have been responsible for the interactions among the modules and the global properties of the assemblage. Historically, architectures have been implicit—accidents of implementation, or legacy systems of the past. Good software developers have often adopted one or several architectural patterns as strategies for system organization, but they use these patterns informally and have no means to make them explicit in the resulting system.

Today, effective software architecture and its explicit representation and design have become dominant themes in software engineering.

14.1.1 What Is Architecture?

When we discuss the architecture of a building, many different attributes come to mind. At the most simplistic level, we consider the overall shape of the physical structure. But in reality, architecture is much more. It is the manner in which the various components of the building are integrated to form a cohesive whole. It is the way in which the building fits into its environment and meshes with other buildings in its vicinity. It is the degree to which the building meets its stated purpose and satisfies the needs of its owner. It is the aesthetic feel of the structure—the visual impact of the building—and the way textures, colors, and materials are combined to create the external facade and the internal "living environment." It is small details—the design of lighting fixtures, the type of flooring, the placement of wall hangings, the list is almost endless. And finally, it is art.

WebRef
A useful list of software architecture resources can be found at **www2.umassd.edu/SECenter/SAResources.html**

But what about software architecture? Bass, Clements, and Kazman [BAS98] define this elusive term in the following way:

> The software architecture of a program or computing system is the structure or structures of the system, which comprise software components, the externally visible properties of those components, and the relationships among them.

The architecture is not the operational software. Rather, it is a representation that enables a software engineer to (1) analyze the effectiveness of the design in meeting its stated requirements, (2) consider architectural alternatives at a stage when making design changes is still relatively easy, and (3) reducing the risks associated with the construction of the software.

Quote:
"The architecture of a system is a comprehensive framework that describes its form and structure—its components and how they fit together."
Jerrold Grochow

This definition emphasizes the role of "software components" in any architectural representation. In the context of architectural design, a software component can be something as simple as a program module, but it can also be extended to include databases and "middleware" that enable the configuration of a network of clients and servers. The properties of components are those characteristics that are necessary to an understanding of how the components interact with other components. At the architectural level, internal properties (e.g., details of an algorithm) are not specified. The relationships between components can be as simple as a procedure call from one module to another or as complex as a database access protocol.

In this book the design of software architecture considers two levels of the design pyramid (Figure 13.1)—data design and architectural design. In the context of the preceding discussion, data design enables us to represent the data component of the architecture. Architectural design focuses on the representation of the structure of software components, their properties, and interactions.

14.1.2 Why Is Architecture Important?

In a book dedicated to software architecture, Bass and his colleagues [BAS98] identify three key reasons that software architecture is important:

KEY POINT
The architectural model provides a Gestalt view of a system, allowing the software engineer to examine it as a whole.

- Representations of software architecture are an enabler for communication between all parties (stakeholders) interested in the development of a computer-based system.
- The architecture highlights early design decisions that will have a profound impact on all software engineering work that follows and, as important, on the ultimate success of the system as an operational entity.
- Architecture "constitutes a relatively small, intellectually graspable model of how the system is structured and how its components work together" [BAS98].

The architectural design model and the architectural patterns contained within it are transferrable. That is, architecture styles and patterns (Section 14.3.1) can be applied to the design of other systems and represent a set of abstractions that enable software engineers to describe architecture in predictable ways.

14.2 DATA DESIGN

Like other software engineering activities, *data design* (sometimes referred to as *data architecting*) creates a model of data and/or information that is represented at a high level of abstraction (the customer/user's view of data). This data model is then refined into progressively more implementation-specific representations that can be processed by the computer-based system. In many software applications, the architecture of the data will have a profound influence on the architecture of the software that must process it.

The structure of data has always been an important part of software design. At the program component level, the design of data structures and the associated algorithms required to manipulate them is essential to the creation of high-quality applications. At the application level, the translation of a data model (derived as part of requirements engineering) into a database is pivotal to achieving the business objectives of a system. At the business level, the collection of information stored in disparate databases and reorganized into a "data warehouse" enables data mining or knowledge discovery that can have an impact on the success of the business itself. In every case, data design plays an important role.

14.2.1 Data Modeling, Data Structures, Databases, and the Data Warehouse

Quote:
"Data quality is the difference between a data warehouse and a data garbage dump."
Jarrett Rosenberg

The data objects defined during software requirements analysis are modeled using entity/relationship diagrams and the data dictionary (Chapter 12). The data design activity translates these elements of the requirements model into data structures at the software component level and, when necessary, a database architecture at the application level.

In years past, data architecture was generally limited to data structures at the program level and databases at the application level. But today, businesses large and small are awash in data. It is not unusual for even a moderately sized business to have dozens of databases serving many applications encompassing hundreds of gigabytes of data. The challenge for a business has been to extract useful information from this data environment, particularly when the information desired is cross-functional (e.g., information that can be obtained only if specific marketing data are cross-correlated with product engineering data).

WebRef
Up-to-date information on data warehouse technologies can be obtained at **www.datawarehouse.com**

To solve this challenge, the business IT community has developed *data mining* techniques, also called *knowledge discovery in databases* (KDD), that navigate through existing databases in an attempt to extract appropriate business-level information. However, the existence of multiple databases, their different structures, the degree of detail contained with the databases, and many other factors make data mining difficult within an existing database environment. An alternative solution, called a *data warehouse,* adds an additional layer to the data architecture.

A data warehouse is a separate data environment that is not directly integrated with day-to-day applications but encompasses all data used by a business [MAT96]. In a sense, a data warehouse is a large, independent database that encompasses some, but not all, of the data that are stored in databases that serve the set of applications required by a business. But many characteristics differentiate a data warehouse from the typical database [INM95]:

Subject orientation. A data warehouse is organized by major business subjects, rather than by business process or function. This leads to the exclusion of data that may be necessary for a particular business function but is generally not necessary for data mining.

KEY POINT
A data warehouse encompasses all data that are used by a business. The intent is to enable access to "knowledge" that might not be otherwise available.

Integration. Regardless of the source, the data exhibit consistent naming conventions, units and measures, encoding structures, and physical attributes, even when inconsistency exists across different application-oriented databases.

Time variancy. For a transaction-oriented application environment, data are accurate at the moment of access and for a relatively short time span (typically 60 to 90 days) before access. For a data warehouse, however, data can be accessed at a specific moment in time (e.g., customers contacted on the date that a new product was announced to the trade press). The typical time horizon for a data warehouse is five to ten years.

Nonvolatility. Unlike typical business application databases that undergo a continuing stream of changes (inserts, deletes, updates), data are loaded into the warehouse, but after the original transfer, the data do not change.

These characteristics present a unique set of design challenges for a data architect.

A detailed discussion of the design of data structures, databases, and the data warehouse is best left to books dedicated to these subjects (e.g., [PRE98], [DAT95], [KIM98]). The interested reader should see the Further Readings and Information Sources section of this chapter for additional references.

14.2.2 Data Design at the Component Level

Data design at the component level focuses on the representation of data structures that are directly accessed by one or more software components. Wasserman [WAS80] has proposed a set of principles that may be used to specify and design such data structures. In actuality, the design of data begins during the creation of the analysis model. Recalling that requirements analysis and design often overlap, we consider the following set of principles [WAS80] for data specification:

? What principles are applicable to data design?

1. *The systematic analysis principles applied to function and behavior should also be applied to data.* We spend much time and effort deriving, reviewing, and specifying functional requirements and preliminary design. Representations of data flow and content should also be developed and reviewed, data

objects should be identified, alternative data organizations should be considered, and the impact of data modeling on software design should be evaluated. For example, specification of a multiringed linked list may nicely satisfy data requirements but lead to an unwieldy software design. An alternative data organization may lead to better results.

2. *All data structures and the operations to be performed on each should be identified.* The design of an efficient data structure must take the operations to be performed on the data structure into account (e.g., see [AHO83]). For example, consider a data structure made up of a set of diverse data elements. The data structure is to be manipulated in a number of major software functions. Upon evaluation of the operations performed on the data structure, an abstract data type is defined for use in subsequent software design. Specification of the abstract data type may simplify software design considerably.
3. *A data dictionary should be established and used to define both data and program design.* The concept of a data dictionary has been introduced in Chapter 12. A data dictionary explicitly represents the relationships among data objects and the constraints on the elements of a data structure. Algorithms that must take advantage of specific relationships can be more easily defined if a dictionarylike data specification exists.
4. *Low-level data design decisions should be deferred until late in the design process.* A process of stepwise refinement may be used for the design of data. That is, overall data organization may be defined during requirements analysis, refined during data design work, and specified in detail during component-level design. The top-down approach to data design provides benefits that are analogous to a top-down approach to software design—major structural attributes are designed and evaluated first so that the architecture of the data may be established.
5. *The representation of data structure should be known only to those modules that must make direct use of the data contained within the structure.* The concept of information hiding and the related concept of coupling (Chapter 13) provide important insight into the quality of a software design. This principle alludes to the importance of these concepts as well as "the importance of separating the logical view of a data object from its physical view" [WAS80].
6. *A library of useful data structures and the operations that may be applied to them should be developed.* Data structures and operations should be viewed as a resource for software design. Data structures can be designed for reusability. A library of data structure templates (abstract data types) can reduce both specification and design effort for data.
7. *A software design and programming language should support the specification and realization of abstract data types.* The implementation of a sophisticated

data structure can be made exceedingly difficult if no means for direct specification of the structure exists in the programming language chosen for implementation.

These principles form a basis for a component-level data design approach that can be integrated into both the analysis and design activities.

14.3 ARCHITECTURAL STYLES

WebRef
The ABLE project at CMU provides useful papers and examples of architectural styles: **tom.cs.cmu.edu/able/**

When a builder uses the phrase "center hall colonial" to describe a house, most people familiar with houses in the United States will be able to conjure a general image of what the house will look like and what the floor plan is likely to be. The builder has used an *architectural style* as a descriptive mechanism to differentiate the house from other styles (e.g., A-frame, raised ranch, Cape Cod). But more important, the architectural style is also a pattern for construction. Further details of the house must be defined, its final dimensions must be specified, customized features may be added, building materials are to be be determined, but the pattern—a "center hall colonial"—guides the builder in his work.

? What is an architectural style?

The software that is built for computer-based systems also exhibits one of many architectural styles.[1] Each style describes a system category that encompasses (1) a set of *components* (e.g., a database, computational modules) that perform a function required by a system; (2) a set of *connectors* that enable "communication, coordinations and cooperation" among components; (3) *constraints* that define how components can be integrated to form the system; and (4) *semantic models* that enable a designer to understand the overall properties of a system by analyzing the known properties of its constituent parts [BAS98]. In the section that follows, we consider commonly used architectural patterns for software.

14.3.1 A Brief Taxonomy of Styles and Patterns

Although millions of computer-based systems have been created over the past 50 years, the vast majority can be categorized (see [SHA96], {BAS98], BUS96]) into one of a relatively small number of architectural styles:

Quote:
"The use of patterns and styles of design is pervasive in engineering disciplines."
Mary Shaw and David Garlan

Data-centered architectures. A data store (e.g., a file or database) resides at the center of this architecture and is accessed frequently by other components that update, add, delete, or otherwise modify data within the store. Figure 14.1 illustrates a typical data-centered style. Client software accesses a central repository. In some cases the data repository is *passive.* That is, client software accesses the data independent of any changes to the data or the actions of other client software. A variation on this approach transforms the repository into a "blackboard" that sends notifications to client software when data of interest to the client change.

1 The terms *styles* and *patterns* are used interchangeably in this discussion.

FIGURE 14.1
Data-centered architecture

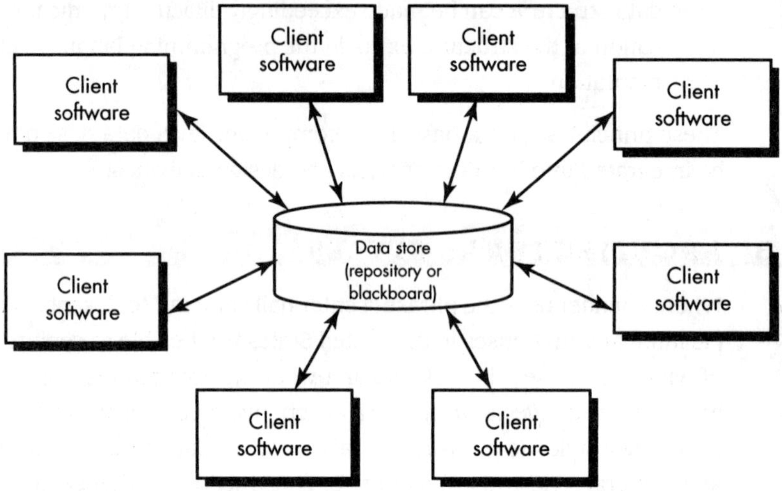

Data-centered architectures promote *integrability* [BAS98]. That is, existing components can be changed and new client components can be added to the architecture without concern about other clients (because the client components operate independently). In addition, data can be passed among clients using the blackboard mechanism (i.e., the blackboard component serves to coordinate the transfer of information between clients). Client components independently execute processes.

Quote:
"A good architect is the principal keeper of the user's vision of the end product."
Norman Simenson

Data-flow architectures. This architecture is applied when input data are to be transformed through a series of computational or manipulative components into output data. A *pipe and filter pattern* (Figure 14.2a) has a set of components, called *filters,* connected by pipes that transmit data from one component to the next. Each filter works independently of those components upstream and downstream, is designed to expect data input of a certain form, and produces data output (to the next filter) of a specified form. However, the filter does not require knowledge of the working of its neighboring filters.

If the data flow degenerates into a single line of transforms, it is termed *batch sequential.* This pattern (Figure 14.2b) accepts a batch of data and then applies a series of sequential components (filters) to transform it.

Call and return architectures. This architectural style enables a software designer (system architect) to achieve a program structure that is relatively easy to modify and scale. A number of substyles [BAS98] exist within this category:

- *Main program/subprogram architectures.* This classic program structure decomposes function into a control hierarchy where a "main" program invokes a number of program components, which in turn may invoke still other components. Figure 13.3 illustrates an architecture of this type.

FIGURE 14.2
Data flow architectures

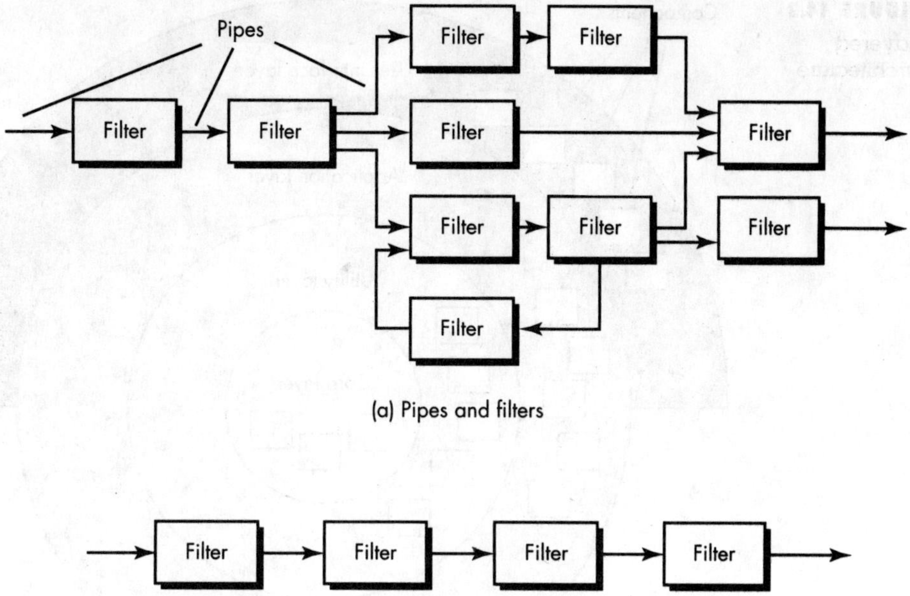

(a) Pipes and filters

(b) Batch sequential

- *Remote procedure call architectures.* The components of a main program/subprogram architecture are distributed across multiple computers on a network

XRef
A detailed discussion of object-oriented architectures is presented in Part Four.

Object-oriented architectures. The components of a system encapsulate data and the operations that must be applied to manipulate the data. Communication and coordination between components is accomplished via message passing.

Layered architectures. The basic structure of a layered architecture is illustrated in Figure 14.3. A number of different layers are defined, each accomplishing operations that progressively become closer to the machine instruction set. At the outer layer, components service user interface operations. At the inner layer, components perform operating system interfacing. Intermediate layers provide utility services and application software functions.

These architectural styles are only a small subset of those available to the software designer.[2] Once requirements engineering uncovers the characteristics and constraints of the system to be built, the architectural pattern (style) or combination of patterns (styles) that best fits those characteristics and constraints can be chosen. In

2 See [SHA96], [SHA97], [BAS98], and [BUS96] for a detailed discussion of architectural styles and patterns.

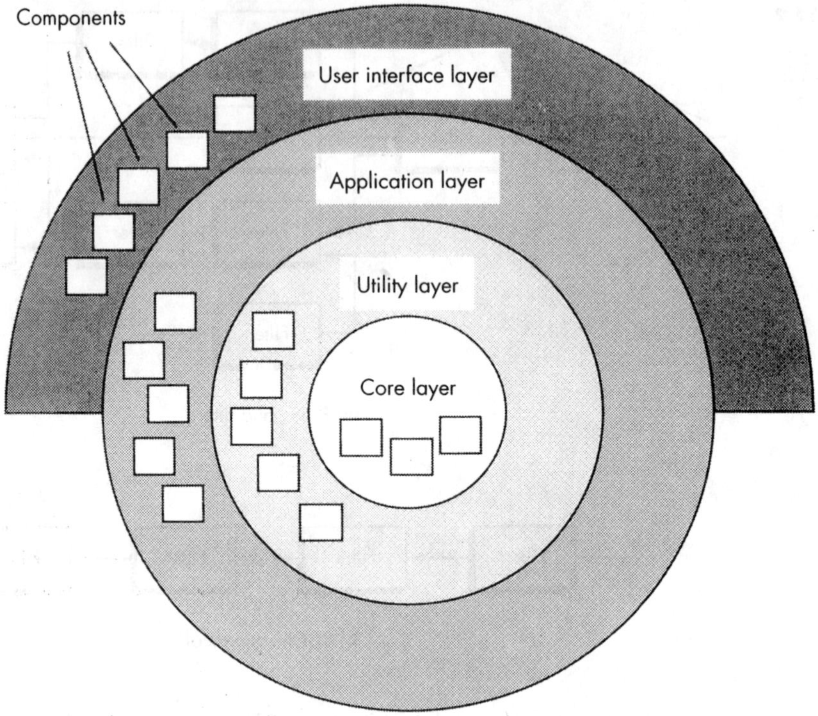

FIGURE 14.3 Layered architecture

many cases, more than one pattern might be appropriate and alternative architectural styles might be designed and evaluated.

14.3.2 Organization and Refinement

Because the design process often leaves a software engineer with a number of architectural alternatives, it is important to establish a set of design criteria that can be used to assess an architectural design that is derived. The following questions [BAS98] provide insight into the architectural style that has been derived:

? How do I assess an architectural style that has been derived?

> **Control.** How is control managed within the architecture? Does a distinct control hierarchy exist, and if so, what is the role of components within this control hierarchy? How do components transfer control within the system? How is control shared among components? What is the control topology (i.e., the geometric form[3] that the control takes)? Is control synchronized or do components operate asynchronously?

3 A hierarchy is one geometric form, but others such as a hub and spoke control mechanism in a client/server system are also encountered.

Data. How are data communicated between components? Is the flow of data continuous, or are data objects passed to the system sporadically? What is the mode of data transfer (i.e., are data passed from one component to another or are data available globally to be shared among system components)? Do data components (e.g., a blackboard or repository) exist, and if so, what is their role? How do functional components interact with data components? Are data components *passive* or *active* (i.e., does the data component actively interact with other components in the system)? How do data and control interact within the system?

These questions provide the designer with an early assessment of design quality and lay the foundation for more-detailed analysis of the architecture.

14.4 ANALYZING ALTERNATIVE ARCHITECTURAL DESIGNS

Quote:

"Maybe it's in the basement, let me go up stairs and check."

M. C. Escher

The questions posed in the preceding section provide a preliminary assessment of the architectural style chosen for a given system. However, a more complete method for evaluating the quality of an architecture is essential if design is to be accomplished effectively. In the sections that follow, we consider two different approaches for the analysis of alternative architectural designs. The first method uses an iterative method to assess design trade-offs. The second approach applies a pseudo-quantitative technique for assessing design quality.

14.4.1 An Architecture Trade-off Analysis Method

The Software Engineering Institute (SEI) has developed an *architecture trade-off analysis method* (ATAM) [KAZ98] that establishes an iterative evaluation process for software architectures. The design analysis activities that follow are performed iteratively:

WebRef

Detailed discussion of software architectural trade-off analysis can be found at **www.sei.cmu.edu/ata/ata_method.html**

1. *Collect scenarios.* A set of use-cases (Chapter 11) is developed to represent the system from the user's point of view.
2. *Elicit requirements, constraints, and environment description.* This information is required as part of requirements engineering and is used to be certain that all customer, user, and stakeholder concerns have been addressed.
3. *Describe the architectural styles/patterns that have been chosen to address the scenarios and requirements.* The style(s) should be described using architectural views such as
   - *Module view* for analysis of work assignments with components and the degree to which information hiding has been achieved.
   - *Process view* for analysis of system performance.
   - *Data flow view* for analysis of the degree to which the architecture meets functional requirements.

XRef
A detailed discussion of quality attributes is presented in Chapters 8 and 19.

4. *Evaluate quality attributes by considering each attribute in isolation.* The number of quality attributes chosen for analysis is a function of the time available for review and the degree to which quality attributes are relevant to the system at hand. Quality attributes for architectural design assessment include reliability, performance, security, maintainability, flexibility, testability, portability, reusability, and interoperability.
5. *Identify the sensitivity of quality attributes to various architectural attributes for a specific architectural style.* This can be accomplished by making small changes in the architecture and determining how sensitive a quality attribute, say performance, is to the change. Any attributes that are significantly affected by variation in the architecture are termed *sensitivity points.*
6. *Critique candidate architectures (developed in step 3) using the sensitivity analysis conducted in step 5.* The SEI describes this approach in the following manner [KAZ98]:

> Once the architectural sensitivity points have been determined, finding trade-off points is simply the identification of architectural elements to which multiple attributes are sensitive. For example, the performance of a client-server architecture might be highly sensitive to the number of servers (performance increases, within some range, by increasing the number of servers). The availability of that architecture might also vary directly with the number of servers. However, the security of the system might vary inversely with the number of servers (because the system contains more potential points of attack). The number of servers, then, is a trade-off point with respect to this architecture. It is an element, potentially one of many, where architectural trade-offs will be made, consciously or unconsciously.

These six steps represent the first ATAM iteration. Based on the results of steps 5 and 6, some architecture alternatives may be eliminated, one or more of the remaining architectures may be modified and represented in more detail, and then the ATAM steps are reapplied.

14.4.2 Quantitative Guidance for Architectural Design

One of the many problems faced by software engineers during the design process is a general lack of quantitative methods for assessing the quality of proposed designs. The ATAM approach discussed in Section 14.4.1 is representative of a useful but undeniably qualitative approach to design analysis.

Work in the area of quantitative analysis of architectural design is still in its formative stages. Asada and his colleagues [ASA96] suggest a number of pseudo-quantitative techniques that can be used to complement the ATAM approach as a method for the analysis of architectural design quality.

Asada proposes a number of simple models that assist a designer in determining the degree to which a particular architecture meets predefined "goodness" criteria.

These criteria, sometimes called *design dimensions,* often encompass the quality attributes defined in the last section: reliability, performance, security, maintainability, flexibility, testability, portability, reusability, and interoperability, among others.

The first model, called *spectrum analysis,* assesses an architectural design on a "goodness" spectrum from the best to worst possible designs. Once the software architecture has been proposed, it is assessed by assigning a "score" to each of its design dimensions. These dimension scores are summed to determine the total score, S, of the design as a whole. Worst-case scores[4] are then assigned to a hypothetical design, and a total score, S_w, for the worst case architecture is computed. A best-case score, S_b, is computed for an optimal design.[5] We then calculate a *spectrum index,* I_s, using the equation

Quote:
"A doctor can bury his mistakes, but an architect can only advise his clients to plant vines."
Frank Lloyd Wright

$$I_s = [(S - S_w)/(S_b - S_w)] \times 100$$

The spectrum index indicates the degree to which a proposed architecture approaches an optimal system within the spectrum of reasonable choices for a design.

If modifications are made to the proposed design or if an entirely new design is proposed, the spectrum indices for both may be compared and an *improvement index,* I_{mp}, may be computed:

$$I_{mp} = I_{s1} - I_{s2}$$

This provides a designer with a relative indication of the improvement associated with architectural changes or a new proposed architecture. If I_{mp} is positive, then we can conclude that system 1 has been improved relative to system 2.

Design selection analysis is another model that requires a set of design dimensions to be defined. The proposed architecture is then assessed to determine the number of design dimensions that it achieves when compared to an ideal (best-case) system. For example, if a proposed architecture would achieve excellent component reuse, and this dimension is required for an idea system, the reusability dimension has been achieved. If the proposed architecture has weak security and strong security is required, that design dimension has not been achieved.

We calculate a *design selection index, d,* as

$$d = (N_s/N_a) \times 100$$

where N_s is the number of design dimensions achieved by a proposed architecture and N_a is the total number of dimensions in the design space. The higher the design selection index, the more closely the proposed architecture approaches an ideal system.

Contribution analysis "identifies the reasons that one set of design choices gets a lower score than another" [ASA96]. Recalling our discussion of quality function deployment (QFD) in Chapter 11, value analysis is conducted to determine the

4 The design must still be applicable to the problem at hand, even if it is not a particularly good solution.

5 The design might be optimal, but constraints, costs, or other factors will not allow it to be built.

relative priority of requirements determined during function deployment, information deployment, and task deployment. A set of "realization mechanisms" (features of the architecture) are identified. All customer requirements (determined using QFD) are listed and a cross-reference matrix is created. The cells of the matrix indicate the relative strength of the relationship (on a numeric scale of 1 to 10) between a realization mechanism and a requirement for each alternative architecture. This is sometimes called a *quantified design space* (QDS). The QDS is relatively easy to implement as a spreadsheet model and can be used to isolate why one set of design choices gets a lower score than another.

14.4.3 Architectural Complexity

A useful technique for assessing the overall complexity of a proposed architecture is to consider dependencies between components within the architecture. These dependencies are driven by information/control flow within the system.

Zhao [ZHA98] suggests three types of dependencies:

> *Sharing dependencies* represent dependence relationships among consumers who use the same resource or producers who produce for the same consumers. For example, for two components *u* and *v*, if *u* and *v* refer to the same global data, then there exists a shared dependence relationship between *u* and *v*.
>
> *Flow dependencies* represent dependence relationships between producers and consumers of resources. For example, for two components *u* and *v*, if *u* must complete before control flows into *v* (prerequisite), or if *u* communicates with *v* by parameters, then there exists a flow dependence relationship between *u* and *v*.
>
> *Constrained dependencies* represent constraints on the relative flow of control among a set of activities. For example, for two components *u* and *v*, *u* and *v* cannot execute at the same time (mutual exclusion), then there exists a constrained dependence relationship between *u* and *v*.

The sharing and flow dependencies noted by Zhao are similar in some ways to the concept of coupling discussed in Chapter 13. Simple metrics for evaluating these dependencies are discussed in Chapter 19.

14.5 MAPPING REQUIREMENTS INTO A SOFTWARE ARCHITECTURE

In Chapter 13 we noted that software requirements can be mapped into various representations of the design model. The architectural styles discussed in Section 14.3.1 represent radically different architectures, so it should come as no surprise that a comprehensive mapping that accomplishes the transition from the requirements model to a variety of architectural styles does not exist. In fact, there is no practical mapping for some architectural styles, and the designer must approach the translation of requirements to design for these styles in an ad hoc fashion.

To illustrate one approach to architectural mapping, we consider the call and return architecture—an extremely common structure for many types of systems.[6] The mapping technique to be presented enables a designer to derive reasonably complex call and return architectures from data flow diagrams within the requirements model. The technique, sometimes called *structured design,* has its origins in earlier design concepts that stressed modularity [DEN73], top-down design [WIR71], and structured programming [DAH72], [LIN79]. Stevens, Myers, and Constantine [STE74] were early proponents of software design based on the flow of data through a system. Early work was refined and presented in books by Myers [MYE78] and Yourdon and Constantine [YOU79].

? What steps should we follow to map DFDs into a call and return architecture?

Structured design is often characterized as a data flow-oriented design method because it provides a convenient transition from a data flow diagram to software architecture.[7] The transition from information flow (represented as a DFD) to program structure is accomplished as part of a six-step process: (1) the type of information flow is established; (2) flow boundaries are indicated; (3) the DFD is mapped into program structure; (4) control hierarchy is defined; (5) resultant structure is refined using design measures and heuristics; and (6) the architectural description is refined and elaborated.

The type of information flow is the driver for the mapping approach required in step 3. In the following sections we examine two flow types.

14.5.1 Transform Flow

XRef
Data flow diagrams are discussed in detail in Chapter 12.

Recalling the fundamental system model (level 0 data flow diagram), information must enter and exit software in an "external world" form. For example, data typed on a keyboard, tones on a telephone line, and video images in a multimedia application are all forms of external world information. Such externalized data must be converted into an internal form for processing. Information enters the system along paths that transform external data into an internal form. These paths are identified as *incoming flow.* At the kernel of the software, a transition occurs. Incoming data are passed through a *transform center* and begin to move along paths that now lead "out" of the software. Data moving along these paths are called *outgoing flow.* The overall flow of data occurs in a sequential manner and follows one, or only a few, "straight line" paths.[8] When a segment of a data flow diagram exhibits these characteristics, *transform flow* is present.

---

6 It is also important to note that the call and return architecture can reside within other more sophisticated architectures discussed earlier in this chapter. For example, the architecture of one or more components of a client/server architecture might be call and return.

7 It should be noted that other elements of the analysis model (e.g., the data dictionary, PSPECs, CSPECs) are also used during the mapping method.

8 An obvious mapping for this type of information flow is the data flow architecture described in Section 14.3.1. There are many cases, however, where the data flow architecture may not be the best choice for a complex system. Examples include systems that will undergo substantial change over time or systems in which the processing associated with the data flow is not necessarily sequential.

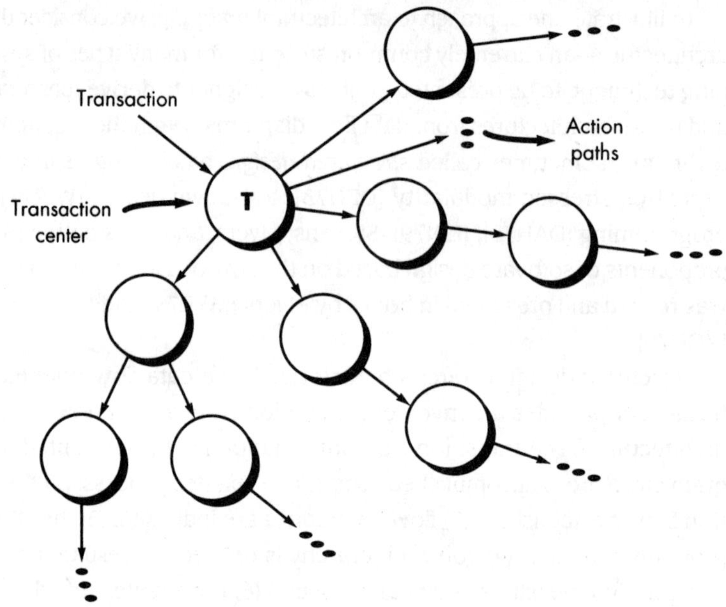

FIGURE 14.4 Transaction flow

14.5.2 Transaction Flow

The fundamental system model implies transform flow; therefore, it is possible to characterize all data flow in this category. However, information flow is often characterized by a single data item, called a *transaction,* that triggers other data flow along one of many paths. When a DFD takes the form shown in Figure 14.4, *transaction flow* is present.

Transaction flow is characterized by data moving along an incoming path that converts external world information into a transaction. The transaction is evaluated and, based on its value, flow along one of many *action paths* is initiated. The hub of information flow from which many action paths emanate is called a *transaction center.*

It should be noted that, within a DFD for a large system, both transform and transaction flow may be present. For example, in a transaction-oriented flow, information flow along an action path may have transform flow characteristics.

14.6 TRANSFORM MAPPING

Transform mapping is a set of design steps that allows a DFD with transform flow characteristics to be mapped into a specific architectural style. In this section transform mapping is described by applying design steps to an example system—a portion of the *SafeHome* security software presented in earlier chapters.

14.6.1 An Example

The *SafeHome* security system, introduced earlier in this book, is representative of many computer-based products and systems in use today. The product monitors the real world and reacts to changes that it encounters. It also interacts with a user through

FIGURE 14.5
Context level DFD for *SafeHome*

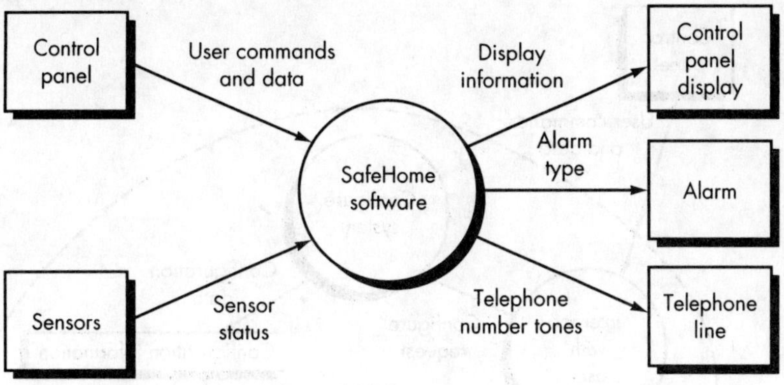

a series of typed inputs and alphanumeric displays. The level 0 data flow diagram for *SafeHome,* reproduced from Chapter 12, is shown in Figure 14.5.

During requirements analysis, more detailed flow models would be created for *SafeHome.* In addition, control and process specifications, a data dictionary, and various behavioral models would also be created.

14.6.2 Design Steps

The preceding example will be used to illustrate each step in transform mapping. The steps begin with a re-evaluation of work done during requirements analysis and then move to the design of the software architecture.

Step 1. Review the fundamental system model. The fundamental system model encompasses the level 0 DFD and supporting information. In actuality, the design step begins with an evaluation of both the *System Specification* and the *Software Requirements Specification.* Both documents describe information flow and structure at the software interface. Figures 14.5 and 14.6 depict level 0 and level 1 data flow for the *SafeHome* software.

ADVICE

If the DFD is refined further at this time, strive to derive bubbles that exhibit high cohesion.

Step 2. Review and refine data flow diagrams for the software. Information obtained from analysis models contained in the *Software Requirements Specification* is refined to produce greater detail. For example, the level 2 DFD for *monitor sensors* (Figure 14.7) is examined, and a level 3 data flow diagram is derived as shown in Figure 14.8. At level 3, each transform in the data flow diagram exhibits relatively high cohesion (Chapter 13). That is, the process implied by a transform performs a single, distinct function that can be implemented as a module[9] in the *SafeHome* software. Therefore, the DFD in Figure 14.8 contains sufficient detail for a "first cut" at the design of architecture for the *monitor sensors* subsystem, and we proceed without further refinement.

9 The use of the term *module* in this chapter is equivalent to *component* as it was used in earlier discussions of software architecture.

FIGURE 14.6
Level 1 DFD for SafeHome

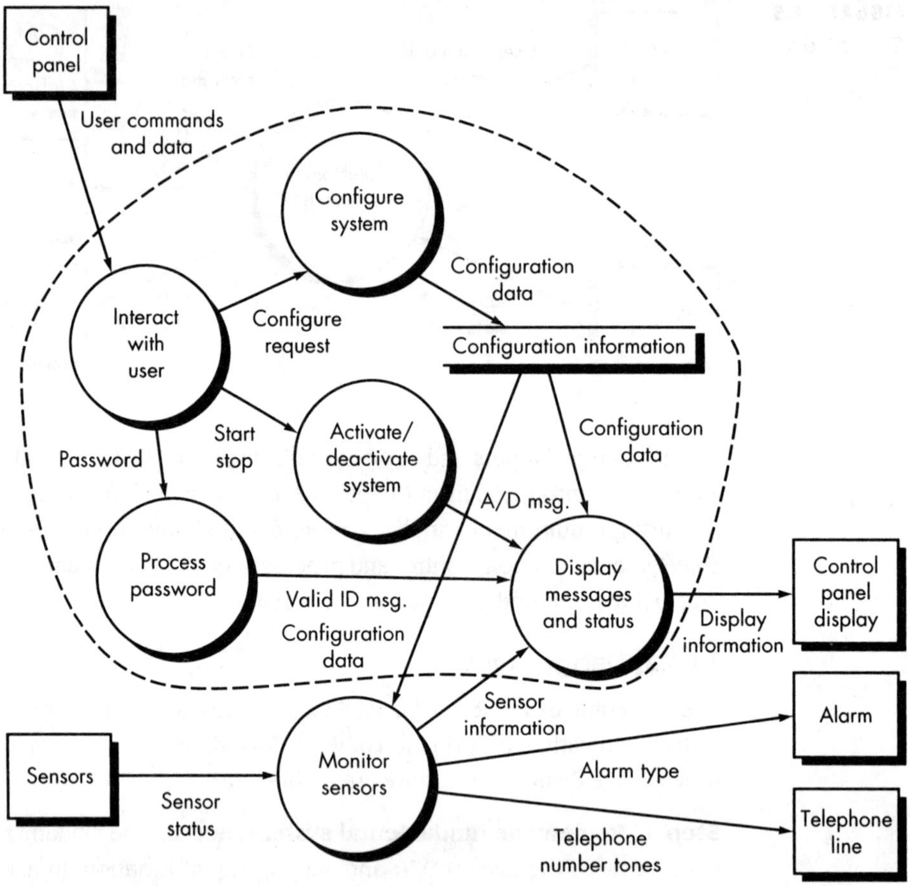

KEY POINT

You will often encounter both types of data flow within the same analysis model. The flows are partitioned and program structure is derived using the appropriate mapping.

Step 3. Determine whether the DFD has transform or transaction flow characteristics. In general, information flow within a system can always be represented as transform. However, when an obvious transaction characteristic (Figure 14.4) is encountered, a different design mapping is recommended. In this step, the designer selects global (softwarewide) flow characteristics based on the prevailing nature of the DFD. In addition, local regions of transform or transaction flow are isolated. These *subflows* can be used to refine program architecture derived from a global characteristic described previously. For now, we focus our attention only on the *monitor sensors* subsystem data flow depicted in Figure 14.8.

Evaluating the DFD (Figure 14.8), we see data entering the software along one incoming path and exiting along three outgoing paths. No distinct transaction center is implied (although the transform establishes alarm conditions that could be perceived as such). Therefore, an overall transform characteristic will be assumed for information flow.

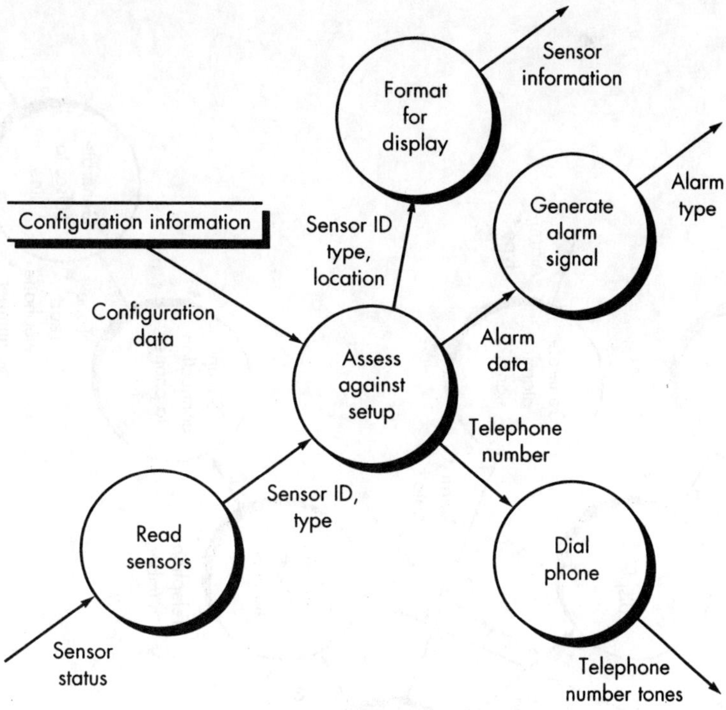

FIGURE 14.7
Level 2 DFD that refines the monitor sensors process

ADVICE

Vary the location of flow boundaries in an effort to explore alternative program structures. This takes very little time and can provide important insight.

Step 4. Isolate the transform center by specifying incoming and outgoing flow boundaries. In the preceding section incoming flow was described as a path in which information is converted from external to internal form; outgoing flow converts from internal to external form. Incoming and outgoing flow boundaries are open to interpretation. That is, different designers may select slightly different points in the flow as boundary locations. In fact, alternative design solutions can be derived by varying the placement of flow boundaries. Although care should be taken when boundaries are selected, a variance of one bubble along a flow path will generally have little impact on the final program structure.

Flow boundaries for the example are illustrated as shaded curves running vertically through the flow in Figure 14.8. The transforms (bubbles) that constitute the transform center lie within the two shaded boundaries that run from top to bottom in the figure. An argument can be made to readjust a boundary (e.g, an incoming flow boundary separating *read sensors* and *acquire response info* could be proposed). The emphasis in this design step should be on selecting reasonable boundaries, rather than lengthy iteration on placement of divisions.

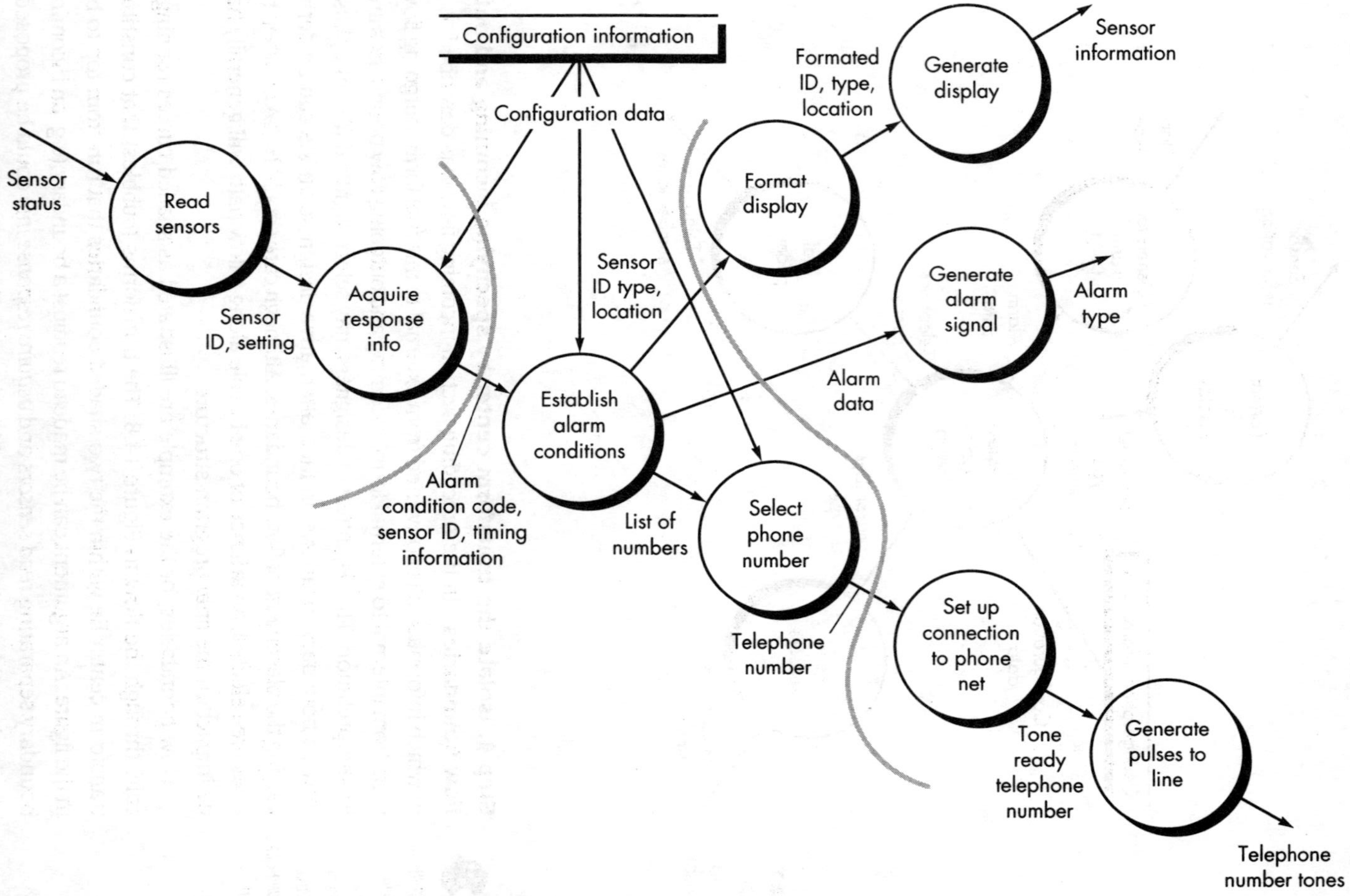

FIGURE 14.8 Level 3 DFD for monitor sensors with flow boundaries

FIGURE 14.9
First-level factoring for monitor sensors

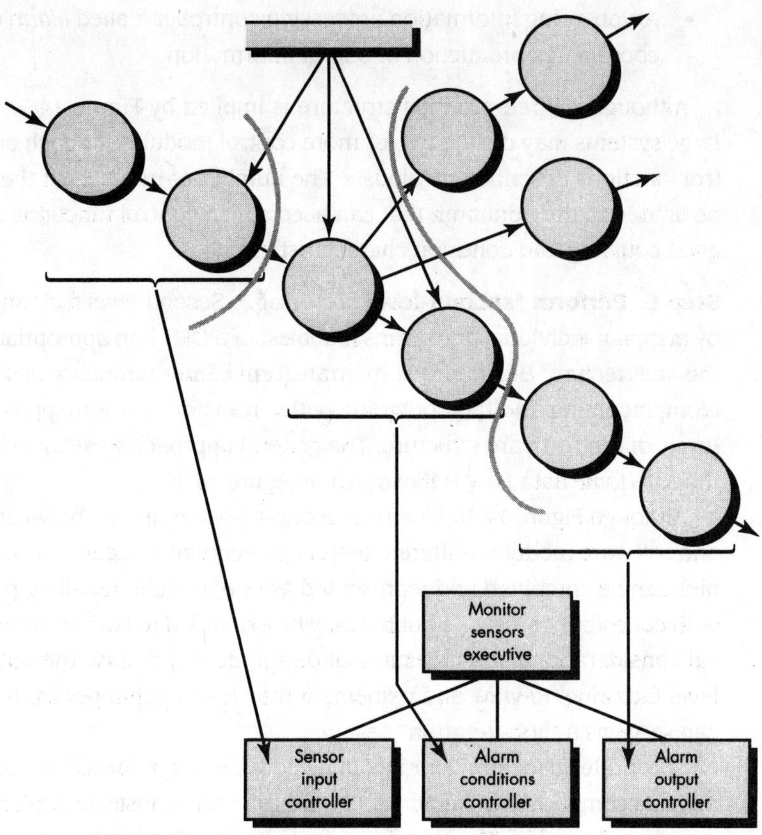

ADVICE

Don't become dogmatic at this stage. It may be necessary to establish two or more controllers for input processing or computation, based on the complexity of the system to be built. If common sense dictates this approach, do it!

Step 5. Perform "first-level factoring." Program structure represents a top-down distribution of control. Factoring results in a program structure in which top-level modules perform decision making and low-level modules perform most input, computation, and output work. Middle-level modules perform some control and do moderate amounts of work.

When transform flow is encountered, a DFD is mapped to a specific structure (a call and return architecture) that provides control for incoming, transform, and outgoing information processing. This first-level factoring for the *monitor sensors* subsystem is illustrated in Figure 14.9. A main controller (called *monitor sensors executive*) resides at the top of the program structure and coordinates the following subordinate control functions:

- An incoming information processing controller, called *sensor input controller,* coordinates receipt of all incoming data.
- A transform flow controller, called *alarm conditions controller,* supervises all operations on data in internalized form (e.g., a module that invokes various data transformation procedures).

- An outgoing information processing controller, called *alarm output controller*, coordinates production of output information.

Although a three-pronged structure is implied by Figure 14.9, complex flows in large systems may dictate two or more control modules for each of the generic control functions described previously. The number of modules at the first level should be limited to the minimum that can accomplish control functions and still maintain good coupling and cohesion characteristics.

Step 6. Perform "second-level factoring." Second-level factoring is accomplished by mapping individual transforms (bubbles) of a DFD into appropriate modules within the architecture. Beginning at the transform center boundary and moving outward along incoming and then outgoing paths, transforms are mapped into subordinate levels of the software structure. The general approach to second-level factoring for the *SafeHome* data flow is illustrated in Figure 14.10.

ADVICE

Keep "worker" modules low in the program structure. This will lead to an architecture that is easier to modify.

Although Figure 14.10 illustrates a one-to-one mapping between DFD transforms and software modules, different mappings frequently occur. Two or even three bubbles can be combined and represented as one module (recalling potential problems with cohesion) or a single bubble may be expanded to two or more modules. Practical considerations and measures of design quality dictate the outcome of second-level factoring. Review and refinement may lead to changes in this structure, but it can serve as a "first-iteration" design.

Second-level factoring for incoming flow follows in the same manner. Factoring is again accomplished by moving outward from the transform center boundary on the incoming flow side. The transform center of *monitor sensors* subsystem software is mapped somewhat differently. Each of the data conversion or calculation transforms of the transform portion of the DFD is mapped into a module subordinate to the transform controller. A completed first-iteration architecture is shown in Figure 14.11.

ADVICE

Eliminate redundant control modules. That is, if a control module does nothing except control one other module, its control function should be imploded at a higher level.

The modules mapped in the preceding manner and shown in Figure 14.11 represent an initial design of software architecture. Although modules are named in a manner that implies function, a brief processing narrative (adapted from the PSPEC created during analysis modeling) should be written for each. The narrative describes

- Information that passes into and out of the module (an interface description).
- Information that is retained by a module, such as data stored in a local data structure.
- A procedural narrative that indicates major decision points and tasks.
- A brief discussion of restrictions and special features (e.g., file I/O, hardware-dependent characteristics, special timing requirements).

The narrative serves as a first-generation *Design Specification*. However, further refinement and additions occur regularly during this period of design.

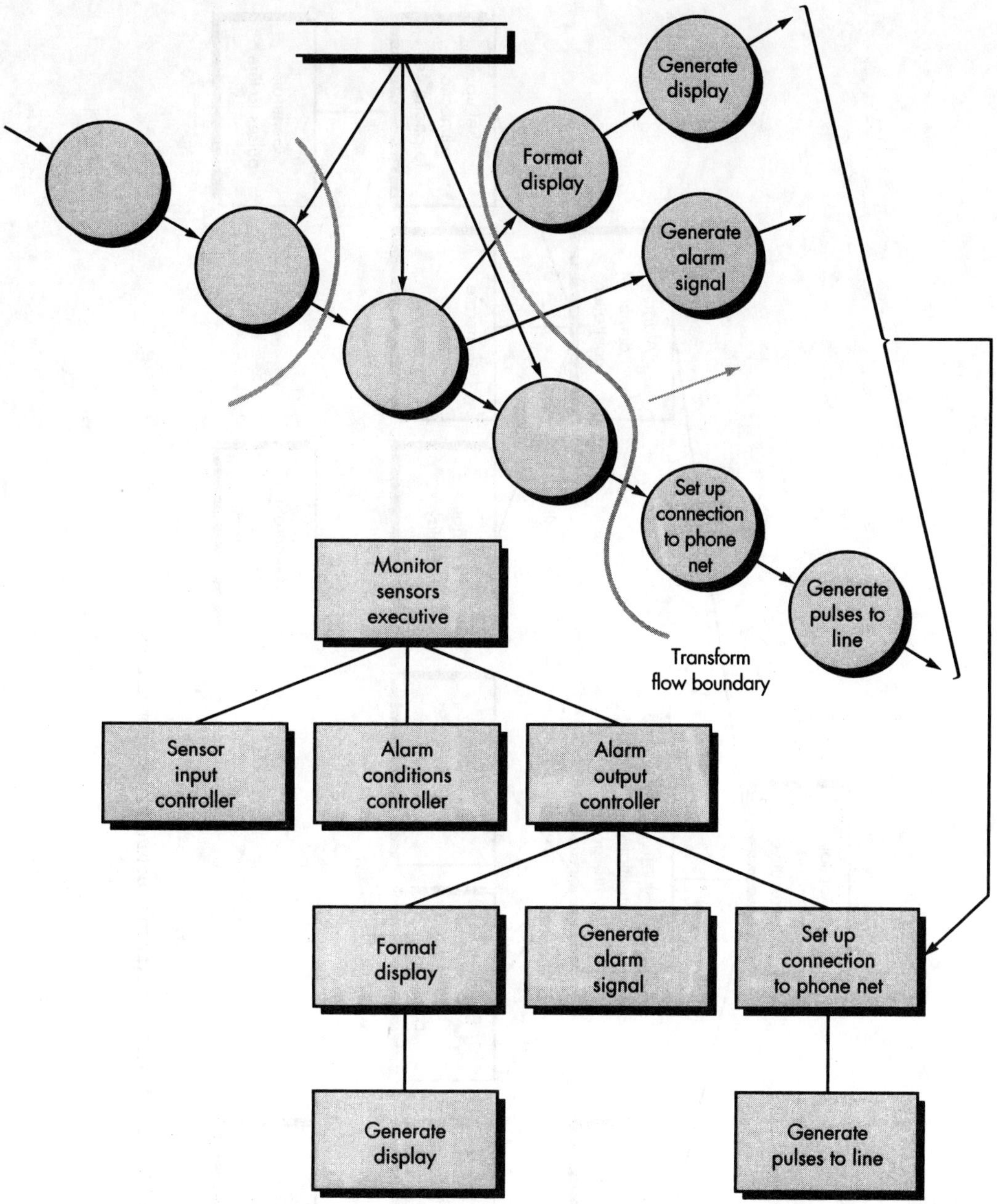

FIGURE 14.10 Second-level factoring for monitor sensors

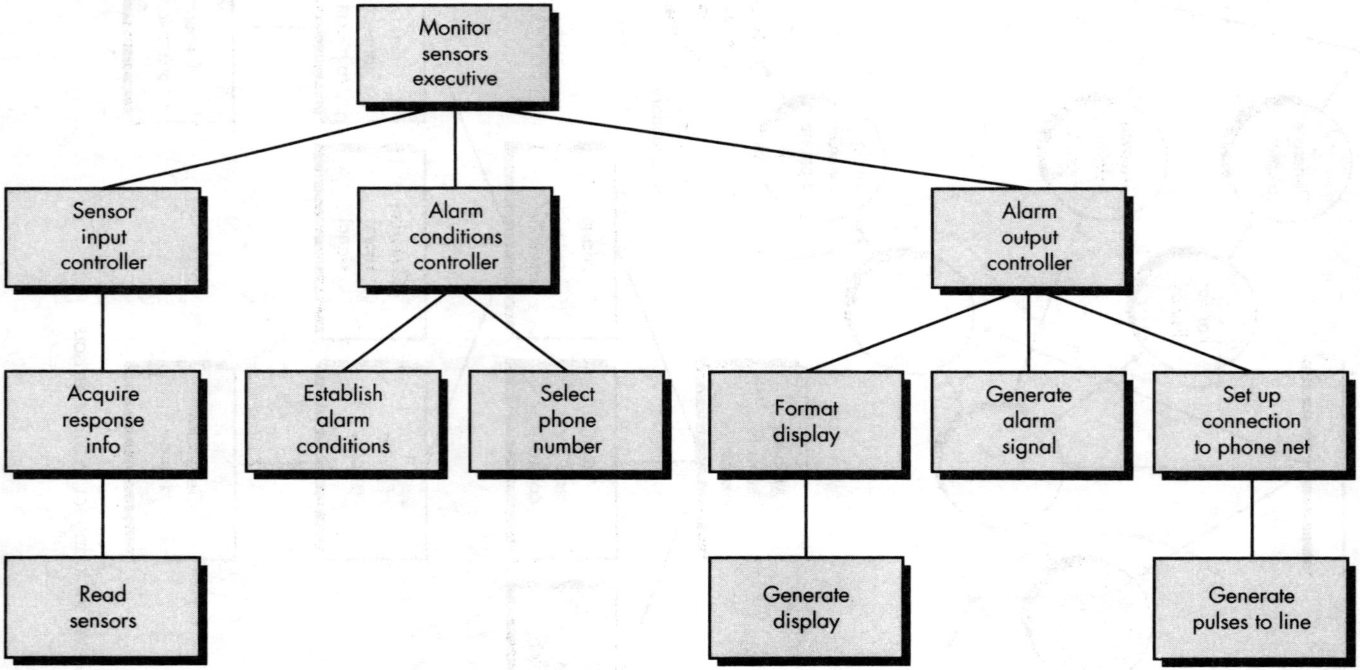

FIGURE 14.11 "First-iteration" program structure for monitor sensors

Step 7. Refine the first-iteration architecture using design heuristics for improved software quality. A first-iteration architecture can always be refined by applying concepts of module independence (Chapter 13). Modules are exploded or imploded to produce sensible factoring, good cohesion, minimal coupling, and most important, a structure that can be implemented without difficulty, tested without confusion, and maintained without grief.

ADVICE

Focus on the functional independence of the modules you've derived. High cohesion and low coupling should be your goal.

Refinements are dictated by the analysis and assessment methods described briefly in Section 14.4, as well as practical considerations and common sense. There are times, for example, when the controller for incoming data flow is totally unnecessary, when some input processing is required in a module that is subordinate to the transform controller, when high coupling due to global data cannot be avoided, or when optimal structural characteristics (see Section 13.6) cannot be achieved. Software requirements coupled with human judgment is the final arbiter.

Many modifications can be made to the first iteration architecture developed for the *SafeHome monitor sensors* subsystem. Among many possibilities,

1. The incoming controller can be removed because it is unnecessary when a single incoming flow path is to be managed.
2. The substructure generated from the transform flow can be imploded into the module *establish alarm conditions* (which will now include the processing implied by *select phone number*). The transform controller will not be needed and the small decrease in cohesion is tolerable.
3. The modules *format display* and *generate display* can be imploded (we assume that display formatting is quite simple) into a new module called *produce display.*

The refined software structure for the monitor sensors subsystem is shown in Figure 14.12.

The objective of the preceding seven steps is to develop an architectural representation of software. That is, once structure is defined, we can evaluate and refine software architecture by viewing it as a whole. Modifications made at this time require little additional work, yet can have a profound impact on software quality.

The reader should pause for a moment and consider the difference between the design approach described and the process of "writing programs." If code is the only representation of software, the developer will have great difficulty evaluating or refining at a global or holistic level and will, in fact, have difficulty "seeing the forest for the trees."

14.7 TRANSACTION MAPPING

In many software applications, a single data item triggers one or a number of information flows that effect a function implied by the triggering data item. The data item,

FIGURE 14.12 Refined program structure for monitor sensors

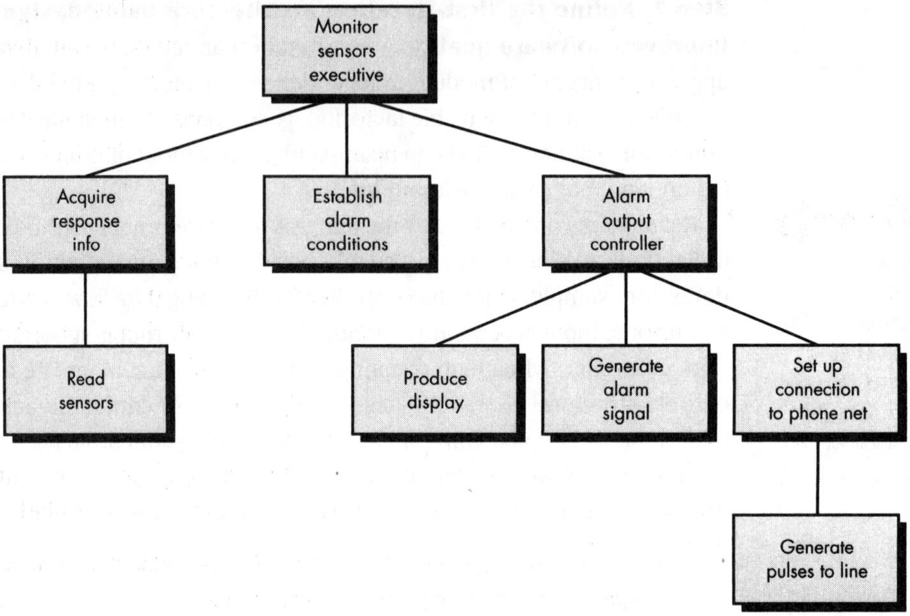

called a *transaction,* and its corresponding flow characteristics are discussed in Section 14.5.2. In this section we consider design steps used to treat transaction flow.

14.7.1 An Example

Transaction mapping will be illustrated by considering the *user interaction* subsystem of the *SafeHome* software. Level 1 data flow for this subsystem is shown as part of Figure 14.6. Refining the flow, a level 2 data flow diagram (a corresponding data dictionary, CSPEC, and PSPECs would also be created) is developed and shown in Figure 14.13.

As shown in the figure, **user commands** flows into the system and results in additional information flow along one of three action paths. A single data item, **command type,** causes the data flow to fan outward from a hub. Therefore, the overall data flow characteristic is transaction oriented.

It should be noted that information flow along two of the three action paths accommodate additional incoming flow (e.g., system parameters and data are input on the "configure" action path). Each action path flows into a single transform, *display messages and status.*

14.7.2 Design Steps

The design steps for transaction mapping are similar and in some cases identical to steps for transform mapping (Section 14.6). A major difference lies in the mapping of DFD to software structure.

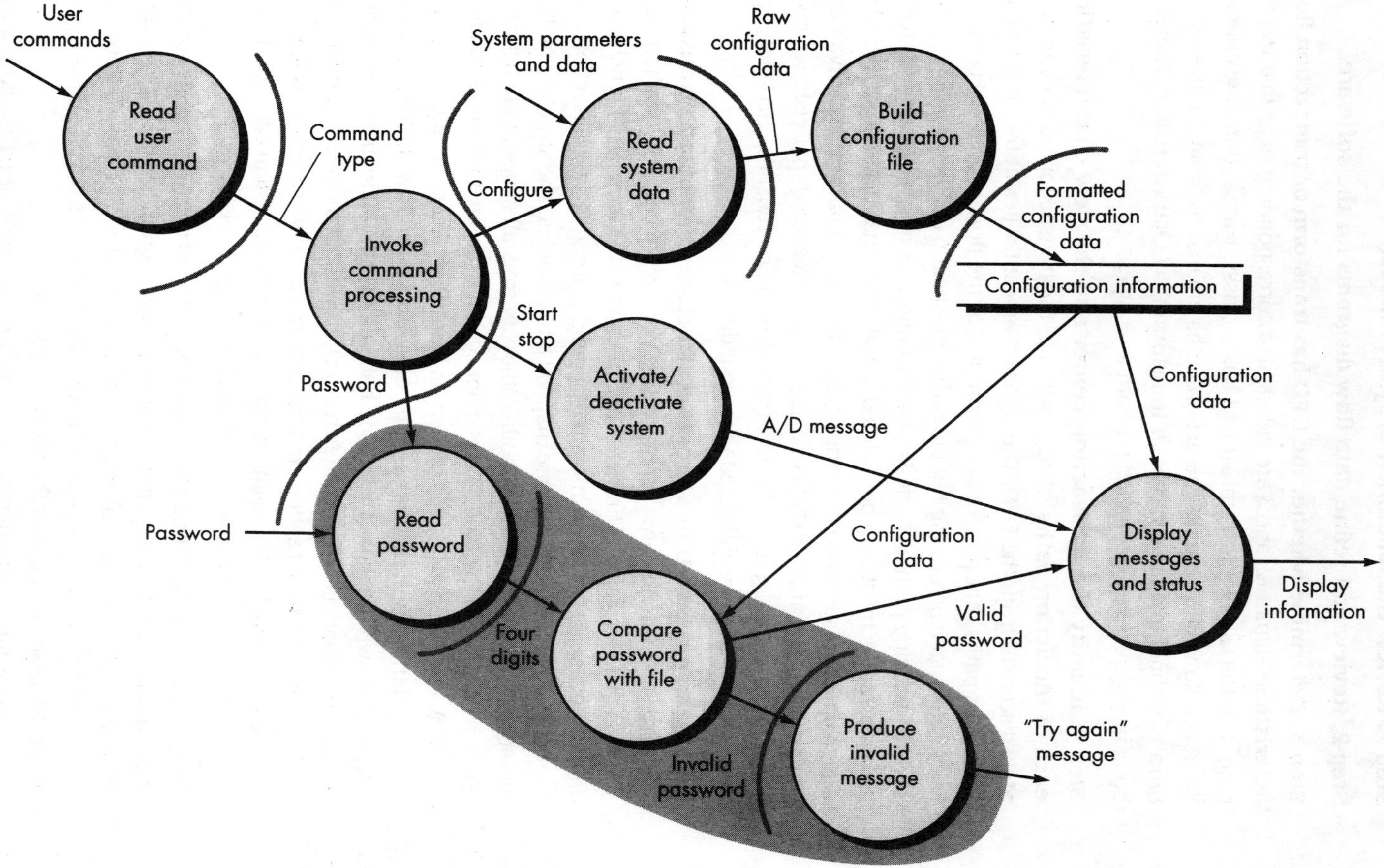

FIGURE 14.13 Level 2 DFD for user interaction subsystem with flow boundaries

Step 1. Review the fundamental system model.

Step 2. Review and refine data flow diagrams for the software.

Step 3. Determine whether the DFD has transform or transaction flow characteristics. Steps 1, 2, and 3 are identical to corresponding steps in transform mapping. The DFD shown in Figure 14.13 has a classic transaction flow characteristic. However, flow along two of the action paths emanating from the *invoke command processing* bubble appears to have transform flow characteristics. Therefore, flow boundaries must be established for both flow types.

Step 4. Identify the transaction center and the flow characteristics along each of the action paths. The location of the transaction center can be immediately discerned from the DFD. The transaction center lies at the origin of a number of actions paths that flow radially from it. For the flow shown in Figure 14.13, the *invoke command processing* bubble is the transaction center.

The incoming path (i.e., the flow path along which a transaction is received) and all action paths must also be isolated. Boundaries that define a reception path and action paths are also shown in the figure. Each action path must be evaluated for its individual flow characteristic. For example, the "password" path (shown enclosed by a shaded area in Figure 14.13) has transform characteristics. Incoming, transform, and outgoing flow are indicated with boundaries.

Step 5. Map the DFD in a program structure amenable to transaction processing. Transaction flow is mapped into an architecture that contains an incoming branch and a dispatch branch. The structure of the incoming branch is developed in much the same way as transform mapping. Starting at the transaction center, bubbles along the incoming path are mapped into modules. The structure of the dispatch branch contains a dispatcher module that controls all subordinate action modules. Each action flow path of the DFD is mapped to a structure that corresponds to its specific flow characteristics. This process is illustrated schematically in Figure 14.14.

KEY POINT

First-level factoring results in the derivation of the control hierarchy for the software. Second-level factoring distributes "worker" modules under the appropriate controller.

Considering the *user interaction* subsystem data flow, first-level factoring for step 5 is shown in Figure 14.15. The bubbles *read user command* and *activate/deactivate system* map directly into the architecture without the need for intermediate control modules. The transaction center, *invoke command processing*, maps directly into a dispatcher module of the same name. Controllers for system configuration and password processing are created as illustrated in Figure 14.14.

Step 6. Factor and refine the transaction structure and the structure of each action path. Each action path of the data flow diagram has its own information flow characteristics. We have already noted that transform or transaction flow may be encountered. The action path-related "substructure" is developed using the design steps discussed in this and the preceding section.

As an example, consider the password processing information flow shown (inside shaded area) in Figure 14.13. The flow exhibits classic transform characteristics. A

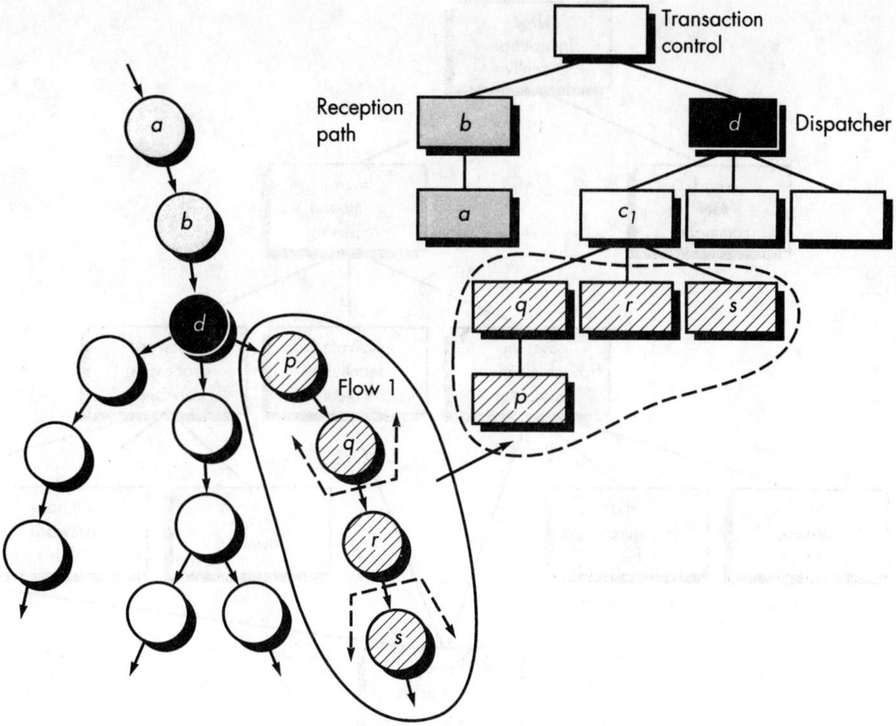

FIGURE 14.14 Transaction mapping

password is input (incoming flow) and transmitted to a transform center where it is compared against stored passwords. An alarm and warning message (outgoing flow) are produced (if a match is not obtained). The "configure" path is drawn similarly using the transform mapping. The resultant software architecture is shown in Figure 14.16.

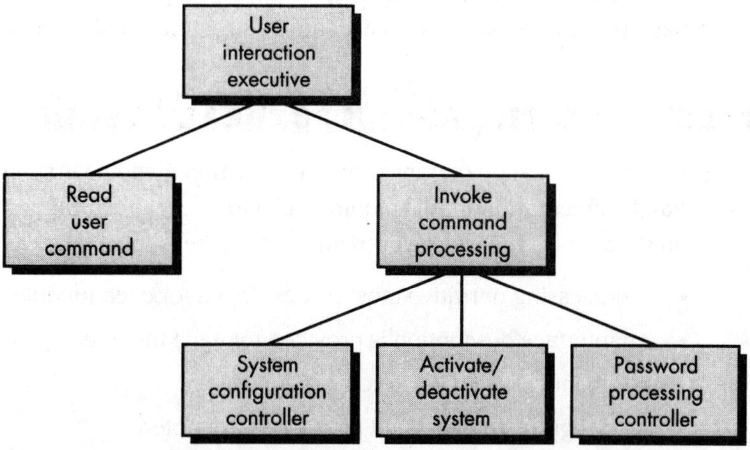

FIGURE 14.15 First-level factoring for user interaction subsystem

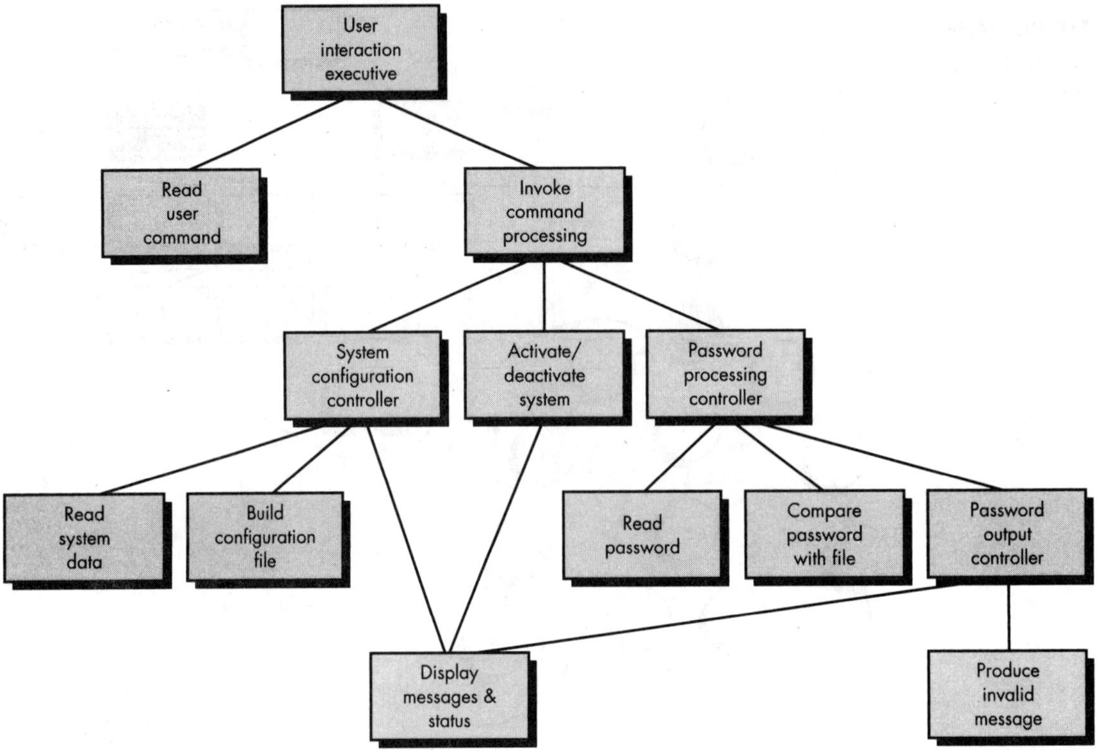

FIGURE 14.16 First-iteration architecture for user interaction subsystem

Step 7. Refine the first-iteration architecture using design heuristics for improved software quality. This step for transaction mapping is identical to the corresponding step for transform mapping. In both design approaches, criteria such as module independence, practicality (efficacy of implementation and test), and maintainability must be carefully considered as structural modifications are proposed.

14.8 REFINING THE ARCHITECTURAL DESIGN

Successful application of transform or transaction mapping is supplemented by additional documentation that is required as part of architectural design. After the program structure has been developed and refined, the following tasks must be completed:

? What happens after the architecture has been created?

- A processing narrative must be developed for each module.
- An interface description is provided for each module.
- Local and global data structures are defined.
- All design restrictions and limitations are noted.

- A set of design reviews are conducted.
- Refinement is considered (if required and justified).

A processing narrative is (ideally) an unambiguous, bounded description of processing that occurs within a module. The narrative describes processing tasks, decisions, and I/O. The interface description describes the design of internal module interfaces, external system interfaces, and the human/computer interface (Chapter 15). The design of data structures can have a profound impact on architecture and the procedural details for each software component. Restrictions and/or limitations for each module are also documented. Typical topics for discussion include restriction on data type or format, memory or timing limitations; bounding values or quantities of data structures; special cases not considered; specific characteristics of an individual module. The purpose of a restrictions and limitations section is to reduce the number of errors introduced because of assumed functional characteristics.

Software Design Specification

Once design documentation has been developed for all modules, one or more design reviews is conducted (see Chapter 8 for review guidelines). The review emphasizes traceability to software requirements, quality of the software architecture, interface descriptions, data structure descriptions, implementation and test practicality, and maintainability.

Any discussion of design refinement should be prefaced with the following comment: "Remember that an 'optimal design' that doesn't work has questionable merit." The software designer should be concerned with developing a representation of software that will meet all functional and performance requirements and merit acceptance based on design measures and heuristics.

Refinement of software architecture during early stages of design is to be encouraged. As we discussed earlier in this chapter, alternative architectural styles may be derived, refined, and evaluated for the "best" approach. This approach to optimization is one of the true benefits derived by developing a representation of software architecture.

It is important to note that structural simplicity often reflects both elegance and efficiency. Design refinement should strive for the smallest number of modules that is consistent with effective modularity and the least complex data structure that adequately serves information requirements.

14.9 SUMMARY

Software architecture provides a holistic view of the system to be built. It depicts the structure and organization of software components, their properties, and the connections between them. Software components include program modules and the various data representations that are manipulated by the program. Therefore, data design is an integral part of the derivation of the software architecture. Architecture highlights early design decisions and provides a mechanism for considering the benefits of alternative system structures.

Data design translates the data objects defined in the analysis model into data structures that reside within the software. The attributes that describe the object, the relationships between data objects and their use within the program all influence the choice of data structures. At a higher level of abstraction, data design may lead to the definition of an architecture for a database or a data warehouse.

A number of different architectural styles and patterns are available to the software engineer. Each style describes a system category that encompasses a set of components that perform a function required by a system, a set of connectors that enable communication, coordination and cooperation among components, constraints that define how components can be integrated to form the system, and semantic models that enable a designer to understand the overall properties of a system.

Once one or more architectural styles have been proposed for a system, an architecture trade-off analysis method may be used to assess the efficacy of each proposed architecture. This is accomplished by determining the sensitivity of selected quality attributes (also called design dimensions) to various realization mechanisms that reflect properties of the architecture.

The architectural design method presented in this chapter uses data flow characteristics described in the analysis model to derive a commonly used architectural style. A data flow diagram is mapped into program structure using one of two mapping approaches—transform mapping or transaction mapping. Transform mapping is applied to an information flow that exhibits distinct boundaries between incoming and outgoing data. The DFD is mapped into a structure that allocates control to input, processing, and output along three separately factored module hierarchies. Transaction mapping is applied when a single information item causes flow to branch along one of many paths. The DFD is mapped into a structure that allocates control to a substructure that acquires and evaluates a transaction. Another substructure controls all potential processing actions based on a transaction.

Once an architecture has been derived, it is elaborated and then analyzed against quality criteria.

Architectural design encompasses the initial set of design activities that lead to a complete design model of the software. In the chapters that follow, the design focus shifts to interfaces and components.

REFERENCES

[AHO83] Aho, A.V., J. Hopcroft, and J. Ullmann, *Data Structures and Algorithms*, Addison-Wesley, 1983.

[ASA96] Asada, T., et al., "The Quantified Design Space," in *Software Architecture* (Shaw, M. and D. Garlan), Prentice-Hall, 1996, pp. 116–127.

[BAS98] Bass, L., P. Clements, and R. Kazman, *Software Architecture in Practice*, Addison-Wesley, 1998.

[BUS96] Buschmann, F., *Pattern-Oriented Software Architecture,* Wiley, 1996.

[DAH72] Dah., O., E. Dijkstra, and C. Hoare, *Structured Programming,* Academic Press, 1972.

[DAT95] Date, C.J., *An Introduction to Database Systems,* 6th ed., Addison-Wesley, 1995.

[DEN73] Dennis, J.B., "Modularity," in *Advanced Course on Software Engineering* (F.L. Bauer, ed.), Springer-Verlag, 1973, pp. 128–182.

[FRE80] Freeman, P., "The Context of Design," in *Software Design Techniques,* 3rd ed. (P. Freeman and A. Wasserman, eds.), IEEE Computer Society Press, 1980, pp. 2–4.

[INM95] Inmon, W.H., "What Is a Data Warehouse?" Prism Solutions, 1995, presented at http://www.cait.wustl.edu/cait/papers/prism/vol1_no1.

[KAZ98] Kazman, R. et al., *The Architectural Tradeoff Analysis Method,* Software Engineering Institute, CMU/SEI-98-TR-008, July 1998.

[KIM98] Kimball, R., L. Reeves, M. Ross, and W. Thornthwaite, *The Data Warehouse Lifecycle Toolkit: Expert Methods for Designing, Developing, and Deploying Data Warehouses,* Wiley, 1998.

[LIN79] Linger, R.C., H.D. Mills, and B.I. Witt, *Structured Programming,* Addison-Wesley, 1979.

[MAT96] Mattison, R., *Data Warehousing: Strategies, Technologies and Techniques,* McGraw-Hill, 1996.

[MYE78] Myers, G., *Composite Structured Design,* Van Nostrand, 1978.

[PRE98] Preiss, B.R., *Data Structures and Algorithms: With Object-Oriented Design Patterns in C++,* Wiley, 1998.

[SHA96] Shaw, M. and D. Garlan, *Software Architecture,* Prentice-Hall, 1996.

[SHA97] Shaw, M. and P. Clements, "A Field Guide to Boxology: Preliminary Classification of Architectural Styles for Software Systems," *Proc. COMPSAC,* Washington, DC, August 1997.

[STE74] Stevens, W., G. Myers, and L. Constantine, "Structured Design," *IBM System Journal,* vol.13, no. 2, 1974, pp.115–139.

[WAS80] Wasserman, A., "Principles of Systematic Data Design and Implementation," in *Software Design Tehcniques* (P. Freeman and A. Wasserman, ed.), 3rd ed., IEEE Computer Society Press, 1980, pp. 287–293.

[WIR71] Wirth, N., "Program Development by Stepwise Refinement," *CACM,* vol. 14, no. 4, 1971, pp. 221–227.

[YOU79] Yourdon, E. and L. Constantine, *Structured Design,* Prentice-Hall, 1979.

[ZHA98] Zhao, J, "On Assessing the Complexity of Software Architectures," *Proc. Intl. Software Architecture Workshop,* ACM, Orlando, FL, 1998, p. 163–167.

PROBLEMS AND POINTS TO PONDER

14.1. Using the architecture of a house or building as a metaphor, draw comparisons with software architecture. How are the disciplines of classical architecture and the software architecture similar? How do they differ?

14.2. Write a three- to five-page paper that presents guidelines for selecting data structures based on the nature of problem. Begin by delineating the classical data structures encountered in software work and then describe criteria for selecting from these for particular types of problems.

14.3. Explain the difference between a database that services one or more conventional business applications and a data warehouse.

14.4. Write a three- to five-page paper that describes how data mining techniques are used in a business context and the current state of KDD techniques.

14.5. Present two or three examples of applications for each of the architectural styles noted in Section 14.3.1.

14.6. Some of the architectural styles noted in Section 14.3.1 are hierarchical in nature and others are not. Make a list of each type. How would the architectural styles that are not hierarchical be implemented?

14.7. Select an application with which you are familiar. Answer each of the questions posed for control and data in Section 14.3.2.

14.8. Research the ATAM (using [KAZ98]) and present a detailed discussion of the six steps presented in Section 14.4.1.

14.9. Select an application with which you are familiar. Using best guesses where required, identify a set of design dimensions and then perform spectrum analysis and design selection analysis.

14.10. Research the QDS (using [ASA96]) and develop a quantified design space for an application with which you are familiar.

14.11. Some designers contend that all data flow may be treated as transform oriented. Discuss how this contention will affect the software architecture that is derived when a transaction-oriented flow is treated as transform. Use an example flow to illustrate important points.

14.12. If you haven't done so, complete problem 12.13. Use the design methods described in this chapter to develop a software architecture for the PHTRS.

14.13. Using a data flow diagram and a processing narrative, describe a computer-based system that has distinct transform flow characteristics. Define flow boundaries and map the DFD into a software structure using the technique described in Section 14.6.

14.14. Using a data flow diagram and a processing narrative, describe a computer-based system that has distinct transaction flow characteristics. Define flow boundaries and map the DFD into a software structure using the technique described in Section 14.7.

14.15. Using requirements that are derived from a classroom discussion, complete the DFDs and architectural design for the *SafeHome* example presented in Sections

14.6 and 14.7. Assess the functional independence of all modules. Document your design.

14.16. Discuss the relative merits and difficulties of applying data flow-oriented design in the following areas: (a) embedded microprocessor applications, (b) engineering/scientific analysis, (c) computer graphics, (d) operating system design, (e) business applications, (f) database management system design, (g) communications software design, (h) compiler design, (i) process control applications, and (j) artificial intelligence applications.

14.17. Given a set of requirements provided by your instructor (or a set of requirements for a problem on which you are currently working) develop a complete architectural design. Conduct a design review (Chapter 8) to assess the quality of your design. This problem may be assigned to a team, rather than an individual.

FURTHER READINGS AND INFORMATION SOURCES

The literature on software architecture has exploded over the past decade. Books by Shaw and Garlan [SHA96], Bass, Clements, and Kazman [BAS98] and Buschmann et al. [BUS96] provide in-depth treatment of the subject. Earlier work by Garlan (*An Introduction to Software Architecture,* Software Engineering Institute, CMU/SEI-94-TR-021, 1994) provides an excellent introduction.

Implementation specific books on architecture address architectural design within a specific development environment or technology. Mowbray (*CORBA Design Patterns,* Wiley, 1997) and Mark et al. (*Object Management Architecture Guide,* Wiley, 1996) provide detailed design guidelines for the CORBA distributed application support framework. Shanley (*Protected Mode Software Architecture,* Addison-Wesley, 1996) provides architectural design guidance for anyone designing PC-based real-time operating systems, multi-task operating systems, or device drivers.

Current software architecture research is documented yearly in the *Proceedings of the International Workshop on Software Architecture,* sponsored by the ACM and other computing organizations, and the *Proceedings of the International Conference on Software Engineering.*

Data modeling is a prerequisite to good data design. Books by Teory (*Database Modeling and Design,* Academic Press, 1998); Schmidt (*Data Modeling for Information Professionals,* Prentice-Hall, 1998); Bobak (*Data Modeling and Design for Today's Architectures,* Artech House, 1997); Silverston, Graziano, and Inmon (*The Data Model Resource Book,* Wiley, 1997); Date [DAT95], Reingruber and Gregory (*The Data Modeling Handbook: A Best-Practice Approach to Building Quality Data Models,* Wiley, 1994); and Hay (*Data Model Patterns: Conventions of Thought,* Dorset House, 1994) contain detailed presentations of data modeling notation, heuristics, and database design approaches. The design of data warehouses has become increasingly important in recent years. Books by Humphreys, Hawkins, and Dy (*Data Warehousing: Architecture and Implementation,* Prentice-Hall, 1999); Kimball et al. [KIM98]; and Inmon [INM95] cover the topic in considerable detail.

Dozens of current books address data design and data structures, usually in the context of a specific programming language. Typical examples are

Horowitz, E. and S. Sahni, *Fundamentals of Data Structures in Pascal,* 4th ed., W.H. Freeman and Co., 1999.

Kingston, J.H., *Algorithms and Data Structures: Design, Correctness, Analysis,* 2nd ed., Addison-Wesley, 1997.

Main, M., *Data Structures and Other Objects Using Java,* Addison-Wesley, 1998.

Preiss, B.R., *Data Structures and Algorithms: With Object-Oriented Design Patterns in C++,* Wiley, 1998.

Sedgewick, R., *Algorithms in C++: Fundamentals, Data Structures, Sorting, Searching,* Addison-Wesley, 1999.

Standish, T.A., *Data Structures in Java,* Addison-Wesley, 1997.

Standish, T.A., *Data Structures, Algorithms, and Software Principles in C,* Addison-Wesley, 1995.

General treatment of software design with discussion of architectural and data design issues can be found in most books dedicated to software engineering. Books by Pfleeger (*Software Engineering: Theory and Practice,* Prentice-Hall, 1998) and Sommerville (*Software Engineering,* 5th ed., Addison-Wesley,1996) are representative of those that cover design issues in some detail.

More rigorous treatments of the subject can be found in Feijs (*Formalization of Design Methods,* Prentice-Hall, 1993), Witt et al. (*Software Architecture and Design Principles,* Thomson Publishing, 1994), and Budgen (*Software Design,* Addison-Wesley, 1994).

Complete presentations of data flow-oriented design may be found in Myers [MYE78], Yourdon and Constantine [YOU79], Buhr (*System Design with Ada,* Prentice-Hall, 1984), and Page-Jones (*The Practical Guide to Structured Systems Design,* 2nd ed., Prentice-Hall, 1988). These books are dedicated to design alone and provide comprehensive tutorials in the data flow approach.

A wide variety of information sources on software design and related subjects is available on the Internet. An up-to-date list of World Wide Web references that are relevant to design concepts and methods can be found at the SEPA Web site:
http://www.mhhe.com/engcs/compsci/pressman/resources/arch-design.mhtml

CHAPTER

15 USER INTERFACE DESIGN

The blueprint for a house (its architectural design) is not complete without a representation of doors, windows, and utility connections for water, electricity, and telephone (not to mention cable TV). The "doors, windows, and utility connections" for computer software make up the interface design of a system.

Interface design focuses on three areas of concern: (1) the design of interfaces between software components, (2) the design of interfaces between the software and other nonhuman producers and consumers of information (i.e., other external entities), and (3) the design of the interface between a human (i.e., the user) and the computer. In this chapter we focus exclusively on the third interface design category—user interface design.

In the preface to his classic book on user interface design, Ben Shneiderman [SHN90] states:

> Frustration and anxiety are part of daily life for many users of computerized information systems. They struggle to learn command language or menu selection systems that are supposed to help them do their job. Some people encounter such serious cases of computer shock, terminal terror, or network neurosis that they avoid using computerized systems.

QUICK LOOK

What is it? User interface design creates an effective communication medium between a human and a computer. Following a set of interface design principles, design identifies interface objects and actions and then creates a screen layout that forms the basis for a user interface prototype.

Who does it? A software engineer designs the user interface by applying an iterative process that draws on predefined design principles.

Why is it important? If software is difficult to use, if it forces you into mistakes, or if it frustrates your efforts to accomplish your goals, you won't like it, regardless of the computational power it exhibits or the functionality it offers. Because it molds a user's perception of the software, the interface has to be right.

What are the steps? User interface design begins with the identification of user, task, and environmental requirements. Once user tasks have been identified, user scenarios are created and analyzed to define a set of interface objects and actions. These form the basis for the creation of screen layout that depicts graphical design and placement of icons, definition of descriptive screen text, specification and titling for windows, and specification of major and minor menu items. Tools are used to prototype and ultimately implement the design model, and the result is evaluated for quality.

QUICK LOOK

What is the work product? User scenarios are created and screen layouts are generated. An interface prototype is developed and modified in an iterative fashion.

How do I ensure that I've done it right? The prototype is "test driven" by the users and feedback from the test drive is used for the next iterative modification of the prototype.

The problems to which Shneiderman alludes are real. It is true that graphical user interfaces, windows, icons, and mouse picks have eliminated many of the most horrific interface problems. But even in a "Windows world," we all have encountered user interfaces that are difficult to learn, difficult to use, confusing, unforgiving, and in many cases, totally frustrating. Yet, someone spent time and energy building each of these interfaces, and it is not likely that the builder created these problems purposely.

User interface design has as much to do with the study of people as it does with technology issues. Who is the user? How does the user learn to interact with a new computer-based system? How does the user interpret information produced by the system? What will the user expect of the system? These are only a few of the many questions that must be asked and answered as part of user interface design.

15.1 THE GOLDEN RULES

In his book on interface design, Theo Mandel [MAN97] coins three "golden rules":

1. Place the user in control.
2. Reduce the user's memory load.
3. Make the interface consistent.

These golden rules actually form the basis for a set of user interface design principles that guide this important software design activity.

15.1.1 Place the User in Control

During a requirements-gathering session for a major new information system, a key user was asked about the attributes of the window-oriented graphical interface.

"What I really would like," said the user solemnly, "is a system that reads my mind. It knows what I want to do before I need to do it and makes it very easy for me to get it done. That's all, just that."

My first reaction was to shake of my head and smile, but I paused for a moment. There was absolutely nothing wrong with the user's request. She wanted a system that reacted to her needs and helped her get things done. She wanted to control the computer, not have the computer control her.

Most interface constraints and restrictions that are imposed by a designer are intended to simplify the mode of interaction. But for whom? In many cases, the designer might introduce constraints and limitations to simplify the implementation of the interface. The result may be an interface that is easy to build, but frustrating to use.

Mandel [MAN97] defines a number of design principles that allow the user to maintain control:

? How do we design interfaces that allow the user to maintain control?

Define interaction modes in a way that does not force a user into unnecessary or undesired actions. An interaction mode is the current state of the interface. For example, if *spell check* is selected in a word-processor menu, the software moves to a spell checking mode. There is no reason to force the user to remain in spell checking mode if the user desires to make a small text edit along the way. The user should be able to enter and exit the mode with little or no effort.

Provide for flexible interaction. Because different users have different interaction preferences, choices should be provided. For example, software might allow a user to interact via keyboard commands, mouse movement, a digitizer pen, or voice recognition commands. But every action is not amenable to every interaction mechanism. Consider, for example, the difficulty of using keyboard command (or voice input) to draw a complex shape.

Quote:

"A common mistake that people make when trying to design something completely foolproof is to underestimate the ingenuity of complete fools."

Douglas Adams

Allow user interaction to be interruptible and undoable. Even when involved in a sequence of actions, the user should be able to interrupt the sequence to do something else (without losing the work that had been done). The user should also be able to "undo" any action.

Streamline interaction as skill levels advance and allow the interaction to be customized. Users often find that they perform the same sequence of interactions repeatedly. It is worthwhile to design a "macro" mechanism that enables an advanced user to customize the interface to facilitate interaction.

Hide technical internals from the casual user. The user interface should move the user into the virtual world of the application. The user should not be aware of the operating system, file management functions, or other arcane computing technology. In essence, the interface should never require that the user interact at a level that is "inside" the machine (e.g., a user should never be required to type operating system commands from within application software).

Design for direct interaction with objects that appear on the screen. The user feels a sense of control when able to manipulate the objects that are necessary to perform a task in a manner similar to what would occur if the object were a physical thing. For example, an application interface that allows a user to "stretch" an object (scale it in size) is an implementation of direct manipulation.

15.1.2 Reduce the User's Memory Load

The more a user has to remember, the more error-prone will be the interaction with the system. It is for this reason that a well-designed user interface does not tax the user's memory. Whenever possible, the system should "remember" pertinent information and assist the user with an interaction scenario that assists recall. Mandel [MAN97] defines design principles that enable an interface to reduce the user's memory load:

How do we design interfaces that reduce the user's memory load?

Reduce demand on short-term memory. When users are involved in complex tasks, the demand on short-term memory can be significant. The interface should be designed to reduce the requirement to remember past actions and results. This can be accomplished by providing visual cues that enable a user to recognize past actions, rather than having to recall them.

Establish meaningful defaults. The initial set of defaults should make sense for the average user, but a user should be able to specify individual preferences. However, a "reset" option should be available, enabling the redefinition of original default values.

Define shortcuts that are intuitive. When mnemonics are used to accomplish a system function (e.g., alt-P to invoke the print function), the mnemonic should be tied to the action in a way that is easy to remember (e.g., first letter of the task to be invoked).

Quote:

"The interface from hell: 'Enter any 11-digit prime number to continue . . .' "

author unknown

The visual layout of the interface should be based on a real world metaphor. For example, a bill payment system should use a check book and check register metaphor to guide the user through the bill paying process. This enables the user to rely on well-understood visual cues, rather than memorizing an arcane interaction sequence.

Disclose information in a progressive fashion. The interface should be organized hierarchically. That is, information about a task, an object, or some behavior should be presented first at a high level of abstraction. More detail should be presented after the user indicates interest with a mouse pick. An example, common to many word-processing applications, is the underlining function. The function itself is one of a number of of functions under a text style menu. However, every underlining capability is not listed. The user must pick underlining, then all underlining options (e.g., single underline, double underline, dashed underline) are presented.

15.1.3 Make the Interface Consistent

The interface should present and acquire information in a consistent fashion. This implies that (1) all visual information is organized according to a design standard that is maintained throughout all screen displays, (2) input mechanisms are constrained to a limited set that are used consistently throughout the application, and (3) mechanisms for navigating from task to task are consistently defined and implemented. Mandel [MAN97] defines a set of design principles that help make the interface consistent:

? How do we design interfaces that are consistent?

Allow the user to put the current task into a meaningful context. Many interfaces implement complex layers of interactions with dozens of screen images. It is important to provide indicators (e.g., window titles, graphical icons, consistent color coding) that enable the user to know the context of the work at hand. In addition, the user should be able to determine where he has come from and what alternatives exist for a transition to a new task.

Maintain consistency across a family of applications. A set of applications (or products) should all implement the same design rules so that consistency is maintained for all interaction.

If past interactive models have created user expectations, do not make changes unless there is a compelling reason to do so. Once a particular interactive sequence has become a de facto standard (e.g., the use of alt-S to save a file), the user expects this in every application he encounters. A change (e.g., using alt-S to invoke scaling) will cause confusion.

The interface design principles discussed in this and the preceding sections provide basic guidance for a software engineer. In the sections that follow, we examine the interface design process itself.

15.2 USER INTERFACE DESIGN

The overall process for designing a user interface begins with the creation of different models of system function (as perceived from the outside). The human- and computer-oriented tasks that are required to achieve system function are then delineated; design issues that apply to all interface designs are considered; tools are used to prototype and ultimately implement the design model; and the result is evaluated for quality.

15.2.1 Interface Design Models

WebRef
An excellent source of GUI design guidelines, methods, and references can be found at **www.ibm.com/ibm/easy/**

Four different models come into play when a user interface is to be designed. The software engineer creates a *design model,* a human engineer (or the software engineer) establishes a *user model,* the end-user develops a mental image that is often called the *user's model* or the *system perception,* and the implementers of the system create a *system image* [RUB88]. Unfortunately, each of these models may differ significantly. The role of interface designer is to reconcile these differences and derive a consistent representation of the interface.

A design model of the entire system incorporates data, architectural, interface, and procedural representations of the software. The requirements specification may establish certain constraints that help to define the user of the system, but the interface design is often only incidental to the design model.[1]

The user model establishes the profile of end-users of the system. To build an effective user interface, "all design should begin with an understanding of the intended users, including profiles of their age, sex, physical abilities, education, cultural or ethnic background, motivation, goals and personality" [SHN90]. In addition, users can be categorized as

Quote:

"USER, n.: The word computer professionals use when they mean 'idiot.'"

Dave Barry

- **Novices.** No *syntactic knowledge*[2] of the system and little *semantic knowledge*[3] of the application or computer usage in general.
- **Knowledgeable, intermittent users.** Reasonable semantic knowledge of the application but relatively low recall of syntactic information necessary to use the interface.
- **Knowledgeable, frequent users.** Good semantic and syntactic knowledge that often leads to the "power-user syndrome"; that is, individuals who look for shortcuts and abbreviated modes of interaction.

The system perception (user's model) is the image of the system that end-users carry in their heads. For example, if the user of a particular word processor were asked to describe its operation, the system perception would guide the response. The accuracy of the description will depend upon the user's profile (e.g., novices would provide a sketchy response at best) and overall familiarity with software in the application domain. A user who understands word processors fully but has worked with the specific word processor only once might actually be able to provide a more complete description of its function than the novice who has spent weeks trying to learn the system.

KEY POINT

When the system image and the system perception coincide, the user can apply the application effectively.

The system image combines the outward manifestation of the computer-based system (the look and feel of the interface), coupled with all supporting information (books, manuals, videotapes, help files) that describe system syntax and semantics. When the system image and the system perception are coincident, users generally feel comfortable with the software and use it effectively. To accomplish this "melding" of the models, the design model must have been developed to accommodate the information contained in the user model, and the system image must accurately reflect syntactic and semantic information about the interface.

The models described in this section are "abstractions of what the user is doing or thinks he is doing or what somebody else thinks he ought to be doing when he

1 Of course, this is not as it should be. For interactive systems, the interface design is as important as the data, architectural, or component-level design.

2 In this context, *syntactic knowledge* refers to the mechanics of interaction that is required to use the interface effectively.

3 *Semantic knowledge* refers to an underlying sense of the application—an understanding of the functions that are performed, the meaning of input and output, and the goals and objectives of the system.

FIGURE 15.1
The user interface design process

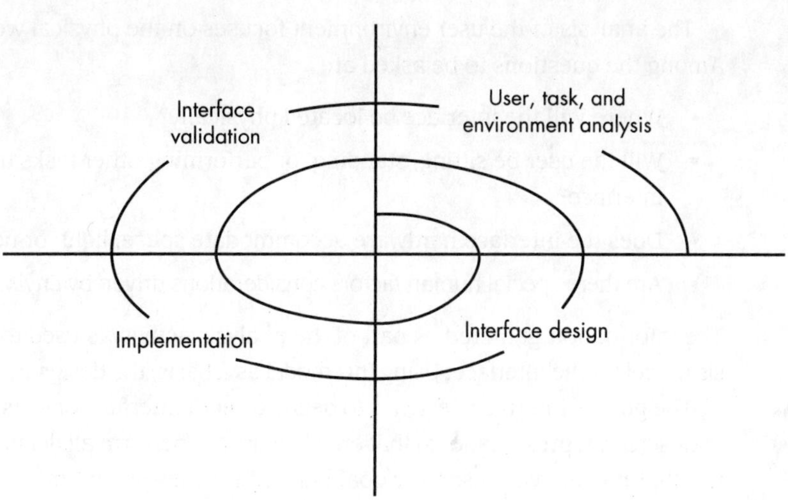

uses an interactive system" [MON84]. In essence, these models enable the interface designer to satisfy a key element of the most important principle of user interface design: "Know the user, know the tasks."

15.2.2 The User Interface Design Process

The design process for user interfaces is iterative and can be represented using a spiral model similar to the one discussed in Chapter 2. Referring to Figure 15.1, the user interface design process encompasses four distinct framework activities [MAN97]:

1. User, task, and environment analysis and modeling
2. Interface design
3. Interface construction
4. Interface validation

The spiral shown in Figure 15.1 implies that each of these tasks will occur more than once, with each pass around the spiral representing additional elaboration of requirements and the resultant design. In most cases, the implementation activity involves prototyping—the only practical way to validate what has been designed.

Quote:
"I never design a building before I've seen the site and met the people who will be using it."
Frank Lloyd Wright

The initial analysis activity focuses on the profile of the users who will interact with the system. Skill level, business understanding, and general receptiveness to the new system are recorded; and different user categories are defined. For each user category, requirements are elicited. In essence, the software engineer attempts to understand the system perception (Section 15.2.1) for each class of users.

Once general requirements have been defined, a more detailed task analysis is conducted. Those tasks that the user performs to accomplish the goals of the system are identified, described, and elaborated (over a number of iterative passes through the spiral). Task analysis is discussed in more detail in Section 15.3.

The analysis of the user environment focuses on the physical work environment. Among the questions to be asked are

- Where will the interface be located physically?
- Will the user be sitting, standing, or performing other tasks unrelated to the interface?
- Does the interface hardware accommodate space, light, or noise constraints?
- Are there special human factors considerations driven by environmental factors?

The information gathered as part of the analysis activity is used to create an analysis model for the interface. Using this model as a basis, the design activity commences.

? What is the goal of user interface design?

The goal of interface design is to define a set of interface objects and actions (and their screen representations) that enable a user to perform all defined tasks in a manner that meets every usability goal defined for the system. Interface design is discussed in more detail in Section 15.4.

The implementation activity normally begins with the creation of a prototype that enables usage scenarios to be evaluated. As the iterative design process continues, a user interface tool kit (Section 15.5) may be used to complete the construction of the interface.

Validation focuses on (1) the ability of the interface to implement every user task correctly, to accommodate all task variations, and to achieve all general user requirements; (2) the degree to which the interface is easy to use and easy to learn; and (3) the users' acceptance of the interface as a useful tool in their work.

As we have already noted, the activities described in this section occur iteratively. Therefore, there is no need to attempt to specify every detail (for the analysis or design model) on the first pass. Subsequent passes through the process elaborate task detail, design information, and the operational features of the interface.

15.3 TASK ANALYSIS AND MODELING

In Chapter 13, we discussed stepwise elaboration (also called functional decomposition or stepwise refinement) as a mechanism for refining the processing tasks that are required for software to accomplish some desired function. Later in this book, we consider object-oriented analysis as a modeling approach for computer-based systems. *Task analysis* for interface design uses either an elaborative or object-oriented approach but applies this approach to human activities.

Task analysis can be applied in two ways. As we have already noted, an interactive, computer-based system is often used to replace a manual or semi-manual activity. To understand the tasks that must be performed to accomplish the goal of the activity, a human engineer[4] must understand the tasks that humans currently perform (when using a manual approach) and then map these into a similar (but not necessarily identical) set of tasks that are implemented in the context of the user interface. Alternatively, the human engineer can study an existing specification for a computer-based solution and derive a set of user tasks that will accommodate the user model, the design model, and the system perception.

KEY POINT

Human tasks are defined and classified as part of task analysis. A process of elaboration is used to refine tasks. Alternatively, objects and actions are identified and refined.

Regardless of the overall approach to task analysis, a human engineer must first define and classify tasks. We have already noted that one approach is stepwise elaboration. For example, assume that a small software company wants to build a computer-aided design system explicitly for interior designers. By observing an interior designer at work, the engineer notices that interior design comprises a number of major activities: furniture layout, fabric and material selection, wall and window coverings selection, presentation (to the customer), costing, and shopping. Each of these major tasks can be elaborated into subtasks. For example, furniture layout can be refined into the following tasks: (1) draw a floor plan based on room dimensions; (2) place windows and doors at appropriate locations; (3) use furniture templates to draw scaled furniture outlines on floor plan; (4) move furniture outlines to get best placement; (5) label all furniture outlines; (6) draw dimensions to show location; (7) draw perspective view for customer. A similar approach could be used for each of the other major tasks.

Subtasks 1–7 can each be refined further. Subtasks 1–6 will be performed by manipulating information and performing actions within the user interface. On the other hand, subtask 7 can be performed automatically in software and will result in little direct user interaction. The design model of the interface should accommodate each of these tasks in a way that is consistent with the user model (the profile of a "typical" interior designer) and system perception (what the interior designer expects from an automated system).

XRef

Object-oriented analysis techniques can be applied during task analysis. These are discussed in Chapter 21.

An alternative approach to task analysis takes an object-oriented point of view. The human engineer observes the physical objects that are used by the interior designer and the actions that are applied to each object. For example, the furniture template would be an object in this approach to task analysis. The interior designer would *select* the appropriate template, *move* it to a position on the floor plan, *trace* the furniture outline and so forth. The design model for the interface would not provide a literal implementation for each of these actions, but it would define user tasks that accomplish the end result (drawing furniture outlines on the floor plan).

4 In many cases the activities described in this section are performed by a software engineer. Ideally, the individual has had some training in human engineering and user interface design.

15.4 INTERFACE DESIGN ACTIVITIES

Once task analysis has been completed, all tasks (or objects and actions) required by the end-user have been identified in detail and the interface design activity commences. The first interface design steps [NOR86] can be accomplished using the following approach:

? What steps do we perform to accomplish interface design?

1. Establish the goals[5] and intentions for each task.
2. Map each goal and intention to a sequence of specific actions.
3. Specify the action sequence of tasks and subtasks, also called a *user scenario,* as it will be executed at the interface level.
4. Indicate the state of the system; that is, what does the interface look like at the time that a user scenario is performed?
5. Define control mechanisms; that is, the objects and actions available to the user to alter the system state.
6. Show how control mechanisms affect the state of the system.
7. Indicate how the user interprets the state of the system from information provided through the interface.

Always following the golden rules discussed in Section 15.1, the interface designer must also consider how the interface will be implemented, the environment (e.g., display technology, operating system, development tools) that will be used, and other elements of the application that "sit behind" the interface.

15.4.1 Defining Interface Objects and Actions

XRef
A complete discussion of the grammatical parse can be found in Section 12.6.2.

An important step in interface design is the definition of interface objects and the actions that are applied to them. To accomplish this, the user scenario is parsed in much the same way as processing narratives were parsed in Chapter 12. That is, a description of a user scenario is written. Nouns (objects) and verbs (actions) are isolated to create a list of objects and actions.

Once the objects and actions have been defined and elaborated iteratively, they are categorized by type. Target, source, and application objects are identified. A *source object* (e.g., a report icon) is dragged and dropped onto a *target object* (e.g., a printer icon). The implication of this action is to create a hard-copy report. An *application object* represents application-specific data that is not directly manipulated as part of screen interaction. For example, a mailing list is used to store names for a mailing. The list itself might be sorted, merged, or purged (menu-based actions) but it is not dragged and dropped via user interaction.

5 Goals include a consideration of the usefulness of the task, its effectiveness in accomplishing the overriding business objective, the degree to which the task can be learned quickly, and the degree to which users will be satisfied with the ultimate implementation of the task.

What is screen layout and how is it applied?

When the designer is satisfied that all important objects and actions have been defined (for one design iteration), *screen layout* is performed. Like other interface design activities, screen layout is an interactive process in which graphical design and placement of icons, definition of descriptive screen text, specification and titling for windows, and definition of major and minor menu items is conducted. If a real world metaphor is appropriate for the application, it is specified at this time and the layout is organized in a manner that complements the metaphor.

To provide a brief illustration of the design steps noted previously, we consider a user scenario for an advanced version of the *SafeHome* system (discussed in earlier chapters). In the advanced version, *SafeHome* can be accessed via modem or through the Internet. A PC application allows the homeowner to check the status of the house from a remote location, reset the *SafeHome* configuration, arm and disarm the system, and (using an extra cost video option[6]) monitor rooms within the house visually. A preliminary user scenario for the interface follows:

XRef
The scenario described here is similar to use-cases described in Chapter 11.

Scenario: The homeowner wishes to gain access to the *SafeHome* system installed in his house. Using software operating on a remote PC (e.g., a notebook computer carried by the homeowner while at work or traveling), the homeowner determines the status of the alarm system, arms or disarms the system, reconfigures security zones, and views different rooms within the house via preinstalled video cameras.

To access *SafeHome* from a remote location, the homeowner provides an identifier and a password. These define levels of access (e.g., all users may not be able to reconfigure the system) and provide security. Once validated, the user (with full access privileges) checks the status of the system and changes status by arming or disarming *SafeHome.* The user reconfigures the system by displaying a floor plan of the house, viewing each of the security sensors, displaying each currently configured zone, and modifying zones as required. The user views the interior of the house via strategically placed video cameras. The user can pan and zoom each camera to provide different views of the interior.

Homeowner tasks:

- *accesses* the *SafeHome* system
- *enters* an **ID** and **password** to allow remote access
- *checks* **system status**
- *arms* or *disarms SafeHome* system
- *displays* **floor plan** and **sensor locations**
- *displays* **zones** on floor plan
- *changes* **zones** on floor plan
- *displays* **video camera locations** on floor plan
- *selects* **video camera** for viewing
- *views* **video images** (4 frames per second)
- *pans* or *zooms* the **video camera**

6 The video option enables the homeowner to place video cameras at key locations throughout a house and peruse the output from a remote location. Big Brother?

Objects (boldface) and actions (italics) are extracted from this list of homeowner tasks. The majority of objects noted are application objects. However, video camera location (a source object) is dragged and dropped onto video camera (a target object) to create a video image (a window with video display).

A preliminary sketch of the screen layout for video monitoring is created (Figure 15.2). To invoke the video image, a **video camera location** icon, *C*, located in **floor plan** displayed in the **monitoring window** is selected. In this case a camera location in the living room, LR, is then dragged and dropped onto the **video camera** icon in the upper left-hand portion of the screen. The **video image window** appears, displaying streaming video from the camera located in the living room (LR). The **zoom** and **pan** control slides are used to control the magnification and direction of the video image. To select a view from another camera, the user simply drags and drops a different **camera location** icon into the **camera** icon in the upper left-hand corner of the screen.

The layout sketch shown would have to be supplemented with an expansion of each menu item within the menu bar, indicating what actions are available for the

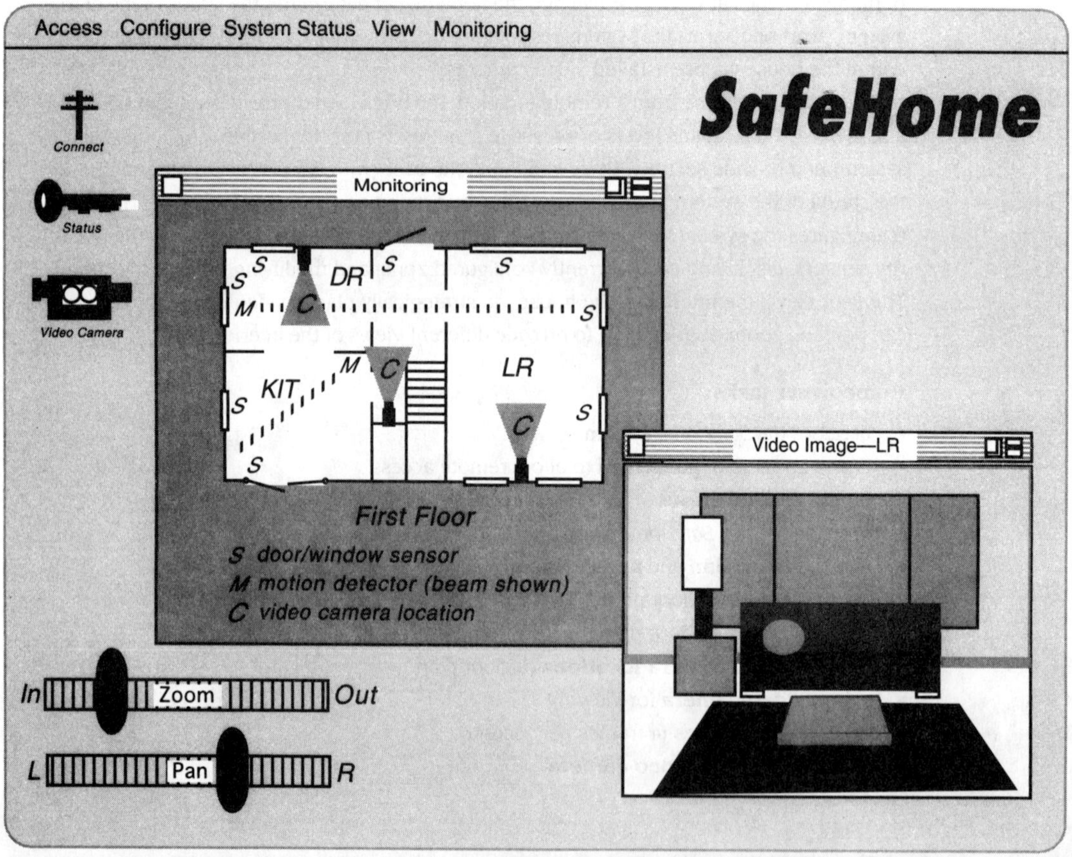

FIGURE 5.2 Preliminary screen layout

video monitoring mode (state). A complete set of sketches for each homeowner task noted in the user scenario would be created during the interface design.

15.4.2 Design Issues

As the design of a user interface evolves, four common design issues almost always surface: system response time, user help facilities, error information handling, and command labeling. Unfortunately, many designers do not address these issues until relatively late in the design process (sometimes the first inkling of a problem doesn't occur until an operational prototype is available). Unnecessary iteration, project delays, and customer frustration often result. It is far better to establish each as a design issue to be considered at the beginning of software design, when changes are easy and costs are low.

System response time is the primary complaint for many interactive applications. In general, system response time is measured from the point at which the user performs some control action (e.g., hits the return key or clicks a mouse) until the software responds with desired output or action.

System response time has two important characteristics: length and variability. If the *length* of system response is too long, user frustration and stress is the inevitable result. However, a very brief response time can also be detrimental if the user is being paced by the interface. A rapid response may force the user to rush and therefore make mistakes.

ADVICE

If variable response is unavoidable, be certain to provide some visual indication of progress, so that the user is aware of what is happening.

Variability refers to the deviation from average response time, and in many ways, it is the most important response time characteristic. Low variability enables the user to establish an interaction rhythm, even if response time is relatively long. For example, a 1-second response to a command is preferable to a response that varies from 0.1 to 2.5 seconds. The user is always off balance, always wondering whether something "different" has occurred behind the scenes.

Almost every user of an interactive, computer-based system requires help now and then. In some cases, a simple question addressed to a knowledgeable colleague can do the trick. In others, detailed research in a multivolume set of "user manuals" may be the only option. In many cases, however, modern software provides on-line help facilities that enable a user to get a question answered or resolve a problem without leaving the interface.

Two different types of help facilities are encountered: integrated and add-on [RUB88]. An *integrated help facility* is designed into the software from the beginning. It is often context sensitive, enabling the user to select from those topics that are relevant to the actions currently being performed. Obviously, this reduces the time required for the user to obtain help and increases the "friendliness" of the interface. An *add-on help facility* is added to the software after the system has been built. In many ways, it is really an on-line user's manual with limited query capability. The user may have to search through a list of hundreds of topics to find appropriate guidance, often making many false starts and receiving much irrelevant information. There is little doubt that the integrated help facility is preferable to the add-on approach.

What design issues should be considered when we build a help facility?

A number of design issues [RUB88] must be addressed when a help facility is considered:

- Will help be available for all system functions and at all times during system interaction? Options include help for only a subset of all functions and actions or help for all functions.
- How will the user request help? Options include a help menu, a special function key, or a HELP command.
- How will help be represented? Options include a separate window, a reference to a printed document (less than ideal), or a one- or two-line suggestion produced in a fixed screen location.
- How will the user return to normal interaction? Options include a return button displayed on the screen, a function key, or control sequence.
- How will help information be structured? Options include a "flat" structure in which all information is accessed through a keyword, a layered hierarchy of information that provides increasing detail as the user proceeds into the structure, or the use of hypertext.

Error messages and warnings are "bad news" delivered to users of interactive systems when something has gone awry. At their worst, error messages and warnings impart useless or misleading information and serve only to increase user frustration. There are few computer users who have not encountered an error of the form:

ADVICE

Spend twice as much effort and expend twice as many words on troubleshooting as you think you'll need for your help facility, and you'll probably get it about right.

SEVERE SYSTEM FAILURE -- 14A

Somewhere, an explanation for error 14A must exist; otherwise, why would the designers have added the identification? Yet, the error message provides no real indication of what is wrong or where to look to get additional information. An error message presented in this manner does nothing to assuage user anxiety or to help correct the problem.

In general, every error message or warning produced by an interactive system should have the following characteristics:

- The message should describe the problem in jargon that the user can understand.
- The message should provide constructive advice for recovering from the error.
- The message should indicate any negative consequences of the error (e.g., potentially corrupted data files) so that the user can check to ensure that they have not occurred (or correct them if they have).
- The message should be accompanied by an audible or visual cue. That is, a beep might be generated to accompany the display of the message, or the message might flash momentarily or be displayed in a color that is easily recognizable as the "error color."
- The message should be "nonjudgmental." That is, the wording should never place blame on the user.

Because no one really likes bad news, few users will like an error message no matter how well designed. But an effective error message philosophy can do much to improve the quality of an interactive system and will significantly reduce user frustration when problems do occur.

The typed command was once the most common mode of interaction between user and system software and was commonly used for applications of every type. Today, the use of window-oriented, point and pick interfaces has reduced reliance on typed commands, but many power-users continue to prefer a command-oriented mode of interaction. A number of design issues arise when typed commands are provided as a mode of interaction:

- Will every menu option have a corresponding command?
- What form will commands take? Options include a control sequence (e.g., alt-P), function keys, or a typed word.
- How difficult will it be to learn and remember the commands? What can be done if a command is forgotten?
- Can commands be customized or abbreviated by the user?

As we noted earlier in this chapter, conventions for command usage should be established across all applications. It is confusing and often error-prone for a user to type alt-D when a graphics object is to be duplicated in one application and alt-D when a graphics object is to be deleted in another. The potential for error is obvious.

15.5 IMPLEMENTATION TOOLS

Once a design model is created, it is implemented as a prototype,[7] examined by users (who fit the user model described earlier) and modified based on their comments. To accommodate this iterative design approach, a broad class of interface design and prototyping tools has evolved. Called *user-interface toolkits* or *user-interface development systems* (UIDS), these tools provide components or objects that facilitate creation of windows, menus, device interaction, error messages, commands, and many other elements of an interactive environment.

Using prepackaged software components to create a user interface, a UIDS provides built-in mechanisms [MYE89] for

CASE Tools
User Interface Design

- managing input devices (such as a mouse or keyboard)
- validating user input
- handling errors and displaying error messages
- providing feedback (e.g., automatic input echo)
- providing help and prompts

---

7 It should be noted that in some cases (e.g., aircraft cockpit displays) the first step might be to simulate the interface on a display device rather than prototyping it.

- handling windows and fields, scrolling within windows
- establishing connections between application software and the interface
- insulating the application from interface management functions
- allowing the user to customize the interface

These functions can be implemented using either a language-based or graphical approach.

15.6 DESIGN EVALUATION

Once an operational user interface prototype has been created, it must be evaluated to determine whether it meets the needs of the user. Evaluation can span a formality spectrum that ranges from an informal "test drive," in which a user provides impromptu feedback to a formally designed study that uses statistical methods for the evaluation of questionnaires completed by a population of end-users.

The user interface evaluation cycle takes the form shown in Figure 15.3. After the design model has been completed, a first-level prototype is created. The prototype is evaluated by the user, who provides the designer with direct comments about the efficacy of the interface. In addition, if formal evaluation techniques are used (e.g., questionnaires, rating sheets), the designer may extract information from these data

FIGURE 15.3
The interface design evaluation cycle

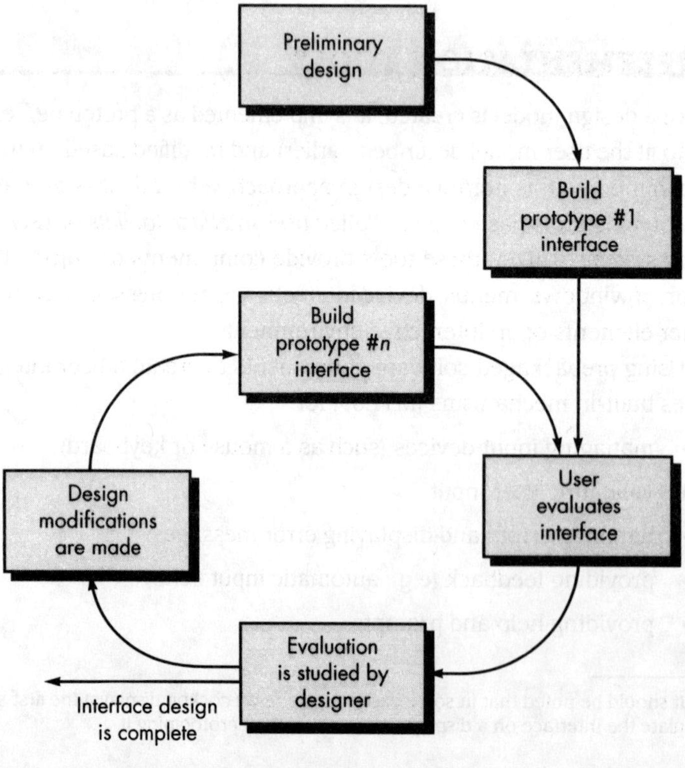

Quote:

"A computer terminal is not some clunky old television with a typewriter in front of it. It is an interface where the mind and body can connect with the universe and move bits of it about."

Douglas Adams

(e.g., 80 percent of all users did not like the mechanism for saving data files). Design modifications are made based on user input and the next level prototype is created. The evaluation cycle continues until no further modifications to the interface design are necessary.

The prototyping approach is effective, but is it possible to evaluate the quality of a user interface before a prototype is built? If potential problems can be uncovered and corrected early, the number of loops through the evaluation cycle will be reduced and development time will shorten. If a design model of the interface has been created, a number of evaluation criteria [MOR81] can be applied during early design reviews:

1. The length and complexity of the written specification of the system and its interface provide an indication of the amount of learning required by users of the system.
2. The number of user tasks specified and the average number of actions per task provide an indication of interaction time and the overall efficiency of the system.
3. The number of actions, tasks, and system states indicated by the design model imply the memory load on users of the system.
4. Interface style, help facilities, and error handling protocol provide a general indication of the complexity of the interface and the degree to which it will be accepted by the user.

Once the first prototype is built, the designer can collect a variety of qualitative and quantitative data that will assist in evaluating the interface. To collect qualitative data, questionnaires can be distributed to users of the prototype. Questions can be all (1) simple yes/no response, (2) numeric response, (3) scaled (subjective) response, or (4) percentage (subjective) response. Examples are

User Interface

1. Were the icons self-explanatory? If not, which icons were unclear?
2. Were the actions easy to remember and to invoke?
3. How many different actions did you use?
4. How easy was it to learn basic system operations (scale 1 to 5)?
5. Compared to other interfaces you've used, how would this rate—top 1%, top 10%, top 25%, top 50%, bottom 50%?

If quantitative data are desired, a form of time study analysis can be conducted. Users are observed during interaction, and data—such as number of tasks correctly completed over a standard time period, frequency of actions, sequence of actions, time spent "looking" at the display, number and types of errors, error recovery time, time spent using help, and number of help references per standard time period—are collected and used as a guide for interface modification.

A complete discussion of user interface evaluation methods is beyond the scope of this book. For further information, see [LEA88] and [MAN97].

15.7 SUMMARY

The user interface is arguably the most important element of a computer-based system or product. If the interface is poorly designed, the user's ability to tap the computational power of an application may be severely hindered. In fact, a weak interface may cause an otherwise well-designed and solidly implemented application to fail.

Three important principles guide the design of effective user interfaces: (1) place the user in control, (2) reduce the user's memory load, and (3) make the interface consistent. To achieve an interface that abides by these principles, an organized design process must be conducted.

User interface design begins with the identification of user, task, and environmental requirements. Task analysis is a design activity that defines user tasks and actions using either an elaborative or object-oriented approach.

Once tasks have been identified, user scenarios are created and analyzed to define a set of interface objects and actions. This provides a basis for the creation of screen layout that depicts graphical design and placement of icons, definition of descriptive screen text, specification and titling for windows, and specification of major and minor menu items. Design issues such as response time, command and action structure, error handling, and help facilities are considered as the design model is refined. A variety of implementation tools are used to build a prototype for evaluation by the user.

The user interface is the window into the software. In many cases, the interface molds a user's perception of the quality of the system. If the "window" is smudged, wavy, or broken, the user may reject an otherwise powerful computer-based system.

REFERENCES

[LEA88] Lea, M., "Evaluating User Interface Designs," *User Interface Design for Computer Systems,* Halstead Press (Wiley), 1988.

[MAN97] Mandel, T., *The Elements of User Interface Design,* Wiley, 1997.

[MON84] Monk, A. (ed.), *Fundamentals of Human-Computer Interaction,* Academic Press, 1984.

[MOR81] Moran, T.P., "The Command Language Grammar: A Representation for the User Interface of Interactive Computer Systems," *Intl. Journal of Man-Machine Studies,* vol. 15, pp. 3–50.

[MYE89] Myers, B.A., "User Interface Tools: Introduction and Survey, *IEEE Software,* January 1989, pp. 15–23.

[NOR86] Norman, D.A., "Cognitive Engineering," in *User Centered Systems Design,* Lawrence Earlbaum Associates, 1986.

[RUB88] Rubin, T., *User Interface Design for Computer Systems,* Halstead Press (Wiley), 1988.

[SHN90] Shneiderman, B., *Designing the User Interface,* 3rd ed., Addison-Wesley, 1990.

PROBLEMS AND POINTS TO PONDER

15.1. Describe the worst interface that you have ever worked with and critique it relative to the concepts introduced in this chapter. Describe the best interface that you have ever worked with and critique it relative to the concepts introduced in this chapter.

15.2. Develop two additional design principles that "place the user in control."

15.3. Develop two additional design principles that "reduce the user's memory load."

15.4. Develop two additional design principles that "make the interface consistent."

15.5. Consider one of the following interactive applications (or an application assigned by your instructor):

a. A desktop publishing system.
b. A computer-aided design system.
c. An interior design system (as described in Section 15.3.2).
d. An automated course registration system for a university.
e. A library management system.
f. An Internet-based polling booth for public elections.
g. A home banking system.
h. An interactive application assigned by your instructor.

Develop a design model, a user model, a system image, and a system perception for any one of these systems.

15.6. Perform a detailed task analysis for any one of the systems listed in Problem 15.5. Use either an elaborative or object-oriented approach.

15.7. Continuing Problem 15.6, define interface objects and actions for the application you have chosen. Identify each object type.

15.8. Develop a set of screen layouts with a definition of major and minor menu items for the system you chose in Problem 15.5.

15.9. Develop a set of screen layouts with a definition of major and minor menu items for the advanced *SafeHome* system described in Section 15.4.1. You may elect to take a different approach than the one shown for the screen layout in Figure 15.2.

15.10. Describe your approach to user help facilities for the task analysis design model and task analysis you have performed as part of Problems 15.5 through 15.8.

15.11. Provide a few examples that illustrate why response time variability can be an issue.

15.12. Develop an approach that would automatically integrate error messages and a user help facility. That is, the system would automatically recognize the error type and provide a help window with suggestions for correcting it. Perform a reasonably complete software design that considers appropriate data structures and algorithms.

15.13. Develop an interface evaluation questionnaire that contains 20 generic questions that would apply to most interfaces. Have ten classmates complete the questionnaire for an interactive system that you all use. Summarize the results and report them to your class.

FURTHER READINGS AND INFORMATION SOURCES

Although his book is not specifically about human/computer interfaces, much of what Donald Norman (*The Design of Everyday Things,* reissue edition, Currency/Doubleday, 1990) has to say about the psychology of effective design applies to the user interface. It is recommended reading for anyone who is serious about doing high-quality interface design.

Dozens of books have been written about interface design over the past decade. However, books by Mandel [MAN97] and Shneiderman [SHN90] continue to provide the most comprehensive (and readable) treatments of the subject. Donnelly (*In Your Face: The Best of Interactive Interface Design,* Rockport Publications, 1998); Fowler, Stanwick, and Smith (*GUI Design Handbook,* McGraw-Hill, 1998); Weinschenk, Jamar, and Yeo (*GUI Design Essentials,* Wiley, 1997); Galitz (*The Essential Guide to User Interface Design: An Introduction to GUI Design Principles and Techniques,* Wiley, 1996); Mullet and Sano (*Designing Visual Interfaces: Communication Oriented Techniques,* PrenticeHall, 1995); and Cooper (*About Face: The Essentials of User Interface Design,* IDG Books, 1995) have written treatments that provide additional design guidelines and principles as well as suggestions for interface requirements elicitation, design modeling, implementation, and testing.

Task analysis and modeling are pivotal interface design activities. Hackos and Redish (*User and Task Analysis for Interface Design,* Wiley, 1998) have written a book dedicated to these subjects and provide a detailed method for approaching task analysis. Wood (*User Interface Design: Bridging the Gap from User Requirements to Design,* CRC Press, 1997) considers the analysis activity for interfaces and the transition to design tasks. One of the first books to present the subject of scenarios in user-interface design has been edited by Carroll *(Scenario-Based Design: Envisioning Work and Technology in System Development,* Wiley, 1995). A formal method for design of user interfaces, based on state-based behavior modeling has been developed by Horrocks (*Constructing the User Interface with Statecharts,* Addison-Wesley, 1998).

The evaluation activity focuses on usability. Books by Rubin (*Handbook of Usability Testing: How to Plan, Design, and Conduct Effective Tests,* Wiley, 1994) and Nielson (*Usability Inspection Methods,* Wiley, 1994) address the topic in considerable detail.

The Apple Macintosh popularized easy to use and solidly designed user interfaces. The Apple staff (*MacIntosh Human Interface Guidelines,* Addison-Wesley, 1993) discusses the now famous (and much copied) Macintosh look and feel. One of the earliest among many books written about the Microsoft Windows interface was produced by the Microsoft staff (*The Windows Interface Guidelines for Software Design: An Application Design Guide,* Microsoft Press, 1995).

In a unique book that may be of considerable interest to product designers, Murphy (*Front Panel: Designing Software for Embedded User Interfaces,* R&D Books, 1998) provides detailed guidance for the design of interfaces for embedded systems and addresses safety hazards inherent in controls, handling heavy machinery, and interfaces for medical or transport systems. Interface design for embedded products is also discussed by Garrett (*Advanced Instrumentation and Computer I/O Design: Real-Time System Computer Interface Engineering,* IEEE, 1994).

A wide variety of information sources on user interface design and related subjects is available on the Internet. An up-to-date list of World Wide Web references that are relevant to interface design issues can be found at the SEPA Web site:
http://www.mhhe.com/engcs/compsci/pressman/resources/interface-design.mhtml

CHAPTER

16 COMPONENT-LEVEL DESIGN

KEY CONCEPTS

Component-level design, also called *procedural design,* occurs after data, architectural, and interface designs have been established. The intent is to translate the design model into operational software. But the level of abstraction of the existing design model is relatively high, and the abstraction level of the operational program is low. The translation can be challenging, opening the door to the introduction of subtle errors that are difficult to find and correct in later stages of the software process. In a famous lecture, Edsgar Dijkstra, a major contributor to our understanding of design, stated [DIJ72]:

> Software seems to be different from many other products, where as a rule higher quality implies a higher price. Those who want really reliable software will discover that they must find a means of avoiding the majority of bugs to start with, and as a result, the programming process will become cheaper . . . effective programmers . . . should not waste their time debugging—they should not introduce bugs to start with.

Although these words were spoken many years ago, they remain true today. When the design model is translated into source code, we must follow a set of design principles that not only perform the translation but also do not "introduce bugs to start with."

QUICK LOOK

What is it? Data, architectural, and interface design must be translated into operational software. To accomplish this, the design must be represented at a level of abstraction that is close to code. Component-level design establishes the algorithmic detail required to manipulate data structures, effect communication between software components via their interfaces, and implement the processing algorithms allocated to each component.

Who does it? A software engineer performs component-level design.

Why is it important? You have to be able to determine whether the program will work before you build it. The component-level design represents the software in a way that allows you to review the details of the design for correctness and consistency with earlier design representations (i.e., the data, architectural, and interface designs). It provides a means for assessing whether data structures, interfaces, and algorithms will work.

What are the steps? Design representations of data, architecture, and interfaces form the foundation for component-level design. The processing narrative for each component is translated into a procedural design model using a set of structured programming constructs. Graphical, tabular, or text-based notation is used to represent the design.

QUICK LOOK

What is the work product? The procedural design for each component, represented in graphical, tabular, or text-based notation, is the primary work product produced during component-level design.

How do I ensure that I've done it right? A design walkthrough or inspection is conducted. The design is examined to determine whether data structures, interfaces, processing sequences, and logical conditions are correct and will produce the appropriate data or control transformation allocated to the component during earlier design steps.

It is possible to represent the component-level design using a programming language. In essence, the program is created using the design model as a guide. An alternative approach is to represent the procedural design using some intermediate (e.g., graphical, tabular, or text-based) representation that can be translated easily into source code. Regardless of the mechanism that is used to represent the component-level design, the data structures, interfaces, and algorithms defined should conform to a variety of well-established procedural design guidelines that help us to avoid errors as the procedural design evolves. In this chapter, we examine these design guidelines.

16.1 STRUCTURED PROGRAMMING

Quote:

"When I'm working on a problem, I never think about beauty. I think only how to solve the problem. But when I have finished, if the solution is not beautiful, I know it is wrong."

R. Buckminster Fuller

The foundations of component-level design were formed in the early 1960s and were solidified with the work of Edsgar Dijkstra and his colleagues ([BOH66], [DIJ65], [DIJ76]). In the late 1960s, Dijkstra and others proposed the use of a set of constrained logical constructs from which any program could be formed. The constructs emphasized "maintenance of functional domain." That is, each construct had a predictable logical structure, was entered at the top and exited at the bottom, enabling a reader to follow procedural flow more easily.

The constructs are sequence, condition, and repetition. *Sequence* implements processing steps that are essential in the specification of any algorithm. *Condition* provides the facility for selected processing based on some logical occurrence, and *repetition* allows for looping. These three constructs are fundamental to *structured programming*—an important component-level design technique.

The structured constructs were proposed to limit the procedural design of software to a small number of predictable operations. Complexity metrics (Chapter 19) indicate that the use of the structured constructs reduces program complexity and thereby enhances readability, testability, and maintainability. The use of a limited number of logical constructs also contributes to a human understanding process that psychologists call *chunking*. To understand this process, consider the way in which you are reading this page. You do not read individual letters but rather recognize patterns or chunks of letters that form words or phrases. The structured constructs are

FIGURE 16.1
Flowchart constructs

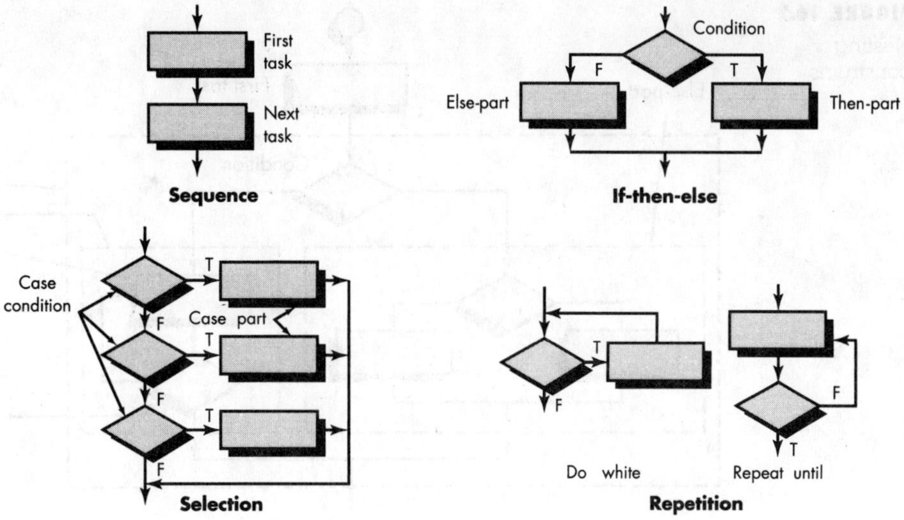

KEY POINT Structured programming provides a designer with useful logical patterns.

logical chunks that allow a reader to recognize procedural elements of a module, rather than reading the design or code line by line. Understanding is enhanced when readily recognizable logical patterns are encountered.

Any program, regardless of application area or technical complexity, can be designed and implemented using only the three structured constructs. It should be noted, however, that dogmatic use of only these constructs can sometimes cause practical difficulties. Section 16.1.1 considers this issue in further detail.

16.1.1 Graphical Design Notation

"A picture is worth a thousand words," but it's rather important to know which picture and which 1000 words. There is no question that graphical tools, such as the flowchart or box diagram, provide useful pictorial patterns that readily depict procedural detail. However, if graphical tools are misused, the wrong picture may lead to the wrong software.

A flowchart is quite simple pictorially. A box is used to indicate a processing step. A diamond represents a logical condition, and arrows show the flow of control. Figure 16.1 illustrates three structured constructs. The *sequence* is represented as two processing boxes connected by an line (arrow) of control. *Condition,* also called *if-then-else,* is depicted as a decision diamond that if true, causes *then-part* processing to occur, and if false, invokes *else-part* processing. *Repetition* is represented using two slightly different forms. The *do while* tests a condition and executes a loop task repetitively as long as the condition holds true. A *repeat until* executes the loop task first, then tests a condition and repeats the task until the condition fails. The selection (or select-case) construct shown in the figure is actually an extension of the

FIGURE 16.2
Nesting constructs

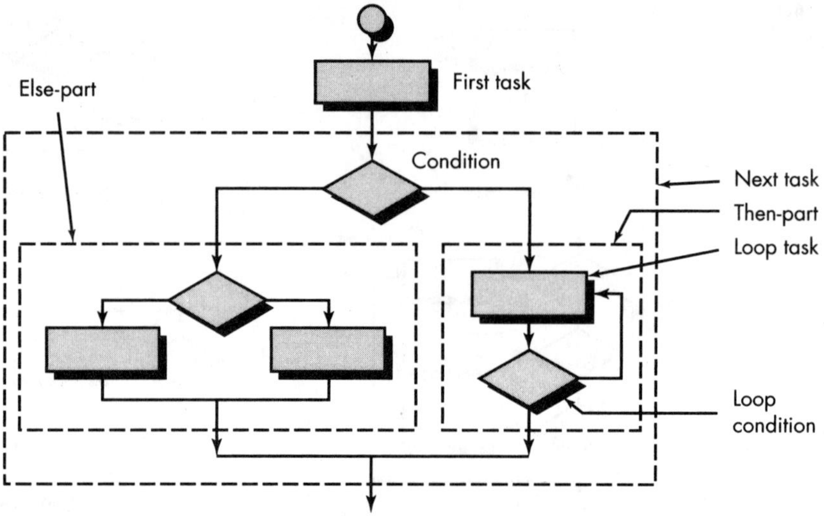

if-then-else. A parameter is tested by successive decisions until a true condition occurs and a case part processing path is executed.

ADVICE
Structured programming constructs should make it easier to understand the design. If using them without "violation" results in unnecessary complexity, it's OK to violate.

The structured constructs may be nested within one another as shown in Figure 16.2. Referring to the figure, repeat-until forms the then part of if-then-else (shown enclosed by the outer dashed boundary). Another if-then-else forms the else part of the larger condition. Finally, the condition itself becomes a second block in a sequence. By nesting constructs in this manner, a complex logical schema may be developed. It should be noted that any one of the blocks in Figure 16.2 could reference another module, thereby accomplishing procedural layering implied by program structure.

In general, the dogmatic use of only the structured constructs can introduce inefficiency when an escape from a set of nested loops or nested conditions is required. More important, additional complication of all logical tests along the path of escape can cloud software control flow, increase the possibility of error, and have a negative impact on readability and maintainability. What can we do?

ADVICE
Both the flowchart and box diagrams no longer are used as widely as they once were. In general, use them to document or evaluate design in specific instances, not to represent an entire system.

The designer is left with two options: (1) The procedural representation is redesigned so that the "escape branch" is not required at a nested location in the flow of control or (2) the structured constructs are violated in a controlled manner; that is, a constrained branch out of the nested flow is designed. Option 1 is obviously the ideal approach, but option 2 can be accommodated without violating of the spirit of structured programming.

Another graphical design tool, the *box diagram,* evolved from a desire to develop a procedural design representation that would not allow violation of the structured constructs. Developed by Nassi and Shneiderman [NAS73] and extended by Chapin [CHA74], the diagrams (also called *Nassi-Shneiderman charts, N-S charts,* or *Chapin charts*) have the following characteristics: (1) functional domain (that is, the scope of

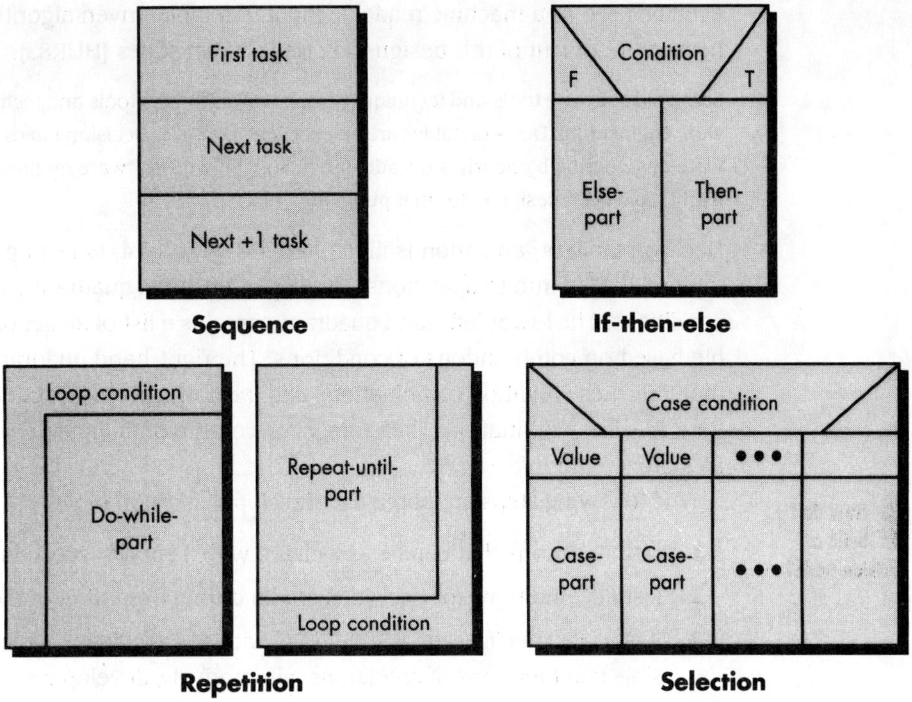

FIGURE 16.3 Box diagram constructs

repetition or if-then-else) is well defined and clearly visible as a pictorial representation, (2) arbitrary transfer of control is impossible, (3) the scope of local and/or global data can be easily determined, (4) recursion is easy to represent.

The graphical representation of structured constructs using the box diagram is illustrated in Figure 16.3. The fundamental element of the diagram is a box. To represent sequence, two boxes are connected bottom to top. To represent if-then-else, a condition box is followed by a then-part and else-part box. Repetition is depicted with a bounding pattern that encloses the process (do-while part or repeat-until part) to be repeated. Finally, selection is represented using the graphical form shown at the bottom of the figure.

Like flowcharts, a box diagram is layered on multiple pages as processing elements of a module are refined. A "call" to a subordinate module can be represented within a box by specifying the module name enclosed by an oval.

ADVICE

Use a decision table when a complex set of conditions and actions is encountered within a component.

16.1.2 Tabular Design Notation

In many software applications, a module may be required to evaluate a complex combination of conditions and select appropriate actions based on these conditions. Decision tables provide a notation that translates actions and conditions (described in a processing narrative) into a tabular form. The table is difficult to misinterpret and may even be used as a machine readable input to a table driven algorithm. In a comprehensive treatment of this design tool, Ned Chapin states [HUR83]:

> Some old software tools and techniques mesh well with new tools and techniques of software engineering. Decision tables are an excellent example. Decision tables preceded software engineering by nearly a decade, but fit so well with software engineering that they might have been designed for that purpose.

Decision table organization is illustrated in Figure 16.4. Referring to the figure, the table is divided into four sections. The upper left-hand quadrant contains a list of all conditions. The lower left-hand quadrant contains a list of all actions that are possible based on combinations of conditions. The right-hand quadrants form a matrix that indicates condition combinations and the corresponding actions that will occur for a specific combination. Therefore, each column of the matrix may be interpreted as a processing *rule.*

How do I build a decision table?

The following steps are applied to develop a decision table:

1. List all actions that can be associated with a specific procedure (or module).
2. List all conditions (or decisions made) during execution of the procedure.
3. Associate specific sets of conditions with specific actions, eliminating impossible combinations of conditions; alternatively, develop every possible permutation of conditions.
4. Define rules by indicating what action(s) occurs for a set of conditions.

Rules

Conditions	1	2	3	4					n
Condition #1	✓			✓	✓				
Condition #2		✓		✓					
Condition #3			✓		✓				
Actions									
Action #1	✓			✓	✓				
Action #2		✓		✓					
Action #3			✓						
Action #4			✓	✓	✓				
Action #5	✓	✓			✓				

FIGURE 16.4 Decision table nomenclature

To illustrate the use of a decision table, consider the following excerpt from a processing narrative for a public utility billing system:

> If the customer account is billed using a fixed rate method, a minimum monthly charge is assessed for consumption of less than 100 KWH (kilowatt-hours). Otherwise, computer billing applies a Schedule A rate structure. However, if the account is billed using a variable rate method, a Schedule A rate structure will apply to consumption below 100 KWH, with additional consumption billed according to Schedule B.

Figure 16.5 illustrates a decision table representation of the preceding narrative. Each of the five rules indicates one of five viable conditions (i.e., a T (true) in both fixed rate and variable rate account makes no sense in the context of this procedure; therefore, this condition is omitted). As a general rule, the decision table can be effectively used to supplement other procedural design notation.

16.1.3 Program Design Language

Program design language (PDL), also called *structured English* or *pseudocode,* is "a pidgin language in that it uses the vocabulary of one language (i.e., English) and the overall syntax of another (i.e., a structured programming language)" [CAI75]. In this chapter, PDL is used as a generic reference for a design language.

At first glance PDL looks like a modern programming language. The difference between PDL and a real programming language lies in the use of narrative text (e.g., English) embedded directly within PDL statements. Given the use of narrative text embedded directly into a syntactical structure, PDL cannot be compiled (at least not yet). However, PDL tools currently exist to translate PDL into a programming lan-

	Rules				
Conditions	**1**	**2**	**3**	**4**	**5**
Fixed rate acct.	T	T	F	F	F
Variable rate acct.	F	F	T	T	F
Consumption <100 kwh	T	F	T	F	
Consumption ≥100 kwh	F	T	F	T	
Actions					
Min. monthly charge	✓				
Schedule A billing		✓	✓		
Schedule B billing				✓	
Other treatment					✓

FIGURE 16.5 Resultant decision table

guage "skeleton" and/or a graphical representation (e.g., a flowchart) of design. These tools also produce nesting maps, a design operation index, cross-reference tables, and a variety of other information.

ADVICE

It's a good idea to use your programming language as the basis for the PDL. This will enable you to generate a code skeleton (mixed with narrative) as you perform component-level design.

A program design language may be a simple transposition of a language such as Ada or C. Alternatively, it may be a product purchased specifically for procedural design. Regardless of origin, a design language should have the following characteristics:

- A fixed syntax of keywords that provide for all structured constructs, data declaration, and modularity characteristics.
- A free syntax of natural language that describes processing features.
- Data declaration facilities that should include both simple (scalar, array) and complex (linked list or tree) data structures.
- Subprogram definition and calling techniques that support various modes of interface description.

A basic PDL syntax should include constructs for subprogram definition, interface description, data declaration, techniques for block structuring, condition constructs, repetition constructs, and I/O constructs. The format and semantics for some of these PDL constructs are presented in the section that follows.

It should be noted that PDL can be extended to include keywords for multitasking and/or concurrent processing, interrupt handling, interprocess synchronization, and many other features. The application design for which PDL is to be used should dictate the final form for the design language.

16.1.4 A PDL Example

To illustrate the use of PDL, we present an example of a procedural design for the *SafeHome* security system software introduced in earlier chapters. The system monitors alarms for fire, smoke, burglar, water, and temperature (e.g., furnace breaks while homeowner is away during winter) and produces an alarm bell and calls a monitoring service, generating a voice-synthesized message. In the PDL that follows, we illustrate some of the important constructs noted in earlier sections.

Recall that PDL is not a programming language. The designer can adapt as required without worry of syntax errors. However, the design for the monitoring software would have to be reviewed (do you see any problems?) and further refined before code could be written. The following PDL defines an elaboration of the procedural design for the *security monitor* component.

```
PROCEDURE security.monitor;
INTERFACE RETURNS system.status;
TYPE signal IS STRUCTURE DEFINED
        name IS STRING LENGTH VAR;
        address IS HEX device location;
```

```
        bound.value IS upper bound SCALAR;
        message IS STRING LENGTH VAR;
END signal TYPE;
TYPE system.status IS BIT (4);
TYPE alarm.type DEFINED
        smoke.alarm IS INSTANCE OF signal;
        fire.alarm IS INSTANCE OF signal;
        water.alarm IS INSTANCE OF signal;
        temp.alarm IS INSTANCE OF signal;
        burglar.alarm IS INSTANCE OF signal;
TYPE phone.number IS area code + 7-digit number;
        •
        •
        •
initialize all system ports and reset all hardware;
CASE OF control.panel.switches (cps):
        WHEN cps = "test" SELECT
            CALL alarm PROCEDURE WITH "on" for test.time in seconds;
        WHEN cps = "alarm-off" SELECT
            CALL alarm PROCEDURE WITH "off";
        WHEN cps = "new.bound.temp" SELECT
        CALL keypad.input PROCEDURE;
        WHEN cps = "burglar.alarm.off" SELECT deactivate signal [burglar.alarm];
        •
        •
        •
        DEFAULT none;
ENDCASE
REPEAT UNTIL activate.switch is turned off
        reset all signal.values and switches;
        DO FOR alarm.type = smoke, fire, water, temp, burglar;
            READ address [alarm.type] signal.value;
            IF signal.value > bound [alarm.type]
            THEN  phone.message = message [alarm.type];
                        set alarm.bell to "on" for alarm.timeseconds;
                        PARBEGIN
                        CALL alarm PROCEDURE WITH "on", alarm.time in seconds;
                        CALL phone PROCEDURE WITH message [alarm.type], phone.number;
                        ENDPAR
            ELSE  skip
            ENDIF
        ENDFOR
ENDREP
END security.monitor
```

Note that the designer for the *security.monitor* component has used a new construct **PARBEGIN . . . ENDPAR** that specifies a parallel block. All tasks specified within the **PARBEGIN** block are executed in parallel. In this case, implementation details are not considered.

16.2 COMPARISON OF DESIGN NOTATION

In the preceding section, we presented a number of different techniques for representing a procedural design. A comparison must be predicated on the premise that any notation for component-level design, if used correctly, can be an invaluable aid in the design process; conversely, even the best notation, if poorly applied, adds little to understanding. With this thought in mind, we examine criteria that may be applied to compare design notation.

Design notation should lead to a procedural representation that is easy to understand and review. In addition, the notation should enhance "code to" ability so that code does, in fact, become a natural by-product of design. Finally, the design representation must be easily maintainable so that design always represents the program correctly.

The following attributes of design notation have been established in the context of the general characteristics described previously:

What criteria can be used to assess design notation?

Modularity. Design notation should support the development of modular software and provide a means for interface specification.

Overall simplicity. Design notation should be relatively simple to learn, relatively easy to use, and generally easy to read.

Ease of editing. The procedural design may require modification as the software process proceeds. The ease with which a design representation can be edited can help facilitate each software engineering task.

Machine readability. Notation that can be input directly into a computer-based development system offers significant benefits.

Maintainability. Software maintenance is the most costly phase of the software life cycle. Maintenance of the software configuration nearly always means maintenance of the procedural design representation.

Structure enforcement. The benefits of a design approach that uses structured programming concepts have already been discussed. Design notation that enforces the use of only the structured constructs promotes good design practice.

Automatic processing. A procedural design contains information that can be processed to give the designer new or better insights into the correctness and quality of a design. Such insight can be enhanced with reports provided via software design tools.

Data representation. The ability to represent local and global data is an essential element of component-level design. Ideally, design notation should represent such data directly.

Logic verification. Automatic verification of design logic is a goal that is paramount during software testing. Notation that enhances the ability to verify logic greatly improves testing adequacy.

"Code-to" ability. The software engineering task that follows component-level design is code generation. Notation that may be converted easily to source code reduces effort and error.

A natural question that arises in any discussion of design notation is: "What notation is really the best, given the attributes noted above?" Any answer to this question is admittedly subjective and open to debate. However, it appears that program design language offers the best combination of characteristics. PDL may be embedded directly into source listings, improving documentation and making design maintenance less difficult. Editing can be accomplished with any text editor or word-processing system, automatic processors already exist, and the potential for "automatic code generation" is good.

However, it does not follow that other design notation is necessarily inferior to PDL or is "not good" in specific attributes. The pictorial nature of flowcharts and box diagrams provide a perspective on control flow that many designers prefer. The precise tabular content of decision tables is an excellent tool for table-driven applications. And many other design representations (e.g., see [PET81], [SOM96]), not presented in this book, offer their own unique benefits. In the final analysis, the choice of a design tool may be more closely related to human factors than to technical attributes.

16.3 SUMMARY

The design process encompasses a sequence of activities that slowly reduces the level of abstraction with which software is represented. Component-level design depicts the software at a level of abstraction that is very close to code.

At the component level, the software engineer must represent data structures, interfaces, and algorithms in sufficient detail to guide in the generation of programming language source code. To accomplish this, the designer uses one of a number of design notations that represent component-level detail in either graphical, tabular, or text-based formats.

Structured programming is a procedural design philosophy that constrains the number and type of logical constructs used to represent algorithmic detail. The intent of structured programming is to assist the designer in defining algorithms that are less complex and therefore easier to read, test, and maintain.

REFERENCES

[BOH66] Bohm, C. and G. Jacopini, "Flow Diagrams, Turing Machines and Languages with Only Two Formation Rules," *CACM,* vol. 9, no. 5, May 1966, pp. 366–371.

[CAI75] Caine, S. and K. Gordon, "PDL—A Tool for Software Design," in *Proc. National Computer Conference,* AFIPS Press, 1975, pp. 271–276.

[CHA74] Chapin, N., "A New Format for Flowcharts," *Software—Practice and Experience,* vol. 4, no. 4 , 1974, pp. 341–357.

[DIJ65] Dijkstra, E., "Programming Considered as a Human Activity," in *Proc. 1965 IFIP Congress,* North-Holland Publishing Co., 1965.

[DIJ72] Dijkstra, E., "The Humble Programmer," 1972 ACM Turing Award Lecture, *CACM,* vol. 15, no. 10, October, 1972, pp. 859–866.

[DIJ76] Dijkstra, E., "Structured Programming," in *Software Engineering, Concepts and Techniques,* (J. Buxton et al., eds.), Van Nostrand-Reinhold, 1976.

[HUR83] Hurley, R.B., *Decision Tables in Software Engineering,* Van Nostrand-Reinhold, 1983.

[LIN79] Linger, R.C., H.D. Mills, and B.I. Witt, *Structured Programming,* Addison-Wesley, 1979.

[NAS73] Nassi, I. and B. Shneiderman, "Flowchart Techniques for Structured Programming," *SIGPLAN Notices,* ACM, August 1973.

[PET81] Peters, L.J., *Software Design: Methods and Techniques,* Yourdon Press, 1981.

[SOM96] Sommerville, I., *Software Engineering,* 5th ed., Addison-Wesley, 1996.

PROBLEMS AND POINTS TO PONDER

16.1. Select a small portion of an existing program (approximately 50–75 source lines). Isolate the structured programming constructs by drawing boxes around them in the source code. Does the program excerpt have constructs that violate the structured programming philosophy? If so, redesign the code to make it conform to structured programming constructs. If not, what do you notice about the boxes that you've drawn?

16.2. All modern programming languages implement the structured programming constructs. Provide examples from three programming languages.

16.3. Why is "chunking" important during the component-level design review process?

Problems 16.4–16.11 may be represented using any one (or more) of the procedural design notations presented in this chapter. Your instructor may assign specific design notation to particular problems.

16.4. Develop a procedural design for components that implement the following sorts: Shell-Metzner sort; heapsort; BSST (tree) sort. Refer to a book on data structures if you are unfamiliar with these sorts.

16.5. Develop a procedural design for an interactive user interface that queries for basic income tax information. Derive your own requirements and assume that all tax computations are performed by other modules.

16.6. Develop a procedural design for a program that accepts an arbitrarily long text as input and produces a list of words and their frequency of occurrence as output.

16.7. Develop a procedural design of a program that will numerically integrate a function *f* in the bounds *a* to *b*.

16.8. Develop a procedural design for a generalized Turing machine that will accept a set of quadruples as program input and produce output as specified.

16.9. Develop a procedural design for a program that will solve the Towers of Hanoi problem. Many books on artificial intelligence discuss this problem in some detail.

16.10. Develop a procedural design for all or major portions of an LR parser for a compiler. Refer to one or more books on compiler design.

16.11. Develop a procedural design for an encryption/decryption algorithm of your choosing.

16.12. Write a one- or two-page argument for the procedural design notation that you feel is best. Be certain that your argument addresses the criteria presented in Section 16.2.

FURTHER READINGS AND INFORMATION SOURCES

The work of Linger, Mills, and Witt (*Structured Programming—Theory and Practice,* Addison-Wesley, 1979) remains a definitive treatment of the subject. The text contains a good PDL as well as detailed discussions of the ramifications of structured programming. Other books that focus on procedural design issues include those by Robertson (*Simple Program Design,* Boyd and Fraser Publishing, 1994), Bentley (*Programming Pearls,* Addison-Wesley, 1986 and *More Programming Pearls,* Addison-Wesley, 1988), and Dahl, Dijkstra, and Hoare (*Structured Programming,* Academic Press, 1972).

Relatively few recent books have been dedicated solely to component-level design. In general, programming language books address procedural design in some detail but always in the context of the language that is introduced by the book. The following books are representative of hundreds of titles that consider procedural design in a programming language context:

[ADA00] Adamson, T.A., K.C. Mansfield, and J.L. Antonakos, *Structured Basic Applied to Technology,* Prentice-Hall, 2000.

[ANT96] Antonakos, J.L. and K. Mansfield, *Application Programming in Structured C,* Prentice-Hall, 1996.

[FOR99] Forouzan, B.A. and R. Gilberg, *Computer Science: A Structured Programming Approach Using C++,* Brooks/Cole Publishing, 1999.

[OBR93] O'Brien, S.K. and S. Nameroff, *Turbo Pascal 7: The Complete Reference,* Osborne McGraw-Hill, 1993.

[WEL95] Welburn, T. and W. Price, *Structured COBOL: Fundamentals and Style,* 4th ed., Mitchell Publishers, 1995.

A wide variety of information sources on software design and related subjects is available on the Internet. An up-to-date list of World Wide Web references that are relevant to design concepts and methods can be found at the SEPA Web site:
http://www.mhhe.com/engcs/compsci/pressman/resources/comp-design.mhtml

CHAPTER

17 SOFTWARE TESTING TECHNIQUES

KEY CONCEPTS

The importance of software testing and its implications with respect to software quality cannot be overemphasized. To quote Deutsch [DEU79],

> The development of software systems involves a series of production activities where opportunities for injection of human fallibilities are enormous. Errors may begin to occur at the very inception of the process where the objectives . . . may be erroneously or imperfectly specified, as well as [in] later design and development stages . . . Because of human inability to perform and communicate with perfection, software development is accompanied by a quality assurance activity.

Software testing is a critical element of software quality assurance and represents the ultimate review of specification, design, and code generation.

The increasing visibility of software as a system element and the attendant "costs" associated with a software failure are motivating forces for well-planned, thorough testing. It is not unusual for a software development organization to expend between 30 and 40 percent of total project effort on testing. In the extreme, testing of human-rated software (e.g., flight control, nuclear reactor monitoring) can cost three to five times as much as all other software engineering steps combined!

QUICK LOOK

What is it? Once source code has been generated, software must be tested to uncover (and correct) as many errors as possible before delivery to your customer. Your goal is to design a series of test cases that have a high likelihood of finding errors—but how? That's where software testing techniques enter the picture. These techniques provide systematic guidance for designing tests that (1) exercise the internal logic of software components, and (2) exercise the input and output domains of the program to uncover errors in program function, behavior. and performance.

Who does it? During early stages of testing, a software engineer performs all tests. However, as the testing process progresses, testing specialists may become involved.

Why is it important? Reviews and other SQA activities can and do uncover errors, but they are not sufficient. Every time the program is executed, the customer tests it! Therefore, you have to execute the program before it gets to the customer with the specific intent of finding and removing all errors. In order to find the highest possible number of errors, tests must be conducted systematically and test cases must be designed using disciplined techniques.

What are the steps? Software is tested from two different perspectives: (1) internal program logic is exercised using "white box" test case design tech-

QUICK LOOK

niques. Software requirements are exercised using "black box" test case design techniques. In both cases, the intent is to find the maximum number of errors with the minimum amount of effort and time.

What is the work product? A set of test cases designed to exercise both internal logic and external requirements is designed and documented, expected results are defined, and actual results are recorded.

How do I ensure that I've done it right? When you begin testing, change your point of view. Try hard to "break" the software! Design test cases in a disciplined fashion and review the test cases you do create for thoroughness.

In this chapter, we discuss software testing fundamentals and techniques for software test case design. Software testing fundamentals define the overriding objectives for software testing. Test case design focuses on a set of techniques for the creation of test cases that meet overall testing objectives. In Chapter 18, testing strategies and software debugging are presented.

17.1 SOFTWARE TESTING FUNDAMENTALS

Quote:
"A working program remains an elusive thing of beauty."
Robert Dunn

Testing presents an interesting anomaly for the software engineer. During earlier software engineering activities, the engineer attempts to build software from an abstract concept to a tangible product. Now comes testing. The engineer creates a series of test cases that are intended to "demolish" the software that has been built. In fact, testing is the one step in the software process that could be viewed (psychologically, at least) as destructive rather than constructive.

Software engineers are by their nature constructive people. Testing requires that the developer discard preconceived notions of the "correctness" of software just developed and overcome a conflict of interest that occurs when errors are uncovered. Beizer [BEI90] describes this situation effectively when he states:

> There's a myth that if we were really good at programming, there would be no bugs to catch. If only we could really concentrate, if only everyone used structured programming, top-down design, decision tables, if programs were written in SQUISH, if we had the right silver bullets, then there would be no bugs. So goes the myth. There are bugs, the myth says, because we are bad at what we do; and if we are bad at it, we should feel guilty about it. Therefore, testing and test case design is an admission of failure, which instills a goodly dose of guilt. And the tedium of testing is just punishment for our errors. Punishment for what? For being human? Guilt for what? For failing to achieve inhuman perfection? For not distinguishing between what another programmer thinks and what he says? For failing to be telepathic? For not solving human communications problems that have been kicked around . . . for forty centuries?

Should testing instill guilt? Is testing really destructive? The answer to these questions is "No!" However, the objectives of testing are somewhat different than we might expect.

17.1.1 Testing Objectives

In an excellent book on software testing, Glen Myers [MYE79] states a number of rules that can serve well as testing objectives:

What are primary objectives when we test software?

1. Testing is a process of executing a program with the intent of finding an error.
2. A good test case is one that has a high probability of finding an as-yet-undiscovered error.
3. A successful test is one that uncovers an as-yet-undiscovered error.

These objectives imply a dramatic change in viewpoint. They move counter to the commonly held view that a successful test is one in which no errors are found. Our objective is to design tests that systematically uncover different classes of errors and to do so with a minimum amount of time and effort.

Quote:
"Errors are more common, more pervasive, and more troublesome in software than with other technologies."
David Parnas

If testing is conducted successfully (according to the objectives stated previously), it will uncover errors in the software. As a secondary benefit, testing demonstrates that software functions appear to be working according to specification, that behavioral and performance requirements appear to have been met. In addition, data collected as testing is conducted provide a good indication of software reliability and some indication of software quality as a whole. But testing cannot show the absence of errors and defects, it can show only that software errors and defects are present. It is important to keep this (rather gloomy) statement in mind as testing is being conducted.

17.1.2 Testing Principles

Before applying methods to design effective test cases, a software engineer must understand the basic principles that guide software testing. Davis [DAV95] suggests a set[1] of testing principles that have been adapted for use in this book:

- **All tests should be traceable to customer requirements.** As we have seen, the objective of software testing is to uncover errors. It follows that the most severe defects (from the customer's point of view) are those that cause the program to fail to meet its requirements.
- **Tests should be planned long before testing begins.** Test planning (Chapter 18) can begin as soon as the requirements model is complete. Detailed definition of test cases can begin as soon as the design model has

1 Only a small subset of Davis's testing principles are noted here. For more information, see [DAV95].

been solidified. Therefore, all tests can be planned and designed before any code has been generated.

- **The Pareto principle applies to software testing.** Stated simply, the Pareto principle implies that 80 percent of all errors uncovered during testing will likely be traceable to 20 percent of all program components. The problem, of course, is to isolate these suspect components and to thoroughly test them.
- **Testing should begin "in the small" and progress toward testing "in the large."** The first tests planned and executed generally focus on individual components. As testing progresses, focus shifts in an attempt to find errors in integrated clusters of components and ultimately in the entire system (Chapter 18).
- **Exhaustive testing is not possible.** The number of path permutations for even a moderately sized program is exceptionally large (see Section 17.2 for further discussion). For this reason, it is impossible to execute every combination of paths during testing. It is possible, however, to adequately cover program logic and to ensure that all conditions in the component-level design have been exercised.
- **To be most effective, testing should be conducted by an independent third party.** By *most effective,* we mean testing that has the highest probability of finding errors (the primary objective of testing). For reasons that have been introduced earlier in this chapter and are considered in more detail in Chapter 18, the software engineer who created the system is not the best person to conduct all tests for the software.

17.1.3 Testability

In ideal circumstances, a software engineer designs a computer program, a system, or a product with "testability" in mind. This enables the individuals charged with testing to design effective test cases more easily. But what is *testability?* James Bach[2] describes testability in the following manner.

WebRef

A useful paper entitled "Improving Software Testability" can be found at **www.stlabs.com/newsletters/testnet/docs/testability.htm**

> Software testability is simply how easily [a computer program] can be tested. Since testing is so profoundly difficult, it pays to know what can be done to streamline it. Sometimes programmers are willing to do things that will help the testing process and a checklist of possible design points, features, etc., can be useful in negotiating with them.
>
> There are certainly metrics that could be used to measure testability in most of its aspects. Sometimes, testability is used to mean how adequately a particular set of

2 The paragraphs that follow are copyright 1994 by James Bach and have been adapted from an Internet posting that first appeared in the newsgroup comp.software-eng. This material is used with permission.

tests will cover the product. It's also used by the military to mean how easily a tool can be checked and repaired in the field. Those two meanings are not the same as *software testability.* The checklist that follows provides a set of characteristics that lead to testable software.

KEY POINT

"Testability" occurs as a result of good design. Data design, architecture, interfaces, and component-level detail can either facilitate testing or make it difficult.

Operability. "The better it works, the more efficiently it can be tested."

- The system has few bugs (bugs add analysis and reporting overhead to the test process).
- No bugs block the execution of tests.
- The product evolves in functional stages (allows simultaneous development and testing).

Observability. "What you see is what you test."

- Distinct output is generated for each input.
- System states and variables are visible or queriable during execution.
- Past system states and variables are visible or queriable (e.g., transaction logs).
- All factors affecting the output are visible.
- Incorrect output is easily identified.
- Internal errors are automatically detected through self-testing mechanisms.
- Internal errors are automatically reported.
- Source code is accessible.

Controllability. "The better we can control the software, the more the testing can be automated and optimized."

- All possible outputs can be generated through some combination of input.
- All code is executable through some combination of input.
- Software and hardware states and variables can be controlled directly by the test engineer.
- Input and output formats are consistent and structured.
- Tests can be conveniently specified, automated, and reproduced.

Decomposability. "By controlling the scope of testing, we can more quickly isolate problems and perform smarter retesting."

- The software system is built from independent modules.
- Software modules can be tested independently.

Simplicity. "The less there is to test, the more quickly we can test it."

- Functional simplicity (e.g., the feature set is the minimum necessary to meet requirements).

- Structural simplicity (e.g., architecture is modularized to limit the propagation of faults).
- Code simplicity (e.g., a coding standard is adopted for ease of inspection and maintenance).

Stability. "The fewer the changes, the fewer the disruptions to testing."

- Changes to the software are infrequent.
- Changes to the software are controlled.
- Changes to the software do not invalidate existing tests.
- The software recovers well from failures.

Understandability. "The more information we have, the smarter we will test."

- The design is well understood.
- Dependencies between internal, external, and shared components are well understood.
- Changes to the design are communicated.
- Technical documentation is instantly accessible.
- Technical documentation is well organized.
- Technical documentation is specific and detailed.
- Technical documentation is accurate.

The attributes suggested by Bach can be used by a software engineer to develop a software configuration (i.e., programs, data, and documents) that is amenable to testing.

And what about the tests themselves? Kaner, Falk, and Nguyen [KAN93] suggest the following attributes of a "good" test:

? What are the attributes of a "good" test?

1. A good test has a high probability of finding an error. To achieve this goal, the tester must understand the software and attempt to develop a mental picture of how the software might fail. Ideally, the classes of failure are probed. For example, one class of potential failure in a GUI (graphical user interface) is a failure to recognize proper mouse position. A set of tests would be designed to exercise the mouse in an attempt to demonstrate an error in mouse position recognition.
2. A good test is not redundant. Testing time and resources are limited. There is no point in conducting a test that has the same purpose as another test. Every test should have a different purpose (even if it is subtly different). For example, a module of the *SafeHome* software (discussed in earlier chapters) is designed to recognize a user password to activate and deactivate the system. In an effort to uncover an error in password input, the tester designs a series of tests that input a sequence of passwords. Valid and invalid passwords (four numeral sequences) are input as separate tests. However, each

valid/invalid password should probe a different mode of failure. For example, the invalid password 1234 should not be accepted by a system programmed to recognize 8080 as the valid password. If it is accepted, an error is present. Another test input, say 1235, would have the same purpose as 1234 and is therefore redundant. However, the invalid input 8081 or 8180 has a subtle difference, attempting to demonstrate that an error exists for passwords "close to" but not identical with the valid password.

3. A good test should be "best of breed" [KAN93]. In a group of tests that have a similar intent, time and resource limitations may mitigate toward the execution of only a subset of these tests. In such cases, the test that has the highest likelihood of uncovering a whole class of errors should be used.
4. A good test should be neither too simple nor too complex. Although it is sometimes possible to combine a series of tests into one test case, the possible side effects associated with this approach may mask errors. In general, each test should be executed separately.

17.2 TEST CASE DESIGN

Quote:

"There is only one rule in designing test cases: cover all features, but do not make too many test cases."
Tsuneo Yamaura

The design of tests for software and other engineered products can be as challenging as the initial design of the product itself. Yet, for reasons that we have already discussed, software engineers often treat testing as an afterthought, developing test cases that may "feel right" but have little assurance of being complete. Recalling the objectives of testing, we must design tests that have the highest likelihood of finding the most errors with a minimum amount of time and effort.

A rich variety of test case design methods have evolved for software. These methods provide the developer with a systematic approach to testing. More important, methods provide a mechanism that can help to ensure the completeness of tests and provide the highest likelihood for uncovering errors in software.

WebRef

The *Testing Techniques Newsletter* is an excellent source of information on testing methods: **www.testworks.com/News/TTN-Online/**

Any engineered product (and most other things) can be tested in one of two ways: (1) Knowing the specified function that a product has been designed to perform, tests can be conducted that demonstrate each function is fully operational while at the same time searching for errors in each function; (2) knowing the internal workings of a product, tests can be conducted to ensure that "all gears mesh," that is, internal operations are performed according to specifications and all internal components have been adequately exercised. The first test approach is called black-box testing and the second, white-box testing.

When computer software is considered, *black-box testing* alludes to tests that are conducted at the software interface. Although they are designed to uncover errors, black-box tests are used to demonstrate that software functions are operational, that input is properly accepted and output is correctly produced, and that the integrity of external information (e.g., a database) is maintained. A black-box test examines some fundamental aspect of a system with little regard for the internal logical structure of the software.

KEY POINT
White-box tests can be designed only after a component-level design (or source code) exists. The logical details of the program must be available.

White-box testing of software is predicated on close examination of procedural detail. Logical paths through the software are tested by providing test cases that exercise specific sets of conditions and/or loops. The "status of the program" may be examined at various points to determine if the expected or asserted status corresponds to the actual status.

At first glance it would seem that very thorough white-box testing would lead to "100 percent correct programs." All we need do is define all logical paths, develop test cases to exercise them, and evaluate results, that is, generate test cases to exercise program logic exhaustively. Unfortunately, exhaustive testing presents certain logistical problems. For even small programs, the number of possible logical paths can be very large. For example, consider the 100 line program in the language C. After some basic data declaration, the program contains two nested loops that execute from 1 to 20 times each, depending on conditions specified at input. Inside the interior loop, four if-then-else constructs are required. There are approximately 10^{14} possible paths that may be executed in this program!

KEY POINT
It is not possible to exhaustively test every program path because the number of paths is simply too large.

To put this number in perspective, we assume that a magic test processor ("magic" because no such processor exists) has been developed for exhaustive testing. The processor can develop a test case, execute it, and evaluate the results in one millisecond. Working 24 hours a day, 365 days a year, the processor would work for 3170 years to test the program. This would, undeniably, cause havoc in most development schedules. Exhaustive testing is impossible for large software systems.

White-box testing should not, however, be dismissed as impractical. A limited number of important logical paths can be selected and exercised. Important data structures can be probed for validity. The attributes of both black- and white-box testing can be combined to provide an approach that validates the software interface and selectively ensures that the internal workings of the software are correct.

17.3 WHITE-BOX TESTING

White-box testing, sometimes called *glass-box testing,* is a test case design method that uses the control structure of the procedural design to derive test cases. Using white-box testing methods, the software engineer can derive test cases that (1) guarantee that all independent paths within a module have been exercised at least once, (2) exercise all logical decisions on their true and false sides, (3) execute all loops at their boundaries and within their operational bounds, and (4) exercise internal data structures to ensure their validity.

A reasonable question might be posed at this juncture: "Why spend time and energy worrying about (and testing) logical minutiae when we might better expend effort ensuring that program requirements have been met?" Stated another way, why don't we spend all of our energy on black-box tests? The answer lies in the nature of software defects (e.g., [JON81]):

- *Logic errors and incorrect assumptions are inversely proportional to the probability that a program path will be executed.* Errors tend to creep into our work when we design and implement function, conditions, or control that are out of the mainstream. Everyday processing tends to be well understood (and well scrutinized), while "special case" processing tends to fall into the cracks.
- *We often believe that a logical path is not likely to be executed when, in fact, it may be executed on a regular basis.* The logical flow of a program is sometimes counterintuitive, meaning that our unconscious assumptions about flow of control and data may lead us to make design errors that are uncovered only once path testing commences.
- *Typographical errors are random.* When a program is translated into programming language source code, it is likely that some typing errors will occur. Many will be uncovered by syntax and type checking mechanisms, but others may go undetected until testing begins. It is as likely that a typo will exist on an obscure logical path as on a mainstream path.

Quote:
"Bugs lurk in corners and congregate at boundaries."
Boris Beizer

Each of these reasons provides an argument for conducting white-box tests. Black-box testing, no matter how thorough, may miss the kinds of errors noted here. White-box testing is far more likely to uncover them.

17.4 BASIS PATH TESTING

Basis path testing is a white-box testing technique first proposed by Tom McCabe [MCC76]. The basis path method enables the test case designer to derive a logical complexity measure of a procedural design and use this measure as a guide for defining a basis set of execution paths. Test cases derived to exercise the basis set are guaranteed to execute every statement in the program at least one time during testing.

17.4.1 Flow Graph Notation

Before the basis path method can be introduced, a simple notation for the representation of control flow, called a *flow graph* (or *program graph*) must be introduced.[3] The flow graph depicts logical control flow using the notation illustrated in Figure 17.1. Each structured construct (Chapter 16) has a corresponding flow graph symbol.

To illustrate the use of a flow graph, we consider the procedural design representation in Figure 17.2A. Here, a flowchart is used to depict program control structure.

3 In actuality, the basis path method can be conducted without the use of flow graphs. However, they serve as a useful tool for understanding control flow and illustrating the approach.

FIGURE 17.1
Flow graph notation

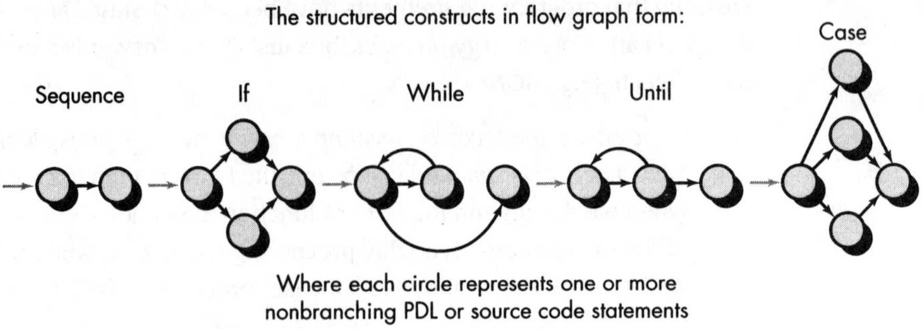

ADVICE

Draw a flow graph when the logical control structure of a module is complex. The flow graph enables you to trace program paths more readily.

Figure 17.2B maps the flowchart into a corresponding flow graph (assuming that no compound conditions are contained in the decision diamonds of the flowchart). Referring to Figure 17.2B, each circle, called a *flow graph node,* represents one or more procedural statements. A sequence of process boxes and a decision diamond can map into a single node. The arrows on the flow graph, called *edges* or *links,* represent flow of control and are analogous to flowchart arrows. An edge must terminate at a node, even if the node does not represent any procedural statements (e.g., see the symbol for the if-then-else construct). Areas bounded by edges and nodes are called *regions.* When counting regions, we include the area outside the graph as a region.[4]

When compound conditions are encountered in a procedural design, the generation of a flow graph becomes slightly more complicated. A compound condition occurs when one or more Boolean operators (logical OR, AND, NAND, NOR) is present in a conditional statement. Referring to Figure 17.3, the PDL segment translates into the flow graph shown. Note that a separate node is created for each of the conditions *a* and *b* in the statement IF *a* OR *b*. Each node that contains a condition is called a *predicate node* and is characterized by two or more edges emanating from it.

17.4.2 Cyclomatic Complexity

Cyclomatic complexity is a software metric that provides a quantitative measure of the logical complexity of a program. When used in the context of the basis path testing method, the value computed for cyclomatic complexity defines the number of independent paths in the basis set of a program and provides us with an upper bound for the number of tests that must be conducted to ensure that all statements have been executed at least once.

An *independent path* is any path through the program that introduces at least one new set of processing statements or a new condition. When stated in terms of a flow

4 A more-detailed discussion of graphs and their use in testing is contained in Section 17.6.1.

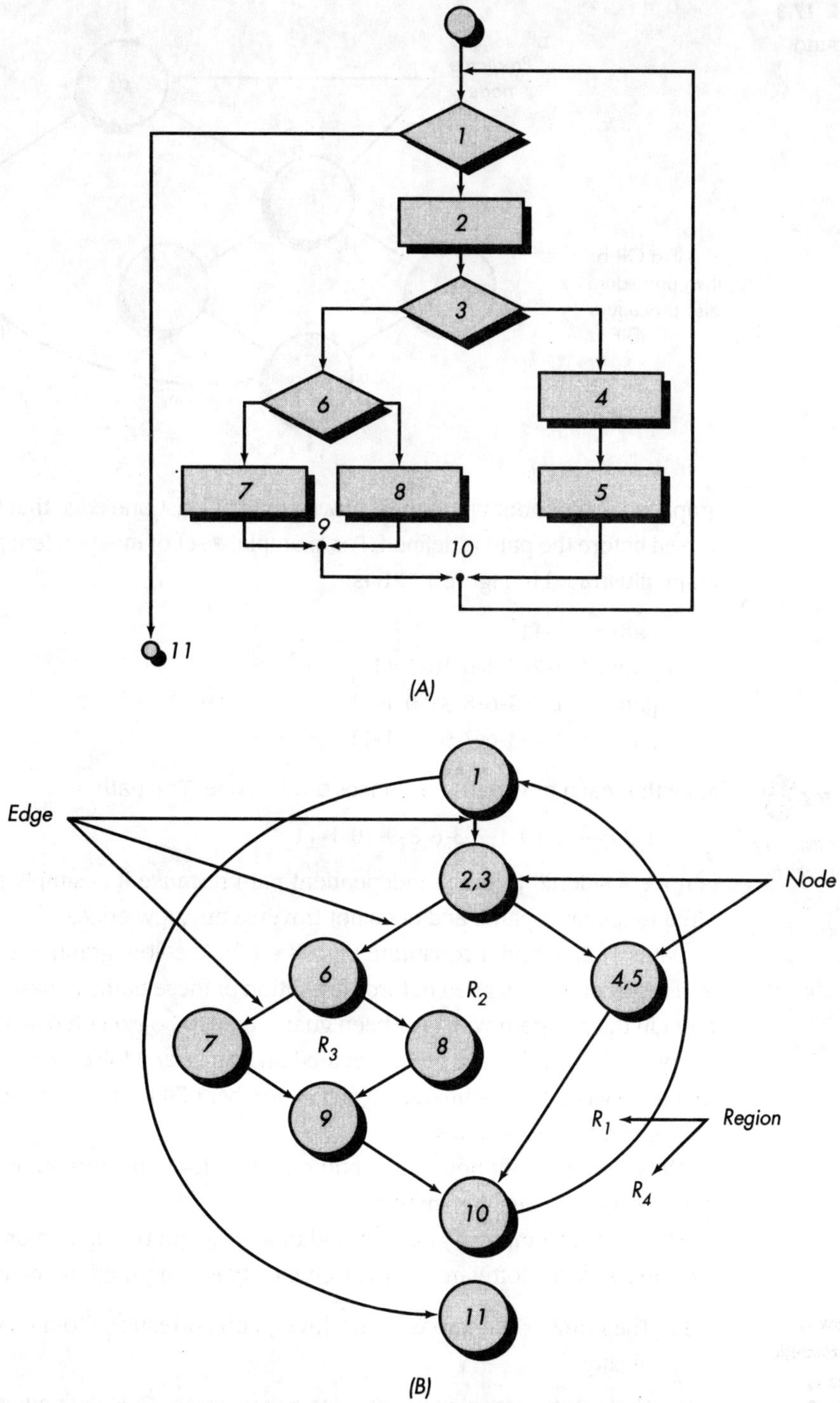

FIGURE 17.2 Flowchart, (A) and flow graph (B)

FIGURE 17.3
Compound logic

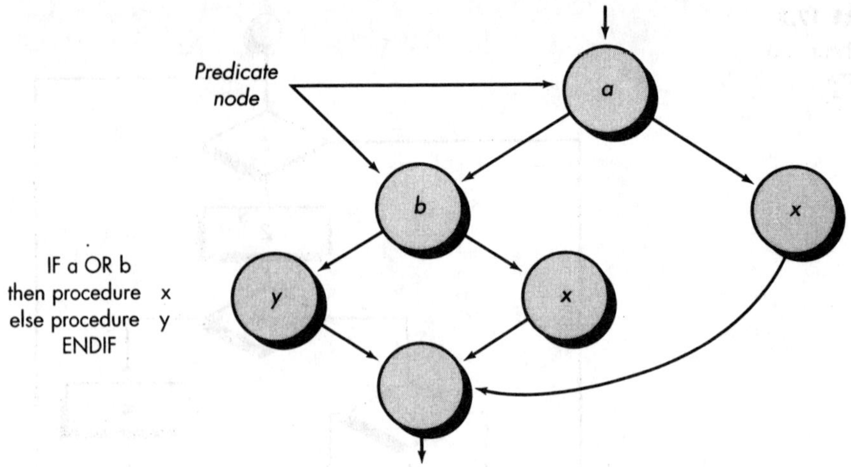

graph, an independent path must move along at least one edge that has not been traversed before the path is defined. For example, a set of independent paths for the flow graph illustrated in Figure 17.2B is

path 1: 1-11
path 2: 1-2-3-4-5-10-1-11
path 3: 1-2-3-6-8-9-10-1-11
path 4: 1-2-3-6-7-9-10-1-11

ADVICE

Cyclomatic complexity is a useful metric for predicting those modules that are likely to be error prone. It can be used for test planning as well as test case design.

Note that each new path introduces a new edge. The path

1-2-3-4-5-10-1-2-3-6-8-9-10-1-11

is not considered to be an independent path because it is simply a combination of already specified paths and does not traverse any new edges.

Paths 1, 2, 3, and 4 constitute a *basis set* for the flow graph in Figure 17.2B. That is, if tests can be designed to force execution of these paths (a basis set), every statement in the program will have been guaranteed to be executed at least one time and every condition will have been executed on its true and false sides. It should be noted that the basis set is not unique. In fact, a number of different basis sets can be derived for a given procedural design.

How do we know how many paths to look for? The computation of cyclomatic complexity provides the answer.

Cyclomatic complexity has a foundation in graph theory and provides us with an extremely useful software metric. Complexity is computed in one of three ways:

? **How is cyclomatic complexity computed?**

1. The number of regions of the flow graph correspond to the cyclomatic complexity.
2. Cyclomatic complexity, $V(G)$, for a flow graph, G, is defined as

$$V(G) = E - N + 2$$

KEY POINT

Cyclomatic complexity provides the upper bound on the number of test cases that must be executed to guarantee that every statement in a component has been executed at least once.

where E is the number of flow graph edges, N is the number of flow graph nodes.

3. Cyclomatic complexity, $V(G)$, for a flow graph, G, is also defined as

$$V(G) = P + 1$$

where P is the number of predicate nodes contained in the flow graph G.

Referring once more to the flow graph in Figure 17.2B, the cyclomatic complexity can be computed using each of the algorithms just noted:

1. The flow graph has four regions.
2. $V(G)$ = 11 edges − 9 nodes + 2 = 4.
3. $V(G)$ = 3 predicate nodes + 1 = 4.

Therefore, the cyclomatic complexity of the flow graph in Figure 17.2B is 4.

More important, the value for $V(G)$ provides us with an upper bound for the number of independent paths that form the basis set and, by implication, an upper bound on the number of tests that must be designed and executed to guarantee coverage of all program statements.

17.4.3 Deriving Test Cases

The basis path testing method can be applied to a procedural design or to source code. In this section, we present basis path testing as a series of steps. The procedure *average,* depicted in PDL in Figure 17.4, will be used as an example to illustrate each step in the test case design method. Note that *average,* although an extremely simple algorithm, contains compound conditions and loops. The following steps can be applied to derive the basis set:

Quote:

"To err is human, to find a bug, devine."

Robert Dunn

1. **Using the design or code as a foundation, draw a corresponding flow graph.** A flow graph is created using the symbols and construction rules presented in Section 16.4.1. Referring to the PDL for average in Figure 17.4, a flow graph is created by numbering those PDL statements that will be mapped into corresponding flow graph nodes. The corresponding flow graph is in Figure 17.5.

2. **Determine the cyclomatic complexity of the resultant flow graph.** The cyclomatic complexity, $V(G)$, is determined by applying the algorithms described in Section 17.5.2. It should be noted that $V(G)$ can be determined without developing a flow graph by counting all conditional statements in the PDL (for the procedure *average,* compound conditions count as two) and adding 1. Referring to Figure 17.5,

   $V(G)$ = 6 regions
   $V(G)$ = 17 edges − 13 nodes + 2 = 6
   $V(G)$ = 5 predicate nodes + 1 = 6

FIGURE 17.4 PDL for test case design with nodes identified

```
PROCEDURE average;

  * This procedure computes the average of 100 or fewer
    numbers that lie between bounding values; it also computes the
    sum and the total number valid.

  INTERFACE RETURNS average, total.input, total.valid;
  INTERFACE ACCEPTS value, minimum, maximum;

  TYPE value[1:100] IS SCALAR ARRAY;
  TYPE average, total.input, total.valid;
     minimum, maximum, sum IS SCALAR;
  TYPE i IS INTEGER;
(1)  i = 1;
(1)  total.input = total.valid = 0;          (2)
(1)  sum = 0;
(1)  DO WHILE value[i] <> -999 AND total.input < 100   (3)
   (4) increment total.input by 1;
(5)    IF value[i] > = minimum AND value[i] < = maximum   (6)
   (7)     THEN increment total.valid by 1;
   (7)          sum = s sum + value[i]
   (7)     ELSE skip
(8)    ENDIF
(8)    increment i by 1;
(9) ENDDO
  IF total.valid > 0   (10)
  (11) THEN average = sum / total.valid;
(12)   ELSE average = -999;
(13) ENDIF
END average
```

3. **Determine a basis set of linearly independent paths.** The value of $V(G)$ provides the number of linearly independent paths through the program control structure. In the case of procedure *average,* we expect to specify six paths:

   path 1: 1-2-10-11-13

   path 2: 1-2-10-12-13

   path 3: 1-2-3-10-11-13

   path 4: 1-2-3-4-5-8-9-2-. . .

   path 5: 1-2-3-4-5-6-8-9-2-. . .

   path 6: 1-2-3-4-5-6-7-8-9-2-. . .

   The ellipsis (. . .) following paths 4, 5, and 6 indicates that any path through the remainder of the control structure is acceptable. It is often worthwhile to identify predicate nodes as an aid in the derivation of test cases. In this case, nodes 2, 3, 5, 6, and 10 are predicate nodes.

4. **Prepare test cases that will force execution of each path in the basis set.** Data should be chosen so that conditions at the predicate nodes are appropriately set as each path is tested. Test cases that satisfy the basis set just described are

FIGURE 17.5
Flow graph for the procedure **average**

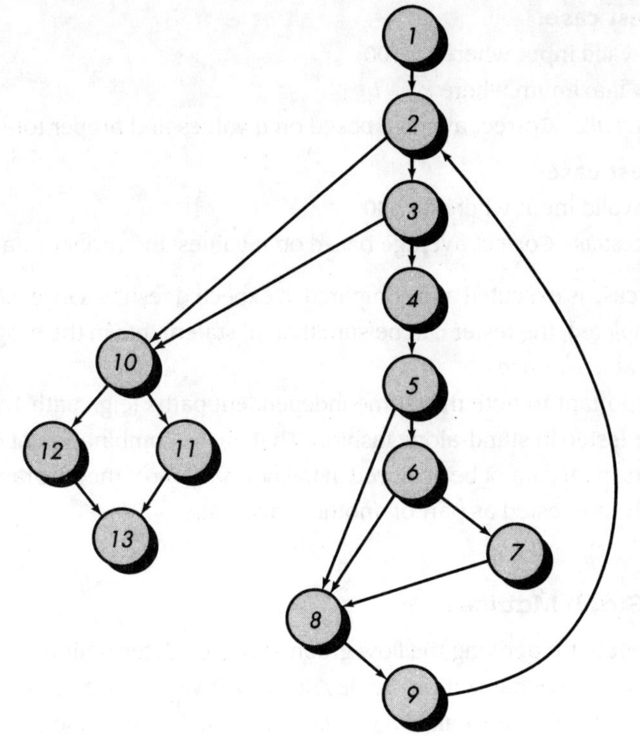

Quote:
"[Software engineers] considerably underestimate the number of tests required to verify a straightforward program."
Martyn Ould and Charles Unwin

Path 1 test case:

value(k) = valid input, where $k < i$ for $2 \le i \le 100$

value(i) = −999 where $2 \le i \le 100$

Expected results: Correct average based on k values and proper totals.

Note: Path 1 cannot be tested stand-alone but must be tested as part of path 4, 5, and 6 tests.

Path 2 test case:

value(1) = −999

Expected results: Average = −999; other totals at initial values.

Path 3 test case:

Attempt to process 101 or more values.

First 100 values should be valid.

Expected results: Same as test case 1.

Path 4 test case:

value(i) = valid input where i < 100

value(k) < minimum where $k < i$

Expected results: Correct average based on k values and proper totals.

Path 5 test case:

value(i) = valid input where $i < 100$

value(k) > maximum where $k <= i$

Expected results: Correct average based on n values and proper totals.

Path 6 test case:

value(i) = valid input where $i < 100$

Expected results: Correct average based on n values and proper totals.

Each test case is executed and compared to expected results. Once all test cases have been completed, the tester can be sure that all statements in the program have been executed at least once.

It is important to note that some independent paths (e.g., path 1 in our example) cannot be tested in stand-alone fashion. That is, the combination of data required to traverse the path cannot be achieved in the normal flow of the program. In such cases, these paths are tested as part of another path test.

17.4.4 Graph Matrices

The procedure for deriving the flow graph and even determining a set of basis paths is amenable to mechanization. To develop a software tool that assists in basis path testing, a data structure, called a *graph matrix,* can be quite useful.

A *graph matrix* is a square matrix whose size (i.e., number of rows and columns) is equal to the number of nodes on the flow graph. Each row and column corresponds to an identified node, and matrix entries correspond to connections (an edge) between nodes. A simple example of a flow graph and its corresponding graph matrix [BEI90] is shown in Figure 17.6.

Referring to the figure, each node on the flow graph is identified by numbers, while each edge is identified by letters. A letter entry is made in the matrix to correspond to a connection between two nodes. For example, node 3 is connected to node 4 by edge *b*.

? What is a graph matrix and how do we extend it for use in testing?

To this point, the graph matrix is nothing more than a tabular representation of a flow graph. However, by adding a *link weight* to each matrix entry, the graph matrix can become a powerful tool for evaluating program control structure during testing. The link weight provides additional information about control flow. In its simplest form, the link weight is 1 (a connection exists) or 0 (a connection does not exist). But link weights can be assigned other, more interesting properties:

- The probability that a link (edge) will be executed.
- The processing time expended during traversal of a link.
- The memory required during traversal of a link.
- The resources required during traversal of a link.

FIGURE 17.6
Graph matrix

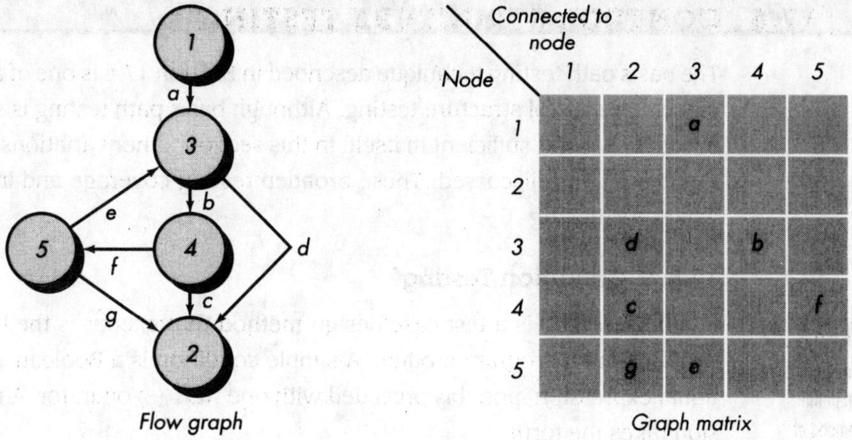

FIGURE 17.7
Connection matrix

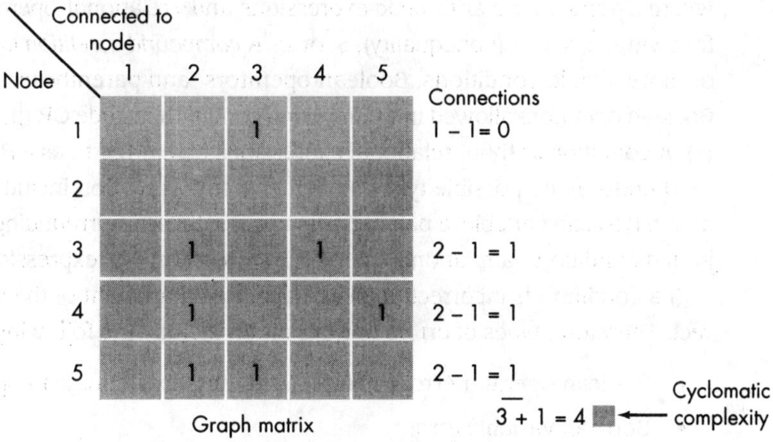

To illustrate, we use the simplest weighting to indicate connections (0 or 1). The graph matrix in Figure 17.6 is redrawn as shown in Figure 17.7. Each letter has been replaced with a 1, indicating that a connection exists (zeros have been excluded for clarity). Represented in this form, the graph matrix is called a *connection matrix.*

Referring to Figure 17.7, each row with two or more entries represents a predicate node. Therefore, performing the arithmetic shown to the right of the connection matrix provides us with still another method for determining cyclomatic complexity (Section 17.4.2).

Beizer [BEI90] provides a thorough treatment of additional mathematical algorithms that can be applied to graph matrices. Using these techniques, the analysis required to design test cases can be partially or fully automated.

17.5 CONTROL STRUCTURE TESTING

The basis path testing technique described in Section 17.4 is one of a number of techniques for control structure testing. Although basis path testing is simple and highly effective, it is not sufficient in itself. In this section, other variations on control structure testing are discussed. These broaden testing coverage and improve quality of white-box testing.

17.5.1 Condition Testing[5]

KEY POINT

Errors are much more common in the neighborhood of logical conditions than they are in the locus of sequential processing statements.

Condition testing is a test case design method that exercises the logical conditions contained in a program module. A simple condition is a Boolean variable or a relational expression, possibly preceded with one NOT (¬) operator. A relational expression takes the form

E_1 <relational-operator> E_2

where E_1 and E_2 are arithmetic expressions and <relational-operator> is one of the following: $<$, $\leq$, $=$, $\neq$ (nonequality), $>$, or $\geq$. A *compound condition* is composed of two or more simple conditions, Boolean operators, and parentheses. We assume that Boolean operators allowed in a compound condition include OR (|), AND (&) and NOT (¬). A condition without relational expressions is referred to as a *Boolean expression.*

Therefore, the possible types of elements in a condition include a Boolean operator, a Boolean variable, a pair of Boolean parentheses (surrounding a simple or compound condition), a relational operator, or an arithmetic expression.

If a condition is incorrect, then at least one component of the condition is incorrect. Therefore, types of errors in a condition include the following:

- Boolean operator error (incorrect/missing/extra Boolean operators).
- Boolean variable error.
- Boolean parenthesis error.
- Relational operator error.
- Arithmetic expression error.

The condition testing method focuses on testing each condition in the program. Condition testing strategies (discussed later in this section) generally have two advantages. First, measurement of test coverage of a condition is simple. Second, the test coverage of conditions in a program provides guidance for the generation of additional tests for the program.

The purpose of condition testing is to detect not only errors in the conditions of a program but also other errors in the program. If a test set for a program *P* is effective

5 Section 17.5.1 and 17.5.2 have been adapted from [TAI89] with permission of Professor K. C. Tai.

for detecting errors in the conditions contained in *P*, it is likely that this test set is also effective for detecting other errors in *P*. In addition, if a testing strategy is effective for detecting errors in a condition, then it is likely that this strategy will also be effective for detecting errors in a program.

A number of condition testing strategies have been proposed. *Branch testing* is probably the simplest condition testing strategy. For a compound condition *C*, the true and false branches of *C* and every simple condition in *C* need to be executed at least once [MYE79].

> **ADVICE**
>
> *Even if you decide against condition testing, you should spend time evaluating each condition in an effort to uncover errors. This is a primary hiding place for bugs!*

Domain testing [WHI80] requires three or four tests to be derived for a relational expression. For a relational expression of the form

E_1 <relational-operator> E_2

three tests are required to make the value of E_1 greater than, equal to, or less than that of E_2 [HOW82]. If <relational-operator> is incorrect and E_1 and E_2 are correct, then these three tests guarantee the detection of the relational operator error. To detect errors in E_1 and E_2, a test that makes the value of E_1 greater or less than that of E_2 should make the difference between these two values as small as possible.

For a Boolean expression with *n* variables, all of 2^n possible tests are required ($n > 0$). This strategy can detect Boolean operator, variable, and parenthesis errors, but it is practical only if *n* is small.

Error-sensitive tests for Boolean expressions can also be derived [FOS84, TAI87]. For a singular Boolean expression (a Boolean expression in which each Boolean variable occurs only once) with *n* Boolean variables ($n > 0$), we can easily generate a test set with less than 2^n tests such that this test set guarantees the detection of multiple Boolean operator errors and is also effective for detecting other errors.

Tai [TAI89] suggests a condition testing strategy that builds on the techniques just outlined. Called *BRO* (branch and relational operator) testing, the technique guarantees the detection of branch and relational operator errors in a condition provided that all Boolean variables and relational operators in the condition occur only once and have no common variables.

The BRO strategy uses condition constraints for a condition *C*. A condition constraint for *C* with *n* simple conditions is defined as $(D_1, D_2, \ldots, D_n)$, where D_i $(0 < i \leq n)$ is a symbol specifying a constraint on the outcome of the *i*th simple condition in condition *C*. A condition constraint *D* for condition *C* is said to be covered by an execution of *C* if, during this execution of *C*, the outcome of each simple condition in *C* satisfies the corresponding constraint in *D*.

For a Boolean variable, *B*, we specify a constraint on the outcome of *B* that states that *B* must be either true (t) or false (f). Similarly, for a relational expression, the symbols >, =, < are used to specify constraints on the outcome of the expression.

As an example, consider the condition

$$C_1: \; B_1 \,\&\, B_2$$

where B_1 and B_2 are Boolean variables. The condition constraint for C_1 is of the form (D_1, D_2), where each of D_1 and D_2 is t or f. The value (t, f) is a condition constraint for C_1 and is covered by the test that makes the value of B_1 to be true and the value of B_2 to be false. The BRO testing strategy requires that the constraint set {(t, t), (f, t), (t, f)} be covered by the executions of C_1. If C_1 is incorrect due to one or more Boolean operator errors, at least one of the constraint set will force C_1 to fail.

As a second example, a condition of the form

$$C_2: \; B_1 \,\&\, (E_3 = E_4)$$

where B_1 is a Boolean expression and E_3 and E_4 are arithmetic expressions. A condition constraint for C_2 is of the form (D_1, D_2), where each of D_1 is t or f and D_2 is >, =, <. Since C_2 is the same as C_1 except that the second simple condition in C_2 is a relational expression, we can construct a constraint set for C_2 by modifying the constraint set {(t, t), (f, t), (t, f)} defined for C_1. Note that t for $(E_3 = E_4)$ implies = and that f for $(E_3 = E_4)$ implies either < or >. By replacing (t, t) and (f, t) with (t, =) and (f, =), respectively, and by replacing (t, f) with (t, <) and (t, >), the resulting constraint set for C_2 is {(t, =), (f, =), (t, <), (t, >)}. Coverage of the preceding constraint set will guarantee detection of Boolean and relational operator errors in C_2.

As a third example, we consider a condition of the form

$$C_3: \; (E_1 > E_2) \,\&\, (E_3 = E_4)$$

where E_1, E_2, E_3, and E_4 are arithmetic expressions. A condition constraint for C_3 is of the form (D_1, D_2), where each of D_1 and D_2 is >, =, <. Since C_3 is the same as C_2 except that the first simple condition in C_3 is a relational expression, we can construct a constraint set for C_3 by modifying the constraint set for C_2, obtaining

{(>, =), (=, =), (<, =), (>, >), (>, <)}

Coverage of this constraint set will guarantee detection of relational operator errors in C_3.

17.5.2 Data Flow Testing

The *data flow testing* method selects test paths of a program according to the locations of definitions and uses of variables in the program. A number of data flow testing strategies have been studied and compared (e.g., [FRA88], [NTA88], [FRA93]).

To illustrate the data flow testing approach, assume that each statement in a program is assigned a unique statement number and that each function does not modify its parameters or global variables. For a statement with S as its statement number,

DEF(*S*) = {*X* | statement *S* contains a definition of *X*}

USE(*S*) = {*X* | statement *S* contains a use of *X*}

If statement *S* is an *if* or *loop* statement, its DEF set is empty and its USE set is based on the condition of statement *S*. The definition of variable *X* at statement *S* is said to be *live* at statement *S'* if there exists a path from statement *S* to statement *S'* that contains no other definition of *X*.

A *definition-use* (DU) *chain* of variable *X* is of the form [*X, S, S'*], where *S* and *S'* are statement numbers, *X* is in DEF(*S*) and USE(*S'*), and the definition of *X* in statement *S* is live at statement *S'*.

ADVICE

It is unrealistic to assume that data flow testing will be used extensively when testing a large system. However, it can be used in a targeted fashion for areas of the software that are suspect.

One simple data flow testing strategy is to require that every DU chain be covered at least once. We refer to this strategy as the *DU testing strategy*. It has been shown that DU testing does not guarantee the coverage of all branches of a program. However, a branch is not guaranteed to be covered by DU testing only in rare situations such as if-then-else constructs in which the *then part* has no definition of any variable and the *else part* does not exist. In this situation, the else branch of the *if* statement is not necessarily covered by DU testing.

Data flow testing strategies are useful for selecting test paths of a program containing nested *if* and *loop* statements. To illustrate this, consider the application of DU testing to select test paths for the PDL that follows:

```
proc x
  B1;
  do while C1
    if C2
      then
        if C4
          then B4;
          else B5;
        endif;
      else
        if C3
          then B2;
          else B3;
        endif;
    endif;
  enddo;
  B6;
end proc;
```

To apply the DU testing strategy to select test paths of the control flow diagram, we need to know the definitions and uses of variables in each condition or block in the PDL. Assume that variable *X* is defined in the last statement of blocks B1, B2, B3, B4, and B5 and is used in the first statement of blocks B2, B3, B4, B5, and B6. The DU testing strategy requires an execution of the shortest path from each of B_i, $0 < i \leq 5$, to each of B_j, $1 < j \le 6$. (Such testing also covers any use of variable X in conditions C1, C2, C3, and C4.) Although there are 25 DU chains of variable X, we need only five paths to cover these DU chains. The reason is that five paths are needed to cover the DU chain of X from B_i, $0 < i \le 5$, to B6 and other DU chains can be covered by making these five paths contain iterations of the loop.

If we apply the branch testing strategy to select test paths of the PDL just noted, we do not need any additional information. To select paths of the diagram for BRO testing, we need to know the structure of each condition or block. (After the selection of a path of a program, we need to determine whether the path is feasible for the program; that is, whether at least one input exists that exercises the path.)

Since the statements in a program are related to each other according to the definitions and uses of variables, the data flow testing approach is effective for error detection. However, the problems of measuring test coverage and selecting test paths for data flow testing are more difficult than the corresponding problems for condition testing.

17.5.3 Loop Testing

ADVICE

Complex loop structures are another hiding place for bugs. It's well worth spending time designing tests that fully exercise loop structures.

Loops are the cornerstone for the vast majority of all algorithms implemented in software. And yet, we often pay them little heed while conducting software tests.

Loop testing is a white-box testing technique that focuses exclusively on the validity of loop constructs. Four different classes of loops [BEI90] can be defined: simple loops, concatenated loops, nested loops, and unstructured loops (Figure 17.8).

Simple loops. The following set of tests can be applied to simple loops, where n is the maximum number of allowable passes through the loop.

1. Skip the loop entirely.
2. Only one pass through the loop.
3. Two passes through the loop.
4. m passes through the loop where $m < n$.
5. $n - 1, n, n + 1$ passes through the loop.

Nested loops. If we were to extend the test approach for simple loops to nested loops, the number of possible tests would grow geometrically as the level of nesting increases. This would result in an impractical number of tests. Beizer [BEI90] suggests an approach that will help to reduce the number of tests:

1. Start at the innermost loop. Set all other loops to minimum values.
2. Conduct simple loop tests for the innermost loop while holding the outer loops at their minimum iteration parameter (e.g., loop counter) values. Add other tests for out-of-range or excluded values.

FIGURE 17.8 Classes of loops

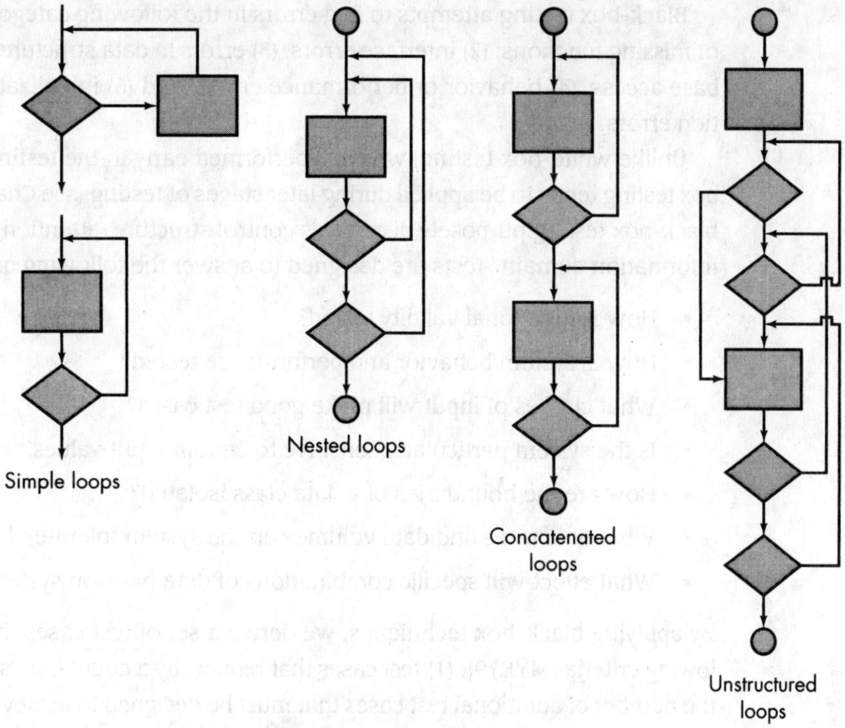

3. Work outward, conducting tests for the next loop, but keeping all other outer loops at minimum values and other nested loops to "typical" values.
4. Continue until all loops have been tested.

ADVICE *You can't test unstructured loops effectively. Redesign them.*

Concatenated loops. Concatenated loops can be tested using the approach defined for simple loops, if each of the loops is independent of the other. However, if two loops are concatenated and the loop counter for loop 1 is used as the initial value for loop 2, then the loops are not independent. When the loops are not independent, the approach applied to nested loops is recommended.

Unstructured loops. Whenever possible, this class of loops should be redesigned to reflect the use of the structured programming constructs (Chapter 16).

17.6 BLACK-BOX TESTING

Black-box testing, also called *behavioral testing,* focuses on the functional requirements of the software. That is, black-box testing enables the software engineer to derive sets of input conditions that will fully exercise all functional requirements for a program. Black-box testing is not an alternative to white-box techniques. Rather, it is a complementary approach that is likely to uncover a different class of errors than white-box methods.

Black-box testing attempts to find errors in the following categories: (1) incorrect or missing functions, (2) interface errors, (3) errors in data structures or external data base access, (4) behavior or performance errors, and (5) initialization and termination errors.

Unlike white-box testing, which is performed early in the testing process, black-box testing tends to be applied during later stages of testing (see Chapter 18). Because black-box testing purposely disregards control structure, attention is focused on the information domain. Tests are designed to answer the following questions:

- How is functional validity tested?
- How is system behavior and performance tested?
- What classes of input will make good test cases?
- Is the system particularly sensitive to certain input values?
- How are the boundaries of a data class isolated?
- What data rates and data volume can the system tolerate?
- What effect will specific combinations of data have on system operation?

By applying black-box techniques, we derive a set of test cases that satisfy the following criteria [MYE79]: (1) test cases that reduce, by a count that is greater than one, the number of additional test cases that must be designed to achieve reasonable testing and (2) test cases that tell us something about the presence or absence of classes of errors, rather than an error associated only with the specific test at hand.

17.6.1 Graph-Based Testing Methods

KEY POINT

A graph represents the relationships between data objects and program objects, enabling us to derive test cases that search for errors associated with these relationships.

The first step in black-box testing is to understand the objects[6] that are modeled in software and the relationships that connect these objects. Once this has been accomplished, the next step is to define a series of tests that verify "all objects have the expected relationship to one another [BEI95]." Stated in another way, software testing begins by creating a graph of important objects and their relationships and then devising a series of tests that will cover the graph so that each object and relationship is exercised and errors are uncovered.

To accomplish these steps, the software engineer begins by creating a *graph*—a collection of *nodes* that represent objects; *links* that represent the relationships between objects; *node weights* that describe the properties of a node (e.g., a specific data value or state behavior); and *link weights* that describe some characteristic of a link.[7]

6 In this context, the term *object* encompasses the data objects that we discussed in Chapters 11 and 12 as well as program objects such as modules or collections of programming language statements.

7 If these concepts seem vaguely familiar, recall that graphs were also used in Section 17.4.1 to create a program graph for the basis path testing method. The nodes of the program graph contained instructions (program objects) characterized as either procedural design representations or source code, and the directed links indicated the control flow between these program objects. Here, the use of graphs is extended to encompass black-box testing as well.

FIGURE 17.9
(A) Graph notation
(B) Simple example

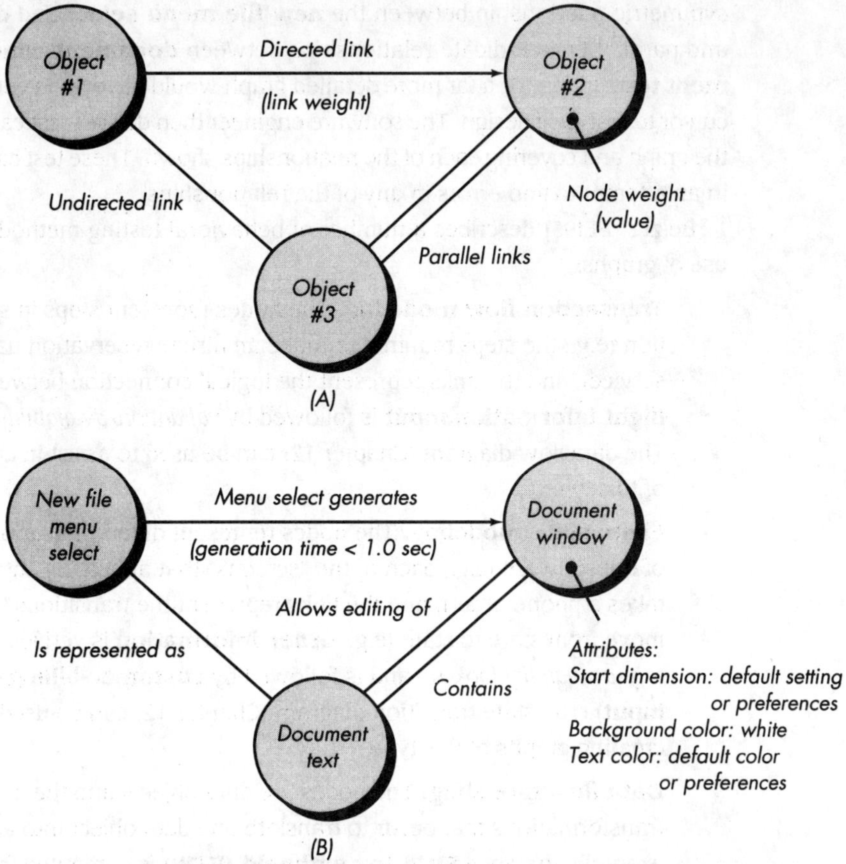

The symbolic representation of a graph is shown in Figure 17.9A. Nodes are represented as circles connected by links that take a number of different forms. A *directed link* (represented by an arrow) indicates that a relationship moves in only one direction. A *bidirectional link,* also called a *symmetric link*, implies that the relationship applies in both directions. *Parallel links* are used when a number of different relationships are established between graph nodes.

As a simple example, consider a portion of a graph for a word-processing application (Figure 17.9B) where

Object #1 = **new file menu select**
Object #2 = **document window**
Object #3 = **document text**

Referring to the figure, a menu select on **new file** generates a **document window.** The node weight of **document window** provides a list of the window attributes that are to be expected when the window is generated. The link weight indicates that the window must be generated in less than 1.0 second. An undirected link establishes a symmetric relationship between the **new file menu select** and **document text,** and parallel links indicate relationships between **document window** and **document text.** In reality, a far more detailed graph would have to be generated as a precursor to test case design. The software engineer then derives test cases by traversing the graph and covering each of the relationships shown. These test cases are designed in an attempt to find errors in any of the relationships.

Beizer [BEI95] describes a number of behavioral testing methods that can make use of graphs:

> **Transaction flow modeling.** The nodes represent steps in some transaction (e.g., the steps required to make an airline reservation using an on-line service), and the links represent the logical connection between steps (e.g., **flight.information.input** is followed by *validation/availability.processing*). The data flow diagram (Chapter 12) can be used to assist in creating graphs of this type.
>
> **Finite state modeling.** The nodes represent different user observable states of the software (e.g., each of the "screens" that appear as an order entry clerk takes a phone order), and the links represent the transitions that occur to move from state to state (e.g., **order-information** is verified during *inventory-availability look-up* and is followed by **customer-billing-information input**). The state transition diagram (Chapter 12) can be used to assist in creating graphs of this type.
>
> **Data flow modeling.** The nodes are data objects and the links are the transformations that occur to translate one data object into another. For example, the node **FICA.tax.withheld (FTW)** is computed from **gross.wages (GW)** using the relationship, FTW = 0.62 × GW.
>
> **Timing modeling.** The nodes are program objects and the links are the sequential connections between those objects. Link weights are used to specify the required execution times as the program executes.

A detailed discussion of each of these graph-based testing methods is beyond the scope of this book. The interested reader should see [BEI95] for a comprehensive discussion. It is worthwhile, however, to provide a generic outline of the graph-based testing approach.

? What generic activities are required during graph-based testing?

Graph-based testing begins with the definition of all nodes and node weights. That is, objects and attributes are identified. The data model (Chapter 12) can be used as a starting point, but it is important to note that many nodes may be program objects (not explicitly represented in the data model). To provide an indication of the start and stop points for the graph, it is useful to define entry and exit nodes.

Once nodes have been identified, links and link weights should be established. In general, links should be named, although links that represent control flow between program objects need not be named.

In many cases, the graph model may have loops (i.e., a path through the graph in which one or more nodes is encountered more than one time). Loop testing (Section 17.5.3) can also be applied at the behavioral (black-box) level. The graph will assist in identifying those loops that need to be tested.

Each relationship is studied separately so that test cases can be derived. The *transitivity* of sequential relationships is studied to determine how the impact of relationships propagates across objects defined in a graph. Transitivity can be illustrated by considering three objects, **X, Y,** and **Z.** Consider the following relationships:

X is required to compute **Y**
Y is required to compute **Z**

Therefore, a transitive relationship has been established between **X** and **Z**:

X is required to compute **Z**

Based on this transitive relationship, tests to find errors in the calculation of **Z** must consider a variety of values for both **X** and **Y.**

The *symmetry* of a relationship (graph link) is also an important guide to the design of test cases. If a link is indeed bidirectional (symmetric), it is important to test this feature. The UNDO feature [BEI95] in many personal computer applications implements limited symmetry. That is, UNDO allows an action to be negated after it has been completed. This should be thoroughly tested and all exceptions (i.e., places where UNDO cannot be used) should be noted. Finally, every node in the graph should have a relationship that leads back to itself; in essence, a "no action" or "null action" loop. These *reflexive* relationships should also be tested.

As test case design begins, the first objective is to achieve *node coverage.* By this we mean that tests should be designed to demonstrate that no nodes have been inadvertently omitted and that node weights (object attributes) are correct.

Next, *link coverage* is addressed. Each relationship is tested based on its properties. For example, a symmetric relationship is tested to demonstrate that it is, in fact, bidirectional. A transitive relationship is tested to demonstrate that transitivity is present. A reflexive relationship is tested to ensure that a null loop is present. When link weights have been specified, tests are devised to demonstrate that these weights are valid. Finally, loop testing is invoked (Section 17.5.3).

17.6.2 Equivalence Partitioning

Equivalence partitioning is a black-box testing method that divides the input domain of a program into classes of data from which test cases can be derived. An ideal test case single-handedly uncovers a class of errors (e.g., incorrect processing of all character data) that might otherwise require many cases to be executed before the general error is observed. Equivalence partitioning strives to define a test case that uncovers classes of errors, thereby reducing the total number of test cases that must be developed.

ADVICE

Input classes are known relatively early in the software process. For this reason, begin thinking about equivalence partitioning as the design is created.

Test case design for equivalence partitioning is based on an evaluation of equivalence classes for an input condition. Using concepts introduced in the preceding section, if a set of objects can be linked by relationships that are symmetric, transitive, and reflexive, an equivalence class is present [BEI95]. An *equivalence class* represents a set of valid or invalid states for input conditions. Typically, an input condition is either a specific numeric value, a range of values, a set of related values, or a Boolean condition. Equivalence classes may be defined according to the following guidelines:

1. If an input condition specifies a *range,* one valid and two invalid equivalence classes are defined.
2. If an input condition requires a specific *value,* one valid and two invalid equivalence classes are defined.
3. If an input condition specifies a member of a *set,* one valid and one invalid equivalence class are defined.
4. If an input condition is *Boolean,* one valid and one invalid class are defined.

As an example, consider data maintained as part of an automated banking application. The user can access the bank using a personal computer, provide a six-digit password, and follow with a series of typed commands that trigger various banking functions. During the log-on sequence, the software supplied for the banking application accepts data in the form

area code—blank or three-digit number
prefix—three-digit number not beginning with 0 or 1
suffix—four-digit number
password—six digit alphanumeric string
commands—check, deposit, bill pay, and the like

The input conditions associated with each data element for the banking application can be specified as

area code: Input condition, *Boolean*—the area code may or may not be present.
Input condition, *range*—values defined between 200 and 999, with specific exceptions.
prefix: Input condition, *range*—specified value >200
Input condition, value—four-digit length
password: Input condition, *Boolean*—a password may or may not be present.
Input condition, *value*—six-character string.
command: Input condition, *set*—containing commands noted previously.

Applying the guidelines for the derivation of equivalence classes, test cases for each input domain data item can be developed and executed. Test cases are selected so that the largest number of attributes of an equivalence class are exercised at once.

17.6.3 Boundary Value Analysis

KEY POINT BVA extends equivalence partitioning by focusing on data at the "edges" of an equivalence class.

For reasons that are not completely clear, a greater number of errors tends to occur at the boundaries of the input domain rather than in the "center." It is for this reason that *boundary value analysis* (BVA) has been developed as a testing technique. Boundary value analysis leads to a selection of test cases that exercise bounding values.

Boundary value analysis is a test case design technique that complements equivalence partitioning. Rather than selecting any element of an equivalence class, BVA leads to the selection of test cases at the "edges" of the class. Rather than focusing solely on input conditions, BVA derives test cases from the output domain as well [MYE79].

Guidelines for BVA are similar in many respects to those provided for equivalence partitioning:

? How do I create BVA test cases?

1. If an input condition specifies a range bounded by values *a* and *b*, test cases should be designed with values *a* and *b* and just above and just below *a* and *b*.
2. If an input condition specifies a number of values, test cases should be developed that exercise the minimum and maximum numbers. Values just above and below minimum and maximum are also tested.
3. Apply guidelines 1 and 2 to output conditions. For example, assume that a temperature vs. pressure table is required as output from an engineering analysis program. Test cases should be designed to create an output report that produces the maximum (and minimum) allowable number of table entries.
4. If internal program data structures have prescribed boundaries (e.g., an array has a defined limit of 100 entries), be certain to design a test case to exercise the data structure at its boundary.

Most software engineers intuitively perform BVA to some degree. By applying these guidelines, boundary testing will be more complete, thereby having a higher likelihood for error detection.

16.6.4 Comparison Testing

There are some situations (e.g., aircraft avionics, automobile braking systems) in which the reliability of software is absolutely critical. In such applications redundant hardware and software are often used to minimize the possibility of error. When redundant software is developed, separate software engineering teams develop independent versions of an application using the same specification. In such situations, each version can be tested with the same test data to ensure that all provide identical output. Then all versions are executed in parallel with real-time comparison of results to ensure consistency.

Using lessons learned from redundant systems, researchers (e.g., [BRI87]) have suggested that independent versions of software be developed for critical applications, even when only a single version will be used in the delivered computer-based system. These independent versions form the basis of a black-box testing technique called *comparison testing* or *back-to-back testing* [KNI89].

When multiple implementations of the same specification have been produced, test cases designed using other black-box techniques (e.g., equivalence partitioning) are provided as input to each version of the software. If the output from each version is the same, it is assumed that all implementations are correct. If the output is different, each of the applications is investigated to determine if a defect in one or more versions is responsible for the difference. In most cases, the comparison of outputs can be performed by an automated tool.

Comparison testing is not foolproof. If the specification from which all versions have been developed is in error, all versions will likely reflect the error. In addition, if each of the independent versions produces identical but incorrect results, condition testing will fail to detect the error.

17.6.5 Orthogonal Array Testing

There are many applications in which the input domain is relatively limited. That is, the number of input parameters is small and the values that each of the parameters may take are clearly bounded. When these numbers are very small (e.g., three input parameters taking on three discrete values each), it is possible to consider every input permutation and exhaustively test processing of the input domain. However, as the number of input values grows and the number of discrete values for each data item increases, exhaustive testing become impractical or impossible.

Orthogonal array testing can be applied to problems in which the input domain is relatively small but too large to accommodate exhaustive testing. The orthogonal array testing method is particularly useful in finding errors associated with *region faults*—an error category associated with faulty logic within a software component.

KEY POINT

Orthogonal array testing enables you to design test cases that provide maximum test coverage with a reasonable number of test cases.

To illustrate the difference between orthogonal array testing and more conventional "one input item at a time" approaches, consider a system that has three input items, *X, Y,* and *Z*. Each of these input items has three discrete values associated with it. There are $3^3 = 27$ possible test cases. Phadke [PHA97] suggests a geometric view of the possible test cases associated with *X, Y,* and *Z* illustrated in Figure 17.10. Referring to the figure, one input item at a time may be varied in sequence along each input axis. This results in relatively limited coverage of the input domain (represented by the left-hand cube in the figure).

When orthogonal array testing occurs, an *L9 orthogonal array* of test cases is created. The L9 orthogonal array has a "balancing property [PHA97]." That is, test cases (represented by black dots in the figure) are "dispersed uniformly throughout the test

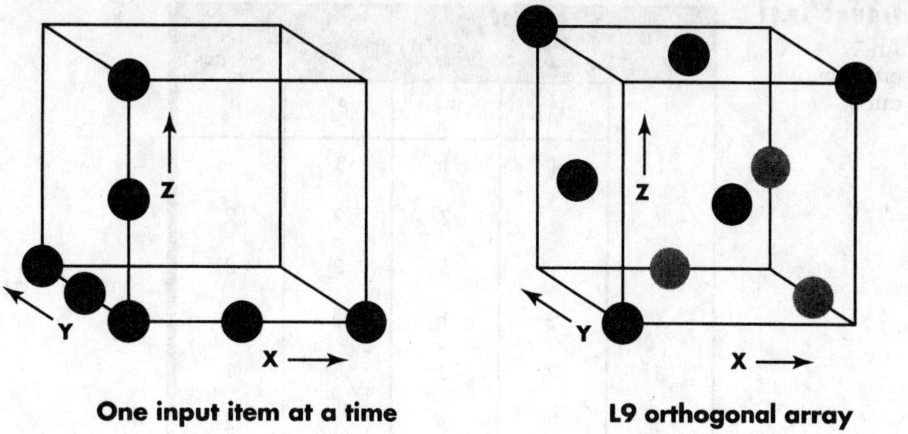

FIGURE 17.10
A geometric view of test cases [PHA97]

domain," as illustrated in the right-hand cube in Figure 17.10. Test coverage across the input domain is more complete.

To illustrate the use of the L9 orthogonal array, consider the *send* function for a fax application. Four parameters, P1, P2, P3, and P4, are passed to the *send* function. Each takes on three discrete values. For example, P1 takes on values:

P1 = 1, send it now
P1 = 2, send it one hour later
P1 = 3, send it after midnight

P2, P3, and P4 would also take on values of 1, 2 and 3, signifying other *send* functions.

If a "one input item at a time" testing strategy were chosen, the following sequence of tests (P1, P2, P3, P4) would be specified: (1, 1, 1, 1), (2, 1, 1, 1), (3, 1, 1, 1), (1, 2, 1, 1), (1, 3, 1, 1), (1, 1, 2, 1), (1, 1, 3, 1), (1, 1, 1, 2), and (1, 1, 1, 3). Phadke [PHA97] assesses these test cases in the following manner:

> Such test cases are useful only when one is certain that these test parameters do not interact. They can detect logic faults where a single parameter value makes the software malfunction. These faults are called *single mode faults*. This method cannot detect logic faults that cause malfunction when two or more parameters simultaneously take certain values; that is, it cannot detect any interactions. Thus its ability to detect faults is limited.

Given the relatively small number of input parameters and discrete values, exhaustive testing is possible. The number of tests required is $3^4 = 81$, large, but manageable. All faults associated with data item permutation would be found, but the effort required is relatively high.

The orthogonal array testing approach enables us to provide good test coverage with far fewer test cases than the exhaustive strategy. An L9 orthogonal array for the fax send function is illustrated in Figure 17.11.

FIGURE 17.11
An L9 orthogonal array

Test case	Test parameters			
	P_1	P_2	P_3	P_4
1	1	1	1	1
2	1	2	2	2
3	1	3	3	3
4	2	1	2	3
5	2	2	3	1
6	2	3	1	2
7	3	1	3	2
8	3	2	1	3
9	3	3	2	1

Phadke [PHA97] assesses the result of tests using the L9 orthogonal array in the following manner:

Detect and isolate all single mode faults. A single mode fault is a consistent problem with level of any single parameter. For example, if all test cases of factor P1 = 1 cause an error condition, it is a single mode failure. In this example tests 1, 2 and 3 [Figure 17.11] will show errors. By analyzing the information about which tests show errors, one can identify which parameter values cause the fault. In this example, by noting that tests 1, 2, and 3 cause an error, one can isolate [logical processing associated with "send it now" (P1 = 1)] as the source of the error. Such an isolation of fault is important to fix the fault.

Detect all double mode faults. If there exists a consistent problem when specific levels of two parameters occur together, it is called a *double mode fault.* Indeed, a double mode fault is an indication of pairwise incompatibility or harmful interactions between two test parameters.

Multimode faults. Orthogonal arrays [of the type shown] can assure the detection of only single and double mode faults. However, many multi-mode faults are also detected by these tests.

A detailed discussion of orthogonal array testing can be found in [PHA89].

17.7 TESTING FOR SPECIALIZED ENVIRONMENTS, ARCHITECTURES, AND APPLICATIONS

As computer software has become more complex, the need for specialized testing approaches has also grown. The white-box and black-box testing methods discussed in Sections 17.5 and 17.6 are applicable across all environments, architectures, and applications, but unique guidelines and approaches to testing are sometimes warranted. In this section we consider testing guidelines for specialized environments, architectures, and applications that are commonly encountered by software engineers.

17.7.1 Testing GUIs

XRef
Guidelines for the design of GUIs are presented in Chapter 15.

Graphical user interfaces (GUIs) present interesting challenges for software engineers. Because of reusable components provided as part of GUI development environments, the creation of the user interface has become less time consuming and more precise. But, at the same time, the complexity of GUIs has grown, leading to more difficulty in the design and execution of test cases.

Because many modern GUIs have the same look and feel, a series of standard tests can be derived. Finite state modeling graphs may be used to derive a series of tests that address specific data and program objects that are relevant to the GUI.

SEPA WEB CHECKLIST
Testing GUIs

Due to the large number of permutations associated with GUI operations, testing should be approached using automated tools. A wide array of GUI testing tools has appeared on the market over the past few years. For further discussion, see Chapter 31.

17.7.2 Testing of Client/Server Architectures

Client/server (C/S) architectures represent a significant challenge for software testers. The distributed nature of client/server environments, the performance issues associated with transaction processing, the potential presence of a number of different hardware platforms, the complexities of network communication, the need to service multiple clients from a centralized (or in some cases, distributed) database, and the coordination requirements imposed on the server all combine to make testing of C/S architectures and the software that reside within them considerably more difficult than stand-alone applications. In fact, recent industry studies indicate a significant increase in testing time and cost when C/S environments are developed.

XRef
Client/server software engineering is presented in Chapter 28.

17.7.3 Testing Documentation and Help Facilities

The term *software testing* conjures images of large numbers of test cases prepared to exercise computer programs and the data that they manipulate. Recalling the definition of *software* presented in the first chapter of this book, it is important to note that testing must also extend to the third element of the software configuration—documentation.

Errors in documentation can be as devastating to the acceptance of the program as errors in data or source code. Nothing is more frustrating than following a user guide or an on-line help facility exactly and getting results or behaviors that do not coincide with those predicted by the documentation. It is for this reason that that documentation testing should be a meaningful part of every software test plan.

Documentation testing can be approached in two phases. The first phase, *review and inspection* (Chapter 8), examines the document for editorial clarity. The second phase, *live test,* uses the documentation in conjunction with the use of the actual program.

Surprisingly, a live test for documentation can be approached using techniques that are analogous to many of the black-box testing methods discussed in Section 17.6. Graph-based testing can be used to describe the use of the program; equivalence partitioning and boundary value analysis can be used to define various classes of input and associated interactions. Program usage is then tracked through the documentation. The following questions should be answered during both phases:

? What questions should be addressed as we test documentation?

- Does the documentation accurately describe how to accomplish each mode of use?
- Is the description of each interaction sequence accurate?
- Are examples accurate?
- Are terminology, menu descriptions, and system responses consistent with the actual program?
- Is it relatively easy to locate guidance within the documentation?
- Can troubleshooting be accomplished easily with the documentation?
- Are the document table of contents and index accurate and complete?
- Is the design of the document (layout, typefaces, indentation, graphics) conducive to understanding and quick assimilation of information?
- Are all software error messages displayed for the user described in more detail in the document? Are actions to be taken as a consequence of an error message clearly delineated?
- If hypertext links are used, are they accurate and complete?
- If hypertext is used, is the navigation design appropriate for the information required?

The only viable way to answer these questions is to have an independent third party (e.g., selected users) test the documentation in the context of program usage. All discrepancies are noted and areas of document ambiguity or weakness are defined for potential rewrite.

17.7.4 Testing for Real-Time Systems

The time-dependent, asynchronous nature of many real-time applications adds a new and potentially difficult element to the testing mix—time. Not only does the test case designer have to consider white- and black-box test cases but also event handling (i.e., interrupt processing), the timing of the data, and the parallelism of the tasks (processes) that handle the data. In many situations, test data provided when a real-time system is in one state will result in proper processing, while the same data provided when the system is in a different state may lead to error.

For example, the real-time software that controls a new photocopier accepts operator interrupts (i.e., the machine operator hits control keys such as RESET or DARKEN) with no error when the machine is making copies (in the "copying" state). These same operator interrupts, if input when the machine is in the "jammed" state, cause a display of the diagnostic code indicating the location of the jam to be lost (an error).

Real-Time Systems

In addition, the intimate relationship that exists between real-time software and its hardware environment can also cause testing problems. Software tests must consider the impact of hardware faults on software processing. Such faults can be extremely difficult to simulate realistically.

Comprehensive test case design methods for real-time systems have yet to evolve. However, an overall four-step strategy can be proposed:

Task testing. The first step in the testing of real-time software is to test each task independently. That is, white-box and black-box tests are designed and executed for each task. Each task is executed independently during these tests. Task testing uncovers errors in logic and function but not timing or behavior.

WebRef

The *Software Testing Discussion Forum* presents topics of interest to testing professionals: **www.ondaweb.com/HyperNews/get.cgi/forums/sti.html**

Behavioral testing. Using system models created with CASE tools, it is possible to simulate the behavior of a real-time system and examine its behavior as a consequence of external events. These analysis activities can serve as the basis for the design of test cases that are conducted when the real-time software has been built. Using a technique that is similar to equivalence partitioning (Section 17.6.1), events (e.g., interrupts, control signals) are categorized for testing. For example, events for the photocopier might be user interrupts (e.g., reset counter), mechanical interrupts (e.g., paper jammed), system interrupts (e.g., toner low), and failure modes (e.g., roller overheated). Each of these events is tested individually and the behavior of the executable system is examined to detect errors that occur as a consequence of processing associated with these events. The behavior of the system model (developed during the analysis activity) and the executable software can be compared for conformance. Once each class of events has been tested, events are presented to the system in random order and with random frequency. The behavior of the software is examined to detect behavior errors.

Intertask testing. Once errors in individual tasks and in system behavior have been isolated, testing shifts to time-related errors. Asynchronous tasks that are known to communicate with one another are tested with different data rates and processing load to determine if intertask synchronization errors will occur. In addition, tasks that communicate via a message queue or data store are tested to uncover errors in the sizing of these data storage areas.

System testing. Software and hardware are integrated and a full range of system tests (Chapter 18) are conducted in an attempt to uncover errors at the software/hardware interface. Most real-time systems process interrupts. Therefore, testing the handling of these Boolean events is essential. Using the state transition diagram and the control specification (Chapter 12), the tester develops a list of all possible interrupts and the processing that occurs as a consequence of the interrupts. Tests are then designed to assess the following system characteristics:

- Are interrupt priorities properly assigned and properly handled?
- Is processing for each interrupt handled correctly?
- Does the performance (e.g., processing time) of each interrupt-handling procedure conform to requirements?
- Does a high volume of interrupts arriving at critical times create problems in function or performance?

In addition, global data areas that are used to transfer information as part of interrupt processing should be tested to assess the potential for the generation of side effects.

17.8 SUMMARY

The primary objective for test case design is to derive a set of tests that have the highest likelihood for uncovering errors in the software. To accomplish this objective, two different categories of test case design techniques are used: white-box testing and black-box testing.

White-box tests focus on the program control structure. Test cases are derived to ensure that all statements in the program have been executed at least once during testing and that all logical conditions have been exercised. Basis path testing, a white-box technique, makes use of program graphs (or graph matrices) to derive the set of linearly independent tests that will ensure coverage. Condition and data flow testing further exercise program logic, and loop testing complements other white-box techniques by providing a procedure for exercising loops of varying degrees of complexity.

Hetzel [HET84] describes white-box testing as "testing in the small." His implication is that the white-box tests that we have considered in this chapter are typically applied to small program components (e.g., modules or small groups of modules). Black-box testing, on the other hand, broadens our focus and might be called "testing in the large."

Black-box tests are designed to validate functional requirements without regard to the internal workings of a program. Black-box testing techniques focus on the information domain of the software, deriving test cases by partitioning the input and output domain of a program in a manner that provides thorough test coverage. Equivalence partitioning divides the input domain into classes of data that are likely to exercise specific software function. Boundary value analysis probes the program's ability to handle data at the limits of acceptability. Orthogonal array testing provides an efficient, systematic method for testing systems will small numbers of input parameters.

Specialized testing methods encompass a broad array of software capabilities and application areas. Testing for graphical user interfaces, client/server architectures, documentation and help facilities, and real-time systems each require specialized guidelines and techniques.

Experienced software developers often say, "Testing never ends, it just gets transferred from you [the software engineer] to your customer. Every time your customer uses the program, a test is being conducted." By applying test case design, the software engineer can achieve more complete testing and thereby uncover and correct the highest number of errors before the "customer's tests" begin.

REFERENCES

[BEI90] Beizer, B., *Software Testing Techniques*, 2nd ed., Van Nostrand-Reinhold, 1990.

[BEI95] Beizer, B., *Black-Box Testing*, Wiley, 1995.

[BRI87] Brilliant, S.S., J.C. Knight, and N.G. Levenson, "The Consistent Comparison Problem in N-Version Software," *ACM Software Engineering Notes*, vol. 12, no. 1, January 1987, pp. 29–34.

[DAV95] Davis, A., *201 Principles of Software Development*, McGraw-Hill, 1995.

[DEU79] Deutsch, M., "Verification and Validation," in *Software Engineering* (R. Jensen and C. Tonies, eds.), Prentice-Hall, 1979, pp. 329–408.

[FOS84] Foster, K.A., "Sensitive Test Data for Boolean Expressions," *ACM Software Engineering Notes*, vol. 9, no. 2, April 1984, pp. 120–125.

[FRA88] Frankl, P.G. and E.J. Weyuker, "An Applicable Family of Data Flow Testing Criteria," *IEEE Trans. Software Engineering*, vol. SE-14, no. 10, October 1988, pp. 1483–1498.

[FRA93] Frankl, P.G. and S. Weiss, "An Experimental Comparison of the Effectiveness of Branch Testing and Data Flow," *IEEE Trans. Software Engineering*, vol. SE-19, no. 8, August 1993, pp. 770–787.

[HET84] Hetzel, W., *The Complete Guide to Software Testing*, QED Information Sciences, 1984.

[HOW82] Howden, W.E., "Weak Mutation Testing and the Completeness of Test Cases," *IEEE Trans. Software Engineering*, vol. SE-8, no. 4, July 1982, pp. 371–379.

[JON81] Jones, T.C., *Programming Productivity: Issues for the 80s*, IEEE Computer Society Press, 1981.

[KAN93] Kaner, C., J. Falk, and H.Q. Nguyen, *Testing Computer Software*, 2nd ed., Van Nostrand-Reinhold, 1993.

[KNI89] Knight, J. and P. Ammann, "Testing Software Using Multiple Versions," Software Productivity Consortium, Report No. 89029N, Reston, VA, June 1989.

[MCC76] McCabe, T., "A Software Complexity Measure," *IEEE Trans. Software Engineering,* vol. SE-2, December 1976, pp. 308–320.

[MYE79] Myers, G., *The Art of Software Testing,* Wiley, 1979.

[NTA88] Ntafos, S.C., A Comparison of Some Structural Testing Strategies," *IEEE Trans. Software Engineering,* vol. SE-14, no. 6, June 1988, pp. 868–874.

[PHA89] Phadke, M.S., *Quality Engineering Using Robust Design,* Prentice-Hall, 1989.

[PHA97] Phadke, M.S., "Planning Efficient Software Tests," *Crosstalk,* vol. 10, no. 10, October 1997, pp. 11–15.

[TAI87] Tai, K.C. and H.K. Su, "Test Generation for Boolean Expressions," *Proc. COMPSAC '87,* October 1987, pp. 278–283.

[TAI89] Tai, K.C., "What to Do Beyond Branch Testing," *ACM Software Engineering Notes,* vol. 14, no. 2, April 1989, pp. 58–61.

[WHI80] White, L.J. and E.I. Cohen, "A Domain Strategy for Program Testing," *IEEE Trans. Software Engineering,* vol. SE-6, no. 5, May 1980, pp. 247–257.

PROBLEMS AND POINTS TO PONDER

17.1. Myers [MYE79] uses the following program as a self-assessment for your ability to specify adequate testing: A program reads three integer values. The three values are interpreted as representing the lengths of the sides of a triangle. The program prints a message that states whether the triangle is scalene, isosceles, or equilateral. Develop a set of test cases that you feel will adequately test this program.

17.2. Design and implement the program (with error handling where appropriate) specified in Problem 1. Derive a flow graph for the program and apply basis path testing to develop test cases that will guarantee that all statements in the program have been tested. Execute the cases and show your results.

17.3. Can you think of any additional testing objectives that are not discussed in Section 17.1.1?

17.4. Apply the basis path testing technique to any one of the programs that you have implemented in Problems 16.4 through 16.11.

17.5. Specify, design, and implement a software tool that will compute the cyclomatic complexity for the programming language of your choice. Use the graph matrix as the operative data structure in your design.

17.6. Read Beizer [BEI95] and determine how the program you have developed in Problem 17.5 can be extended to accommodate various link weights. Extend your tool to process execution probabilities or link processing times.

17.7. Use the condition testing approach described in Section 17.5.1 to design a set of test cases for the program you created in Problem 17.2.

17.8. Using the data flow testing approach described in Section 17.5.2, make a list of definition-use chains for the program you created in Problem 17.2.

17.9. Design an automated tool that will recognize loops and categorize them as indicated in Section 17.5.3.

17.10. Extend the tool described in Problem 17.9 to generate test cases for each loop category, once encountered. It will be necessary to perform this function interactively with the tester.

17.11. Give at least three examples in which black-box testing might give the impression that "everything's OK," while white-box tests might uncover an error. Give at least three examples in which white-box testing might give the impression that "everything's OK," while black-box tests might uncover an error.

17.12. Will exhaustive testing (even if it is possible for very small programs) guarantee that the program is 100 percent correct?

17.13. Using the equivalence partitioning method, derive a set of test cases for *SafeHome* system described earlier in this book.

17.14. Using boundary value analysis, derive a set of test cases for the PHTRS system described in Problem 12.13.

17.15. Do a bit of outside research and write a brief paper that discusses the mechanics for generating orthogonal arrays for test data.

17.16. Select a specific GUI for a program with which you are familiar and design a series of tests to exercise the GUI.

17.17. Do some research on a client/server system with which you are familiar. Develop a set of user scenarios and then create an operational profile for the system.

17.18. Test a user manual (or help facility) for an application that you use frequently. Find at least one error in the documentation.

FURTHER READINGS AND INFORMATION SOURCES

Software engineering presents both technical and management challenges. Books by Black (*Managing the Testing Process,* Microsoft Press, 1999); Dustin, Rashka, and Paul (*Test Process Improvement: Step-by-Step Guide to Structured Testing,* Addison-Wesley, 1999); Perry (*Surviving the Top Ten Challenges of Software Testing: A People-Oriented Approach,* Dorset House, 1997); and Kit and Finzi (*Software Testing in the Real World: Improving the Process,* Addison-Wesley, 1995) address management and process issues.

A number of excellent books are now available for those readers who desire additional information on software testing technology. Kaner, Nguyen, and Falk (*Testing Computer Software,* Wiley, 1999); Hutcheson (*Software Testing Methods and Metrics: The Most Important Tests,* McGraw-Hill, 1997); Marick (*The Craft of Software Testing: Subsystem Testing Including Object-Based and Object-Oriented Testing,* Prentice-Hall, 1995); Jorgensen (*Software Testing : A Craftsman's Approach,* CRC Press, 1995) present treatments of the subject that consider testing methods and strategies.

Myers [MYE79] remains a classic text, covering black-box techniques in considerable detail. Beizer [BEI90] provides comprehensive coverage of white-box techniques, introducing a level of mathematical rigor that has often been missing in other treatments of testing. His later book [BEI95] presents a concise treatment of important methods. Perry (*Effective Methods for Software Testing,* Wiley-QED, 1995) and Friedman and Voas (*Software Assessment: Reliability, Safety, Testability,* Wiley, 1995) present good introductions to testing strategies and tactics. Mosley (*The Handbook of MIS Application Software Testing,* Prentice-Hall, 1993) discusses testing issues for large information systems, and Marks (*Testing Very Big Systems,* McGraw-Hill, 1992) discusses the special issues that must be considered when testing major programming systems.

Software testing is a resource-intensive activity. It is for this reason that many organizations automate parts of the testing process. Books by Dustin, Rashka, and Poston (*Automated Software Testing: Introduction, Management, and Performance,* Addison-Wesley, 1999) and Poston (*Automating Specification-Based Software Testing,* IEEE Computer Society, 1996) discuss tools, strategies, and methods for automated testing. An excellent source of information on automated tools for software testing is the *Testing Tools Reference Guide* (Software Quality Engineering, Jacksonville, FL, updated yearly). This directory contains descriptions of hundreds of testing tools, categorized by testing activity, hardware platform, and software support.

A number of books consider testing methods and strategies in specialized application areas. Gardiner (*Testing Safety-Related Software: A Practical Handbook,* Springer-Verlag, 1999) has edited a book that addresses testing of safety-critical systems. Mosley (*Client/Server Software Testing on the Desk Top and the Web,* Prentice-Hall, 1999) discusses the test process for clients, servers, and network components. Rubin (*Handbook of Usability Testing,* Wiley, 1994) has written a useful guide for those who must exercise human interfaces.

A wide variety of information sources on software testing and related subjects is available on the Internet. An up-to-date list of World Wide Web references that are relevant to testing concepts, methods, and strategies can be found at the SEPA Web site:

http://www.mhhe.com/engcs/compsci/sepa/resources/test-techniques.mhtml

CHAPTER

18 SOFTWARE TESTING STRATEGIES

KEY CONCEPTS

A strategy for software testing integrates software test case design methods into a well-planned series of steps that result in the successful construction of software. The strategy provides a road map that describes the steps to be conducted as part of testing, when these steps are planned and then undertaken, and how much effort, time, and resources will be required. Therefore, any testing strategy must incorporate test planning, test case design, test execution, and resultant data collection and evaluation.

A software testing strategy should be flexible enough to promote a customized testing approach. At the same time, it must be rigid enough to promote reasonable planning and management tracking as the project progresses. Shooman [SHO83] discusses these issues:

> In many ways, testing is an individualistic process, and the number of different types of tests varies as much as the different development approaches. For many years, our only defense against programming errors was careful design and the native intelligence of the programmer. We are now in an era in which modern design techniques [and formal technical reviews] are helping us to reduce the number of initial errors that are inherent in the code. Similarly, different test methods are beginning to cluster themselves into several distinct approaches and philosophies.

QUICK LOOK

What is it? Designing effective test cases (Chapter 17) is important, but so is the strategy you use to execute them. Should you develop a formal plan for your tests? Should you test the entire program as a whole or run tests only on a small part of it? Should you rerun tests you've already conducted as you add new components to a large system? When should you involve the customer? These and many other questions are answered when you develop a software testing strategy.

Who does it? A strategy for software testing is developed by the project manager, software engineers, and testing specialists.

Why is it important? Testing often accounts for more project effort than any other software engineering activity. If it is conducted haphazardly, time is wasted, unnecessary effort is expended, and even worse, errors sneak through undetected. It would therefore seem reasonable to establish a systematic strategy for testing software.

What are the steps? Testing begins "in the small" and progresses "to the large." By this we mean that early testing focuses on a single component and applies white- and black-box tests to uncover errors in program logic and function. After individual components are tested they must be integrated. Testing continues as the software is constructed. Finally, a series of high-order tests are executed once the full program is operational.

QUICK LOOK

These tests are designed to uncover errors in requirements.

What is the work product? A Test Specification documents the software team's approach to testing by defining a plan that describes an overall strategy and a procedure that defines specific testing steps and the tests that will be conducted.

How do I ensure that I've done it right? By reviewing the Test Specification prior to testing, you can assess the completeness of test cases and testing tasks. An effective test plan and procedure will lead to the orderly construction of the software and the discovery of errors at each stage in the construction process.

These "approaches and philosophies" are what we shall call *strategy*. In Chapter 17, the technology of software testing was presented.[1] In this chapter, we focus our attention on the strategy for software testing.

18.1 A STRATEGIC APPROACH TO SOFTWARE TESTING

Testing is a set of activities that can be planned in advance and conducted systematically. For this reason a template for software testing—a set of steps into which we can place specific test case design techniques and testing methods—should be defined for the software process.

A number of software testing strategies have been proposed in the literature. All provide the software developer with a template for testing and all have the following generic characteristics:

WebRef
Useful information on software testing strategies is provided by the *Software Testing Newsletter* at **www.ondaweb.com/sti/newsltr.htm**

- Testing begins at the component level[2] and works "outward" toward the integration of the entire computer-based system.
- Different testing techniques are appropriate at different points in time.
- Testing is conducted by the developer of the software and (for large projects) an independent test group.
- Testing and debugging are different activities, but debugging must be accommodated in any testing strategy.

A strategy for software testing must accommodate low-level tests that are necessary to verify that a small source code segment has been correctly implemented as well as high-level tests that validate major system functions against customer requirements. A strategy must provide guidance for the practitioner and a set of milestones for the manager. Because the steps of the test strategy occur at a time when dead-

1 Testing for object-oriented systems is discussed in Chapter 23.

2 For object-oriented systems, testing begins at the class or object level. See Chapter 23 for details.

line pressure begins to rise, progress must be measurable and problems must surface as early as possible.

18.1.1 Verification and Validation

Software testing is one element of a broader topic that is often referred to as *verification and validation* (V&V). *Verification* refers to the set of activities that ensure that software correctly implements a specific function. *Validation* refers to a different set of activities that ensure that the software that has been built is traceable to customer requirements. Boehm [BOE81] states this another way:

Verification: "Are we building the product right?"
Validation: "Are we building the right product?"

XRef
SQA activities are discussed in detail in Chapter 8.

The definition of V&V encompasses many of the activities that we have referred to as *software quality assurance* (SQA).

Verification and validation encompasses a wide array of SQA activities that include formal technical reviews, quality and configuration audits, performance monitoring, simulation, feasibility study, documentation review, database review, algorithm analysis, development testing, qualification testing, and installation testing [WAL89]. Although testing plays an extremely important role in V&V, many other activities are also necessary.

Quote:
"Testing is an unavoidable part of any responsible effort to develop a software system."
William Howden

Testing does provide the last bastion from which quality can be assessed and, more pragmatically, errors can be uncovered. But testing should not be viewed as a safety net. As they say, "You can't test in quality. If it's not there before you begin testing, it won't be there when you're finished testing." Quality is incorporated into software throughout the process of software engineering. Proper application of methods and tools, effective formal technical reviews, and solid management and measurement all lead to quality that is confirmed during testing.

Miller [MIL77] relates software testing to quality assurance by stating that "the underlying motivation of program testing is to affirm software quality with methods that can be economically and effectively applied to both large-scale and small-scale systems."

18.1.2 Organizing for Software Testing

For every software project, there is an inherent conflict of interest that occurs as testing begins. The people who have built the software are now asked to test the software. This seems harmless in itself; after all, who knows the program better than its developers? Unfortunately, these same developers have a vested interest in demonstrating that the program is error free, that it works according to customer requirements, and that it will be completed on schedule and within budget. Each of these interests mitigate against thorough testing.

From a psychological point of view, software analysis and design (along with coding) are *constructive* tasks. The software engineer creates a computer program, its documentation, and related data structures. Like any builder, the software engineer is proud of the edifice that has been built and looks askance at anyone who attempts to tear it down. When testing commences, there is a subtle, yet definite, attempt to "break" the thing that the software engineer has built. From the point of view of the builder, testing can be considered to be (psychologically) *destructive*. So the builder treads lightly, designing and executing tests that will demonstrate that the program works, rather than uncovering errors. Unfortunately, errors will be present. And, if the software engineer doesn't find them, the customer will!

KEY POINT

An independent test group does not have the "conflict of interest" that builders of the software have.

There are often a number of misconceptions that can be erroneously inferred from the preceeding discussion: (1) that the developer of software should do no testing at all, (2) that the software should be "tossed over the wall" to strangers who will test it mercilessly, (3) that testers get involved with the project only when the testing steps are about to begin. Each of these statements is incorrect.

The software developer is always responsible for testing the individual units (components) of the program, ensuring that each performs the function for which it was designed. In many cases, the developer also conducts integration testing—a testing step that leads to the construction (and test) of the complete program structure. Only after the software architecture is complete does an independent test group become involved.

ADVICE

If an ITG does not exist within your organization, you'll have to take its point of view. When you test, try to break the software.

The role of an *independent test group* (ITG) is to remove the inherent problems associated with letting the builder test the thing that has been built. Independent testing removes the conflict of interest that may otherwise be present. After all, personnel in the independent group team are paid to find errors.

However, the software engineer doesn't turn the program over to ITG and walk away. The developer and the ITG work closely throughout a software project to ensure that thorough tests will be conducted. While testing is conducted, the developer must be available to correct errors that are uncovered.

The ITG is part of the software development project team in the sense that it becomes involved during the specification activity and stays involved (planning and specifying test procedures) throughout a large project. However, in many cases the ITG reports to the software quality assurance organization, thereby achieving a degree of independence that might not be possible if it were a part of the software engineering organization.

18.1.3 A Software Testing Strategy

The software engineering process may be viewed as the spiral illustrated in Figure 18.1. Initially, system engineering defines the role of software and leads to software requirements analysis, where the information domain, function, behavior, performance, constraints, and validation criteria for software are established. Moving

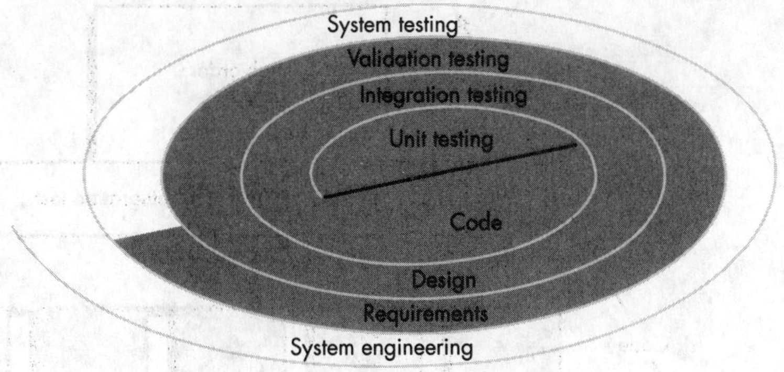

FIGURE 18.1 Testing strategy

inward along the spiral, we come to design and finally to coding. To develop computer software, we spiral inward along streamlines that decrease the level of abstraction on each turn.

What is the overall strategy for software testing?

A strategy for software testing may also be viewed in the context of the spiral (Figure 18.1). *Unit testing* begins at the vortex of the spiral and concentrates on each unit (i.e., component) of the software as implemented in source code. Testing progresses by moving outward along the spiral to *integration testing,* where the focus is on design and the construction of the software architecture. Taking another turn outward on the spiral, we encounter *validation testing,* where requirements established as part of software requirements analysis are validated against the software that has been constructed. Finally, we arrive at *system testing,* where the software and other system elements are tested as a whole. To test computer software, we spiral out along streamlines that broaden the scope of testing with each turn.

Considering the process from a procedural point of view, testing within the context of software engineering is actually a series of four steps that are implemented sequentially. The steps are shown in Figure 18.2. Initially, tests focus on each component individually, ensuring that it functions properly as a unit. Hence, the name *unit testing*. Unit testing makes heavy use of white-box testing techniques, exercising specific paths in a module's control structure to ensure complete coverage and maximum error detection. Next, components must be assembled or integrated to form the complete software package. Integration testing addresses the issues associated with the dual problems of verification and program construction. Black-box test case design techniques are the most prevalent during integration, although a limited amount of white-box testing may be used to ensure coverage of major control paths. After the software has been integrated (constructed), a set of high-order tests are conducted. Validation criteria (established during requirements analysis) must be tested. Validation testing provides final assurance that software meets all functional, behavioral, and performance requirements. Black-box testing techniques are used exclusively during validation.

XRef
Black-box and white-box testing techniques are discussed in Chapter 17.

FIGURE 18.2
Software testing steps

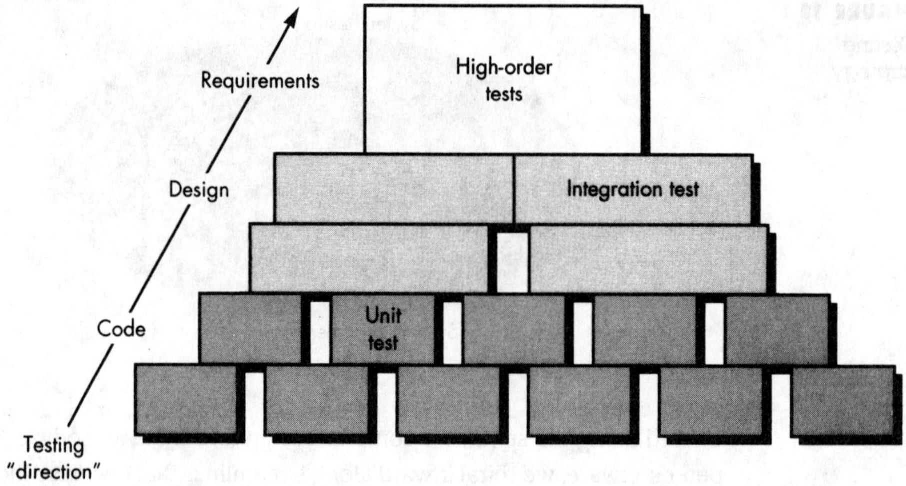

The last high-order testing step falls outside the boundary of software engineering and into the broader context of computer system engineering. Software, once validated, must be combined with other system elements (e.g., hardware, people, databases). System testing verifies that all elements mesh properly and that overall system function/performance is achieved.

18.1.4 Criteria for Completion of Testing

A classic question arises every time software testing is discussed: "When are we done testing—how do we know that we've tested enough?" Sadly, there is no definitive answer to this question, but there are a few pragmatic responses and early attempts at empirical guidance.

When are we done testing?

One response to the question is: "You're never done testing, the burden simply shifts from you (the software engineer) to your customer." Every time the customer/user executes a computer program, the program is being tested. This sobering fact underlines the importance of other software quality assurance activities. Another response (somewhat cynical but nonetheless accurate) is: "You're done testing when you run out of time or you run out of money."

Although few practitioners would argue with these responses, a software engineer needs more rigorous criteria for determining when sufficient testing has been conducted. Musa and Ackerman [MUS89] suggest a response that is based on statistical criteria: "No, we cannot be absolutely certain that the software will never fail, but relative to a theoretically sound and experimentally validated statistical model, we have done sufficient testing to say with 95 percent confidence that the probability of 1000 CPU hours of failure free operation in a probabilistically defined environment is at least 0.995."

FIGURE 18.3
Failure intensity as a function of execution time

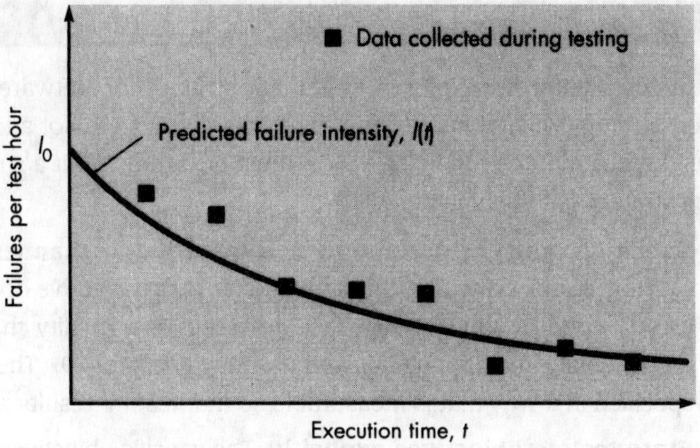

Using statistical modeling and software reliability theory, models of software failures (uncovered during testing) as a function of execution time can be developed [MUS89]. A version of the failure model, called a *logarithmic Poisson execution-time model,* takes the form

$$f(t) = (1/p) \ln [l_0 pt + 1] \tag{18-1}$$

where $f(t)$ = cumulative number of failures that are expected to occur once the software has been tested for a certain amount of execution time, t,

l_0 = the initial software failure intensity (failures per time unit) at the beginning of testing,

p = the exponential reduction in failure intensity as errors are uncovered and repairs are made.

The instantaneous failure intensity, $l(t)$ can be derived by taking the derivative of $f(t)$

$$l(t) = l_0 / (l_0 pt + 1) \tag{18-2}$$

Using the relationship noted in Equation (18-2), testers can predict the drop-off of errors as testing progresses. The actual error intensity can be plotted against the predicted curve (Figure 18.3). If the actual data gathered during testing and the logarithmic Poisson execution time model are reasonably close to one another over a number of data points, the model can be used to predict total testing time required to achieve an acceptably low failure intensity.

By collecting metrics during software testing and making use of existing software reliability models, it is possible to develop meaningful guidelines for answering the question: "When are we done testing?" There is little debate that further work remains to be done before quantitative rules for testing can be established, but the empirical approaches that currently exist are considerably better than raw intuition.

18.2 STRATEGIC ISSUES

Later in this chapter, we explore a systematic strategy for software testing. But even the best strategy will fail if a series of overriding issues are not addressed. Tom Gilb [GIL95] argues that the following issues must be addressed if a successful software testing strategy is to be implemented:

What guidelines lead to a successful testing strategy?

Specify product requirements in a quantifiable manner long before testing commences. Although the overriding objective of testing is to find errors, a good testing strategy also assesses other quality characteristics such as portability, maintainability, and usability (Chapter 19). These should be specified in a way that is measurable so that testing results are unambiguous.

State testing objectives explicitly. The specific objectives of testing should be stated in measurable terms. For example, test effectiveness, test coverage, mean time to failure, the cost to find and fix defects, remaining defect density or frequency of occurrence, and test work-hours per regression test all should be stated within the test plan [GIL95].

XRef
Use-cases describe a scenario for software use and are discussed in Chapter 11.

Understand the users of the software and develop a profile for each user category. Use-cases that describe the interaction scenario for each class of user can reduce overall testing effort by focusing testing on actual use of the product.

Develop a testing plan that emphasizes "rapid cycle testing." Gilb [GIL95] recommends that a software engineering team "learn to test in rapid cycles (2 percent of project effort) of customer-useful, at least field 'trialable,' increments of functionality and/or quality improvement." The feedback generated from these rapid cycle tests can be used to control quality levels and the corresponding test strategies.

Quote:
"Testing only to end-user perceived requirements is like inspecting a building based on the work done by the interior decorator at the expense of the foundations, girders, and plumbing."
Boris Beizer

Build "robust" software that is designed to test itself. Software should be designed in a manner that uses antibugging (Section 18.3.1) techniques. That is, software should be capable of diagnosing certain classes of errors. In addition, the design should accommodate automated testing and regression testing.

Use effective formal technical reviews as a filter prior to testing. Formal technical reviews (Chapter 8) can be as effective as testing in uncovering errors. For this reason, reviews can reduce the amount of testing effort that is required to produce high-quality software.

Conduct formal technical reviews to assess the test strategy and test cases themselves. Formal technical reviews can uncover inconsistencies, omissions, and outright errors in the testing approach. This saves time and also improves product quality.

Develop a continuous improvement approach for the testing process. The test strategy should be measured. The metrics collected during testing should be used as part of a statistical process control approach for software testing.

18.3 UNIT TESTING

Unit testing focuses verification effort on the smallest unit of software design—the software component or module. Using the component-level design description as a guide, important control paths are tested to uncover errors within the boundary of the module. The relative complexity of tests and uncovered errors is limited by the constrained scope established for unit testing. The unit test is white-box oriented, and the step can be conducted in parallel for multiple components.

18.3.1 Unit Test Considerations

Unit Testing

The tests that occur as part of unit tests are illustrated schematically in Figure 18.4. The module interface is tested to ensure that information properly flows into and out of the program unit under test. The local data structure is examined to ensure that data stored temporarily maintains its integrity during all steps in an algorithm's execution. Boundary conditions are tested to ensure that the module operates properly at boundaries established to limit or restrict processing. All independent paths (basis paths) through the control structure are exercised to ensure that all statements in a module have been executed at least once. And finally, all error handling paths are tested.

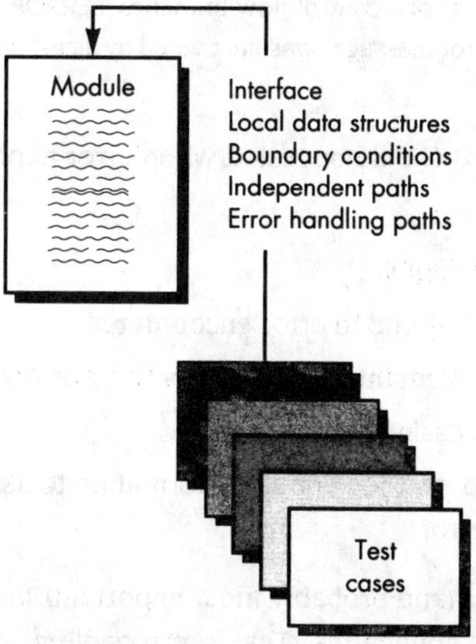

FIGURE 18.4
Unit test

Tests of data flow across a module interface are required before any other test is initiated. If data do not enter and exit properly, all other tests are moot. In addition, local data structures should be exercised and the local impact on global data should be ascertained (if possible) during unit testing.

Selective testing of execution paths is an essential task during the unit test. Test cases should be designed to uncover errors due to erroneous computations, incorrect comparisons, or improper control flow. Basis path and loop testing are effective techniques for uncovering a broad array of path errors.

? What errors are commonly found during unit testing?

Among the more common errors in computation are (1) misunderstood or incorrect arithmetic precedence, (2) mixed mode operations, (3) incorrect initialization, (4) precision inaccuracy, (5) incorrect symbolic representation of an expression. Comparison and control flow are closely coupled to one another (i.e., change of flow frequently occurs after a comparison). Test cases should uncover errors such as (1) comparison of different data types, (2) incorrect logical operators or precedence, (3) expectation of equality when precision error makes equality unlikely, (4) incorrect comparison of variables, (5) improper or nonexistent loop termination, (6) failure to exit when divergent iteration is encountered, and (7) improperly modified loop variables.

Good design dictates that error conditions be anticipated and error-handling paths set up to reroute or cleanly terminate processing when an error does occur. Yourdon [YOU75] calls this approach *antibugging.* Unfortunately, there is a tendency to incorporate error handling into software and then never test it. A true story may serve to illustrate:

> A major interactive design system was developed under contract. In one transaction processing module, a practical joker placed the following error handling message after a series of conditional tests that invoked various control flow branches: ERROR! THERE IS NO WAY YOU CAN GET HERE. This "error message" was uncovered by a customer during user training!

ADVICE

Be sure that you design tests to execute every error-handling path. If you don't, the path may fail when it is invoked, exacerbating an already dicey situation.

Among the potential errors that should be tested when error handling is evaluated are

1. Error description is unintelligible.
2. Error noted does not correspond to error encountered.
3. Error condition causes system intervention prior to error handling.
4. Exception-condition processing is incorrect.
5. Error description does not provide enough information to assist in the location of the cause of the error.

Boundary testing is the last (and probably most important) task of the unit test step. Software often fails at its boundaries. That is, errors often occur when the *n*th element of an *n*-dimensional array is processed, when the *i*th repetition of a loop with

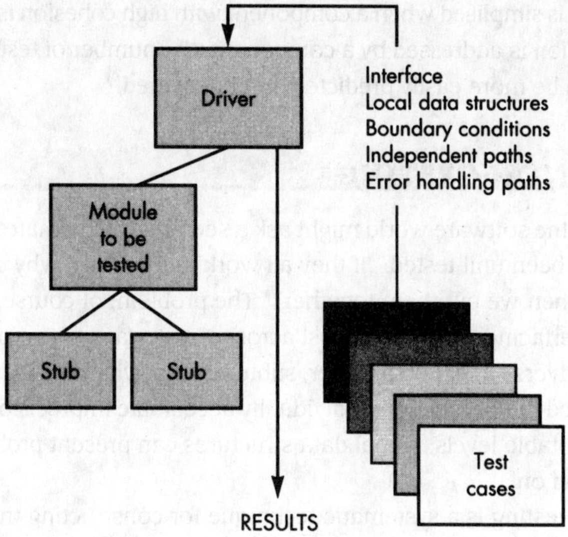

FIGURE 18.5 Unit test environment

i passes is invoked, when the maximum or minimum allowable value is encountered. Test cases that exercise data structure, control flow, and data values just below, at, and just above maxima and minima are very likely to uncover errors.

18.3.2 Unit Test Procedures

ADVICE

There are some situations in which you will not have the resources to do comprehensive unit testing. Select critical modules and those with high cyclomatic complexity and unit test only them.

Unit testing is normally considered as an adjunct to the coding step. After source level code has been developed, reviewed, and verified for correspondence to component-level design, unit test case design begins. A review of design information provides guidance for establishing test cases that are likely to uncover errors in each of the categories discussed earlier. Each test case should be coupled with a set of expected results.

Because a component is not a stand-alone program, driver and/or stub software must be developed for each unit test. The unit test environment is illustrated in Figure 18.5. In most applications a *driver* is nothing more than a "main program" that accepts test case data, passes such data to the component (to be tested), and prints relevant results. *Stubs* serve to replace modules that are subordinate (called by) the component to be tested. A stub or "dummy subprogram" uses the subordinate module's interface, may do minimal data manipulation, prints verification of entry, and returns control to the module undergoing testing.

Drivers and stubs represent overhead. That is, both are software that must be written (formal design is not commonly applied) but that is not delivered with the final software product. If drivers and stubs are kept simple, actual overhead is relatively low. Unfortunately, many components cannot be adequately unit tested with "simple" overhead software. In such cases, complete testing can be postponed until the integration test step (where drivers or stubs are also used).

Unit testing is simplified when a component with high cohesion is designed. When only one function is addressed by a component, the number of test cases is reduced and errors can be more easily predicted and uncovered.

18.4 INTEGRATION TESTING[3]

A neophyte in the software world might ask a seemingly legitimate question once all modules have been unit tested: "If they all work individually, why do you doubt that they'll work when we put them together?" The problem, of course, is "putting them together"—interfacing. Data can be lost across an interface; one module can have an inadvertent, adverse affect on another; subfunctions, when combined, may not produce the desired major function; individually acceptable imprecision may be magnified to unacceptable levels; global data structures can present problems. Sadly, the list goes on and on.

Integration testing is a systematic technique for constructing the program structure while at the same time conducting tests to uncover errors associated with interfacing. The objective is to take unit tested components and build a program structure that has been dictated by design.

ADVICE

Taking the big bang approach to integration is a lazy strategy that is doomed to failure. Integration testing should be conducted incrementally.

There is often a tendency to attempt nonincremental integration; that is, to construct the program using a "big bang" approach. All components are combined in advance. The entire program is tested as a whole. And chaos usually results! A set of errors is encountered. Correction is difficult because isolation of causes is complicated by the vast expanse of the entire program. Once these errors are corrected, new ones appear and the process continues in a seemingly endless loop.

Incremental integration is the antithesis of the big bang approach. The program is constructed and tested in small increments, where errors are easier to isolate and correct; interfaces are more likely to be tested completely; and a systematic test approach may be applied. In the sections that follow, a number of different incremental integration strategies are discussed.

18.4.1 Top-down Integration

ADVICE

When you develop a detailed project schedule you have to consider the manner in which integration will occur so that components will be available when needed.

Top-down integration testing is an incremental approach to construction of program structure. Modules are integrated by moving downward through the control hierarchy, beginning with the main control module (main program). Modules subordinate (and ultimately subordinate) to the main control module are incorporated into the structure in either a depth-first or breadth-first manner.

Referring to Figure 18.6, *depth-first integration* would integrate all components on a major control path of the structure. Selection of a major path is somewhat arbitrary and depends on application-specific characteristics. For example, selecting the left-hand path, components M_1, M_2, M_5 would be integrated first. Next, M_8 or (if neces-

3 Integration strategies for object-oriented systems are discussed in Chapter 23.

FIGURE 18.6
Top-down integration

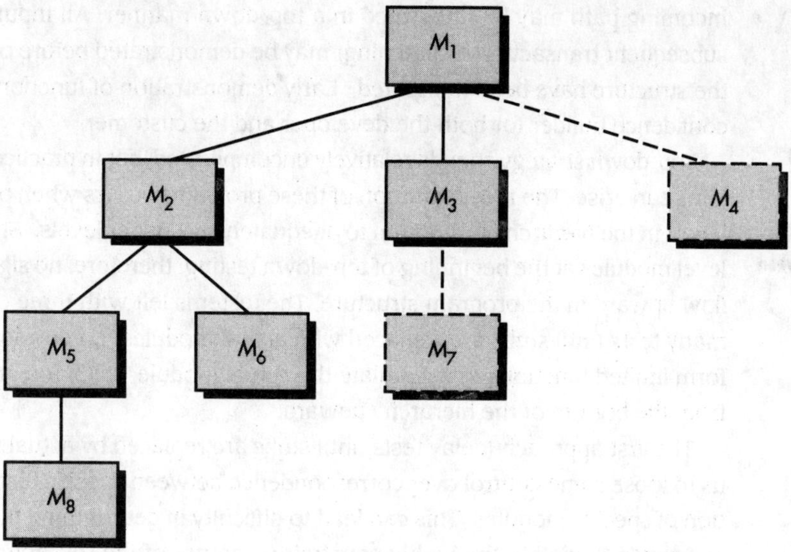

sary for proper functioning of M_2) M_6 would be integrated. Then, the central and right-hand control paths are built. *Breadth-first integration* incorporates all components directly subordinate at each level, moving across the structure horizontally. From the figure, components M_2, M_3, and M_4 (a replacement for stub S_4) would be integrated first. The next control level, M_5, M_6, and so on, follows.

The integration process is performed in a series of five steps:

What are the steps for top-down integration?

1. The main control module is used as a test driver and stubs are substituted for all components directly subordinate to the main control module.
2. Depending on the integration approach selected (i.e., depth or breadth first), subordinate stubs are replaced one at a time with actual components.
3. Tests are conducted as each component is integrated.
4. On completion of each set of tests, another stub is replaced with the real component.
5. Regression testing (Section 18.4.3) may be conducted to ensure that new errors have not been introduced.

The process continues from step 2 until the entire program structure is built.

XRef
Factoring is important for certain architectural styles. See Chapter 14 for additional details.

The top-down integration strategy verifies major control or decision points early in the test process. In a well-factored program structure, decision making occurs at upper levels in the hierarchy and is therefore encountered first. If major control problems do exist, early recognition is essential. If depth-first integration is selected, a complete function of the software may be implemented and demonstrated. For example, consider a classic transaction structure (Chapter 14) in which a complex series of interactive inputs is requested, acquired, and validated via an incoming path. The incoming path may be integrated in a top-down manner. All input processing (for subsequent transaction dispatching) may be demonstrated before other elements of the structure have been integrated. Early demonstration of functional capability is a confidence builder for both the developer and the customer.

What problems may be encountered when the top-down integration strategy is chosen?

Top-down strategy sounds relatively uncomplicated, but in practice, logistical problems can arise. The most common of these problems occurs when processing at low levels in the hierarchy is required to adequately test upper levels. Stubs replace low-level modules at the beginning of top-down testing; therefore, no significant data can flow upward in the program structure. The tester is left with three choices: (1) delay many tests until stubs are replaced with actual modules, (2) develop stubs that perform limited functions that simulate the actual module, or (3) integrate the software from the bottom of the hierarchy upward.

The first approach (delay tests until stubs are replaced by actual modules) causes us to loose some control over correspondence between specific tests and incorporation of specific modules. This can lead to difficulty in determining the cause of errors and tends to violate the highly constrained nature of the top-down approach. The second approach is workable but can lead to significant overhead, as stubs become more and more complex. The third approach, called *bottom-up testing*, is discussed in the next section.

18.4.2 Bottom-up Integration

Bottom-up integration testing, as its name implies, begins construction and testing with *atomic modules* (i.e., components at the lowest levels in the program structure). Because components are integrated from the bottom up, processing required for components subordinate to a given level is always available and the need for stubs is eliminated.

A bottom-up integration strategy may be implemented with the following steps:

What are the steps for bottom-up integration?

1. Low-level components are combined into clusters (sometimes called *builds*) that perform a specific software subfunction.
2. A driver (a control program for testing) is written to coordinate test case input and output.
3. The cluster is tested.
4. Drivers are removed and clusters are combined moving upward in the program structure.

KEY POINT
Bottom-up integration eliminates the need for complex stubs.

Integration follows the pattern illustrated in Figure 18.7. Components are combined to form clusters 1, 2, and 3. Each of the clusters is tested using a driver (shown as a dashed block). Components in clusters 1 and 2 are subordinate to M_a. Drivers D_1 and D_2 are removed and the clusters are interfaced directly to M_a. Similarly, driver D_3 for cluster 3 is removed prior to integration with module M_b. Both M_a and M_b will ultimately be integrated with component M_c, and so forth.

FIGURE 18.7
Bottom-up integration

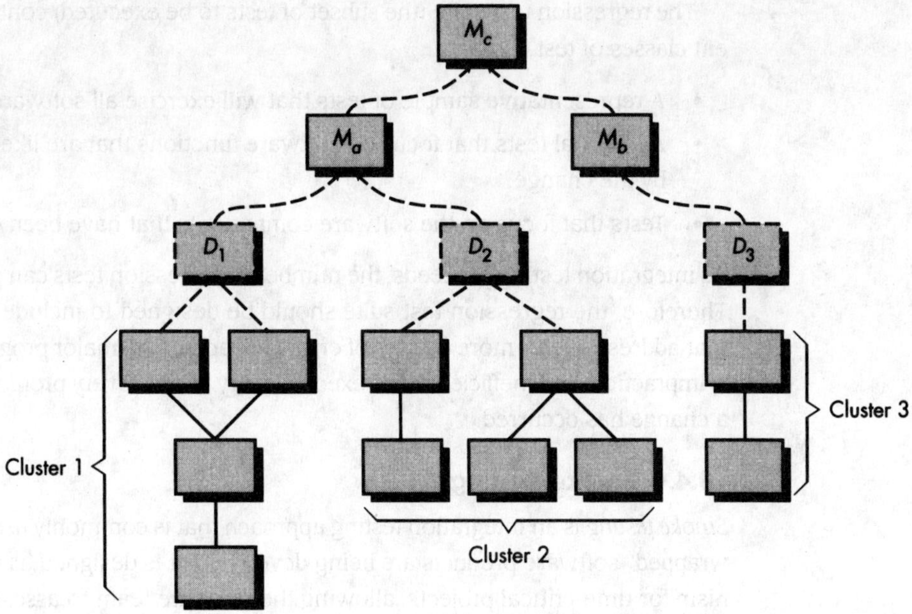

As integration moves upward, the need for separate test drivers lessens. In fact, if the top two levels of program structure are integrated top down, the number of drivers can be reduced substantially and integration of clusters is greatly simplified.

18.4.3 Regression Testing

Each time a new module is added as part of integration testing, the software changes. New data flow paths are established, new I/O may occur, and new control logic is invoked. These changes may cause problems with functions that previously worked flawlessly. In the context of an integration test strategy, *regression testing* is the re-execution of some subset of tests that have already been conducted to ensure that changes have not propagated unintended side effects.

ADVICE *Regression testing is an important strategy for reducing "side effects." Run regression tests every time a major change is made to the software (including the integration of new modules).*

In a broader context, successful tests (of any kind) result in the discovery of errors, and errors must be corrected. Whenever software is corrected, some aspect of the software configuration (the program, its documentation, or the data that support it) is changed. Regression testing is the activity that helps to ensure that changes (due to testing or for other reasons) do not introduce unintended behavior or additional errors.

Regression testing may be conducted manually, by re-executing a subset of all test cases or using automated *capture/playback tools.* Capture/playback tools enable the software engineer to capture test cases and results for subsequent playback and comparison.

The regression test suite (the subset of tests to be executed) contains three different classes of test cases:

- A representative sample of tests that will exercise all software functions.
- Additional tests that focus on software functions that are likely to be affected by the change.
- Tests that focus on the software components that have been changed.

As integration testing proceeds, the number of regression tests can grow quite large. Therefore, the regression test suite should be designed to include only those tests that address one or more classes of errors in each of the major program functions. It is impractical and inefficient to re-execute every test for every program function once a change has occurred.

18.4.4 Smoke Testing

Smoke testing is an integration testing approach that is commonly used when "shrinkwrapped" software products are being developed. It is designed as a pacing mechanism for time-critical projects, allowing the software team to assess its project on a frequent basis. In essence, the smoke testing approach encompasses the following activities:

KEY POINT

Smoke testing might be characterized as a rolling integration strategy. The software is rebuilt (with new components added) and exercised every day.

1. Software components that have been translated into code are integrated into a "build." A build includes all data files, libraries, reusable modules, and engineered components that are required to implement one or more product functions.
2. A series of tests is designed to expose errors that will keep the build from properly performing its function. The intent should be to uncover "show stopper" errors that have the highest likelihood of throwing the software project behind schedule.
3. The build is integrated with other builds and the entire product (in its current form) is smoke tested daily. The integration approach may be top down or bottom up.

The daily frequency of testing the entire product may surprise some readers. However, frequent tests give both managers and practitioners a realistic assessment of integration testing progress. McConnell [MCO96] describes the smoke test in the following manner:

> The smoke test should exercise the entire system from end to end. It does not have to be exhaustive, but it should be capable of exposing major problems. The smoke test should be thorough enough that if the build passes, you can assume that it is stable enough to be tested more thoroughly.

Smoke testing provides a number of benefits when it is applied on complex, time-critical software engineering projects:

- *Integration risk is minimized.* Because smoke tests are conducted daily, incompatibilities and other show-stopper errors are uncovered early, thereby reducing the likelihood of serious schedule impact when errors are uncovered.
- *The quality of the end-product is improved.* Because the approach is construction (integration) oriented, smoke testing is likely to uncover both functional errors and architectural and component-level design defects. If these defects are corrected early, better product quality will result.
- *Error diagnosis and correction are simplified.* Like all integration testing approaches, errors uncovered during smoke testing are likely to be associated with "new software increments"—that is, the software that has just been added to the build(s) is a probable cause of a newly discovered error.
- *Progress is easier to assess.* With each passing day, more of the software has been integrated and more has been demonstrated to work. This improves team morale and gives managers a good indication that progress is being made.

Quote:

"Treat the daily build as the heartbeat of the project. If there's no heartbeat, the project is dead."
Jim McCarthy

18.4.5 Comments on Integration Testing

There has been much discussion (e.g., [BEI84]) of the relative advantages and disadvantages of top-down versus bottom-up integration testing. In general, the advantages of one strategy tend to result in disadvantages for the other strategy. The major disadvantage of the top-down approach is the need for stubs and the attendant testing difficulties that can be associated with them. Problems associated with stubs may be offset by the advantage of testing major control functions early. The major disadvantage of bottom-up integration is that "the program as an entity does not exist until the last module is added" [MYE79]. This drawback is tempered by easier test case design and a lack of stubs.

Selection of an integration strategy depends upon software characteristics and, sometimes, project schedule. In general, a combined approach (sometimes called *sandwich testing*) that uses top-down tests for upper levels of the program structure, coupled with bottom-up tests for subordinate levels may be the best compromise.

What is a critical module and why should we identify it?

As integration testing is conducted, the tester should identify *critical modules.* A critical module has one or more of the following characteristics: (1) addresses several software requirements, (2) has a high level of control (resides relatively high in the program structure), (3) is complex or error prone (cyclomatic complexity may be used as an indicator), or (4) has definite performance requirements. Critical modules should be tested as early as is possible. In addition, regression tests should focus on critical module function.

18.4.6 Integration Test Documentation

An overall plan for integration of the software and a description of specific tests are documented in a *Test Specification.* This document contains a test plan, and a test procedure, is a work product of the software process, and becomes part of the software configuration.

Test Specification

The test plan describes the overall strategy for integration. Testing is divided into phases and builds that address specific functional and behavioral characteristics of the software. For example, integration testing for a CAD system might be divided into the following test phases:

- User interaction (command selection, drawing creation, display representation, error processing and representation).
- Data manipulation and analysis (symbol creation, dimensioning; rotation, computation of physical properties).
- Display processing and generation (two-dimensional displays, three-dimensional displays, graphs and charts).
- Database management (access, update, integrity, performance).

Each of these phases and subphases (denoted in parentheses) delineates a broad functional category within the software and can generally be related to a specific domain of the program structure. Therefore, program builds (groups of modules) are created to correspond to each phase. The following criteria and corresponding tests are applied for all test phases:

Interface integrity. Internal and external interfaces are tested as each module (or cluster) is incorporated into the structure.

Functional validity. Tests designed to uncover functional errors are conducted.

Information content. Tests designed to uncover errors associated with local or global data structures are conducted.

Performance. Tests designed to verify performance bounds established during software design are conducted.

A schedule for integration, the development of overhead software, and related topics is also discussed as part of the test plan. Start and end dates for each phase are established and "availability windows" for unit tested modules are defined. A brief description of overhead software (stubs and drivers) concentrates on characteristics that might require special effort. Finally, test environment and resources are described. Unusual hardware configurations, exotic simulators, and special test tools or techniques are a few of many topics that may also be discussed.

The detailed testing procedure that is required to accomplish the test plan is described next. The order of integration and corresponding tests at each integration step are described. A listing of all test cases (annotated for subsequent reference) and expected results is also included.

A history of actual test results, problems, or peculiarities is recorded in the *Test Specification.* Information contained in this section can be vital during software maintenance. Appropriate references and appendixes are also presented.

Like all other elements of a software configuration, the test specification format may be tailored to the local needs of a software engineering organization. It is important to note, however, that an integration strategy (contained in a test plan) and testing details (described in a test procedure) are essential ingredients and must appear.

18.5 VALIDATION TESTING

At the culmination of integration testing, software is completely assembled as a package, interfacing errors have been uncovered and corrected, and a final series of software tests—*validation testing*—may begin. Validation can be defined in many ways, but a simple (albeit harsh) definition is that validation succeeds when software functions in a manner that can be reasonably expected by the customer. At this point a battle-hardened software developer might protest: "Who or what is the arbiter of reasonable expectations?"

KEY POINT

Like all other testing steps, validation tries to uncover errors, but the focus is at the requirements level—on things that will be immediately apparent to the end-user.

Reasonable expectations are defined in the *Software Requirements Specification*—a document (Chapter 11) that describes all user-visible attributes of the software. The specification contains a section called *Validation Criteria.* Information contained in that section forms the basis for a validation testing approach.

18.5.1 Validation Test Criteria

Software validation is achieved through a series of black-box tests that demonstrate conformity with requirements. A test plan outlines the classes of tests to be conducted and a test procedure defines specific test cases that will be used to demonstrate conformity with requirements. Both the plan and procedure are designed to ensure that all functional requirements are satisfied, all behavioral characteristics are achieved, all performance requirements are attained, documentation is correct, and human-engineered and other requirements are met (e.g., transportability, compatibility, error recovery, maintainability).

After each validation test case has been conducted, one of two possible conditions exist: (1) The function or performance characteristics conform to specification and are accepted or (2) a deviation from specification is uncovered and a *deficiency list* is created. Deviation or error discovered at this stage in a project can rarely be corrected prior to scheduled delivery. It is often necessary to negotiate with the customer to establish a method for resolving deficiencies.

18.5.2 Configuration Review

An important element of the validation process is a *configuration review.* The intent of the review is to ensure that all elements of the software configuration have been properly developed, are cataloged, and have the necessary detail to bolster the support phase of the software life cycle. The configuration review, sometimes called an *audit,* has been discussed in more detail in Chapter 9.

18.5.3 Alpha and Beta Testing

It is virtually impossible for a software developer to foresee how the customer will really use a program. Instructions for use may be misinterpreted; strange combinations of data may be regularly used; output that seemed clear to the tester may be unintelligible to a user in the field.

When custom software is built for one customer, a series of *acceptance tests* are conducted to enable the customer to validate all requirements. Conducted by the end-user rather than software engineers, an acceptance test can range from an informal "test drive" to a planned and systematically executed series of tests. In fact, acceptance testing can be conducted over a period of weeks or months, thereby uncovering cumulative errors that might degrade the system over time.

If software is developed as a product to be used by many customers, it is impractical to perform formal acceptance tests with each one. Most software product builders use a process called alpha and beta testing to uncover errors that only the end-user seems able to find.

The *alpha test* is conducted at the developer's site by a customer. The software is used in a natural setting with the developer "looking over the shoulder" of the user and recording errors and usage problems. Alpha tests are conducted in a controlled environment.

The *beta test* is conducted at one or more customer sites by the end-user of the software. Unlike alpha testing, the developer is generally not present. Therefore, the beta test is a "live" application of the software in an environment that cannot be controlled by the developer. The customer records all problems (real or imagined) that are encountered during beta testing and reports these to the developer at regular intervals. As a result of problems reported during beta tests, software engineers make modifications and then prepare for release of the software product to the entire customer base.

18.6 SYSTEM TESTING

At the beginning of this book, we stressed the fact that software is only one element of a larger computer-based system. Ultimately, software is incorporated with other system elements (e.g., hardware, people, information), and a series of system integration and validation tests are conducted. These tests fall outside the scope of the software process and are not conducted solely by software engineers. However, steps taken during software design and testing can greatly improve the probability of successful software integration in the larger system.

A classic system testing problem is "finger-pointing." This occurs when an error is uncovered, and each system element developer blames the other for the problem. Rather than indulging in such nonsense, the software engineer should anticipate potential interfacing problems and (1) design error-handling paths that test all information coming from other elements of the system, (2) conduct a series of tests that simulate bad data or other potential errors at the software interface, (3) record the results of tests to use as "evidence" if finger-pointing does occur, and (4) participate in planning and design of system tests to ensure that software is adequately tested.

Quote:
"Like death and taxes, testing is both unpleasant and inevitable."
Ed Yourdon

System testing is actually a series of different tests whose primary purpose is to fully exercise the computer-based system. Although each test has a different purpose, all work to verify that system elements have been properly integrated and perform allocated functions. In the sections that follow, we discuss the types of system tests [BEI84] that are worthwhile for software-based systems.

18.6.1 Recovery Testing

Many computer based systems must recover from faults and resume processing within a prespecified time. In some cases, a system must be fault tolerant; that is, processing faults must not cause overall system function to cease. In other cases, a system failure must be corrected within a specified period of time or severe economic damage will occur.

WebRef
Extensive information on software testing and related quality issues can be obtained at **www.stqe.net**

Recovery testing is a system test that forces the software to fail in a variety of ways and verifies that recovery is properly performed. If recovery is automatic (performed by the system itself), reinitialization, checkpointing mechanisms, data recovery, and restart are evaluated for correctness. If recovery requires human intervention, the mean-time-to-repair (MTTR) is evaluated to determine whether it is within acceptable limits.

18.6.2 Security Testing

Any computer-based system that manages sensitive information or causes actions that can improperly harm (or benefit) individuals is a target for improper or illegal penetration. Penetration spans a broad range of activities: hackers who attempt to penetrate systems for sport; disgruntled employees who attempt to penetrate for revenge; dishonest individuals who attempt to penetrate for illicit personal gain.

Security testing attempts to verify that protection mechanisms built into a system will, in fact, protect it from improper penetration. To quote Beizer [BEI84]: "The system's security must, of course, be tested for invulnerability from frontal attack—but must also be tested for invulnerability from flank or rear attack."

During security testing, the tester plays the role(s) of the individual who desires to penetrate the system. Anything goes! The tester may attempt to acquire passwords through external clerical means; may attack the system with custom software designed to breakdown any defenses that have been constructed; may overwhelm the system, thereby denying service to others; may purposely cause system errors, hoping to penetrate during recovery; may browse through insecure data, hoping to find the key to system entry.

Given enough time and resources, good security testing will ultimately penetrate a system. The role of the system designer is to make penetration cost more than the value of the information that will be obtained.

18.6.3 Stress Testing

During earlier software testing steps, white-box and black-box techniques resulted in thorough evaluation of normal program functions and performance. Stress tests are designed to confront programs with abnormal situations. In essence, the tester who performs stress testing asks: "How high can we crank this up before it fails?"

> **Quote:**
> "If you're trying to find true system bugs and have never subjected your software to a real stress test, then it is high time you started."
> **Boris Beizer**

Stress testing executes a system in a manner that demands resources in abnormal quantity, frequency, or volume. For example, (1) special tests may be designed that generate ten interrupts per second, when one or two is the average rate, (2) input data rates may be increased by an order of magnitude to determine how input functions will respond, (3) test cases that require maximum memory or other resources are executed, (4) test cases that may cause thrashing in a virtual operating system are designed, (5) test cases that may cause excessive hunting for disk-resident data are created. Essentially, the tester attempts to break the program.

A variation of stress testing is a technique called *sensitivity testing.* In some situations (the most common occur in mathematical algorithms), a very small range of data contained within the bounds of valid data for a program may cause extreme and even erroneous processing or profound performance degradation. Sensitivity testing attempts to uncover data combinations within valid input classes that may cause instability or improper processing.

18.6.4 Performance Testing

For real-time and embedded systems, software that provides required function but does not conform to performance requirements is unacceptable. *Performance testing* is designed to test the run-time performance of software within the context of an integrated system. Performance testing occurs throughout all steps in the testing process. Even at the unit level, the performance of an individual module may be assessed as white-box tests are conducted. However, it is not until all system elements are fully integrated that the true performance of a system can be ascertained.

Performance tests are often coupled with stress testing and usually require both hardware and software instrumentation. That is, it is often necessary to measure resource utilization (e.g., processor cycles) in an exacting fashion. External instru-

FIGURE 18.8
The debugging process

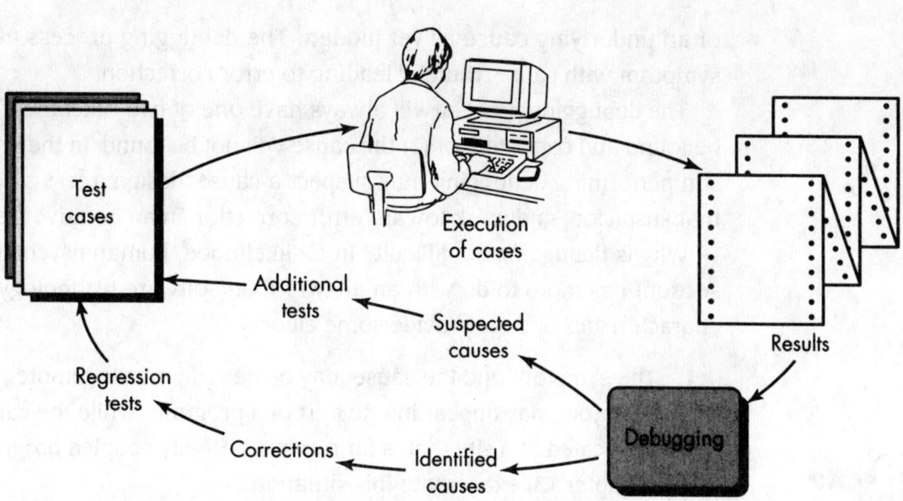

mentation can monitor execution intervals, log events (e.g., interrupts) as they occur, and sample machine states on a regular basis. By instrumenting a system, the tester can uncover situations that lead to degradation and possible system failure.

18.7 THE ART OF DEBUGGING

Software testing is a process that can be systematically planned and specified. Test case design can be conducted, a strategy can be defined, and results can be evaluated against prescribed expectations.

WebRef
BugNet tracks security problems and bugs in PC-based software and provides useful information on debugging topics:
www.bugnet.com

Debugging occurs as a consequence of successful testing. That is, when a test case uncovers an error, debugging is the process that results in the removal of the error. Although debugging can and should be an orderly process, it is still very much an art. A software engineer, evaluating the results of a test, is often confronted with a "symptomatic" indication of a software problem. That is, the external manifestation of the error and the internal cause of the error may have no obvious relationship to one another. The poorly understood mental process that connects a symptom to a cause is debugging.

18.7.1 The Debugging Process

Debugging is not testing but always occurs as a consequence of testing.[4] Referring to Figure 18.8, the debugging process begins with the execution of a test case. Results are assessed and a lack of correspondence between expected and actual performance is encountered. In many cases, the noncorresponding data are a symptom

4 In making this statement, we take the broadest possible view of testing. Not only does the developer test software prior to release, but the customer/user tests software every time it is used!

of an underlying cause as yet hidden. The debugging process attempts to match symptom with cause, thereby leading to error correction.

The debugging process will always have one of two outcomes: (1) the cause will be found and corrected, or (2) the cause will not be found. In the latter case, the person performing debugging may suspect a cause, design a test case to help validate that suspicion, and work toward error correction in an iterative fashion.

Why is debugging so difficult? In all likelihood, human psychology (see the next section) has more to do with an answer than software technology. However, a few characteristics of bugs provide some clues:

Quote:

"The variety within all computer programs that must be diagnosed [for debugging] is probably greater than the variety within all other examples of systems that are regularly diagnosed."

John Gould

1. The symptom and the cause may be geographically remote. That is, the symptom may appear in one part of a program, while the cause may actually be located at a site that is far removed. Highly coupled program structures (Chapter 13) exacerbate this situation.
2. The symptom may disappear (temporarily) when another error is corrected.
3. The symptom may actually be caused by nonerrors (e.g., round-off inaccuracies).
4. The symptom may be caused by human error that is not easily traced.
5. The symptom may be a result of timing problems, rather than processing problems.
6. It may be difficult to accurately reproduce input conditions (e.g., a real-time application in which input ordering is indeterminate).
7. The symptom may be intermittent. This is particularly common in embedded systems that couple hardware and software inextricably.
8. The symptom may be due to causes that are distributed across a number of tasks running on different processors [CHE90].

During debugging, we encounter errors that range from mildly annoying (e.g., an incorrect output format) to catastrophic (e.g. the system fails, causing serious economic or physical damage). As the consequences of an error increase, the amount of pressure to find the cause also increases. Often, pressure sometimes forces a software developer to fix one error and at the same time introduce two more.

18.7.2 Psychological Considerations

Unfortunately, there appears to be some evidence that debugging prowess is an innate human trait. Some people are good at it and others aren't. Although experimental evidence on debugging is open to many interpretations, large variances in debugging ability have been reported for programmers with the same education and experience.

Commenting on the human aspects of debugging, Shneiderman [SHN80] states:

Debugging is one of the more frustrating parts of programming. It has elements of problem solving or brain teasers, coupled with the annoying recognition that you have made a mistake. Heightened anxiety and the unwillingness to accept the possibility of errors increases the task difficulty. Fortunately, there is a great sigh of relief and a lessening of tension when the bug is ultimately . . . . corrected.

Although it may be difficult to "learn" debugging, a number of approaches to the problem can be proposed. We examine these in the next section.

18.7.3 Debugging Approaches

Regardless of the approach that is taken, debugging has one overriding objective: to find and correct the cause of a software error. The objective is realized by a combination of systematic evaluation, intuition, and luck. Bradley [BRA85] describes the debugging approach in this way:

> Debugging is a straightforward application of the scientific method that has been developed over 2,500 years. The basis of debugging is to locate the problem's source [the cause] by binary partitioning, through working hypotheses that predict new values to be examined.
>
> Take a simple non-software example: A lamp in my house does not work. If nothing in the house works, the cause must be in the main circuit breaker or outside; I look around to see whether the neighborhood is blacked out. I plug the suspect lamp into a working socket and a working appliance into the suspect circuit. So goes the alternation of hypothesis and test.

In general, three categories for debugging approaches may be proposed [MYE79]: (1) brute force, (2) backtracking, and (3) cause elimination.

ADVICE

Set a time limit, say two hours, on the amount of time you spend trying to debug a problem on your own. After that, get help!

The *brute force* category of debugging is probably the most common and least efficient method for isolating the cause of a software error. We apply brute force debugging methods when all else fails. Using a "let the computer find the error" philosophy, memory dumps are taken, run-time traces are invoked, and the program is loaded with WRITE statements. We hope that somewhere in the morass of information that is produced we will find a clue that can lead us to the cause of an error. Although the mass of information produced may ultimately lead to success, it more frequently leads to wasted effort and time. Thought must be expended first!

Backtracking is a fairly common debugging approach that can be used successfully in small programs. Beginning at the site where a symptom has been uncovered, the source code is traced backward (manually) until the site of the cause is found. Unfortunately, as the number of source lines increases, the number of potential backward paths may become unmanageably large.

The third approach to debugging—*cause elimination*—is manifested by induction or deduction and introduces the concept of binary partitioning. Data related to the error occurrence are organized to isolate potential causes. A "cause hypothesis" is devised and the aforementioned data are used to prove or disprove the hypothesis. Alternatively, a list of all possible causes is developed and tests are conducted to eliminate each. If initial tests indicate that a particular cause hypothesis shows promise, data are refined in an attempt to isolate the bug.

CASE Tools
Testing and Debugging

Each of these debugging approaches can be supplemented with debugging tools. We can apply a wide variety of debugging compilers, dynamic debugging aids ("tracers"), automatic test case generators, memory dumps, and cross-reference maps. However, tools are not a substitute for careful evaluation based on a complete software design document and clear source code.

Any discussion of debugging approaches and tools is incomplete without mention of a powerful ally—other people! Each of us can recall puzzling for hours or days over a persistent bug. A colleague wanders by and in desperation we explain the problem and throw open the listing. Instantaneously (it seems), the cause of the error is uncovered. Smiling smugly, our colleague wanders off. A fresh viewpoint, unclouded by hours of frustration, can do wonders. A final maxim for debugging might be: "When all else fails, get help!"

Once a bug has been found, it must be corrected. But, as we have already noted, the correction of a bug can introduce other errors and therefore do more harm than good. Van Vleck [VAN89] suggests three simple questions that every software engineer should ask before making the "correction" that removes the cause of a bug:

When I correct an error, what questions should I ask myself?

1. **Is the cause of the bug reproduced in another part of the program?** In many situations, a program defect is caused by an erroneous pattern of logic that may be reproduced elsewhere. Explicit consideration of the logical pattern may result in the discovery of other errors.
2. **What "next bug" might be introduced by the fix I'm about to make?** Before the correction is made, the source code (or, better, the design) should be evaluated to assess coupling of logic and data structures. If the correction is to be made in a highly coupled section of the program, special care must be taken when any change is made.
3. **What could we have done to prevent this bug in the first place?** This question is the first step toward establishing a statistical software quality assurance approach (Chapter 8). If we correct the process as well as the product, the bug will be removed from the current program and may be eliminated from all future programs.

18.8 SUMMARY

Software testing accounts for the largest percentage of technical effort in the software process. Yet we are only beginning to understand the subtleties of systematic test planning, execution, and control.

The objective of software testing is to uncover errors. To fulfill this objective, a series of test steps—unit, integration, validation, and system tests—are planned and executed. Unit and integration tests concentrate on functional verification of a component and incorporation of components into a program structure. Validation testing demonstrates traceability to software requirements, and system testing validates software once it has been incorporated into a larger system.

Each test step is accomplished through a series of systematic test techniques that assist in the design of test cases. With each testing step, the level of abstraction with which software is considered is broadened.

Unlike testing (a systematic, planned activity), debugging must be viewed as an art. Beginning with a symptomatic indication of a problem, the debugging activity must track down the cause of an error. Of the many resources available during debugging, the most valuable is the counsel of other members of the software engineering staff.

The requirement for higher-quality software demands a more systematic approach to testing. To quote Dunn and Ullman [DUN82],

> What is required is an overall strategy, spanning the strategic test space, quite as deliberate in its methodology as was the systematic development on which analysis, design and code were based.

In this chapter, we have examined the strategic test space, considering the steps that have the highest likelihood of meeting the overriding test objective: to find and remove errors in an orderly and effective manner.

REFERENCES

[BEI84] Beizer, B., *Software System Testing and Quality Assurance,* Van Nostrand-Reinhold, 1984.

[BOE81] Boehm, B., *Software Engineering Economics,* Prentice-Hall, 1981, p. 37.

[BRA85] Bradley, J.H., "The Science and Art of Debugging," *Computerworld,* August 19, 1985, pp. 35–38.

[CHE90] Cheung, W.H., J.P. Black, and E. Manning, "A Framework for Distributed Debugging," *IEEE Software,* January 1990, pp. 106–115.

[DUN82] Dunn, R. and R. Ullman, *Quality Assurance for Computer Software,* McGraw-Hill, 1982, p. 158.

[GIL95] Gilb, T., "What We Fail to Do in Our Current Testing Culture," *Testing Techniques Newsletter,* (on-line edition, ttn@soft.com), Software Research, January 1995.

[MCO96] McConnell, S., "Best Practices: Daily Build and Smoke Test", *IEEE Software,* vol. 13, no. 4, July 1996, 143–144.

[MIL77] Miller, E., "The Philosophy of Testing," in *Program Testing Techniques,* IEEE Computer Society Press, 1977, pp. 1–3.

[MUS89] Musa, J.D. and Ackerman, A.F., "Quantifying Software Validation: When to Stop Testing?" *IEEE Software*, May 1989, pp. 19–27.

[MYE79] Myers, G., *The Art of Software Testing*, Wiley, 1979.

[SHO83] Shooman, M.L., *Software Engineering*, McGraw-Hill, 1983.

[SHN80] Shneiderman, B., *Software Psychology*, Winthrop Publishers, 1980, p. 28.

[VAN89] Van Vleck, T., "Three Questions About Each Bug You Find," *ACM Software Engineering Notes*, vol. 14, no. 5, July 1989, pp. 62–63.

[WAL89] Wallace, D.R. and R.U. Fujii, "Software Verification and Validation: An Overview," *IEEE Software*, May 1989, pp. 10–17.

[YOU75] Yourdon, E., *Techniques of Program Structure and Design*, Prentice-Hall, 1975.

PROBLEMS AND POINTS TO PONDER

18.1. Using your own words, describe the difference between verification and validation. Do both make use of test case design methods and testing strategies?

18.2. List some problems that might be associated with the creation of an independent test group. Are an ITG and an SQA group made up of the same people?

18.3. Is it always possible to develop a strategy for testing software that uses the sequence of testing steps described in Section 18.1.3? What possible complications might arise for embedded systems?

18.4. If you could select only three test case design methods to apply during unit testing, what would they be and why?

18.5. Why is a highly coupled module difficult to unit test?

18.6. The concept of "antibugging" (Section 18.2.1) is an extremely effective way to provide built-in debugging assistance when an error is uncovered:

a. Develop a set of guidelines for antibugging.
b. Discuss advantages of using the technique.
c. Discuss disadvantages.

18.7. Develop an integration testing strategy for the any one of the systems implemented in Problems 16.4 through 16.11. Define test phases, note the order of integration, specify additional test software, and justify your order of integration. Assume that all modules (or classes) have been unit tested and are available. Note: it may be necessary to do a bit of design work first.

18.8. How can project scheduling affect integration testing?

18.9. Is unit testing possible or even desirable in all circumstances? Provide examples to justify your answer.

18.10. Who should perform the validation test—the software developer or the software user? Justify your answer.

18.11. Develop a complete test strategy for the *SafeHome* system discussed earlier in this book. Document it in a *Test Specification.*

18.12. As a class project, develop a *Debugging Guide* for your installation. The guide should provide language and system-oriented hints that have been learned through the school of hard knocks! Begin with an outline of topics that will be reviewed by the class and your instructor. Publish the guide for others in your local environment.

FURTHER READINGS AND INFORMATION RESOURCES

Books by Black (*Managing the Testing Process,* Microsoft Press, 1999); Dustin, Rashka, and Paul (*Test Process Improvement: Step-by-Step Guide to Structured Testing,* Addison-Wesley, 1999); Perry (*Surviving the Top Ten Challenges of Software Testing: A People-Oriented Approach,* Dorset House, 1997); and Kit and Finzi (*Software Testing in the Real World: Improving the Process,* Addison-Wesley, 1995) address software testing strategies.

Kaner, Nguyen, and Falk (*Testing Computer Software,* Wiley, 1999); Hutcheson (*Software Testing Methods and Metrics: The Most Important Tests* McGraw-Hill, 1997); Marick (*The Craft of Software Testing: Subsystem Testing Including Object-Based and Object-Oriented Testing,* Prentice-Hall, 1995); Jorgensen (*Software Testing: A Craftsman's Approach,* CRC Press, 1995) present treatments of the subject that consider testing methods and strategies.

In addition, older books by Evans *(Productive Software Test Management,* Wiley-Interscience, 1984), Hetzel (*The Complete Guide to Software Testing,* QED Information Sciences, 1984), Beizer [BEI84], Ould and Unwin (*Testing in Software Development,* Cambridge University Press, 1986), Marks (*Testing Very Big Systems,* McGraw-Hill, 1992, and Kaner et al. (*Testing Computer Software,* 2nd ed., Van Nostrand-Reinhold, 1993), delineate the steps of an effective testing strategy, provide a set of techniques and guidelines, and suggest procedures for controlling and tracking the testing process. Hutcheson (*Software Testing Methods and Metrics,* McGraw-Hill, 1996) presents testing methods and strategies but also provides a detailed discussion of how measurement can be used to achieve efficient testing.

Guidelines for debugging are contained in a book by Dunn (*Software Defect Removal,* McGraw-Hill, 1984). Beizer [BEI84] presents an interesting "taxonomy of bugs" that can lead to effective methods for test planning. McConnell (*Code Complete,* Microsoft Press, 1993) presents pragmatic advice on unit and integration testing as well as debugging.

A wide variety of information sources on software testing and related subjects is available on the Internet. An up-to-date list of World Wide Web references that are relevant to testing concepts, methods, and strategies can be found at the SEPA Website:
http://www.mhhe.com/engcs/compsci/pressman/resources/test-strategy.mhtml

CHAPTER

19 TECHNICAL METRICS FOR SOFTWARE

KEY CONCEPTS

A key element of any engineering process is measurement. We use measures to better understand the attributes of the models that we create and to assess the quality of the engineered products or systems that we build. But unlike other engineering disciplines, software engineering is not grounded in the basic quantitative laws of physics. Absolute measures, such as voltage, mass, velocity, or temperature, are uncommon in the software world. Instead, we attempt to derive a set of indirect measures that lead to metrics that provide an indication of the quality of some representation of software. Because software measures and metrics are not absolute, they are open to debate. Fenton [FEN91] addresses this issue when he states:

> Measurement is the process by which numbers or symbols are assigned to the attributes of entities in the real world in such a way as to define them according to clearly defined rules. . . . In the physical sciences, medicine, economics, and more recently the social sciences, we are now able to measure attributes that we previously thought to be unmeasurable. . . . Of course, such measurements are not as refined as many measurements in the physical sciences . . ., but they exist [and important decisions are made based on them]. We feel that the obligation to attempt to "measure the unmeasurable" in order to improve our understanding of particular entities is as powerful in software engineering as in any discipline.

QUICK LOOK

What is it? By its nature, engineering is a quantitative discipline. Engineers use numbers to help them design and assess the product to be built. Until recently, software engineers had little quantitative guidance in their work—but that's changing. Technical metrics help software engineers gain insight into the design and construction of the products they build.

Who does it? Software engineers use technical metrics to help them build higher-quality software.

Why is it important? There will always be a qualitative element to the creation of computer software. The problem is that qualitative assessment may not be enough. A software engineer needs objective criteria to help guide the design of data, architecture, interfaces, and components. The tester needs quantitative guidance that will help in the selection of test cases and their targets. Technical metrics provide a basis from which analysis, design, coding, and testing can be conducted more objectively and assessed more quantitatively.

What are the steps? The first step in the measurement process is to derive the software measures and metrics that are appropriate for the representation of software that is being considered. Next, data required to derive the formulated metrics are collected. Once computed, appropriate metrics are analyzed based on pre-established ▶

QUICK LOOK

guidelines and past data. The results of the analysis are interpreted to gain insight into the quality of the software, and the results of the interpretation lead to modification of work products arising out of analysis, design, code, or test.

What is the work product? Software metrics that are computed from data collected from the analysis and design models, source code, and test cases.

How do I ensure that I've done it right? You should establish the objectives of measurement before data collection begins, defining each technical metric in an unambiguous manner. Define only a few metrics and then use them to gain insight into the quality of a software engineering work product.

But some members of the software community continue to argue that software is unmeasurable or that attempts at measurement should be postponed until we better understand software and the attributes that should be used to describe it. This is a mistake.

Although technical metrics for computer software are not absolute, they provide us with a systematic way to assess quality based on a set of clearly defined rules. They also provide the software engineer with on-the-spot, rather than after-the-fact insight. This enables the engineer to discover and correct potential problems before they become catastrophic defects.

In Chapter 4, we discussed software metrics as they are applied at the process and project level. In this chapter, our focus shifts to measures that can be used to assess the quality of the product as it is being engineered. These measures of internal product attributes provide the software engineer with a real-time indication of the efficacy of the analysis, design, and code models; the effectiveness of test cases; and the overall quality of the software to be built.

19.1 SOFTWARE QUALITY

Even the most jaded software developers will agree that high-quality software is an important goal. But how do we define *quality?* In Chapter 8, we proposed a number of different ways to look at software quality and introduced a definition that stressed conformance to explicitly stated functional and performance requirements, explicitly documented development standards, and implicit characteristics that are expected of all professionally developed software.

Quote:

"Every program does something right, it just may not be the thing that we want it to do."

author unknown

There is little question that the preceding definition could be modified or extended and debated endlessly. For the purposes of this book, the definition serves to emphasize three important points:

1. Software requirements are the foundation from which quality is measured. Lack of conformance to requirements is lack of quality.[1]

1 It is important to note that quality extends to the technical attributes of the analysis, design, and code models. Models that exhibit high quality (in the technical sense) will lead to software that exhibits high quality from the customer's point of view.

2. Specified standards define a set of development criteria that guide the manner in which software is engineered. If the criteria are not followed, lack of quality will almost surely result.
3. There is a set of implicit requirements that often goes unmentioned (e.g., the desire for ease of use). If software conforms to its explicit requirements but fails to meet implicit requirements, software quality is suspect.

Software quality is a complex mix of factors that will vary across different applications and the customers who request them. In the sections that follow, software quality factors are identified and the human activities required to achieve them are described.

19.1.1 McCall's Quality Factors

KEY POINT

It's interesting to note that McCall's quality factors are as valid today as they were when they were first proposed in the 1970s. Therefore, it's reasonable to assert that the factors that affect software quality do not change.

The factors that affect software quality can be categorized in two broad groups: (1) factors that can be directly measured (e.g., defects per function-point) and (2) factors that can be measured only indirectly (e.g., usability or maintainability). In each case measurement must occur. We must compare the software (documents, programs, data) to some datum and arrive at an indication of quality.

McCall, Richards, and Walters [MCC77] propose a useful categorization of factors that affect software quality. These software quality factors, shown in Figure 19.1, focus on three important aspects of a software product: its operational characteristics, its ability to undergo change, and its adaptability to new environments.

Referring to the factors noted in Figure 19.1, McCall and his colleagues provide the following descriptions:

Correctness. The extent to which a program satisfies its specification and fulfills the customer's mission objectives.

Reliability. The extent to which a program can be expected to perform its intended function with required precision. [It should be noted that other, more complete definitions of reliability have been proposed (see Chapter 8).]

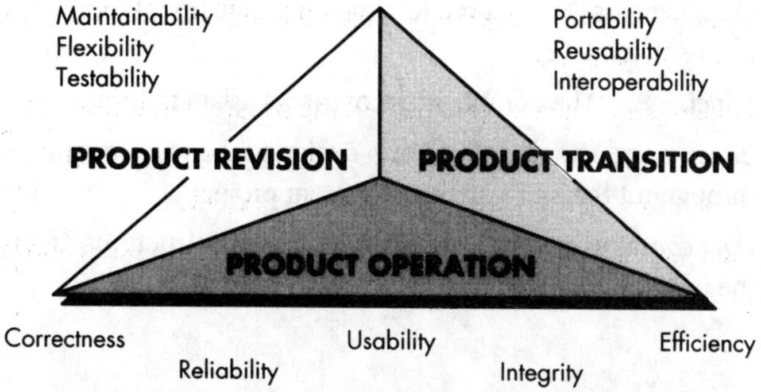

FIGURE 19.1 McCall's software quality factors

Efficiency. The amount of computing resources and code required by a program to perform its function.

Integrity. Extent to which access to software or data by unauthorized persons can be controlled.

Quote:

"A product's quality is a function of how much it changes the world for the better."

Tom DeMarco

Usability. Effort required to learn, operate, prepare input, and interpret output of a program.

Maintainability. Effort required to locate and fix an error in a program. [This is a very limited definition.]

Flexibility. Effort required to modify an operational program.

Testability. Effort required to test a program to ensure that it performs its intended function.

Portability. Effort required to transfer the program from one hardware and/or software system environment to another.

Reusability. Extent to which a program [or parts of a program] can be reused in other applications—related to the packaging and scope of the functions that the program performs.

Interoperability. Effort required to couple one system to another.

It is difficult, and in some cases impossible, to develop direct measures of these quality factors. Therefore, a set of metrics are defined and used to develop expressions for each of the factors according to the following relationship:

$$F_q = c_1 \times m_1 + c_2 \times m_2 + \ldots + c_n \times m_n$$

where F_q is a software quality factor, c_n are regression coefficients, m_n are the metrics that affect the quality factor. Unfortunately, many of the metrics defined by McCall et al. can be measured only subjectively. The metrics may be in the form of a checklist that is used to "grade" specific attributes of the software [CAV78]. The grading scheme proposed by McCall et al. is a 0 (low) to 10 (high) scale. The following metrics are used in the grading scheme:

Auditability. The ease with which conformance to standards can be checked.

Accuracy. The precision of computations and control.

Communication commonality. The degree to which standard interfaces, protocols, and bandwidth are used.

XRef

The metrics noted can be assessed during formal technical reviews discussed in Chapter 8.

Completeness. The degree to which full implementation of required function has been achieved.

Conciseness. The compactness of the program in terms of lines of code.

Consistency. The use of uniform design and documentation techniques throughout the software development project.

Data commonality. The use of standard data structures and types throughout the program.

Error tolerance. The damage that occurs when the program encounters an error.

Execution efficiency. The run-time performance of a program.

Expandability. The degree to which architectural, data, or procedural design can be extended.

Generality. The breadth of potential application of program components.

Hardware independence. The degree to which the software is decoupled from the hardware on which it operates.

Instrumentation. The degree to which the program monitors its own operation and identifies errors that do occur.

Modularity. The functional independence (Chapter 13) of program components.

Operability. The ease of operation of a program.

Quality Factors

Security. The availability of mechanisms that control or protect programs and data.

Self-documentation. The degree to which the source code provides meaningful documentation.

Simplicity. The degree to which a program can be understood without difficulty.

Software system independence. The degree to which the program is independent of nonstandard programming language features, operating system characteristics, and other environmental constraints.

Traceability. The ability to trace a design representation or actual program component back to requirements.

Training. The degree to which the software assists in enabling new users to apply the system.

The relationship between software quality factors and these metrics is shown in Figure 19.2. It should be noted that the weight given to each metric is dependent on local products and concerns.

19.1.2 FURPS

The quality factors described by McCall and his colleagues [MCC77] represent one of a number of suggested "checklists" for software quality. Hewlett-Packard [GRA87] developed a set of software quality factors that has been given the acronym FURPS—

FIGURE 19.2
Quality factors and metrics

Quality factor \ Software quality metric	Correctness	Reliability	Efficiency	Integrity	Maintainability	Flexibility	Testability	Portability	Reusability	Interoperability	Usability
Auditability				x			x				
Accuracy		x									
Communication commonality										x	
Completeness	x										
Complexity		x				x	x				
Concision			x		x	x					
Consistency	x	x			x	x					
Data commonality										x	
Error tolerance		x									
Execution efficiency			x								
Expandability						x					
Generality						x		x	x	x	
Hardware Indep.								x	x		
Instrumentation				x	x		x				
Modularity		x			x	x	x	x	x	x	
Operability			x								x
Security				x							
Self-documentation					x	x	x	x	x		
Simplicity		x			x	x	x				
System Indep.								x	x		
Traceability	x										
Training											x

(Adapted from Arthur, L. A., *Measuring Programmer Productivity and Software Quality*, Wiley-Interscience, 1985.)

functionality, usability, reliability, performance, and supportability. The FURPS quality factors draw liberally from earlier work, defining the following attributes for each of the five major factors:

- *Functionality* is assessed by evaluating the feature set and capabilities of the program, the generality of the functions that are delivered, and the security of the overall system.
- *Usability* is assessed by considering human factors (Chapter 15), overall aesthetics, consistency, and documentation.
- *Reliability* is evaluated by measuring the frequency and severity of failure, the accuracy of output results, the mean-time-to-failure (MTTF), the ability to recover from failure, and the predictability of the program.
- *Performance* is measured by processing speed, response time, resource consumption, throughput, and efficiency.

- *Supportability* combines the ability to extend the program (extensibility), adaptability, serviceability—these three attributes represent a more common term, maintainability—in addition, testability, compatibility, configurability (the ability to organize and control elements of the software configuration, Chapter 9), the ease with which a system can be installed, and the ease with which problems can be localized.

The FURPS quality factors and attributes just described can be used to establish quality metrics for each step in the software engineering process.

19.1.3 ISO 9126 Quality Factors

The ISO 9126 standard was developed in an attempt to identify the key quality attributes for computer software. The standard identifies six key quality attributes:

Functionality. The degree to which the software satisfies stated needs as indicated by the following subattributes: suitability, accuracy, interoperability, compliance, and security.

Reliability. The amount of time that the software is available for use as indicated by the following subattributes: maturity, fault tolerance, recoverability.

Quote:
"Any activity becomes creative when the doer cares about doing it right, or better."
John Updike

Usability. The degree to which the software is easy to use as indicated by the following subattributes: understandability, learnability, operability.

Efficiency. The degree to which the software makes optimal use of system resources as indicated by the following subattributes: time behavior, resource behavior.

Maintainability. The ease with which repair may be made to the software as indicated by the following subattributes: analyzability, changeability, stability, testability.

Portability. The ease with which the software can be transposed from one environment to another as indicated by the following subattributes: adaptability, installability, conformance, replaceability.

Like other software quality factors discussed in Sections 19.1.1 and 19.1.2, the ISO 9126 factors do not necessarily lend themselves to direct measurement. However, they do provide a worthwhile basis for indirect measures and an excellent checklist for assessing the quality of a system.

19.1.4 The Transition to a Quantitative View

In the preceding sections, a set of qualitative factors for the "measurement" of software quality was discussed. We strive to develop precise measures for software quality and are sometimes frustrated by the subjective nature of the activity. Cavano and McCall [CAV78] discuss this situation:

> The determination of quality is a key factor in every day events—wine tasting contests, sporting events [e.g., gymnastics], talent contests, etc. In these situations, quality is judged in the most fundamental and direct manner: side by side comparison of objects under identical conditions and with predetermined concepts. The wine may be judged according to clarity, color, bouquet, taste, etc. However, this type of judgement is very subjective; to have any value at all, it must be made by an expert.
>
> Subjectivity and specialization also apply to determining software quality. To help solve this problem, a more precise definition of software quality is needed as well as a way to derive quantitative measurements of software quality for objective analysis . . . Since there is no such thing as absolute knowledge, one should not expect to measure software quality exactly, for every measurement is partially imperfect. Jacob Bronkowski described this paradox of knowledge in this way: "Year by year we devise more precise instruments with which to observe nature with more fineness. And when we look at the observations we are discomfited to see that they are still fuzzy, and we feel that they are as uncertain as ever."

In the sections that follow, we examine a set of software metrics that can be applied to the quantitative assessment of software quality. In all cases, the metrics represent indirect measures; that is, we never really measure quality but rather some manifestation of quality. The complicating factor is the precise relationship between the variable that is measured and the quality of software.

19.2 A FRAMEWORK FOR TECHNICAL SOFTWARE METRICS

As we noted in the introduction to this chapter, measurement assigns numbers or symbols to attributes of entities in the real word. To accomplish this, a measurement model encompassing a consistent set of rules is required. Although the theory of measurement (e.g., [KYB84]) and its application to computer software (e.g., [DEM81], [BRI96], [ZUS97]) are topics that are beyond the scope of this book, it is worthwhile to establish a fundamental framework and a set of basic principles for the measurement of technical metrics for software.

Quote:

"Just as temperature measurement began with an index finger . . . and grew to sophisticated scales, tools and techniques, so too is software measurement maturing . . ."

Shari Pfleeger

19.2.1 The Challenge of Technical Metrics

Over the past three decades, many researchers have attempted to develop a single metric that provides a comprehensive measure of software complexity. Fenton [FEN94] characterizes this research as a search for "the impossible holy grail." Although dozens of complexity measures have been proposed [ZUS90], each takes a somewhat different view of what complexity is and what attributes of a system lead to complexity. By analogy, consider a metric for evaluating an attractive car. Some observers might emphasize body design, others might consider mechanical characteristics, still others might tout cost, or performance, or fuel economy, or the ability to recycle when the car is junked. Since any one of these characteristics may be at odds with others, it is difficult to derive a single value for "attractiveness." The same problem occurs with computer software.

WebRef
Voluminous information on technical metrics has been compiled by Horst Zuse:
irb.cs.tu-berlin.de/~zuse/

Yet there is a need to measure and control software complexity. And if a single value of this quality metric is difficult to derive, it should be possible to develop measures of different internal program attributes (e.g., effective modularity, functional independence, and other attributes discussed in Chapters 13 through 16). These measures and the metrics derived from them can be used as independent indicators of the quality of analysis and design models. But here again, problems arise. Fenton [FEN94] notes this when he states:

> The danger of attempting to find measures which characterize so many different attributes is that inevitably the measures have to satisfy conflicting aims. This is counter to the representational theory of measurement.

Although Fenton's statement is correct, many people argue that technical measurement conducted during the early stages of the software process provides software engineers with a consistent and objective mechanism for assessing quality.

It is fair to ask, however, just how valid technical metrics are. That is, how closely aligned are technical metrics to the long-term reliability and quality of a computer-based system? Fenton [FEN91] addresses this question in the following way:

> In spite of the intuitive connections between the internal structure of software products [technical metrics] and its external product and process attributes, there have actually been very few scientific attempts to establish specific relationships. There are a number of reasons why this is so; the most commonly cited is the impracticality of conducting relevant experiments.

Each of the "challenges" noted here is a cause for caution, but it is no reason to dismiss technical metrics.[2] Measurement is essential if quality is to be achieved.

19.2.2 Measurement Principles

Before we introduce a series of technical metrics that (1) assist in the evaluation of the analysis and design models, (2) provide an indication of the complexity of procedural designs and source code, and (3) facilitate the design of more effective testing, it is important to understand basic measurement principles. Roche [ROC94] suggests a measurement process that can be characterized by five activities:

? What are the steps of an effective measurement process?

- *Formulation*. The derivation of software measures and metrics that are appropriate for the representation of the software that is being considered.
- *Collection*. The mechanism used to accumulate data required to derive the formulated metrics.
- *Analysis*. The computation of metrics and the application of mathematical tools.

---

2 A vast literature on software metrics (e.g., see [FEN94], [ROC94], [ZUS97] for extensive bibliographies) has been spawned, and criticism of specific metrics (including some of those presented in this chapter) is common. However, many of the critiques focus on esoteric issues and miss the primary objective of measurement in the real world: to help the engineer establish a systematic and objective way to gain insight into his or her work and to improve product quality as a result.

- *Interpretation*. The evaluation of metrics results in an effort to gain insight into the quality of the representation.
- *Feedback*. Recommendations derived from the interpretation of technical metrics transmitted to the software team.

The principles that can be associated with the formulation of technical metrics are [ROC94]

What rules should we observe when we establish technical measures?

- The objectives of measurement should be established before data collection begins.
- Each technical metric should be defined in an unambiguous manner.
- Metrics should be derived based on a theory that is valid for the domain of application (e.g., metrics for design should draw upon basic design concepts and principles and attempt to provide an indication of the presence of an attribute that is deemed desirable).
- Metrics should be tailored to best accommodate specific products and processes [BAS84].

Although formulation is a critical starting point, collection and analysis are the activities that drive the measurement process. Roche [ROC94] suggests the following principles for these activities:

ADVICE

Above all, keep your early attempts at technical measurement simple. Don't obsess over the "perfect" metric because it doesn't exist.

- Whenever possible, data collection and analysis should be automated.
- Valid statistical techniques should be applied to establish relationships between internal product attributes and external quality characteristics (e.g., is the level of architectural complexity correlated with the number of defects reported in production use?).
- Interpretative guidelines and recommendations should be established for each metric.

In addition to these principles, the success of a metrics activity is tied to management support. Funding, training, and promotion must all be considered if a technical measurement program is to be established and sustained.

19.2.3 The Attributes of Effective Software Metrics

Hundreds of metrics have been proposed for computer software, but not all provide practical support to the software engineer. Some demand measurement that is too complex, others are so esoteric that few real world professionals have any hope of understanding them, and others violate the basic intuitive notions of what high-quality software really is.

Ejiogu [EJI91] defines a set of attributes that should be encompassed by effective software metrics. The derived metric and the measures that lead to it should be

? How should we assess the quality of a proposed software metric?

- *Simple and computable.* It should be relatively easy to learn how to derive the metric, and its computation should not demand inordinate effort or time.
- *Empirically and intuitively persuasive.* The metric should satisfy the engineer's intuitive notions about the product attribute under consideration (e.g., a metric that measures module cohesion should increase in value as the level of cohesion increases).
- *Consistent and objective.* The metric should always yield results that are unambiguous. An independent third party should be able to derive the same metric value using the same information about the software.

ADVICE

Experience indicates that a technical metric will be used only if it is intuitive and easy to compute. If dozens of "counts" have to be made and complex computations are required, it's unlikely that the metric will be widely applied.

- *Consistent in its use of units and dimensions.* The mathematical computation of the metric should use measures that do not lead to bizarre combinations of units. For example, multiplying people on the project teams by programming language variables in the program results in a suspicious mix of units that are not intuitively persuasive.
- *Programming language independent.* Metrics should be based on the analysis model, the design model, or the structure of the program itself. They should not be dependent on the vagaries of programming language syntax or semantics.
- *An effective mechanism for high-quality feedback.* That is, the metric should provide a software engineer with information that can lead to a higher-quality end product.

Although most software metrics satisfy these attributes, some commonly used metrics may fail to satisfy one or two of them. An example is the function point (discussed in Chapter 4 and again in this chapter). It can be argued[3] that the consistent and objective attribute fails because an independent third party may not be able to derive the same function point value as a colleague using the same information about the software. Should we therefore reject the FP measure? The answer is: "Of course not!" FP provides useful insight and therefore provides distinct value, even if it fails to satisfy one attribute perfectly.

19.3 METRICS FOR THE ANALYSIS MODEL

XRef

Data, functional, and behavioral models are discussed in Chapters 11 and 12.

Technical work in software engineering begins with the creation of the analysis model. It is at this stage that requirements are derived and that a foundation for design is established. Therefore, technical metrics that provide insight into the quality of the analysis model are desirable.

---

3 Please note that an equally vigorous counterargument can be made. Such is the nature of software metrics.

FIGURE 19.3 Part of the analysis model for SafeHome software

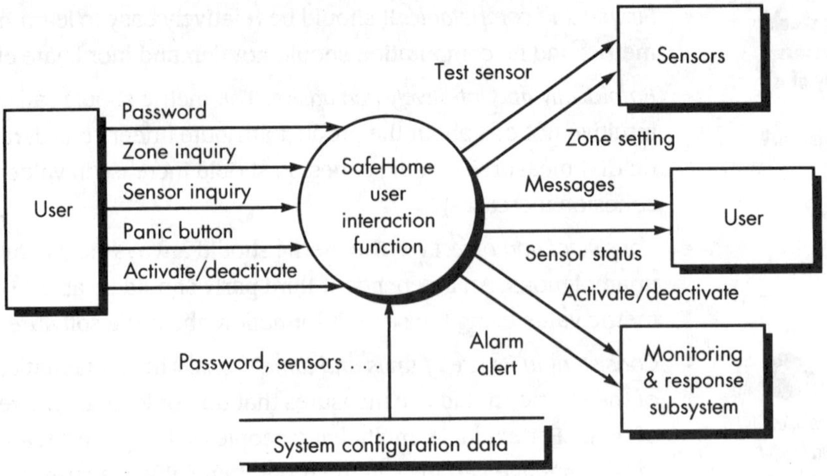

Although relatively few analysis and specification metrics have appeared in the literature, it is possible to adapt metrics derived for project application (Chapter 4) for use in this context. These metrics examine the analysis model with the intent of predicting the "size" of the resultant system. It is likely that size and design complexity will be directly correlated.

19.3.1 Function-Based Metrics

ADVICE: *To be useful for technical work, measures that will assist technical decision making (e.g., errors found during unit testing) must be collected and then normalized using the FP metric.*

The function point metric (Chapter 4) can be used effectively as a means for predicting the size of a system that will be derived from the analysis model. To illustrate the use of the FP metric in this context, we consider a simple analysis model representation, illustrated in Figure 19.3. Referring to the figure, a data flow diagram (Chapter 12) for a function within the *SafeHome* software[4] is represented. The function manages user interaction, accepting a user password to activate or deactivate the system, and allows inquiries on the status of security zones and various security sensors. The function displays a series of prompting messages and sends appropriate control signals to various components of the security system.

The data flow diagram is evaluated to determine the key measures required for computation of the function point metric (Chapter 4):

- number of user inputs
- number of user outputs
- number of user inquiries
- number of files
- number of external interfaces

4 *SafeHome* is a home security system that has been used as an example application in earlier chapters.

Measurement parameter	Count		Weighting Factor: Simple	Average	Complex		
Number of user inputs	3	×	(3)	4	6	=	9
Number of user outputs	2	×	(4)	5	7	=	8
Number of user inquiries	2	×	(3)	4	6	=	6
Number of files	1	×	(7)	10	15	=	7
Number of external interfaces	4	×	(5)	7	10	=	20
Count total →							50

FIGURE 19.4 Computing function points for a SafeHome function

Three user inputs—**password, panic button,** and **activate/deactivate**—are shown in the figure along with two inquires—**zone inquiry** and **sensor inquiry.** One file (**system configuration file**) is shown. Two user outputs (**messages** and **sensor status**) and four external interfaces (**test sensor, zone setting, activate/deactivate,** and **alarm alert**) are also present. These data, along with the appropriate complexity, are shown in Figure 19.4.

The *count total* shown in Figure 19.4 must be adjusted using Equation (4-1):

WebRef

A useful introduction on FP has been prepared by Capers Jones and may be obtained at **www.spr.com/library/0funcmet.htm**

$$FP = \text{count total} \times [0.65 + 0.01 \times \Sigma\,(F_i)]$$

where count total is the sum of all FP entries obtained from Figure 19.3 and F_i (i = 1 to 14) are "complexity adjustment values." For the purposes of this example, we assume that $\Sigma\,(F_i)$ is 46 (a moderately complex product). Therefore,

$$FP = 50 \times [0.65 + (0.01 \times 46)] = 56$$

Based on the projected FP value derived from the analysis model, the project team can estimate the overall implemented size of the *SafeHome* user interaction function. Assume that past data indicates that one FP translates into 60 lines of code (an object-oriented language is to be used) and that 12 FPs are produced for each person-month of effort. These historical data provide the project manager with important planning information that is based on the analysis model rather than preliminary estimates. Assume further that past projects have found an average of three errors per function point during analysis and design reviews and four errors per function point during unit and integration testing. These data can help software engineers assess the completeness of their review and testing activities.

19.3.2 The Bang Metric

Like the function point metric, the *bang metric* can be used to develop an indication of the size of the software to be implemented as a consequence of the analysis model. Developed by DeMarco [DEM82], the bang metric is "an implementation independent indication of system size." To compute the bang metric, the software engineer must first evaluate a set of *primitives*—elements of the analysis model that are not further subdivided at the analysis level. Primitives [DEM82] are determined by evaluating the analysis model and developing counts for the following forms:[5]

Quote:

"Rather than just musing on what 'new metric' might apply . . . we should also be asking ourselves the more basic question, 'What will we do with metrics.'"

Michael Mah and Larry Putnam

Functional primitives (FuP). The number of transformations (bubbles) that appear at the lowest level of a data flow diagram (Chapter 12).

Data elements (DE). The number of attributes of a data object, data elements are not composite data and appear within the data dictionary.

Objects (OB). The number of data objects as described in Chapter 12.

Relationships (RE). The number of connections between data objects as described in Chapter 12.

States (ST). The number of user observable states in the state transition diagram (Chapter 12).

Transitions (TR). The number of state transitions in the state transition diagram (Chapter 12).

In addition to these six primitives, additional counts are determined for

Modified manual function primitives (FuPM). Functions that lie outside the system boundary but must be modified to accommodate the new system.

Input data elements (DEI). Those data elements that are input to the system.

Output data elements. (DEO). Those data elements that are output from the system.

Retained data elements. (DER). Those data elements that are retained (stored) by the system.

Data tokens (TC_i). The data tokens (data items that are not subdivided within a functional primitive) that exist at the boundary of the *i*th functional primitive (evaluated for each primitive).

Relationship connections (RE_i). The relationships that connect the *i*th object in the data model to other objects.

DeMarco [DEM82] suggests that most software can be allocated to one of two domains: *function strong* or *data strong,* depending upon the ratio RE/FuP. Function-strong

5 The acronym noted in parentheses following the primitive is used to denote the count of the particular primitive, e,g., FuP indicates the number of functional primitives present in an analysis model.

applications (often encountered in engineering and scientific applications) emphasize the transformation of data and do not generally have complex data structures. Data-strong applications (often encountered in information systems applications) tend to have complex data models.

RE/FuP < 0.7 implies a function-strong application.
0.8 < RE/FuP < 1.4 implies a hybrid application.
RE/FuP > 1.5 implies a data-strong application.

Because different analysis models will partition the model to greater or lessor degrees of refinement, DeMarco suggests that an average token count per primitive is

$$TC_{avg} = \Sigma\, TC_i / FuP$$

be used to control uniformity of partitioning across many different models within an application domain.

To compute the bang metric for function-strong applications, the following algorithm is used:

```
set initial value of bang = 0;
do while functional primitives remain to be evaluated
    Compute token-count around the boundary of primitive i
    Compute corrected FuP increment (CFuPI)
    Allocate primitive to class
    Assess class and note assessed weight
    Multiply CFuPI by the assessed weight
    bang = bang + weighted CFuPI
enddo
```

The token-count is computed by determining how many separate tokens are "visible" [DEM82] within the primitive. It is possible that the number of tokens and the number of data elements will differ, if data elements can be moved from input to output without any internal transformation. The corrected CFuPI is determined from a table published by DeMarco. A much abbreviated version follows:

TC_i	CFuPI
2	1.0
5	5.8
10	16.6
15	29.3
20	43.2

The assessed weight noted in the algorithm is determined from 16 different classes of functional primitives defined by DeMarco. A weight ranging from 0.6 (simple data routing) to 2.5 (data management functions) is assigned, depending on the class of the primitive.

For data-strong applications, the bang metric is computed using the following algorithm:

```
set initial value of bang = 0;
do while objects remain to be evaluated in the data model
    compute count of relationships for object i
    compute corrected OB increment (COBI)
    bang = bang + COBI
enddo
```

The COBI is determined from a table published by DeMarco. An abbreviated version follows:

RE_i	COBI
1	1.0
3	4.0
6	9.0

Once the bang metric has been computed, past history can be used to associate it with size and effort. DeMarco suggests that an organization build its own versions of the CFuPI and COBI tables using calibration information from completed software projects.

19.3.3 Metrics for Specification Quality

KEY POINT

By measuring characteristics of the specification, it is possible to gain quantitative insight into specificity and completeness.

Davis and his colleagues [DAV93] propose a list of characteristics that can be used to assess the quality of the analysis model and the corresponding requirements specification: *specificity* (lack of ambiguity), *completeness, correctness, understandability, verifiability, internal and external consistency, achievability, concision, traceability, modifiability, precision,* and *reusability.* In addition, the authors note that high-quality specifications are electronically stored, executable or at least interpretable, annotated by relative importance and stable, versioned, organized, cross-referenced, and specified at the right level of detail.

Although many of these characteristics appear to be qualitative in nature, Davis et al. [DAV93] suggest that each can be represented using one or more metrics.[6] For example, we assume that there are n_r requirements in a specification, such that

$$n_r = n_f + n_{nf}$$

where n_f is the number of functional requirements and n_{nf} is the number of nonfunctional (e.g., performance) requirements.

To determine the *specificity* (lack of ambiguity) of requirements, Davis et al. suggest a metric that is based on the consistency of the reviewers' interpretation of each requirement:

$$Q_1 = n_{ui}/n_r$$

6 A complete discussion of specification quality metrics is beyond the scope of this chapter. See [DAV93] for more details.

where n_{ui} is the number of requirements for which all reviewers had identical interpretations. The closer the value of Q to 1, the lower is the ambiguity of the specification.

The *completeness* of functional requirements can be determined by computing the ratio

$$Q_2 = n_u/[n_i \times n_s]$$

where n_u is the number of unique function requirements, n_i is the number of inputs (stimuli) defined or implied by the specification, and n_s is the number of states specified. The Q_2 ratio measures the percentage of necessary functions that have been specified for a system. However, it does not address nonfunctional requirements. To incorporate these into an overall metric for completeness, we must consider the degree to which requirements have been validated:

$$Q_3 = n_c/[n_c + n_{nv}]$$

where n_c is the number of requirements that have been validated as correct and n_{nv} is the number of requirements that have not yet been validated.

19.4 METRICS FOR THE DESIGN MODEL

> **Quote:**
> "Measure what is measurable, and what is not measurable, make measurable."
> Galileo

It is inconceivable that the design of a new aircraft, a new computer chip, or a new office building would be conducted without defining design measures, determining metrics for various aspects of design quality, and using them to guide the manner in which the design evolves. And yet, the design of complex software-based systems often proceeds with virtually no measurement. The irony of this is that design metrics for software are available, but the vast majority of software engineers continue to be unaware of their existence.

Design metrics for computer software, like all other software metrics, are not perfect. Debate continues over their efficacy and the manner in which they should be applied. Many experts argue that further experimentation is required before design measures can be used. And yet, design without measurement is an unacceptable alternative.

In the sections that follow, we examine some of the more common design metrics for computer software. Each can provide the designer with improved insight and all can help the design to evolve to a higher level of quality.

19.4.1 Architectural Design Metrics

Architectural design metrics focus on characteristics of the program architecture (Chapter 14) with an emphasis on the architectural structure and the effectiveness of modules. These metrics are black box in the sense that they do not require any knowledge of the inner workings of a particular software component.

Card and Glass [CAR90] define three software design complexity measures: structural complexity, data complexity, and system complexity.

Structural complexity of a module *i* is defined in the following manner:

$$S(i) = f^2_{out}(i) \qquad (19\text{-}1)$$

KEY POINT

Metrics can provide insight into structural, data and system complexity associated with the architectural design.

where $f_{out}(i)$ is the fan-out[7] of module *i*.

Data complexity provides an indication of the complexity in the internal interface for a module *i* and is defined as

$$D(i) = v(i)/[f_{out}(i) + 1] \qquad (19\text{-}2)$$

where *v(i)* is the number of input and output variables that are passed to and from module *i*.

Finally, *system complexity* is defined as the sum of structural and data complexity, specified as

$$C(i) = S(i) + D(i) \qquad (19\text{-}3)$$

As each of these complexity values increases, the overall architectural complexity of the system also increases. This leads to a greater likelihood that integration and testing effort will also increase.

? Is there a way to assess the complexity of certain architectural models?

An earlier high-level architectural design metric proposed by Henry and Kafura [HEN81] also makes use the fan-in and fan-out. The authors define a complexity metric (applicable to call and return architectures) of the form

$$\text{HKM} = \text{length}(i) \times [f_{in}(i) + f_{out}(i)]^2 \qquad (19\text{-}4)$$

where length*(i)* is the number of programming language statements in a module *i* and $f_{in}(i)$ is the fan-in of a module *i*. Henry and Kafura extend the definitions of *fan-in* and *fan-out* presented in this book to include not only the number of module control connections (module calls) but also the number of data structures from which a module *i* retrieves (fan-in) or updates (fan-out) data. To compute HKM during design, the procedural design may be used to estimate the number of programming language statements for module *i*. Like the Card and Glass metrics noted previously, an increase in the Henry-Kafura metric leads to a greater likelihood that integration and testing effort will also increase for a module.

Fenton [FEN91] suggests a number of simple *morphology* (i.e., shape) metrics that enable different program architectures to be compared using a set of straightforward dimensions. Referring to Figure 19.5, the following metrics can be defined:

$$\text{size} = n + a$$

7 Recalling the discussion presented in Chapter 13, fan-out indicates the number of modules immediately subordinate to module *i*; that is, the number of modules that are directly invoked by module *i*.

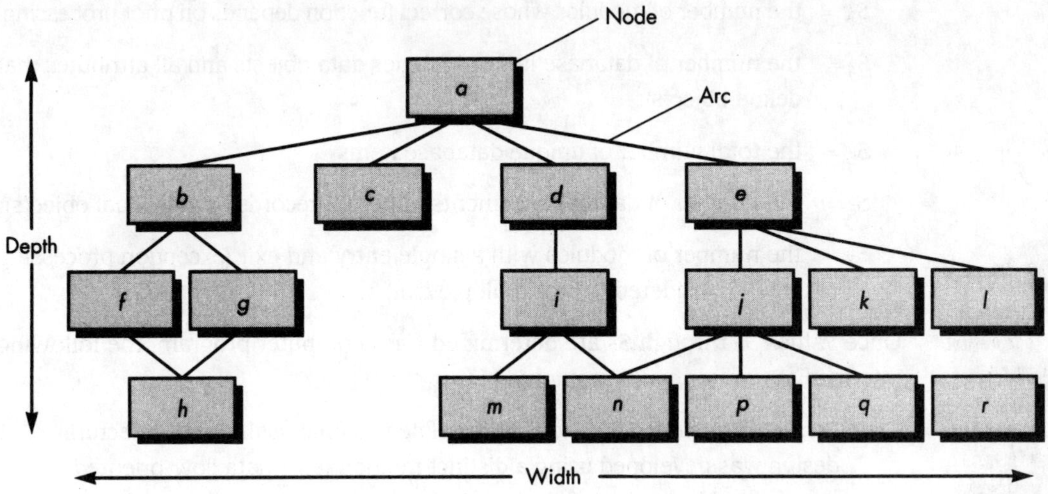

FIGURE 19.5 Morphology metrics

where n is the number of nodes and a is the number of arcs. For the architecture shown in Figure 19.5,

size = 17 + 18 = 35

depth = the longest path from the root (top) node to a leaf node. For the architecture shown in Figure 19.5, depth = 4.

width = maximum number of nodes at any one level of the architecture. For the architecture shown in Figure 19.5, width = 6.

arc-to-node ratio, $r = a/n$,

which measures the connectivity density of the architecture and may provide a simple indication of the coupling of the architecture. For the architecture shown in Figure 19.5, r = 18/17 = 1.06.

The U.S. Air Force Systems Command [USA87] has developed a number of software quality indicators that are based on measurable design characteristics of a computer program. Using concepts similar to those proposed in IEEE Std. 982.1-1988 [IEE94], the Air Force uses information obtained from data and architectural design to derive a *design structure quality index* (DSQI) that ranges from 0 to 1. The following values must be ascertained to compute the DSQI [CHA89]:

S_1 = the total number of modules defined in the program architecture.

S_2 = the number of modules whose correct function depends on the source of data input or that produce data to be used elsewhere (in general, control modules, among others, would not be counted as part of S_2).

S_3 = the number of modules whose correct function depends on prior processing.

S_4 = the number of database items (includes data objects and all attributes that define objects).

S_5 = the total number of unique database items.

S_6 = the number of database segments (different records or individual objects).

S_7 = the number of modules with a single entry and exit (exception processing is not considered to be a multiple exit).

Quote:
"Measurement can be seen as a detour. This detour is necessary because humans mostly are not able to make clear and objective decisions [without quantitative support]."
Horst Zuse

Once values S_1 through S_7 are determined for a computer program, the following intermediate values can be computed:

Program structure: D_1, where D_1 is defined as follows: If the architectural design was developed using a distinct method (e.g., data flow-oriented design or object-oriented design), then $D_1 = 1$, otherwise $D_1 = 0$.

Module independence: $D_2 = 1 - (S_2/S_1)$

Modules not dependent on prior processing: $D_3 = 1 - (S_3/S_1)$

Database size: $D_4 = 1 - (S_5/S_4)$

Database compartmentalization: $D_5 = 1 - (S_6/S_4)$

Module entrance/exit characteristic: $D_6 = 1 - (S_7/S_1)$

With these intermediate values determined, the DSQI is computed in the following manner:

$$\text{DSQI} = \Sigma\, w_i D_i \tag{19-5}$$

where i = 1 to 6, w_i is the relative weighting of the importance of each of the intermediate values, and $\Sigma\, w_i = 1$ (if all D_i are weighted equally, then $w_i = 0.167$).

The value of DSQI for past designs can be determined and compared to a design that is currently under development. If the DSQI is significantly lower than average, further design work and review are indicated. Similarly, if major changes are to be made to an existing design, the effect of those changes on DSQI can be calculated.

19.4.2 Component-Level Design Metrics

Component-level design metrics focus on internal characteristics of a software component and include measures of the "three Cs"—module cohesion, coupling, and complexity. These measures can help a software engineer to judge the quality of a component-level design.

The metrics presented in this section are glass box in the sense that they require knowledge of the inner working of the module under consideration. Component-level design metrics may be applied once a procedural design has been developed. Alternatively, they may be delayed until source code is available.

KEY POINT

It is possible to compute measures of the functional independence—coupling and cohesion—of a component and to use these to assess the quality of the design.

Cohesion metrics. Bieman and Ott [BIE94] define a collection of metrics that provide an indication of the cohesiveness (Chapter 13) of a module. The metrics are defined in terms of five concepts and measures:

Data slice. Stated simply, a data slice is a backward walk through a module that looks for data values that affect the module location at which the walk began. It should be noted that both program slices (which focus on statements and conditions) and data slices can be defined.

Data tokens. The variables defined for a module can be defined as data tokens for the module.

Glue tokens. This set of data tokens lies on one or more data slice.

Superglue tokens. These data tokens are common to every data slice in a module.

Stickiness. The relative stickiness of a glue token is directly proportional to the number of data slices that it binds.

Bieman and Ott develop metrics for *strong functional cohesion* (SFC), *weak functional cohesion* (WFC), and *adhesiveness* (the relative degree to which glue tokens bind data slices together). These metrics can be interpreted in the following manner [BIE94]:

> All of these cohesion metrics range in value between 0 and 1. They have a value of 0 when a procedure has more than one output and exhibits none of the cohesion attribute indicated by a particular metric. A procedure with no superglue tokens, no tokens that are common to all data slices, has zero strong functional cohesion—there are no data tokens that contribute to all outputs. A procedure with no glue tokens, that is no tokens common to more than one data slice (in procedures with more than one data slice), exhibits zero weak functional cohesion and zero adhesiveness—there are no data tokens that contribute to more than one output.

Strong functional cohesion and adhesiveness are encountered when the Bieman and Ott metrics take on a maximum value of 1.

A detailed discussion of the Bieman and Ott metrics is best left to the authors [BIE94]. However, to illustrate the character of these metrics, consider the metric for strong functional cohesion:

$$\text{SFC}(i) = \text{SG}\ [\text{SA}(i))/(\text{tokens}(i)] \qquad (19\text{-}6)$$

where SG[SA(*i*)] denotes superglue tokens—the set of data tokens that lie on all data slices for a module *i*. As the ratio of superglue tokens to the total number of tokens in a module *i* increases toward a maximum value of 1, the functional cohesiveness of the module also increases.

Coupling metrics. Module coupling provides an indication of the "connectedness" of a module to other modules, global data, and the outside environment. In Chapter 13, coupling was discussed in qualitative terms.

Dhama [DHA95] has proposed a metric for module coupling that encompasses data and control flow coupling, global coupling, and environmental coupling. The measures required to compute module coupling are defined in terms of each of the three coupling types noted previously.

WebRef
A paper, "A Software Metric System for Module Coupling," can be downloaded from **www.isse.gmu.edu/faculty/ofut/rsrch/abstracts/mj-coupling.html**

For data and control flow coupling,

d_i = number of input data parameters
c_i = number of input control parameters
d_o = number of output data parameters
c_o = number of output control parameters

For global coupling,

g_d = number of global variables used as data
g_c = number of global variables used as control

For environmental coupling,

w = number of modules called (fan-out)
r = number of modules calling the module under consideration (fan-in)

Using these measures, a module coupling indicator, m_c, is defined in the following way:

$$m_c = k/M$$

where k = 1, a proportionality constant[8] and

$$M = d_i + (a \times c_i) + d_o + (b \times c_o) + g_d + (c \times g_c) + w + r$$

where $a = b = c = 2$.

The higher the value of m_c, the lower is the overall module coupling. For example, if a module has single input and output data parameters, accesses no global data, and is called by a single module,

$$m_c = 1/(1 + 0 + 1 + 0 + 0 + + 0 + 1 + 0) = 1/3 = 0.33$$

We would expect that such a module exhibits low coupling. Hence, a value of m_c = 0.33 implies low coupling. Alternatively, if a module has five input and five output data parameters, an equal number of control parameters, accesses ten items of global data, has a fan-in of 3 and a fan-out of 4,

$$m_c = 1/[5 + (2 \times 5) + 5 + (2 \times 5) + 10 + 0 + 3 + 4] = 0.02$$

and the implied coupling would be high.

8 The author [DHA95] notes that the values of *k* and *a, b,* and *c* (discussed in the next equation) may be adjusted as more experimental verification occurs.

In order to have the coupling metric move upward as the degree of coupling increases (an important attribute discussed in Section 18.2.3), a revised coupling metric may be defined as

$$C = 1 - m_C$$

where the degree of coupling increases nonlinearly between a minimum value in the range 0.66 to a maximum value that approaches 1.0.

Complexity metrics. A variety of software metrics can be computed to determine the complexity of program control flow. Many of these are based on the flow graph. As we discussed in Chapter 17, a graph is a representation composed of nodes and links (also called *edges*). When the links (edges) are *directed,* the flow graph is a directed graph.

McCabe and Watson [MCC94] identify a number of important uses for complexity metrics:

> Complexity metrics can be used to predict critical information about reliability and maintainability of software systems from automatic analysis of source code [or procedural design information]. Complexity metrics also provide feedback during the software project to help control the [design activity]. During testing and maintenance, they provide detailed information about software modules to help pinpoint areas of potential instability.

KEY POINT

Cyclomatic complexity is only one of a large number of complexity metrics.

The most widely used (and debated) complexity metric for computer software is cyclomatic complexity, originally developed by Thomas McCabe [MCC76], [MCC89] and discussed in detail in Section 17.4.2.

The McCabe metric provides a quantitative measure of testing difficulty and an indication of ultimate reliability. Experimental studies indicate distinct relationships between the McCabe metric and the number of errors existing in source code, as well as time required to find and correct such errors.

McCabe also contends that cyclomatic complexity may be used to provide a quantitative indication of maximum module size. Collecting data from a number of actual programming projects, he has found that cyclomatic complexity = 10 appears to be a practical upper limit for module size. When the cyclomatic complexity of modules exceeded this number, it became extremely difficult to adequately test a module. See Chapter 17 for a discussion of cyclomatic complexity as a guide for the design of white-box test cases.

Zuse ([ZUS90], [ZUS97]) presents an encyclopedic discussion of no fewer that 18 different categories of software complexity metrics. The author presents the basic definitions for metrics in each category (e.g., there are a number of variations on the cyclomatic complexity metric) and then analyzes and critiques each. Zuse's work is the most comprehensive published to date.

19.4.3 Interface Design Metrics

Although there is significant literature on the design of human/computer interfaces (see Chapter 15), relatively little information has been published on metrics that would provide insight into the quality and usability of the interface.

Sears [SEA93] suggests that *layout appropriateness* (LA) is a worthwhile design metric for human/computer interfaces. A typical GUI uses *layout entities*—graphic icons, text, menus, windows, and the like—to assist the user in completing tasks. To accomplish a given task using a GUI, the user must move from one layout entity to the next. The absolute and relative position of each layout entity, the frequency with which it is used, and the "cost" of the transition from one layout entity to the next all contribute to the appropriateness of the interface.

Quote: "Beauty—the adjustment of all parts proportionately so that one cannot add or subtract or change without impairing the harmony of the whole." **Leon Alberti (1404–1472)**

For a specific layout (i.e., a specific GUI design), cost can be assigned to each sequence of actions according to the following relationship:

$$\text{cost} = \Sigma\ [\text{frequency of transition}(k) \times \text{cost of transition}(k)] \tag{19-7}$$

where k is a specific transition from one layout entity to the next as a specific task is accomplished. The summation occurs across all transitions for a particular task or set of tasks required to accomplish some application function. Cost may be characterized in terms of time, processing delay, or any other reasonable value, such as the distance that a mouse must travel between layout entities. Layout appropriateness is defined as

$$\text{LA} = 100 \times [(\text{cost of LA} - \text{optimal layout})/(\text{cost of proposed layout})] \tag{19-8}$$

where LA = 100 for an optimal layout.

To compute the optimal layout for a GUI, interface real estate (the area of the screen) is divided into a grid. Each square of the grid represents a possible position for a layout entity. For a grid with N possible positions and K different layout entities to place, the number of possible layouts is represented in the following manner [SEA93]:

$$\text{number of possible layouts} = [N!/(K! \times (N-K)!)] \times K! \tag{19-9}$$

ADVICE *Interface design metrics are fine, but above all else, be absolutely sure that your end-users like the interface and are comfortable with the interactions required.*

As the number of layout positions increases, the number of possible layouts grows very large. To find the optimal (lowest cost) layout, Sears [SEA93] proposes a tree searching algorithm.

LA is used to assess different proposed GUI layouts and the sensitivity of a particular layout to changes in task descriptions (i.e., changes in the sequence and/or frequency of transitions). The interface designer can use the change in layout appropriateness, ΔLA, as a guide in choosing the best GUI layout for a particular application.

It is important to note that the selection of a GUI design can be guided with metrics such as LA, but the final arbiter should be user input based on GUI prototypes. Nielsen and Levy [NIE94] report that "one has a reasonably large chance of success if one chooses between interface [designs] based solely on users' opinions. Users' average task performance and their subjective satisfaction with a GUI are highly correlated."

19.5 METRICS FOR SOURCE CODE

Quote:

"The Human Brain follows a more rigid set of rules [in developing algorithms] than it has been aware of."
Maurice Halstead

Halstead's theory of software science [HAL77] is one of "the best known and most thoroughly studied . . . composite measures of (software) complexity" [CUR80]. Software science proposed the first analytical "laws" for computer software.[9]

Software science assigns quantitative laws to the development of computer software, using a set of primitive measures that may be derived after code is generated or estimated once design is complete. These follow:

n_1 = the number of distinct operators that appear in a program.
n_2 = the number of distinct operands that appear in a program.
N_1 = the total number of operator occurrences.
N_2 = the total number of operand occurrences.

Halstead uses these primitive measures to develop expressions for the overall *program length, potential minimum volume* for an algorithm, the *actual volume* (number of bits required to specify a program), the *program level* (a measure of software complexity), the *language level* (a constant for a given language), and other features such as development effort, development time, and even the projected number of faults in the software.

ADVICE

Operators include all flow of control constructs, conditionals, and math operations. Operands encompass all program variables and constants.

Halstead shows that length *N* can be estimated

$$N = n_1 \log_2 n_1 + n_2 \log_2 n_2 \qquad (19\text{-}10)$$

and program volume may be defined

$$V = N \log_2 (n_1 + n_2) \qquad (19\text{-}11)$$

It should be noted that *V* will vary with programming language and represents the volume of information (in bits) required to specify a program.

Theoretically, a minimum volume must exist for a particular algorithm. Halstead defines a volume ratio *L* as the ratio of volume of the most compact form of a program to the volume of the actual program. In actuality, *L* must always be less than 1. In terms of primitive measures, the volume ratio may be expressed as

$$L = 2/n_1 \times n_2/N_2 \qquad (19\text{-}12)$$

9 It should be noted that Halstead's "laws" have generated substantial controversy and that not everyone agrees that the underlying theory is correct. However, experimental verification of Halstead's findings have been made for a number of programming languages (e.g., [FEL89]).

Halstead's work is amenable to experimental verification and a large body of research has been conducted to investigate software science. A discussion of this work is beyond the scope of this text, but it can be said that good agreement has been found between analytically predicted and experimental results. For further information, see [ZUS90], [FEN91], and [ZUS97].

19.6 METRICS FOR TESTING

Although much has been written on software metrics for testing (e.g., [HET93]), the majority of metrics proposed focus on the process of testing, not the technical characteristics of the tests themselves. In general, testers must rely on analysis, design, and code metrics to guide them in the design and execution of test cases.

KEY POINT

Testing metrics fall into two broad categories: (1) metrics that attempt to predict the likely number of tests required at various testing levels and (2) metrics that focus on test coverage for a given component.

Function-based metrics (Section 19.3.1) can be used as a predictor for overall testing effort. Various project-level characteristics (e.g., testing effort and time, errors uncovered, number of test cases produced) for past projects can be collected and correlated with the number of FP produced by a project team. The team can then project "expected values" of these characteristics for the current project.

The bang metric can provide an indication of the number of test cases required by examining the primitive measures discussed in Section 19.3.2. The number of functional primitives (FuP), data elements (DE), objects (OB), relationships (RE), states (ST), and transitions (TR) can be used to project the number and types of black-box and white-box tests for the software. For example, the number of tests associated with the human/computer interface can be estimated by (1) examining the number of transitions (TR) contained in the state transition representation of the HCI and evaluating the tests required to exercise each transition; (2) examining the number of data objects (OB) that move across the interface, and (3) the number of data elements that are input or output.

Architectural design metrics provide information on the ease or difficulty associated with integration testing (Chapter 18) and the need for specialized testing software (e.g., stubs and drivers). Cyclomatic complexity (a component-level design metric) lies at the core of basis path testing, a test case design method presented in Chapter 17. In addition, cyclomatic complexity can be used to target modules as candidates for extensive unit testing (Chapter 18). Modules with high cyclomatic complexity are more likely to be error prone than modules whose cyclomatic complexity is lower. For this reason, the tester should expend above average effort to uncover errors in such modules before they are integrated in a system. Testing effort can also be estimated using metrics derived from Halstead measures (Section 19.5). Using the definitions for program volume, V, and program level, PL, software science effort, e, can be computed as

$$\mathrm{PL} = 1/[(n_1/2)\bullet(N_2/n_2)] \qquad \text{(19-13a)}$$

$$e = V/\mathrm{PL} \qquad \text{(19-13b)}$$

The percentage of overall testing effort to be allocated to a module k can be estimated using the following relationship:

$$\text{percentage of testing effort }(k) = e(k)/\sum e(i) \qquad (19\text{-}14)$$

where $e(k)$ is computed for module k using Equations (19-13) and the summation in the denominator of Equation (19-14) is the sum of software science effort across all modules of the system.

As tests are conducted, three different measures provide an indication of testing completeness. A measure of the breath of testing provides an indication of how many requirements (of the total number of requirements) have been tested. This provides an indication of the completeness of the test plan. Depth of testing is a measure of the percentage of independent basis paths covered by testing versus the total number of basis paths in the program. A reasonably accurate estimate of the number of basis paths can be computed by adding the cyclomatic complexity of all program modules. Finally, as tests are conducted and error data are collected, fault profiles may be used to rank and categorize errors uncovered. Priority indicates the severity of the problem. Fault categories provide a description of an error so that statistical error analysis can be conducted.

19.7 METRICS FOR MAINTENANCE

All of the software metrics introduced in this chapter can be used for the development of new software and the maintenance of existing software. However, metrics designed explicitly for maintenance activities have been proposed.

IEEE Std. 982.1-1988 [IEE94] suggests a *software maturity index* (SMI) that provides an indication of the stability of a software product (based on changes that occur for each release of the product). The following information is determined:

M_T = the number of modules in the current release
F_c = the number of modules in the current release that have been changed
F_a = the number of modules in the current release that have been added
F_d = the number of modules from the preceding release that were deleted in the current release

The software maturity index is computed in the following manner:

$$\text{SMI} = [M_T - (F_a + F_c + F_d)]/M_T \qquad (19\text{-}15)$$

As SMI approaches 1.0, the product begins to stabilize. SMI may also be used as metric for planning software maintenance activities. The mean time to produce a release of a software product can be correlated with SMI and empirical models for maintenance effort can be developed.

19.8 SUMMARY

Software metrics provide a quantitative way to assess the quality of internal product attributes, thereby enabling the software engineer to assess quality before the product is built. Metrics provide the insight necessary to create effective analysis and design models, solid code, and thorough tests.

To be useful in a real world context, a software metric must be simple and computable, persuasive, consistent, and objective. It should be programming language independent and provide effective feedback to the software engineer.

Metrics for the analysis model focus on function, data, and behavior—the three components of the analysis model. The function point and the bang metric each provide a quantitative means for evaluating the analysis model. Metrics for design consider architecture, component-level design, and interface design issues. Architectural design metrics consider the structural aspects of the design model. Component-level design metrics provide an indication of module quality by establishing indirect measures for cohesion, coupling, and complexity. Interface design metrics provide an indication of layout appropriateness for a GUI.

Software science provides an intriguing set of metrics at the source code level. Using the number of operators and operands present in the code, software science provides a variety of metrics that can be used to assess program quality.

Few technical metrics have been proposed for direct use in software testing and maintenance. However, many other technical metrics can be used to guide the testing process and as a mechanism for assessing the maintainability of a computer program.

REFERENCES

[BAS84] Basili, V.R. and D.M. Weiss, "A Methodology for Collecting Valid Software Engineering Data," *IEEE Trans. Software Engineering,* vol. SE-10, 1984, pp. 728–738.

[BIE94] Bieman, J.M. and L.M. Ott, "Measuring Functional Cohesion," *IEEE Trans. Software Engineering,* vol. SE-20, no. 8, August 1994, pp. 308–320.

[BRI96] Briand, L.C., S. Morasca, and V.R. Basili, "Property-Based Software Engineering Measurement," *IEEE Trans. Software Engineering,* vol. SE-22, no. 1, January 1996, pp. 68–85.

[CAR90] Card, D.N. and R.L. Glass, *Measuring Software Design Quality,* Prentice-Hall, 1990.

[CAV78] Cavano, J.P. and J.A. McCall, "A Framework for the Measurement of Software Quality," *Proc. ACM Software Quality Assurance Workshop,* November 1978, pp. 133–139.

[CHA89] Charette, R.N., *Software Engineering Risk Analysis and Management,* McGraw-Hill/Intertext, 1989.

[CUR80] Curtis, W. "Management and Experimentation in Software Engineering," *Proc. IEEE,* vol. 68, no. 9, September 1980.

[DAV93] Davis, A., et al., "Identifying and Measuring Quality in a Software Requirements Specification, *Proc. First Intl. Software Metrics Symposium,* IEEE, Baltimore, MD, May 1993, pp. 141–152.

[DEM81] DeMillo, R.A. and R.J. Lipton, "Software Project Forecasting," in *Software Metrics* (A.J. Perlis, F.G. Sayward, and M. Shaw, eds.), MIT Press, 1981, pp. 77–89.

[DEM82] DeMarco, T., *Controlling Software Projects,* Yourdon Press, 1982.

[DHA95] Dhama, H., "Quantitative Models of Cohesion and Coupling in Software," *Journal of Systems and Software,* vol. 29, no. 4, April 1995.

[EJI91] Ejiogu, L., *Software Engineering with Formal Metrics,* QED Publishing, 1991.

[FEL89] Felican, L. and G. Zalateu, "Validating Halstead's Theory for Pascal Programs," *IEEE Trans. Software Engineering,* vol. SE-15, no. 2, December 1989, pp. 1630–1632.

[FEN91] Fenton, N., *Software Metrics,* Chapman and Hall, 1991.

[FEN94] Fenton, N., "Software Measurement: A Necessary Scientific Basis," *IEEE Trans. Software Engineering,* vol. SE-20, no. 3, March 1994, pp. 199–206.

[GRA87] Grady, R.B. and D.L. Caswell, *Software Metrics: Establishing a Company-Wide Program,* Prentice-Hall, 1987.

[HAL77] Halstead, M., *Elements of Software Science,* North-Holland, 1977.

[HEN81] Henry, S. and D. Kafura, "Software Structure Metrics Based on Information Flow," *IEEE Trans. Software Engineering,* vol. SE-7, no. 5, September 1981, pp. 510–518.

[HET93] Hetzel, B., *Making Software Measurement Work,* QED Publishing, 1993.

[IEE94] *Software Engineering Standards,* 1994 edition, IEEE, 1994.

[KYB84] Kyburg, H.E., *Theory and Measurement,* Cambridge University Press, 1984.

[MCC76] McCabe, T.J., "A Software Complexity Measure," *IEEE Trans. Software Engineering,* vol. SE-2, December 1976, pp. 308–320.

[MCC77] McCall, J., P. Richards, and G. Walters, "Factors in Software Quality," three volumes, NTIS AD-A049-014, 015, 055, November 1977.

[MCC89] McCabe, T.J. and C.W. Butler, "Design Complexity Measurement and Testing," *CACM,* vol. 32, no. 12, December 1989, pp. 1415–1425.

[MCC94] McCabe, T.J. and A.H. Watson, "Software Complexity," *Crosstalk,* vol. 7, no. 12, December 1994, pp. 5–9.

[NIE94] Nielsen, J., and J. Levy, "Measuring Usability: Preference vs. Performance," *CACM,* vol. 37, no. 4, April 1994, pp. 65–75.

[ROC94] Roche, J.M., "Software Metrics and Measurement Principles," *Software Engineering Notes,* ACM, vol. 19, no. 1, January 1994, pp. 76–85.

[SEA93] Sears, A., "Layout Appropriateness: A Metric for Evaluating User Interface Widget Layout, *IEEE Trans. Software Engineering,* vol. SE-19, no. 7, July 1993, pp. 707–719.

[USA87] *Management Quality Insight,* AFCSP 800-14 (U.S. Air Force), January 20, 1987.

[ZUS90] Zuse, H., *Software Complexity: Measures and Methods,* DeGruyter, 1990.

[ZUS97] Zuse, H., *A Framework of Software Measurement,* DeGruyter, 1997.

PROBLEMS AND POINTS TO PONDER

19.1. Measurement theory is an advanced topic that has a strong bearing on software metrics. Using [ZUS97], [FEN91], [ZUS90], [KYB84] or some other source, write a brief paper that outlines the main tenets of measurement theory. Individual project: Develop a presentation on the subject and present it to your class.

19.2. McCall's quality factors were developed during the 1970s. Almost every aspect of computing has changed dramatically since the time that they were developed, and yet, McCall's factors continue to apply to modern software. Can you draw any conclusions based on this fact?

19.3. Why is it that a single, all-encompassing metric cannot be developed for program complexity or program quality?

19.4. Review the analysis model you developed as part of Problem 12.13. Using the guidelines presented in Section 19.3.1, develop an estimate for the number of function points associated with PHTRS.

19.5. Review the analysis model you developed as part of Problem 12.13. Using the guidelines presented in Section 19.3.2, develop primitive counts for the bang metric. Is the PHTRS system function strong or data strong?

19.6. Compute the value of the bang metric using the measures you developed in Problem 19.5.

19.7. Create a complete design model for a system that is proposed by your instructor. Compute structural and data complexity using the metrics described in Section 19.4.1. Also compute the Henry-Kafura and morphology metrics for the design model.

19.8. A major information system has 1140 modules. There are 96 modules that perform control and coordination functions and 490 modules whose function depends on prior processing. The system processes approximately 220 data objects that each have an average of three attributes. There are 140 unique data base items and 90 different database segments. Finally, 600 modules have single entry and exit points. Compute the DSQI for this system.

19.9. Research Bieman and Ott's [BIE94] paper and develop a complete example that illustrates the computation of their cohesion metric. Be sure to indicate how data slices, data tokens, glue, and superglue tokens are determined.

19.10. Select five modules in an existing computer program. Using Dhama's metric described in Section 19.4.2, compute the coupling value for each module.

19.11. Develop a software tool that will compute cyclomatic complexity for a programming language module. You may choose the language.

19.12. Develop a software tool that will compute layout appropriateness for a GUI. The tool should enable you to assign the transition cost between layout entities. (Note: Recognize that the size of the potential population of layout alternatives grows very large as the number of possible grid positions grows.)

19.13. Develop a small software tool that will perform a Halstead analysis on programming language source code of your choosing.

19.14. Research the literature and write a paper on the relationship of Halstead's metric and McCabe's metric on software quality (as measured by error count). Are the data compelling? Recommend guidelines for the application of these metrics.

19.15. Research the literature for any recent papers on metrics specifically developed to assist in test case design. Present your findings to the class.

19.16. A legacy system has 940 modules. The latest release required that 90 of these modules be changed. In addition, 40 new modules were added and 12 old modules were removed. Compute the software maturity index for the system.

FURTHER READING AND INFORMATION SOURCES

There are a surprisingly large number of books that are dedicated to software metrics, although the majority focus on process and project metrics to the exclusion of technical metrics. Zuse [ZUS97] has written the most thorough treatment of technical metrics published to date.

Books by Card and Glass [CAR90], Zuse [ZUS90], Fenton {FEN91], Ejiogu [EJI91], Moeller and Paulish *(Software Metrics,* Chapman and Hall, 1993), and Hetzel [HET93] all address technical metrics in some detail. Oman and Pfleeger (*Applying Software Metrics,* IEEE Computer Society Press, 1997) have edited an anthology of important papers on software metrics. In addition, the following books are worth examining:

Conte, S.D., H.E. Dunsmore, and V.Y. Shen. *Software Engineering Metrics and Models,* Benjamin/Cummings, 1984.

Fenton, N.E. and S.L. Pfleeger, *Software Metrics: A Rigorous and Practical Approach,* 2nd ed., PWS Publishing Co., 1998.

Grady, R.B. *Practical Software Metrics for Project Management and Process Improvement,* Prentice-Hall, 1992.

Perlis, A., et al., *Software Metrics: An Analysis and Evaluation,* MIT Press, 1981.

Sheppard, M., *Software Engineering Metrics,* McGraw-Hill, 1992.

The theory of software measurement is presented by Denvir, Herman, and Whitty in an edited collection of papers (*Proceedings of the International BCS-FACS Workshop: Formal Aspects of Measurement,* Springer-Verlag, 1992). Shepperd (*Foundations of Software Measurement,* Prentice-Hall, 1996) also addresses measurement theory in some detail.

CHAPTER

20 OBJECT-ORIENTED CONCEPTS AND PRINCIPLES

We live in a world of objects. These objects exist in nature, in human-made entities, in business, and in the products that we use. They can be categorized, described, organized, combined, manipulated, and created. Therefore, it is no surprise that an object-oriented view would be proposed for the creation of computer software—an abstraction that enables us to model the world in ways that help us to better understand and navigate it.

An object-oriented approach to the development of software was first proposed in the late 1960s. However, it took almost 20 years for object technologies to become widely used. Throughout the 1990s, object-oriented software engineering became the paradigm of choice for many software product builders and a growing number of information systems and engineering professionals. As time passes, object technologies are replacing classical software development approaches. An important question is why?

The answer (like many answers to questions about software engineering) is not a simple one. Some people would argue that software professionals simply yearned for a "new" approach, but that view is overly simplistic. Object technologies do lead to a number of inherent benefits that provide advantage at both the management and technical levels.

QUICK LOOK

What is it? There are many ways to look at a problem to be solved using a software-based solution. One widely used approach to problem solving takes an object-oriented viewpoint. The problem domain is characterized as a set of objects that have specific attributes and behaviors. The objects are manipulated with a collection of functions (called methods, operations, or services) and communicate with one another through a messaging protocol. Objects are categorized into classes and subclasses.

Who does it? The definition of objects encompasses a description of attributes, behaviors, operations, and messages. This activity is performed by a software engineer.

Why is it important? An object encapsulates both data and the processing that is applied to the data. This important characteristic enables classes of objects to be built and inherently leads to libraries of reusable classes and objects. Because reuse is a critically important attribute of modern software engineering, the object-oriented paradigm is attractive to many software development organizations. In addition, the software components derived using the object-oriented paradigm exhibit design characteristics (e.g., functional independence, information hiding) that are associated with high-quality software.

What are the steps? Object-oriented software engineering follows the same steps as conventional approaches. Analysis identifies objects and classes

QUICK LOOK

that are relevant to the problem domain; design provides the architecture, interface, and component-level detail; implementation (using an object-oriented language) transforms design into code; and testing exercises the object-oriented architecture, interfaces and components.

What is the work product? A set of object oriented models is produced. These models describe the requirements, design, code, and test process for a system or product.

How do I ensure that I've done it right? At each stage, object-oriented work products are reviewed for clarity, correctness, completeness, and consistency with customer requirements and with one another.

Object technologies lead to reuse, and reuse (of program components) leads to faster software development and higher-quality programs. Object-oriented software is easier to maintain because its structure is inherently decoupled. This leads to fewer side effects when changes have to be made and less frustration for the software engineer and the customer. In addition, object-oriented systems are easier to adapt and easier to scale (i.e., large systems can be created by assembling reusable subsystems).

In this chapter we introduce the basic principles and concepts that form a foundation for the understanding of object technologies. Throughout the remainder of Part Four of this book, we consider methods that form the basis for an engineering approach to the creation of object-oriented products and systems.

20.1 THE OBJECT-ORIENTED PARADIGM

For many years, the term *object oriented* (OO) was used to denote a software development approach that used one of a number of object-oriented programming languages (e.g., Ada95, Java, C++, Eiffel, Smalltalk). Today, the OO paradigm encompasses a complete view of software engineering. Edward Berard notes this when he states [BER93]:

> **Quote:**
> "With objects, it's actually easier to build models [for complex systems] than to engage in sequential programming."
> **David Taylor**

> The benefits of object-oriented technology are enhanced if it is addressed early-on and throughout the software engineering process. Those considering object-oriented technology must assess its impact on the entire software engineering process. Merely employing object-oriented programming (OOP) will not yield the best results. Software engineers and their managers must consider such items as object-oriented requirements analysis (OORA), object-oriented design (OOD), object-oriented domain analysis (OODA), object-oriented database systems (OODBMS) and object-oriented computer aided software engineering (OOCASE).

A reader who is familiar with the conventional approach to software engineering (presented in Part Three of this book) might react to this statement with a shrug: "What's the big deal? We use analysis, design, programming, testing, and related tech-

FIGURE 20.1
The OO process model

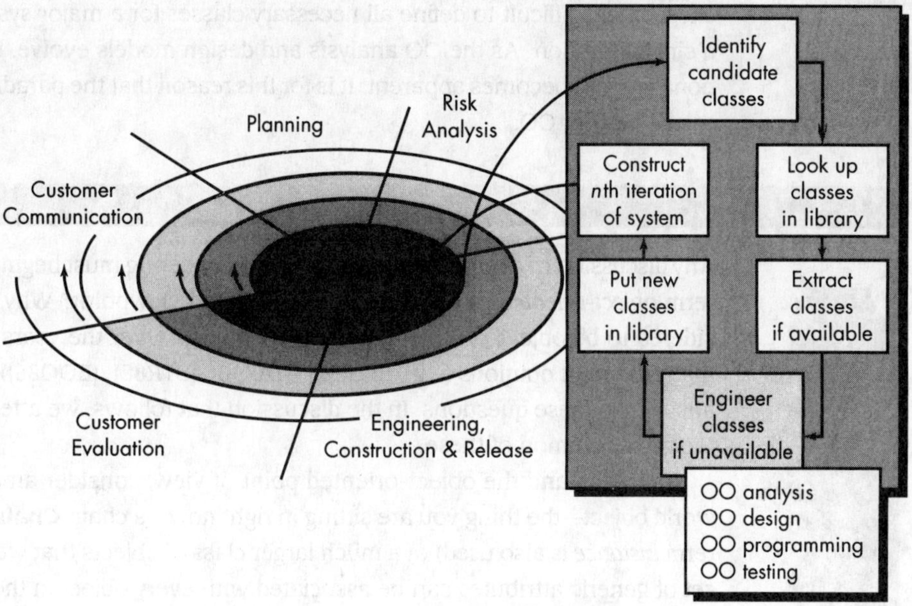

nologies when we engineer software using the classical methods. Why should OO be any different?" Indeed, why should OO be any different? In short, it shouldn't!

KEY POINT

OO systems are engineered using an evolutionary process model. Later in this chapter, it will be referred to as a *recursive parallel model.*

In Chapter 2, we discussed a number of different process models for software engineering. Although any one of these models could be adapted for use with OO, the best choice would recognize that OO systems tend to evolve over time. Therefore, an evolutionary process model, coupled with an approach that encourages component assembly (reuse), is the best paradigm for OO software engineering. Referring to Figure 20.1, the component-based development process model (Chapter 2) has been tailored for OO software engineering.

The OO process moves through an evolutionary spiral that starts with customer communication. It is here that the problem domain is defined and that basic problem classes (discussed later in this chapter) are identified. Planning and risk analysis establish a foundation for the OO project plan. The technical work associated with OO software engineering follows the iterative path shown in the shaded box. OO software engineering emphasizes reuse. Therefore, classes are "looked up" in a library (of existing OO classes) before they are built. When a class cannot be found in the library, the software engineer applies object-oriented analysis (OOA), object-oriented design (OOD), object-oriented programming (OOP), and object-oriented testing (OOT) to create the class and the objects derived from the class. The new class is then put into the library so that it may be reused in the future.

WebRef

One of the Web's most extensive lists of OO resources can be found at **mini.net/cetus/software.html**

The object-oriented view demands an evolutionary approach to software engineering. As we will see throughout this and the following chapters, it would be exceedingly difficult to define all necessary classes for a major system or product in a single iteration. As the OO analysis and design models evolve, the need for additional classes becomes apparent. It is for this reason that the paradigm just described works best for OO.

20.2 OBJECT-ORIENTED CONCEPTS

Quote:

"Object-oriented programming is not so much a coding technique as it is a code packaging technique, a way for code suppliers to encapsulate functionality for delivery to customers."

Brad Cox

Any discussion of object-oriented software engineering must begin by addressing the term *object-oriented.* What is an object-oriented viewpoint? Why is a method considered to be object-oriented? What is an object? Over the years, there have been many different opinions (e.g., [BER93], [TAY90], [STR88], [BOO86]) about the correct answers to these questions. In the discussion that follows, we attempt to synthesize the most common of these.

To understand the object-oriented point of view, consider an example of a real world object—the thing you are sitting in right now—a chair. **Chair** is a member (the term *instance* is also used) of a much larger class of objects that we call **furniture**. A set of generic attributes can be associated with every object in the class **furniture**. For example, all furniture has a cost, dimensions, weight, location, and color, among many possible *attributes.* These apply whether we are talking about a table or a chair, a sofa or an armoire. Because **chair** is a member of **furniture, chair** *inherits* all attributes defined for the class. This concept is illustrated schematically in Figure 20.2.

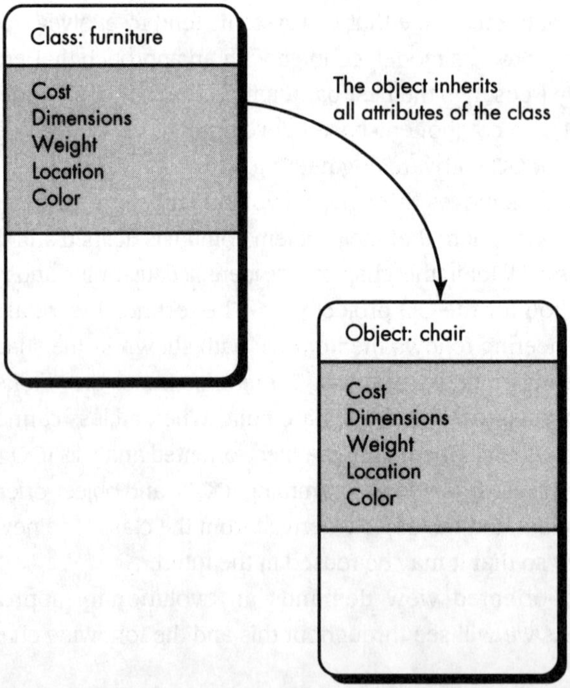

FIGURE 20.2
Inheritance from class to object

Once the class has been defined, the attributes can be reused when new instances of the class are created. For example, assume that we were to define a new object called a **chable** (a cross between a chair and a table) that is a member of the class **furniture. Chable** inherits all of the attributes of **furniture**.

We have attempted an anecdotal definition of a class by describing its attributes, but something is missing. Every object in the class **furniture** can be manipulated in a variety of ways. It can be bought and sold, physically modified (e.g., you can saw off a leg or paint the object purple) or moved from one place to another. Each of these *operations* (other terms are *services* or *methods*) will modify one or more attributes of the object. For example, if the attribute **location** is a composite data item defined as

XRef
Data modeling notation can be used to represent objects and their attributes. See Chapter 12 for details.

location = building + floor + room

then an operation named *move* would modify one or more of the data items (**building, floor,** or **room**) that form the attribute **location**. To do this, *move* must have "knowledge" of these data items. The operation *move* could be used for a chair or a table, as long as both are instances of the class **furniture**. All valid operations (e.g., *buy, sell, weigh*) for the class **furniture** are "connected" to the object definition as shown in Figure 20.3 and are inherited by all instances of the class.

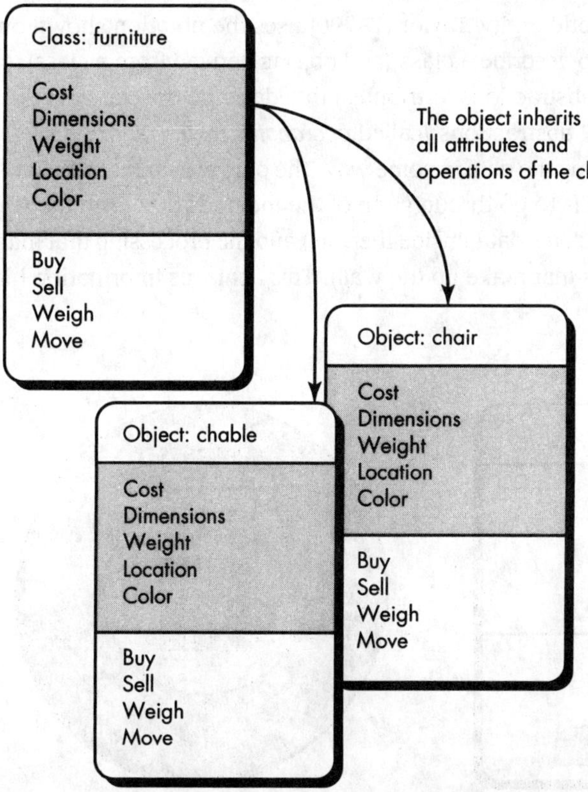

FIGURE 20.3
Inheritance of operations from class to object

Quote:

"Encapsulation prevents a program from becoming so interdependent that a small change has massive ripple effects."

Jim Rumbaugh et al.

The object **chair** (and all objects in general) encapsulates data (the attribute values that define the chair), operations (the actions that are applied to change the attributes of chair), other objects (composite objects can be defined [EVB89]), constants (set values), and other related information. *Encapsulation* means that all of this information is packaged under one name and can be reused as one specification or program component.

Now that we have introduced a few basic concepts, a more formal definition of object-oriented will prove more meaningful. Coad and Yourdon [COA91] define the term this way:

object-oriented = objects + classification + inheritance + communication

Three of these concepts have already been introduced. We postpone a discussion of communication until later.

20.2.1 Classes and Objects

The fundamental concepts that lead to high-quality design (Chapter 13) apply equally to systems developed using conventional and object-oriented methods. For this reason, an OO model of computer software must exhibit data and procedural abstractions that lead to effective modularity. A class is an OO concept that encapsulates the data and procedural abstractions required to describe the content and behavior of some real world entity. Taylor {TAY90] uses the notation shown on the right side of Figure 20.4 to describe a class (and objects derived from a class).

KEY POINT

An object encapsulates both data (attributes) and the functions (operation, methods, or services) that manipulate the data.

The data abstractions (attributes) that describe the class are enclosed by a "wall" of procedural abstractions (called *operations, methods,* or *services*) that are capable of manipulating the data in some way. The only way to reach the attributes (and operate on them) is to go through one of the methods that form the wall. Therefore, the class encapsulates data (inside the wall) and the processing that manipulates the data (the methods that make up the wall). This achieves information hiding and reduces

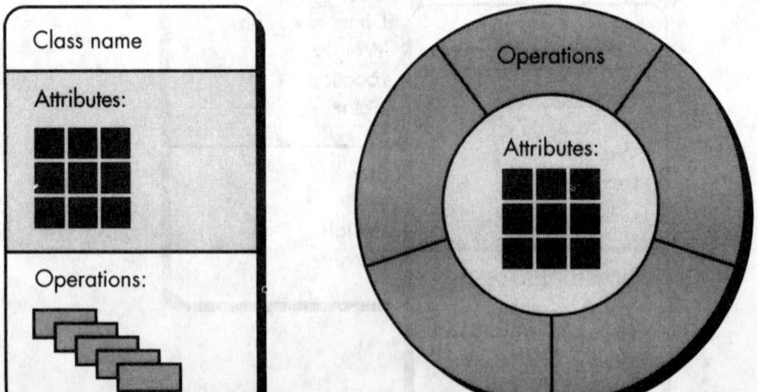

FIGURE 20.4
An alternative representation of an object-oriented class

the impact of side effects associated with change. Since the methods tend to manipulate a limited number of attributes, they are cohesive; and because communication occurs only through the methods that make up the "wall," the class tends to be decoupled from other elements of a system. All of these design characteristics lead to high-quality software.

> **ADVICE**
> *One of the first things to think about when building an OO system is how to classify the objects that are to be manipulated by the system.*

Stated another way, a class is a *generalized description* (e.g., a template, pattern, or blueprint) that describes a collection of similar objects. By definition, all objects that exist within a class inherit its attributes and the operations that are available to manipulate the attributes. A *superclass* is a collection of classes, and a *subclass* is a specialized instance of a class.

These definitions imply the existence of a class hierarchy in which the attributes and operations of the superclass are inherited by subclasses that may each add additional "private" attributes and methods. A class hierarchy for the class **furniture** is illustrated in Figure 20.5.

20.2.2 Attributes

We have already seen that attributes are attached to classes and objects, and that they describe the class or object in some way. A discussion of attributes is presented by de Champeaux, Lea, and Favre [CHA93]:

> Real life entities are often described with words that indicate stable features. Most physical objects have features such as shape, weight, color, and type of material. People have features including date of birth, parents, name, and eye color. A feature may be seen as a binary relation between a class and a certain domain.

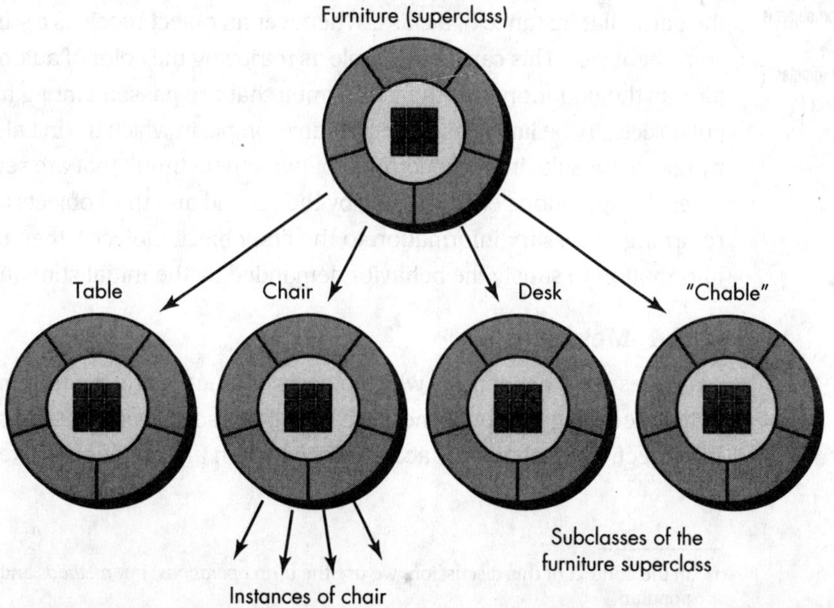

FIGURE 20.5
A class hierarchy

The "binary relation" implies that an attribute can take on a value defined by an enumerated domain. In most cases, a domain is simply a set of specific values. For example, assume that a class **automobile** has an attribute **color**. The domain of values for **color** is {**white, black, silver, gray, blue, red, yellow, green**}. In more complex situations, the domain can be a set of classes. Continuing the example, the class **automobile** also has an attribute **power train** that encompasses the following domain of classes: {**16-valve economy option, 16-valve sport option, 24-valve sport option, 32-valve luxury option**}. Each of the options noted has a set of specific attributes of its own.

KEY POINT
The values assigned to an object's attributes make that object unique.

The features (values of the domain) can be augmented by assigning a default value (feature) to an attribute. For example, the **power train** attribute defaults to **16-valve sport option**. It may also be useful to associate a probability with a particular feature by assigned {value, probability} pairs. Consider the **color** attribute for **automobile**. In some applications (e.g., manufacturing planning) it might be necessary to assign a probability to each of the colors (white and black are highly probable as automobile colors).

20.2.3 Operations, Methods, and Services

An object encapsulates data (represented as a collection of attributes) and the algorithms that process the data. These algorithms are called operations, methods, or services[1] and can be viewed as modules in a conventional sense.

KEY POINT
Whenever an object is stimulated by a message, it initiates some behavior by executing an operation.

Each of the operations that is encapsulated by an object provides a representation of one of the behaviors of the object. For example, the operation *GetColor* for the object **automobile** will extract the color stored in the **color** attribute. The implication of the existence of this operation is that the class **automobile** has been designed to receive a stimulus [JAC92] (we call the stimulus a *message*) that requests the color of the particular instance of a class. Whenever an object receives a stimulus, it initiates some behavior. This can be as simple as retrieving the color of automobile or as complex as the initiation of a chain of stimuli that are passed among a variety of different objects. In the latter case, consider an example in which the initial stimulus received by object 1 results in the generation of two other stimuli that are sent to object 2 and object 3. Operations encapsulated by the second and third objects act on the stimuli, returning necessary information to the first object. Object 1 then uses the returned information to satisfy the behavior demanded by the initial stimulus.

20.2.4 Messages

Messages are the means by which objects interact. Using the terminology introduced in the preceding section, a message stimulates some behavior to occur in the receiving object. The behavior is accomplished when an operation is executed.

---

1 In the context of this discussion, we use the term *operations,* but *methods* and *services* are equally popular.

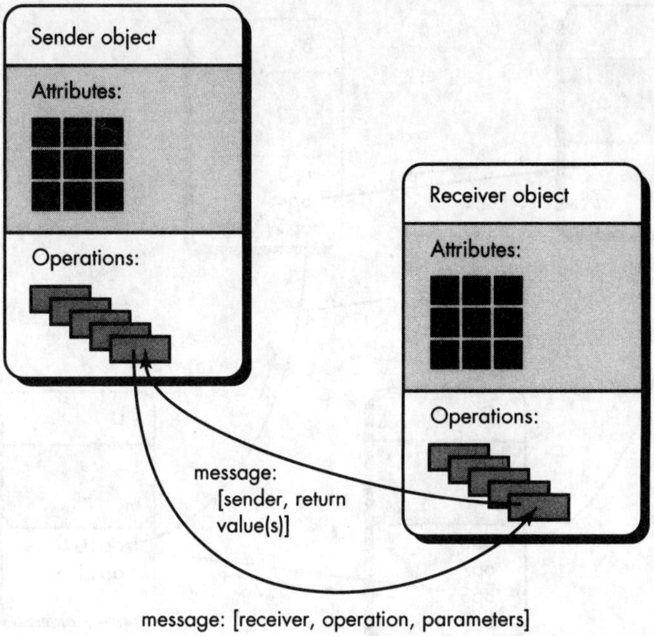

FIGURE 20.6 Message passing between objects

The interaction between messages is illustrated schematically in Figure 20.6. An operation within a sender object generates a message of the form

Message: [destination, operation, parameters]

where *destination* defines the *receiver object* that is stimulated by the message, *operation* refers to the operation that is to receive the message, and *parameters* provides information that is required for the operation to be successful.

> **Quote:**
> "Messages and methods [operations] are two sides of the same coin. Methods are the procedures that are invoked when an object receives a message."
> Greg Voss

As an example of message passing within an OO system, consider the objects shown in Figure 20.7. Four objects, **A, B, C,** and **D** communicate with one another by passing messages. For example, if object **B** requires processing associated with operation *op10* of object **D**, it would send **D** a message of the form

message: [**D**, *op10,* {data}]

As part of the execution of *op10*, object **D** may send a message to object **C** of the form

message: (**C**, *op08*, {data})

Then **C** finds *op08*, performs it, and sends an appropriate return value to **D**. Operation *op10* completes and sends a return value to **B**.

Cox [COX86] describes the interchange between objects in the following manner:

> An object is requested to perform one of its operations by sending it a message telling the object what to do. The receiver [object] responds to the message by first choosing the operation that implements the message name, executing this operation, and then returning control to the caller.

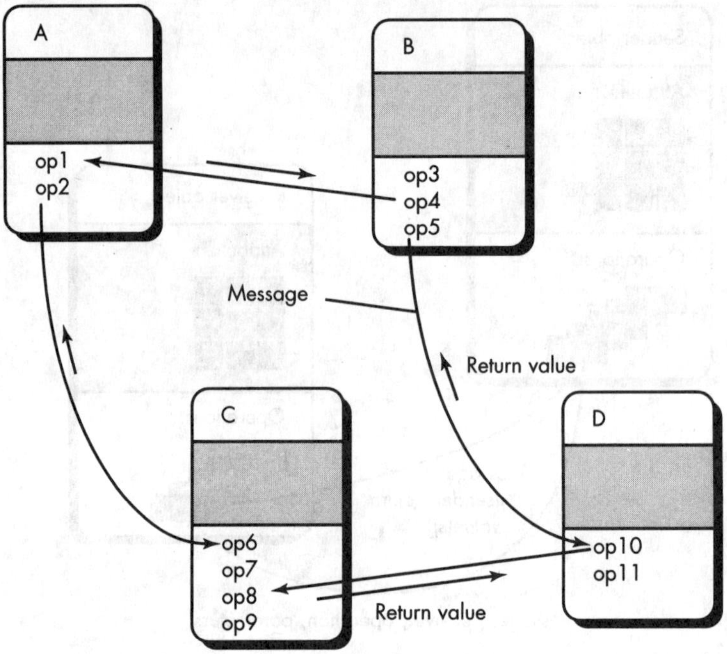

FIGURE 20.7 Message passing example

Messaging ties an object-oriented system together. Messages provide insight into the behavior of individual objects and the OO system as a whole.

20.2.5 Encapsulation, Inheritance, and Polymorphism

Although the structure and terminology introduced in Sections 20.2.1 through 20.2.4 differentiate OO systems from their conventional counterparts, three characteristics of object-oriented systems make them unique. As we have already noted, the OO class and the objects spawned from the class encapsulate data and the operations that work on the data in a single package. This provides a number of important benefits:

? What are the primary benefits of an OO architecture?

- The internal implementation details of data and procedures are hidden from the outside world (information hiding). This reduces the propagation of side effects when changes occur.
- Data structures and the operations that manipulate them are merged in a single named entity—the class. This facilitates component reuse.
- Interfaces among encapsulated objects are simplified. An object that sends a message need not be concerned with the details of internal data structures. Hence, interfacing is simplified and the system coupling tends to be reduced.

Inheritance is one of the key differentiators between conventional and OO systems. A subclass **Y** inherits all of the attributes and operations associated with its superclass, **X**. This means that all data structures and algorithms originally designed and implemented for **X** are immediately available for **Y**—no further work need be done. Reuse has been accomplished directly.

Any change to the data or operations contained within a superclass is immediately inherited by all subclasses that have inherited from the superclass.[2] Therefore, the class hierarchy becomes a mechanism through which changes (at high levels) can be immediately propagated through a system.

It is important to note that, at each level of the class hierarchy, new attributes and operations may be added to those that have been inherited from higher levels in the hierarchy. In fact, whenever a new class is to be created, the software engineer has a number of options:

- The class can be designed and built from scratch. That is, inheritance is not used.
- The class hierarchy can be searched to determine if a class higher in the hierarchy contains most of the required attributes and operations. The new class inherits from the higher class and additions may then be added, as required.
- The class hierarchy can be restructured so that the required attributes and operations can be inherited by the new class.
- Characteristics of an existing class can be overridden and private versions of attributes or operations are implemented for the new class.

Quote:
"Whereas an object is a concrete entity that exists in time and space, a class represents only an abstraction, the 'essence' of an object, as it were."
Grady Booch

To illustrate how restructuring of the class hierarchy might lead to a desired class, consider the example shown in Figures 20.8. The class hierarchy illustrated in Figure 20.8A enables us to derive classes **X3** and **X4** with characteristics 1, 2, 3, 4, 5 and 6 and 1, 2, 3, 4, 5, and 7, respectively.[3] Now, suppose that a new class with only characteristics 1, 2, 3, 4, and 8 is desired. To derive this class, called **X2b** in the example, the hierarchy may be restructured as shown in Figure 20.8B. It is important to note that restructuring the hierarchy can be difficult, and for this reason, *overriding* is sometimes used.

In essence, overriding occurs when attributes and operations are inherited in the normal manner but are then modified to the specific needs of the new class. As Jacobson notes, when overriding is used "inheritance is not transitive" [JAC92].

In some cases, it is tempting to inherit some attributes and operations from one class and others from another class. This is called *multiple inheritance,* and it is controversial. In general, multiple inheritance complicates the class hierarchy and creates potential problems in configuration control (Chapter 9). Because multiple inheritance sequences are more difficult to trace, changes to the definition of a class that resides high in the hierarchy may have an unintended impact on classes defined lower in the architecture.

---

2 The terms *descendants* and *ancestors* [JAC92] are sometimes used to replace *subclass* and *superclass*, respectively.

3 For the purposes of this example, "characteristics" may be either attributes or operations.

FIGURE 20.8 Class hierarchy: original (A), restructured (B)

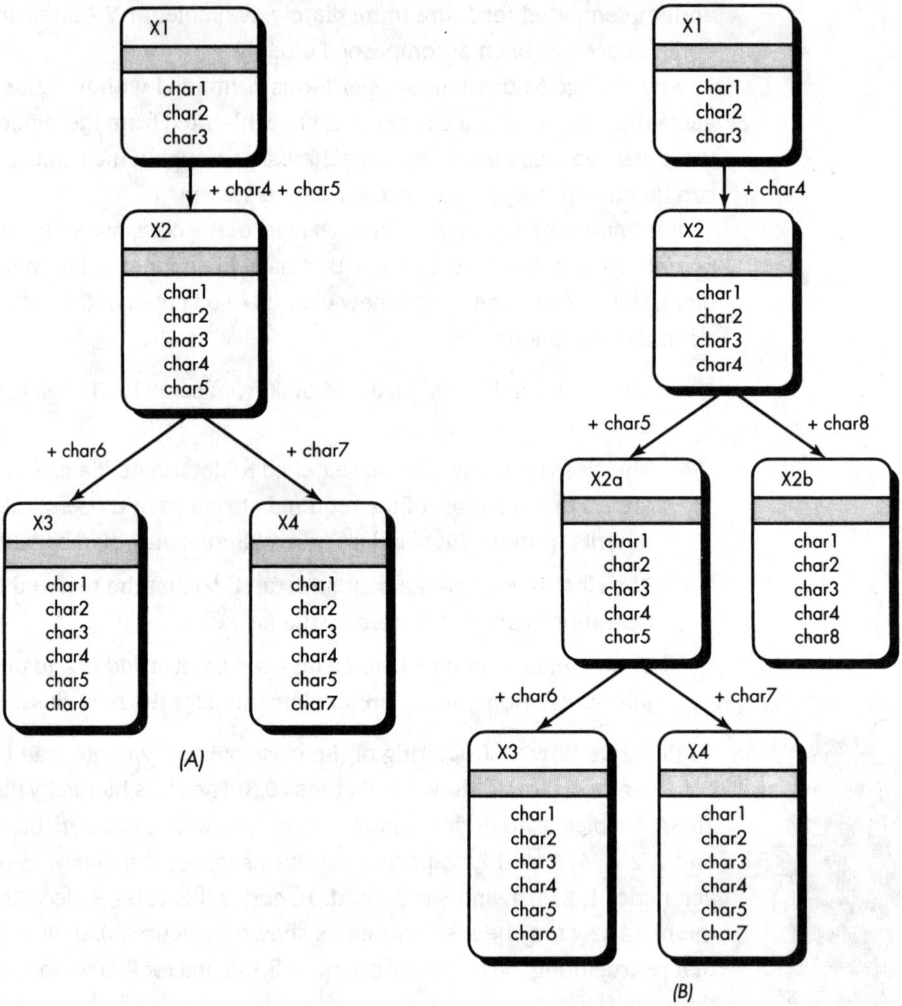

Quote:

"The name [polymorphism] may be awkward, but the mechanism is sheer elegance."
David Taylor

Polymorphism is a characteristic that greatly reduces the effort required to extend an existing OO system. To understand polymorphism, consider a conventional application that must draw four different types of graphs: line graphs, pie charts, histograms, and Kiviat diagrams. Ideally, once data are collected for a particular type of graph, the graph should draw itself. To accomplish this in a conventional application (and maintain module cohesion), it would be necessary to develop drawing modules for each type of graph. Then, within the design for each graph type, control logic similar to the following would have to be embedded:

```
case of graphtype:
    if graphtype = linegraph then DrawLineGraph (data);
    if graphtype = piechart then DrawPieChart (data);
```

```
    if graphtype = histogram then DrawHisto (data);
    if graphtype = kiviat then DrawKiviat (data);
end case;
```

Although this design is reasonably straightforward, adding new graph types could be tricky. A new drawing module would have to be created for each graph type and then the control logic would have to be updated for each graph.

To solve this problem, all of the graphs become subclasses of a general class called **graph**. Using a concept called *overloading* [TAY90], each subclass defines an operation called *draw*. An object can send a *draw* message to any one of the objects instantiated from any one of the subclasses. The object receiving the message will invoke its own *draw* operation to create the appropriate graph. Therefore, the design is reduced to

```
graphtype draw
```

When a new graph type is to be added to the system, a subclass is created with its own *draw* operation. But no changes are required within any object that wants a graph drawn because the message **graphtype draw** remains unchanged. To summarize, polymorphism enables a number of different operations to have the same name. This in turn decouples objects from one another, making each more independent.

20.3 IDENTIFYING THE ELEMENTS OF AN OBJECT MODEL

The elements of an object model—classes and objects, attributes, operations, and messages—were each defined and discussed in the preceding section. But how do we go about identifying these elements for an actual problem? The sections that follow present a series of informal guidelines that will assist in the identification of the elements of the object model.

20.3.1 Identifying Classes and Objects

> **Quote:**
> "The really hard problem [in OO] is discovering what are the 'right' objects in the first place."
> **Carl Argila**

If you look around a room, there is a set of physical objects that can be easily identified, classified, and defined (in terms of attributes and operations). But when you "look around" the problem space of a software application, the objects may be more difficult to comprehend.

We can begin to identify objects[4] by examining the problem statement or (using the terminology from Chapter 12) by performing a "grammatical parse" on the processing narrative for the system to be built. Objects are determined by underlining each noun or noun clause and entering it in a simple table. Synonyms should be

4 In reality, OOA actually attempts to define classes from which objects are instantiated. Therefore, when we isolate potential objects, we also identify members of potential classes.

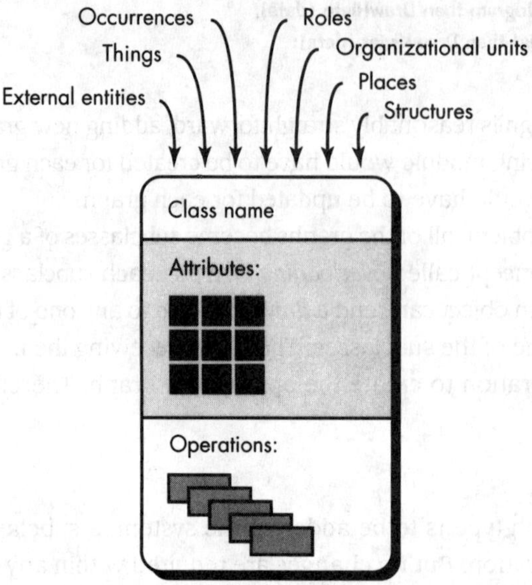

FIGURE 20.9 How objects manifest themselves

noted. If the object is required to implement a solution, then it is part of the solution space; otherwise, if an object is necessary only to describe a solution, it is part of the problem space. What should we look for once all of the nouns have been isolated?

Objects manifest themselves in one of the ways represented in Figure 20.9. Objects can be

? How do I pick out objects as I study the problem to be solved?

- *External entities* (e.g., other systems, devices, people) that produce or consume information to be used by a computer-based system.
- *Things* (e.g, reports, displays, letters, signals) that are part of the information domain for the problem.
- *Occurrences* or *events*[5] (e.g., a property transfer or the completion of a series of robot movements) that occur within the context of system operation.
- *Roles* (e.g., manager, engineer, salesperson) played by people who interact with the system.
- *Organizational units* (e.g., division, group, team) that are relevant to an application.
- *Places* (e.g., manufacturing floor or loading dock) that establish the context of the problem and the overall function of the system.
- *Structures* (e.g., sensors, four-wheeled vehicles, or computers) that define a class of objects or in the extreme, related classes of objects.

5 In this context, the term *event* connotes any occurrence. It does not necessarily imply control as it did in Chapter 12.

This categorization is but one of many that have been proposed in the literature. For example, Budd [BUD96] suggests a taxonomy of classes that includes producers (sources) and consumers (sinks) of data, data managers, view or observer classes, and helper classes.

It is also important to note what objects are not. In general, an object should never have an "imperative procedural name" [CAS89]. For example, if the developers of software for a medical imaging system defined an object with the name **image inversion**, they would be making a subtle mistake. The image obtained from the software could, of course, be an object (it is a thing that is part of the information domain). Inversion of the image is an operation that is applied to the object. It is likely that *inversion* would be defined as an operation for the object **image**, but it would not be defined as a separate object to connote "image inversion." As Cashman [CAS89] states: "the intent of object-orientation is to encapsulate, but still keep separate, data and operations on the data."

To illustrate how objects might be defined during the early stages of analysis, we return to the *SafeHome* security system example. In Chapter 12, we performed a "grammatical parse" on a processing narrative for the *SafeHome* system. The processing narrative is reproduced:

> *SafeHome* software enables the homeowner to configure the security system when it is installed, monitors all sensors connected to the security system, and interacts with the homeowner through a keypad and function keys contained in the *SafeHome* control panel shown in Figure 11.2.
>
> During installation, the *SafeHome* control panel is used to "program" and configure the system. Each sensor is assigned a number and type, a master password is programmed for arming and disarming the system, and telephone number(s) are input for dialing when a sensor event occurs.
>
> When a sensor event is sensed by the software, it rings an audible alarm attached to the system. After a delay time that is specified by the homeowner during system configuration activities, the software dials a telephone number of a monitoring service, provides information about the location, reporting and the nature of the event that has been detected. The number will be redialed every 20 seconds until telephone connection is obtained.
>
> All interaction with *SafeHome* is managed by a user-interaction subsystem that reads input provided through the keypad and function keys, displays prompting messages on the LCD display, displays system status information on the LCD display. Keyboard interaction takes the following form . . .

KEY POINT
A grammatical parse can be used to isolate potential objects (nouns) and operations (verbs).

Extracting the nouns, we can propose a number of potential objects:

Potential Object/Class	General Classification
homeowner	role or external entity
sensor	external entity
control panel	external entity
installation	occurrence
system (alias security system)	thing
number, type	not objects, attributes of sensor

Potential Object/Class	General Classification
master password	thing
telephone number	thing
sensor event	occurrence
audible alarm	external entity
monitoring service	organizational unit or external entity

The list would be continued until all nouns in the processing narrative have been considered. Note that we call each entry in the list a *potential* object. We must consider each further before a final decision is made.

Coad and Yourdon [COA91] suggest six selection characteristics that should be used as an analyst considers each potential object for inclusion in the analysis model:

How do I know whether a potential object is a good candidate for use in an OO system?

1. **Retained information.** The potential object will be useful during analysis only if information about it must be remembered so that the system can function.
2. **Needed services.** The potential object must have a set of identifiable operations that can change the value of its attributes in some way.
3. **Multiple attributes.** During requirement analysis, the focus should be on "major" information; an object with a single attribute may, in fact, be useful during design, but is probably better represented as an attribute of another object during the analysis activity.
4. **Common attributes.** A set of attributes can be defined for the potential object and these attributes apply to all occurrences of the object.
5. **Common operations.** A set of operations can be defined for the potential object and these operations apply to all occurrences of the object.
6. **Essential requirements.** External entities that appear in the problem space and produce or consume information essential to the operation of any solution for the system will almost always be defined as objects in the requirements model.

KEY POINT
A potential object should satisfy most or all of these characteristics if it is to be used in the analysis model.

To be considered a legitimate object for inclusion in the requirements model, a potential object should satisfy all (or almost all) of these characteristics. The decision for inclusion of potential objects in the analysis model is somewhat subjective, and later evaluation may cause an object to be discarded or reinstated. However, the first step of OOA must be a definition of objects, and decisions (even subjective ones) must be made. With this in mind, we apply the selection characteristics to the list of potential *SafeHome* objects:

Potential Object/Class	Characteristic Number That Applies
homeowner	rejected: 1, 2 fail even though 6 applies
sensor	accepted: all apply
control panel	accepted: all apply
installation	rejected
system (alias security system)	accepted: all apply

number, type	rejected: 3 fails, attributes of sensor
master password	rejected: 3 fails
telephone number	rejected: 3 fails
sensor event	accepted: all apply
audible alarm	accepted: 2, 3, 4, 5, 6 apply
monitoring service	rejected: 1, 2 fail even though 6 applies

It should be noted that (1) the preceding list is not all-inclusive, additional objects would have to be added to complete the model; (2) some of the rejected potential objects will become attributes for those objects that were accepted (e.g., **number** and **type** are attributes of **sensor**, and **master password** and **telephone number** may become attributes of **system**); (3) different statements of the problem might cause different "accept or reject" decisions to be made (e.g., if each homeowner had an individual password or was identified by voice print, the **homeowner** object would satisfy characteristics 1 and 2 and would have been accepted).

20.3.2 Specifying Attributes

Attributes describe an object that has been selected for inclusion in the analysis model. In essence, it is the attributes that define the object—that clarify what is meant by the object in the context of the problem space. For example, if we were to build a system that tracks baseball statistics for professional baseball players, the attributes of the object **player** would be quite different than the attributes of the same object when it is used in the context of the professional baseball pension system. In the former, attributes such as **name, position, batting average, fielding percentage, years played,** and **games played** might be relevant. For the latter, some of these attributes would be meaningful, but others would be replaced (or augmented) by attributes like **average salary, credit toward full vesting, pension plan options chosen, mailing address,** and the like.

KEY POINT

Attributes are chosen by examining the problem statement, looking for things that fully define an object and make it unique.

To develop a meaningful set of attributes for an object, the analyst can again study the processing narrative (or statement of scope) for the problem and select those things that reasonably "belong" to the object. In addition, the following question should be answered for each object: "What data items (composite and/or elementary) fully define this object in the context of the problem at hand?"

To illustrate, we consider the **system** object defined for *SafeHome.* We noted earlier in the book that the homeowner can configure the security system to reflect sensor information, alarm response information, activation/deactivation information, identification information, and so forth. Using the content description notation defined for the data dictionary and presented in Chapter 12, we can represent these composite data items in the following manner:

sensor information = sensor type + sensor number + alarm threshold
alarm response information = delay time + telephone number + alarm type
activation/deactivation information = master password + number of allowable tries + temporary password
identification information = system ID + verification phone number + system status

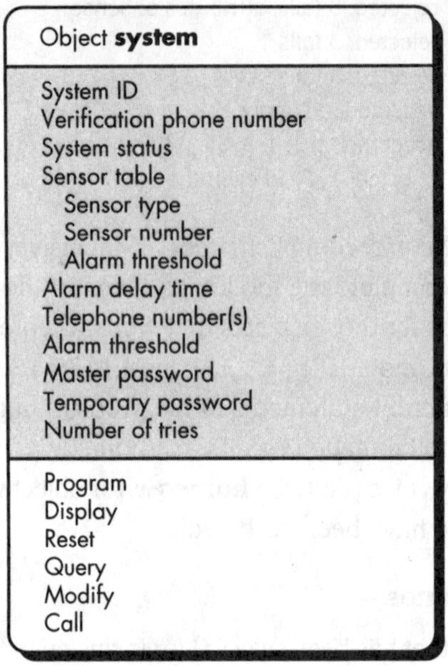

FIGURE 20.10 The **system** object with operations attached

Each of the data items to the right of the equal sign could be further defined to an elementary level, but for our purposes, they constitute a reasonable list of attributes for the system object (shaded portion of Figure 20.10).

20.3.3 Defining Operations

Operations define the behavior of an object and change the object's attributes in some way. More specifically, an operation changes one or more attribute values that are contained within the object. Therefore, an operation must have "knowledge" of the nature of the object's attributes and must be implemented in a manner that enables it to manipulate the data structures that have been derived from the attributes.

Is there a reasonable way to categorize an object's operations?

Although many different types of operations exist, they can generally be divided into three broad categories: (1) operations that manipulate data in some way (e.g., adding, deleting, reformatting, selecting), (2) operations that perform a computation, and (3) operations that monitor an object for the occurrence of a controlling event.

As a first iteration at deriving a set of operations for the objects of the analysis model, the analyst can again study the processing narrative (or statement of scope) for the problem and select those operations that reasonably belong to the object. To accomplish this, the grammatical parse is again studied and verbs are isolated. Some of these verbs will be legitimate operations and can be easily connected to a specific object. For example, from the *SafeHome* processing narrative presented earlier in this chapter, we see that "sensor is assigned a number and type" or that "a master password is programmed for arming and disarming the system." These two phrases indicate a number of things:

- That an *assign* operation is relevant for the **sensor** object.
- That a *program* operation will be applied to the **system** object.
- That *arm* and *disarm* are operations that apply to **system** (also that **system status** may ultimately be defined (using data dictionary notation) as

  system status = [armed | disarmed]

Upon further investigation, it is likely that the operation *program* will be divided into a number of more specific suboperations required to configure the system. For example, *program* implies specifying phone numbers, configuring system characteristics (e.g., creating the sensor table, entering alarm characteristics), and entering password(s). But for now, we specify *program* as a single operation.

In addition to the grammatical parse, we can gain additional insight into other operations by considering the communication that occurs between objects. Objects communicate by passing messages to one another. Before continuing with the specification of operations, we explore this matter in a bit more detail.

20.3.4 Finalizing the Object Definition

The definition of operations is the last step in completing the specification of an object. In Section 20.3.3, operations were culled from a grammatical parse of the processing narrative for the system. Additional operations may be determined by considering the "life history" [COA91] of an object and the messages that are passed among objects defined for the system.

The generic life history of an object can be defined by recognizing that the object must be created, modified, manipulated or read in other ways, and possibly deleted. For the **system** object, this can be expanded to reflect known activities that occur during its life (in this case, during the time that *SafeHome* is operational). Some of the operations can be ascertained from likely communication between objects. For example, **sensor event** will send a message to **system** to *display* the **event location** and **number**; **control panel** will send **system** a *reset* message to update **system status**; the **audible alarm** will send a *query* message; the **control panel** will send a *modify* message to change one or more attributes without reconfiguring the entire system object; **sensor event** will also send a message to *call* the **phone number(s)** contained in the object. Other messages can be considered and operations derived. The resulting object definition is shown in Figure 20.10.

A similar approach would be used for each of the objects defined for *SafeHome*. After attributes and operations are defined for each of the objects identified to this point, the beginnings of an OOA model would be created. A more detailed discussion of the analysis model that is created as part of OOA is presented in Chapter 21.

20.4 MANAGEMENT OF OBJECT-ORIENTED SOFTWARE PROJECTS

ADVICE

OO projects require as much or more management planning and oversight as conventional software projects. Do not assume that OO somehow relieves you of this responsibility.

As we discussed in Parts One and Two of this book, modern software project management can be subdivided into the following activities:

1. Establishing a common process framework for a project.
2. Using the framework and historical metrics to develop effort and time estimates.
3. Establishing deliverables and milestones that will enable progress to be measured.
4. Defining checkpoints for risk management, quality assurance, and control.
5. Managing the changes that invariably occur as the project progresses.
6. Tracking, monitoring, and controlling progress.

WebRef

An extensive OO project management tutorial and set of pointers can be found at **mini.net/cetus/oo_project_mngt.html**

The technical manager who is faced with an object-oriented project applies these six activities. But, because of the unique nature of object-oriented software, each of these management activities has a subtly different feel and must be approached using a somewhat different mind-set.

In the sections that follow, we explore software project management for object-oriented projects. The fundamental principles of management stay the same, but the technique must be adapted so that an OO project is properly managed.

20.4.1 The Common Process Framework for OO

A common process framework defines an organization's approach to software engineering. It identifies the paradigm that is applied to build and maintain software and the tasks, milestones, and deliverables that will be required. It establishes the degree of rigor with which different kinds of projects will be approached. The CPF is always adaptable so it can meet the individual needs of a project team. This is its single most important characteristic.

XRef

The common process framework defines basic software engineering activities. It is described in Chapter 2.

As we noted earlier in this chapter, object-oriented software engineering applies a process model that encourages iterative development. That is, OO software evolves through a number of cycles. The common process framework that is used to manage an OO project must be evolutionary in nature.

Ed Berard [BER93] and Grady Booch [BOO91] among others suggest the use of a "recursive/parallel model" for object-oriented software development. In essence the recursive/parallel model works in the following way:

- Do enough analysis to isolate major problem classes and connections.
- Do a little design to determine whether the classes and connections can be implemented in a practical way.

How do we apply a recursive/parallel model for OO software engineering?

- Extract reusable objects from a library to build a rough prototype.
- Conduct some tests to uncover errors in the prototype.
- Get customer feedback on the prototype.
- Modify the analysis model based on what you've learned from the prototype, from doing design, and from customer feedback.
- Refine the design to accommodate your changes.
- Code special objects (that are not available from the library).
- Assemble a new prototype using objects from the library and the new objects you've created.
- Conduct some tests to uncover errors in the prototype.
- Get customer feedback on the prototype.

This approach continues until the prototype evolves into a production application.

The recursive/parallel model is quite similar to the spiral or evolutionary paradigm. Progress occurs iteratively. What makes the recursive/parallel model different is (1) the recognition that analysis and design modeling for OO systems cannot be accomplished at an even level of abstraction and (2) analysis and design can be applied to independent system components concurrently. Berard [BER93] describes the model in the following manner:

- Systematically decompose the problem into highly independent components.
- Reapply the decomposition process to each of the independent components to decompose each further (the recursive part).
- Conduct this reapplication of decomposition concurrently on all components (the parallel part).
- Continue this process until completion criteria are attained.

It's important to note that this decomposition process is discontinued if the analyst/designer recognizes that the component or subcomponent required is available in a reuse library.

ADVICE

In many ways, the architecture of an OO system makes it easier to initiate work in parallel. However, be certain that each parallel task is defined so that progress can be assessed.

To control the recursive/parallel process framework, the project manager must recognize that progress is planned and measured incrementally. That is, project tasks and the project schedule are tied to each of the "highly independent components," and progress is measured for each of these components individually.

Each iteration of the recursive/parallel process requires planning, engineering (analysis, design, class extraction, prototyping, and testing), and evaluation activities (Figure 20.11). During planning, activities associated with each of the independent program components are planned and scheduled. (Note: With each iteration, the schedule is adjusted to accommodate changes associated with the preceding iteration.) During early stages of engineering, analysis and design occur iteratively. The

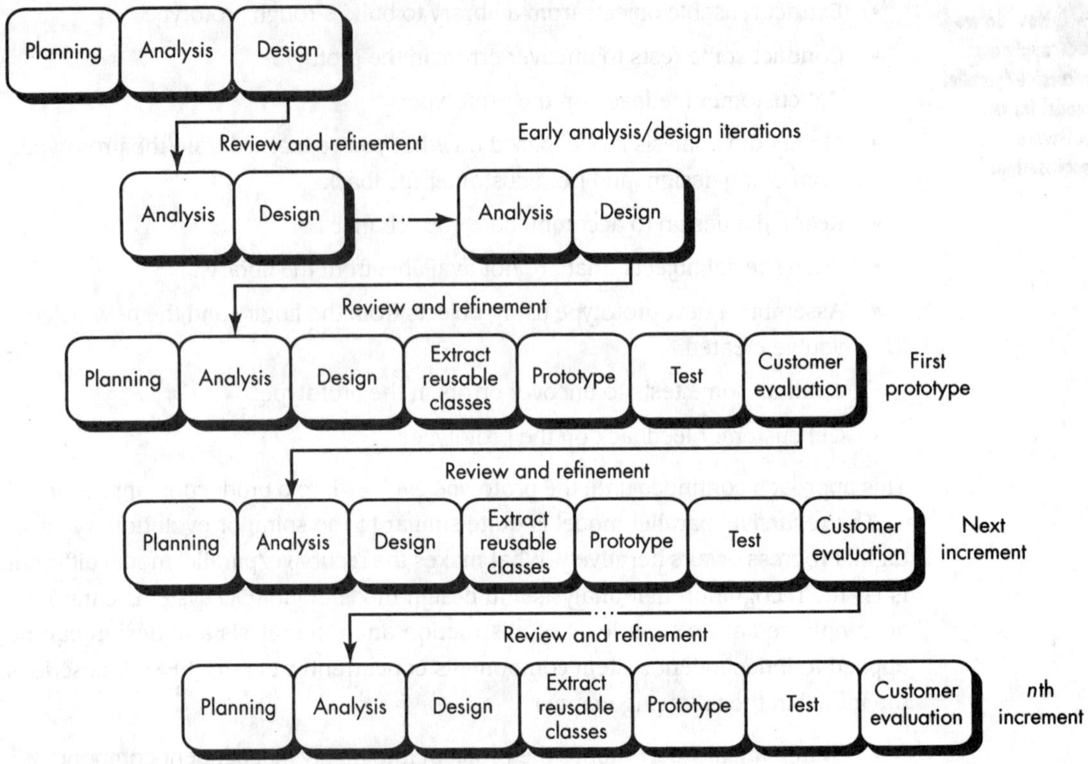

FIGURE 20.11 Typical process sequence for an OO project

intent is to isolate all important elements of the OO analysis and design models. As engineering work proceeds, incremental versions of the software are produced. During evaluation, reviews, customer evaluation, and testing are performed for each increment, with feedback affecting the next planning activity and subsequent increment.

20.4.2 OO Project Metrics and Estimation

Conventional software project estimation techniques require estimates of lines-of-code (LOC) or function points (FP) as the primary driver for estimation. Because an overriding goal for OO projects should be reuse, LOC estimates make little sense. FP estimates can be used effectively because the information domain counts that are required are readily obtainable from the problem statement. FP analysis may provide value for estimating OO projects, but the FP measure does not provide enough granularity for the schedule and effort adjustments that are required as we iterate through the recursive/parallel paradigm.

ADVICE

These metrics can be used to supplement the FP metric. They provide a way to "size" an OO project.

Lorenz and Kidd [LOR94] suggest the following set of project metrics:[6]

Number of scenario scripts. A *scenario script* (analogous to use-cases discussed in Chapter 11) is a detailed sequence of steps that describe the interaction between the user and the application. Each script is organized into triplets of the form

{**initiator,** *action,* **participant**}

where **initiator** is the object that requests some service (that initiates a message); *action* is the result of the request; and **participant** is the server object that satisfies the request. The number of scenario scripts is directly correlated to the size of the application and to the number of test cases that must be developed to exercise the system once it is constructed.

XRef

A detailed discussion of OO metrics is presented in Chapter 24.

Number of key classes. *Key classes* are the "highly independent components" [LOR94] that are defined early in OOA. Because key classes are central to the problem domain, the number of such classes is an indication of the amount of effort required to develop the software and also an indication of the potential amount of reuse to be applied during system development.

Number of support classes. *Support classes* are required to implement the system but are not immediately related to the problem domain. Examples might be GUI classes, database access and manipulation classes, and computation classes. In addition, support classes can be developed for each of the key classes. Support classes are defined iteratively throughout the recursive/parallel process.

The number of support classes is an indication of the amount of effort required to develop the software and also an indication of the potential amount of reuse to be applied during system development.

Average number of support classes per key class. In general, key classes are known early in the project. Support classes are defined throughout. If the average number of support classes per key class were known for a given problem domain, estimating (based on total number of classes) would be much simplified. Lorenz and Kidd suggest that applications with a GUI have between two and three times the number of support classes as key classes. Non-GUI applications have between one and two times the number of support classes as key classes.

Number of subsystems. A *subsystem* is an aggregation of classes that support a function that is visible to the end-user of a system. Once subsystems are identified, it is easier to lay out a reasonable schedule in which work on subsystems is partitioned among project staff.

6 Technical metrics for OO systems are discussed in detail in Chapter 24.

20.4.3 An OO Estimating and Scheduling Approach

Software project estimation remains more art than science. However, this in no way precludes the use of a systematic approach. To develop reasonable estimates it is essential to develop multiple data points. That is, estimates should be derived using a number of different techniques. Effort and duration estimates used for conventional software development are applicable to the OO world, but the historical database for OO projects is relatively small for many organizations. Therefore, it is worthwhile to supplement conventional software cost estimation with an approach that has been designed explicitly for OO software. Lorenz and Kidd [LOR94] suggest the following approach:

1. Develop estimates using effort decomposition, FP analysis, and any other method that is applicable for conventional applications.
2. Using OOA (Chapter 21), develop scenario scripts (use-cases) and determine a count. Recognize that the number of scenario scripts may change as the project progresses.
3. Using OOA, determine the number of key classes.
4. Categorize the type of interface for the application and develop a multiplier for support classes:

XRef
A number of software project estimation techniques are considered in detail in Chapter 5.

Interface type	**Multiplier**
No GUI	2.0
Text-based user interface	2.25
GUI	2.5
Complex GUI	3.0

Multiply the number of key classes (step 3) by the multiplier to obtain an estimate for the number of support classes.

5. Multiply the total number of classes (key + support) by the average number of work-units per class. Lorenz and Kidd suggest 15 to 20 person-days per class.
6. Cross check the class-based estimate by multiplying the average number of work-units per scenario script.

Scheduling for object-oriented projects is complicated by the iterative nature of the process framework. Lorenz and Kidd suggest a set of metrics that may assist during project scheduling:

Number of major iterations. Thinking back to the spiral model (Chapter 2), a major iteration would correspond to one 360° traversal of the spiral. The recursive/parallel process model would spawn a number of mini-spirals (localized iterations) that occur as the major iteration progresses. Lorenz and

Kidd suggest that iterations of between 2.5 and 4 months in length are easiest to track and manage.

Number of completed contracts. A *contract* is "a group of related public responsibilities that are provided by subsystems and classes to their clients" [LOR94]. A contract is an excellent milestone and at least one contract should be associated with each project iteration. A project manager can use completed contracts as a good indicator of progress on an OO project.

20.4.4 Tracking Progress for an OO Project

Although the recursive/parallel process model is the best framework for an OO project, task parallelism makes project tracking difficult. The project manager can have difficulty establishing meaningful milestones for an OO project because a number of different things are happening at once. In general, the following major milestones can be considered "completed" when the criteria noted have been met.

Technical milestone: OO analysis completed

- All classes and the class hierarchy have been defined and reviewed.
- Class attributes and operations associated with a class have been defined and reviewed.
- Class relationships (Chapter 21) have been established and reviewed.
- A behavioral model (Chapter 21) has been created and reviewed.
- Reusable classes have been noted.

Technical milestone: OO design completed

- The set of subsystems (Chapter 22) has been defined and reviewed.
- Classes are allocated to subsystems and reviewed.
- Task allocation has been established and reviewed.
- Responsibilities and collaborations (Chapter 22) have been identified.
- Attributes and operations have been designed and reviewed.
- The messaging model has been created and reviewed.

Technical milestone: OO programming completed

- Each new class has been implemented in code from the design model.
- Extracted classes (from a reuse library) have been implemented.
- Prototype or increment has been built.

Technical milestone: OO testing

- The correctness and completeness of OO analysis and design models has been reviewed.

- A class-responsibility-collaboration network (Chapter 23) has been developed and reviewed.
- Test cases are designed and class-level tests (Chapter 23) have been conducted for each class.
- Test cases are designed and cluster testing (Chapter 23) is completed and the classes are integrated.
- System level tests have been completed.

Recalling the recursive/parallel process model discussed earlier in this chapter, it is important to note that each of these milestones may be revisited as different increments are delivered to the customer.

20.5 SUMMARY

Object-oriented technologies reflect a natural view of the world. Objects are categorized into classes and class hierarchies. Each class contains a set of attributes that describe it and a set of operations that define its behavior. Objects model almost any identifiable aspect of the problem domain. External entities, things, occurrences, roles, organizational units, places, and structures can all be represented as objects. As important, objects (and the classes from which they are derived) encapsulate both data and process. Processing operations are part of the object and are initiated by passing the object a message. A class definition, once defined, forms the basis for reusability at the modeling, design, and implementation levels. New objects can be instantiated from a class.

Three important concepts differentiate the OO approach from conventional software engineering. Encapsulation packages data and the operations that manipulate the data into a single named object. Inheritance enables the attributes and operations of a class to be inherited by all subclasses and the objects that are instantiated from them. Polymorphism enables a number of different operations to have the same name, reducing the number of lines of code required to implement a system and facilitating changes when they are made.

Object-oriented products and systems are engineered using an evolutionary model, sometimes called a recursive/parallel model. OO software evolves iteratively and must be managed with the recognition that the final product will be developed over a series of increments.

REFERENCES

[BER93] Berard, E.V., *Essays on Object-Oriented Software Engineering,* Addison-Wesley, 1993.

[BOO86] Booch, G., "Object-Oriented Development," *IEEE Trans. Software Engineering,* vol. SE-12, no. 2, February 1986, pp. 211ff.

[BOO91] Booch, G., *Object-Oriented Design,* Benjamin Cummings, 1991.

[BUD96] Budd, T., *An Introduction to Object-Oriented Programming,* 2nd ed., Addison-Wesley, 1996.

[CAS89] Cashman, M., "Object Oriented Domain Analysis," *ACM Software Engineering Notes,* vol. 14, no. 6, October 1989, p. 67.

[CHA93] de Champeaux, D., D. Lea, and P. Faure, *Object-Oriented System Development,* Addison-Wesley, 1993.

[COA91] Coad, P. and E. Yourdon, *Object-Oriented Analysis,* 2nd ed., Prentice-Hall, 1991.

[COX86] Cox, B.J., *Object-Oriented Programming,* Addison-Wesley, 1986.

[EVB89] *Object-Oriented Requirements Analysis* (course notebook), EVB Software Engineering, 1989.

[JAC92] Jacobson, I., *Object-Oriented Software Engineering,* Addison-Wesley, 1992.

[LOR94] Lorenz, M. and J. Kidd, *Object-Oriented Software Metrics,* Prentice-Hall, 1994.

[STR88] Stroustrup, B., "What Is Object-Oriented Programming?" *IEEE Software,* vol. 5, no. 3, May 1988, pp. 10–20.

[TAY90] Taylor, D.A., *Object-Oriented Technology: A Manager's Guide,* Addison-Wesley, 1990.

PROBLEMS AND POINTS TO PONDER

20.1. Object-oriented software engineering is rapidly displacing conventional software development approaches. Yet, like all technologies, OO has flaws. Using the Internet and hard-copy sources from your library, write a brief paper summarizing what critics have to say about OO and why they believe care must be taken when applying the OO paradigm.

20.2. In this chapter we did not consider the case in which a new object requires an attribute or operation that is not contained in the class from which it inherited all other attributes and operations. How do you think this is handled?

20.3. Do some research and find the real answer to Problem 20.2.

20.4. Using your own words and a few examples, define the terms *class, encapsulation, inheritance,* and *polymorphism.*

20.5. Review the objects defined for the *SafeHome* system. Are there other objects that you feel should be defined as modeling begins?

20.6. Consider a typical graphical user interface. Define a set of classes (and subclasses) for the interface entities that typically appear in the GUI. Be sure to define appropriate attributes and operations.

20.7. Provide an example of a composite object.

20.8. You have been assigned the job of engineering new word-processing software. A class named **document** is identified. Define the attributes and operations that are relevant for **document.**

20.9. Research two different OO programming languages and show how messages are implemented in the language syntax. Provide a few examples for each language.

20.10. Provide a concrete example of class hierarchy restructuring as described in the discussion of Figure 20.8.

20.11. Provide a concrete example of multiple inheritance. Research one or more papers on this subject and provide the pro and con arguments for multiple inheritance.

20.12. Develop a statement of scope for a system requested by your instructor. Use the grammatical parse to isolate candidate classes, attributes, and operations for the system. Apply the selection criteria discussed in Section 20.3.1 to determine whether the class should be used in the analysis model.

20.13. In your own words, describe why the recursive/parallel process model is appropriate for OO systems.

20.14. Provide three or four specific examples of the key class and support class described in Section 20.4.2.

FURTHER READINGS AND INFORMATION SOURCES

The explosion of interest in object-technologies has resulted in the publication of literally hundreds of books during the past 15 years. Taylor's abbreviated treatment [TAY90] remains a classic introduction to the subject. In addition, books by Ambler (*The Object Primer: The Application Developer's Guide to Object-Orientation,* SIGS Books, 1998), Gossain and Graham (*Object Modeling and Design Strategies,* SIGS Books, 1998), Bahar (*Object Technology Made Simple,* Simple Software Publishing, 1996), and Singer (*Object Technology Strategies and Tactics,* Cambridge University Press, 1996) are worthwhile introductions to object-oriented concepts and methods.

Zamir (*Handbook of Object Technology,* CRC Press, 1998) has edited a voluminous treatment that covers every aspect of object technologies. Fayad and Laitnen (*Transition to Object-Oriented Software Development,* Wiley, 1998) use case studies to identify technical, management, and cultural challenges that must be overcome when an organization makes the transition to object technologies. Gardner et al. (*Cognitive Patterns: Problem-Solving Frameworks for Object Technology,* Cambridge University Press, 1998) provide the reader with a basic introduction to problem-solving concepts and terminology associated with cognitive patterns and cognitive modeling as they are applied to OO systems.

The unique nature of the OO paradigm poses special challenges to project managers. Books by Cockburn (*Surviving Object-Oriented Projects: A Manager's Guide,* Addison-Wesley, 1998), Booch (*Object Solutions: Managing the Object-Oriented Project,* Addison-Wesley, 1995), Goldberg and Rubin (*Succeeding with Objects: Decision Frameworks for Project Management,* Addison-Wesley, 1995), and Meyer (*Object-Success: A Manager's Guide to Object-Orientation,* Prentice-Hall, 1995) consider strategies for planning, tracking, and controlling OO projects.

Eeles and Sims (*Building Business Objects,* Wiley, 1998), Carmichael (*Developing Business Objects,* SIGS Books, 1998), Fingar (*The Blueprint for Business Objects,* Cambridge University Press, 1996), and Taylor (*Business Engineering with Object Technology,* Wiley, 1995) address object technology as it is applied in a business context. Their books address methods for expressing business concepts and requirements directly as objects and object-oriented applications.

A wide variety of information sources on object technologies and related subjects is available on the Internet. An up-to-date list of World Wide Web references that are relevant to OO can be found at the SEPA Web site:

http://www.mhhe.com/engcs/compsci/pressman/resources/OO-concepts.mhtml

CHAPTER

21 OBJECT-ORIENTED ANALYSIS

KEY CONCEPTS

When a new product or system is to be built, how do we characterize it in a way that is amenable to object-oriented software engineering? Are there special questions that we need to ask the customer? What are the relevant objects? How do they relate to one another? How do objects behave in the context of the system? How do we specify or model a problem so that we can create an effective design?

Each of these questions is answered within the context of *object-oriented analysis* (OOA)—the first technical activity that is performed as part of OO software engineering. Instead of examining a problem using the classic information flow model, OOA introduces a number of new concepts. Coad and Yourdon [COA91] consider this issue when they write:

> OOA—object-oriented analysis—is based upon concepts that we first learned in kindergarten: objects and attributes, classes and members, wholes and parts. Why it has taken us so long to apply these concepts to the analysis and specification of information systems is anyone's guess . . .

OOA is grounded in a set of basic principles that were introduced in Chapter 11. In order to build an analysis model, five basic principles were applied: (1) the information domain is modeled; (2) function is described; (3) behavior is

QUICK LOOK

What is it? Before you can build an object-oriented system, you have to define the classes (objects) that represent the problem to be solved, the manner in which the classes relate to and interact with one another, the inner workings (attributes and operations) of objects, and the communication mechanisms (messages) that allow them to work together. All of these things are accomplished during object-oriented analysis (OOA).

Who does it? The definition of an object-oriented analysis model encompasses a description of the static and dynamic characteristics of classes that describe a system or product. This activity is performed by a software engineer.

Why is it important? You can't build software (object-oriented or otherwise) until you have a reasonable understanding of the system or product. OOA provides you with a concrete way to represent your understanding of requirements and then test that understanding against the customer's perception of the system to be built.

What are the steps? OOA begins with a description of use-cases—a scenario-based description of how actors (people, machines, other systems) interact with the product to be built. Class-responsibility-collaborator (CRC) modeling translates the information contained in use-cases into a representation of classes and their collaborations with other classes. The static and dynamic characteristics of classes are then modeled using ▶

QUICK LOOK

a unified modeling language (or some other method).

What is the work product? An object-oriented analysis model is created. The OO analysis model is composed of graphical or language-based representations that define class attributes, relationships, and behaviors, as well as interclass communication and a depiction of class behavior over time.

How do I ensure that I've done it right? At each stage, the elements of the object-oriented analysis model are reviewed for clarity, correctness, completeness, and consistency with customer requirements and with one another.

represented; (4) data, functional, and behavioral models are partitioned to expose greater detail; and (5) early models represent the essence of the problem while later models provide implementation details. These principles form the foundation for the approach to OOA presented in this chapter.

The intent of OOA is to define all classes that are relevant to the problem to be solved—the operations and attributes associated with them, the relationships between them, and behavior they exhibit. To accomplish this, a number of tasks must occur:

> **Quote:**
> "A problem well-stated is a problem half-solved."
> **Charles Kettering**

1. Basic user requirements must be communicated between the customer and the software engineer.
2. Classes must be identified (i.e., attributes and methods are defined).
3. A class hierarchy must be specified.
4. Object-to-object relationships (object connections) should be represented.
5. Object behavior must be modeled.
6. Tasks 1 through 5 are reapplied iteratively until the model is complete.

It is important to note that there is no universal agreement on the "concepts" that serve as a foundation for OOA. But a limited number of key ideas appear repeatedly, and it is these that we will consider in this chapter.

21.1 OBJECT-ORIENTED ANALYSIS

The objective of object-oriented analysis is to develop a model that describes computer software as it works to satisfy a set of customer-defined requirements. OOA, like the conventional analysis methods described in Chapter 12, builds a multipart analysis model to satisfy this objective. The analysis model depicts information, function, and behavior within the context of the elements of the object model described in Chapter 20.

21.1.1 Conventional vs. OO Approaches

Is object-oriented analysis really different from the structured analysis approach that was presented in Chapter 12? Fichman and Kemerer [FIC92] address the question head-on:

> We conclude that the object-oriented analysis approach . . . represents a radical change over process oriented methodologies such as structured analysis, but only an incremental change over data oriented methodologies such as information engineering. Process-oriented methodologies focus attention away from the inherent properties of objects during the modeling process and lead to a model of the problem domain that is orthogonal to the three essential principles of object-orientation: encapsulation, classification of objects, and inheritance.

Stated simply, structured analysis (SA) takes a distinct input-process-output view of requirements. Data are considered separately from the processes that transform the data. System behavior, although important, tends to play a secondary role in structured analysis. The structured analysis approach makes heavy use of functional decomposition (partitioning of the data flow diagram, Chapter 12).

Fichman and Kemerer [FIC92] suggest 11 "modeling dimensions" that may be used to compare various conventional and object-oriented analysis methods:

What criteria can be used to compare conventional and OOA methods?

1. Identification/classification of entities[1]
2. General-to-specific and whole-to-part entity relationships
3. Other entity relationships
4. Description of attributes of entities
5. Large-scale model partitioning
6. States and transitions between states
7. Detailed specification for functions
8. Top-down decomposition
9. End-to-end processing sequences
10. Identification of exclusive services
11. Entity communication (via messages or events)

Because many variations exist for structured analysis and dozens of OOA methods (see Section 21.1.2) have been proposed over the years, it is difficult to develop a generalized comparison between the two methods. It can be stated, however, that modeling dimensions 8 and 9 are always present with SA and never present when OOA is used.

21.1.2 The OOA Landscape

The popularity of object technologies spawned dozens of OOA methods during the late 1980s and into the 1990s.[2] Each of these introduced a process for the analysis

1 In this context, *entity* refers to either a data object (in the structured analysis sense) or an object (in the OOA sense).

2 A detailed discussion of these methods and their differences is beyond the scope of this book. In addition, the industry is moving toward a unified method of analysis modeling, making a detailed discussion of older methods useful for historical purposes only. The interested reader should refer to Berard [BER99] and Graham [GRA94] for detailed comparisons.

of a product or system, a set of diagrams that evolved out of the process, and a notation that enabled the software engineer to create the analysis model in a consistent manner. Among the most widely used were[3]

The Booch method. The Booch method [BOO94] encompasses both a "micro development process" and a "macro development process." The micro level defines a set of analysis tasks that are reapplied for each step in the macro process. Hence, an evolutionary approach is maintained. Booch's OOA micro development process identifies classes and objects and the semantics of classes and objects and defines relationships among classes and objects and conducts a series of refinements to elaborate the analysis model.

Quote:
"The central activity of working with objects is not so much a matter of programming as it is representation."
David Taylor

The Rumbaugh method. Rumbaugh [RUM91] and his colleagues developed the *object modeling technique* (OMT) for analysis, system design, and object-level design. The analysis activity creates three models: the object model (a representation of objects, classes, hierarchies, and relationships), the dynamic model (a representation of object and system behavior), and the functional model (a high-level DFD-like representation of information flow through the system).

The Jacobson method. Also called OOSE (object-oriented software engineering), the Jacobson method [JAC92] is a simplified version of the proprietary objectory method, also developed by Jacobson. This method is differentiated from others by heavy emphasis on the use-case—a description or scenario that depicts how the user interacts with the product or system.

The Coad and Yourdon method. The Coad and Yourdon method [COA91] is often viewed as one of the easiest OOA methods to learn. Modeling notation is relatively simple and guidelines for developing the analysis model are straightforward. A brief outline of Coad and Yourdon's OOA process follows:

- Identify objects using "what to look for" criteria.
- Define a generalization/specification structure.
- Define a whole/part structure.
- Identify subjects (representations of subsystem components).
- Define attributes.
- Define services.

The Wirfs-Brock method. Wirfs-Brock, Wilkerson, and Weiner [WIR90] do not make a clear distinction between analysis and design tasks. Rather a continuous process that begins with the assessment of a customer specification and ends with design is proposed. A brief outline of Wirfs-Brock et al.'s analysis-related tasks follows:

3 In general, OOA methods are identified using the name(s) of the developer of the method, even if the method has been given a unique name or acronym.

- Evaluate the customer specification.
- Extract candidate classes from the specification via grammatical parsing.
- Group classes in an attempt to identify superclasses.
- Define responsibilities for each class.
- Assign responsibilities to each class.
- Identify relationships between classes.
- Define collaboration between classes based on responsibilities.
- Build hierarchical representations of classes.
- Construct a collaboration graph for the system.

Although the terminology and process steps for each of these OOA methods differ, the overall OOA processes are really quite similar. To perform object-oriented analysis, a software engineer should perform the following generic steps:

KEY POINT

A set of generic steps are applied during OOA, regardless of the analysis method that is chosen.

1. Elicit customer requirements for the system.
2. Identify scenarios or use-cases.
3. Select classes and objects using basic requirements as a guide.
4. Identify attributes and operations for each system object.
5. Define structures and hierarchies that organize classes.
6. Build an object-relationship model.
7. Build an object-behavior model.
8. Review the OO analysis model against use-cases or scenarios.

These generic steps are considered in greater detail in Sections 21.3 and 21.4.

21.1.3 A Unified Approach to OOA

Quote:

"UML has unified some of the existing OO notations, thus creating a single point of reference for many important concepts."

Peter Hruschka

Over the past decade, Grady Booch, James Rumbaugh, and Ivar Jacobson have collaborated to combine the best features of their individual object-oriented analysis and design methods into a unified method. The result, called the *Unified Modeling Language* (UML), has become widely used throughout the industry.[4]

UML allows a software engineer to express an analysis model using a modeling notation that is governed by a set of syntactic, semantic, and pragmatic rules. Eriksson and Penker [ERI98] explain these rules in the following way:

> The syntax tells us how the symbols should look and how the symbols are combined. The syntax is compared to words in natural language; it is important to know how to spell them correctly and how to put different words together to form a sentence. The semantic rules tell us what each symbol means and how it should be interpreted by itself and in the context of other symbols; they are compared to the meanings of words in a natural language.

---

4 Booch, Rumbaugh, and Jacobson have written a set of three definitive books on UML. The interested reader should see [BOO99], [RUM99], and [JAC99].

The pragmatic rules define the intentions of the symbols through which the purpose of the model is achieved and becomes understandable for others. This corresponds in natural language to the rules for constructing sentences that are clear and understandable.

In UML, a system is represented using five different "views" that describe the system from distinctly different perspectives. Each view is defined by a set of diagrams. The following views [ALH98] are present in UML:

ADVICE

Like all analysis approaches, requirements elicitation is key. Be certain that you get the user model view right. The rest will follow.

User model view. This view represents the system (product) from the user's (called *actors* in UML) perspective. The use-case is the modeling approach of choice for the user model view. This important analysis representation describes a usage scenario from the end-user's perspective and has been discussed in detail in Chapter 11.[5]

Structural model view. Data and functionality are viewed from inside the system. That is, static structure (classes, objects, and relationships) is modeled.

Behavioral model view. This part of the analysis model represents the dynamic or behavioral aspects of the system. It also depicts the interactions or collaborations between various structural elements described in the user model and structural model views.

Implementation model view. The structural and behavioral aspects of the system are represented as they are to be built.

Environment model view. The structural and behavioral aspects of the environment in which the system is to be implemented are represented.

WebRef

An extensive tutorial and listing of UML resources including tools, papers, and examples can be found at **mini.net/cetus/oo_uml.html**

In general, UML analysis modeling focuses on the user model and structural model views of the system. UML design modeling (considered in Chapter 22) addresses the behavioral model, implementation model, and environmental model views.

21.2 DOMAIN ANALYSIS

KEY POINT

The objective of domain analysis is to define a set of classes (objects) that are encountered throughout an application domain. These can then be reused in many applications.

Analysis for object-oriented systems can occur at many different levels of abstraction. At the business or enterprise level, the techniques associated with OOA can be coupled with a business process engineering approach (Chapter 10) in an effort to define classes, objects, relationships, and behaviors that model the entire business. At the business area level, an object model that describes the workings of a particular business area (or a category of products or systems) can be defined. At an application level, the object model focuses on specific customer requirements as those requirements affect an application to be built.

OOA at the highest level of abstraction (the enterprise level) is beyond the scope of this book. Interested readers should see [EEL98], [CAR98], [FIN96], [TAY95], [MAT94],

5 If you have not already done so, please read Section 11.2.4 for a detailed discussion of use-cases.

and [SUL94] for detailed discussions of enterprise-level modeling. OOA at the lowest level of abstraction falls within the general purview of object-oriented software engineering and is the focus of all other sections of this chapter. In this section, we conducted OOA at a middle level of abstraction. This activity, called *domain analysis,* is performed when an organization wants to create a library of reusable classes (components) that will be broadly applicable to an entire category of applications.

21.2.1 Reuse and Domain Analysis

Object-technologies are leveraged through reuse. Consider a simple example. The analysis of requirements for a new application indicates that 100 classes are needed. Two teams are assigned to build the application. Each will design and construct a final product. Each team is populated by people with the same skill levels and experience.

Team A does not have access to a class library, and therefore, it must develop all 100 classes from scratch. Team B uses a robust class library and finds that 55 classes already exist. It is highly likely that

ADVICE

Other benefits derived from reuse are consistency and familiarity. Patterns within the software will become more consistent, leading to better maintainability. Be certain to establish a set of reuse "design rules" so that these benefits are achieved.

1. Team B will finish the project much sooner than Team A.
2. The cost of Team B's product will be significantly lower than the cost of Team A's product.
3. The product produced by Team B will have fewer delivered defects than Team A's product.

Although the margin by which Team B's work would exceed Team A's accomplishments is open to debate, few would argue that reuse provides Team B with a substantial advantage.

But where did the "robust class library" come from? How were the entries in the library determined to be appropriate for use in new applications? To answer these questions, the organization that created and maintained the library had to apply domain analysis.

21.2.2 The Domain Analysis Process

Firesmith [FIR93] describes software domain analysis in the following way:

> Software domain analysis is the identification, analysis, and specification of common requirements from a specific application domain, typically for reuse on multiple projects within that application domain . . . [Object-oriented domain analysis is] the identification, analysis, and specification of common, reusable capabilities within a specific application domain, in terms of common objects, classes, subassemblies, and frameworks . . .

XRef

Reuse is the cornerstone of component-based software engineering, a topic discussed in Chapter 27.

The "specific application domain" can range from avionics to banking, from multimedia video games to applications within an MRI device. The goal of domain analysis is straightforward: to find or create those classes that are broadly applicable, so that they may be reused.

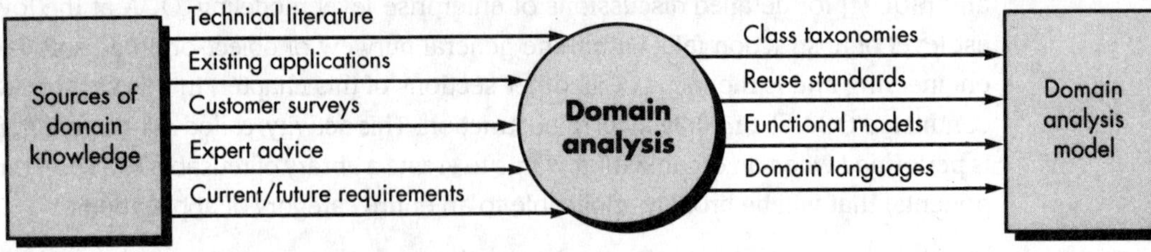

FIGURE 21.1 Input and output for domain analysis

Using terminology that was introduced earlier in this book, domain analysis may be viewed as an umbrella activity for the software process. By this we mean that domain analysis is an ongoing software engineering activity that is not connected to any one software project. In a way, the role of a domain analyst is similar to the role of a master toolsmith in a heavy manufacturing environment. The job of the toolsmith is to design and build tools that may be used by many people doing similar but not necessarily the same jobs. The role of the domain analyst is to design and build reusable components that may be used by many people working on similar but not necessarily the same applications.

Quote: "If an organization is to make a major investment in software reuse, it needs to know what components to consider in the development of such a model." **David Rine**

Figure 21.1 [ARA89] illustrates key inputs and outputs for the domain analysis process. Sources of domain knowledge are surveyed in an attempt to identify objects that can be reused across the domain. In essence domain analysis is quite similar to knowledge engineering. The knowledge engineer investigates a specific area of interest in an attempt to extract key facts that may be of use in creating an expert system or artificial neural network. During domain analysis, *object* (and class) *extraction* occurs.

The domain analysis process can be characterized by a series of activities that begin with the identification of the domain to be investigated and end with a specification of the objects and classes that characterize the domain. Berard [BER93] suggests the following activities:

XRef A complete domain analysis strategy must consider architecture as well as components. A detailed discussion of software architecture is presented in Chapter 14.

Define the domain to be investigated. To accomplish this, the analyst must first isolate the business area, system type, or product category of interest. Next, both OO and non-OO "items" must be extracted. OO items include specifications, designs, and code for existing OO application classes; support classes (e.g., GUI classes or database access classes); commercial off-the-shelf (COTS) component libraries that are relevant to the domain; and test cases. Non-OO items encompass policies, procedures, plans, standards, and guidelines; parts of existing non-OO applications (including specification, design, and test information); metrics; and COTS non-OO software.

Categorize the items extracted from the domain. The items are organized into categories and the general defining characteristics of the category are defined. A classification scheme for the categories is proposed and naming conventions for each item are defined. When appropriate, classification hierarchies are established.

Collect a representative sample of applications in the domain. To accomplish this activity, the analyst must ensure that the application in question has items that fit into the categories that have already been defined. Berard [BER93] notes that during the early stages of use of object-technologies, a software organization will have few if any OO applications. Therefore, the domain analyst must "identify the conceptual (as opposed to physical) objects in each [non-OO] application."

Analyze each application in the sample. The following steps [BER93] are followed by the analyst:

- Identify candidate reusable objects.
- Indicate the reasons that the object has been identified for reuse.
- Define adaptations to the object that may also be reusable.
- Estimate the percentage of applications in the domain that might make reuse of the object.
- Identify the objects by name and use configuration management techniques (Chapter 9) to control them. In addition, once the objects have been defined, the analyst should estimate what percentage of a typical application could be constructed using the reusable objects.

Develop an analysis model for the objects. The analysis model will serve as the basis for design and construction of the domain objects.

WebRef
A worthwhile tutorial on domain analysis can be found at **www.sei.cmu.edu/str/descriptions/deda.html**

In addition to these steps, the domain analyst should also create a set of reuse guidelines and develop an example that illustrates how the domain objects could be used to create a new application.

Domain analysis is the first technical activity in a broader discipline that some call *domain engineering.* When a business, system, or product domain is defined to be business strategic in the long term, a continuing effort to create a robust reuse library can be undertaken. The goal is to be able to create software within the domain with a very high percentage of reusable components. Lower cost, higher quality, and improved time to market are the arguments in favor of a dedicated domain engineering effort.

21.3 GENERIC COMPONENTS OF THE OO ANALYSIS MODEL

The object-oriented analysis process conforms to the basic analysis concepts and principles discussed in Chapter 11. Although the terminology, notation, and activities differ from conventional methods, OOA (at its kernel) addresses the same underlying objectives. Rumbaugh et al. [RUM91] discuss this when they state:

> Analysis . . . is concerned with devising a precise, concise, understandable, and correct model of the real world. . . . The purpose of object-oriented analysis is to model the real world so that it can be understood. To do this, you must examine requirements, analyze their implications, and restate them rigorously. You must abstract real-world features first, and defer small details until later.

To develop a "precise, concise, understandable, and correct model of the real world," a software engineer must select a notation that implements a set of generic components of an OO analysis model. Monarchi and Puhr [MON92] define a set of generic representational components that appear in all OO analysis models.[6] *Static components* are structural in nature and indicate characteristics that hold throughout the operational life of an application. These characteristics distinguish one object from other objects. *Dynamic components* focus on control and are sensitive to timing and event processing. They define how one object interacts with other objects over time. The following components are identified [MON92]:

What are the key components of an OOA model?

Static view of semantic classes. A taxonomy of typical classes was identified in Chapter 20. Requirements are assessed and classes are extracted (and represented) as part of the analysis model. These classes persist throughout the life of the application and are derived based on the semantics of the customer requirements.

Static view of attributes. Every class must be explicitly described. The attributes associated with the class provide a description of the class, as well as a first indication of the operations that are relevant to the class.

KEY POINT
Static components do not change as the application is executed. Dynamic components are influenced by timing and events.

Static view of relationships. Objects are "connected" to one another in a variety of ways. The analysis model must represent these relationships so that operations (that affect these connections) can be identified and the design of a messaging approach can be accomplished.

Static view of behaviors. The relationships just noted define a set of behaviors that accommodate the usage scenario (use-cases) of the system. These behaviors are implemented by defining a sequence of operations that achieve them.

Dynamic view of communication. Objects must communicate with one another and do so based on a series of events that cause transition from one state of a system to another

Dynamic view of control and time. The nature and timing of events that cause transitions among states must be described.

6 The authors [MON92] also provide an analysis of 23 early OOA methods and indicate how they address these components.

De Champeaux, Lea, and Faure [CHA93] define a slightly different view of OOA representations. Static and dynamic components are identified for object internals and for interobject representations. A dynamic view of object internals can be characterized as an *object life history;* that is, the states of the object change over time as various operations are performed on its attributes.

21.4 THE OOA PROCESS

The OOA process does not begin with a concern for objects. Rather, it begins with an understanding of the manner in which the system will be used—by people, if the system is human-interactive; by machines, if the system is involved in process control; or by other programs, if the system coordinates and controls applications. Once the scenario of usage has been defined, the modeling of the software begins.

The sections that follow define a series of techniques that may be used to gather basic customer requirements and then define an analysis model for an object-oriented system.

21.4.1 Use-Cases

As we noted in Chapter 11, use-cases model the system from the end-user's point of view. Created during requirements elicitation, use-cases should achieve the following objectives:

XRef
Use-cases are an excellent requirements elicitation tool, regardless of the analysis method that is used. See Chapter 11 for additional information.

- To define the functional and operational requirements of the system (product) by defining a scenario of usage that is agreed upon by the end-user and the software engineering team.
- To provide a clear and unambiguous description of how the end-user and the system interact with one another.
- To provide a basis for validation testing.

During OOA, use-cases serve as the basis for the first element of the analysis model.

Using UML notation, a diagrammatic representation of a use-case, called a *use-case diagram,* can be created. Like many elements of the analysis model, the use-case diagram can be represented at many levels of abstraction. The use-case diagram contains actors and use-cases. *Actors* are entities that interact with the system. They can be human users or other machines or systems that have defined interfaces to the software.

To illustrate the development of a use-case diagram, we consider the use-cases for the *SafeHome* security system described in Section 11.2.4. Three actors were identified: the **homeowner, sensors,** and the **monitoring and response subsystem**. For the purpose of this example, only the homeowner is considered.

Figure 21.2A depicts a high-level use-case diagram for the **homeowner**. Referring to Figure 21.2A, two use-cases are identified (represented by ovals). Each of the high-level use-cases may be elaborated with lower-level use-case diagrams. For

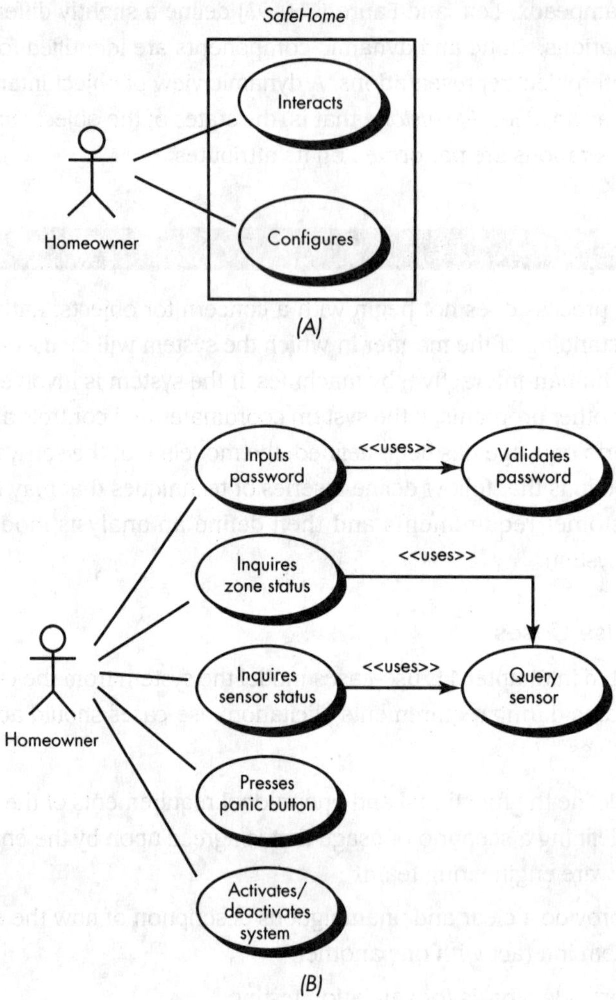

FIGURE 21.2 (A) High-level use-case diagram, (B) elaborated use-case diagram

example, Figure 21.2B represents a use-case diagram that elaborates the *interacts* function. A complete set of use-case diagrams is created for all actors. A detailed discussion of use-case modeling using UML is best left to books (e.g., [ERI98], [ALH98]) dedicated to this OOA method.

21.4.2 Class-Responsibility-Collaborator Modeling

Once basic usage scenarios have been developed for the system, it is time to identify candidate classes and indicate their responsibilities and collaborations. *Class-responsibility-collaborator* (CRC) modeling [WIR90] provides a simple means for identifying and organizing the classes that are relevant to system or product requirements. Ambler [AMB95] describes CRC modeling in the following way:

A CRC model is really a collection of standard index cards that represent classes. The cards are divided into three sections. Along the top of the card you write the name of the class. In the body of the card you list the class responsibilities on the left and the collaborators on the right.

In reality, the CRC model may make use of actual or virtual *index cards.* The intent is to develop an organized representation of classes. *Responsibilities* are the attributes and operations that are relevant for the class. Stated simply, a responsibility is "anything the class knows or does" [AMB95]. *Collaborators* are those classes that are required to provide a class with the information needed to complete a responsibility. In general, a collaboration implies either a request for information or a request for some action.

Classes

Basic guidelines for identifying classes and objects were presented in Chapter 20. To summarize, objects manifest themselves in a variety of forms (Section 20.3.1): external entities, things, occurrences, or events; roles; organizational units; places; or structures. One technique for identifying these in the context of a software problem is to perform a grammatical parse on the processing narrative for the system. All nouns become potential objects. However, not every potential object makes the cut. Six selection characteristics were defined:

How do I determine whether a potential object is worthy of inclusion on a CRC index card?

1. **Retained information.** The potential object will be useful during analysis only if information about it must be remembered so that the system can function.
2. **Needed services.** The potential object must have a set of identifiable operations that can change the value of its attributes in some way.
3. **Multiple attributes.** During requirements analysis, the focus should be on "major" information; an object with a single attribute may, in fact, be useful during design but is probably better represented as an attribute of another object during the analysis activity.
4. **Common attributes.** A set of attributes can be defined for the potential object and these attributes apply to all occurrences of the object.
5. **Common operations.** A set of operations can be defined for the potential object and these operations apply to all occurrences of the object.
6. **Essential requirements.** External entities that appear in the problem space and produce or consume information that is essential to the operation of any solution for the system will almost always be defined as objects in the requirements model.

A potential object should satisfy all six of these selection characteristics if it is to be considered for inclusion in the CRC model.

Firesmith [FIR93] extends this taxonomy of class types by suggesting the following additions:

Is there a way to categorize classes, and what characteristics help us do this?

> **Device classes** model external entities such as sensors, motors, keyboards.
>
> **Property classes** represent some important property of the problem environment (e.g., credit rating within the context of a mortgage loan application).
>
> **Interaction classes** model interactions that occur among other objects (e.g., a purchase or a license).

In addition, objects and classes may be categorized by a set of characteristics:

> **Tangibility.** Does the class represent a tangible thing (e.g., a keyboard or sensor) or does it represent more abstract information (e.g., a predicted outcome)?
>
> **Inclusiveness.** Is the class *atomic* (i.e., it includes no other classes) or is it *aggregate* (it includes at least one nested object)?
>
> **Sequentiality.** Is the class concurrent (i.e., it has its own thread of control) or sequential (it is controlled by outside resources)?
>
> **Persistence.** Is the class *transient* (i.e., it is created and removed during program operation), *temporary* (it is created during program operation and removed once the program terminates), or *permanent* (it is stored in a database)?
>
> **Integrity.** Is the class *corruptible* (i.e., it does not protect its resources from outside influence) or *guarded* (i.e., the class enforces controls on access to its resources)?

Using these class categories, the "index card" created as part of the CRC model might be extended to include the type of class and its characteristics (Figure 21.3).

Responsibilities

KEY POINT
The responsibilities of a class encompass both attributes and operations.

Basic guidelines for identifying responsibilities (attributes and operations) were also presented in Chapter 20. To summarize, attributes represent stable features of a class; that is, information about the class that must be retained to accomplish the objectives of the software specified by the customer. Attributes can often be extracted from the statement of scope or discerned from an understanding of the nature of the class. Operations can be extracted by performing a grammatical parse on the processing narrative for the system. All verbs become candidate operations. Each operation that is chosen for a class exhibits a behavior of the class.

Wirfs-Brock and her colleagues [WIR90] suggest five guidelines for allocating responsibilities to classes:

FIGURE 21.3
A CRC model index card

Class name:	
Class type: (e.g., device, property, role, event)	
Class characteristic: (e.g., tangible, atomic, concurrent)	
responsibilities:	collaborations:

How do I allocate responsibilities to a class?

1. **System intelligence should be evenly distributed.** Every application encompasses a certain degree of intelligence; that is, what the system knows and what it can do. This intelligence can be distributed across classes in a number of different ways. "Dumb" classes (those that have few responsibilities) can be modeled to act as servants to a few "smart" classes (those having many responsibilities. Although this approach makes the flow of control in a system straightforward, it has a few disadvantages: (1) It concentrates all intelligence within a few classes, making changes more difficult, and (2) it tends to require more classes, hence more development effort.

   Therefore, system intelligence should be evenly distributed across the classes in an application. Because each object knows about and does only a few things (that are generally well focused), the cohesiveness of the system is improved. In addition, side effects due to change tend to be dampened because system intelligence has been decoupled across many objects.

   ADVICE

   If a class has an extraordinarily long list of responsibilities, you should consider partitioning its definition into more than one class.

   To determine whether system intelligence is evenly distributed, the responsibilities noted on each CRC model index card should be evaluated to determine if any class has an extraordinarily long list of responsibilities. This indicates a concentration of intelligence. In addition, the responsibilities for each class should exhibit the same level of abstraction. For example, among the operations listed for an aggregate class called **checking account** a reviewer notes two responsibilities: *balance-the-account* and *check-off-*

cleared-checks. The first operation (responsibility) implies a complex mathematical and logical procedure. The second is a simple clerical activity. Since these two operations are not at the same level of abstraction, *check-off-cleared-checks* should be placed within the responsibilities of **check-entry**, a class that is encompassed by the aggregate class **checking account**.

2. **Each responsibility should be stated as generally as possible.** This guideline implies that general responsibilities (both attributes and operations) should reside high in the class hierarchy (because they are generic, they will apply to all subclasses). In addition, polymorphism (Chapter 20) should be used in an effort to define operations that generally apply to the superclass but are implemented differently in each of the subclasses.
3. **Information and the behavior related to it should reside within the same class.** This achieves the OO principle that we have called *encapsulation* (Chapter 20). Data and the processes that manipulate the data should be packaged as a cohesive unit.
4. **Information about one thing should be localized with a single class, not distributed across multiple classes.** A single class should take on the responsibility for storing and manipulating a specific type of information. This responsibility should not, in general, be shared across a number of classes. If information is distributed, software becomes more difficult to maintain and more challenging to test.
5. **Responsibilities should be shared among related classes, when appropriate.** There are many cases in which a variety of related objects must all exhibit the same behavior at the same time. As an example, consider a video game that must display the following objects: **player, player-body, player-arms, player-legs, player-head.** Each of these objects has its own attributes (e.g., **position, orientation, color, speed**) and all must be updated and displayed as the user manipulates a joy stick. The responsibilities *update* and *display* must therefore be shared by each of the objects noted. **Player** knows when something has changed and *update* is required. It collaborates with the other objects to achieve a new position or orientation, but each object controls its own display.

Collaborations

Classes fulfill their responsibilities in one of two ways: (1) A class can use its own operations to manipulate its own attributes, thereby fulfilling a particular responsibility, or (2) a class can collaborate with other classes.

Wirfs-Brock and her colleagues [WIR90] define collaborations in the following way:

> Collaborations represent requests from a client to a server in fulfillment of a client responsibility. A collaboration is the embodiment of the contract between the client and the server. . . . We say that an object collaborates with another object if, to fulfill a responsibility, it

needs to send the other object any messages. A single collaboration flows in one direction—representing a request from the client to the server. From the client's point of view, each of its collaborations are associated with a particular responsibility implemented by the server.

KEY POINT

A server object collaborates with a client object in an effort to fulfill some responsibility. The collaboration involves the passing of messages.

Collaborations identify relationships between classes. When a set of classes all collaborate to achieve some requirement, they can be organized into a subsystem (a design issue).

Collaborations are identified by determining whether a class can fulfill each responsibility itself. If it cannot, then it needs to interact with another class. Hence, a collaboration.

As an example, consider the *SafeHome* application.[7] As part of the activation procedure (see the use-case for *activation* in Section 11.2.4), the **control panel** object must determine whether any sensors are open. A responsibility named *determine-sensor-status* is defined. If sensors are open **control panel** must set a **status** attribute to "not ready." Sensor information can be acquired from the **sensor** object. Therefore, the responsibility *determine-sensor-status* can be fulfilled only if **control panel** works in collaboration with **sensor**.

To help in the identification of collaborators, the analyst can examine three different generic relationships between classes [WIR90]: (1) the *is-part-of* relationship, (2) the *has-knowledge-of* relationship, and (3) the *depends-upon* relationship. By creating a class-relationship diagram (Section 21.4.4), the analyst develops the connections necessary to identify these relationships. Each of the three generic relations is considered briefly in the paragraphs that follow.

All classes that are part of an aggregate class are connected to the aggregate class via an is-part-of relationship. Consider the classes defined for the video game noted earlier, the class **player-body** is-part-of **player,** as are **player-arms, player-legs,** and **player-head.**

When one class must acquire information from another class, the has-knowledge-of relationship is established. The *determine-sensor-status* responsibility noted earlier is an example of a has-knowledge-of relationship.

The depends-upon relationship implies that two classes have a dependency that is not achieved by has-knowledge-of or is-part-of. For example, **player-head** must always be connected to **player-body** (unless the video game is particularly violent), yet each object could exist without direct knowledge of the other. An attribute of the **player-head** object called **center-position** is determined from the center position of **player-body**. This information is obtained via a third object, **player**, that acquires it from **player-body**. Hence, **player-head** depends-upon **player-body**.

In all cases, the collaborator class name is recorded on the CRC model index card next to the responsibility that has spawned the collaboration. Therefore, the index card contains a list of responsibilities and the corresponding collaborations that enable the responsibilities to be fulfilled (Figure 21.3).

---

7 See Section 20.3 for a delineation of classes for *SafeHome*.

When a complete CRC model has been developed, the representatives from the customer and software engineering organizations can review the model using the following approach [AMB95]:

What is an effective approach for reviewing a CRC model?

1. All participants in the review (of the CRC model) are given a subset of the CRC model index cards. Cards that collaborate should be separated (i.e., no reviewer should have two cards that collaborate).
2. All use-case scenarios (and corresponding use-case diagrams) should be organized into categories.
3. The review leader reads the use-case deliberately. As the review leader comes to a named object, she passes a token to the person holding the corresponding class index card. For example, a use-case for *SafeHome* contains the following narrative:

   The homeowner observes the *SafeHome* control panel to determine if the system is ready for input. If the system is not ready, the homeowner must physically close windows/doors so that the ready indicator is present. [A not-ready indicator implies that a sensor is open, i.e., that a door or window is open.]

   When the review leader comes to "control panel," in the use-case narrative, the token is passed to the person holding the **control panel** index card. The phrase "implies that a sensor is open" requires that the index card contains a responsibility that will validate this implication (the responsibility *determine-sensor-status* accomplishes this). Next to the responsibility on the index card is the collaborator **sensor**. The token is then passed to the **sensor** object.
4. When the token is passed, the holder of the class card is asked to describe the responsibilities noted on the card. The group determines whether one (or more) of the responsibilities satisfies the use-case requirement.
5. If the responsibilities and collaborations noted on the index cards cannot accommodate the use-case, modifications are made to the cards. This may include the definition of new classes (and corresponding CRC index cards) or the specification of new or revised responsibilities or collaborations on existing cards.

This modus operandi continues until the use-case is finished. When all use-cases (or use-case diagrams) have been reviewed, OOA continues.

21.4.3 Defining Structures and Hierarchies

Once classes and objects have been identified using the CRC model, the analyst begins to focus on the structure of the class model and the resultant hierarchies that arise as classes and subclasses emerge. Using UML notation, a variety of class diagrams can be created. *Generalization/specialization* class structures can be created for identified classes.

To illustrate, consider the **sensor** object defined for *SafeHome*, shown in Figure 21.4. Here, the generalization class, **sensor**, is refined into a set of specializations—

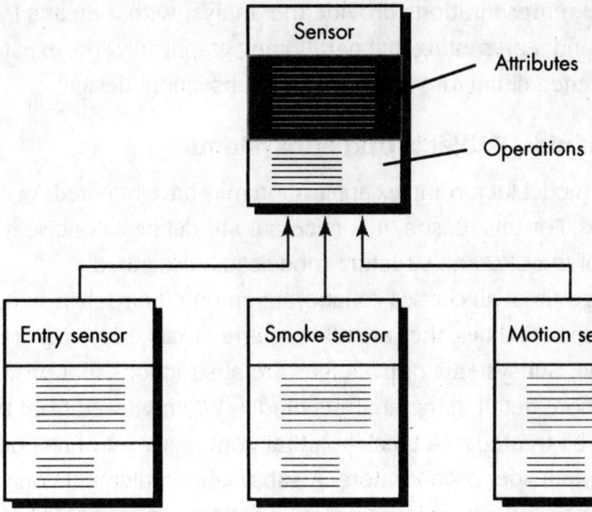

FIGURE 21.4 Class diagram for generalization/ specialization

entry sensor, smoke sensor, and **motion sensor**. The attributes and operations noted for the **sensor** class are inherited by the specializations of the class. We have created a simple class hierarchy.

In other cases, an object represented in the initial model might actually be composed of a number of component parts that could themselves be defined as objects. These aggregate objects can be represented as a *composite aggregate* [ERI98] and are defined using the notation represented in Figure 21.5. The diamond implies an assembly relationship. It should be noted that the connecting lines may be augmented with additional symbols (not shown) to represent cardinality. These are adapted from the entity/relationship modeling notation discussed in Chapter 12.

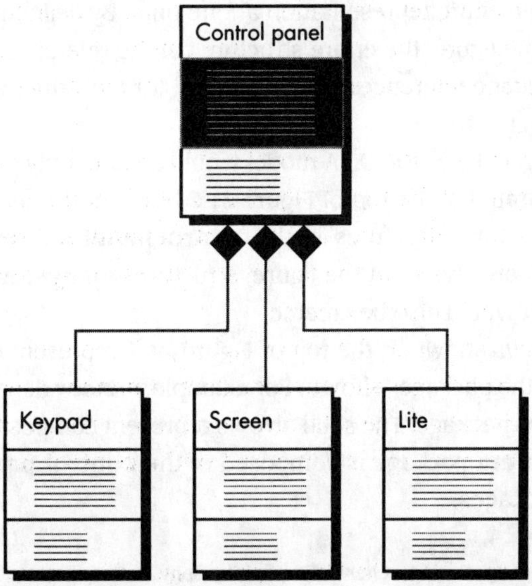

FIGURE 21.5 Class diagram for composite aggregates

Structure representations provide the analyst with a means for partitioning the CRC model and representing that partitioning graphically. The expansion of each class provides needed detail for review and for subsequent design.

21.4.4 Defining Subjects and Subsystems

An analysis model for a complex application may have hundreds of classes and dozens of structures. For this reason, it is necessary to define a concise representation that is a digest of the CRC and structure models just described.

KEY POINT

A subsystem (UML package) points to a more-detailed class hierarchy.

When a group of all classes collaborate among themselves to accomplish a set of cohesive responsibilities, they are often referred to as *subsystems* or *packages* (in UML terminology). Subsystems or packages are abstractions that provide a reference or pointer to more detail in the analysis model. When viewed from the outside, a subsystem can be treated as a black box that contains a set of responsibilities and that has its own (outside) collaborators. A subsystem implements one or more *contracts* [WIR90] with its outside collaborators. A contract is a specific list of requests that collaborators can make of the subsystem.[8]

Subsystems can be represented with the context of CRC modeling by creating a subsystem index card. The subsystem index card indicates the name of the subsystem, the contracts that the subsystem must accommodate, and the classes or (other) subsystems that support the contract.

Packages are identical to subsystems in intent and content but are represented graphically in UML. For example, assume that the control panel for *SafeHome* is considerably more complex that the one implied by Figure 21.5, containing multiple display areas, a sophisticated key arrangement, and other features. It might be modeled as the composite aggregate structure shown in Figure 21.6. If the overall requirements model contains dozens of these structures (*SafeHome* would not), it would be difficult to absorb the entire representation at one time. By defining a package reference as shown in the figure, the entire structure can be referenced by a single icon (the file folder). Package references can be created for any structure that has multiple objects.

At the most abstract level, the OOA model would contain only package references such as those illustrated at the top of Figure 21.7. Each of the references would be expanded into a structure. Structures for the **control panel** and **sensor** objects (Figures 21.5 and 21.6) are shown in the figure; structures for **system, sensor event** and **audible alarm** would also be created.

The dashed arrows shown at the top of Figure 21.7 represent dependence relationships between the packages shown. For example, **sensor** depends on the status of the **sensor event** package. The solid arrows represent composition. In the example shown, the **system** package is composed of the **control panel, sensor,** and **audible alarm** packages.

8 Recall that classes interact using a client/server philosophy. In this case, the subsystem is the server and outside collaborators are clients.

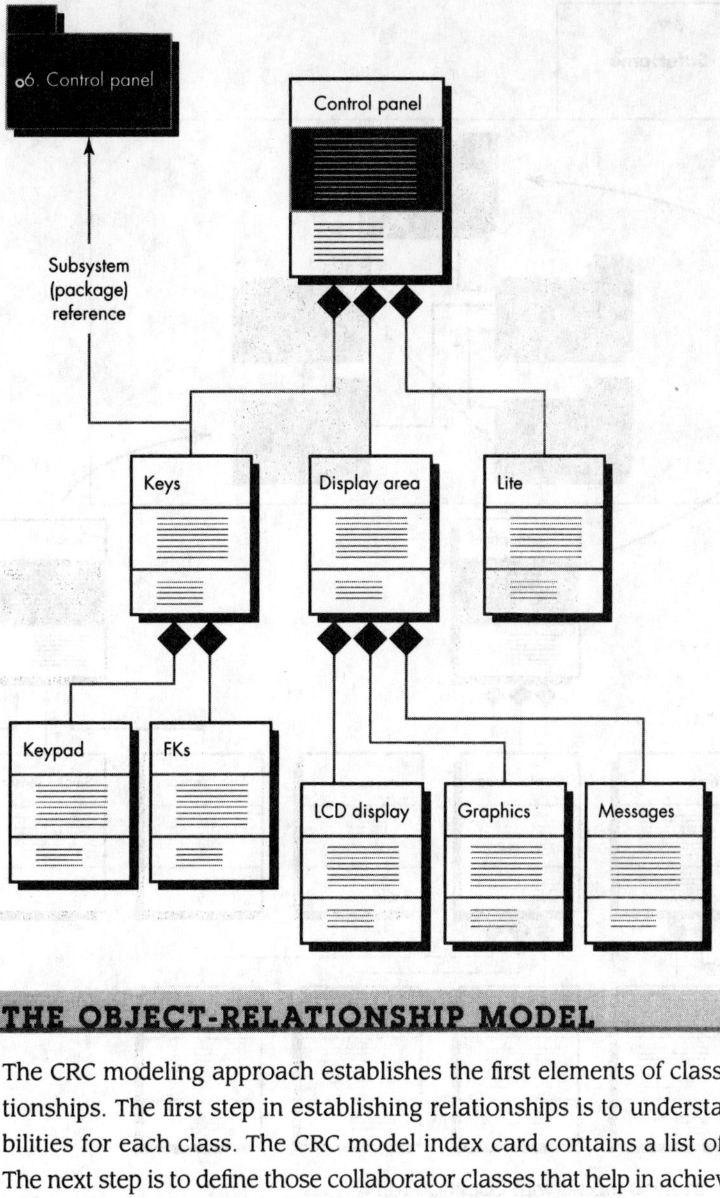

FIGURE 21.6
Package (subsystem) reference

21.5 THE OBJECT-RELATIONSHIP MODEL

The CRC modeling approach establishes the first elements of class and object relationships. The first step in establishing relationships is to understand the responsibilities for each class. The CRC model index card contains a list of responsibilities. The next step is to define those collaborator classes that help in achieving each responsibility. This establishes the "connection" between classes.

A relationship exists between any two classes that are connected.[9] Therefore, collaborators are always related in some way. The most common type of relationship is binary—a connection exists between two classes. When considered within the context of an OO system, a binary relationship has a specific direction[10] that is defined based on which class plays the role of the client and which acts as a server.

9 Other terms for relationship are *association* [RUM91] and *connection* [COA91].

10 It is important to note that this is a departure from the bidirectional nature of relationships used in data modeling (Chapter 12).

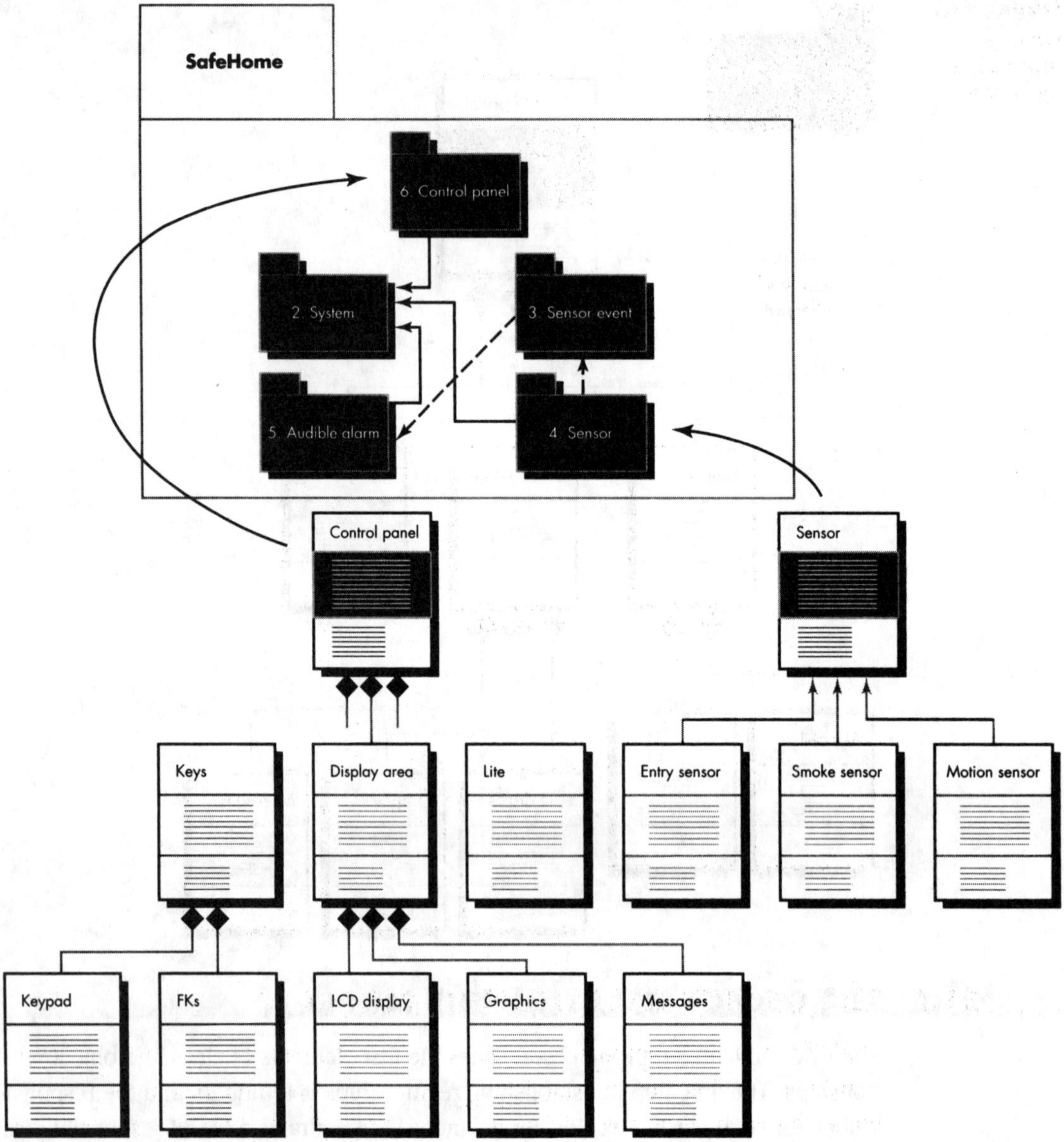

FIGURE 21.7 An analysis model with package references

Rumbaugh and his colleagues [RUM91] suggest that relationships can be derived by examining the stative verbs or verb phrases in the statement of scope or use-cases for the system. Using a grammatical parse, the analyst isolates verbs that indicate physical location or placement (next to, part of, contained in), communications (transmits to, acquires from), ownership (incorporated by, is composed of), and satisfaction of a condition (manages, coordinates, controls). These provide an indication of a relationship.

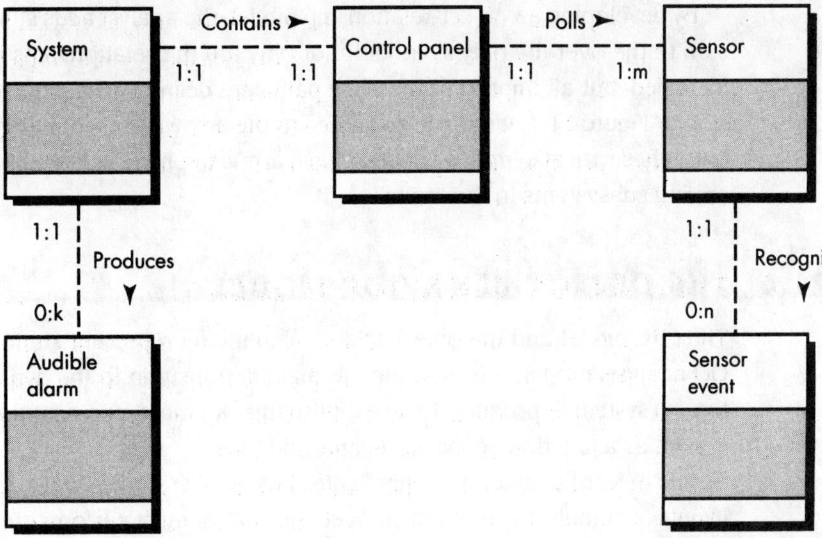

FIGURE 21.8 Relationships between objects

The Unified Modeling Language notation for the object-relationship model makes use of a symbology that has been adapted from the entity-relationship modeling techniques discussed in Chapter 12. In essence, objects are connected to other objects using named relationships. The cardinality of the connection (see Chapter 12) is specified and an overall network of relationships is established.

The object relationship model (like the entity relationship model) can be derived in three steps:

How is an object-relationship model derived?

1. **Using the CRC index cards, a network of collaborator objects can be drawn.** Figure 21.8 represents the class connections for *SafeHome* objects. First the objects are drawn, connected by unlabeled lines (not shown in the figure) that indicate some relationship exists between the connected objects.
2. **Reviewing the CRC model index card, responsibilities and collaborators are evaluated and each unlabeled connected line is named.** To avoid ambiguity, an arrow head indicates the "direction" of the relationship (Figure 21.8).
3. **Once the named relationships have been established, each end is evaluated to determine cardinality** (Figure 21.8). Four options exist: 0 to 1, 1 to 1, 0 to many, or 1 to many. For example, the *SafeHome* system contains a single control panel (the 1:1 cardinality notation indicates this). At least one sensor must be present for polling by the control panel. However, there may be many sensors present (the 1:m notation indicates this). One sensor can recognize from 0 to many sensor events (e.g., smoke is detected or a break-in has occurred).

The steps just noted continue until a complete object-relationship model has been produced.

By developing an object-relationship model, the analyst adds still another dimension to the overall analysis model. Not only are the relationships between objects identified, but all important message paths are defined (Chapter 20). In our discussion of Figure 21.7, we made reference to the arrows that connected package symbols. These are also message paths. Each arrow implies the interchange of messages among subsystems in the model.

21.6 THE OBJECT-BEHAVIOR MODEL

The CRC model and the object-relationship model represent static elements of the OO analysis model. It is now time to make a transition to the dynamic behavior of the OO system or product. To accomplish this, we must represent the behavior of the system as a function of specific events and time.

The object-behavior model indicates how an OO system will respond to external events or stimuli. To create the model, the analyst must perform the following steps:

? What are the steps required to build an object-behavior model?

1. Evaluate all use-cases (Section 21.4.1) to fully understand the sequence of interaction within the system.
2. Identify events that drive the interaction sequence and understand how these events relate to specific objects.
3. Create an event trace [RUM91] for each use-case.
4. Build a state transition diagram for the system.
5. Review the object-behavior model to verify accuracy and consistency.

Each of these steps is discussed in the sections that follow.

21.6.1 Event Identification with Use-Cases

As we noted in Section 21.4.1, the use-case represents a sequence of activities that involves actors and the system. In general, an event occurs whenever an OO system and an actor (recall that an actor can be a person, a device, or even an external system) exchange information. Recalling the discussion presented in Chapter 12, it is important to note that an event is Boolean. That is, an event is *not* the information that has been exchanged but rather the fact that information has been exchanged.

A use-case is examined for points of information exchange. To illustrate, reconsider the use-case for *SafeHome* described in Section 11.2.4:

1. The homeowner observes the *SafeHome* control panel (Figure 11.2) to determine if the system is ready for input. If the system is *not ready*, the homeowner must physically close windows/doors so that the *ready* indicator is present. [A *not-ready* indicator implies that a sensor is open, i.e., that a door or window is open.]

2. The homeowner uses the keypad to key in a four-digit password. The password is compared with the valid password stored in the system. If the password is incorrect, the control panel will beep once and reset itself for additional input. If the password is correct, the control panel awaits further action.

3. The homeowner selects and keys in *stay* or *away* to activate the system. *Stay* activates only perimeter sensors (inside motion detecting sensors are deactivated). *Away* activates all sensors.

4. When activation occurs, a red alarm light can be observed by the homeowner.

The underlined portions of the use-case scenario indicate events. An actor should be identified for each event; the information that is exchanged should be noted; and any conditions or constraints should be listed.

As an example of a typical event, consider the underlined use-case phrase "homeowner uses the keypad to key in a four-digit password." In the context of the OO analysis model, the object, **homeowner,** transmits an event to the object **control panel.** The event might be called *password entered.* The information transferred is the four digits that constitute the password, but this is not an essential part of the behavioral model. It is important to note that some events have an explicit impact on the flow of control of the use-case, while others have no direct impact on the flow of control. For example, the event *password entered* does not explicitly change the flow of control of the use-case, but the results of the event *compare password* (derived from the interaction "password is compared with the valid password stored in the system") will have an explicit impact on the information and control flow of the *SafeHome* software.

Once all events have been identified, they are allocated to the objects involved. Objects can be responsible for generating events (e.g., **homeowner** generates the *password entered* event) or recognizing events that have occurred elsewhere (e.g., **control panel** recognizes the binary result of the *compare password* event).

21.6.2 State Representations

In the context of OO systems, two different characterizations of states must be considered: (1) the state of each object as the system performs its function and (2) the state of the system as observed from the outside as the system performs its function.

ADVICE

As you begin to identify states, focus on externally observable modes of behavior. Later, you may refine these states into behaviors that are not evident from outside the system.

The state of an object takes on both passive and active characteristics [CHA93]. A *passive state* is simply the current status of all of an object's attributes. For example, the passive state of the aggregate object **player** (in the video game application discussed earlier) would include the current **position** and **orientation** attributes of **player** as well as other features of player that are relevant to the game (e.g., an attribute that indicates **magic wishes remaining**). The *active state* of an object indicates the current status of the object as it undergoes a continuing transformation or processing. The object **player** might have the following active states: *moving, at rest, injured, being cured; trapped, lost,* and so forth. An event (sometimes called a *trigger*) must occur to force an object to make a transition from one active state to another. One component of

FIGURE 21.9
A representation of active state transitions

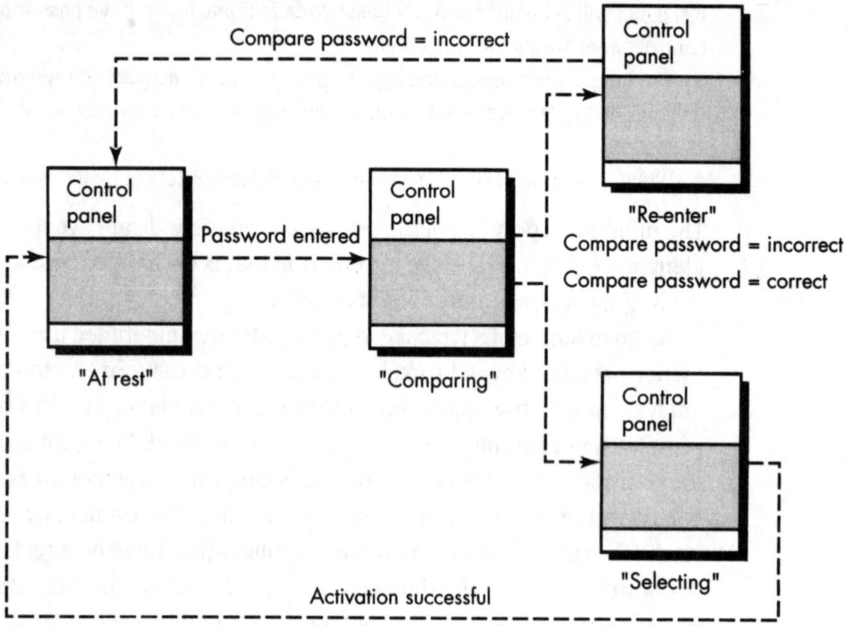

an object-behavior model is a simple representation of the active states for each object and the events (triggers) that cause changes between these active states. Figure 21.9 illustrates a simple representation of active states for the **control panel** object in the *SafeHome* system.

Each arrow shown in Figure 21.9 represents a transition from one active state of an object to another. The labels shown for each arrow represent the event that triggers the transition. Although the active state model provides useful insight into the "life history" of an object, it is possible to specify additional information to provide more depth in understanding the behavior of an object. In addition to specifying the event that causes the transition to occur, the analyst can specify a guard and an action [CHA93]. A *guard* is a Boolean condition that must be satisfied in order for the transition to occur. For example, the guard for the transition from the "at rest" state to the "comparing state" in Figure 21.9 can be determined by examining the use-case:

if (password input = 4 digits) then make transition to comparing state;

In general, the guard for a transition usually depends upon the value of one or more attributes of an object. In other words, the guard depends on the passive state of the object.

An *action* occurs concurrently with the state transition or as a consequence of it and generally involves one or more operations (responsibilities) of the object. For example, the action connected to the *password entered* event (Figure 21.9) is an operation that accesses a password object and performs a digit-by-digit comparison to validate the entered password.

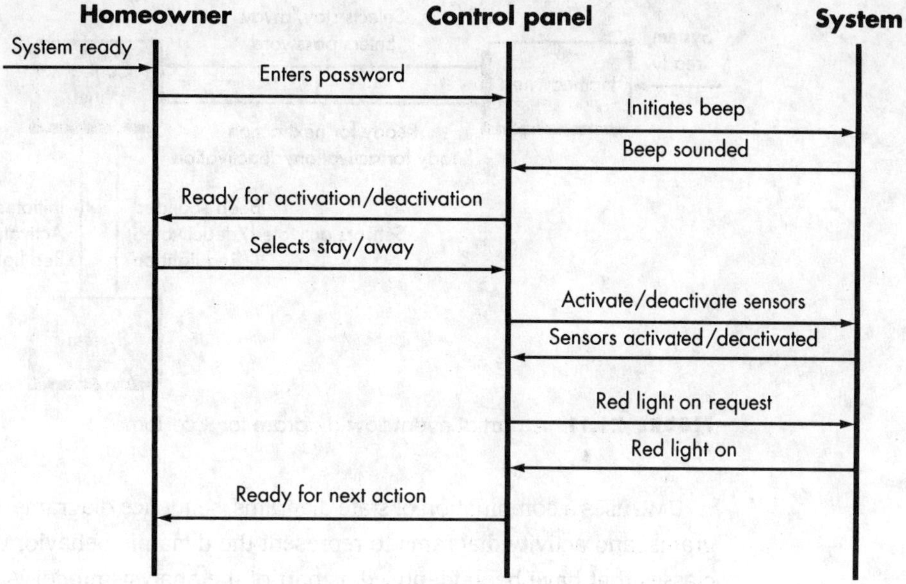

FIGURE 21.10 A partial event trace for SafeHome

The second type of behavioral representation for OOA considers a state representation for the overall product or system. This representation encompasses a simple *event trace model* [RUM91] that indicates how events cause transitions from object to object and a state transition diagram that depicts the processing behavior of each object.

KEY POINT
A transition from one state to another requires that an event occur. Events are Boolean in nature and often occur when objects communicate with one another.

Once events have been identified for a use-case, the analyst creates a representation of how events cause flow from one object to another. Called an *event trace,* this representation is a shorthand version of the use-case. It represents key objects and the events that cause behavior to flow from object to object.

Figure 21.10 illustrates a partial event trace for the *SafeHome* system. Each of the arrows represents an event (derived from a use-case) and indicates how the event channels behavior between *SafeHome* objects. The first event, *system ready,* is derived from the external environment and channels behavior to the **homeowner** object. The homeowner enters a password. The event initiates *beep* and "beep sounded" and indicates how behavior is channeled if the password is invalid. A valid password results in flow back to **homeowner.** The remaining events and traces follow the behavior as the system is activated or deactivated.

Once a complete event trace has been developed, all of the events that cause transitions between system objects can be collated into a set of input events and output events (from an object). This can be represented using an event flow diagram [RUM91]. All events that flow into and out of an object are noted as shown in Figure 21.11. A state transition diagram (Chapter 12) can then be developed to represent the behavior associated with responsibilities for each class.

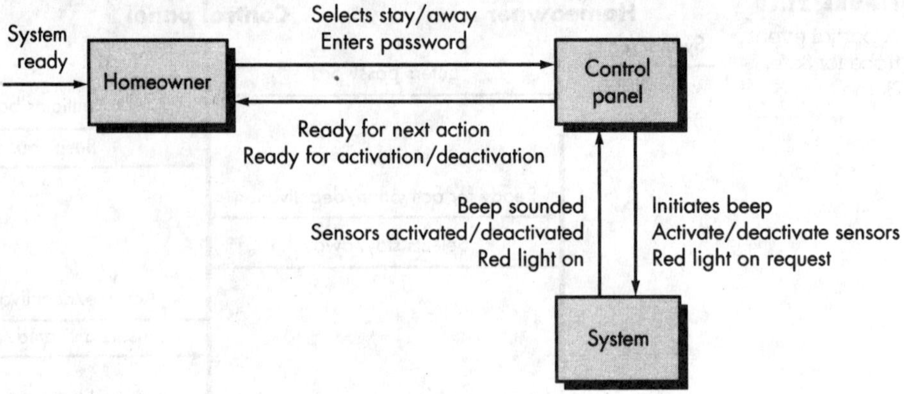

FIGURE 21.11 A partial event flow diagram for SafeHome

UML uses a combination of state diagrams, sequence diagrams, collaboration diagrams, and activity diagrams to represent the dynamic behavior of the objects and classes that have been identified as part of the analysis model. A complete discussion of these graphical representations and the language descriptions that underlie them is beyond the scope of this book. The interested reader should see [BOO99], [BEN99], [ALH98], and [ERI98] for additional detail.

21.7 SUMMARY

Object-oriented analysis methods enable a software engineer to model a problem by representing both static and dynamic characteristics of classes and their relationships as the primary modeling components. Like earlier OO analysis methods, the Unified Modeling Language builds an analysis model that has the following characteristics: (1) representation of classes and class hierarchies, (2) creation of object-relationship models, and (3) derivation of object-behavior models.

Analysis for object-oriented systems occurs at many different levels of abstraction. At the business or enterprise level, the techniques associated with OOA can be coupled with a business process engineering approach. This technique is often called domain analysis. At an application level, the object model focuses on specific customer requirements as those requirements affect the application to be built.

The OOA process begins with the definition of use-cases—scenarios that describe how the OO system is to be used. The class-responsibility-collaborator modeling technique is then applied to document classes and their attributes and operations. It also provides an initial view of the collaborations that occur among objects. The next step in the OOA process is classification of objects and the creation of a class hierarchy. Subsystems (packages) can be used to encapsulate related objects. The object-relationship model provides an indication of how classes are connected to one another, and the object-behavior model indicates the behavior of individual objects and the overall behavior of the OO system.

REFERENCES

[ALH98] Alhir, S.S., *UML in a Nutshell,* O'Reilly & Associates, 1998.

[AMB95] Ambler, S., "Using Use-Cases," *Software Development,* July 1995, pp. 53–61.

[ARA89] Arango, G. and R. Prieto-Diaz, "Domain Analysis: Concepts and Research Directions," *Domain Analysis: Acquisition of Reusable Information for Software Construction,* (Arango, G. and R. Prieto-Diaz, eds.), IEEE Computer Society Press, 1989.

[BEN99] Bennett, S., S. McRobb, and R. Farmer, *Object Oriented System Analysis and Design Using UML,* McGraw-Hill, 1999.

[BER93] Berard, E.V., *Essays on Object-Oriented Software Engineering,* Addison-Wesley, 1993.

[BOO94] Booch, G., *Object-Oriented Analysis and Design,* 2nd ed., Benjamin Cummings, 1994.

[BOO99] Booch, G., I. Jacobson, J. Rumbaugh, *The Unified Modeling Language User Guide,* Addison-Wesley, 1999.

[CAR98] Carmichael, A., *Developing Business Objects,* SIGS Books, 1998).

[CHA93] De Champeaux, D., D. Lea, and P. Faure, *Object-Oriented System Development,* Addison-Wesley, 1993.

[COA91] Coad, P. and E. Yourdon, *Object-Oriented Analysis,* 2nd ed., Prentice-Hall, 1991.

[EEL98] Eeles, P. and O. Sims, *Building Business Objects,* Wiley, 1998.

[ERI98] Eriksson, H.E. and M. Penker, *UML Toolkit,* Wiley, 1998.

[FIC92] Fichman, R.G. and C.F. Kemerer, "Object-Oriented and Conventional Analysis and Design Methodologies," *Computer,* vol. 25, no. 10, October 1992, pp. 22–39.

[FIN96] Fingar, P., *The Blueprint for Business Objects,* Cambridge University Press, 1996.

[FIR93] Firesmith, D.G., *Object-Oriented Requirements Analysis and Logical Design,* Wiley, 1993.

[GRA94] Graham, I., *Object-Oriented Methods,* Addison-Wesley, 1994.

[JAC92] Jacobson, I., *Object-Oriented Software Engineering,* Addison-Wesley, 1992.

[JAC99] Jacobson, I., G. Booch, J. Rumbaugh, *Unified Software Development Process,* Addison-Wesley, 1999.

[MAT94] Mattison, R., *The Object-Oriented Enterprise,* McGraw-Hill, 1994.

[MON92] Monarchi, D.E. and G.I. Puhr, "A Research Typology for Object-Oriented Analysis and Design," *CACM,* vol. 35, no. 9, September 1992, pp. 35–47.

[RUM91] Rumbaugh, J., et al., *Object-Oriented Modeling and Design,* Prentice-Hall, 1991.

[RUM99] Rumbaugh, J., I. Jacobson, and G. Booch, *The Unified Modeling Language Reference Manual,* Addison-Wesley, 1999.

[SUL94] Sullo, G.C., *Object Engineering,* Wiley, 1994.

[TAY95] Taylor, D.A., *Business Engineering with Object Technology,* Wiley, 1995.

[WIR90] Wirfs-Brock, R., B. Wilkerson, and L. Weiner, *Designing Object-Oriented Software,* Prentice-Hall, 1990.

PROBLEMS AND POINTS TO PONDER

21.1. Obtain one or more books dedicated to the Unified Modeling Language and compare it to structured analysis (Chapter 12) using the modeling dimensions proposed by Fichman and Kemerer [FIC92] in Section 21.1.1.

21.2. Develop a classroom presentation on one static or dynamic modeling diagram used in UML. Present the diagram in the context of a simple example, but provide enough detail to demonstrate most important aspects of the diagrammatic form.

21.3. Conduct an abbreviated domain analysis for one of the following areas:

a. A university student record-keeping system.

b. An e-commerce application (e.g., clothes, books, electronic gear).

c. Customer service for a bank.

d. A video game developer.

e. An application area suggested by your instructor.

Be sure to isolate classes that can be used for a number of applications in the domain.

21.4. In your own words describe the difference between static and dynamic views of an OO system.

21.5. Write a use-case for the *SafeHome* system discussed in this book. The use-case should address the scenario required to define a security zone. A security zone encompasses a set of sensors can be addressed, activated, and deactivated as a set rather than individually. As many as ten security zones can be defined. Be creative here but stay within the bounds of the *SafeHome* control panel as it is defined earlier in the book.

21.6. Develop a set of use-cases for the PHTRS system introduced in Problem 12.13. You'll have to make a number of assumptions about the manner in which a user interacts with this system.

21.7. Develop a set of use-cases for any one of the following applications:

a. Software for a general-purpose personal digital assistant.

b. Software for a video game of your choosing.

c. Software that sits inside a climate control system for a car.

d. Software for a navigation system for a car.

e. A system (product) suggested by your instructor.

Do a few hours of research on the application area and conduct a FAST meeting (Chapter 11) with your fellow students to develop basic requirements (your instructor will help you coordinate this).

21.8. Develop a complete set of CRC model index cards on the product or system you chose as part of Problem 21.7.

21.9. Conduct a review of the CRC index cards with your colleagues. How many additional classes, responsibilities, and collaborators were added as a consequence of the review?

21.10. Develop a class hierarchy for the product or system you chose as part of Problem 21.7.

21.11. Develop a set of subsystems (packages) for the product or system you chose as part of Problem 21.7.

21.12. Develop an object-relationship model for the product or system you chose as part of Problem 21.7.

21.13. Develop an object-behavior model for the product or system you chose as part of Problem 21.7. Be sure to list all events, provide an event trace, develop an event flow diagram, and define state diagram for each class.

21.14. In your own words, describe how collaborators for a class are determined.

21.15. What strategy would you propose for defining subsystems for a collection of classes?

21.16 What role does cardinality play in the development of an object-relationship model?

21.17. What is the difference between an active and a passive state for an object?

FURTHER READINGS AND INFORMATION SOURCES

Use-cases form the foundation of object-oriented analysis, regardless of the OOA method that is chosen. Books by Rosenberg and Scott (*Use Case Driven Object Modeling with UML: A Practical Approach,* Addison-Wesley, 1999); Schneider, Winters, and Jacobson (*Applying Use Cases: A Practical Guide,* Addison-Wesley, 1998); and Texel and Williams (*Use Cases Combined With Booch/OMT/UML: Process and Products,* Prentice-Hall, 1997) provide worthwhile guidance in the creation and use of this important requirements elicitation and representation mechanism.

Virtually every recent book published on object-oriented analysis and design emphasizes UML. Those serious about applying UML in their work should acquire [BOO99], [RUM99], and [JAC99]. In addition, the following books are representative of dozens written on UML technology:

Douglass, B., *Real-Time UML: Developing Efficient Objects for Embedded Systems,* Addison-Wesley, 1999.

Fowler, M. and K. Scott, *UML Distilled,* 2nd ed., Addison-Wesley, 2000.

Odell, J.J. and M. Fowler, *Advanced Object-Oriented Analysis and Design Using UML,* SIGS Books, 1998.

Oestereich, B., *Developing Software with UML: Object-Oriented Analysis and Design in Practice,* Addison-Wesley, 1999.

A wide variety of information sources on object-oriented analysis and related subjects is available on the Internet. An up-to-date list of World Wide Web references that are relevant to OOA can be found at the SEPA Web site:

http://www.mhhe.com/engcs/compsci/pressman/resources/OOA.mhtml

CHAPTER

22 OBJECT-ORIENTED DESIGN

KEY CONCEPTS

Object-oriented design transforms the analysis model created using object-oriented analysis (Chapter 21) into a design model that serves as a blueprint for software construction. Yet, the job of the software designer can be daunting. Gamma and his colleagues [GAM95] provide a reasonably accurate picture of OOD when they state:

> Designing object-oriented software is hard, and designing reusable object-oriented software is even harder. You must find pertinent objects, factor them into classes at the right granularity, define class interfaces and inheritance hierarchies, and establish key relationships among them. Your design should be specific to the problem at hand but also general enough to address future problems and requirements. You also want to avoid redesign, or at least minimize it. Experienced object-oriented designers will tell you that a reusable and flexible design is difficult if not impossible to get "right" the first time. Before a design is finished, they usually try to reuse it several times, modifying it each time.

Unlike conventional software design methods, OOD results in a design that achieves a number of different levels of modularity. Major system components are organized into subsystems, a system-level "module." Data and the operations that manipulate the data are encapsulated into objects—a modular form

QUICK LOOK

What is it? The design of object-oriented software requires the definition of a multilayered software architecture, the specification of subsystems that perform required functions and provide infrastructure support, a description of objects (classes) that form the building blocks of the system, and a description of the communication mechanisms that allow data to flow between layers, subsystems, and objects. Object-oriented design accomplishes all of these things.

Who does it? OOD is performed by a software engineer.

Why is it important? An object-oriented system draws upon class definitions that are derived from the analysis model. Some of these definitions will have to be built from scratch, but many others may be reused if appropriate design patterns are recognized. OOD establishes a design blueprint that enables a software engineer to define the OO architecture in a manner that maximizes reuse, thereby improving development speed and end-product quality.

What are the steps? OOD is divided into two major activities: system design and object design. System design creates the product architecture, defining a series of "layers" that accomplish specific system functions and identifying the classes that are encapsulated by subsystems that reside at each layer. In addition, system design considers the specification of three components: the user interface, data management functions, and task

QUICK LOOK

management facilities. Object design focuses on the internal detail of individual classes, defining attributes, operations, and message detail.

What is the work product? An OO design model encompasses software architecture, user interface description, data management components, task management facilities, and detailed descriptions of each class to be used in the system.

How do I ensure that I've done it right? At each stage, the elements of the object-oriented design model are reviewed for clarity, correctness, completeness, and consistency with customer requirements and with one another.

that is the building block of an OO system. In addition, OOD must describe the specific data organization of attributes and the procedural detail of each individual operation. These represent data and algorithmic pieces of an OO system and are contributors to overall modularity.

The unique nature of object-oriented design lies in its ability to build upon four important software design concepts: abstraction, information hiding, functional independence, and modularity (Chapter 13). All design methods strive for software that exhibits these fundamental characteristics, but only OOD provides a mechanism that enables the designer to achieve all four without complexity or compromise.

Object-oriented design, object-oriented programming, and object-oriented testing are construction activities for OO systems. In this chapter, we consider the first step in construction.

22.1 DESIGN FOR OBJECT-ORIENTED SYSTEMS

In Chapter 13, we introduced the concept of a design pyramid for conventional software. Four design layers—data, architectural, interface, and component level—were defined and discussed. For object-oriented systems, we can also define a design pyramid, but the layers are a bit different. Referring to Figure 22.1, the four layers of the OO design pyramid are

Quote:
"In design, we shape the system and find its form . . ."
Ivar Jacobson, Grady Booch, and James Rumbaugh

The subsystem layer contains a representation of each of the subsystems that enable the software to achieve its customer-defined requirements and to implement the technical infrastructure that supports customer requirements.

The class and object layer contains the class hierarchies that enable the system to be created using generalizations and increasingly more targeted specializations. This layer also contains representations of each object.

The message layer contains the design details that enable each object to communicate with its collaborators. This layer establishes the external and internal interfaces for the system.

The responsibilities layer contains the data structure and algorithmic design for all attributes and operations for each object.

FIGURE 22.1
The OO design pyramid

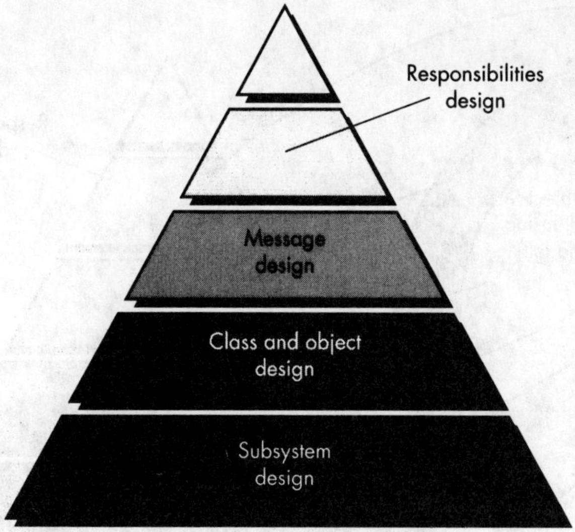

The design pyramid focuses exclusively on the design of a specific product or system. It should be noted, however, that another "layer" of design exists, and this layer forms the foundation on which the pyramid rests. The foundation layer focuses on the design of *domain objects* (called *design patterns* later in this chapter). Domain objects play a key role in building the infrastructure for the OO system by providing support for human/computer interface activities, task management, and data management. Domain objects can also be used to flesh out the design of the application itself.

22.1.1 Conventional vs. OO Approaches

Conventional approaches to software design apply a distinct notation and set of heuristics to map the analysis model into a design model. Recalling Figure 13.1, each element of the conventional analysis model maps into one or more layers of the design model. Like conventional software design, OOD applies data design when attributes are represented, interface design when a messaging model is developed, and component-level (procedural) design for the design of operations. It is important to note that the architecture of an OO design has more to do with the collaborations among objects than with the flow of control between components of the system.

Although similarity between the conventional and OO design models does exist, we have chosen to rename the layers of the design pyramid to reflect more accurately the nature of an OO design. Figure 22.2 illustrates the relationship between the OO analysis model (Chapter 21) and design model that will be derived from it.[1]

---

1 It is important to note that the derivation is not always straightforward. For further discussion, see [DAV95].

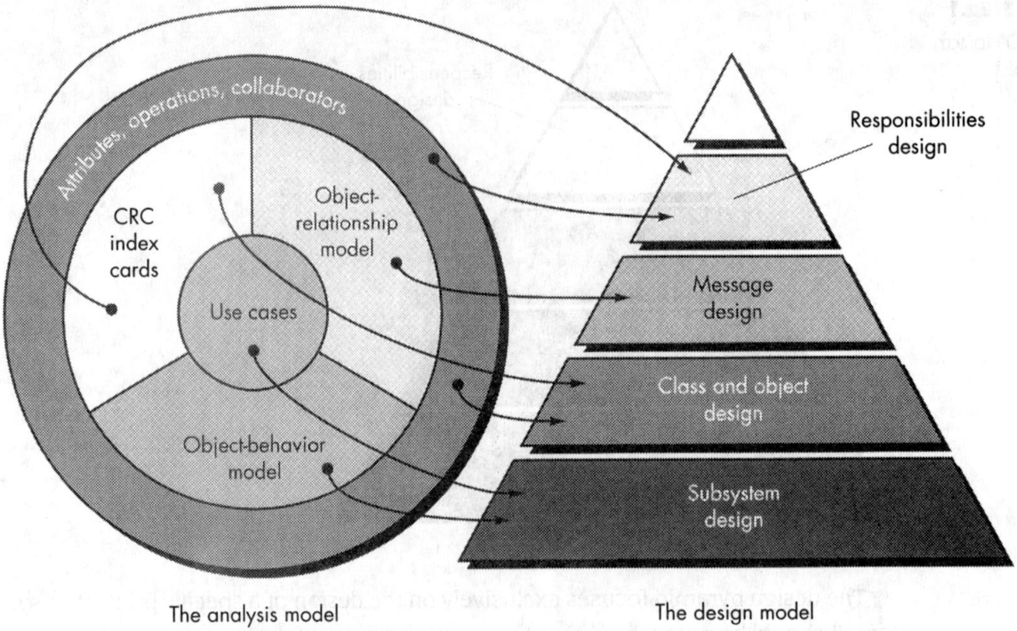

FIGURE 22.2 Translating an OOA model into an OOD model

The subsystem design is derived by considering overall customer requirements (represented with use-cases) and the events and states that are externally observable (the object-behavior model). Class and object design is mapped from the description of attributes, operations, and collaborations contained in the CRC model. Message design is driven by the object-relationship model, and responsibilities design is derived using the attributes, operations, and collaborations described in the CRC model.

Fichman and Kemerer [FIC92] suggest ten design modeling components that may be used to compare various conventional and object-oriented design methods:

? What criteria can be used to compare conventional and OOD methods?

1. Representation of hierarchy of modules.
2. Specification of data definitions.
3. Specification of procedural logic.
4. Indication of end-to-end processing sequences.
5. Representation of object states and transitions.
6. Definition of classes and hierarchies.
7. Assignment of operations to classes.
8. Detailed definition of operations.
9. Specification of message connections.
10. Identification of exclusive services.

Because many conventional and object-oriented design approaches are available, it is difficult to develop a generalized comparison between the two methods. It can be stated, however, that modeling dimensions 5 through 10 are not supported using structured design (Chapter 14) or its derivatives.

22.1.2 Design Issues

Bertrand Meyer [MEY90] suggests five criteria for judging a design method's ability to achieve modularity and relates these to object-oriented design:

WebRef
A discussion that addresses the question "What makes a good object-oriented design?" can be found at **www.kinetica.com/ootips/ood-principles.html**

- *Decomposability*—the facility with which a design method helps the designer to decompose a large problem into subproblems that are easier to solve.
- *Composability*—the degree to which a design method ensures that program components (modules), once designed and built, can be reused to create other systems.
- *Understandability*—the ease with which a program component can be understood without reference to other information or other modules.
- *Continuity*—the ability to make small changes in a program and have these changes manifest themselves with corresponding changes in just one or a very few modules.
- *Protection*—an architectural characteristic that will reduce the propagation of side effects if an error does occur in a given module.

What basic principles guide us in the design of modular architectures?

From these criteria, Meyer [MEY90] suggests five basic design principles that can be derived for modular architectures: (1) linguistic modular units, (2) few interfaces, (3) small interfaces (weak coupling), (4) explicit interfaces, and (5) information hiding.

Modules are defined as *linguistic modular units* when they "correspond to syntactic units in the language used" [MEY90]. That is, the programming language to be used should be capable of supporting the modularity defined directly. For example, if the designer creates a subroutine, any of the older programming languages (e.g., FORTRAN, C, Pascal) could implement it as a syntactic unit. But if a package that contains data structures and procedures and identifies them as a single unit were defined, a language such as Ada (or another object-oriented language) would be necessary to directly represent this type of component in the language syntax.

To achieve low coupling (a design concept introduced in Chapter 13), the number of interfaces between modules should be minimized ("few interfaces") and the amount of information that moves across an interface should be minimized ("small interfaces"). Whenever components do communicate, they should do so in an obvious and direct way ("explicit interfaces"). For example, if component X and component Y communicate through a global data area (what we called *common coupling* in Chapter 13), they violate the principle of explicit interfaces because the communication between the components is not obvious to an outside observer. Finally, we achieve the principle of information hiding when all information about a component is hidden from outside access, unless that information is specifically defined as *public information*.

The design criteria and principles presented in this section can be applied to any design method (e.g., we can apply them to structured design). As we will see, however, the object-oriented design method achieves each of the criteria more efficiently than other approaches and results in modular architectures that allow us to meet each of the modularity criteria most effectively.

22.1.3 The OOD Landscape

As we noted in Chapter 21, a wide variety of object-oriented analysis and design methods were proposed and used during the 1980s and 1990s. These methods established the foundation for modern OOD notation, design heuristics, and models. A brief overview of the most important early OOD methods follows:

Quote:
"There is no reason why the transition from requirements to design should be any easier in software engineering than it is in any other engineering discipline. Design is hard."
Alan Davis

The Booch method. As we noted in Chapter 21, the Booch method [BOO94] encompasses both a "micro development process" and a "macro development process." In the design context, macro development encompasses an architectural planning activity that clusters similar objects in separate architectural partitions, layers objects by level of abstraction, identifies relevant scenarios, creates a design prototype, and validates the design prototype by applying it to usage scenarios. Micro development defines a set of "rules" that govern the use of operations and attributes and the domain-specific policies for memory management, error handling, and other infrastructure functions; develops scenarios that describe the semantics of the rules and policies; creates a prototype for each policy; instruments and refines the prototype; and reviews each policy so that it "broadcasts its architectural vision" [BOO94].

The Rumbaugh method. The *object modeling technique* [RUM91] encompasses a design activity that encourages design to be conducted at two different levels of abstraction. *System design* focuses on the layout for the components that are needed to construct a complete product or system. The analysis model is partitioned into subsystems, which are then allocated to processors and tasks. A strategy for implementing data management is defined and global resources and the control mechanisms required to access them are identified.

Object design emphasizes the detailed layout of an individual object. Operations are selected from the analysis model and algorithms are defined for each operation. Data structures that are appropriate for attributes and algorithms are represented. Classes and class attributes are designed in a manner that optimizes access to data and improves computational efficiency. A messaging model is created to implement the object relationships (associations).

The Jacobson method. The design activity for OOSE (object-oriented software engineering) [JAC92] is a simplified version of the proprietary *objectory method,* also developed by Jacobson. The design model emphasizes traceability to the OOSE analysis model. First, the idealized analysis model is adapted to fit the real world environment. Then primary design objects, called *blocks,*[2] are created and categorized as interface blocks, entity blocks, and control blocks. Communication between blocks during execution is defined and the blocks are organized into subsystems.

The Coad and Yourdon method. The Coad and Yourdon method for OOD [COA91] was developed by studying how "effective object-oriented designers" do their design work. The design approach addresses not only the application but also the infrastructure for the application and focuses on the representation of four major system components: the problem domain component, the human interaction component, the task management component, and the data management component.

ADVICE

Although it is not nearly as robust as UML, the Wirfs-Brock method has a simple elegance that makes it an interesting alternative approach to OOD.

The Wirfs-Brock method. Wirfs-Brock, Wilkerson, and Weiner [WIR90] define a continuum of technical tasks in which analysis leads seamlessly into design. *Protocols*[3] for each class are constructed by refining contracts between objects. Each operation (responsibility) and protocol (interface design) is designed at a level of detail that will guide implementation. Specifications for each class (defining private responsibilities and detail for operations) and each subsystem (identifying all encapsulated classes and the interaction between subsystems) are developed.

Although the terminology and process steps for each of these OOD methods differ, the overall OOD processes are reasonably consistent. To perform object-oriented design, a software engineer should perform the following generic steps:

KEY POINT

A set of generic steps are applied during OOD, regardless of the design method that is chosen.

1. Describe each subsystem and allocate it to processors and tasks.
2. Choose a design strategy for implementing data management, interface support, and task management.
3. Design an appropriate control mechanism for the system.
4. Perform object design by creating a procedural representation for each operation and data structures for class attributes.
5. Perform message design using collaborations between objects and object relationships.
6. Create the messaging model.
7. Review the design model and iterate as required.

2 A *block* is the design abstraction that allows for the representation of an aggregate object.

3 A *protocol* is a formal description of the messages to which a class will respond.

It is important to note that the design steps discussed in this section are iterative. That is, they may be executed incrementally, along with additional OOA activities, until a completed design is produced.

22.1.4 A Unified Approach to OOD

In Chapter 21, we noted that Grady Booch, James Rumbaugh, and Ivar Jacobson combined the best features of their individual object-oriented analysis and design methods into a unified method. The result, called the *Unified Modeling Language* has become widely used throughout the industry.[4]

WebRef
An extensive tutorial and listing of UML resources including tools, papers, and examples can be found at **mini.net/cetus/oo_uml.html**

During analysis modeling (Chapter 21), the user model and structural model views are represented. These provide insight into the usage scenarios for the system (providing guidance for behavioral modeling) and establish a foundation for the implementation and environment model views by identifying and describing the static structural elements of the system.

UML is organized into two major design activities: system design and object design. The primary objective of UML *system design* is to represent the software architecture. Bennett, McRobb, and Farmer [BEN99] discuss this issue in the following way:

> In terms of object-oriented development, the conceptual architecture is concerned with the structure of the static class model and the connections between components of the model. The module architecture describes the way the system is divided into subsystems or modules and how they communicate by exporting and importing data. The code architecture defines how the program code is organized into files and directories and grouped into libraries. The execution architecture focuses on the dynamic aspects of the system and the communication between components as tasks and operations execute.

KEY POINT
System design focuses on software architecture and the definition of subsystems. Object design describes objects at a level of detail that can be implemented in a programming language.

The definition of the "subsystems" noted by Bennett et al. is a primary concern during UML system design.

UML *object design* focuses on a description of objects and their interactions with one another. A detailed specification of attribute data structures and a procedural design of all operations are created during object design. The visibility[5] for all class attributes is defined and interfaces between objects are elaborated to define the details of a complete messaging model.

System and object design in UML are extended to consider the design of user interfaces, data management with the system to be built, and task management for the subsystems that have been specified. User interface design in UML draws on the same concepts and principles discussed in Chapter 15. The user model view drives the user interface design process, providing a scenario that is elaborated iteratively to become a set of interface classes.[6]

---

4 Booch, Rumbaugh, and Jacobson have written a set of three definitive books on UML. The interested reader should see [BOO99], [RUM99], and [JAC99].

5 *Visibility* indicates whether an attribute is public (available across all instantiations of the class), private (available only for the class that specifies it), or protected (an attribute that may be used by the class that specifies it and its subclasses).

6 Today, most interface classes are part of a library of reusable software components. This expedites the design and implementation of GUIs.

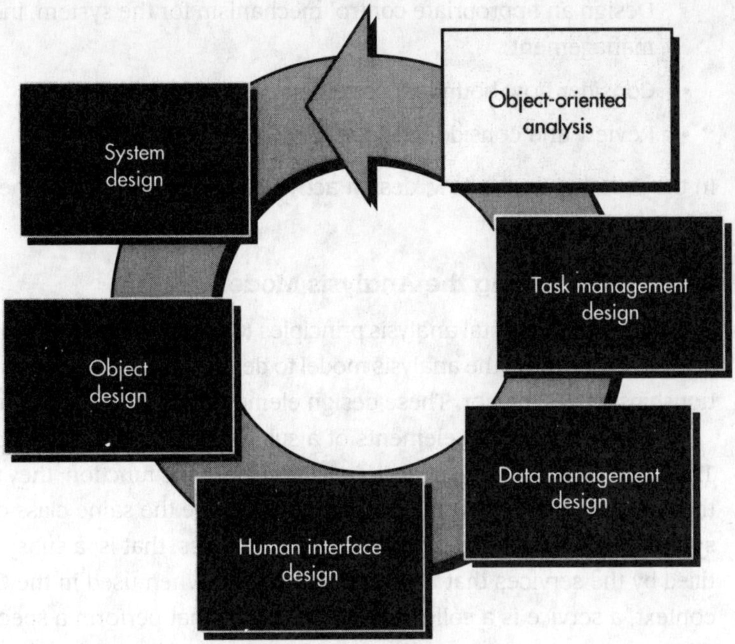

FIGURE 22.3 Process flow for OOD

Data management design establishes a set of classes and collaborations that allow the system (product) to manage persistent data (e.g., files and databases). Task management design establishes the infrastructure that organizes subsystems into tasks and then manages task concurrency. The process flow for design is illustrated in Figure 22.3.[7]

Throughout the UML design process, the user model view and structure model view are elaborated into the design representation outlined above. This elaboration activity is discussed in the sections that follow.

22.2 THE SYSTEM DESIGN PROCESS

System design develops the architectural detail required to build a system or product. The system design process encompasses the following activities:

What are the steps of the system design process?

- Partition the analysis model into subsystems.
- Identify concurrency that is dictated by the problem.
- Allocate subsystems to processors and tasks.
- Develop a design for the user interface.
- Choose a basic strategy for implementing data management.
- Identify global resources and the control mechanisms required to access them.

7 Recall that OOA is an iterative activity. It is entirely possible that the analysis model will be revised as a consequence of design work.

- Design an appropriate control mechanism for the system, including task management.
- Consider how boundary conditions should be handled.
- Review and consider trade-offs.

In the sections that follow, design activities related to each of these steps are considered in more detail.

22.2.1 Partitioning the Analysis Model

ADVICE

The concepts of coupling and cohesion (Chapter 13) can be applied at the subsystem level. Strive to achieve good functional independence as you design subsystems.

One of the fundamental analysis principles (Chapter 11) is partitioning. In OO system design, we partition the analysis model to define cohesive collections of classes, relationships, and behavior. These design elements are packaged as a subsystem.

In general, all of the elements of a subsystem share some property in common. They all may be involved in accomplishing the same function; they may reside within the same product hardware, or they may manage the same class of resources. Subsystems are characterized by their responsibilities; that is, a subsystem can be identified by the services that it provides [RUM91]. When used in the OO system design context, a service is a collection of operations that perform a specific function (e.g., managing word-processor files, producing a three-dimensional rendering, translating an analog video signal into a compressed digital image).

As subsystems are defined (and designed), they should conform to the following design criteria:

? What criteria guide us in the design of subsystems?

- The subsystem should have a well-defined interface through which all communication with the rest of the system occurs.
- With the exception of a small number of "communication classes," the classes within a subsystem should collaborate only with other classes within the subsystem.
- The number of subsystems should be kept low.
- A subsystem can be partitioned internally to help reduce complexity.

When two subsystems communicate with one another, they can establish a client/server link or a peer-to-peer link [RUM91]. In a client/server link, each of the subsystems takes on one of the roles implied by client and server. Service flows from server to client in only one direction. In a peer-to-peer link, services may flow in either direction.

When a system is partitioned into subsystems, another design activity, called *layering,* also occurs. Each layer [BUS96] of an OO system contains one or more subsystems and represents a different level of abstraction of the functionality required to accomplish system functions. In most cases, the levels of abstraction are determined by the degree to which the processing associated with a subsystem is visible to an end-user.

For example, a four-layer architecture might might include (1) a presentation layer (the subsystems associated with the user interface), (2) an application layer (the subsystems that perform the processing associated with the application), (3) a data formatting layer (the subsystems that prepare the data for processing), and (4) a database layer (the subsystems associated with data management). Each layer moves deeper into the system, representing increasingly more environment-specific processing.

Buschmann and his colleagues [BUS96] suggest the following design approach for layering:

How do I create a layered design?

1. Establish layering critèria. That is, decide how subsystems will be grouped in a layered architecture.
2. Determine the number of layers. Too many introduce unnecessary complexity; too few may harm functional independence.
3. Name the layers and allocate subsystems (with their encapsulated classes) to a layer. Be certain that communication between subsystems (classes) on one layer and other subsystems (classes) at another layer follow the design philosophy for the architecture.[8]
4. Design interfaces for each layer.
5. Refine the subsystems to establish the class structure for each layer.
6. Define the messaging model for communication between layers.
7. Review the layer design to ensure that coupling between layers is minimized (a client/server protocol can help accomplish this).
8. Iterate to refine the layered design.

22.2.2 Concurrency and Subsystem Allocation

ADVICE

In most cases, a multiprocessor implementation increases complexity and technical risk. Whenever possible, choose the simplest processor architecture that will get the job done.

The dynamic aspect of the object-behavior model provides an indication of concurrency among classes (or subsystems). If classes (or subsystems) are not active at the same time, there is no need for concurrent processing. This means that the classes (or subsystems) can be implemented on the same processor hardware. On the other hand, if classes (or subsystems) must act on events asynchronously and at the same time, they are viewed as concurrent. When subsystems are concurrent, two allocation options exist: (1) Allocate each subsystem to an independent processor or (2) allocate the subsystems to the same processor and provide concurrency support through operating system features.

Concurrent tasks are defined [RUM91] by examining the state diagram for each object. If the flow of events and transitions indicates that only a single object is active at any one time, a thread of control has been established. The thread of control

8 In a *closed* architecture, messages from one layer may be sent only to the adjacent lower layer. In an *open* architecture, messages may be sent to any lower layer.

continues even when one object sends a message to another object, as long as the first object waits for a response. If, however, the first object continues processing after sending a message, the thread of control splits.

Tasks in an OO system are designed by isolating threads of control. For example, while the *SafeHome* security system is monitoring its sensors, it can also be dialing the central monitoring station for verification of connection. Since the objects involved in both of these behaviors are active at the same time, each represents a separate thread of control and each can be defined as a separate task. If the monitoring and dialing activities occur sequentially, a single task could be implemented.

To determine which of the processor allocation options is appropriate, the designer must consider performance requirements, costs, and the overhead imposed by interprocessor communication.

22.2.3 The Task Management Component

Coad and Yourdon [COA91] suggest the following strategy for the design of the objects that manage concurrent tasks:

- The characteristics of the task are determined.
- A coordinator task and associated objects are defined.
- The coordinator and other tasks are integrated.

Quote:

"Discipline and focused awareness . . . contribute to the act of creation."

John Poppy

The characteristics of a task are determined by understanding how the task is initiated. Event-driven and clock-driven tasks are the most commonly encountered. Both are activated by an interrupt, but the former receives an interrupt from some outside source (e.g., another processor, a sensor) while that latter is governed by a system clock.

In addition to the manner in which a task is initiated, the priority and criticality of the task must also be determined. High-priority tasks must have immediate access to system resources. High-criticality tasks must continue to operate even if resource availability is reduced or the system is operating in a degraded state.

Once the characteristics of the task have been determined, object attributes and operations required to achieve coordination and communication with other tasks are defined. The basic task template (for a task object) takes the form [COA91]

Task name—the name of the object
Description—a narrative describing the purpose of the object
Priority—task priority (e.g., low, medium, high)
Services—a list of operations that are responsibilities of the object
Coordinates by—the manner in which object behavior is invoked
Communicates via—input and output data values relevant to the task

This template description can then be translated into the standard design model (incorporating representation of attributes and operations) for the task object(s).

22.2.4 The User Interface Component

Although the user interface component is implemented within the context of the problem domain, the interface itself represents a critically important subsystem for most modern applications. The OO analysis model (Chapter 21) contains usage scenarios (called *use-cases*) and a description of the roles that users play (called *actors*) as they interact with the system. These serve as input to the user interface design process.

XRef
Most of the classes necessary to build a modern interface already exist and are available to the designer. The design of the interface follows the approach defined in Chapter 15.

Once the actor and its usage scenario are defined, a command hierarchy is identified. The command hierarchy defines major system menu categories (the menu bar or tool palette) and all subfunctions that are available within the context of a major system menu category (the menu windows). The command hierarchy is refined iteratively until every use-case can be implemented by navigating the hierarchy of functions.

Because a wide variety of user interface development environments already exist, the design of GUI elements is not necessary. Reusable classes (with appropriate attributes and operations) already exist for windows, icons, mouse operations, and a wide variety of other interaction functions. The implementer need only instantiate objects that have appropriate characteristics for the problem domain.

22.2.5 The Data Management Component

Data management encompasses two distinct areas of concern: (1) the management of data that are critical to the application itself and (2) the creation of an infrastructure for storage and retrieval of objects. In general, data management is designed in a layered fashion. The idea is to isolate the low-level requirements for manipulating data structures from the higher-level requirements for handling system attributes.

Within the system context, a database management system is often used as a common data store for all subsystems. The objects required to manipulate the database are members of reusable classes that are identified using domain analysis (Chapter 21) or are supplied directly by the database vendor. A detailed discussion of database design for OO systems is beyond the scope of this book.[9]

The design of the data management component includes the design of the attributes and operations required to manage objects. The relevant attributes are appended to every object in the problem domain and provide information that answers the question, "How do I store myself?" Coad and Yourdon [COA91] suggest the creation of an object-server class "with services to (a) tell each object to save itself and (b) retrieve stored objects for use by other design components."

As an example of data management for the **sensor** object discussed as part of the *SafeHome* security system, the design could specify a flat file called "sensor." Each record would correspond to a named instance of **sensor** and would contain the values of each **sensor** attribute for that named instance. Operations within the object-server class would enable a specific object to be stored and retrieved when it is needed

9 Interested readers should refer to [BRO91], [TAY92], or [RAO94].

FIGURE 22.4
A model of collaboration between subsystems

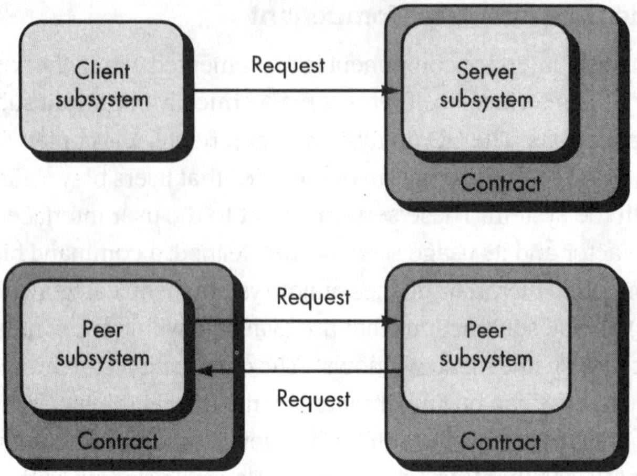

by the system. For more complex objects, it might be necessary to specify a relational database or an object-oriented database to accomplish the same function.

22.2.6 The Resource Management Component

A variety of different resources are available to an OO system or product; and in many instances, subsystems compete for these resources at the same time. Global system resources can be external entities (e.g., a disk drive, processor, or communication line) or abstractions (e.g., a database, an object). Regardless of the nature of the resource, the software engineer should design a control mechanism for it. Rumbaugh and his colleagues [RUM91] suggest that each resource should be owned by a "guardian object." The guardian object is the gatekeeper for the resource, controlling access to it and moderating conflicting requests for it.

22.2.7 Intersubsystem Communication

Once each subsystem has been specified, it is necessary to define the collaborations that exist between the subsystems. The model that we use for object-to-object collaboration can be extended to subsystems as a whole. Figure 22.4 illustrates a collaboration model. As we noted earlier in this chapter, communication can occur by establishing a client/server link or a peer-to-peer link. Referring to the figure, we must specify the contract that exists between subsystems. Recall that a contract provides an indication of the ways in which one subsystem can interact with another.

? What design steps are required to specify a "contract" for a subsystem?

The following design steps can be applied to specify a contract for a subsystem [WIR90]:

1. **List each request that can be made by collaborators of the subsystem.** Organize the requests by subsystem and define them within one or more appropriate contracts. Be sure to note contracts that are inherited from superclasses.

Contract	Type	Collaborators	Class(es)	Operation(s)	Message Format

FIGURE 22.5 Subsystem collaboration table

2. **For each contract, note the operations (both inherited and private) that are required to implement the responsibilities implied by the contract.** Be sure to associate the operations with specific classes that reside within a subsystem.

KEY POINT
Every contract between subsystems is manifested by one or more messages that move between objects within the subsystems.

3. **Considering one contract at a time, create a table of the form shown in Figure 22.5.** For each contract, the following entries are made in the table:

   Type—the type of contract (i.e., client/server or peer-to-peer).

   Collaborators—the names of the subsystems that are parties to the contract.

   Class—the names of the classes (contained within a subsystem) that support services implied by the contract.

   Operation—the names of the operations (within the class) that implement the services.

   Message format—the message format required to implement the interaction between collaborators.

   Draft an appropriate message description for each interaction between the subsystems.

4. **If the modes of interaction between subsystems are complex, a subsystem-collaboration diagram, illustrated in Figure 22.6 is created.** The collaboration graph is similar in form to the event flow diagram discussed in Chapter 21. Each subsystem is represented along with its interactions with other subsystems. The contracts that are invoked during an interaction are noted as shown. The details of the interaction are determined by looking up the contract in the subsystem collaboration table (Figure 22.5)

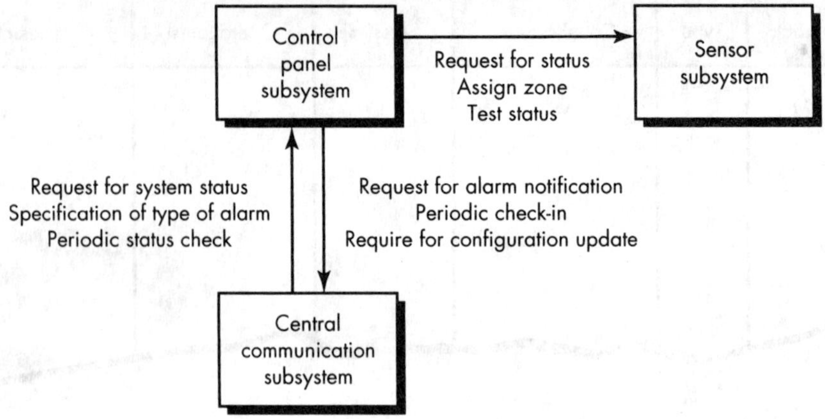

FIGURE 22.6 Abbreviated subsystem collaboration graph for SafeHome

22.3 THE OBJECT DESIGN PROCESS

Borrowing from a metaphor that was introduced earlier in this book, the OO system design might be viewed as the floor plan of a house. The floor plan specifies the purpose of each room and the architectural features that connect the rooms to one another and to the outside environment. It is now time to provide the details that are required to build each room. In the context of OOD, object design focuses on the "rooms."

Bennett and his colleagues [BEN99] discuss object design in the following way:

> Object design is concerned with the detailed design of the objects and their interactions. It is completed within the overall architecture defined during system design and according to agreed design guidelines and protocols. Object design is particularly concerned with the specification of attribute types, how operations function, and how objects are linked to other objects.

It is at this stage that the basic concepts and principles associated with component-level design (Chapter 16) come into play. Local data structures are defined (for attributes) and algorithms (for operations) are designed.

22.3.1 Object Descriptions

ADVICE *Be sure that the architecture has been defined before you begin working on object design. Don't let the architecture just happen.*

A design description of an object (an instance of a class or subclass) can take one of two forms [GOL83]: (1) a *protocol description* that establishes the interface of an object by defining each message that the object can receive and the related operation that the object performs when it receives the message or (2) an *implementation description* that shows implementation details for each operation implied by a message that is passed to an object. Implementation details include information about the object's private part; that is, internal details about the data structures that describe the object's attributes and procedural details that describe operations.

The protocol description is nothing more than a set of messages and a corresponding comment for each message. For example, a portion of the protocol description for the object **motion sensor** (described earlier) might be

MESSAGE (motion.sensor) --> read: RETURNS sensor.ID, sensor.status;

This describes the message required to read the sensor. Similarly,

MESSAGE (motion.sensor) --> set: SENDS sensor.ID, sensor.status;

sets or resets the status of the sensor.

For a large system with many messages, it is often possible to create message categories. For example, message categories for the *SafeHome* **system** object might include system configuration messages, monitoring messages, event messages, and so forth.

KEY POINT

To achieve the benefits of information hiding (Chapter 13), anyone who intends to use an object needs only the protocol description. The implementation description contains detail that should be "hidden" from those with no need to know.

An implementation description of an object provides the internal ("hidden") details that are required for implementation but are not necessary for invocation. That is, the designer of the object must provide an implementation description and must therefore create the internal details of the object. However, another designer or implementer who uses the object or other instances of the object requires only the protocol description but not the implementation description.

An implementation description is composed of the following information: (1) a specification of the object's name and reference to class; (2) a specification of private data structure with indication of data items and types; (3) a procedural description of each operation or, alternatively, pointers to such procedural descriptions. The implementation description must contain sufficient information to provide for proper handling of all messages described in the protocol description.

Cox [COX85] characterizes the difference between the information contained in the protocol description and that contained in the implementation description in terms of "users" and "suppliers" of services. A user of the service provided by an object must be familiar with the protocol for invoking the service; that is, for specifying what is desired. The supplier of the service (the object itself) must be concerned with how the service is to be supplied to the user; that is, with implementation details.

22.3.2 Designing Algorithms and Data Structures

A variety of representations contained in the analysis model and the system design provide a specification for all operations and attributes. Algorithms and data structures are designed using an approach that differs little from the data design and component-level design approaches discussed for conventional software engineering.

XRef

Virtually every concept presented in Chapter 13 is applicable here. Be sure you're familiar with the topics presented there.

An algorithm is created to implement the specification for each operation. In many cases, the algorithm is a simple computational or procedural sequence that can be implemented as a self-contained software module. However, if the specification of the operation is complex, it may be necessary to modularize the operation. Conventional component-level design techniques can be used to accomplish this.

Data structures are designed concurrently with algorithms. Since operations invariably manipulate the attributes of a class, the design of the data structures that best reflect the attributes will have a strong bearing on the algorithmic design of the corresponding operations.

? Is there a way to categorize operations (methods)?

Although many different types of operations exist, they can generally be divided into three broad categories: (1) operations that manipulate data in some way (e.g., adding, deleting, reformatting, selecting), (2) operations that perform a computation, and (3) operations that monitor an object for the occurrence of a controlling event.

For example, the *SafeHome* processing narrative contains the sentence fragments: "sensor is assigned a number and type" and "a master password is programmed for arming and disarming the system." These two phrases indicate a number of things:

- That an *assign* operation is relevant for the **sensor** object.
- That a *program* operation will be applied to the **system** object.
- That *arm* and *disarm* are operations that apply to **system** (also that **system status** may ultimately be defined (using data dictionary notation) as

system status = [armed | disarmed]

ADVICE

An operation is refined in much the same way that we refine a function in conventional design. Write a processing narrative, do a grammatical parse, and isolate new operations at a lower level of abstraction.

The operation *program* is allocated during OOA, but during object design it will be refined into a number of more specific operations that are required to configure the system. For example, after discussions with product engineering, the analyst, and possibly the marketing department, the designer might elaborate the original processing narrative and write the following for *program* (potential operations—verbs—are underlined):

Program enables the *SafeHome* user to configure the system once it has been installed. The user can (1) install phone numbers; (2) define delay times for alarms; (3) build a sensor table that contains each sensor ID, its type, and location; and (4) load a master password.

Therefore, the designer has refined the single operation *program* and replaced it with the operations: *install, define, build,* and *load*. Each of these new operations becomes part of the **system** object, has knowledge of the internal data structures that implement the object's attributes, and is invoked by sending the object messages of the form

```
MESSAGE (system) --> install: SENDS telephone.number;
```

This implies that, to provide the system with an emergency phone number, an *install* message will be sent to system.

Verbs connote actions or occurrences. In the context of object design formalization, we consider not only verbs but also descriptive verb phrases and predicates (e.g., "is equal to") as potential operations. The grammatical parse is applied recursively until each operation has been refined to its most-detailed level.

Once the basic object model is created, optimization should occur. Rumbaugh and his colleagues [RUM91] suggest three major thrusts for OOD design optimization:

- Review the object-relationship model to ensure that the implemented design leads to efficient utilization of resources and ease of implementation. Add redundancy where necessary.
- Revise attribute data structures and corresponding operation algorithms to enhance efficient processing.
- Create new attributes to save derived information, thereby avoiding recomputation.

A detailed discussion of OO design optimization is beyond the scope of this book. The interested reader should refer to [RUM91] and [CHA93]. For a discussion of how these concepts translate into the UML process, the reader should examine [JAC99] and [RUM99].

22.3.3 Program Components and Interfaces

An important aspect of software design quality is modularity; that is, the specification of program components (modules) that are combined to form a complete program. The object-oriented approach defines the object as a program component that is itself linked to other components (e.g., private data, operations). But defining objects and operations is not enough. During design, we must also identify the interfaces between objects and the overall structure (considered in an architectural sense) of the objects.

Although a program component is a design abstraction, it should be represented in the context of the programming language used for implementation. To accommodate OOD, the programming language to be used for implementation should be capable of creating the following program component (modeled after Ada):

```
PACKAGE program-component-name IS
   TYPE specification of data objects
        •
        •
        •
   PROC specification of related operations . . .
PRIVATE
   data structure details for objects
PACKAGE BODY program-component-name IS
   PROC operation.1 (interface description) IS
        •
        •
        •
   END
   PROC operation.n (interface description) IS
        •
        •
        •
   END
END program-component-name
```

Referring to the Ada-like PDL (program design language) just shown, a program component is specified by indicating both data objects and operations. The *specification part* of the component indicates all data objects (declared with the **TYPE** statement) and the operations (**PROC** for procedure) that act on them. The *private part* (**PRIVATE**) of the component provides otherwise hidden details of data structure and processing. In the context of our earlier discussion, the **PACKAGE** is conceptually similar to objects discussed throughout this chapter.

The first program component to be identified should be the highest-level module from which all processing originates and all data structures evolve. Referring once again to the *SafeHome* example, we can define the highest-level program component as

```
PROCEDURE SafeHome software
```

The *SafeHome* software component can be coupled with a preliminary design for the following packages (objects):

```
PACKAGE system IS
    TYPE system data
    PROC install, define, build, load
    PROC display, reset, query, modify, call
    PRIVATE
        PACKAGE BODY system IS
        PRIVATE
            system.id IS STRING LENGTH (8);
            verification phone.number, telephone.number, ...
            IS STRING LENGTH (8);
            sensor.table DEFINED
                sensor.type IS STRING LENGTH (2),
                sensor.number, alarm.threshold IS NUMERIC;
        PROC install RECEIVES (telephone.number)
            {design detail for operation install}
        •
        •
        •
END system
PACKAGE sensor IS
    TYPE sensor data
    PROC read, set, test
    PRIVATE
        PACKAGE BODY sensor IS
        PRIVATE
            sensor.id IS STRING LENGTH (8);
            sensor.status IS STRING LENGTH (8);
            alarm.characteristics DEFINED
                threshold, signal type, signal level IS NUMERIC,
            hardware.interface DEFINED
                type, a/d.characteristics, timing.data IS NUMERIC,
```

```
END sensor
   :
   :
END SafeHome software
```

Data objects and corresponding operations are specified for each of the program components for *SafeHome* software. The final step in the object design process completes all information required to fully implement data structure and types contained in the **PRIVATE** portion of the package and all procedural detail contained in the **PACKAGE BODY**.

To illustrate the detail design of a program component, we reconsider the **sensor** package described earlier. The data structures for **sensor** attributes have already been defined. Therefore, the first step is to define the interfaces for each of the operations attached to **sensor:**

```
PROC read (sensor.id, sensor.status: OUT);
PROC set (alarm.characteristics, hardware.interface: IN)
PROC test (sensor.id, sensor.status, alarm.characteristics: OUT);
```

KEY POINT

Stepwise refinement and structured programming (Chapter 16) are used at this stage to complete the design of each operation.

The next step requires stepwise refinement of each operation associated with the **sensor** package. To illustrate the refinement, we develop a processing narrative (an informal strategy) for *read:*

> When the sensor object receives a *read* message, the *read* process is invoked. The process determines the interface and signal type, polls the sensor interface, converts A/D characteristics into an internal signal level, and compares the internal signal level to a threshold value. If the threshold is exceeded, the sensor status is set to "event." Otherwise, the sensor status is set to "no event." If an error is sensed while polling the sensor, the sensor status is set to "error."

Given the processing narrative, a PDL description of the *read* process can be developed:

```
PROC read (sensor.id, sensor.status: OUT);
   raw.signal IS BIT STRING
   IF (hardware.interface.type = "s" & alarm.characteristics.signal.type = "B"
   THEN
      GET (sensor, exception: sensor.status := error) raw.signal;
      CONVERT raw.signal TO internal.signal.level;
      IF internal.signal.level > threshold
         THEN sensor.status := "event";
         ELSE sensor.status := "no event";
      ENDIF
   ELSE {processing for other types of s interfaces would be specified}
   ENDIF
   RETURN sensor.id, sensor.status;
END read
```

The PDL representation of the *read* operation can be translated into the appropriate implementation language. The functions **GET** and **CONVERT** are assumed to be available as part of a run-time library.

22.4 DESIGN PATTERNS

The best designers in any field have an uncanny ability to see patterns that characterize a problem and corresponding patterns that can be combined to create a solution. Gamma and his colleagues [GAM95] discuss this when they state:

XRef
Patterns exist at the architecture and the component levels. For further discussion, see Chapter 14.

> [Y]ou'll find recurring patterns of classes and communicating objects in many object-oriented systems. These patterns solve specific design problems and make object-oriented design more flexible, elegant, and ultimately reusable. They help designers reuse successful designs by basing new designs on prior experience. A designer who is familiar with such patterns can apply them immediately to design problems without having to rediscover them.

Throughout the OOD process, a software engineer should look for every opportunity to reuse existing design patterns (when they meet the needs of the design) rather than creating new ones.

WebRef
An excellent paper entitled "Non-Software Examples of Software Design Patterns" provides insight:
www.agcs.com/patterns/papers/patexamples.htm

22.4.1 Describing a Design Pattern

Mature engineering disciplines make use of thousands of design patterns. For example, a mechanical engineer uses a two-step, keyed shaft as a design pattern. Inherent in the pattern are attributes (the diameters of the shaft, the dimensions of the keyway, etc.) and operations (e.g., shaft rotation, shaft connection). An electrical engineer uses an integrated circuit (an extremely complex design pattern) to solve a specific element of a new problem. All design patterns can be described by specifying the following information [GAM95]:

Quote:
"[Patterns] constitute a 'grass roots' effort to build on the collective experience of skilled designers and software engineers."
Frank Buschmann et al.

- the name of the pattern
- the intent of the pattern
- the "design forces" that motivate the pattern
- the solution that mitigates these forces
- the classes that are required to implement the solution
- the responsibilities and collaboration among solution classes
- guidance that leads to effective implementation
- example source code or source code templates
- cross-references to related design patterns

The design pattern name is itself an abstraction that conveys significant meaning once the applicability and intent are understood. *Design forces* describe the data, functional, or behavioral requirements associated with part of the software for which the pattern is to be applied. In addition forces define the constraints that may restrict the manner in which the design is to be derived. In essence, design forces describe the environment and conditions that must exist to make the design pattern applicable. The pattern characteristics (classes, responsibilities, and collaborations) indicate the attributes of the design that may be adjusted to enable the pattern to accommodate a variety of problems. These attributes represent characteristics of the design that can be searched (e.g., via a database) so that an appropriate pattern can be found. Finally, guidance associated with the use of a design pattern provides an indication of the ramifications of design decisions.

Quote:

"A design pattern becomes an AntiPattern when it creates more problems than it solves."

William Brown et al.

The names of objects and subsystems (potential design patterns) should be chosen with care. As we discuss in Chapter 27, one of the key technical problems in software reuse is simply the inability to find existing reusable patterns when hundreds or thousands of candidate patterns exist. The search for the "right" pattern is aided immeasurably by a meaningful pattern name along with a set of characteristics that help in classifying the object [PRE95].

22.4.2 Using Patterns in Design

WebRef

The Portland Pattern Repository publishes an evolving collection of design patterns at: **c2.com/ppr**

In an object-oriented system, design patterns[10] can be used by applying two different mechanisms: inheritance and composition. Inheritance is a fundamental OO concept and was described in detail in Chapter 20. Using inheritance, an existing design pattern becomes a template for a new subclass. The attributes and operations that exist in the pattern become part of the subclass.

Composition is a concept that leads to aggregate objects. That is, a problem may require objects that have complex functionality (in the extreme, a subsystem accomplishes this). The complex object can be assembled by selecting a set of design patterns and composing the appropriate object (or subsystem). Each design pattern is treated as a black box, and communication among the patterns occurs only via well-defined interfaces.

ADVICE

Good design always strives for simplicity. Therefore, opt for composition when it leads to simpler inheritance structures.

Gamma and his colleagues [GAM95] suggest that object composition should be favored over inheritance when both options exist. Rather than creating large and sometimes unmanageable class hierarchies (the consequence of the overuse of inheritance), composition favors small class hierarchies and objects that remain focused on one objective. Composition uses existing design patterns (reusable components) in an unaltered form.

22.5 OBJECT-ORIENTED PROGRAMMING

Although all areas of object technologies have received significant attention within the software community, no subject has produced more books, more discussion, and

10 Buschmann [BUS96] and Gamma et al. [GAM95] among many others have written catalogs of design patterns for use in OO systems.

more debate than *object-oriented programming* (OOP). Hundreds of books have been written on C++ and Java programming, and hundreds more are dedicated to less widely used OO languages.

The software engineering viewpoint stresses OOA and OOD and considers OOP (coding) an important, but secondary, activity that is an outgrowth of analysis and design. The reason for this is simple. As the complexity of systems increases, the design architecture of the end product has a significantly stronger influence on its success than the programming language that has been used. And yet, "language wars" continue to rage.

The details of OOP are best left to books dedicated to the subject. The interested reader should refer to one or more of the OOP books noted in the Further Readings and Information Sources section at the end of this chapter.

22.6 SUMMARY

Object-oriented design translates the OOA model of the real world into an implementation-specific model that can be realized in software. The OOD process can be described as a pyramid composed of four layers. The foundation layer focuses on the design of subsystems that implement major system functions. The class layer specifies the overall object architecture and the hierarchy of classes required to implement a system. The message layer indicates how collaboration between objects will be realized, and the responsibilities layer identifies the attributes and operations that characterize each class.

Like OOA, there are many different OOD methods. UML is an attempt to provide a single approach to OOD that is applicable in all application domains. UML and other methods approach the design process through two levels of abstraction—design of subsystems (architecture) and design of individual objects.

During system design, the architecture of the object-oriented system is developed. In addition to developing subsystems, their interactions, and their placement in architectural layers, system design considers the user interaction component, a task management component, and a data management component. These subsystem components provide a design infrastructure that enables the application to operate effectively. The object design process focuses on the description of data structures that implement class attributes, algorithms that implement operations, and messages that enable collaborations and object relationships.

Design patterns allow the designer to create the system architecture by integrating reusable components. Object-oriented programming extends the design model into the executable domain. An OO programming language is used to translate the classes, attributes, operations, and messages into a form that can be executed by a machine.

REFERENCES

[BEN99] Bennett, S., S. McRobb, and R. Farmer, *Object Oriented System Analysis and Design Using UML,* McGraw-Hill, 1999.

[BIH92] Bihari, T. and P. Gopinath, "Object-Oriented Real-Time Systems: Concepts and Examples," *Computer,* vol. 25, no. 12, December 1992, pp. 25–32.

[BOO94] Booch, G., *Object-Oriented Analysis and Design,* 2nd ed., Benjamin Cummings, 1994.

[BOO99] Booch, G., I. Jacobson, J. Rumbaugh, *The Unified Modeling Language User Guide,* Addison-Wesley, 1999.

[BRO91] Brown, A.W., *Object-Oriented Databases,* McGraw-Hill, 1991.

[BUS96] Buschmann, F., et al., *A System of Patterns: Pattern Oriented System Architecture,* Wiley, 1996.

[CHA93] De Champeaux, D., D. Lea, and P. Faure, *Object-Oriented System Development,* Addison-Wesley, 1993.

[COA91] Coad, P. and E. Yourdon, *Object-Oriented Design,* Prentice-Hall, 1991.

[COX85] Cox, B., "Software ICs and Objective-C," *UnixWorld,* Spring 1985.

[DAV95] Davis, A., "Object-Oriented Requirements to Object-Oriented Design: An Easy Transition?" *Journal of Systems Software,* vol. 30, 1995, pp. 151–159.

[DOU99] Douglass, B., *Real-Time UML: Developing Efficient Objects for Embedded Systems,* Addison-Wesley, 1999.

[FIC92] Fichman, R. and C. Kemerer, "Object-Oriented and Conceptual Design Methodologies," *Computer,* vol. 25, no. 10, October 1992, pp. 22–39.

[GAM95] Gamma, E., et al., *Design Patterns,* Addison-Wesley, 1995.

[GOL83] Goldberg, A. and D. Robson, *Smalltalk-80: The Language and Its Implementation,* Addison-Wesley, 1983.

[JAC92] Jacobson, I., *Object-Oriented Software Engineering,* Addison-Wesley, 1992.

[JAC99] Jacobson, I., G. Booch, J. Rumbaugh, *Unified Software Development Process,* Addison-Wesley, 1999.

[MEY90] Meyer, B., *Object-Oriented Software Construction,* 2nd ed., Prentice-Hall, 1988.

[PRE95] Pree, W., *Design Patterns for Object-Oriented Software Development,* Addison-Wesley, 1995.

[RUM91] Rumbaugh, J., et al., *Object-Oriented Modeling and Design,* Prentice-Hall, 1991.

[RUM99] Rumbaugh, J., I. Jacobson, and G. Booch, *The Unified Modeling Language Reference Manual,* Addison-Wesley, 1999.

[RAO94] Rao, B.A., *Object-Oriented Databases: Technology, Applications and Products,* McGraw-Hill, 1994.

[TAY92] Taylor, D.A., *Object-Oriented Information Systems,* Wiley, 1992.

[WIR90] Wirfs-Brock, R., B. Wilkerson, and L. Weiner, *Designing Object-Oriented Software,* Prentice-Hall, 1990.

PROBLEMS AND POINTS TO PONDER

22.1. The design pyramid for OOD differs somewhat from the pyramid described for conventional software design (Chapter 13). Discuss the differences and similarities of the two pyramids.

22.2. How do OOD and structured design differ? What aspects of these two design methods are the same?

22.3. Review the five criteria for effective OO modularity discussed in Section 22.1.2. Using the design approach described later in the chapter, demonstrate how these five criteria are achieved.

22.4. Using outside references on UML, prepare a one-hour tutorial for your class. Be sure to show all important diagrammatic modeling conventions used in UML.

22.5. Select an older OOD method presented in Section 22.1.3 and prepare a one-hour tutorial for your class. Be sure to show all important diagrammatic modeling conventions that the authors suggest.

22.6. Discuss how the use-case can serve as an important source of information for design.

22.7. Research a GUI development environment and show how the user interaction component is implemented in the real world. What design patterns are offered and how are they used?

22.8. Task management for OO systems can be quite complex. Do some research of OOD methods for real-time systems (e.g., [BIH92] or [DOU99]) and determine how task management is achieved in that context.

22.9. Discuss how the data management component is implemented in a typical OO development environment.

22.10. Write a two- or three-page paper on object-oriented databases and discuss how they might be used to develop the data management component.

22.11. How does a designer recognize tasks that must be concurrent?

22.12. Apply the OOD approach discussed in this chapter to flesh out the design for the *SafeHome* system. Define all relevant subsystems and develop object designs for important classes.

22.13. Apply OOD approach discussed in this chapter to the PHTRS system described in Problem 12.13.

22.14. Describe a video game and apply OOD approach discussed in this chapter to represent its design.

22.15. You are responsible for the development of an electronic mail (e-mail) system to be implemented on a PC network. The e-mail system will enable users to create letters to be mailed to another user, general distribution, or a specific address list. Letters can be read, copied, stored, and the like. The e-mail system will use existing word-processing capability to create letters. Using this description as a starting point, derive a set of requirements and apply OOD techniques to create a top-level design for the e-mail system.

22.16. A small island nation has decided to build an air traffic control (ATC) system for its one airport. The system is specified as follows:

> All aircraft landing at the airport must have a transponder that transmits aircraft type and flight data in high-density packed format to the ATC ground station. The ATC ground station can query an aircraft for specific information. When the ATC ground station receives data, it is unpacked and stored in an aircraft database. A computer graphics display is created from the stored information and displayed for an air traffic controller. The display is updated every 2 seconds. All information is analyzed to determine if "dangerous situations" are present. The air traffic controller can query the database for specific information about any plane displayed on the screen.

Using OOD, create a design for the ATC system. Do not attempt to implement it!

FURTHER READINGS AND INFORMATION SOURCES

In addition to the many references in this chapter, books by Gossain and Graham (*Object Modeling and Design Strategies,* SIGS Books, 1998); Meyer (*Object-Oriented Software Construction,* 2nd ed., Prentice-Hall, 1997); Reil (*Object-Oriented Design Through Heuristics,* Addison-Wesley, 1996); and Walden and Nerson (*Seamless Object-Oriented Software Architecture: Analysis and Design of Reliable Systems,* Prentice-Hall, 1995) cover OOD in considerable detail. Fowler (*Refactoring: Improving the Design of Existing Code,* Addison-Wesley, 1999) addresses the use of object-oriented techniques to redesign and rebuild old programs to improve their design quality.

Many recent books published on object-oriented design emphasize UML. Those serious about applying UML in their work should acquire [BOO99], [RUM99], and [JAC99]. In addition, many of the books referenced in the Further Reading and Information Sources section of Chapter 21 also address design in considerable detail.

The use of design patterns for the development of object-oriented software has important implications for component-based software engineering, reusability in general, and the overall quality of resultant systems. In addition to [BUS96] and [GAM95], many recent books are dedicated to the subject:

Ambler, S.W., *Process Patterns: Building Large-Scale Systems Using Object Technology,* Cambridge University Press, 1999.

Coplien, J.O. and D.C. Schmidt, *Pattern Languages of Program Design,* Addison-Wesley, 1995.

Fowler, M., *Analysis Patterns: Reusable Object Models,* Addison-Wesley, 1996.

Larman, C., *Applying UML and Patterns: An Introduction to Object-Oriented Analysis and Design,* Prentice-Hall, 1997.

Martin, R.C., et al., *Pattern Languages of Program Design 3,* Addison-Wesley, 1997.

Rising, L. and J. Coplien (eds.), *The Patterns Handbook: Techniques, Strategies, and Applications,* SIGS Books, 1998.

Pree, W., *Design Patterns for Object-Oriented Software Development,* Addison-Wesley, 1995.

Vlissides, J., Pattern Hatching: *Design Patterns Applied,* Addison-Wesley, 1998.

Vlissides, J.M., J.O. Coplien, and N. Kerth, *Pattern Languages of Program Design 2,* Addison-Wesley, 1996.

Hundreds of books have been published on object-oriented programming. A sampling of OOP language-specific books follows:

C++: Cohoon, J.P., *C++ Program Design: An Introduction to Programming and Object-Oriented Design,* McGraw Hill, 1998.

Barclay, K. and J. Savage, *Object-Oriented Design with C++,* Prentice-Hall, 1997.

Eiffel: Thomas, P. and R. Weedon, *Object-Oriented Programming in Eiffel,* Addison-Wesley, 1997.

Jezequel, J.M., *Object-Oriented Software Engineering with Eiffel,* Addison-Wesley, 1996.

Java: Coad, P., M. Mayfield, and J. Kern, *Java Design: Building Better Apps and Applets,* 2nd ed., Prentice-Hall, 1998.

Lewis, J. and W. Loftus, *Java Software Solutions: Foundations of Program,* Addison-Wesley, 1997.

Smalltalk: Sharp, A., *Smalltalk by Example: The Developer's Guide,* McGraw-Hill, 1997.

LaLonde, W.R. and J.R. Pugh, *Programming in Smalltalk,* Prentice-Hall, 1995.

Books that cover OOD topics using two or more OO programming languages provide insight and comparison of language features. Titles include:

Drake, C., *Object-Oriented Programming With C++ and Smalltalk,* Prentice-Hall, 1998.

Joyner, I., *Objects Unencapsulated: Java, Eiffel and C++,* Prentice-Hall, 1999.

Zeigler, B.P., *Objects and Systems: Principled Design with Implementations in C++ and Java,* Springer-Verlag, 1997.

A wide variety of information sources on object-oriented design and related subjects is available on the Internet. An up-to-date list of World Wide Web references that are relevant to OOD can be found at the SEPA Web site:

http://www.mhhe.com/engcs/compsci/pressman/resources/OOD.mhtml

CHAPTER

23 OBJECT-ORIENTED TESTING

KEY CONCEPTS

The objective of testing, stated simply, is to find the greatest possible number of errors with a manageable amount of effort applied over a realistic time span. Although this fundamental objective remains unchanged for object-oriented software, the nature of OO programs changes both testing strategy and testing tactics.

It might be argued that, as OOA and OOD mature, greater reuse of design patterns will mitigate the need for heavy testing of OO systems. Exactly the opposite is true. Binder [BIN94b] discusses this when he states:

> [E]ach reuse is a new context of usage and retesting is prudent. It seems likely that more, not less, testing will be needed to obtain high reliability in object-oriented systems.

The testing of OO systems presents a new set of challenges to the software engineer. The definition of testing must be broadened to include error discovery techniques (formal technical reviews) applied to OOA and OOD models. The completeness and consistency of OO representations must be assessed as they are built. Unit testing loses much of its meaning, and integration strategies change significantly. In summary, both testing strategies and testing tactics must account for the unique characteristics of OO software.

QUICK LOOK

What is it? The architecture of object-oriented software results in a series of layered subsystems that encapsulate collaborating classes. Each of these system elements (subsystems and classes) perform functions that help to achieve system requirements. It is necessary to test an OO system at a variety of different levels in an effort to uncover errors that may occur as classes collaborate with one another and subsystems communicate across architectural layers.

Who does it? Object-oriented testing is performed by software engineers and testing specialists.

Why is it important? You have to execute the program before it gets to the customer with the specific intent of removing all errors, so that the customer will not experience the frustration associated with a poor-quality product. In order to find the highest possible number of errors, tests must be conducted systematically and test cases must be designed using disciplined techniques.

What are the steps? OO testing is strategically similar to the testing of conventional systems, but it is tactically different. Because the OO analysis and design models are similar in structure and content to the resultant OO program, "testing" begins with the review of these models. Once code has been generated, OO testing begins "in the small" with class testing. A series of tests are designed that exercise class operations and examine

QUICK LOOK

whether errors exist as one class collaborates with other classes. As classes are integrated to form a subsystem, thread-based, use-based, and cluster testing, along with fault-based approaches, are applied to fully exercise collaborating classes. Finally, use-cases (developed as part of the OO analysis model) are used to uncover errors at the software validation level.

What is the work product? A set of test cases to exercise classes, their collaborations, and behaviors is designed and documented; expected results defined; and actual results recorded.

How do I ensure that I've done it right? When you begin testing, change your point of view. Try hard to "break" the software! Design test cases in a disciplined fashion and review the test cases you do create for thoroughness.

23.1 BROADENING THE VIEW OF TESTING

The construction of object-oriented software begins with the creation of analysis and design models (Chapters 21 and 22). Because of the evolutionary nature of the OO software engineering paradigm, these models begin as relatively informal representations of system requirements and evolve into detailed models of classes, class connections and relationships, system design and allocation, and object design (incorporating a model of object connectivity via messaging). At each stage, the models can be tested in an attempt to uncover errors prior to their propagation to the next iteration.

Quote:

"Because of their ability to detect and correct defects in upstream work products, technical reviews are at least as important in controlling cost and schedule as testing."

Steve McConnell

It can be argued that the review of OO analysis and design models is especially useful because the same semantic constructs (e.g., classes, attributes, operations, messages) appear at the analysis, design, and code levels. Therefore, a problem in the definition of class attributes that is uncovered during analysis will circumvent side effects that might occur if the problem were not discovered until design or code (or even the next iteration of analysis).

For example, consider a class in which a number of attributes are defined during the first iteration of OOA. An extraneous attribute is appended to the class (due to a misunderstanding of the problem domain). Two operations are then specified to manipulate the attribute. A review is conducted and a domain expert points out the error. By eliminating the extraneous attribute at this stage, the following problems and unnecessary effort may be avoided during analysis:

1. Special subclasses may have been generated to accommodate the unnecessary attribute or exceptions to it. Work involved in the creation of unnecessary subclasses has been avoided.
2. A misinterpretation of the class definition may lead to incorrect or extraneous class relationships.

3. The behavior of the system or its classes may be improperly characterized to accommodate the extraneous attribute.

If the error is not uncovered during analysis and propagated further, the following problems could occur (and will have been avoided because of the earlier review) during design:

1. Improper allocation of the class to subsystem and/or tasks may occur during system design.
2. Unnecessary design work may be expended to create the procedural design for the operations that address the extraneous attribute.
3. The messaging model will be incorrect (because messages must be designed for the operations that are extraneous).

ADVICE

There's an old saying about "nipping problems in the bud." If you spend time reviewing the OOA and OOD models, that's what you'll do.

If the error remains undetected during design and passes into the coding activity, considerable effort will be expended to generate code that implements an unnecessary attribute, two unnecessary operations, messages that drive interobject communication, and many other related issues. In addition, testing of the class will absorb more time than necessary. Once the problem is finally uncovered, modification of the system must be carried out with the ever-present potential for side effects that are caused by change.

During later stages of their development, OOA and OOD models provide substantial information about the structure and behavior of the system. For this reason, these models should be subjected to rigorous review prior to the generation of code.

All object-oriented models should be tested (in this context, the term *testing* is used to incorporate formal technical reviews) for correctness, completeness, and consistency [MGR94] within the context of the model's syntax, semantics, and pragmatics [LIN94].

23.2 TESTING OOA AND OOD MODELS

Analysis and design models cannot be tested in the conventional sense, because they cannot be executed. However, formal technical reviews (Chapter 8) can be used to examine the correctness and consistency of both analysis and design models.

23.2.1 Correctness of OOA and OOD Models

The notation and syntax used to represent analysis and design models will be tied to the specific analysis and design method that is chosen for the project. Hence, syntactic correctness is judged on proper use of the symbology; each model is reviewed to ensure that proper modeling conventions have been maintained.

During analysis and design, semantic correctness must be judged based on the model's conformance to the real world problem domain. If the model accurately reflects the real world (to a level of detail that is appropriate to the stage of development at which the model is reviewed), then it is semantically correct. To determine whether the model does, in fact, reflect the real world, it should be presented to problem domain experts, who will examine the class definitions and hierarchy for omissions and ambiguity. Class relationships (instance connections) are evaluated to determine whether they accurately reflect real world object connections.[1]

23.2.2 Consistency of OOA and OOD Models

The consistency of OOA and OOD models may be judged by "considering the relationships among entities in the model. An inconsistent model has representations in one part that are not correctly reflected in other portions of the model" [MGR94].

OOA Models

To assess consistency, each class and its connections to other classes should be examined. The class-responsibility-collaboration model and an object-relationship diagram can be used to facilitate this activity. As we noted in Chapter 21, the CRC model is composed on CRC index cards. Each CRC card lists the class name, its responsibilities (operations), and its collaborators (other classes to which it sends messages and on which it depends for the accomplishment of its responsibilities). The collaborations imply a series of relationships (i.e., connections) between classes of the OO system. The object-relationship model provides a graphic representation of the connections between classes. All of this information can be obtained from the OOA model (Chapter 21).

To evaluate the class model the following steps have been recommended [MGR94]:

What steps should we take to review the class model?

1. **Revisit the CRC model and the object-relationship model.** Cross check to ensure that all collaborations implied by the OOA model are properly represented.
2. **Inspect the description of each CRC index card to determine if a delegated responsibility is part of the collaborator's definition.** For example, consider a class defined for a point-of-sale checkout system, called *credit sale.* This class has a CRC index card illustrated in Figure 23.1. For this collection of classes and collaborations, we ask whether a responsibility (e.g., *read credit card*) is accomplished if delegated to the named collaborator (**credit card**). That is, does the class **credit card** have an operation that enables it to be read? In this case the answer is, "Yes." The object-relationship is traversed to ensure that all such connections are valid.
3. **Invert the connection to ensure that each collaborator that is asked for service is receiving requests from a reasonable source.** For example, if the **credit card** class receives a request for **purchase amount** from the **credit sale** class, there would be a problem. **Credit card** does not know the **purchase amount.**

XRef
Additional suggestions for conducting a CRC model review are presented in Chapter 21.

---

1 Use-cases can be invaluable in tracking analysis and design models against real world usage scenarios for the OO system.

Class name: Credit sale	
Class type: Transaction event	
Class characteristics: Nontangible, atomic, sequential, permanent, guarded	
Responsibilities:	Collaborators:
Read credit card	Credit card
Get authorization	Credit authority
Post purchase amount	Product ticket
	Sales ledger
	Audit file
Generate bill	Bill

FIGURE 23.1 An example CRC index card used for review

4. **Using the inverted connections examined in step 3, determine whether other classes might be required and whether responsibilities are properly grouped among the classes.**
5. **Determine whether widely requested responsibilities might be combined into a single responsibility.** For example, *read credit card* and *get authorization* occur in every situation. They might be combined into a *validate credit request* responsibility that incorporates getting the credit card number and gaining authorization.
6. **Steps 1 through 5 are applied iteratively to each class and through each evolution of the OOA model.**

OOD Model

Once the OOD model (Chapter 22) is created, reviews of the system design and the object design should also be conducted. The system design depicts the overall product architecture, the subsystems that compose the product, the manner in which subsystems are allocated to processors, the allocation of classes to subsystems, and the design of the user interface. The object model presents the details of each class and the messaging activities that are necessary to implement collaborations between classes.

The system design is reviewed by examining the object-behavior model developed during OOA and mapping required system behavior against the subsystems designed to accomplish this behavior. Concurrency and task allocation are also reviewed within the context of system behavior. The behavioral states of the system are evaluated to determine which exist concurrently. Use-case scenarios are used to exercise the user interface design.

The object model should be tested against the object-relationship network to ensure that all design objects contain the necessary attributes and operations to implement the collaborations defined for each CRC index card. In addition, the detailed specification of operation details (i.e., the algorithms that implement the operations) are reviewed using conventional inspection techniques.

23.3 OBJECT-ORIENTED TESTING STRATEGIES

Quote:

"The best tester isn't the one who finds the most bugs . . . The best tester is the one who gets the most bugs fixed."

Cem Kaner et al.

The classical strategy for testing computer software begins with "testing in the small" and works outward toward "testing in the large." Stated in the jargon of software testing (Chapter 18), we begin with unit testing, then progress toward integration testing, and culminate with validation and system testing. In conventional applications, unit testing focuses on the smallest compilable program unit—the subprogram (e.g., module, subroutine, procedure, component). Once each of these units has been tested individually, it is integrated into a program structure while a series of regression tests are run to uncover errors due to interfacing between the modules and side effects caused by the addition of new units. Finally, the system as a whole is tested to ensure that errors in requirements are uncovered.

23.3.1 Unit Testing in the OO Context

When object-oriented software is considered, the concept of the unit changes. Encapsulation drives the definition of classes and objects. This means that each class and each instance of a class (object) packages attributes (data) and the operations (also known as *methods* or *services*) that manipulate these data. Rather than testing an individual module, the smallest testable unit is the encapsulated class or object. Because a class can contain a number of different operations and a particular operation may exist as part of a number of different classes, the meaning of unit testing changes dramatically.

KEY POINT

Class testing for OO software is equivalent to module unit testing for conventional software. It is not advisable to test operations in isolation.

We can no longer test a single operation in isolation (the conventional view of unit testing) but rather as part of a class. To illustrate, consider a class hierarchy in which an operation *X* is defined for the superclass and is inherited by a number of subclasses. Each subclass uses operation *X*, but it is applied within the context of the private attributes and operations that have been defined for the subclass. Because the context in which operation *X* is used varies in subtle ways, it is necessary to test operation *X* in the context of each of the subclasses. This means that testing operation *X* in a vacuum (the traditional unit testing approach) is ineffective in the object-oriented context.

Class testing for OO software is the equivalent of unit testing for conventional software.[2] Unlike unit testing of conventional software, which tends to focus on the algorithmic detail of a module and the data that flow across the module interface, class

2 Test case design methods for OO classes are discussed in Sections 23.4 through 23.6.

testing for OO software is driven by the operations encapsulated by the class and the state behavior of the class.

23.3.2 Integration Testing in the OO Context

Because object-oriented software does not have a hierarchical control structure, conventional top-down and bottom-up integration strategies have little meaning. In addition, integrating operations one at a time into a class (the conventional incremental integration approach) is often impossible because of the "direct and indirect interactions of the components that make up the class" [BER93].

KEY POINT

The OO testing integration strategy focuses on groups of classes that collaborate or communicate in some manner.

There are two different strategies for integration testing of OO systems [BIN94a]. The first, *thread-based testing,* integrates the set of classes required to respond to one input or event for the system. Each *thread* is integrated and tested individually. Regression testing is applied to ensure that no side effects occur. The second integration approach, *use-based testing,* begins the construction of the system by testing those classes (called *independent classes*) that use very few (if any) of server classes. After the independent classes are tested, the next layer of classes, called *dependent classes,* that use the independent classes are tested. This sequence of testing layers of dependent classes continues until the entire system is constructed. Unlike conventional integration, the use of drivers and stubs (Chapter 18) as replacement operations is to be avoided, when possible.

Cluster testing [MGR94] is one step in the integration testing of OO software. Here, a cluster of collaborating classes (determined by examining the CRC and object-relationship model) is exercised by designing test cases that attempt to uncover errors in the collaborations.

23.3.3 Validation Testing in an OO Context

At the validation or system level, the details of class connections disappear. Like conventional validation, the validation of OO software focuses on user-visible actions and user-recognizable output from the system. To assist in the derivation of validation tests, the tester should draw upon the use-cases (Chapter 20) that are part of the analysis model. The use-case provides a scenario that has a high likelihood of uncovered errors in user interaction requirements.

XRef

Virtually all of the black-box testing methods discussed in Chapter 17 are applicable for OO.

Conventional black-box testing methods can be used to drive validations tests. In addition, test cases may be derived from the object-behavior model and from event flow diagram created as part of OOA.

23.4 TEST CASE DESIGN FOR OO SOFTWARE

Test case design methods for OO software are still evolving. However, an overall approach to OO test case design has been defined by Berard [BER93]:

1. Each test case should be uniquely identified and explicitly associated with the class to be tested.

2. The purpose of the test should be stated.
3. A list of testing steps should be developed for each test and should contain [BER93]:
   a. A list of specified states for the object that is to be tested.
   b. A list of messages and operations that will be exercised as a consequence of the test.
   c. A list of exceptions that may occur as the object is tested.
   d. A list of external conditions (i.e., changes in the environment external to the software that must exist in order to properly conduct the test).
   e. Supplementary information that will aid in understanding or implementing the test.

Unlike conventional test case design, which is driven by an input-process-output view of software or the algorithmic detail of individual modules, object-oriented testing focuses on designing appropriate sequences of operations to exercise the states of a class.

23.4.1 The Test Case Design Implications of OO Concepts

As we have already seen, the OO class is the target for test case design. Because attributes and operations are encapsulated, testing operations outside of the class is generally unproductive. Although encapsulation is an essential design concept for OO, it can create a minor obstacle when testing. As Binder [BIN94a] notes, "Testing requires reporting on the concrete and abstract state of an object." Yet, encapsulation can make this information somewhat difficult to obtain. Unless built-in operations are provided to report the values for class attributes, a snapshot of the state of an object may be difficult to acquire.

WebRef
An excellent collection of papers, resources, and a bibliography on OO testing can be found at **www.rbsc.com**

Inheritance also leads to additional challenges for the test case designer. We have already noted that each new context of usage requires retesting, even though reuse has been achieved. In addition, multiple inheritance[3] complicates testing further by increasing the number of contexts for which testing is required [BIN94a]. If subclasses instantiated from a superclass are used within the same problem domain, it is likely that the set of test cases derived for the superclass can be used when testing the subclass. However, if the subclass is used in an entirely different context, the superclass test cases will have little applicability and a new set of tests must be designed.

23.4.2 Applicability of Conventional Test Case Design Methods

The white-box testing methods described in Chapter 17 can be applied to the operations defined for a class. Basis path, loop testing, or data flow techniques can help to ensure that every statement in an operation has been tested. However, the con-

3 An OOD concept that should be used with extreme care.

cise structure of many class operations causes some to argue that the effort applied to white-box testing might be better redirected to tests at a class level.

Black-box testing methods are as appropriate for OO systems as they are for systems developed using conventional software engineering methods. As we noted earlier in this chapter, use-cases can provide useful input in the design of black-box and state-based tests [AMB95].

KEY POINT

The strategy is to hypothesize a set of plausible faults and then derive tests to prove the hypothesis.

23.4.3 Fault-Based Testing[4]

The object of *fault-based testing* within an OO system is to design tests that have a high likelihood of uncovering plausible faults. Because the product or system must conform to customer requirements, the preliminary planning required to perform fault-based testing begins with the analysis model. The tester looks for plausible faults (i.e., aspects of the implementation of the system that may result in defects). To determine whether these faults exist, test cases are designed to exercise the design or code.

Consider a simple example.[5] Software engineers often make errors at the boundaries of a problem. For example, when testing a SQRT operation that returns errors for negative numbers, we know to try the boundaries: a negative number close to zero and zero itself. "Zero itself" checks whether the programmer made a mistake like

```
if (x > 0) calculate_the_square_root();
```

instead of the correct

```
if (x >= 0) calculate_the_square_root();
```

ADVICE

Because fault-based testing occurs at a detailed level, it is best reserved for operations and classes that are critical or suspect.

As another example, consider a Boolean expression:

```
if (a && !b || c)
```

Multicondition testing and related techniques probe for certain plausible faults in this expression, such as

&& should be **||**

! was left out where it was needed

There should be parentheses around **!b || c**

For each plausible fault, we design test cases that will force the incorrect expression to fail. In the previous expression, **(a=0, b=0, c=0)** will make the expression as given evaluate *false*. If the **&&** should have been **||**, the code has done the wrong thing and might branch to the wrong path.

---

4 Sections 23.4.3 through 23.4.7 have been adapted from an article by Brian Marick posted on the Internet newsgroup comp.testing. This adaptation is included with the permission of the author. For further discussion of these topics, see [MAR94].

5 The code presented in this and the following sections uses C++ syntax. For further information, see any good book on C++.

Of course, the effectiveness of these techniques depends on how testers perceive a "plausible fault." If real faults in an OO system are perceived to be "implausible," then this approach is really no better than any random testing technique. However, if the analysis and design models can provide insight into what is likely to go wrong, then fault-based testing can find significant numbers of errors with relatively low expenditures of effort.

What types of faults are encountered in operation calls and message connections?

Integration testing looks for plausible faults in operation calls or message connections. Three types of faults are encountered in this context: unexpected result, wrong operation/message used, incorrect invocation. To determine plausible faults as functions (operations) are invoked, the behavior of the operation must be examined.

Integration testing applies to attributes as well as to operations. The "behaviors" of an object are defined by the values that its attributes are assigned. Testing should exercise the attributes to determine whether proper values occur for distinct types of object behavior.

It is important to note that integration testing attempts to find errors in the client object, not the server. Stated in conventional terms, the focus of integration testing is to determine whether errors exist in the calling code, not the called code. The operation call is used as a clue, a way to find test requirements that exercise the calling code.

23.4.4 The Impact of OO Programming on Testing

Quote:

"If you want and expect a program to work, you will be more likely to see a working program—you will miss failures."

Cem Kaner et al.

There are several ways object-oriented programming can have an impact on testing. Depending on the approach to OOP,

- Some types of faults become less plausible (not worth testing for).
- Some types of faults become more plausible (worth testing now).
- Some new types of faults appear.

When an operation is invoked, it may be hard to tell exactly what code gets exercised. That is, the operation may belong to one of many classes. Also, it can be hard to determine the exact type or class of a parameter. When the code accesses it, it may get an unexpected value. The difference can be understood by considering a conventional function call:

```
x = func (y);
```

For conventional software, the tester need consider all behaviors attributed to **func** and nothing more. In an OO context, the tester must consider the behaviors of **base::func()**, of **derived::func()**, and so on. Each time **func** is invoked, the tester must consider the union of all distinct behaviors. This is easier if good OO design practices are followed and the difference between superclasses and subclasses (in C++ jargon, these are called *base classes* and *derived classes*) are limited. The testing approach for base and derived classes is essentially the same. The difference is one of bookkeeping.

Testing OO class operations is analogous to testing code that takes a function parameter and then invokes it. Inheritance is a convenient way of producing polymorphic operations. At the call site, what matters is not the inheritance, but the polymorphism. Inheritance does make the search for test requirements more straightforward.

By virtue of OO software architecture and construction, are some types of faults more plausible for an OO system and others less plausible? The answer is, "Yes." For example, because OO operations are generally smaller, more time tends to be spent on integration because there are more opportunities for integration faults. Therefore, integration faults become more plausible.

23.4.5 Test Cases and the Class Hierarchy

As noted earlier in this chapter, inheritance does not obviate the need for thorough testing of all derived classes. In fact, it can actually complicate the testing process.

Consider the following situation. A class **base** contains operations *inherited* and *redefined*. A class **derived** redefines *redefined* to serve in a local context. There is little doubt the **derived::redefined()** has to be tested because it represents a new design and new code. But does **derived::inherited()** have to be retested?

KEY POINT

Even though a base class has been thoroughly tested, you will still have to test all classes derived from it.

If **derived::inherited()** calls *redefined* and the behavior of *redefined* has changed, **derived::inherited()** may mishandle the new behavior. Therefore, it needs new tests even though the design and code have not changed. It is important to note, however, that only a subset of all tests for **derived::inherited()** may have to be conducted. If part of the design and code for *inherited* does not depend on *redefined* (i.e., that does not call it nor call any code that indirectly calls it), that code need not be retested in the derived class.

Base::redefined() and **derived::redefined()** are two different operations with different specifications and implementations. Each would have a set of test requirements derived from the specification and implementation. Those test requirements probe for plausible faults: integration faults, condition faults, boundary faults, and so forth. But the operations are likely to be similar. Their sets of test requirements will overlap. The better the OO design, the greater is the overlap. New tests need to be derived only for those **derived::redefined()** requirements that are not satisfied by the **base::redefined()** tests.

To summarize, the **base::redefined()** tests are applied to objects of class **derived**. Test inputs may be appropriate for both base and derived classes, but the expected results may differ in the derived class.

23.4.6 Scenario-Based Test Design

Fault-based testing misses two main types of errors: (1) incorrect specifications and (2) interactions among subsystems. When errors associated with incorrect specification occur, the product doesn't do what the customer wants. It might do the wrong thing or it might omit important functionality. But in either circumstance, quality (conformance to requirements) suffers. Errors associated with subsystem interaction occur when the behavior of one subsystem creates circumstances (e.g., events, data flow) that cause another subsystem to fail.

KEY POINT

Scenario-based testing will uncover errors that occur when any actor interacts with the OO software.

Scenario-based testing concentrates on what the user does, not what the product does. This means capturing the tasks (via use-cases) that the user has to perform, then applying them and their variants as tests.

Scenarios uncover interaction errors. But to accomplish this, test cases must be more complex and more realistic than fault-based tests. Scenario-based testing tends to exercise multiple subsystems in a single test (users do not limit themselves to the use of one subsystem at a time).

As an example, consider the design of scenario-based tests for a text editor. Use cases follow:

Use-Case: *Fix the Final Draft*

Background: It's not unusual to print the "final" draft, read it, and discover some annoying errors that weren't obvious from the on-screen image. This use-case describes the sequence of events that occurs when this happens.

1. Print the entire document.
2. Move around in the document, changing certain pages.
3. As each page is changed, it's printed.
4. Sometimes a series of pages is printed.

This scenario describes two things: a test and specific user needs. The user needs are obvious: (1) a method for printing single pages and (2) a method for printing a range of pages. As far as testing goes, there is a need to test editing after printing (as well as the reverse). The tester hopes to discover that the *printing* function causes errors in the *editing* function; that is, that the two software functions are not properly independent.

ADVICE

Although scenario-based testing has merit, you will get a higher return on time invested by reviewing use-cases when they are developed during OOA.

Use-Case: *Print a New Copy*

Background: Someone asks the user for a fresh copy of the document. It must be printed.

1. Open the document.
2. Print it.
3. Close the document.

Again, the testing approach is relatively obvious. Except that this document didn't appear out of nowhere. It was created in an earlier task. Does that task affect this one?

In many modern editors, documents remember how they were last printed. By default, they print the same way next time. After the *Fix the Final Draft* scenario, just selecting "Print" in the menu and clicking the "Print" button in the dialog box will cause the last corrected page to print again. So, according to the editor, the correct scenario should look like this:

Use-Case: *Print a New Copy*

1. Open the document.
2. Select "Print" in the menu.
3. Check if you're printing a page range; if so, click to print the entire document.
4. Click on the Print button.
5. Close the document.

But this scenario indicates a potential specification error. The editor does not do what the user reasonably expects it to do. Customers will often overlook the check noted in step 3 above. They will then be annoyed when they trot off to the printer and find one page when they wanted 100. Annoyed customers signal specification bugs.

A test case designer might miss this dependency in test design, but it is likely that the problem would surface during testing. The tester would then have to contend with the probable response, "That's the way it's supposed to work!"

23.4.7 Testing Surface Structure and Deep Structure

Surface structure refers to the externally observable structure of an OO program. That is, the structure that is immediately obvious to an end-user. Rather than performing functions, the users of many OO systems may be given objects to manipulate in some way. But whatever the interface, tests are still based on user tasks. Capturing these tasks involves understanding, watching, and talking with representative users (and as many nonrepresentative users as are worth considering).

KEY POINT

Structure testing occurs at two levels: (1) tests that exercise the structure observable by the end-user and (2) tests designed to exercise the internal program structure.

There will surely be some difference in detail. For example, in a conventional system with a command-oriented interface, the user might use the list of all commands as a testing checklist. If no test scenarios existed to exercise a command, testing has likely overlooked some user tasks (or the interface has useless commands). In a object-based interface, the tester might use the list of all objects as a testing checklist.

The best tests are derived when the designer looks at the system in a new or unconventional way. For example, if the system or product has a command-based interface, more thorough tests will be derived if the test case designer pretends that operations are independent of objects. Ask questions like, "Might the user want to use this operation—which applies only to the **Scanner** object—while working with the printer?" Whatever the interface style, test case design that exercises the surface structure should use both objects and operations as clues leading to overlooked tasks.

Deep structure refers to the internal technical details of an OO program. That is, the structure that is understood by examining the design and/or code. Deep structure testing is designed to exercise dependencies, behaviors, and communication mechanisms that have been established as part of the system and object design (Chapter 22) of OO software.

The analysis and design models are used as the basis for deep structure testing. For example, the object-relationship diagram or the subsystem collaboration diagram depicts collaborations between objects and subsystems that may not be externally visible. The test case design then asks: "Have we captured (as a test) some task that exercises the collaboration noted on the object-relationship diagram or the subsystem collaboration diagram? If not, why not?"

Design representations of class hierarchy provide insight into inheritance structure. Inheritance structure is used in fault-based testing. Consider a situation in which an operation named *caller* has only one argument and that argument is a reference to a base class. What might happen when *caller* is passed a derived class? What are the differences in behavior that could affect *caller?* The answers to these questions might lead to the design of specialized tests.

23.5 TESTING METHODS APPLICABLE AT THE CLASS LEVEL

In Chapter 17, we noted that software testing begins "in the small" and slowly progresses toward testing "in the large." Testing in the small focuses on a single class and the methods that are encapsulated by the class. Random testing and partitioning are methods that can be used to exercise a class during OO testing [KIR94].

23.5.1 Random Testing for OO Classes

To provide brief illustrations of these methods, consider a banking application in which an **account** class has the following operations: *open, setup, deposit, withdraw, balance, summarize, creditLimit,* and *close* [KIR94]. Each of these operations may be applied for **account**, but certain constraints (e.g., the account must be opened before other operations can be applied and closed after all operations are completed) are implied by the nature of the problem. Even with these constraints, there are many permutations of the operations. The minimum behavioral life history of an instance of **account** includes the following operations:

ADVICE

The number of possible permutations for random testing can grow quite large. A strategy similar to orthogonal array testing (Chapter 17) can be used to improve testing efficiency.

open•setup•deposit•withdraw•close

This represents the minimum test sequence for account. However, a wide variety of other behaviors may occur within this sequence:

open•setup•deposit•[deposit|withdraw|balance|summarize|creditLimit]^n•withdraw•close

A variety of different operation sequences can be generated randomly. For example:

Test case r_1: **open•setup•deposit•deposit•balance•summarize•withdraw•close**
Test case r_2: **open•setup•deposit•withdraw•deposit•balance•creditLimit•withdraw•close**

These and other random order tests are conducted to exercise different class instance life histories.

23.5.2 Partition Testing at the Class Level

Partition testing reduces the number of test cases required to exercise the class in much the same manner as equivalence partitioning (Chapter 17) for conventional software. Input and output are categorized and test cases are designed to exercise each category. But how are the partitioning categories derived?

What testing options are available at the class level?

State-based partitioning categorizes class operations based on their ability to change the state of the class. Again considering the **account** class, state operations include *deposit* and *withdraw*, whereas nonstate operations include *balance, summarize,* and *creditLimit.* Tests are designed in a way that exercises operations that change state and those that do not change state separately. Therefore,

Test case p_1: **open•setup•deposit•deposit•withdraw•withdraw•close**

Test case p_2: **open•setup•deposit•summarize•creditLimit•withdraw•close**

Test case p_1 changes state, while test case p_2 exercises operations that do not change state (other than those in the minimum test sequence).

Attribute-based partitioning categorizes class operations based on the attributes that they use. For the **account** class, the attributes **balance** and **creditLimit** can be used to define partitions. Operations are divided into three partitions: (1) operations that use **creditLimit**, (2) operations that modify **creditLimit**, and (3) operations that do not use or modify **creditLimit**. Test sequences are then designed for each partition.

Category-based partitioning categorizes class operations based on the generic function that each performs. For example, operations in the **account** class can be categorized in initialization operations (*open, setup*), computational operations (*deposit, withdraw*). queries (*balance, summarize, creditLimit*) and termination operations (*close*).

23.6 INTERCLASS TEST CASE DESIGN

Test case design becomes more complicated as integration of the OO system begins. It is at this stage that testing of collaborations between classes must begin. To illustrate "interclass test case generation" [KIR94], we expand the banking example introduced in Section 23.5 to include the classes and collaborations noted in Figure 23.2. The direction of the arrows in the figure indicates the direction of messages and the labeling indicates the operations that are invoked as a consequence of the collaborations implied by the messages.

Like the testing of individual classes, class collaboration testing can be accomplished by applying random and partitioning methods, as well as scenario-based testing and behavioral testing.

23.6.1 Multiple Class Testing

Kirani and Tsai [KIR94] suggest the following sequence of steps to generate multiple class random test cases:

1. For each client class, use the list of class operations to generate a series of random test sequences. The operations will send messages to other server classes.

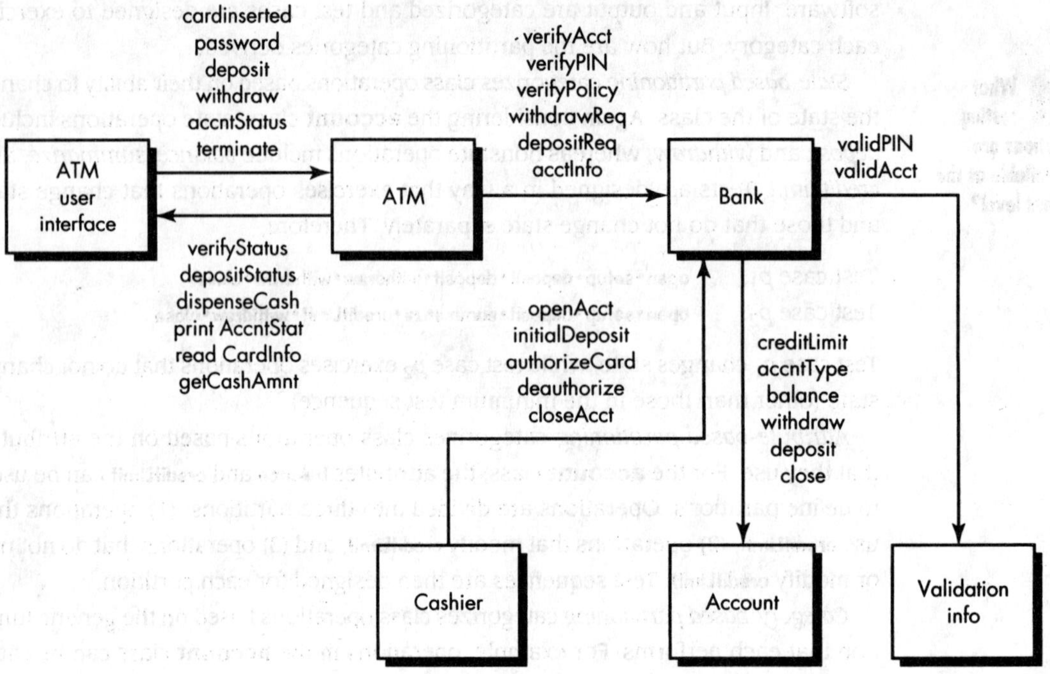

FIGURE 23.2 Class collaboration diagram for banking application [KIR94]

2. For each message that is generated, determine the collaborator class and the corresponding operation in the server object.
3. For each operation in the server object (that has been invoked by messages sent from the client object), determine the messages that it transmits.
4. For each of the messages, determine the next level of operations that are invoked and incorporate these into the test sequence.

To illustrate [KIR94], consider a sequence of operations for the **bank** class relative to an **ATM** class (Figure 23.2):

verifyAcct•verifyPIN•[[verifyPolicy•withdrawReq]|depositReq|acctInfoREQ]^n

A random test case for the **bank** class might be

test case r_3 = **verifyAcct•verifyPIN•depositReq**

In order to consider the collaborators involved in this test, the messages associated with each of the operations noted in test case r_3 is considered. **Bank** must collaborate with **ValidationInfo** to execute the *verifyAcct* and *verifyPIN*. **Bank** must collaborate with **account** to execute *depositReq*. Hence, a new test case that exercises these collaborations is

$$\text{test case } r_4 = \textbf{verifyAcct}_{\textbf{Bank}}[\textbf{validAcct}_{\textbf{ValidationInfo}}]\bullet\textbf{verifyPIN}_{\textbf{Bank}}\bullet[\textbf{validPin}_{\textbf{ValidationInfo}}]\bullet\textbf{depositReq}\bullet[\textbf{deposit}_{\textbf{account}}]$$

FIGURE 23.3
State transition diagram for account class [KIR94]

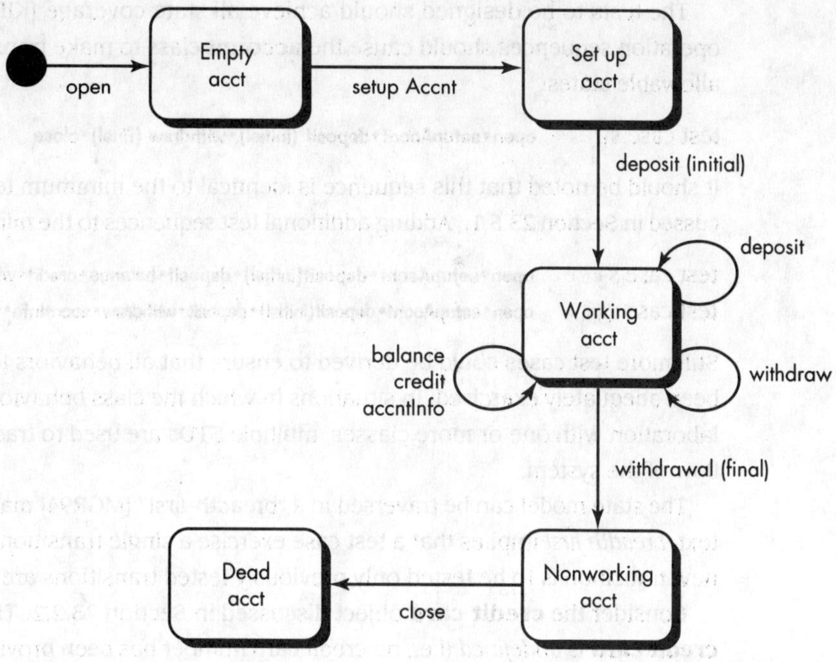

The approach for multiple class partition testing is similar to the approach used for partition testing of individual classes. A single class is partitioned as discussed in Section 23.4.5. However, the test sequence is expanded to include those operations that are invoked via messages to collaborating classes. An alternative approach partitions tests based on the interfaces to a particular class. Referring to Figure 23.2, the **bank** class receives messages from the **ATM** and **cashier** classes. The methods within **bank** can therefore be tested by partitioning them into those that serve **ATM** and those that serve **cashier**. State-based partitioning (Section 23.4.9) can be used to refine the partitions further.

23.6.2 Tests Derived from Behavior Models

In Chapter 21, we discussed the use of the state transition diagram as a model that represents the dynamic behavior of a class. The STD for a class can be used to help derive a sequence of tests that will exercise the dynamic behavior of the class (and those classes that collaborate with it). Figure 23.3 [KIR94] illustrates an STD for the **account** class discussed earlier.[6] Referring to the figure, initial transitions move through the *empty acct* and *setup acct* states. The majority of all behavior for instances of the class occurs while in the *working acct* state. A final withdrawal and close cause the account class to make transitions to the *nonworking acct* and *dead acct* states, respectively.

6 UML symbology is used for the STD shown in Figure 23.3. It differs slightly from the symbology used for STDs in Part Three of this book.

The tests to be designed should achieve all state coverage [KIR94]. That is, the operation sequences should cause the **account** class to make transition through all allowable states:

test case s_1: **open•setupAccnt•deposit (initial)•withdraw (final)•close**

It should be noted that this sequence is identical to the minimum test sequence discussed in Section 23.5.1. Adding additional test sequences to the minimum sequence,

test case s_2: **open•setupAccnt•deposit(initial)•deposit•balance•credit•withdraw (final)•close**

test case s_3: **open•setupAccnt•deposit(initial)•deposit•withdraw•accntInfo•withdraw (final)•close**

Still more test cases could be derived to ensure that all behaviors for the class have been adequately exercised. In situations in which the class behavior results in a collaboration with one or more classes, multiple STDs are used to track the behavioral flow of the system.

The state model can be traversed in a "breadth-first" [MGR94] manner. In this context, *breadth first* implies that a test case exercise a single transition and that when a new transition is to be tested only previously tested transitions are used.

Consider the **credit card** object discussed in Section 23.2.2. The initial state of **credit card** is *undefined* (i.e., no credit card number has been provided). Upon reading the credit card during a sale, the object takes on a *defined* state; that is, the attributes **card number** and **expiration date**, along with bank specific identifiers are defined. The credit card is *submitted* when it is sent for authorization and it is *approved* when authorization is received. The transition of **credit card** from one state to another can be tested by deriving test cases that cause the transition to occur. A breadth-first approach to this type of testing would not exercise *submitted* before it exercised *undefined* and *defined*. If it did, it would make use of transitions that had not been previously tested and would therefore violate the breadth-first criterion.

23.7 SUMMARY

The overall objective of object-oriented testing—to find the maximum number of errors with a minimum amount of effort—is identical to the objective of conventional software testing. But the strategy and tactics for OO testing differ significantly. The view of testing broadens to include the review of both the analysis and design model. In addition, the focus of testing moves away from the procedural component (the module) and toward the class.

Because the OO analysis and design models and the resulting source code are semantically coupled, testing (in the form of formal technical reviews) begins during these engineering activities. For this reason, the review of CRC, object-relationship, and object-behavior models can be viewed as first stage testing.

Once OOP has been accomplished, unit testing is applied for each class. The design of tests for a class uses a variety of methods: fault-based testing, random testing, and partition testing. Each of these methods exercises the operations encapsulated by the class. Test sequences are designed to ensure that relevant operations are exercised. The state of the class, represented by the values of its attributes, is examined to determine if errors exist.

Integration testing can be accomplished using a thread-based or use-based strategy. Thread-based testing integrates the set of classes that collaborate to respond to one input or event. Use-based testing constructs the system in layers, beginning with those classes that do not use server classes. Integration test case design methods can also use random and partition tests. In addition, scenario-based testing and tests derived from behavioral models can be used to test a class and its collaborators. A test sequence tracks the flow of operations across class collaborations.

OO system validation testing is black-box oriented and can be accomplished by applying the same black-box methods discussed for conventional software. However, scenario-based testing dominates the validation of OO systems, making the use-case a primary driver for validation testing.

REFERENCES

[AMB95] Ambler, S., "Using Use Cases," *Software Development,* July 1995, pp. 53–61.

[BER93] Berard, E.V., *Essays on Object-Oriented Software Engineering,* vol. 1, Addison-Wesley, 1993.

[BIN94a] Binder, R.V., "Testing Object-Oriented Systems: A Status Report," *American Programmer,* vol. 7, no. 4, April 1994, pp. 23–28.

[BIN94b] Binder, R.V., "Object-Oriented Software Testing," *CACM,* vol. 37, no. 9, September 1994, p. 29.

[KIR94] Kirani, S. and W.T. Tsai, "Specification and Verification of Object-Oriented Programs," Technical Report TR 94-64, Computer Science Department, University of Minnesota, December 1994.

[LIN94] Lindland, O.I., et al., "Understanding Quality in Conceptual Modeling," *IEEE Software,* vol. 11, no 4, July 1994, pp. 42–49.

[MAR94] Marick, B., *The Craft of Software Testing,* Prentice-Hall, 1994.

[MGR94] McGregor, J.D. and T.D. Korson, "Integrated Object-Oriented Testing and Development Processes," *CACM,* vol. 37, no. 9, September 1994, pp. 59–77.

PROBLEMS AND POINTS TO PONDER

23.1. In your own words, describe why the class is the smallest reasonable unit for testing within an OO system.

23.2. Why do we have to retest subclasses that are instantiated from an existing class, if the existing class has already been thoroughly tested? Can we use the test cases designed for the existing class?

23.3. Why should "testing" begin with the OOA and OOD activities?

23.4. Derive a set of CRC index cards for *SafeHome* and conduct the steps noted in Section 23.2.2 to determine if inconsistencies exist.

23.5. What is the difference between thread-based and use-based strategies for integration testing? How does cluster testing fit in?

23.6. Apply random testing and partitioning to three classes defined in the design for the *SafeHome* system that you produced for Problem 22.12. Produce test cases that indicate the operation sequences that will be invoked.

23.7. Apply multiple class testing and tests derived from the behavioral model to the *SafeHome* design.

23.8. Derive tests using methods noted in Problems 23.6 and 23.7 for the PHTRS system described in Problem 12.13.

23.9. Derive tests using methods noted in Problems 23.6 and 23.7 for the video game considered in Problem 22.14.

23.10. Derive tests using methods noted in Problems 23.6 and 23.7 for the e-mail system considered in Problem 22.15.

23.11. Derive tests using methods noted in Problems 23.6 and 23.7 for the ATC system considered in Problem 22.16.

23.12. Derive four additional tests using each of the methods noted in Problems 23.6 and 23.7 for the banking application presented in Sections 23.5 and 23.6.

FURTHER READINGS AND INFORMATION SOURCES

The literature for object-oriented testing is relatively sparse, although it has expanded somewhat in recent years. Binder (*Testing Object-Oriented Systems: Models, Patterns, and Tools,* Addison-Wesley, 2000) has written the most comprehensive treatment of the subject published to date. Siegel and Muller (*Object Oriented Software Testing: A Hierarchical Approach,* Wiley, 1996) proposed a practical testing strategy for OO systems. Marick (*The Craft of Software Testing: Subsystem Testing Including Object-Based and Object-Oriented Testing,* Prentice-Hall, 1995) covers testing for both conventional and OO software.

Anthologies of important papers on OO testing have been edited by Kung et al. (*Testing Object-Oriented Software,* IEEE Computer Society, 1998) and Braude (*Object Oriented Analysis, Design and Testing: Selected Readings,* IEEE Computer Society, 1998).

These IEEE tutorials provide an interesting historical perspective on development in OO testing.

Jorgensen *(Software Testing: A Craftsman's Approach,* CRC Press, 1995) and McGregor and Sykes (*Object-Oriented Software Development,* Van Nostrand-Reinhold, 1992) present chapters dedicated to the topic. Beizer (*Black-Box Testing,* Wiley, 1995) discusses a variety of test case design methods that are appropriate in an OO context. Binder (*Testing Object-Oriented Systems,* Addison-Wesley, 1996) and Marick [MAR94] present detailed treatments of OO testing. In addition, many of the sources noted for Chapter 17 are generally applicable to OO testing.

A wide variety of information sources on object-oriented testing and related subjects is available on the Internet. An up-to-date list of World Wide Web references that are relevant to OO testing can be found at the SEPA Web site:
http://www.mhhe.com/engcs/compsci/pressman/resources/OOT.mhtml

CHAPTER

24 TECHNICAL METRICS FOR OBJECT-ORIENTED SYSTEMS

KEY CONCEPTS

Early in this book we noted that measurement and metrics are key components of any engineering discipline—and object-oriented software engineering is no exception. Sadly, the use of metrics for OO systems has progressed much more slowly than the use of other OO methods. Ed Berard [BER95] notes the irony of measurement when he states:

> Software people seem to have a love-hate relationship with metrics. On one hand, they despise and distrust anything that sounds or looks like a measurement. They are quick to point out the "flaws" in the arguments of anyone who talks about measuring software products, software processes, and (especially) software people. On the other hand, these same people seem to have no problems identifying which programming language is the best, the stupid things that managers do to "ruin" projects, and who's methodology works in what situations.

The "love-hate relationship" that Berard notes is real. And yet, as OO systems become more pervasive, it is essential that software engineers have quantitative measurements for assessing the quality of designs at both the architectural and component levels. These measures enable an engineer to assess the software early in the process, making changes that will reduce complexity and improve the long-term viability of the end product.

QUICK LOOK

What is it? Building OO software has been an engineering activity that relies more on collective wisdom, folklore, and qualitative guidance than on quantitative evaluation. OO metrics have been introduced to help a software engineer use quantitative analysis to assess the quality of the design before a system is built. The focus of OO metrics is on the class—the fundamental building block of the OO architecture.

Who does it? Software engineers use OO metrics to help them build higher-quality software.

Why is it important? As we stated in the Quick Look for Chapter 19, qualitative assessment of computer software must be complemented with quantitative analysis. A software engineer needs objective criteria to help guide the design of the OO architecture, the classes and subsystems that populate the architecture, and the operations and attributes that constitute a class. The tester needs quantitative guidance that will help in the selection of test cases and their targets. Technical metrics provide a basis from which analysis, design, and testing can be conducted more objectively and assessed more quantitatively.

What are the steps? The first step in the measurement process is to derive the software measures and metrics that are appropriate for the representation of software that is being considered. Next, data required to derive the formulated metrics are ▶

QUICK LOOK

collected. Once computed, appropriate metrics are analyzed based on pre-established guidelines and past data. The results of the analysis are interpreted to gain insight into the quality of the software, and the results of the interpretation lead to modification of work products arising out of analysis, design, code, or test.

What is the work product? Software metrics that are computed using data collected from the analysis and design models, source code, and test cases.

How do I ensure that I've done it right? You should establish the objectives of measurement before the data collection begins, defining each OO metric in an unambiguous manner. Define only a few metrics and then use them to gain insight into the quality of a software engineering work product.

24.1 THE INTENT OF OBJECT-ORIENTED METRICS

The primary objectives for object-oriented metrics are no different than those for metrics derived for conventional software:

- to better understand the quality of the product
- to assess the effectiveness of the process
- to improve the quality of work performed at a project level

Each of these objectives is important, but for the software engineer, product quality must be paramount. But how do we measure the quality of an OO system? What characteristics of the design model can be assessed to determine whether the system will be easy to implement, amenable to test, simple to modify, and most important, acceptable to end-users? These questions are addressed throughout the remainder of this chapter.

24.2 THE DISTINGUISHING CHARACTERISTICS OF OBJECT-ORIENTED METRICS

Metrics for any engineered product are governed by the unique characteristics of the product. For example, it would be meaningless to compute miles per gallon for an electric automobile. The metric is sound for conventional (i.e., gasoline powered) cars but it does not apply when the mode of propulsion changes radically. Object-oriented software is fundamentally different than software developed using conventional methods. For this reason, the metrics for OO systems must be tuned to the characteristics that distinguish OO from conventional software.

Berard [BER95] defines five characteristics that lead to specialized metrics: localization, encapsulation, information hiding, inheritance, and object abstraction techniques. Each of these characteristics is discussed briefly in the sections that follow.[1]

1 This discussion has been adapted from [BER95].

24.2.1 Localization

Localization is a characteristic of software that indicates the manner in which information is concentrated within a program. For example, conventional methods for functional decomposition localize information around functions, which are typically implemented as procedural modules. Data-driven methods localize information around specific data structures. In the OO context, information is concentrated by encapsulating both data and process within the bounds of a class or object.

XRef
Technical metrics for conventional software are discussed in Chapter 19.

Because conventional software emphasizes function as a localization mechanism, software metrics have focused on the internal structure or complexity of functions (e.g., module length, cohesion or cyclomatic complexity) or the manner in which functions connect to one another (e.g., module coupling).

Since the class is the basic unit of an OO system, localization is based on objects. Therefore, metrics should apply to the class (object) as a complete entity. In addition, the relationship between operations (functions) and classes is not necessarily one to one. Therefore, metrics that reflect the manner in which classes collaborate must be capable of accommodating one-to-many and many-to-one relationships.

24.2.2 Encapsulation

Berard [BER95] defines encapsulation as "the packaging (or binding together) of a collection of items. Low-level examples of encapsulation [for conventional software] include records and arrays, [and] subprograms (e.g., procedures, functions, subroutines, and paragraphs) are mid-level mechanisms for encapsulation."

XRef
Basic design concepts are discussed in Chapter 13. Their application to OO software is discussed in Chapter 20.

For OO systems, encapsulation encompasses the responsibilities of a class, including its attributes (and other classes for aggregate objects) and operations, and the states of the class, as defined by specific attribute values.

Encapsulation influences metrics by changing the focus of measurement from a single module to a package of data (attributes) and processing modules (operations). In addition encapsulation encourages measurement at a higher level of abstraction. For example, later in this chapter metrics associated with the number of operations per class will be introduced. Contrast this level of abstraction to conventional metrics that focus on counts of Boolean conditions (cyclomatic complexity) or line of code counts.

24.2.3 Information Hiding

Information hiding suppresses (or hides) the operational details of a program component. Only the information necessary to access the component is provided to those other components that wish to access it.

A well-designed OO system should encourage information hiding. Therefore, metrics that provide an indication of the degree to which hiding has been achieved should provide an indication of the quality of the OO design.

24.2.4 Inheritance

Inheritance is a mechanism that enables the responsibilities of one object to be propagated to other objects. Inheritance occurs throughout all levels of a class hierarchy. In general, conventional software does not support this characteristic.

Because inheritance is a pivotal characteristic in many OO systems, many OO metrics focus on it. Examples (discussed later in this chapter) include number of *children* (number of immediate instances of a class), number of *parents* (number of immediate generalizations), and class hierarchy *nesting level* (depth of a class in an inheritance hierarchy).

24.2.5 Abstraction

Abstraction is a mechanism that enables the designer to focus on the essential details of a program component (either data or process) with little concern for lower-level details. As Berard states: "Abstraction is a relative concept. As we move to higher levels of abstraction we ignore more and more details, i.e., we provide a more general view of a concept or item. As we move to lower levels of abstraction, we introduce more details, i.e., we provide a more specific view of a concept or item."

Because a class is an abstraction that can be viewed at many different levels of detail and in a number of different ways (e.g., as a list of operations, as a sequence of states, as a series of collaborations), OO metrics represent abstractions in terms of measures of a class (e.g., number of instances per class per application, number or parameterized classes per application, and ratio of parameterized classes to nonparameterized classes).

24.3 METRICS FOR THE OO DESIGN MODEL

There is much about object-oriented design that is subjective—an experienced designer "knows" how to characterize an OO system so that it will effectively implement customer requirements. But, as an OO design model grows in size and complexity, a more objective view of the characteristics of the design can benefit both the experienced designer (who gains additional insight) and the novice (who obtains an indication of quality that would otherwise be unavailable).

In a detailed treatment of software metrics for OO systems, Whitmire [WHI97] describes nine distinct and measurable characteristics of an OO design:

What characteristics can be measured when we assess an OO design?

Size. Size is defined in terms of four views: population, volume, length, and functionality. *Population* is measured by taking a static count of OO entities such as classes or operations. *Volume* measures are identical to population measures but are collected dynamically—at a given instant of time. *Length* is a measure of a chain of interconnected design elements (e.g., the depth of an inheritance tree is a measure of length). *Functionality* metrics provide an indirect indication of the value delivered to the customer by an OO application.

Complexity. Like size, there are many differing views of software complexity [ZUS97]. Whitmire views complexity in terms of structural characteristics by examining how classes of an OO design are interrelated to one another.

Coupling. The physical connections between elements of the OO design (e.g., the number of collaborations between classes or the number of messages passed between objects) represent coupling within an OO system.

Sufficiency. Whitmire defines *sufficiency* as "the degree to which an abstraction possesses the features required of it, or the degree to which a design component possesses features in its abstraction, from the point of view of the current application." Stated another way, we ask: "What properties does this abstraction (class) need to possess to be useful to me?" [WHI97]. In essence, a design component (e.g., a class) is sufficient if it fully reflects all properties of the application domain object that it is modeling—that is, that the abstraction (class) possesses the features required of it.

Quote:

"Many of the design decisions for which I had to rely on folklore and myth can now be made using quantitative data."

Scott Whitmire

Completeness. The only difference between completeness and sufficiency is "the feature set against which we compare the abstraction or design component [WHI97]." Sufficiency compares the abstraction from the point of view of the current application. Completeness considers multiple points of view, asking the question: "What properties are required to fully represent the problem domain object?" Because the criterion for completeness considers different points of view, it has an indirect implication about the degree to which the abstraction or design component can be reused.

Cohesion. Like its counterpart in conventional software, an OO component should be designed in a manner that has all operations working together to achieve a single, well-defined purpose. The cohesiveness of a class is determined by examining the degree to which "the set of properties it possesses is part of the problem or design domain" [WHI97].

WebRef

A NASA technical report addressing quality metrics for OO systems can be downloaded from **satc.gsfc.nasa.gov/support/index.html**

Primitiveness. A characteristic that is similar to simplicity, primitiveness (applied to both operations and classes) is the degree to which an operation is *atomic*—that is, the operation cannot be constructed out of a sequence of other operations contained within a class. A class that exhibits a high degree of primitiveness encapsulates only primitive operations.

Similarity. The degree to which two or more classes are similar in terms of their structure, function, behavior, or purpose is indicated by this measure.

Volatility. As we have seen earlier in this book, design changes can occur when requirements are modified or when modifications occur in other parts of an application, resulting in mandatory adaptation of the design component in question. Volatility of an OO design component measures the likelihood that a change will occur.

Whitmire's derivation of metrics for these design characteristics is beyond the scope of this book. Interested readers should see [WHI97] for more detail.

In reality, technical metrics for OO systems can be applied not only to the design model, but also the analysis model. In the sections that follow, we explore metrics that provide an indication of quality at the OO class level and the operation level. In addition, metrics applicable for project management and testing are also explored.

24.4 CLASS-ORIENTED METRICS

The class is the fundamental unit of an OO system. Therefore, measures and metrics for an individual class, the class hierarchy, and class collaborations will be invaluable to a software engineer who must assess design quality. In earlier chapters, we saw that the class encapsulates operations (processing) and attributes (data). The class is often the "parent" for subclasses (sometimes called *children*) that inherit its attributes and operations. The class often collaborates with other classes. Each of these characteristics can be used as the basis for measurement.[2]

24.4.1 The CK Metrics Suite

One of the most widely referenced sets of OO software metrics has been proposed by Chidamber and Kemerer [CHI94]. Often referred to as the *CK metrics suite,* the authors have proposed six class-based design metrics for OO systems.[3]

Weighted methods per class (WMC). Assume that n methods of complexity c_1, $c_2, \ldots, c_n$ are defined for a class **C**. The specific complexity metric that is chosen (e.g., cyclomatic complexity) should be normalized so that nominal complexity for a method takes on a value of 1.0.

$$\text{WMC} = \Sigma\, c_i$$

for $i = 1$ to n. The number of methods and their complexity are reasonable indicators of the amount of effort required to implement and test a class. In addition, the larger the number of methods, the more complex is the inheritance tree (all subclasses inherit the methods of their parents). Finally, as the number of methods grows for a given class, it is likely to become more and more application specific, thereby limiting potential reuse. For all of these reasons, WMC should be kept as low as is reasonable.

KEY POINT The number of methods and their complexity are directly correlated to the effort required to test a class.

2 It should be noted that the validity of some of the metrics discussed in this chapter is currently debated in the technical literature. Those who champion measurement theory demand a degree of formalism that some of the OO metrics do not provide. However, it is reasonable to state that all of the metrics noted provide useful insight for the software engineer.

3 Chidamber, Darcy, and Kemerer use the term *methods* rather than *operations*. Their usage of the term is reflected in this section.

Although it would seem relatively straightforward to develop a count for the number of methods in a class, the problem is actually more complex than it seems. Churcher and Shepperd [CHU95] discuss this issue when they write:

> In order to count methods, we must answer the fundamental question "Does a method belong only to the class which defines it, or does it also belong to every class which inherits it directly or indirectly?" Questions such as this may seem trivial since the runtime system will ultimately resolve them. However, the implications for metrics may be significant.
>
> One possibility is to restrict counting to the current class, ignoring inherited members. The motivation for this would be that inherited members have already been counted in the classes where they are defined, so the class increment is the best measure of its functionality—what it does reflects its reason for existing. In order to understand what a class does, the most important source of information is its own operations. If a class cannot respond to a message (i.e., it lacks a corresponding method of its own) then it will pass the message on to its parent(s).
>
> At the other extreme, counting could include all methods defined in the current class, together with all inherited methods. This approach emphasizes the importance of the state space, rather than the class increment, in understanding a class.
>
> Between these extremes lie a number of other possibilities. For example, one could restrict counting to the current class and members inherited directly from parent(s). This approach would be based on the argument that the specialization of parent classes is the most directly relevant to the behavior of a child class.

Like most counting conventions in software metrics, any of the approaches just outlined is acceptable, as long as the counting approach is applied consistently whenever metrics are collected.

ADVICE

Inheritance is an extremely powerful feature that can get you into trouble, if you use it without care. Use DIT and other related metrics to give yourself a reading on the complexity of class hierarchies.

Depth of the inheritance tree (DIT). This metric is "the maximum length from the node to the root of the tree" [CHI94]. Referring to Figure 24.1, the value of DIT for the class-hierarchy shown is 4. As DIT grows, it is likely that lower-level classes will inherit many methods. This leads to potential difficulties when attempting to predict the behavior of a class. A deep class hierarchy (DIT is large) also leads to greater design complexity. On the positive side, large DIT values imply that many methods may be reused.

Number of children (NOC). The subclasses that are immediately subordinate to a class in the class hierarchy are termed its *children*. Referring to Figure 24.1, class $\mathbf{C_2}$ has three children—subclasses $\mathbf{C_{21}}$, $\mathbf{C_{22}}$, and $\mathbf{C_{23}}$. As the number of children grows, reuse increases but also, as NOC increases, the abstraction represented by the parent class can be diluted. That is, some of the children may not really be appropriate members of the parent class. As NOC increases, the amount of testing (required to exercise each child in its operational context) will also increase.

FIGURE 24.1
A class hierarchy

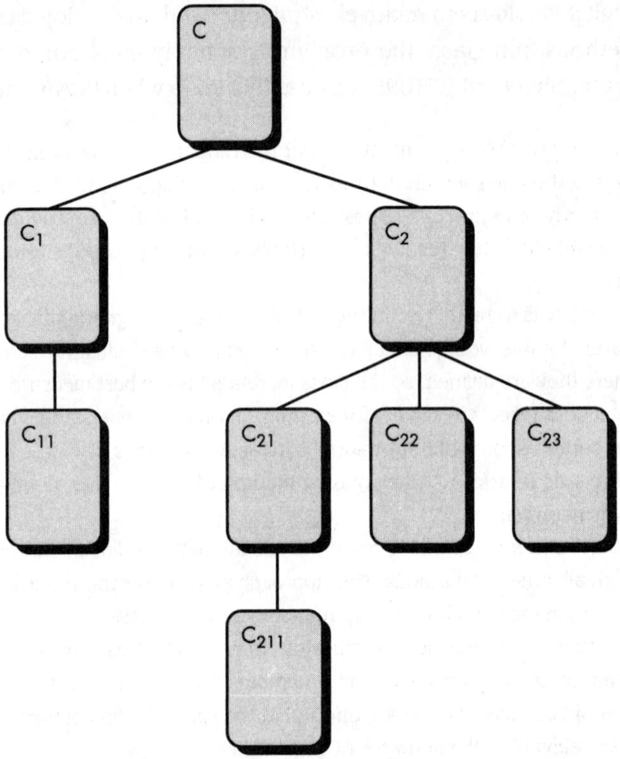

Coupling between object classes (CBO). The CRC model (Chapter 21) may be used to determine the value for CBO. In essence, CBO is the number of collaborations listed for a class on its CRC index card. As CBO increases, it is likely that the reusability of a class will decrease. High values of CBO also complicate modifications and the testing that ensues when modifications are made. In general, the CBO values for each class should be kept as low as is reasonable. This is consistent with the general guideline to reduce coupling in conventional software.

ADVICE
The concepts of coupling and cohesion apply to both conventional and OO software. Keep class coupling low and class and operation cohesion high.

Response for a class (RFC). The response set of a class is "a set of methods that can potentially be executed in response to a message received by an object of that class" [CHI94]. RFC is the number of methods in the response set. As RFC increases, the effort required for testing also increases because the test sequence (Chapter 23) grows. It also follows that, as RFC increases, the overall design complexity of the class increases.

Lack of cohesion in methods (LCOM). Each method within a class, **C,** accesses one or more attributes (also called *instance variables*). LCOM is the number of methods that access one or more of the same attributes.[4] If no methods access the same

4 The formal definition is a bit more complex. See [CHI94] for details.

attributes, then LCOM = 0. To illustrate the case where LCOM ≠ 0, consider a class with six methods. Four of the methods have one or more attributes in common (i.e., they access common attributes). Therefore, LCOM = 4. If LCOM is high, methods may be coupled to one another via attributes. This increases the complexity of the class design. In general, high values for LCOM imply that the class might be better designed by breaking it into two or more separate classes. Although there are cases in which a high value for LCOM is justifiable, it is desirable to keep cohesion high; that is, keep LCOM low.

Quote:

"Object-oriented measures are an integral part of object technology and of good software engineering."

Brian Henderson-Sellers

24.4.2 Metrics Proposed by Lorenz and Kidd

In their book on OO metrics, Lorenz and Kidd [LOR94] divide class-based metrics into four broad categories: size, inheritance, internals, and externals. Size-oriented metrics for the OO class focus on counts of attributes and operations for an individual class and average values for the OO system as a whole. Inheritance-based metrics focus on the manner in which operations are reused through the class hierarchy. Metrics for class internals look at cohesion (Section 24.4.1) and code-oriented issues, and external metrics examine coupling and reuse. A sampling of metrics proposed by Lorenz and Kidd follows:[5]

Class size (CS). The overall size of a class can be measured by determining the following measures:

- The total number of operations (both inherited and private instance operations) that are encapsulated within the class.
- The number of attributes (both inherited and private instance attributes) that are encapsulated by the class.

ADVICE

During review of the OOA model, the CRC index cards will provide a reasonable indication of expected values for CS. If you encounter a class with a large responsibility count during OOA, consider partitioning it.

The WMC metric proposed by Chidamber and Kemerer (Section 24.4.1) is also a weighted measure of class size. As we noted earlier, large values for CS indicate that a class may have too much responsibility. This will reduce the reusability of the class and complicate implementation and testing. In general, inherited or public operations and attributes should be weighted more heavily in determining class size [LOR94]. Private operations and attributes enable specialization and are more localized in the design. Averages for the number of class attributes and operations may also be computed. The lower the average values for size, the more likely that classes within the system can be reused widely.

Number of operations overridden by a subclass (NOO). There are instances when a subclass replaces an operation inherited from its superclass with a specialized version

5 For a complete discussion, see [LOR94].

for its own use. This is called *overriding*. Large values for NOO generally indicate a design problem. As Lorenz and Kidd point out:

> Since a subclass should be a specialization of its superclasses, it should primarily extend the services [operations] of the superclasses. This should result in unique new method names.

If NOO is large, the designer has violated the abstraction implied by the superclass. This results in a weak class hierarchy and OO software that can be difficult to test and modify.

Number of operations added by a subclass (NOA). Subclasses are specialized by adding private operations and attributes. As the value for NOA increases, the subclass drifts away from the abstraction implied by the superclass. In general, as the depth of the class hierarchy increases (DIT becomes large), the value for NOA at lower levels in the hierarchy should go down.

Specialization index (SI). The specialization index provides a rough indication of the degree of specialization for each of the subclasses in an OO system. Specialization can be achieved by adding or deleting operations or by overriding.

$$SI = [NOO \times level]/M_{total}$$

where *level* is the level in the class hierarchy at which the class resides and M_{total} is the total number of methods for the class. The higher is the value of SI, the more likely the class hierarchy has classes that do not conform to the superclass abstraction.

24.4.3 The MOOD Metrics Suite

Harrison, Counsell, and Nithi [HAR98] propose a set of metrics for object-oriented design that provide quantitative indicators for OO design characteristics. A sampling of MOOD metrics follows:

Quote:
"Analyzing OO software in order to evaluate its quality is becoming increasingly important as the paradigm continues to increase in popularity."
Rachel Harrison, et al.

Method inheritance factor (MIF). The degree to which the class architecture of an OO system makes use of inheritance for both methods (operations) and attributes is defined as

$$MIF = \Sigma\, M_i(C_i)/\Sigma\, M_a(C_i)$$

where the summation occurs over $i = 1$ to TC. TC is defined as the total number of classes in the architecture, C_i is a class within the architecture, and

$$M_a(C_i) = M_d(C_i) + M_i(C_i)$$

where

$M_a(C_i)$ = the number of methods that can be invoked in association with C_i.
$M_d(C_i)$) = the number of methods declared in the class C_i.
$M_i(C_i)$ = the number of methods inherited (and not overridden) in C_i.

The value of MIF (the *attribute inheritance factor,* AIF, is defined in an analogous manner) provides an indication of the impact of inheritance on the OO software.

Coupling factor (CF). Earlier in this chapter we noted that coupling is an indication of the connections between elements of the OO design. The MOOD metrics suite defines coupling in the following way:

$$CF = \Sigma_i \Sigma_j \, is\_client\, (C_i, C_j)] / (TC^2 - TC)$$

where the summations occur over $i = 1$ to TC and $j = 1$ to TC. The function

is_client = 1, *if and only if* a relationship exists between the client class, C_c and the server class, C_s, and $C_c \neq C_s$
= 0, otherwise

Although many factors affect software complexity, understandability, and maintainability, it is reasonable to conclude that, as the value for CF increases, the complexity of the OO software will also increase and understandability, maintainability, and the potential for reuse may suffer as a result.

Polymorphism factor (PF). Harrison and her colleagues [HAR98] define PF as "the number of methods that redefine inherited methods, divided by the maximum number of possible distinct polymorphic situations . . . [t]hus, PF is an indirect measure of the relative amount of dynamic binding in a system." The MOOD metrics suite defines PF in the following manner:

$$MIF = \Sigma_i M_o(C_i) / \Sigma_i [M_n(C_i) \times DC(C_i)]$$

where the summations occur over $i = 1$ to TC and

$$M_d(C_i) = M_n(C_i) + M_o(C_i)$$

Also,

$M_n(C_i)$ = the number of new methods.
$M_o(C_i)$ = the number of overriding methods.
$DC(C_i)$ = the descendants count (the number of descendant classes of a base class).

Harrison and her colleagues [HAR98] present a detailed analysis of MIF, CF, and PF along with other metrics and examine their validity for use in the assessment of design quality.

24.5 OPERATION-ORIENTED METRICS

Because the class is the dominant unit in OO systems, fewer metrics have been proposed for operations that reside within a class. Churcher and Shepperd [CHU95] discuss this when they state:

> Results of recent studies indicate that methods tend to be small, both in terms of number of statements and in logical complexity [WIL93], suggesting that connectivity structure of a system may be more important than the content of individual modules.

However, some insights can be gained by examining average characteristics for methods (operations). Three simple metrics, proposed by Lorenz and Kidd [LOR94], are noted next:

XRef
Metrics that can be applied at the component level can also be applied to operations. See Chapter 19 for details.

Average operation size (OS_{avg}). Although lines of code could be used as an indicator for operation size, the LOC measure suffers from all the problems discussed in Chapter 4. For this reason, the number of messages sent by the operation provides an alternative for operation size. As the number of messages sent by a single operation increases, it is likely that responsibilities have not been well-allocated within a class.

Operation complexity (OC). The complexity of an operation can be computed using any of the complexity metrics (Chapter 19) proposed for conventional software [ZUS90]. Because operations should be limited to a specific responsibility, the designer should strive to keep OC as low as possible.

Average number of parameters per operation (NP_{avg}). The larger the number of operation parameters, the more complex the collaboration between objects. In general, NP_{avg} should be kept as low as possible.

24.6 METRICS FOR OBJECT-ORIENTED TESTING

The design metrics noted in Sections 24.4 and 24.5 provide an indication of design quality. They also provide a general indication of the amount of testing effort required to exercise an OO system.

Binder [BIN94] suggests a broad array of design metrics that have a direct influence on the "testability" of an OO system. The metrics are organized into categories that reflect important design characteristics.

Encapsulation

Lack of cohesion in methods (LCOM).[6] The higher the value of LCOM, the more states must be tested to ensure that methods do not generate side effects.

6 See Section 24.4.1 for a description of LCOM.

Percent public and protected (PAP). Public attributes are inherited from other classes and therefore visible to those classes. Protected attributes are a specialization and private to a specific subclass. This metric indicates the percentage of class attributes that are public. High values for PAP increase the likelihood of side effects among classes. Tests must be designed to ensure that such side effects are uncovered.

ADVICE

OO testing can be quite complex. Metrics can assist you in targeting testing resources at threads, scenarios, and class clusters that are "suspect" based on measured characteristics. Use them.

Public access to data members (PAD). This metric indicates the number of classes (or methods) that can access another class's attributes, a violation of encapsulation. High values for PAD lead to the potential for side effects among classes. Tests must be designed to ensure that such side effects are uncovered.

Inheritance

Number of root classes (NOR). This metric is a count of the distinct class hierarchies that are described in the design model. Test suites for each root class and the corresponding class hierarchy must be developed. As NOR increases, testing effort also increases.

Fan-in (FIN). When used in the OO context, fan-in is an indication of multiple inheritance. FIN > 1 indicates that a class inherits its attributes and operations from more than one root class. FIN > 1 should be avoided when possible.

Number of children (NOC) and depth of the inheritance tree (DIT).[7] As we discussed in Chapter 23, superclass methods will have to be retested for each subclass.

In addition to these metrics, Binder [BIN94] defines metrics for class complexity and polymorphism. The metrics defined for class complexity include three CK metrics (Section 24.4.1): weighted methods per class, coupling between object classes, and response for a class. In addition, metrics associated with method counts are defined. The metrics associated with polymorphism are highly specialized. A discussion of them is best left to Binder.

24.7 METRICS FOR OBJECT-ORIENTED PROJECTS

As we discovered in Part Two of this book, the job of the project manager is to plan, coordinate, track, and control a software project. In Chapter 20, we discussed some of the special issues associated with management of OO projects. But what about measurement? Are there specialized OO metrics that can be used by the project manager to provide additional insight into progress?[8] The answer, of course, is, "Yes."

---

7 See Section 24.4.1 for a description of NOC and DIT.

8 A worthwhile discussion of the CK metrics suite (Section 24.4.1) for use in management decision-making can be found in [CHI98].

XRef
The applicability of an evolutionary process model, called the recursive/parallel model, is discussed in Chapter 20.

The first activity performed by the project manager is planning, and one of the early planning tasks is estimation. Recalling the evolutionary process model, planning is revisited after each iteration of the software. Therefore, the plan (and its project estimates) are revisited after each iteration of OOA, OOD, and even OOP.

A key issue that faces a project manager during planning is an estimate of the implemented size of the software. Size is directly proportional to effort and duration. The following OO metrics [LOR94] can provide insight into software size:

Number of scenario scripts (NSS). The number of scenario scripts or use-cases (Chapters 11 and 21) is directly proportional to the number of classes required to meet requirements; the number of states for each class; and the number of methods, attributes, and collaborations. NSS is a strong indicator of program size.

Number of key classes (NKC). A key class focuses directly on the business domain for the problem and will have a lower probability of being implemented via reuse.[9] For this reason, high values for NKC indicate substantial development work. Lorenz and Kidd [LOR94] suggest that between 20 and 40 percent of all classes in a typical OO system are key classes. The remainder support infrastructure (GUI, communications, databases, etc.).

Number of subsystems (NSUB). The number of subsystems provides insight into resource allocation, scheduling (with particular emphasis on parallel development) and overall integration effort.

The metrics NSS, NKC, and NSUB can be collected for past OO projects and are related to the effort expended on the project as a whole and on individual process activities (e.g., OOA, OOD, OOP, and OOT). These data can also be used along with the design metrics discussed earlier in this chapter to compute "productivity metrics" such as average number of classes per developer or average methods per person-month. Collectively, these metrics can be used to estimate effort, duration, staffing, and other information for the current project.

24.8 SUMMARY

Object-oriented software is fundamentally different than software developed using conventional methods. Therefore, the metrics for OO systems focus on measurement that can be applied to the class and the design characteristics—localization, encapsulation, information hiding, inheritance, and object abstraction techniques—that make the class unique.

The CK metrics suite defines six class-oriented software metrics that focus on the class and the class hierarchy. The metrics suite also develops metrics to assess the

9 This will be true only until a robust library of reusable components is developed for a particular domain.

collaborations between classes and the cohesion of methods that reside within a class. At a class-oriented level, the CK metrics suite can be augmented with metrics proposed by Lorenz and Kidd and the MOOD metrics suite. These include measures of class "size" and metrics that provide insight into the degree of specialization for subclasses.

Operation-oriented metrics focus on the size and complexity of individual operations. It is important to note, however, the the primary thrust for OO design metrics is at the class level.

A wide variety of OO metrics have been proposed to assess the testability of an OO system. These metrics focus on encapsulation, inheritance, class complexity, and polymorphism. Many of these metrics have been adapted from the CK metrics suite and metrics proposed by Lorenz and Kidd. Others have been proposed by Binder.

Measurable characteristics of the analysis and design model can assist the project manager for an OO system in planning and tracking activities. The number of scenario scripts (use-cases), key classes, and subsystems provide information about the level of effort required to implement the system.

REFERENCES

[BER95] Berard, E., *Metrics for Object-Oriented Software Engineering,* an Internet posting on comp.software-eng, January 28, 1995.

[BIN94] Binder, R.V., "Object-Oriented Software Testing," *CACM,* vol. 37, no,. 9, September 1994, p. 29.

[CHI94] Chidamber, S.R. and C.F. Kemerer, "A Metrics Suite for Object-Oriented Design," *IEEE Trans. Software Engineering,* vol. SE-20, no. 6, June 1994, pp. 476–493.

[CHI98] Chidamber, S.R., D.P. Darcy, and C.F. Kemerer, "Management Use of Metrics for Object-Oriented Software: An Exploratory Analysis," *IEEE Trans. Software Engineering,* vol. SE-24, no. 8, August 1998, pp. 629–639.

[CHU95] Churcher, N.I. and M.J. Shepperd, "Towards a Conceptual Framework for Object-Oriented Metrics," *ACM Software Engineering Notes,* vol. 20, no. 2, April 1995, pp. 69–76.

[HAR98] Harrison, R., S.J. Counsell, and R.V. Nithi, "An Evaluation of the MOOD Set of Object-Oriented Software Metrics," *IEEE Trans. Software Engineering,* vol. SE-24, no. 6, June 1998, pp. 491–496.

[LOR94] Lorenz, M. and J. Kidd, *Object-Oriented Software Metrics,* Prentice-Hall, 1994.

[WHI97] Whitmire, S., *Object-Oriented Design Measurement,* Wiley, 1997.

[WIL93] Wilde, N. and R. Huitt, "Maintaining Object-Oriented Software," *IEEE Software,* January 1993, pp. 75–80.

[ZUS90] Zuse, H., *Software Complexity: Measures and Methods,* DeGruyter, 1990.

[ZUS97] Zuse, H., *A Framework of Software Measurement,* DeGruyter, 1997.

PROBLEMS AND POINTS TO PONDER

24.1. Review the metrics presented in this chapter and in Chapter 19. How would you characterize the syntactic and semantic differences between metrics for conventional and OO software?

24.2. How does localization affect metrics developed for conventional and OO software?

24.3. Why isn't more emphasis given to OO metrics that address the specific characteristics of operations within a class?

24.4. Review the metrics discussed in this chapter and suggest a few that directly or indirectly address the information hiding design characteristic.

24.5. Review the metrics discussed in this chapter and suggest a few that directly or indirectly address the abstraction design characteristic.

24.6. A class, **X**, has 12 operations. Cyclomatic complexity has been computed for all operations in the OO system and the average value of module complexity is 4. For class **X,** the complexity for operations 1 to 12 is 5, 4, 3, 3, 6, 8, 2, 2, 5, 5, 4, 4, respectively. Compute the weighted methods per class.

24.7. Referring to Figure 20.8, compute the value of DIT for each inheritance tree. What is the value of NOC for the class **X2** for both trees?

24.8. Refer to [CHI94] and present a one-page discussion of the formal definition of the LCOM metric.

24.9. Referring to Figure 20.8B, what is the value of NOA for classes **X3** and **X4**?

24.10. Referring to Figure 20.8B, assume that four operations have been overridden in the inheritance tree (class hierarchy), what is the value of SI for the hierarchy?

24.11. A software team has completed five OO projects to date. The following data have been collected for all size projects:

Project	NSS	NKC	NSUB	Effort (days)
1	34	60	3	900
2	55	75	6	1575
3	122	260	8	4420
4	45	66	2	990
5	80	124	6	2480

A new project is in early stages of OOA. It is estimated that 95 use-cases will be developed for the project. Estimate

a. The total number of classes that will be required to implement the system.

b. The total amount of effort required to implement the system.

24.12. Your instructor will provide you with a list of OO metrics from this chapter. Compute the values of these metrics for one or more of these problems:

a. The design model for the *SafeHome* design.
b. The design model for the PHTRS system described in Problem 12.13.
c. The design model for the video game considered in Problem 22.14.
d. The design model for the e-mail considered in Problem 22.15.
e. The design model for the ATC system considered in Problem 22.16.

FURTHER READINGS AND INFORMATION SOURCES

A variety of books on OOA, OOD, and OOT (see Further Readings and Information Sources in Chapters 20, 21, and 22) make passing reference to OO metrics, but few address the subject in any detail. Books by Jacobson (*Object-Oriented Software Engineering,* Addison-Wesley, 1994) and Graham (*Object-Oriented Methods,* Addison-Wesley, 2nd ed., 1993) provide more treatment than most.

Whitmire [WHI97] presents the most comprehensive and mathematically sophisticated treatment of OO metrics published to date. Lorenz and Kidd [LOR94] and Hendersen-Sellers (*Object-Oriented Metrics: Measures of Complexity,* Prentice-Hall, 1996) offer the only other books dedicated to OO metrics. Other books dedicated to conventional software metrics (see Further Readings and Information Sources for Chapters 4 and 19) contain limited discussions of OO metrics.

A wide variety of information sources on object-oriented metrics and related subjects is available on the Internet. An up-to-date list of World Wide Web references that are relevant to OO metrics can be found at the SEPA Web site:
http://www.mhhe.com/engcs/compsci/pressman/resources/OOM.mhtml

PART

Five

ADVANCED TOPICS IN SOFTWARE ENGINEERING

In this part of *Software Engineering: A Practitioner's Approach,* we consider a number of advanced topics that will extend your understanding of software engineering. In the chapters that follow, we address the following questions:

- What notation and mathematical preliminaries ("formal methods") are required to formally specify software?
- What key technical activities are conducted during the cleanroom software engineering process?
- How is component-based software engineering used to create systems from reusable components?
- How does the client/server architecture affect the way in which software is engineered?
- Are software engineering concepts and principles applicable for Web-based applications and products?
- What key technical activities are required for software reengineering?
- What are the architectural options for establishing a CASE tools environment?
- What are the future directions of software engineering?

Once these questions are answered, you'll understand topics that may have a profound impact on software engineering over the next decade.

CHAPTER

25 FORMAL METHODS

KEY CONCEPTS

Software engineering methods can be categorized on a "formality" spectrum that is loosely tied to the degree of mathematical rigor applied during analysis and design. For this reason, the analysis and design methods discussed earlier in this book fall at the informal end of the spectrum. A combination of diagrams, text, tables, and simple notation is used to create analysis and design models, but little mathematical rigor has been applied.

We now consider the other end of the formality spectrum. Here, a specification and design are described using a formal syntax and semantics that specify system function and behavior. The specification is mathematical in form (e.g., predicate calculus can be used as the basis for a formal specification language).

In his introductory discussion of formal methods, Anthony Hall [HAL90] states:

> Formal methods are controversial. Their advocates claim that they can revolutionize [software] development. Their detractors think they are impossibly difficult. Meanwhile, for most people, formal methods are so unfamiliar that it is difficult to judge the competing claims.

In this chapter, we explore formal methods and examine their potential impact on software engineering in the years to come.

QUICK LOOK

What is it? Formal methods allow a software engineer to create a specification that is more complete, consistent, and unambiguous than those produced using conventional or object-oriented methods. Set theory and logic notation are used to create a clear statement of facts (requirements). This mathematical specification can then be analyzed to prove correctness and consistency. Because the specification is created using mathematical notation, it is inherently less ambiguous than informal modes of representation.

Who does it? A specially trained software engineer creates a formal specification.

Why is it important? In safety-critical or mission-critical systems, failure can have a high price. Lives may be lost or severe economic consequences can arise when computer software fails. In such situations, it is essential that errors are uncovered before software is put into operation. Formal methods reduce specification errors dramatically and, as a consequence, serve as the basis for software that has very few errors once the customer begins using it.

What are the steps? The first step in the application of formal methods is to define the data invariant, state, and operations for a system function. The data invariant is a condition that is true throughout the execution of a function that contains a collection of data. The state is the stored data that a

QUICK LOOK

function accesses and alters; and operations are actions that take place in a system as it reads or writes data to a state. An operation is associated with two conditions: a precondition and a postcondition. The notation and heuristics of sets and constructive specification—set operators, logic operators, and sequences—form the basis of formal methods.

What is the work product? A specification represented in a formal language such as Z or VDM is produced when formal methods are applied.

How do I ensure that I've done it right? Because formal methods use discrete mathematics as the specification mechanism, logic proofs can be applied to each system function to demonstrate that the specification is correct.

25.1 BASIC CONCEPTS

The *Encyclopedia of Software Engineering* [MAR94] defines *formal methods* in the following manner:

> Formal methods used in developing computer systems are mathematically based techniques for describing system properties. Such formal methods provide frameworks within which people can specify, develop, and verify systems in a systematic, rather than ad hoc manner.
>
> A method is formal if it has a sound mathematical basis, typically given by a formal specification language. This basis provides a means of precisely defining notions like consistency and completeness, and more relevantly, specification, implementation and correctness.

Quote:
"[F]ormal methods have tremendous potential for improving the clarity and precision of requirements specifications, and in finding important and subtle errors.
Steve Easterbrook et al.

The desired properties of a formal specification—consistency, completeness, and lack of ambiguity—are the objectives of all specification methods. However, the use of formal methods results in a much higher likelihood of achieving these ideals. The formal syntax of a specification language (Section 25.4) enables requirements or design to be interpreted in only one way, eliminating ambiguity that often occurs when a natural language (e.g., English) or a graphical notation must be interpreted by a reader. The descriptive facilities of set theory and logic notation (Section 25.2) enable clear statement of facts (requirements). To be consistent, facts stated in one place in a specification should not be contradicted in another place. Consistency is ensured by mathematically proving that initial facts can be formally mapped (using inference rules) into later statements within the specification.

Completeness is difficult to achieve, even when formal methods are used. Some aspects of a system may be left undefined as the specification is being created; other characteristics may be purposely omitted to allow designers some freedom in choosing an implementation approach; and finally, it is impossible to consider every operational scenario in a large, complex system. Things may simply be omitted by mistake.

Although the formalism provided by mathematics has an appeal to some software engineers, others (some would say, the majority) look askance at a mathematical view of software development. To understand why a formal approach has merit, we must first consider the deficiencies associated with less formal approaches.

25.1.1 Deficiencies of Less Formal Approaches[1]

The methods discussed for analysis and design in Parts Three and Four of this book made heavy use of natural language and a variety of graphical notations. Although careful application of analysis and design methods, coupled with thorough review can and does lead to high-quality software, sloppiness in the application of these methods can create a variety of problems. A system specification can contain contradictions, ambiguities, vagueness, incomplete statements, and mixed levels of abstraction.

ADVICE

Although a good document index cannot eliminate contradictions, it can help to uncover them. Spend the time to create a comprehensive index for specifications and other documents.

Contradictions are sets of statements that are at variance with each other. For example, one part of a system specification may state that the system must monitor all the temperatures in a chemical reactor while another part, perhaps written by another member of staff, may state that only temperatures occurring within a certain range are to be monitored. Normally, contradictions that occur on the same page of a system specification can be detected easily. However, contradictions are often separated by a large number of pages.

Ambiguities are statements that can be interpreted in a number of ways. For example, the following statement is ambiguous:

> The operator identity consists of the operator name and password; the password consists of six digits. It should be displayed on the security VDU and deposited in the login file when an operator logs into the system.

In this extract, does the word *it* refer to the password or the operator identity?

Quote:

"Making mistakes is human, Repeating 'em is too."
Malcolm Forbes

Vagueness often occurs because a system specification is a very bulky document. Achieving a high level of precision consistently is an almost impossible task. It can lead to statements such as "The interface to the system used by radar operators should be user-friendly" or "The virtual interface shall be based on simple overall concepts that are straightforward to understand and use and few in number." A casual perusal of these statements might not detect the underlying lack of any useful information.

Incompleteness is probably one of the most frequently occurring problems with system specifications. For example, consider the functional requirement:

> The system should maintain the hourly level of the reservoir from depth sensors situated in the reservoir. These values should be stored for the past six months.

1 This section and others in the first part of this chapter have been adapted from work contributed by Darrel Ince for the European version of the fourth edition of *Software Engineering: A Practitioner's Approach.*

ADVICE

Effective use of formal technical reviews during specification can eliminate many of these problems. However, some will not be uncovered. Therefore, be on the lookout for deficiencies during design, code, and test.

This describes the main data storage part of a system. If one of the commands for the system was

The function of the AVERAGE command is to display on a PC the average water level for a particular sensor between two times.

Assuming that no more detail was presented for this command, the details of the command would be seriously incomplete. For example, the description of the command does not include what should happen if a user of a system specifies a time that was more than six months before the current hour.

Mixed levels of abstraction occur when very abstract statements are intermixed randomly with statements that are at a much lower level of detail. For example, statements such as

The purpose of the system is to track the stock in a warehouse.

might be intermixed with

When the loading clerk types in the *withdraw* command he or she will communicate the order number, the identity of the item to be removed, and the quantity removed. The system will respond with a confirmation that the removal is allowable.

While such statements are important in a system specification, specifiers often manage to intermix them to such an extent that it becomes very difficult to see the overall functional architecture of a system.

Each of these problems is more common than we would like to believe. And each represents a potential deficiency in conventional and object-oriented methods for specification.

25.1.2 Mathematics in Software Development

Mathematics has many useful properties for the developers of large systems. One of its most useful properties is that it is capable of succinctly and exactly describing a physical situation, an object, or the outcome of an action. Ideally, the software engineer should be in the same position as the applied mathematician. A mathematical specification of a system should be presented, and a solution developed in terms of a software architecture that implements the specification should be produced.[2]

Another advantage of using mathematics in the software process is that it provides a smooth transition between software engineering activities. Not only functional specifications but also system designs can be expressed in mathematics, and of course, the program code is a mathematical notation—albeit a rather long-winded one.

---

2 A word of caution is appropriate at this point. The mathematical system specifications that are presented in this chapter are not as succinct as a simple mathematical expression. Software systems are notoriously complex, and it would be unrealistic to expect that they could be specified in one line of mathematics.

The major property of mathematics is that it supports abstraction and is an excellent medium for modeling. Because it is an exact medium there is little possibility of ambiguity: Specifications can be mathematically validated for contradictions and incompleteness, and vagueness disappears completely. In addition, mathematics can be used to represent levels of abstraction in a system specification in an organized way.

Mathematics is an ideal tool for modeling. It enables the bare bones of a specification to be exhibited and helps the analyst and system specifier to validate a specification for functionality without intrusion of such issues as response time, design directives, implementation directives, and project constraints. It also helps the designer, because the system design specification exhibits the properties of a model, providing only sufficient details to enable the task in hand to be carried out.

Finally, mathematics provides a high level of validation when it is used as a software development medium. It is possible to use a mathematical proof to demonstrate that a design matches a specification and that some program code is a correct reflection of a design. This is preferable to current practice, where often little effort is put into early validation and where much of the checking of a software system occurs during system and acceptance testing.

25.1.3 Formal Methods Concepts

The aim of this section is to present the main concepts involved in the mathematical specification of software systems, without encumbering the reader with too much mathematical detail. To accomplish these, we use a few simple examples.

Example 1: A Symbol Table. A program is used to maintain a symbol table. Such a table is used frequently in many different types of applications. It consists of a collection of items without any duplication. An example of a typical symbol table is shown in Figure 25.1. It represents the table used by an operating system to hold the names of the users of the system. Other examples of tables include the collection of names of staff in a payroll system, the collection of names of computers in a network communications system, and the collection of destinations in a system for producing railway timetables.

KEY POINT

A data invariant is a set of conditions that are true throughout the execution of the system that contains a collection of data.

Assume that the table presented in this example consists of no more than *MaxIds* members of staff. This statement, which places a constraint on the table, is a component of a condition known as a *data invariant*—an important idea that we shall return to throughout this chapter.

A data invariant is a condition that is true throughout the execution of the system that contains a collection of data. The data invariant that holds for the symbol table just discussed has two components: (1) that the table will contain no more than *MaxIds* names and (2) that there will be no duplicate names in the table. In the case of the symbol table program, this means that, no matter when the symbol table

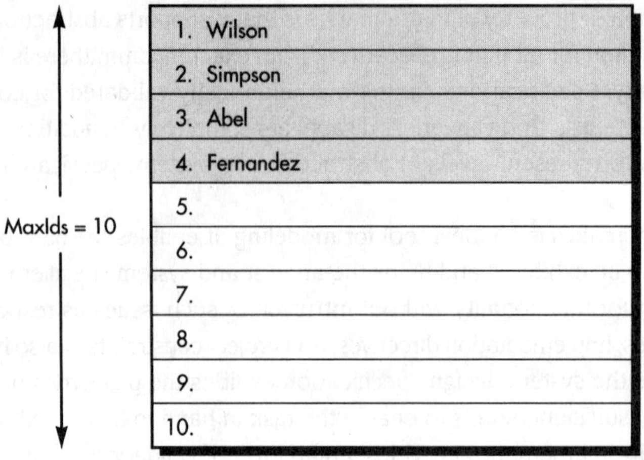

FIGURE 25.1 A symbol table used for an operating system

KEY POINT In formal methods, a "state" is stored data that the system accesses and alters. An "operation" is an action that reads or writes data to a state.

is examined during execution of the system, it will always contain no more than *MaxIds* staff identifiers and will contain no duplicates.

Another important concept is that of a *state.* In the context of formal methods,[3] a state is the stored data that a system accesses and alters. In the example of the symbol table program, the state is the symbol table.

The final concept is that of an *operation*. This is an action that takes place in a system and reads or writes data to a state. If the symbol table program is concerned with adding and removing staff names from the symbol table, then it will be associated with two operations: an operation to add a specified name to the symbol table and an operation to remove an existing name from the table. If the program provides the facility to check whether a specific name is contained in the table, then there would be an operation that would return some indication of whether the name is in the table.

KEY POINT A "precondition" defines the circumstances in which a particular operation is valid. A "postcondition" defines what happens when an operation has completed its action.

An operation is associated with two conditions: a precondition and a postcondition. A *precondition* defines the circumstances in which a particular operation is valid. For example, the precondition for an operation that adds a name to the staff identifier symbol table is valid only if the name that is to be added is not contained in the table and also if there are fewer than MaxIds staff identifiers in the table. The *postcondition* of an operation defines what happens when an operation has completed its action. This is defined by its effect on the state. In the example of an operation that adds an identifier to the staff identifier symbol table, the postcondition would specify mathematically that the table has been augmented with the new identifier.

3 Recall that the term *state* has also been used in Chapters 12 and 21 as a representation of the behavior of a system or objects.

FIGURE 25.2
A block handler

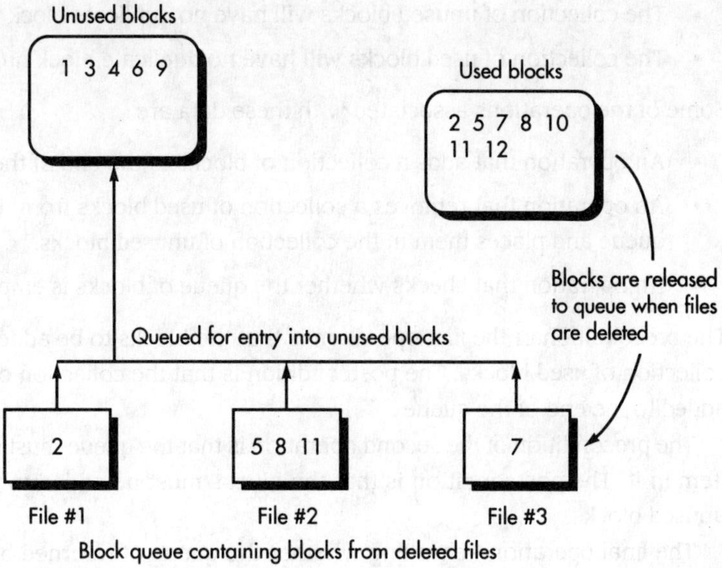

Example 2: A Block Handler. One of the more important parts of a computer's operating system is the subsystem that maintains files created by users. Part of the filing subsystem is the *block handler.* Files in the file store are composed of blocks of storage that are held on a file storage device. During the operation of the computer, files will be created and deleted, requiring the acquisition and release of blocks of storage. In order to cope with this, the filing subsystem will maintain a reservoir of unused (free) blocks and keep track of blocks that are currently in use. When blocks are released from a deleted file they are normally added to a queue of blocks waiting to be added to the reservoir of unused blocks. This is shown in Figure 25.2. In this figure, a number of components are shown: the reservoir of unused blocks, the blocks that currently make up the files administered by the operating system, and those blocks that are waiting to be added to the reservoir. The waiting blocks are held in a queue, with each element of the queue containing a set of blocks from a deleted file.

ADVICE
Brainstorming techniques can work well when you need to develop a data invariant for a reasonably complex function. Have a number of people write down bounds, restrictions, and limitations for the function and then combine and edit.

For this subsystem the state is the collection of free blocks, the collection of used blocks, and the queue of returned blocks. The data invariant, expressed in natural language, is

- No block will be marked as both unused and used.
- All the sets of blocks held in the queue will be subsets of the collection of currently used blocks.
- No elements of the queue will contain the same block numbers.
- The collection of used blocks and blocks that are unused will be the total collection of blocks that make up files.

- The collection of unused blocks will have no duplicate block numbers.
- The collection of used blocks will have no duplicate block numbers.

Some of the operations associated with these data are

- An operation that adds a collection of blocks to the end of the queue.
- An operation that removes a collection of used blocks from the front of the queue and places them in the collection of unused blocks.
- An operation that checks whether the queue of blocks is empty.

The precondition of the first operation is that the blocks to be added must be in the collection of used blocks. The postcondition is that the collection of blocks must be added to the end of the queue.

The precondition of the second operation is that the queue must have at least one item in it. The postcondition is that the blocks must be added to the collection of unused blocks.

The final operation—checking whether the queue of returned blocks is empty—has no precondition. This means that the operation is always defined, regardless of what value the state has. The postcondition delivers the value *true* if the queue is empty and *false* otherwise.

Example 3: A Print Spooler. In multitasking operating systems, a number of tasks make requests to print files. Often, there are not enough printing devices to satisfy all current print requests simultaneously. Any print request that cannot be immediately satisfied is placed in a queue awaiting printing. The part of an operating system that deals with the administration of such queues is known as a *print spooler.*

In this example we assume that the operating system can employ no more than *MaxDevs* output devices and that each device has a queue associated with it. We will also assume that each device is associated with a limit of lines in a file which it will print. For example, an output device that has a limit of 1000 lines of printing will be associated with a queue that contains only files having no more than 1000 lines of text. Print spoolers sometimes impose this constraint in order to forbid large print jobs that may occupy slow printing devices for exceptionally long periods. A schematic representation of a print spooler is shown in Figure 25.3.

Referring to the figure, spooler state consists of four components: the queues of files waiting to be printed, each queue being associated with a particular output device; the collection of output devices controlled by the spooler; the relationship between the output devices and the maximum file size that each can print; and the relationship between the files awaiting printing and their size in lines. For example, Figure 25.3 shows that the output device LP1 which has a print limit of 750 lines has two files **ftax** and **persons** awaiting printing, and that the size of the files are 650 lines and 700 lines, respectively.

FIGURE 25.3
A print spooler

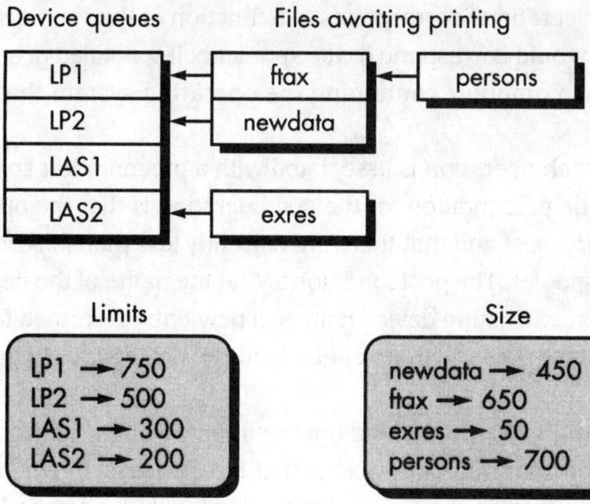

The state of the spooler is represented by the four components: queues, output devices, limits, and sizes. The data invariant has five components:

- Each output device is associated with an upper limit on print lines.
- Each output device is associated with a possibly nonempty queue of files awaiting printing.
- Each file is associated with a size.
- Each queue associated with an output device contains files that have a size less than the upper limit of the output device.
- There will be no more than *MaxDevs* output devices administered by the spooler.

KEY POINT

States and operations are analogous in many ways to the class definition for OO systems. States represents the data domain (attributes) and operations are the processes (methods) that manipulate the data.

A number of operations can be associated with the spooler. For example,

- An operation that adds a new output device to the spooler together with its associated print limit.
- An operation that removes a file from the queue associated with a particular output device.
- An operation that adds a file to the queue associated with a particular output device.
- An operation that alters the upper limit of print lines for a particular output device.
- An operation that moves a file from a queue associated with an output device to another queue associated with a second output device.

Each of these operations corresponds to a function of the spooler. For example, the first operation would correspond to the spooler being notified of a new device being attached to the computer containing the operating system that administers the spooler.

As before, each operation is associated with a precondition and a postcondition. For example, the precondition for the first operation is that the output device name does not already exist and that there are currently less than *MaxDevs* output devices known to the spooler. The postcondition is that the name of the new device is added to the collection of existing device names, a new entry is formed for the device with no files being associated with its queue, and the device is associated with its print limit.

The precondition for the second operation (removing a file from a queue associated with a particular output device) is that the device is known to the spooler and that at least one entry in the queue is associated with the device. The postcondition is that the head of the queue associated with the output device is removed and its entry in the part of the spooler that keeps tracks of file sizes is deleted.

The precondition for the fifth operation described (moving a file from a queue associated with an output device to another queue associated with a second output device) is

- The first output device is known to the spooler.
- The second output device is known to the spooler.
- The queue associated with the first device contains the file to be moved.
- The size of the file is less than or equal to the print limit associated with the second output device.

The postcondition is that the file is removed from one queue and added to another queue.

In each of the examples noted in this section, we introduce the key concepts of formal specification. But we do so without emphasizing the mathematics that are required to make the specification formal. In the next section, we consider these mathematics.

25.2 MATHEMATICAL PRELIMINARIES

To apply formal methods effectively, a software engineer must have a working knowledge of the mathematical notation associated with sets and sequences and the logical notation used in predicate calculus. The intent of the section is to provide a brief introduction. For a more detailed discussion the reader is urged to examine books dedicated to these subjects (e.g., [WIL87], [GRI93], and [ROS95]).

25.2.1 Sets and Constructive Specification

A set is a collection of objects or elements and is used as a cornerstone of formal methods. The elements contained within a set are unique (i.e., no duplicates are allowed). Sets with a small number of elements are written within curly brackets (braces) with the elements separated by commas. For example, the set

{C++, Pascal, Ada, COBOL, Java}

contains the names of five programming languages.

The order in which the elements appear within a set is immaterial. The number of items in a set is known as its *cardinality*. The # operator returns a set's cardinality. For example, the expression

$\#\{A, B, C, D\} = 4$

implies that the cardinality operator has been applied to the set shown with a result indicating the number of items in the set.

? What is constructive set specification?

There are two ways of defining a set. A set may be defined by enumerating its elements (this is the way in which the sets just noted have been defined). The second approach is to create a *constructive set specification*. The general form of the members of a set is specified using a Boolean expression. Constructive set specification is preferable to enumeration because it enables a succinct definition of large sets. It also explicitly defines the rule that was used in constructing the set.

Consider the following constructive specification example:

$\{n : \mathbb{N} \mid n < 3 \cdot n\}$

This specification has three components, a signature, $n : \mathbb{N}$, a predicate $n < 3$, and a term, *n*. The *signature* specifies the range of values that will be considered when forming the set, the *predicate* (a Boolean expression) defines how the set is to be constricted, and, finally, the *term* gives the general form of the item of the set. In the example above, $\mathbb{N}$ stands for the natural numbers; therefore, natural numbers are to be considered. The predicate indicates that only natural numbers less than 3 are to be included; and the term specifies that each element of the set will be of the form *n*. Therefore, this specification defines the set

{0, 1, 2}

When the form of the elements of a set is obvious, the term can be omitted. For example, the preceding set could be specified as

$(n : \mathbb{N} \mid n < 3\}$

All the sets that have been described here have elements that are single items. Sets can also be made from elements that are pairs, triples, and so on. For example, the set specification

$$\{x, y : \mathbb{N} \mid x + y = 10 \cdot (x, y^2)\}$$

describes the set of pairs of natural numbers that have the form (x, y^2) and where the sum of x and y is 10. This is the set

$$\{ (1, 81), (2, 64), (3, 49), \ldots\}$$

Obviously, a constructive set specification required to represent some component of computer software can be considerably more complex than those noted here. However, the basic form and structure remain the same.

25.2.2 Set Operators

A specialized set of symbology is used to represent set and logic operations. These symbols must be understood by the software engineer who intends to apply formal methods.

ADVICE

Knowledge of set operations is indispensible when formal specifications are developed. Spend the time to familiarize yourself with each, if you intend to apply formal methods.

The $\in$ operator is used to indicate membership of a set. For example, the expression

$$x \in X$$

has the value *true* if x is a member of the set X and the value *false* otherwise. For example, the predicate

$$12 \in \{6, 1, 12, 22\}$$

has the value *true* since 12 is a member of the set.

The opposite of the $\in$ operator is the $\notin$ operator. The expression

$$x \notin X$$

has the value *true* if x is not a member of the set X and *false* otherwise. For example, the predicate

$$13 \notin \{13, 1, 124, 22\}$$

has the value *false*.

The operators $\subset$ and $\subseteq$ take sets as their operands. The predicate

$$A \subset B$$

has the value *true* if the members of the set A are contained in the set B and has the value *false* otherwise. Thus, the predicate

$$\{1, 2\} \subset \{4, 3, 1, 2\}$$

has the value *true*. However, the predicate

$$\{HD1, LP4, RC5\} \subset \{HD1, RC2, HD3, LP1, LP4, LP6\}$$

has a value of *false* because the element RC5 is not contained in the set to the right of the operator.

The operator $\subseteq$ is similar to $\subset$. However, if its operands are equal, it has the value *true.* Thus, the value of the predicate

{HD1, LP4, RC5} $\subseteq$ {HD1, RC2, HD3, LP1, LP4, LP6}

is *false,* and the predicate

{HD1, LP4, RC5} $\subseteq$ {HD1, LP4, RC5}

is *true.*

A special set is the empty set $\varnothing$. This corresponds to zero in normal mathematics. The empty set has the property that it is a subset of every other set. Two useful identities involving the empty set are

$\varnothing \cup A = A$ and $\varnothing \cap A = \varnothing$

for any set *A,* where $\cup$ is known as the *union operator,* sometimes known as *cup*; $\cap$ is the *intersection operator,* sometimes known as *cap.*

> **Quote:**
> "Mathematical structures are among the most beautiful discoveries made by the human mind."
> **Douglas Hofstadter**

The union operator takes two sets and forms a set that contains all the elements in the set with duplicates eliminated. Thus, the result of the expression

{File1, File2, Tax, Compiler} $\cup$ {NewTax, D2, D3, File2}

is the set

{Filel, File2, Tax, Compiler, NewTax, D2, D3}

The intersection operator takes two sets and forms a set consisting of the common elements in each set. Thus, the expression

{12, 4, 99, 1} $\cap$ {1, 13, 12, 77}

results in the set {12, 1}.

The *set difference* operator, \, as the name suggests, forms a set by removing the elements of its second operand from the elements of its first operand. Thus, the value of the expression

{New, Old, TaxFile, Sysparam} \ {Old, SysParam}

results in the set {New, TaxFile}.

The value of the expression

{a, b, c, d} $\cap$ {x, y}

will be the empty set $\varnothing$. The operator always delivers a set; however, in this case there are no common elements between its operands so the resulting set will have no elements.

The final operator is the *cross product,* $\times$, sometimes known as the *Cartesian product.* This has two operands which are sets of pairs. The result is a set of pairs where each pair consists of an element taken from the first operand combined with an released from a deleted file they are normally added to a queue of blocks waiting to be added to the reservoir of unused blocks. This has been depicted schematically in Figure 25.2.[4]

How can I represent states and data invariants using the set and logic operators that have already been introduced?

A set named *BLOCKS* will consist of every block number. *AllBlocks* is a set of blocks that lie between 1 and *MaxBlocks*. The state will be modeled by two sets and a sequence. The two sets are *used* and *free*. Both contain blocks—the *used* set contains the blocks that are currently used in files and the *free* set contains blocks that are available for new files. The sequence will contain sets of blocks that are ready to be released from files that have been deleted. The state can be described as

$$used, free: \mathbb{P}\ BLOCKS$$
$$BlockQueue: \text{seq}\ \mathbb{P}\ BLOCKS$$

This is very much like the declaration of program variables. It states that *used* and *free* will be sets of blocks and that *BlockQueue* will be a sequence, each element of which will be a set of blocks. The data invariant can be written as

$$used \cap free = \varnothing \wedge$$
$$used \cup free = AllBlocks \wedge$$
$$\forall i: \text{dom}\ BlockQueue \cdot BlockQueue\ i \subseteq used \wedge$$
$$\forall i, j: \text{dom}\ BlockQueue \cdot i \neq j \Rightarrow BlockQueue\ i \cap BlockQueue\ j = \varnothing$$

WebRef
Extensive information on formal methods can be found at **archive.comlab.ox.ac.uk/formal-methods.html**

The mathematical components of the data invariant match four of the bulleted, natural-language components described earlier. The first line of the data invariant states that there will be no common blocks in the used collection and free collections of blocks. The second line states that the collection of used blocks and free blocks will always be equal to the whole collection of blocks in the system. The third line indicates the *i*th element in the block queue will always be a subset of the used blocks. The final line states that, for any two elements of the block queue that are not the same, there will be no common blocks in these two elements. The final two natural language components of the data invariant are implemented by virtue of the fact that used and free are sets and therefore will not contain duplicates.

The first operation we shall define is one that removes an element from the head of the block queue. The precondition is that there must be at least one item in the queue:

$$\#BlockQueue > 0,$$

The postcondition is that the head of the queue must be removed and placed in the collection of free blocks and the queue adjusted to show the removal:

4 If your recollection of the block handler example is hazy, please return to Section 25.1.3 to review the data invariant, operations, preconditions, and postconditions associated with the block handler.

$$used' = used \setminus head\ BlockQueue\ \wedge$$
$$free' = free \cup head\ BlockQueue\ \wedge$$
$$BlockQueue' = tail\ BlockQueue$$

A convention used in many formal methods is that the value of a variable after an operation is primed. Hence, the first component of the preceding expression states that the new used blocks (*used'*) will be equal to the old used blocks minus the blocks that have been removed. The second component states that the new free blocks (*free'*) will be the old free blocks with the head of the block queue added to it. The third component states that the new block queue will be equal to the tail of the old value of the block queue; that is, all elements in the queue apart from the first one. A second operation adds a collection of blocks, *Ablocks,* to the block queue. The precondition is that *Ablocks* is currently a set of used blocks:

How do I represent pre- and post-conditions?

$$Ablocks \subseteq used$$

The postcondition is that the set of blocks is added to the end of the block queue and the set of used and free blocks remains unchanged:

$$BlockQueue' = BlockQueue \frown \langle Ablocks \rangle\ \wedge$$
$$used' = used\ \wedge$$
$$free' = free$$

There is no question that the mathematical specification of the block queue is considerably more rigorous that a natural language narrative or a graphical model. The additional rigor requires effort, but the benefits gained from improved consistency and completeness can be justified for many types of applications.

25.4 FORMAL SPECIFICATION LANGUAGES

A formal specification language is usually composed of three primary components: (1) a syntax that defines the specific notation with which the specification is represented, (2) semantics to help define a "universe of objects" [WIN90] that will be used to describe the system, and (3) a set of relations that define the rules that indicate which objects properly satisfy the specification.

The *syntactic domain* of a formal specification language is often based on a syntax that is derived from standard set theory notation and predicate calculus. For example, variables such as *x, y,* and *z* describe a set of objects that relate to a problem (sometimes called the *domain of discourse*) and are used in conjunction with the operators described in Section 25.2. Although the syntax is usually symbolic, icons (e.g., graphical symbols such as boxes, arrows, and circles) can also be used, if they are unambiguous.

The *semantic domain* of a specification language indicates how the language represents system requirements. For example, a programming language has a set of formal semantics that enables the software developer to specify algorithms that transform input to output. A formal grammar (such as BNF) can be used to describe the syntax of the programming language. However, a programming language does not make a good specification language because it can represent only computable functions. A specification language must have a semantic domain that is broader; that is, the semantic domain of a specification language must be capable of expressing ideas such as, "For all *x* in an infinite set *A*, there exists a *y* in an infinite set *B* such that the property *P* holds for *x* and *y*" [WIN90]. Other specification languages apply semantics that enable the specification of system behavior. For example, a syntax and semantics can be developed to specify states and state transition, events and their effect on state transition, synchronization and timing.

It is possible to use different semantic abstractions to describe the same system in different ways. We did this in a less formal fashion in Chapters 12 and 21. Data flow and corresponding processing were described using the data flow diagram, and system behavior was depicted with the state transition diagram. Analogous notation was used to describe object-oriented systems. Different modeling notation can be used to represent the same system. The semantics of each representation provides complementary views of the system. To illustrate this approach when formal methods are used, assume that a formal specification language is used to describe the set of events that cause a particular state to occur in a system. Another formal relation depicts all functions that occur within a given state. The intersection of these two relations provides an indication of the events that will cause specific functions to occur.

A variety of formal specification languages are in use today. CSP ([HIN95], [HOR85]), LARCH [GUT93], VDM [JON91], and Z ([SPI88], [SPI92]) are representative formal specification languages that exhibit the characteristics noted previously. In this chapter, the Z specification language is used for illustrative purposes. Z is coupled with an automated tool that stores axioms, rules of inference, and application-oriented theorems that lead to mathematical proof of correctness of the specification.

25.5 USING Z TO REPRESENT AN EXAMPLE SOFTWARE COMPONENT

Z specifications are structured as a set of schemas—a boxlike structure that introduces variables and specifies the relationship between these variables. A schema is essentially the formal specification analog of the programming language subroutine or procedure. In the same way that procedures and subroutines are used to structure a system, schemas are used to structure a formal specification.

In this section, we use the Z specification language to model the block handler example, introduced in Section 25.1.3 and discussed further in Section 25.3. A summary of Z language notation is presented in Table 25.1. The following example of a schema describes the state of the block handler and the data invariant:

TABLE 25.1 Summary of Z Notation

Z notation is based on typed set theory and first-order logic. Z provides a construct, called a *schema*, to describe a specification's state space and operations. A schema groups variable declarations with a list of predicates that constrain the possible value of a variable. In Z, the schema X is defined by the form

```
——X——————————————
  declarations
—————————————————
  predicates
—————————————————
```

Global functions and constants are defined by the form

```
  declarations
—————————————————
  predicates
```

The declaration gives the type of the function or constant, while the predicate gives it value. Only an abbreviated set of Z symbols is presented in this table.

Sets:

$S : \mathbb{P}\, X$	S is declared as a set of Xs.
$x \in S$	x is a member of S.
$x \notin S$	x is not a member of S.
$S \subseteq T$	S is a subset of T: Every member of S is also in T.
$S \cup T$	The union of S and T: It contains every member of S or T or both.
$S \cap T$	The intersection of S and T: It contains every member of both S and T.
$S \setminus T$	The difference of S and T: It contains every member of S except those also in T.
$\varnothing$	Empty set: It contains no members.
$\{x\}$	Singleton set: It contains just x.
$\mathbb{N}$	The set of natural numbers 0, 1, 2, ...
$S : \mathbb{F}\, X$	S is declared as a finite set of Xs.
$\max(S)$	The maximum of the nonempty set of numbers S.

Functions:

$f : X ⤔ Y$	f is declared as a partial injection from X to Y
$\operatorname{dom} f$	The domain of f: the set of values x for which $f(x)$ is defined.
$\operatorname{ran} f$	The range of f: the set of values taken by $f(x)$ as x varies over the domain of f.
$f \oplus \{x \mapsto y\}$	A function that agrees with f except that x is mapped to y.
$\{x\} \trianglelefteq f$	A function like f, except that x is removed from its domain.

Logic:

$P \wedge Q$	P and Q: It is true if both P and Q are true.
$P \Rightarrow Q$	P implies Q: It is true if either Q is true or P is false.
$\theta S' = \theta S$	No components of schema S change in an operation.

——*BlockHandler*——————————

$used, free : \mathbb{P}\ BLOCKS$

$BlockQueue : \text{seq}\ \mathbb{P}\ BLOCKS$

——————————————

$used \cap free = \varnothing \wedge$

$used \cup free = AllBlocks \wedge$

$\forall i : \text{dom}\ BlockQueue \cdot BlockQueue\ i \subseteq \text{used} \wedge$

$\forall i, j : \text{dom}\ BlockQueue \cdot i \neq j \Rightarrow$

$BlockQueue\ i \cap BlockQueue\ j = \varnothing$

——————————————

WebRef
Detailed information on the Z language, including FAQ, can be found at **archive.comlab.ox.ac.uk/z.html**

The schema consists of two parts. The part above the central line represents the variables of the state, while the part below the central line describes the data invariant. Whenever the schema representing the data invariant and state is used in another schema it is preceded by the Δ symbol. Therefore, if the preceding schema is used in a schema that, for example, describes an operation, then it would be written as Δ*BlockHandler.* As the last sentence implies, schemas can be used to describe operations. The following example of a schema describes the operation that removes an element from the block queue:

——*RemoveBlock*——————————

$\Delta BlockHandler$

——————————————

$\#BlockQueue > 0,$

$used' = used \setminus head\ BlockQueue \wedge$

$free' = free \cup head\ BlockQueue \wedge$

$BlockQueue' = tail\ BlockQueue$

——————————————

The inclusion of Δ*BlockHandler* results in all variables that make up the state being available for the *RemoveBlock* schema and ensures that the data invariant will hold before and after the operation has been executed.

The second operation, which adds a collection of blocks to the end of the queue, is represented as

——*AddBlock*——————————

$\Delta BlockHandler$

$Ablocks? : \ BLOCKS$

——————————————

$Ablocks? \subseteq used$

$BlockQueue' = BlockQueue \frown \langle Ablocks? \rangle$

$used' = used \wedge$

$free' = free$

——————————————

By convention in Z, an input variable that is read from and does not form part of the state is terminated by a question mark. Thus, *Ablocks*?, which acts as an input parameter, is terminated by a question mark.

25.6 THE TEN COMMANDMENTS OF FORMAL METHODS

The decision to use of formal methods in the real world is not one that is taken lightly. Bowan and Hinchley [BOW95] have coined "the ten commandments of formal methods" as a guide for those who are about to apply this important software engineering approach.[5]

ADVICE

The decision to use formal methods should not be taken lightly. Follow these "commandments" and be sure that everyone has received proper training.

1. **Thou shalt choose the appropriate notation.** In order to choose effectively from the wide array of formal specification languages, a software engineer should consider language vocabulary, application type to be specified, and breadth of usage of the language.
2. **Thou shalt formalize but not overformalize.** It is generally not necessary to apply formal methods to every aspect of a major system. Those components that are safety critical are first choices, followed by components whose failure cannot be tolerated (for business reasons).
3. **Thou shalt estimate costs.** Formal methods have high startup costs. Training staff, acquisition of support tools, and use of contract consultants result in high first-time costs. These costs must be considered when examining the return on investment associated with formal methods.
4. **Thou shalt have a formal methods guru on call.** Expert training and ongoing consulting is essential for success when formal methods are used for the first time.
5. **Thou shalt not abandon thy traditional development methods.** It is possible, and in many cases desirable, to integrate formal methods with conventional or object-oriented methods (Chapters 12 and 21). Each has strengths and weakness. A combination, if properly applied, can produce excellent results.[6]
6. **Thou shalt document sufficiently.** Formal methods provide a concise, unambiguous, and consistent method for documenting system requirements. However, it is recommended that a natural language commentary accompany the formal specification to serve as a mechanism for reinforcing the reader's understanding of the system.

WebRef

Useful information on formal methods can be obtained at **www.cl.cam.uk/users/mgh1001**

5 This treatment is a much abbreviated version of [BOW95].

6 Cleanroom software engineering (Chapter 26) is an example of an integrated approach that uses formal methods and more conventional development methods.

7. **Thou shalt not compromise thy quality standards.** "There is nothing magical about formal methods" [BOW95] and for this reason, other SQA activities (Chapter 8) must continue to be applied as systems are developed.
8. **Thou shalt not be dogmatic.** A software engineer must recognize that formal methods are not a guarantee of correctness. It is possible (some would say, likely) that the final system, even when developed using formal methods, may have small omissions, minor bugs, and other attributes that do not meet expectations.
9. **Thou shalt test, test, and test again.** The importance of software testing has been discussed in Chapters 17, 18, and 23. Formal methods do not absolve the software engineer from the need to conduct well-planned, thorough tests.
10. **Thou shalt reuse.** Over the long term, the only rational way to reduce software costs and increase software quality is through reuse (Chapter 27). Formal methods do not change this reality. In fact, it may be that formal methods are an appropriate approach when components for reuse libraries are to be created.

25.7 FORMAL METHODS—THE ROAD AHEAD

Although formal, mathematically based specification techniques are not as yet used widely in the industry, they do offer substantial advantages over less formal techniques. Liskov and Bersins [LIS86] summarize these in the following way:

> Formal specifications can be studied mathematically while informal specifications cannot. For example, a correct program can be proved to meet its specifications, or two alternative sets of specifications can be proved equivalent . . . Certain forms of incompleteness or inconsistency can be detected automatically.

In addition, formal specification removes ambiguity and encourages greater rigor in the early stages of the software engineering process.

But problems remain. Formal specification focuses primarily on function and data. Timing, control, and behavioral aspects of a problem are more difficult to represent. In addition, some elements of a problem (e.g., human/machine interfaces) are better specified using graphical techniques or prototypes. Finally, specification using formal methods is more difficult to learn than methods such as structured analysis and represents a significant "culture shock" for some software practitioners. For this reason, it is likely that formal, mathematical specification techniques will form the foundation for a future generation of CASE tools. When and if this occurs, mathematically based specification may be adopted by a wider segment of the software engineering community.[7]

7 It is important to note that others disagree. See [YOU94].

25.8 SUMMARY

Formal methods provide a foundation for specification environments leading to analysis models that are more complete, consistent, and unambiguous than those produced using conventional or object-oriented methods. The descriptive facilities of set theory and logic notation enable a software engineer to create a clear statement of facts (requirements).

The underlying concepts that govern formal methods are, (1) the data invariant, a condition true throughout the execution of the system that contains a collection of data; (2) the state, the stored data that a system accesses and alters; and (3) the operation, an action that takes place in a system and reads or writes data to a state. An operation is associated with two conditions: a precondition and a postcondition.

Discrete mathematics—the notation and heuristics associated with sets and constructive specification, set operators, logic operators, and sequences—forms the basis of formal methods. Discrete mathematics is implemented in the context of a formal specification language, such as Z.

Z, like all formal specification languages, has both syntactic and semantic domains. The syntactic domain uses a symbology that is closely aligned with the notation of sets and predicate calculus. The semantic domain enables the language to express requirements in a concise manner. The structure of Z incorporates schemas—box-like structures that introduce variables and specify the relationship between these variables.

A decision to use formal methods must consider startup costs as well as the cultural changes associated with a radically different technology. In most instances, formal methods have highest payoff for safety-critical and business-critical systems.

REFERENCES

[BOW95] Bowan, J.P. and M.G. Hinchley, "Ten Commandments of Formal Methods," *Computer,* vol. 28, no. 4, April 1995.

[GRI93] Gries, D. and F.B. Schneider, *A Logical Approach to Discrete Math,* Springer-Verlag, 1993.

[GUT93] Guttag, J.V., and J.J. Horning, *Larch: Languages and Tools for Formal Specification,* Springer-Verlag, 1993.

[HAL90] Hall, A., "Seven Myths of Formal Methods," *IEEE Software,* September 1990, pp. 11–20.

[HIN95] Hinchley, M.G. and S.A. Jarvis, *Concurrent Systems: Formal Development in CSP,* McGraw-Hill, 1995.

[HOR85] Hoare, C.A.R., *Communicating Sequential Processes,* Prentice-Hall International, 1985.

[JON91] Jones, C.B., *Systematic Software Development Using VDM,* 2nd ed., Prentice-Hall, 1991.

[LIS86] Liskov, B.H., and V. Berzins, "An Appraisal of Program Specifications," in *Software Specification Techniques,* N. Gehani and A.T. McKittrick (eds.), Addison-Wesley, 1986, p. 3.

[MAR94] Marciniak, J.J. (ed.), *Encyclopedia of Software Engineering,* Wiley, 1994.

[ROS95] Rosen, K.H., *Discrete Mathematics and Its Applications,* 3rd ed., McGraw-Hill, 1995.

[SPI88] Spivey, J.M., *Understanding Z: A Specification Language and Its Formal Semantics,* Cambridge University Press, 1988.

[SPI92] Spivey, J.M., *The Z Notation: A Reference Manual,* Prentice-Hall, 1992.

[WIL87] Wiltala, S.A., *Discrete Mathematics: A Unified Approach,* McGraw-Hill, 1987.

[WIN90] Wing, J.M., "A Specifier's Introduction to Formal Methods," *Computer,* vol. 23, no. 9, September 1990, pp. 8–24.

[YOU94] Yourdon, E., "Formal Methods," *Guerrilla Programmer,* Cutter Information Corp., October 1994.

PROBLEMS AND POINTS TO PONDER

25.1. Review the types of deficiencies associated with less formal approaches to software engineering in Section 25.1.1. Provide three examples of each from your own experience.

25.2. The benefits of mathematics as a specification mechanism have been discussed at length in this chapter. Is there a downside?

25.3. You have been assigned to a team that is developing software for a fax modem. Your job is to develop the "phone book" portion of the application. The phone book function enables up to *MaxNames* people to be stored along with associated company names, fax numbers, and other related information. Using natural language, define

a. The data invariant.

b. The state.

c. The operations that are likely.

25.4. You have been assigned to a software team that is developing software, called *MemoryDoubler,* that provides greater apparent memory for a PC than physical memory. This is accomplished by identifying, collecting, and reassigning blocks of memory that have been assigned to an existing application but are not being used. The unused blocks are reassigned to applications that require additional memory. Making appropriate assumptions and using natural language, define

a. The data invariant.

b. The state.

c. The operations that are likely.

25.5. Develop a constructive specification for a set that contains tuples of natural numbers of the form (x, y, z^2) such that the sum of x and y equals z.

25.6. The installer for a PC-based application first determines whether an acceptable set of hardware and systems resources is present. It checks the hardware configuration to determine whether various devices (of many possible devices) are present, and determines whether specific versions of system software and drivers are already installed. What set operator could be used to accomplish this? Provide an example in this context.

25.7. Attempt to develop a expression using logic and set operators for the following statement: "For all x and y, if x is the parent of y and y is the parent of z, then x is the grandparent of z. Everyone has a parent." Hint: Use the function $P(x, y)$ and $G(x, z)$ to represent parent and grandparent functions, respectively.

25.8. Develop a constructive set specification of the set of pairs where the first element of each pair is the sum of two nonzero natural numbers and the second element is the difference between the same numbers. Both numbers should be between 100 and 200 inclusive.

25.9. Develop a mathematical description for the state and data invariant for Problem 25.3. Refine this description in the Z specification language.

25.10. Develop a mathematical description for the state and data invariant for Problem 25.4. Refine this description in the Z specification language.

25.11. Using the Z notation presented in Table 25.1, select some part of the *SafeHome* security system described earlier in this book and attempt to specify it with Z.

25.12. Using one or more of the information sources noted in the references to this chapter or Further Readings and Information Sources, develop a half-hour presentation on the basic syntax and semantics of a formal specification language other than Z.

FURTHER READINGS AND INFORMATION SOURCES

In addition to the books used as references in this chapter, a fairly large number of books on formal methods topics have been published over the past decade. A listing of some of the more useful offerings follows:

Bowan, J., *Formal Specification and Documentation using Z: A Case Study Approach,* International Thomson Computer Press, 1996.

Casey, C., *A Programming Approach to Formal Methods,* McGraw-Hill, 2000.

Cooper, D. and R. Barden, *Z in Practice,* Prentice-Hall, 1995.

Craigen, D., S. Gerhart, and T. Ralston, *Industrial Application of Formal Methods to Model, Design and Analyze Computer Systems,* Noyes Data Corp., 1995.

Diller, A., *Z: An Introduction to Formal Methods,* 2nd ed., Wiley, 1994.

Harry, A., *Formal Methods Fact File: VDM and Z,* Wiley, 1997.

Hinchley, M. and J. Bowan, *Applications of Formal Methods,* Prentice-Hall, 1995.

Hinchley, M. and J. Bowan, *Industrial Strength Formal Methods,* Academic Press, 1997.

Hussmann, H., *Formal Foundations for Software Engineering Methods,* Springer-Verlag, 1997.

Jacky, J., *The Way of Z: Practical Programming with Formal Methods,* Cambridge University Press, 1997.

Lano, J. and H. Haughton (eds.), *Object-Oriented Specification Case Studies,* Prentice-Hall, 1993.

Rann, D., J. Turner, and J. Whitworth, *Z: A Beginner's Guide,* Chapman and Hall, 1994.

Ratcliff, B., *Introducing Specification Using Z: A Practical Case Study Approach,* McGraw-Hill, 1994.

D. Sheppard, *An Introduction to Formal Specification with Z and VDM,* McGraw-Hill, 1995.

The September 1990, issues of *IEEE Transactions on Software Engineering, IEEE Software,* and *IEEE Computer* were dedicated to formal methods. They remain an excellent source of useful information.

Schuman (*Formal Object-Oriented Development,* Springer-Verlag, 1996) has edited a book that addresses formal methods and object technologies, providing guidelines on the selective use of formal methods, and showing how such methods can be used in conjunction with OO approaches. Bowman and Derrick (*Formal Methods for Open Object-Based Distributed Systems,* Kluwer Academic Publishers, 1997) address the use of formal methods when coupled with OO applications in a distributed environment.

A wide variety of information sources on formal methods and related subjects is available on the Internet. An up-to-date list of World Wide Web references that are relevant to formal methods can be found at the SEPA Web site:
http://www.mhhe.com/engcs/compsci/pressman/resources/formal-methods.mhtml

CHAPTER

26 CLEANROOM SOFTWARE ENGINEERING

KEY CONCEPTS

The integrated use of conventional software engineering modeling (and possibly formal methods), program verification (correctness proofs), and statistical SQA have been combined into a technique that can lead to extremely high-quality software. *Cleanroom software engineering* is an approach that emphasizes the need to build correctness into software as it is being developed. Instead of the classic analysis, design, code, test, and debug cycle, the cleanroom approach suggests a different point of view [LIN94]:

> The philosophy behind cleanroom software engineering is to avoid dependence on costly defect removal processes by writing code increments right the first time and verifying their correctness before testing. Its process model incorporates the statistical quality certification of code increments as they accumulate into a system.

In many ways, the cleanroom approach elevates software engineering to another level. Like the formal methods presented in Chapter 25, the cleanroom process emphasizes rigor in specification and design, and formal verification of each design element using correctness proofs that are mathematically based. Extending the approach taken in formal methods, the cleanroom approach also emphasizes techniques for statistical quality control, including testing that is based on the anticipated use of the software by customers.

QUICK LOOK

What is it? How many times have you heard someone say "Do it right the first time"? That's the overriding philosophy of cleanroom software engineering—a process that emphasizes mathematical verification of correctness before program construction commences and certification of software reliability as part of the testing activity. The bottom line is extremely low failure rates that would be difficult or impossible to achieve using less formal methods.

Who does it? A specially trained software engineer.

Why is it important? Mistakes create rework. Rework takes time and increases costs. Wouldn't it be nice if we could dramatically reduce the number of mistakes (bugs) introduced as the software is designed and built? That's the premise of cleanroom software engineering.

What are the steps? Analysis and design models are created using box structure representation. A "box" encapsulates the system (or some aspect of the system) at a specific level of abstraction. Correctness verification is applied once the box structure design is complete. Once correctness has been verified for each box structure, statistical usage testing commences. The software is tested by defining a set of usage scenarios, determining the probability of use for each scenario, and then defining random tests that conform to the probabilities. The

QUICK LOOK

error records that result are analyzed to enable mathematical computation of projected reliability for the software component.

What is the work product? Black-box, state-box, and clear-box specifications are developed. The results of formal correctness proofs and statistical use tests are recorded.

How do I ensure that I've done it right? Formal proof of correctness is applied to the box structure specification. Statistical use testing exercises usage scenarios to ensure that errors in user functionality are uncovered and corrected. Test data are used to provide an indication of software reliability.

When software fails in the real world, immediate and long-term hazards abound. The hazards can be related to human safety, economic loss, or effective operation of business and societal infrastructure. Cleanroom software engineering is a process model that removes defects before they can precipitate serious hazards.

26.1 THE CLEANROOM APPROACH

The philosophy of the "cleanroom" in hardware fabrication technologies is really quite simple: It is cost-effective and time-effective to establish a fabrication approach that precludes the introduction of product defects. Rather than fabricating a product and then working to remove defects, the cleanroom approach demands the discipline required to eliminate defects in specification and design and then fabricate in a "clean" manner.

Quote:

"Cleanroom engineering achieves statistical quality control over software development by strictly separating the design process from the testing process in a pipeline of incremental software development."

Harlan Mills

The cleanroom philosophy was first proposed for software engineering by Mills, Dyer, and Linger [MIL87] during the 1980s. Although early experiences with this disciplined approach to software work showed significant promise [HAU94], it has not gained widespread usage. Henderson [HEN95] suggests three possible reasons:

1. A belief that the cleanroom methodology is too theoretical, too mathematical, and too radical for use in real software development.
2. It advocates no unit testing by developers but instead replaces it with correctness verification and statistical quality control—concepts that represent a major departure from the way most software is developed today.
3. The maturity of the software development industry. The use of cleanroom processes requires rigorous application of defined processes in all life cycle phases. Since most of the industry is still operating at the ad hoc level (as defined by the Software Engineering Institute Capability Maturity Model), the industry has not been ready to apply those techniques.

Despite elements of truth in each of these concerns, the potential benefits of cleanroom software engineering far outweigh the investment required to overcome the cultural resistance that is at the core of these concerns.

26.1.1 The Cleanroom Strategy

The cleanroom approach makes use of a specialized version of the incremental software model (Chapter 2). A "pipeline of software increments" [LIN94] is developed by small independent software engineering teams. As each increment is certified, it is integrated in the whole. Hence, functionality of the system grows with time.

The sequence of cleanroom tasks for each increment is illustrated in Figure 26.1. Overall system or product requirements are developed using the system engineering methods discussed in Chapter 10. Once functionality has been assigned to the software element of the system, the pipeline of cleanroom increments is initiated. The following tasks occur:

What are the major tasks conducted as part of cleanroom software engineering?

Increment planning. A project plan that adopts the incremental strategy is developed. The functionality of each increment, its projected size, and a cleanroom development schedule are created. Special care must be taken to ensure that certified increments will be integrated in a timely manner.

Requirements gathering. Using techniques similar to those introduced in Chapter 11, a more-detailed description of customer-level requirements (for each increment) is developed.

Box structure specification. A specification method that makes use of box structures [HEV93] is used to describe the functional specification. Conforming

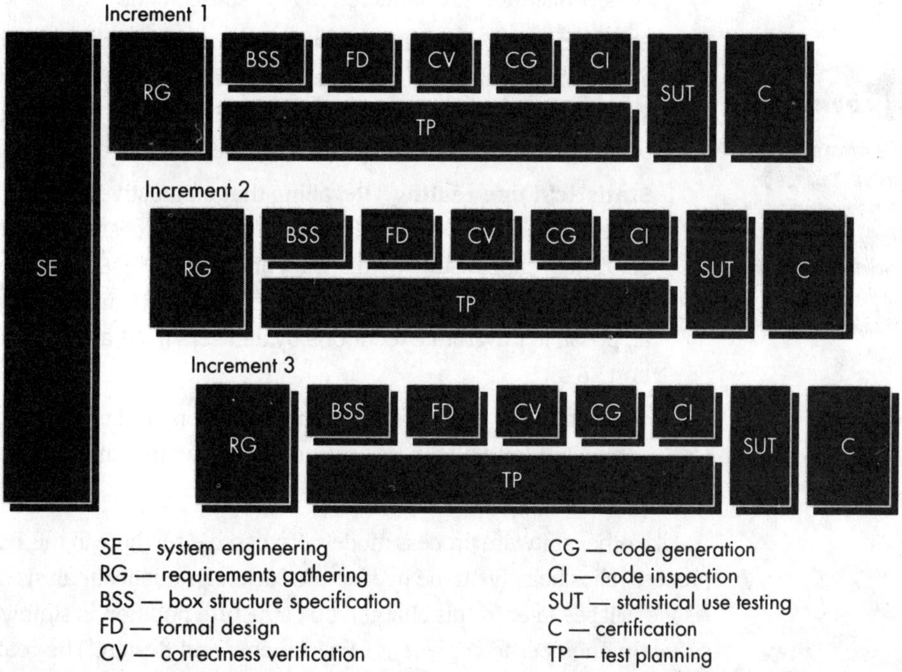

FIGURE 26.1 The cleanroom process model

to the operational analysis principles discussed in Chapter 11, box structures "isolate and separate the creative definition of behavior, data, and procedures at each level of refinement."

WebRef
An excellent source of information and resources for cleanroom software engineering can be found at **www.cleansoft.com**

Formal design. Using the box structure approach, cleanroom design is a natural and seamless extension of specification. Although it is possible to make a clear distinction between the two activities, specifications (called *black boxes*) are iteratively refined (within an increment) to become analogous to architectural and component-level designs (called *state boxes* and *clear boxes,* respectively).

Correctness verification. The cleanroom team conducts a series of rigorous correctness verification activities on the design and then the code. Verification (Sections 26.3 and 26.4) begins with the highest-level box structure (specification) and moves toward design detail and code. The first level of correctness verification occurs by applying a set of "correctness questions" [LIN88]. If these do not demonstrate that the specification is correct, more formal (mathematical) methods for verification are used.

Quote:
"Quality is not an act. It is a habit."
Aristotle

Code generation, inspection, and verification. The box structure specifications, represented in a specialized language, are translated into the appropriate programming language. Standard walkthrough or inspection techniques (Chapter 8) are then used to ensure semantic conformance of the code and box structures and syntactic correctness of the code. Then correctness verification is conducted for the source code.

Statistical test planning. The projected usage of the software is analyzed and a suite of test cases that exercise a "probability distribution" of usage are planned and designed (Section 26.4). Referring to Figure 26.1, this cleanroom activity is conducted in parallel with specification, verification, and code generation.

ADVICE
Cleanroom emphasizes tests that exercise the way the software is really used. Use-cases provide excellent input to the statistical test planning process.

Statistical use testing. Recalling that exhaustive testing of computer software is impossible (Chapter 17), it is always necessary to design a finite number of test cases. Statistical use techniques [POO88] execute a series of tests derived from a statistical sample (the probability distribution noted earlier) of all possible program executions by all users from a targeted population (Section 26.4).

Certification. Once verification, inspection, and usage testing have been completed (and all errors are corrected), the increment is certified as ready for integration.

Like other software process models discussed elsewhere in this book, the cleanroom process relies heavily on the need to produce high-quality analysis and design models. As we will see later in this chapter, box structure notation is simply another way for a software engineer to represent requirements and design. The real distinction of the cleanroom approach is that formal verification is applied to engineering models.

26.1.2 What Makes Cleanroom Different?

Dyer [DYE92] alludes to the differences of the cleanroom approach when he defines the process:

> Cleanroom represents the first practical attempt at putting the software development process under statistical quality control with a well-defined strategy for continuous process improvement. To reach this goal, a cleanroom unique life cycle was defined which focused on mathematics-based software engineering for correct software designs and on statistics-based software testing for certification of software reliability.

KEY POINT
The most important distinguishing characteristics of cleanroom are proof of correctness and statistical use testing.

Cleanroom software engineering differs from the conventional and object-oriented views presented in Parts Three and Four of this book because

1. It makes explicit use of statistical quality control.
2. It verifies design specification using a mathematically based proof of correctness.
3. It relies heavily on statistical use testing to uncover high-impact errors.

Obviously, the cleanroom approach applies most, if not all, of the basic software engineering principles and concepts presented throughout this book. Good analysis and design procedures are essential if high quality is to result. But cleanroom engineering diverges from conventional software practices by deemphasizing (some would say, eliminating) the role of unit testing and debugging and dramatically reducing (or eliminating) the amount of testing performed by the developer of the software.[1]

Quote:
"It's a funny thing about life: if you refuse to accept anything but the best, you very often get it."
W. Somerset Maugham

In conventional software development, errors are accepted as a fact of life. Because errors are deemed to be inevitable, each program module should be unit tested (to uncover errors) and then debugged (to remove errors). When the software is finally released, field use uncovers still more defects and another test and debug cycle begins. The rework associated with these activities is costly and time consuming. Worse, it can be degenerative—error correction can (inadvertently) lead to the introduction of still more errors.

In cleanroom software engineering, unit testing and debugging are replaced by correctness verification and statistically based testing. These activities, coupled with the record keeping necessary for continuous improvement, make the cleanroom approach unique.

26.2 FUNCTIONAL SPECIFICATION

Regardless of the analysis method that is chosen, the operational principles presented in Chapter 11 apply. Data, function, and behavior are modeled. The resultant

1 Testing is conducted but by an independent testing team.

models must be partitioned (refined) to provide increasingly greater detail. The overall objective is to move from a specification that captures the essence of a problem to a specification that provides substantial implementation detail.

Cleanroom software engineering complies with the operational analysis principles by using a method called *box structure specification.* A "box" encapsulates the system (or some aspect of the system) at some level of detail. Through a process of stepwise refinement, boxes are refined into a hierarchy where each box has *referential transparency.* That is, "the information content of each box specification is sufficient to define its refinement, without depending on the implementation of any other box" [LIN94]. This enables the analyst to partition a system hierarchically, moving from essential representation at the top to implementation-specific detail at the bottom. Three types of boxes are used:

How is refinement accomplished as part of box structure specification?

Black box. The black box specifies the behavior of a system or a part of a system. The system (or part) responds to specific stimuli (events) by applying a set of transition rules that map the stimulus into a response.

State box. The state box encapsulates state data and services (operations) in a manner that is analogous to objects. In this specification view, inputs to the state box (stimuli) and outputs (responses) are represented. The state box also represents the "stimulus history" of the black box; that is, the data encapsulated in the state box that must be retained between the transitions implied.

Clear box. The transition functions that are implied by the state box are defined in the clear box. Stated simply, a clear box contains the procedural design for the state box.

Figure 26.2 illustrates the refinement approach using box structure specification. A black box (BB_1) defines responses for a complete set of stimuli. BB_1 can be refined into a set of black boxes, $BB_{1.1}$ to $BB_{1.n}$, each of which addresses a class of behavior. Refinement continues until a cohesive class of behavior is identified (e.g., $BB_{1.1.1}$). A state box ($SB_{1.1.1}$) is then defined for the black box ($BB_{1.1.1}$). In this case, $SB_{1.1.1}$ contains all data and services required to implement the behavior defined by $BB_{1.1.1}$. Finally, $SB_{1.1.1}$ is refined into clear boxes ($CB_{1.1.1.n}$) and procedural design details are specified.

KEY POINT

Box structure refinement and verification of correctness occur simultaneously.

As each of these refinement steps occurs, verification of correctness also occurs. State-box specifications are verified to ensure that each conforms to the behavior defined by the parent black-box specification. Similarly, clear-box specifications are verified against the parent state box.

It should be noted that specification methods based on formal methods (Chapter 25) can be used in lieu of the box structure specification approach. The only requirement is that each level of specification can be formally verified.

FIGURE 26.2
Box structure refinement

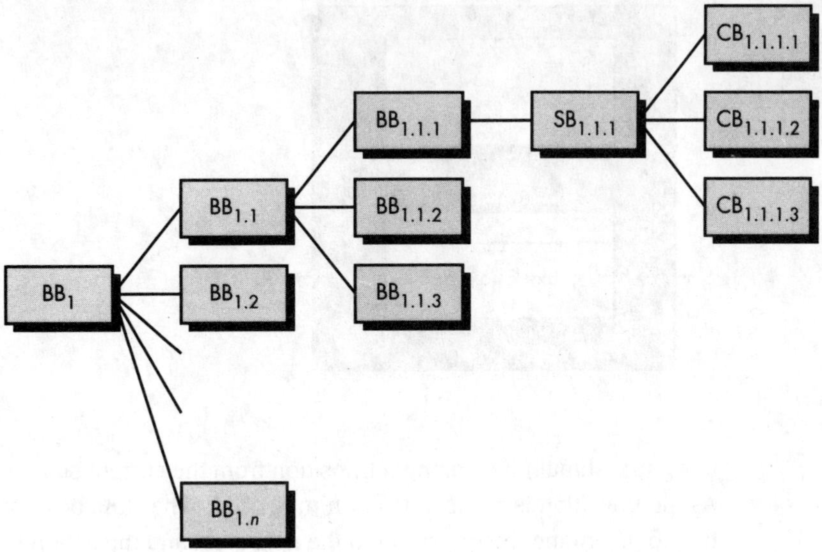

26.2.1 Black-Box Specification

A black-box specification describes an abstraction, stimuli, and response using the notation shown in Figure 26.3 [MIL88]. The function *f* is applied to a sequence, *S**, of inputs (stimuli), *S*, and transforms them into an output (response), *R*. For simple software components, *f* may be a mathematical function, but in general, *f* is described using natural language (or a formal specification language).

XRef
Object-oriented concepts are discussed in Chapter 20.

Many of the concepts introduced for object-oriented systems are also applicable for the black box. Data abstractions and the operations that manipulate those abstractions are encapsulated by the black box. Like a class hierarchy, the black box specification can exhibit usage hierarchies in which low-level boxes inherit the properties of those boxes higher in the tree structure.

26.2.2 State-Box Specification

The state box is "a simple generalization of a state machine" [MIL88]. Recalling the discussion of behavioral modeling and state transition diagrams in Chapter 12, a state is some observable mode of system behavior. As processing occurs, a system responds

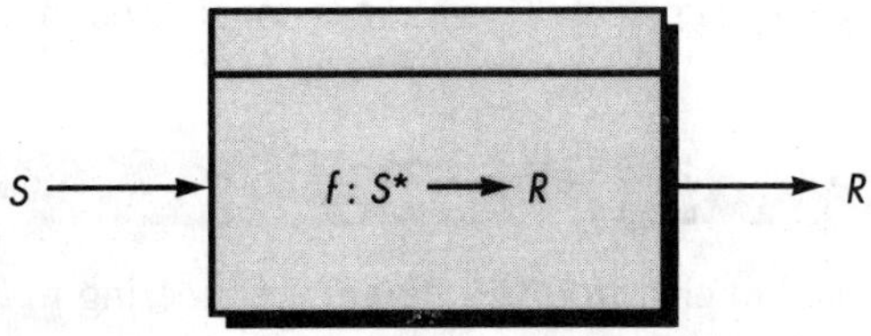

FIGURE 26.3
A black-box specification

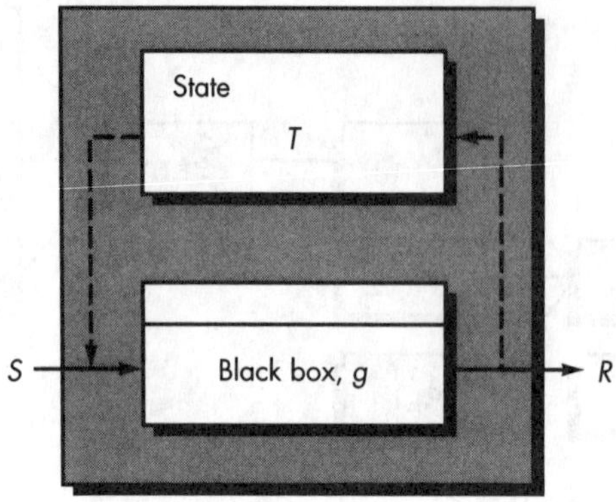

FIGURE 26.4
A state box specification

to events (stimuli) by making a transition from the current state to some new state. As the transition is made, an action may occur. The state box uses a data abstraction to determine the transition to the next state and the action (response) that will occur as a consequence of the transition.

Referring to Figure 26.4, the state box incorporates a black box. The stimulus, *S*, that is input to the black box arrives from some external source and a set of internal system states, *T*. Mills [MIL88] provides a mathematical description of the function, *f*, of the black box contained within the state box:

$$g : S^* \times T^* \text{—>} R \times T$$

where *g* is a subfunction that is tied to a specific state, *t*. When considered collectively, the state-subfunction pairs (*t*, *g*) define the black box function *f*.

26.2.3 Clear-Box Specification

> **XRef**
> Procedural design and structured programming are discussed in Chapter 16.

The clear-box specification is closely aligned with procedural design and structured programming. In essence, the subfunction *g* within the state box is replaced by the structured programming constructs that implement *g*.

As an example, consider the clear box shown in Figure 26.5. The black box, *g*, shown in Figure 26.4, is replaced by a sequence construct that incorporates a conditional. These, in turn, can be refined into lower-level clear boxes as stepwise refinement proceeds.

It is important to note that the procedural specification described in the clear-box hierarchy can be proved to be correct. This topic is considered in the next section.

26.3 CLEANROOM DESIGN

The design approach used in cleanroom software engineering makes heavy use of the structured programming philosophy. But in this case, structured programming is applied far more rigorously.

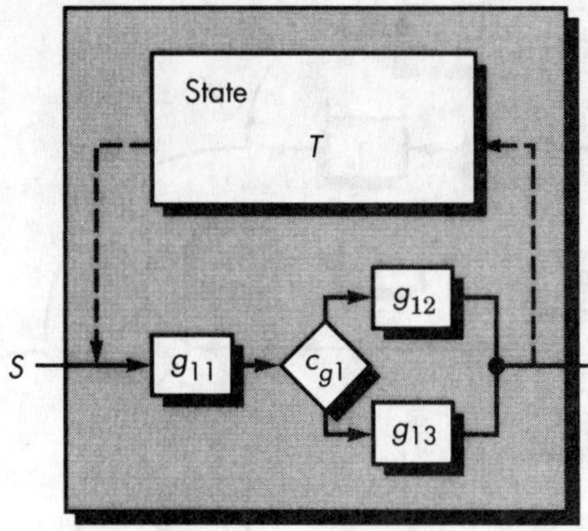

FIGURE 26.5
A clear-box specification

WebRef
The DoD STARS program has developed a variety of cleanroom guides and documents: **ftp.cdrom.com/pub/ada/docs/cleanrm/**

Basic processing functions (described during earlier refinements of the specification) are refined using a "stepwise expansion of mathematical functions into structures of logical connectives [e.g., *if-then-else*] and subfunctions, where the expansion [is] carried out until all identified subfunctions could be directly stated in the programming language used for implementation" [DYE92].

The structured programming approach can be used effectively to refine function, but what about data design? Here a number of fundamental design concepts (Chapter 13) come into play. Program data are encapsulated as a set of abstractions that are serviced by subfunctions. The concepts of data encapsulation, information hiding, and data typing are used to create the data design.

26.3.1 Design Refinement and Verification

Each clear-box specification represents the design of a procedure (subfunction) required to accomplish a state box transition. With the clear box, the structured programming constructs and stepwise refinement are used as illustrated in Figure 26.6. A program function, *f*, is refined into a sequence of subfunctions *g* and *h*. These in turn are refined into conditional constructs (*if-then-else* and *do-while*). Further refinement illustrates continuing logical refinement.

? What conditions are applied to prove structured constructs correct?

At each level of refinement, the cleanroom team[2] performs a formal correctness verification. To accomplish this, a set of generic *correctness conditions* are attached to the structured programming constructs. If a function *f* is expanded into a sequence *g* and *h*, the correctness condition for all input to *f* is

- **Does *g* followed by *h* do *f*?**

When a function *p* is refined into a conditional of the form, if ⟨ c ⟩ then *q*, else *r*, the correctness condition for all input to *p* is

2 Because the entire team is involved in the verification process, it is less likely that an error will be made in conducting the verification itself.

FIGURE 26.6
Stepwise refinement

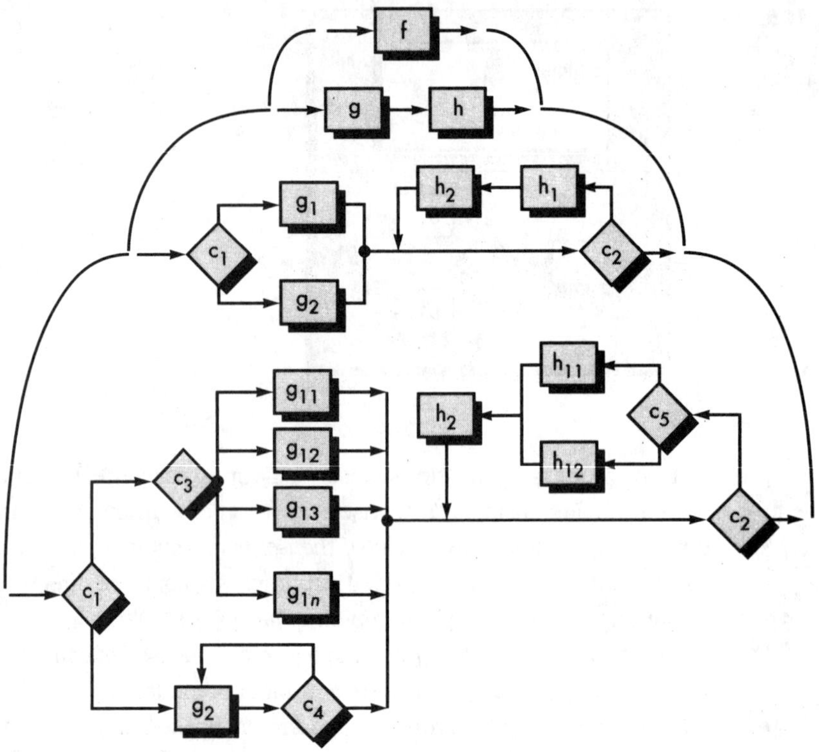

- **Whenever condition ⟨c⟩ is true, does *q* do *p*; and whenever ⟨c⟩ is false, does *r* do *p*?**

When function *m* is refined as a loop, the correctness conditions for all input to *m* are

- **Is termination guaranteed?**
- **Whenever ⟨c⟩ is true, does *n* followed by *m* do *m*; and whenever ⟨c⟩ is false, does skipping the loop still do *m*?**

ADVICE

If you limit yourself to just the structured constructs as you create a procedural design, proof of correctness is straightforward. If you "violate" the constructs, correctness proofs are difficult or impossible.

Each time a clear box is refined to the next level of detail, these correctness conditions are applied.

It is important to note that the use of the structured programming constructs constrains the number of correctness tests that must be conducted. A single condition is checked for sequences; two conditions are tested for if-then-else, and three conditions are verified for loops.

To illustrate correctness verification for a procedural design, we use a simple example first introduced by Linger, Mills, and Witt [LIN79]. The intent is to design and verify a small program that finds the integer part, *y*, of a square root of a given integer, *x*. The procedural design is represented using the flowchart in Figure 26.7.

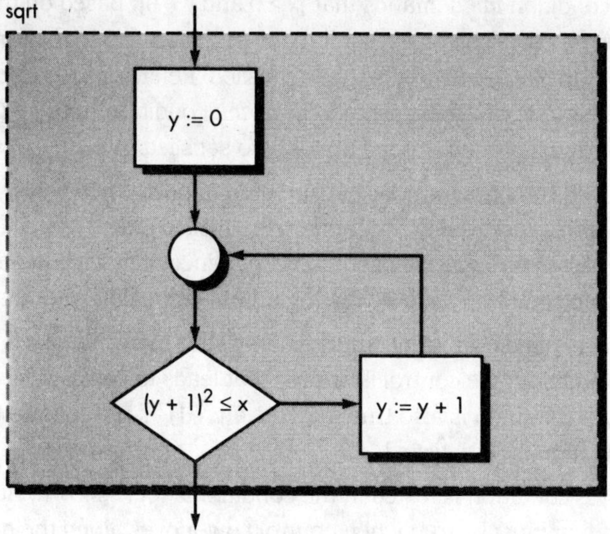

FIGURE 26.7 Computing the integer part of a square root [LIN79]

To verify the correctness of this design, we must define entry and exit conditions as noted in Figure 26.8. The entry condition notes that x must be greater than or equal to 0. The exit condition requires that x remain unchanged and take on a value within the range noted in the figure. To prove the design to be correct, it is necessary to prove the conditions *init, loop, cont, yes,* and *exit* shown in Figure 26.8 are true in all cases. These are sometimes called *subproofs.*

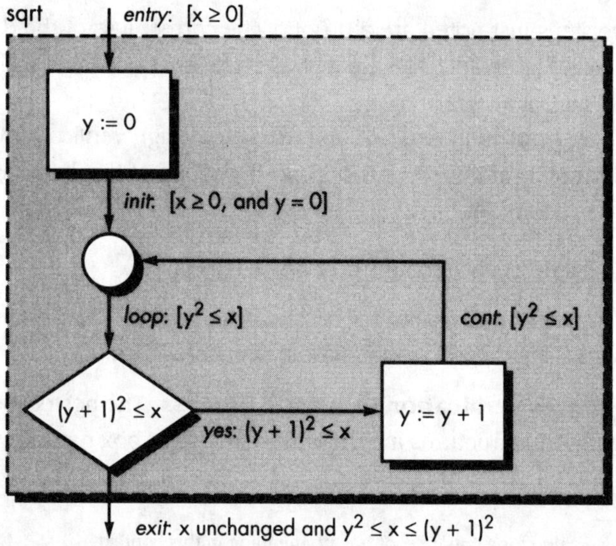

FIGURE 26.8 Proving the design correct [LIN79]

1. The condition *init* demands that [$x \geq 0$ and $y = 0$]. Based on the requirements of the problem, the entry condition is assumed correct.[3] Therefore, the first part of the *init* condition, $x \geq 0$, is satisfied. Referring to the flowchart, the statement immediately preceding the *init* condition, sets $y = 0$. Therefore, the second part of the *init* condition is also satisfied. Hence, *init* is true.

KEY POINT

To prove a design correct, you must first identify all conditions and then prove that each takes on the appropriate Boolean value. These are called *subproofs*.

2. The *loop* condition may be encountered in one of two ways: (1) directly from *init* (in this case, the *loop* condition is satisfied directly) or via control flow that passes through the condition *cont*. Since the *cont* condition is identical to the *loop* condition, *loop* is true regardless of the flow path that leads to it.
3. The *cont* condition is encountered only after the value of y is incremented by 1. In addition, the control flow path that leads to *cont* can be invoked only if the *yes* condition is also true. Hence, if $(y + 1)^2 \leq x$, it follows that $y^2 \leq x$. The *cont* condition is satisfied.
4. The *yes* condition is tested in the conditional logic shown. Hence, the *yes* condition must be true when control flow moves along the path shown.
5. The *exit* condition first demands that x remain unchanged. An examination of the design indicates that x appears nowhere to the left of an assignment operator. There are no function calls that use x. Hence, it is unchanged. Since the conditional test $(y + 1)^2 \leq x$ must fail to reach the *exit* condition, it follows that $(y + 1)^2 \leq x$. In addition, the loop condition must still be true (i.e., $y^2 \leq x$). Therefore, $(y + 1)^2 > x$ and $y^2 \leq x$ can be combined to satisfy the *exit* condition.

We must further ensure that the loop terminates. An examination of the loop condition indicates that, because y is incremented and $x \geq 0$, the loop must eventually terminate.

The five steps just noted are a proof of the correctness of the design of the algorithm noted in Figure 26.7. We are now certain that the design will, in fact, compute the integer part of a square root.

A more rigorous mathematical approach to design verification is possible. However, a discussion of this topic is beyond the scope of this book. Interested readers should refer to [LIN79].

26.3.2 Advantages of Design Verification[4]

Rigorous correctness verification of each refinement of the clear-box design has a number of distinct advantages. Linger [LIN94] describes these in the following manner:

? What do we gain by doing correctness proofs?

- **It reduces verification to a finite process.** The nested, sequential way that control structures are organized in a clear box naturally defines a hierar-

3 A negative value for a square root has no meaning in this context.

4 This section and Figures 26.7 through 26.9 have been adapted from [LIN94]. Used with permission.

FIGURE 26.9
A design with subproofs [LIN94]

```
[f1]                    Subproofs:
 DO                     f1 = [DO g1; g2; [f2] END] ?
  g1
  g2
  [f2]                  f2 = [WHILE p1 DO [f3] END] ?
   WHILE
    p1
   DO [f3]              f3 = [DO g3; [f4]; g8 END] ?
    g3
    [f4]                f4 = [IF p2; THEN [f5] ELSE [f6] END] ?
    IF
     p2
    THEN [f5]           f5 = [DO g4; g5 END] ?
     g4
     g5
    ELSE [f6]           f6 = [DO g6; g7 END] ?
     g6
     g7
    END
    g8
   END
END
```

chy that reveals the correctness conditions that must be verified. An axiom of replacement [LIN79] lets us substitute intended functions with their control structure refinements in the hierarchy of subproofs. For example, the subproof for the intended function f1 in Figure 26.9 requires proving that the composition of the operations g1 and g2 with the intended function f2 has the same effect on data as f1. Note that f2 substitutes for all the details of its refinement in the proof. This substitution localizes the proof argument to the control structure at hand. In fact, it lets the software engineer carry out the proofs in any order.

KEY POINT
Despite the extremely large number of execution paths in a program, the number of steps to prove the program correct is quite small.

- **It is impossible to overemphasize the positive effect that reducing verification to a finite process has on quality.** Even though all but the most trivial programs exhibit an essentially infinite number of execution paths, they can be verified in a finite number of steps.
- **It lets cleanroom teams verify every line of design and code.** Teams can carry out the verification through group analysis and discussion on the basis of the correctness theorem, and they can produce written proofs when extra confidence in a life- or mission-critical system is required.
- **It results in a near zero defect level.** During a team review, every correctness condition of every control structure is verified in turn. Every team member must agree that each condition is correct, so an error is possible

only if every team member incorrectly verifies a condition. The requirement for unanimous agreement based on individual verification results in software that has few or no defects before first execution.

- **It scales up.** Every software system, no matter how large, has top-level, clear-box procedures composed of sequence, alternation, and iteration structures. Each of these typically invokes a large subsystem with thousands of lines of code—and each of those subsystems has its own top-level intended functions and procedures. So the correctness conditions for these high-level control structures are verified in the same way as are those of low-level structures. Verification at high levels may take, and well be worth, more time, but it does not take more theory.
- **It produces better code than unit testing.** Unit testing checks the effects of executing only selected test paths out of many possible paths. By basing verification on function theory, the cleanroom approach can verify every possible effect on all data, because while a program may have many execution paths, it has only one function. Verification is also more efficient than unit testing. Most verification conditions can be checked in a few minutes, but unit tests take substantial time to prepare, execute, and check.

It is important to note that design verification must ultimately be applied to the source code itself. In this context, it is often called *correctness verification.*

26.4 CLEANROOM TESTING

The strategy and tactics of cleanroom testing are fundamentally different from conventional testing approaches. Conventional methods derive a set of test cases to uncover design and coding errors. The goal of cleanroom testing is to validate software requirements by demonstrating that a statistical sample of use-cases (Chapter 11) have been executed successfully.

26.4.1 Statistical Use Testing

The user of a computer program rarely needs to understand the technical details of the design. The user-visible behavior of the program is driven by inputs and events that are often produced by the user. But in complex systems, the possible spectrum of input and events (i.e., the use-cases) can be extremely wide. What subset of use-cases will adequately verify the behavior of the program? This is the first question addressed by statistical use testing.

Statistical use testing "amounts to testing software the way users intend to use it" [LIN94]. To accomplish this, *cleanroom testing teams* (also called *certification teams*) must determine a usage probability distribution for the software. The specification (black box) for each increment of the software is analyzed to define a set of stimuli (inputs or events) that cause the software to change its behavior. Based on interviews with potential users, the creation of usage scenarios, and a general understanding of the application domain, a probability of use is assigned to each stimuli.

Test cases are generated for each stimuli[5] according to the usage probability distribution. To illustrate, consider the *SafeHome* security system discussed earlier in this book. Cleanroom software engineering is being used to develop a software increment that manages user interaction with the security system keypad. Five stimuli have been identified for this increment. Analysis indicates the percent probability distribution of each stimulus. To make selection of test cases easier, these probabilities are mapped into intervals numbered between 1 and 99 [LIN94] and illustrated in the following table:

Program Stimulus	Probability	Interval
Arm/disarm (AD)	50%	1–49
Zone set (ZS)	15%	50–63
Query (Q)	15%	64–78
Test (T)	15%	79–94
Panic alarm	5%	95–99

To generate a sequence of usage test cases that conform to the usage probability distribution, a series of random numbers between 1 and 99 is generated. The random number corresponds to an interval on the preceding probability distribution. Hence, the sequence of usage test cases is defined randomly but corresponds to the appropriate probability of stimuli occurrence. For example, assume the following random number sequences are generated:

13-94-22-24-45-56
81-19-31-69-45-9
38-21-52-84-86-4

Selecting the appropriate stimuli based on the distribution interval shown in the table, the following use-cases are derived:

AD–T–AD–AD–AD–ZS
T–AD–AD–AD–Q–AD–AD
AD–AD–ZS–T–T–AD

The testing team executes these use-cases and verifies software behavior against the specification for the system. Timing for tests is recorded so that interval times may be determined. Using interval times, the certification team can compute mean-time-to-failure. If a long sequence of tests is conducted without failure, the MTTF is low and software reliability may be assumed high.

---

5 Automated tools are used to accomplish this. For further information, see [DYE92].

26.4.2 Certification

The verification and testing techniques discussed earlier in this chapter lead to software components (and entire increments) that can be certified. Within the context of the cleanroom software engineering approach, *certification* implies that the reliability (measured by mean-time-to-failure, MTTF) can be specified for each component.

The potential impact of certifiable software components goes far beyond a single cleanroom project. Reusable software components can be stored along with their usage scenarios, program stimuli, and probability distributions. Each component would have a certified reliability under the usage scenario and testing regime described. This information is invaluable to others who intend to use the components.

The certification approach involves five steps [WOH94]:

How do we certify a software component?

1. Usage scenarios must be created.
2. A usage profile is specified.
3. Test cases are generated from the profile.
4. Tests are executed and failure data are recorded and analyzed.
5. Reliability is computed and certified.

Steps 1 through 4 have been discussed in an earlier section. In this section, we concentrate on reliability certification.

Certification for cleanroom software engineering requires the creation of three models [POO93]:

Sampling model. Software testing executes *m* random test cases and is certified if no failures or a specified numbers of failures occur. The value of *m* is derived mathematically to ensure that required reliability is achieved.

Component model. A system composed of *n* components is to be certified. The component model enables the analyst to determine the probability that component *i* will fail prior to completion.

Certification model. The overall reliability of the system is projected and certified.

At the completion of statistical use testing, the certification team has the information required to deliver software that has a certified MTTF computed using each of these models.

A detailed discussion of the computation of the sampling, component, and certification models is beyond the scope of this book. The interested reader should see [MUS87], [CUR86], and [POO93] for additional detail.

26.5 SUMMARY

Cleanroom software engineering is a formal approach to software development that can lead to software that has remarkably high quality. It uses box structure specification (or formal methods) for analysis and design modeling and emphasizes correctness verification, rather than testing, as the primary mechanism for finding and removing errors. Statistical use testing is applied to develop the failure rate information necessary to certify the reliability of delivered software.

The cleanroom approach begins with analysis and design models that use a box structure representation. A "box" encapsulates the system (or some aspect of the system) at a specific level of abstraction. Black boxes are used to represent the externally observable behavior of a system. State boxes encapsulate state data and operations. A clear box is used to model the procedural design that is implied by the data and operations of a state box.

Correctness verification is applied once the box structure design is complete. The procedural design for a software component is partitioned into a series of subfunctions. To prove the correctness of the subfunctions, exit conditions are defined for each subfunction and a set of subproofs is applied. If each exit condition is satisfied, the design must be correct.

Once correctness verification is complete, statistical use testing commences. Unlike conventional testing, cleanroom software engineering does not emphasize unit or integration testing. Rather, the software is tested by defining a set of usage scenarios, determining the probability of use for each scenario, and then defining random tests that conform to the probabilities. The error records that result are combined with sampling, component, and certification models to enable mathematical computation of projected reliability for the software component.

The cleanroom philosophy is a rigorous approach to software engineering. It is a software process model that emphasizes mathematical verification of correctness and certification of software reliability. The bottom line is extremely low failure rates that would be difficult or impossible to achieve using less formal methods.

REFERENCES

[CUR86] Curritt, P.A., M. Dyer, and H.D. Mills, "Certifying the Reliability of Software," *IEEE Trans, Software Engineering,* vol. SE-12, no. 1, January 1994.

[DYE92] Dyer, M., *The Cleanroom Approach to Quality Software Development,* Wiley, 1992.

[HAU94] Hausler, P.A., R. Linger, and C. Trammel, "Adopting Cleanroom Software Engineering with a Phased Approach," *IBM Systems Journal,* vol. 33, no.1, January 1994, pp. 89–109.

[HEN95] Henderson, J., "Why Isn't Cleanroom the Universal Software Development Methodology?" *Crosstalk,* vol. 8, No. 5, May 1995, pp. 11–14.

[HEV93] Hevner, A.R. and H.D. Mills, "Box Structure Methods for System Development with Objects," *IBM Systems Journal,* vol. 31, no.2, February 1993, pp. 232–251.

{LIN79] Linger, R.M., H.D. Mills, and B.I. Witt, *Structured Programming: Theory and Practice,* Addison-Wesley, 1979.

[LIN88] Linger, R.M. and H.D. Mills, "A Case Study in Cleanroom Software Engineering: The IBM COBOL Structuring Facility," *Proc. COMPSAC '88,* Chicago, October 1988.

[LIN94] Linger, R., "Cleanroom Process Model," *IEEE Software,* vol. 11, no. 2, March 1994, pp. 50–58.

[MIL87] Mills, H.D., M. Dyer, and R. Linger, "Cleanroom Software Engineering," *IEEE Software,* vol. 4, no. 5, September 1987, pp. 19–24.

[MIL88] Mills, H.D., "Stepwise Refinement and Verification in Box Structured Systems," *Computer,* vol. 21, no. 6, June 1988, pp. 23–35.

[MUS87] Musa, J.D., A. Iannino, and K. Okumoto, *Engineering and Managing Software with Reliability Measures,* McGraw-Hill, 1987.

[POO88] Poore, J.H. and H.D. Mills, "Bringing Software Under Statistical Quality Control," *Quality Progress,* November 1988, pp. 52–55.

[POO93] Poore, J.H., H.D. Mills, and D. Mutchler, "Planning and Certifying Software System Reliability," *IEEE Software,* vol. 10, no. 1, January 1993, pp. 88–99.

[WOH94] Wohlin, C. and P. Runeson, "Certification of Software Components," *IEEE Trans. Software Engineering,* vol. SE-20, no. 6, June 1994, pp. 494–499.

PROBLEMS AND POINTS TO PONDER

26.1. If you had to pick one aspect of cleanroom software engineering that makes it radically different from conventional or object-oriented software engineering approaches, what would it be?

26.2. How do an incremental process model and certification work together to produce high-quality software?

26.3. Using box structure specification, develop "first-pass" analysis and design models for the *SafeHome* system.

26.4. Develop a box structure specification for a portion of the PHTRS system introduced in Problem 12.13.

26.5. Develop a box structure specification for the e-mail system presented in Problem 21.15.

26.6. A bubble sort algorithm is defined in the following manner:

```
procedure bubblesort;
   var i, t, integer;
   begin
   repeat until t=a[1]
      t:=a[1];
      for j:= 2 to n do
         if a[j-1] > a[j] then begin
            t:=a[j-1];
```

```
            a[j-1]:=a[j];
            a[j]:=t;
            end
    endrep
end
```

Partition the design into subfunctions and define a set of conditions that would enable you to prove that this algorithm is correct.

26.7. Document a correctness verification proof for the bubble sort discussed in Problem 26.6.

26.8. Select a program component that you have designed in another context (or one assigned by your instructor) and develop a complete proof of correctness for it.

26.9. Select a program that you use regularly (e.g., an e-mail handler, a word processor, a spreadsheet program). Create a set of usage scenarios for the program. Define the probability of use for each scenario and then develop a program stimuli and probability distribution table similar to the one shown in Section 26.4.1.

26.10. For the program stimuli and probability distribution table developed in Problem 26.9, use a random number generator to develop a set of test cases for use in statistical use testing.

26.11. In your own words, describe the intent of certification in the cleanroom software engineering context.

26.12. Write a short paper that describes the mathematics used to define the certification models described briefly in Section 26.4.2. Use [MUS87], [CUR86], and [POO93] as a starting point.

FURTHER READINGS AND INFORMATION SOURCES

Prowell et al. (*Cleanroom Software Engineering: Technology and Process,* Addison-Wesley, 1999) provides an in-depth treatment of all important aspects of the cleanroom approach. Useful discussions of cleanroom topics have been edited by Poore and Trammell *(Cleanroom Software Engineering: A Reader,* Blackwell Publishing, 1996). Becker and Whittaker (*Cleanroom Software Engineering Practices,* Idea Group Publishing, 1996) present an excellent overview for those who are unfamiliar with cleanroom practices.

The Cleanroom Pamphlet (Software Technology Support Center, Hill AF Base, April 1995) contains reprints of a number of important articles. Linger [LIN94] produced one of the better introductions to the subject. *Asset Source for Software Engineering Technology,* ASSET, (United States Department of Defense) offers an excellent six volume set of *Cleanroom Engineering Handbooks.* ASSET can be contacted at info@source.asset.com. Lockheed Martin's *Guide to the Integration of Object-Oriented*

Methods and Cleanroom Software Engineering (1997) contains a generic cleanroom process for OO systems and is available at http://www.asset.com/stars/loral/cleanroom/oo/guidhome.htm.

Linger and Trammell (*Cleanroom Software Engineering Reference Model,* SEI Technical Report CMU/SEI-96-TR-022, 1996) have defined a set of 14 cleanroom processes and 20 work products that form the basis for the SEI CMM for cleanroom software engineering (CMU/SEI-96-TR-023).

Michael Deck of Cleanroom Software Engineering has prepared a bibliography on cleanroom topics. Among the references are the following:

General and Introductory

Deck, M.D., "Cleanroom Software Engineering Myths and Realities," *Quality Week 1997,* May 1997.

Deck, M.D, and J. A. Whittaker, "Lessons Learned from Fifteen Years of Cleanroom Testing," *Software Testing, Analysis, and Review (STAR) '97,* San Jose, CA, May 5–9, 1997.

Lokan, C.J., "The Cleanroom Process for Software Development," *The Australian Computer Journal,* vol. 25, no. 4, November 1993.

Linger, Richard C., "Cleanroom Software Engineering for Zero-Defect Software," *Proc. 15th International Conference on Software Engineering,* May 1993.

Keuffel, W., "Clean Your Room: Formal Methods for the '90s," *Computer Language,* July 1992, pp. 39–46.

Hevner, A.R., S.A. Becker, and L.B. Pedowitz, "Integrated CASE for Cleanroom Development," *IEEE Software,* March 1992, pp. 69–76.

Cobb, R.H. and H.D. Mills, "Engineering Software under Statistical Quality Control," *IEEE Software,* November 1990, pp. 44–54.

Management Practices

Becker, S.A., Deck, M.D., and Janzon, T., "Cleanroom and Organizational Change," *Proc. 14th Pacific Northwest Software Quality Conference,* Portland, OR, October 29–30, 1996.

Linger, R.C., "Cleanroom Process Model," *IEEE Software.* March 1994, pp. 50–58.

Linger, R.C. and R.A. Spangler, "The IBM Cleanroom Software Engineering Technology Transfer Program," *Sixth SEI Conference on Software Engineering Education,* San Diego, CA, October 1992.

Specification, Design, and Review

Deck, M.D., "Cleanroom and Object-Oriented Software Engineering: A Unique Synergy," *1996 Software Technology Conference,* Salt Lake City, UT, April 24, 1996.

Deck, M.D., "Using Box Structures to Link Cleanroom and Object-Oriented Software Engineering," Technical Report 94.01b, Cleanroom Software Engineering, 1994.

Dyer, M., "Designing Software for Provable Correctness: The Direction for Quality Software," *Information and Software Technology,* vol. 30 no. 6, July–August 1988, pp. 331–340.

Testing and Certification

Dyer, M., "An Approach to Software Reliability Measurement," *Information and Software Technology,* vol. 29 no. 8, October 1987, pp. 415–420.

Head, G.E., "Six-Sigma Software Using Cleanroom Software Engineering Techniques," *Hewlett-Packard Journal,* June 1994, pp. 40–50.

Oshana, R., "Quality Software via a Cleanroom Methodology," *Embedded Systems Programming,* September. 1996, pp. 36–52.

Whittaker, J.A. and M.G. Thomason, "A Markov Chain Model for Statistical Software Testing," *IEEE Trans. Software Engineering,* vol. SE-20 October 1994, pp. 812–824.

Case Studies and Experience Reports

Head, G.E., "Six-Sigma Software Using Cleanroom Software Engineering Techniques," *Hewlett-Packard Journal,* June 1994, pp. 40–50.

Hevner, A.R. and H.D. Mills, "Box-Structured Methods for Systems Development with Objects," *IBM Systems Journal,* vol. 32, no. 2, 1993, p. 232–251.

Tann, L-G., "OS32 and Cleanroom," *Proc. First Annual European Industrial Symposium on Cleanroom Software Engineering,* Copenhagen, Denmark, 1993, pp. 1–40.

Hausler, P.A., "A Recent Cleanroom Success Story: The Redwing Project," *Proc. 17th Annual Software Engineering Workshop,* NASA Goddard Space Flight Center, December 1992.

Trammel, C.J., L.H. Binder, and C.E. Snyder, "The Automated Production Control Documentation System: A Case Study in Cleanroom Software Engineering," *ACM Trans. on Software Engineering and Methodology,* vol. 1, no. 1, January 1992, pp. 81–94.

Design verification via proof of correctness lies at the heart of the cleanroom approach. Books by Baber (*Error-Free Software,* Wiley, 1991) and Schulmeyer (*Zero Defect Software,* McGraw-Hill, 1990) discuss proof of correctness in considerable detail.

A wide variety of information sources on cleanroom software engineering and related subjects is available on the Internet. An up-to-date list of World Wide Web references that are relevant to cleanroom software engineering can be found at the SEPA Web site:

http://www.mhhe.com/engcs/compsci/pressman/resources/cleanroom.mhtml

CHAPTER

27 COMPONENT-BASED SOFTWARE ENGINEERING

KEY CONCEPTS

In the software engineering context, reuse is an idea both old and new. Programmers have reused ideas, abstractions, and processes since the earliest days of computing, but the early approach to reuse was ad hoc. Today, complex, high-quality computer-based systems must be built in very short time periods. This mitigates toward a more organized approach to reuse.

Component-based software engineering (CBSE) is a process that emphasizes the design and construction of computer-based systems using reusable software "components." Clements [CLE95] describes CBSE in the following way:

> [CBSE] is changing the way large software systems are developed. [CBSE] embodies the "buy, don't build" philosophy espoused by Fred Brooks and others. In the same way that early subroutines liberated the programmer from thinking about details, [CBSE] shifts the emphasis from programming software to composing software systems. Implementation has given way to integration as the focus. At its foundation is the assumption that there is sufficient commonality in many large software systems to justify developing reusable components to exploit and satisfy that commonality.

But a number of questions arise. Is it possible to construct complex systems by assembling them from a catalog of reusable software components? Can this

QUICK LOOK

What is it? You purchase a "stereo system" and bring it home. Each component has been designed to fit a specific architectural style—connections are standardized, communication protocol has be preestablished. Assembly is easy because you don't have to build the system from hundreds of discrete parts. Component-based software engineering strives to achieve the same thing. A set of prebuilt, standardized software components are made available to fit a specific architectural style for some application domain. The application is then assembled using these components, rather than the "discrete parts" of a conventional programming language.

Who does it? Software engineers apply the CBSE process.

Why is it important? It takes only a few minutes to assemble the stereo system because the components are designed to be integrated with ease. Although software is considerably more complex, it follows that component-based systems are easier to assemble and therefore less costly to build than systems constructed from discrete parts. In addition, CBSE encourages the use of predictable architectural patterns and standard software infrastructure, thereby leading to a higher-quality result.

What are the steps? CBSE encompasses two parallel engineering activities: domain engineering and ▶

QUICK LOOK

component-based development. Domain engineering explores an application domain with the specific intent of finding functional, behavioral, and data components that are candidates for reuse. These components are placed in reuse libraries. Component-based development elicits requirements from the customer, selects an appropriate architectural style to meet the objectives of the system to be built, and then (1) selects potential components for reuse, (2) qualifies the components to be sure that they properly fit the architecture for the system, (3) adapts components if modifications must be made to properly integrate them, and (4) integrates the components to form subsystems and the application as a whole. In addition, custom components are engineered to address those aspects of the system that cannot be implemented using existing components.

What is the work product? Operational software, assembled using existing and newly developed software components, is the result of CBSE.

How do I ensure that I've done it right? Use the same SQA practices that are applied in every software engineering process—formal technical reviews assess the analysis and design models, specialized reviews consider issues associated with acquired components, testing is applied to uncover errors in newly developed software and in reusable components that have been integrated into the architecture.

be accomplished in a cost- and time-effective manner? Can appropriate incentives be established to encourage software engineers to reuse rather than reinvent? Is management willing to incur the added expense associated with creating reusable software components? Can the library of components necessary to accomplish reuse be created in a way that makes it accessible to those who need it? Can components that do exist be found by those who need them?

These and many other questions continue to haunt the community of researchers and industry professionals who are striving to make software component reuse a mainstream approach to software engineering. We look at some of the answers in this chapter.

27.1 ENGINEERING OF COMPONENT-BASED SYSTEMS

On the surface, CBSE seems quite similar to conventional or object-oriented software engineering. The process begins when a software team establishes requirements for the system to be built using conventional requirements elicitation techniques (Chapters 10 and 11). An architectural design (Chapter 14) is established, but rather than moving immediately into more detailed design tasks, the team examines requirements to determine what subset is directly amenable to *composition,* rather than construction. That is, the team asks the following questions for each system requirement:

- Are commercial off-the-shelf (COTS) components available to implement the requirement?
- Are internally developed reusable components available to implement the requirement?

- Are the interfaces for available components compatible within the architecture of the system to be built?

The team attempts to modify or remove those system requirements that cannot be implemented with COTS or in-house components.[1] If the requirement(s) cannot be changed or deleted, conventional or object-oriented software engineering methods are applied to develop those new components that must be engineered to meet the requirement(s). But for those requirements that are addressed with available components, a different set of software engineering activities commences:

What are the CBSE framework activities?

Component qualification. System requirements and architecture define the components that will be required. Reusable components (whether COTS or in-house) are normally identified by the characteristics of their interfaces. That is, "the services that are provided, and the means by which consumers access these services" [BRO96] are described as part of the component interface. But the interface does not provide a complete picture of the degree to which the component will fit the architecture and requirements. The software engineer must use a process of discovery and analysis to qualify each component's fit.

Component adaptation. In Chapter 14, we noted that software architecture represents design patterns that are composed of components (units of functionality), connections, and coordination. In essence the architecture defines the design rules for all components, identifying modes of connection and coordination. In some cases, existing reusable components may be mismatched to the architecture's design rules. These components must be adapted to meet the needs of the architecture or discarded and replaced by other, more suitable components.

Quote:

"[I]t seems clear that in the near future most software applications will be assembled from components rather than being constructed from scratch."

Paul Allen and Stuart Frost

Component composition. Architectural style again plays a key role in the way in which software components are integrated to form a working system. By identifying connection and coordination mechanisms (e.g., run-time properties of the design), the architecture dictates the composition of the end product.

Component update. When systems are implemented with COTS components, update is complicated by the imposition of a third party (i.e., the organization that developed the reusable component may be outside the immediate control of the software engineering organization).

Each of these CBSE activities is discussed in more detail in Section 27.4.

---

1 The implication is that the organization adjust its business or product requirements so that component-based implementation can be achieved without the need for custom engineering. This approach reduces system cost and improves time to market but is not always possible.

In the first part of this section, the term *component* has been used repeatedly, yet a definitive description of the term is elusive. Brown and Wallnau [BRO96] suggest the following possibilities:

- *Component*—a nontrivial, nearly independent, and replaceable part of a system that fulfills a clear function in the context of a well-defined architecture.
- *Run-time software component*—a dynamic bindable package of one or more programs managed as a unit and accessed through documented interfaces that can be discovered in run time.
- *Software component*—a unit of composition with contractually specified and explicit context dependencies only.
- *Business component*—the software implementation of an "autonomous" business concept or business process.

In addition to these descriptions, software components can also be characterized based on their use in the CBSE process. In addition to COTS components, the CBSE process yields:

XRef
Certification of software components can be accomplished using cleanroom methods. See Chapter 26 for details.

- *Qualified components*—assessed by software engineers to ensure that not only functionality, but performance, reliability, usability, and other quality factors (Chapter 19) conform to the requirements of the system or product to be built.
- *Adapted components*—adapted to modify (also called *mask* or *wrap*) [BRO96] unwanted or undesirable characteristics.
- *Assembled components*—integrated into an architectural style and interconnected with an appropriate infrastructure that allows the components to be coordinated and managed effectively.
- *Updated components*—replacing existing software as new versions of components become available.

Because CBSE is an evolving discipline, it is unlikely that a unifying definition will emerge in the near term.

27.2 THE CBSE PROCESS

In Chapter 2, a "component-based development model" (Figure 2.11) was used to illustrate how a library of reusable "candidate components" can be integrated into a typical evolutionary process model. The CBSE process, however, must be characterized in a manner that not only identifies candidate components but also qualifies each component's interface, adapts components to remove architectural mismatches, assembles components into a selected architectural style, and updates components as requirements for the system change [BRO96].

FIGURE 27.1
A process model that supports CBSE

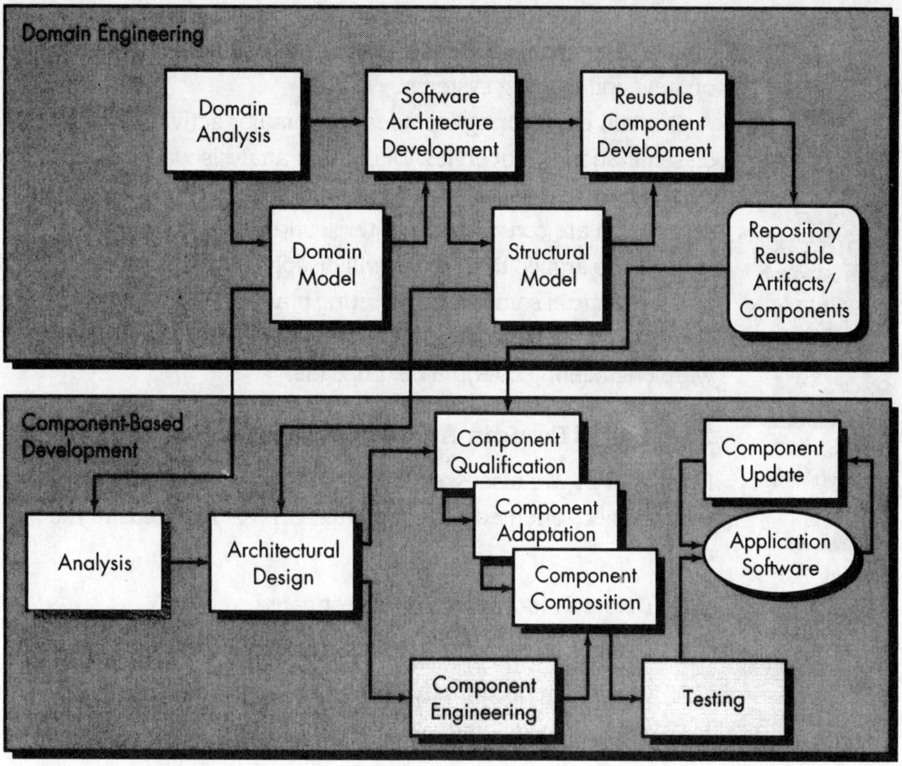

The process model for component-based software engineering emphasizes parallel tracks in which domain engineering (Section 27.3) occurs concurrently with component-based development. *Domain engineering* performs the work required to establish a set of software components that can be reused by the software engineer. These components are then transported across a "boundary" that separates domain engineering from component-based development.

WebRef
The component technology homepage provides useful information for CBSE: **www.odateam.com/cop/**

Figure 27.1 illustrates a typical process model that explicitly accommodates CBSE [CHR95]. Domain engineering creates a model of the application domain that is used as a basis for analyzing user requirements in the software engineering flow. A generic software architecture (and corresponding structure points, see Section 27.3.3) provide input for the design of the application. Finally, after reusable components have been purchased, selected from existing libraries, or constructed (as part of domain engineering), they are made available to software engineers during component-based development.

27.3 DOMAIN ENGINEERING

The intent of domain engineering is to identify, construct, catalog, and disseminate a set of software components that have applicability to existing and future software in a particular application domain. The overall goal is to establish mechanisms that enable software engineers to share these components—to reuse them—during work on new and existing systems.

Quote:

"Domain engineering is about finding commonalities among systems to identify components that can be applied to many systems, and to identify program families that are positioned to take fullest advantage of those components."

Paul Clements

Domain engineering includes three major activities—analysis, construction, and dissemination. An overview of domain analysis was presented in Chapter 21. However, the topic is revisited in the sections that follow. Domain construction and dissemination are considered in later sections in this chapter.

It can be argued that "reuse will disappear, not by elimination, but by integration" into the fabric of software engineering practice [TRA95]. As greater emphasis is placed on reuse, some believe that domain engineering will become as important as software engineering over the next decade.

27.3.1 The Domain Analysis Process

In Chapter 21, we discussed the overall approach to domain analysis within the context of object-oriented software engineering. The steps in the process were defined as:

1. Define the domain to be investigated.
2. Categorize the items extracted from the domain.
3. Collect a representative sample of applications in the domain.
4. Analyze each application in the sample.
5. Develop an analysis model for the objects.

It is important to note that domain analysis is applicable to any software engineering paradigm and may be applied for conventional as well as object-oriented development.

Prieto-Diaz [PRI87] expands the second domain analysis step and suggests an eight-step approach to the identification and categorization of reusable components:

? How can we identify and categorize reusable components?

1. Select specific functions or objects.
2. Abstract functions or objects.
3. Define a taxonomy.
4. Identify common features.
5. Identify specific relationships.
6. Abstract the relationships.
7. Derive a functional model.
8. Define a domain language.

A *domain language* enables the specification and later construction of applications within the domain.

Although the steps just noted provide a useful model for domain analysis, they provide no guidance for deciding which software components are candidates for reuse. Hutchinson and Hindley [HUT88] suggest the following set of pragmatic questions as a guide for identifying reusable software components:

? Which components identified during domain analysis will be candidates for reuse?

- Is component functionality required on future implementations?
- How common is the component's function within the domain?
- Is there duplication of the component's function within the domain?
- Is the component hardware dependent?
- Does the hardware remain unchanged between implementations?
- Can the hardware specifics be removed to another component?
- Is the design optimized enough for the next implementation?
- Can we parameterize a nonreusable component so that it becomes reusable?
- Is the component reusable in many implementations with only minor changes?
- Is reuse through modification feasible?
- Can a nonreusable component be decomposed to yield reusable components?
- How valid is component decomposition for reuse?

An in-depth discussion of domain analysis methods is beyond the scope of this book. For additional information on domain analysis, see [PRI93].

27.3.2 Characterization Functions

It is sometimes difficult to determine whether a potentially reusable component is in fact applicable in a particular situation. To make this determination, it is necessary to define a set of domain characteristics that are shared by all software within a domain. A domain characteristic defines some generic attribute of all products that exist within the domain. For example, generic characteristics might include the importance of safety/reliability, programming language, concurrency in processing, and many others.

A set of domain characteristics for a reusable component can be represented as $\{D_p\}$, where each item, D_{pi}, in the set represents a specific domain characteristic. The value assigned to D_{pi} represents an ordinal scale that is an indication of the relevance of the characteristic for component p. A typical scale [BAS94] might be

1: not relevant to whether reuse is appropriate

2: relevant only under unusual circumstances

3: relevant—the component can be modified so that it can be used, despite differences

TABLE 27.1 Domain Characteristics Affecting Reuse [BAS94]

Product	**Process**	**Personnel**
Requirements stability	Process model	Motivation
Concurrent software	Process conformance	Education
Memory constraints	Project environment	Experience/training
Application size	Schedule constraints	• application domain
User interface complexity	Budget constraints	• process
Programming language(s)	Productivity	• platform
Safety/reliability		• language
Lifetime requirements		Development team
Product quality		productivity
Product reliability		

4: clearly relevant, and if the new software does not have this characteristic, reuse will be inefficient but may still be possible

5: clearly relevant, and if the new software does not have this characteristic, reuse will be ineffective and reuse without the characteristic is not recommended

WebRef
A worthwhile report addressing object technology, architectures, and domain analysis can be found at **www.sei.cmu.edu/mbse/wisr_report.html**

When new software, *w*, is to be built within the application domain, a set of domain characteristics is derived for it. A comparison is then made between D_{pi} and D_{wi} to determine whether the existing component *p* can be effectively reused in application *w*.

Table 27.1 [BAS94] lists typical domain characteristics that can have an impact of software reuse. These domain characteristics must be taken into account in order to reuse a component effectively.

Even when software to be engineered clearly exists within an application domain, the reusable components within that domain must be analyzed to determine their applicability. In some cases (ideally, a limited number), "reinventing the wheel" may still be the most cost-effective choice.

27.3.3 Structural Modeling and Structure Points

When domain analysis is applied, the analyst looks for repeating patterns in the applications that reside within a domain. *Structural modeling* is a pattern-based domain engineering approach that works under the assumption that every application domain has repeating patterns (of function, data, and behavior) that have reuse potential.

Pollak and Rissman [POL94] describe structural models in the following way:

> Structural models consist of a small number of structural elements manifesting clear patterns of interaction. The architectures of systems using structural models are characterized by multiple ensembles that are composed from these model elements. Many architectural units emerge from simple patterns of interaction among this small number of elements.

Each application domain can be characterized by a structural model (e.g., aircraft avionics systems differ greatly in specifics, but all modern software in this domain has the same structural model). Therefore, the structural model is an architectural style (Chapter 14) that can and should be reused across applications within the domain.

McMahon [MCM95] describes a *structure point* as "a distinct construct within a structural model." Structure points have three distinct characteristics:

What is a "structure point" and what are its characteristics?

1. A structure point is an abstraction that should have a limited number of instances. Restating this in object-oriented jargon (Chapter 20), the size of the class hierarchy should be small. In addition, the abstraction should recur throughout applications in the domain. Otherwise, the cost to verify, document, and disseminate the structure point cannot be justified.
2. The rules that govern the use of the structure point should be easily understood. In addition, the interface to the structure point should be relatively simple.
3. The structure point should implement information hiding by isolating all complexity contained within the structure point itself. This reduces the perceived complexity of the overall system.

As an example of structure points as architectural patterns for a system, consider the domain of software for alarm systems. This domain might encompass systems as simple as *SafeHome* (discussed in earlier chapters) or as complex as the alarm system for an industrial process. In every case, however, a set of predictable structural patterns are encountered:

KEY POINT
A structure point can be viewed as a design pattern that can be found repeatedly in applications within a specific domain.

- An *interface* that enables the user to interact with the system.
- A *bounds setting mechanism* that allows the user to establish bounds on the parameters to be measured.
- A *sensor management mechanism* that communicates with all monitoring sensors.
- A *response mechanism* that reacts to the input provided by the sensor management system.
- A *control mechanism* that enables the user to control the manner in which monitoring is carried out.

Each of these structure points is integrated into a domain architecture.

It is possible to define generic structure points that transcend a number of different application domains [STA94]:

- *Application front end*—the GUI including all menus, panels and input and command editing facilities.
- *Database*—the repository for all objects relevant to the application domain.

- *Computational engine*—the numerical and nonnumerical models that manipulate data.
- *Reporting facility*—the function that produces output of all kinds.
- *Application editor*—the mechanism for customizing the application to the needs of specific users.

Structure points have been suggested as an alternative to lines of code and function points for software cost estimation [MCM95]. A brief discussion of costing using structure points is presented in Section 27.6.2.

27.4 COMPONENT-BASED DEVELOPMENT

Component-based development is a CBSE activity that occurs in parallel with domain engineering. Using analysis and architectural design methods discussed earlier in this book, the software team refines an architectural style that is appropriate for the analysis model created for the application to be built.[2]

Once the architecture has been established, it must be populated by components that (1) are available from reuse libraries and/or (2) are engineered to meet custom needs. Hence, the task flow for component-based development has two parallel paths (Figure 27.1). When reusable components are available for potential integration into the architecture, they must be qualified and adapted. When new components are required, they must be engineered. The resultant components are then "composed" (integrated) into the architecture template and tested thoroughly.

27.4.1 Component Qualification, Adaptation, and Composition

As we have already seen, domain engineering provides the library of reusable components that are required for component-based software engineering. Some of these reusable components are developed in-house, others can be extracted from existing applications, and still others may be acquired from third parties.

Unfortunately, the existence of reusable components does not guarantee that these components can be integrated easily or effectively into the architecture chosen for a new application. It is for this reason that a sequence of component-based development activities are applied when a component is proposed for use.

Component Qualification

Component qualification ensures that a candidate component will perform the function required, will properly "fit" into the architectural style specified for the system, and will exhibit the quality characteristics (e.g., performance, reliability, usability) that are required for the application.

2 It should be noted that the architectural style is often influenced by the generic structural model created during domain engineering (see Figure 27.1).

The interface description provides useful information about the operation and use of a software component, but it does not provide all of the information required to determine if a proposed component can, in fact, be reused effectively in a new application. Among the many factors considered during component qualification are [BRO96]:

? What factors are considered during component qualification?

- Application programming interface (API).
- Development and integration tools required by the component.
- Run-time requirements, including resource usage (e.g., memory or storage), timing or speed, and network protocol.
- Service requirements, including operating system interfaces and support from other components.
- Security features, including access controls and authentication protocol.
- Embedded design assumptions, including the use of specific numerical or nonnumerical algorithms.
- Exception handling.

Each of these factors is relatively easy to assess when reusable components that have been developed in-house are proposed. If good software engineering practices were applied during their development, answers to the questions implied by the list can be developed. However, it is much more difficult to determine the internal workings of COTS or third-party components because the only available information may be the interface specification itself.

Component Adaptation

Quote: "Component integrators need to discover the function and form of software components." **Alan Brown and Kurt Wallnau**

In an ideal setting, domain engineering creates a library of components that can be easily integrated into an application architecture. The implication of "easy integration" is that (1) consistent methods of resource management have been implemented for all components in the library, (2) common activities such as data management exist for all components, and (3) interfaces within the architecture and with the external environment have been implemented in a consistent manner.

In reality, even after a component has been qualified for use within an application architecture, it may exhibit conflict in one or more of the areas just noted. To mitigate against these conflicts, an adaptation technique called *component wrapping* [BRO96] is often used. When a software team has full access to the internal design and code for a component (often not the case when COTS components are used) white-box wrapping is applied. Like its counterpart in software testing (Chapter 17), *white-box wrapping* examines the internal processing details of the component and makes code-level modifications to remove any conflict. *Gray-box wrapping* is applied when the component library provides a component extension language or API that enables conflicts to be removed or masked. *Black-box wrapping* requires the introduction of pre- and postprocessing at the component interface to remove or mask conflicts. The software team must determine whether the effort required to adequately wrap a component is justified or whether a custom component (designed to eliminate the conflicts encountered) should be engineered instead.

Component Composition

The *component composition* task assembles qualified, adapted, and engineered components to populate the architecture established for an application. To accomplish this, an infrastructure must be established to bind the components into an operational system. The infrastructure (usually a library of specialized components) provides a model for the coordination of components and specific services that enable components to coordinate with one another and perform common tasks.

Among the many mechanisms for creating an effective infrastructure is a set of four "architectural ingredients" [ADL95] that should be present to achieve component composition:

What ingredients are necessary to achieve component composition?

Data exchange model. Mechanisms that enable users and applications to interact and transfer data (e.g., drag and drop, cut and paste) should be defined for all reusable components. The data exchange mechanisms not only allow human-to-software and component-to-component data transfer but also transfer among system resources (e.g., dragging a file to a printer icon for output).

Automation. A variety of tools, macros, and scripts should be implemented to facilitate interaction between reusable components.

Structured storage. Heterogeneous data (e.g., graphical data, voice/video, text, and numerical data) contained in a "compound document" should be organized and accessed as a single data structure, rather than a collection of separate files. "Structured data maintains a descriptive index of nesting structures that applications can freely navigate to locate, create, or edit individual data contents as directed by the end user" [ADL95].

Underlying object model. The object model ensures that components developed in different programming languages that reside on different platforms can be interoperable. That is, objects must be capable of communicating across a network. To achieve this, the object model defines a standard for component interoperability.

Because the potential impact of reuse and CBSE on the software industry is enormous, a number of major companies and industry consortia[3] have proposed standards for component software:

---

3 An excellent discussion of the "distributed objects" standards is presented in [ORF96] and [YOU98].

WebRef
The latest information on CORBA can be obtained at **www.omg.org**

- **OMG/CORBA.** The Object Management Group has published a *common object request broker architecture* (OMG/CORBA). An object request broker (ORB) provides a variety on services that enable reusable components (objects) to communicate with other components, regardless of their location within a system. When components are built using the OMG/CORBA standard, integration of those components (without modification) within a system is assured if an *interface definition language* (IDL) interface is created for every component. Using a client/server metaphor, objects within the client application request one or more services from the ORB server. Requests are made via an IDL or dynamically at run time. An interface repository contains all necessary information about the service's request and response formats. CORBA is discussed further in Chapter 28.

WebRef
The latest information on COM can be obtained at **www.microsoft.com/COM**

- **Microsoft COM.** Microsoft has developed a component object model (COM) that provides a specification for using components produced by various vendors within a single application running under the Windows operating system. COM encompasses two elements: COM interfaces (implemented as COM objects) and a set of mechanisms for registering and passing messages between COM interfaces. From the point of view of the application, "the focus is not on how [COM objects are] implemented, only on the fact that the object has an interface that it registers with the system, and that it uses the component system to communicate with other COM objects" [HAR98].

WebRef
The latest information on Javabeans can be obtained at **java.sun.com/beans**

- **Sun JavaBean Components.** The JavaBean component system is a portable, platform independent CBSE infrastructure developed using the Java programming language. The JavaBean system extends the Java applet[4] to accommodate the more sophisticated software components required for component-based development. The JavaBean component system encompasses a set of tools, called the *Bean Development Kit* (BDK), that allows developers to (1) analyze how existing Beans (components) work, (2) customize their behavior and appearance, (3) establish mechanisms for coordination and communication, (4) develop custom Beans for use in a specific application, and (5) test and evaluate Bean behavior.

Which of these standards will dominate the industry? There is no easy answer at this time. Although many developers have standardized on one of the standards, it is likely that large software organizations may choose to use all three standards, depending on the application categories and platforms that are chosen.

4 In this context, an applet may be viewed as a simple component.

27.4.2 Component Engineering

As we noted earlier in this chapter, the CBSE process encourages the use of existing software components. However, there are times when components must be engineered. That is, new software components must be developed and integrated with existing COTS and in-house components. Because these new components become members of the in-house library of reusable components, they should be engineered for reuse.

Nothing is magical about creating software components that can be reused. Design concepts such as abstraction, hiding, functional independence, refinement, and structured programming, along with object-oriented methods, testing, SQA, and correctness verification methods, all contribute to the creation of software components that are reusable.[5] In this section we will not revisit these topics. Rather, we consider the reuse-specific issues that are complementary to solid software engineering practices.

27.4.3 Analysis and Design for Reuse

The components of the analysis model were discussed in detail in Parts Three and Four of this book. Data, functional, and behavioral models (represented in a variety of different notations) can be created to describe what a particular application must accomplish. Written specifications are then used to describe these models. A complete description of requirements is the result.

ADVICE

Even if your organization doesn't do domain engineering, do it informally as you work. As you build the analysis model ask yourself, "Is it likely that this object or function has been encountered in other applications of this type?" If the answer is, "Yes;" a component may already exist.

Ideally, the analysis model is analyzed to determine those elements of the model that point to existing reusable components. The problem is extracting information from the requirements model in a form that can lead to "specification matching." Bellinzoni, Gugini, and Pernici [BEL95] describe one approach for object-oriented systems:

> Components are defined and stored as specification, design, and implementation classes at various levels of abstraction—with each class being an engineered description of a product from previous applications. The specification knowledge—development knowledge—is stored in the form of reuse-suggestion classes, which contain directions for retrieving reusable components on the basis of their description and for composing and tailoring them after retrieval.

Automated tools are used to browse a repository in an attempt to match the requirement noted in the current specification with those described for existing reusable components (classes). Characterization functions (Section 27.3.2) and keywords are used to help find potentially reusable components.

If specification matching yields components that fit the needs of the current application, the designer can extract these components from a reuse library (repository) and use them in the design of new systems. If design components cannot be found, the software engineer must apply conventional or OO design methods to create them.

---

5 To learn more about these topics, see Chapters 13 through 16 and 20 through 22.

It is at this point—when the designer begins to create a new component—that *design for reuse* (DFR) should be considered.

ADVICE

Although special issues must be considered when reuse is an objective, focus on the basic principles of good design. If you follow them, your chances of reuse increase significantly.

As we have already noted, DFR requires the software engineer to apply solid software design concepts and principles (Chapter 13). But the characteristics of the application domain must also be considered. Binder [BIN93] suggests a number of key issues[6] that form a basis for design for reuse:

Standard data. The application domain should be investigated and standard global data structures (e.g., file structures or a complete database) should be identified. All design components can then be characterized to make use of these standard data structures.

Standard interface protocols. Three levels of interface protocol should be established: the nature of intramodular interfaces, the design of external technical (nonhuman) interfaces, and the human/machine interface.

Program templates. The structure model (Section 27.3.3) can serve as a template for the architectural design of a new program.

Once standard data, interfaces, and program templates have been established, the designer has a framework in which to create the design. New components that conform to this framework have a higher probability for subsequent reuse.

Like design, the construction of reusable components draws on software engineering methods that have been discussed elsewhere in this book. Construction can be accomplished using conventional third generation programming languages, fourth generation languages and code generators, visual programming techniques, or more advanced tools.

27.5 CLASSIFYING AND RETRIEVING COMPONENTS

Quote:

"The next best thing to knowing something, is knowing where to find it."
Samuel Johnson

Consider a large university library. Tens of thousands of books, periodicals, and other information resources are available for use. But to access these resources, a categorization scheme must be developed. To navigate this large volume of information, librarians have defined a classification scheme that includes a Library of Congress classification code, keywords, author names, and other index entries. All enable the user to find the needed resource quickly and easily.

Now, consider a large component repository. Tens of thousands of reusable software components reside in it. But how does a software engineer find the one she needs? To answer this question, another question arises: How do we describe software components in unambiguous, classifiable terms? These are difficult questions, and no definitive answer has yet been developed. In this section we explore current directions that will enable future software engineers to navigate reuse libraries.

---

6 In general, the design for reuse preparations should be undertaken as part of domain engineering (Section 27.3).

27.5.1 Describing Reusable Components

KEY POINT

In order to describe a reusable component, the component's concept, content, and context should be described.

A reusable software component can be described in many ways, but an ideal description encompasses what Tracz [TRA90] has called the *3C model*—concept, content, and context.

The *concept* of a software component is "a description of what the component does" [WHI95]. The interface to the component is fully described and the semantics—represented within the context of pre- and postconditions—are identified. The concept should communicate the intent of the component.

The *content* of a component describes how the concept is realized. In essence, the content is information that is hidden from casual users and need be known only to those who intend to modify or test the component.

The *context* places a reusable software component within its domain of applicability. That is, by specifying conceptual, operational, and implementation features, the context enables a software engineer to find the appropriate component to meet application requirements.

WebRef

A detailed guide for component reuse can be downloaded from **web1.ssg.gunter.af.mil/sep/SEPver40/Main.html#GD**

To be of use in a pragmatic setting, concept, content, and context must be translated into a concrete specification scheme. Dozens of papers and articles have been written about classification schemes for reusable software components (e.g., [WHI95] contains an extensive bibliography). The methods proposed can be categorized into three major areas: library and information science methods, artificial intelligence methods, and hypertext systems. The vast majority of work done to date suggests the use of library science methods for component classification.

Figure 27.2 presents a taxonomy of library science indexing methods. *Controlled indexing vocabularies* limit the terms or syntax that can be used to classify an object (component). *Uncontrolled indexing vocabularies* place no restrictions on the nature

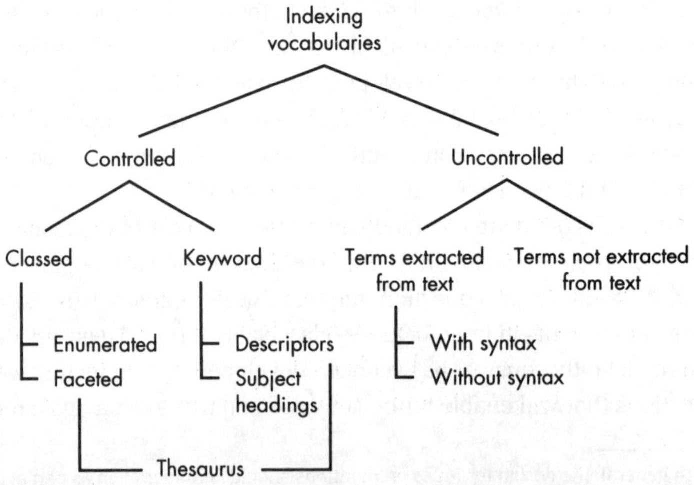

FIGURE 27.2
A taxonomy of indexing methods [FRA94]

of the description. The majority of classification schemes for software components fall into three categories:

What options are available for classifying components?

Enumerated classification. Components are described by a hierarchical structure in which classes and varying levels of subclasses of software components are defined. Actual components are listed at the lowest level of any path in the enumerated hierarchy. For example, an enumerated hierarchy for window operations[7] might be

```
window operations
    display
        open
            menu-based
                openWindow
            system-based
                sysWindow
        close
            via pointer
                ...
    resize
        via command
            setWindowSize, stdResize, shrinkWindow
        via drag
            pullWindow, stretchWindow
    up/down shuffle
                ...
    move
                ...
    close
                ...
```

The hierarchical structure of an enumerated classification scheme makes it easy to understand and to use. However, before a hierarchy can be built, domain engineering must be conducted so that sufficient knowledge of the proper entries in the hierarchy is available.

Faceted classification. A domain area is analyzed and a set of basic descriptive features are identified. These features, called *facets,* are then ranked by importance and connected to a component. A facet can describe the function that the component performs, the data that are manipulated, the context in which they are applied, or any other feature. The set of facets that describe a component is called the *facet descriptor.* Generally, the facet description is limited to no more than seven or eight facets.

7 Only a small subset of all possible operations is noted.

As a simple illustration of the use of facets in component classification, consider a scheme [LIA93] that makes use of the following facet descriptor:

{function, object type, system type}

Each facet in the facet descriptor takes on one or more values that are generally descriptive keywords. For example, if *function* is a facet of a component, typical values assigned to this facet might be

function = (*copy, from*) or (*copy, replace, all*)

The use of multiple facet values enables the primitive function *copy* to be refined more fully. *Keywords* (values) are assigned to the set of facets for each component in a reuse library. When a software engineer wants to query the library for possible components for a design, a list of values is specified and the library is searched for matches. Automated tools can be used to incorporate a thesaurus function. This enables the search to encompass not only the keyword specified by the software engineer but also technical synonyms for those keywords. A faceted classification scheme gives the domain engineer greater flexibility in specifying complex descriptors for components [FRA94]. Because new facet values can be added easily, the faceted classification scheme is easier to extend and adapt than the enumeration approach.

Attribute-value classification. A set of attributes is defined for all components in a domain area. Values are then assigned to these attributes in much the same way as faceted classification. In fact, attribute value classification is similar to faceted classification with the following exceptions: (1) no limit is placed on the number of attributes that can be used; (2) attributes are not assigned priorities, and (3) the thesaurus function is not used.

Based on an empirical study of each of these classification techniques, Frakes and Pole [FRA94] indicate that there is no clear "best" technique and that "no method did more than moderately well in search effectiveness . . ." It would appear that further work remains to be done in the development of effective classification schemes for reuse libraries.

27.5.2 The Reuse Environment

Software component reuse must be supported by an environment that encompasses the following elements:

- A component database capable of storing software components and the classification information necessary to retrieve them.
- A library management system that provides access to the database.

- A software component retrieval system (e.g., an object request broker) that enables a client application to retrieve components and services from the library server.
- CBSE tools that support the integration of reused components into a new design or implementation.

Each of these functions interact with or is embodied within the confines of a reuse library.

The reuse library is one element of a larger CASE repository (Chapter 31) and provides facilities for the storage of software components and a wide variety of reusable artifacts (e.g., specifications, designs, code fragments, test cases, user guides). The library encompasses a database and the tools that are necessary to query the database and retrieve components from it. A component classification scheme (Section 27.5.1) serves as the basis for library queries.

Queries are often characterized using the context element of the 3C model described earlier in this section. If an initial query results in a voluminous list of candidate components, the query is refined to narrow the list. Concept and content information are then extracted (after candidate components are found) to assist the developer in selecting the proper component.

A detailed discussion of the structure of reuse libraries and the tools that manage them is beyond the scope of this book. The interested reader should see [HOO91] and [LIN95] for additional information.

27.6 ECONOMICS OF CBSE

Component-based software engineering has an intuitive appeal. In theory, it should provide a software organization with advantages in quality and timeliness. And these should translate into cost savings. But are there hard data that support our intuition?

To answer this question we must first understand what actually can be reused in a software engineering context and then what the costs associated with reuse really are. As a consequence, it is possible to develop a cost/benefit analysis for component reuse.

27.6.1 Impact on Quality, Productivity, and Cost

ADVICE

CBSE is an economic "no brainer" if the components available are right for the job. If reuse demands customization, proceed with caution.

Considerable evidence from industry case studies (e.g., [HEN95], [MCM95], [LIM94]) indicates substantial business benefits can be derived from aggressive software reuse. Product quality, development productivity, and overall cost are all improved.

Quality. In an ideal setting, a software component that is developed for reuse would be verified to be correct (see Chapter 26) and would contain no defects. In reality, formal verification is not carried out routinely, and defects can and do occur. However, with each reuse, defects are found and eliminated, and a component's quality improves as a result. Over time, the component becomes virtually defect free.

KEY POINT

Although empirical data vary, industry evidence indicates that reuse does provide substantial cost benefit.

In a study conducted at Hewlett Packard, Lim [LIM94] reports that the defect rate for reused code is 0.9 defects per KLOC, while the rate for newly developed software is 4.1 defects per KLOC. For an application that was composed of 68 percent reused code, the defect rate was 2.0 defects per KLOC—a 51 percent improvement from the expected rate, had the application been developed without reuse. Henry and Faller [HEN95] report a 35 percent improvement in quality. Although anecdotal reports span a reasonably wide spectrum of quality improvement percentages, it is fair to state that reuse provides a nontrivial benefit in terms of the quality and reliability for delivered software.

Productivity. When reusable components are applied throughout the software process, less time is spent creating the plans, models, documents, code, and data that are required to create a deliverable system. It follows that the same level of functionality is delivered to the customer with less input effort. Hence, productivity is improved. Although percentage productivity improvement reports are notoriously difficult to interpret,[8] it appears that 30 to 50 percent reuse can result in productivity improvements in the 25–40 percent range.

Cost. The net cost savings for reuse are estimated by projecting the cost of the project if it were developed from scratch, C_s, and then subtracting the sum of the costs associated with reuse, C_r, and the actual cost of the software as delivered, C_d.

C_s can be determined by applying one or more of the estimation techniques discussed in Chapter 5. The costs associated with reuse, C_r, include [CHR95]

What costs are associated with software reuse?

- Domain analysis and modeling.
- Domain architecture development.
- Increased documentation to facilitate reuse.
- Support and enhancement of reuse components.
- Royalties and licenses for externally acquired components.
- Creation or acquisition and operation of a reuse repository.
- Training of personnel in design and construction for reuse.

Although costs associated with domain analysis (Section 27.4) and the operation of a reuse repository can be substantial, many of the other costs noted here address issues that are part of good software engineering practice, whether or not reuse is a priority.

8 Many extenuating circumstances (e.g., application area, problem complexity, team structure and size, project duration, technology applied) can have an impact on the productivity of a project team.

27.6.2 Cost Analysis Using Structure Points

In Section 27.3.3, we defined a structure point as an architectural pattern that recurs throughout a particular application domain. A software designer (or system engineer) can develop an architecture for a new application, system, or product by defining a domain architecture and then populating it with structure points. These structure points are either individual reusable components or packages of reusable components.

Even though structure points are reusable, their qualification, adaptation, integration, and maintenance costs are nontrivial. Before proceeding with reuse, the project manager must understand the costs associated with the use of structure points.

Since all structure points (and reusable components in general) have a past history, cost data can be collected for each. In an ideal setting, the qualification, adaptation, integration, and maintenance costs associated with each component in a reuse library is maintained for each instance of usage. These data can then be analyzed to develop projected costs for the next instance of reuse.

As an example, consider a new application, *X*, that requires 60 percent new code and the reuse of three structure points, SP_1, SP_2, and SP_3. Each of these reusable components has been used in a number of other applications and average costs for qualification, adaptation, integration, and maintenance are available.

? Is there a quick calculation that allows us to estimate the cost benefit of component reuse?

To estimate the effort required to deliver *X*, the following must be determined:

$$\text{overall effort} = E_{new} + E_{qual} + E_{adapt} + E_{int}$$

where

E_{new} = effort required to engineer and construct new software components (determined using techniques described in Chapter 5).

E_{qual} = effort required to qualify SP_1, SP_2, and SP_3.

E_{adapt} = effort required to adapt SP_1, SP_2, and SP_3.

E_{int} = effort required to integrate SP_1, SP_2, and SP_3.

The effort required to qualify, adapt, and integrate SP_1, SP_2 and SP_3 is determined by taking the average of historical data collected for qualification, adaptation, and integration of the reusable components in other applications.

27.6.3 Reuse Metrics

A variety of software metrics have been developed in an attempt to measure the benefits of reuse within a computer-based system. The benefit associated with reuse within a system *S* can be expressed as a ratio

$$R_b(S) = [C_{noreuse} - C_{reuse}]/C_{noreuse} \qquad (27\text{-}1)$$

where

$C_{noreuse}$ is the cost of developing S with no reuse.
C_{reuse} is the cost of developing S with reuse.

It follows that $R_b(S)$ can be expressed as a nondimensional value in the range

$$0 \le R_b(S) \le 1 \tag{27-2}$$

Devanbu and his colleagues [DEV95] suggest that (1) R_b will be affected by the design of the system; (2) since R_b is affected by the design, it is important to make R_b a part of an assessment of design alternatives; and (3) the benefits associated with reuse are closely aligned to the cost benefit of each individual reusable component.

A general measure of reuse in object-oriented systems, termed *reuse leverage* [BAS94], is defined as

$$R_{lev} = OBJ_{reused}/OBJ_{built} \tag{27-3}$$

where

OBJ_{reused} is the number of objects reused in a system.
OBJ_{built} is the number of objects built for a system.

27.7 SUMMARY

Component-based software engineering offers inherent benefits in software quality, developer productivity, and overall system cost. And yet, many roadblocks remain to be overcome before the CBSE process model is widely used throughout the industry.

In addition to software components, a variety of reusable artifacts can be acquired by a software engineer. These include technical representations of the software (e.g., specifications, architectural models, designs), documents, test data, and even process-related tasks (e.g., inspection techniques).

The CBSE process encompasses two concurrent subprocesses—domain engineering and component-based development. The intent of domain engineering is to identify, construct, catalog, and disseminate a set of software components in a particular application domain. Component-based development then qualifies, adapts, and integrates these components for use in a new system. In addition, component-based development engineers new components that are based on the custom requirements of a new system,

Analysis and design techniques for reusable components draw on the same principles and concepts that are part of good software engineering practice. Reusable components should be designed within an environment that establishes standard data structures, interface protocols, and program architectures for each application domain.

Component-based software engineering uses a data exchange model, tools, structured storage, and an underlying object model to construct applications. The object model generally conforms to one or more component standards (e.g., OMG/CORBA) that define the manner in which an application can access reusable objects. Classification schemes enable a developer to find and retrieve reusable components and conform to a model that identifies concept, content, and context. Enumerated classification, faceted classification, and attribute-value classification are representative of many component classification schemes.

The economics of software reuse are addressed by a single question: Is it cost effective to build less and reuse more? In general, the answer is, "Yes," but a software project planner must consider the nontrivial costs associated with the qualification, adaptation, and integration of reusable components.

REFERENCES

[ADL95] Adler, R.M., "Emerging Standards for Component Software, *Computer,* vol. 28, no. 3, March 1995, pp. 68–77.

[BAS94] Basili, V.R., L.C. Briand, and W.M. Thomas, "Domain Analysis for the Reuse of Software Development Experiences," *Proc. of the 19th Annual Software Engineering Workshop,* NASA/GSFC, Greenbelt, MD, December 1994.

[BEL95] Bellinzona R., M.G. Gugini, and B. Pernici, "Reusing Specifications in OO Applications," *IEEE Software,* March 1995, pp. 65–75.

[BIN93] Binder, R., "Design for Reuse Is for Real," *American Programmer,* vol. 6, no. 8, August 1993, pp. 30–37.

[BRO96] Brown, A.W. and K.C. Wallnau, "Engineering of Component Based Systems," *Component-Based Software Engineering,* IEEE Computer Society Press, 1996, pp. 7–15.

[CHR95] Christensen, S.R., "Software Reuse Initiatives at Lockheed," *CrossTalk,* vol. 8, no. 5, May 1995, pp. 26–31.

[CLE95] Clements, P.C., "From Subroutines to Subsystems: Component Based Software Development," *American Programmer,* vol. 8, No. 11, November 1995.

[DEV95] Devanbu, P., et al., "Analytical and Empirical Evaluation of Software Reuse Metrics," Technical Report, Computer Science Department, University of Maryland, August 1995.

[FRA94] Frakes, W.B. and T.P. Pole, "An Empirical Study of Representation Methods for Reusable Software Components," *IEEE Trans. Software Engineering,* vol. SE-20, no. 8, August 1994, pp. 617–630.

[HAR98] Harmon, P., "Navigating the Distributed Components Landscape," *Cutter IT Journal,* vol. 11, no. 2, December 1998, pp. 4–11.

[HEN95] Henry, E. and B. Faller, "Large Scale Industrial Reuse to Reduce Cost and Cycle Time," *IEEE Software,* September 1995, pp. 47–53.

[HOO91] Hooper, J.W. and R.O. Chester, *Software Reuse: Guidelines and Methods,* Plenum Press, 1991.

[HUT88] Hutchinson, J.W. and P.G. Hindley, "A Preliminary Study of Large Scale Software Reuse," *Software Engineering Journal,* vol. 3, no. 5, 1988, pp. 208–212.

[LIA93] Liao, H. and Wang, F., "Software Reuse Based on a Large Object-Oriented Library," *ACM Software Engineering Notes,* vol. 18, no. 1, January 1993, pp. 74–80.

[LIM94] Lim, W.C., "Effects of Reuse on Quality, Productivity, and Economics," *IEEE Software,* September 1994, pp. 23–30.

[LIN95] Linthicum, D.S., "Component Development (a Special Feature)," *Application Development Trends,* June 1995, pp. 57–78.

[MCM95] McMahon, P.E., "Pattern-Based Architecture: Bridging Software Reuse and Cost Management," *Crosstalk,* vol. 8, no. 3, March 1995, pp. 10–16.

[ORF96] Orfali, R., D. Harkey, and J. Edwards, *The Essential Distributed Objects Survival Guide,* Wiley, 1996.

[PRI87] Prieto-Diaz, R., "Domain Analysis for Reusability," *Proc. COMPSAC '87,* Tokyo, October 1987, pp. 23–29.

[PRI93] Prieto-Diaz, R., "Issues and Experiences in Software Reuse," *American Programmer,* vol. 6, no. 8, August 1993, pp. 10–18.

[POL94] Pollak, W. and M. Rissman, "Structural Models and Patterned Architectures," *Computer,* vol. 27, no. 8, August 1994, pp. 67–68.

[STA94] Staringer, W., "Constructing Applications from Reusable Components," *IEEE Software,* September 1994, pp. 61–68.

[TRA90] Tracz, W., "Where Does Reuse Start?" *Proc. Realities of Reuse Workshop,* Syracuse University CASE Center, January 1990.

[TRA95] Tracz, W., "Third International Conference on Software Reuse—Summary," *ACM Software Engineering Notes,* vol. 20, no. 2, April 1995, pp. 21–22.

[WHI95] Whittle, B., "Models and Languages for Component Description and Reuse," *ACM Software Engineering Notes,* vol. 20, no. 2, April 1995, pp. 76–89.

[YOU98] Yourdon, E. (ed.), "Distributed Objects," *Cutter IT Journal,* vol. 11, no. 12, December 1998.

PROBLEMS AND POINTS TO PONDER

27.1. One of the key roadblocks to reuse is getting software developers to consider reusing existing components, rather than reinventing new ones (after all, building things is fun!). Suggest three or four different ways that a software organization can provide incentives for software engineers to reuse. What technologies should be in place to support the reuse effort?

27.2. Although software components are the most obvious reusable "artifact," many other entities produced as part of software engineering can be reused. Consider project plans and cost estimates. How can these be reused and what is the benefit of doing so?

27.3. Do a bit of research on domain engineering and flesh out the process model outlined in Figure 27.1. Identify the tasks that are required for domain analysis and software architecture development.

27.4. How are characterization functions for application domains and component classification schemes the same? How are they different?

27.5. Develop a set of domain characteristics for information systems that are relevant to a university's student data processing.

27.6. Develop a set of domain characteristics that are relevant for word-processing/desktop-publishing software.

27.7. Develop a simple structural model for an application domain assigned by your instructor or one with which you are familiar.

27.8. What is a structure point?

27.9. Acquire information on the most recent CORBA or COM or JavaBeans standard and prepare a three- to five-page paper that discusses its major highlights. Get information on an object request broker tool and illustrate how the tool achieves the standard.

27.10. Develop an enumerated classification for an application domain assigned by your instructor or one with which you are familiar.

27.11. Develop a faceted classification scheme for an application domain assigned by your instructor or one with which you are familiar.

27.12. Research the literature to acquire recent quality and productivity data that support the use of CBSE. Present the data to your class.

27.13. An object-oriented system is estimated to require 320 objects, when complete. It is further estimated that 190 objects can be acquired from an existing repository. What is the reuse leverage? Assume that new objects cost $1000 each and that the cost to adapt an object is $600 and to integrate each object is $400. What is the estimated cost of the system. What is the value for R_b?

FURTHER READINGS AND INFORMATION SOURCES

Many books on component-based development and component reuse have been published in recent years. Allen, Frost, and Yourdon (*Component-Based Development for Enterprise Systems: Applying the Select Perspective,* Cambridge University Press, 1998) cover the entire CBSE process, using UML (Chapters 21 and 22) as the basis for their modeling approach. Books by Lim (*Managing Software Reuse: A Comprehensive Guide to Strategically Reengineering the Organization for Reusable Components,* Prentice-Hall, 1998); Coulange (*Software Reuse,* Springer-Verlag, 1998); Reifer (*Practical Software Reuse,* Wiley, 1997); and Jacobson, Griss, and Jonsson (*Software Reuse: Architecture Process and Organization for Business Success,* Addison-Wesley, 1997) address many CBSE topics. Fowler (*Analysis Patterns: Reusable Object Models,* Addison-Wesley, 1996) considers the application of architectural patterns within the CBSE process and provides many useful examples. Tracz (*Confessions of a Used Program Salesman: Institutionalizing Software Reuse,* Addison-Wesley, 1995) presents a sometimes lighthearted, but meaningful, discussion of the issues associated with creating a reuse culture.

Leach (*Software Reuse: Methods, Models, and Costs,* McGraw-Hill, 1997) provides a detailed analysis of cost issues associated with CBSE and reuse. Poulin (*Measuring Software Reuse: Principles, Practices, and Economic Models,* Addison-Wesley, 1996) suggests a number of quantitative methods for assessing the benefits of software reuse.

Dozens of books describing the industry's component-based standards have been published in recent years. These address the inner workings of the standards themselves but also consider many important CBSE topics. A sampling for the three standards discussed in this chapter follows:

CORBA

Doss, G.M., *CORBA Networking With Java,* Wordware Publishing, 1999.

Hoque, R., *CORBA for Real Programmers,* Academic Press/Morgan Kaufmann, 1999.

Siegel, J., *CORBA 3 Fundamentals and Programming,* Wiley, 1999.

Slama, D., J. Garbis, and P. Russell, *Enterprise CORBA,* Prentice-Hall, 1999.

COM

Box, D., K. Brown, T. Ewald, and C. Sells, *Effective COM: 50 Ways to Improve Your COM- and MTS-Based Applications,* Addison-Wesley, 1999.

Kirtland, M., *Designing Component-Based Applications,* Microsoft Press, 1999.

Many organizations apply a combination of component standards. Books by Geraghty et al. (*COM-CORBA Interoperability,* Prentice-Hall, 1999), Pritchard (*COM and CORBA Side by Side: Architectures, Strategies, and Implementations,* Addison-Wesley, 1999), and Rosen et al. (*Integrating CORBA and COM Applications,* Wiley, 1999) consider the issues associated with the use of both CORBA and COM as the basis for component-based development.

JavaBeans

Asbury, S. and S.R. Weiner, *Developing Java Enterprise Applications,* Wiley, 1999.

Valesky, T.C., *Enterprise Javabeans: Developing Component-Based Distributed Applications,* Addison-Wesley, 1999.

Vogel, A. and M. Rangarao, *Programming with Enterprise JavaBeans, JTS, and OTS,* Wiley, 1999.

A wide variety of information sources on component-based software engineering and component reuse is available on the Internet. An up-to-date list of World Wide Web references that are relevant to CBSE can be found at the SEPA Web site: **http://www.mhhe.com/engcs/compsci/pressman/resources/cbse.mhtml**

CHAPTER

28 CLIENT/SERVER SOFTWARE ENGINEERING

KEY CONCEPTS

At the turn of the twentieth century, the development of a new generation of machine tools capable of holding very tight tolerances empowered the engineers who designed a new factory process called *mass production.* Before the advent of this advanced machine tool technology, machines could not hold tight tolerances. But with it, easily assembled interchangeable parts—the cornerstone of mass production—could be built.

When a new computer-based system is to be developed, a software engineer is constrained by the limitations of existing computing technology and empowered when new technologies provide capabilities that were unavailable to earlier generations of engineers. The evolution of distributed computer architectures has enabled system and software engineers to develop new approaches to how work is structured and how information is processed within an organization.

New organization structures and new information processing approaches (e.g., intra- and Internet technologies, decision support systems, groupware, and imaging) represent a radical departure from the earlier mainframe- and minicomputer-based technologies. New computing architectures have provided the technology that has enabled organizations to reengineer their business processes (Chapter 30).

QUICK LOOK

What is it? Client/server (c/s) architectures dominate the landscape of computer-based systems. Everything from automatic teller networks to the Internet exist because software residing on one computer—the client—requests services and/or data from another computer—the server. Client/server software engineering blends conventional principles, concepts, and methods discussed earlier in this book with elements of object-oriented and component-based software engineering to create c/s systems.

Who does it? Software engineers perform the analysis, design, implementation, and testing of c/s systems.

Why is it important? The impact of c/s systems on business, commerce, government, and science is pervasive. As technological advances (e.g., component-based development, object request brokers, Java) change the way in which c/s systems are built, a solid software engineering process must be applied to their construction.

What are the steps? The steps involved in the engineering of c/s systems are similar to those applied during OO and component-based software engineering. The process model is evolutionary, beginning with requirements elicitation. Functionality is allocated to subsystems of components, which are then assigned to either the client or the server side of the c/s architecture.

QUICK LOOK

Design focuses on integration of existing components and the creation of new components. Implementation and testing strive to exercise both client and server functionality within the context of component integration standards and the architecture.

What is the work product? A high-quality client/server system is the outcome of c/s software engineering. Other software work products (discussed earlier in this book) are also produced.

How do I ensure that I've done it right? Use the same SQA practices that are applied in every software engineering process—formal technical reviews assess the analysis and design models, specialized reviews consider issues associated with component integration and middleware, and testing is applied to uncover errors at the component, subsystem, client, and server levels.

In this chapter, we examine a dominant architecture for information processing—*client/server* (c/s) systems. Client/server systems have evolved in conjunction with advances in desktop computing, component-based software engineering, new storage technologies, improved network communications, and enhanced database technology. The objective of this chapter[1] is to present a brief overview of client/server systems with an emphasis on the special software engineering issues that must be addressed when such c/s systems are analyzed, designed, tested, and supported.

28.1 THE STRUCTURE OF CLIENT/SERVER SYSTEMS

Quote:

"The c/s computing model represents a specific instance of distributed cooperative processing, where the relationship between clients and servers is the relationship of both hardware and software components."

Alex Berson

Hardware, software, database, and network technologies all contribute to distributed and cooperative computer architectures. In its most general form, a distributed and cooperative computer architecture is as illustrated in Figure 28.1. A *root system,* sometimes a mainframe, serves as the repository for corporate data. The root system is connected to servers (typically powerful workstations or PCs) that play a dual role. The servers update and request corporate data maintained by the root system. They also maintain local departmental systems and play a key role in networking user-level PCs via a local area network (LAN).

In a c/s structure, the computer that resides above another computer (in Figure 28.1) is called the *server,* and the computer(s) at the level below is called the *client.* The client requests services,[2] and the server provides them. However, within the context of the the architecture represented in Figure 28.2, a number of different implementations can be achieved [ORF99]:

1 Portions of this chapter have been adapted from course material developed by John Porter for the client/server curriculum offered at The BEI Engineering School of Fairfield University. Used with permission.

2 In this context, *services* can be broadly interpreted to mean data, processing, or a combination of the two.

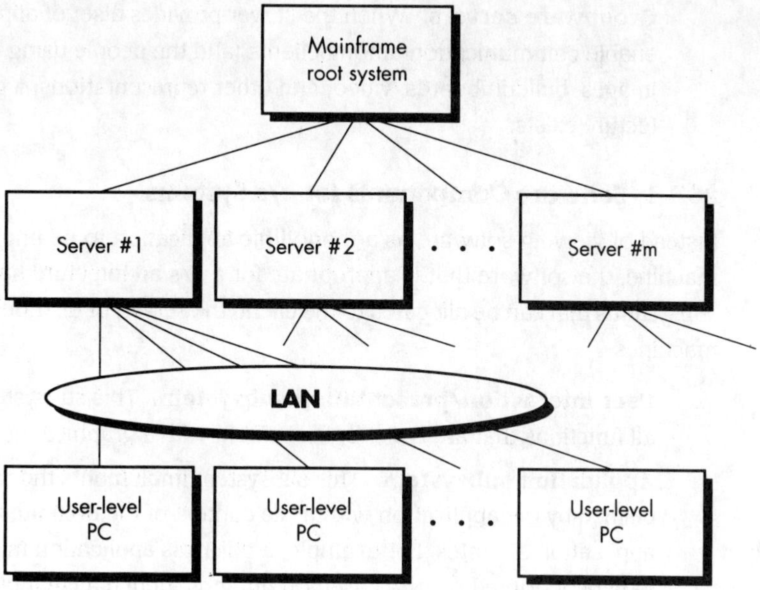

FIGURE 28.1 Distributed, cooperative computer architectures in a corporate setting

File servers. The client requests specific records from a file. The server transmits these records to the client across the network.

Database servers. The client sends *structured query language* (SQL) requests to the server. These are transmitted as messages across the network. The server processes the SQL request and finds the requested information, passing back the results only to the client.

Transaction servers. The client sends a request that invokes remote procedures at the server site. The remote procedures are a set of SQL statements. A *transaction* occurs when a request results in the execution of the remote procedure with the result transmitted back to the client.

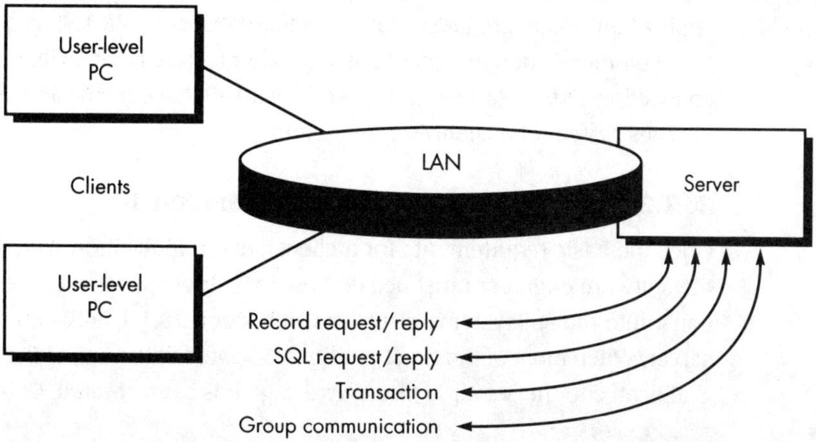

FIGURE 28.2 Client/server options

Groupware servers. When the server provides a set of applications that enable communication among clients (and the people using them) using text, images, bulletin boards, video, and other representations, a groupware architecture exists.

28.1.1 Software Components for c/s Systems

Instead of viewing software as a monolithic application to be implemented on one machine, the software that is appropriate for a c/s architecture has several distinct subsystems that can be allocated to the client, the server, or distributed between both machines:

WebRef
The FAQ for the **comp.client-server** newsgroup can be found at **www.faqs.org/faqs/client-server-faq/**

User interaction/presentation subsystem. This subsystem implements all functions that are typically associated with a graphical user interface.

Application subsystem. This subsystem implements the requirements defined by the application within the context of the domain in which the application operates. For example, a business application might produce a variety of printed reports based on numeric input, calculations, database information, and other considerations. A groupware application might provide the facilities for enabling bulletin board communication or e-mail. In both cases, the application software may be partitioned so that some components reside on the client and others reside on the server.

Database management subsystem. This subsystem performs the data manipulation and management required by an application. Data manipulation and management may be as simple as the transfer of a record or as complex as the processing of sophisticated SQL transactions.

KEY POINT
Middleware establishes the infrastructure that enables c/s software components to interoperate.

In addition to these subsystems, another software building block, often called *middleware*, exists in all c/s systems. Middleware comprises software components that exist on both the client and the server and includes elements of network operating systems as well as specialized application software that supports database-specific applications, object request broker standards (Section 28.1.5), groupware technologies, communication management, and other features that facilitate the client/server connection. Orfali, Harkey, and Edwards [ORF99] have referred to middleware as "the nervous system of a client/server system."

28.1.2 The Distribution of Software Components

Once the basic requirements for a client/server application have been determined, the software engineer must decide how to distribute the software components that constitute the subsystems discussed in Section 28.1.1 between the client and the server. When most of the functionality associated with each of the three subsystems is allocated to the server, a *fat server* design has been created. Conversely, when the client implements most of the user interaction/presentation, application, and database components, a *fat client* design has been created.

KEY POINT

A "fat" client implements most application-specific functions at the client. A "thin" client relegates most processing to the server.

Fat clients are commonly encountered when file server and database server architectures are implemented. In this case, the server provides data management support, but all application and GUI software resides at the client. Fat servers are often designed when transaction and groupware systems are implemented. The server provides application support required to respond to transactions and communication from the clients. The client software focuses on GUI and communication management.

Fat clients and fat servers can be used to illustrate the general approach for the allocation of client/server software systems. However, a more granular approach to software component allocation defines five different configurations:

What are configuration options for c/s software components?

Distributed presentation. In this rudimentary client/server approach, database logic and the application logic remain on the server, typically a mainframe. The server also contains the logic for preparing screen information, using software such as CICS. Special PC-based software is used to convert character-based screen information transmitted from the server into a GUI presentation on a PC.

Remote presentation. An extension of the distributed presentation approach, primary database and application logic remain on the server, and data sent by the server is used by the client to prepare the user presentation.

Distributed logic. The client is assigned all user presentation tasks and the processes associated with data entry, such as field-level validation, server query formulation, and server update information and requests. The server is assigned database management tasks and the processes for client queries, server file updates, client version control, and enterprise-wide applications.

Remote data management. Applications on the server create a new data source by formatting data that have been extracted from elsewhere (e.g., from a corporate level source). Applications allocated to the client are used to exploit the new data that has been formatted by the server. Decision support systems are included in this category.

Distributed databases. The data forming the database is spread across multiple servers and clients. Therefore, the client must support data management software components as well as application and GUI components.

In recent years, there has also been considerable emphasis on thin-client technology. A *thin client* is a so-called "network computer" that relegates all application processing to a fat server. Thin clients (network computers) offer substantially lower per unit cost at little or no significant performance loss when compared to desktop machines.

28.1.3 Guidelines for Distributing Application Subsystems

While no absolute rules cover the distribution of application subsystems between the client and server, the following guidelines are generally followed:

Quote:

"Some analysts view client/server computing as the fourth wave of [change in the history of] computing."

Bernard Boar

The presentation/interaction subsystem is generally placed on the client. The availability of PC-based, Windows-based environments and the computing power required for a graphical user interface makes this approach cost effective.

If the database is to be shared by multiple users connected by the LAN, it is typically located on the server. The database management system and the database access capability are also located on the server together with the physical database.

Static data that are used for reference should be allocated to the client. This places the data closest to the users that require them and minimizes unnecessary network traffic and loading on the server.

The balance of the application subsystem is distributed between the client and server based on the distribution that optimizes the server and client configurations and the network that connects them. For example, the implementation of a mutually exclusive relationship typically involves a search of the database to determine if there is a record that matches the parameters for a search pattern. If no match is found, an alternate search pattern is used. If the application that controls this search pattern is contained fully on the server, network traffic is minimized. The first network transmission from the client to the server would contain the parameters for both the primary and secondary search patterns. Application logic on the server would determine if the secondary search is required. The response message to the client would contain the record found as a result of either the primary or the secondary search. The alternate approach of placing on the client the logic to determine if a second search is required would involve a message for the first record retrieval, a response over the network if the record is not found, a second message containing the parameters for the second search, and a final response with the retrieved record. If the second search is required 50 percent of the time, placing the logic on the server to evaluate the first search and initiate the second search, if necessary, would reduce network traffic by 33 percent.

ADVICE

Although distribution guidelines are worthwhile, every system must be considered on its own merits. For every benefit derived from, say, a fat client, the designer must contend with an equal set of negatives.

The final decision on subsystem distribution should be based not only on the individual application but on the mix of applications operating on the system. For example, an installation might contain some applications that require extensive GUI processing and little central database processing. This would lead to the use of powerful workstations on the client side, and a bare bones server. With this configuration in place, other applications would favor the fat client approach so that the capabilities of the server do not need to be upgraded.

As the use of the client/server architecture has matured, the trend is to place volatile application logic on the server. This simplifies deployment of software updates as changes are made to the application logic [PAU95].

28.1.4 Linking c/s Software Subsystems

A number of different mechanisms are used to link the various subsystems of the client/server architecture. These mechanisms are incorporated into the network and operating system structure and are transparent to the end-user at the client site. The most common types of linking mechanisms are:

? What options are available for linking subsystems?

- *Pipes.* Widely used in UNIX-based systems, pipes permit messaging between different machines running on different operating systems.
- *Remote procedure calls.* These permit one process to invoke the execution of another process or module which resides on a different machine.
- *Client/server SQL interaction.* This is used to pass SQL requests and associated data from one component (typically on the client) to another component (typically the DBMS on the server). This mechanism is limited to relational database management system (RDBMS) applications.

In addition, object-oriented implementation of the c/s software subsystems results in "linkage" using an object request broker. This approach is discussed in the following section.

28.1.5 Middleware and Object Request Broker Architectures

KEY POINT
An ORB enables an object that resides on a client to send a message to a method encapsulated by an object that resides on a server.

The c/s software subsystems discussed in the preceding sections are implemented by components (objects) that must be capable of interacting with one another within a single machine (either client or server) or across the network. An *object request broker* is middleware that enables an object that resides on a client to send a message to a method that is encapsulated by an object that resides on a server. In essence, the ORB intercepts the message and handles all communication and coordination activities required to find the object to which the message was addressed, invoke its method, pass appropriate data to the object, and transfer the resulting data back to the object that generated the message in the first place.

WebRef
The latest information on component standards can be obtained at **www.omg.com, www.microsoft.com/COM,** and **java.sun.com/beans**

Three widely used standards that implement an object request broker philosophy—CORBA, COM, and JavaBeans—were discussed briefly in Chapter 27. CORBA will be used to illustrate the use of ORB middleware.

The basic structure of a CORBA architecture is illustrated in Figure 28.3. When CORBA is implemented in a client/server system, objects and object classes (Chapter 20) on both the client and the server are defined using an *interface description language*, a declarative language that allows a software engineer to define objects,

FIGURE 28.3
The basic CORBA architecture

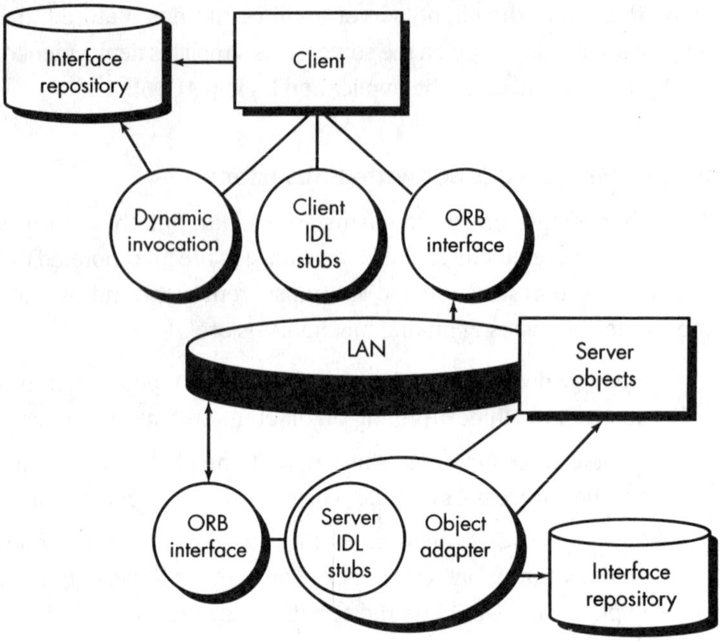

attributes, methods, and the messages required to invoke them. In order to accommodate a request for a server-resident method by a client-resident object, client and server IDL stubs are created. The stubs provide the gateway through which requests for objects across the c/s system are accommodated.

Because requests for objects across the network occur at run time, a mechanism for storing the object description must be established so that pertinent information about the object and its location are available when needed. The interface repository accomplishes this.

Quote:
"Adoption of CORBA is a positive step, but it is not enough to resolve the most critical software challenges."
Thomas Mowbray and Raphael Malveau

When a client application must invoke a method contained within an object elsewhere in the system, CORBA uses dynamic invocation to (1) obtain pertinent information about the desired method from the interface repository, (2) create a data structure with parameters to be passed to the object, (3) create a request for the object, and (4) invoke the request. The request is then passed to the *ORB core*—an implementation-specific part of the network operating system that manages requests—and the request is fulfilled.

The request is passed through the core and is processed by the server. At the server site, an *object adapter* stores class and object information in a server-resident interface repository, accepts and manages incoming requests from the client, and performs a variety of other object management functions [ORF99]. At the server, IDL stubs that are similar to those defined at the client machine are used as the interface to the actual object implementation resident at the server site.

Software development for a modern c/s system is object oriented. Using the CORBA architecture described briefly in this section, software developers can create an environment in which objects can be reused throughout a large network environment. For further information on CORBA and its overall impact on software engineering for c/s systems, the interested reader should refer to [HOQ99] and [SIE99].

28.2 SOFTWARE ENGINEERING FOR C/S SYSTEMS

A number of different software process models were introduced in Chapter 2. Although any of them could be adapted for use during the development of software for c/s systems, two approaches are most commonly used: (1) an evolutionary paradigm that makes use of event-based and/or object-oriented software engineering and (2) component-based software engineering (Chapter 27) that draws on a library of COTS and in-house software components.

Client/server systems are developed using the classic software engineering activities—analysis, design, construction, and testing—as the system evolves from a set of general business requirements to a collection of validated software components that have been implemented on client and server machines.

28.3 ANALYSIS MODELING ISSUES

The requirements modeling activity for c/s systems differs little from the analysis modeling methods applied to more conventional computer architectures. Therefore, the basic analysis principles discussed in Chapter 11 and the analysis modeling methods presented in Chapters 12 and 21 apply equally well to c/s software. It should be noted, however, that, because many modern c/s systems make use of reusable components, the qualification activities associated with CBSE (Chapter 27) also apply.

Because analysis modeling avoids specification of implementation detail, issues associated with the allocation of software components to client and server are considered only as the transition is made to design.[3] However, because an evolutionary approach to software engineering is applied for c/s systems, implementation decisions on the overall c/s approach (e.g., fat client vs. fat server) may be made during early analysis and design iterations.

28.4 DESIGN FOR C/S SYSTEMS

When software is being developed for implementation using a specific computer architecture, the design approach must consider the specific construction environment. In essence, the design should be customized to accommodate the hardware architecture.

3 For example, a CORBA-compliant c/s architecture (Section 28.1.5) will have a profound impact on design and implementation decisions.

When software is designed for implementation using client/server architecture, the design approach must be "customized" to accommodate the following issues:

- Data and architectural design (Chapter 14) dominate the design process. To effectively use the capabilities of a relational database management system (RDBMS) or object-oriented database management system (OODBMS) the design of the data becomes even more significant than in conventional applications.
- When the event-driven paradigm is chosen, behavioral modeling (an analysis activity, Chapters 12 and 21) should be conducted and the control-oriented aspects implied by the behavioral model should be translated into the design model.
- The user interaction/presentation component of a c/s system implements all functions that are typically associated with a graphical user interface. Therefore, interface design (Chapter 15) is elevated in importance.
- An object-oriented view of design (Chapter 22) is often chosen. Instead of the sequential structure provided by a procedural language, an object structure is provided by the linkage between an event initiated at the GUI and an event handling function within the client-based software.

ADVICE

Although c/s software is different, you can use conventional or OO design methods with very few modifications.

Although debate continues on the best analysis and design approach for c/s systems, object-oriented methods (Chapters 21 and 22) appear to have the best combination of features. However, conventional methods (Chapters 12 through 16) can also be adopted.

28.4.1 Architectural Design for Client/Server Systems

The architectural design of a client/server system is often characterized as a *communicating processes* style. Bass, Clements, and Kazman [BAS98] describe this architecture in the following way:

> The goal is to achieve the quality of scalability. A server exists to serve data to one or more clients, which are typically located across a network. The client originates a call to the server, which works, synchronously or asynchronously, to serve the client's request. If the server works synchronously, it returns control to the client at the same time it returns data. If the server works asynchronously, it returns only data to the client (which has its own thread of control).

XRef

A detailed discussion of architecture is presented in Chapter 14.

Because modern c/s systems are component based, an object request broker architecture (Figure 28.3) is used to implement this synchronous or asynchronous communication.

At the architectural level, the CORBA[4] interface description language is used to specify interface details. The use of IDL allows application software components to access ORB services (components) without knowledge of their internal workings.

---

4 An analogous approach is used in COM and JavaBeans.

The ORB also has the responsibility for coordinating communication among components for both the client and server. To accomplish this, the designer specifies an *object adapter* (also called a *wrapper*) that provides the following services [BAS98]:

- Component (object) implementations are registered.
- All component (object) references are interpreted and reconciled.
- Component (object) references are mapped to the corresponding component implementation.
- Objects are activated and deactivated.
- Methods (operations) are invoked when messages are transmitted.
- Security features are implemented.

To accommodate COTS components supplied by different vendors and in-house components that may have been implemented using different technologies, the ORB architecture must be designed to achieve interoperability among components. To accomplish this CORBA uses a bridging concept.

Assume that a client has been implemented using ORB protocol *X* and the server has been implemented using ORB protocol *Y*. Both protocols are CORBA compliant, but because of internal implementation differences, they must communicate to a "bridge" that provides a mechanism for translation between internal protocols [BAS98]. The bridge translates messages so that client and server can communicate smoothly.

28.4.2 Conventional Design Approaches for Application Software

In client/server systems, the data flow diagram (Chapters 12 and 14) can be used to establish the scope of a system, identify the high-level functions and subject data areas (data stores), and permit the decomposition of the high-level functions. In a departure from the traditional DFD approach, however, decomposition stops at the level of an elementary business process rather than continuing to the level of an atomic process.

In the c/s context, an *elementary business process* (EBP) can be defined as a set of tasks performed without a break by one user at a client site. The tasks are either performed fully or not at all.

The entity relationship diagram also assumes an expanded role. It continues to be used to decompose the subject data areas (data stores) of the DFD in order to establish a high-level view of a database that is to be implemented using an RDBMS. Its new role is to provide the structure for defining high-level business objects (Section 28.4.3).

Instead of serving as a tool for functional decomposition, the structure chart is now used as an assembly diagram to show the components involved in the solution for an elementary business process. These components, consisting of interface objects, application objects, and database objects, establish how the data are to be processed.

28.4.3 Database Design

Database design is used to define and then specify the structure of business objects used in the client/server system. The analysis required to identify business objects is accomplished using business process engineering methods discussed in Chapter 10. Conventional analysis modeling notation (Chapter 12), such as the ERD, can be used to define business objects, but a database repository should be established in order to capture the additional information that cannot be fully documented using a graphic notation such as an ERD.

In this repository, a *business object* is defined as information that is visible to the purchasers and users of the system, not its implementers. This information, implemented using a relational database, can be maintained in a design repository. The following design information is collected for the client/server database [POR94]:

Quote:

"The organization of data in a database has to represent the underlying meaning or semantics of the data correctly and efficiently."

Gio Wiederhold

- *Entities* are identified within the ERD for the new system.
- *Files* implement the entities identified within the ERD.
- *File-to-field relationships* establish the layout for the files by identifying which fields are included in which files.
- *Fields* define the fields in the design (the data dictionary).
- *File-to-file relationships* identify related files that can be joined to create logical views or queries.
- *Relationship validation* identifies the type of file-to-file or file-to-field relationships used for validation.
- *Field type* is used to permit inheritance of field characteristics from field superclasses (e.g., date, text, number, value, price).
- *Data type* specifies the characteristics of the data contained in a field.
- *File type* is used to identify the location of the file.
- *Field functions* include key, foreign key, attribute, virtual field, derived field, and the like.
- *Allowed values* identify values allowed for status type fields.
- *Business rules* are the rules for editing, calculating derived fields, and so on.

The trend toward distributed data management has accelerated as c/s architectures have become more pervasive. In c/s systems that implement this approach, the data management component resides on both the client and the server. Within the context of database design, a key issue is data distribution. That is, how are data distributed between the client and server and dispersed across the nodes of a network?

A relational database system enables easy access to distributed data through the use of structured query language. The advantage of SQL in a c/s architecture is that it is "nonnavigational" [BER92]. In an RDBMS, the type of data is specified using SQL, but no navigational information is required. Of course, the implication of this is that the RDBMS must be sophisticated enough to maintain the location of all data and be capable of defining the best path to it. In less sophisticated database systems, a request for data must indicate what is to be accessed and where it is. If application software must maintain navigational information, data management becomes much more complicated for c/s systems.

It should be noted that other data distribution and management techniques are also available to the designer [BER92]:

? What options exist for distributing data within a c/s system?

Manual extract. The user is allowed to manually copy appropriate data from a server to a client. This approach is useful when static data are required by a user and the control of the extract can be left in the user's hands.

Snapshot. This technique automates the manual extract by specifying a "snapshot" of data that should be transferred from a server to a client at predefined intervals. This approach is useful for distributing relatively static data that require only infrequent update.

Replication. This technique can be used when multiple copies of data must be maintained at different sites (e.g., different servers or clients and servers). Here, the level of complexity escalates because data consistency, updates, security, and processing must all be coordinated at multiple sites.

Fragmentation. In this approach, the system database is fragmented across multiple machines. Although intriguing in theory, fragmentation is exceptionally difficult to implement and is not encountered frequently.

Database design and, more specifically, database design for c/s systems are topics that are beyond the scope of this book. The interested reader should see [BRO91], [BER92], [VAS93], and [ORF99] for additional discussion.

28.4.4 An Overview of a Design Approach

Porter [POR95] suggests a set of steps for designing an elementary business process that combines elements of conventional design with elements of object-oriented design. It is assumed that a requirements model which defines business objects has been developed and refined prior to the start of the design of elementary business processes. The following steps are then used to derive the design:

1. For each elementary business process, identify the files that are created, updated, referenced, or deleted.
2. Use the files identified in step 1 as the basis for defining components or objects.

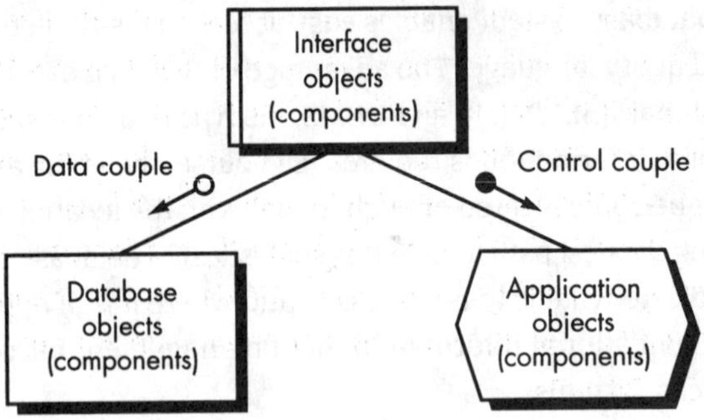

FIGURE 28.4 Structure chart notation for c/s components

3. For each component, retrieve the business rules and other business object information that has been established for the relevant file.
4. Determine which rules are relevant to the process, and decompose the rules down to a method level.
5. As required, define any additional components that are needed to implement the methods.

Porter [POR95] suggests a structure chart notation (Figure 28.4) for representing the component structure of an elementary business process. However, a different symbology is used so that the chart will conform to the object-oriented nature of c/s software. Referring to the figure, five different symbols are encountered:

Interface object. This type of component, also called the *user interaction/presentation component,* is typically built over a single file and related files that have been joined through a query. It includes methods for formatting the GUI interface and client-resident related application logic. It also includes embedded SQL that specifies database processing performed on the primary file over which the interface is built. If application logic normally associated with an interface object is implemented on a server instead, typically through the use of the middleware tools, the application logic operating on the server should be identified as a separate application object.

Database object. This type of component is used to identify database processing such as record creation or selection based on a file other than the primary file over which an interface object is built. It should be noted that, if the primary file over which an interface object is built is processed in a different manner, using a second SQL statement to retrieve a file in an alternate sequence. For example, the second file processing technique should be identified separately on the structure chart as a separate database object.

Application object. Used by either an interface object or a database object, this component is invoked by either a database trigger or a remote procedure call. It can also be used to identify business logic normally associated with interface processing that has been moved to the server for operation.

Data couple. When one object invokes another independent object, a message is passed between the two objects. The data couple symbol is used to denote this occurrence.

Control couple. When one object invokes another independent object and no data are passed between the two objects, a control couple symbol is used.

28.4.5 Process Design Iteration

The design repository (Section 28.4.3) used to represent business objects is also used to represent interface, application, and database objects. The following entities are identified:

- *Methods* describe how a business rule is to be implemented.
- *Elementary processes* define the elementary business processes identified in the analysis model.
- *Process/component link* identifies the components that make up the solution for an elementary business process.
- *Components* describe the components shown on the structure chart.
- *Business rule/component link* identifies the components that are significant to the implementation of a given business rule.

If a repository is implemented using an RDBMS, the designer will have access to a useful design tool that provides reporting to aid both construction and future maintenance of a c/s system.

28.5 TESTING ISSUES[5]

The distributed nature of client/server systems pose a set of unique problems for software testers. Binder [BIN92] suggests the following areas of focus:

WebRef
Useful c/s testing information and resources are presented at **www.icon-stl.net/~djmosley/**

- Client GUI considerations.
- Target environment and platform diversity considerations.
- Distributed database considerations (including replicated data).
- Distributed processing considerations (including replicated processes).
- Nonrobust target environment.
- Nonlinear performance relationships.

The strategy and tactics associated with c/s testing must be designed in a manner that allows each of these issues to be addressed.

5 This section is a much abbreviated and adapted version of an unpublished paper written by Daniel Mosley (used with the author's permission). An updated an expanded discussion can be found in [MOS99].

28.5.1 Overall c/s Testing Strategy

In general, the testing of client/server software occurs at three different levels: (1) individual client applications are tested in a "disconnected" mode, the operation of the server and the underlying network are not considered; (2) the client software and associated server applications are tested in concert, but network operations are not explicitly exercised; (3) the complete c/s architecture, including network operation and performance, is tested.

Although many different types of tests are conducted at each of these levels of detail, the following testing approaches are commonly encountered for c/s applications:

What types of tests are conducted for c/s systems?

Application function tests. The functionality of client applications is tested using the methods discussed in Chapter 17. In essence, the application is tested in stand-alone fashion in an attempt to uncover errors in its operation.

Server tests. The coordination and data management functions of the server are tested. Server performance (overall response time and data throughput) is also considered.

Database tests. The accuracy and integrity of data stored by the server is tested. Transactions posted by client applications are examined to ensure that data are properly stored, updated, and retrieved. Archiving is also tested.

Transaction tests. A series of tests are created to ensure that each class of transactions is processed according to requirements. Tests focus on the correctness of processing and also on performance issues (e.g., transaction processing times and transaction volume).

Network communication tests. These tests verify that communication among the nodes of the network occurs correctly and that message passing, transactions, and related network traffic occur without error. Network security tests may also be conducted as part of these tests.

XRef
Requirements elicitation techniques and use-cases are discussed in Chapter 11.

To accomplish these testing approaches, Musa [MUS93] recommends the development of operational profiles derived from client/server usage scenarios. An *operational profile* indicates how different types of users interoperate with the c/s system. That is, the profiles provide a "pattern of usage" that can be applied when tests are designed and executed. For example, for a particular type of user, what percentage of transactions will be inquiries? updates? orders?

To develop the operational profile, it is necessary to derive a set of user scenarios [BIN95] that are similar to use-cases discussed earlier in this book. Each scenario addresses who, where, what, and why. That is, who the user is, where (in the physical c/s architecture) the system interaction occurs, what the transaction is, and why it has occurred. Scenarios can be derived using requirements elicitation techniques or through less formal discussions with end-users. The result, however, should be the same. Each scenario should provide an indication of the system functions that will be required to service a particular user, the order in which those functions are required, the timing and response that is expected, and the frequency with which each function is used. These data are then combined (for all users) to create the operational profile.

Quote:
"The topic of testing is one area in which a good deal of commonality exists between traditional systems and client/server-based systems."
Kelley Bourne

The strategy for testing c/s architectures is analogous to the testing strategy for software-based systems described in Chapter 18. Testing begins with testing in the small. That is, a single client application is tested. Integration of the clients, the server, and the network are tested progressively. Finally, the entire system is tested as an operational entity.

Traditional testing views module/subsystem/system integration and testing (Chapter 18) as top down, bottom up, or some variation of the two. Module integration in c/s development may have some top-down or bottom-up aspects, but integration in c/s projects tends more toward parallel development and integration of modules across all design levels. Therefore, integration testing in c/s projects is sometimes best accomplished using a nonincremental or "big bang" approach.

The fact that the system is not being built to use prespecified hardware and software affects system testing. The networked cross-platform nature of c/s systems requires that we pay considerably more attention to configuration testing and compatibility testing.

Configuration testing doctrine forces testing of the system in all of the known hardware and software environments in which it will operate. Compatibility testing ensures a functionally consistent interface across hardware and software platforms. For example, a Windows-type interface may be visually different depending on the implementation environment, but the same basic user behaviors should produce the same results regardless of the client interface standard.

28.5.2 c/s Testing Tactics

Even if the c/s system has not been implemented using object technology, object-oriented testing techniques (Chapter 23) make good sense because the replicated data and processes can be organized into classes of objects that share the same set of properties. Once test cases have been derived for a class of objects (or their equivalent in a conventionally developed system), those test cases should be broadly applicable for all instances of the class.

The OO point of view is particularly valuable when the graphical user interface of modern c/s systems is considered. The GUI is inherently object oriented and departs from traditional interfaces because it must operate on many platforms. In addition, testing must explore a large number of logic paths because the GUI creates, manipulates, and modifies a broad range of graphical objects. Testing is further complicated because the objects can be present or absent, they may exist for a length of time, and they can appear anywhere on the desktop.

What this means is that the traditional capture/playback approach for testing conventional character-based interfaces must be modified in order to handle the complexities of the GUI environment. A functional variation of the capture/playback paradigm called *structured capture/playback* [FAR93] has evolved for GUI testing.

Traditional capture/playback records input as keystrokes and output as screen images, which are saved and compared against inputs and output images of subsequent tests. Structured capture/playback is based on an internal (logical) view of external activities. The application program's interactions with the GUI are recorded as internal events, which can be saved as "scripts" written in Microsoft's Visual Basic, one of the C variants, or in the vendor's proprietary language.

Tools that exercise GUIs do not address traditional data validation or path testing needs. The black-box and white-box testing methods discussed in Chapter 17 are applicable in many instances and the special object-oriented tactics presented in Chapter 23 are appropriate for both client and server software.

28.6 SUMMARY

Although client/server systems can adopt one or more of the software process models and many of the analysis, design, and testing methods described earlier in this book, the special architectural features of c/s require customization of the software engineering approach. In general, the software process model applied for c/s systems is evolutionary in nature and the technical methods often gravitate toward object-oriented or component-based approaches. The developer must describe objects that result in the implementation of user interaction/presentation, database, and application subsystems. The components (objects) defined for these subsystems must be allocated to either the client or server machines and can be linked via an object request broker.

Object request broker architectures support c/s designs in which client objects send messages to server objects. The CORBA standard makes use of interface definition language, and interface repositories manage requests for objects regardless of their location on the network.

Analysis and design for client/server systems make use of data flow and entity relationship diagrams, modified structure charts, and other notation that is encountered in the development of conventional applications. Testing strategies must be modified to accommodate tests that examine network communication and the interplay between software that resides on client and server.

REFERENCES

[BAS98] Bass, L., P. Clements, and R. Kazman, *Software Architecture in Practice,* Addison-Wesley, 1998.

[BER92] Berson, Alex, *Client/Server Architecture,* McGraw-Hill, 1992.

[BIN92] Binder, R., "A CASE-Based Systems Engineering Approach to Client-Server Development," *CASE Trends,* 1992.

[BIN95] Binder, R., "Scenario-Based Testing for Client Server Systems," *Software Development,* vol. 3, no. 8, August 1995, pp. 43–49.

[BRO91] Brown, A.W., *Object-Oriented Databases,* McGraw-Hill, 1991.

[FAR93] Farley, K.J., "Software Testing for Windows Developers," *Data Based Advisor,* November 1993, pp. 45–46, 50–52.

[HOQ99] Hoque, R., *CORBA for Real Programmers,* Academic Press/Morgan Kaufmann, 1999.

[ORF99] Orfali, R., D. Harkey, and J. Edwards, *Essential Client/Server Survival Guide,* 3rd ed., Wiley, 1999.

[MOS99] Mosley, D., *Client Server Software Testing on the Desk Top and the Web,* Prentice-Hall, 1999.

[MUS93] Musa, J., "Operational Profiles in Software Reliability Engineering," *IEEE Software,* March 1993, pp. 14–32.

[PAU95] L.G. Paul, "Client/Server Deployment," *Computerworld,* December 18, 1995.

[POR94] Porter, J., *O-DES Design Manual,* Fairfield University, 1994.

[POR95] Porter, J., *Synon Developer's Guide,* McGraw-Hill, 1995.

[SIE99] Siegel, J., *CORBA 3 Fundamentals and Programming,* Wiley, 1999.

[VAS93] Vaskevitch, D., *Client/Server Strategies,* IDG Books, 1993.

PROBLEMS AND POINTS TO PONDER

28.1. Using trade publications or Internet resources for background information, define a set of criteria for evaluating tools for c/s software engineering.

28.2. Suggest five applications in which a fat server would seem to be an appropriate design strategy.

28.3. Suggest five applications in which a fat client would seem to be an appropriate design strategy.

28.4. Do some additional research on the CORBA standard and determine how the latest release of the standard addresses interoperability among different ORBs provided by different vendors.

28.5. Research a structured query language and provide a brief example of how a transaction might be characterized using the language.

28.6. Research the latest advances in groupware and develop a brief presentation for your class. Your instructor may assign a specific function to different presenters.

28.7. A company is establishing a new e-commerce division to sell casual apparel and outdoor merchandise. The e-catalog will be published on the World Wide Web and orders can be placed via the Web site, by e-mail, or via telephone or fax. A client/server system will be built to support order processing at the company site. Define a set of high-level objects that would be required for the order-processing system and organize these objects into three component categories: the user interaction/presentation, database, and application.

28.8. Define business rules to establish when a shipment can be made if payment is by credit card for the system described in Problem 28.7. Add additional rules if payment is by check.

28.9. Develop a state transition diagram (Chapter 12) that defines the events and states that would be visible to an order entry clerk working at a client PC within the e-commerce sales division (Problem 28.7).

28.10. Provide examples of three or four messages that might result in a request from a client for a method maintained on the server.

FURTHER READINGS AND INFORMATION SOURCES

Although software engineering methods for client/server systems are quite similar to conventional and OO systems, specialized knowledge and techniques are required. Worthwhile introductions to basic concepts have been written by Lowe and Helda (*Client/Server Computing for Dummies,* 3rd ed., IDG Books Worldwide, 1999) and Zantinge and Adriaans (*Managing Client/Server,* Addison-Wesley, 1997). At an intermediate level, McClanahan (*Developing Client-Server Applications,* IDG Books Worldwide, 1999) covers a broad range of c/s topics. On a more sophisticated level, Orfali and his colleagues [ORF99] and Linthicum (*Guide to Client/Server and Intranet Development,* Wiley, 1997) provide detailed guidelines for engineering c/s applications. Berson (*Client/Server Architecture,* 2nd ed., McGraw-Hill, 1996) discusses component and architecture issues.

Network computers have become a hot technology topic (and a risky business strategy) in recent years. Sinclair and Merkow (*Thin Clients Clearly Explained,* Morgan Kaufmann, 1999), Friedrichs and Jubin (*Java Thin-Client Programming for a Network Computing Environment,* Prentice-Hall, 1999), Dewire (*Thin Clients,* McGraw-Hill, 1998), and Kanter (*Understanding Thin-Client/Server Computing,* Microsoft Press, 1998) provide worthwhile guidance on how to design, build, deploy, and support thin-client systems.

Beginning with the modeling of business events, Ruble (*Practical Analysis and Design for Client/Server and GUI Systems,* Yourdon Press, 1997) provides an in-depth discussion of techniques for the analysis and design of c/s systems. Books by Goldman, Rawles, and Mariga (*Client/Server Information Systems: A Business-Oriented Approach,* Wiley, 1999); Shan, Earle, and Lenzi (*Enterprise Computing with Objects: From Client/Server Environments to the Internet,* Addison-Wesley, 1997); and Gold-Bernstein and Marca (*Designing Enterprise Client/Server Systems,* Prentice-Hall, 1997) consider c/s in a broader enterprise context.

Loosley and Douglas (*High-Performance Client/Server,* Wiley, 1997) explain the principles of software performance engineering and apply them to distributed systems architecture and design. Heinckiens and Loomis (*Building Scalable Database Applications: Object-Oriented Design, Architectures, and Implementations,* Addison-Wesley, 1998) emphasize database design in their guide for building client/server applications. Ligon (*Client/Server Communications Services: A Guide for the Applications Developer,* McGraw-Hill, 1997) considers a wide variety of communication-related topics including TCP/IP, ATM, EDI, CORBA, messaging, and encryption. Schneberger (*Client/Server Software Maintenance,* McGraw-Hill, 1997) presents a framework for controlling c/s software maintenance costs and optimizing user support.

Hundreds of books address vendor-specific c/s systems development. The following represents a small sampling:

Anderson, G.W., *Client/Server Database Design with Sybase: A High-Performance and Fine-Tuning Guide,* McGraw-Hill, 1997.

Barlotta, M.J., *Distributed Application Development with Powerbuilder 6,* Manning Publications, 1998.

Bates, R.J., *Hands-on Client/Server Internetworking,* McGraw-Hill, 1997.

Mahmoud, Q.H., *Distributed Programming with Java,* Manning, 1998.

Orfali, R. and D. Harkey, *Client/Server Programming with JavaBeans,* Wiley, 1999.

Sankar, K., *Building Internet Client/Server Systems,* McGraw-Hill, 1999.

Detailed guidebooks for c/s testing have been written by Mosley [MOS99] and Bourne (*Testing Client/Server Systems,* McGraw-Hill, 1997). Both authors provide in-depth discussion of testing strategies, tactics, and tools.

A wide variety of information sources on client/server software engineering is available on the Internet. An up-to-date list of World Wide Web references that are relevant to c/s systems can be found at the SEPA Web site:

http://www.mhhe.com/engcs/compsci/pressman/resources/client-server.mhtml

CHAPTER

29 WEB ENGINEERING

KEY CONCEPTS

The World Wide Web and the Internet have drawn the general populace into the world of computing. We purchase stock and mutual funds, download music, view movies, get medical advice, book hotel rooms, sell personal items, schedule airline flights, meet people, do our banking, take college courses, buy groceries—we do just about anything and everything in the virtual world of the Web. Arguably, the Web and the Internet that empowers it are the most important developments in the history of computing. These computing technologies have drawn us all (with billions more who will eventually follow) into the information age. They have become integral to daily life in the first years of the twenty-first century.

For those of us who can remember a world without the Web, the chaotic growth of the technology harkens back to another era—the early days of software. It was a time of little discipline, but enormous enthusiasm and creativity. It was a time when programmers often hacked together systems—some good, some bad. The prevailing attitude seemed to be "Get it done fast, and get it into the field, we'll clean it up (and better understand what we really need to build) as we go." Sound familiar?

In a virtual round table published in *IEEE Software* [PRE98], I staked out my position with regard to Web engineering:

QUICK LOOK

What is it? Web-based systems and applications (WebApps) deliver a complex array of content and functionality to a broad population of end-users. Web engineering is the process used to create high-quality WebApps. Web engineering is not a perfect clone of software engineering, but it borrows many of software engineering's fundamental concepts and principles, emphasizing the same technical and management activities. There are subtle differences in the way these activities are conducted, but an overriding philosophy that dictates a disciplined approach to the development of a computer-based system is identical.

Who does it? Web engineers and nontechnical content developers create the WebApp.

Why is it important? As WebApps become increasing integrated in business strategies for small and large companies (e.g., e-commerce), the need to build reliable, usable, and adaptable systems grows in importance. That's why a disciplined approach to WebApp development is necessary.

What are the steps? Like any engineering discipline, Web engineering applies a generic approach that is tempered with specialized strategies, tactics, and methods. The Web engineering process begins with a formulation of the problem to be solved by the WebApp. The project is planned, and the

QUICK LOOK

requirements of the WebApp are analyzed. Architectural, navigational, and interface design are conducted. The system is implemented using specialized languages and tools associated with the Web, and testing commences. Because WebApps evolve continuously, mechanisms for configuration control, quality assurance, and ongoing support are needed.

What is the work product? A variety of Web engineering work products (e.g., analysis models, design models, test procedures) are produced. The final output is the operational WebApp.

How do I ensure that I've done it right? Use the same SQA practices that are applied in every software engineering process—formal technical reviews assess the analysis and design models, specialized reviews consider usability; testing is applied to uncover errors in content, functionality, and compatibility.

It seems to me that just about any important product or system is worth engineering. Before you start building it, you'd better understand the problem, design a workable solution, implement it in a solid way, and test it thoroughly. You should probably also control changes to it as you work and have some mechanism for ensuring the end result's quality. Many Web developers don't argue with this; they just think their world is really different and that conventional software engineering approaches simply don't apply.

This leads us to a pivotal question: Can software engineering principles, concepts, and methods be applied to Web development? Many of them can, but their application may require a somewhat different spin.

But what if the current ad hoc approach to Web development persists? In the absence of a disciplined process for developing Web-based systems, there is increasing concern that we may face serious problems in the successful development, deployment, and "maintenance" of these systems. In essence, the application infrastructure that we are creating today may lead to something that might be called a *tangled Web* as we move further into this new century. This phrase connotes a morass of poorly developed Web-based applications that have too high a probability of failure. Worse, as Web-based systems grow more complex, a failure in one can and will propagate broad-based problems across many. When this happens, confidence in the entire Internet may be shaken irreparably. Worse, it may lead to unnecessary and ill-conceived government regulation, leading to irreparable harm to these unique technologies.

> **Quote:**
> "The engineering principles of planning before designing and designing before building have withstood every prior technology transition; they'll survive this transition as well."
> **Watts Humphrey**

In order to avoid a tangled Web and achieve greater success in development and application of large-scale, complex Web-based systems, there is a pressing need for disciplined Web engineering approaches and new methods and tools for development, deployment, and evaluation of Web-based systems and applications. Such approaches and techniques must take into account the special features of the new medium, the operational environments and scenarios, and the multiplicity of user profiles that pose additional challenges to Web-based application development.

Web Engineering (WebE) is concerned with the establishment and use of sound scientific, engineering, and management principles and disciplined and systematic approaches to the successful development, deployment, and maintenance of high-quality Web-based systems and applications [MUR99].

29.1 THE ATTRIBUTES OF WEB-BASED APPLICATIONS

There is little debate that Web-based systems and applications[1] (we will refer to these collectively as *WebApps*) are different than the many other categories of computer software discussed in Chapter 1. Powell summarizes the primary differences when he states that Web-based systems "involve a mixture between print publishing and software development, between marketing and computing, between internal communications and external relations, and between art and technology" [POW98]. The following attributes are encountered in the vast majority of WebApps:[2]

KEY POINT

WebApps are network intensive, content driven, and continuously evolving. These attributes have a profound impact on the way in which WebE is conducted.

Network intensive. By its nature, a WebApp is network intensive. It resides on a network and must serve the needs of a diverse community of clients. A WebApp may reside on the Internet (thereby enabling open worldwide communication). Alternatively, an application may be placed on an intranet (implementing communication across an organization) or an Extranet (internetwork communication).

Content driven. In many cases, the primary function of a WebApp is to use hypermedia to present text, graphics, audio, and video content to the end-user.

Continuous evolution. Unlike conventional application software that evolves over a series of planned, chronologically spaced releases, Web applications evolve continuously. It is not unusual for some WebApps (specifically, their content) to be updated on an hourly schedule.

Some argue that the continuous evolution of WebApps makes the work performed on them analogous to gardening. Lowe {LOW99] discusses this when he writes:

> Engineering is about adopting a consistent and scientific approach, tempered by a specific practical context, to development and commissioning of systems or applications. Web site development is often much more about creating an infrastructure (laying out the garden) and then "tending" the information which grows and blooms within this garden. Over time the garden (i.e., Web site) will continue to evolve, change, and grow. A good initial architecture should allow this growth to occur in a controlled and consistent manner . . . we could have "tree surgeons" that prune "trees" (i.e., sections of the site) within the "garden"

---

1 Included within this category are complete Web sites, specialized functionality within Web sites, and information processing applications that reside on the Internet or on an intranet or Extranet.

2 In the context of this chapter, the term *Web application* encompasses everything from a simple Web page that might help a consumer compute an automobile lease payment to a comprehensive Web site that provides complete travel services for business people and vacationers.

(the site itself) while ensuring cross-referential integrity. We could have "garden nurseries" where young plants (i.e., design patterns for Web sites) are "grown." I probably should stop this analogy before I get too carried away!

Continual care and feeding allows a Web site to grow (in robustness and importance). But, unlike a garden, Web applications must serve (and adapt to) the needs of more than the gardener. The following WebApp characteristics drive the process:

ADVICE

There is little doubt that immediacy often holds sway in WebApp development, but be careful! Just because you have to get it done quickly does not mean that you have the luxury of doing a poorly engineered job. Quick and wrong are rarely an acceptable result.

Immediacy. Web-based applications have an immediacy [NOR99] that is not found in any other type of software. That is, the time to market for a complete Web site can be a matter of a few days or weeks.[3] Developers must use methods for planning, analysis, design, implementation, and testing that have been adapted to the compressed time schedules required for WebApp development.

Security. Because WebApps are available via network access, it is difficult, if not impossible, to limit the population of end-users who may access the application. In order to protect sensitive content and provide secure modes of data transmission, strong security measures must be implemented throughout the infrastructure that supports a WebApp and within the application itself.

Aesthetics. An undeniable part of the appeal of a WebApp is its look and feel. When an application has been designed to market or sell products or ideas, aesthetics may have as much to do with success as technical design.

These general characteristics apply to all WebApps but with different degrees of influence. The following application categories are most commonly encountered in WebE work [DAR99]:

? How can we categorize WebApps?

- *Informational.* Read-only content is provided with simple navigation and links.
- *Download.* A user downloads information from the appropriate server.
- *Customizable.* The user customizes content to specific needs.
- *Interaction.* Communication among a community of users occurs via chatroom, bulletin boards, or instant messaging.
- *User input.* Forms-based input is the primary mechanism for communicating need.
- *Transaction oriented.* The user makes a request (e.g., places an order) that is fulfilled by the WebApp.
- *Service oriented.* The application provides a service to the user (e.g., assists the user in determining a mortgage payment).
- *Portal.* The application channels the user to other Web content or services outside the domain of the portal application.

3 Reasonably sophisticated Web pages can be produced in only a few hours.

- *Database access*. The user queries a large database and extracts information.
- *Data warehousing*. The user queries a collection of large databases and extracts information.

The characteristics noted earlier in this section and the application categories just noted represent facts of life for Web engineers. The key is living within the constraints imposed by the characteristics and still producing a successful WebApp.

29.1.1 Quality Attributes

Every person who has surfed the Web or used a corporate intranet has an opinion about what makes a "good" WebApp. Individual viewpoints vary widely. Some users enjoy flashy graphics, others want simple text. Some demand copious information, others desire an abbreviated presentation. In fact, the user's perception of "goodness" (and the resultant acceptance or rejection of the WebApp as a consequence) might be more important that any technical discussion of WebApp quality.

But how is WebApp quality perceived? What attributes must be exhibited to achieve goodness in the eyes of end-users and at the same time exhibit the technical characteristics of quality that will enable a Web engineer to correct, adapt, enhance, and support the application over the long term?

In reality, all of the general characteristics of software quality discussed in Chapters 8, 19, and 24 apply to WebApps. However, the most relevant of these characteristics—usability, functionality, reliability, efficiency, and maintainability—provide a useful basis for assessing the quality of Web-based systems.

SEPA WEB CHECKLIST

Detailed quality requirement tree for WebApps

Olsina and his colleagues [OLS99] has prepared a "quality requirement tree" that identifies a set of attributes that lead to high-quality WebApps. Figure 29.1 summarizes their work.

29.1.2 The Technologies

The design and implementation of Web-based systems and applications incorporates three important enabling technologies: component-based development, security, and Internet standards. A Web engineer must be familiar with all three in order to build high-quality WebApps.

Component-Based Development

The component technologies discussed in Chapters 27 and 28 have evolved in large part because of the explosive growth of Web-based systems and applications. Recalling our discussion from the preceding chapters, three major infrastructure standards are available for Web engineers: CORBA, COM/DCOM, and JavaBeans. These standards (accompanied by prebuilt components, tools, and techniques) provide an infrastructure that enables developers to deploy third party and custom developed components and allow them to communicate with one another and with system-level services.

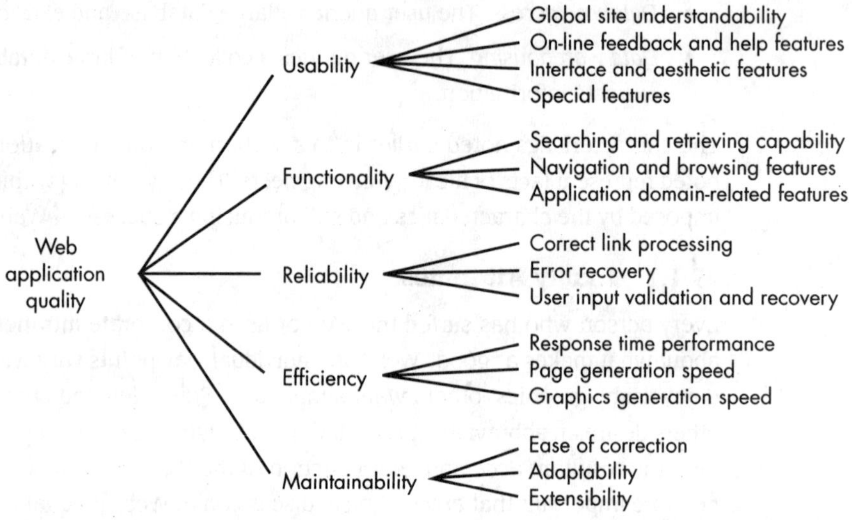

FIGURE 29.1 Quality requirements tree [OLS99]

Security

Quote: "The Internet is a risky place to conduct business or store assets. Hackers, crackers, snoops, spoofers, spammers, scammers, shammers, jammers, intruders, thieves, purloiners, conspirators, vandals, Trojan horse dealers, virus launchers and rouge program purveyors run loose." **Dorothy Denning and Peter Denning**

If a WebApp resides on a network, it is open to unauthorized access. In some cases, unauthorized access may be attempted by internal personnel. In others, outsiders (hackers) may attempt access for sport, for profit, or with more malevolent intent. A variety of security measures are provided by the network infrastructure, encryption techniques, firewalls, and other measures. A comprehensive discussion of this important topic is beyond the scope of this book. For more information, the interested reader should see [ATK97], [KAE99], and [BRE99].

Internet Standards

For the last decade the dominant standard for the creation of WebApp content and structure has been HTML, a markup language that enables the developer to provide a series of tags that describe the appearance of a wide array of data objects (text, graphics, audio/video, forms, etc.). However, as the size and complexity of applications grow, a new standard—XML— has been adopted for the next generation of WebApps. XML (extensible markup language) is a strictly defined subset of the metalanguage SGML [BRA97], allowing developers to define custom tags within Web page descriptions. Using an XML meta-language description, the meaning of the custom tags is defined in the information transmitted to the client site. For more information on XML, the interested reader should see [PAR99] and [STL99].

29.2 THE WEBE PROCESS

The characteristics of Web-based systems and applications have a profound influence on the WebE process. Immediacy and continuous evolution dictate an iter-

KEY POINT
WebE demands an evolutionary, incremental software process.

ative, incremental process model (Chapter 2) that produces WebApp releases in rapid fire sequence. The network-intensive nature of applications in this domain suggests a population of users that is diverse (thereby making special demands on requirements elicitation and modeling) and an application architecture that can be highly specialized (thereby making demands on design). Because WebApps are often content driven with an emphasis on aesthetics, it is likely that parallel development activities will be scheduled within the WebE process and involve a team of both technical and non-technical people (e.g., copywriters, graphic designers).

29.3 A FRAMEWORK FOR WEBE

As WebApps evolve from static, content-directed information sources to dynamic, user-directed application environments, the need to apply solid management and engineering principles grows in importance. To accomplish this, it is necessary to develop a WebE framework that encompasses an effective process model, populated by framework activities[4] and engineering tasks. A process model for WebE is suggested in Figure 29.2.

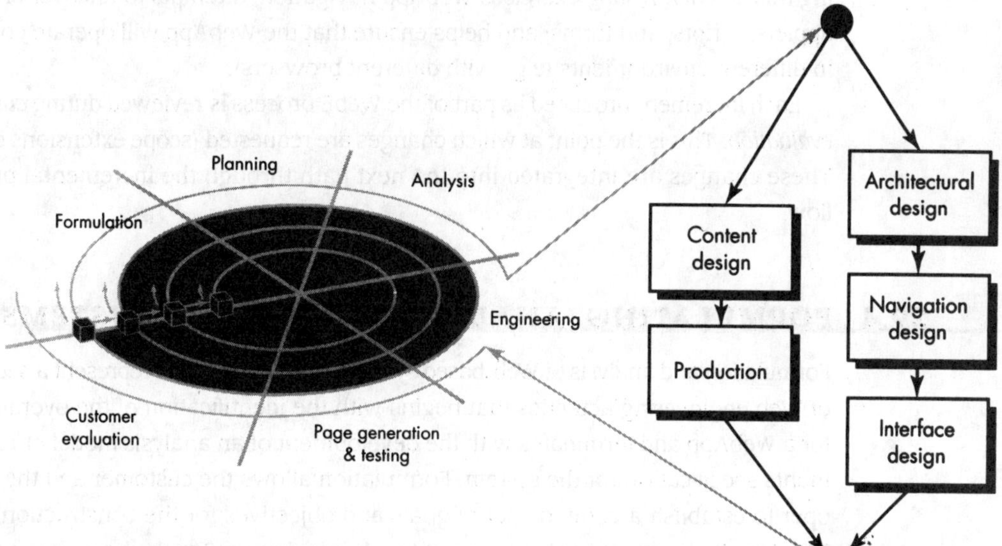

FIGURE 29.2 The WebE process model

4 Recalling the discussion of process models in Chapter 2, framework activities are performed for all WebApps, while engineering tasks are adapted to the size and complexity of the WebApp to be developed.

The WebE process begins with a *formulation*—an activity that identifies the goals and objectives of the WebApp and establishes the scope for the first increment. *Planning* estimates overall project cost, evaluates risks associated with the development effort, and defines a finely granulated development schedule for the initial WebApp increment, with a more coarsely granulated schedule for subsequent increments. *Analysis* establishes technical requirements for the WebApp and identifies the content items that will be incorporated. Requirements for graphic design (aesthetics) are also defined.

WebRef

W3C, an industry consortium that provides access to WWW information of interest to Web engineers can be accessed at **www.w3.org**

The *engineering* activity incorporates two parallel tasks illustrated on the right side of Figure 29.2. *Content design* and *production* are tasks performed by nontechnical members of the WebE team. The intent of these tasks is to design, produce, and/or acquire all text, graphics, audio, and video content that are to become integrated into the WebApp. At the same time, a set of technical design tasks (Section 29.5) are conducted.

Page generation is a construction activity that makes heavy use of automated tools for WebApp creation. The content defined in the engineering activity is merged with the architectural, navigation, and interface designs to produce executable Web pages in HTML, XML, and other process-oriented languages (e.g., Java). Integration with component middleware (i.e., CORBA, DCOM, or JavaBeans) is also accomplished during this activity. *Testing* exercises WebApp navigation; attempts to uncover errors in applets, scripts, and forms; and helps ensure that the WebApp will operate correctly in different environments (e.g., with different browsers).

Each increment produced as part of the WebE process is reviewed during *customer evaluation*. This is the point at which changes are requested (scope extensions occur). These changes are integrated into the next path through the incremental process flow.

29.4 FORMULATING/ANALYZING WEB-BASED SYSTEMS

Formulation and analysis of Web-based systems and applications represent a sequence of Web engineering activities that begins with the identification of the overall goals for a WebApp and terminates with the development of an analysis model or requirements specification for the system. Formulation allows the customer and the developer to establish a common set of goals and objectives for the construction of the WebApp. It also identifies the scope of the development effort and provides a means for determining a successful outcome. Analysis is a technical activity that identifies the data, functional, and behavioral requirements for the WebApp.

29.4.1 Formulation

Powell [POW98] suggests a set of questions that should be answered at the beginning of the formulation step:

What questions should be asked to formulate the problem?

- What is the main motivation for the WebApp?
- Why is the WebApp needed?
- Who will use the WebApp?

The answer to each of these simple questions should be stated as succinctly as possible. For example, assume that the manufacturer of home security systems has decided to establish an e-commerce Web site to sell its products directly to consumers. A statement describing the motivation for the WebApp might be

SafeHomeInc.com[5] will allow consumers to configure and purchase all components required to install a home/business security system.

It is important to note that detail is not provided in this statement. The objective is to bound the overall intent of the site.

After discussion with various constituencies within SafeHome Inc., an answer to the second question is stated:

SafeHomeInc.com will allow us to sell directly to consumers, thereby eliminating retailer costs and improving our profit margins. It will also allow us to increase sales by a projected 25 percent over current annual sales and will allow us to penetrate geographic regions where we currently do not have sales outlets.

Finally, the company defines the demographic for the WebApp: "Projected users of SafeHomeInc.com are homeowners and owners of small businesses."

KEY POINT

Both informational and applicative goals should be defined for every WebApp.

These answers imply specific goals for the SafeHomeInc.com Web site. In general, two categories of goals [GNA99] are identified:

- *Informational goals*. Indicate an intention to provide specific content and/or information to the end-user.
- *Applicative goals*. Indicate the ability to perform some task within the WebApp.

In the content of the SafeHomeInc.com WebApp, one informational goal might be

The site will provide users with detailed product specifications, including technical description, installation instructions, and pricing information.

Examination of the answers to the questions just posed might lead to the statement of an applicative goal:

SafeHomeInc.com will query the user about the facility (i.e., house, office/retail space) that is to be protected and make customized recommendations about the product and configuration to be used.

Once all informational and applicative goals have been identified, a user profile is developed. The user profile captures "relevant features related to potential users

5 *SafeHome* has been used as a continuing example earlier in this book.

including their background, knowledge, preferences and even more" [GNA99]. In the case of SafeHomeInc.com, a user profile would identify the characteristics of a typical purchaser of security systems (this information would be supplied by the SafeHome Inc. marketing department).

Once goals and user profiles have been developed, the formulation activity focuses on a statement of scope (Chapter 5) for the WebApp. In many cases, the goals already developed are integrated into the statement of scope. In addition, however, it is useful to indicate the degree of integration to be expected of the WebApp. That is, it is often necessary to integrate existing information systems (e.g., an existing database application) with a Web-based front end. Connectivity issues are considered at this stage.

29.4.2 Analysis

The concepts and principles discussed for software requirements analysis (Chapter 11) apply without revision for the Web engineering analysis activity. Scope defined during the formulation activity is elaborated to create a complete analysis model for the WebApp. Four different types of analysis are conducted during WebE:

> **Quote:**
> "Successful knowledge products [WebApps] allow customers to meet their needs better, faster, or cheaper themselves, rather than working through employee end-users. The Internet's ability to connect customers directly with companies provides an infrastructure for knowledge products."
> **Mark McDonald**

Content analysis. The full spectrum of content to be provided by the WebApp is identified. Content includes text, graphics and images, video and audio data. Data modeling (Chapter 12) can be used to identify and describe each of the data objects to be used within the WebApp.

Interaction analysis. The manner in which the user interacts with the WebApp is described in detail. Use-cases (Chapter 11) can be developed to provide detailed descriptions of this interaction.

Functional analysis. The usage scenarios (use-cases) created as part of interaction analysis define the operations that will be applied to WebApp content and imply other processing functions. All operations and functions are described in detail.

Configuration analysis. The environment and infrastructure in which the WebApp resides are described in detail. The WebApp can reside on the Internet, an intranet, or an Extranet. In addition, the infrastructure (i.e., the component infrastructure and the degree to which a database will be used to generate content) for the WebApp should be identified at this stage.

Although a detailed requirements specification is recommended for large, complex WebApps, such documents are rare. It can be argued that the continuous evolution of WebApp requirements may make obsolete any document before it is finished. Although this may be true in the extreme, it is necessary to define an analysis model that can serve as a foundation for the design activity that follows. At a minimum, the information collected during the preceding four analysis tasks should be reviewed, modified as required, and then organized into a document that can be passed to WebApp designers.

29.5 DESIGN FOR WEB-BASED APPLICATIONS

WebRef
A worthwhile source of practical guidelines for Web site design can be found at **www.ibm.com/ibm/easy/design/lower/f060100.html**

The immediate nature of Web-based applications coupled with the pressure for continuous evolution forces a Web engineer to establish a design that solves the immediate business problem while at the same time defining an application architecture that has the ability to evolve rapidly over time. The problem, of course, is that solving the immediate problem (quickly) can result in compromises that affect the ability of the application to evolve over time. This is the designer's dilemma.

In order to perform Web-based design effectively, a Web engineer should work to reuse four technical elements [NAN98]:

Design principles and methods. It is important to note that the design concepts and principles discussed in Chapter 13 apply to all WebApps. Effective modularity (exhibited by high cohesion and low coupling), information hiding, stepwise elaboration, and other software design heuristics lead to Web-based systems and applications that are easier to adapt, enhance, test, and use.

Quote:
"To some, Web design focuses on visual look and feel . . . To others, Web design is about the structuring of information and the navigation through the document space. Others might even consider Web design to be about the technology used to build interactive Web applications. In reality, design includes all of these things and maybe more."
Thomas Powell

Design methods for object-oriented systems discussed earlier in this book can be reused when Web-applications are created. Hypermedia defines "objects" that interact via a communication protocol that is loosely analogous to messaging. In fact the diagrammatic notation proposed for UML (Chapters 21 and 22) can be adapted for use in design activities for WebApps. In addition, a variety of hypermedia design methods have been proposed (e.g., [ISA95], [SCH96]).

Golden rules. Interactive hypermedia applications (WebApps) have been constructed for more than a decade. Over that time, designers have developed a set of design heuristics (*golden rules*) that can be reapplied during the design of new applications.

Design patterns. As we noted earlier in this book, design patterns are a generic approach for solving some small problems that can be adapted to a much wider variety of specific problems. In the context of WebApps, design patterns can be applied not only to the functional elements of an application, but to documents, graphics, and general aesthetics for a Web site.

Templates. A template can be used to provide a skeletal framework for any design pattern or document that is to be used within a WebApp. Nanard and Kahn [NAN98] describe this reusable design element in the following way:

> Once a template is specified, any part of a hypermedia structure that conforms to this template can be automatically generated or updated just by calling the template with relevant data [to flesh out the skeleton]. The use of constructive templates implicitly relies on the separation of hypermedia document contents from the specification of its presentation: source data are mapped into the hypertext structure as specified in the template.

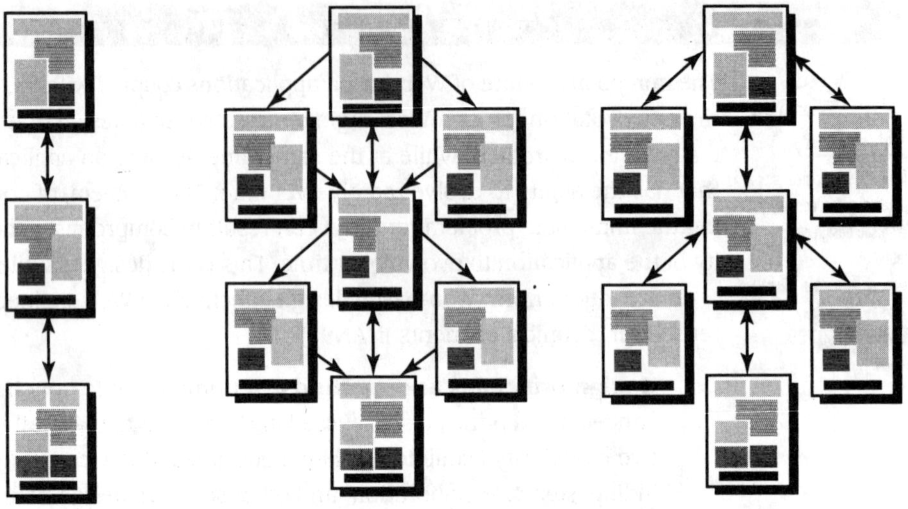

FIGURE 29.3 Linear structures

Each of the four reusable design elements is discussed in greater detail in the sections that follow.

ADVICE *Most WebApp structures just happen. Avoid this trap. Layout the WebApp structural design explicitly before you begin developing navigation or page detail.*

29.5.1 Architectural Design

Architectural design for Web-based systems and applications focuses on the definition of the overall hypermedia structure of the WebApp and the application of design patterns and constructive templates to populate the structure (and achieve reuse). A parallel activity, called *content design*,[6] derives the overall structure and detailed layout of the information content that will be presented as part of the WebApp.

WebApp Structures

Overall architectural structure is tied to the goals established for a WebApp, the content to be presented, the users who will visit, and the navigation philosophy (Section 29.5.3) that has been established. The architectural designer can choose from four different structures [POW98] when developing the design for a typical WebApp.

? What structural options are available for WebApp design?

Linear structures (Figure 29.3) are encountered when a predictable sequence of interactions (with some variation or diversion) is common. A classic example might be a tutorial presentation in which pages of information along with related graphics, short videos, or audio are presented only after prerequisite information has been pre-

6 Content design is a nontechnical activity that is performed by copywriters, artists, graphic designers, and others who generate Web-based content. For further detail, see [DIN98] and [LYN99].

FIGURE 29.4
Grid Structure

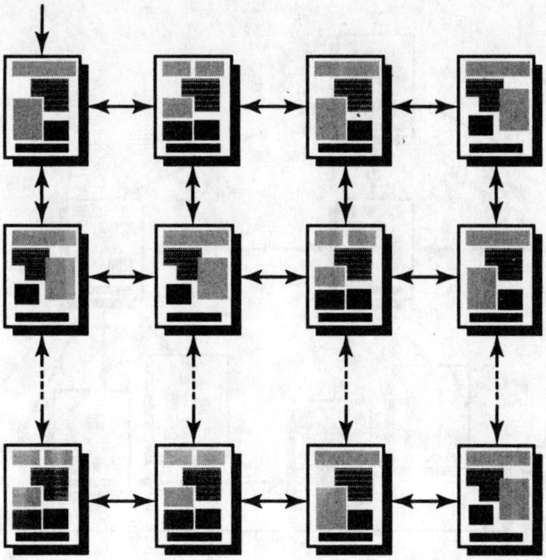

sented. The sequence of content presentation is predefined and generally linear. Another example might be a product order entry sequence in which specific information must be specified in a specific order. In such cases, the structures shown in Figure 29.3 are appropriate. As content and processing become more complex, the purely linear flow shown on the left of the figure gives way to more sophisticated linear structures in which alternative content may be invoked or a diversion to acquire complementary content (structure shown on the right side of Figure 29.3) occurs.

KEY POINT
Grid structures work well when content can be organized categorically in two or more dimensions.

Grid structures (Figure 29.4) are an architectural option that can be applied when WebApp content can be organized categorically in two (or more) dimensions. For example, consider a situation in which an e-commerce site sells golf clubs. The horizontal dimension of the grid represents the type of club to be sold (e.g., woods, irons, wedges, putters). The vertical dimension represents the offerings provided by various golf club manufacturers. Hence, a user might navigate the grid horizontally to find the putters column and then vertically to examine the offerings provided by those manufacturers that sell putters. This WebApp architecture is useful only when highly regular content is encountered [POW98].

ADVICE
Coupling is a tricky issue for WebApp architectures. On one hand, it facilitates navigation. But it can also cause the user to "get lost." Don't overdo horizontal connections within a hierarchy.

Hierarchical structures (Figure 29.5) are undoubtedly the most common WebApp architecture. Unlike the partitioned software hierarchies discussed in Chapter 14 which encourage flow of control only along vertical branches of the hierarchy, a WebApp hierarchical structure can be designed in a manner that enables (via hypertext branching) flow of control horizontally, across vertical branches of the structure. Hence, content presented on the far left-hand branch of the hierarchy can have hypertext links that lead to content that exists in the middle or right-hand branch of the structure. It should be noted, however, that although such branching allows rapid navigation across WebApp content, it can lead to confusion on the part of the user.

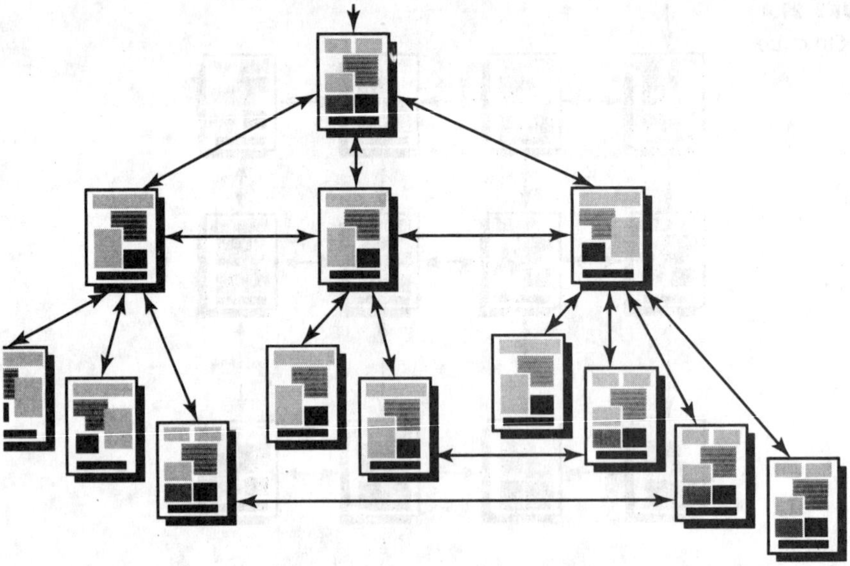

FIGURE 29.5
Hierarchical structures

A *networked,* or "pure Web," structure (Figure 29.6) is similar in may ways to the architecture that evolves for object-oriented systems. Architectural components (in this case, Web pages) are designed so that they may pass control (via hypertext links) to virtually every other component in the system. This approach allows considerable navigation flexibility, but at the same time, can be confusing to a user.

The architectural structures discussed in the preceding paragraphs can be combined to form composite structures. The overall architecture of a WebApp may be hierarchical, but one part of the structure may exhibit linear characteristics, while

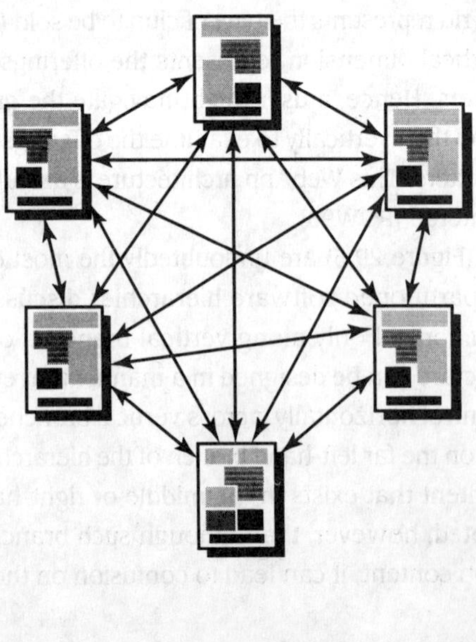

FIGURE 29.6
Networked, or "pure Web," structure

another part of the architecture may be networked. The goal for the architectural designer is to match the WebApp structure to the content to be presented and the processing to be conducted.

Design Patterns

XRef
Further discussion of design patterns may be found in Chapters 14 and 22.

As we noted earlier in this book, design patterns are a generic approach for solving some small problem that can be adapted to a much wider variety of specific problems. In the context of Web-based systems and applications, design patterns can be applied at the architectural level, the component-level, and at the hypertext (navigational) level.

When data processing functionality is required within a WebApp, the architectural and component-level design patterns proposed by [BUS96], [GAM95], and others are applicable. Hypertext-level design patterns focus on the design of navigation features that allow a user to move through WebApp content in a facile manner. Among many hypertext design patterns proposed in the literature are [BER98]:

Quote:
"Each pattern is a three-part rule, which expresses a relation between a certain context, a problem, and a solution."
Christopher Alexander

- *Cycle*—a pattern that returns the user to a previously visited content node.
- *Web ring*—a pattern that implements a "grand cycle that links entire hypertexts in a tour of a subject" [BER98].
- *Contour*—a pattern that occurs when cycles impinge upon one another, allowing navigation across paths defined by the cycles.
- *Counterpoint*—a pattern that adds hypertext commentary, which interrupts content narrative to provide additional information or insight.
- *Mirrorworld*—content is presented using different narrative threads, each with a different point of view or perspective. For example, content that describes a personal computer might allow the user to select a "technical" or "nontechnical" narrative that describes the machine.
- *Sieve*—a pattern that guides a user through a series of options (decisions) in order to direct the user to specific content indicated by the sequence of options chosen or decisions made.
- *Neighborhood*—a pattern that overlays a uniform navigational frame across all Web pages in order to allow a user to have consistent navigation guidance regardless of location within the WebApp.

These hypertext design patterns can be reused as content is translated into a format that allows navigation through a WebApp.

29.5.2 Navigation Design

Once the WebApp architecture has been established and the components (pages, scripts, applets, and other processing functions) of the architecture have been identified, the designer must define navigation pathways that enable a user to access

WebApp content and services. To accomplish this, the designer must (1) identify the semantics of navigation for different users of the site and (2) define the mechanics (syntax) of achieving the navigation.

A large WebApp will often have a variety of different user roles. For example, roles might be *visitor, registered customer,* or *privileged user.* Each of these roles can be associated with different levels of content access and different services. A *visitor* may have access to only limited content while a *registered customer* may have access to a much broader range of information and services. The semantics of navigation for each of these two roles would be different.

The WebApp designer creates a *semantic navigation unit* (SNU) for each goal associated with each user role [GNA99]. For example, a *registered customer* may have six different goals, all resulting in access to different information and services. A SNU is created for each goal. Gnaho and Larcher [GNA99] describe the SNU in the following way:

KEY POINT

A SNU is composed of a set of navigational substructures called *ways of navigating* (WoN). The SNU represents a specific navigational goal for a specific type of user.

> The structure of an SNU is composed of a set of navigational sub-structures that we call *ways of navigating* (WoN). A WoN represents the best navigation way or path for users with certain profiles to achieve their desired goal or sub-goal. Therefore, the concept of WoN is associated to the concept of User Profile.
>
> The structure of a WoN is made out of a set of relevant *navigational nodes* (NN) connected by *navigational links,* including sometimes other SNUs. That means that SNUs may themselves be aggregated to form a higher-level SNU, or may be nested to any depth.

During the initial stages of navigation design, the WebApp structure (architecture and components) is assessed to determine one or more WoN for each user goal. As noted, a WoN identifies navigation nodes (e.g., Web pages) and then links that enable navigation between them. The WoN are then organized into SNUs.

As design proceeds, the mechanics of each navigation link are identified. Among many possible options are text-based links, icons, buttons and switches, and graphical metaphors. The designer must choose navigation links that are appropriate for the content and consistent with the heuristics that lead to high-quality interface design.

In addition to choosing the mechanics of navigation, the designer should also establish appropriate navigation conventions and aids. For example, icons and graphical links should look "clickable" by beveling the edges to give the image a three-dimensional look. Audio or visual feedback should be designed to provide the user with an indication that a navigation option has been chosen. For text-based navigation, color should be used to indicate navigation links and to provide an indication of links already traveled. These are but a few of dozens of design conventions that make navigation user-friendly. In addition to conventions, navigation aids such as site maps, tables of contents, indexes, search mechanisms, and dynamic help facilities should also be designed at this time.

29.5.3 Interface Design

Quote:
"People have very little patience for poorly designed WWW sites."
Jakob Nielsen and Annette Wagner

The interface design concepts, principles, and methods presented in Chapter 15 are all applicable to the design of user interfaces for WebApps. However, the special characteristics of Web-based systems and applications require a number of additional considerations.

The user interface of a WebApp is its "first impression." Regardless of the value of its content, the sophistication of its processing capabilities and services, and the overall benefit of the WebApp itself, a poorly designed interface will disappoint the potential user and may, in fact, cause the user to go elsewhere. Because of the sheer volume of competing WebApps in virtually every subject area, the interface must "grab" a potential user immediately. Nielsen and Wagner [NIE96] suggest a few simple guidelines based on their redesign of a major WebApp:

? What are some basic guidelines for the design of a Web site's look and feel?

- Server errors, even minor ones, are likely to cause a user to leave the Web site and look elsewhere for information or services.
- Reading speed on a computer monitor is approximately 25 percent slower than reading speed for hard copy. Therefore, do not force the user to read voluminous amounts of text, particularly when the text explains the operation of the WebApp or assists in navigation.
- Avoid "under construction" signs—they raise expectations and cause an unnecessary link that is sure to disappoint.
- Users prefer not to scroll. Important information should be placed within the dimensions of a typical browser window.
- Navigation menus and headbars should be designed consistently and should be available on all pages that are available to the user. The design should not rely on browser functions to assist in navigation.
- Aesthetics should never supersede functionality. For example, a simple button might be a better navigation option than an aesthetically pleasing, but vague image or icon whose intent is unclear.
- Navigation options should be obvious, even to the casual user. The user should not have to search the screen to determine how to link to other content or services.

WebRef
One of the Web's best collections of usability resources has been assembled by The Usability Group and can be found at **www.usability.com/umi_links.htm**

A well-designed interface improves the user's perception of the content or services provided by the site. It need not be flashy, but it should always be well structured and ergonomically sound. A comprehensive discussion of WebApp user interfaces is beyond the scope of this book. Interested readers should see [SAN96], [SPO98], [ROS98], or [LYN99] among hundreds of offerings for additional guidance.

29.6 TESTING WEB-BASED APPLICATIONS

In Chapter 17, we noted that testing is the process of exercising software with the intent of finding (and ultimately correcting) errors. This fundamental philosophy does not change for WebApps. In fact, because Web-based systems and applications reside on a network and interoperate with many different operating systems, browsers, hardware platforms, and communications protocols, the search for errors represents a significant challenge for Web engineers.

The approach for WebApp testing adopts the basic principles for all software testing (Chapter 17) and applies a strategy and tactics that have been recommended for object-oriented systems (Chapter 23). The following steps summarize the approach:

? **What steps do we follow to test a WebApp?**

1. **The content model for the WebApp is reviewed to uncover errors.** This "testing" activity is similar in many respects to copy editing a written document. In fact, a large Web-site might enlist the services of a professional copy editor to uncover typographical errors, grammatical mistakes, errors in content consistency, errors in graphical representations, and cross-referencing errors.
2. **The design model for the WebApp is reviewed to uncover navigation errors.** Use-cases, derived as part of the analysis activity, allow a Web engineer to exercise each usage scenario against the architectural and navigation design. In essence, these nonexecutable tests help uncover errors in navigation (e.g., a case where the user cannot reach a navigation node). In addition, the navigation links (Section 29.5.2) are reviewed to ensure that they correspond with those specified in each SNU for each user role.

Quote:

"Innovation is a bittersweet deal for software testers. Just when it seems that we know how to test a particular technology, a new one [the Internet and WebApps] comes along and all bets are off."

James Bach

3. **Selected processing components and Web pages are unit tested.** When WebApps are considered, the concept of the unit changes. Each Web page encapsulates content, navigation links, and processing elements (forms, scripts, applets). It is not always possible or practical to test each of these characteristics individually. In many cases, the smallest testable unit is the Web page. Unlike unit testing of conventional software, which tends to focus on the algorithmic detail of a module and the data that flow across the module interface, page-level testing for WebApps is driven by the content, processing, and links encapsulated by the Web page.
4. **The architecture is constructed and integration tests are conducted.** The strategy for integration testing depends on the architecture that has been chosen for the WebApp. If the WebApp has been designed with a linear, grid, or simple hierarchical structure, it is possible to integrate Web pages in much the same way as we integrate modules for conventional software. However, if a mixed hierarchy or network (Web) architecture is used, integration testing is similar to the approach used for OO systems. Thread-based testing (Chapter 23) can be used to integrate the set of Web pages (a SNU may be used to define the appropriate set) required to respond to a user event. Each thread is

XRef

Integration strategies are discussed in Chapters 18 and 23.

integrated and tested individually. Regression testing is applied to ensure that no side effects occur. Cluster testing integrates a set of collaborating pages (determined by examining the the use-cases and SNU). Test cases are derived to uncover errors in the collaborations.

5. **The assembled WebApp is tested for overall functionality and content delivery.** Like conventional validation, the validation of Web-based systems and applications focuses on user-visible actions and user-recognizable output from the system. To assist in the derivation of validation tests, the tester should draw upon use-cases. The use-case provides a scenario that has a high likelihood of uncovering errors in user interaction requirements.
6. **The WebApp is implemented in a variety of different environmental configurations and is tested for compatibility with each configuration.** A cross-reference matrix that defines all probable operating systems, browsers,[7] hardware platforms, and communications protocols is created. Tests are then conducted to uncover errors associated with each possible configuration.
7. **The WebApp is tested by a controlled and monitored population of end-users.** A population of users that encompasses every possible user role is chosen. The WebApp is exercised by these users and the results of their interaction with the system are evaluated for content and navigation errors, usability concerns, compatibility concerns, and WebApp reliability and performance.

Because many WebApps evolve continuously, the testing process is an ongoing activity, conducted by Web support staff who use regression tests derived from the tests developed when the WebApp was first engineered.

29.7 MANAGEMENT ISSUES

Given the immediacy of WebApps, it is reasonable to ask: "Do we really need to spend time managing a WebApp effort? Shouldn't we just let a WebApp evolve naturally, with little or no explicit management?" More than a few Web developers would opt for little or no management, but that doesn't make them right!

XRef
The activities associated with software project management are discussed in Part Two of this book.

Web engineering is a complicated technical activity. Many people are involved, often working in parallel. The combination of technical and nontechnical tasks that must occur (on time and within budget) to produce a high-quality WebApp represents a challenge for any group of professionals. In order to avoid confusion, frustration, and failure, planning must occur, risks must be considered, a schedule must be established and tracked, and controls must be defined. These are the core activities that we have called *project management.*

7 Browsers are notorious for implementing their own subtly different "standard" interpretations of HTML and Javascript. See www.browsercaps.com for a discussion of compatibility issues.

29.7.1 The WebE Team

Quote: "In today's net-centric and Web-enabled world, one now needs to know a lot about a lot." **Scott Tilly and Shihoug Huang**

The creation of a successful Web application demands a broad array of skills. Tilley and Huang [TIL99] address this issue when they state: "There are so many different aspects to [Web] application software that there is a (re)emergence of the renaissance person, one who is comfortable operating in several disciplines . . ." While the authors are absolutely correct, "renaissance" people are in relatively short supply; and given the demands associated with major WebApp development projects, the diverse skill set required might be better distributed over a WebE team.

WebE teams can be organized in much the same way as the software teams discussed in Chapter 3. However, the players and their roles are often quite different. Among the many skills that must be distributed across WebE team members are component-based software engineering, networking, architectural and navigational design, Internet standards/languages, human interface design, graphic design, content layout, and WebApp testing. The following roles[8] should be distributed among the members of the WebE team:

? **What roles do people play on a WebE team?**

Content developer and providers. Because WebApps are inherently content driven, one WebE team member role must focus on the generation or collection of content. Recalling that content spans a broad array of data objects, content developers and providers may come from diverse (non-software) backgrounds. For example, marketing or sales staff may provide product information and graphical images, media producers may provide video and audio, graphic designers may provide layout design and aesthetic content, copywriters may provide text-based content. In addition, research staff may be required to find and format external content for placement or reference within the WebApp.

Web publisher. The diverse content generated by content developers and providers must be organized for inclusion within the WebApp. In addition, someone must act as liaison between technical staff that engineers the WebApp and nontechnical content developers and providers. This role is filled by the Web publisher, who must understand both content and WebApp technology including HTML (or its next generation extensions, such as XML), database functionality, scripts, and general Web-site navigation.

Web engineer. A Web engineer becomes involved in a wide range of activities during the development of a WebApp including requirements elicitation; analysis modeling; architectural, navigational, and interface design; WebApp implementation; and testing. The Web engineer should also have a solid understanding of component technologies, client/server architectures, HTML/XML, and database technologies as well as a working knowledge of

8 These roles have been adapted from Hansen, Deshpande, and Murgusan [HAN99].

multi-media concepts, hardware/software platforms, network security, and Web-site support issues.

Support specialist. This role is assigned to the person (people) who has responsibility for continuing WebApp support. Because WebApps continuously evolve, the support specialist is responsible for corrections, adaptations, and enhancements to the site, including updates to content, implementation of new procedures and forms, and changes to the navigation pattern.

Administrator. Often called the *Web master,* this person has responsibility for the day-to-day operation of the WebApp, including

- Development and implementation of policies for the operation of the WebApp.
- Establishment of support and feedback procedures.
- Implementation of security procedures and access rights.
- Measurement and analysis of Web-site traffic.
- Coordination of change control procedures (Section 29.7.3).
- Coordination with support specialists.

The administrator may also be involved in the technical activities performed by Web engineers and support specialists.

29.7.2 Project Management

In Part Two of this book, we considered each of the activities that are collectively called *project management.*[9] Process and project metrics, project planning (and estimation), risk analysis and management, scheduling and tracking, SQA and SCM were all considered in some detail. In theory, most (if not all) of the the project management activities discussed in earlier chapters apply to WebE projects. But in practice, the WebE approach to project management is considerably different.

First, a substantial percentage[10] of WebApps are outsourced to vendors who (purportedly) specialize in the development of Web-based systems and applications. In such cases, a business (the customer) asks for a fixed price quote for WebApp development from two or more vendors, evaluates competing quotes, and then selects a vendor to do the work. But what does the contracting organization look for? How is the competence of a WebApp vendor determined? How does one know whether a price quote is reasonable? What degree of planning, scheduling, and risk assessment can be expected as an organization (and its outsourcing contractor) embarks on a major WebApp development effort?

---

9 Readers who are unfamiliar with basic project management concepts are urged to review Chapter 3 at this time.

10 Although reliable industry data are difficult to find, it is safe to say that this percentage is considerably higher than the one encountered in conventional software work.

Second, WebApp development is a relatively new application area and there is little historical data to use for estimation. To date, virtually no WebE metrics have been published in the literature. In fact, relatively little discussion has emerged on what those metrics might be. Therefore, estimation is purely qualitative—based on past experience with similar projects. But almost every WebApp wants to be innovative—offering something new and different to those that use it. Hence, experiential estimation, although useful, is open to considerable error. Therefore, how are reliable estimates derived? What degree of assurance can be given that defined schedules will be met?

Third, estimation, risk analysis, and scheduling are all predicated on a clear understanding of project scope. And yet, the "continuous evolution" characteristic discussed in Section 29.1 suggests that WebApp scope will be fluid. How can the contracting organization and the outsourcing vendor control costs and schedule when requirements are likely to change dramatically as a project progresses? How can scope creep be controlled, and more important, should it be controlled, given the unique nature of Web-based systems and applications?

At this stage in the history of project management for WebApps, the questions precipitated by the differences just noted are not easy to answer. However, a few guidelines are worth considering.

Quote:

"My advice to builders [of WebApps]? 1. State your quality requirements quantitatively. 2. Get contractual guarantees . . . 3. Use proven track record suppliers . . . 4. Build and expand the system in evolutionary stages. 5. Consider appropriate systematic redundancy at many levels to allow some degree of operation when failures occur."

Tom Gilb

Initiating a project. Even if outsourcing is the strategy to be chosen for WebApp development, an organization must perform a number of tasks before searching for an outsourcing vendor to do the work:

1. *Many of the analysis activities discussed in Section 29.3 should be performed internally.* The audience for the WebApp is identified; internal stakeholders who may have interest in the WebApp are listed; the overall goals for the WebApp are defined and reviewed; the information and services to be delivered by the WebApp are specified; competing Web sites are noted; and qualitative and quantitative "measures" of a successful WebApp are defined. This information should be documented in a product specification.
2. *A rough design for the WebApp should be developed internally.* Obviously, an expert Web developer will create a complete design, but time and cost can be saved if the general look and feel of the WebApp is identified for the outsourcing vendor (this can always be modified during preliminary stages of the project). The design should include an indication of the type and volume of content to be presented by the WebApp and the types of interactive processing (e.g., forms, order entry) to be performed. This information should be added to the product specification.
3. *A rough project schedule, including not only final delivery dates but also milestone dates, should be developed.* Milestones should be attached to deliverable versions of the WebApp as it evolves.

4. *The degree of oversight and interaction by the contractor with the vendor should be identified.* This should include the naming of a vendor liaison and the identification of the liaison's responsibilities and authority, the definition of quality review points as development proceeds, and the vendor's responsibilities with respect to interorganizational communication.

All of the information developed during these steps should be organized into a *request for quote* that is transmitted to candidate vendors.[11]

Selection of candidate outsourcing vendors. In recent years, thousands of "Web design" companies have emerged to help businesses establish a Web presence or engage in e-commerce. Many have become adept at the WebE process, but many others are little more than hackers. In order to select candidate Web developers, the contractor must perform due diligence: (1) interview past clients to determine the Web vendor's professionalism, ability to meet schedule and cost commitments, and ability to communicate effectively; (2) determine the name of the vendor's chief Web engineer(s) for successful past projects (and, later, be certain that this person is contractually obligated to be involved in your project); and (3) carefully examine samples of the vendor's work that are similar in look and feel (and business area) to the WebApp that is to be contracted. Even before a request for quote is offered, a face-to-face meeting may provide substantial insight into the "fit" between contractor and vendor.

Quote:

"If you're only willing to pay peanuts, you get monkeys."

from "The A Team"

Assessing the validity of price quotes and the reliability of estimates. Because relatively little historical data exist and the scope of WebApps is notoriously fluid, estimation is inherently risky. For this reason, some vendors will embed substantial safety margins into the cost quoted for a project. This is both understandable and appropriate. The question is *not* "Have we gotten the best bang for our buck?" Rather, the questions should be

- Does the quoted cost of the WebApp provide a direct or indirect return on investment that justifies the project?
- Does the vendor that has provided the quote exhibit the professionalism and experience we require?

If the answers to these questions are, "Yes," the price quote is fair.

The degree of project management you can expect or perform. The formality associated with project management tasks (performed by both the vendor and the contractor) is directly proportional to the size, cost, and complexity of the WebApp. For large, complex projects, a detailed project schedule that defines work tasks, SQA

11 If WebApp development work is to be conducted by an internal group, nothing changes! The project is initiated in the same manner.

checkpoints, engineering work products, customer review points, and major milestones should be developed. The vendor and contractor should assess risk jointly and develop plans for mitigating, monitoring, and managing those risks that are deemed important. Mechanisms for quality assurance and change control should be explicitly defined in writing. Methods for effective communication between the contractor and the vendor should be established.

Assessing the development schedule. Because WebApp development schedules span a relatively short period of time (often less than one or two months), the development schedule should have a high degree of granularity. That is, work tasks and minor milestones should be scheduled on a daily timeline. This fine granularity allows both the contractor and the vendor to recognize schedule slippage before it threatens the final completion date.

Managing scope. Because it is highly likely that scope will change as a WebApp project moves forward, the WebE process model should be incremental (Chapter 2). This allows the development team to "freeze" the scope for one increment so that an operational WebApp release can be created. The next increment may address scope changes suggested by a review of the preceding increment, but once the second increment commences, scope is again frozen temporarily. This approach enables the WebApp team to work without having to accommodate a continual stream of changes but still recognizes the continuous evolution characteristic of most WebApps.

These guidelines are not intended to be a foolproof cookbook for the production of low-cost, on-time WebApps. However, they will help both the contractor and the vendor initiate work smoothly with a minimum of misunderstandings.

29.7.3 SCM Issues for WebE

> **Quote:**
> "The most effective way to cope with change is to help create it."
> L. W. Lynett

Over the past decade, WebApps have evolved from informal devices for information dissemination to sophisticated sites for e-commerce. As WebApps become increasingly important to business survival and growth, the need for configuration control grows. Why? Because, without effective controls, improper changes to a WebApp (recall that immediacy and continuous evolution are the dominant attributes of many WebApps) can lead to (1) unauthorized posting of new product information, (2) erroneous or poorly tested functionality that frustrates visitors to a Web site, (3) security holes that jeopardize internal company systems, and other economically unpleasant or even disastrous consequences.

The general strategies for software configuration management (SCM) described in Chapter 9 are applicable, but tactics and tools must be adapted to conform to the unique nature of WebApps. Four issues [DAR99] should be considered when developing tactics for WebApp configuration management—content, people, scalability, and politics.

Content. A typical WebApp contains a vast array of content—text, graphics, applets, scripts, audio and video files, forms, active page elements, tables, streaming data, and many others. The challenge is to organize this sea of content into a rational set of configuration objects (Chapter 9) and then establish appropriate configuration control mechanisms for these objects. One approach is to model the WebApp content using conventional data modeling techniques (Chapter 11), attaching a set of specialized properties to each object. The static or dynamic nature of each object and its projected longevity (e.g., temporary, fixed existence, or permanent object) are examples of properties that are required to establish an effective SCM approach. For example, if a content item is changed hourly, it has *temporary longevity.* The control mechanisms for this item would be different (less formal) than those applied for a forms component that is a permanent object.

People. Because a significant percentage of WebApp development continues to be conducted in an ad hoc manner, any person involved in the WebApp can (and often does) create content. Many content creators have no software engineering background and are completely unaware of the need for configuration management. The application grows and changes in an uncontrolled fashion.

ADVICE

Controlling change during WebE projects is essential, but it can be overdone. Begin with relatively informal change control procedures (Chapter 9). Your initial goal should be to avoid the ratcheting effects of uncontrolled change.

Scalability. The techniques and controls applied to small WebApps do not scale upward well. It is not uncommon for a simple WebApp to grow significantly as interconnections with existing information systems, databases, data warehouses, and portal gateways are implemented. As size and complexity grows, small changes can have far-reaching and unintended effects that can be problematic. Therefore, the rigor of configuration control mechanisms should be directly proportional to application scale.

Politics. Who "owns" a WebApp? This question is argued in companies large and small, and its answer has a significant impact on the management and control activities associated with WebE. In some instances Web developers are housed outside the IT organization, creating potential communication difficulties. Dart [DAR99] suggests the following questions to help understand the politics associated with WebE: Who assumes responsibility for the accuracy of the information on the Web site? Who ensures that quality control processes have been followed before information is published to the site? Who is responsible for making changes? Who assumes the cost of change? The answers to these questions help determine the people within an organization who must adopt a configuration management process for WebApps.

Configuration management for WebE is in its infancy. A conventional SCM process may be too cumbersome. The vast majority of SCM tools lack the features that allow them to be adapted easily to WebE. Among the issues that remain to be addressed are [DAR99]

- How can we create a configuration management process that is nimble enough to accommodate the immediacy and continuous evolution of WebApps?
- How can we best introduce configuration management concepts and tools to developers who are completely unfamiliar with the technology?
- How can we provide support for distributed WebApp development teams?
- How can we provide control in a quasi-publishing environment where content changes on a nearly continuous basis?
- How can we attain the granularity required to control a large array of configuration objects?
- How can we incorporate configuration management functionality into existing WebE tools?
- How can we manage changes to objects that contain links to other objects?

These and many other issues must be addressed before effective configuration management is available for WebE.

29.8 SUMMARY

The impact of Web-based systems and applications is arguably the single most significant event in the history of computing. As WebApps grow in importance, a disciplined Web engineering approach—based on the principles, concepts, process, and methods that have been developed for software engineering—has begun to evolve.

WebApps are different from other categories of computer software. They are network intensive, content driven, and continuously evolving. The immediacy that drives their development, the overriding need for security in their operation, and the demand for aesthetic as well as functional content delivery are additional differentiating factors. Three technologies—component-based development, security, and Internet standard markup languages—are integrated with more conventional software engineering technologies during WebApp development.

The Web engineering process begins with formulation—an activity that identifies the goals and objectives of the WebApp. Planning estimates overall project cost, evaluates risks associated with the development effort, and defines a development schedule. Analysis establishes technical requirements for the WebApp and identifies the content items that will be incorporated. The engineering activity incorporates two parallel tasks: content design and technical design. Page generation is a construction activity that makes heavy use of automated tools for WebApp creation; and testing exercises WebApp navigation, attempting to uncover errors in function and content, while ensuring that the WebApp will operate correctly in different environments. Web engineering makes use of an iterative, incremental process model because the development timeline for WebApps is very short. The umbrella activities applied during software engineering work—SQA, SCM, project management—apply to all Web engineering projects.

REFERENCES

[ATK97] Atkins, D., et al., *Internet Security: Professional Reference,* New Riders Publishing, 2nd ed., 1997.

[BER98] Bernstein, M., "Patterns in Hypertext," *Proc. 9th ACM Conf. Hypertext,* ACM Press, 1998, pp. 21–29.

[BRA97] Bradley, N., *The Concise SGML Companion,* Addison-Wesley, 1997.

[BRE99] Brenton, C., *Mastering Network Security,* Sybex, 1999.

[BUS96] Buschmann, F., et al., *Pattern-Oriented Software Architecture,* Wiley, 1996.

[DAR99] Dart, S., "Containing the Web Crisis Using Configuration Management," *Proc. First ICSE Workshop on Web Engineering,* ACM, Los Angeles, May 1999. (The proceedings of the First ICSE Workshop on Web Engineering are published on-line at http://fistserv.macarthur.uws.edu.au/san/icse99-WebE/ICSE99-WebE-Proc/default.htm).

[DIN98] Dinucci, D., M. Giudice, and L. Stiles, *Elements of Web Design: The Designer's Guide to a New Medium,* 2nd ed., Peachpit Press, 1998.

[GAM95] Gamma, E., et al., *Design Patterns,* Addison-Wesley, 1995.

[GNA99] Gnaho, C. and F. Larcher, "A User Centered Methodology for Complex and Customizable Web Applications Engineering," *Proc. First ICSE Workshop on Web Engineering,* ACM, Los Angeles, May 1999.

[HAN99] Hansen, S., Y. Deshpande, and S. Murugesan, "A Skills Hierarchy for Web Information System Development," *Proc. First ICSE Workshop on Web Engineering,* ACM, Los Angeles, May 1999.

[ISA95] Isakowitz, T., et al., "RMM: A Methodology for Structured Hypermedia Design," *CACM,* vol. 38., no. 8, August 1995, pp. 34–44.

[KAE99] Kaeo, M., *Designing Network Security,* Cisco Press, 1999.

[LOW99] Lowe, D., "Web Engineering or Web Gardening?" *WebNet Journal,* vol. 1, no. 2, January–March 1999.

[LYN99] Lynch, P.J. and S. Horton, *Web Style Guide: Basic Design Principles for Creating Web Sites,* Yale University Press, 1999.

[MUR99] Murugesan, S., WebE home page, http://fistserv.macarthur.uws.edu.au/san/WebEHome, July 1999.

[NAN98] Nanard, M. and P. Kahn, "Pushing Reuse in Hypermedia Design: Golden Rules, Design Patterns and Constructive Templates," *Proc. Ninth ACM Conf. on Hypertext and Hypermedia,* ACM Press, 1998, pp. 11–20.

[NIE96] Nielsen, J. and A. Wagner, "User Interface Design for the WWW," *Proc. CHI '96 Conference on Human Factors in Computing Systems,* ACM Press, 1996, pp. 330–331.

[NOR99] Norton, K., "Applying Cross Functional Evolutionary Methodologies to Web Development," *Proc. First ICSE Workshop on Web Engineering,* ACM, Los Angeles, May 1999.

[OLS99] Olsina, L., et al., "Specifying Quality Characteristics and Attributes for Web Sites," *Proc. First ICSE Workshop on Web Engineering,* ACM, Los Angeles, May 1999.

[PAR99] Pardi, W.J., *XML in Action,* Microsoft Press, 1999.

[POW98] Powell, T.A., *Web Site Engineering,* Prentice-Hall, 1998.

[PRE98] Pressman, R.S. (moderator), "Can Internet-Based Applications Be Engineered?" *IEEE Software,* September 1998, pp. 104–110.

[ROS98] Rosenfeld, L. and P. Morville, *Information Architecture for the World Wide Web,* O'Reilly and Associates, 1998.

[SAN96] Sano, D., *Designing Large-Scale Web Sites: A Visual Design Methodology,* Wiley, 1996.

[SCH96] Schwabe, D., G. Rossi, and S. Barbosa, "Systematic Hypermedia Application Design with OOHDM," *Proc. Hypertext '96,* pp. 116–128.

[SPO98] Spool, J.M., et al., *Web Site Usability: A Designer's Guide,* Morgan Kaufmann, 1998.

[STL99] St. Laurent, S. and E. Cerami, *Building XML Applications,* McGraw-Hill, 1999.

[TIL99] Tilley, S. and S. Huang, "On the Emergence of the Renaissance Software Engineer," *Proc. First ICSE Workshop on Web Engineering,* ACM, Los Angeles, May 1999.

PROBLEMS AND POINTS TO PONDER

29.1. Are there other generic attributes that differentiate WebApps for more conventional software applications? Try to name two or three.

29.2. How do you judge the "quality" of a Web site? Make a ranked list of ten quality attributes that you believe are most important.

29.3. Do a bit of research and write a two- or three-page paper that summarizes one of the three technologies noted in Section 29.1.2.

29.4. Using an actual Web site as an example, illustrate the different manifestations of WebApp "content."

29.5. Answer the three formulation questions for a Web site that you're familiar with. Develop a statement of scope for the Web site.

29.6. Develop a set of user profiles for SafeHomeInc.com or a Web site assigned by your instructor.

29.7. Develop a complete list of informational and applicative goals for SafeHome-Inc.com or a Web site assigned by your instructor.

29.8. Produce a set of use-cases for SafeHomeInc.com or a Web site assigned by your instructor.

29.9. How does content analysis differ from interaction and functional analysis?

29.10. Conduct a content analysis for SafeHomeInc.com or a Web site assigned by your instructor.

29.11. Suggest three "golden rules" that would help guide the design of WebApps.

29.12. How does a WebApp design pattern differ from a template?

29.13. Select a Web site with which you are familiar and develop a reasonably complete architectural design for the site. What architectural structure did the site designers select?

29.14. Do a bit of research and write a two- or three-page paper that summarizes current work in WebApp design patterns.

29.15. Develop an architectural design for SafeHomeInc.com or a Web site assigned by your instructor.

29.16. Develop SNUs for SafeHomeInc.com or a Web site assigned by your instructor.

29.17. Using an actual Web site as an example, develop a critique of its user interface and make recommendations that would improve it.

29.18. Describe how project management for Web-based systems and applications differs from project management for conventional software. How is it similar?

FURTHER READINGS AND INFORMATION SOURCES

Hundreds of books that discuss one or more Web engineering topics have been published in recent years, although relatively few address all aspects of Web engineering. Lowe and Hall (*Hypertext and the Web: An Engineering Approach,* Wiley, 1999) and Powell [POW98] provide reasonably complete coverage. Norris, West, and Watson (*Media Engineering: A Guide to Developing Information Products,* Wiley, 1997); Navarro and Khan (*Effective Web Design: Master the Essentials,* Sybex, 1998); Fleming and Koman (*Web Navigation: Designing the User Experience,* O'Reilly and Associates, 1998); and Sano [SAN96] also cover important aspects of the engineering process.

In addition to [LYN99] and [DIN98], the following books provide useful guidance for technical and nontechnical (content and aesthetic) aspects of WebApp design:

Baumgardt, M., *Creative Web Design: Tips and Tricks Step by Step,* Springer-Verlag, 1998.

Donnelly, D., et al., *Cutting Edge Web Design: The Next Generation,* Rockport Publishing, 1998.

Holzschlag, M.E., *Web by Design: The Complete Guide,* Sybex, 1998.

Niederst, J. and R. Koman, *Web Design in a Nutshell: A Desktop Quick Reference,* O'Reilly and Associates, 1998.

Nielsen, J., *Designing Web Usability,* New Riders Publishing, 2000.

Weinman, L. and R. Pirouz, *Click Here: Web Communication Design,* New Riders Publishing, 1997.

Menasce and Almeida (*Capacity Planning for Web Performance: Metrics, Models, and Methods,* Prentice-Hall, 1998) address the quantitative assessment of WebApp performance. Amoroso (*Intrusion Detection: An Introduction to Internet Surveillance, Correlation, Trace Back, Traps, and Response,* Intrusion.Net Books, 1999) provides detailed guidance for those Web engineers who specialize in security issues. Umar (*Application (Re)Engineering: Building Web-Based Applications and Dealing with Legacies,* Prentice-Hall, 1997) discusses strategies for the transformation (reengineering) of legacy systems into Web-based applications. Mosley (*Client Server Software Testing on the Desk Top and the Web,* Prentice-Hall, 1999) has written one of the few books that address testing issues associated with WebApps.

Haggard (*Survival Guide to Web Site Development,* Microsoft Press, 1998) and Siegel (*Secrets of Successful Web Sites: Project Management on the World Wide Web,* Hayden Books, 1997) provide guidance to managers who must control and track WebApp development.

A wide variety of information sources on Web engineering is available on the Internet. An up-to-date list of World Wide Web references can be found at the SEPA Web site:

http://www.mhhe.com/engcs/compsci/pressman/resources/webe.mhtml

CHAPTER

30 REENGINEERING

KEY CONCEPTS

In a seminal article written for the *Harvard Business Review,* Michael Hammer [HAM90] laid the foundation for a revolution in management thinking about business processes and computing:

> It is time to stop paving the cow paths. Instead of embedding outdated processes in silicon and software, we should obliterate them and start over. We should "reengineer" our businesses: use the power of modern information technology to radically redesign our business processes in order to achieve dramatic improvements in their performance.
>
> Every company operates according to a great many unarticulated rules . . . Reengineering strives to break away from the old rules about how we organize and conduct our business.

Like all revolutions, Hammer's call to arms resulted in both positive and negative changes. During the 1990s, some companies made a legitimate effort to reengineer, and the results led to improved competitiveness. Others relied solely on downsizing and outsourcing (instead of reengineering) to improve their bottom line. "Mean" organizations with little potential for future growth often resulted [DEM95].

During this first decade of the twenty-first century, the hype associated with reengineering has waned, but the process itself continues in companies large

QUICK LOOK

What is it? Consider any technology product that has served you well. You use it regularly, but it's getting old. It breaks too often, takes longer to repair than you'd like, and no longer represents the newest technology. What to do? If the product is hardware, you'll likely throw it away and buy a newer model. But if it's custom-built software, that option may not be available. You'll need to rebuild it. You'll create a product with added functionality, better performance and reliability, and improved maintainability. That's what we call reengineering.

Who does it? At a business level, reengineering is performed by business specialists (often consulting companies). At the software level, reengineering is performed by software engineers.

Why is it important? We live in a rapidly changing world. The demands on business functions and the information technology that supports them are changing at a pace that puts enormous competitive pressure on every commercial organization. Both the business and the software that supports (or is) the business must be reengineered to keep pace.

What are the steps? Business process reengineering (BPR) defines business goals, identifies and evaluates existing business processes, and creates revised business processes that better meet current goals. The software reengineering process

QUICK LOOK

encompasses inventory analysis, document restructuring, reverse engineering, program and data restructuring, and forward engineering. The intent of these activities is to create versions of existing programs that exhibit higher quality and better maintainability.

What is the work product? A variety of reengineering work products (e.g., analysis models, design models, test procedures) are produced. The final output is the reengineered business process and/or the reengineered software that supports it.

How do I ensure that I've done it right? Use the same SQA practices that are applied in every software engineering process—formal technical reviews assess the analysis and design models, specialized reviews consider business applicability and compatibility, testing is applied to uncover errors in content, functionality, and interoperability.

and small. The nexus between business reengineering and software engineering lies in a "system view."

Software is often the realization of the business rules that Hammer discusses. As these rules change, software must also change. Today, major companies have tens of thousands of computer programs that support the "old business rules." As managers work to modify the rules to achieve greater effectiveness and competitiveness, software must keep pace. In some cases, this means the creation of major new computer-based systems.[1] But in many others, it means the modification or rebuilding of existing applications.

In this chapter, we examine reengineering in a top-down manner, beginning with a brief overview of business process reengineering and proceeding to a more detailed discussion of the technical activities that occur when software is reengineered.

30.1 BUSINESS PROCESS REENGINEERING

Quote:
"To face tomorrow with the thought of using the methods of yesterday is to envision life at a standstill."
James Bell

Business process reengineering (BPR) extends far beyond the scope of information technologies and software engineering. Among the many definitions (most somewhat abstract) that have been suggested for BPR is one published in Fortune magazine [STE93]: "the search for, and the implementation of, radical change in business process to achieve breakthrough results." But how is the search conducted, and how is the implementation achieved? More important, how can we ensure that the "radical change" suggested will in fact lead to "breakthrough results" instead of organizational chaos?

30.1.1 Business Processes

A *business process* is "a set of logically related tasks performed to achieve a defined business outcome" [DAV90]. Within the business process, people, equipment, mate-

1 The Web-based systems and applications discussed in Chapter 29 are contemporary examples.

rial resources, and business procedures are combined to produce a specified result. Examples of business processes include designing a new product, purchasing services and supplies, hiring a new employee, and paying suppliers. Each demands a set of tasks and each draws on diverse resources within the business.

Every business process has a defined customer—a person or group that receives the outcome (e.g., an idea, a report, a design, a product). In addition, business processes cross organizational boundaries. They require that different organizational groups participate in the "logically related tasks" that define the process.

ADVICE

As a software engineer, your reengineering work occurs at the bottom of this hierarchy. Be sure, however, that someone has given serious thought to the level above. If this hasn't been done, your work is at risk.

In Chapter 10, we noted that every system is actually a hierarchy of subsystems. A business is no exception. The overall business is segmented in the following manner:

- The business
  - business systems
    - business process
      - business subprocesses

Each business system (also called *business function*) is composed of one or more business processes, and each business process is defined by a set of subprocesses.

BPR can be applied at any level of the hierarchy, but as the scope of BPR broadens (i.e., as we move upward in the hierarchy), the risks associated with BPR grow dramatically. For this reason, most BPR efforts focus on individual processes or subprocesses.

30.1.2 Principles of Business Process Reengineering

In many ways, BPR is identical in focus and scope to business process engineering (Chapter 10). In an ideal setting, BPR should occur in a top-down manner, beginning with the identification of major business objectives and goals and culminating with a much more detailed specification of the tasks that define a specific business process.

WebRef

Extensive information on business process reengineering can be found at **www.brint.com/BPR.htm**

Hammer [HAM90] suggests a number of principles that guide BPR activities when they begin at the top (business) level:

Organize around outcomes, not tasks. Many companies have compartmentalized business activities so that no single person (or organization) has responsibility (or control) of a business outcome. It such cases, it is difficult to determine the status of work and even more difficult to debug process problems if they do occur. BPR should design processes that avoid this problem.

Have those who use the output of the process perform the process. The intent of this recommendation is to allow those who need business output to control all of the variables that allow them to get the output in a timely manner. The fewer separate constituencies involved in a process, the smoother is the road to a rapid outcome.

Incorporate information processing work into the real work that produces the raw information. As IT becomes more distributed, it is possible to locate most information processing within the organization that produces the raw data. This localizes control, reduces communication time, and puts computing power in the hands of those that have a vested interest in the information that is produced.

> **Quote:**
> "As soon as we are shown the existence of something old in a new thing, we are pacified."
> **Friedrich Wilhelm Nietzsche**

Treat geographically dispersed resources as though they were centralized. Computer-based communications have become so sophisticated that geographically diverse groups can be placed in the same "virtual office." For example, instead of running three engineering shifts at a single location, a global company can run one shift in Europe, a second shift in North America, and a third shift in Asia. In each case, engineers will work during daylight hours and communicate via high-bandwidth networks.

Link parallel activities instead of integrating their results. When different constituencies perform work in parallel, it is essential to design a process that demands continuing communication and coordination. Otherwise, integration problems are sure to result.

Put the decision point where the work is performed, and build control into the process. Using software design jargon, this principle suggests a flatter organizational architecture with reduced factoring.

Capture data once, at its source. Data should be stored on-line so that once collected it need never be re-entered.

Each of these principles represents a "big picture" view of BPR. Guided by these principles, business planners and process designers must begin process redesign. In the next section, we examine the process of BPR in a bit more detail.

30.1.3 A BPR Model

Like most engineering activities, business process reengineering is iterative. Business goals and the processes that achieve them must be adapted to a changing business environment. For this reason, there is no start and end to BPR—it is an evolutionary process. A model for business process reengineering is depicted in Figure 30.1. The model defines six activities:

Business definition. Business goals are identified within the context of four key drivers: *cost reduction, time reduction, quality improvement,* and *personnel development and empowerment.* Goals may be defined at the business level or for a specific component of the business.

Process identification. Processes that are critical to achieving the goals defined in the business definition are identified. They may then be ranked by importance, by need for change, or in any other way that is appropriate for the reengineering activity.

FIGURE 30.1
A BPR model

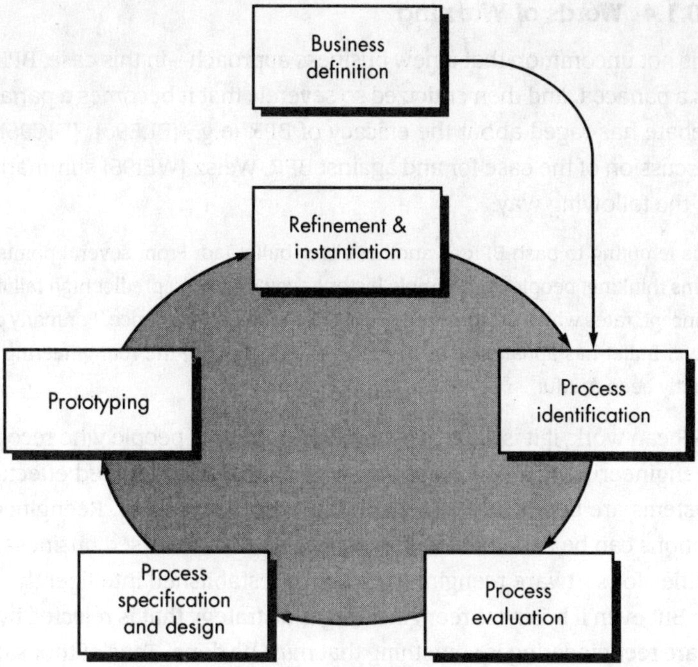

Process evaluation. The existing process is thoroughly analyzed and measured. Process tasks are identified; the costs and time consumed by process tasks are noted; and quality/performance problems are isolated.

Process specification and design. Based on information obtained during the first three BPR activities, use-cases (Chapter 11) are prepared for each process that is to be redesigned. Within the context of BPR, use-cases identify a scenario that delivers some outcome to a customer. With the use-case as the specification of the process, a new set of tasks (which conform to the principles noted in Section 30.2.1) are designed for the process.

Prototyping. A redesigned business process must be prototyped before it is fully integrated into the business. This activity "tests" the process so that refinements can be made.

Refinement and instantiation. Based on feedback from the prototype, the business process is refined and then instantiated within a business system.

These BPR activities are sometimes used in conjunction with workflow analysis tools. The intent of these tools is to build a model of existing workflow in an effort to better analyze existing processes. In addition, the modeling techniques commonly associated with business process engineering activities such as information strategy planning and business area analysis (Chapter 10) can be used to implement the first four activities described in the process model.

30.1.4 Words of Warning

It is not uncommon that a new business approach—in this case, BPR—is at first hyped as a panacea, and then criticized so severely that it becomes a pariah. Over the years, debate has raged about the efficacy of BPR (e.g., [BLE93], [DIC95]). In an excellent discussion of the case for and against BPR, Weisz [WEI95] summarizes the argument in the following way:

> It is tempting to bash BPR as another silver-bullet fad. From several points of view—systems thinking, peopleware, simple history—you'd have to predict high failure rates for the concept, rates which seem to be borne out by empirical evidence. For many companies, the silver bullet has apparently missed. For others, though, the reengineering effort has evidently been fruitful.

BPR can work, if it is applied by motivated, trained people who recognize that process reengineering is a continuous activity. If BPR is conducted effectively, information systems are better integrated into the business process. Reengineering older applications can be examined in the context of a broad-based business strategy, and priorities for software reengineering can be established intelligently.

But even if business reengineering is a strategy that is rejected by a company, software reengineering is something that *must* be done. Tens of thousands of legacy systems—applications that are crucial to the success of businesses large and small—are in dire need of refurbishing or rebuilding.

30.2 SOFTWARE REENGINEERING

WebRef
The SEI offers a variety of software reengineering resources at **www.sei.cmu.edu/reengineering/**

The scenario is all too common: An application has served the business needs of a company for 10 or 15 years. During that time it has been corrected, adapted, and enhanced many times. People approached this work with the best intentions, but good software engineering practices were always shunted to the side (the press of other matters). Now the application is unstable. It still works, but every time a change is attempted, unexpected and serious side effects occur. Yet the application must continue to evolve. What to do?

Unmaintainable software is not a new problem. In fact, the broadening emphasis on software reengineering has been spawned by a software maintenance "iceberg" that has been building for more than three decades.

30.2.1 Software Maintenance

Thirty years ago, software maintenance was characterized [CAN72] as an "iceberg." We hope that what was immediately visible is all there is to it, but we know that an enormous mass of potential problems and cost lies under the surface. In the early 1970s, the maintenance iceberg was big enough to sink an aircraft carrier. Today, it could easily sink the entire navy!

The maintenance of existing software can account for over 60 percent of all effort expended by a development organization, and the percentage continues to rise as more software is produced [HAN93]. Uninitiated readers may ask why so much maintenance is required and why so much effort is expended. Osborne and Chikofsky [OSB90] provide a partial answer:

> Much of the software we depend on today is on average 10 to 15 years old. Even when these programs were created using the best design and coding techniques known at the time [and most were not], they were created when program size and storage space were principle concerns. They were then migrated to new platforms, adjusted for changes in machine and operating system technology and enhanced to meet new user needs—all without enough regard to overall architecture.
>
> The result is the poorly designed structures, poor coding, poor logic, and poor documentation of the software systems we are now called on to keep running . . .

The ubiquitous nature of change underlies all software work. Change is inevitable when computer-based systems are built; therefore, we must develop mechanisms for evaluating, controlling, and making modifications.

Quote:

"Program maintainability and program understandability are parallel concepts: the more difficult a program is to understand, the more difficult it is to maintain."

Gerald Berns

Upon reading the preceding paragraphs, a reader may protest: "but I don't spend 60 percent of my time fixing mistakes in the programs I develop." Software maintenance is, of course, far more than "fixing mistakes." We may define maintenance by describing four activities [SWA76] that are undertaken after a program is released for use. In Chapter 2, we defined four different maintenance activities: *corrective maintenance, adaptive maintenance, perfective maintenance* or *enhancement,* and *preventive maintenance* or *reengineering.* Only about 20 percent of all maintenance work is spent "fixing mistakes." The remaining 80 percent is spent adapting existing systems to changes in their external environment, making enhancements requested by users, and reengineering an application for future use. When maintenance is considered to encompass all of these activities, it is relatively easy to see why it absorbs so much effort.

30.2.2 A Software Reengineering Process Model

Reengineering takes time; it costs significant amounts of money; and it absorbs resources that might be otherwise occupied on immediate concerns. For all of these reasons, reengineering is not accomplished in a few months or even a few years. Reengineering of information systems is an activity that will absorb information technology resources for many years. That's why every organization needs a pragmatic strategy for software reengineering.

A workable strategy is encompassed in a reengineering process model. We'll discuss the model later in this section, but first, some basic principles.

Reengineering is a rebuilding activity, and we can better understand the reengineering of information systems if we consider an analogous activity: the rebuilding of a house. Consider the following situation.

You have purchased a house in another state. You've never actually seen the property, but you acquired it at an amazingly low price, with the warning that it might have to be completely rebuilt. How would you proceed?

- Before you can start rebuilding, it would seem reasonable to inspect the house. To determine whether it is in need of rebuilding, you (or a professional inspector) would create a list of criteria so that your inspection would be systematic.

ADVICE

The steps noted here for a house are "obvious." Be sure that your consideration of legacy software applies steps that are just as obvious. Think about it. A lot more money is at stake.

- Before you tear down and rebuild the entire house, be sure that the structure is weak. If the house is structurally sound, it may be possible to "remodel" without rebuilding (at much lower cost and in much less time).
- Before you start rebuilding be sure you understand how the original was built. Take a peek behind the walls. Understand the wiring, the plumbing, and the structural internals. Even if you trash them all, the insight you'll gain will serve you well when you start construction.
- If you begin to rebuild, use only the most modern, long-lasting materials. This may cost a bit more now, but it will help you to avoid expensive and time-consuming maintenance later.
- If you decide to rebuild, be disciplined about it. Use practices that will result in high quality—today and in the future.

Although these principles focus on the rebuilding of a house, they apply equally well to the reengineering of computer-based systems and applications.

To implement these principles, we apply a software reengineering process model that defines six activities, shown in Figure 30.2. In some cases, these activities occur in a linear sequence, but this is not always the case. For example, it may be that reverse engineering (understanding the internal workings of a program) may have to occur before document restructuring can commence.

The reengineering paradigm shown in the figure is a cyclical model. This means that each of the activities presented as a part of the paradigm may be revisited. For any particular cycle, the process can terminate after any one of these activities.

SEPA WEB CHECKLIST

Inventory Analysis

Inventory analysis. Every software organization should have an inventory of all applications. The inventory can be nothing more than a spreadsheet model containing information that provides a detailed description (e.g., size, age, business criticality) of every active application. By sorting this information according to business criticality, longevity, current maintainability, and other locally important criteria, candidates for reengineering appear. Resources can then be allocated to candidate applications for reengineering work.

It is important to note that the inventory should be revisited on a regular cycle. The status of applications (e.g., business criticality) can change as a function of time, and as a result, priorities for reengineering will shift.

FIGURE 30.2
A software reengineering process model

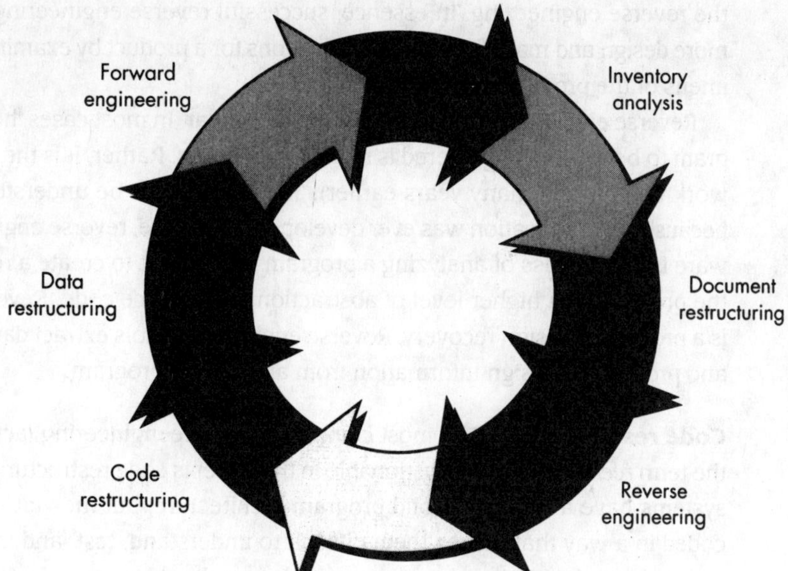

Document restructuring. Weak documentation is the trademark of many legacy systems. But what do we do about it? What are our options?

1. *Creating documentation is far too time consuming. If the system works, we'll live with what we have.* In some cases, this is the correct approach. It is not possible to re-create documentation for hundreds of computer programs. If a program is relatively static, is coming to the end of its useful life, and is unlikely to undergo significant change, let it be!

ADVICE
Create only as much documentation as is required to enhance understanding of the software, not one page more.

2. *Documentation must be updated, but we have limited resources. We'll use a "document when touched" approach.* It may not be necessary to fully redocument an application. Rather, those portions of the system that are currently undergoing change are fully documented. Over time, a collection of useful and relevant documentation will evolve.
3. *The system is business critical and must be fully redocumented.* Even in this case, an intelligent approach is to pare documentation to an essential minimum.

Each of these options is viable. A software organization must choose the one that is most appropriate for each case.

Reverse engineering. The term *reverse engineering* has its origins in the hardware world. A company disassembles a competitive hardware product in an effort to understand its competitor's design and manufacturing "secrets." These secrets could be easily understood if the competitor's design and manufacturing specifications were obtained. But these documents are proprietary and unavailable to the company doing the reverse engineering. In essence, successful reverse engineering derives one or more design and manufacturing specifications for a product by examining actual specimens of the product.

Reverse engineering for software is quite similar. In most cases, however, the program to be reverse engineered is not a competitor's. Rather, it is the company's own work (often done many years earlier). The "secrets" to be understood are obscure because no specification was ever developed. Therefore, reverse engineering for software is the process of analyzing a program in an effort to create a representation of the program at a higher level of abstraction than source code. Reverse engineering is a process of design recovery. Reverse engineering tools extract data, architectural, and procedural design information from an existing program.

Code restructuring. The most common type of reengineering (actually, the use of the term *reengineering* is questionable in this case) is code restructuring. Some legacy systems have a relatively solid program architecture, but individual modules were coded in a way that makes them difficult to understand, test, and maintain. In such cases, the code within the suspect modules can be restructured.

To accomplish this activity, the source code is analyzed using a restructuring tool. Violations of structured programming constructs are noted and code is then restructured (this can be done automatically). The resultant restructured code is reviewed and tested to ensure that no anomalies have been introduced. Internal code documentation is updated.

WebRef

A vast array of resources for the reengineering community can be obtained at **www.comp.lancs.ac.uk/projects/RenaissanceWeb/**

Data restructuring. A program with weak data architecture will be difficult to adapt and enhance. In fact, for many applications, data architecture has more to do with the long-term viability of a program that the source code itself.

Unlike code restructuring, which occurs at a relatively low level of abstraction, data structuring is a full-scale reengineering activity. In most cases, data restructuring begins with a reverse engineering activity. Current data architecture is dissected and necessary data models are defined (Chapter 12). Data objects and attributes are identified, and existing data structures are reviewed for quality.

When data structure is weak (e.g., flat files are currently implemented, when a relational approach would greatly simplify processing), the data are reengineered.

Because data architecture has a strong influence on program architecture and the algorithms that populate it, changes to the data will invariably result in either architectural or code-level changes.

Forward engineering. In an ideal world, applications would be rebuilt using a automated "reengineering engine." The old program would be fed into the engine, analyzed, restructured, and then regenerated in a form that exhibited the best aspects of software quality. In the short term, it is unlikely that such an "engine" will appear, but CASE vendors have introduced tools that provide a limited subset of these capabilities that addresses specific application domains (e.g., applications that are implemented using a specific database system). More important, these reengineering tools are becoming increasingly more sophisticated.

Forward engineering, also called *renovation* or *reclamation* [CHI90], not only recovers design information from existing software, but uses this information to alter or reconstitute the existing system in an effort to improve its overall quality. In most cases, reengineered software reimplements the function of the existing system and also adds new functions and/or improves overall performance.

30.3 REVERSE ENGINEERING

Reverse engineering conjures an image of the "magic slot." We feed an unstructured, undocumented source listing into the slot and out the other end comes full documentation for the computer program. Unfortunately, the magic slot doesn't exist. Reverse engineering can extract design information from source code, but the abstraction level, the completeness of the documentation, the degree to which tools and a human analyst work together, and the directionality of the process are highly variable [CAS88].

XRef
The notation discussed here is explained in detail in Chapter 12.

The *abstraction level* of a reverse engineering process and the tools used to effect it refers to the sophistication of the design information that can be extracted from source code. Ideally, the abstraction level should be as high as possible. That is, the reverse engineering process should be capable of deriving procedural design representations (a low-level abstraction), program and data structure information (a somewhat higher level of abstraction), data and control flow models (a relatively high level of abstraction), and entity relationship models (a high level of abstraction). As the abstraction level increases, the software engineer is provided with information that will allow easier understanding of the program.

KEY POINT
Three reverse engineering issues must be addressed: abstraction level, completeness, and directionality.

The *completeness* of a reverse engineering process refers to the level of detail that is provided at an abstraction level. In most cases, the completeness decreases as the abstraction level increases. For example, given a source code listing, it is relatively easy to develop a complete procedural design representation. Simple data flow representations may also be derived, but it is far more difficult to develop a complete set of data flow diagrams or entity-relationship models.

Completeness improves in direct proportion to the amount of analysis performed by the person doing reverse engineering. *Interactivity* refers to the degree to which the human is "integrated" with automated tools to create an effective reverse engineering process. In most cases, as the abstraction level increases, interactivity must increase or completeness will suffer.

If the *directionality* of the reverse engineering process is one way, all information extracted from the source code is provided to the software engineer who can then use it during any maintenance activity. If directionality is two way, the information is

FIGURE 30.3
The reverse engineering process

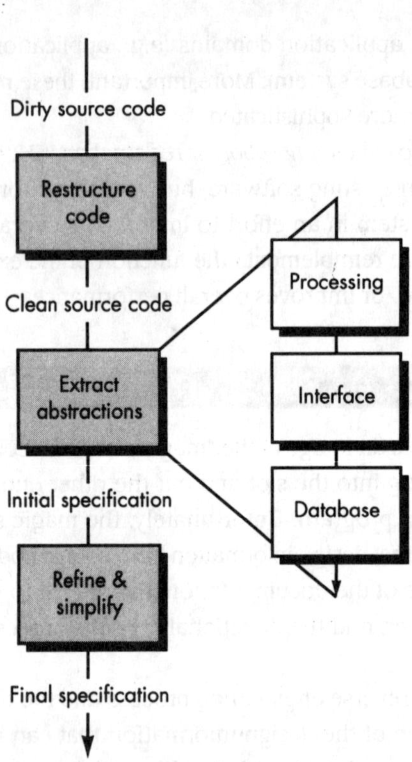

fed to a reengineering tool that attempts to restructure or regenerate the old program.

WebRef
The Design Recovery and Program Understanding page provides useful resources for reengineering work: **wwwsel.iit.nrc.ca/projects/dr/dr.html**

The reverse engineering process is represented in Figure 30.3. Before reverse engineering activities can commence, unstructured ("dirty") source code is *restructured* (Section 30.4.1) so that it contains only the structured programming constructs.[2] This makes the source code easier to read and provides the basis for all the subsequent reverse engineering activities.

The core of reverse engineering is an activity called *extract abstractions.* The engineer must evaluate the old program and from the (often undocumented) source code, extract a meaningful specification of the processing that is performed, the user interface that is applied, and the program data structures or database that is used.

30.3.1 Reverse Engineering to Understand Processing

The first real reverse engineering activity begins with an attempt to understand and then extract procedural abstractions represented by the source code. To understand procedural abstractions, the code is analyzed at varying levels of abstraction: system, program, component, pattern, and statement.

2 Code can be restructured automatically using a "restructuring engine"—a CASE tool that restructures source code.

The overall functionality of the entire application system must be understood before more detailed reverse engineering work occurs. This establishes a context for further analysis and provides insight into interoperability issues among applications within the system. Each of the programs that make up the application system represents a functional abstraction at a high level of detail. A block diagram, representing the interaction between these functional abstractions, is created. Each component performs some subfunction and represents a defined procedural abstraction. A processing narrative for each component is created. In some situations, system, program and component specifications already exist. When this is the case, the specifications are reviewed for conformance to existing code.[3]

Quote:

"There exists a passion for comprehension, just as there exists a passion for music. That passion is rather common in children, but gets lost in most people later on."

Albert Einstein

Things become more complex when the code inside a component is considered. The engineer looks for sections of code that represent generic procedural patterns. In almost every component, a section of code prepares data for processing (within the module), a different section of code does the processing, and another section of code prepares the results of processing for export from the component. Within each of these sections, we can encounter smaller patterns; for example, data validation and bounds checking often occur within the section of code that prepares data for processing.

For large systems, reverse engineering is generally accomplished using a semi-automated approach. CASE tools are used to "parse" the semantics of existing code. The output of this process is then passed to restructuring and forward engineering tools to complete the reengineering process.

30.3.2 Reverse Engineering to Understand Data

Reverse engineering of data occurs at different levels of abstraction. At the program level, internal program data structures must often be reverse engineered as part of an overall reengineering effort. At the system level, global data structures (e.g., files, databases) are often reengineered to accommodate new database management paradigms (e.g., the move from flat file to relational or object-oriented database systems). Reverse engineering of the current global data structures sets the stage for the introduction of a new systemwide database.

Internal data structures. Reverse engineering techniques for internal program data focus on the definition of classes of objects.[4] This is accomplished by examining the program code with the intent of grouping related program variables. In many cases, the data organization within the code identifies abstract data types. For example, record structures, files, lists, and other data structures often provide an initial indicator of classes.

---

3 Often, specifications written early in the life history of a program are never updated. As changes are made, the code no longer conforms to the specification.

4 For a complete discussion of these object-oriented concepts, see Part Four of this book.

ADVICE

Relatively insignificant compromises in data structures can lead to potentially catastrophic problems in future years. Consider the Y2K problem as an example.

Breuer and Lano [BRE91] suggest the following approach for reverse engineering of classes:

1. Identify flags and local data structures within the program that record important information about global data structures (e.g., a file or database).
2. Define the relationship between flags and local data structures and the global data structures. For example, a flag may be set when a file is empty; a local data structure may serve as a buffer that contains the last 100 records acquired from a central database.
3. For every variable (within the program) that represents an array or file, list all other variables that have a logical connection to it.

These steps enable a software engineer to identify classes within the program that interact with the global data structures.

Database structure. Regardless of its logical organization and physical structure, a database allows the definition of data objects and supports some method for establishing relationships among the objects. Therefore, reengineering one database schema into another requires an understanding of existing objects and their relationships.

The following steps [PRE94] may be used to define the existing data model as a precursor to reengineering a new database model:

? What steps can be applied to reverse engineer an existing database structure?

1. **Build an initial object model.** The classes defined as part of the model may be acquired by reviewing records in a flat file database or tables in a relational schema. The items contained in records or tables become attributes of a class.
2. **Determine candidate keys.** The attributes are examined to determine whether they are used to point to another record or table. Those that serve as pointers become candidate keys.
3. **Refine the tentative classes.** Determine whether similar classes can be combined into a single class.
4. **Define generalizations.** Examine classes that have many similar attributes to determine whether a class hierarchy should be constructed with a generalization class at its head.
5. **Discover associations.** Use techniques that are analogous to the CRC approach (Chapter 21) to establish associations among classes.

Once information defined in the preceding steps is known, a series of transformations [PRE94] can be applied to map the old database structure into a new database structure.

30.3.3 Reverse Engineering User Interfaces

Sophisticated GUIs have become de rigueur for computer-based products and systems of every type. Therefore, the redevelopment of user interfaces has become one of the most common types of reengineering activity. But before a user interface can be rebuilt, reverse engineering should occur.

To fully understand an existing user interface (UI), the structure and behavior of the interface must be specified. Merlo and his colleagues [MER93] suggest three basic questions that must be answered as reverse engineering of the UI commences:

? How do I understand the workings of an existing user interface?

- What are the basic actions (e.g., keystrokes and mouse clicks) that the interface must process?
- What is a compact description of the behavioral response of the system to these actions?
- What is meant by a "replacement," or more precisely, what concept of equivalence of interfaces is relevant here?

Behavioral modeling notation (Chapter 12) can provide a means for developing answers to the first two questions. Much of the information necessary to create a behavioral model can be obtained by observing the external manifestation of the existing interface. But additional information necessary to create the behavioral model must extracted from the code.

It is important to note that a replacement GUI may not mirror the old interface exactly (in fact, it may be radically different). It is often worthwhile to develop new interaction metaphors. For example, an old UI requests that a user provide a scale factor (ranging from 1 to 10) to shrink or magnify a graphical image. A reengineered GUI might use a slide-bar and mouse to accomplish the same function.

30.4 RESTRUCTURING

Software restructuring modifies source code and/or data in an effort to make it amenable to future changes. In general, restructuring does not modify the overall program architecture. It tends to focus on the design details of individual modules and on local data structures defined within modules. If the restructuring effort extends beyond module boundaries and encompasses the software architecture, restructuring becomes forward engineering (Section 30.5).

Arnold [ARN89] defines a number of benefits that can be achieved when software is restructured:

? What benefits are derived from restructuring?

- Programs have higher quality—better documentation, less complexity, and conformance to modern software engineering practices and standards.
- Frustration among software engineers who must work on the program is reduced, thereby improving productivity and making learning easier.
- Effort required to perform maintenance activities is reduced.
- Software is easier to test and debug.

Restructuring occurs when the basic architecture of an application is solid, even though technical internals need work. It is initiated when major parts of the software are serviceable and only a subset of all modules and data need extensive modification.[5]

30.4.1 Code Restructuring

ADVICE

Although code restructuring can alleviate immediate problems associated with debugging or small changes, it is not reengineering. Real benefit is achieved only when data and architecture are restructured.

Code restructuring is performed to yield a design that produces the same function but with higher quality than the original program. In general, code restructuring techniques (e.g., Warnier's logical simplification techniques [WAR74]) model program logic using Boolean algebra and then apply a series of transformation rules that yield restructured logic. The objective is to take "spaghetti-bowl" code and derive a procedural design that conforms to the structured programming philosophy (Chapter 16).

Other restructuring techniques have also been proposed for use with reengineering tools. A *resource exchange diagram* maps each program module and the resources (data types, procedures and variables) that are exchanged between it and other modules. By creating representations of resource flow, the program architecture can be restructured to achieve minimum coupling among modules.

30.4.2 Data Restructuring

Before data restructuring can begin, a reverse engineering activity called *analysis of source code* must be conducted. All programming language statements that contain data definitions, file descriptions, I/O, and interface descriptions are evaluated. The intent is to extract data items and objects, to get information on data flow, and to understand the existing data structures that have been implemented. This activity is sometimes called *data analysis* [RIC89].

Once data analysis has been completed, *data redesign* commences. In its simplest form, a *data record standardization* step clarifies data definitions to achieve consistency among data item names or physical record formats within an existing data structure or file format. Another form of redesign, called *data name rationalization,* ensures that all data naming conventions conform to local standards and that aliases are eliminated as data flow through the system.

When restructuring moves beyond standardization and rationalization, physical modifications to existing data structures are made to make the data design more effective. This may mean a translation from one file format to another, or in some cases, translation from one type of database to another.

30.5 FORWARD ENGINEERING

A program with control flow that is the graphic equivalent of a bowl of spaghetti, with "modules" that are 2,000 statements long, with few meaningful comment lines in

5 It is sometimes difficult to make a distinction between extensive restructuring and redevelopment. Both are reengineering.

290,000 source statements and no other documentation must be modified to accommodate changing user requirements. We have the following options:

What options exist when we're faced with a poorly designed and implemented program?

1. We can struggle through modification after modification, fighting the implicit design and source code to implement the necessary changes.
2. We can attempt to understand the broader inner workings of the program in an effort to make modifications more effectively.
3. We can redesign, recode, and test those portions of the software that require modification, applying a software engineering approach to all revised segments.
4. We can completely redesign, recode, and test the program, using CASE (reengineering) tools to assist us in understanding the current design.

There is no single "correct" option. Circumstances may dictate the first option even if the others are more desirable.

Rather than waiting until a maintenance request is received, the development or support organization uses the results of inventory analysis to select a program that (1) will remain in use for a preselected number of years, (2) is currently being used successfully, and (3) is likely to undergo major modification or enhancement in the near future. Then, option 2, 3, or 4 is applied.

This preventative maintenance approach was pioneered by Miller [MIL81] under the title *structured retrofit.* This concept is defined as "the application of today's methodologies to yesterday's systems to support tomorrow's requirements."

At first glance, the suggestion that we redevelop a large program when a working version already exists may seem quite extravagant. Before passing judgment, consider the following points:

ADVICE

Reengineering is a lot like getting your teeth cleaned. You can think of a thousand reasons to delay it, and you'll get away with procrastinating for quite a while. But eventually, your delaying tactics will come back to haunt you.

1. The cost to maintain one line of source code may be 20 to 40 times the cost of initial development of that line.
2. Redesign of the software architecture (program and/or data structure), using modern design concepts, can greatly facilitate future maintenance.
3. Because a prototype of the software already exists, development productivity should be much higher than average.
4. The user now has experience with the software. Therefore, new requirements and the direction of change can be ascertained with greater ease.
5. CASE tools for reengineering will automate some parts of the job.
6. A complete software configuration (documents, programs, and data) will exist upon completion of preventive maintenance.

When a software development organization sells software as a product, preventive maintenance is seen in "new releases" of a program. A large in-house software developer (e.g., a business systems software development group for a large consumer products company) may have 500–2000 production programs within its domain of responsibility. These programs can be ranked by importance and then reviewed as candidates for preventive maintenance.

The forward engineering process applies software engineering principles, concepts, and methods to re-create an existing application. In most cases, forward engineering does not simply create a modern equivalent of an older program. Rather, new user and technology requirements are integrated into the reengineering effort. The redeveloped program extends the capabilities of the older application.

30.5.1 Forward Engineering for Client/Server Architectures

XRef

Client/server software engineering is discussed in Chapter 28.

Over the past decade many mainframe applications have been reengineered to accommodate client/server architectures. In essence, centralized computing resources (including software) are distributed among many client platforms. Although a variety of different distributed environments can be designed, the typical mainframe application that is reengineered into a client/server architecture has the following features:

- Application functionality migrates to each client computer.
- New GUI interfaces are implemented at the client sites.
- Database functions are allocated to the server.
- Specialized functionality (e.g., compute-intensive analysis) may remain at the server site.
- New communications, security, archiving, and control requirements must be established at both the client and server sites.

It is important to note that the migration from mainframe to c/s computing requires both business and software reengineering. In addition, an "enterprise network infrastructure" [JAY94] should be established.

ADVICE

In some cases, c/s or OO systems designed to replace a legacy application should be approached as a new development project.. Reengineering enters the picture only when elements of an old system are to be integrated with the new architecture. In some cases, you may be better off rejecting the old and creating identical new functionality.

Reengineering for c/s applications begins with a thorough analysis of the business environment that encompasses the existing mainframe. Three layers of abstraction (Figure 30.4) can be identified. The database sits at the foundation of a client/server architecture and manages transactions and queries from server applications. Yet these transactions and queries must be controlled within the context of a set of business rules (defined by an existing or reengineered business process). Client applications provide targeted functionality to the user community.

The functions of the existing database management system and the data architecture of the existing database must be reverse engineered as a precursor to the redesign of the database foundation layer. In some cases a new data model (Chapter 12) is created. In every case, the c/s database is reengineered to ensure that transactions are executed in a consistent manner, that all updates are performed only by authorized users, that core business rules are enforced (e.g., before a vendor record is deleted, the server ensures that no related accounts payable, contracts, or com-

FIGURE 30.4 Reengineering mainframe applications to client/server

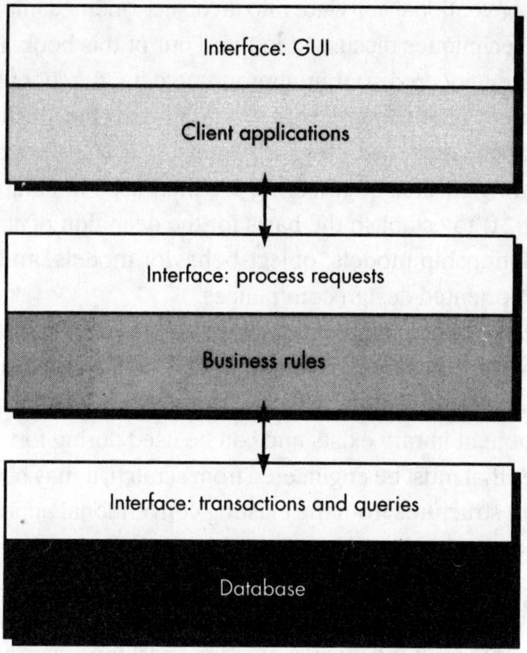

munications exist for that vendor), that queries can be accommodated efficiently, and that full archiving capability has been established.

The business rules layer represents software resident at both the client and the server. This software performs control and coordination tasks to ensure that transactions and queries between the client application and the database conform to the the established business process.

The client applications layer implements business functions that are required by specific groups of end-users. In many instances, a mainframe application is segmented into a number of smaller, reengineered desktop applications. Communication among the desktop applications (when necessary) is controlled by the business rules layer.

A comprehensive discussion of client/server software design and reengineering is best left to books dedicated to the subject. The interested reader should see [VAS93], [INM93], and [BER92].

30.5.2 Forward Engineering for Object-Oriented Architectures

Object-oriented software engineering has become the development paradigm of choice for many software organizations. But what about existing applications that were developed using conventional methods? In some cases, the answer is to leave such applications "as is." In others, older applications must be reengineered so that they can be easily integrated into large, object-oriented systems.

Reengineering conventional software into an object-oriented implementation uses many of the same techniques discussed in Part Four of this book. First, the existing software is reverse engineered so that appropriate data, functional, and behavioral models can be created. If the reengineered system extends the functionality or behavior of the original application, use-cases (Chapters 11 and 21) are created. The data models created during reverse engineering are then used in conjunction with CRC modeling (Chapter 21) to establish the basis for the definition of classes. Class hierarchies, object-relationship models, object-behavior models, and subsystems are defined, and object-oriented design commences.

As object-oriented forward engineering progresses from analysis to design, a CBSE process model (Chapter 27) can be invoked. If the existing application exists within a domain that is already populated by many object-oriented applications, it is likely that a robust component library exists and can be used during forward engineering.

For those classes that must be engineered from scratch, it may be possible to reuse algorithms and data structures from the existing conventional application. However, these must be redesigned to conform to the object-oriented architecture.

30.5.3 Forward Engineering User Interfaces

As applications migrate from the mainframe to the desktop, users are no longer willing to tolerate arcane, character-based user interfaces. In fact, a significant portion of all effort expended in the transition from mainframe to client/server computing can be spent in the reengineering of client application user interfaces.

Merlo and his colleagues [MER95] suggest the following model for reengineering user interfaces:

? What steps should we follow to reengineer a user interface?

1. **Understand the original interface and the data that move between it and the remainder of the application.** The intent is to understand how other elements of a program interact with existing code that implements the interface. If a new GUI is to be developed, the data that flow between the GUI and the remaining program must be consistent with the data that currently flow between the character-based interface and the program.
2. **Remodel the behavior implied by the existing interface into a series of abstractions that have meaning in the context of a GUI.** Although the mode of interaction may be radically different, the business behavior exhibited by users of the old and new interfaces (when considered in terms of a usage scenario) must remain the same. A redesigned interface must still allow a user to exhibit the appropriate business behavior. For example, when a database query is to be made, the old interface may require a long series of text-based commands to specify the query. The reengineered GUI may streamline the query to a small sequence of mouse picks, but the intent and content of the query remain unchanged.

3. **Introduce improvements that make the mode of interaction more efficient.** The ergonomic failings of the existing interface are studied and corrected in the design of the new GUI.
4. **Build and integrate the new GUI.** The existence of class libraries and fourth generation tools can reduce the effort required to build the GUI significantly. However, integration with existing application software can be more time consuming. Care must be taken to ensure that the GUI does not propagate adverse side effects into the remainder of the application.

30.6 THE ECONOMICS OF REENGINEERING

In a perfect world, every unmaintainable program would be retired immediately, to be replaced by high-quality, reengineered applications developed using modern software engineering practices. But we live in a world of limited resources. Reengineering drains resources that can be used for other business purposes. Therefore, before an organization attempts to reengineer an existing application, it should perform a cost/benefit analysis.

A cost/benefit analysis model for reengineering has been proposed by Sneed [SNE95]. Nine parameters are defined:

Quote:

"You can pay us a little now, or pay us a lot more later."

Sign in auto dealership suggesting a tune-up

P_1 = current annual maintenance cost for an application.
P_2 = current annual operation cost for an application.
P_3 = current annual business value of an application.
P_4 = predicted annual maintenance cost after reengineering.
P_5 = predicted annual operations cost after reengineering.
P_6 = predicted annual business value after reengineering.
P_7 = estimated reengineering costs.
P_8 = estimated reengineering calendar time.
P_9 = reengineering risk factor ($P_9 = 1.0$ is nominal).
L = expected life of the system.

The cost associated with continuing maintenance of a candidate application (i.e., reengineering is not performed) can be defined as

$$C_{\text{maint}} = [P_3 - (P_1 + P_2)] \times L \tag{30-1}$$

The costs associated with reengineering are defined using the following relationship:

$$C_{\text{reeng}} = [P_6 - (P_4 + P_5) \times (L - P_8) - (P_7 \times P_9)] \tag{30-2}$$

Using the costs presented in equations (30-1) and (30-2), the overall benefit of reengineering can be computed as

$$\text{cost benefit} = C_{\text{reeng}} - C_{\text{maint}} \tag{30-3}$$

The cost/benefit analysis presented in the equations can be performed for all high-priority applications identified during inventory analysis (Section 30.2.2). Those applications that show the highest cost/benefit can be targeted for reengineering, while work on others can be postponed until resources are available.

30.7 SUMMARY

Reengineering occurs at two different levels of abstraction. At the business level, reengineering focuses on the business process with the intent of making changes to improve competitiveness in some area of the business. At the software level, reengineering examines information systems and applications with the intent of restructuring or reconstructing them so that they exhibit higher quality.

Business process reengineering defines business goals, identifies and evaluates existing business processes (in the context of defined goals), specifies and designs revised processes, and prototypes, refines, and instantiates them within a business. BPR has a focus that extends beyond software. The result of BPR is often the definition of ways in which information technologies can better support the business.

Software reengineering encompasses a series of activities that include inventory analysis, document restructuring, reverse engineering, program and data restructuring, and forward engineering. The intent of these activities is to create versions of existing programs that exhibit higher quality and better maintainability—programs that will be viable well into the twenty-first century.

Inventory analysis enables an organization to assess each application systematically, with the intent of determining which are candidates for reengineering. Document restructuring creates a framework of documentation that is necessary for the long-term support of an application. Reverse engineering is the process of analyzing a program in an effort to extract data, architectural, and procedural design information. Finally, forward engineering reconstructs a program using modern software engineering practices and information learned during reverse engineering.

The cost/benefit of reengineering can be determined quantitatively. The cost of the status quo, that is, the cost associated with ongoing support and maintenance of an existing application, is compared to the projected costs of reengineering and the resultant reduction in maintenance costs. In almost every case in which a program has a long life and currently exhibits poor maintainability, reengineering represents a cost-effective business strategy.

REFERENCES

[ARN89] Arnold, R.S., "Software Restructuring," *Proc. IEEE*, vol. 77, no. 4, April 1989, pp. 607–617.

[BER92] Berson, A., *Client/Server Architecture*, McGraw-Hill, 1992.

[BLE93] Bleakley, F.R., "The Best Laid Plans: Many Companies Try Management Fads, Only to See Them Flop," *The Wall Street Journal,* July 6, 1993, p. 1.

[BRE91] Breuer, P.T. and K. Lano, "Creating Specification From Code: Reverse-Engineering Techniques," *Journal of Software Maintenance: Research and Practice,* vol. 3, 1991, pp. 145–162.

[CAN72] Canning, R., "The Maintenance 'Iceberg'," *EDP Analyzer,* vol. 10, no. 10, October 1972.

[CAS88] "Case Tools for Reverse Engineering," *CASE Outlook,* CASE Consulting Group, vol. 2, no. 2, 1988, pp. 1–15.

[CHI90] Chikofsky, E.J., and J.H. Cross, II, "Reverse Engineering and Design Recovery: A Taxonomy," *IEEE Software,* January 1990, pp. 13–17.

[DAV90] Davenport, T.H. and J.E. Young, "The New Industrial Engineering: Information Technology and Business Process Redesign," *Sloan Management Review,* Summer 1990, pp. 11–27.

[DEM95] DeMarco, T., "Lean and Mean," *IEEE Software,* November 1995, pp. 101–102.

[DIC95] Dickinson, B., *Strategic Business Reengineering,* LCI Press, 1995.

[HAM90] Hammer, M., "Reengineer Work: Don't Automate, Obliterate," *Harvard Business Review,* July–August 1990, pp. 104–112.

[HAN93] Manna, M., "Maintenance Burden Begging for a Remedy," *Datamation,* April 1993, pp. 53–63.

[INM93] Inmon, W.H., *Developing Client Server Applications,* QED Publishing, 1993.

[JAY94] Jaychandra, Y., *Re-engineering the Networked Enterprise,* McGraw-Hill, 1994.

[MER93] Merlo, E., et al., "Reverse Engineering of User Interfaces," *Proc. Working Conference on Reverse Engineering,* IEEE, Baltimore, May 1993, pp. 171–178.

[MER95] Merlo, E., et al., "Reengineering User Interfaces," *IEEE Software,* January 1995, pp. 64–73.

[MIL81] Miller, J., in *Techniques of Program and System Maintenance,* (G. Parikh, ed.) Winthrop Publishers, 1981.

[OSB90] Osborne, W.M. and E.J. Chikofsky, "Fitting Pieces to the Maintenance Puzzle," *IEEE Software,* January 1990, pp. 10–11.

[PRE94] Premerlani,W.J., and M.R. Blaha, "An Approach for Reverse Engineering of Relational Databases," *CACM,* vol. 37, no. 5, May 1994, pp. 42–49.

[RIC89] Ricketts, J.A., J.C. DelMonaco, and M.W. Weeks, "Data Reengineering for Application Systems," *Proc. Conf. Software Maintenance—1989,* IEEE, 1989, pp. 174–179.

[SNE95] Sneed, H., "Planning the Reengineering of Legacy Systems," *IEEE Software,* January 1995, pp. 24–25.

[STE93] Stewart, T.A., "Reengineering: The Hot New Managing Tool," *Fortune,* August 23, 1993, pp. 41–48.

[SWA76] Swanson, E.B., "The Dimensions of Maintenance,"*Proc. Second Intl. Conf. Software Engineering,* IEEE, October 1976, pp. 492–497.

[VAS93] Vaskevitch, D., *Client/Server Strategies,* IDG Books, 1993.

[WAR74] Warnier, J.D., *Logical Construction of Programs,* Van Nostrand-Reinhold, 1974.

[WEI95] Weisz, M., "BPR Is Like Teenage Sex," *American Programmer,* vol. 8, no. 6, June 1995, pp. 9–15.

PROBLEMS AND POINTS TO PONDER

30.1. Consider any job that you've held in the last five years. Describe the business process in which you played a part. Use the BPR model described in Section 30.1.3 to recommend changes to the process in an effort to make it more efficient.

30.2. Do some research on the efficacy of business process reengineering. Present pro and con arguments for this approach.

30.3. Your instructor will select one of the programs that everyone in the class has developed during this course. Exchange your program randomly with someone else in the class. Do not explain or walk through the program. Now, implement an enhancement (specified by your instructor) in the program you have received.

a. Perform all software engineering tasks including a brief walkthrough (but not with the author of the program).

b. Keep careful track of all errors encountered during testing.

c. Discuss your experiences in class.

30.4. Explore the inventory analysis checklist presented at the SEPA Web site and attempt to develop a quantitative software rating system that could be applied to existing programs in an effort to pick candidate programs for reengineering. Your system should extend beyond economic analysis presented in Section 30.6.

30.5. Suggest alternatives to paper and ink or conventional electronic documentation that could serve as the basis for document restructuring. (Hint: Think of new descriptive technologies that could be used to communicate the intent of the software.)

30.6. Some people believe that artificial intelligence technology will increase the abstraction level of the reverse engineering process. Do some research on this subject (i.e., the use of AI for reverse engineering) and write a brief paper that takes a stand on this point.

30.7. Why is completeness difficult to achieve as abstraction level increases?

30.8. Why must interactivity increase if completeness is to increase?

30.9. Get product literature on three reverse engineering tools and present their characteristics in class.

30.10. There is a subtle difference between restructuring and forward engineering What is it?

30.11. Research the literature to find one or more papers that discuss case studies of mainframe to client/server reengineering. Present a summary.

30.12. How would you determine P_4 through P_7 in the cost-benefit model presented in Section 30.6?

FURTHER READINGS AND INFORMATION SOURCES

Like many hot topics in the business community, the hype surrounding business process reengineering has given way to a more pragmatic view of the subject. Hammer and Champy (*Reengineering the Corporation,* HarperCollins, 1993) precipitated early interest with their best selling book. Later, Hammer (*Beyond Reengineering: How the Processed-Centered Organization Is Changing Our Work and Our Lives,* HarperCollins 1997) refined his view by focusing on "process-centered" issues.

Books by Andersen (*Business Process Improvement Toolbox,* American Society for Quality, 1999), Harrington et al. (*Business Process Improvement Workbook,* McGraw-Hill, 1997), Hunt (*Process Mapping: How to Reengineer Your Business Processes,* Wiley, 1996), and Carr and Johansson (*Best Practices in Reengineering: What Works and What Doesn't in the Reengineering Process,* McGraw-Hill, 1995) present case studies and detailed guidelines for BPR.

Feldmann (*The Practical Guide to Business Process Reengineering Using IDEF0,* Dorset House, 1998) discusses a modeling notation that assists in BPR. Berztiss (*Software Methods for Business Reengineering,* Springer, 1996) and Spurr et al. (*Software Assistance for Business Reengineering,* Wiley, 1994) discuss tools and techniques that facilitate BPR.

Relatively few books have been dedicated to software reengineering. Rada (*Reengineering Software: How to Reuse Programming to Build New, State-of-the-Art Software,* Fitzroy Dearborn Publishers, 1999) focuses on reengineering at a technical level. Miller (*Reengineering Legacy Software Systems,* Digital Press, 1998) "provides a framework for keeping application systems synchronized with business strategies and technology changes." Umar (*Application (Re)Engineering: Building Web-Based Applications and Dealing with Legacies,* Prentice-Hall, 1997) provides worthwhile guidance for organizations that want to transform legacy systems into a Web-based environment. Cook (*Building Enterprise Information Architectures: Reengineering Information Systems,* Prentice-Hall, 1996) discusses the bridge between BPR and information technology. Aiken (*Data Reverse Engineering,* McGraw-Hill, 1996) discusses how to reclaim, reorganize, and reuse organizational data. Arnold (*Software Reengineering,* IEEE Computer Society Press, 1993) has put together an excellent anthology of early papers that focus on software reengineering technologies.

A wide variety of information sources on business process reengineering and software reengineering is available on the Internet. An up-to-date list of World Wide Web references can be found at the SEPA Web site:
http://www.mhhe.com/engcs/compsci/pressman/resources/reengineering.mhtml

CHAPTER

31 COMPUTER-AIDED SOFTWARE ENGINEERING

KEY CONCEPTS

Everyone has heard the old saying about the shoemaker's children: The shoemaker is so busy making shoes for others that his children don't have shoes of their own. Prior to the 1990s, many software developers were the "shoemaker's children." Although these technical professionals built complex systems and products that automated the work of others, they used very little automation themselves.

Today, software engineers have their first new pair of shoes—computer-aided software engineering (CASE). The shoes don't come in as many varieties as they would like, haven't lived up to the many exaggerated promises made by their manufacturers, are often a bit stiff and sometimes uncomfortable, don't provide enough sophistication for those who are stylish, and don't always match other garments that software developers use, but they provide an absolutely essential piece of apparel for the software engineer's wardrobe and will, over time, become more comfortable, more useable, and more adaptable to the needs of individual practitioners.

In earlier chapters of this book we have attempted to provide a reasonable understanding of the underpinnings of software engineering technology. In this chapter, the focus shifts to the tools and environments that will help to automate the software process.

QUICK LOOK

What is it? Computer-aided software engineering (CASE) tools assist software engineering managers and practitioners in every activity associated with the software process. They automate project management activities, manage all work products produced throughout the process, and assist engineers in their analysis, design, coding and test work. CASE tools can be integrated within a sophisticated environment.

Who does it? Project managers and software engineers use CASE.

Why is it important? Software engineering is difficult. Tools that reduce the amount of effort required to produce a work product or accomplish some project milestone have substantial benefit. But there's something that's even more important. Tools can provide new ways of looking at software engineering information—ways that improve the insight of the engineer doing the work. This leads to better decisions and higher software quality.

What are the steps? CASE is used in conjunction with the process model that is chosen. If a full tool set is available, CASE will be used during virtually every step of the software process.

What is the work product? CASE tools assist a software engineer in producing high-quality work products. In addition, the availability of automation allows the CASE user to produce additional customized work products that could not be

QUICK LOOK

easily or practically produced without tool support.

How do I ensure that I've done it right? Use tools to complement solid software engineering practices—not to replace them. Before tools can be used effectively, a software process framework must be established, software engineering concepts and methods must be learned, and software quality must be emphasized. Only then will CASE provide benefit.

31.1 WHAT IS CASE?

A good workshop for any craftsperson—a mechanic, a carpenter, or a software engineer—has three primary characteristics: (1) a collection of useful tools that will help in every step of building a product, (2) an organized layout that enables tools to be found quickly and used efficiently, and (3) a skilled artisan who understands how to use the tools in an effective manner. Software engineers now recognize that they need more and varied tools along with an organized and efficient workshop in which to place the tools.

The workshop for software engineering has been called an *integrated project support environment* (discussed later in this chapter) and the tools that fill the workshop are collectively called *computer-aided software engineering*.

CASE provides the software engineer with the ability to automate manual activities and to improve engineering insight. Like computer-aided engineering and design tools that are used by engineers in other disciplines, CASE tools help to ensure that quality is designed in before the product is built.

31.2 BUILDING BLOCKS FOR CASE

Computer aided software engineering can be as simple as a single tool that supports a specific software engineering activity or as complex as a complete "environment" that encompasses tools, a database, people, hardware, a network, operating systems, standards, and myriad other components. The building blocks for CASE are illustrated in Figure 31.1. Each building block forms a foundation for the next, with tools sitting at the top of the heap. It is interesting to note that the foundation for effective CASE environments has relatively little to do with software engineering tools themselves. Rather, successful environments for software engineering are built on an environment architecture that encompasses appropriate hardware and systems software. In addition, the environment architecture must consider the human work patterns that are applied during the software engineering process.

> **Quote:** "The most valuable CASE tools are those that contribute information to the development process."
> **Robert Dixon**

The environment architecture, composed of the hardware platform and system support (including networking software, database management, and object management services), lays the ground work for CASE. But the CASE environment itself

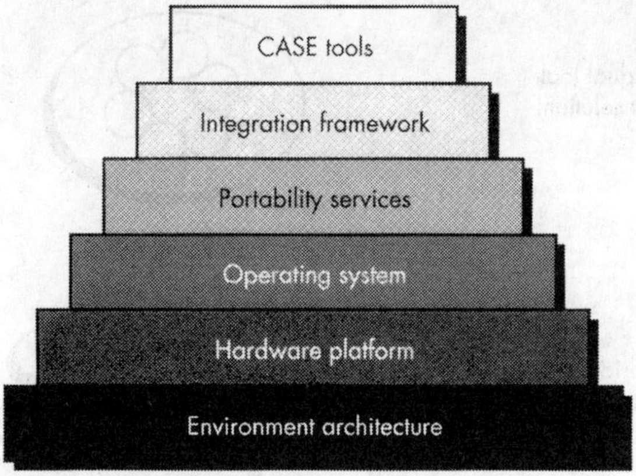

FIGURE 31.1
CASE building blocks

demands other building blocks. A set of *portability services* provides a bridge between CASE tools and their integration framework and the environment architecture. The *integration framework* is a collection of specialized programs that enables individual CASE tools to communicate with one another, to create a project database, and to exhibit the same look and feel to the end-user (the software engineer). Portability services allow CASE tools and their integration framework to migrate across different hardware platforms and operating systems without significant adaptive maintenance.

The building blocks depicted in Figure 31.1 represent a comprehensive foundation for the integration of CASE tools. However, most CASE tools in use today have not been constructed using all these building blocks. In fact, some CASE tools remain "point solutions." That is, a tool is used to assist in a particular software engineering activity (e.g., analysis modeling) but does not directly communicate with other tools, is not tied into a project database, is not part of an *integrated CASE environment* (I-CASE). Although this situation is not ideal, a CASE tool can be used quite effectively, even if it is a point solution.

ADVICE

Point-solution CASE tools can provide substantial individual benefit, but a software team needs tools that talk to one another. Integrated tools help the team develop, organize, and control work products. Use them.

The relative levels of CASE integration are shown in Figure 31.2. At the low end of the integration spectrum is the individual (point solution) tool. When individual tools provide facilities for data exchange (most do), the integration level is improved slightly. Such tools produce output in a standard format that should be compatible with other tools that can read the format. In some cases, the builders of complementary CASE tools work together to form a bridge between the tools (e.g., an analysis and design tool that is coupled with a code generator). Using this approach, the synergy between the tools can produce end products that would be difficult to create using either tool separately. *Single-source integration* occurs when a single CASE tools vendor integrates a number of different tools and sells them as a package. Although this approach is quite effective, the closed architecture of most single-source environments precludes easy addition of tools from other vendors.

FIGURE 31.2
Integration options

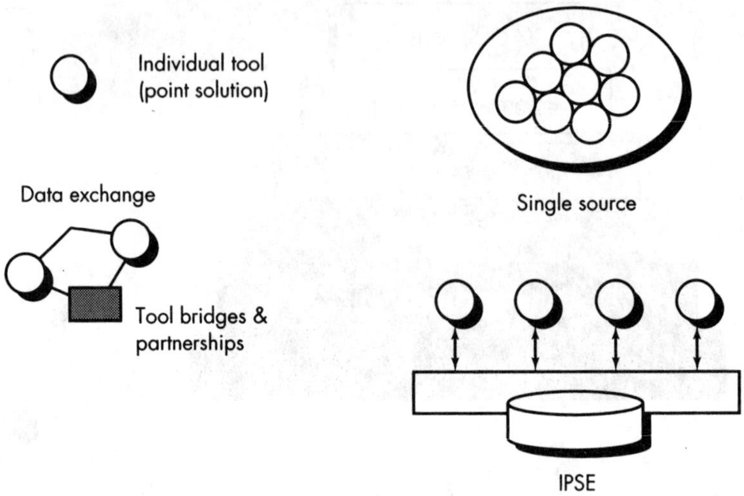

At the high end of the integration spectrum is the *integrated project support environment* (IPSE). Standards for each of the building blocks described previously have been created. CASE tool vendors use IPSE standards to build tools that will be compatible with the IPSE and therefore compatible with one another.

31.3 A TAXONOMY OF CASE TOOLS

A number of risks are inherent whenever we attempt to categorize CASE tools. There is a subtle implication that to create an effective CASE environment, one must implement all categories of tools—this is simply not true. Confusion (or antagonism) can be created by placing a specific tool within one category when others might believe it belongs in another category. Some readers may feel that an entire category has been omitted—thereby eliminating an entire set of tools for inclusion in the overall CASE environment. In addition, simple categorization tends to be flat—that is, we do not show the hierarchical interaction of tools or the relationships among them. But even with these risks, it is necessary to create a taxonomy of CASE tools—to better understand the breadth of CASE and to better appreciate where such tools can be applied in the software engineering process.

CASE Tools

CASE tools can be classified by function, by their role as instruments for managers or technical people, by their use in the various steps of the software engineering process, by the environment architecture (hardware and software) that supports them, or even by their origin or cost [QED89]. The taxonomy presented here uses function as a primary criterion.

Business process engineering tools. By modeling the strategic information requirements of an organization, business process engineering tools provide a "meta-model" from which specific information systems are derived. Rather than focusing on the requirements of a specific application, business information is modeled as it moves between various organizational entities within a company. The primary objective for tools in this category is to represent business data objects, their relationships, and how these data objects flow between different business areas within a company.

> **XRef**
> Business process engineering is discussed in Chapter 10.

Process modeling and management tools. If an organization works to improve a business (or software) process, it must first understand it. Process modeling tools (also called *process technology* tools) are used to represent the key elements of a process so that it can be better understood. Such tools can also provide links to process descriptions that help those involved in the process to understand the work tasks that are required to perform it. Process management tools provide links to other tools that provide support to defined process activities.

> **XRef**
> The elements of the software process are discussed in Chapter 2.

Project planning tools. Tools in this category focus on two primary areas: software project effort and cost estimation and project scheduling. Estimation tools compute estimated effort, project duration, and recommended number of people for a project. Project scheduling tools enable the manager to define all project tasks (the work breakdown structure), create a task network (usually using graphical input), represent task interdependencies, and model the amount of parallelism possible for the project.

> **XRef**
> Estimation techniques are presented in Chapter 5. Scheduling methods are discussed in Chapter 7.

Risk analysis tools. Identifying potential risks and developing a plan to mitigate, monitor, and manage them is of paramount importance in large projects. Risk analysis tools enable a project manager to build a risk table by providing detailed guidance in the identification and analysis of risks.

> **XRef**
> Risk analysis and management are discussed in Chapter 6.

Project management tools. The project schedule and project plan must be tracked and monitored on a continuing basis. In addition, a manager should use tools to collect metrics that will ultimately provide an indication of software product quality. Tools in the category are often extensions to project planning tools.

> **XRef**
> Tracking and monitoring are discussed in Chapter 7.

Requirements tracing tools. When large systems are developed, things "fall into the cracks." That is, the delivered system does not fully meet customer specified requirements. The objective of requirements tracing tools is to provide a systematic approach to the isolation of requirements, beginning with the customer request for proposal or specification. The typical requirements tracing tool combines human-interactive text evaluation with a database management system that stores and categorizes each system requirement that is "parsed" from the original RFP or specification.

> **XRef**
> Requirements engineering methods are discussed in Chapter 10.

Metrics and management tools. Software metrics improve a manager's ability to control and coordinate the software engineering process and a practitioner's ability

XRef
Metrics are presented in Chapters 4, 19, and 24.

to improve the quality of the software that is produced. Today's metrics or measurement tools focus on process and product characteristics. Management-oriented tools capture project specific metrics (e.g., LOC/person-month, defects per function point) that provide an overall indication of productivity or quality. Technically oriented tools determine technical metrics that provide greater insight into the quality of design or code.

XRef
Documentation is discussed throughout the book. More detail is presented at the SEPA Web site.

Documentation tools. Document production and desktop publishing tools support nearly every aspect of software engineering and represent a substantial "leverage" opportunity for all software developers. Most software development organizations spend a substantial amount of time developing documents, and in many cases the documentation process itself is quite inefficient. It is not unusual for a software development organization to spend as much as 20 or 30 percent of all software development effort on documentation. For this reason, documentation tools provide an important opportunity to improve productivity.

XRef
See Chapters 27, 28, and 29 for limited discussion of these topics.

System software tools. CASE is a workstation technology. Therefore, the CASE environment must accommodate high-quality network system software, object management services, distributed component support, electronic mail, bulletin boards, and other communication capabilities.

XRef
SQA is presented in Chapter 8.

Quality assurance tools. The majority of CASE tools that claim to focus on quality assurance are actually metrics tools that audit source code to determine compliance with language standards. Other tools extract technical metrics (Chapters 19 and 24) in an effort to project the quality of the software that is being built.

XRef
The software repository is discussed in Chapter 9.

Database management tools. Database management software serves as a foundation for the establishment of a CASE database (repository) that we have called the *project database.* Given the emphasis on configuration objects, database management tools for CASE are evolving from relational database management systems to object-oriented database management systems.

XRef
SCM activities, including identification, version control, change control, auditing, and status accounting, are discussed in Chapter 9.

Software configuration management tools. Software configuration management lies at the kernel of every CASE environment. Tools can assist in all five major SCM tasks—identification, version control, change control, auditing, and status accounting. The CASE database provides a mechanism for identifying each configuration item and relating it to other items; the change control process can be implemented with the aid of specialized tools; easy access to individual configuration items facilitates the auditing process; and CASE communication tools can greatly improve status accounting (reporting information about changes to all who need to know).

Analysis and design tools. Analysis and design tools enable a software engineer to create models of the system to be built. The models contain a representation of data, function, and behavior (at the analysis level) and characterizations of data, archi-

XRef
Analysis and design are discussed throughout Parts Three and Four of this book.

tectural, component-level, and interface design.[1] By performing consistency and validity checking on the models, analysis and design tools provide a software engineer with some degree of insight into the analysis representation and help to eliminate errors before they propagate into the design, or worse, into implementation itself.

XRef
Prototyping and simulation are discussed briefly in Chapter 10.

PRO/SIM tools. PRO/SIM (prototyping and simulation) tools [NIC90] provide the software engineer with the ability to predict the behavior of a real-time system prior to the time that it is built. In addition, these tools enable the software engineer to develop mock-ups of the real-time system, allowing the customer to gain insight into the function, operation and response prior to actual implementation.

XRef
The elements of user interface design are presented in Chapter 15.

Interface design and development tools. Interface design and development tools are actually a tool kit of software components (classes) such as menus, buttons, window structures, icons, scrolling mechanisms, device drivers, and so forth. However, these tool kits are being replaced by interface prototyping tools that enable rapid on-screen creation of sophisticated user interfaces that conform to the interfacing standard that has been adopted for the software.

XRef
Prototyping is discussed in Chapters 2 and 11.

Prototyping tools. A variety of different prototyping tools can be used. *Screen painters* enable a software engineer to define screen layout rapidly for interactive applications. More sophisticated CASE prototyping tools enable the creation of a data design, coupled with both screen and report layouts. Many analysis and design tools have extensions that provide a prototyping option. PRO/SIM tools generate skeleton Ada and C source code for engineering (real-time) applications. Finally, a variety of fourth generation tools have prototyping features.

Programming tools. The programming tools category encompasses the compilers, editors, and debuggers that are available to support most conventional programming languages. In addition, object-oriented programming environments, fourth generation languages, graphical programming environments, application generators, and database query languages also reside within this category.

XRef
WebE is discussed in Chapter 29.

Web development tools. The activities associated with Web engineering are supported by a variety of tools for WebApp development. These include tools that assist in the generation of text, graphics, forms, scripts, applets, and other elements of a Web page.

XRef
Software testing is discussed in Chapters 17, 18, and 23 as well as 28 and 29.

Integration and testing tools. In their directory of software testing tools, Software Quality Engineering [SQE95] defines the following testing tools categories:

- *Data acquisition*—tools that acquire data to be used during testing.
- *Static measurement*—tools that analyze source code without executing test cases.

1 Analogous representations are provided by object-oriented analysis and design tools.

- *Dynamic measurement*—tools that analyze source code during execution.
- *Simulation*—tools that simulate function of hardware or other externals.
- *Test management*—tools that assist in the planning, development, and control of testing.
- *Cross-functional tools*—tools that cross the bounds of the preceding categories.

It should be noted that many testing tools have features that span two or more of the categories.

XRef
White-box testing methods are discussed in Chapter 17.

Static analysis tools. Static testing tools assist the software engineer in deriving test cases. Three different types of static testing tools are used in the industry: code-based testing tools, specialized testing languages, and requirements-based testing tools. *Code-based testing tools* accept source code (or PDL) as input and perform a number of analyses that result in the generation of test cases. *Specialized testing languages* (e.g., ATLAS) enable a software engineer to write detailed test specifications that describe each test case and the logistics for its execution. *Requirements-based testing tools* isolate specific user requirements and suggest test cases (or classes of tests) that will exercise the requirements.

Dynamic analysis tools. Dynamic testing tools interact with an executing program, checking path coverage, testing assertions about the value of specific variables, and otherwise instrumenting the execution flow of the program. Dynamic tools can be either intrusive or nonintrusive. An *intrusive tool* changes the software to be tested by inserting probes (extra instructions) that perform the activities just mentioned. *Nonintrusive testing tools* use a separate hardware processor that runs in parallel with the processor containing the program that is being tested.

XRef
Test strategies are discussed in Chapter 18.

Test management tools. Test management tools are used to control and coordinate software testing for each of the major testing steps. Tools in this category manage and coordinate regression testing, perform comparisons that ascertain differences between actual and expected output, and conduct batch testing of programs with interactive human/computer interfaces. In addition to the functions noted, many test management tools also serve as generic test drivers. A test driver reads one or more test cases from a testing file, formats the test data to conform to the needs of the software under test, and then invokes the software to be tested.

XRef
c/s testing is discussed in Chapter 28.

Client/server testing tools. The c/s environment demands specialized testing tools that exercise the graphical user interface and the network communications requirements for client and server.

Reengineering tools. Tools for legacy software address a set of maintenance activities that currently absorb a significant percentage of all software-related effort. The reengineering tools category can be subdivided into the following functions:

XRef
Reengineering methods are discussed in Chapter 30.

- *Reverse engineering to specification tools* take source code as input and generate graphical structured analysis and design models, where-used lists, and other design information.
- *Code restructuring and analysis tools* analyze program syntax, generate a control flow graph, and automatically generate a structured program.
- *On-line system reengineering tools* are used to modify on-line database systems (e.g., convert IDMS or DB2 files into entity-relationship format).

These tools are limited to specific programming languages (although most major languages are addressed) and require some degree of interaction with the software engineer.

31.4 INTEGRATED CASE ENVIRONMENTS

What are the benefits of integrated CASE?

Although benefits can be derived from individual CASE tools that address separate software engineering activities, the real power of CASE can be achieved only through integration. The benefits of integrated CASE (I-CASE) include (1) smooth transfer of information (models, programs, documents, data) from one tool to another and one software engineering step to the next; (2) a reduction in the effort required to perform umbrella activities such as software configuration management, quality assurance, and document production; (3) an increase in project control that is achieved through better planning, monitoring, and communication; and (4) improved coordination among staff members who are working on a large software project.

KEY POINT
CASE tools integration demands a database that contains consistent representations of software engineering information.

But I-CASE also poses significant challenges. Integration demands consistent representations of software engineering information, standardized interfaces between tools, a homogeneous mechanism for communication between the software engineer and each tool, and an effective approach that will enable I-CASE to move among various hardware platforms and operating systems. Comprehensive I-CASE environments have emerged more slowly than originally expected. However, integrated environments do exist and are becoming more powerful as the years pass.

The term *integration* implies both *combination* and *closure*. I-CASE combines a variety of different tools and a spectrum of information in a way that enables closure of communication among tools, between people, and across the software process. Tools are integrated so that software engineering information is available to each tool that needs it; usage is integrated so that a common look and feel is provided for all tools; a development philosophy is integrated, implying a standardized software engineering approach that applies modern practice and proven methods.

To define integration in the context of the software engineering process, it is necessary to establish a set of requirements [FOR89a] for I-CASE: An integrated CASE environment should

- Provide a mechanism for sharing software engineering information among all tools contained in the environment.
- Enable a change to one item of information to be tracked to other related information items.
- Provide version control and overall configuration management for all software engineering information.
- Allow direct, nonsequential access to any tool contained in the environment.
- Establish automated support for the software process model that has been chosen, integrating CASE tools and software configuration items (SCIs) into a standard work breakdown structure.
- Enable the users of each tool to experience a consistent look and feel at the human/computer interface.
- Support communication among software engineers.
- Collect both management and technical metrics that can be used to improve the process and the product.

XRef

Process-related issues are discussed in Chapters 2, 4, and 7. SCIs are presented in Chapter 9.

To achieve these requirements, each of the building blocks of a CASE architecture (Figure 31.1) must fit together in a seamless fashion. The foundation building blocks—environment architecture, hardware platform, and operating system—must be "joined" through a set of portability services to an integration framework that achieves these requirements.

31.5 THE INTEGRATION ARCHITECTURE

SEPA WEB DOCUMENT

A list of all software engineering information items can be found under SCIs

A software engineering team uses CASE tools, corresponding methods, and a process framework to create a pool of software engineering information. The integration framework facilitates transfer of information into and out of the pool. To accomplish this, the following architectural components must exist: a database must be created (to store the information); an object management system must be built (to manage changes to the information); a tools control mechanism must be constructed (to coordinate the use of CASE tools); a user interface must provide a consistent pathway between actions made by the user and the tools contained in the environment. Most models (e.g., [FOR90], [SHA95]) of the integration framework represent these components as layers. A simple model of the framework, depicting only the components just noted is shown in Figure 31.3.

The *user interface layer* (Figure 31.3) incorporates a standardized interface tool kit with a common presentation protocol. The interface tool kit contains software for human/computer interface management and a library of display objects. Both provide a consistent mechanism for communication between the interface and individual CASE tools. The *presentation protocol* is the set of guidelines that gives all CASE

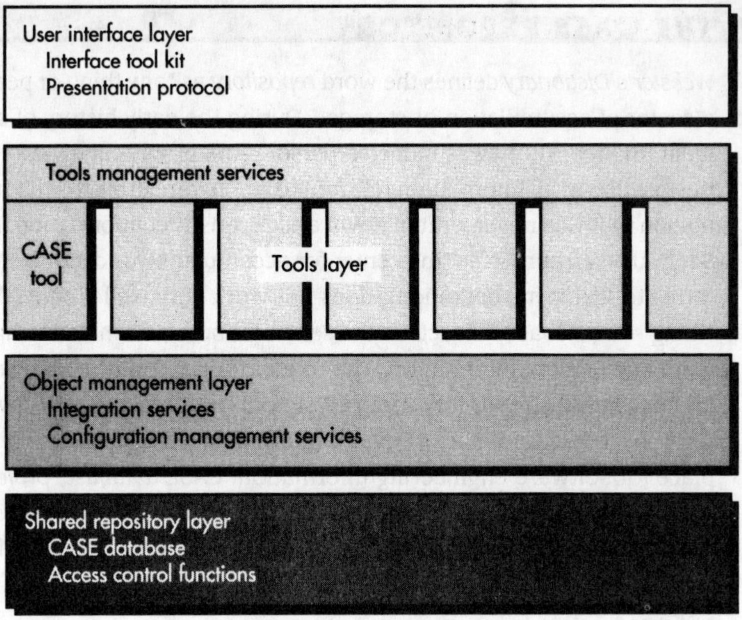

FIGURE 31.3 Architectural model for the integration framework

tools the same look and feel. Screen layout conventions, menu names and organization, icons, object names, the use of the keyboard and mouse, and the mechanism for tools access are all defined as part of the presentation protocol.

The *tools layer* incorporates a set of tools management services with the CASE tools themselves. *Tools management services* (TMS) control the behavior of tools within the environment. If multitasking is used during the execution of one or more tools, TMS performs multitask synchronization and communication, coordinates the flow of information from the repository and object management system into the tools, accomplishes security and auditing functions, and collects metrics on tool usage.

WebRef
Resources for CASE tool integration and integrated software engineering environments can be obtained at **see.cs.flinders.edu.au/seweb/ti/**

The *object management layer* (OML) performs the configuration management functions described in Chapter 9. In essence, software in this layer of the framework architecture provides the mechanism for tools integration. Every CASE tool is "plugged into" the object management layer. Working in conjunction with the CASE repository, the OML provides integration services—a set of standard modules that couple tools with the repository. In addition, the OML provides configuration management services by enabling the identification of all configuration objects, performing version control, and providing support for change control, audits, and status accounting.

The *shared repository layer* is the CASE database and the access control functions that enable the object management layer to interact with the database. Data integration is achieved by the object management and shared repository layers and is discussed in greater detail later in this chapter.

31.6 THE CASE REPOSITORY

Webster's Dictionary defines the word *repository* as "any thing or person thought of as a center of accumulation or storage." During the early history of software development, the repository was indeed a person—the programmer who had to remember the location of all information relevant to a software project, who had to recall information that was never written down and reconstruct information that had been lost. Sadly, using a person as "the center for accumulation and storage" (although it conforms to Webster's definition), does not work very well. Today, the repository is a "thing"—a database that acts as the center for both accumulation and storage of software engineering information. The role of the person (the software engineer) is to interact with the repository using CASE tools that are integrated with it.

In this book, a number of different terms have been used to refer to the storage place for software engineering information: *CASE database, project database, integrated project support environment (IPSE) database, requirements dictionary* (a limited database), and *repository.* Although there are subtle differences between some of these terms, all refer to the center for accumulation and storage.

31.6.1 The Role of the Repository in I-CASE

The repository for an I-CASE environment is the set of mechanisms and data structures that achieve data/tool and data/data integration. It provides the obvious functions of a database management system, but in addition, the repository performs or precipitates the following functions [FOR89b]:

? What functions are performed by the services that are coupled with the CASE repository?

- *Data integrity* includes functions to validate entries to the repository, ensure consistency among related objects, and automatically perform "cascading" modifications when a change to one object demands some change to objects related to it.
- *Information sharing* provides a mechanism for sharing information among multiple developers and between multiple tools, manages and controls multi-user access to data and locks or unlocks objects so that changes are not inadvertently overlaid on one another.
- *Data/tool integration* establishes a data model that can be accessed by all tools in the I-CASE environment, controls access to the data, and performs appropriate configuration management functions.
- *Data/data integration* is the database management system that relates data objects so that other functions can be achieved.
- *Methodology enforcement* defines an entity-relationship model stored in the repository that implies a specific paradigm for software engineering; at a minimum, the relationships and objects define a set of steps that must be conducted to build the contents of the repository.

- *Document standardization* is the definition of objects in the database that leads directly to a standard approach for the creation of software engineering documents.

To achieve these functions, the repository is defined in terms of a meta-model. The *meta-model* determines how information is stored in the repository, how data can be accessed by tools and viewed by software engineers, how well data security and integrity can be maintained, and how easily the existing model can be extended to accommodate new needs [WEL89].

The meta-model is the template into which software engineering information is placed. A detailed discussion of these models is beyond the scope of this book. For further information, the interested reader should see [WEL89], [SHA95], and [GRI95].

31.6.2 Features and Content

The features and content of the repository are best understood by looking at it from two perspectives: what is to be stored in the repository and what specific services are provided by the repository. In general, the types of things to be stored in the repository include

- The problem to be solved.
- Information about the problem domain.
- The system solution as it emerges.
- Rules and instructions pertaining to the software process (methodology) being followed.
- The project plan, resources, and history.
- Information about the organizational context.

A detailed list of types of representations, documents and deliverables that are stored in the CASE repository is included in Table 31.1.

A robust CASE repository provides two different classes of services: (1) the same types of services that might be expected from any sophisticated database management system and (2) services that are specific to the CASE environment.

Many repository requirements are the same as those of typical applications built on a commercial database management system (DBMS). In fact, most of today's CASE repositories employ a DBMS (usually relational or object oriented) as the basic data management technology. The DBMS features that support the management of software development information include

? What typical DBMS features support CASE?

- *Nonredundant data storage.* Each object is stored only once, but is accessible by all CASE tools that need it.
- *High-level access.* A common data access mechanism is implemented so data handling facilities do not have to be duplicated in each CASE tool.

TABLE 31.1 Case Repository Contents [FOR89B]

Enterprise information	**Construction**
Organizational structure	Source code; Object code
Business area analyses	System build instructions
Business functions	Binary images
Business rules	Configuration dependencies
Process models (scenarios)	Change information
Information architecture	
	Validation and verification
Application design	Test plan; Test data cases
Methodology rules	Regression test scripts
Graphical representations	Test results
System diagrams	Statistical analyses
Naming standards	Software quality metrics
Referential integrity rules	
Data structures	**Project management information**
Process definitions	Project plans
Class definitions	Work breakdown structure
Menu trees	Estimates; Schedules
Performance criteria	Resource loading; Problem reports
Timing constraints	Change requests; Status reports
Screen definitions	Audit information
Report definitions	
Logic definitions	**System documentation**
Behavioral logic	Requirements documents
Algorithms	External/internal designs
Transformation rules	User manuals

- *Data independence.* CASE tools and the target applications are isolated from physical storage so they are not affected when the hardware configuration is changed.
- *Transaction control.* The repository implements record locking, two-stage commits, transaction logging, and recovery procedures to maintain the integrity of the data when there are concurrent users.
- *Security.* The repository provides mechanisms to control who can view and modify information contained within it.
- *Ad hoc data queries and reports.* The repository allows direct access to its contents through a convenient user interface such as SQL or a forms-oriented "browser," enabling user-defined analysis beyond the standard reports provided with the CASE tool set.
- *Openness.* Repositories usually provide a simple import/export mechanism to enable bulk loading or transfer.
- *Multiuser support.* A robust repository must permit multiple developers to work on an application at the same time. It must manage concurrent access to the database by multiple tools and users with access arbitration and lock-

ing at the file or record level. For environments based on networking, multi-user support also implies that the repository can interface with common networking protocols (object request brokers) and facilities.

The CASE environment also places special demands on the repository that go beyond what is directly available in a commercial DBMS. The special features of CASE repositories include

What special features are exhibited by the CASE repository?

- *Storage of sophisticated data structures.* The repository must accommodate complex data types such as diagrams, documents, and files, as well as simple data elements. A repository also includes an information model (or meta-model) describing the structure, relationships and semantics of the data stored in it. The meta-model must be extensible so that new representations and unique organizational information can be accommodated. The repository not only stores models and descriptions of systems under development, but also associated meta-data (i.e., additional information describing the software engineering data itself, such as when a particular design component was created, what its current status is, and what other components it depends upon).
- *Integrity enforcement.* The repository information model also contains rules, or policies, describing valid business rules and other constraints and requirements on information being entered into the repository (directly or via a CASE tool). A facility called a *trigger* may be employed to activate the rules associated with an object whenever it is modified, making it possible to check the validity of design models in real time.

WebRef
A detailed tutorial and list of resources for OO repositories (which can be used for CASE environments) can be found at **mini.net/cetus/oo_db_systems_1.html**

- *Semantics-rich tool interface.* The repository information model (meta-model) contains semantics that enable a variety of tools to interpret the meaning of the data stored in the repository. For example, a data flow diagram created by a CASE tool is stored in the repository in a form based on the information model and independent of any internal representations used by the tool itself. Another CASE tool can then interpret the contents of the repository and use the information as needed for its task. Thus, the semantics stored in the repository permit data sharing among a variety of tools, as opposed to specific tool-to-tool conversions or "bridges."
- *Process/project management.* A repository contains information not only about the software application itself, but also about the characteristics of each particular project and the organization's general process for software development (phases, tasks, and deliverables). This opens up possibilities for automated coordination of technical development activity with the project management activity. For example, updating the status of project tasks could be done automatically or as a by-product of using the CASE tools. Status updating can be made very easy for developers to perform without having to

leave the normal development environment. Task assignment and queries can also be handled by e-mail. Problem reports, maintenance tasks, change authorization, and repair status can be coordinated and monitored via tools accessing the repository.

The following repository features are all encompassed by software configuration management (Chapter 9). They are re-examined here to emphasize their interrelationship to I-CASE environments:

? How does the repository assist in SCM?

Versioning. As a project progresses, many versions of individual work products will be created. The repository must be able to save all of these versions to enable effective management of product releases and to permit developers to go back to previous versions during testing and debugging.

The CASE repository must be able to control a wide variety of object types, including text, graphics, bit maps, complex documents, and unique objects like screen and report definitions, object files, test data, and results. A mature repository tracks versions of objects with arbitrary levels of granularity, for example, a single data definition or a cluster of modules can be tracked.

To support parallel development, the version control mechanism should permit multiple derivatives (variants) from a single predecessor. Thus, a developer could be working on two possible solutions to a design problem at the same time, both generated from the same starting point.

Dependency tracking and change management. The repository manages a wide variety of relationships among the data elements stored in it. These include relationships between enterprise entities and processes, among the parts of an application design, between design components and the enterprise information architecture, between design elements and deliverables, and so on. Some of these relationships are merely associations, and some are dependencies or mandatory relationships. Maintaining these relationships among development objects is called *link management.*

KEY POINT

The repository's ability to track relationships among configuration objects is one of its most important features. The impact of change can be tracked if this feature is available.

The ability to keep track of all of these relationships is crucial to the integrity of the information stored in the repository and to the generation of deliverables based on it, and it is one of the most important contributions of the repository concept to the improvement of the software development process. Among the many functions that link management supports is the ability to identify and assess the effects of change. As designs evolve to meet new requirements, the ability to identify all objects that might be affected enables more accurate assessment of cost, downtime, and degree of difficulty. It also helps prevent unexpected side effects that would otherwise lead to defects and system failures.

Link management helps the repository mechanism ensure that design information is correct by keeping the various portions of a design synchronized. For example, if a data flow diagram is modified, the repository can detect whether related data dictionaries, screen definitions, and code modules also require modification and can bring affected components to the developer's attention.

Requirements tracing. This special function depends on link management and provides the ability to track all the design components and deliverables that result from a specific requirement specification (forward tracking). In addition, it provides the ability to identify which requirement generated any given deliverable (backward tracking).

Configuration management. A configuration management facility works closely with the link management and versioning facilities to keep track of a series of configurations representing specific project milestones or production releases. Version management provides the needed versions, and link management keeps track of interdependencies.

Audit trails. An audit trail establishes additional information about when, why, and by whom changes are made. Information about the source of changes can be entered as attributes of specific objects in the repository. A repository trigger mechanism is helpful for prompting the developer or the tool that is being used to initiate entry of audit information (such as the reason for a change) whenever a design element is modified.

31.7 SUMMARY

Computer-aided software engineering tools span every activity in the software process and those umbrella activities that are applied throughout the process. CASE combines a set of building blocks that begin at the hardware and operating system software level and end with individual tools.

In this chapter, we consider a taxonomy of CASE tools. Categories encompass both management and technical activities that span most software application areas. Each category of tool is considered a "point solution."

The I-CASE environment combines integration mechanisms for data, tools, and human/computer interaction. Data integration can be achieved through direct exchange of information, through common file structures, by data sharing or interoperability, or through the use of a full I-CASE repository. Tools integration can be custom designed by vendors who work together or achieved through management software provided as part of the repository. Human/computer integration is achieved through interface standards that have become commonplace throughout the industry. An integration architecture is designed to facilitate the integration of users with tools, tools with tools, tools with data, and data with data.

The CASE repository has been referred to as a "software bus." Information moves through it, passing from tool to tool as software engineering progresses. But the repository is much more than a "bus." It is also a storage place that combines sophisticated mechanisms for integrating CASE tools and thereby improving the process through which software is developed. The repository is a relational or object-oriented database that is "the center of accumulation and storage" for software engineering information.

REFERENCES

[FOR89a] Forte, G., "In Search of the Integrated Environment," *CASE Outlook*, March–April 1989, pp. 5–12.

[FOR89b] Forte, G., "Rally Round the Repository," *CASE Outlook*, December 1989, pp. 5–27.

[FOR90] Forte, G., "Integrated CASE: A Definition," *Proc. 3rd Annual TEAMWORKERS Intl. User's Group Conference*, Cadre Technologies, Providence, RI, March 1990.

[GRI95] Griffen, J., "Repositories: Data Dictionary Descendant Can Extend Legacy Code Investment," *Application Development Trends*, April 1995, pp. 65–71.

[NIC90] Nichols, K.M., "Performance Tools," *IEEE Software*, May 1990, pp. 21–23.

[QED89] *CASE: The Potential and the Pitfalls*, QED Information Sciences,1989.

[SQE95] *Testing Tools Reference Guide*, Software Quality Engineering, 1995.

[SHA95] Sharon, D. and R. Bell, "Tools That Bind: Creating Integrated Environments," *IEEE Software*, March 1995, pp. 76–85.

[WEL89] Welke, R.J., "Meta Systems on Meta Models," *CASE Outlook*, December 1989, pp. 35–45.

PROBLEMS AND POINTS TO PONDER

31.1. Make a list of all software development tools that you use. Organize them according to the taxonomy presented in this chapter.

31.2. Using the ideas introduced in Chapters 13 through 16, how would you suggest that portability services be built?

31.3. Build a paper prototype for a project management tool that encompasses the categories noted in Section 31.3. Use Part Two of this book for additional guidance.

31.4. Do some research on object-oriented database management systems. Discuss why OODMS would be ideal for SCM tools.

31.5. Gather product information on at least three CASE tools in a category specified by your instructor. Develop a matrix that compares features.

31.6. Are there situations in which dynamic testing tools are "the only way to go"? If so, what are they?

31.7. Discuss other human activities in which the integration of a set of tools has provided substantially more benefit than the use of each of the tools individually. Do not use examples from computing.

31.8. Describe what is meant by data/tool integration in your own words.

31.9. In a number of places in this chapter, the terms meta-model and meta-data are used. Describe what these terms mean in your own words.

31.10. Can you think of additional configuration items that might be included in the repository contents shown in Table 31.1? Make a list.

FURTHER READINGS AND INFORMATION SOURCES

A number of books on CASE were published in the 1980s and early 1990s in an effort to capitalize on the high degree of interest in the industry at that time. Subsequently, few books on the subject have appeared. Among the early offerings that still have value are

Bergin, T. et al., *Computer-Aided Software Engineering: Issues and Trends for the 1990s and Beyond,* Idea Group Publishing, 1993.

Braithwaite, K.S., *Application Development Using CASE Tools,* Academic Press, 1990.

Brown, A.W., D.J. Carney, and E.J. Morris, *Principles of CASE Tool Integration,* Oxford University Press, 1994.

Clegg, D. and R. Barker, *CASE Method Fast-Track: A RAD Approach,* Addison-Wesley, 1994.

Lewis, T.G., *Computer-Aided Software Engineering,* Van Nostrand-Reinhold, 1990.

Mylls, R., *Information Engineering: CASE Practices and Techniques,* Wiley, 1993.

An anthology by Chikofsky (*Computer-Aided Software Engineering,* 2nd ed., IEEE Computer Society, 1992) contains a useful collection of early papers on CASE and software development environments. Muller and his colleagues (*Computer-Aided Software Engineering,* Kluwer Academic Publishers, 1996) have edited a collection of that describes CASE research in the mid-1990s. The best sources of current information on CASE tools are the Internet, technical periodicals, and industry newsletters.

IEEE Standard 1209 (*Evaluation and Selection of CASE Tools*) presents a set of guidelines for evaluating CASE tools for "project management processes, pre-development processes, development processes, post-development processes, and integral processes." A detailed report by Wallnau and Feiler (*Tool Integration and Environment Architectures, Software Engineering Institute,* CMU/SEI-91-TR-11, May 1991), although dated, remains one of the best discussions of CASE environments readily available.

A wide variety of information sources on CASE is available on the Internet. An up-to-date list of World Wide Web references can be found at the SEPA Web site:
http://www.mhhe.com/engcs/compsci/pressman/resources/CASE.mhtml

CHAPTER

32 THE ROAD AHEAD

KEY CONCEPTS

In the 31 chapters that have preceded this one, we explored a process for software engineering. We presented both management procedures and technical methods, basic principles and specialized techniques, people-oriented activities and tasks that are amenable to automation, paper and pencil notation and CASE tools. We argued that measurement, discipline, and an overriding focus on quality will result in software that meets the customer's needs, software that is reliable, software that is maintainable, software that is *better.* Yet, we have never promised that software engineering is a panacea.

As we begin our journey through a new century, software and systems technologies remain a challenge for every software professional and every company that builds computer-based systems. Although he wrote these words more than a decade ago, Max Hopper [HOP90] describes the current state of affairs:

> Because changes in information technology are becoming so rapid and unforgiving, and the consequences of falling behind are so irreversible, companies will either master the technology or die . . . Think of it as a technology treadmill. Companies will have to run harder and harder just to stay in place.

Changes in software engineering technology are indeed "rapid and unforgiving," but at the same time progress is often quite slow. By the time a decision

QUICK LOOK

What is it? The future is never easy to predict—pundits, talking heads, and industry experts notwithstanding. The road ahead is littered with the carcasses of exciting new technologies that never really made it (despite the hype) and is often shaped by more modest technologies that somehow modify the direction and width of the thoroughfare. Therefore, we won't try to predict the future. Rather we'll discuss some of the issues that you'll need to consider to understand how software and software engineering will change in the years ahead.

Who does it? Everyone!

Why is it important? Why did ancient kings hire soothsayers? Why do major multinational corporations hire consulting firms and think tanks to prepare forecasts? Why does a substantial percentage of the public read horoscopes? We want to know what's coming so we can ready ourselves.

What are the steps? There is no formula for predicting the road ahead. We attempt to do this by collecting data, organizing it to provide useful information, examining subtle associations to extract knowledge, and from this knowledge, suggest probable occurrences that predict how things will be at some future time.

What is the work product? A view of the near-term future that may or may not be correct.

QUICK LOOK

How do I ensure that I've done it right? Predicting the road ahead is an art, not a science. In fact, it's quite rare when a serious prediction about the future is absolutely right or unequivocally wrong (with the exception, thankfully, of predictions of the end of the world). We look for trends and try to extrapolate them ahead in time. We can assess the correctness of the extrapolation only as time passes.

is made to adopt a new method (or a new tool), conduct the training necessary to understand its application, and introduce the technology into the software development culture, something newer (and even better) has come along, and the process begins anew.

In this chapter, we examine the road ahead. Our intent is not to explore every area of research the holds promise. Nor is it to gaze into a "crystal ball" and prognosticate about the future. Rather, we explore the scope of change and the way in which change itself will affect the software engineering process in the years ahead.

32.1 THE IMPORTANCE OF SOFTWARE—REVISITED

The importance of computer software can be stated in many ways. In Chapter 1, software was characterized as a *differentiator.* The function delivered by software differentiates products, systems, and services and provides competitive advantage in the marketplace. But software is more that a differentiator. The programs, documents, and data that are software help to generate the most important commodity that any individual, business, or government can acquire—information. Pressman and Herron [PRE91] describe software in the following way:

> Computer software is one of only a few key technologies that will have a significant impact on nearly every aspect of modern society . . . It is a mechanism for automating business, industry, and government, a medium for transferring new technology, a method of capturing valuable expertise for use by others, a means for differentiating one company's products from its competitors, and a window into a corporation's collective knowledge. Software is pivotal to nearly every aspect of business. But in many ways, software is also a hidden technology. We encounter software (often without realizing it) when we travel to work, make any retail purchase, stop at the bank, make a phone call, visit the doctor, or perform any of the hundreds of day-to-day activities that reflect modern life.
>
> Software is pervasive, and yet, many people in positions of responsibility have little or no real understanding of what it really is, how it's built, or what it means to the institutions that they (and it) control. More importantly, they have little appreciation of the dangers and opportunities that software offers.

The pervasiveness of software leads us to a simple conclusion: Whenever a technology has a broad impact—an impact that can save lives or endanger them, build businesses or destroy them, inform government leaders or mislead them—it must be "handled with care."

32.2 THE SCOPE OF CHANGE

The changes in computing over the past 50 years have been driven by advances in the "hard sciences"—physics, chemistry, materials science, engineering. During the next few decades, revolutionary advances in computing may well be driven by "soft sciences"—human psychology, biology, neurophysiology, sociology, philosophy, and others. The gestation period for the computing technologies that may be derived from these disciplines is very difficult to predict.

> **Quote:**
> "The best thing about the future is that it comes one day at a time."
> Abraham Lincoln

The influence of the soft sciences may help mold the direction of computing research in the hard sciences. For example, the design of "future computers" may be guided more by an understanding of brain physiology than an understanding of conventional microelectronics.

The changes that will affect software engineering over the next decade will be influenced from four simultaneous sources: (1) the people who do the work, (2) the process that they apply, (3) the nature of information, and (4) the underlying computing technology. In the sections that follow, each of these components—people, the process, information, and the technology—is examined in more detail.

32.3 PEOPLE AND THE WAY THEY BUILD SYSTEMS

The software required for high-technology systems becomes more and more complex with each passing year, and the size of resultant programs increases proportionally. The rapid growth in the size of the "average" program would present us with few problems if it wasn't for one simple fact: As program size increases, the number of people who must work on the program must also increase.

Experience indicates that, as the number of people on a software project team increases, the overall productivity of the group may suffer. One way around this problem is to create a number of software engineering teams, thereby compartmentalizing people into individual working groups. However, as the number of software engineering teams grows, communication between them becomes as difficult and time consuming as communication between individuals. Worse, communication (between individuals or teams) tends to be inefficient—that is, too much time is spent transferring too little information content, and all too often, important information "falls into the cracks."

If the software engineering community is to deal effectively with the communication dilemma, the road ahead for software engineers must include radical changes in the way individuals and teams communicate with one another. E-mail, bulletin boards, and centralized video conferencing are now commonplace as mechanisms for connecting a large number of people to an information network. The importance of these tools in the context of software engineering work cannot be overemphasized. With an effective electronic mail or bulletin board system, the problem encountered by a software engineer in New York City may be solved with the help of a colleague in Tokyo. In a very real sense, bulletin boards and specialized newsgroups become knowledge repositories that allow the collective wisdom of a large group of technologists to be brought to bear on a technical problem or management issue.

Video personalizes the communication. At its best, it enables colleagues at different locations (or on different continents) to "meet" on a regular basis. But video also provides another benefit. It can be used as a repository for knowledge about the software and to train newcomers on a project.

Quote:
"Future shock [is] the shattering stress and disorientation that we induce in individuals by subjecting them to too much change in too short a time."
Alvin Toffler

The evolution of intelligent agents will also change the work patterns of a software engineer by dramatically extending the capabilities of software tools. Intelligent agents will enhance the engineer's ability by cross-checking engineering work products using domain-specific knowledge, performing clerical tasks, doing directed research, and coordinating human-to-human communication.

Finally, the acquisition of knowledge is changing in profound ways. On the Internet, a software engineer can subscribe to newsgroups that focus on technology areas of immediate concern. A question posted within a newsgroup precipitates answers from other interested parties around the globe. The World Wide Web provides a software engineer with the world's largest library of research papers and reports, tutorials, commentary, and references in software engineering.[1]

If past history is any indication, it is fair to say that people themselves will not change. However, the ways in which they communicate, the environment in which they work, the way in which they acquire knowledge, the methods and tools that they use, the discipline that they apply, and therefore, the overall culture for software development will change in significant and even profound ways.

32.4 THE "NEW" SOFTWARE ENGINEERING PROCESS

It is reasonable to characterize the first two decades of software engineering practice as the era of "linear thinking." Fostered by the classic life cycle model, software engineering was approached as a linear activity in which a series of sequential steps could be applied in an effort to solve complex problems. Yet, linear approaches to software development run counter to the way in which most systems are actually built. In reality, complex systems evolve iteratively, even incrementally. It is for this reason that a large segment of the software engineering community is moving toward evolutionary models for software development.

Evolutionary process models recognize that uncertainty dominates most projects, that timelines are often impossibly short, and that iteration provides the ability to

1 The SEPA Web site can provide you with electronic links to most important subjects presented in this book.

deliver a partial solution, even when a complete product is not possible within the time allotted. Evolutionary models emphasize the need for incremental work products, risk analysis, planning and then plan revision, and customer feedback.

What activities must populate the evolutionary process? Over the past decade, the Capability Maturity Model developed by the Software Engineering Institute [PAU93] has had a substantial impact on efforts to improve software engineering practices. The CMM has generated much debate (e.g., [BOL91], [GIL96]), and yet, it provides a good indicator of the attributes that must exist when solid software engineering is practiced.

Quote:
"The best preparation for good work tomorrow is to do good work today."
Elbert Hubbard

Object technologies, coupled with component-based software engineering (Chapter 27), are a natural outgrowth of the trend toward evolutionary process models. Both will have a profound impact on software development productivity and product quality. Component reuse provides immediate and compelling benefits. When reuse is coupled with CASE tools for application prototyping, program increments can be built far more rapidly than through the use of conventional approaches. Prototyping draws the customer into the process. Therefore, it is likely that customers and users will become much more involved in the development of software. This, in turn, may lead to higher end-user satisfaction and better software quality overall.

The rapid growth in Web-based applications (WebApps) is changing both the software engineering process and its participants. Again, we encounter an incremental, evolutionary paradigm. But in the case of WebApps, immediacy, security, and aesthetics become dominant concerns. A Web engineering team melds technologists with content specialists (e.g., artists, musicians, videographers) to build an information source for a community of users that is both large and unpredictable. The software that has grown out of Web engineering work has already resulted in radical economic and cultural change. Although the basic concepts and principles discussed in this book are applicable, the software engineering process must adapt to accommodate the Web.

32.5 NEW MODES FOR REPRESENTING INFORMATION

Over the past two decades, a subtle transition has occurred in the terminology that is used to describe software development work performed for the business community. Thirty years ago, the term *data processing* was the operative phrase for describing the use of computers in a business context. Today, data processing has given way to another phrase—*information technology*—that implies the same thing but presents a subtle shift in focus. The emphasis is not merely to process large quantities of data but rather to extract meaningful information from this data. Obviously, this was always the intent, but the shift in terminology reflects a far more important shift in management philosophy.

When software applications are discussed today, the words *data* and *information* occur repeatedly. We encounter the word *knowledge* in some artificial intelligence

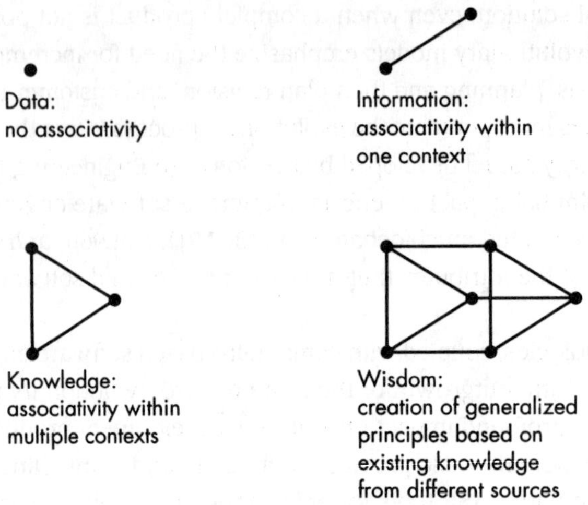

FIGURE 32.1 An "information" spectrum

applications, but its use is relatively rare. Virtually no one discusses *wisdom* in the context of computer software applications.

Data is raw information—collections of facts that must be processed to be meaningful. Information is derived by associating facts within a given context. Knowledge associates information obtained in one context with other information obtained in a different context. Finally, wisdom occurs when generalized principles are derived from disparate knowledge. Each of these four views of "information" is represented schematically in Figure 32.1.

> **Quote:**
> "Wisdom is the power that enables us to use knowledge for the benefit of ourselves and others."
> **Thomas J. Watson**

To date, the vast majority of all software has been built to process data or information. Software engineers are now equally concerned with systems that process knowledge.[2] Knowledge is two-dimensional. Information collected on a variety of related and unrelated topics is connected to form a body of fact that we call *knowledge.* The key is our ability to associate information from a variety of different sources that may not have any obvious connection and combine it in a way that provides us with some distinct benefit.

To illustrate the progression from data to knowledge, consider census data indicating that the birthrate in 1996 in the United States was 4.9 million. This number represents a data value. Relating this piece of data with birthrates for the preceding 40 years, we can derive a useful piece of information—aging "baby boomers" of the 1950s and early 1960s made a last gasp effort to have children prior to the end of their child-bearing years. In addition "gen-Xers" have begun their childbearing years. The census data can then be connected to other seemingly unrelated pieces of information. For example, the current number of elementary school teachers who will retire during the next decade, the number of college students graduating with degrees

2 The rapid growth in data mining and data warehousing technologies reflects this growing trend.

in primary and secondary education, the pressure on politicians to hold down taxes and therefore limit pay increases for teachers.

All of these pieces of information can be combined to formulate a representation of knowledge—there will be significant pressure on the education system in the United States in the first decade of the twenty-first century and this pressure will continue for over a decade. Using this knowledge, a business opportunity may emerge. There may be significant opportunity to develop new modes of learning that are more effective and less costly than current approaches.

The road ahead for software leads toward systems that process knowledge. We have been processing data for 50 years and extracting information for almost three decades. One of the most significant challenges facing the software engineering community is to build systems that take the next step along the spectrum—systems that extract knowledge from data and information in a way that is practical and beneficial.

32.6 TECHNOLOGY AS A DRIVER

The people who build and use software, the software engineering process that is applied, and the information that is produced are all affected by advances in hardware and software technology. Historically, hardware has served as the technology driver in computing. A new hardware technology provides potential. Software builders then react to customer demands in an attempt to tap the potential.

> **Quote:**
> "The new electronic independence recreates the world in the image of a global village."
> **Marshall McLuhan**

The road ahead for hardware technology is likely to progress along two parallel paths. Along one path, hardware technologies will continue to evolve at a rapid pace. With greater capacity provided by traditional hardware architectures, the demands on software engineers will continue to grow.

But the real changes in hardware technology may occur along another path. The development of nontraditional hardware architectures (e.g., massively parallel machines, optical processors, neural network machines) may cause radical changes in the kind of software that we build and fundamental changes in our approach to software engineering. Since these nontraditional approaches are not yet mature, it is difficult to determine which will survive and even more difficult to predict how the world of software will change to accommodate them.

The road ahead for software engineering is driven by software technologies. Reuse and component-based software engineering (technologies that are not yet mature) offer the best opportunity for order of magnitude improvements in system quality and time to market. In fact, as time passes, the software business may begin to look very much like the hardware business of today. There may be vendors that build discrete devices (reusable software components), other vendors that build system components (e.g., a set of tools for human/computer interaction) and system integrators that provide solutions (products and custom-built systems) for the end-user.

Software engineering will change—of that we can be certain. But regardless of how radical the changes are, we can be assured that quality will never lose its importance and that effective analysis and design and competent testing will always have a place in the development of computer-based systems.

32.7 A CONCLUDING COMMENT

It has been 20 years since the first edition of this book was written. I can still recall sitting at my desk as a young professor, writing the manuscript (by hand) for a book on a subject that few people cared about and even fewer really understood. I remember the rejection letters from publishers, who argued (politely, but firmly) that there would never be a market for a book on "software engineering." Luckily, McGraw-Hill decided to give it a try,[3] and the rest, as they say, is history.

Over the past 20 years, this book has changed dramatically—in scope, in size, in style, and in content. Like software engineering, it has grown and (I hope) matured over the years.

An engineering approach to the development of computer software is now conventional wisdom. Although debate continues on the "right paradigm," the degree of automation, and the most effective methods, the underlying principles of software engineering are now accepted throughout the industry. Why, then, are we seeing their broad adoption only recently?

The answer, I think, lies in the difficulty of technology transition and the cultural change that accompanies it. Even though most of us appreciate the need for an engineering discipline for software, we struggle against the inertia of past practice and face new application domains (and the developers who work in them) that appear ready to repeat the mistakes of the past.

To ease the transition we need many things—an adaptable and sensible software process, more effective methods, more powerful tools, better acceptance by practitioners and support from managers, and no small dose of education and "advertising." Software engineering has not had the benefit of massive advertising, but as time passes, the concept sells itself. In a way, this book is an "advertisement" for the technology.

You may not agree with every approach described in this book. Some of the techniques and opinions are controversial; others must be tuned to work well in different software development environments. It is my sincere hope, however, that *Software Engineering: A Practitioner's Approach* has delineated the problems we face, demonstrated the strength of software engineering concepts, and provided a framework of methods and tools.

As we begin a new millennium, software has become the most important product and the most important industry on the world stage. Its impact and importance

3 Actually, credit should go to Peter Freeman and Eric Munson, who convinced McGraw-Hill it was worth a shot.

have come a long, long way. And yet, a new generation of software developers must meet many of the same challenges that faced earlier generations. Let us hope that the people who meet the challenge—software engineers—will have the wisdom to develop systems that improve the human condition.

REFERENCES

[BOL91] Bollinger, T. and C. McGowen, "A Critical Look at Software Capability Evaluations," *IEEE Software,* July 1991, pp. 25–41.

[GIL96] Gilb, T., "What Is Level Six?" *IEEE Software,* January 1996, pp. 97–98, 103.

[HOP90] Hopper, M.D., "Rattling SABRE, New Ways to Compete on Information," *Harvard Business Review,* May–June 1990.

[PAU93] Paulk, M., et al., *Capability Maturity Model for Software,* Software Engineering Institute, Carnegie Mellon University, 1993.

[PRE91] Pressman, R.S., and S.R. Herron, *Software Shock,* Dorset House, 1991.

PROBLEMS AND POINTS TO PONDER

32.1. Get a copy of this week's major business and news magazines (e.g., *Newsweek, Time, Business Week*). List every article or news item that can be used to illustrate the importance of software.

32.2. One of the hottest software application domains is Web-based systems and applications (Chapter 29). Discuss how people, communication, and process has to evolve to accommodate the development of "next generation" WebApps.

32.3. Write a brief description of an ideal software engineer's development environment circa 2010. Describe the elements of the environment (hardware, software, and communications technologies) and their impact on quality and time to market.

32.4. Review the discussion of the evolutionary process models in Chapter 2. Do some research and collect recent papers on the subject. Summarize the strengths and weaknesses of evolutionary paradigms based on experiences outlined in the papers.

32.5. Attempt to develop an example that begins with the collection of raw data and leads to acquisition of information, then knowledge, and finally, wisdom.

32.6. Select a current "hot" technology (it need not be a software technology) that is being discussed in the popular media and describe how software enables its evolution and impact.

FURTHER READINGS AND INFORMATION SOURCES

Books that discuss the road ahead for software and computing span a vast array of technical, scientific, economic, political, and social issues. Robertson (*The New*

Renaissance: Computers and the Next Level of Civilization, Oxford University Press 1998) argues that the computer revolution may be the single most significant advance in the history of civilization. Dertrouzos and Gates (*What Will Be: How the New World of Information Will Change Our Lives,* HarperBusiness, 1998) provide a thoughtful discussion of some of the directions that information technologies may take in the first few decades of this century. Barnatt (*Valueware: Technology, Humanity and Organization,* Praeger Publishing, 1999) presents an intriguing discussion of an "ideas economy" and how economic value will be created as cyber-business evolves. Negroponte's (*Being Digital,* Alfred A. Knopf, 1995) was a best seller in the mid-1990s and continues to provide an interesting view of computing and its overall impact.

Kroker and Kroker (*Digital Delirium,* New World Perspectives, 1997) have edited a controversial collection of essays, poems, and humor that examines the impact of digital technologies on people and society. Brin (*The Transparent Society: Will Technology Force Us to Choose Between Privacy and Freedom?* Perseus Books, 1999) revisits the continuing debate associated with the inevitable loss of personal privacy that accompanies the growth of information technologies. Shenk (*Data Smog: Surviving the Information Glut,* HarperCollins, 1998) discusses the problems associated with an "information-infested society" that is suffocating from the volume of information that information technologies produce.

Miller, Michalski, and Stevens (*21st Century Technologies: Promises and Perils of a Dynamic Future,* Brookings Institution Press, 1999) have edited a collection of papers and essays on the impact of technology on social, business, and economic structures. For those interested in technical issues, Luryi, Xu, and Zaslavsky (*Future Trends in Microelectronics,* Wiley, 1999) have edited a collection of papers on probable directions for computer hardware. Hayzelden and Bigham (*Software Agents for Future Communication Systems,* Springer-Verlag, 1999) have edited a collection that discusses trends in the development of intelligent software agents.

Kurzweil (*The Age of Spiritual Machines, When Computers Exceed Human Intelligence,* Viking/Penguin Books, 1999) argues that, within 20 years, hardware technology will have the capacity to fully model the human brain. Borgmann (*Holding on to Reality: The Nature of Information at the Turn of the Millennium,* University of Chicago Press, 1999) has written a intriguing history of information, tracing its role in the transformation of culture. Devlin (*InfoSense: Turning Information into Knowledge,* W. H. Freeman & Co., 1999) tries to make sense of the constant flow of information that bombards us on a daily basis. Gleick (*Faster: The Acceleration of Just About Everything,* Pantheon Books, 2000) discusses the ever-accelerating rate of technological change and its impact on every aspect of modern life. Jonscher (*The Evolution of Wired Life: From the Alphabet to the Soul-Catcher Chip—How Information Technologies Change Our World,* Wiley, 2000) argues that human thought and interaction transcend the importance of technology.

A wide variety of information sources on future trends in computing is available on the Internet. An up-to-date list of World Wide Web references can be found at the SEPA Web site:

http://www.mhhe.com/engcs/compsci/pressman/resources/future.mhtml

INDEX

清华大学出版社影印版图书目录

大学计算机教育丛书

1. *Computer Networks 3rd ed*. 1996/**Andrew S. Tanenbaum** (计算机网络 第3版 832页)
2. *Distributed Operating Systems* 1995/**Andrew S. Tanenbaum** (分布式操作系统 628页)
3. *The C Programming Language 2nd ed*. 1988/**Brian W. Kernighan, Dennis M. Ritchie** (C程序设计语言 第2版 284页)
4. *The C Answer Book*: **Solutions to the Exercises in The C programming Languange, second edition by Brian W. Kernighan & Dennis M. Ritchie** *2nd ed*. 1989/**Clovis L. Tondo, Scott E. Gimpel** (C程序设计语言第2版习题解答 第2版 216页)
5. *Multimedia*: **Computing, Communications & Applications** 1995/**Ralf Steinmetz, Klara Nahrstedt** (多媒体技术:计算,通信及应用 876页)
6. *Data Structure with C++* 1996/**William Ford, William Topp** (数据结构 C++语言描述 916页)
7. *Computer Organization And Architecture*: **Designing for Performance** *4th ed*. 1996/**William Stallings** (计算机组织与结构:性能设计 第4版 696页)
8. *Use Case Maps for Object-Oriented Systems* 1996/**R. J. A. Buhr, R. S. Casselman** (用于面向对象系统开发的使用实例图 326页)
9. *Operating Systems*: **Design and Implementation 2nd ed**. 1997/**Andrew S. Tanenbaum, Albert S. Woodhull** (操作系统:设计与实现 第2版 960页 附光盘)
10. *Data And Computer Communications 5th ed*. 1997/**William Stallings** (数据通信与计算机通信 第5版 820页)
11. *Digital Logic Circuit Analysis & Design* 1995/**Victor P. Nelson, H. Troy Nagle, Bill D. Carroll, J. David Irwin** (数字逻辑电路分析与设计 868页)
12. *Discrete Mathematical Structures 3rd ed*. 1996/**Bernard Kolman, Robert C. Busby, Sharon Ross** (离散数学结构 第3版 544页)
13. *Computer graphics C Version 2nd ed*. 1997/**Donald Hearn, M. Pauline Baker** (计算机图形学 C语言版 第2版 864页 附彩插)
14. *Computer Networks and Internets* 1997/**Douglas E. Comer** (计算机网络与因特网 530页 附光盘)
15. *A First Course in Database Systems* 1997/**Jeffrey D. Ullman, Jennifer Widom** (数据库系统基础教程 484页)
16. *Digital Image Processing* 1996/**Kenneth R. Castleman** (数字图象处理 686页)
17. *Business Data Communications 3rd ed*. 1998/**William Stallings, Richard Van Slyke** (事务数据通信 第3版 578页)
18. *Software Architecture*: **Perspectives on an Emerging Discipline** 1996/**Mary Shaw, David Garlan** (软件体系结构 264页)
19. *Digital Video Processing* 1995/**A. Murat Tekalp** (数字视频处理 548页)
20. *IBM PC Assembly Language and Programming 4th ed*. 1998/**PETER ABEL** (*IBM PC* 汇编语言与程序设计 第4版 622页)
21. *Operating Systems*: **Internals and Design Principles** *3rd ed*. 1998/**William Stallings** (操作系统:精髓与设计原理 第3版 800页)
22. *Programming Languages*: **Design and Implementation** *3rd ed*. 1996/**Terrence W. Pratt, Marvin V. Zelkowitz** (程序设计语言:设计与实现 第3版 570页)
23. *Computer System Architecture 3rd ed*. 1993/**M. Morris Mano** (计算机系统体系结构 第3版 542页)
24. *Object-Oriented Systems Analysis and Design* 1996/**Ronald J. Norman** (面向对象系统分析与设计 456页)
25. *Digital and Analog Communication Systems 5th ed*. 1997/**Leon W. Couch Ⅱ** (数字及模拟通信系统 第5版 776页)
26. *Data Structures & Program Design in C 2nd ed*. 1997/**Robert Kruse, C. L. Tondo, Bruce Leung** (数据结构与程序设计 C语言描述 692页)
27. *UNIX Network Programming Volume I 2nd ed*. 1998/**W. Richard Stevens** (UNIX往络编程 卷1 第2版 1038页)

28. *Object-Oriented Software Construction 2nd ed*. 1997/**Bertrand Meyer** (面向对象软件构造第 2 版 1288 页 附光盘)
29. *Elements of The Theory of Computation 2nd ed*. 1998/**Harry R. Lewis, Christos H. Papadimitriou** (计算理论基础第 2 版 376 页)
30. *Fundamentals of Speech Recognition* 1993/**Lawrence Rabiner, Biing-Hwang Juang** (语音识别基本原理 544 页)
31. *Java Structures*: ***Data structures in Java for the Principled Programmer*** 1999/**Duane A. Bailey** (数据结构 Java 描述:数据结构的设计原则与 Java 实现 382 页)
32. *Database Management Systems 2nd ed*. 2000/**Raghu Ramakrishnan, Johannes Gehrke** (数据库管理系统第 2 版 934 页)
33. *In-line/On-line*: ***Fundamentals of the Internet and the World Wide Web*** 1999/**Raymond Greenlaw, Ellen Hepp** (因特网与万维网基本原理与技术 574 页)
34. *Student Solutions Manual to Accompany In-line/On-line*: ***Fundamentals of the Internet and the World Wide Web*** 1999/**Raymond Greenlaw, Ellen Hepp** (因特网与万维网基本原理与技术学生解题手册 164 页)
35. *TCP/IP Protocol Suite* 2000/**Behrouz A. Forouzan** (TCP/IP 协议族 856 页)
36. *Practical Object-Oriented Design with UML* 2000/**Mark Priestley** (面向对象设计的 UML 实践 352 页)
37. *Software Engineering*: ***A Practitioner's Approach 5th ed***. 2001/**Roger S. Pressman** (软件工程:实践者之路第 5 版 888 页)
38. *Communication Networks*: ***Fundamental Concepts and key Architectures*** 2000/**Alberto Leon-GarCia, Indra Widjaja** (通信网:基本概念与主体结构)

ATM 与 B-ISDN 技术丛书

1. *Emerging Communications technologies 2nd ed*, 1997/**Uyless Black** (现代通信最新技术 第 2 版 468 页)
2. *ATM: Foundation for Broadband Networks*, 1995/**Uyless Black** (宽带网络技术基础 448 页)
3. *ATM: Signaling in Broadband Networks*, 1998/**Uyless Black** (宽带网络信令 209 页)
4. *Broadband Integrated Networks*, 1996/**Mischa Schwartz** (宽带网络性能分析 383 页)
5. *ATM: Internetworking with ATM*, 1998/**Uyless Black** (ATM 网互通技术 254 页)
6. *Planning and Managing ATM Networks*, 1997/**Dan Minoli** (ATM 网络规划与管理 338 页)
7. *ATM: The New Paradigm for Internet, Intranet & Residential Broadband Services & Applications*, 1998/**Timothy Kwok** (解决因特网、企业网和居民宽带的新途径 381 页)

网络互连技术系列

1. *Internetworking with TCP/IP Vol. Ⅰ*: ***Principles, Protocols, and Architecture***, 3rd ed., 1995/**Douglas E. Comer** (TCP/IP 网络互连技术卷Ⅰ:原理,协议和体系结构,第 3 版 636 页)
2. *Internetworking with TCP/IP Vol. Ⅱ*: ***Design, Implementation, and Internals***, 2nd ed. 1994/**Douglas E. Comer, David L. Stevens** (TCP/IP 网络互连技术卷Ⅱ:设计与实现,第 2 版 630 页)
3. *Internetworking with TCP/IP Vol. Ⅲ*: ***Client-Server Programming and Applications, BSD Socket Version***, 2nd ed. 1996/**Douglas E. Comer, David L. Stevens**(TCP/IP 网络互连技术卷Ⅲ:客户服务器编程和应用,BSD 套接字版,第 2 版 536 页)
4. *Internetworking with TCP/IP Vol. Ⅲ*: ***Client-Server Programming and Applications, Windows Sockets Version*** 1997/**Douglas E. Comer, David L. Stevens**(TCP/IP 网络互连技术卷Ⅲ:客户服务器编程和应用,Windows 套接字版,532 页)
5. *IPv6 The New Internet Protocol 2nd ed*. 1998/**Christian Huitema** (新因特网协议 IPv6 第 2 版 256 页)

电子工程技术系列丛书

1. *Signals & Systems 2nd ed*. 1997/**Alan V. Oppenheim, Alan S. Willsky** (信号与系统,第 2 版,983 页)
2. *Introduction to Signal Processing*, 1996/**Sophocles J. Orfanidis** (信号处理导论,814 页)
3. *Digital Integrated Circuits*: ***A Design Perspective***, 1996/**Jan M. Rabaey** (数字集成电路:设计透视,724 页)

CISCO 系列丛书

1. *Introduction to Cisco Router Configuration*, 1998/**Edited by Laura Chappell** (Cisco 路由器配置导论,560 页)
2. *IP Routing Primer*, 1998/**Robert Wright** (IP 路由技术基础,318 页)

3. *Routing TCP/IP Vol*. Ⅰ 1998/**Jeff Doyle**（TCP/IP 路由技术卷Ⅰ,1055 页）
4. *Internetworking Troubleshooting Handbook*, 1999/**H. Kim Lew, Spank McCoy, Tim Stevenson, Kathleen Wallace, Kevin Downes**（网络互联排错手册,736 页）
5. *IP Routing Fundamentals*, 1999/**Mark A. Sportack**（IP 路由技术原理,528 页）
6. *CCNA Exam Certification Guide*, 1999/**Wendell Odom**(CCNA 资格认证考试及培训必读,640 页 附光盘)
7. *Network Design and Case Studies*, 1998/**Cisco Systems, Inc.**（网络设计与个案分析 862 页）
8. *Advanced Cisco Router Configuration* 1999 /**Edited by Laura Chappell**(**Cisco** 高级路由器配置技术 670 页)
9. *Internet Routing Architectures* 1997/**Bassam Halabi**(**Internet** 路由结构 496 页）

网络新技术系列丛书

1. *Gigabit Ethernet Networking* 1999/**David G. Cunningham, William G. Lane**（千兆以太网　592 页）
2. *Virtual LANs* 1999/**Marina Smith**（虚拟局域网　429 页）
3. *Switched LANs* 1999/**John J. Roese**（交换式局域网　415 页）
4. *Mobile IP*: ***the Internet Unplugged*** 1998/**James D. Solomon**（移动 IP　377 页）
5. *XDSL Architecture* 2000/**Padmanand Warrier, Balaji Kumar**（XDSL 体系结构）
6. *Telecommunication Protocols second Edition* 2000/**Travis Russell**（电信协议(第 2 版)）
7. *QoS & Traffic Management in IP & ATM Networks* 2000/**David McDysan**（IP 与 ATM 网络中的 QoS 和业务量管理）
8. *Managing Dynamic IP Networks* 2000/**Paul T. Ammann**（管理动态 IP 网络）

The ESE Components

1	**Software Engineering Overview**	Thorough discussion of basic concepts and principles, software engineering process models and software process improvement. 3 modules.
2	**Software Project Management**	Detailed coverage of measurement and metrics, project estimation and planning, risk analysis, and scheduling, tracking and control. 4 modules.
3	**Information Engineering** Structured Analysis	In-depth discussion of information engineering, analysis principles, design principles, methods for structured analysis and design. 7 modules.
4	**Reengineering Techniques**	Thorough treatment of business process reengineering as it related to IT and software reengineering techniques. 2 modules.
5	**Object-Oriented Methods**	Detailed coverage of concepts and principles, OO analysis, OO design, reuse, project management and OO testing. 4 modules
6	**Software Testing**	In-depth training that covers basic testing concepts and principles, white box and black box test case design methods, and testing strategies. 3 modules
7	**Software Quality Assurance**	Detailed coverage of proactive SQA practices including quality factors and metrics, SQA tasks, and guidelines for reviews and inspections. 3 modules
8	**Software Configuration Management**	Thorough treatment of SCM concepts and tasks including identification and version control, change control, auditing and reporting. 4 modules
9	**ISO 9000 Software Development**	In-depth discussion of the strategy required to develop an ISO 9000 compliant software process including ISO 9001 and ISO 9000-3. 4 modules Advanced ESE component.

Place postage here to obtain your ESE video sampler

R.S. Pressman & Associates, Inc.
6425 Via Rosa
Boca Raton, FL 33433

